West's Law School Advisory Board

INTERNATIONAL L
AND LITIGATION IN THE U.S.

Second Edition

By

Jordan J. Paust
Mike and Teresa Baker Professor
Law Center, University of Houston

Jon M. Van Dyke
Professor of Law
William S. Richardson School of Law, University of Hawaii at Manoa

Linda A. Malone
Marshall-Wythe Foundation Professor of Law
College of William and Mary, Marshall-Wythe School of Law

AMERICAN CASEBOOK SERIES®

THOMSON
WEST

Mat #40393345

610 Opperman Drive
P.O. Box 64526
St. Paul, MN 55164–0526
1–800–328–9352

Printed in the United States of America

ISBN–13: 978–0–314–16269–4
ISBN–10: 0–314–16269–0

TEXT IS PRINTED ON 10% POST CONSUMER RECYCLED PAPER

We dedicate this book to:

Paula, Christine and Erik

Sherry, Jesse, Eric and Michelle

Erin and Corey

with special rememberance of

Joan M. Fitzpatrick

*

Preface

This coursebook is designed for a first or introductory course in international law, sometimes referred to as Public International Law. Most of the traditional topics covered in an initial or primary course are addressed in this book. However, this book also provides a more detailed focus on the use, and possibilities of use, of international law in U.S. domestic legal processes than most general international law coursebooks. Thus, we pay more attention to various forms of incorporation of international law into U.S. federal and state legal processes, questions of federal and state jurisdictional competencies regarding civil and criminal sanctions, hurdles concerning actual litigation and prosecution, extradition, cooperation in transnational law enforcement (civil and criminal), and related matters.

Most U.S. students who take an international law course are likely to practice international law in U.S. domestic legal processes. Indeed, with growing global interdependence and transnational impacts in all sectors of public life and legal practice, it is increasingly difficult to practice law, especially in the federal system, without familiarity with the nature, relevance, proof, and forms of incorporation of international law; issues concerning jurisdiction under international law; relevant defenses; and issues concerning relative immunities. We note, for example, that the United States is a signatory to over 14,000 international agreements that, as supreme law of the land, raise questions concerning their direct and indirect use to create, enhance or delimit various governmental and private powers, duties and rights. The practice of law in the U.S. increasingly involves attention to such questions, whether one specializes in corporate, contracting, commercial, criminal, civil rights, energy, environmental, family, immigration, torts, property (including intellectual property), transportation, or governmental legal processes.

This book will more adequately prepare students for such a practice of international law, while also covering traditional topics such as the nature, sources, and evidences of international law; the law of the sea, airspace and outer space law, and the use of armed force. Where appropriate, traditional topics have been addressed also with reference to U.S. domestic legal processes and trends. For example, Chapter 8, addressing the use of force, also pays detailed attention to the allocation of war powers within our federal system and to trends in relevant U.S. litigation. Students who use this book will have both traditional and relevant U.S.-incorporation bases of knowledge useful in all other international law and related courses they might pursue, such as: international environmental law, human rights, international criminal law, foreign affairs and national security law, alien-immigration law, international contracting, international litigation and arbitration, international energy law, international trade, international commercial law, and specialty courses and seminars on topics addressed in various chapters in this book. Similarly, the Documents Supplement will be useful in specialty courses, especially human rights courses or seminars.

Sometimes a series of short extracts from judicial decisions and opinions of Attorneys General are set forth merely to demonstrate patterns of legal expectation and trends in decision on specific points or issues. They are not set forth as typical ìcasesî with detailed fact patterns. Footnote numbers in this book do not correspond to those in relevant extracts from cases or materials.

JORDAN J. PAUST
Houston

JON M. VAN DYKE
Honolulu

LINDA A. MALONE
Williamsburg

October 2005

Acknowledgements

We gratefully acknowledge permission to reprint extracts from the following;

American Bar Association Journal:
Bernard H. Oxman, *The New Law of the Sea*, 69 A.B.A. J. 156 (February 1983)
American Law Institute:
RESTATEMENT OF THE FOREIGN RELATIONS LAW OF THE UNITED STATES (3 ed. 1987), Copyright 1988 by the American Law Institute, reprinted with permission
American Society of International Law:
Hilary Charlesworth, Christine Chinkin, Shelley Wright, *Feminist Approaches to International Law*, 85 AM. J. INT'L L. 613 (1991)
Gunther Handl, remarks, in 82 PROC., AM. SOC. INT'L L. 371, 372 (1988)
W. Michael Reisman, remarks, in 82 PROC., AM. SOC. INT'L L. 374 (1988)
Alan Kreczko, testimony, in Contemporary Practice of the United States Relating to International Law, 86 AM. J. INT'L L. 548 (1992)
Commission on the Responsibilities of the Authors of the War and on Enforcement of Penalties, Report Presented to the Preliminary Peace Conference, March 29, 1919, in 14 AM. J. INT'L L. 95 (1920)
Asia Foundation Center for Asian Pacific Affairs:
Onuma, Yasuaki, *In Quest of Intercivilizational Human Rights: 'Universal' vs. 'Relative' Human Rights Viewed from an Asian Perspective*, Occasional Paper No. 2 (March 1996)
Carolina Academic Press:
Jordan J. Paust, INTERNATIONAL LAW AS LAW OF THE UNITED STATES (1996)
Connecticut Journal of International Law:
Anthony D'Amato, *It's a Bird, It's a Plane, It's Jus Cogens*, 6 CONN. J. INT'L L. 1 (1990)
Jordan J. Paust, *The Reality of Jus Cogens*, 7 CONN. J. INT'L L. 81 (1991)
Elsevier Science (Oxford):
Jon M. Van Dyke, *The Aegean Sea Dispute: Opinions and Avenues*, 20 MARINE POLICY 398 (1996)
Georgia Journal of International and Comparative Law:
Jordan J. Paust, *The Complex Nature, Sources and Evidences of Customary Human Rights*, 25 GA. J. INT'L & COMP. L. 147 (1995–96)
Jordan J. Paust, *U.N. Peace and Security Powers and Related Presidential Powers,* 26 GA. J. INT'L & COMP. L. 15 (1996)

German Yearbook of International Law:

Jordan J. Paust, *Customary International Law in the United States: Clean and Dirty Laundry*, 40 GERMAN Y.B. INT'L L. 78 (1997)

Harvard Human Rights Journal:

Jordan J. Paust, *The Other Side of Right: Private Duties Under Human Rights Law*, 5 HARV. H.R.J. 51 (1992)

International Law Association:

Report of the Committee on International Law in National Courts, in REPORT OF THE SIXTY-SEVENTH CONFERENCE, HELSINKI 570 (1996)

International Law Reports (Cambridge):

Attorney General of Israel v. Eichmann (Jerusalem d. ct. 1961 and S. Ct. 1962), reprinted in 36 INT'L L. RPTS. 277 (1968)

X v. Empire of Iran, German Federal Constitutional Court (30 April 1963), reprinted in 45 INT'L L. RPTS. 57 (1972)

Kluwer Law International:

Gunther Handl, *Regional Arrangements and Third State Vessels: Is the Pacta Tertiis Principle Being Modified?*, in CONTEMPORARY NORMS IN THE LAW OF MARINE ENVIRONMENTAL PROTECTION–FOCUS ON SHIP AND SAFETY POLLUTION PREVENTION 217 (Henrik Ringbohm ed. 1997)

Jon M. Van Dyke, *The Straddling and Migratory Stocks Agreement and the Pacific*, 11 INT'L J. MARINE & COASTAL L. 406 (1996)

Jon M. Van Dyke, *Sharing Ocean Resources...in a time of Scarcity and Selfishness*, ___ (Harry Scheiber ed. 2000)

Law and Contemporary Problems (Duke University):

Michael Scharf, *Beyond the Rhetoric of Comparative Interest Balancing*, 50 L. & CONTEMP. PROBS. 95 (1987)

Michigan Journal of International Law:

Jordan J. Paust, *Customary International Law: Its Nature, Sources and Status as Law of the United States*, 12 MICH. J. INT'L L. 59 (1990)

Jordan J. Paust, *Race-Based Affirmative Action and International Law*, 18 MICH. J. INT'L L. 659 (1997)

Jordan J. Paust, *Customary International Law and Human Rights Treaties Are Law of the United States*, 20 MICH. J. INT'L L. 301 (1999)

Review of European Community & International Environmental Law (RECIEL):

Duncan E.J. Currie & John M. Van Dyke, *Recent Developments in the International Law Governing Shipments of Nuclear Materials and Wastes and Their Implications for SIDS*, 14:2 REVIEW OF EUROPEAN COMMUNITY & INTERNATIONAL ENVIRONMENTAL LAW (RECIEL) 117 (2005)

Saint John's Law Review:

Jordan J. Paust, *After Alvarez-Machain: Abduction, Standing, Denials of Justice, and Unaddressed Human Rights Claims*, 67 ST. JOHN'S L. REV. 551 (1993)

San Diego Law Review:

Jon M. Van Dyke, Christopher Yuen, *'Common Heritage' v. 'Freedom of the High Seas': Which Governs the Seabed?*, 19 SAN DIEGO L. REV. 493 (1982)

University of Hawaii Law Review:

Jon M. Van Dyke, *The Role of Customary International Law in Federal and State Court Litigation*, 26 U. HAWAII L. REV. 361 (2004)

Virginia Journal of International Law:

Jordan J. Paust, *Federal Jurisdiction Over Extraterritorial Acts of Terrorism and Nonimmunity for Violators of International Law Under the FSIA and the Act of State Doctrine*, 23 VA. J. INT'L L. 191 (1983)

Yale University Press:

Lung-chu Chen, INTRODUCTION TO CONTEMPORARY INTERNATIONAL LAW (1989)

W. Michael Reisman, NULLITY AND REVISION 559–562 (1971)

*

Summary of Contents

Table of Contents

CHAPTER TWO. DOMESTIC INCORPORATION

CHAPTER FIVE. COOPERATION IN TRANSNATIONAL ENFORCEMENT

CHAPTER SIX. LAW OF THE SEA

CHAPTER SEVEN. LAW OF AIRSPACE AND OUTER SPACE

*

Table of Cases

The principal cases are in bold type. Cases cited or discussed in the text are roman type. References are to pages. Cases cited in principal cases and within other quoted materials are not included.

INTERNATIONAL LAW AND LITIGATION IN THE U.S.

Second Edition

*

Chapter One

NATURE, SOURCES AND EVIDENCES OF INTERNATIONAL LAW

SECTION 1. THE NATURE OF INTERNATIONAL LAW

Introductory Problem

Knaunstait Aktor, a charismatic leader of an unsuccessful insurgent effort to overthrow the government of a foreign country, was sued in a federal district court while vacationing in the United States by fellow nationals who claim to be victims and surviving relatives of victims of various "torts" committed or ordered by Aktor in violation of the law of nations and treaties of the United States. Among the alleged violations are claims concerning war crimes, genocide, and human rights, especially human rights involving summary execution of persons detained by Aktor's insurgent group.

Defendant Aktor has moved for dismissal with prejudice on the following grounds:

(a) international law only applies to states and relations between states, not to private individuals or insurgent groups;

(b) alternatively, international law only applies additionally to relations between a state and persons—not between or among private persons;

(c) Aktor's government, his insurgent group, and all other governments in the long history of his state's existence have engaged in conduct such as that alleged and view it as culturally acceptable for the maintenance of "public order"; they have never consented to the existence of any law proscribing such conduct; and international law only binds those who have consented to it;

(d) conduct such as that alleged occurs elsewhere each year, thus demonstrating that there are no such prohibitions under international law;

(e) international agreements that do not mention individuals or individual liability cannot bind individuals or form the basis for a domestic lawsuit; and

(f) only norms *jus cogens* [which are peremptory norms that preempt other international law] are actionable in U.S. courts and none of the alleged infractions are norms *jus cogens*.

After reviewing the materials in this section, how would you rule on the defense motion? Why?

A. *Basic Types of International Law*

There are two basic types of international law: (1) international agreements, and (2) customary international law. International agreements are technically binding only upon the signatories to such agreements (which in the past have included states, nations, international organizations, and other entities) and, in the case of states or nations, their nationals (and possibly also those with a significant nexus with a signatory[1] to an agreement). In general, it does not matter that the international agreement is termed a treaty, charter, convention, covenant, protocol, or something else. It is an international agreement, subject to international law concerning such agreements. Customary international law, unlike agreements as such, is universally obligatory. What might have been merely an international agreement at the time it was formed can later become customary international law for the entire community. A well-known example of this transformation involved the recognition by the International Military Tribunal at Nuremberg that the 1907 Hague Convention No. IV Respecting the Laws and Customs of War on Land, which had not been ratified by Germany, had become part of customary international law by 1939 (some 32 years later) and had thus become binding on Germany and its nationals.

It should also be noted that the phrase "international law" does not seem to have been used in U.S. courts prior to 1813, when it appeared in The Aurora, 2 F. Cas. 227, 228 (D.C.D.R.I. 1813) (No. 660). The "law of nations" was used earlier to identify what we term international law, although most cases using the phrase and applying the law of nations had in mind what we term customary international law as opposed to treaty-based international law. Ever since, courts in the United States have used the phrases "international law" and the "law of nations" interchangeably. *See, e.g.*, JORDAN J. PAUST, INTERNATIONAL LAW AS LAW OF THE UNITED STATES 3, 17–18, *passim* (2 ed. 2003).

Introductory Remarks of Professor Van Dyke*

International law has been evolving for centuries to provide a framework for international and transnational activities. Like other areas of the law, one of its major purposes is to allow participants to deal with each other with some level of predictability and, thus, to reduce misunderstandings and avoid conflicts and confrontations.

1. By signatory we mean those states or other entities that are parties to an international agreement, for example, upon ratification as opposed to some initial signature prior to ratification.

* Extract reprinted with permission from Jon M. Van Dyke, *The Role of Customary International Law in Federal and State Court Litigation,* 26 U. HAWAII L. REV. 361 (2004).

But international law is a more primitive system of law than the domestic legal systems found in advanced nations. It does not have a legislative body with the capacity to enact laws binding on all nations, an executive branch or military or police force that can enforce the laws that do exist, or judicial tribunals that have broad jurisdiction or the power to issue binding and enforceable decrees. Although early versions of such bodies can be found in the United Nations and in emerging regional organizations, the process of constructing institutions that enjoy widespread support and can meet the challenges presented by a deeply divided world is just beginning.

Some have argued that because international law cannot be enforced by a superior body it is not law at all. But most commentators contend that because most states and nations follow international law most of the time, and because those that violate its norms frequently suffer consequences, it should be viewed as a system of law.

International law is less developed than other systems of law because the larger and more powerful nations do not always accept that it is in their interest to subordinate their self-interest to an international or multinational goal. Although smaller nations will see the benefit of an international structure that protects the weak against the powerful, the stronger nations do not always agree that such a structure is beneficial. The foundations of international law have always been, therefore, reciprocity and enlightened self-interest. "For example, the increasing cost of war, or perhaps the infeasibility of a major war, makes a legal settlement of conflicting interests more attractive. At any rate, war costs diminish the types of interests over which states are willing to fight a war." WERNER LEVI, CONTEMPORARY INTERNATIONAL LAW: A CONCISE INTRODUCTION 4 (2nd ed. 1991).

One of the primary sources of international law is customary international law. The "practices" of states are usually found in actions taken by a country, but sometimes can be discovered in the statements their diplomats or leaders issue or in their votes at international organizations or diplomatic conferences. To become "custom," a practice must have the widespread (but not necessarily universal) support of countries concerned with the issue and must usually have continued for a period of time long enough to signify understanding and acquiescence. Occasionally a regional custom can emerge, if the countries of a certain part of the world order their affairs in a certain manner. Customary international law can emerge from agreements, practices, and understandings to become universally obligatory. In recent years, it has become accepted that some principles of customary international law are so important that they are called "peremptory norms" or "*jus cogens*" (commanding law) of international law, and that no nation is permitted to depart from these principles. *See, e.g.*, Section 1 F 3, *infra*. Among these norms are the prohibitions on aggression, genocide, crimes against humanity, slavery, extrajudicial murder, prolonged arbitrary detention, torture, and racial discrimination.

Although most historical summaries of the development of international law focus on its growth in Europe and the West, the reality is more complex. Practices governing interactions among nations and peoples also developed in Asia and elsewhere, and these norms have been merging with those that came to be accepted in the West.

Statute of the International Court of Justice, Article 38

1. The Court, whose function is to decide in accordance with international law such disputes as are submitted to it, shall apply:

(a) international conventions, whether general or particular, establishing rules expressly recognized by the contesting states;

(b) international custom, as evidence of a general practice accepted as law;

(c) the general principles of law recognized by civilized nations;

(d) ... judicial decisions and the teachings of the most highly qualified publicists of the various nations, as subsidiary means for the determination of rules of law.

2. This provision shall not prejudice the power of the Court to decide a case *ex aequo et bono*, if the parties agree thereto.

Restatement of the Foreign Relations Law of the United States § 102 (3 ed. 1987)

(1) A rule of international law is one that has been accepted as such by the international community of states

(a) in the form of customary law;

(b) by international agreement; or

(c) by derivation from general principles common to the major legal systems of the world.

(2) Customary international law results from a general and consistent practice of states followed by them from a sense of legal obligation.

(3) International agreements create law for the states parties thereto and may lead to the creation of customary international law when such agreements are intended for adherence by states generally and are in fact widely accepted.

(4) General principles common to the major legal systems, even if not incorporated or reflected in customary international law or international agreement, may be invoked as supplementary rules of international law where appropriate.

Notes and Questions

1. How are the I.C.J. Statute and the U.S. Restatement different? Does Article 38 (1) (b) of the Statute use the word "states"? The phrase "contesting states" appears in Article 38 (1) (a) because only states can be parties to cases before the I.C.J., although advisory jurisdiction can extend to requests

from various U.N. entities such as the Security Council and General Assembly. Note that Article 38 (1) (c) and (d) use the term "nations".

2. What is the difference between the I.C.J. Statute Article 38 (1) (c) and the Restatement Section 102 (1) (c)? Is Article 38 (1) (c) of the Statute consistent with the Restatement Section 102 (4)? Is Section 102 (4) of the Restatement conditioned by 102 (1)? How can general principles of domestic law be "rules" of international law if they are not incorporated or reflected in customary international law or international agreements?

3. The United States has argued that a norm concerning fair, prompt and adequate compensation for property expropriated by a state is now a norm of customary international law reflected in a web of bilateral international agreements to which the United States is a party (i.e., that such bilateral agreements reflect current general practice and general patterns of legal expectation). Is this claim consistent with Article 38 (1) (b) of the Statute? with the Restatement Section 102 (3)? Which approach seems correct?

4. It should be noted that "usage" as such is merely long-term practice, not law (unless combined with relevant patterns of legal expectation or *opinio juris*). Further, the word "comity" is not the equivalent of law or legal obligation. Something granted as a matter of comity is granted basically as a matter of grace or discretion. *See* Verlinden B.V. v. Central Bank of Nigeria, 461 U.S. 480, 486 (1983); The Paquete Habana, 175 U.S. 677, 719 (1900) (Fuller, C.J., dissenting) (disagreeing that relevant treatment of alien vessels was required as a matter of law and noting the distinction that if it is "essentially an act of grace, and not a matter of right.... It is, said Sir William Scott, 'a rule of comity only, and not of legal decision.' "); *cf.* Hilton v. Guyot, 159 U.S. 113, 163–64 (1895); Russian Republic v. Cibrario, 235 N.Y. 255, 139 N.E. 259 (Ct. of App. N.Y. 1923).

5. The International Court of Justice (I.C.J.) is the judicial branch of the United Nations. Its permanent seat is at The Hague, The Netherlands. The Court consists of fifteen jurists reflective of the varied legal systems and regions of the world, plus any *ad hoc* judges sitting on a particular case (since States have a right to the appointment of an *ad hoc* judge of their nationality in a case to which they are a party if there is not already a judge of their nationality among the fifteen members of the Court. I.C.J. Stat. art. 31 (2)-(3)). The jurisdiction of the I.C.J. is both advisory (of U.N. bodies) and contentious (concerning cases between states), as specified in its Statute. Article 59 of the Statute states that decisions are binding only on "parties in respect of that particular case," but the Court often cites its prior opinions in other cases. Only states can be parties in cases before the I.C.J., although primary organs of the United Nations (such as the Security Council and General Assembly) can request advisory opinions. See U.N. Charter, arts. 7, 92–93, 96. How might decisions of the I.C.J. ultimately be enforced? See *id.* art. 94.

The I.C.J. exercises "consensual" jurisdiction, because countries must agree to participate in cases before it. Such agreement can exist either through (1) a special *ad hoc* agreement between the parties as to the particular dispute at issue, (2) a declaration of compulsory jurisdiction stating that a country will allow the Court to adjudicate any dispute with another country that also accepts such compulsory jurisdiction (a general declaration of acceptance), or (3) a treaty that states, for example, that disputes over the interpretation or implementation of the treaty will be resolved by the Court (a special declaration of acceptance). If the Court decides it has jurisdiction over a dispute by virtue of the second or third avenues, it can proceed to decide a case even if one party refuses to participate. *See, e.g.*, Fisheries Jurisdiction Case (United Kingdom v. Iceland), 1974 I.C.J. 3; Case Concerning United States Diplomatic and Consular Staff in Tehran (United States v. Iran), 1980 I.C.J. 3; Case Concerning Military and Paramilitary Activities In and Against Nicaragua (Nicaragua v. United States), 1986 I.C.J. 14.

B. Definitions and Actors

Is there an adequate definition of international law? Who are the actors in the international legal process? What type of actors can have rights or duties under international law? Some of the following materials offer inconsistent views concerning the nature, definition, and reach of international law. For example, the opinion of Judge Edwards in *Tel-Oren* claiming the individuals do not have duties under international law is out of line with significant trends in decision. Which views seem more realistic? What sort of consequences might result from incomplete or less realistic viewpoints?

THE S.S. LOTUS (FRANCE v. TURKEY)

[1927] P.C.I.J., Ser. A, No. 10, at 4, 18.

International law governs relations between independent States. The rules of law binding upon States therefore emanate from their own free will as expressed in conventions or by usages generally accepted as expressing principles of law and established in order to regulate the relations between these co-existing independent communities or with a view to the achievement of common aims. Restrictions upon the independence of States cannot therefore be presumed.

[Having decided that international law was not violated in this case, the Permanent Court of International Justice (P.C.I.J.), the predecessor to the International Court of Justice (I.C.J.), added that it did not have to decide "[w]hat pecuniary reparations are due to M. Demons," a French individual that France had argued had been arrested by Turkey in violation of international law, a statement that implies that individuals can have rights under international law. The Court had ruled that no rule of international law prohibited Turkey from exercising jurisdiction over Lieutenant Demons with respect to negligence on board a French vessel that caused the vessel to collide with a Turkish vessel and led to the death of several persons on board the Turkish vessel. We consider this case again in connection with objective territorial jurisdiction in Chapter 3 and also in Chapter 6.]

TEL–OREN, *ET AL.* v. LIBYAN ARAB REPUBLIC, *ET AL.*

726 F.2d 774 (D.C.Cir.1984).

PER CURIAM opinion.

Plaintiffs in this action, mostly Israeli citizens, are survivors and representatives of persons murdered in an armed attack on a civilian bus in Israel in March 1978. They filed suit for compensatory and punitive damages in the District Court, naming as defendants the Libyan Arab Republic, the Palestine Liberation Organization, the Palestine Information Office, the National Association of Arab Americans, and the Palestine Congress of North America.

In their complaint, plaintiffs alleged that defendants were responsible for multiple tortious acts in violation of the law of nations, treaties of the United States, and criminal laws of the United States, as well as the common law. Jurisdiction was claimed under four separate statutes: 28 U.S.C. § 1331 (federal question jurisdiction); 28 U.S.C. § 1332 (diversity jurisdiction); 28 U.S.C. § 1350 [the Alien Tort Claims Act (ATCA), which some term the Alien Tort Statute (ATS), see Chapter 2, Section 2 D 2] (providing jurisdiction over actions by an alien alleging a tort committed in violation of the law of nations or a treaty of the United States); and the Foreign Sovereign Immunities Act of 1976, 28 U.S.C. §§ 1330, 1602–1611. For purposes of our jurisdictional analysis, we assume plaintiffs' allegations to be true.

The District Court dismissed the action both for lack of subject matter jurisdiction and as barred by the applicable statute of limitations. Hanoch Tel–Oren v. Libyan Arab Republic, 517 F. Supp. 542 (D.D.C. 1981). Plaintiffs appeal the District Court's rulings on two of their claimed jurisdictional bases, 28 U.S.C. §§ 1331, 1350, and on the statute of limitations issue.

We affirm the dismissal of this action. [There are] separate concurring statements of Judge Edwards, Judge Bork, and Senior Judge Robb, indicating different reasons for affirming the result reached by the District Court. [Editors' note: In Chapter 2, concerning human rights litigation, students will revisit points made by Judge Edwards and discover some of those made by Judge Bork. Judge Robb sought to dismiss under a claim that the political question required that result.]

EDWARDS, J., concurring

. . . I do not believe the law of nations imposes the same responsibility or liability on non-state actors, such as the PLO, as it does on states and persons acting under color of state law. Absent direction from the Supreme Court on the proper scope of the obscure section 1350, I am therefore not prepared to extend . . . construction of section 1350 to encompass this case. . . .

. . . The Palestine Liberation Organization is not a recognized state, and it does not act under color of any recognized state's law. . . .

Plaintiffs in the case before us do not allege facts to show that official or state-initiated torture is implicated in this action. Nor do I think they could, so long as the PLO is not a recognized member of the community of nations.... [opinion's fn. 21: ... To qualify as a state under international law, there must be a people, a territory, a government and a capacity to enter into relations with other states....]

The question therefore arises whether to ... incorporate [within 28 U.S.C. § 1350] torture perpetrated by a party other than a recognized state or one of its officials acting under color of state law. The extension would require this court to venture out of the comfortable realm of established international law ... in which states are the actors. It would require an assessment of the extent to which international law imposes not only rights but also obligations on individuals. It would require a determination of where to draw a line between persons or groups who are or are not bound by dictates of international law, and what the groups look like. Would terrorists be liable, because numerous international documents recognize their existence and proscribe their acts? *See generally* R. LILLICH, TRANSNATIONAL TERRORISM: CONVENTIONS AND COMMENTARY (1982) (reprinting numerous international anti-terrorism accords); see also Lauterpacht, *The Subjects of the Law of Nations* (pt. 1), 63 L.Q. REV. 438, 444–45 (discussing international obligations of insurgents). Would all organized political entities be obliged to abide by the law of nations? Would everybody be liable? ...

While I do not believe that international harmony exists on the liability of private individuals, it is worth noting that a number of jurists and commentators either have assumed or urged that the individual is a subject of international law. See Lopes v. Reederei Richard Schroder, 225 F. Supp. 292, 297 (E.D.Pa.1963) (violation of law of nations, in section 1350, means, "at least a violation by one or more individuals"); Adra v. Clift, 195 F. Supp. 857 (D.Md.1961) (individual violation of law of nations); Judgment of the International Military Tribunal, 22 Trial of the Major War Criminals Before the International Military Tribunal, Proceedings, 441, 465–66 (1948), 41 AM. J. INT'L L. 172, 220–21 (1947) (international law "imposes duties and liabilities upon individuals as well as upon States"), *reprinted in* The Nurnberg Trial 1946, 6 F.R.D. 69, 110–11 (1947); G.A. Res. 95, U.N. Doc. A/64/Add. 1, at 188 (1947) (affirming Nuremberg principles).... Confusion arises because the term "individual liability" denotes two distinct forms of liability. The first, now well-implanted in the law of nations, refers to individuals acting under color of state law. Commentators routinely place the origin of this development at the Nuremberg Trials ... and it was in this context that the International Military Tribunal wrote of individual responsibility for war crimes. The second, currently less-established meaning addresses the responsibility of individuals acting separate from any state's authority or direction....

Even in the truly private arena there is support for the concept of individual responsibility. Inferences from case law suggest that courts over the years have toyed with the notion of truly individual liability both under section 1350 and more generally. Section 1350 case law, unfortunately, is sparse. Other than *Filartiga* [630 F.2d 876 (2d Cir. 1980)], only two cases brought under section 1350 have established jurisdiction. Both involved private-party defendants. In one, Bolchos v. Darrel, 1 Bee 74, 3 Fed. Cas. 810 (D.S.C. 1795) (No. 1607), a predecessor to section 1350 provided jurisdiction for an action, grounded on a treaty violation, involving a title dispute concerning neutral property on a captured enemy vessel. It is worthwhile to note that, although *Bolchos* involved a treaty obligation, at the time of the *Bolchos* case individual defendants were in fact found to violate the law of nations, although not necessarily in actions based on section 1350. *See, e.g.*, United States v. Smith, 18 U.S. (5 Wheat.) 153 ... (1820) (indictment for crime of piracy, as defined by the law of nations). In a more recent case, Adra v. Clift, 195 F. Supp. 857 (D.Md.1961), an individual was in fact found to have violated the law of nations, and section 1350 jurisdiction was thereby established. The action ... involved a child custody suit between two aliens; the court found that defendant's wrongful withholding of custody was a tort and that her misuse of passports to bring the child into the United States violated international law. To reach this conclusion on individual responsibility, the court relied primarily on one commentator, who asserted that some acts violate the law of nations and may be prosecuted when committed by a private offender, *Adra*, 195 F. Supp. at 863–64 (*citing* 1 C. HYDE [INTERNATIONAL LAW CHIEFLY AS INTERPRETED AND APPLIED BY THE UNITED STATES (2d ed. rev. 1945)] § 11A, at 33–34); it then leapt to a conclusion that passport violations are among such acts. *Id.* at 864–65. As I shall demonstrate, *infra*, Hyde's position, while certainly compelling, is not so widely accepted doctrinally or practically as to represent the consensus among nations.

That the individual's status in international law has been in flux since section 1350 was drafted explains in part the current mix of views about private party liability. Through the 18th century and into the 19th, writers and jurists believed that rules of international law bound individuals as well as states. *See, e.g.*, United States v. Smith, 18 U.S. (5 Wheat.) 153 ... (1820) (piracy violates law of nations; individual liable); Respublica v. DeLongchamps, 1 U.S. (1 Dall.) 111 ... (1784) (assault on French consul-general violates law of nations; individual liable); 4 BLACKSTONE'S COMMENTARIES 66–73 (Welsby ed. 1854) (recounting various offenses against law of nations, committed by private persons, punishable under English statutory law); *see generally* Dickinson, ... [*The Law of Nations as Part of the National Law of the United States* (pt. 1), 101 U. PA. L. REV. 26 (1952)], at 26–27, 29–30; Dickinson, *The Law of Nations as Part of the National Law of the United States* (pt. 2), 101 U. PA. L. REV. 792, 792–95 (1953); Korowicz, *The Problem of the International Personality of Individuals*, 50 AM. J. INT'L L. 533, 534 (1956). In the 19th century, the view emerged that states alone were subjects of international law, and they alone were able to assert rights and be held to duties devolved from the law of nations. Under that view—which became firmly entrenched both in doctrine and in practice, see Korowicz, *supra*, 50 AM.

J. INT'L L. at 535, 541—individual rights existed only as rights of the state, see Lauterpacht, *The Subjects of the Law of Nations* (Pt. 1), 63 L.Q. REV. 438, 439–40 (1947), and could be asserted, defended or withdrawn by the state.... [Editors' note: After reviewing the applicable legal principles, Judge Edwards reached the conclusion that the plaintiffs' complaint must be dismissed because in his view the actions of private parties unconnected with a government to terrorize and murder other individuals did not constitute a violation of international law.]

RESTATEMENT OF THE FOREIGN RELATIONS LAW OF THE UNITED STATES § 101 (3 ed. 1987)**

International law, as used in this Restatement, consists of rules and principles of general application dealing with the conduct of states and of international organizations and with their relations *inter se*, as well as with some of their relations with persons, whether natural or juridical.

Part II—Persons in International Law

The principal persons under international law are states ... individuals and private juridical entities can have any status, capacity, rights, or duties given them by international law or agreement, and increasingly individuals and private entities have been accorded such aspects of personality in varying measures. For example, international law and numerous international agreements now recognize human rights of individuals and sometimes give individuals remedies before international bodies.... Individuals may be held liable for offenses against international law, such as piracy, war crimes, or genocide.

Notes and Questions

1. In view of the preceding materials, how would you rule on Aktor's claims in paras. a and b in the Introductory Problem?

2. In *Tel–Oren*, Judge Bork also embraced the theory of a few textwriters that rights and duties under international law are those of states alone. See 726 F.2d at 805–06, 817 (Bork, J.: "the general rule that international law imposes duties only on states and on their agents or officials ... international law protections of persons [exist] solely in terms of state obligations".... " 'As a rule, the subjects of the rights and duties arising from the Law of Nations are States solely and exclusively.' "). Professor Paust has responded: "Interestingly, even some of the 'supporting' material that [Judge Bork] used contains sufficient qualifying language to alert one to the fact that international law does address private rights and duties. Although Judge Edwards also argued that the 'states alone' view became 'firmly entrenched' by the early twentieth century, such a view was not correct, and was always challenged by other textwriters of that period, if not in relevant judicial decisions. Additionally, the inhibiting myth that Judge Bork would resurrect had rested on theories about the functioning of law at the state-to-state level, not the trends in actual decision at the domestic

level. In sum, it was, and is, simply not true that individuals could not benefit directly from international law or be subject either to civil or criminal sanctions for violations of international law." JORDAN J. PAUST, INTERNATIONAL LAW AS LAW OF THE UNITED STATES 235–36, with supporting cites at 317–92 (2 ed. 2003). Professor Paust's treatise also documents historic recognition and trends in use of human rights in the United States from the early 1700s. See *id.* at 195–223, 240–84, *passim*. These historic recognitions demonstrate that far too common notions that human rights precepts are relatively new to international law (*e.g.*, since the end of World War II) and did not involve rights against one's own state are simplistic and false.

In La Abra Silver Mining Co. v. United States, 175 U.S. 423, 458, 461 (1899), it was recognized at the turn of the century that although claims before a U.S.-Mexican Commission were those of governments, a private company had a claim of right under a "treaty and the award of the commission" and such rights were undoubtedly "susceptible of judicial determination" domestically. Contrary to such a recognition by the Supreme Court, some have assumed that the fact that an individual might not be able to present a claim directly at the international level (*e.g.*, through diplomatic negotiation or before an international institution) meant that the individual had no claim of right under international law.

In 1907, an Opinion of the Attorney General recognized that a Texas dredging company had violated a treaty and was liable to other private actors in Mexico. See 26 Op. Att'y Gen. 250 (1907).

3. In 1795, an Opinion of U.S. Attorney General Bradford recognized:

> "It is stated ... that certain American citizens trading to the coast of Africa [in Sierra Leone] ... voluntarily joined, conducted, aided, and abetted a French fleet in attacking the settlement, and plundering or destroying the property of British subjects on that coast.... [A]cts of hostility committed by American citizens against such as are in amity with us, being in violation of a treaty, and against the public peace, are offenses against the United States ... and, as such, are punishable by indictment in the district or circuit courts.... [T]here can be no doubt that the company or individuals who have been injured by these acts of hostility have a remedy by civil suit in the courts of the United States; jurisdiction being expressly given to these courts [under what is now 28 U.S.C. § 1350, the Alien Tort Claims Act (ATCA)] in all cases where an alien sues for a tort only, in violation of the law of nations, or a treaty of the United States...." 1 Op. Att'y Gen. 57, 58–59 (1795).

Does this historic recognition of the Attorney General comply with the Restatement's notion of "international law"? Would you choose a different definition of international law?

4. In United States v. Haun, 26 F. Cas. 227, 231 (C.C.S.D.Ala.1860) (No. 15,329), Justice Campbell recognized: "Unquestionably, President Jefferson, when he congratulated congress at the approach of the period at which they might interpose their authority constitutionally to withdraw the citizens of the United States from all further violations of human rights which have been so long continued on the unoffending inhabitants of Africa ... supposed that something beyond a regulation of commerce was concerned in the action to be taken ...," *e.g.*, the Act of 1808 punishing the

importation of Africans as slaves and the purchasing of them from the importer. Note the recognition of private violations of human rights, *e.g.*, by "citizens of the United States." President Jefferson made such remarks in his Sixth Annual Message to Congress in 1806. See PAUST, *supra* at 202.

5. Blackstone had written in the 1760s:

> The law of nations is a system of rules, deducible by natural reason, and *established by* universal consent among the civilized *inhabitants* of the world; in order to decide all disputes, to regulate all ceremonies and civilities, and to ensure the observance of justice and good faith, in that intercourse which must frequently occur between two or more independent states, and the individuals belonging to each.

4 WILLIAM BLACKSTONE, COMMENTARIES ON THE LAWS OF ENGLAND 66 (1765–1769) (emphasis added). Nonetheless, it is widely recognized that relevant expectations need not be "universal" and that "consent" is not required. *See, e.g.*, J.L. BRIERLY, THE LAW OF NATIONS 55 (5th ed. 1955) ("a customary rule is observed, not because it has been consented to, but because it is believed to be binding ... [and such] does not depend ... on the approval of the individual or the state...."); *id.* at 61–62 (adding: "what is sought for is a general recognition among states of a certain practice as obligatory."); PAUST, *supra* at 3–5, 18–19.

6. Clearly some perpetrators of international crime are private actors. *See, e.g.*, United States v. Arjona, 120 U.S. 479 (1887) (counterfeiting of foreign currency); United States v. The Cargo of the Brig Malek Adhel, 43 U.S. (2 How.) 210, 232, 235 (1844) (piracy); United States v. Morris, 39 U.S. (14 Pet.) 464 (1840) (slave trade); United States v. The Garonne, 36 U.S. (11 Pet.) 73 (1837) (same); United States v. Ortega, 24 U.S. (11 Wheat.) 467 (1826) (violence against *chargé d' affaires*); United States v. Smith, 18 U.S. (5 Wheat.) 153 (1820) (piracy); Talbot v. Janson, 3 U.S. (3 Dall.) 133, 159 (1795) (Iredell, J., concurring) ("all piracies and trespasses committed against the general law of nations"); Respublica v. De Longchamps, 1 U.S. (1 Dall.) 111, 116–17 (1784) (assault on foreign consul); Charge to Grand Jury, 30 F. Cas. 1026 (C.C.D.Ga.1859) (No. 18,269a) (slave trade); United States v. Smith, 27 F. Cas. 1192 (C.C.N.Y. 1806) (No. 16,342) (private war, breach of neutrality); United States v. Liddle, 26 F. Cas. 936 (C.C.D.Pa.1808) (No. 15,598) (assault on a foreign minister (secretary of a legation)); United States v. Haun, 26 F. Cas. 227 (C.C.S.D.Ala.1860) (No. 15,329) (slave trade, also recognized as "violations of human rights" by private individuals); United States v. Hand, 26 F. Cas. 103 (C.C.D.Pa.1810) (No. 15,297) (assault on *chargé d' affaires*); Henfield's Case, 11 F. Cas. 1099 (C.C.D.Pa.1793) (No. 6,360) (breach of neutrality); 1 Op. Att'y Gen. 68, 69 (1797) (violation of territorial rights); 1 Op. Att'y Gen. 61, 62 (1796) (breach of neutrality); 1 Op. Att'y Gen. 57, 58 (1795) ("acts of hostility," breach of neutrality, offense "against the public peace"); ALBERICO GENTILI, DE JURE BELLI LIBRI TRES (1612) (lst ed. 1598); EMERICH DE VATTEL, LE DROIT DES GENS (LAW OF NATIONS) (1758) 464–65 (J. Chitty ed. 1883); 4 WILLIAM BLACKSTONE, COMMENTARIES ON THE LAWS OF ENGLAND 68 (1765); Jordan J. Paust, *Federal Jurisdiction Over Extraterritorial Acts of Terrorism and Nonimmunity for Foreign Violators of International Law Under the FSIA and the Act of State Doctrine*, 23 VA. J. INT'L L. 191, 211–12 ns.76–80 (1983) (violence against ambassadors, pirates, poison-

ers, assassins, incendiaries, banditti, brigands, slave trade, breaches of neutrality). Additionally, offenses against human rights recognized in particular treaties often reach private perpetrators (as well as private victims). *United States v. Haun* is an interesting case in this regard. It is addressed in more detail in Chapter 2.

Concerning private actor responsibility for international crimes, see also the many relevant international criminal law treaties and instruments in the Documents Supplement.

7. Under Article 101 of the 1982 Convention on the Law of the Sea (U.N. LOSC), "piracy" includes:

> "(a) any illegal acts of violence or detention, or any act of depredation, committed for private ends by the crew or the passengers of a private ship or a private aircraft, and directed:
>
> (i) on the high seas, against another ship or aircraft, or against persons or property on board such ship or aircraft.... "

Can the LOSC definition reach acts of private (nonstate) perpetrators against private (nonstate) victims on board a private vessel? If so, can international law deal with the relations of persons between or among themselves?

In the *S.S. Lotus* case, Judge Moore added with respect to the nature of piracy: "Piracy by law of nations, in its jurisdictional aspects, is *sui generis*. Though statutes may provide for its punishment, it is an offense against the law of nations; and as the scene of the pirate's operations is the high seas, which is not the right or duty of any nation to police, he is denied the protection of the flag which he may carry, and is treated as an outlaw, as the enemy of all mankind—*hostis humani generis*—whom any nation may in the interest of all capture and punish...." From the above, is piracy merely a "relation" between a state and an individual, within the meaning of Section 101 of the Restatement?

8. If a private individual can sue another private individual in a domestic tribunal to recover property taken by an act of piracy, or for money damages with respect to property destroyed by an act of piracy in violation of international law, does such a reach and application of international law fit within the statement in the *S.S. Lotus* case? Did the Court state that international law only governs the relations between states? the approach of Judge Edwards in *Tel-Oren*? the Restatement's definitional scheme? If not the reach of international law, its application in domestic fora? For an example of such a case, see Davison v. Seal–Skins, 7 F. Cas. 192 (C.C.D.Conn.1835); *see also* 3 Op. Att'y Gen. 484, 490 (1839); JORDAN J. PAUST, INTERNATIONAL LAW AS LAW OF THE UNITED STATES 300 n.526 (2 ed. 2003).

Further, since piracy and war crimes could be committed by private individuals in the 18th, 19th and 20th centuries, was Judge Edwards correct when he stated that the view that "states alone ... were able to ... be held to duties devolved from the law of nations" had become firmly entrenched in the 20th century?

9. Some state-oriented writers, in particular those writing in the 20th century before Word War II, have assumed that a proper definition of international law focuses exclusively on rules applicable between states

within the international legal process, *i.e.*, that international law is merely a system of rules binding on states in their relations with each other. *See, e.g.*, 1 HACKWORTH, DIGEST OF INTERNATIONAL LAW 1 (1940); J.L. BRIERLY, THE LAW OF NATIONS 1 (5 ed. 1955); 1 L. OPPENHEIM, INTERNATIONAL LAW: A TREATISE 362–69 (2 ed. 1912). Such an approach, often based in British positivism (which tends to focus on law as abstract rules and then as rules coming down from the "state" or state elites to the populace and/or law based merely on the "consent" of states), was always opposed and never universally accepted. *See, e.g.*, OPPENHEIM, *supra* at 367 ("Several writers," including Bonfils, Bluntschli, Fiore, and Martens, opposed such a theory even in the early 20th Century). Proponents normally claimed that individuals were not "subjects" of international law, but might be "objects" of such law (*e.g.*, if in an international agreement states consented to a duty to protect certain individuals or to prosecute them, the duty was that of state signatories and individuals had no corresponding rights or duties). How is such a definitional orientation different from that of the U.S. Restatement? Given the existence of human rights law and international criminal law, which more adequately reflects reality?

10. Concerning the status of international organizations as actors, see also FREDERIC L. KIRGIS, INTERNATIONAL ORGANIZATIONS IN THEIR LEGAL SETTING 1–53 (2 ed. 1993).

11. *Nations*. Technically, the word "nation" is different than the word "state," although some writers mix the terms. The state-oriented focus to international law addressed in *Tel-Oren* is ahistorial, since international law was applied early in U.S. history also to relations among nations or to states and nations. The state-oriented focus fails to reflect the fact that a "nation" (or a relevant group of people) need not have a territorial base or its own state, that the "law of nations" has never been so state-oriented, and, for example, that states like the United States and Canada have had treaties with various Indian nations and consider these to be part of international law. Also *see generally*, J.L. BRIERLY, THE LAW OF NATIONS 118–19 (5 ed. 1955); H. WHEATON, ELEMENTS OF INTERNATIONAL LAW 27 (2 ed. 1880); Siegfried Wiessner, *Rights and Status of Indigenous Peoples: A Global Comparative and International Legal Analysis*, 12 HARV. H.R. J. 57 (1999); United States v. Kusche, 56 F.Supp. 201, 207 (S.D.Cal.1944). In 1873, some Modoc Indians were convicted in a U.S. military tribunal for violations of the laws of war, thus demonstrating the reach of international law to nations and individuals. See 14 Ops. Att'y Gen. 249 (1873).

12. *Peoples*. Does Section 101 of the Restatement reflect the fact that the right of self-determination which has been recognized, for example, in Article 1 (2) of the United Nations Charter, as well as in Article 1 of the 1966 International Covenant on Civil and Political Rights (ICCPR) and Article 1 of the 1966 International Covenant on Economic, Social, and Cultural Rights (ICESCR), is that of "peoples" and not states? Here, we also note that there can be many forms and permissible consequences of processes of self-determination, but that they are related directly to rights of a given people. *See also* Jon M. Van Dyke, Camen Di Amore–Siah, Gerald W. Berkley–Coats, *Self-Determination for Nonself-governing Peoples and for Indigenous Peoples: The Cases of Guam and Hawaii*, 18 HAW. L. REV. 623 (1996), adding that native or indigenous peoples have a right of self-

determination under international law that is different from the right of self-determination that non-self-governing peoples have.

13. Unrealistic Public—Private Dichotomy. Among the critiques by feminist scholars of certain conceptualizations of international law, one finds criticism of the emphasis that some place on so-called "public" and state-oriented conduct or processes and certain consequences that might follow. For example, consider the following: "The structure of the international legal order reflects a male perspective and ensures its continued dominance. The primary subjects of international law are states and, increasingly, international organizations. In both states and international organizations the invisibility of women is striking. Power structures within governments are overwhelmingly masculine: women have significant positions of power in very few states, and in those where they do, their numbers are minuscule. Women are either unrepresented or under represented in the national and global decision-making processes....

> "Since the primary subjects of international law are states, it is sometimes assumed that the impact of international law falls on the state and not directly on individuals. In fact, the application of international law does affect individuals, which has been recognized by the International Court in several cases. International jurisprudence assumes that international law norms directed at individuals within states are universally applicable and neutral. It is not recognized, however, that such principles may impinge differently on men and women; consequently, women's experiences of the operation of these laws tend to be silenced or discounted.
>
> The normative structure of international law has allowed issues of particular concern to women to be either ignored or undermined. For example, modern international law rests on and reproduces various dichotomies between the public and private spheres, and the "public" sphere is regarded as the province of international law. One such distinction is between public international law, the law governing the relations between nation-states, and private international law, the rules about conflicts between national legal systems. Another is the distinction between matters of international "public" concern and matters "private" to states that are considered within their domestic jurisdiction, in which the international community has no recognized legal interest. Yet another is the line drawn between law and other forms of "private" knowledge such as morality.
>
> At a deeper level one finds a public/private dichotomy based on gender. One explanation feminist scholars offer for the dominance of men and the male voice in all areas of power and authority in the western liberal tradition is that a dichotomy is drawn between the public sphere and the private or domestic one. The public realm of the work place, the law, economics, politics and intellectual and cultural life, where power and authority are exercised, is regarded as the natural province of men; while the private world of the home, the hearth and children is seen as the appropriate domain of women. The public/private distinction has a normative, as well as a descriptive, dimension. Traditionally, the two spheres are accorded asymmetrical value: greater

significance is attached to the public, male world than to the private, female one. The distinction drawn between the public and the private thus vindicates and makes natural the division of labor and allocation of rewards between the sexes. Its reproduction and acceptance in all areas of knowledge have conferred primacy on the male world and supported the dominance of men." Hilary Charlsworth, Christine Chinkin, Shelley Wright, *Feminist Approaches to International Law*, 85 AM. J. INT'L L. 613 (1991).

JORDAN J. PAUST, *THE OTHER SIDE OF RIGHT: PRIVATE DUTIES UNDER HUMAN RIGHTS LAW*

5 HARV. H.R. J. 51, 51–54, 56–61 (1992).

Today, it should be beyond doubt that private individuals can have duties under treaty-based and customary international law and such duties can recognizably implicate human rights. These general points have been affirmed in numerous judicial decisions and, more recently, by the United States executive branch. Increasingly, textwriters affirm that human rights law can place duties on private individuals and groups, not just on states. Thus, the issue is not whether treaties can bind private individuals but whether private duties can result from the language of a particular treaty even though there is no express mention of individuals or individual duties....

[H]uman rights instruments demonstrate the existence of private duties in at least two ways. First, provisions in various instruments explicitly affirm, or at least imply, that individuals can owe duties. Second, rights are generally set forth without any reference to those who owe a corresponding duty and can be understood to impose duties on individuals. Courts that limit the scope of application of human rights instruments by adding limiting words, such as "the state" or "state action," improperly insert terms that the treatymakers did not choose. In particular, United States courts that rely on "state action" read into international human rights law a phrase peculiar to the domestic law of the United States.

One can recognize both of these points when examining the Universal Declaration of Human Rights. Most of the Articles in the Declaration speak generally of the right of each person or of everyone without any mention of which person or entity might owe a corresponding duty. The implication of such language is that most of the human rights listed in the Declaration can be claimed not merely against the state but also against groups or individuals, *i.e.*, against private actors.

Such an implication is even more evident in the preamble of the Universal Declaration, which states: "This universal declaration of human rights ... [is proclaimed] a common standard of achievement for all peoples and all nations, to the end that every individual and every organ of society" shall strive to secure respect for and observance of the standards therein set forth. Article 1 recognizes that certain precepts should apply to private relations: all human beings "should act towards one another in a spirit of brotherhood." Furthermore, there is no mention of the state, state action or color of law when Article 28 proclaims that "[e]veryone is entitled to a social ... order in which the rights and freedoms set forth in this Declaration can be fully realized." Significantly, paragraph 1 of Article 29 also recognizes private, nonstate duties when it affirms: "Everyone has duties to the community...." Finally, Article 30 proclaims that nothing in the Declaration "may be interpreted as implying for any State, group or person any right to engage in any activity or to perform any act aimed at the destruction of any of the rights and freedoms set forth herein." Article 30 thus ties the rights and freedoms enumerated in the Declaration to private duties. The duties implied are duties not to engage in action aimed at the destruction of the human rights of others.... [The essay proceeds to address other human rights instruments.]

The growing panoply of treaties recognizing individual criminal responsibility for human rights violations affirms that individual duties exist with respect to human rights and, indeed, that the most serious forms of sanctions can attach to private violations of international law. There is simply no question whether the 1926 Slavery Convention; the Supplementary Convention on the Abolition of Slavery, the Slave Trade, and Institutions and Practices Similar to Slavery; the 1948 Convention on the Prevention and Punishment of the Crime of Genocide; the 1973 International Convention on the Suppression and Punishment of the Crime of Apartheid; and the 1979 International Convention Against the Taking of Hostages, for example, implicate human rights and attempt to regulate private (if not also public) actor behavior. Article IV of the Genocide Convention is quite specific: "Persons committing genocide ... shall be punished, whether they are constitutionally responsible rulers, public officials or private individuals." Additionally, the 1985 General Assembly Resolution on Measures to Prevent International Terrorism "[u]nequivocally condemns, as criminal, all acts, methods and practices of terrorism wherever and by whomever committed...." As with human rights instruments more generally, the proscriptions of the anti-terrorism resolution are not limited to activities of the state, state action or color of law....

Some human rights instruments do set certain limitations with respect to the scope of corresponding duties, at least in relation to the guarantee of particular rights....

Rarely is a human rights instrument directed, expressly or implicitly, merely to obligations of the state or government officials. Article 1, paragraph 1, of the 1984 Convention Against Torture and Other Cruel, Inhuman or Degrading Treatment or Punishment restricts the Convention's application to acts of torture committed "by or at the instigation of or with the consent or acquiescence of a public official or other person acting in an official capacity." The second paragraph of the article, however, implicitly recognizes that other acts of torture are covered in other human rights instruments, which, as noted above, can indeed reach private actor conduct. Article 1, paragraph 2, of the Convention Against Torture reads in pertinent part: "This article is without prejudice to any international instrument ... which does or may contain provisions of wider application."

Moreover, even if the person committing torture "by or at the instigation of or with the consent or acquiescence of" a public official is not a public official or "person acting in an official capacity," that person will nevertheless be covered by the Convention. Thus, even under this treaty one can recognize the possibility that private duties will be implicated. The same point follows with respect to the limitations found in the regional Inter–American Convention to Prevent and Punish Torture, the preamble of which also reaffirms "that *all* acts of torture or *any* other cruel, inhuman, or degrading treatment or punishment constitute an offense against human dignity ... and are violations of the fundamental human rights and freedoms proclaimed in the American Declaration ... and the Universal Declaration of Human Rights" (emphasis added).

Notes and Questions

1. When interpreting Article 7 of the International Covenant on Civil and Political Rights (ICCPR), the Human Rights Committee created by the Covenant declared: "Complaints about ill-treatment must be investigated.... Those found guilty must be held responsible, and the alleged victims must themselves have effective remedies at their disposal, including the right to obtain compensation." General Comment No. 7, para. 1, Report of the H.R. Comm., 37 U.N. GAOR, Supp. No. 40, Annex V, U.N. Doc. E/CN.4/Sub.2/Add.1/963 (1982). General Comment No. 20 (1992) replaced No. 7 and recognized that "it is not sufficient" merely to make violations "a crime" (para. 8), states should report "the provisions of their criminal law which penalize torture and cruel, inhuman and degrading treatment or punishment, specifying the penalties applicable to such acts, whether committed by public officials or other persons acting on behalf of the State, or by private persons. Those who violate article 7, whether by encouraging, ordering, tolerating or perpetrating prohibited acts, must be held responsible" (para. 13), states have a duty to afford protection against such acts "whether inflicted by people acting in their official capacity, outside their official capacity or in a private capacity" (para. 2), and "[a]mnesties are generally incompatible with" such duties and "States must not deprive individuals of the right to an effective remedy...." (para. 15), in International Human Rights Instruments, U.N. Doc. HRI/GEN/1 (4 Sept. 1992), at 29–32.

The preamble to the International Covenant on Civil and Political Rights (ICCPR) expressly affirms "that the individual, *having duties* to other individuals and to the community to which he belongs, *is under a responsibility* to strive for the promotion and observance of the rights recognized in the present Covenant." Thus, at a minimum, individuals have duties to not violate human rights. Article 5, paragraph 1, like Article 30 of the Universal Declaration, also affirms the lack of a right of "any ... group or person ... to engage in any activity or to perform any act aimed at the destruction of any of the rights and freedoms set forth" in the Covenant "or at their limitation to a greater extent than is provided," and thus impliedly affirms the correlative duty of any group or person to not destroy or limit human rights.

Private duties are also expressly recognized in the preamble to and Articles 27–29 of the African Charter on Human and Peoples' Rights. The preamble to the American Declaration of the Rights and Duties of Man acknowledges that "the fulfillment of duty by each individual is a prerequisite to the rights of all. Rights and duties are interrelated...."; and Articles XXIX through XXXVIII set forth several express duties of private actors. Indeed, the very title of the American Declaration is an express affirmation of private human rights duties. The American Convention on Human Rights also contains express recognition in Article 32 (1) that "[e]very person has responsibilities to ... his community, and mankind," and Article 29 (a) commands that the treaty not be interpreted to allow "any ... group, or person to suppress the enjoyment or exercise of the rights and freedoms recognized ... or to restrict them to a greater extent than is provided for" in the Convention, and thus an implied duty of groups and persons exists to not suppress or restrict human rights. Article 17 of the European Convention for the Protection of Human Rights and Fundamental Freedoms contains a "group or person" provision similar to that in the International Covenant and the American Convention.

2. Is there any reason why duties of private individuals under international law cannot reach juridic persons such as corporations? For example, can corporations be responsible for violations of the laws of war, human rights law, international environmental standards, the law of the sea (see Chapter 6), air and space law (see Chapter 7)? Can corporate vessel owners be liable for infracting the law of nations? What types of sanctions are more likely, civil or criminal? Also *see generally* Wiwa v. Royal Dutch Petroleum Co., 226 F.3d 88, 92 (2d Cir. 2000) (human rights claims re: killing, imprisonment, torture); Weisshaus v. Swiss Bankers Ass'n, 225 F.3d 191 (2d Cir. 2000); Vietnam Ass'n for Victims of Agent Orange/Dioxin v. Dow Chemical Co. (*In re* Agent Orange Prod. Liab. Litg.), 373 F.Supp.2d 7 (E.D.N.Y. 2005); Estate of Rodriquez v. Drummond Co., Inc., 256 F.Supp.2d 1250 (N.D. Ala. 2003); Sinaltrainal v. Coca Cola Co., 256 F.Supp.2d 1345 (S.D. Fla. 2003); Presbyterian Church of Sudan v. Talisman Energy, Inc., 374 F.Supp.2d 331 (S.D.N.Y. 2005); *id.*, 244 F.Supp.2d at 305, 308–20, 328, 333 (S.D.N.Y. 2003); *In re* World War II Era Japanese Forced Labor Litigation, 114 F.Supp.2d 939 (N.D. Cal. 2000); Bodner, *et al.* v. Banque Paribas, *et al.*, 114 F.Supp.2d 117 (E.D.N.Y. 2000); *In re* Holocaust Victim Assets Litigation, 105 F.Supp.2d 139 (E.D.N.Y. 2000); Iwanowa v. Ford Motor Co., 57 F.Supp.2d 41, 60–62 (D.N.J. 1999), amended, 67 F.Supp.2d 424, 443–46 & n.26 (1999); Burger–Fischer v. DeGussa Corp., 65 F.Supp.2d 248, 272–73 (D.N.J. 1999); Eastman Kodak Co. v. Kavlin, 978 F.Supp. 1078, 1090–95 (S.D. Fla. 1997); Doe v. Unocal Corp., 963 F.Supp. 880 (C.D.Cal. 1997) (a case also addressed in Chapter 4 that involved claims made by farmers from Burma against a private corporation, UNOCAL, for violations of international law, including impermissible violence, torture, cruel and inhuman treatment, forced labor, slavery, and other crimes against humanity done in complicity with or through the Burmese military, intelligence

groups and police); Aquinda v. Texaco, Inc., 945 F.Supp. 625 (S.D.N.Y.1996) (a case dismissed on forum non conveniens grounds, and which dismissal was later reversed in Jota v. Texaco, Inc., 157 F.3d 153 (2d Cir.1998)); 26 Op. Att'y Gen. 250, 252–53 (1907) (agreeing with the International Water Boundary Commission that a private U.S. company had violated a treaty by dredging activities and explaining that the Alien Tort Claims act (ATCA), 28 U.S.C. § 1350, provided a rights of action against the company); RESTATEMENT § 213, Reporters' Note [hereinafter RN] 7 ("Multinational enterprises have been under increasing scrutiny by international bodies.... The product of this scrutiny thus far has been the development of codes of conduct for multinational enterprises."); 3 INTERNATIONAL CRIMINAL LAW: ENFORCEMENT 21, 104, 230 (M. Cherif Bassiouni ed. 1987); HENRY WHEATON, ELEMENTS OF INTERNATIONAL LAW 28 (6th ed. 1855) ("Private individuals, or public and private corporations may ..., incidentally, become the subjects of this law in regard to rights growing out of their international relations with foreign sovereigns and states, or their subjects and citizens.").

For a Japanese case, see Chapter 2, Section 1, Note 9 (ruling that a Japanese store was liable for discrimination against foreign nationals). For an English case, see Johnson v. Unisys, Ltd., [2001] UKHL/13, at [37] (22 Mar. 2001) (Lord Hoffmann) (explaining that responsibilities of private companies under domestic employment law are also "[s]ubject to observance of fundamental human rights"). In 1998, the Supreme Court of Canada also recognized that it is possible "for a non-state actor to perpetuate human rights violations on a scale amounting to persecution" within the reach of the Refugee Convention and, thus more generally, that private actors can engage in human rights violations. Pushpanathan v. Canada, 160 D.L.R. (4th) 193, 231 (S. Ct. Canada 1998), also noting a related practice of Australia. The Court addressed whether private violations of human rights fell within the scope of Article 1 F (c) of the Convention Relating to the Status of Refugees, 189 U.N.T.S. 150, which deals with denial of refugee protections to persons "guilty of acts contrary to the purposes and principles of the United Nations." The European Court of Human Rights has also stated that private "terrorist activities ... of individuals or groups ... are in clear disregard of human rights." See Ireland v. United Kingdom, Eur. Ct. H.R., Ser. A, No. 25, para. 149 (13 Dec. 1977). Other U.S. cases and opinions recognizing responsibilities of non-state or private entities include: Linder v. Portocarrero, 963 F.2d 332, 336–37 (11th Cir. 1992) (the Contras can be civilly liable for torture and unlawful killing); Klinghoffer v. S.N.C. Achille Lauro, 937 F.2d 44, 49 (2d Cir. 1991) (the PLO and various organizations can be civilly liable for murder); *id.*, 739 F.Supp. 854, 858, 860 (S.D.N.Y. 1990); Bolchos v. Darrel, 3 F. Cas. 810 (D.S.C. 1795) (No. 1,607); Jama v. U.S. I.N.S., 22 F.Supp.2d 353, 362–63 (D.N.J. 1998); Doe I v. Islamic Salvation Front, 993 F.Supp. 3, 8 (D.D.C. 1998); Mushikiwabo v. Barayagwiza, 1996 WL 164496 (S.D.N.Y. 1996); Adra v. Clift, 195 F.Supp. 857, 864 (D.Md. 1961); 1 Op. Att'y Gen. 57, 58 (1795); *see also* M'Grath v. Candalero, 16 F. Cas. 128 (D.C.D. S.C. 1794) (No. 8,810); Jordan J. Paust, *Human Rights Responsibilities of Private Corporations*, 35 VAND. J. TRANSNAT'L. L. 801 (2002).

3. Human rights law also applies during war or armed conflicts. *See, e.g.*, JEAN-MARIE HENCKAERTS & LOUISE DOSWALD-BECK, CUSTOMARY INTERNATIONAL

Humanitarian Law, Volume 1: Rules 299–306 (ICRC 2005); Jordan J. Paust, *Judicial Power to Determine the Status and Rights of Persons Detained Without Trial*, 44 Harv. Int'l L.J. 503, 505–06 n.5 (2003); Alfred de Zayas, *The Status of Guantanamo Bay and the Status of Detainees*, 37 U.B.C. L. Rev. 277, 281–82, 309–10 (2004); see also *Ex parte* Milligan, 71 U.S. (4 Wall.) 2, 119 (1866) ("human rights"); The Julia, 12 U.S. (8 Cranch) 181, 193 (1814) ("rights of humanity" pertain in war); Kadic v. Karadzic, 70 F.3d 232, 242–44 (2d Cir. 1995), *cert. denied*, 518 U.S. 1005 (1996); 11 Op. Att'y Gen. 19, 21 (1864) ("human rights"); U.N. G.A. Res. 59/182, Torture and other cruel, inhuman or degrading treatment or punishment, preamble and paras. 1–2, U.N. Doc. A/RES/59/182 (20 Dec. 2004).

KADIC v. KARADZIC

70 F.3d 232, 239–43 (2d Cir.1995), *cert. denied*, 518 U.S. 1005 (1996).

[Editors' note: this case significantly reaffirms the underlying theme of this section, that individuals who are not necessarily acting in connection with a state can be liable for violations of international law. Plaintiff-appellants filed claims under at least two federal statutes, one of which was the Alien Tort Claims Act (ATCA) also known as the Alien Tort Statute (ATS), 28 U.S.C. § 1350, which reads: "The district courts shall have original jurisdiction of any civil action by an alien for a tort only, committed in violation of the law of nations or a treaty of the United States." The statute was enacted by the first Congress in 1789 but was used only in a few cases prior to a landmark decision of the Second Circuit in *Filartiga v. Pena–Irala* in 1980 (see Chapter 2, Section 2 D 2, also containing a number of other cases and other portions of this case). Some professors may wish to assign the second part of *Kadic* (p. 391) also at this point in the course. Others may wish to assign the second part after taking up the Torture Victim Protection Act and other cases. Several relevant law of war documents are in the Documents Supplement.]

Newman, J.

Background

The plaintiffs-appellants are Croat and Muslim citizens of the internationally recognized nation of Bosnia–Herzegovina, formerly a republic of Yugoslavia. Their complaints, which we accept as true for purposes of this appeal, allege that they are victims, and representatives of victims, of various atrocities, including brutal acts of rape, forced prostitution, forced impregnation, torture, and summary execution, carried out by Bosnian–Serb military forces as part of a genocidal campaign conducted in the course of the Bosnian civil war. Karadzic, formerly a citizen of Yugoslavia and now a citizen of Bosnia–Herzegovina, is the President of a three-man presidency of the self-proclaimed Bosnian–Serb republic within Bosnia–Herzegovina, sometimes referred to as "Srpska," which claims to exercise lawful authority, and does in fact exercise actual control, over large parts of the territory of Bosnia–Herzegovina. In his capacity as President, Karadzic possesses ultimate command authority over the Bosnian–Serb military forces, and the injuries perpetrated upon plaintiffs were committed as part of a pattern of systematic human rights violations that was directed by Karadzic and carried out by the military forces under his command. The complaints allege that Karadzic acted in an official capacity either as the titular head of Srpska or in collaboration with the government of the recognized nation of the former Yugoslavia and its dominant constituent republic, Serbia.

The two groups of plaintiffs asserted causes of action for genocide, rape, forced prostitution and impregnation, torture and other cruel, inhuman, and degrading treatment, assault and battery, sex and ethnic inequality, summary execution, and wrongful death. They sought compensatory and punitive damages, attorney's fees, and, in one of the cases, injunctive relief. Plaintiffs grounded subject-matter jurisdiction in the Alien Tort Act, the Torture Victim Protection Act of 1991 ("Torture Victim Act"), Pub. L. No. 102–256, 106 Stat. 73 (1992), codified at 28 U.S.C. § 1350 note (Supp. V 1993), the general federal-question jurisdictional statute, 28 U.S.C. § 1331 (1988), and principles of supplemental jurisdiction, 28 U.S.C. § 1367 (Supp. V 1993). . . .

Karadzic contends that appellants have not alleged violations of the norms of international law because such norms bind only states and persons acting under color of a state's law, not private individuals. In making this contention, Karadzic advances the contradictory positions that he is not a state actor . . . , even as he asserts that he is the President of the self-proclaimed Republic of Srpska. . . . For their part, the Kadic appellants also take somewhat inconsistent positions in pleading defendant's role as President of Srpska . . . , and also contending that "Karadzic is not an official of any government." . . .

Judge Leisure accepted Karadzic's contention that "acts committed by non-state actors do not violate the law of nations," Doe, 866 F. Supp. at 739, and considered him to be a non-state actor. The Judge appears to have deemed state action required primarily on the basis of cases determining the need for state action as to claims of official torture, *see, e.g.*, Carmichael v. United Technologies Corp., 835 F.2d 109 (5th Cir. 1988), without consideration of the substantial body of law, discussed below, that renders private individuals liable for some international law violations.

We do not agree that the law of nations, as understood in the modern era, confines its reach to state action. Instead, we hold that certain forms of conduct violate the law of nations whether undertaken by those acting under the auspices of a state or only as private individuals. An early example of the application of the law of nations to the acts of private individuals is the prohibition against piracy. See United States v. Smith, 18 U.S. (5 Wheat.) 153, 161 . . . (1820); United States v. Furlong, 18 U.S. (5 Wheat.) 184, 196–97 . . . (1820). In The Brig Malek Adhel, 43 U.S. (2 How.) 210, 232 . . . (1844), the Supreme Court observed that pirates were "hostis humani generis" (an enemy of all mankind) in part because they acted "without . . . any pretense of public authority." *See generally* 4 WILLIAM BLACKSTONE, COMMENTARIES ON THE LAWS OF ENGLAND 68 (facsimile of 1st ed. 1765–1769, Univ. of Chi. ed., 1979). Later examples are prohibitions against the slave trade and certain war crimes. See M. CHERIF BASSIOUNI, CRIMES AGAINST HUMANITY IN INTERNATIONAL CRIMINAL LAW 193 (1992); Jordan Paust, *The Other Side of Right: Private Duties Under Human Rights Law*, 5 HARV. HUM. RTS. J. 51 (1992).

The liability of private persons for certain violations of customary international law and the availability of the Alien Tort Act to remedy such violations was early recognized by the Executive Branch in an opinion of Attorney General Bradford in reference to acts of American citizens aiding the French fleet to plunder British property off the coast of Sierra Leone in 1795. See Breach of Neutrality, 1 Op. Att'y Gen. 57, 59 (1795). The Executive Branch has emphatically restated in this litigation its position that private persons may be found liable under the Alien Tort Act for acts of genocide, war crimes, and other violations of international humanitarian law. See Statement of Interest of the United States at 5–13.

The RESTATEMENT (THIRD) OF THE FOREIGN RELATIONS LAW OF THE UNITED STATES (1986) ("Restatement (Third)") proclaims: "Individuals may be held liable for offenses against international law, such as piracy, war crimes, and genocide." Restatement (Third) pt. II, introductory note. The Restatement is careful to identify those violations that are actionable when committed by a state, Restatement (Third) § 702, and a more limited category of violations of "universal concern," *id.* § 404, partially overlapping with those listed in Section 702. Though the immediate focus of Section 404 is to identify those offenses for which a state has jurisdiction to punish without regard to territoriality or the nationality of the offenders, *cf. id.* § 402(1)(a), (2), the inclusion of piracy and slave trade from an earlier era and aircraft hijacking from the modern era demonstrates that the offenses of "universal concern" include those capable of being committed by non-state actors. Although the jurisdiction authorized by Section 404 is usually exercised by application of criminal law, international law also permits states to establish appropriate civil remedies, *id.* § 404, Comment [hereinafter cmt.] b, such as the tort actions authorized by the Alien Tort Act. Indeed, the two cases invoking the Alien Tort Act prior to *Filartiga* both applied the civil remedy to private action. See Adra v. Clift, 195 F. Supp. 857 (D.Md. 1961); Bolchos v. Darrel, 3 F. Cas. 810, 1 Bee 74 (D.S.C.1795) (No. 1,607)....

SPECIFIC APPLICATION OF ALIEN TORT ACT TO APPELLANTS' CLAIMS

In order to determine whether the offenses alleged by the appellants in this litigation are violations of the law of nations that may be the subject of Alien Tort Act claims against a private individual, we must make a particularized examination of these offenses, mindful of the important precept that "evolving standards of international law govern who is within the [Alien Tort Act's] jurisdictional grant." Amerada Hess,

830 F.2d at 425. In making that inquiry, it will be helpful to group the appellants' claims into three categories: (a) genocide, (b) war crimes, and (c) other instances of inflicting death, torture, and degrading treatment.

(a) *Genocide*. In the aftermath of the atrocities committed during the Second World War, the condemnation of genocide as contrary to international law quickly achieved broad acceptance by the community of nations. In 1946, the General Assembly of the United Nations declared that genocide is a crime under international law that is condemned by the civilized world, whether the perpetrators are "private individuals, public officials or statesmen." G.A. Res. 96 (I), 1 U.N. GAOR, U.N. Doc. A/64/Add.1, at 188–89 (1946). The General Assembly also affirmed the principles of Article 6 of the Agreement and Charter Establishing the Nuremberg War Crimes Tribunal for punishing " 'persecutions on political, racial, or religious grounds,' "regardless of whether the offenders acted " 'as individuals or as members of organizations,' " *In re* Extradition of Demjanjuk, 612 F. Supp. 544, 555 n. 11 (N.D.Ohio 1985) (quoting Article 6). See G.A. Res. 95 (I), 1 U.N. GAOR, U.N. Doc. A/64/Add.1, at 188 (1946).

The Convention on the Prevention and Punishment of the Crime of Genocide, 78 U.N.T.S. 277, entered into force Jan. 12, 1951, for the United States Feb. 23, 1989 (hereinafter "Convention on Genocide"), provides a more specific articulation of the prohibition of genocide in international law. The Convention, which has been ratified by more than 120 nations, including the United States, see U.S. Dept. of State, Treaties in Force 345 (1994), defines "genocide" to mean any of the following acts committed with intent to destroy, in whole or in part, a national, ethnical, racial or religious group, as such:

(a) Killing members of the group;

(b) Causing serious bodily or mental harm to members of the group;

(c) Deliberately inflicting on the group conditions of life calculated to bring about its physical destruction in whole or in part;

(d) Imposing measures intended to prevent births with the group;

(e) Forcibly transferring children of the group to another group.

Convention on Genocide art. II. Especially pertinent to the pending appeal, the Convention makes clear that "persons committing genocide . . . shall be punished, whether they are constitutionally responsible rulers, public officials or private individuals." *Id.* art. IV (emphasis added). These authorities unambiguously reflect that, from its incorporation into international law, the proscription of genocide has applied equally to state and non-state actors.

The applicability of this norm to private individuals is also confirmed by the Genocide Convention Implementation Act of 1987, 18 U.S.C. § 1091 (1988), which criminalizes acts of genocide without regard to whether the offender is acting under color of law, see *id.* § 1091(a) ("whoever" commits genocide shall be punished), if the crime is committed within the United States or by a U.S. national, *id.* § 1091(d). Though

Congress provided that the Genocide Convention Implementation Act shall not "be construed as creating any substantive or procedural right enforceable by law by any party in any proceeding," *id.* § 1092, the legislative decision not to create a new private remedy does not imply that a private remedy is not already available under the Alien Tort Act. Nothing in the Genocide Convention Implementation Act or its legislative history reveals an intent by Congress to repeal the Alien Tort Act insofar as it applies to genocide, and the two statutes are surely not repugnant to each other. Under these circumstances, it would be improper to construe the Genocide Convention Implementation Act as repealing the Alien Tort Act by implication. See Rodriguez v. United States, 480 U.S. 522, 524 . . . (1987) ("Repeals by implication are not favored and will not be found unless an intent to repeal is clear and manifest.") (citations and internal quotation marks omitted); United States v. Cook, 922 F.2d 1026, 1034 (2d Cir.) ("mutual exclusivity" of statutes is required to demonstrate Congress's "clear, affirmative intent to repeal"), *cert. denied*, 500 U.S. 941 (1991).

Appellants' allegations that Karadzic personally planned and ordered a campaign of murder, rape, forced impregnation, and other forms of torture designed to destroy the religious and ethnic groups of Bosnian Muslims and Bosnian Croats clearly state a violation of the international law norm proscribing genocide, regardless of whether Karadzic acted under color of law or as a private individual. The District Court has subject-matter jurisdiction over these claims pursuant to the Alien Tort Act.

(b) *War crimes*. Plaintiffs also contend that the acts of murder, rape, torture, and arbitrary detention of civilians, committed in the course of hostilities, violate the law of war. Atrocities of the types alleged here have long been recognized in international law as violations of the law of war. See *In re* Yamashita, 327 U.S. 1, 14 . . . (1946). Moreover, international law imposes an affirmative duty on military commanders to take appropriate measures within their power to control troops under their command for the prevention of such atrocities. *Id.* at 15–16.

After the Second World War, the law of war was codified in the four Geneva Conventions, which have been ratified by more than 180 nations, including the United States, see Treaties in Force, *supra*, at 398–99. Common article 3, which is substantially identical in each of the four Conventions, applies to "armed conflicts not of an international character" and binds "each Party to the conflict . . . to apply, as a minimum, the following provisions":

> Persons taking no active part in the hostilities . . . shall in all circumstances be treated humanely, without any adverse distinction founded on race, colour, religion or faith, sex, birth or wealth, or any other similar criteria.
>
> To this end, the following acts are and shall remain prohibited at any time and in any place whatsoever with respect to the above-mentioned persons:

> (a) violence to life and person, in particular murder of all kinds, mutilation, cruel treatment and torture;
>
> (b) taking of hostages;
>
> (c) outrages upon personal dignity, in particular humiliating and degrading treatment;
>
> (d) the passing of sentences and carrying out of executions without previous judgment pronounced by a regularly constituted court. . . .

Geneva Convention I art. 3 (1). Thus, under the law of war as codified in the Geneva Conventions, all "parties" to a conflict—which includes insurgent military groups—are obliged to adhere to these most fundamental requirements of the law of war. [Editors' note: today it is well recognized that the customary rights, duties and protections mirrored in common Article 3 also apply as a minimum set of rules during an international armed conflict and that they apply to all detained persons regardless of their status. That Article 3 provides such "a minimum yardstick" was recognized by the I.C.J. in Nicaragua v. United States, 1986 I.C.J. 4, paras. 218, 255.]

The offenses alleged by the appellants, if proved, would violate the most fundamental norms of the law of war embodied in common article 3, which binds parties to internal conflicts regardless of whether they are recognized nations or roving hordes of insurgents. The liability of private individuals for committing war crimes has been recognized since World War I and was confirmed at Nuremberg after World War II, see Telford Taylor, *Nuremberg Trials: War Crimes and International Law*, 450 INT'L CONCILIATION 304 (April 1949) (collecting cases), and remains today an important aspect of international law, see Jordan Paust, *After My Lai: The Case for War Crimes Jurisdiction Over Civilians in Federal District Courts*, in 4 THE VIETNAM WAR AND INTERNATIONAL LAW 447 (R. Falk ed., 1976). The District Court has jurisdiction pursuant to the Alien Tort Act over appellants' claims of war crimes and other violations of international humanitarian law.

(c) *Torture and summary execution.* In *Filartiga*, we held that official torture is prohibited by universally accepted norms of international law, see 630 F.2d at 885, and the Torture Victim Act confirms this holding and extends it to cover summary execution. Torture Victim Act Secs. 2 (a), 3 (a). However, torture and summary execution—when not perpetrated in the course of genocide or war crimes—are proscribed by international law only when committed by state officials or under color of law. See Declaration on Torture art. 1 (defining torture as being "inflicted by or at the instigation of a public official"); Convention Against Torture and Other Cruel, Inhuman, or Degrading Treatment or Punishment pt. I, art. 1, 23 I.L.M. 1027 (1984), as modified, 24 I.L.M. 535 (1985), entered into force June 26, 1987, ratified by United States Oct. 21, 1994, 34 I.L.M. 590, 591 (1995) (defining torture as "inflicted by or at the instigation of or with the consent or acquiescence of a public official or other person acting in an official capacity"); Torture Victim

Act § 2(a) (imposing liability on individuals acting "under actual or apparent authority, or color of law, of any foreign nation").

In the present case, appellants allege that acts of rape, torture, and summary execution were committed during hostilities by troops under Karadzic's command and with the specific intent of destroying appellants' ethnic-religious groups. Thus, many of the alleged atrocities are already encompassed within the appellants' claims of genocide and war crimes. Of course, at this threshold stage in the proceedings it cannot be known whether appellants will be able to prove the specific intent that is an element of genocide, or prove that each of the alleged torts were committed in the course of an armed conflict, as required to establish war crimes. It suffices to hold at this stage that the alleged atrocities are actionable under the Alien Tort Act, without regard to state action, to the extent that they were committed in pursuit of genocide or war crimes, and otherwise may be pursued against Karadzic to the extent that he is shown to be a state actor.... [Other portions of this case appear in Chapter 2, Section 2 D 2. Several international instruments addressing war crimes are in the Documents Supplement.]

RESOLUTION OF 1781

21 Journals of the Continental Congress 1136–37.

On a report of a committee, consisting of Mr. [Edmund] Randolph, Mr. [James] Duane, Mr. [John] Witherspoon, appointed to prepare a recommendation to the states to enact laws for punishing infractions of the laws of nations:

The committee, to whom was referred the motion for a recommendation to the several legislatures to enact punishments against violators of the law of nations, report:

That the scheme of criminal justice in the several states does not sufficiently comprehend offenses against the law of nations:

That a prince, to whom it may be hereafter necessary to disavow any transgression of that law by a citizen of the United States, will receive such disavowal with reluctance and suspicion, if regular and adequate punishment shall not have been provided against the transgressor:

That as instances may occur, in which, for the avoidance of war, it may be expedient to repair out of the public treasury injuries committed by individuals, and the property of the innocent to be exposed to reprisal, the author of those injuries should compensate the damage out of his private fortune.

Resolved, That it be recommended to the legislatures of the several states to provide expeditious, exemplary and adequate punishment:

First. For the violation of safe conducts or passports, expressly granted under the authority of Congress to the subjects of a foreign power in time of war:

Secondly. For the commission of acts of hostility against such as are in amity, league or truce with the United States, or who are within the same, under a general implied safe conduct:

Thirdly. For the infractions of the immunities of ambassadors and other public ministers, authorised and received as such by the United States in Congress assembled, by animadverting on violence offered to their persons, houses, carriages and property, under the limitations allowed by the usages of nations; and on disturbance given to the free exercise of their religion: by annulling all writs and processes, at any time sued forth against an ambassador, or other public minister, or against their goods and chattels, or against their domestic servants, whereby his person may be arrested: and,

Fourthly. For infractions of treaties and conventions to which the United States are a party.

The preceding being only those offences against the law of nations which are most obvious, and public faith and safety requiring that punishment should be co-extensive with such crimes:

Resolved, That it be farther recommended to the several states to erect a tribunal in each State, or to vest one already existing with power to decide on offences against the law of nations, not contained in the foregoing enumeration, under convenient restrictions.

Resolved, That it be farther recommended to authorise suits to be instituted for damages by the party injured, and for compensation to the United States for damage sustained by them from an injury done to a foreign power by a citizen.

JUDGEMENT AND OPINION, INTERNATIONAL MILITARY TRIBUNAL (NUREMBERG)

Oct. 1, 1946.

[Editors' note: the I.M.T. at Nuremberg was an international criminal tribunal set up by four of the victors after World War II, the U.S., France, Great Britain, and the Soviet Union to prosecute certain German nationals accused of crimes against peace, crimes against humanity, and/or war crimes. See Charter of the International Military Tribunal at Nuremberg, extract in the Documents Supplement.]

It was submitted that international law is concerned with the actions of sovereign States, and provides no punishment for individuals; and further, that where the act in question is an act of state, those who carry it out are not personally responsible, but are protected by the doctrine of sovereignty of the State. In the opinion of the Tribunal, both of these submissions must be rejected. That international law imposes duties and liabilities on individuals as well as upon States has long been recognized. In the recent case of *Ex parte* Quirin, 317 U.S. 1 (1942), before the Supreme Court of the United States, . . . the Court, said:

> "From the very beginning of its history this Court has applied the law of war as including that part of the law of nations which

prescribes for the conduct of war, the status, rights and duties of enemy nations as well as enemy individuals."

.... Many other authorities could be cited, but enough has been said to show that individuals can be punished for violations of international law. Crimes against international law are committed by men, not by abstract entities, and only by punishing individuals who commit such crimes can the provisions of international law be enforced.

The principle of international law, which under certain circumstances, protects representatives of a state, cannot be applied to acts which are condemned as criminal by international law. The authors of these acts cannot shelter themselves behind their official position.... He who violates the laws of war cannot obtain immunity while acting in pursuance of the authority of the State if the State in authorising action moves outside its competence under international law.

UNITED STATES v. VON LEEB (THE HIGH COMMAND CASE)

U.S. Military Tribunal, 1948, XI Trials of War Criminals 462, 487–88, 490 (1950).

[Editors' note: this tribunal was a military commission created by the United States in accordance with Control Council Law No. 10 (see Documents Supplement) that operated in war-related occupied territory at Nuremberg after World War II, as part of what became known as the Subsequent Nuremberg Proceedings.]

Since international common law grows out of the common reactions and the composite thinking with respect to recurring situations by the various states composing the family of nations, it is pertinent to consider the general attitude of the citizens of states with respect to their military commanders and their obligations when their nations plan, prepare for and initiate or engage in war.

While it is undoubtedly true that international common law in case of conflict with state law takes precedence over it and while it is equally true that absolute unanimity among all states in the family of nations is not required to bring an international common law into being, it is scarcely a tenable proposition that international common law will run counter to the consensus within any considerable number of nations. ... We may safely assume that the general and considered opinions of the people within states—the source from which international common law springs....

International law operates as a restriction and limitation on the sovereignty of nations. It may also limit the obligations which individuals owe to their states, and create for them international obligations which are binding on them to an extent that they must be carried out even if to do so violates a positive law or directive of the state. But the limitation which international common law imposes on national sovereignty, or on individual obligations, is a limitation self-imposed or imposed by the composite thinking in the international community, for it is by such democratic processes that common law comes into being. If there is no generality of opinion among the nations of the world as to a particular restriction on national sovereignty or on the obligations of individuals toward their own state, there then is no international common law on such matter.

PRINCIPLES OF THE NUREMBERG CHARTER AND JUDGMENT

formulated by the International Law Commission, and adopted by G.A. Res. 177 (II)(a), U.N. Doc. A/1316 (1950).

I. Any person who commits an act which constitutes a crime under international law is responsible therefor and liable to punishment.

II. The fact that internal law does not impose a penalty for an act which constitutes a crime under international law does not relieve the person who committed the act from responsibility under international law.

III. The fact that a person who committed an act which constitutes a crime under international law acted as Head of State or responsible Government official does not relieve him from responsibility under international law.

IV. The fact that a person acted pursuant to order of his Government or of a superior does not relieve him from responsibility under international law, provided a moral choice was in fact possible to him....

Notes and Questions

1. Do the last five documents and cases cause you to reconsider your definition of "international law"? Is the Restatement's notion of international law, which includes attention to a state's "relations with persons," a sufficient focus? Do these documents suggest that individual duties exist under international law regardless of an individual's relations with a state?

Does the Resolution of 1781 recognize private duties under the law of nations? What type of crimes are recognized? Was there an expectation that "infractions of treaties" could lead to criminal sanctions? Was there an expectation that there should be a right of access to courts and civil remedies for violations of the law of nations? When reading Chapter 2, consider how this has been implemented. Also consider what constitutes an actionable "wrong" or crime under the law of nations.

2. Does the Restatement's notion of international law adequately reflect the fact that the International Criminal Tribunals for the Former Yugoslavia (ICTY) and for Rwanda (ICTR), which were created by the U.N. Security Council, have indicted and tried various individuals or nonstate actors who had no formal connection with any state's government (as well as state actors) for international crimes of genocide, crimes against humanity, and war crimes committed against other nonstate actors? The ICTY and ICTR were the first international criminal tribunals to be established after the International Military Tribunals at Nuremberg and the Far East in the

late 1940s. They were created by the U.N. Security Council in the 1990s to prosecute the major perpetrators of atrocities in the former Yugoslavia and during the acts of genocide and other crimes committed in 1994 in Rwanda. These innovative tribunals have indicted and tried nonstate (and state) actors for international crimes of genocide, crimes against humanity, and war crimes committed against other nonstate actors. Concerning the legality of the creation of such tribunals and powers of the Security Council, *see, e.g.*, The Prosecutor of the Tribunal v. Dusko Tadic, Decision on the Defence Motion on Jurisdiction (Aug. 10, 1995), ICTY, reprinted in part in Chapter 8, and JORDAN J. PAUST, M. CHERIF BASSIOUNI, SHARON A. WILLIAMS, MICHAEL SCHARF, JIMMY GURULÉ, BRUCE ZAGARIS, INTERNATIONAL CRIMINAL LAW 672–97 (2 ed. 2000). Concerning genocide, crimes against humanity, and war crimes, *see, e.g., id.* at 803–958; several international legal instruments in the Documents Supplement; the 1919 Report of the Responsibilities Commission, in Chapter 8 (regarding war crimes and offenses against the laws of humanity). Under instruments that today at least reflect customary international law, such as the Charters of the I.M.T.s at Nuremberg and at Tokyo, would the September 11, 2001 al Qaeda attacks on the World Trade Center in New York in 2001 be covered?

The International Criminal Tribunal for Rwanda convicted Jean–Paul Akayesu (a former mayor of a small town in Rwanda) in 1998 for genocide and crimes against humanity. The specific acts for which he was convicted included murder, torture, and rape. The specific number of direct victims under certain counts included as few as 3, 5, and 8 persons. *See* The Prosecutor v. Akayesu, ICTR–96–4–T (2 Sept. 1998), *reprinted in* 37 I.L.M. 1401 (1998). He was also convicted of direct and public incitement to commit genocide. *Id.* at paras. 47, and findings re: Count 4; *see also* Convention on the Prevention and Punishment of the Crime of Genocide, art. III (c) (1948), in the Documents Supplement. The Tribunal found that an "armed conflict not of an international character" (within the meaning of common Article 3 of the 1949 Geneva Conventions) existed in Rwanda. Yet, the Tribunal would not convict Akayesu on charges of violating common Article 3 on the mistaken ground that it was not proven that he "was a member of the armed forces and that he was duly mandated and expected ... to support and carry out the war effort" (*id.* at para. 64). Perhaps inconsistently, the Tribunal found that the accused "belongs to a category of individuals who could be held responsible" for such crimes and a violation of common Article 3 "may, in principle, commit criminal responsibility of civilians" (*id.* at para. 49). However, civilian status had never been a defense to war crimes and civilians have often been prosecuted for war crimes. *See, e.g.*, PAUST, BASSIOUNI, *ET AL.*, *supra* at 27–33, 40 (*Borkum Island* case), 42, 46–47 (Judgment of the I.M.T. for the Far East), 53 (Trial of *Koiso*, an Ex–Prime Minister), 58–59, 67–69, 74–75, 88 (ICTY Indictment of Karadzic), 230, 255–58, 260, 278–82, 286–91 (including Subsequent Nuremberg Trials), 691, 821–22; U.S. DEP'T OF ARMY FIELD MANUAL 27–10, THE LAW OF LAND WARFARE paras. 498–499 (1956) [hereinafter FM 27–10].

The Statutes of the ICTY and ICTR were the first statutes to define violations of common Article 3 committed during an insurgency explicitly as "war crimes," although states, courts, military manuals, textwriters, and others had already recognized this fact. *See, e.g., The Prosecutor of the*

Tribunal v. Dusko Tadic, *supra* at paras. 60–74; PAUST, BASSIOUNI, *ET AL.*, *supra* at 691–95, 698, 826–27, 829–33; FM 27–10, *supra* at paras. 11 b, 499 ("The term 'war crime' is the technical expression for a violation of the law of war by any person or persons, military or civilian. Every violation of the law of war is a war crime."). Article 8 (c) and (e) of the 1998 "Rome Statute" for the International Criminal Court (ICC) also recognizes that violations of the laws of war committed during an internal insurgency are war crimes. Who is protected under common Article 3? Would alleged terrorists captured during wars in Afghanistan or Iraq be covered? Would members of al Qaeda found in Canada? What type of protections would exist? Are U.S. Executive and/or military approved interrogation tactics such as stripping a person naked for interrogation, use of hoods, and use of dogs violations of common Article 3? *See, e.g.*, Paust, *Executive Plans and Authorizations to Violate International Law Concerning Treatment and Interrogation of Detainees*, 43 COLUMBIA J. TRANSNAT'L L. 811 (2005).

In the ICTY, as of August 2004:

* 82 individuals had been indicted
* 20 remained at large
* 56 were currently incarcerated (5 were on provisional release)
* 2 had been discharged
* 3 had been released
* 1 had died
* 47 cases remained active.

Illustrative of the decisions are the convictions of Maj. Gen. Radislav Krstic for genocide with regard to his role in directing the 1995 Serbian attack on Srebrenica, in which 7,000 Bosnian Muslim men were marched off to their deaths, and Anto Furundzija, a 29–year-old Bosnian Croat for aiding and abetting torture and rape by persons under his command (he was standing by in 1993 while a subordinate repeatedly raped at knifepoint a naked Muslim woman during interrogation). Krstic was sentenced to 46 years in prison and Furundzija was sentenced to a ten-year prison term. The trial of the Serbian leader Slobodan Milosovic has been going on for more than two years as of this writing, and is expected to continue for another two years. Among those formally indicted but not yet apprehended are Radovan Karadzic and Ratko Mladic, the civilian and military leaders of the Bosnian Serbs.

In the ICTR, as of February 2005,

* Judgments had been issued against 25 defendants.
    ** 5 were released.
    ** 20 were convicted (9 were on appeal).
* Trials were ongoing regarding 26 others.
* 17 were in custody awaiting trial.
* 9 accused were still at large.

Among the prominent convictions was that of Jean Kambanda, who had been Prime Minister of Rwanda during the three months in 1994 when 800,000–1,000,000 people were killed. He had made speeches encouraging killing of Tutsi, had signed directives legalizing the militia, and had distributed arms to them. He pled guilty to six counts of genocide and crimes against humanity and was sentenced to life imprisonment.

4. An *ad hoc* criminal tribunal has also been established to prosecute violators of international law during the recent conflict in Sierra Leone. Domestic tribunals were also created to address crimes committed during conflicts in East Timor and Cambodia. The Special Court for War Crimes in Sierra Leone differs from the Yugoslav and Rwanda Tribunals in that it has both international and local judges. As of February 2005, 11 persons associated with all three of the country's former warring factions had been indicted by the Special Court. They were charged with war crimes and crimes against humanity, based on acts of murder, rape, extermination, acts of terror, enslavement, looting and burning, sexual slavery, conscription of children into an armed force, and attacks on UN peacekeepers and humanitarian workers.

East Timor was granted its independence from Indonesia in 1999, after which Indonesian militias killed about 1,400 people, mainly independence supporters, and tortured and raped an unknown number of people. More than a quarter of a million people, or some 30 per cent of East Timor's population, were forcibly deported or fled across the border to West Timor in Indonesia where around 28,000 remained in early 2005. The United Nations coordinated with local courts to support and staff a Special Panel for Serious Crimes, and this process led to the jailing of 75 persons for their involvement in the events of 1999. This Special Panel completed its business in 2005. Some crimes were addressed in local Indonesian courts, but in June 2005 a group of U.N. experts expressed serious concern about the failure to adequately prosecute and convict all who have been reasonably accused of international crimes.

During the Cambodian genocide of 1975–79, some 1.7 million people lost their lives, constituting 21% of the country's population. The Khmer Rouge regime headed by Pol Pot combined extremist ideology with ethnic animosity and a diabolical disregard for human life to produce repression, misery, and murder on a massive scale. In late 2004, after six years of deliberation, the Cambodian National Assembly ratified an agreement with the United Nations to establish a tribunal utilizing both international and national judges to try the Khmer Rouge leaders.

5. With respect to individual duties under international law, consider also the following statement of Justice Wilson on circuit in Henfield's Case, 11 F. Cas. 1099, 1107 (C.C.D.Pa.1793) (No. 6,360): "Under all the obligations due to the universal society of the human race, the citizens of a state still continue. To this universal society it is the duty that each nation should contribute to the welfare, the perfection and the happiness of the others. If so, the first degree of this duty is to do no injury. Among states as well as among men, justice is a sacred law.... On states as well as individuals the duties of humanity are strictly incumbent; what each is obliged to perform for others, from others it is entitled to receive." As noted later in this book, *Henfield's Case* involved direct incorporation of treaty law and customary international law termed the "law of nations" for criminal sanction purposes, that is, prosecution of an individual for alleged violations of interna-

tional law without a federal criminal statute forming the basis for prosecution. *Henfield's Case* also recognized that private duties may pertain even when a treaty makes no express mention of individuals or individual duties. *Id.* at 1120 (Wilson, J.).

6. With respect to the universal nature of customary international law, also consider: The Public Prosecutor v. Dusko Tadic, International Tribunal for the Former Yugoslavia, IT–94–1–AR72, Decision on the Defence Motion for Interlocutory Appeal on Jurisdiction (Appeals Chamber 2 Oct. 1995), in which Judge Cassese quoted from a 1950 case against General Wagener in the Supreme Military Tribunal of Italy: " 'Crimes against the laws and customs of war cannot be considered political offences, as they do not harm a political interest of a particular State, nor a political right of a particular citizen. They are, instead, crimes of *lese-humanite* (*reati di lesa umanita*) and . . . the norms prohibiting them have a universal character, not simply a territorial one.' "

7. *Monist theory* (often related to a naturalist theory of law), at its extreme, considers that only one system of human law exists, with international law at its apex. *Dualist theory* (often related to a state-oriented definitional theory), at its extreme, considers that there are two entirely separate systems of law that are not interconnected, *i.e.*, international law and domestic law. Thus, dualist theory assumes that violations of international law are not actionable or directly relevant domestically unless implemented by a domestic legal system (usually, the legislature). To generalize, positivist theories have adopted both monist and dualist approaches, although state-oriented positivism tends to view law as coming from the "consent" of states and is often dualist in nature. *See, e.g.*, J.L. Brierly, The Law of Nations 52 (5th ed. 1955) ("positivism . . . teaches that international law is the sum of the rules by which states have consented to be bound, and that nothing can be law to which they have not consented."). The phrase "natural law" generally refers to an approach that stresses the primacy of unchanging universal norms and naturalist views tend to be monist in orientation. Realist theories, stressing the need to focus on how law is really created and operates, tend to abandon both monist and dualist extremes and to identify interconnections and interaffectations where, how and when they actually exist. Such theories can also be relevant to one's view of how international law is incorporated into a domestic legal process, a process examined in the next chapter.

LUNG–CHU CHEN, AN INTRODUCTION TO CONTEMPORARY INTERNATIONAL LAW

23, 76, 79–80 (1989).*

In recent decades, participation in the global constitutive process of authoritative decision has been greatly democratized. All participants—conveniently categorized as nation-states, international governmental organizations, nongovernmental organizations and associations (including political parties, pressure groups, and private associations), and individual human beings—now openly or recognizably play important roles and perform numerous functions. The role of nation-states has been, and continues to be, predominant at the international level. International governmental organizations, now recognized as appropriate "subjects" of international law, participate in all functions. Political parties, though often receiving no formal recognition, exert effective influence on many authoritative decisions. Pressure groups actively seek to promote and influence the decision making. Multiplying hosts of private associations, dedicated to values other than power, are increasingly transnational in membership, goals, organizational structure, spheres of activity, and influence. Individuals, acting both alone and as representatives of groups, have ample opportunity to participate in all activities that comprise the making and application of law. Indeed, individuals are the ultimate participants in the international legal process and in each organization or association mentioned above. Such a realistic role has been recognized at various times but appears to be increasingly evident in the latter part of the twentieth century....

Individual human beings, acting through all the group and institutional forms already mentioned, communicate and collaborate continuously in every phase of effective and authoritative decision as well as in the shaping and sharing of all values.... Whatever their multiple identifications, individuals are the ultimate actors in all social process. In addition to their common roles in effective power, individuals increasingly are achieving recognized roles in the processes of authoritative decision and review....

Transnational structures of authority and procedures for application have been established and maintained to supplement long-standing domestic procedures and to secure greater compliance with the high legal standards set forth in the global bill of human rights. More importantly, individuals and private groups are given increased, though still limited, access to arenas of transnational authority to bring complaints about human rights deprivations against even their own governments. The capacity of individuals and private groups to invoke human rights prescriptions before appropriate transnational decision makers is so enhanced that the subject-object theory cannot explain or wish it away. Indeed, a state-centered international law is being transformed into an international law of homocentricity....

Viewed comprehensively and realistically, international law is a continuing process of decision and review aimed at identifying, clarifying, and securing the common interest of the members of the world community. It is a process in which various participants (actors) play various roles in making and applying international law and the related decision functions.... The meaningful inquiry concerns not who are technically subjects and objects for a body of static rules but who actually participate in the global process of decision making and perform what functions.

Notes and Questions

1. Is it necessary to be a monist in order to identify actual constitutive processes, normative interconnections, or systems? Is it realistic to conceive of a global system that is indivisible? Is it preferable? After investigating materials in several chapters in this book, consider whether there are various processes of interaction and interaffectation in which various actors can participate. Indeed, is there one "international law"?

2. Consider the following remarks adapted from Professor Van Dyke's article *The Role of Customary International Law in Federal and State Court Litigation,* 26 U. HAWAII L. REV. 361 (2004):

During the nineteenth and early twentieth centuries, some European and U.S. scholars and judges viewed international law as applying only to "civilized nations," and they used this term almost exclusively to refer to Christian nations. [However, as demonstrated in Chapter 2 and elsewhere in this casebook, other writers and judges addressed the law of nations as universal law.] The influential treatise written in the late nineteenth century by the President of Yale University contains a typical Eurocentric and politically-incorrect explanation of this phenomenon, explaining that Christians were "the first to elaborate a system of international law" for the same reasons that "have enabled Christian states to reach a higher point of civilization than any other." THEODORE D. WOOLSEY, INTRODUCTION TO THE STUDY OF INTERNATIONAL LAW 22 (4 ed. 1874). These reasons include "the high moral standards of the religion . . . which cultivates alike the sentiments of justice and humanity" as well as the Roman law heritage. *Id.* Christian nations, he explained, had shared "religious and jural views" and "a similar historical development," but "[n]o such common feeling, but quite the opposite, existed between them and their Mohammedan neighbors; and hence the latter were long shut out from the pale of their international law." *Id.*

One of the major disputes of the early colonial period was whether the colonized peoples had any rights of any sort under international law. The generally-accepted view was that "peoples overseas could be subjected to European rule and their territories annexed through effective occupation by the conquering state," and "[t]he territory then became subject to treatment or mistreatment without protection of international law or, indeed, with its approval. Rules legitimizing imperialism and its means . . . endured well into the twentieth century, until most colonies became independent." WERNER LEVI, CONTEMPORARY INTERNATIONAL LAW: A CONCISE INTRODUCTION 9 (2 ed 1991).

The first major writer to oppose this view was a Spanish professor of theology Francisco Vitoria (1480–1546), who defended Spain's right to conquer lands in the new world, but recognized that the native people had inherent rights that needed to be recognized by the conquerers. In his book DE INDIS, Vitoria explained that the natives had souls and were part of the fundamental unity of the human race, and were entitled to the protections of the ethically-based principles of international law.

During the nineteenth century, Western states were forced to realize that non-Christian countries such as Turkey, Persia, Siam, Japan, and China needed to be included within the international legal structure. It was never exactly clear what was needed to be admitted to the family of nations. The British scholar T.J. Lawrence wrote in 1895 that "a certain degree of civilization is necessary, though it is difficult to define the exact amount." T.J. LAWRENCE, THE PRINCIPLES OF INTERNATIONAL LAW 58 (1895). "It would, for instance, be absurd to expect the king of Dahomey to establish a Prize Court, or to require the dwarfs of the central African forest to receive a permanent diplomatic mission." *Id.* In 1856, the European nations formally admitted Turkey into their "family of nations" in the Treaty of Paris, after the Crimean War, which had been concluded to maintain the balance of power in Europe. Western countries started dealing with China as a "state" for at least certain purposes because of the relationships that developed after China's defeats in the Opium Wars of 1840 and 1856.

Japan forced itself into the family of nations by defeating China in 1894 and Russia in 1904. As a Japanese diplomat later put it: "We show ourselves equal to you in scientific butchery, and at once we are admitted to your council tables as civilized men." B.V.A. ROLING, INTERNATIONAL LAW IN AN EXPANDED WORLD 27 (1960). In 1900, the U.S. Supreme Court referred to "the Empire of Japan" as "the last state admitted into the rank of civilized nations." The Paquete Habana, 175 U.S. 677, 700 (1900). Africa continued to be completely excluded in a formal sense, and at the Berlin Conference on Africa in 1884–85, where European nations established rules for dividing up distant territories that had not yet been conquered or even explored, no African representative was invited. But the colonial process forced Europeans to come to grips with the rest of world, and, as Professor Anghie has explained, "[i]t was principally through colonial expansion in the nineteenth century that international law became universal. . . ." Antony Anghie, *Colonialism and the Birth of International Institutions: Sovereignty, Economy, and the Mandate System of the League of Nations*, 34 N.Y.U. J. INT'L L. & POL. 513, 516 (2002).

Writing in 1905, Oppenheim declared that 72 European and 21 American states were in the family of nations, but that "in Asia only Japan is a full and real member of the Family of Nations. Persia, Korea, China, Siam and Tibet are, for some parts, only within the family." OPPENHEIM, INTERNATIONAL LAW 37 (1 ed. 1905)). The Western countries negotiated a wide series of multilateral treaties in the second half of the nineteenth century, but Asian countries were not centrally involved in any of these negotiations. China did not begin participating in the Universal Postal Union until 1897, 20 years after it was established, and this entry marked China's first involvement with any public international organization.

3. Professor Onuma, Yasuaki, from the University of Tokyo has offered a different perspective regarding the interaction of legal perspectives from Europe and Asia, which he terms an "intercivilizational" approach. "The term 'intercivilizational,'" he writes, "refers to a perspective seeking to overcome a perspective which is assumed by, and framed within, a particular civilization. It seeks to reach a more widely shared perspective by bringing into intellectual discourses plural ways of thinking based not only on modern Western civilization but on other civilizations as well. It is a methodological as well as strategic concept to overcome a predominant Westcentric universalist discourse on one hand, yet to prevent intellectual discourses from falling into a one-sided criticism based on some particular non-Western civilization on the other. . . . One purpose of the intercivilizational approach is to gauge the bases and extent of universality of the ideas and institutions

of the predominant Western civilization. One should not deny the universal validity of an idea or institution simply because of its Western origin. At the same time, however, one should not assume that an idea or institution of some non-Western civilization is relative or particular simply because of its non-Western origin. . . ." Onuma Yasuaki, *In Quest of Intercivilizational Human Rights: "Universal" vs. "Relative" Human Rights Viewed from an Asian Perspective,* The Asia Foundation Center for Asian Pacific Affairs, Occasional Paper No. 2, at 14 (Mar. 1996). Professor Onuma highlights "fundamental problems such as (1) contradictions between the globalization of economic and information activities and the nation state system; (2) contradictions between the emergence of non-Western powers in Asia and the persistence of Westcentric power structures of information and culture in international society; and (3) contradictions between a sincere quest for a more humane and less violent world and a deep resentment against the colonial past and present inequality among nations in international society." *Id.* at 1.

Nonetheless, he continues: "one must admit that human rights are universally valid at least to the extent that most nations are committed to the universal notion of human rights in international conventions and in some other forms. Some may argue that most nations are committed to human rights because they represent genuine human aspirations regardless of differences in culture, religion and other factors. Thus, it may be argued, the universalist claim of human rights is theoretically correct.

"However, the very claim of universal human rights is characterized by, and forms a part of, the existing international hierarchy of information and culture. It cannot be denied that a part of the strength of this claim derives from the Westcentric power structure of information and culture. Many among the Third World population, though attracted to modern Western notions, cultures and institutions, are at the same time resentful of the huge gap between the rich North and the poor South. They are also critical of the hierarchical and often biased structure of information and culture, and of the colonialist and imperialist history of the North. They are further resentful of successive interventions by the Western powers under various beautiful slogans: humanity, democracy, civilization, and so forth. No wonder that claims of universal human rights are often received with suspicion and defiance, and criticized as a form of cultural imperialism. . . . To secure the willingness to accept human rights in developing countries, those who claim the value and universality of human rights must also give due weight to the virtue of modesty and self-criticism." *Id.* at 10.

The broad intercivilizational acceptance of human rights is reflected in the near universal ratification of the United Nations Charter (see preamble and Articles 1 (3), 55 (c), 56) and the International Covenant on Civil and Political Rights (see preamble and Article 2 (1)) (both are in the Documents Supplement). In the Vienna Declaration and Programme of Action, § 1, paras. 1, 5, U.N. Doc. A/CONF.157/23 (1993), produced after a contentious United Nations meeting on human rights, the "universal nature" of human rights was stressed and it was agreed that "all human rights are universal, indivisible and interdependent and interrelated," but one should take into account "national and regional particularities and various historical, cultural and religious backgrounds"). Should one try to identify a core of generally shared and stable content?

4. If there are any natural laws in the universe, will they shape the nature and content of international law? If we encounter life elsewhere in the universe, will such an event change the nature of international law? See also M. Scharf & L. Roberts, *The Interstellar Relations of the Federation: International Law and "Star Trek: The Next Generation,"* 25 Toledo L. Rev. 577 (1995). Will human international norms, if adopted, allow us to coexist in other worlds with other species or to manage and share resources? With respect to resources, consider also the materials in this book on the law of the sea, space law, and environmental law.

5. Rules often have general opposites (*i.e.*, complementary opposites, rule complementarity). Rules are often easy to identify, but are not self-applicative. Consider, for example, domestic prohibitions of "murder" (with their often conclusory or circular definitions, such as the "unlawful" killing of a human being) and their opposites, which tolerate "self-defense" and "defense of others." How should one decide whether a killing is "murder" or "self-defense"? In the domestic legal process, who realistically can make a claim that a killing is "murder" or "self-defense" or, thus, invoke rules, who can apply them (formally and informally), who realistically can review even formal applications? Consider also the extract from Professor Chen's treatise, below, on the inadequacies of a mere rule-oriented approach to inquiry concerning the nature and content of law or its application to a particular human event.

6. Is international law merely a set of rules? Does awareness merely of rules provide much insight into the functioning of the international legal process, currently or through time? Consider the insights that are possible when viewing law as rules as opposed to law as process. Recall the earlier excerpts from Charlesworth, Chinkin & Shelley; and Chen. Does a focus merely on current rules allow adequate awareness of context and consequences, actual patterns and trends, conditioning factors, or the development of rules, exceptions to rules, and historic methods of challenge to rules and possibilities for change? From a realist-oriented law as process focus, with respect to the creation, shaping and termination of law, also consider, for example, who participates, with what sort of claims and expectations, in what arenas, marshaling what resources, using what strategies, how, and with what consequences.

LUNG-CHU CHEN, AN INTRODUCTION TO CONTEMPORARY INTERNATIONAL LAW

11–13 (1989).*

International law has its origins in the natural law school and has been influenced in varying degrees by all major schools of jurisprudence. The past influence of the positivist (analytical) school lingers, despite recent signs of growing receptivity to new, more pragmatic theories. The late nineteenth and early twentieth-century approaches to international law, as dominated by the positivist school, were rule-oriented, conceiving international law as a body of rules—indeed, often unrealistically as rules merely between states.

The rule-oriented approaches tend to view international law dogmatically as a static body of auto-operational rules—rules that are given and self-contained and operate automatically. The judicial task is said to be to discover and enforce, in particular cases, extant "correct rules." Logical derivation is the intellectual task stressed: when behavior can be sustained by statements logically derived from existing rules, it is regarded as "legal" or "lawful." In this perspective, international law operates automatically within its autonomous realm of self-contained rules, within its own internal logical mechanism.

Such rule-oriented approaches to international law have several inadequacies: (1) failure to grip the notions of decision (choice) in the legal process; (2) insufficient attention to the goals (policies) for which rules are devised and to value consequences of particular applications of rules; (3) failure to relate rules to the dynamic context of interaction involving the international and domestic social processes and to the ongoing process of decision making; (4) failure to grasp the normative ambiguity involved in rules; (5) failure to come to grips with the generality and complementarity involved in rules; and (6) failure to develop and employ adequate intellectual skills in problem solving....

Making choices (decisions) inevitably involves policy considerations—what are policy purposes for which certain rules are developed and maintained—and involves considerations of alternatives—what are alternative value consequences in making one choice or another.... Decisions ... cannot be made by neutral decision makers (neutral human beings) neutrally applying neutral rules that are neutrally derived. Rules simply do not decide cases, people decide, and rules may provide only minimal guidance in decision making.

Indeed, rules are not autonomous absolutes and do not exist in a vacuum. Divorced from policy and context, rules are skeletons without body and soul. Rules cannot make much sense without reference to policy or the purposes for which they are created and maintained. Rules cannot be meaningfully understood without reference to the context of interaction that gives rise to legal controversies and to the ongoing process of decision making in which rules are made and remade, applied and reapplied, by human decision makers in response to changing demands and expectations under the ever-changing context of conditions. The dynamism of the law in real life cannot be grasped by mere reference to law in the abstract. Law in the social process is dynamic and based on what real human beings think and do.

Notes and Questions

1. With respect to historic developments and certain differences between positivist and naturalist views, consider also the following adapted

from Professor Van Dyke, *The Role of Customary International Law in Federal and State Court Litigation,* 26 U. HAWAII L. REV. 361 (2004):

Commentators trying to describe the nature of international law have noted a tension between the "positivistic" view (expressed in *S.S.Lotus*, here at p. 6) that international law comes from the consent of governments and the "natural law" view that the standards of international law emerge from a moralistic or ethical sense of how nations should behave. International law started to be seen as a coherent legal system around the time of the Peace of Westphalia, which ended the Thirty Years War (1618–48) and gave formal recognition to the sovereign state system. This treaty-based system was designed, in part, to allow Catholic and Protestant states to coexist in Europe. International law became necessary to confirm the boundaries among these states, to promote adherence to treaties and other agreements, and to bring some order to their dealings with each other. During the years that followed, citizen participation in government emerged in England and then in France through the French Revolution, and as monarchies crumbled the "state" began to be seen as linked to the people or a nation rather than the monarch.

The Final Act of the Congress of Vienna (1815), signed by Austria, France, Great Britain, Portugal, Prussia, Russia, and Sweden, which formally ended the Napoleonic Wars, was another significant event, because it created a system of political and economic cooperation in Europe and announced norms of international law. Among the principles that emerged from this Congress were a set of rules governing diplomatic protocol, a condemnation of the slave trade, the principle of free navigation (not only for the riparian states but for all states) on the major rivers of Europe (the Rhine, the Neckar, the Mayne, the Moselle, the Meuse, and the Scheldt), and the neutrality of Switzerland. Treaties, both bilateral and multilateral, began to cover a wide range of topics, supplementing and sometimes replacing custom as a source of law.

The second half of the nineteenth century in Europe was a period of numerous conferences and treaties, with particularly significant meetings taking place in The Hague in 1899 and again in 1907. Twenty-five nations attended the 1899 conference, which was convened by Czar Nicholas II of Russia, and a larger number ratified the documents produced by the meeting, which included conventions for the Peaceful Settlement of International Disputes, on the Laws and Customs of War on Land, for the Adaptation to Maritime Warfare of the Principles of the Geneva Convention of 1864, Prohibiting the Launching of Projectiles and Explosives from Balloons and declarations on the use of projectiles to transmit poisonous gases, and on the prohibition of dum-dum bullets. Although European nations dominated the negotiations, 19 Latin American nations signed or ratified one or more of the documents, as did China, Japan, Korea, Persia, Siam, and Turkey.

The 1907 Hague conference, called again by the Russian Czar Nicholas II upon the initiative of President Theodore Roosevelt, produced conventions on the Pacific Settlement of International Disputes, the Limitation of Employment of Force for Recovery of Contract Debts, the Opening of Hostilities, the Laws and Customs of War on Land, the Rights and Duties of Neutral Powers and Persons in Case of War on Land, the Status of Enemy

Merchant Ships at the Outbreak of Hostilities, the Conversion of Merchant Ships into War–Ships, the Laying of Automatic Submarine Contact Mines, Bombardment by Naval Forces in Time of War, Adaptation to Maritime War of the Principles of the Geneva Convention, Certain Restrictions with Regard to the Exercise of the Right of Capture in Naval War, the Creation of an International Prize Court (Never Ratified), and the Rights and Duties of Neutral Powers in Naval War. The European nations again dominated the negotiations, but 18 Latin American nations signed or ratified one of more of the conventions as did China, Japan, Persia, Siam, and Turkey. Liberia also adhered to many of the conventions.

The nature of the international legal system that was being built was thought by many to be one of consent—or "positivism"—wherein only those norms agreed upon by the states could be enforced against them. But perhaps because of the theocracies that had governed many parts of Europe in previous centuries, the Canon law that had developed during that period, and the religious fervor that still burned brightly for many, others contended that certain inherent principles also governed nations. Tension emerged between this "natural law" formula for the basis of international law and the perspective of "positivism" promoted by others, and this tension still exists today.

The Dutch diplomat Hugo de Groot, who wrote under the Latin name Grotius [in the 1600s], is often called the "father" or "founder" of modern international law because he tried to reconcile the conflicting sources of international law. His analysis of the laws of war, the law of the sea, and the protection owed to diplomats laid the framework for modern thinking on these topics. He believed that a "law of nature" could be deduced by logical reasoning, rather than by resort to divine sources, and thus tried to formulate principles that could be acceptable to every nation.

2. With respect to a "process of review" involving many participants, consider Jordan J. Paust, *The Complex Nature, Sources and Evidences of Customary Human Rights*, 25 GA. J. INT'L & COMP. L. 147, 156–58 (1995–96)*:

Individual participation in the creation and shaping of customary human rights is less well-perceived, but no less real. All human beings recognizably participate in a dynamic process of acceptance or expectation which leads to patterns of *opinio juris* [*i.e.*, one element of customary international law involving expectations generally shared about what is legally appropriate or required] measurable at various moments. Participation in the shaping of attitudes is a social fact, whether or not such participation is actually recognized by each individual or is as effective as it might otherwise be (*e.g.*, even if apathetic "inaction" is the form of participation for some, a form that simply allows others a more significant role). Actors may also have a more significant role in any given social context because of relatively higher respect, power, enlightenment, skill, wealth, and so forth; but such relative outcomes (or "value positions" at any given moment) are tied to the dynamics of the social process in which all participate, however directly or indirectly or seemingly integrated, dominated or

* This article was originally published in 25 GA. J. INT'L L. 15 (1995–96) and is reprinted with permission.

alienated. The same can be said of state actors. Indeed, the same recognitions apply to participation in the creation of patterns of human practice or behavior, the other element of customary law.

Since each nation-state, indeed each human being, is a participant in both the attitudinal and behavioral aspects of dynamic customary human rights law, each may initiate a change in such law, or, with others, reaffirm its validity. Indeed, such a law at least, born of what people think and do, is constantly reviewed and "re-enacted" in the social process, changed, or terminated. The decisions of governmental elites are especially subject to a constant "process of review" in which all can participate. As Myres McDougal, Harold Lasswell, and Michael Reisman remarked:

> Most of us are performing ... these ... roles without being fully aware of the scope and consequences of our acts. Because of this, our participation is often considerably less effective than it might be. Every individual cannot, of course, realistically expect or demand to be a decisive factor in every major decision. Yet the converse feeling of pawnlike political impotence, of being locked out of effective decisions, is an equally unwarranted orientation. The limits of the individual's role ... are as much a function of his passive acquiescence and ignorance of the potentialities of his participation as of the structures of the complex human organizations of the contemporary world.

Moreover, it is the reality of participation in processes of expectation and practice which allows one to recognize that individuals are not merely objects of customary international law, but are also participants in the creation, shaping and termination of such law; that patterns of "domestic" practice are relevant, not merely practice state-to-state or at the international level; and that the related pretense of British positivism at the start of the twentieth century, widely opposed but adopting several false myths, was perhaps substantially as unreal then as it would be now despite the many more formal institutional arrangements for individual and group participation at the international level and recognition today of a growing interaction and interdependence of individuals, groups, and public and private institutions in all social, economic, and political sectors. Need one stress, customary human rights law is neither made purely by actions, and/or the *opinio*, of "States," nor merely by national governmental actors within a federated system. Similarly, the international legal process is not simplistically a purely horizontal system or radically decentralized.

For additional attention to the process of review, *see, e.g.*, W. M. REISMAN, NULLITY AND REVISION: THE REVIEW AND ENFORCEMENT OF INTERNATIONAL JUDGMENTS AND AWARDS 4, 239 (1971); Myres S. McDougal, Harold D. Lasswell, W. Michael Reisman, *Theories About International Law: Prologue to a Configurative Jurisprudence*, 8 VA. J. INT'L L. 183, 193 (1968); Myres S. McDougal, Harold D. Lasswell, W. Michael Reisman, *The World Constitutive Process of Authoritative Decision*, 19 J. LEGAL EDU. 253, 424–26, 436–37 (1967); Jordan J. Paust, *The Concept of Norm: Toward a Better Understanding of Content, Authority, and Constitutional Choice*, 53 TEMPLE L.Q. 226, 231–37 (1980).

3. What types of sanctions are available with respect to violations of international law? Do they include political sanctions (*e.g.*, world public

opinion, use of the media), diplomatic sanctions, military sanctions, and economic sanctions? Does it matter that there is no world police force, no world jail, and limited access to international courts for civil or criminal sanctions? What institutional processes are available for victims to pursue sanctions other than criminal penalties, money damages, or injunctive relief? What actors (state and nonstate) might engage in sanction strategies and processes, *e.g.*, who might invoke international law claims in domestic contexts; who might monitor implementation; who might engage in sanctions efforts involving the shaping of public opinion; who might participate and shape the efficacy of boycotts and economic embargoes? Did you consider possible roles of private individuals, groups, corporations, governments (national and sub-national), international organizations? *See generally* MYRES S. MCDOUGAL, HAROLD D. LASSWELL, LUNG-CHU CHEN, HUMAN RIGHTS AND WORLD PUBLIC ORDER 219–47, 551–60, *passim* (1980); MYRES S. MCDOUGAL, FLORENTINO P. FELICIANO, LAW AND MINIMUM WORLD PUBLIC ORDER 309–32 (1961) (identifying categories of diplomatic, ideologic, economic, and military sanction in terms of the following strategies: prevention, deterrence, restoration or rehabilitation, reconstruction, and correction); Jordan J. Paust, *The Complex Nature, Sources and Evidences of Customary Human Rights,* 25 GA. J. INT'L & COMP. L. 147, 160–61 (1995–96); Jordan J. Paust, *Response to Terrorism: A Prologue to Decision Concerning Private Measures of Sanction,* 12 STAN. J. INT'L STUD. 79 (1977).

4. Some commentators differentiate between "hard" and "soft" law, but there is no general agreement as to what these terms mean. For example, some consider that "soft" law is not law, some that it is too vague for adequate application, some that there are not sufficiently intense and or widespread patterns of supportive expectation, some that it is less stable or secure or that it is "weak," some that it is not related to normal and effective sanctions, some that it is not mirrored in "traditionally" (or formalistically) correct instruments (*e.g.*, not in treaties), some that it relates to a new form of law-making. An informative panel discussion of various meanings, factors and concerns appears at *A Hard Look at Soft Law*, 82 PROC., AM. SOC. INT'L L. 371–95 (1988) (especially by Professors Günther Handl, W. Michael Reisman, Bruno Sima, Pierre Marie Dupuy, Christine Chinkin, Lung-chu Chen).* Professor Handl remarked: "We are all ... familiar with examples of formal international law such as treaties, whose ineffectiveness relegates them to the ranks of nonlegal norms, or, if you will, soft norms, notwithstanding their formal status. And vice versa, there is an abundance of, formally speaking, nonnormative documents such as resolutions and declarations of international organizations or conferences, which have proved to be highly effective internationally and must be deemed part and parcel of the international normative order." *Id.* at 372. Professor Reisman added: "soft law has come to refer to a diverse range of phenomena related to lawmaking and frequently presented as law. For some scholars, the phenomenon is supposedly so lacking in the third component, control intention, as to be mislabeled law. These same scholars are apparently unaware that scholars in many weak and small states view some very 'hard'

* Reproduced with permission from 82 Proc., ASIL 372 and 374 (1988), © The American Society of International Law.

law, that is, communications backed by compelling control intention but of questionable authority, as naked power. In fact, law can be soft in all its dimensions: in terms of its content, in terms of its authority, and in terms of control intention." *Id.* at 374.

Read the full discussion in the Proceedings, which is also online, and consider what, if anything, might appropriately be considered "soft" law. For further guidance, *see, e.g.*, ANTHONY D'AMATO, INTERNATIONAL LAW ANTHOLOGY 148–57 (1994); *Environmental Law: When Does It Make Sense to Negotiate International Agreements?*, 87 PROC., AM. SOC. INT'L L. 377 (1993); José E. Alvarez, *Organizational Insights*, *id.* at 403–04; Geoffrey Palmer, *New Ways to Make International Environmental Law*, 86 AM. J. INT'L L. 259 (1992); Pierre–Marie Dupuy, *Soft Law and the International Law of the Environment*, 12 MICH. J. INT'L L. 420 (1991); Günther Handl, *National Uses of Transboundary Air Resources: The International Entitlement Issue Reconsidered*, 26 NAT. RESOURCES J. 405, 407–09 (1986); Prosper Weil, *Towards Relative Normativity in International Law?*, 77 AM. J. INT'L L. 413 (1983); Ignaz Seidl–Hohenveldern, *International Economic "Soft Law,"* 163 RECUEIL DES COURS 169 (1979 II).

5. Counsel arguing in The Nereide, 13 U.S. (9 Cranch) 388 (1815) claimed: "Reciprocity is the permanent basis of the law of nations." In Hilton v. Guyot, 159 U.S. 113, 228 (1895), Justice Gray added: "international law is founded upon mutuality and reciprocity." Viewed contextually and comprehensively, what is involved in a process of reciprocity? How might patterns of *opinio juris* be related to such a process? In particular, what actors, in what arenas, with what claims and counterclaims, sharing what expectations, from what levels or bases of power (and enlightenment, respect, wealth, skill, well-being, rectitude, and affection), using what strategies, with what outcomes and effects might be involved in processes of reciprocity? If one started with a focus on power as a process, but viewed power realistically and comprehensively, would one eventually identify similar actors, arenas, and so forth? *See generally* materials cited in notes 5–8 above, especially writings of Professors Chen and McDougal and Reisman.

C. United Nations Resolutions

Does Article 38 of the Statute of the I.C.J. or Section 102 of the Restatement mention international law reflected in a U.N. Security Council resolution or a General Assembly resolution?

Both the United Nations Security Council and General Assembly function under a process constituted by treaty, the U.N. Charter. Each signatory to the Charter has representation within the General Assembly on the basis of one state one vote. The primary base for General Assembly authority or competence is found in Article 13 of the Charter, which recognizes the competence of the General Assembly to "initiate studies and make recommendations" for certain purposes. It also has recommendatory powers under Article 14. See Documents Supplement. The powers of the Security Council under Articles 24–25, 39, 41–42 and 48 (for example, involving threats to the peace, breaches of the peace and acts of aggression) are far more extensive. We pay particular attention to such powers in Chapter 8. The Council is presently composed of five permanent members that each possess a power to veto potential decisions of the Council (the U.S., China, France, Great Britain, Russia). The ten other members of the Council are elected by the General Assembly for a period of two years. Indeed, the Security Council can make binding "decisions" and either authorize or order sanctions of various sorts, at least if the decisions are made in compliance with the Charter. *See* Articles 1, 24(2), 25, 55. In contrast, the General Assembly does not expressly have the power to enact legislation, to make such decisions, to condemn a state for violating international law, or to order sanctions. However, subsequent practice demonstrates a growing competence of the General Assembly to make legally relevant determinations and to condemn violations of the Charter and international law more generally. As recognized in Article 31 of the Vienna Convention on the Law of Treaties, the meaning of a treaty, such as the U.N. Charter, can be influenced in part by subsequent practice of the signatories.

The short extracts from the following cases, an international and a U.S. case, are set forth merely to demonstrate the accepted legal relevance of certain General Assembly resolutions. Each case is addressed more fully in another chapter.

CASE CONCERNING MILITARY AND PARAMILITARY ACTIVITIES IN AND AGAINST NICARAGUA (NICARAGUA v. UNITED STATES)

1986 I.C.J. 14.

191. As regards certain particular aspects of the principle in question [concerning permissible use of armed force under international law], it will be necessary to distinguish the most grave forms of the use of force ... [under customary international law and] in determining the legal rule, ... the Court can again draw on the formulations contained in the [1970] Declaration on Principles of International Law concerning Friendly Relations and Co–Operation among States in accordance with the Charter of the United Nations (General Assembly resolution 2625 (XXV)) [a resolution 25 years in the making that provides agreed detail concerning basic principles or norms contained in the U.N. Charter, *e.g.*, on the use of armed force, human rights duties of states, and self-determination–see the Documents Supplement].... The adoption by States of this text affords an indication of their *opinio juris* as to customary international law on the question....

193. ... [T]he [United Nations] Charter itself testifies to the existence of the right of collective self-defense in customary international law. Moreover, just as the wording of certain General Assembly declarations adopted by States demonstrates their recognition of the principle of the prohibition of force as definitely a matter of customary international law, some of the wording in those declarations operates similarly in respect of the right of self-defence....

195. ... There appears not to be general agreement on the nature of the acts which can be treated as constituting armed attacks [in

violation of international law and authorizing responsive force in self-defense].... This description, contained in Article 3, paragraph (g), of the Definition of Aggression annexed to General Assembly resolution 3314 (XXIX) [in the Documents Supplement], may be taken to reflect customary international law....

228. ... [T]he Court finds that ... the United States has committed a prima facie violation of that principle [of non-use of armed force] by its assistance to the *Contras* in Nicaragua, by "organizing or encouraging the organization of irregular forces or armed bands ... for incursion into the territory of another State," and "participating in acts of civil strife ... in another State," in the terms of General Assembly resolution 2625 (XXV). According to that resolution, participation of this kind is contrary to the principle of the prohibition of the use of force when the acts of civil strife referred to "involve a threat or use of force."

...

FILARTIGA v. PENA–IRALA

630 F.2d 876, 881–84 (2d Cir.1980).

[Editors' note: the rest of the opinion is in Chapter 2, Section 2 D 2.]

While this broad mandate [in the U.N. Charter, arts. 55 (c) and 56, to respect and ensure respect for human rights] has been held not to be wholly self-executing, ... this observation does not end our inquiry. For although there is no universal agreement as to the precise extent of the "human rights and fundamental freedoms" guaranteed to all by the Charter, there is at present no dissent from the view that the guarantees include, at a bare minimum, the right to be free from torture. This prohibition has become part of customary international law, as evidenced and defined by the Universal Declaration of Human Rights, General Assembly Resolution 217 (III) (A) (Dec. 10, 1948) which states in the plainest of terms, "no one shall be subjected to torture." The General Assembly has declared that the Charter precepts embodied in this Universal Declaration "constitute basic principles of international law." G.A. Res. 2625 (XXV) (Oct. 24, 1970) [the 1970 Declaration on Principles of International Law].

Particularly relevant is the Declaration on the Protection of All Persons from Being Subjected to Torture, General Assembly Resolution 3452 (1975).... This Declaration, like the Declaration of Human Rights before it, was adopted without dissent by the General Assembly....

These U.N. declarations are significant because they specify with great precision the obligations of member nations under the Charter. Since their adoption, "[m]embers can no longer contend that they do not know what human rights they promised in the Charter to promote".... [T]he Universal Declaration ... "is ... an authoritative statement of the international community." ...

Having examined the sources from which customary international law is derived—the usage of nations, judicial opinions and the works of jurists—we conclude that official torture is now prohibited by the law of nations.

Restatement of the Foreign Relations Law of the United States § 102, RN 2 (3 ed. 1987).

... The practice of states that builds customary law takes many forms and includes what states do in or through international organizations.... The United Nations General Assembly in particular has adopted resolutions, declarations, and other statements of principles that in some circumstances contribute to the process of making customary law, insofar as statements and votes of governments are kinds of state practice ... and may be expressions of *opinio juris*.... The contributions of such resolutions and of the statements and votes supporting them to the lawmaking process will differ widely, depending on factors such as the subject of the resolution, whether it purports to reflect legal principles, how large a majority it commands and how numerous and important are the dissenting states, whether it is widely supported (including in particular the states principally affected), and whether it is later confirmed by other practice. "Declarations of principles" may have greater significance than ordinary resolutions ... "in view of the greater solemnity and significance of a 'declaration,' it may be considered to impart ... a strong expectation that Members of the international community will abide by it." ...

UNITED STATES v. STEINBERG

478 F.Supp. 29, 31, 33 (N.D.Ill.1979).

The United Nations Charter, a treaty ratified by the United States, is a part of the supreme law of this land.... This country has a continuing obligation to observe with entire good faith and scrupulous care all of its undertakings under this treaty, including support of the resolutions adopted by the Security Council.

Of course, a treaty, either by its terms or in its application, cannot run counter to the provisions of the constitution of this country.... Therefore, the government through its officials could not choose between respecting the constitutional rights of a citizen and adhering to the provisions of a treaty....

Notes and Questions

1. Concerning the authoritativeness of U.N. Security Council resolutions, see United States v. Toscanino, 500 F.2d 267, 277–78 (2d Cir.1974); Diggs v. Schultz, 470 F.2d 461, 465–66 (D.C.Cir.1972), *cert. denied*, 411 U.S. 931 (1973).

2. Read U.N. Charter, Articles 24–25, 39, 41–42, 48–49. What do you suspect is a "decision" of the Security Council? Must all "decisions" of the Security Council be accepted and carried out? Could particular decisions be *ultra vires*? If so, what guidance is there in the U.N. Charter concerning standards and norms that might limit the power of the Security Council? See Articles 1, 2, 24, 25.

For further consideration, *see, e.g.*, MYRES S. McDOUGAL, HAROLD D. LASSWELL, LUNG-CHU CHEN, HUMAN RIGHTS AND WORLD PUBLIC ORDER 332–34 (1980); David Caron, *The Legitimacy of the Collective Authority of the Security Council,* 87 AM. J. INT'L L. 552 (1993); Thomas M. Franck, *The "Powers of Appreciation": Who Is the Ultimate Guardian of UN Legality?,* 86 AM. J. INT'L L. 519 (1992); Vera Gowlland–Debbas, *Security Council Enforcement Action and Issues of State Responsibility*, 43 INT'L & COMP. L.Q. 55 (1994); Jordan J. Paust, *U.N. Peace and Security Powers and Related Presidential Powers*, 26 GA. J. INT'L & COMP. L. 15 (1996); Michael Reisman, *The Constitutional Crisis in the United Nations*, 87 AM. J. INT'L L. 83 (1993).

3. Concerning the legal relevance of U.N. General Assembly resolutions, *see also* ANTHONY D'AMATO, INTERNATIONAL LAW ANTHOLOGY 104–07 (1994); JORDAN J. PAUST, INTERNATIONAL LAW AS LAW OF THE UNITED STATES 6, 34–36 (2 ed. 2003), extract of lst edition reprinted below in Section 2 B; Christopher C. Joyner, *U.N. General Assembly Resolutions and International Law: Rethinking the Contemporary Dynamics of Norm–Creation*, 11 CAL. W. INT'L L.J. 445 (1981); Oscar Schachter, *International Law in Theory and Practice*, 178 REC. DES COURS 111–21 (1982–V). More particularly, concerning the growth of the Universal Declaration of Human Rights into an authoritative exposition of human rights guaranteed by the U.N. Charter and as an evidence of customary human rights, as addressed in *Filartiga*, *see, e.g.*, MYRES S. McDOUGAL, HAROLD D. LASSWELL, LUNG-CHU CHEN, HUMAN RIGHTS AND WORLD PUBLIC ORDER 272–74, 302, 325–30 (1980); PAUST, *supra* at 207, 217, 224, 254, 273, 284; Richard B. Lillich, *The Current Status of the Law of State Responsibility for Injuries to Aliens*, in INTERNATIONAL LAW OF STATE RESPONSIBILITY FOR INJURY TO ALIENS 1, 28–29 (1983); Hurst Hannum, *The Status of the Universal Declaration of Human Rights in National and International Law*, 25 GA. J. INT'L & COMP. L. 287 (1995/96); W. Michael Reisman, *Sovereignty and Human Rights in Contemporary International Law*, 84 AM. J. INT'L L. 866, 867 (1990).

4. Although Article 13 of the U.N. Charter is at best silent concerning condemnatory powers, beginning early in its history the General Assembly condemned states for violations of human rights law. *See, e.g.*, the 1949 Russian Wives "case," reported in RICHARD B. LILLICH, INTERNATIONAL HUMAN RIGHTS 49 (2 ed. 1991). What is the relevance of such practice?

5. A remarkable General Assembly resolution in 1984 recalled that the Security Council had rejected "the so-called 'new constitution' [of the apartheid regime of South Africa] and declared it null and void," commended "the united resistance of the oppressed people of South Africa ... and recogniz[ed] the legitimacy of their struggle to eliminate apartheid and establish a society based on majority rule with equal participation of all the people of South Africa ... ," urged "all governments and organizations ... to assist the oppressed people of South Africa in their legitimate struggle for national liberation," and condemned "the South African racist regime for ... persisting with the further entrenchment of apartheid, a system declared a crime against humanity and a threat to international peace and security." U.N. G.A. Res. 39/2 (28 Sept. 1984) (vote: 133–0–2 abstentions).

6. A 1989 U.N. G.A. resolution on Large–Scale Pelagic Driftnet Fishing recalled "the relevant principles elaborated in the United Nations Conven-

tion on the Law of the Sea," which some states have not ratified, and recalled "that, in accordance with the relevant articles of the Convention, it is the responsibility of all members of the international community to ensure the conservation and management of living marine resources and the protection and preservation of the living marine environment within their exclusive economic zones." U.N. G.A. Res. 225 (22 Dec. 1989). Can a treaty create responsibilities for nonsignatories (either those that have not signed awaiting ratification or those that have not ratified)? Is that how the responsibilities arise? What treaty is most relevant as a basis of responsibility, the U.N. Charter or the Law of the Sea Convention? *See also* Günther Handl, *Regional Arrangements and Third State Vessels: Is the* Pacta Tertiis *Principle Being Modified?*, in COMPETING NORMS IN THE LAW OF MARINE ENVIRONMENTAL PROTECTION—FOCUS ON SHIP SAFETY AND POLLUTION PREVENTION 217 (Henrik Ringbom ed. 1997), extract reprinted below in Section 2 A 2.

The 1989 resolution proceeds by declaring that the General Assembly "Calls upon all members of the international community" to do certain things and "recommends that all members ... should" do certain things. See *id.* paras. 1 and 4 (a)-(c). Does the phrase "calls upon" imply more than a recommendation? Is it stronger than "urges" or "requests"? Does the word "should," when following the word "recommends," imply a duty? Does the resolution appear in part to be a "law-making" resolution? Does the General Assembly have the power to create law?

A similar 1991 resolution "Calls upon all members of the international community to implement resolutions 44/225 and 45/197 by, *inter alia*, taking the following actions," and then lists such actions in para. 3 (a)-(c). This paragraph does not contain the word "should," nor the word "recommends." Is this a "law-making" resolution? Is the authority of the General Assembly in this instance enhanced by the Law of the Sea Convention? Does it function beyond what appears in the words of either the U.N. Charter or the Law of the Sea Convention?

7. A number of international agreements create international institutions with law-making and/or regulative powers. The Restatement notes that, under their constitutive instruments, the International Monetary Fund has power to prescribe rules concerning the maintenance or change of exchange rates or depreciation of currency and the International Civil Aviation Organization (ICAO) can set binding standards in addition to recommended guidelines concerning air navigation. RESTATEMENT, § 102, cmt. g. See also Convention on International Civil Aviation (the Chicago Convention), arts. 37–38 (in the Documents Supplement). The International Maritime Organization (I.M.O.) also has related powers which have influenced the law of the sea (see Chapter 6). The Council of the European Economic Community set up under the Treaty of Rome also has power to make decisions and to create regulations and directives binding on states as well as individuals. See Treaty of Rome of the European Union, art. 189.

8. The Ad Hoc International Criminal Tribunals for Former Yugoslavia and for Rwanda were set up by Security Council resolutions. *See, e.g.*, JORDAN J. PAUST, M. CHERIF BASSIOUNI, *ET AL.*, INTERNATIONAL CRIMINAL LAW 665, 679–87, 699, *passim* (2 ed. 2000). Do provisions in the U.N. Charter support these exercises of substantial sanction powers? What articles seem relevant?

The International Criminal Court

Although the *ad hoc* criminal tribunals established to prosecute those who violated international law in the recent conflicts in Yugoslavia, Rwanda, Sierra Leone, East Timor, and Cambodia have made important contributions to justice and accountability, the process of developing a new court for every situation has been time-consuming, expensive, and exhausting. Both the lessons learned from these efforts and frustrations involved in each separate situation led many governments to decide that the time had come to develop a permanent International Criminal Court. Various textwriters (including Professor Cherif Bassiouni and Benjamin Ferencz) had also demonstrated why a permanent international criminal court was needed. In 1998, the International Criminal Court (ICC) was created by the "Rome Statute" adopted by the United Nations Diplomatic Conference on Plenipotentiaries on the Establishment of an International Criminal Court on 17 July 1998. The "Rome Statute" creating the ICC is part of a new treaty that as of April 2005 has been ratified by ninety-eight states (and had been signed while awaiting ratification by another 41 states). The Court formally came into being on July 1, 2002, after the 60th state ratified the treaty. Of those ratifying, 26 were from the Western Europe and Other regional group (including every nation in Western Europe except a couple of the ministates), 15 were from Eastern Europe, 19 were from Latin America and the Caribbean, 26 were from Africa, and 11 were from Asia. In February 2003, the contracting parties elected seven females and eleven males representing the geographical variety of the global community to serve as the initial judges on the court.

The International Criminal Court has limited jurisdiction over three so-called "core" crimes under customary international law: (1) genocide, (2) some crimes against humanity, and (3) some war crimes (see Articles 12–15 of the treaty, in the Documents Supplement–with respect to crimes against humanity, compare the broader definitions in the Charter of the I.M.T. at Nuremberg, Charter of the I.M.T. for the Far East, and Control Council Law No. 10), and will have jurisdiction over "aggression" when the contracting parties are able to define the crime and amend the treaty (see Article 5(2)). The ICC has a form of limited universal jurisdiction in certain situations where national courts are unable or unwilling to prosecute these crimes. Under special provisions, cases can be brought to the Court by the Security Council (acting under Chapter VII of the UN Charter), or by a contracting party, or by the Court's Prosecutor, if such a proceeding is approved by the Court's "Pre–Trial Chamber." *See* Articles 12–15. Under Article 12(2), unless the matter has been referred to the Prosecutor by the Security Council, either the state on whose territory (or vessel or aircraft) an alleged crime has occurred or the state of nationality of the accused must have ratified the treaty. Due process guarantees include those in Articles 21(3) (human rights law is incorporated by reference and prevails) and 66–69. Are they consistent with the customary rights to due process mirrored in Articles 9 and 14 of the ICCPR?

The United States was a major participant in the 1998 drafting sessions that produced the treaty but expressed doubts about the Court almost immediately. During the Clinton Administration, David Scheffer (the U.S. Ambassador at Large for War Crimes Issues) led the U.S. effort to raise questions about the proper role of the Court. The Clinton Administration was comfortable with the listing of war crimes and their elements, but was concerned that politics (perhaps related to the Middle East peace process) might lead to "political" prosecutions with regard to an occupying power's transfer of its own population into occupied territory (in violation of customary laws of war). The U.S. was also concerned that the crime of aggression might be poorly defined and could interfere with "the need for the international community to respond to humanitarian and other crises without being harassed and much worse, charged with violations of the Statute." U.S. Statement before the U.N. General Assembly Sixth Committee: The Rome Treaty on the International Criminal Court, Oct. 21, 1999, http://www.igc.apc.org/icc/html/us19991021.html; *see generally* David Scheffer, *The United States and the International Criminal Court*, 93 AM. J. INT'L L. 12 (1999). Another political concern of the U.S. involves the possibility that a crime within the competence of the ICC will be committed by a U.S. soldier (perhaps while on a peacekeeping mission in a country that has accepted the jurisdiction of the ICC). In such a situation, the United States would have a responsibility under international law to either initiate prosecution of or to extradite the soldier (*aut dedere aut judicare*). The state where the crime took place would have the same responsibility and would have jurisdiction under international law under two principles addressed in Chapter 3 (*i.e.*, territorial and universal jurisdiction). Yet, could the state where the crime occurred extradite or transfer the U.S. soldier to the ICC? *See* Articles 12(2)(a), 13(a), 89–90. In general, under the principle of universal jurisdiction (discussed in detail in Chapter 3) any state can prosecute any individual reasonably accused of having committed any of the core crimes that are also within the treaty-based competence of the ICC and any state could extradite such an accused to any other state (since each state has such a universal jurisdictional competence). Ambassador Scheffer argued vigorously, however, that the territorial state's territorial jurisdiction as such cannot be "delegated," which misses the point that the ICC has been created by a multilateral treaty and can exercise a form of limited universal jurisdiction much like the International Military Tribunals at Nuremberg and the Far East. *See also* Demjanjuk v. Petrovsky, 776 F.2d 571, 582 (6th Cir. 1985), quoted in Chapter 3. Scheffer quoted Duke Law Professor Madeline Morris for the proposition that "territorial jurisdiction [as such] is not 'a form of negotiable instrument' " and has offered her hypothetical that the country where the atrocity took place might transfer jurisdiction to Libya (in exchange for Libya's transferring jurisdiction over a national of the country where the atrocity occurred. *See* Address by Ambassador David Scheffer, remarks, *International Criminal Court: The Challenge of Jurisdiction*, 93 PROC., AM. SOC. INT'L L.68 (1999); see also Scheffer, remarks, 92 PROC., AM. SOC. INT'L L. (1998); *The United States and the*

International Criminal Court, 93 AM. J. INT'L L. 12 (1999); *but see* Jordan J. Paust, *The Reach of ICC Jurisdiction Over Non–Signatory Nationals*, 33 VAND. J. TRANSNAT'L. L. 1 (2000) (in certain situations, the ICC can obtain jurisdiction under the terms of the treaty over nationals of a state that has not ratified the treaty–*see, e.g.*, ICC Statute, arts. 12, 89–90).

President Clinton "signed" the Rome Statute at the end of his Administration in 2001, but President Bush withdrew the U.S. signature within a few months, which is the prerogative of a state that has signed a treaty while awaiting ratification. President Bush denounced the Court on a number of occasions and spoke proudly of his decision to reject the Court in his second debate with John Kerry on October 8, 2004 in St. Louis:

> "I made a decision not to join the International Criminal Court in The Hague, which is where our troops could be brought to—brought in front of a judge, an unaccounted judge.
>
> "I don't think we ought to join that. That [decision] was unpopular....
>
> "You don't want to join the International Criminal Court just because it's popular in certain capitals in Europe."

As of April 2005, the ICC had been authorized to investigate cases from the Central African Republic, Democratic Republic of Congo, Ivory Coast, and the Republic of Uganda. The Uganda referral stemmed from the civil war in northern Uganda that has led to 100,000 dead and 1,500,000 refugees. In February 2005, a spokesperson for the Court announced that arrest warrants would issue for up to a dozen suspects, which would be the first arrest warrants issued by the Court.

A defining moment for the Court also involved alleged war crimes committed during the crisis in Darfur, Sudan. Reports exist of indiscriminate attacks by Sudanese government forces and militias (including the killing of civilians, genocide, torture, enforced disappearances, destruction of villages, rape and other forms of sexual violence, pillaging and forced displacement) which have produced some 300,000 deaths and left some 2,000,000 persons homeless. A U.N. commission released a report in early 2005 identifying 51 suspects (including members of the Sudanese government) and explaining the evidence against them. In February 2005, Louise Arbour, the U.N. High Commissioner for Human Rights, emphasized that such crimes must be referred to the ICC, explaining that "[t]here is no hope for sustainable peace in Darfur without immediate access to justice." U.N. Secretary–General Kofi Annan added that "[i]t is vital that these crimes are not left unpunished." However, the Bush Administration, because of its opposition to the ICC, took a different view and advocated the creation of an *ad hoc* international court for Darfur to be established in Arusha, Tanzania (where the ICTR Trial Chambers operate). China and Algeria took a third view, opposing international adjudication, and arguing that Sudan's own courts should try those who have been implicated. In the face of a united European view favoring referral of these cases to the ICC, the U.S. finally abandoned its opposition on March 31, 2005 and agreed not to veto the U.N. Security Council's referral of the Darfur crimes to the ICC. The Council's vote was 11–0, with Algeria, Brazil, China, and the United States abstaining. The United States was persuaded to abstain after it received assurances that any U.S. citizens accused of war crimes in the Sudan would not be handed over to the ICC or to any non-U.S. court. The Acting U.S. Ambassador to the United Nations reiterated that the U.S. still "fundamentally objects" to the ICC but had abstained because "[i]t is important that the international community speak with one voice in order to help promote effective accountability."

D. *Equity and Justice*

Recall that Article 38 (2) of the Statute of the I.C.J. notes that the Court might have "power to decide a case *ex aequo et bono*, if the parties agree thereto." It is widely expected that the Court has no power to make principles of equity and goodness or justice the primary bases of its decision, unless the parties to a case agree thereto (which apparently has not happened at the Court), but that the Court may use such principles indirectly as aids to interpret treaty-based or customary international law (*e.g.*, the use of equity *praeter legem* or partly in between the law, as opposed to equity *infra legem* (when use of equity is clearly within or allowed by the law)). *See also* RESTATEMENT OF THE FOREIGN RELATIONS LAW OF THE UNITED STATES §§ 102, cmt. m, and 903, RN 9 (3 ed. 1987).

The precursor to the I.C.J. was the Permanent Court of International Justice (P.C.I.J.) set up under the Charter of the League of Nations. Sitting on the P.C.I.J., Judge Hudson, in The Diversion of Water from the Muese (Netherlands v. Belgium), P.C.I.J., Ser. A/B, No. 70, at 76 (1937), made somewhat different statements: "What are widely known as principles of equity have long been considered to constitute a part of international law, and as such they have often been applied by international tribunals.... The Court has not been expressly authorized by its Statute [which was basically the same as that of the I.C.J.] to apply equity as distinguished from law.... [,however, ' "general principles of law recognized by civilized nations" ' can also be applied,] and in more than one nation principles of equity have an established place in the legal system. The Court's recognition of equity as a part of international law is in no way restricted by the special power conferred upon it 'to decide a case *ex aequo et bono*, if the parties agree thereto.' ... It must be concluded, therefore, that under Article 38 of the Statute, if not independently of the Article, the Court has some freedom to consider principles of equity as part of the international law which it must apply." He added: "One result of applying the principle will be that even if the Court should be of the opinion that ... [one state's] action ... is contrary to the Treaty of 1863, it should nevertheless refuse in this case to order ... [that state] to discontinue that action. In equity, the ... [other state involved] is not in a position to have such relief decreed to her." See also MARK W. JANIS & JOHN E. NOYES, INTERNATIONAL LAW 126–29 (1997).

In a given case, a treaty may incorporate principles of equity and/or justice as relevant standards. *See, e.g.*, U.N. Charter, preamble ("to establish conditions under which justice ... can be maintained"), art. 2 (3) (settle disputes "in such a manner that international peace, security, and justice, are not endangered"); Charter of the Organization of American States, Apr. 30, 1948, 119 U.N.T.S. 3, art. 1 (the O.A.S. was established in part to achieve "an order of peace and justice"), art. 3 ((c) "Good faith shall govern the relations between States," (h) "Social justice," (*l*) "education of peoples should be directed toward social justice...."), art. 14 (states are not authorized "to commit unjust acts against another State"), art. 16 (each state shall respect "the principles of universal morality"), art. 29 (pledge "to a united effort to ensure social justice in the Hemisphere"), art. 31 (basic goals: (b) "[e]quitable distribution of national income," (c) "equitable systems of taxation," (d) "equitable" land tenure, (f) "social justice," (g) "[f]air wages"), art. 37 (b)(i) ("prices ... fair to consumers"), art. 43 ("a just social order," including principles of (b) "fair wages" and (d) "fair and efficient systems and procedures ... of production"), art. 100 ("social justice"); 1969 American Convention on Human Rights, preamble ("social justice"); the North Atlantic Treaty, Apr. 4, 1949, 34 U.N.T.S. 243, T.I.A.S. No. 164, art. 1 (settle disputes "in such a manner that international peace and security, and justice, are not endangered...."); the 1794 Jay Treaty between Great Britain and the United States, 1 Malloy 596 ("justice, equity and the laws of nations"); 1982 Convention on the Law of the Sea, preamble ("justice"), arts. 59 (conflicts regarding delimitation of Exclusive Economic Zones "should be resolved on the basis of equity and in light of all relevant circumstances"), 74 (1) (delimitation of Exclusive Economic Zone Between States with Opposite or Adjacent Coasts "in order to achieve and equitable solution"), 83 (1) (delimitation of shelf areas "in order to achieve an equitable solution"); The North Sea Continental Shelf Cases (Federal Republic of Germany v. Denmark) (Federal Republic of Germany v. the Netherlands), 1969 I.C.J. 3.

W. MICHAEL REISMAN, NULLITY AND REVISION

559–62 (1971).*

... [M]ost of the basic principles of Anglo–American equity have counterparts in most legal systems and are regularly applied in international law, either unconsciously as weighted inferences or unenunciated presumptions, or consciously as "general principles"....

... International law not only allows, but demands, that the most equitable construction of past communications [*e.g.*, in an international instrument] be chosen, so long as it is not contrary to the purport of the communication in question. Where the manifest purport allows for two or more constructions, that which is equitable is to be chosen: *interpretatio infra legem*. Where the manifest purport would, in the circumstances of the case, be inequitable, yet an alternate interpretation that is more equitable but not contradictory to the purport is possible, the latter is to be chosen: *interpretatio praeter* or *secundem legem*.

The doctrinal controversy attaches to the third possibility: any interpretation conforming to the purport of the past communication would, in the circumstances of the case, lead to an inequitable result. In these circumstances, is a tribunal authorized to adopt an interpretation *contra legem*? ... [T]he test of the decision's lawfulness is ... its consonance with the fundamental goals of the international community. It is according to this latter criterion that its ultimate lawfulness and effectiveness will be tested in social process....

No attempt is made to minimize the difficulties involved in the application of international equity.... [It] is not the visceral law of the legal realist, nor is it a modality for the expression of unpoliced personal preferences. It involves clarification and satisfaction of the basic minimum and maximum goals of the international community....

Notes

1. Concerning these concepts more generally, *see, e.g.*, D'AMATO, INTERNATIONAL LAW ANTHOLOGY, *supra* at 102–03; MARK W. JANIS, AN INTRODUCTION TO INTERNATIONAL LAW 54–66 (1988); 1 OPPENHEIM'S INTERNATIONAL LAW 43–45 (Robert Jennings & Arthur Watts eds., 9 ed. 1992). Concerning use of equitable principles as law, *see also* Grisbadarna Case (Norway v. Sweden), Permanent Court of Arbitration (23 Oct. 1909) (maritime boundary dispute), *reprinted in* 4 AM. J. INT'L L. 226, 233 (1910); addressed in Sang-Myon Rhee, *Sea Boundary Delimitation Between States Before World War II*, 76 AM. J. INT'L L. 555, 571 (1982).

2. In Thirty Hogsheads of Sugar v. Boyle, 13 U.S. (9 Cranch) 191, 198 (1815), Chief Justice Marshall declared: "The law of nations ... is in part unwritten, and in part conventional. To ascertain that which is unwritten, we resort to the great principles of reason and justice ... being, in some degree, fixed and rendered stable by a series of judicial decisions. The decisions of the Courts of every country, so far as they are founded upon a law common to every country, will be received, not as authority, but with respect." For related judicial and other recognitions of "natural reason and justice," "principles of equity and natural justice" in connection with efforts to clarify the content of the law of nations, *see, e.g.*, JORDAN J. PAUST, INTERNATIONAL LAW AS LAW OF THE UNITED STATES 29 (2 ed. 2003).

E. General Principles of Domestic Law

Recall that Article 38 (1) (c) of the Statute of the I.C.J. refers to the competence of the International Court of Justice to use general principles of domestic law as bases for decision. Although such principles are rarely used, the Permanent Court of International Justice (P.C.I.J.) recognized in the Factory at Chorzow Case, P.C.I.J., Ser. A., No. 17

(1928), that there is "a general conception of law that every violation of an engagement involves an obligation to make reparation," *i.e.*, that for every wrong there should be a remedy. The Court also recognized that a state must not benefit from an illegality. See Factory at Chorzow Case, P.C.I.J., Ser. A, No. 9, at 31 (1927). In the Corfu Channel Case (United Kingdom v. Albania), 1949 I.C.J. 1, the I.C.J. noted that the use of "indirect evidence is admitted in all systems of law and its use is recognized by international decisions." The principle common to most legal systems sometimes termed estoppel was recognized by the I.C.J. in Case of the Temple of Preah Vihear (Cambodia v. Thailand), 1962 I.C.J. 6, 23, 31–32, 42, 61–65, and the French Nuclear Test Cases (New Zealand v. France) (Australia v. France), 1974 I.C.J. 253, 268, 457, 473; *see also* Eastern Greenland Case (Denmark v. Norway), P.C.I.J., Ser. A/B, No. 53, at 71 (1933) (unilateral declaration).

Notes and Questions

1. Is the use of general principles of domestic law during international decisional processes consistent with the view that there are basically two types of international law, international agreements and customary law?

2. In Case Concerning Barcelona Traction Light and Power Company, Ltd., 1970 I.C.J. 3, 34–35, 38, paras. 37–40, 50, the Court recognized a general principle in domestic processes whereby the corporate entity is a recognized institution.

3. What other general principles might be useful for decisional application? *See also* RESTATEMENT, § 102, cmt. l and RN 7; BIN CHENG, GENERAL PRINCIPLES OF LAW AS APPLIED BY INTERNATIONAL COURTS AND TRIBUNALS (1953); 1 OPPENHEIM'S INTERNATIONAL LAW 36–40 (Robert Jennings & Arthur Watts eds., 9 ed. 1992); OSCAR SCHACHTER, INTERNATIONAL LAW IN THEORY AND PRACTICE 50–55 (1991); MALCOLM N. SHAW, INTERNATIONAL LAW 81–84 (2 ed. 1986).

F. Hierarchic Categories of International Law

Although textwriters disagree, in the case of an unavoidable clash between an ordinary international agreement and ordinary customary international law, the international community has not definitely resolved which form of international law should prevail.

Section 102, comment j of the Restatement declares: "Customary law and law made by international agreement have equal authority as international law. Unless the parties evince a contrary intention, a rule established by agreement supersedes for them a prior inconsistent rule of customary international law. However, an agreement will not supersede a prior rule of customary international law that is a peremptory norm of international law...." This formulation, however, is far too simplistic. First, an ordinary bilateral treaty should not have the same status as a norm of customary international law, much less the same status as an important multilateral treaty. Second, as materials that follow demonstrate, it is obvious that certain forms of international law are of greater significance to the international community and have a higher status than ordinary international law; even the Restatement pays some attention to the preemption of an international agreement by a peremptory norm. When considering these higher forms, do they cause you to reconsider the nature of or your definition of international law?

1. The U.N. Charter

UNITED NATIONS CHARTER, ARTICLE 103.

> In the event of a conflict between the obligations of the Members of the United Nations under the present Charter and their obligations under any other international agreement, their obligations under the present Charter shall prevail.

Does Article 103 place the U.N. Charter in a new category of international law? Is the primacy of U.N. Charter obligations consistent with a theory that international agreements generally rest on the consent of signatories thereto? Does the primacy of the U.N. Charter pertain in the case of an unavoidable clash with obligations under customary international law? *See also* Judge Lauterpacht, separate opinion, in Case Concerning Application of the Convention on the Prevention of the Crime of Genocide (Bosnia and Herzegovina v. Yugoslavia (Serbia and Montenegro)), Further Requests for the Indication of Provisional Measures, 1993 I.C.J. 325, para. 100 (*jus cogens* norms, such as the prohibition of genocide, will trump Article 103–thus, even the Security Council could not authorize genocide); W. Czaplinski, G. Danilenko, *Conflicts of Norms in International Law*, 21 NETHERLANDS Y.B. INT'L L. 14–15 (1990). Consider these points again when reading materials in Chapter 8 with respect to the use of force, Security Council powers, and regional treaty arrangements such as NATO.

Professor Seidl–Hohenveldern writes that generally there is no hierarchy between treaties, but there are at least three exceptional circumstances: (1) amendments to treaties "are subordinated to the basic agreement unless the parties intend them to be autonomous, (2) treaties concluded by international organizations are subordinated to the organization's constitutive instrument, and (3) Article 103 of the U.N. Charter renders the Charter hierarchially superior to any other treaty." See Ignaz Seidl–Hohenveldern, *Hierarchy of Treaties*, in ESSAYS ON THE LAW OF TREATIES 7, 9 (J. Klabbers & R. Lefeber eds. 1998). He adds: "The impact of Article 103 is somewhat obfuscated by the fact that many of the rules of the Charter could claim superiority already on account of their *jus cogens* or *erga omnes* character." *Id.* at 16. Should amendments, which express the last pattern of expectations of the signatories, have a presumptive priority? Should one's choice depend on the nature of the agreements and other legal policies at stake?

2. Obligatio Erga Omnes

CASE CONCERNING THE BARCELONA TRACTION, LIGHT AND POWER COMPANY, LTD.

(Belgium v. Spain), 1970 I.C.J. 3, 32, Paras. 33–34.

In particular, an essential distinction should be drawn between the obligations of a State towards the international community as a whole, and those arising vis-a-vis another State in the field of diplomatic protection. By their very nature, the former are the concern of all States. In view of the importance of the rights involved, all States can be held to have a legal interest in their protection; they are obligations *erga omnes*.

Such obligations derive, for example, in contemporary international law, from the outlawing of acts of aggression, and of genocide, as also from the principles and rules concerning the basic rights of the human person, including protection from slavery and racial discrimination. Some of the corresponding rights of protection have entered into the body of general international law . . .; others are conferred by international instruments of a universal or quasi-universal character.

Notes and Questions

1. *Obligatio erga omnes* are obligations owing not merely to certain states and their nationals but to and among all of humankind. Are they another category of international law? Are they a type of customary international law, but of greater primacy than ordinary customary law? Can they be reflected in treaties?

The High Court of the Netherlands refused to extradite a U.S. serviceperson to the U.S. despite a requirement to do so under a NATO SOFA agreement in view of the Court's conclusion that the European Convention for the Protection of Human Rights and Fundamental Freedoms and Protocol No. 6 thereto concerning the propriety of the death penalty (see Documents Supplement) took precedence over the NATO treaty obligations. The Netherlands, High Ct., Neth. v. Short (30 March 1990), in 29 I.L.M. 1376 (1990).

2. Article 60(5) of the Vienna Convention on the Law of Treaties, May 22, 1969, U.N. Doc. A/CONF./39/27, 1155 U.N.T.S. 331, states that paragraphs addressing the possibility for one party of termination or suspension of performance in the case of a material breach of a treaty by another party "do not apply to provisions relating to the protection of the human person contained in treaties of a humanitarian character, in particular to provisions prohibiting any form of reprisals against persons protected by such treaties."

Is the *erga omnes* nature of such treaties evident from the fact that neither termination nor suspension of performance is available and that these are normal responsive options with respect to a material breach of an international agreement?

3. Common Article 1 of the 1949 Geneva Conventions, humanitarian treaties applicable in times of armed conflict, states: "The High Contracting Parties undertake to respect and to ensure respect for the present Conven-

tion in all circumstances." It is recognized that signatories and their nationals are thus bound to respect and ensure respect for the Conventions even in case of a material breach by another signatory, *i.e.,* that the obligations are owing not merely between one signatory (and its nationals) and another (and its nationals), but also among all or to all of the others. For example, a material breach by an enemy in time of war does not allow suspension of performance by another signatory. See JORDAN J. PAUST, M. CHERIF BASSIOUNI, *ET AL.*, INTERNATIONAL CRIMINAL LAW 130–31, 142–43, 170, 172, 650–51 (2 ed. 2000). In this sense, the treaty creates its own process of *obligatio erga omnes*. *See also* Case Concerning Military and Paramilitary Activities in and Against Nicaragua (Nicaragua v. United States), 1986 I.C.J. 14, para. 220 (the obligation in Article 1 "does not derive only from the Conventions themselves, but from the general principles of humanitarian law to which the Conventions merely give specific expression.").

Are obligations of members of the United Nations under Articles 55(c) and 56 of the U.N. Charter to achieve "universal respect for, and observance of, human rights" of a similar nature?

4. In 1841, in the case *The Schooner Amistad*, the Supreme Court recognized the primacy of fundamental human rights over ordinary treaty law. Control of the Spanish vessel *Amistad* had been taken over by a group of Africans who were being transported to Cuba as slaves and the vessel and the Africans had come to the United States. One issue before the Court was whether a treaty between the U.S. and Spain required the U.S. to return the Spanish "cargo." Former President John Quincy Adams was counsel for the Africans and made the argument that persons held as slaves ("but kidnapped and free") on board a Spanish vessel that was later captured by them and taken to our shores must be set free or the U.S. executive and courts would become complicitors in the deprivation of fundamental human rights. The Supreme Court ordered the Executive to release them. See The Schooner Amistad, 40 U.S. (15 Pet.) 518, 553 (1841) (argument of counsel, John Quincy Adams, asking whether "the people of the United States whose government is based on the great principles of the Revolution, proclaimed the Declaration of Independence, confer upon the federal executive, or judicial tribunals, the power of making our nation accessories to such atrocious violations of human right?"); JORDAN J. PAUST, INTERNATIONAL LAW AS LAW OF THE UNITED STATES 210–11, 258 (2 ed. 2003). The Court, per Justice Story, responded less directly but with implicit attention to a hierarchy of norms: "where human life and human liberty are in issue, and constitute the very essence of the controversy, a [treaty between the U.S. and Spain concerning documents pertaining to ships and their 'cargo'] never could have intended to take away the equal rights of all foreigners who should contest their claims before any of our courts to equal justice; or to deprive such foreigners of the protection given them by other treaties, or by the general law of nations. Upon the merits of the case, then, there does not seem to us to be any ground for doubt that these negroes ought to be deemed free; and that the Spanish Treaty interposes no obstacle to the just assertion of their rights." *Id.* at 595–96, also referring to "eternal principles of justice and international law." *Id.* at 595. Story also noted that Spain had "utterly abolished" the slave trade and made it a heinous crime. *Id.* at 593. More generally, the U.S. Founders and many U.S. judicial opinions confirmed a

primacy for human rights as inalienable rights. *See, e.g.*, PAUST, *supra* at 196–202, 208–15, 219, 222.

5. The right of a people to self-determination was recognized as an obligation *erga omnes* in The East Timor Case (Portugal v. Australia), 1995 I.C.J. 90.

3. Peremptory Norms Jus Cogens

Read Articles 53 and 64 of the Vienna Convention on the Law of Treaties (in the Documents Supplement).

RESTATEMENT OF THE FOREIGN RELATIONS LAW OF THE UNITED STATES § 702 (3 ed. 1987)

A state violates international law if, as a matter of state policy, it practices, encourages, or condones

(a) genocide,

(b) slavery or slave trade,

(c) the murder or causing the disappearance of individuals,

(d) torture or other cruel, inhuman, or degrading treatment or punishment,

(e) prolonged arbitrary detention,

(f) systematic racial discrimination, or

(g) a consistent pattern of gross violations of internationally recognized human rights.

Comment *n. Customary law of human rights and* jus cogens. Not all human rights norms are peremptory norms (*jus cogens*), but those in clauses (a) to (f) of this section are, and an international agreement that violates them is void. See § 331 (2).

HUMAN RIGHTS COMMITTEE, GENERAL COMMENT ON ISSUES RELATING TO RESERVATIONS MADE UPON RATIFICATION OR ACCESSION TO THE COVENANT AND OPTIONAL PROTOCOLS

U.N. DOC. CCPR/C/21/REV.1/add.6, General Comment No. 24, Para. 8 (Nov. 2, 1994).

[Editors' note: The Human Rights Committee has been established under the International Covenant on Civil and Political Rights. See Articles 28–46 in the Documents Supplement.]

8. Reservations that offend peremptory norms would not be compatible with the object and purpose of the Covenant [on Civil and Political Rights]. Although treaties that are mere exchanges of obligations between States allow them to reserve *inter se* application of rules of general international law, it is otherwise in human rights treaties, which are for the benefit of persons within their jurisdiction. Accordingly, provisions in the Covenant that represent customary international

law (and *a fortiori* when they have the character of peremptory norms) may not be the subject of reservations. Accordingly, a State may not reserve the right to engage in slavery, to torture, to subject persons to cruel, inhuman or degrading treatment or punishment, to arbitrarily deprive persons of their lives, to arbitrarily arrest and detain persons, to deny freedom of thought, conscience and religion, to presume a person guilty unless he proves his innocence, to execute pregnant women or children, to permit the advocacy of national, racial or religious hatred, to deny to persons of marriageable age the right to marry, or to deny to minorities the right to enjoy their own culture, profess their own religion, or use their own language. And while reservations to particular clauses of Article 14 may be acceptable, a general reservation to the right to a fair trial would not be.

JOHANN BLUNTSCHLI, MODERN LAW OF NATIONS OF CIVILIZED STATES

(1867).

. . . [T]reaties the contents of which violate the generally recognized human right . . . are invalid.

Notes and Questions

1. Reporters' Note 6 to Section 102 of the Restatement states that the notion of norms *jus cogens* is now widely accepted as a principle of customary international law. Some term these norms "commanding law."

2. "A treaty can never bind parties to do an unlawful act. . . . Thus, . . . a combination to commit injustice, for example, to put down liberty or religion . . . is a crime which no formalities of treaty can sanction." THEODORE DWIGHT WOOLSEY, INTRODUCTION TO THE STUDY OF INTERNATIONAL LAW 163 (6th ed. 1901).

3. What is the ultimate criterion or test concerning *jus cogens* status evident in Article 53 of the Vienna Convention? Is it similar to a criterion or factor concerning the formation of customary international law? How is it different?

4. Should states be permitted to enter into an international agreement authorizing the commission of any international crime (*e.g.*, any of those not mentioned above)? Why? *See also* RESTATEMENT, § 102, RN 6.

5. The Restatement adds that "principles of the United Nations Charter prohibiting the use of force" are norms *jus cogens*. *Id.* § 102, cmt. k and RN 6; *see also id.* § 331 (2) (a); Vienna Convention on the Law of Treaties, art. 52; Carin Kahgan, Jus Cogens *and the Inherent Right to Self-Defense,* 3 ILSA J. INT'L & COMP. L. 767 (1997). What principles of the Charter prohibit the use of force? See U.N. Charter, preamble and arts. 1, 2(4), 33, 42, 51, 52–53; Chapter 8, Section 1.

6. U.S. cases identifying norms *jus cogens* include: United States v. Matta–Ballesteros, 71 F.3d 754, 764 n. 5 (9th Cir.1995) (also evidencing confusion regarding directly incorporable customary international law);

Princz v. Federal Republic of Germany, 26 F.3d 1166, 1173 (D.C.Cir.1994); *In re* Estate of Marcos, 25 F.3d 1467, 1472 (9th Cir.1994); *In re* Estate of Marcos Human Rights Litigation, 978 F.2d 493, 500 (9th Cir.1992); Siderman de Blake v. Republic of Argentina, 965 F.2d 699, 714–717 (9th Cir. 1992) (an important opinion otherwise misconstruing the universal obligatory nature of customary international law and assuming incorrectly that such law is based on "consent"); Committee of U.S. Citizens in Nicaragua v. Reagan, 859 F.2d 929, 940–41 (D.C.Cir.1988); Presbyterian Church of Sudan v. Talisman Energy Co., Inc., 374 F.Supp.2d 331 (S.D.N.Y. 2005), *id.* , 244 F.Supp.2d 289, 305 (S.D.N.Y. 2003); Iwanowa v. Ford Motor Co., 67 F.Supp.2d 424, 440–41 & n.18 (D.N.J. 1999); Hirsh v. State of Israel, 962 F.Supp. 377, 381 (S.D.N.Y. 1997) ("state violates *jus cogens* when it participates in such blatant violations of human rights as genocide, slavery, murder, torture, prolonged arbitrary detention, and racial discrimination."); White v. Paulsen, 997 F.Supp. 1380, 1383 (E.D.Wash.1998); Alejandre v. Republic of Cuba, 996 F.Supp. 1239, 1252 (S.D.Fla.1997); Doe v. Unocal Corp., 963 F.Supp. 880, 890, 894 (C.D.Cal.1997) (settled out of court Dec. 2004); Denegri v. Republic of Chile, 1992 WL 91914 (D.D.C.1992).

It would be improper for a court to state that only *jus cogens* norms can be litigated under the Alien Tort Clams Act (ATCA), 28 U.S.C. § 1350, since: (1) it would be an improper attempt by the judiciary to rewrite a federal statute that contains no such limitation and that expressly applies to "any" civil action for a tort in violation of the law of nations or treaties of the U.S., thus constituting a violation of the separation of powers, and (2) cases have addressed other violations. See Chapter 2, Section 2.

7. Should norms *jus cogens* have greater effect in domestic legal processes than ordinary treaty-based or customary international legal norms? Consider this question also in connection with Chapter 2.

8. Are there other categories of *jus cogens*? How would you attempt to prove their existence? Do norms *jus cogens* trump more ordinary customary international law? How does the existence of norms *jus cogens* impact on notions of state "sovereignty" or state "consent"?

9. The Inter–American Court of Human Rights has stated that judicial guarantees essential for the protection of nonderogable human rights under the American Convention on Human Rights are also nonderogable in time of public emergency. Judicial Guarantees in States of Emergency (Arts. 27(2), 25, and 8 of the American Convention on Human Rights), Advisory Opinion OC–9/97, Inter–Am. Ct. H.R., Ser. A, No. 9 (1987). Additionally, the Inter–American Court has recognized that the human right to be brought promptly before a judge must be subject to judicial control and that judicial protection must include the right to habeas corpus petitions and cannot be suspended during an emergency. See Castillo Petruzzi, Merits, Judgment, Inter–Am. Ct. Hum. Rts., Ser. C, No. 52 (30 May 1999), addressed in J. Becherer, 'International Decisions,' 95 Am. J. Int'l L. 171 *ff* (2001). Are such judicial guarantees effectively *jus cogens* norms as well?

10. Concerning the nature, sources and evidences of *jus cogens*, consider Anthony D'Amato, The Concept of Custom in International Law 111, 132 n.73 (1971); Ian Brownlie, Principles of Public International Law 513 (3 ed. 1979); Lung-chu Chen, An Introduction to Contemporary International Law: A

POLICY-ORIENTED PERSPECTIVE 179, 214–15, 268, 274, 276, 286, 389–90 (1989); MARK W. JANIS, AN INTRODUCTION TO INTERNATIONAL LAW 53 (1988); 1 OPPENHEIM'S INTERNATIONAL LAW 7–8 (Robert Jennings & Arthur Watts eds., 9 ed. 1992); Gordon A. Christenson, *The World Court and* Jus Cogens, 81 AM. J. INT'L L. 93 (1987); Anthony D'Amato, *It's a Bird, It's a Plane, It's* Jus Cogens!, 6 CONN. J. INT'L L. 1 (1990); Ronald St.J. Macdonald, *Fundamental Norms in Contemporary International Law*, 25 CAN. Y.B. INT'L L. 115 (1987); Jordan J. Paust, *The Reality of* Jus Cogens, 7 CONN. J. INT'L L. 81 (1991).

SECTION 2. SOURCES AND EVIDENCES

A. *International Agreements*

1. *The Nature of Treaties*

VIENNA CONVENTION ON THE LAW OF TREATIES

Article 2

1. For the purposes of the present Convention:

(a) "treaty" means an international agreement concluded between States in written form and governed by international law, whether embodied in a single instrument or in two or more related instruments and whatever its particular designation.

Article 18

A State is obligated to refrain from acts which would defeat the object and purpose of a treaty when:

(a) it has signed the treaty or has exchanged instruments constituting the treaty subject to ratification, acceptance or approval, until it shall have made its intention clear not to become a party to the treaty....

Article 26. *Pacta Sunt Servanda*

Every treaty in force is binding upon the parties to it and must be performed by them in good faith.

Article 27. Internal Law and Observance of Treaties

A party may not invoke the provisions of its internal law as justification for its failure to perform a treaty....

RESTATEMENT OF THE FOREIGN RELATIONS LAW OF THE UNITED STATES

§ 301(1) (3 ed. 1987).

As used in this Restatement, (1) "international agreement" means an agreement between two or more states or international organizations that is intended to be legally binding and is governed by international law.

Comment *a*. *Various designations of agreements*. The terminology used for international agreements is varied. Among the terms used are: treaty, convention, agreement, protocol, covenant, charter, statute, act, declaration, *concordat*, exchange of notes, agreed minute, and *modus vivendi*. Whatever their designation, all agreements have the same legal status, except as their provisions or circumstances of their conclusion indicate otherwise.

b. Form of agreement. ...[W]ritten form is not essential to their binding character ... oral agreements are no less binding....

c. Unilateral declarations. Since an international agreement does not require consideration ... its obligations may be wholly unilateral, flowing from one party only, as in a peace treaty following unconditional surrender. A unilateral statement is not an agreement, but may have legal consequences and may become a source of rights and obligations on principles analogous to estoppel....

d. Commercial agreements. An international agreement ... does not include a contract by a state, even with another state, that is essentially commercial in character and is intended to be governed by some national or other body of contract law. Examples include a loan agreement, a lease of a building, or a sale of goods.

Reporters' Note 4. *Oral agreements.* In Legal Status of Eastern Greenland [Denmark v. Norway], P.C.I.J. ser. A/B, No. 53 p. 71 (1933), ... the Court held that an agreement arose from an oral undertaking by a foreign minister from Norway not to interfere with another state's claim to sovereignty over territory.

Notes and Questions

1. The Vienna Convention on the Law of Treaties has not been ratified by the United States. Nonetheless, it is cited by U.S. courts and the Executive view is that much of the treaty on treaties is customary international law. *See, e.g.*, Restatement, Introduction at pp. 145–46, § 325, cmt. a and RN 4; Ehrlich v. American Airlines, Inc., 360 F.3d 366, 373 n.5 (2d Cir. 2004); Fujitsu Ltd. v. Federal Express Corp., 247 F.3d 423, 433 (2d Cir. 2001), *cert. denied*, 534 U.S. 891 (2001).

2. In 1993, a Declaration of Principles on Interim Self–Government Arrangements between Israel and the P.L.O. was created and signed by the parties, *reprinted in* 32 I.L.M. 1525 (1993). At that time, there was no Palestinian state. Is the Declaration a treaty within the meaning of the Vienna Convention? the U.S. Restatement? international law more generally? Consider also the 1995 Israel–Palestine Liberation Organization Interim Agreement on the West Bank and the Gaza Strip, *reprinted in* 36 I.L.M. 551 (1997).

3. Are treaties between the United States and various Indian nations "treaties" within the meaning of the Vienna Convention? the U.S. Restatement?

4. Are any of the following international agreements that are governed by relevant international law?

a. an agreement between East and West Germany concerning German reunification.

b. an agreement between the Republic of Texas and the United States concerning admission of Texas into the Union and its status.

c. an agreement between Great Britain and the Confederate States of America during the U.S. Civil War concerning commerce. Great Britain had recognized the Confederacy as a "belligerent" involved in a civil war, but not as an independent state. Once a state of "belligerency" occurs, all of the laws of war apply between the "belligerent" and its former government. *See generally* Jordan J. Paust, M. Cherif Bassiouni, *et al.*, International Criminal Law 809, 812–15, 818–19, *passim* (2 ed. 2000). An "insurgent" status is less than that of a "belligerent," which in turn is less than that of a state. Concerning "insurgent" civil war status, *see, e.g., id.* at 810–12, 815, 818–19, *passim*. Both belligerents and insurgents will have: (1) a government, (2) represent a given people, (3) be able to field military forces, and (4) have significant control of certain territory as its own. Concerning insurgencies, see also Protocol II to the 1949 Geneva Conventions, art. 1(1). A belligerent will also have outside recognition as a belligerent or nation or state. Do you think that al Qaeda every reached the level of an insurgent?

d. an agreement between an insurgent group led by Radovan Karadzic in Bosnia–Herzegovina and certain states concerning suspension of active hostilities.

e. an agreement between an insurgent group and the International Committee of the Red Cross (a private nongovernmental organization based in Geneva) attempting to facilitate the efficacy of humanitarian law, laws of war. As common Article 3 of the 1949 Geneva Conventions states: "An impartial humanitarian body, such as the International Committee of the Red Cross, may offer its services to the Parties to the conflict" having the status of an insurgency.

f. a 1989 agreement between the Ministry of Foreign Affairs of Mexico and the University of Houston (a state university), termed a "Cooperation Agreement" and containing a preamble and four "articles" concerning the exchange of students and related matters. If so, what constitutional issues might arise? Consider the U.S. Constitution, art. I, § 9.

g. an agreement between the City of Houston and Mexico City concerning commerce.

Would there be probable deleterious consequences if any of these are not considered to be international agreements governed by relevant international law?

5. If the President of the United States and the Prime Minister of Canada orally agree that importation of potatoes into the United States from Canada shall be free from any tariffs, taxes, or monetary restrictions, is such an agreement a "treaty" within the meaning of the Vienna Convention? the U.S. Restatement?

6. Article XXI of the General Agreement on Tariffs and Trade, 1947, allows the following "escape" clauses: "Nothing in this Agreement shall be construed (a) to require any contracting party to furnish any information the

disclosure of which it considers contrary to its essential security interests; or (b) to prevent any contracting party from taking any action which it considers necessary for the protection of its essential security interests."

Do the escape clauses noted above render the GATT nonbinding because, in effect, the language "which it considers" renders the agreement an agreement only if a state later agrees (*i.e.*, the escape clauses, with unilateral determinations concerning a continuing obligation, render the obligations specious or illusory)? or is it binding until such determinations are made? or is it binding and unilateral determinations will be subject to review by the international community? Also recall Vienna Convention on the Law of Treaties, arts. 26–27.

7. Would your answer be the same with respect to the 1963 Nuclear Test Ban Treaty and the 1968 Treaty on the Non–Proliferation of Nuclear Weapons, 729 U.N.T.S. 161, art. X. 1., which contain the following: "Each Party shall in exercising its national sovereignty have the right to withdraw from the Treaty if it decides that extraordinary events ... have jeopardized the supreme interests of its country"? Would your answer be the same with respect to a U.S. Reservation to the Convention on the Prevention and Punishment of the Crime of Genocide, 78 U.N.T.S. 277, which states: "(2) ... nothing in the Convention requires or authorizes legislation or other action by the United States of America prohibited by the Constitution of the United States as interpreted by the United States"? Also recall Vienna Convention on the Law of Treaties, arts. 26–27.

Consider also Case of Certain Norwegian Loans (France v. Norway), 1957 I.C.J. 9, Separate Opinion of Judge Hersch Lauterpacht, stating that a French Declaration of Acceptance of the general competence of the I.C.J. which stated that the "declaration does not apply to differences relating to matters which are essentially within the national jurisdiction as understood by the Government of the French Republic" "is incapable of giving rise to a legal obligation inasmuch as it claims, and effectively secures, the right of unilateral determination of the extent and of the existence of the obligation...." Do you agree?

8. The United States has signed but not yet ratified the American Convention on Human Rights. What is the obligation of the United States in connection with that treaty? *See also* Case of Certain German Interests in Polish Upper Silesia, P.C.I.J., Ser. A, No. 7, at 30 (1926).

9. A listing, citation, and list of contracting parties or signatories to many of the treaties that the United States is a signatory to can be found in a U.S. Department of State publication, Treaties in Force. The International Legal Materials (I.L.M.) produced by the American Society of International Law also contain several copies of such instruments and an update of new signatories. It can also be accessed through Westlaw. On the web, one can find many treaties in the United Nations Treaty Series (U.N.T.S.) at www.un.org/Depts/Treaty/overview. Signatories to some treaties can also be found at www.unhchr.ch.

2. *Interpretation of Treaties*

VIENNA CONVENTION ON THE LAW OF TREATIES

Article 31. General Rule of Interpretation

1. A treaty shall be interpreted in good faith in accordance with the ordinary meaning to be given to the terms of the treaty in their context and in light of its object and purpose.

2. The context for the purpose of the interpretation of a treaty shall comprise, in addition to the text, including its preamble and annexes:

> (a) any agreement relating to the treaty which was made between all the parties in connexion with the conclusion of the treaty;
>
> (b) any instrument which was made by one or more parties in connexion with the conclusion of the treaty and accepted by the other parties as an instrument related to the treaty.

3. There shall be taken into account, together with the context:

> (a) any subsequent agreement made between the parties regarding the interpretation of the treaty or the application of its provisions;
>
> (b) any subsequent practice in the application of the treaty which establishes the agreement of the parties regarding its interpretation;
>
> (c) any relevant rules of international law applicable in the relations between the parties.

4. A special meaning shall be given to a term if it is established that the parties so intended.

Article 32. Supplementary Means of Interpretation

Recourse may be had to supplementary means of interpretation, including the preparatory work of the treaty and the circumstances of its conclusion, in order to confirm the meaning resulting from the application of Article 31, or to determine the meaning when the interpretation according to Article 31:

> (a) leaves the meaning ambiguous or obscure; or
>
> (b) leads to a result which is manifestly absurd or unreasonable.

Restatement of the Foreign Relations Law of the United States § 325 (3 ed. 1987)

Comment *e. Recourse to* travaux préparatoires. The Vienna Convention ... requires the interpreting body to conclude that the "ordinary meaning" of the text either is obscure or unreasonable before it can look to "supplementary means." Some interpreting bodies are more willing to come to that conclusion than others.... Article 32 ... reflects reluctance to permit the use of materials constituting the development and negotiation of an agreement (*travaux préparatoires*) as a guide to the interpretation of the agreement. The Convention's inhospitality to *travaux* is not wholly consistent with the attitude of the International Court of Justice and not at all with that of United States courts.

f. Interpretation of agreements authenticated in two or more languages. When an international agreement has been authenticated in two or more languages, the text in each language is equally authoritative, unless it has been agreed that a particular text will prevail....

g. Interpretation by United States courts. ...Courts in the United States are generally more willing than those of other states to look outside the instrument to determine its meaning....

Notes and Questions

1. What is the "ordinary" meaning of a term? For example, is it the special meaning given to a term by the parties to a bilateral treaty, but not set forth in the instrument as a special meaning, or the meaning that generally pertains in the international community? By analogy to contracts law, is it the subjective or objective meaning of a term that should prevail? What evidence might be relevant concerning the "ordinary" meaning of a term? Does the phrase "ordinary meaning" open the interpretive task up to any evidence of generally shared meaning in the international community?

2. For an example of a reversal of judicial interpretation of a treaty on the basis of the meaning of *será* in Spanish, see United States v. Percheman, 32 U.S. (7 Pet.) 51, 89 (1833) (Marshall, C.J.) (the "Spanish part of the treaty was not ... [first] brought to our view.... [It shows a] difference of expression in the same instrument, drawn up in the language of each party" and shows a mandatory "shall" quality of the obligation of the U.S. to protect titles to land held by the residents of Spanish Florida) (reversing the outcome previously reached concerning the same treaty in Foster v. Neilson, 27 U.S. (2 Pet.) 253 (1829) (Marshall, C.J.)).

3. Is the meaning of a treaty subject to evolution? What portions of the Vienna Convention point to such a conclusion? If so, is the content of treaty law significantly different than that of customary international law? Consider especially the interplay between paragraphs 1 and 3 (b) and (c) of Article 31. Is "consent" only generally relevant to the objective and evolving meaning of a treaty?

4. Is customary international law background for interpretive purposes? What provision of the Vienna Convention seems relevant? Do Articles 53 and 64 of the Vienna Convention supplement your answer?

5. Since the U.N. Charter, under Article 103, prevails over other treaties in case of an unavoidable clash, should other treaties be interpreted consistently with obligations of states under the U.N. Charter?

6. Article 34 of the Vienna Convention declares: "A treaty does not create either obligations or rights for a third State without its consent." This is termed the *pacta tertiis* principle. Some have claimed that a "constitutive treaty" creating an "objective regime" or process leading to newer rules and regulations poses an exception to the principle mirrored in Article 34. In a sense, by consenting to a process that will produce newer, more specific

rules, one is predisposed to expect that they are valid and may generally expect that each is valid when created. If third, non-party states also generally expect that they are valid, the constitutive process can enjoy an expanded authority beyond signatories. Lord McNair, in a separate opinion in the Advisory Opinion on the International Status of South West Africa, explained:

> "[F]rom time to time it happens that a group of great Powers, or a large number of States both great and small, assume a power to create by a multi-party treaty some new international regime or status, which soon acquires a degree of acceptance and durability extending beyond the limits of the actual contracting parties, and giving it an objective existence."

1950 I.C.J. 153. Yet, if the "objective existence" of a process is based on "a degree of acceptance and durability," does such a base seem to rest on new patterns of generally shared *opinio juris* and general practice? *See, e.g.*, Luke T. Lee, *The Law of the Sea Convention and Third States*, 77 AM. J. INT'L L. 541, 568 (1983).

Professor Günther Handl cautiously explores claims and counterclaims concerning the reach of the Law of the Sea Convention regarding marine environmental protection and vessel safety, but more confidently concludes:

> "[T]he emergence of sophisticated 'rules of recognition,' a dense matrix of decisions, standards and rules evincing the contours of a constitutive process by which the law of the oceans is being made, [is] a process that is ultimately backed by the Convention's compulsory dispute settlement procedures. These emerging 'rules of recognition' reflect the fact that increasingly treaty-based general law is the preferred, indeed only conceivable tool for the management of the multifaceted issues arising from global interdependence, be that in the environmental, the oceans, human rights or international security context.
>
> "In this changing normative system, at the end of the day, the principle of consent is being honoured by individual states' validating the basic process of law-making and the fundamental principles of international governance, rather than by retaining a say on each and every aspect of normative development, *i.e.*, on every individual rule emanating therefrom. In such a world, although decision-making by majority and delegated law-making may be the rule, the *pacta tertiis* rule is still a valid international constitutional concept, albeit in a significantly different sense from that earlier one, the cornerstone of classic international law."

Günther Handl, *Regional Arrangements and Third State Vessels: Is the* Pacta Tertiis *Principle Being Modified?*, in COMPETING NORMS IN THE LAW OF MARINE ENVIRONMENTAL PROTECTION—FOCUS ON SHIP SAFETY AND POLLUTION PREVENTION 217, 240 (Henrik Ringbom ed. 1997).*

In a sense, does every treaty constitute a process whereby its meaning, though conditioned partly by a range of theoretically possible meanings regarding each term used in the treaty, is subject to decisionmaking by a majority? to development of a core of generally shared meaning? *See* Vienna Convention, art. 31 (1) and (3)(b).

7. Several international institutions, some with rule-making or clarifying powers and some with rule invoking or applicative powers, are created by international agreements. Consider, for example, the U.N. Security Council created by the U.N. Charter. In Chapter 7, there is attention to the International Civil Aviation Organization (ICAO) created by the Chicago Convention. Consider also: the Human Rights Committee created under the International Covenant on Civil and Political Rights; the Inter–American Commission on Human Rights and the Inter–American Court of Human Rights created under the American Convention on Human Rights; the European Commission of Human Rights and the European Court of Human Rights created under the European Convention on Human Rights; and the newer African Commission on Human and Peoples' Rights created under the African [Banjul] Charter on Human and Peoples' Rights–each in the Documents Supplement.

8. Professor Maria Frankowska disagrees with the Restatement with respect to use of the *travaux*. She prefers an interpretation of Article 32 of the Vienna Convention that "permits recourse to the *travaux* [merely] to confirm the meaning of the terms of the treaty...." *See* Maria Frankowska, *The Vienna Convention on the Law of Treaties Before United States Courts*, 28 VA. J. INT'L L. 281, 335 (1988). Who is correct? Do the commas point to a particular interpretation of Article 32?

9. Why might resort to the *travaux* or "legislative" history be misleading or dangerous? Consider Sale v. Haitian Centers Council, Inc., *et al.*, 509 U.S. 155 (1993) (Blackmun, J., dissenting), reprinted below; United States v. Stuart, 489 U.S. 353, 371–74 (1989) (Scalia, J., concurring). Justice Scalia stated that use of "extratextual materials" or "preratification extrinsic materials" should be used "[o]nly when a treaty provision is ambiguous." *Id.* at 373, adding:

> Even, however, if one generally regards the use of preratification extrinsic materials to confirm an unambiguous text as an innocuous practice, there is special reason to object to that superfluous reference in the present case. What is distinctive here is the nature of the extratextual materials to which the Court unnecessarily refers. To discover Canada's and the United States' "intent and expectations," the Court looks solely to the United States Senate floor debates that preceded the President's ratification of the treaty.... The use of such materials is unprecedented. Even where the terms of the treaty are ambiguous, and resort to preratification materials is therefore appropriate, I have been unable to discover a single case in which this Court has consulted the Senate debate, committee hearings, or committee reports. It would be no more appropriate for me than it is for the Court to use the present case as the occasion for pronouncing upon the legitimacy of using such materials, but it is permissible to suggest some of the arguments against it. Using preratification Senate materials, it may be said, is rather like determining the meaning of a bilateral contract between two corporations on the basis of what the board of directors of one of them thought it meant when authorizing the chief executive officer to conclude it. The question before us in a treaty case is what the two or more sovereigns agreed to, rather than what a single one of them, or the legislature of a single one of them, thought it agreed to. And to answer that question accurately, it can reasonably be said, whatever extratextual materials are consulted must be

materials that reflect the mutual agreement (for example, the negotiating history) rather than a unilateral understanding. Thus, we have declined to give effect, not merely to Senate debates and committee reports, but even to an explicit condition of ratification adopted by the full Senate, when the President failed to include that in his ratification. We said:

"The power to make treaties is vested by the Constitution in the President and Senate, and, while this proviso was adopted by the Senate, there is no evidence that it ever received the sanction or approval of the President. It cannot be considered as a legislative act, since the power to legislate is vested in the President, Senate and House of Representatives. There is something, too, which shocks the conscience in the idea that a treaty can be put forth as embodying the terms of an arrangement with a foreign power or an Indian tribe, a material provision of which is unknown to one of the contracting parties, and is kept in the background to be used by the other only when the exigencies of a particular case may demand it." New York Indians v. United States, 170 U.S. 1, 23 (1898).

10. If the *travaux* should not be resorted to in a particular case, should what is merely the domestic "legislative" history leading up to ratification be consulted? Would that tend to reflect merely one signatory's pre-ratification view of the meaning of a treaty?

11. Is one state's interpretation of a bilateral agreement binding on the other? Consider Jesse Lewis Claim (The David J. Adams Claim) (United States v. Great Britain), 1921, 6 U.N.R.I.A.A. 85. There, a Canadian court had determined that actions of a U.S. fishing vessel, The David J. Adams, violated the Treaty of London of 1818. The Arbitral Tribunal found that Great Britain and Canada had been acting under "proper judicial authority as was established by their municipal law ... to interpret and apply" the treaty, but "[t]he fundamental principle of juridical equality of States is opposed to ... the subjection of one State to an interpretation of a Treaty asserted by another State. There is no reason why one more than the other should impose such an unilateral interpretation of a contract with is essentially bilateral." Yet, the Tribunal later held that the Canadian court's interpretation was not erroneous. See Louis Henkin, Richard Crawford Pugh, Oscar Schachter, Hans Smit, International Law 471–72 (3 ed. 1993).

12. How does one identify and clarify the object and purpose of a treaty? Having identified the object and purpose of a treaty, should one consider the probable consequences of adoption of various interpretations of words or phrases contained within the treaty, *e.g.*, whether a particular interpretation would be thwarting or generally serving of the object and purpose of a treaty?

Consider the 1966 International Covenant on Civil and Political Rights (in the Documents Supplement). Should the human rights treaty be interpreted in ways that best facilitate human dignity and a fuller participation by each human being in various civil and political processes?

13. For a recent Supreme Court opinion using the object and purpose of a treaty when the text and legislative history of the treaty are ambiguous, see El Al Airlines, Ltd. v. Tseng, 525 U.S. 155 (1999), in Chapter 7.

SALE v. HAITIAN CENTERS COUNCIL, INC., *ET AL.*

509 U.S. 155 (1993).

[Editors' note: Under the Refugee Convention addressed in this case, a "refugee" is "[a]ny person who, owing to a well-founded fear of being persecuted for reasons of race, religion, nationality, membership of a particular social group, or political opinion, is outside the country of his nationality and is unable or, owing to such fear, is unwilling to avail himself of the protection of that country." *Id.* art. 1 (A) (2)]

STEVENS, J.

The President has directed the Coast Guard to intercept vessels illegally transporting passengers from Haiti to the United States and to return those passengers to Haiti without first determining whether they may qualify as refugees. The question presented in this case is whether such forced repatriation, "authorized to be undertaken only beyond the territorial sea of the United States," violates § 243(h)(1) of the Immigration and Nationality Act of 1952 (INA or Act). We hold that neither § 243(h) nor Article 33 of the United Nations Protocol Relating to the Status of Refugees applies to action taken by the Coast Guard on the high seas.

Aliens residing illegally in the United States are subject to deportation after a formal hearing. Aliens arriving at the border, or those who are temporarily paroled into the country, are subject to an exclusion hearing, the less formal process by which they, too, may eventually be removed from the United States. In either a deportation or exclusion proceeding the alien may seek asylum as a political refugee for whom removal to a particular country may threaten his life or freedom.... The INA offers these statutory protections only to aliens who reside in or have arrived at the border of the United States. For 12 years, in one form or another, the interdiction program challenged here has prevented Haitians such as respondents from reaching our shores and invoking those protections....

Like the text and the history of § 243(h), the text and negotiating history of Article 33 of the United Nations Convention are both completely silent with respect to the Article's possible application to actions taken by a country outside its own borders. Respondents argue that the Protocol's broad remedial goals require that a nation be prevented from repatriating refugees to their potential oppressors whether or not the refugees are within that nation's borders. In spite of the moral weight of that argument, both the text and negotiating history of Article 33 affirmatively indicate that it was not intended to have extraterritorial effect....

Two aspects of Article 33's text are persuasive. The first is the explicit reference in Article 33.2 to the country in which the alien is located; the second is the parallel use of the terms "expel or return," the latter term explained by the French word "*refouler*."

The full text of Article 33 reads as follows:

"Article 33.—Prohibition of expulsion or return ('*refoulement*')

"1. No Contracting State shall expel or return ('*refouler*') a refugee in any manner whatsoever to the frontiers of territories where his life or freedom would be threatened on account of his race, religion, nationality, membership of a particular social group or political opinion.

"2. The benefit of the present provision may not, however, be claimed by a refugee whom there are reasonable grounds for regarding as a danger to the security of the country in which he is, or who, having been convicted by a final judgment of a particularly serious crime, constitutes a danger to the community of that country." Convention Relating to the Status of Refugees, July 28, 1951, 19 U.S.T. 6259, 6276, T. I. A. S. No. 6577....

Under the second paragraph of Article 33 an alien may not claim the benefit of the first paragraph if he poses a danger to the country in which he is located. If the first paragraph did apply on the high seas, no nation could invoke the second paragraph's exception with respect to an alien there: an alien intercepted on the high seas is in no country at all. If Article 33.1 applied extraterritorially, therefore, Article 33.2 would create an absurd anomaly: dangerous aliens on the high seas would be entitled to the benefits of 33.1 while those residing in the country that sought to expel them would not. It is more reasonable to assume that the coverage of 33.2 was limited to those already in the country because it was understood that 33.1 obligated the signatory state only with respect to aliens within its territory.

Article 33.1 uses the words "expel or return ('*refouler*')" as an obvious parallel to the words "deport or return" in § 243(h)(1). There is no dispute that "expel" has the same meaning as "deport"; it refers to the deportation or expulsion of an alien who is already present in the host country. The dual reference identified and explained in our opinion in *Leng May Ma v. Barber*, suggests that the term "return ('*refouler*')" refers to the exclusion of aliens who are merely " 'on the threshold of initial entry.' "357 U.S. at 187 (*quoting* Shaughnessy v. United States *ex rel.* Mezei, 345 U.S. 206, 212 ... (1953)).

This suggestion—that "return" has a legal meaning narrower than its common meaning—is reinforced by the parenthetical reference to "*refouler*", a French word that is not an exact synonym for the English word "return." Indeed, neither of two respected English–French Dictionaries mentions "*refouler*" as one of many possible French translations of "return." Conversely, the English translations of "*refouler*" do not include the word "return." They do, however, include words like "repulse," "repel," "drive back," and even "expel." To the extent that they are relevant, these translations imply that "return" means a defensive act of resistance or exclusion at a border rather than an act of transporting someone to a particular destination. In the context of the Convention, to "return" means to "repulse" rather than to "reinstate."

The text of Article 33 thus fits with Judge Edwards' understanding "that 'expulsion' would refer to a 'refugee already admitted into a country' and that 'return' would refer to a 'refugee already within the territory but not yet resident there.' Thus, the Protocol was not intended to govern parties' conduct outside of their national borders." Haitian Refugee Center v. Gracey, 257 U.S. App. D.C. at 413, 809 F.2d at 840 (footnotes omitted). From the time of the Convention, commentators have consistently agreed with this view.

The drafters of the Convention and the parties to the Protocol—like the drafters of § 243(h)—may not have contemplated that any nation would gather fleeing refugees and return them to the one country they had desperately sought to escape; such actions may even violate the spirit of Article 33; but a treaty cannot impose uncontemplated extraterritorial obligations on those who ratify it through no more than its general humanitarian intent. Because the text of Article 33 cannot reasonably be read to say anything at all about a nation's actions toward aliens outside its own territory, it does not prohibit such actions....

In early drafts of the Convention, what finally emerged as Article 33 was numbered 28. At a negotiating conference of plenipotentiaries held in Geneva, Switzerland on July 11, 1951, the Swiss delegate explained his understanding that the words "expel" and "return" covered only refugees who had entered the host country....

No one expressed disagreement with the position of the Swiss delegate on that day or at the session two weeks later when Article 28 was again discussed. At that session, the delegate of the Netherlands recalled the Swiss delegate's earlier position....

Therefore, even if we believed that Executive Order 12807 violated the intent of some signatory states to protect all aliens, wherever they might be found, from being transported to potential oppressors, we must acknowledge that other signatory states carefully—and successfully—sought to avoid just that implication. The negotiating history, which suggests that the Convention's limited reach resulted from a deliberate bargain, is not dispositive, but it solidly supports our reluctance to interpret Article 33 to impose obligations on the contracting parties that are broader than the text commands. We do not read that text to apply to aliens interdicted on the high seas.

BLACKMUN, J., dissenting.

... I believe that the duty of nonreturn expressed in both the Protocol and the statute is clear. The majority finds it "extraordinary," ... that Congress would have intended the ban on returning "any alien" to apply to aliens at sea. That Congress would have meant what it said is not remarkable. What is extraordinary in this case is that the Executive, in disregard of the law, would take to the seas to intercept fleeing refugees and force them back to their persecutors—and that the Court would strain to sanction that conduct.

I begin with the Convention, for it is undisputed that the Refugee Act of 1980 was passed to conform our law to Article 33, and that "the nondiscretionary duty imposed by § 243(h) parallels the United States' mandatory non*refoulement* obligations under Article 33.1...." INS v. Doherty, 502 U.S. 314, 331 (1992) (Scalia, J., concurring in the judgment in part and dissenting in part). See also Cardoza–Fonseca, 480 U.S. at 429, 436–437, 440; Stevic, 467 U.S. at 418, 421. The Convention thus constitutes the backdrop against which the statute must be understood.

Article 33.1 of the Convention states categorically and without geographical limitation:

> "No Contracting State shall expel or return ('*refouler*') a refugee in any manner whatsoever to the frontiers of territories where his life or freedom would be threatened on account of his race, religion, nationality, membership of a particular social group or political opinion."

The terms are unambiguous. Vulnerable refugees shall not be returned. The language is clear, and the command is straightforward; that should be the end of the inquiry. Indeed, until litigation ensued, see Haitian Refugee Center v. Gracey, 257 U.S. App. D.C. 367, 809 F.2d 794 (1987), the Government consistently acknowledged that the Convention applied on the high seas.

The majority, however, has difficulty with the Treaty's use of the term "return ('*refouler*')." "Return," it claims, does not mean return, but instead has a distinctive legal meaning.... For this proposition the Court relies almost entirely on the fact that American law makes a general distinction between deportation and exclusion. Without explanation, the majority asserts that in light of this distinction the word "return" as used in the Treaty somehow must refer only to "the exclusion of aliens who are ... 'on the threshold of initial entry' "....

Setting aside for the moment the fact that respondents in this case seem very much "on the threshold of initial entry"—at least in the eyes of the Government that has ordered them seized for "attempting to come to the United States by sea without necessary documentation," Preamble to Executive Order No. 12,807, 57 Fed. Reg. 23133 (1992)—I find this tortured reading unsupported and unnecessary. The text of the Convention does not ban the "exclusion" of aliens who have reached some indeterminate "threshold"; it bans their "return." It is well settled that a treaty must first be construed according to its "ordinary meaning." Article 31.1 of the Vienna Convention on the Law of Treaties ... (1969). The ordinary meaning of "return" is "to bring, send, or put (a person or thing) back to or in a former position." Webster's Third New International Dictionary 1941 (1986). That describes precisely what petitioners are doing to the Haitians. By dispensing with ordinary meaning at the outset, and by taking instead as its starting point the assumption that "return," as used in the Treaty, "has a legal meaning narrower than its common meaning," the majority leads itself astray.

The straightforward interpretation of the duty of nonreturn is strongly reinforced by the Convention's use of the French term "*refouler.*" The ordinary meaning of "*refouler,*" as the majority concedes ... is "to repulse, ... ; to drive back, to repel." *Dictionnaire Larousse* 631 (1981). Thus construed, Article 33.1 of the Convention reads: "No contracting state shall expel or [repulse, drive back, or repel] a refugee in any manner whatsoever to the frontiers of territories where his life or freedom would be threatened...." That, of course, is exactly what the Government is doing. It thus is no surprise that when the French press has described the very policy challenged here, the term it has used is "*refouler.*" *See, e.g., Le bourbier hatien, Le Monde,* May 31–June 1, 1992 ("*Les Etats–Unis ont decide de refouler directement les refugies recueillis par la garde cotire.*" (The United States has decided [*de refouler*] directly the refugees picked up by the Coast Guard)).

And yet the majority insists that what has occurred is not, in fact, "*refoulement.*" It reaches this conclusion in a peculiar fashion. After acknowledging that the ordinary meaning of "*refouler*" is "repulse," "repel," and "drive back," the majority without elaboration declares: "To the extent that they are relevant, these translations imply that 'return' means a defensive act of resistance or exclusion at a border...." I am at a loss to find the narrow notion of "exclusion at a border" in broad terms like "repulse," "repel," and "drive back." Gage was repulsed (initially) at Bunker Hill. Lee was repelled at Gettysburg. Rommel was driven back across North Africa. The majority's puzzling progression ("*refouler*" means repel or drive back; therefore "return" means only exclude at a border; therefore the treaty does not apply) hardly justifies a departure from the path of ordinary meaning. The text of Article 33.1 is clear, and whether the operative term is "return" or "*refouler,*" it prohibits the Government's actions.

Article 33.1 is clear not only in what it says, but also in what it does not say: it does not include any geographical limitation. It limits only where a refugee may be sent "to", not where he may be sent from. This is not surprising, given that the aim of the provision is to protect refugees against persecution.

Article 33.2, by contrast, does contain a geographical reference, and the majority seizes upon this as evidence that the section as a whole applies only within a signatory's borders. That inference is flawed. Article 33.2 states that the benefit of Article 33.1

> "may not ... be claimed by a refugee whom there are reasonable grounds for regarding as a danger to the security of the country in which he is, or who, having been convicted by a final judgment of a particularly serious crime, constitutes a danger to the community of that country."

The signatories' understandable decision to allow nations to deport criminal aliens who have entered their territory hardly suggests an intent to permit the apprehension and return of noncriminal aliens who have not entered their territory, and who may have no desire ever to enter it. One wonders what the majority would make of an exception that removed from the Article's protection all refugees who "constitute a danger to their families." By the majority's logic, the inclusion of such an exception presumably would render Article 33.1 applicable only to refugees with families....

The majority further relies on a remark by Baron van Boetzelaer, the Netherlands' delegate at the Convention's negotiating conference, to support its contention that Article 33 does not apply extraterritorially. This reliance, for two reasons, is misplaced. First, the isolated statement of a delegate to the Convention cannot alter the plain meaning of the Treaty itself. Second, placed in its proper context, van Boetzelaer's comment does not support the majority's position.

It is axiomatic that a treaty's plain language must control absent "extraordinarily strong contrary evidence." Sumitomo Shoji America, Inc. v. Avagliano, 457 U.S. 176, 185 ... (1982). See also United States v. Stuart, 489 U.S. 353, 371 ... (1989) (Scalia, J., concurring in the judgment); *id.*, at 370 (Kennedy, J., concurring in part and concurring in the judgment). Reliance on a treaty's negotiating history (*travaux préparatoires*) is a disfavored alternative of last resort, appropriate only where the terms of the document are obscure or lead to "manifestly absurd or unreasonable" results. See Vienna Convention on the Law of Treaties, Art. 32.... Moreover, even the general rule of treaty construction allowing limited resort to *travaux préparatoires* "has no application to oral statements made by those engaged in negotiating the treaty which were not embodied in any writing and were not communicated to the government of the negotiator or to its ratifying body." Arizona v. California, 292 U.S. 341, 360 ... (1934). There is no evidence that the comment on which the majority relies was ever communicated to the United States' Government or to the Senate in connection with the ratification of the Convention.

The pitfalls of relying on the negotiating record are underscored by the fact that Baron van Boetzelaer's remarks almost certainly represent, in the words of the United Nations High Commissioner for Refugees, a mere "parliamentary gesture by a delegate whose views did not prevail upon the negotiating conference as a whole." ... Brief for Office of the United Nations High Commissioner for Refugees as Amicus Curiae 24. The Baron, like the Swiss delegate whose sentiments he restated, expressed a desire to reserve the right to close borders to large groups of refugees. "According to [the Swiss delegate's] interpretation, States were not compelled to allow large groups of persons claiming refugee status to cross [their] frontiers." Conference of Plenipotentiaries on the Status of Refugees and Stateless Persons, Summary Record of the Sixteenth Meeting, U.N. Doc. A/CONF.2/SR.16, p.6 (July 11, 1951). Article 33, van Boetzelaer maintained, "would not have involved any obligations in the possible case of mass migrations across frontiers or of attempted mass migrations" and this was important because "the Netherlands could not accept any legal obligations in respect of large groups of refugees seeking access to its territory." Conference of Plenipotentiaries on the Status of

Refugees and Stateless Persons, Summary Record of the Thirty–Fifth Meeting, U.N. Doc. A/CONF.2/SR.35, pp. 21–22 (Dec. 3, 1951). Yet no one seriously contends that the Treaty's protections depend on the number of refugees who are fleeing persecution. Allowing a state to disavow "any obligations" in the case of mass migrations or attempted mass migrations would eviscerate Article 33, leaving it applicable only to "small" migrations and "small" attempted migrations.

There is strong evidence as well that the Conference rejected the right to close land borders where to do so would trap refugees in the persecutors' territory. Indeed, the majority agrees that the Convention does apply to refugees who have reached the border. The majority thus cannot maintain that van Boetzelaer's interpretation prevailed....

In sum, the fragments of negotiating history upon which the majority relies are not entitled to deference, were never voted on or adopted, probably represent a minority view, and in any event do not address the issue in this case. It goes without saying, therefore, that they do not provide the "extraordinarily strong contrary evidence," Sumitomo Shoji America, Inc., 457 U.S. at 185, required to overcome the Convention's plain statement: "No Contracting State shall expel or return (*'refouler'*) a refugee in any manner whatsoever to the frontiers of territories where his life or freedom would be threatened....''....

Notes and Questions

1. Did the majority or dissent have the better view?

2. Is it appropriate to consult dictionaries in view of the approach to interpretation adopted in Article 31 of the Vienna Convention?

3. Knowing that under customary international law a U.S. flag vessel, such as a U.S. Coast Guard cutter, is the equivalent of U.S. territory for jurisdictional purposes, would you decide the case differently, at least with respect to some Haitians? Did the Court "miss the boat"?

3. Reservations, Understandings, and Such

VIENNA CONVENTION ON THE LAW OF TREATIES

Article 2

1. For the purposes of the present Convention:

(d) "reservation" means a unilateral statement, however phrased or named, made by a State, when signing, ratifying, accepting, approving or acceding to a treaty, whereby it purports to exclude or to modify the legal effect of certain provisions of the treaty in their application to that State.

Article 19

A State may, when signing, ratifying, accepting, approving or acceding to a treaty, formulate a reservation unless:

(a) the reservation is prohibited by the treaty;

(b) the treaty provides that only specified reservations, which do not include the reservation in question, may be made; or

(c) in cases not falling under sub-paragraphs (a) and (b), the reservation is incompatible with the object and purpose of the treaty.

Article 20

1. A reservation expressly authorized by a treaty does not require any subsequent acceptance by the other contracting States unless the treaty so provides.

2. When it appears from the limited number of the negotiating States and the object and purpose of a treaty that the application of the treaty in its entirety between all the parties is an essential condition of the consent of each one to be bound by the treaty, a reservation requires acceptance by all the parties . . .

4. In cases not falling under the preceding paragraphs and unless the treaty otherwise provides:

(a) acceptance by another contracting State of a reservation constitutes the reserving State a party to the treaty in relation to that other State if or when the treaty is in force for those States . . .

5. For the purposes of paragraphs 2 and 4 and unless the treaty otherwise provides, a reservation is considered to have been accepted by a State if it shall have raised no objection to the reservation by the end of a period of twelve months after it was notified of the reservation or by the date on which it expressed its consent to be bound by the treaty, whichever is later.

Restatement of the Foreign Relations Law of the United States § 313 (3 ed. 1987)

Comment *g. Declarations and understandings.*

. . . [A] state may make a unilateral declaration that does not purport to be a reservation. Whatever it is called, it constitutes a reservation in fact if it purports to exclude, limit, or modify the state's legal obligation. Sometimes, however, a declaration purports to be an "understanding," an interpretation of the agreement in a particular respect. Such an interpretive declaration is not a reservation if it reflects the accepted view of the agreement. But another contracting party may challenge the expressed understanding, treating it as a reservation which it is not prepared to accept.

Reporters' Note 1

. . . In the Advisory Opinion on Reservations to the Genocide Convention . . . , a majority of the International Court of Justice concluded that, when a reservation was not incompatible with the object and purpose of the agreement, obligations might be created between the reserving state and those parties that accepted the reservation, and that the reserving state could be considered a party to the agreement. . . .

The American Convention on Human Rights provides that the Convention "shall be subject to reservations only in conformity with the provisions of the Vienna Convention...." In an Advisory Opinion, the Inter–American Court of Human Rights declared that such a treaty was designed to enhance the protection of individuals rather than to give states reciprocal rights against each other. Accordingly, since reservations that would be impermissible because they frustrate the object and purpose of the treaty were rare, the Convention would enter into force ... without the necessity of acceptance ... [of a putative reservation] by other states.

RESERVATIONS TO THE CONVENTION ON GENOCIDE

Advisory Opinion, 1951 I.C.J. 15.

[Editors' note: The extract of the Court's opinion below was in response to the following question posed by the U.N. General Assembly while seeking an advisory opinion: "Can the reserving State be regarded as being a party to the Convention while still maintaining its reservation if the reservation is objected to by one or more of the parties to the Convention but not by others?"]

It is well established that in its treaty relations a State cannot be bound without its consent, and that consequently, no reservation can be effective against any State, without its agreement thereto. It is also a generally recognized principle that a multilateral convention is the result of an agreement freely concluded upon its clauses and that consequently none of the contracting parties is entitled to frustrate or impair, by means of unilateral decisions or particular agreements, the purposes and *raison d'être* of the convention. To this principle was linked the notion of the integrity of the convention as adopted, a notion which in its traditional concept involved the proposition that no reservation was valid unless it was accepted by all the contracting parties without exception....

This concept, which is directly inspired by the notion of contract, is of undisputed value as a principle. However, as regards the Genocide Convention, it is proper to refer to a variety of circumstances which would lead to a more flexible application of this principle....

The objects of such a convention must also be considered. The Convention was manifestly adopted for a purely humanitarian and civilizing purpose. It is indeed difficult to imagine a convention that might have this dual character to a greater degree, since its object on the one hand is to safeguard the very existence of certain human groups and on the other hand to confirm and endorse the most elementary principles of morality. In such a convention the contracting States do not have any interests of their own; they merely have, one and all, a common interest, namely, the accomplishment of those high purposes which are the *raison d'être* of the convention. Consequently, in a convention of this type one cannot speak of individual advantages or disadvantages to

States, or of the maintenance of a perfect contractual balance between rights and duties. The high ideals inspired by the Convention provide, by virtue of the common will of the parties, the foundation and measure of all its provisions.

The object and purpose of the Genocide Convention imply that it was the intention ... that as many States as possible should participate.... The object and purpose of the Convention thus limit both the freedom of making reservations and that of objecting to them....

It has nevertheless been argued that any State entitled to become a party to the Genocide Convention may do so while making any reservation it chooses by virtue of its sovereignty. The Court cannot share this view. It is obvious that so extreme an application of the idea of State sovereignty could lead to a complete disregard of the object and purpose of the Convention.... [Editors' note: the Court also recognized that a reservation incompatible with the object and purpose of a treaty is legally unacceptable, a rule reflected subsequently in Article 19(c) of the Vienna Convention on the Law of Treaties.]

It results from the foregoing considerations that ... [the question noted above], on account of its abstract character, cannot be given an absolute answer. The appraisal of a reservation and the effect of objections that might be made to it depend upon the particular circumstances of each individual case.

HUMAN RIGHTS COMMITTEE, GENERAL COMMENT ON ISSUES RELATING TO RESERVATIONS MADE UPON RATIFICATION OR ACCESSION TO THE COVENANT OR THE OPTIONAL PROTOCOLS

General Comment No. 24 (2 Nov. 1994).

7. In an instrument which articulates very many civil and political rights, each of the many articles, and indeed their interplay, secures the objectives of the Covenant. The object and purpose of the Covenant is to create legally binding standards for human rights by defining certain civil and political rights and placing them in a framework of obligations which are legally binding for those States which ratify; and to provide an efficacious supervisory machinery for the obligations undertaken.

8. [reproduced on pages 61–62 concerning norms *jus cogens*]

9. Applying more generally the object and purpose test to the Covenant, the Committee notes that, for example, reservation to Article 1 denying peoples the right to determine their own political status and to pursue their economic, social and cultural development, would be incompatible with the object and purpose of the Covenant. Equally, a reservation to the obligation to respect and ensure the rights, and to do so on a nondiscriminatory basis (Article 2 (1)) would not be acceptable. Nor may a State reserve an entitlement not to take necessary steps at the

domestic level to give effect to the rights of the Covenant (Article 2 (2))....

11. The Covenant consists not just of the specified rights, but of important supportive guarantees. These guarantees provide the necessary framework for securing the rights in the Covenant and are thus essential to its object and purpose. Some operate at the national level and some at the international level. Reservations designed to remove these guarantees are thus not acceptable. Thus, a State could not make a reservation to Article 2, paragraph 3, of the Covenant, indicating that it intends to provide no remedies for human rights violations. Guarantees such as these are an integral part of the structure of the Covenant and underpin its efficacy. The Covenant also envisages, for the better attainment of its stated objectives, a monitoring role for the Committee. Reservations that purport to evade that essential element in the design of the Covenant, which is also directed to securing the enjoyment of the rights, are also incompatible with its object and purpose. A State may not reserve the right not to present a report and have it considered by the Committee. The Committee's role under the Covenant, whether under Article 40 or under the Optional Protocols, necessarily entails interpreting the provisions of the Covenant and the development of a jurisprudence. Accordingly, a reservation that rejects the Committee's competence to interpret the requirements of any provisions of the Covenant would also be contrary to the object and purpose of that treaty.

12. The intention of the Covenant is that the rights contained therein should be ensured to all those under a State party's jurisdiction. To this end certain attendant requirements are likely to be necessary. Domestic laws may need to be altered properly to reflect the requirements of the Covenant; and mechanisms at the domestic level will be needed to allow the Covenant rights to be enforceable at the local level. Reservations often reveal a tendency of States not to want to change a particular law. And sometimes that tendency is elevated to a general policy. Of particular concern are widely formulated reservations which essentially render ineffective all Covenant rights which would require any change in national law to ensure compliance with Covenant obligations. No real international rights or obligations have thus been accepted. And when there is an absence of provisions to ensure that Covenant rights may be sued on in domestic courts, and, further, a failure to allow individual complaints to be brought to the Committee under the first Optional Protocol, all the essential elements of the Covenant guarantees have been removed....

17. ... [T]he Committee believes that ... [Vienna Convention Article 20] provisions on the role of State objections in relation to reservations are inappropriate to address the problem of reservations to human rights treaties. Such treaties, and the Covenant specifically, are not a web of inter-State exchanges of mutual obligations. They concern the endowment of individuals with rights. The principle of inter-State reciprocity has no place, save perhaps in the limited context of reservations to declarations on the Committee's competence under Article

41. . . . The absence of protest by States cannot imply that a reservation is either compatible or incompatible with the object and purpose of the Covenant. . . .

18. It necessarily falls to the Committee to determine whether a specific reservation is compatible with the object and purpose of the Covenant. This is in part because . . . it is an inappropriate task for States parties in relation to human rights treaties, and in part because it is a task that the Committee cannot avoid in the performance of its functions. . . . Because of the special character of a human rights treaty, the compatibility of a reservation with the object and purpose of the Covenant must be established objectively, by reference to legal principles, and the Committee is particularly well placed to perform this task. The normal consequence of an unacceptable reservation is not that the Covenant will not be in effect at all for a reserving party. Rather, such a reservation will generally be severable, in the sense that the Covenant will be operative for the reserving party without benefit of the reservation.

Notes and Questions

1. Logically, can there be a reservation to a bilateral agreement? See also Restatement § 313, cmt. f, adding: "If a reservation is attached at ratification, it constitutes in effect a rejection of the original tentative agreement and a counter-offer of a new agreement." *See also id.* § 314, RN 1, adding: "in bilateral treaties, the United States has made it a practice to include in the Protocol of Exchange of the instruments of ratification a statement by each party expressly stipulating its acceptance of the reservations, declarations, understandings, etc. of the other." For the U.S., after the President has obtained advice and consent from the Senate concerning the initial draft, can the President simply accept changes suggested by the other state? See also *id.* RN 4.

2. If an "understanding" does not purport to be a reservation, is the difference between a reservation and an understanding primarily a difference in intended legal effect, *i.e.*, that an "understanding" as such does not attempt to exclude, modify, or limit the legal effect of a treaty? If otherwise appropriate, over time can an "understanding" nevertheless shape attitudes and thus influence the shared meaning of a treaty provision?

3. Can acceptance of a reservation logically occur under Article 20 (5) of the Vienna Convention if the reservation is void *ab initio* under Article 19 (c)? Who decides whether a reservation is void *ab initio* as a matter of law? Who might review that decision?

4. If a reservation is void *ab initio* under Article 19(c) of the Vienna Convention, is the reserving state still bound by the agreement? Is it relevant that the agreement is an international criminal law instrument or a human rights treaty protecting basic rights of the human person? Is consent the only criterion? What information would you like in order to decide whether a void reservation is severable? *See also* materials cited in notes 6 and 7 below.

5. Although generally quite authoritative, the Human Rights Committee's General Comment No. 24 has stimulated controversy concerning its power to express its view concerning the admissibility of particular reservations. The International Law Commission (ILC) undertook a study of the law and practice of reservations to treaties in 1994, and Special Rapporteur Alain Pellet had submitted three reports by 1998. See Third Report on Reservations to Treaties, U.N. Doc. A/CN.4/491 (1998). The ILC has tentatively agreed that the Vienna Convention should not be revised despite some confusion concerning matters such as the consequences of the inadmissibility of a reservation to a multilateral treaty that is void *ab initio*. The ILC preliminarily concluded that the Vienna Convention regime is suitable to normative multilateral treaties, including human rights treaties. The question whether human rights treaty bodies may express a view as to the admissibility of reservations, or whether this authority is exclusively vested in the other states parties, has been contested in the Sixth Committee of the General Assembly during debates on the ILC's reports, with opinion there apparently divided in half. See Report of the International Law Commission at Its Fiftieth Session, U.N. Doc. A/53/10 (1999), at para. 484. The ILC has accepted that human rights monitoring bodies are competent to comment upon and to express recommendations with regard to the permissibility of reservations and to call upon reserving states to give due consideration to these recommendations. Some members of the ILC would recognize that human rights treaty bodies may authoritatively pronounce upon the admissibility of reservations and specify whether the purportedly reserving state is bound to the treaty without the reservation. *Id.* at para. 483.

The European Court of Human Rights has held that a certain reservation, styled an interpretive declaration, is void and severable from the reserving state's instrument of ratification. Belilos v. Switzerland, 132 Eur. Ct. H.R. (Ser. A) at 28 (1988). The Special Rapporteur is consulting with members of human rights treaty bodies as well as states in preparing a guide to practices with respect to reservations.

6. U.S. instruments of ratification concerning the 1966 International Covenant on Civil and Political Rights and the 1965 Convention on Elimination of Racial Discrimination, with Senate approval, do not contain a "proviso" concerning applicability of the U.S. Constitution (see Chapter 2). The "provisos" are found in the Senate's resolutions providing advice and consent to the President. Do the provisos have any direct legal effect internationally or in the U.S. domestic legal process? Also recall Justice Scalia's quotation from *New York Indians v. United States*, *supra* pp. 71–72. Why might they have been added to the Senate's resolutions? Should they have been reservations? See Chapter 2, Section 2 C 1 d.

7. When ratifying the 1966 International Covenant on Civil and Political Rights, the United States added the following "Declaration": "... the United States declares that the provisions of Articles 1 through 27 of the Covenant are not self-executing." In its explanation of the suggested declaration of partial non-self-execution, the Executive explained: "For reasons of prudence, we recommend including a declaration that the substantive provisions of the Covenant are not self-executing. The intent is to clarify that the Covenant will not create a private cause of action in U.S. courts ... existing U.S. law generally complies with the Covenant; hence, implementing legisla-

tion is not contemplated." See Report on the International Covenant on Civil and Political Rights, Explanation of Proposed Reservations, Understandings and Declarations, at 19, 102d Cong., 2d Sess., Mar. 24, 1992, *reprinted in* 31 I.L.M. 645 (1992). As noted in Chapter 2, a treaty that is generally (as opposed to partly) non-self-executing generally does not operate directly to create a cause of action or provide a remedy. *But see* U.S. Constitution, Article VI, clause 2 (in the Documents Supplement).

If operative, would the declaration have a special meaning, *e.g.*, would it operate merely to preclude creation of a private cause of action directly under the treaty? If so, what other uses can be made of the Covenant even without specific congressional implementing legislation, Executive regulations, etc.? For example, can it be used to interpret other laws, defensively in civil or criminal contexts, or for supremacy and preemptive purposes? See United States v. Duarte–Acero, 208 F.3d 1282, 1284 (11th Cir. 2000) (despite declaration, ICCPR is supreme law of the land); *id.*, 132 F.Supp.2d 1036, 1040 n.8 (S.D. Fla. 2001) (declaration does not apply when raising "ICCPR claims defensively"); United States v. Bakeas, 987 F.Supp. 44 (D. Mass. 1997); Connie de la Vega, *Civil Rights During the 1990s: New Treaty Law Could Help Immensely*, 65 U. CINN. L. REV. 423, 467, 470 (1997); Jordan J. Paust, *Race-Based Affirmative Action and International Law*, 18 MICH. J. INT'L L. 659, 672 n.45 (1997); Paust, *Customary International Law and Human Rights Treaties* Are *Law of the United States*, 20 MICH. J. INT'L L. 301, 325–27 (1999); Thomas M. McDonnell, *Defensively Invoking Treaties in American Courts—Jurisdictional Challenges Under the U.N. Drug Trafficking Convention by Foreign Defendants Kidnapped Abroad by U.S. Agents,* 37 WM. & MARY L. REV. 1401 (1996); John Quigley, *Human Rights Defenses in U.S. Courts*, 20 HUM. RTS. Q. 555 (1998); Kristen B. Rosati, *The United Nations Convention Against Torture: A Self-Executing Treaty That Prevents the Removal of Persons Ineligible for Asylum and Withholding of Removal*, 26 DENV. J. INT'L L. & POL. 533, 562–63 (1998); David Sloss, *Ex parte Young and Federal Remedies for Human Rights Treaty Violations*, 75 WASH. L. REV. 1103, 1108 & n.19, 1121 & n.79, 1123 & n.85, 1129–30, 1141–42, 1199, 1203 n.114 (2000); Ruth Wedgwood, remarks, 85 PROC., AM. SOC. INT'L L. 139, 141 (1991); *see also* JORDAN J. PAUST, INTERNATIONAL LAW AS LAW OF THE UNITED STATES 361–62, 371–74, 379–80 (2 ed. 2003); Chapter 2. With respect to the U.S. declaration of non-self-execution concerning the International Convention on the Elimination of All Forms of Racial Discrimination, the Executive explained: "The intent is to clarify that the treaty will not create a new or independently enforceable private cause of action in U.S. courts." S. Exec. Rep. No. 103–29, at 25–26 (1994).

Read preambular paragraph 3 and Articles 2, 4 (2), 9 (5), 14 (1) and (6), and 50 of the Covenant. Also read Article 8 of the Universal Declaration of Human Rights in connection with Articles 55 (c) and 56 of the United Nations Charter. Note that the U.S. declaration is not a general declaration of non-self-execution. It expressly does not reach Article 50 of the International Covenant; and Article 50 mandates that "[t]he provisions of the present Covenant shall extend to all parts of federal states without any limitations or exceptions." See also the Executive Explanation concerning Article 50, in Chapter 2, Section 2 C 1 d and 2 F 2; U.S. Constitution, Art. VI, cl. 2. Professor Paust has noted: "the declaration ... is expressly limited.... Article 50 reaches back to all '[t]he provisions' of the Covenant and mandates, consistently with the command of the U.S. Constitution: 'The provisions of the present Covenant shall extend to all parts of federal States without any limitations or exceptions.' Such 'shall' language is mandatory and self-executory. Moreover, the declaration should be interpreted consistently with Article 50 of the Covenant to preserve rights, since treaties are to be construed in a broad manner to protect express and implied rights.... Thus, even if the declaration of non-self-execution were operative, the treaty is partly self-executing, has the force and effect of law, and is supreme federal law." Paust, *Customary International Law*, *supra*; PAUST, INTERNATIONAL LAW AS LAW OF THE UNITED STATES 361–62 (2 ed. 2003). See also Thomas Buergenthal, *Modern Constitutions and Human Rights Treaties*, 26 COLUM. J. TRANSNAT'L. L. 211, 221 (1997).

Is the U.S. Declaration nonetheless void *ab initio* as a matter of law? *See, e.g.*, Human Rights Committee, General Comment No. 24, *supra*; FRANK NEWMAN & DAVID WEISSBRODT, INTERNATIONAL HUMAN RIGHTS 589–91 (1990); PAUST, *supra* at 363–68; Louis Henkin, *The Covenant on Civil and Political Rights*, in U.S. RATIFICATION OF THE HUMAN RIGHTS TREATIES: WITH OR WITHOUT RESERVATIONS? 20, 22 (R. Lillich ed. 1981); Lori Fisler Damrosch, *The Role of the United States Senate Concerning "Self–Executing" and "Non–Self–Executing" Treaties*, 67 CHI.-KENT L. REV. 515 (1991); Louis Henkin, *U.S. Ratification of Human Rights Conventions: The Ghost of Senator Bricker*, 89 AM. J. INT'L L. 341 (1995); Hurst Hannum, remarks, *id.* at 69; Paust, *Race-Based Affirmative Action*, *supra* at 671; John Quigley, *The International Covenant on Civil and Political Rights and the Supremacy Clause*, 42 DEPAUL L. REV. 1287 (1993); Stefan A. Riesenfeld & Fred M. Abbott, *The Scope of U.S. Senate Control Over the Conclusion and Operation of Treaties*, 67 CHI.-KENT L. REV. 571 (1991); William A. Schabas, *Invalid Reservations to the International Covenant on Civil and Political Rights: Is the United States Still a Party?*, 21 BROOKLYN J. INT'L L. 277 (1995); Oscar Schachter, *The Obligations of the Parties to Give Effect to the Covenant on Civil and Political Rights*, 73 AM. J. INT'L L. 462 (1979); David P. Stewart, *U.S. Ratification of the Covenant on Civil and Political Rights: The Significance of the Reservations, Understandings, and Declarations*, 42 DEPAUL L. REV. 1183 (1993); *see also* Malvina Halberstam, *United States Ratification of the Convention on the Elimination of All Forms of Discrimination Against Women*, 31 G.W. J. INT'L L. & ECON. 49, 64, 67–69 (1997) (declarations of non-self-execution are "inconsistent with the language, history, and purpose of Article VI of the U.S. Constitution" and are constitutionally suspect); John Quigley, *The International Covenant on Civil and Political Rights and the Supremacy Clause*, 42 DEPAUL L. REV. 1287 (1993).

8. Professor Schabas, with support from conclusions of the Covenant's Committee, argues that a U.S. reservation concerning the execution of juveniles [found in Chapter 2, Section 2 C 1 d] is incompatible with the object and purpose of the Covenant and, thus, void. He also argues that the U.S. reservation is severable. See Schabas, *supra*; *see also* Human Rights Committee, Annual Report of the Human Rights Committee, Oct. 3, 1995, 50 U.N. GAOR, Supp. No. 40, U.N. Doc. A/50/40, at para. 279 (U.S. reservation to Article 6 (5) is "incompatible with the object and purpose of the Covenant."); General Comment Adopted by the Human Rights Committee Under

Article 40, Paragraph 4, of the International Covenant on Civil and Political Rights, Addendum, Hum. Rts. Comm., General Comment No. 24 (52), para. 8, U.N. Doc. CCPR/C/21/Rev. 1/Add.6 (1994) (reservations regarding execution of children are void and also conflict with a peremptory norm *jus cogens* under international law); Report of the Special Rapporteur on Extrajudicial,Summary or Arbitrary Executions, Addendum, Mission to the United States of America, U.N. Doc. E/CN.4/1998/68/Add.3, paras. 29, 49–56 (22 Jan. 1998). Cases in the U.S. have not been following this approach and have relied on the U.S. reservation concerning execution of juveniles. *See* Beazley v. Johnson, 242 F.3d 248, 264–69 (5th Cir.2001); *Ex parte* Pressley, 770 So.2d 143, 148 (Ala. 2000), *cert. denied*, 531 U.S. 931 (2000); Domingues v. Nevada, 114 Nev. 783, 961 P.2d 1279 (1998), *cert. denied*, 528 U.S. 963 (1999). Nonetheless, in 2005 the Supreme Court found that juvenile executions violate the 8th Amendment to the U.S. Constitution. See Roper v. Simmons, ___ U.S. ___, 125 S.Ct. 1183 (2005). Writing for the majority of Justices Stevens, Souther, Ginsburg, and Breyer, Justice Kennedy concluded that the United States "stands alone in a world that has turned its face against the death penalty." Although noting that the "overwhelming weight of international opinion against the juvenile death penalty is not controlling," the majority in *Roper* acknowledged that the Supreme Court has referred to laws of other countries and international authorities to interpret the Eighth Amendment's prohibition on cruel and unusual punishment. *Id.* at 1198–99. Dissenting Justices Scalia, Chief Justice Rehnquist, and Thomas found insufficient evidence of a national consensus against the juvenile death penalty and, even more unequivocally, that "... the basic premise of the Court's argument–that American law should conform to the laws of the rest of the world–ought to be rejected out of hand." *Id.* at 1226. Justice O'Connor, in a separate dissent found a national consensus against the juvenile death penalty to be lacking, but nevertheless disagreed with the other dissenting Justices that foreign and international law "have no place in our Eighth Amendment jurisprudence." *Id.* at 1215. *See generally* Linda A. Malone, *From* Breard *to* Atkins *to* Malvo: *Legal Incompetency and Human Rights Norms on the Fringes of the Death Penalty*, 13 Wm. & Mary Bill of Rights J. 363(2004).

Generally, a reservation to a treaty can be severable if its deletion does not unalterably condition or substantially interfere with overall consent to ratification. Yet, severability from a human rights treaty does not even depend upon impacts on state consent. *See* General Comment Adopted by the Human Rights Committee Under Article 40, Paragraph 4, of the International Covenant on Civil and Political Rights, Addendum, Hum. Rts. Comm., General Comment No. 24 (52), para. 20, U.N. Doc. CCPR/C/21/Rev.1/Add.6 (1994); Paust, *supra* at 368–70, 378, 386 n.30, 400, 413; *see also Advisory Opinion on Reservations to the Convention on Genocide*, 1951 I.C.J. 1, 15; *Loizidou v. Turkey*, 310 Eur. Ct. H.R. (ser. A) (1995) [in 90 Am. J. Int'l L. 98 (1996)]; *Belilos v. Switzerland*, 132 Eur. Ct. H.R. (ser. A) (1988). The Human Rights Committee created by the International Covenant provides authoritative interpretation of the treaty. See Report of the Committee, 1994 Report, vol. 1, 49 U.N. GAOR, Supp. No. 40, U.N. Doc. A/49/40, para. 50 ("General comments ... are intended ... [among other purposes] to clarify the requirements of the Covenant...."); Richard B. Lillich & Hurst Hannum,

INTERNATIONAL HUMAN RIGHTS LAW 224 (3 ed. 1995) ("the Human Rights Committee from time to time has issued general comments about the nature of the obligations states have assumed under particular articles of the Covenant.... they are ... the gloss ... put on the Covenant's substantive provisions...."); Maria v. McElroy, 68 F.Supp.2d 206, 232 (E.D.N.Y. 1999); United States v. Bakeas, 987 F.Supp. 44, 46 n. 4 (D.Mass.1997) ("the Human Rights Committee has the ultimate authority to decide whether parties' clarifications or reservations have any effect."); see also United States v. Duarte–Acero, 208 F.3d 1282, 1285 n.12, 1287–88 (11th Cir. 2000).

More generally, note the argument that a putative reservation is not of great import to the reserving state (so it is severable) but is of such import to the community that it is thwarting of the object and purpose of a treaty and, thus, void. Does acceptance of the argument impact on the notion that international agreements are based on "consent"? Consider also the next subsection.

4. Other Aspects of Void and Voidable Status

Read Articles 49–52 and 75 of the Vienna Convention on the Law of Treaties (in the Documents Supplement)

Notes and Questions

1. Does the fact that some treaties are only voidable, not void, and that Article 75 impacts detrimentally on aggressor states indicate that "consent" is not the only criterion concerning obligations under international agreements? With respect to aggressor states, is true consent less important than peace, security and other community interests? RESTATEMENT § 331, cmt. d, notes that some coercion is "privileged" under the U.N. Charter (*e.g.*, art. 51 re: self-defense) and that when a victim state imposes a peace treaty on an aggressor, the treaty can be valid.

2. Are unjust treaties "imposed" on former colonies of a colonial power void or voidable under the Vienna Convention? Does a 1903 Lease of Lands for Coaling and Naval Stations (Feb. 23, 1903, T.S. No. 418, extended by a 1934 Treaty Defining Relations with Cuba, T.S. No. 866, 48 Stat. 1683) that "leases" "complete jurisdiction and control" of Guantanamo Bay, Cuba to the United States as a coal-powered vessel refueling station fit this scenario? If the 1934 agreement extends the "lease" for "[s]o long as the United States of America shall not abandon the ... naval station of Guantanamo," absent modification or termination of the agreement, is the present use of the area by the U.S. consistent with the object and purpose of the 1903 treaty?

3. If a state splits into two or more states, are the prior treaty obligations of the former state binding on the new states? There are different views. On this issue, the Restatement differs from the Vienna Convention on Succession of States in Respect of Treaties, U. N. Doc. A/CONF. 80/31 (1978), *reprinted in* 17 I.L.M. 1488 (1978), the Restatement preferring that a new state does not succeed to the international agreements of the predecessor state, "unless, expressly or by implication, it accepts such agreements and the other party or parties thereto agree or acquiesce." RESTATEMENT § 210 (3). This "clean slate" approach is applied to "both newly

independent states and to a state separated from another by secession or other circumstances." See *id.* cmt. f. The Restatement "rejects a distinction, made in the Vienna Convention on State Succession . . . , between newly independent states emerging from colonialism and states arising from secession or other separation of parts of a state," the Vienna Convention preferring that former colonies have a "clean slate" and not be bound, but that all others be bound by the treaties of the former state until they express a formal and otherwise permissible claim to the contrary. See *id.* RN 4; Vienna Convention, arts. 34–35. *See also* Detlev F. Vagts, *State Succession: The Codifiers' View*, 33 VA. J. INT'L L. 275, 289–94 (1993). The Restatement adds that customary international law is binding on all new states. RESTATEMENT § 210, cmt. i.

What approach do you prefer? Why? Should it matter that the treaties are significant multilateral treaties proscribing genocide, war crimes, or violations of basic human rights?

4. Are Articles 51 and 52 of the Vienna Convention on the Law of Treaties self-operative in the sense that treaties are void *ab initio* as a matter of law? Can private claimants properly raise this point domestically in a court of law in the absence of official recognition by political branches? If the political branches choose to ignore the coercion and go on with the agreement, is that legally possible? Is there a new agreement evidenced by the subsequent conduct and expectations of the parties? The International Law Commission noted in 1966: "Even if it were conceivable that after being liberated from the influence of a threat or of a use of force a State might wish to allow a treaty procured from it by such means, the Commission considered it essential that the treaty should be regarded in law as void *ab initio*. . . . If, therefore, the treaty were [later] maintained . . . , it would in effect be by the conclusion of a new treaty. . . ." [1966] II Y.B.I.L.C. 247.

5. Why do you suppose any coercion of a representative of a state voids a treaty, but only coercion of a state in violation of the U.N. Charter voids a treaty? Is some coercion of states normal or tolerated?

6. If coercion occurs in violation of the principles of the U.N. Charter, does such require the conclusion that a relevant agreement was "procured by" such coercion?

7. If the 1995 Dayton Peace Accords (the General Framework Agreement for Peace in Bosnia–Herzegovina, completed in Dayton, Ohio), were arguably imposed upon Bosnia–Herzegovina in view of U.N. Security Council arms embargoes and other pressures from states, would they be void or voidable under the Vienna Convention? Does the phrase coercion of a state in violation of international law include coercion by the Security Council? coercion in violation of a state's "inherent right of individual or collective self-defense" under Article 51 of the U.N. Charter? coercion of an economic nature? What articles of the U.N. Charter are relevant to Article 52 of the Vienna Convention when it refers to "the threat or use of force in violation of the principles of international law embodied in the Charter"? Are Articles 1, 2 (4), 2 (7), 24 (2), 25, and 51 relevant?

8. RESTATEMENT § 331, cmt. d, declares that only coercion by military force, not economic or political coercion, vitiates an agreement. Is this consistent with Article 2 (4) of the U.N. Charter? Does it matter that Article

2 (4) uses the word "force" (and not the more specific phrase "armed force") while Article 51 of the Charter refers to an "armed attack"? Reporters' Note 3 of § 331 of the Restatement notes that there was a significant split among the conferees during formal drafting of the Vienna Convention whether the word "force" should include economic force. Nonetheless, as a "compromise," a declaration was unanimously adopted and was annexed to the Final Act of the Conference which condemned the threat or use of pressure "in any form" by a state to coerce any other state in order to conclude a treaty. *See also* Richard D. Kearney & Robert E. Dalton, *The Treaty on Treaties*, 64 Am. J. Int'l L. 495, 533–35 (1970).

9. Some forms of economic coercion (retaliation, reprisals) are tolerated. Since formation of the Vienna Convention, have other forms of economic coercion been recognizably of such intensity and/or of such impact as to thwart the legal policies at stake in Articles 2 (4) and 2 (7) of the U.N. Charter? *See, e.g.*, Richard B. Lillich, Economic Coercion and the New International Economic Order (1976); Jordan J. Paust & Albert P. Blaustein, The Arab Oil Weapon (1977).

5. *Breach of Treaties*

VIENNA CONVENTION ON THE LAW OF TREATIES

Article 60

1. A material breach of a bilateral treaty by one of the parties entitles the other to invoke the breach as a ground for terminating the treaty or suspending its operation in whole or in part.

2. A material breach of a multilateral treaty by one of the parties entitles:

(a) the other parties by unanimous agreement to suspend the operation of the treaty in whole or in part or to terminate it either:

(i) in the relations between themselves and the defaulting State, or

(ii) as between all the parties;

(b) a party specially affected by the breach to invoke it as a ground for suspending the operation of the treaty in whole or in part in the relations between itself and the defaulting State; . . .

3. A material breach of a treaty . . . consists in:

(a) a repudiation of the treaty not sanctioned by the present Convention; or

(b) the violation of a provision essential to the accomplishment of the object or purpose of the treaty. . . .

5. Paragraphs 1 to 3 do not apply to provisions relating to the protection of the human person contained in treaties of a humanitarian character, in particular to provisions prohibiting any form of reprisals against persons protected by such treaties.

Notes and Questions

1. Is termination or suspension automatic in case of a material breach?

2. Who decides whether a material breach has occurred? Does the non-breaching state make a provisional determination, subject to review (both formal and informal) by the international community including, in some contexts, review by the U.N. Security Council under Article 39 of the Charter? With respect to choice in the United States, see Chapter 2.

3. If the U.S. and France are parties to a bilateral air transport agreement allowing the air carriers of each country rights to fly into, land, and transport passengers and cargo for hire and France refuses U.S. air carriers such rights, is the French refusal a material breach of the treaty?

4. If a material breach occurs, can any non-breaching state choose either to terminate or suspend performance? Can a state with such an option choose merely to suspend performance of parts of the treaty and continue with the remainder of the agreement? *See also* Vienna Convention, art. 44.

5. If a treaty contains a provision for dispute settlement, does a material breach by one party still allow the other party(ies) to suspend performance while pursuing, in good faith, the dispute settlement process(es)? See Case Concerning the Air Services Agreement between France and the United States, Award of 9 Dec. 1978, 18 U.N.R.I.A.A. 417.

6. In view of previous portions of this chapter, what provisions of humanitarian law are likely to be covered under Article 60 (5) of the Vienna Convention? Unlike coverage under Article 60 (5) of the Vienna Convention, do *erga omnes* obligations only exist under multilateral agreements and customary international law?

6. *Impossibility and Change of Circumstances*

Read Articles 61 and 62 of the Vienna Convention on the Law of Treaties (in the Documents Supplement)

Notes and Questions

1. If two countries have a bilateral trade agreement concerning the supply of weapons, a war involving one of the countries breaks out, and the U.N. Security Council orders an arms embargo on shipments to the warring parties, does the doctrine of fundamental change of circumstances (*rebus sic stantibus*) apply? Does the doctrine of impossibility? Is there any other override of the bilateral treaty obligations?

2. If both parties to a bilateral agreement have contributed to the impossibility or to a fundamental change of circumstances vitiating an essential basis of consent to be bound, should they be bound to perform the agreement?

3. Does impossibility relate only to "disappearance or destruction of an object" and not to impossibility created elsewise by acts of God, war, or other actions? See RESTATEMENT § 336, RN 3. Can the latter acts be covered under the doctrine of fundamental change of circumstances?

B. Customary International Law

What is "custom" or the customary law of nations? Article 38 of the Statute of the International Court of Justice recognizes that customary international law is evidenced by "a general practice accepted as law." Thus, custom is comprised of two elements: (a) general patterns of practice or behavior (what people do), and (b) general acceptance as law (what people think) or general patterns of legal expectation or *opinio juris* (*i.e.*, expectations generally shared that something is legally required or appropriate). Both elements or patterns must exist or coincide at a relevant moment. *See generally* North Sea Continental Shelf Cases (Federal Republic of Germany v. Denmark) (Federal Republic of Germany v. the Netherlands), 1969 I.C.J. 3, 44, para. 77: "Not only must the acts concerned amount to a settled practice, but they must also be such, or be carried out in such a way, as to be evidence of a rule of law requiring it. The need for such a belief, *i.e.*, the existence of a subjective element, is implicit in the very notion of the *opinio juris sive necessitatis*. The States concerned must therefore feel that they are conforming to what amounts to a legal obligation. The frequency, or even habitual character of the acts is not in itself enough. There are many international acts, *e.g.*, in the field of ceremonial and protocol, which are performed almost invariably, but which are motivated only by considerations of courtesy, convenience or tradition, and not by any sense of legal duty."

Fairly obviously, customary law can be dynamic—a law reflected in a dynamic process of behavior and expectation. What once was custom can change to non-custom if one or both of the elements are no longer extant, and what once was not customary law can grow into customary law recognizable, for example, by a judicial tribunal. Moreover, the traditional view is that custom rests upon the general consent or expectations of humankind, not merely that of their representatives (*i.e.*, nation-states). *See, e.g.*, The Scotia, 81 U.S. (14 Wall.) 170, 187–88 (1871) (below); The Prize Cases, 67 U.S. (2 Black) 635, 670 (1862) ("founded on the common consent as well as the common sense of the world"); Ware v. Hylton, 3 U.S. (3 Dall.) 199, 227 (1796) ("established by the general consent of mankind"); 4 W. Blackstone, Commentaries on the Law of England 66 (1765). The preamble to the 1907 Hague Convention No. IV Respecting the Laws and Customs of War on Land contained an early recognition that the "law of nations ... [results] from the usages established among civilized peoples, from the laws of humanity, and from the dictates of the public conscience." T.S. No. 539; League of Nations Treaty Series vol. XCIV (1929), No. 2138; 36 Stat. 2277 (18 Oct. 1907). Similar phrases appear in the 1949 Geneva Conventions. *See, e.g.*, Article 158 of the 1949 Geneva Convention Relative to the Protection of Civilian Persons in Time of War, 75 U.N.T.S. 287, 6 U.S.T. 3516 (1955).

THE SCOTIA

81 U.S. (14 Wall.) 170 (1871).

[Editors' note: a U.S. vessel collided with a British on the high seas. The British owners, who were the defendants, claimed that the U.S. vessel neglected to show colored lights as required by both British and U.S. law. The Court concluded that the regulations found in British and U.S. laws governing colored lights had become part of binding customary international law.]

... The question still remains, what was the law of the place where the collision occurred [on the high seas], and at the time when it occurred. Conceding that it was not the law of the United States, nor that of Great Britain [whose flag vessels collided], nor the concurrent regulations of the two governments, but that it was the law of the sea, was it the ancient ... [law], or the law changed after ... [British regulations of 1863 and an Act of Congress of 1864]? Undoubtedly, no single nation can change the law of the sea. That law is of universal obligation, and no statute of one or two nations can create obligations for the world. Like all the laws of nations, it rests upon the common consent of civilized communities. It is of force, not because it was prescribed by any superior power, but because it has been generally accepted as a rule of conduct. Whatever may have been its origin, whether in the usages of navigation or in the ordinances of maritime states, or in both, it has become the law of the sea only by the concurrent sanction of those nations who may be said to constitute the commercial world.... They all became the law of the sea, not on account of their origin, but by reason of their acceptance as such.... Changes in nautical rules have taken place. How have they been accomplished, if not by the concurrent assent, express or understood, of maritime nations? ...

This is not giving to the statutes of any nation extraterritorial effect. It is not treating them as general maritime laws, but it is recognition of the historical fact that by common consent of mankind, these rules have been acquiesced in as of general obligation. Of that fact we think we may take judicial notice. Foreign municipal laws must indeed be proved as facts, but it is not so with the law of nations.

THE PAQUETE HABANA

175 U.S. 677 (1900).

[Editors' note: Portions of this case also appear in Chapter 2, Section 2 D 1 concerning the limitation of Executive acts by customary international law.]

GRAY, J.

These are two appeals from decrees of the District Court of the United States for the Southern District of Florida, condemning two fishing vessels and their cargoes as prize of war. [Editors' note: the law of prize is part of the law of war and, as the Court notes below, international law.]

Each vessel was a fishing smack, running in and out of Havana, and regularly engaged in fishing on the coast of Cuba; sailed under the Spanish flag; was owned by a Spanish subject of Cuban birth, living in the city of Havana; was commanded by a subject of Spain, also residing in Havana; and her master and crew had no interest in the vessel, but were entitled to shares, amounting in all to two thirds, of her catch, the other third belonging to her owner. Her cargo consisted of fresh fish, caught by her crew from the sea, put on board as they were caught, and kept and sold alive. Until stopped by the blockading squadron, she had no knowledge of the existence of the war, or of any blockade. She had no arms or ammunition on board, and made no attempt to run the blockade after she knew of its existence, nor any resistance at the time of the capture.

The Paquete Habana was a sloop, 43 feet long on the keel, and of 25 tons burden, and had a crew of three Cubans, including the master, who had a fishing license from the Spanish Government, and no other commission or license. She left Havana March 25, 1898; sailed along the coast of Cuba to Cape San Antonio at the western end of the island, and there fished for twenty-five days, lying between the reefs off the cape, within the territorial waters of Spain; and then started back for Havana, with a cargo of about 40 quintals of live fish. On April 25, 1898, about two miles off Mariel, and eleven miles from Havana, she was captured by the United States gunboat Castine.

The Lola was a schooner, 51 feet long on the keel, and of 35 tons burden, and had a crew of six Cubans, including the master, and no commission or license. She left Havana April 11, 1898, and proceeded to Campeachy Sound off Yucatan, fished there eight days, and started back for Havana with a cargo of about 10,000 pounds of live fish. On April 26, 1898, near Havana, she was stopped by the United States steamship Cincinnati, and was warned not to go into Havana, but was told that she would be allowed to land at Bahia Honda. She then changed her course, and put for Bahia Honda, but on the next morning, when near that port, was captured by the United States steamship Dolphin.

Both the fishing vessels were brought by their captors into Key West. A libel for the condemnation of each vessel and her cargo as prize of war was there filed on April 27, 1898; a claim was interposed by her master, on behalf of himself and the other members of the crew, and of her owner; evidence was taken, showing the facts above stated; and on May 30, 1898, a final decree of condemnation and sale was entered, "the court not being satisfied that as a matter of law, without any ordinance, treaty or proclamation, fishing vessels of this class are exempt from seizure." . . .

We are then brought to the consideration of the question whether, upon the facts appearing in these records, the fishing smacks were subject to capture by the armed vessels of the United States during the recent war with Spain.

By an ancient usage among civilized nations, beginning centuries ago, and gradually ripening into a rule of international law, coast fishing vessels, pursuing their vocation of catching and bringing in fresh fish, have been recognized as exempt, with their cargoes and crews, from capture as prize of war.

This doctrine, however, has been earnestly contested at the bar; and no complete collection of the instances illustrating it is to be found, so far as we are aware, in a single published work, although many are referred to and discussed by the writers on international law, notably in 2 Ortolan, *Regles Internationales et Diplomatie de la Mer*, (4th ed.) lib. 3, c. 2, pp. 51–56; in 4 Calvo, *Droit International*, (5th ed.) §§ 2367–2373; in De Boeck, *Propriete Privee Ennemie sous Pavillon Ennemi*, §§ 191–196; and in Hall, International Law, (4th. ed.) § 148. It is therefore worth the while to trace the history of the rule, from the earliest accessible sources, through the increasing recognition of it, with occasional setbacks, to what we may now justly consider as its final establishment in our own country and generally throughout the civilized world.

The earliest acts of any government on the subject, mentioned in the books, either emanated from, or were approved by, a King of England.

In 1403 and 1406, Henry IV issued orders to his admirals and other officers, entitled "Concerning Safety for Fishermen—*De Securitate pro Piscatoribus*."....

The treaty made October 2, 1521, between the Emperor Charles V and Francis I of France....

The herring fishery was permitted, in time of war, by French and Dutch edicts in 1536. Bynkershoek, *Quaestiones Juris Publicae*, lib. 1, c. 3; 1 *Emerigon des Assurances*, c. 4, sect. 9; c. 12, sect. 19, § 8.

[Editors' note: The Court next addressed French practice and writers such as Cleirac, Pardessus, Ortolan, and Froissart, from 1543 to 1661.]

The same custom would seem to have prevailed in France until towards the end of the seventeenth century. For example, in 1675, Louis XIV and the States General of Holland, by mutual agreement, granted to Dutch and French fishermen the liberty, undisturbed by their vessels of war, of fishing along the coasts of France, Holland and England. D'Hauterive et De Cussy, *Traites de Commerce*, pt. 1, vol. 2, p. 278. But by the ordinances of 1681 and 1692 the practice was discontinued, because, Valin says, of the faithless conduct of the enemies of France, who, abusing the good faith with which she had always observed the treaties, habitually carried off her fishermen, while their own fished in safety. 2 Valin *sur l'Ordonnance de la Marine*, (1776) 689, 690; 2 Ortolan, 52; De Boeck, § 192.

The doctrine which exempts coast fishermen with their vessels and cargoes from capture as prize of war has been familiar to the United States from the time of the War of Independence.

[Editors' note: The Court next addressed a letter of the French King to his admiral in 1779 and a royal order of 1780.]

Among the standing orders made by Sir James Marriott, Judge of the English High Court of Admiralty, was one of April 11, 1780....

In the treaty of 1785 between the United States and Prussia, article 23, (which was proposed by the American Commissioners, John Adams, Benjamin Franklin and Thomas Jefferson, and is said to have been drawn up by Franklin,)....

Since the United States became a nation, the only serious interruptions, so far as we are informed, of the general recognition of the exemption of coast fishing vessels from hostile capture, arose out of the mutual suspicions and recriminations of England and France during the wars of the French Revolution.

In the first years of those wars, England having authorized the capture of French fishermen, a decree of the French National Convention of October, 2, 1793, directed the executive power "to protest against this conduct, theretofore without example; to reclaim the fishing boats seized; and, in case of refusal, to resort to reprisals." But in July, 1796, the Committee of Public Safety ordered the release of English fishermen seized under the former decree, "not considering them as prisoners of war." La Nostra Segnora de la Piedad, (1801) cited below; 2 De Cussy, *Droit Maritime*, 164, 165; 1 Masse, *Droit Commercial*, (2d ed.) 266, 267.

On January 24, 1798, the English Government, by express order, instructed the commanders of its ships to seize French and Dutch fishermen with their boats. 6 Martens, *Recueil des Traites*, (2d ed.) 505; 6 Schoell, *Histoire des Traites*, 119; 2 Ortolan, 53. After the promulgation of that order, Lord Stowell (then Sir William Scott) in the High Court of Admiralty of England condemned small Dutch fishing vessels as prize of war. In one case, the capture was in April, 1798, and the decree was made November 13, 1798. The Young Jacob and Johanna, 1 C. Rob. 20. In another case, the decree was made August 23, 1799. The Noydt Gedacht, 2 C. Rob. 137, note.

[Editors' note: The Court next addressed various English and French orders and correspondence between them evidenced, for example, in works by Martens, Schoell, and Ortolan.] ...

Lord Stowell's judgment in The Young Jacob and Johanna, 1 C. Rob. 20, above cited, was much relied on by the counsel for the United States, and deserves careful consideration.... The opinion begins by admitting the known custom in former wars not to capture such vessels—adding, however, "but this was a rule of comity only, and not of legal decision." Assuming the phrase "legal decision" to have been there used, in the sense in which courts are accustomed to use it, as equivalent to "judicial decision," it is true that, so far as appears, there had been no such decision on the point in England. The word "comity" was apparently used by Lord Stowell as synonymous with courtesy or good will. But the period of a hundred years which has since elapsed is amply sufficient to have enabled what originally may have rested in custom or comity, courtesy or concession, to grow, by the general assent of civilized nations, into a settled rule of international law. As well said by Sir James Mackintosh: "In the present century a slow and silent, but very substantial mitigation has taken place in the practice of war; and in proportion as that mitigated practice has received the sanction of time, it is raised from the rank of mere usage, and becomes part of the law of nations." Discourse on the Law of Nations, 38; 1 Miscellaneous Works, 360.

The French prize tribunals, both before and after Lord Stowell's decision, took a wholly different view of the general question. In 1780, as already mentioned, an order in council of Louis XVI had declared illegal the capture by a French cruiser of The John and Sarah, an English vessel, coming from Holland, laden with fresh fish. And on May 17, 1801, where a Portuguese fishing vessel, with her cargo of fish, having no more crew than was needed for her management, and for serving the nets, on a trip of several days, had been captured in April, 1801, by a French cruiser, three leagues off the coast of Portugal, the Council of Prizes held that the capture was contrary to "the principles of humanity, and the maxims of international law," and decreed that the vessel, with the fish on board, or the net proceeds of any that had been sold, should be restored to her master. La Nostra Segnora de la Piedad, 25 Merlin, Jurisprudence, *Prise Maritime*, § 3, art. 1, 3; S.C. 1 Pistoye et Duverdy, *Prises Maritimes*, 331; 2 De Cussy, *Droit Maritime*, 166.

The English government, soon afterwards, more than once unqualifiedly prohibited the molestation of fishing vessels employed in catching and bringing to market fresh fish. . . .

[Editors' note: The Court next cited works by Wheaton, Ortolan, De Boeck and Hall.]

In the war with Mexico in 1846, the United States recognized the exemption of coast fishing boats from capture. In proof of this, counsel have referred to records of the Navy Department, which this court is clearly authorized to consult upon such a question. Jones v. United States, 137 U.S. 202; Underhill v. Hernandez, 168 U.S. 250, 253. . . .

. . . General Halleck, in the preface to his work on International Law or Rules Regulating the Intercourse of States in Peace and War, published in 1861. . . .

That edition was the only one sent out under the author's own auspices, except an abridgment, entitled Elements of International Law and the Law of War, which he published in 1866, as he said in the preface, to supply a suitable textbook for instruction upon the subject, "not only in our colleges, but also in our two great national schools—the Military and Naval Academies." In that abridgment, the statement as to fishing boats was condensed, as follows:

> "Fishing boats have also, as a general rule, been exempted from the effects of hostilities. French writers consider this exemption as an

established principle of the modern law of war, and it has been so recognized in the French courts, which have restored such vessels when captured by French cruisers." Halleck's Elements, c. 20, § 21.

In the treaty of peace between the United States and Mexico in 1848 were inserted the very words of the earlier treaties with Prussia, already quoted, forbidding the hostile molestation or seizure in time of war of the persons, occupations, houses or goods of fishermen. 9 Stat. 939, 940.

Wharton's Digest of the International Law of the United States, published by authority of Congress in 1886 and 1887, embodies General Halleck's fuller statement, above quoted, and contains nothing else upon the subject. 3 Whart. Int. Law Dig. § 345, p. 315; 2 Halleck, (Eng. eds. 1873 and 1878) p. 151.

France, in the Crimean War in 1854, and in her wars with Austria in 1859 and with Germany in 1870, by general orders, forbade her cruisers to trouble the coast fisheries, or to seize any vessel or boat engaged therein, unless naval or military operations should make it necessary. Calvo, § 2372; Hall, § 148; 2 Ortolan, (4th ed.) 449; 10 *Revue de Droit International*, (1878) 399.

Calvo says that in the Crimean War, "notwithstanding her alliance with France and Italy, England did not follow the same line of conduct, and her cruisers in the Sea of Azof destroyed the fisheries, nets, fishing implements, provisions, boats, and even the cabins, of the inhabitants of the coast." Calvo, § 2372. And a Russian writer on Prize Law remarks that those depredations, "having brought ruin on poor fishermen and inoffensive traders, could not but leave a painful impression on the minds of the population, without impairing in the least the resources of the Russian government." Katchenovsky, (Pratt's ed.) 148. But the contemporaneous reports of the English naval officers put a different face on the matter, by stating that the destruction in question was part of a military measure, conducted with the cooperation of the French ships, and pursuant to instructions of the English admiral "to clear the seaboard of all fish stores, all fisheries and mills, on a scale beyond the wants of the neighboring population, and indeed of all things destined to contribute to the maintenance of the enemy's army in the Crimea;" and that the property destroyed consisted of large fishing establishments and storehouses of the Russian government, numbers of heavy launches, and enormous quantities of nets and gear, salted fish, corn and other provisions, intended for the supply of the Russian army. United Service Journal of 1855, pt. 3, pp. 108–112.

Since the English orders in council of 1806 and 1810, before quoted, in favor of fishing vessels employed in catching and bringing to market fresh fish, no instance has been found in which the exemption from capture of private coast fishing vessels, honestly pursuing their peaceful industry, has been denied by England, or by any other nation. And the Empire of Japan, (the last State admitted into the rank of civilized nations,) by an ordinance promulgated at the beginning of its war with China in August, 1894, established prize courts, and ordained that "the following enemy's vessels are exempt from detention"—including in the exemption "boats engaged in coast fisheries," as well as "ships engaged exclusively on a voyage of scientific discovery, philanthropy or religious mission." Takahashi, International Law, 11, 178.

International law is part of our law, and must be ascertained and administered by the courts of justice of appropriate jurisdiction, as often as questions of right depending upon it are duly presented for their determination. For this purpose, where there is no treaty, and no controlling executive or legislative act or judicial decision, resort must be had to the customs and usages of civilized nations; and, as evidence of these, to the works of jurists and commentators, who by years of labor, research and experience, have made themselves peculiarly well acquainted with the subjects of which they treat. Such works are resorted to by judicial tribunals, not for the speculations of their authors concerning what the law ought to be, but for trustworthy evidence of what the law really is. Hilton v. Guyot, 159 U.S. 113, 163, 164, 214, 215.

Wheaton places, among the principal sources of international law, "Text-writers of authority, showing what is the approved usage of nations, or the general opinion respecting their mutual conduct, with the definitions and modifications introduced by general consent." As to these he forcibly observes: "Without wishing to exaggerate the importance of these writers, or to substitute, in any case, their authority for the principles of reason, it may be affirmed that they are generally impartial in their judgment. They are witnesses of the sentiments and usages of civilized nations, and the weight of their testimony increases every time that their authority is invoked by statesmen, and every year that passes without the rules laid down in their works being impugned by the avowal of contrary principles." Wheaton's International Law, (8th ed.) § 15.

Chancellor Kent says: "In the absence of higher and more authoritative sanctions, the ordinances of foreign States, the opinions of eminent statesmen, and the writings of distinguished jurists, are regarded as of great consideration on questions not settled by conventional law. In cases where the principal jurists agree, the presumption will be very great in favor of the solidity of their maxims; and no civilized nation, that does not arrogantly set all ordinary law and justice at defiance, will venture to disregard the uniform sense of the established writers on international law." 1 Kent Com. 18.

It will be convenient, in the first place, to refer to some leading French treatises on international law, which deal with the question now before us, not as one of the law of France only, but as one determined by the general consent of civilized nations. . . .

No international jurist of the present day has a wider or more deserved reputation than Calvo, who, though writing in French, is a citizen of the Argentine Republic, employed in its diplomatic service abroad. In the fifth edition of his great work on international law, published in 1896, he observes, in § 2366, that the international authority of decisions in particular cases by the prize courts of France, of England, and of the United States, is lessened by the fact that the principles on which they are based are largely derived from the internal legislation of each country; and yet the peculiar character of maritime wars, with other considerations, gives to prize jurisprudence a force and importance reaching beyond the limits of the country in which it has prevailed. He therefore proposes here to group together a number of particular cases proper to serve as precedents for the solution of grave questions of maritime law in regard to the capture of private property as prize of war. Immediately, in § 2367, he goes on to say: "Notwithstanding the hardships to which maritime wars subject private property, notwithstanding the extent of the recognized rights of belligerents, there are generally exempted, from seizure and capture, fishing vessels." In the next section he adds: "This exception is perfectly justiciable—*Cette exception est parfaitement justiciable*"—that is to say, belonging to judicial jurisdiction or cognizance. Littre, *Dict. voc. Justiciable*; Hans v. Louisiana, 134 U.S. 1, 15. Calvo then quotes Ortolan's description, above cited, of the nature of the coast fishing industry; and proceeds to refer, in detail, to some of the French precedents, to the acts of the French and English governments in the times of Louis XVI and of the French Revolution, to the position of the United States in the war with Mexico, and of France in later wars, and to the action of British cruisers in the Crimean War. And he concludes his discussion of the subject, in § 2373, by affirming the exemption of the coast fishery, and pointing out the distinction in this regard between the coast fishery and what he calls the great fishery, for cod, whales or seals, as follows: "The privilege of exemption from capture, which is generally acquired by fishing vessels plying their industry near the coasts, is not extended in any country to ships employed on the high sea in what is called the great fishery, such as that for the cod, for the whale or the sperm whale, or for the seal or sea calf. These ships are, in effect, considered as devoted to operations which are at once commercial and industrial—*Ces navires sont en effect consideres comme adonnes a des operations a la fois commerciales et industrielles*." The distinction is generally recognized. 2 Ortolan, 54; De Boeck, § 196; Hall, § 148. See also The Susa, 2 C. Rob. 251; The Johan, Edw. Adm. 275, and appx. L.

The modern German books on international law, cited by the counsel for the appellants, treat the custom, by which the vessels and implements of coast fishermen are exempt from seizure and capture, as well established by the practice of nations. Heffter, § 137; 2 Kaltenborn, § 237, p. 480; Bluntschli, § 667; Perels, § 37, p. 217.

De Boeck, in his work on Enemy Private Property under Enemy Flag—*de la Propriēte Privėe Ennemie sous Pavillon Ennemi*—published in 1882,and the only continental treatise cited by the counsel for the United States, says in § 191: "A usage very ancient, if not universal, withdraws from the right of capture enemy vessels engaged in the coast fishery. The reason of this exception is evident; it would have been too hard to snatch from poor fishermen the means of earning their bread."

"The exemption includes the boats, the fishing implements and the cargo of fish." Again, in § 195: "It is to be observed that very few treaties sanction in due form this immunity of the coast fishery." "There is, then, only a custom. But what is its character? It is so fixed and general that it can be raised to the rank of a positive and formal rule of international law?" After discussing the statements of other writers, he approves the opinion of Ortolan (as expressed in the last sentence above quoted from his work) and says that, at bottom, it differs by a shade only from that formulated by Calvo and by some of the German jurists, and that "it is more exact, without ignoring the imperative character of the humane rule in question—*elle est plus exacte, sans méconnaitre le caractere imperatif de la regle d'humanité dont il s'agit*." And, in § 196, he defines the limits of the rule as follows: "But the immunity of the coast fishery must be limited by the reasons that justify it. The reasons of humanity and of harmlessness—*les raisons d'humanité et d'innocuité*—which militate in its favor do not exist in the great fishery, such as the cod fishery; ships engaged in that fishery devote themselves to truly commercial operations, which employ a large number of seamen. And these same reasons cease to be applicable to fishing vessels employed for a warlike purpose, to those which conceal arms, or which exchange signals of intelligence with ships of war; but only those taken in the fact can be rigorously treated; to allow seizure by way of prevention would open the door to every abuse, and would be equivalent to a suppression of the immunity."

[Editors' note: The Court next addressed partly conflicting but mostly supporting views of textwriters from England, the Netherlands, Austria, Spain, France, and Italy from the 1870s to the 1880s: Hall, Lawrence, Attlmayr, de Negrin, Testa, and Fiore.] . . .

This review of the precedents and authorities on the subject appears to us abundantly to demonstrate that at the present day, by the general consent of the civilized nations of the world, and independently of any express treaty or other public act, it is an established rule of international law, founded on considerations of humanity to a poor and industrious order of men, and of the mutual convenience of belligerent States, that coast fishing vessels, with their implements and supplies, cargoes and crews, unarmed, and honestly pursuing their peaceful calling of catching and bringing in fresh fish, are exempt from capture as prize of war.

Notes and Questions

1. Concerning proof of the content of a customary norms, one need only demonstrate a core of generally expected meaning and cases recognize that normative content need only be "sufficiently" defined. *See, e.g.*, Alvarez–Machain v. United States, 331 F.3d 604, 612 (9th Cir. 2003) ("sufficient consensus," " 'sufficiently . . . defined,' " *quoting* United States v. Smith, 18 U.S. (5 Wheat.) 153, 162 (1820)); *id.* 266 F.3d 1045, 1050–53 (9th Cir. 2001) (norm need not be specific in human rights instruments); Hilao v. Estate of Marcos (*In re* Estate of Ferdinand Marcos Human Rights Litig.), 25 F.3d 1467, 1475 (9th Cir. 1994) (" 'definable' "); Tel–Oren v. Libyan Arab Repub-

lic, 726 F.2d at 781 (Edwards, J.) ("definable"); Filartiga v. Pena–Irala, 630 F.2d at 880–82 ("sufficiently determinate," " 'sufficiently ... defined,' " *quoting Smith*); Xuncax v. Gramajo, 886 F.Supp. at 185 ("adequately defined"), 187 ("not necessary that every aspect ... be fully defined"); Forti v. Suarez–Mason, 672 F.Supp. 1531, 1540–42 (N.D. Cal. 1987) ("definable," "sufficient consensus to evince"); *id.*, 694 F.Supp. 707, 709–11 (N.D. Cal. 1988) ("general recognition," "sufficient to establish"); *see also* The Paquete Habana, 175 U.S. at 700 ("must be ascertained and administered by the courts"); Hilton v. Guyot, 159 U.S. at 163 (same); The Nereide, 13 U.S. (9 Cranch) at 422; Kadic v. Karadzic, 70 F.3d at 238 (courts ascertain the evolving content of the law of nations); *cf id.* at 239 ("well-established"). This approach to normative identification is consistent with judicial power, since the judiciary has the primary competence to identify and clarify the content of international law and that power is constitutionally based because customary international law is part of the "laws of the United States" within the meaning of Articles III, § 2, and VI, cl. 2 of the U.S. Constitution.

2. Note the extensive array of textwriter opinions and other evidences of practice and *opinio juris* addressed in the extract from *The Paquete Habana*. Some were even deleted from the extract. It was not unusual to cite foreign textwriters as proof of the content of customary international law. *See also* United States v. Smith, 18 U.S. (5 Wheat.) 153 (1820); The Nereide, 13 U.S. (9 Cranch) 388 (1815); Ware v. Hylton, 3 U.S. (3 Dall.) 199 (1796); Henfield's Case, 11 F. Cas. 1099 (C.C.D.Pa.1793) (No. 6,360), in Chapter 2; 1 Op. Att'y Gen. 509 (1821). How many foreign textwriters were cited in Kadic v. Karadzic, 70 F.3d 232 (2d Cir.1995), *supra*, or Filartiga v. Pena–Irala, 630 F.2d 876 (2d Cir.1980), see the more extensive extract in Chapter 2? Have General Assembly resolutions replaced significant reliance on foreign textwriters? How many U.S. lawyers are familiar with French, German, Italian, Japanese, Russian, Spanish, or other foreign languages?

Filartiga is also informing concerning the proof of customary international law through attention to several other evidences of such law, including the use of affidavits. See the extensive extract in Chapter 2.

3. In *Paquete Habana*, was there consideration of relevant treaties as well as other evidences of customary international law? What do you suspect the meaning of the phrase "where there is no treaty" might be, given the fact that treaties were considered? Does the word "must" appearing twice in the same paragraph aid in determining Justice Gray's probable meaning?

4. In Hilton v. Guyot, 159 U.S. 113 (1895) (Gray, J., opinion), cited by Justice Gray at the end of the paragraph in *Paquete* noted above, Justice Gray had written:

"International law in its widest and most comprehensive sense ... is part of our law, and must be ascertained and administered by the courts of justice, as often as such questions are presented in litigation between man and man, duly submitted to their determination.

"The most certain guide, no doubt, ... is a treaty or a statute of this country. But when, as is the case here, there is no written law upon the subject, the duty still rests upon the judicial tribunals of ascertaining and declaring what the law is, whenever it becomes necessary to do so in order to determine the rights of parties to suits regularly brought before them. In doing this, the courts must obtain such aid as they can from judicial decisions, from the works of jurists and commentators, and from the acts and usages of civilized nations." *Id.* at 163.

Do these extracts provide guidance concerning the meaning of Justice Gray's statements in *Paquete*?

The primary focus of the litigation was whether a judgment of a French court should be enforced. Defendant argued that it should not, since it had been obtained fraudulently. This involved inquiry into what the Court termed " 'private international law,' or the 'conflict of laws,' and concerning the rights of private persons within the territory and dominion of one nation, by reason of acts, private or public, done within the dominions of another nation." *Id.* at 163. Justice Gray then proceeded (as he did later in *Paquete*) to undertake in an extensive survey of international-law treatises on the question whether the courts of one nation need to give full faith to the decisions of the courts of another nation, which is followed by an equally extensive survey of judicial decisions from other countries on this question. These foreign decisions are primarily from European sources, but the Court also referred to a decision from Egypt and several from Latin America. From these many sources, the Court determined that so-called "private international law" recognized a "rule of reciprocity" that "has worked itself firmly into the structure of international jurisprudence" (*id.* at 227), but that, in the absence of a reciprocal agreement to give the decisions of each other's courts full faith and credit, the decision of a foreign court is only *prima facie* evidence which can be challenged by a showing of fraud or prejudice. In summarizing the ruling, Justice Gray explained that "international law is founded upon mutuality and reciprocity" (*id.* at 228), and that, because French courts would reexamine a U.S. judgment, it is only appropriate for a U.S. court to reexamine a French decision. "If we should hold this judgment to be conclusive, we should allow it an effect to which ... it would ... be entitled in hardly any other country in Christendom, except the country in which it was rendered." *Id.*

5. Importantly, in the Executive briefs before the Supreme Court in *Paquete Habana*, the Executive had argued a certain content of customary international law (that enemy fishing vessels were not immune from seizure in time of war) and lost. The Executive view of international law, then, was not controlling. Moreover, the Executive seizure of the vessels was declared to be illegal under international law. The Executive never argued that it had authority to violate international law, and a presidential proclamation during the war had expressly noted that the U.S. would maintain its blockade "in pursuance of the laws of the United States, and the law of nations applicable to such cases." *See generally* Jordan J. Paust, International Law as Law of the United States 174–76, 183–84, 189–90 (2 ed. 2003). We will revisit the case later when considering the incorporation of customary international law into the domestic legal process and whether the President of the United States is and should be bound by customary international law.

Restatement of the Foreign Relations Law of the United States § 102 (3 ed. 1987)

Comment *b*. *Practice as customary law*. "Practice of states" ... includes diplomatic acts and instructions as well as public measures and other governmental acts and official statements of policy, whether they are unilateral or undertaken in cooperation with other states, for example in organizations such as the Organization for Economic Cooperation and Development (OECD). Inaction may constitute state practice, as when a state acquiesces in acts of another state that affect its legal rights. The practice necessary to create customary law may be of comparatively short duration, but ... must be "general and consistent." A practice can be general even if it is not universally followed; there is no precise formula to indicate how widespread a practice must be, but it should reflect wide acceptance among the states particularly involved in the relevant activity. Failure of a significant number of important states to adopt a practice can prevent a principle from becoming general customary law though it might become "particular customary law" for the participating states....

Comment *c. Opinio juris*. For a practice of states to become a rule of customary international law it must appear that the states follow the practice from a sense of legal obligation (*opinio juris sive necessitatis*); a practice that is generally followed but which states feel legally free to disregard does not contribute to customary law. A practice initially followed by states as a matter of courtesy or habit may become law when states generally come to believe that they are under a legal obligation to comply with it. It is often difficult to determine when that transformation into law has taken place. Explicit evidence of a sense of legal obligation (*e.g.*, by official statements) is not necessary; *opinio juris* may be inferred from acts or omissions.

JORDAN J. PAUST, *CUSTOMARY INTERNATIONAL LAW: ITS NATURE, SOURCES AND STATUS AS LAW OF THE UNITED STATES*

12 MICH. J. INT'L L. 59, 63–74 (1990), revised in INTERNATIONAL LAW AS LAW OF THE UNITED STATES 1 (1996) and (2 ed. 2003).

Of further significance is the fact that relevant patterns of legal expectation, perhaps contrary to Blackstone, need only be generally shared in the international community. Universality or unanimity are not required. Yet, for fuller exposition and understanding it is suggested that the researcher identify not merely how widespread a particular pattern of expectation is or has been, but also how intensely held or demanded a particular norm is or has been within the community. Awareness of the *degree* and *intensity* of general acceptance provides a more realistic approach to the identification and clarification of normative content and should aid those who must apply customary international law in making informed and rational choices. It would also be useful to know how long such patterns of expectation have existed, although a prior stability evident through time is no guarantee of continued acceptance in the future and time is not otherwise a determinative factor. It is possible, of course, to have a relatively recently widespread and intensely held expectation that something is legally appropriate or required and that such a pattern of *opinio juris* could form one of the components of a new rule of customary international law, one that will even be more stable in the future.

It is also significant that the behavioral element of custom (*i.e.*, general practice) is similarly free from the need for total conformity, and it rests not merely upon the practice of States as such but ultimately upon the practice of all participants in the international legal process. Thus, a particular nation-state might disagree whether a particular norm is customary and might even violate such a norm, but it would still be bound if the norm is supported by patterns of generally shared legal expectation and conforming behavior extant in the community. If the patterns of violation become too widespread, however, one of the primary bases of customary law can be lost. Similarly, if it is no longer generally expected that a norm is legally appropriate or required, the other base of customary law can be lost. When either base is no longer generally extant, there can be no conjoining of general patterns of legal expectation and behavior and, for such a social moment at least, a prior customary law will no longer be operative.

Since each nation-state, indeed each human being, is a participant in both the attitudinal and behavioral aspects of dynamic customary international law, each may initiate a change in such law or, with others, reaffirm its validity. Indeed, such a law at least, born of what people think and do is constantly reviewed and "re-enacted" in the social process, changed, or terminated. In the long-term, one wants to view such law with a movie camera; and yet at any given social moment (or at the time of a particular decision or activity), the existence of a customary international law will be dependent upon relevant patterns of expectation and behavior then extant.

These recognitions are also critical for the researcher's task. In one sense, they simplify that task since one need only identify patterns of what real people generally think and do. Yet, in another sense, researching customary law is significantly complicated by the fact that each person ultimately is a participant in the shaping of customary law and thus each viewpoint and every sort of human interaction could be relevant. But relevance is also a delimiting criterion. What patterns of expectation and which patterns of action and inaction are to be investigated will depend in part on choice about relevance. And there are additional limitations and even acceptable substitutes for full inquiry.

For example, it is often impossible for one researcher to identify every relevant pattern of expectation and behavior. However, far less than perfect investigation has been accepted by courts and others, especially if documentation of such patterns is with reference to "judicial decisions, . . . the works of jurists and commentators, and [documented] . . . acts and usages of . . . nations." Any evidence of customary norms and relevant patterns of expectation or behavior can be useful. In fact, in addition to judicial opinions and the works of textwriters, U.S. courts have considered treaties and other international agreements; domestic constitutions or legislation; executive orders, declarations or recognitions; draft conventions or codes; reports, resolutions or decisions of international organizations; and even the testimony or affidavits of textwriters.

Since any such evidence of expectation and behavior can be useful, it is also particularly misleading to ask whether a United Nations General Assembly resolution can be a source of customary law. A more realistic question, for example, might be whether a nearly unanimous resolution concerning the content or application of a norm of international law evidences a pattern of generally shared legal expectation or *opinio juris*. The very act of voting on a resolution is in some sense also an instance of behavior, but the most relevant forms of behavior will probably involve other patterns of action and inaction outside the U.N. plaza. Importantly also, U.N. resolutions have been utilized by U.S. courts as aids in identifying the content of customary international law.

Notes and Questions

1. Professor Paust's treatise documents an extensive array of cases using each of the forms of proof of the content of customary international law mentioned above. It also documents the historic reach of the law of nations:

"By the time of the formation of the Constitution and within a generation of so thereafter, it was apparent that customary international law was relevant to various powers, rights and duties in civil, criminal, prize and admiralty, and other types of cases.... [C]ustomary international law pertained with respect to constitutional and jurisdictional questions and could reach governmental and private conduct.... Most generally, the Supreme Court noted that 'all ... trespasses committed against the general law of nations, are enquirable....' More specifically, earliest subjects included piracy, acts of hostility or breaches of neutrality, assaults on foreign governmental personnel, terroristic publications, prizes of war and unlawful captures, the laws of war, slave trading, territorial infractions, 'poisoners, assassins, and incendiaries by profession,' violation of passports, violation of safe-conducts, extradition and 'refuge' or asylum, human rights (itself of rich and of varied orientation), denials of justice to aliens, remedies, jurisdiction, nonimmunity, confiscation of property, war, reprisals, lawful intervention, oppression, tyrannicide, revolution, title to land by discovery and conquest, settlement of controversies between nations, and the law concerning treaties, including the primacy of the law of nations over treaties. Since that early period, the subjects addressed have grown."

2. When considering cases identifying and clarifying the content of customary international law later in this book, do such cases tend to identify indicia of *opinio juris* more than indicia of actual patterns of practice? What patterns are more likely to be available to lawyers in law libraries and/or on computer-based research systems? Some textwriters argue that *opinio juris* "is not an essential element of custom" *See, e.g.*, J. STARKE, INTRODUCTION TO INTERNATIONAL LAW 38 (9th ed. 1984); Bruno Simma & Philip Alston, *The Sources of Human Rights Law: Custom,* Jus Cogens, *and General Principles*, 12 AUSTRL. Y.B. INT'L L. 82, 88–89, 107 (1989) (past practice is supposedly

determinative of future practice and more important than actual human demands and expectations). Others seem to stress *opinio juris* over practice. *See, e.g.*, J. BRIERLY, THE OUTLOOK FOR INTERNATIONAL LAW 4–5 (1944); M. Akehurst, *Custom as a Source of International Law*, 47 BRIT. Y.B. INT'L L. 1 (1974–75).

3. Some cases have suggested that patterns of legal expectation must be "universal," *i.e.*, that all expect that something is legally appropriate or required. *See, e.g.*, *In re* Estate of Ferdinand Marcos Human Rights Litigation, 25 F.3d 1467, 1475 (9th Cir.1994); Xuncax v. Gramajo, 886 F.Supp. 162, 180 (D.Mass.1995) ("the standard can be said to be 'universal, definable and obligatory.' Forti I, 672 F.Supp. at 1540. These qualifications essentially require that ... no state condone the act in question and there is a recognizable 'universal' consensus of prohibition against it.... "). Other cases seem to use phrases like "universal condemnation" as mere rhetorical flourish to make the point that widespread patterns of *opinio juris* exist to support a particular norm.

It is worth stressing that *opinio juris* is not the equivalent of "consent." For example, one might strongly disagree that a particular rule should be law, but still expect that it is present law. Also, neither "universal" consent nor "universal" expectation is required for the formation or continued validity of a customary norm. *See, e.g.*, *The Scotia*; *The Paquete Habana*.

4. The Restatement and a few other textwriters argue that "[a] principle of customary law is not binding on a state that declares its dissent from the principle during its development." RESTATEMENT § 102, cmt. b. The Restatement adds: "Although customary law may be built by the acquiescence as well as by the actions of states ... and become generally binding on all states, in principle a state that indicates its dissent from a practice while the law is still in the process of development is not bound by that rule even after it matures.... A state that enters the international system after a practice has ripened into a rule of international law is bound by that rule." *Id.*, cmt. d. The Restatement does not offer a logical explanation of this theory or use of its phrase "in principle". When justifications are attempted, they usually rest on a premise that positivist notions of state "consent" are the only basis for creation of binding customary law.

The so-called persistent-objector "rule" is not reflected in any known treaties or General Assembly resolutions and it is not based in general patterns of state practice and *opinio juris*. Thus, it is not a rule of customary international law concerning the nature or reach of customary international law. It is basically the preference of a few professors and the Restatement that seems to have generally arisen in the 1980s. *See* RESTATEMENT, *supra* § 102, cmts. b & d ("in principle" although "historically, such ... exemption ... has been rare"–citing no actual case or incident, but misconstruing what was involved in the 1951 Fisheries Case (U.K. v. Norway), see below); PAUST, INTERNATIONAL LAW AS LAW OF THE UNITED STATES 22–26 n.14 (2 ed. 2003). Although there is extremely rare dictum in some cases, we know of no case actually using the persistent objector minority preference to decide a case or that customary international law is not binding on a so-called persistent objector. *Cf* Alvarez–Machain v. United States, 331 F.3d 604, 613 (9th Cir. 2003) (dictum); Princz v. Federal Republic of Germany, 26 F.3d 1166, 1181

(D.C.Cir.1994) (Wald, J., dissenting), extract in Chapter 4; Siderman de Blake v. Republic of Argentina, 965 F.2d 699, 715 (9th Cir. 1992) (dictum, citing merely the Restatement and stating in significant error that customary international law rests on "consent"). Moreover, the theory known as the "dissenter view" or the "persistent objector" principle is inconsistent with predominant trends in U.S. and other judicial opinions and is theoretically unsound since customary international law rests upon general assent or general patterns of expectation (not unanimous consent) and, as the U.S. Supreme Court has declared emphatically, "[t]hat law is of universal obligation." The Scotia, 81 U.S. (14 Wall.) 170, 187 (1871). *Also see* J.L. Brierly, The Law of Nations 62 (5 ed. 1955) (one need only identify "general recognition among states of a certain practice as obligatory ... it is not necessary, to show that every state has recognized.... This test of *general* recognition") (emphasis in original); Lung-chu Chen, An Introduction to Contemporary International Law 345 (2 ed. 2000) ("The requisite patterns in past behavior and subjectivities are *generality*, not universality.... The express consent of every nation-state is not a prerequisite to the authority of a particular customary law.... the function of customary international law is precisely to vitiate the requirement of specific consent as the basis of international obligation."); Paust, *supra* at 4–5, 21–22 n.11, 23–26 n.14, and the many cases cited (also quoting Professor Reisman, *International Lawmaking: A Process of Communication*, 75 Proc., Am. Soc. Int'l L. 101, 111 (1981) ("norms are prescribed because they are policies which part of the community does not voluntarily or spontaneously support")); W. Michael Reisman, Nullity and Revision 556 (1971) (customary international law "is a set of shared subjectivities about normative behavior.... [A] majority of the nations of the world may ... make law for all states of the globe, they may do the same by custom. In this regard, ... unanimity is not required."); Jonathan I. Charney, *Universal International Law*, 87 Am. J. Int'l L. 529, 538–40 (1993) (it is rarely claimed, it is not supported by state practice, the I.C.J. mentioned it only twice in *dicta*, "[t]hus, state practice and other evidence do not support the existence of the persistent objector rule."); Myres S. McDougal, remarks, 64 Proc., Am. Soc. Int'l L. 57 (1970) ("The realistic function of customary law has been to get rid of minority veto, either in the making or the termination of a principle.")). The 1951 Fisheries case did not address objection to the existence of a customary rule of law concerning a coastal state's right to a territorial sea. Instead, the Court addressed the necessary circumstance at the time for extension of the Norwegian territorial sea up to four nautical miles and its control of that area without significant interruption or objection over a long period of time (*i.e.*, factors of control and intent that are relevant to the reach of a particular territorial sea, not to the existence of the particular rule of customary law as such). *See* Fisheries Case (United Kingdom v. Norway), 1951 I.C.J. 116, extract reprinted in Chapter 6.

Under such a theory, if a lone but persistent dissenter during the formation of a rule is not bound, why would one who persistently dissents after the formation of a norm still be bound? Customary international law is not based on "consent," but patterns of legal expectation. Is the dissenter view an attempt to partially change the nature of customary international law and require that some customary international obligations rest on consent? If you consider that states are not the only actors in the international legal process, what sort of consequences might follow if the dissenter view is adopted? Does any domestic legal system allow a "dissenter" to opt out of legal requirements created elsewise in the domestic legal process? More generally, see ANTHONY D'AMATO, INTERNATIONAL LAW ANTHOLOGY 110–15 (1994), reproducing excerpts from Jonathan I. Charney, *The Persistent Objector Rule and the Development of Customary International Law*, 56 BRIT. Y.B. INT'L L. 1 (1986), and Ted Stein, *The Approach of the Different Drummer: The Principle of the Persistent Objector in International Law*, 26 HARV. INT'L L. J. 457 (1985); PAUST, *supra*.

5. One clear example of the world community rejecting a claim of a "persistent objector" is the near universal condemnation of South Africa's system of *apartheid* or racist segregation, which it institutionalized formally in 1948. South Africa argued for several decades that it was a persistent objector to the customary human rights norm of racial equality, which had emerged after World War II, and should be allowed to separate its racial groups. The U.N. General Assembly and Security Council acted repeatedly to reject this claim, making it clear that a state could not opt out of such a customary norm. After substantial international pressure, South Africa finally abandoned its *apartheid* system in 1990.

6. Concerning law violations and violators, the International Court of Justice adds: "It is not to be expected that in the practice of States the application of the rules in question should have been perfect ..., with complete consistency.... In order to deduce the existence of customary rules, ... it [is] sufficient that the conduct of States should, in general, be consistent with such rules, and that instances of State conduct inconsistent with a given rule should generally have been treated as breaches of that rule, not as indications of the recognition of a new rule. If a State acts in a way prima facie incompatible with a recognized rule, but defends its conduct by appealing to exceptions or justifications contained within the rule itself, ... the significance of that attitude is to confirm rather than to weaken the rule." Case Concerning Military and Paramilitary Activities In and Against Nicaragua (Nicaragua v. United States), 1986 I.C.J. 14, para. 186.

Are these recognitions consistent with the view expressed by a few textwriters that violations of international law should be tolerated as mere claims for change? *See, e.g.*, Phillip R. Trimble, *A Revisionist View of Customary International Law*, 33 UCLA L. REV. 665 (1986) (adding: a system of evolving customary international law "must be constructed so as to accept the possibility of illegal conduct by states. To accomplish this it is simply declared acceptable that at a time of change a state may deviate from the legal course of action.... this explanation seems eminently sensible ... [one should] concede that states may act illegally ... [and there is a supposed] necessity of accommodating change in customary international law...."); *but see* JORDAN J. PAUST, INTERNATIONAL LAW AS LAW OF THE UNITED STATES 4–7 (2 ed. 2003); Jordan J. Paust, *The Complex Nature, Sources and Evidences of Customary Human Rights*, 25 GA. J. INT'L & COMP. L. 147, 162–64 (1995–96). In the latter article, Professor Paust raises the following hypothetical:

"Suppose, for example, that genocidal violations of human rights law [or war crimes] are occurring in four countries with either the conspiratorial or complicitous involvement of three other States. Assume also that most private and official perpetrators know or should know that such acts are illegal under customary international law and that, once caught, they could even suffer criminal sanctions. Additionally, the general populations in such countries are split as to whether or not such conduct should be supported, but a majority supports genocide [or war crimes] in only three of the seven countries, and in all but two the majority expects that genocide [or a war crime] is unlawful. Further, the official elites in these countries are divided as to whether or not such acts should be lawful in the future, but a majority of officials from two States openly and formally presses two sorts of claim: (1) that their actions are recognized exceptions, and (2) that there should be such exceptions in the future. The United Nations General Assembly has formally condemned genocide [and war crimes] and singled out actions in one such country. Similarly, the U.N. Security Council has issued resolutions condemning such acts in the same country, imposing economic sanctions, and calling for an end to such acts and the complicitous, if not conspiratorial, acts of two outside States. To date, genocide [and war crime activity] continues in each of the four countries.

"Given widespread and intensely held expectations among humankind (even in some of the countries where violations occur) that genocidal violations of human rights [and war crimes] are unlawful under customary international law and the patterns of general practice within and outside the United Nations (including patterns of public and private compliance with the prohibition of genocide), it would be, to say the least, unreal to conclude that the unabated actions of a few violators has led to the demise of a customary norm prohibiting genocide [or war crimes] or that the violators have somehow opted out or can lawfully avoid the reach of such law and various future sanctions. The actions of perpetrators and complicitors from seven States certainly cannot be controlling patterns of practice, nor do they mirror general and controlling patterns of *opinio juris* in a community of some one hundred and eighty States unless they happen to represent the majority of humankind.

"Even if there were no 'coercive' efforts made by States or official state elites at the United Nations or elsewhere to oppose such genocidal [or war crime] acts and official elite actions were cynical, hypocritical, and even functionally complicitous in part, the facts of general practice in compliance and widespread *opinio juris* would remain and the customary norm would retain its validity. Additionally, the fact that such violators and their supporters are (along with all other actors in the international legal process) law creators does not simplistically compel the conclusion that those who participate in the creation of law are not bound by law currently extant."

Which approach do you prefer? Why? What are the two types of general patterns necessary to support a customary norm? Is it necessary that a state violate customary international law in order to communicate its desire to change it? Does it make a difference that genocide is a prohibition *jus cogens*, but that some war crimes are violations of *obligatio erga omnes* while some may be merely violations of more ordinary customary international law?

Chapter Two

DOMESTIC INCORPORATION

SECTION 1. GENERAL TRENDS

REPORT OF THE COMMITTEE ON INTERNATIONAL LAW IN NATIONAL COURTS

International Law Association, Report of the Sixty–Seventh Conference, Helsinki 570, 572–77, 582, 587–90 (1996).*

Customary international law becomes automatically part of national law by reason of the provisions of some constitutions. For example, the Constitution of Austria (1920) provides that "the generally recognized rules of international law are regarded as integral parts of federal law." The preamble to the French Constitution provides that "*la république francaise se conforme aux regles du droit public international*", and courts have consequently applied customary international law in a number of cases. The [older] Constitution of the Philippines (1946) contains a similar provision. What happens in the case of a conflict between customary international law and national law is not always stated in constitutions. The South African Constitution of 1993 gives in that event priority to national law: "The rules of customary international law binding on the Republic shall, unless inconsistent with this Constitution or an Act of Parliament, form part of the law of the Republic." By contrast, the Constitution of the Federal Republic of Germany (1949) provides in art. 25 that "the general rules of international law are an integral part of federal law. They have priority over statutes and give rise directly to rights and obligations for inhabitants of the federal territory." This provision thus renders a statute inoperative to the extent that it conflicts with a general rule of international law.

Most states do not have a provision in their constitutions or laws relating to the application of customary international law. Such application takes place by way of judicial recognition and enforcement, which, as for example in the case of China (Taiwan), "is taken for granted".

* Reprinted with permission.

Specific judicial statements of high authority may also confirm automatic incorporation of a relevant rule of customary international law, for example in the practice of the High Court and Supreme Court of Ireland, which have affirmed on several occasions that principles of international law are part of the law of Ireland and are to be applied as they change and develop from time to time in accordance with modifications in the practice of states.

Where there arises a clear conflict between a prescription of national law and a relevant rule of international law, some national courts are obliged to follow national law. This is so in those countries for general constitutional reasons: the courts are obliged to give effect to the will of the national legislative authority, whether it accords with international law or not. By contrast, the newly accepted doctrine in Swiss law is that the peremptory norms of customary international law (*jus cogens*) prevail over the Constitution and all other laws; constitutional initiatives approved by a vote of the people and of the Cantons resulting in a violation of *jus cogens* will be declared void by the National Assembly, and other such laws will be set aside by the Tribunal *fédéral*.

In courts of the Common Law tradition (except the United States) there is a continuing debate as to whether customary international law is automatically incorporated into national law, or whether that law requires some positive act of incorporation by way of "adoption" or "transformation", either by the legislature or by the judiciary. The former view has been taken in the United Kingdom, but clearly stated only in the Court of Appeal (by Lord Denning in the *Trendtex* case, 1977), not by the House of Lords, the supreme appellate body. [*Cf* note 9 below] The High Court of Australia leans to the view that customary international law is a source, but not automatically part, of Australian law; however, it has stated that clearly established rules of international law would always be accepted by the courts, subject to the superior force of statute law. . . .

Another common problem is where a doubt arises as to whether a conflict exists between the prescriptions of international law and national law. There is a tendency of courts, where national law is capable of more than one interpretation, to resolve such questions in favour of an interpretation of national law so as to be consistent with international law. Another consideration may be said to underlie this "harmonisation" approach: that the judicial arm of government should endeavour not to embarrass the executive arm in its conduct of international relations, especially those aspects of international relations involving rights and duties under international law. . . .

International conventions as a source of international law applicable in national proceedings raise two kinds of questions. The first is whether the executive government is free to conclude any international agreements it wishes, or whether constitutional or other limitations are imposed on this power. The second is whether validly concluded international agreements operate automatically as part of national law, or do so only after legislative approval.

For states of the Common Law tradition there is in principle no limitation of general application on the power of the executive to conclude international agreements. The power of making treaties is seen as an aspect of executive power, and legislative involvement in the process is only by way of tabling such instruments in Parliament for information. Where, however, the treaty requires something to be done by or in relation to individuals, or to be prohibited, not warranted by existing law, or the expenditure of funds not already appropriated under existing law, legislative action is required to give effect to the treaty as part of national law. If the executive government does not have a sufficient number of supporters in the legislature it could, unless it had taken the precaution of delaying ratification of the treaty, find itself in the position of being bound by the treaty but lacking the means to give effect to it. An exception to the Common Law position is the United States [where a treaty can be self-executing–see this chapter, Section 2 C 1 c]. . . . In view of the enormous increase in treaty-making by the executive in recent years, especially multilateral conventions on such subjects as human rights, there are current political moves in Australia to attempt to secure greater "transparency" in the treaty-negotiation and-conclusion processes, and for greater involvement by the federal Parliament. The decision of the High Court of Australia in *Teoh v. Minister for Immigration* (1995) to the effect that a ratified but unincorporated treaty (the International Convention on the Rights of the Child), although not made part of Australian law, nonetheless raised legitimate expectations on the part of citizens and residents that it would be taken into account by decision-makers in deportation cases, has led to indications by the executive that it might seek legislation to reverse any such "legitimate expectation".

Countries of the Civil Law tradition recognise the right of the executive to conclude treaties, which enter into force after appropriate procedures. They recognise the automatic applicability of those treaties in national law on the same level as, or even at a higher level than, statute law, provided that the operative provisions of the treaty are apt for direct application. Automatic applicability of treaties, duly concluded, on the same level as statute law gives the treaty a force superior to prior conflicting law, as is made express, *e.g.*, in Article 134 of the Constitution of Croatia. In countries where treaties have a higher rank than statute law, they take precedence also over subsequent conflicting law. Article 55 of the French Constitution, for example, stipulates that "treaties or agreements properly ratified or approved have, as from their publication (in the *Journal officiel de la République française*) an authority superior to that of statutes, subject to its application by the other party in the case of each agreement or treaty." It is, however, doubtful whether this "reciprocity condition" was ever imposed in practice. After considerable discussion, it is now clear in French law that, under this constitutional provision, a treaty prevails over a subsequent statute. The same is true

. . . for the Constitution of the Netherlands, which provides in Article 93 that "Statutory regulations in force within the Kingdom shall not be applicable if such application is in conflict with the provisions of treaties that are binding on all persons or of resolutions by international institutions."

A related problem is the relation between treaties and the national constitution. As a rule, treaties do not rank above the constitution, although in some cases they may have equal rank, as for example, the European Convention on Human Rights in Austria. Advisory opinions from Supreme or Constitutional Courts, where available . . . , may conclude that a treaty could only be ratified or approved after amendment of the Constitution (*cf.* Article 54 of the French Constitution). A unique clause, which effectively gives superiority of certain treaties (peace settlements or treaties serving the defence of the country) over the Constitution, is contained in Article 79 sect. 1 of the German Constitution, which provides that "it shall be sufficient, in order to make clear that the provisions of this Constitution do not preclude the conclusion and entry into force of such treaties, to supplement the text of this Constitution and to confine the supplement to such clarification."

There are a number of other kinds of qualification to be noted. The Constitutions of Austria and Germany, for example, require the consent of the national legislature for political treaties and treaties that would have the effect of changing or extending existing statutes or relate to matters of federal legislation. In Switzerland certain treaties have to be submitted to a referendum of the people.

The practice of China (Taiwan) and of Japan should be noted, as falling into traditions of their own, albeit influenced to an extent by the Civil Law. For China (Taiwan), although the President has power to conclude treaties the Constitution assigns to both the Executive Yüan Council and to the Legislative Yüan roles in the approval of treaties. In practice these bodies exercise those roles, and thus it can be concluded that treaties are in general not effective without the sanction of the legislature, and rank together with legislation. For Japan, not all treaties require approval of the Diet (the Parliament), but treaties containing as their substance an engagement touching upon the legislative power of the Diet, relating to budgetary matters not already sanctioned, or relating to basic relations between Japan and other States, require legislative approv[al] before entry into force. . . .

In all jurisdictions the normal appellate process was seen as generally effective to ensure that mistakes were not made or perpetuated. But practice divided on the obligation to refer doubtful questions to a higher court, and on the availability of a path of voluntary reference to a higher court. So far as an obligation is concerned, practice does not support a general compulsory reference. An exception is within the European Union: those courts of Member States, against whose decisions there is no appeal in national law, are obliged, by Article 177 of the EC Treaty, to request a (binding) preliminary ruling of the European Court of Justice on any doubtful question of interpretation of that Treaty or on the validity and interpretation of acts of the institutions of the Community. All other courts and tribunals of Member States may voluntarily request the European Court to give such a ruling. Additional exceptions are Germany, where courts must refer doubtful questions of international law to the Federal Constitutional Court for decision, and Austria, whose Constitutional Court must consider any special federal statute, the provisions of which appear to be in contravention of international law. . . .

An additional consideration is whether the executive branch of government should have a role to play in the interpretation and application of treaties by national courts. In most national legal systems formal guidance is not sought by the courts from the executive, nor is it regarded as decisive where offered (such as in cases to which the government is itself a party). Exceptions are France, before 1990, and the United States. . . .

. . . [O]n occasion national courts do justify their decisions by additional reference to international law. This may be by way of confirming that national law already reflects, or is in accordance with, international law. . . . Or it may be by way of pointing out that the national rule being applied has a parallel in international law. An exceptional reason may be where national law is comprehensive and sufficient, as where the law of Israel justified the trial of Adolf Eichmann for crimes against humanity, yet where, in view of the intense international interest in the case, the court felt it desirable to justify its assumption of jurisdiction on international law grounds also.

The first type of occasion is where national law contains an ambiguity or a "gap" which can be resolved or filled by the courts in the exercise of their interstitial power to shape and develop law. Courts in several Common Law countries have used human rights instruments in this way as justifying a development or extension of national law in a similar direction. Recent decisions of the High Court of Australia (*Dietrich*, 1992) and the House of Lords [U.K.] (*Derbyshire County Council*, 1993) can be cited as examples. This is less common a case in countries of the Civil Law tradition where there is a keener sense of the automatic application of international law by national courts.

The second type of occasion can also be linked especially to human rights, where a comprehensive code of rights, such as the Canadian Charter of Rights and Freedoms, can be supplemented or further developed through reference to the similar International Covenant on Civil and Political Rights, or to decisions of the European Court of Human Rights on the European Convention. Another illustration is where the High Court of Australia decided a question of the river boundary between the States of Australian federation partly by reference to an analogy with international law (which was not in principle applicable at all). . . .

Gaps are one thing; contrary provisions of national law another. Here there is a fairly sharp division between the approaches of the Civil Law and most Common Law countries. In the Civil Law countries it is not at all unusual for the courts to disregard or overrule a provision of national law found to be in conflict with a rule of international law. This is said to be a matter of "everyday occurrence" in France. In other Civil Law countries the answer to the question may depend upon the respective hierarchical positions of the conflicting prescriptions. In most Common Law countries clear conflict between international law and national law must be resolved in favour of the latter, since an essentially dualist approach is taken towards the relationship between the two legal orders. However, the higher courts, which have the power of overruling past judicial decisions (but not statutes) in developing the common law, would regard a conflicting rule of international law as constituting good reason for at least reconsidering the existing law. There is also always the possibility that the legislature would make the necessary changes to the law in order to bring it into line with international law (*e.g.*, the statutes of various Common Law countries on the subject of state immunity)....

Generally speaking, the judges of the Civil Law countries are more likely to have studied international law as a compulsory part of their legal studies than their Common Law colleagues. This is in part a reflection of the more monistic conceptions of the relationship between international law and national law prevailing in countries of the Civil Law tradition. Awareness is, however, growing in the Common Law world....

Notes and Questions

1. What countries tend to incorporate international law more freely and fully? What countries seem far less attentive to international law? Which trends are preferable, why? Which approaches to incorporation should be improved? How and why? *See generally* Benedetto Conforti, Francesco Francioni, Enforcing International Human Rights in Domestic Courts (1997).

2. Should the ease of incorporation and the status of international law domestically depend upon its hierarchic status internationally, its subject matter, or its character as custom or agreement-based? Why?

3. In 1971, the Belgian Court of Cassation recognized with respect to the E.E.C. treaty that in the event of a conflict with domestic law, a norm of international law which produces direct effects in the internal legal system shall prevail, adding: "The primacy of the treaty results from the very nature of international treaty law ... [especially with respect to 'a norm of Community law']. The reason is that the treaties which have created Community law have instituted a new legal system in whose favour the member-States have restricted the exercise of their sovereign powers in the areas determined by those treaties. Article 12 of the Treaty establishing the European Economic Community is immediately effective and confers on individual persons rights which national courts are bound to uphold." Minister for Economic Affairs v. S.A. Fromagerie Fanco–Suisee "Le Ski", Common Mark. Rep. 330 (1972).

4. Unlike, for example, the United States and Mexico, most countries ratify treaties by an act of legislation. Some, like Austria, indicate the domestic rank of an agreement at the time of such legislative ratification (*e.g.*, as having a constitutional, federal, or local level status). Does such a process of ratification make it less likely that there will be a conflict with domestic law?

5. In view of the ILA Report's consideration of Article 79 of the German Constitution, if a Constitution states that treaties shall have a higher status than other constitutional norms, does a treaty really prevail "over" "the Constitution"? What is the source of such a supremacy?

6. In 1977, the Constitutional Court of Yugoslavia stated that based on Section VII, para. 2 of the preamble to the 1974 Constitution, the generally recognized norms of international law form part of the law of Yugoslavia, and, as evidence of binding international law, it listed the U.N. Charter, the Universal Declaration of Human Rights, the International Covenant on Civil and Political Rights, and the Helsinki Final Act. See Int'l Comm. of Jurists, STATES OF EMERGENCY: THEIR IMPACT ON HUMAN RIGHTS 84 (1983).

7. In 1959, the Court of Cassation of Italy recognized that domestic legislation in conflict with customary international law does not prevail. See *Re* Martinez, 28 INT'L L. REP. 170 (1963).

8. In Trendtex Trading Corporation v. Central Bank of Nigeria, 1 Q.B. 529, 553–54 (U.K. 1977), Lord Denning recognized that under "the doctrine of incorporation ... rules of international law are incorporated into English law automatically and considered to be part of English law unless they are in conflict with an Act of Parliament.... Under the doctrine of incorporation, when the rules of international law change, our English law changes with them.... Seeing that the rules of international law have changed—and do change—and that the courts have given effect to the changes without an Act of Parliament, it follows to my mind inexorably that the rules of international law, as existing from time to time, do form part of our English law...." He also noted: "The other school of thought holds to the doctrine of transformation. It says that the rules of international law are not to be considered as part of English law except in so far as they have been already adopted and made part of our law by the decisions of the judges, or by Act of Parliament, or long established custom. The difference is vital when you are faced with a change in the rules of international law." Direct incorporation of customary international law in England actually has significant early precedent. *See, e.g.*, Heathfield v. Chilton, 4 Burrow 2015, 2016, 98 Eng. Rep. 50 (K.B. 1767) (Lord Mansfield) ("law of nations ... is part of the common law" of England and cannot be altered by an act of Parliament); Triquet v. Bath, 3 Burrow 1478, 1481, 97 Eng. Rep. 936, 937–38 (K.B. 1764) (Lord Mansfield); Buvot v. Barbut (Barbuit's Case), 3 Burrow 1481, 25 Eng. Rep. 777 (K.B. 1736) (Lord Talbot).

9. In 1999, Judge Tetsuro So, who presides in a Japanese district court, ruled that the Convention on the Elimination of All Forms of Racial Discrimination provides a basis for damages with respect to "an illegal act against an individual" by a jewelry store in Hamamatsu City when the store ejected a Brazilian, Ms. Bortz, because of her nationality. A sign in another Japanese store is depicted in the news story and reads "*proibido a entrada*

de estrangeiros, foreigners are not allowed inside." See Howard W. French, *Fed-up foreigners in Japan fight back, win court ruling*, HOUS. CHRON., Nov. 15, 1999, at 15A. She was awarded 1,500,000 yen for the store's violation of the treaty. Read Article 6 of the Convention. Does it appear to be directly operable, allowing courts to fashion a remedy?

10. In Australia, federal legislation implementing treaty law prevails over state or local powers. See Koowarta v. Bjelke–Petersen, 153 CLR 168 (1982) (re: legislation implementing the International Convention on the Elimination of All Forms of Racial Discrimination).

11. Articles 6 and 133 of the Constitution of Mexico are similar to provisions in the U.S. Constitution that expressly incorporate treaties as domestic law and recognize supremacy over inconsistent law of governmental entities, at least, below the federal level. In Mexico, in case of an unavoidable clash between a treaty and the Constitution, the Constitution has primacy domestically.

If you were an adviser to a Canadian or U.S. corporation with a contract for investment and operation of corporate activities in Mexico that is also protected by a treaty, is the contract necessarily going to be fully effective in Mexico? What more would you like to know?

Concerning the incorporation of international law generally in Mexico, *see, e.g.*, Jorge Cicero, *International Law in Mexican Courts*, 30 VAND. J. TRANSNAT'L L. 1035 (1997).

12. Article 28 (1) of the Greek Constitution assures that a generally accepted rule of international law forms an integral part of the Greek legal order and supersedes any inconsistent domestic legislation.

13. Some non-U.S. trends or decisions are also mentioned in the next section.

ATTORNEY GENERAL OF ISRAEL v. EICHMANN

[1965] 45 Pesakim Mehoziim 3 (Israel, Jerusalem d. ct. 1961); 36 INT'L L. REP. 18 (1968), *aff'd*, [1962] 16 Piske Din 2033 (Israel Supreme Court), 36 INT'L L. REP. 277 (1968).

[Editors' note: Adolf Eichmann was charged with crimes against the Jewish people, crimes against humanity, war crimes, and membership in hostile organizations, all contrary to the 1950 Israeli Nazi and Nazi Collaborators (Punishment) Law. He was convicted and sentenced to death.]

Our jurisdiction to try this case is based on the Nazis and Nazi Collaborators (Punishment) Law, *a statutory law the provisions of which are unequivocal*. The Court has to give effect to the law of the Knesset, and we cannot entertain the contention that this law conflicts with the principles of international law. For this reason alone Counsel's first contention must be rejected. . . .

But we have also perused the sources of international law, including the numerous authorities mentioned by learned Counsel in his comprehensive written brief upon which he based his oral pleadings, and by the learned Attorney–General in his comprehensive oral pleadings, and failed to find any foundation for the contention that Israeli law is in conflict with the principles of international law. On the contrary, we have reached the conclusion that the law in question conforms to the best traditions of the law of nations.

The power of the State of Israel to enact the law in question or Israel's right to punish is based, with respect to the offences in question, from the point of view of international law, on a dual foundation: The universal character of the crimes in question and their specific character as being designated to exterminate the Jewish people. In what follows we shall deal with each of these two aspects separately....

The abhorrent crimes defined in this law are crimes not under Israel law alone. These crimes which afflicted the whole of mankind and shocked the conscience of nations are grave offenses against the law of nations itself ("*delicta juris gentium*"). Therefore, so far from international law negating or limiting the jurisdiction of countries with respect to such crimes, in the absence of an International Court the international law is in need of the judicial and legislative authorities of every country, to give effect to its penal injunctions and to bring criminals to trial. The authority and jurisdiction to try crimes under international law are universal....

[The District Court then addressed whether the Israeli incorporation of international law in its statute violated the prohibition of *ex post facto* laws. The opinion stressed that the statute was valid because it did not create new crimes, but incorporated or mirrored international law that had already proscribed the conduct at issue. Additionally, Israel could apply its statute to acts committed abroad and before the state of Israel existed, since it had universal jurisdiction. See Chapter 3. The court next addressed forms of incorporation adopted in The Netherlands and Germany after World War II.]

The Netherlands Law of July 10, 1947, which amends the preceding Law (of October 22, 1943) may serve as an example of *municipal retroactive legislation*, in adding Article 27A, which provides:

> "Any person who, during the present war, while in the military service of the enemy, is guilty of a war crime or any crime against humanity as defined in Article 6, subsection (b) or (c), of the Charter [of the IMT at Nuremberg] annexed to the London Agreement of August 8, 1945 ... shall, if such crime contains at the same time the elements of an act punishable according to Netherlands law, receive the punishment laid down for such act."

On the strength of such retroactive adoption of the definition of crimes contained in the Nuremberg Charter, the Senior Commander of the S.S. and Police in Holland, one Rauter, was sentenced to death by a special tribunal, and his appeal was dismissed in 1949 by the Special Court of Cassation (see L.R.T.W.C., XIV, pp. 89 *ff*). The double plea of "*nullum crimen, nulla poena sine lege*" was dismissed by the Court of Cassation on the grounds that the Netherlands legislator had abrogated this rule (which is expressly laid down in Section I of the Netherlands Criminal Law) with respect to crimes of this kind, and that indeed the rule was not adequate for these crimes. At p. 120 (*ibid.*) it is stated:

> "From what appears above it follows that neither Article 27(A) of the Extraordinary Penal Law Decree nor Article 6 of the Charter of London (to which the said Netherlands provision refers) had, as the result of a change of view as to its legality, declared *after the event* to be a crime an act which was hitherto permitted; ... These provisions have merely defined in more detail the jurisdiction, as well as the limits of penal liability and the imposition of punishment, in respect of acts which already before their commission were not permitted by international law but were regarded as crimes....
>
> "In so far as the appellant considers punishment unlawful because his actions, although illegal and criminal, lacked a legal sanction provided against them precisely outlined and previously prescribed, this objection also fails....
>
> "These latter interests do not tolerate that extremely serious violations of the generally accepted principles of international law, the criminal ... character of which was already established beyond doubt at the time they were committed, should not be considered punishable on the sole ground that a previous threat of punishment was lacking. It is for this reason that neither the London Charter of 1945 nor the Judgment of the International Military Tribunal (at Nuremberg) in the case of the Major German War Criminals have accepted this plea, which is contrary to the international concept of justice, and which has since been also rejected by the Netherlands legislator, as appears from Article 27(A) of the Extraordinary Penal Law Decree."

The courts in Germany, too, have rejected the contention that the crimes of the Nazis were not prohibited at the time and that their perpetrators did not have the requisite criminal intent. The judgment of the Supreme Federal Tribunal of January 29, 1952 (I St/R 563/51 (BGH 562 234)) declares that the expulsion of the Jews, the object of which was the death of the deportees, was a continuous crime of murder committed by the principal planners and executants, a matter of which all other executants must have been conscious, since it cannot be accepted that they were unaware of the basic principles on which human society is based and which are the common legacy of all civilized nations.

See also BGH I St.R 404/60 (NIV 1961, 276), a judgment of December 6, 1960, which deals with the murder of mentally-sick persons on Hitler's orders. The judgment says, *inter alia* (pp. 277, 278) that in 1940 at the latest, it was clear to every person not too naive, and certainly to all who were part of the leadership establishment, that the Nazi regime did not shrink from the commission of crimes, and that whoever took part in these crimes could not argue that he had mistakenly assumed that a forbidden act was permissible, when these crimes violated basic principles of the rule of law.

[On appeal, the Supreme Court of Israel stated in 1962:]

Most of the legal contentions of counsel for the appellant revolve around the argument that in assuming jurisdiction to try the appellant the District Court acted contrary to the principles of international law. These contentions are as follows:

> (1) The Law of 1950, which is the only source of the jurisdiction of the Court in this case, constitutes ex post facto penal legislation which prescribes as offences acts that were committed before the State of Israel came into existence; therefore the validity of this Law is confined to its citizens alone.
>
> (2) The offences for which the appellant was tried are "extra-territorial offences", that is to say, offences that were committed outside the territory of Israel by a citizen of a foreign State, and even though the Law confers jurisdiction in respect of such offences, it conflicts in so doing with the principle of territorial sovereignty, which postulates that only the country within whose territory the offence was committed or to which the offender belongs—in this case, Germany—has the right to punish therefor....

We have thus far stated our reasons for dismissing the first two contentions of counsel for the appellant in reliance upon the rules that determine the relationship between Israel municipal law and international law. Our principal object was to make it clear—and this by way of a negative approach—that under international law no *prohibition* whatsoever falls upon the enactment of the Law of 1950 either because it created *ex post facto* offences or because such offences are of an extra-territorial character. Nevertheless, like the District Court, we too do not content ourselves with this solution but have undertaken the task of showing that it is impossible to justify these contentions even from a positive approach—that in enacting the said Law the Knesset only sought to set out the principles of international law and embody its aims. The two propositions on which we propose to rely will therefore be as follows:

(1) The crimes created by the Law and of which the appellant was convicted must be deemed today as having always borne the stamp of international crimes, banned by the law of nations and entailing individual criminal responsibility.

(2) It is the peculiarly universal character of these crimes that vests in every State the authority to try and punish anyone who participated in their commission.

SECTION 2. U.S. INCORPORATION

A. *The United States Constitution*

UNITED STATES CONSTITUTION

[read the extracts in the Documents Supplement]

Notes and Questions

1. In Ware v. Hylton, 3 U.S. (3 Dall.) 199, 237, 244 (1796), the Supreme Court declared: "national or federal judges are bound by duty and oath to the same conduct" as state judges under Art. VI, cl. 2. Five years later, the Court recognized that "where a treaty ... affects the rights of parties litigating in court, the treaty as much binds those rights and is as much to be regarded by the court as an act of Congress." The Schooner Peggy, 5 U.S. (1 Cranch) 103, 110 (1801). *See also* Owings v. Norwood's Lessee, 9 U.S. (5 Cranch) 344 (1809), quoted *infra*. p. 252.

2. Article I, Section 1 declares: "All legislative Powers herein granted...." Does this imply that "legislative" powers are also granted elsewhere in the Constitution? What other lawmaking powers might there be?

3. Treaties are mentioned in several parts of the U.S. Constitution. The "law of nations," a phrase used as an equivalent to "international law," is mentioned once. Does this mean that customary laws of nations (as opposed to treaty-based international law) are not operative through the Constitution except where the phrase is expressly mentioned or do not relate to provisions such as Articles III and VI which contain the phrase "treaties"? Is there another phrase within Articles III and VI that can apply to customary law? See JORDAN J. PAUST, INTERNATIONAL LAW AS LAW OF THE UNITED STATES 7–11 (2 ed. 2003).

4. An early draft of Article III of the U.S. Constitution also declared that "the Judiciary [shall] have authority to hear and determine ... by Way of Appeal ... all cases in which foreigners may be interested in the Construction of any Treaty ... or on the Law of Nations...." Document VII of the Committee of Detail, reproduced in II THE RECORDS OF THE FEDERAL CONVENTION OF 1787, at 157 (M. Farrand ed. 1937). The draft was dropped, possibly because the federal judiciary was given far more than mere appellate jurisdiction and Document VII was conditioned on an appellate competence. *See also id.* vol. III, at 608 (appeal of "all Causes wherein Questions shall arise on the Construction of Treaties made by U.S.—or on the Law of Nations") (the Pinckney Plan), 117 ("as well as the trial of questions arising on the law of nations, the construction of treaties, or ...") (1787 Pinckney plan); vol. II, at 136 (the Pinckney Plan), 143 (legislative power to punish "offences against the law of nations"), 168 (same in Committee of detail Doc. IX), 182 (Madison's report), 316, 570, 595, 614–15; vol. I, at 292, 244, 238 ("foreigners where treaties are in their favor"), 22. See also Alexander Hamilton, THE FEDERALIST NO. 80 (1788) ("cases arising upon treaties and the laws of nations" are appropriate); Preyer, *Jurisdiction to Punish: Federal Authority, Federalism and the Common Law of Crimes in the Early Republic*,

4 LAW & HIST. REV. 223, 232 (1986) ("law of nations" was "within the federal judicial power ... within the language of Article III...."); Palmer, *The Federal Common Law of Crime*, 4 LAW & HIST. REV. 267, 276–78 (1986) (adding: "Livermore stated that the only reason why inferior federal courts should be established was to enforce the law of nations").

5. Concerning early views about the incorporation of treaties and federal judicial power, consider also: THE FEDERALIST NO. 22 (1787) ("treaties of the United States, to have any force at all, must be considered as part of the law of the land. Their true import, as far as respects individuals, must, like all other laws, be ascertained by judicial determinations."); IV J. ELLIOT, THE DEBATES IN THE SEVERAL STATE CONVENTIONS ON THE ADOPTION OF THE FEDERAL CONSTITUTION, AS RECOMMENDED BY THE GENERAL CONVENTION AT PHILADELPHIA IN 1787 158 (1901) (Davie in North Carolina in 1788: "It was necessary that treaties should operate as laws on individuals. They ought to be binding upon us the moment they are made. They involve in their nature not only our own rights, but those of foreigners" and should be protected by the federal judiciary); *id.* at 267 (Rutledge in South Carolina in 1788: "every treaty was law paramount, and must operate ... this treaty is binding in our courts and in England" regarding private duties); *id.* at 277–79 (Pinckney: treaties are "paramount to the laws of the land," create individual rights and duties, and have the force of law); *id.*, vol II, at 490 (Wilson: by "the provision for judicial power over cases arising under treaties, ... we make the faith of treaties a constitutional part of the character of the United States; ... [to] secure its performance ... the judges of the United States will be enabled to carry it into effect."

B. General Types of Incorporation

There are various types of incorporation of international law into domestic legal processes. One primary form is direct incorporation or the use of international law directly, for example, as the basis for a civil cause of action or for criminal prosecution. In such cases, direct incorporation occurs whether or not there is a specific statutory basis for the cause of action or crime. Direct incorporation of customary international law for civil sanctions and jurisdictional purposes has occurred throughout U.S. history. Another primary form of incorporation is indirect incorporation involving the use of international law as an interpretive aid. In the case of indirect incorporation, international law is used indirectly to clarify or supplement the meaning of, for example, the U.S. Constitution, a federal statute, common law, or other legal provision. Some constitutional provisions, like the Ninth Amendment to the U.S. Constitution, were also meant to mirror portions of international law—in the case of the Ninth Amendment, human rights were expected to be among the unenumerated rights protected by the amendment. *See, e.g.*, JORDAN J. PAUST, INTERNATIONAL LAW AS LAW OF THE UNITED STATES 9, 323–25, *passim* (2 ed. 2003). However phrased, it is important to note how each form of incorporation might operate.

1. *Federal Judicial Competence*

a. *General Judicial Power*

[see U.S. Constitution, Articles III and VI]

Notes and Questions

1. As noted above, Articles III and VI of the U.S. Constitution expressly refer to a general judicial competence with respect to treaties of the United States.

2. Are there constitutional bases for judicial incorporation of customary international law? Are there constitutionally-based competencies for direct incorporation of customary international law without some statutory base? Consider JORDAN J. PAUST, INTERNATIONAL LAW AS LAW OF THE UNITED STATES 7–13 (2 ed. 2003) [numerous cases and materials are cited in endnotes in the original work and can be consulted there]:

> Although customary international law has been incorporated both directly and indirectly in civil and criminal cases from the beginning of the United States, the only express reference to the "law of nations" found in the Constitution is that aligned with a congressional power (*i.e.*, Article I, section 8, clause 10). It would be incorrect to assume, however, that incorporation of customary international law has no other adequate constitutional base. Indeed, as explained below, there are several relevant textual bases.... [Further], it is evident that several of the amendments to the U.S. Constitution (especially the Ninth Amendment) have as one of their purposes the object to serve human rights reflected in customary international law and, therefore, that incorporation of several customary rights is possible through the use of certain constitutional amendments. Thus, in these instances there are both different constitutional bases for incorporation and a status far different than that of mere common law or even an implementing statute. And there are other textual bases for the incorporation of customary international law.
>
> Since it was recognized early that customary international law in general is part of the laws of the United States, customary international law is relevant both with respect to the duty and the power of the Executive under Article II, section 3 to "take care that the Laws be faithfully executed." Supreme Court and other opinions have also recognized that while exercising presidential war powers, the Executive is bound by customary international law. Additionally, judicial opinions and the opinions of Attorneys General have recognized that customary international law can limit the exercise of an otherwise appropriate congressional power and thus can function partly as an aid for interpreting the extent of constitutional grants of power. And, of course, customary international law may be relevant to an adequate interpretation of various sorts of congressional power in order functionally to enhance such powers. Significantly, the latter process of incorporation might include an enhancement of the power of Congress under Article I, section 8, clause 18 to enact legislation "necessary and proper for carrying into Execution ... all other Powers vested by this Constitution in the Government of the United States, or in any Department or Officer thereof."

Though not widely understood, the judicial power to identify, clarify and apply customary international law in cases otherwise properly before the courts also has a constitutional base. Under Article III, section 2, clause 1 of the Constitution, not only might matters involving customary international law arise under other parts of the Constitution as such (as noted above) or treaties, but they can also arise under "the Laws of the United States." Indeed, as recognized by the first Chief Justice of the U.S. Supreme Court, this same phrase, "the laws of the United States," includes the customary "law of nations."* Thus, although treaties have an express constitutional

* [Edited] *See* Henfield's Case, 11 F. Cas. 1099, 1101 (C.C.D.Pa.1793) (No. 6,360) (Jay, C.J.). *See also id.* at 1103–04, 1112, 1115; Chief Justice Jay, Charge to the Grand Jury for the District of Virginia (May 22, 1793) ("The Constitution, the statutes of Congress, the laws of nations, and treaties constitutionally made compose the laws of the United States"), in 3 THE CORRESPONDENCE AND PUBLIC PAPERS OF JOHN JAY 479 (H. Johnston ed. 1891); New York Life Insurance Co. v. Hendren, 92 U.S. 286, 287–88 (1875) (Bradley, J., dissenting) ("unwritten international law" is among the "laws of the United States") *(cf. id.* at 286–87—majority opinion is unclear, finding the laws of war not "modified or suspended by ... laws ... of the United States," but perhaps implicitly disagreeing with the dissent that they are also laws of the United States); Caperton v. Bowyer, 81 U.S. (14 Wall.) 216, 226 (1872) (argument of counsel: "law of nations, part of the law of the United States."); United States v. Ravara, 2 U.S. (2 Dall.) 297, 299 n. * (C.C.D.Pa.1793) ("law of nations is part of the law of the United States"); *id.* at 298 (Wilson, J., declaring that the Supreme Court has original jurisdiction "in cases like the present" and Congress can nevertheless provide a concurrent jurisdiction in lower federal courts); Demjanjuk v. Petrovsky, 776 F.2d 571, 582 (6th Cir.1985), *cert. denied,* 475 U.S. 1016 (1986) ("law of the United States includes international law"); Laker Airways Ltd. v. Sabena, Belgian World Airlines, 731 F.2d 909, 951 n. 159 (D.C.Cir.1984) ("part of United States laws"); Filartiga v. Pena-Irala, 630 F.2d 876, 886 (2d Cir.1980) (re: claim as to "part of the laws of the United States"); District of Columbia v. International Distributing Corp., 331 F.2d 817, 820 n. 4 (D.C.Cir.1964) ("It has long been recognized that international law is part of the law of the United States."); Warren County, Pa. v. Southern Surety Co., 34 F.2d 168, 170 (E.D.Pa.1929) ("The laws of the United States are found in ... treaties ... and international law...."); Waite v. The Antelope, 28 F. Cas. 1341, 1341 (D.C.D. S. Car. 1807) (No. 17,045) ("courts ... [i]n this country ... are bound, by the Constitution of the United States, to determine according to treaties and the law of nations, wherever they apply"); United States v. The Ariadne, 24 F. Cas. 851, 856 (D.C.D. Pa. 1812) (No. 14,465) ("the laws of the United States (the laws of nations being included in them)"); Zamora–Trevino v. Barton, 727 F.Supp. 589, 591 (D.Kan.1989) ("laws of the United States (international law)," implicitly referring to customary law when citing *Paquete Habana* and no relevant treaty); Ahmad v. Wigen, 726 F.Supp. 389, 414 (E.D.N.Y.1989) *(quoting Demjanjuk)*; Ishtyaq v. Nelson, 627 F.Supp. 13, 27 (E.D.N.Y.1983) ("international law is a part of the laws of the United States that federal courts are bound to ascertain and apply in appropriate cases"); United States v. Crews, 605 F.Supp. 730, 734 n.1 (S.D. Fla. 1985) ("is incorporated into the law of the United States"); Lareau v. Manson, 507 F.Supp. at 1188 n.9 ("customary international law is part of the law of the United States"); Banco Nacional De Cuba v. Sabbatino, 193 F.Supp. 375, 381–82 (S.D.N.Y. 1961) (courts "have the obligation to respect and enforce international law ... because international law is a part of the law of the United States"); 11 Op. Att'y Gen. 297, 299–300 (1865) ("the law of the land"); 1 Op. Att'y Gen. 566, 570–71(1822) ("the laws of the country"); 1 Op. Att'y Gen. 26, 27 (1792) ("the law of the land"); *Ex parte* Bushnell, 9 Ohio St. 77, 189 (1859) ("The constitution of the United States was framed ... subordinate to, and without violating the fundamental law of nations...."); Dickinson, *The Law of Nations as Part of the Law of the United States,* 101 U. PA. L. REV. 26, 46, 55–56 (1952), adding (*id.* at 48): "the Constitution accepted the Law of Nations as national law.... "; ... T. MERON, HUMAN RIGHTS AND HUMANITARIAN NORMS AS CUSTOMARY LAW 114 (1989) (customary international law "is a part of the law of the United States"); *cf.* Trimble, [*A Revisionist View of Customary International Law,* 33 UCLA L. REV. 665,] 677 [1986] (downplaying the significance of customary international law although conceding that it is a part of U.S. law); *but see* Caperton v. Bowyer, 81 U.S. (14 Wall.) at 228 (argu-

base in Article III, a primary base for judicial incorporation of customary international law can be found in the phrase "Laws of the United States" contained in the same Article and also in Article VI, clause 2 of the Constitution, which affirms that both treaties and "the Laws of the United States" are "the supreme Law of the Land." ...

For these reasons also, customary international law has been directly incorporable, at least for civil sanction and jurisdictional purposes, without the need for some other statutory base. Indeed, direct incorporation by the Supreme Court, at least while exercising its original jurisdiction, can rest on Articles III and VI alone. While customary international law had also been directly incorporable for criminal sanctions early in our history and such incorporation is still theoretically possible, the matter is not beyond dispute. Another form of direct incorporation has also recognizably enhanced and/or limited the jurisdiction of federal courts. Customary principles of jurisdictional competence (*e.g.*, jurisdiction to prescribe) have been used in this manner precisely because such competencies and requirements under international law, being also law of the United States, are relevant to full inquiry about judicial power under Article III of the Constitution and the reach and limits of federal court jurisdiction.

Since international law is law of the United States in several senses noted above, the judiciary also has the power to take judicial notice of and, thus, to identify and clarify customary international law. More importantly, such attributes of international law and judicial power compel recognition that the judiciary is bound to identify, clarify and apply customary international law in cases or controversies otherwise properly before the courts....

b. *Federal Question Jurisdiction*

28 U.S.C. § 1331

The district courts shall have original jurisdiction of all civil actions arising under the Constitution, laws, or treaties of the United States.

ment of counsel: "international law ... can give this court no jurisdiction. The law of nations is not embodied in any provision of the Constitution...." *Cf. id.*: "It is true that the courts of the United States ... recognize the law of nations as binding upon them....."); United States v. Williams, 617 F.2d 1063, 1089 (5th Cir. 1980) (although "international law is a factor suggesting that a search or seizure is reasonable within the meaning of the fourth amendment," a violation "may yet be both constitutional and permissible under the laws of the United States," also *citing* United States v. Postal, 589 F.2d 862, 884 (5th Cir.), *cert. denied,* 444 U.S. 832 (1979) (re: non-self-executing treaty), *but see id.* at 1093–94 (Rubin, J., dissenting)); ... In *Respublica v. De Longchamps,* there had been use of the related phrases "the law of this state" and "part of the municipal law." 1 U.S. (1 Dall.) 111, 113, 115 (Pa. 1784). In Commonwealth v. Schaffer, 4 U.S. (4 Dall.) xxvi (Mayor's Ct. of Phila. 1797), Ingersoll and Thomas had recognized that a breach of neutrality [in *Henfield's Case*] "was contrary to the law of nations, to the treaty, and against the constitution of the United States," though not resulting from an act of Congress. *Id.* at xxxi. And in *Littlejohn & Co. v. United States,* counsel had argued that if a congressional resolution confers a "confiscation" it "is unconstitutional because it violates international law." 270 U.S. 215, 219 (1926). Nonetheless, the Court found that there had been no violation of international law. *Id.* at 226–27.

18 U.S.C. § 3231

The district courts of the United States shall have original jurisdiction, exclusive of the courts of the States, of all offenses against the laws of the United States.

Restatement of the Foreign Relations Law of the United States § 111 (3 ed. 1987)

(1) International law and international agreements of the United States are law of the United States and supreme over the law of the several States.

(2) Cases arising under international law or international agreements of the United States are within the Judicial Power of the United States and, subject to Constitutional and statutory limitations and requirements of justiciability, are within the jurisdiction of the federal courts.

(3) Courts in the United States are bound to give effect to international law and to international agreements of the United States, except that a "non-self-executing" agreement will not be given effect as law in the absence of necessary implementation.

(4) An international agreement of the United States is "non-self-executing"

(a) if the agreement manifests an intention that it shall not become effective as domestic law without enactment of implementing legislation,

(b) if the Senate in giving consent to a treaty, or Congress by resolution, requires implementing legislation, or

(c) if implementing legislation is constitutionally required.

Comment *c*. *International law and agreements as law of the United States*. The proposition that international law and agreements are law in the United States is addressed largely to the courts. In appropriate cases they apply international law or agreements without the need of enactment by Congress or proclamation by the President....

That international law and agreements of the United States are law of the United States means also that the President has the obligation and the necessary authority to take care that they be faithfully executed.... But ... the President has the power to take various measures including some that might constitute violations of international law by the United States.

d. *International law and agreements as supreme federal law*. Treaties made under the authority of the United States, like the Constitution itself and the laws of the United States, are expressly declared to be "supreme Law of the Land" by Article VI of the Constitution. International agreements of the United States other than treaties ... and customary international law ... are also federal law and as such are supreme over State law. Interpretations of international agreements by the United States Supreme Court are binding on the States. Customary international law is considered to be like common law in the United States, but it is federal law. A determination of international law by the Supreme Court is binding on States and on State courts....

Questions under international law or international agreements of the United States often arise in State courts. As law of the United States, international law is also the law of every State, is a basis for the exercise of judicial authority by State courts, and is cognizable in cases in State courts, in the same way as other United States law....

e. Federal jurisdiction over cases "arising under" international law and agreements. Cases arising under treaties to which the United States is a party, as well as cases arising under customary international law, or under international agreements of the United States other than treaties, are "Cases ... arising under ... the Laws of the United States, and Treaties made ... under their Authority," and therefore within the Judicial Power of the United States under Article III, Section 2 of the Constitution. Civil actions arising under international law or under a treaty or other international agreement of the United States are within the jurisdiction of the United States district courts. 28 U.S.C. § 1331.... For the purpose of Section 1331, all valid international agreements of the United States, whatever their designation and whatever the form by which they are concluded ..., are "treaties of the United States." Customary international law, like other federal law, is part of the "laws ... of the United States." ...

Reporters' Note

4. ... The statutory provision in 28 U.S.C. § 1331 gives the district courts original jurisdiction (but not exclusive of State courts) "of all civil actions arising under the Constitution, laws, or treaties of the United States." ...

Matters arising under customary international law also arise under "the laws of the United States," since international law is "part of our law" (*The Paquete Habana* ... [see below]) and is federal law....

c. *Subject Matter Jurisdiction*

[see cases in Section 2 D 2, Litigating Human Rights and Related Claims]

JORDAN J. PAUST, INTERNATIONAL LAW AS LAW OF THE UNITED STATES

6–7 (1996), 10 (2 ed. 2003).

As the *Restatement* ... recognizes: "Matters arising under customary international law also arise under 'the laws of the United States,' since international law is 'part of our law' ... and is federal law." Thus, cases "arising under customary international law" are "within the Judicial Power of the United States under Article III, section 2 of the

Constitution;" and such law, "while not mentioned explicitly in the Supremacy Clause," is supreme federal law within the meaning of Article VI, clause 2. For these reasons, the phrase "laws ... of the United States" contained in 28 U.S.C. § 1331 gives the district courts original jurisdiction over all civil cases arising under customary international law. Thus, a general jurisdictional competence exists to address and apply customary international law as law of the United States (including "substantive" rights, duties, causes of action, and rights to remedies thereunder) under 28 U.S.C. § 1331 whether or not other statutes, such as the Alien Tort Statute (Alien Tort Claims Act)[28 U.S.C. § 1350], refer expressly to the "law of nations" or to customary international law and thus provide additional bases for federal jurisdiction or additional substantive law. To stress a point, customary international law that provides rights or remedies, as law of the United States, is federal substantive law and federal courts have subject matter jurisdiction with respect to such law. Further, customary international law is federal law and supreme law of the land whether or not other more technical jurisdictional competencies also pertain (such as diversity or admiralty jurisdiction).

Notes and Questions

1. Consider these constitutional and statutory bases for incorporation of customary international law also in Section 2 D 2 below concerning litigation of human rights and related claims. First, there is a general federal judicial power or competence to address international law that is based in the Constitution and, second, with respect to civil sanctions, 28 U.S.C. § 1331 provides federal question jurisdiction. Other federal statutes may also provide federal question jurisdiction. *See, e.g.*, Restatement § 111, cmt. f.

2. Although the Alien Tort Claims Act (ATCA), 28 U.S.C. § 1350, has been found to supply both federal question and subject matter jurisdiction (see cases in Section 2 D 2 below), the Torture Victim Protection Act (TVPA), 106 Stat. 73 (1992), has been said to be not a "jurisdictional" statute. *See, e.g.*, Kadic v. Karadzic, 70 F.3d 232, 246 (2d Cir.1995), relevant excerpt in this chapter, Section 2 D 2. If not, what federal statute forms a statutory base for federal question jurisdiction regarding the TVPA?

3. With respect to subject matter jurisdiction as such, cases have held that 28 U.S.C. § 1331 also provides subject matter jurisdiction in federal courts. *See, e.g.*, Abebe–Jiri v. Negewo, 1993 WL 814304 (N.D. Ga. 1993), *aff'd*, 72 F.3d 844 (11th Cir. 1996) (but focusing on the ATCA re: subject matter jurisdiction, *id.* at 846–48); Xuncax v. Gramajo, 886 F.Supp. 162, 178 (D.Mass.1995) (re: § 1331 plus the TVPA); Forti v. Suarez–Mason, 672 F.Supp. 1531, 1544 (N.D.Cal.1987); *see also* Filartiga v. Pena–Irala, 630 F.2d 876, 887 n. 22 (2d. Cir.1980) ("We recognize that our reasoning might also sustain jurisdiction under the general federal question jurisdiction provision, 28 U.S.C. § 1331. We prefer, however, to rest our decision upon the Alien Tort Statute, in light of that provision's close coincidence with the jurisdictional facts presented in this case."). This point was addressed but not decided in Kadic v. Karadzic, 70 F.3d at 246 (the "causes of action [in this

case] are statutorily authorized, and ... we need not rule definitely on whether any causes of action not specifically authorized by statute may be implied by international law ... as incorporated into United States law and grounded on section 1331 jurisdiction."), the court agreeing nonetheless that a more specific statute, the ATCA, provides subject matter jurisdiction and that "jurisdiction" can rest on § 1331 or the ATCA.

4. For controversial minority views attacking the well-recognized nature of customary international law, especially human rights, as law of the United States for use both in federal courts and for supremacy purposes, *see, e.g.*, Curtis A. Bradley, Jack L. Goldsmith, *Federal Courts and the Incorporation of International Law*, 111 HARV. L. REV. 2260 (1998); *Customary International Law as Federal Common Law: A Critique of the Modern Position*, 110 HARV. L. REV. 815 (1997); Curtis A. Bradley, Breard, *Our Dualist Constitution, and the Internationalist Conception*, 51 STAN. L. REV. 529 (1999); *see also* Phillip R. Trimble, *A Revisionist View of Customary International Law*, 33 U.C.L.A. L. REV. 665, 707–09, 713–16, 721–23, 731 (1985). Such views have been widely criticized. *See, e.g.*, Harold Hongju Koh, *Is International Law Really State Law?*, 111 HARV. L. REV. 1824 (1998); Jordan J. Paust, *Customary International Law and Human Rights Treaties* Are *Law of the United States*, 20 MICH. J. INT'L L. 301 (1999), where it is explained that:

> ... [A]t the time of the formation of the Constitution John Jay had written: "Under the national government ... the laws of nations, will always be expounded in one sense ... [and there is] wisdom ... in committing such questions to the jurisdiction and judgment of courts appointed by and responsible only to one national government...." [THE FEDERALIST NO. 3, at 62 (J.C. Hamilton ed. 1868)] In 1792, the supremacy of the customary law of nations within the United States was affirmed in *Ross v. Rittenhouse* [2 U.S. (2 Dall.) 160, 162 (Pa.1792)]; and Attorney General Randolph declared: "The law of nations, although not specially adopted ... is essentially a part of the law of the land." [1 Op. Att'y Gen. 26, 27 (1792); *see also* 1 Op. Att'y Gen. 68, 69 (1797).]
>
> In 1793, then Chief Justice Jay recognized that "the laws of the United States," the same phrase found in Article III, section 2, clause 1 and in Article VI, clause 2 of the Constitution, includes the customary "law of nations" and that such law was directly incorporable for the purpose of criminal sanctions. [*Henfield's Case*, extract *infra* this chapter] Also in 1793, the Chief Justice stated that prior to the Constitution:
>
>> the United States had ... become amenable to the laws of nations; and it was their interest as well as their duty to provide, that those laws should be respected and obeyed; in their national character and capacity, the United States were responsible to foreign nations for the conduct of each state, relative to the laws of nations, and the performance of treaties; and there the inexpediency of referring all such questions to State Courts, and particularly to the Courts of delinquent States, became apparent.... These were among the evils which it was proper for the nation ... to provide by a national judiciary. [Chisholm v. Georgia, 2 U.S. (2 Dall.) 419, 474 (1793)]

That same year it was affirmed that the "law of nations is part of the law of the United States." [United States v. Ravara, 2 U.S. (2 Dall.) 297, 299 n. * (C.C.D.Pa.1793)] Justice Wilson also declared that the Supreme Court has original jurisdiction in certain cases addressing such law, but that Congress can nevertheless provide a concurrent jurisdiction in lower federal courts. [*Id.* at 298] Chief Justice Jay had also charged a grand jury in Virginia that year in markedly familiar words: "The Constitution, the statutes of Congress, the law of nations, and treaties constitutionally made compose the laws of the United States." [May 22, 1793)] In that year also, Secretary of State Thomas Jefferson reassured the French Minister Genet that the law of nations is an "integral part" of the law of the land [Letter of June 5, 1793)], and in his home state of Virginia it was declared in *Page v. Pendleton* [1 Va. Rep. (Wythe) 211 (Ch. 1793)]: "[T]he legislature ... admitted, that the law and usages of nations require ... the legislature could not retract their consent to observe the praecepts of the law, and conform to the usages, of nations...." [*Id.*] In 1795, Justice Iredell addressed direct incorporation of customary international law and affirmed the fact of incorporation with or without a statutory base in a consistent and telling fashion: "This is so palpable a violation of our own law ... of which the law of nations is a part, as it subsisted either before the act of Congress on the subject, or since...." [Talbot v. Janson, 3 U.S. (3 Dall.) 133, 159–61 (1795)] With respect to the broad range of matters subject to incorporation, he added: "[A]ll ... trespasses committed against the general law of nations, are enquirable...." [*Id.* at 159–60] An early case had also expressly related the duty to incorporate customary international law to the Constitution: "[C]ourts ... [i]n this country ... are bound, by the Constitution of the United States, to determine according to treaties and the law of nations, wherever they apply." [Waite v. The Antelope, 28 F. Cas. 1341 (D.C.D. S. Car. 1807)]

Similar recognitions had occurred previously and would occur throughout our history.

Id. at 301–03 (footnotes, in brackets, highly edited).

5. Other examples of U.S. courts utilizing and recognizing the importance of international law in the early years of U.S. history are described in Jon M. Van Dyke, *The Role of Customary International Law in Federal and State Court Litigation*, 26 U. Hawaii L. Rev. 361 (2004) (footnotes revised; reprinted with permission):

When the United States emerged from the Revolutionary War as an independent country, our early leaders and judges accepted international law as a source of law that governed our country and our people. The first U.S. Congress enacted in 1789 the statute that has become known as the Alien Tort Claims Act, which gives aliens the right to bring claims in U.S. courts for torts committed in violation of the law of nations....

The first decisions handed down by the courts of the United States treated international law with deference and respect.... Chief Justice John Marshall explained in an early case that "[a]n act of Congress ought never to be construed to violate the law of nations if any other possible construction remains, and consequently can never be construed to violate ... rights ... further than is warranted by the law of nations as understood in this country.'' Murray v. The Charming Betsy, 6 U.S. (2 Cranch) 64, 118 (1804). The United States was worried about its precarious status in world affairs, particularly in light of the constant European wars of the time and Britain's invasion of the United States in 1812. Chief Justice Marshall explained forcefully in a difficult 1825 case that: ''no principle of general law is more universally acknowledged, than the perfect equality of nations. Russia and Geneva have equal rights.'' The Antelope, 23 U.S. 66, 122 (1825). That case was difficult because it involved the slave trade, and Chief Justice Marshall's opinion protected the rights of the slave traders to their slaves, ruling that although trading in humans is contrary to the law of nature, it cannot be said to be contrary to international law because of the long practice of trading in slaves sanctioned by universal assent and carried on without much opposition and without censure for two centuries.

Chief Justice Marshall also turned to international law for his seminal analysis of native rights in the 1832 case of Worcestor v. Georgia, 31 U.S. 515 (1832), where he relied upon the international law scholar Vattel to explain that under the law of nations the relationship between natives and the United States government was comparable to that of the weaker and stronger powers in Europe:

> the settled doctrine of the law of nations is, that a weaker power does not surrender its independence–its right to self government, by associating with a stronger, and taking its protection. A weak state, in order to provide for its safety, may place itself under the protection of one more powerful, without stripping itself of the right of government, and ceasing to be a state.

The basic doctrine of native autonomy in the United States is thus based on an explicit invocation and understanding of international law.

Sixteen years after Chief Justice Marshall's opinion involving slavery in *The Antelope*, the Supreme Court once again examined the international law principles applicable to this topic in The Amistad, 40 U.S. (1 Pet.) 518 (1841). But this time the Court reached a different result, refusing to return the Africans to Spain, despite a treaty that seemed to support such a result, because the Africans' claims to liberty based on the eternal principles of justice and international law were deemed to override the treaty. In an opinion by Justice Joseph Story, the Court pointed out that Spain had ''utterly abolished'' the slave trade and made it ''a heinous crime.'' The kidnapped Africans on the ship must thus be viewed ''by the laws of Spain itself'' as individuals ''entitled to their freedom.'' As ''free negroes, the treaty with Spain cannot be obligatory upon them; and the United States are bound to respect their rights as much as those of Spanish subjects.'' The conflict of rights between the Spanish claimants and the kidnapped Africans therefore ''must be decided upon the eternal principles of justice and international law,'' especially because ''human life and liberty are in issue.'' ''The treaty with Spain never could have intended to take away the equal rights of all foreigners . . . to equal justice; or to deprive such foreigners of the protection given them by other treaties, *or by the general law of nations*.'' (emphasis added.) The Court thus concluded ''that these negroes ought to be free; and that the Spanish treaty interposes no obstacle to the just assertion of their rights.'' This important opinion is sometimes viewed as an early example of a court recognizing that a "peremptory norm" or "*jus cogens*" principle of international law will override a contrary treaty provision. The slave trade was also viewed as violative of evolved customary international law in United States v. Haun, 26 F.Cas. 227 (C.C.S.D. Ala. 1860)(No. 15,329).

2. *Direct Incorporation*

a. *The Founders and Early Cases*

RESPUBLICA v. DE LONGCHAMPS

1 U.S. (1 Dall.) 111, 113, 115 (Pa. 1784).

[Editors' note: While on the streets of Philadelphia (which at the time was the capital of the United States, one De Longchamps (a Frenchman) became embroiled in a heated argument with the Consul of France over a financial matter. During the argument, De Longchamps struck the cane of the foreign consul, for which he was charged in the following indictment: assault on a French Minister "in violation of the laws of nations, against the peace and dignity of the United States and of the commonwealth of Pennsylvania."]

M'KEAN, C.J.

This is a case of the first impression in the United States. It must be determined on the principles of the laws of nations, which form a part of the municipal laws of Pennsylvania....

The first crime in the indictment is an infraction of the law of nations. This law, in its full extent, is part of the law of this state, and is to be collected from the practice of different nations, and the authority of writers.

The person of a public minister is sacred and inviolable. Whoever offers any violence to him, not only affronts the sovereign he represents, but also hurts the common safety and well-being of nations;—he is guilty of a crime against the whole world.

All the reasons [apply likewise to the Minister's house] ... to invade its freedom is a crime against the state and all other nations.

Notes and Questions

1. De Longchamps was convicted and given a criminal fine and jail sentence (of two years with seven years probation). He also had to post a security bond. See *id.* at 111, 117. Also prior to the creation of the U.S. Constitution, in Nathan v. Commonwealth of Virginia, 1 U.S. (1 Dall.) 77, 78 (Common Pleas, Philadelphia County 1781), the Pennsylvania Attorney General had argued that an English statute had reflected the law of nations and was incorporated directly into local domestic law for criminal sanction purposes (*i.e.*, prosecuting and punishing "infractors of the law of nations").

2. After the decision in *De Longchamps*, a resolution of the Continental Congress did "highly approve the action." See 27 J. CONT. CONG. 502–04. Recall the resolution of the Continental Congress in Chapter 1, Section 1 A.

3. Was the early expectation that written laws are necessary for prosecution of violators of the customary laws of nations?

4. After ratification of the U.S. Constitution, was an infraction of the law of nations still indictable in our courts? In U.S. courts?

5. In Sosa v. Alvarez–Machain, 542 U.S. 692 (2004), the Court's majority rejected the controversial minority viewpoint that customary international law should not be viewed as law of the United States. Justice Souter, writing for the majority, stated that there are "actionable international norms" and "[f]or two centuries we have affirmed that the domestic law of the United States recognizes the law of nations." 124 S.Ct. at 2764. Justice Breyer, concurring in part and concurring the judgment, affirmed that "torture, genocide, crimes against humanity, and war crimes" implicate universal jurisdictional competence. *Id.* at 2783.

1 **OP. ATT'Y GEN.** 26, 27 (June 26, 1792) (Randolph, Att'y Gen.)

The law of nations, although not specially adopted by the constitution or any municipal act, is essentially a part of the law of the land. Its obligation commences and runs with the existence of a nation, subject to modifications on some points of indifference. Indeed a people may regulate it so as to be binding upon the departments of their own government, in any form whatever; but with regard to foreigners, every change is at the peril of the nation which makes it. Impliedly, however, the law of nations is considered by the act affixing penalties to certain crimes as being in force, and some of its subjects are thrown under particular provisions ... what would be the consequence of finding this to be the case; and what ought to be done to avenge an infraction of the law of nations, which may not be punishable under any merely municipal law? ... [here] The arrest of the domestic servant of a public minister is declared illegal by the act ... [and here] Congress appear to have excluded every resort to the law of nations. This must be the effect of their regulations, or else the offender would be punishable both under that and the law of nations; or at least under either, at the will of the prosecutor. But this cannot be conceived [here] as the sense of the legislature....

Notes and Questions

1. Does the above opinion of Attorney General Randolph indicate that Congress has the power to immunize or obviate altogether a crime under the law of nations? What is the relevant constitutional power of Congress? In his view, can a persons be prosecuted for an international crime even if Congress has not explicitly enacted a statute authorizing such a prosecution?

2. During the debates concerning ratification, James Wilson was reported to have stated: "To pretend to define the law of nations which depended on the authority of all the Civilized Nations of the World, would have a look of arrogance." See 2 FARRAND, RECORDS, at 65. See also Palmer, *The Federal Common Law of Crime*, 4 LAW & HIST. REV. 267, 277 n.63 (1986):

"Allowing the judiciary to punish offenses against the law of nations without prior congressional definition was congruent with constitutional original intent," also *quoting* Representative John Marshall in 10 ANNALS OF CONG. 607 (Mar. 7, 1800) re: Art. I, sec. 8, cl. 10: ' "[T]his clause of the Constitution cannot be considered, [...] as affecting acts which are piracy under the law of nations' "(Marshall adding that "the judicial power of the United States [under Art. III] extends to ... piracy under the law of nations ..., punishable by every nation" and that such power had been exercised by courts "under the Confederation ... although there was no express power in Congress to define and punish the offence."

3. When courts and others had stated that the law of nations has been a part of the "common" or "municipal" law and part of the "law of the land," was its status merely that of common law? Does the law of nations bind the government, including Congress, in addition to individuals? In addition to materials above, consider the following excerpts from early cases and Opinions of Attorney Generals:

UNITED STATES v. SMITH

18 U.S. (5 Wheat.) 153, 161 (1820).

The common law ... recognizes and punishes piracy as an offence, not against its own municipal code, but as an offence against the law of nations....

ROSS v. RITTENHOUSE

2 U.S. (2 Dall.) 160, 162 (Pa.1792).

[A resolution of the Continental Congress of January 15, 1780 had resolved] "that the trials in the Court of Appeals be according to the usage of nations, *and not by Jury*." This has been the practice in most nations, but the law of nations ... is enforced by ... the *municipal law* of the country; which ... may ... facilitate or improve the execution of its decisions, by any means they shall think best, provided the great universal law remains unaltered. (emphasis in original)

11 **OP. ATT'Y GEN.** 297, 299–300 (1865) (Speed, Att'y Gen.)

That the law of nations constitutes a part of the laws of the land, must be admitted. The laws of nations are expressly made laws of the land by the Constitution, when it says that "Congress shall have power to define and punish piracies and felonies committed on the high seas, and offences against the laws of nations." To *define* is to give the limits or precise meaning of a word or thing in being; to make is to call into being. Congress has power to *define*, not to make, the laws of nations; but Congress has the power to make rules for the government of the army and navy. From the very face of the Constitution, then, it is evident that the laws of nations do constitute a part of the laws of the land. But very soon after the organization of the federal government, Mr. Randolph, the Attorney General, said: "The law of nations, although not specifically adopted by the Constitution, is essentially a part of the law of the land. Its obligation commences and runs with the existence of a nation, subject to modification on some points of indifference." (See

Opin. Attorney General, vol. 1, p.27.) The framers of the Constitution knew that a nation could not maintain an honorable place amongst the nations of the world that does not regard the great and essential principles of the law of nations as a part of the law of the land. Hence Congress may define those laws, but cannot abrogate them, or, as Mr. Randolph says, may "modify on some points of indifference."

That the laws of nations constitute a part of the laws of the land is established from the face of the Constitution, upon principle and by authority.

But the laws of war constitute much the greater part of the law of nations. Like the other laws of nations, they exist and are of binding force upon the departments and citizens of the Government, though not defined by any law of Congress. No one that has ever glanced at the many treatises that have been published in different ages of the world by great, good, and learned men, can fail to know that the laws of war constitute a part of the law of nations, and that those laws have been prescribed with tolerable accuracy.

Congress can declare war. When war is declared, it must be, under the Constitution, carried on according to the known laws and usages of war amongst civilized nations. Under the power to define those laws, Congress cannot abrogate them or authorize their infraction. The Constitution does not permit this Government to prosecute a war as an uncivilized and barbarous people.

As war is required by the framework of our Government to be prosecuted according to the known usages of war amongst the civilized nations of the earth, it is important to understand what are the obligations, duties, and responsibilities imposed by war upon the military. Congress, not having defined, as under the Constitution it might have done, the laws of war, we must look to the usage of nations to ascertain the powers conferred in war, on whom the exercise of such powers devolve, over whom, and to what extent do those powers reach, and in how far the citizen and the soldier are bound by the legitimate use thereof.

9 **OP. ATT'Y GEN.** 356, 362–63 (1859) (Black, Att'y Gen.)

[The public law of nations] must be paramount to local law in every question where local laws are in conflict [and] [w]hat you [the President] will do must of course depend upon the law of our own country, as controlled and modified by the law of nations.

1 **OP. ATT'Y GEN.** 566, 570–71 (1821) (Wirt, Att'y Gen.)

The President is the executive officer of the laws of the country; these laws are not merely the constitution, statutes, and treaties of the United States, but those general laws of nations which ... impose on them, in common with other nations, the strict observance of a respect for their natural rights and sovereignties ... This obligation becomes one of the laws of the country; to the enforcement of which, the

President, charged by his office with the execution of all our laws, ... is bound to look.

4. *See also* III ELLIOT, DEBATES, *supra*, at 502 (Nicholas in Virginia, 1788: "the law of nations ... was superior to any act or law of any nation"); Shanks v. Dupont, 28 U.S. (3 Pet.) 242, 248 (1830) (Story, J., op.); Heathfield v. Chilton, 4 Burrow 2015, 98 E.R. 50 (K.B. 1767) (an act of Parliament cannot "alter" the law of nations, which is part of English law); RESTATEMENT §§ 102, 103, 111, 114–115, 702 & cmt. c, RN 12 (3 ed. 1987); JORDAN J. PAUST, INTERNATIONAL LAW AS LAW OF THE UNITED STATES 7–9, 38–43, *passim* (2 ed. 2003); Louis Henkin, *The President and International Law*, 80 AM. J. INT'L L. 930, 933 (1986), *citing* Louis Henkin, *International Law as Law in the United States*, 82 MICH. L. REV. 1555, 1561 (1984) (not mere "common law"); Jules L. Lobel, *The Limits of Constitutional Power: Conflicts Between Foreign Policy and International Law*, 71 VA. L. REV. 1071, 1089, *passim* (1985); Jordan J. Paust, *Rediscovering the Relationship Between Congressional Power and International Law: Exceptions to the Last in Time Rule and the Primacy of Custom,* 28 VA. J. INT'L L. 393 (1988), revised in JORDAN J. PAUST, INTERNATIONAL LAW AS LAW OF THE UNITED STATES chpt. 3 (2 ed. 2003); *Customary International Law: Its Nature, Sources and Status as Law of the United States*, 12 MICH. J. INT'L L. 59 (1990).

5. Concerning the powers of Congress, the year before he joined the Supreme Court Representative Marshall had recognized that Article I, Section 8, clause 10 of the Constitution "cannot be considered, as affecting acts which are piracy under the law of nations" and that where, under customary international law, the people of the United States themselves have no competence to act, "that clause [10] can never be construed to make to the Government a grant of power, which the people making it do not themselves possess," and thus that Congress has no power to act in violation of the law of nations, nor "consequently ... [could such power be transferred] to their courts...." 10 ANNALS OF CONG. 607. *See also id.* at 611; The Antelope, 23 U.S. (10 Wheat.) 66, 99 & n. 6 (1825) (argument of counsel, *citing* House committee reports) (congressional act cannot "increase or diminish the list of offenses punishable by the law of nations"); Miller v. The Ship Resolution, 2 U.S. (2 Dall.) 1, 3–4 (1781) (congressional act "cannot change the law of nations"); Justice Wilson's 1791 charge to a grand jury (customary law of nations cannot be altered or abrogated by domestic law), in II THE WORKS OF JAMES WILSON 803, 813–14 (R. McCloskey ed. 1967).

6. Justice Story stated in 1814 that a penalty of "forfeiture under the ... act [of Congress], was absorbed in the more general operation of the law of war." See The Sally, 12 U.S. (8 Cranch) 382, 384 (1814) (Story, J., opinion). Does this mean that the customary law of war has a higher status domestically than congressional legislation? and an "absorbing" effect?

HENFIELD'S CASE

11 F. Cas. 1099 (C.C.D.Pa.1793) (No. 6,360).

[Editors' note: The British Minister Plenipotentiary to the United States, Mr. Hammond, sent a letter to Secretary of State Jefferson complaining of the outfitting of two privateers in Charleston, South Carolina under French Commissions, carrying six guns, and being navigated by forty-fifty men, "for the most part, citizens of the United States," which constitute alleged breaches of neutrality. He also asked the Executive to repress such practices. Thereafter, Secretary Jefferson wrote to Mr. Rawle to apprehend and prosecute such U.S. citizens according to law. In turn, Mr. Rawle wrote to Mr. Baker that he had received information that one Gideon Henfield of Massachusetts was an officer of a privateer fitted out in Charleston that had been a British vessel taken as prize and stated that he had "received orders to prosecute, in every instance, those who commit breaches of the neutrality, declared to exist on the part of the United States, during the present war between the European powers," and that he should prosecute Henfield if the information is correct.]

This charge, though not delivered to the particular grand jury by whom the bill against Henfield was found, was prepared for the purpose of settling the law generally as applying to the class of offenders, of whom Henfield was one, and in this light it is here introduced....

A charge delivered by the Honourable JOHN JAY, Esquire, Chief Justice of the United States, to the grand jury impanelled for the court of the United States, holden for the Middle circuit in the district of Virginia, at the capitol in the city of Richmond, on the 22d day of May, 1793.

Gentlemen of the Grand Jury: That citizens and nations should [so] use their own as not to injure others, is an ancient and excellent maxim; and is one of those plain precepts of common justice, which it is the interest of all, and the duty of each to obey, and that not only in the use they may make of their property, but also of their liberty, their power and other blessings of every kind....

By their constitution and laws, the people of the United States have expressed their will, and their will so expressed, must sway and rule supreme in our republic. It is in obedience to their will, and in pursuance of their authority, that this court is now to dispense their justice in this district; and they have made it your duty, gentlemen, to inquire whether any and what infractions of their laws have been committed in this district, or on the seas, by persons in or belonging to it. Proceed, therefore, to inquire accordingly, and to present such as either have, or shall come to your knowledge. That you may perceive more clearly the extent and objects of your inquiries, it may be proper to observe, that the laws of the United States admit of being classed under three heads of descriptions. 1st. All treaties made under the authority of the United

States. 2d. The laws of nations. 3dly. The constitution, and statutes of the United States.

Treaties between independent nations, are contracts or bargains which derive all their force and obligation from mutual consent and agreement; and, consequently, when once fairly made and properly concluded, cannot be altered or annulled by one of the parties, without the consent and concurrence of the other. Wide is the difference between treaties and statutes—we may negotiate and make contracts with other nations, but we can neither legislate for them, nor they for us; we may repeal or alter our statutes, but no nation can have authority to vacate or modify treaties at discretion. Treaties, therefore, necessarily become the supreme law of the land, and so they are very properly declared to be by the sixth article of the constitution. Whenever doubts and questions arise relative to the validity, operation or construction of treaties, or of any articles in them, those doubts and questions must be settled according to the maxims and principles of the laws of nations applicable to the case. The peace, prosperity, and reputation of the United States, will always greatly depend on their fidelity to their engagements; and every virtuous citizen (for every citizen is a party to them) will concur in observing and executing them with honour and good faith....

As to the laws of nations—they are those laws by which nations are bound to regulate their conduct towards each other, both in peace and war. Providence has been pleased to place the United States among the nations of the earth, and therefore, all those duties, as well as rights, which spring from the relation of nation to nation, have devolved upon us. We are with other nations, tenants in common of the sea—it is a highway for all, and all are bound to exercise that common right, and use that common highway in the manner which the laws of nations and treaties require. On this occasion, it is proper to observe to you, gentlemen, that various circumstances and considerations now unite in urging the people of the United States to be particularly exact and circumspect in observing the obligation of treaties, and the laws of nations, which as has been already remarked, form a very important part of the laws of our nation. I allude to the facts and injunctions specified in the president's late proclamation; it is in these words: "Whereas, it appears that a state of war exists between Austria, Prussia, Sardinia, Great Britain, and the United Netherlands of the one part, and France of the other, and the duty and interest of the United States, require that they should with sincerity and good faith, adopt and pursue a conduct friendly and impartial towards the belligerent powers: I have, therefore, thought fit by these presents, to declare the disposition of the United States to observe the conduct aforesaid towards these powers respectively, and to exhort and warn the citizens of the United States, carefully to avoid all acts and proceedings whatsoever, which may in any manner tend to contravene such disposition. I do hereby make known, that whosoever of the citizens of the United States, shall render himself liable to punishment or forfeiture, under the law of nations, by committing, aiding, or abetting hostilities against any of the said powers, or by carrying to them those articles which are deemed contraband, by the modern usage of nations, will not receive the protection of the United States against such punishment or forfeiture; and further, that I have given instructions to those officers to whom it belongs, to cause prosecutions to be instituted against all persons who shall within the cognizance of the courts of the United States, violate the law of nations, with respect to the powers at war, or any of them."

By this proclamation, authentic and official information is given to the citizens of the United States:—That war actually exists between the nations mentioned in it: That they are to observe a conduct friendly and impartial towards the belligerent powers: That offenders will not be protected, but on the contrary, prosecuted and punished. The law of nations, considers those as neutral nations "who take no part in the war, remaining friends to both parties, and not favouring the arms of one to the detriment of the other;" and it declares that a "nation, desirous safely to enjoy the conveniences of neutrality, is in all things to show an exact impartiality between the parties at war; for should he, when under no obligation, favour one to the detriment of the other, he cannot complain of being treated as an adherent and confederate of his enemy, of which no nation would be the dupe if able to resent it." The proclamation is exactly consistent with and declaratory of the conduct enjoined by the law of nations. It is worthy of remark that we are at peace with all these belligerent powers not only negatively in having war with none of them, but also in a more positive and particular sense by treaties with four of them.

By the first article of our treaty with France it is stipulated that "there shall be a firm, inviolable and universal peace, and true and sincere friendship between his Most Christian Majesty, his heirs and successors, and the United States; and between the countries, islands, cities and towns situate under the jurisdiction of his Most Christian Majesty and of the United States, and the people and inhabitants of every degree, without exception of persons or places." By the first article of our treaty with the United Netherlands, it is stipulated that "there shall be a firm, inviolable and universal peace, and sincere friendship between their High Mightinesses, the Lords and States General of the United Netherlands and the United States of America, and between the subjects and inhabitants of the said parties, and between the countries, islands and places situate under the jurisdiction of the said United Netherlands and the United States of America, their subjects and inhabitants of every degree, without exception of persons or places." The definitive treaty of peace with Great Britain begins with great solemnity, in the words following: "In the name of the most holy and undivided Trinity." By the seventh article of this treaty it is stipulated that "there shall be a firm and perpetual peace between his Britannic Majesty, and the United States, and between the subjects of the one and the citizens of the other." By the first article of our treaty with Prussia it is stipulated that "there shall be a firm, inviolable and universal peace and sincere friendship between his Majesty, the King of Prussia, his heirs, successors and subjects on the one part, and the United States of America and their citizens on the other, without exception of persons or places." ...

While the people of other nations do no violence or injustice to our citizens, it would certainly be criminal and wicked in our citizens, for the sake of plunder, to do violence and injustice to any of them. The president, therefore, has with great propriety declared "that the duty and interest of the United States require that they should, with sincerity and good faith, adopt and pursue a conduct friendly and impartial towards the belligerent powers." ...

It is on these and similar principles that whoever shall render himself liable to punishment or forfeiture, under the law of nations, by committing, aiding or abetting hostilities forbidden by his country, ought to lose the protection of his country against such punishment or forfeiture. But this is not all, it is not sufficient that a nation should only withdraw its protection from such offenders, it ought also to prosecute and punish them....

From the observations which have been made, this conclusion appears to result, viz.: That the United States are in a state of neutrality relative to all the powers at war, and that it is their duty, their interest, and their disposition to maintain it: that, therefore, they who commit, aid, or abet hostilities against these powers, or either of them, offend against the laws of the United States, and ought to be punished; and consequently, that it is your duty, gentlemen, to inquire into and present all such of these offences, as you shall find to have been committed within this district. What acts amount to committing or aiding, or abetting hostilities, must be determined by the laws and approved practice of nations, and by the treaties and other laws of the United States relative to such cases....

Charge of Judge WILSON, as president of a special court of the United States, for the Middle circuit and Pennsylvania district, holden at the court house, in the city of Philadelphia, on the 22d day of July, 1793, to the grand jury of said court:

Gentlemen of the Grand Jury: It is my duty to explain to you the very important occasion on which this court is specially convened, and to state the points of law not less important to the application of which that occasion gives rise.

To the judge of the Pennsylvania district information was given on oath, that certain citizens of the United States had acted in several capacities as officers on board an armed schooner, said to be commissioned by France as a cruiser or private ship-of-war; and with others on board that schooner did capture and make prize of several ships or vessels belonging to his Britannic Majesty, and otherwise assist in an hostile manner in annoying the commerce of the subjects of his said Britannic Majesty, who is at peace with the United States, contrary to their duty as citizens of the United States. On receiving this information the judge issued his warrant for apprehending the persons against whom complaint was made, that they might answer for their doings in the premises, and be dealt with according to law. That legal proceedings in this and some other business might be had speedily, one of the judges of the supreme court of the United States and the judge of the Pennsylvania district issued their warrant, directing that on this day, and at this place a special session of the circuit court for this district should be held, and that grand and traverse jurors should be summoned to attend it. As the court however is authorized generally to try criminal causes, if any other crimes or offences cognizable in it be laid before you or are in your knowledge, it is your duty to present them ... under our national constitution, treaties compose a portion of the public and supreme law of the land, and for their construction and enforcement are brought openly before the tribunals of our country. Of those tribunals juries form an essential part; under the construction given by those juries, treaties will suffer neither in their importance nor in their sanctity....

Under all the obligations due to the universal society of the human race, the citizens of a state still continue. To this universal society it is a duty that each nation should contribute to the welfare, the perfection and the happiness of the others. If so, the first degree of this duty is to do no injury. Among states as well as among men, justice is a sacred law. This sacred law prohibits one state from exciting disturbances in another, from depriving it of its natural advantages, from calumniating its reputation, from seducing its citizens, from debauching the attachment of its allies, from fomenting or encouraging the hatred of its enemies. Vatt. Law Nat. 127 [E. DE VATTEL, THE LAW OF NATIONS (1758)]. But nations are not only prohibited from doing evil, they are also commanded to do good to one another. On states as well as individuals the duties of humanity are strictly incumbent; what each is obliged to perform for others, from others it is entitled to receive. Hence the advantage as well as the duty of humanity.... Let such be held responsible, when they can be rendered amenable for the consequences of their crimes and disorders. If the offended nation have the criminal in its power, it may without difficulty punish him, and oblige him to make satisfaction. Vatt. Law Nat. 145. When the offending citizen escapes into his own country, his nation should oblige him to repair the damage, if reparation can be made, or should punish him according to the measure of his offence. Vatt. Law Nat. 75; Burrows, 1480; 4 Bl. Comm. 68, 69 [W. BLACKSTONE, COMMENTARIES ON THE LAWS OF ENGLAND (1765)]. If the nation refuse to do either, it renders itself in some measure an accomplice in the guilt, and becomes responsible for the injury. Vatt. Law Nat. 145. To what does this responsibility lead? To reprisal certainly (Vatt. Law Nat. 251); and if so, probably to war (*Id.* 2; 4 Bl. Comm. 68, 69). And should the fortunes or the lives of millions be placed in either of those predicaments by the conduct of one citizen, or of a few citizens? Vatt. Law Nat. 2, 89. Humanity and reason say no. The constitution of the United States says no....

Judge WILSON (with whom were Judge IREDELL and Judge PETERS) charged the jury as follows:

. . . It is the joint and unanimous opinion of the court, that the United States, being in a state of neutrality relative to the present war, the acts of hostility committed by Gideon Henfield are an offence against this country, and punishable by its laws. It has been asked by his counsel, in their address to you, against what law has he offended? The answer is, against many and binding laws. As a citizen of the United States, he was bound to act no part which could injure the nation; he was bound to keep the peace in regard to all nations with whom we are at peace. This is the law of nations; not an ex post facto law, but a law that was in existence long before Gideon Henfield existed. There are also, positive laws, existing previous to the offence committed, and expressly declared to be part of the supreme law of the land. The constitution of the United States has declared that all treaties made, or to be made, under the authority of the United States, shall be part of the supreme law of the land. I will state to you, gentlemen, so much of the several treaties in force between American and any of the powers at war with France, as applies to the present case.... [The charge then addressed the treaties with the United Netherlands, Great Britain, and Prussia.] It may be observed, that the treaty would not be less sufficient in relation to the present question, if "subjects" and "citizens" had not been mentioned. These treaties were in the most public, the most notorious existence, before the act for which the prisoner is indicted was committed.

The jury retired about nine on Saturday evening, and came into court again about half-past eleven, when they informed the court they had not agreed. They were desired to retire again, which they did, and returned on Monday morning, having delivered into the hands of Judge Wilson a privy verdict on Sunday morning, soon after the adjournment of the court.

One of the jurymen now expressed some doubts, which occasioned the judges separately to deliver their sentiments on the points of law adverted to in the charge on Saturday evening, each of them assenting to the same, particularly as to the change of political relation in the defendant, from his having been some time absent from home previous to his entering on board the privateer.

The jury again retired, and the court adjourned. At half-past four the court was convened, and the jury presented a written verdict, which the court refused to receive, as being neither general nor special. Another adjournment took place, and about seven o'clock a verdict of "not guilty" was delivered.[7]

7. Chief Justice Marshall (Life of Washington, vol. 2, pp. 273, 274) thus notices the result: "The administration received additional evidence of the difficulty that would attend an adherence to the system which had been commenced in the acquittal of Gideon Henfield. A prosecution had been instituted against this person, who had enlisted in Charleston on Board a French privateer equipped in the port, which had

Notes and Questions

1. Duponceau, who had argued for the defense, made the following statement after the case:

> Judge Wilson, who presided at this trial, in his charge to the jury, took the ground of its being also an offence at common law, of which the law of nations was a part, and maintained the doctrine that the common law was to be looked to for the definition and punishment of the offence. This ground had not been adverted to in argument, or, at least, very slightly. But it would seem that the common law considered as a municipal system had nothing to do with this case. The law of nations, being the common law of the civilized world, may be said, indeed, to be a part of the law of every civilized nation; but it stands on other and higher grounds than municipal customs, statutes, edicts, or ordinances. It is binding on every people and on every government. It is to be carried into effect at all times under the penalty of being thrown out of the pale of civilization, or involving the country into a war. Every branch of the national administration, each within its district and its particular jurisdiction, is bound to administer it. It defines offences and affixes punishments, and acts everywhere *proprio rigore*, whenever it is not altered or modified by particular national statutes, or usages not inconsistent with its great and fundamental principles. Whether there is or not a national common law in other respects this universal common law can never cease to be the rule of executive and judicial proceedings until mankind shall return to the savage state. Judge Wilson, therefore, in my opinion, rather weakened than strengthened the ground of the prosecution in placing the law of nations on the same footing with the municipal or local common law and deriving its authority exclusively from the latter. It was considering the subject in its narrowest point of view.

Reprinted in 11 F. Cas. at 1122. Do you agree with Mr. Duponceau? Note that Chief Justice Jay and Justice Wilson gave separate charges and Duponceau was responding to Wilson's in Philadelphia. Both also addressed treaties as supreme federal law.

brought her prizes into the port of Philadelphia. This prosecution had been directed under the advice of the attorney general, who was of opinion that persons of this description were punishable for having violated subsisting treaties, which by the constitution are the supreme law of the land, and that they were also indictable at common law, for disturbing the peace of the United States. It could not be expected that the Democratic party would be inattentive to an act so susceptible of misrepresentation. Their papers sounded the alarm, and it was universally asked, 'What law had been offended, and under what statute was the indictment supported? Were the American people already prepared to give to a proclamation the force of a legislative act, and to subject themselves to the will of the executive? But if they were already sunk to such a state of degradation, were they to be punished for violating a proclamation which had not been published when the offence was committed, if indeed it could be termed an offence to engage with France, combating for liberty against the combined despots of Europe.' "“As the trial approached, a great degree of sensibility was displayed, and the verdict in favour of Henfield was celebrated with extravagant marks of joy and exultation. It bereaved the executive of the strength to be derived from an opinion, that punishment might be legally inflicted on those who should openly violate the rules prescribed for the preservation of neutrality; and exposed that department to the obloquy of having attempted a measure which the laws would not justify." The verdict was considered by Washington of such moment, as to lead him to enumerate it as a principal reason to be considered in the question of calling an extra session of congress, respecting which he asked the opinion of his cabinet on August 3, 1793. See 10 Wash. Writ. by Sparks. 362.

2. Chief Justice Jay's recognition that customary laws of nations are a necessary background for the interpretation ("validity, operation or construction") of treaties has generally been followed. *See, e.g.,* McCulloch v. Sociedad Nacional de Marineros de Honduras, 372 U.S. 10, 20–21 & n. 12 (1963); Santovincenzo v. Egan, 284 U.S. 30, 40 (1931); De Geofroy v. Riggs, 133 U.S. 258, 271 (1890); United States v. Rauscher, 119 U.S. 407, 419–20, 429 (1886); The Pizarro, 15 U.S. (2 Wheat.) 227, 245–46 (1817) ("the language of the law of nations, which is always to be consulted in the interpretation of treaties"); Ware v. Hylton, 3 U.S. (3 Dall.) 199, 261 (1796) ("The subject of treaties ... is to be determined by the law of nations"); *see also* Trans World Airlines v. Franklin Mint Corp., 466 U.S. 243, 261 (1984); Jordan v. Tashiro, 278 U.S. 123, 127 (1928); Tucker v. Alexandroff, 183 U.S. 424, 437 (1902); Society for the Propagation of the Gospel in Foreign Parts v. New Haven, 21 U.S. (8 Wheat.) 464, 490 (1823).

3. It is of interest that Justice Wilson's charge to the grand jury and the indictment recognized that private violations of the law of nations can constitute an act of "aggression" and a crime against "peace." See 11 F. Cas. at 1108–15. *See also id.* at 117 (points of Rawle, dist. att'y: his "aggression" on them, "actual aggression is charged"); 1 Op. Att'y Gen. 68, 69 (1797) ("the peace of Mankind"); 1 Op. Att'y Gen. 57, 58 (1795) ("against the public peace"). Consider these points again in connection with materials in Chapter 8, Section 1.

4. In 1794, Congress passed the Neutrality Act to provide criminal sanctions for such offenses against the law of nations. 18 U.S.C.§ 25, now § 960, reads:

> "Expedition against friendly nation
>
> "Whoever, within the United States, knowingly begins or sets on foot or provides or prepares a means for or furnishes the money for, or takes part in, any military or naval expedition or enterprise to be carried on from thence against the territory or dominion of any foreign prince or state, or of any colony, district, or people with whom the United States is at peace, shall be fined not more than $3,000 or imprisoned not more than three years, or both."

Other sections that may be relevant include §§ 956–959 and 961–967.

5. 18 U.S.C. § 960 does not mention "treaties" or the "law of nations." Nonetheless, are such laws relevant to an adequate interpretation of the statute? Also compare the following:

1 **OP. ATT'Y GEN.** 57, 58 (July 6, 1795) (Bradford, Att'y Gen.)

... [A]cts of hostility committed by American citizens against such as are in amity with us, being in violation of a treaty, and against the public peace, are offences against the United States, so far as they were committed within the territory or jurisdiction thereof; and, as such, are punishable by indictment in the district or circuit courts.

... [T]here can be no doubt that the company or individuals who have been injured by these acts of hostility have a remedy by a civil suit in the courts of the United States; jurisdiction being expressly given to these courts [by the ATCA] in all cases where an alien sues for a tort only, in violation of the law of nations, or a treaty of the United States....

... President [Washington] ... , by his proclamation of the 22d of April, 1793 [Proc. of Neutrality, No. 3, *reprinted in* 11 Stat. 753 (App. 1859)], warned all of the United States against all such proceedings; declaring that all those who should render themselves liable to punishment under the laws of nations, by committing, aiding, or abetting hostilities against any of the said parties, would not receive the protection of the United States against such punishment; and that he had given instructions to those officers to whom it belongs to cause proceedings to be instituted against all persons who should, within the [jurisdictional] cognizance of the courts of the United States, violate the laws of nations with respect to the powers at war, or any of them.

1 **OP. ATT'Y GEN.** 61, 62 (Jan. 20, 1796) (Lee, Att'y Gen.)

[re: breach of neutrality by an individual:] Forfeiture of the goods and ship, is the penalty annexed to such acts by the law of nations....

1 **OP. ATT'Y GEN.** 68, 69 (Jan. 26, 1797) (Lee, Att'y Gen.)

The constitution [art. I, sec. 8, cl. 10] gives to Congress, in express words, the power of passing a law for punishing a violation of territorial rights, it being an offence against the law of nations, and of a nature very serious in its consequence. That the peace of mankind may be preserved, it is the interest as well as the duty of every government to punish with becoming severity all the individuals of the State who commit this offence. Congress has passed no act yet upon the subject, and Jones and his associates are only liable to be prosecuted in our courts at common law for the misdemeanor; and if convicted, to be fined and imprisoned. The common law has adopted the law of nations in its fullest extent, and made it a part of the law of the land.

6. Had legislation been necessary in *Henfield's Case* to incorporate relevant laws of nations? or treaties? Did Justice Wilson's statement that treaties, "for their construction and enforcement [,] are brought openly before the tribunals of our country" reflect Chief Justice Jay's approach to such a question and the meaning of Article III, Section 2, clause 1 of the Constitution?

7. What was the intent and effect of the President's proclamation? What is the relevant power of the President under Article II of the Constitution?

8. Was it thought to be necessary that treaties or laws of nations mention individual duties, elements of crimes, or even the possibility of criminal (or civil) sanctions?

b. Prosecuting Without an Implementing Statute

Today, is a statute that incorporates customary or treaty-based international law necessary for criminal sanction purposes? Despite earlier cases noted above, today must Congress exercise its power "to define and punish'' before lawful prosecution can commence? Consider the following cases and materials.

(1) CUSTOM

THE THREE FRIENDS

166 U.S. 1, 53 (1897).

FULLER, C.J.

The act of 1794, which has been generally recognized as the first instance of municipal legislation in support of the obligations of neutrality.... And though [the] law of nations had been declared by Chief Justice Jay, in his charge to the grand jury at Richmond, May 22, 1793 (Whart. St. Tr. 49, 56), and by Mr. Justice Wilson, Mr. Justice Iredell, and Judge Peters, on the trial of Henfield in July of that year (Whart. St. Tr. 66, 84) to be capable of being enforced in the courts of the United States criminally, as well as civilly, without further legislation, yet it was deemed advisable to pass the act in view of controversy over that position, and, moreover, in order to provide a comprehensive code in prevention of acts by individuals....

Notes

1. By 1812, the United States Supreme Court had ruled that there were to be no "common law" crimes. See United States v. Hudson & Goodwin, 11 U.S. (7 Cranch) 32, 32–3 (1812); 1 Op. Att'y Gen. 209, 210 (1818) (same re: fraud case). In no such case, however, was there any mention of treaties or the law of nations. Further, as noted above, customary international law, although a part of the law of the land and common law, was considered to be more than mere common law, of a higher transnational status, and of significant federal concern and even constitutionally based. Recall the 1865 opinion of the Attorney General and the Supreme Court's dictum in United States v. Smith (1820), *supra*. Chief Justice Fuller, however, recognizes a prior "controversy" over the matter around 1794. Yet cases and opinions after that date (as noted above and in subsequent pages) continued to apply customary international law or to recognize its potential application without reference to a statute. In most cases since the early 1800s, however, criminal prosecution has also been supported by statute. Yet in some cases, U.S. courts allowed indictments alternatively under a statute or under the law of nations. For example in United States v. Hand, 26 F. Cas. 103 (C.C.D. Pa. 1810) (No. 15,297), the accused was found not guilty of an assault on the *chargé d' affaires* of Russia but had been indicted both under a statute and for "infracting the law of nations." For other relevant cases, *see, e.g.*, United States v. Liddle, 26 F. Cas. 936 (C.C.D.Pa.1808) (assault; statute & law of nations); *id.* at 938 (degree of punishment rests with the court); United States v. Ortega, 24 U.S. (11 Wheat.) 467 (1826) (circuit court has jurisdiction, not U.S. Supreme Court (because the victim was not an ambassador), over the defendant for violating law of nations by offering violence to the King of Spain's charge d' affairs—the defendant was indicted for "infracting the law of nations" and a statute).

2. There was certainly no mention of a controversy concerning direct incorporation of customary international law for criminal sanction purposes in Attorney General Lee's opinion of 1797 or in the following judicial opinion:

TALBOT v. JANSON

3 U.S. (3 Dall.) 133, 159–61 (1795).

IREDELL, J., concurring

. . . [A]ll piracies and trespasses committed against the general law of nations, are enquirable, and may be proceeded against, in any nation where no special exemption can be maintained, either by the general law of nations, or by some treaty which forbids or restrains it . . .

. . . [Such] is not merely an offence against the nation of the individual committing the injury, but also against the law of nations, and, of course, cognizable in other countries . . .

This is so palpable a violation of our own law (I mean the common law, of which the law of nations is a part, as it subsisted either before the act of Congress on the subject, or since that has provided a particular manner of enforcing it,) as well as the law of nations generally; that I cannot entertain the slightest doubt, but that upon the case of the libel, *prima facie*, the District Court has jurisdiction.

3. Consider also the following:

MORRIS v. UNITED STATES

161 F. 672, 675 (8th Cir.1908).

Without reviewing the authorities, as this would be but a work of supererogation, the following summary may be regarded as the settled law within the federal jurisdiction: (1) There are no crimes or offenses cognizable in the federal courts, outside of maritime or international law or treaties, except such as are created and defined by acts of Congress. . . .

14 **OP. ATT'Y GEN.** 249 (1873)

[A military tribunal convicted some Modoc Indians for law of war violations though Congress had not enacted a statute, the Attorney General adding:]

All the laws and customs of civilized warfare may not be applicable to an armed conflict with the Indian tribes upon our Western frontiers, but the circumstances attending the assassination of Canby and Thomas are such as to make their murder as much a violation of the laws of savage as of civilized warfare, and the Indians concerned in it fully understood the baseness and treachery of their act.

U.S. DEP'T OF ARMY FIELD MANUAL **FM 27–10, THE LAW OF LAND WARFARE**, para. 505(e) (1956)

Law Applied. As the international law of war is part of the law of the land in the United States, enemy personnel charged with war crimes are tried directly under international law without recourse to the statutes of the United States.

(2) TREATIES

Can a federally prosecutable crime be created by treaty alone, without additional domestic legislation? The answer hinges on whether the congressional power listed in Article I, § 8, cl. 10, to "define and punish" offenses against international law is an exclusive or concurrent power. If it is exclusive, Congress must exercise the power, since then "implementing legislation is constitutionally required." RESTATEMENT § 111 (4) (c) and cmt. i. If it is merely concurrent or shared, federally prosecutable crimes could be created by other directly operative law, such as a treaty, and treaties would not be inherently non-self-executing for criminal sanction purposes merely because a concurrent congressional power exists to enact relevant legislation. Today, most seem to think that a treaty cannot be directly operative for criminal prosecutions, and the editors are split on this issue. The Restatement adds: "An international agreement cannot ... [be self-executing] without implementation by Congress if the agreement would achieve what lies within the exclusive law-making power of Congress under the Constitution.... It has been commonly assumed that an international agreement ... could not itself become part of the criminal law of the United States, but would require Congress to enact an appropriate statute before an individual could be tried or punished for the offense." *Id.* cmt. i. For some, it is nevertheless arguable that the question remains open. In early cases such as *Respublica v. De Longchamps* and *Henfield's Case* (with three Supreme Court Justices in agreement), the direct incorporation of international law, without congressional or other implementing legislation, was entirely permissible and expected. Further, the Supreme Court has not specifically ruled on direct incorporation of treaties for criminal prosecutions. For different views, consider:

THE OVER THE TOP

5 F.2d 838, 845 (D.Conn.1925).

THOMAS, J.

In support of its contention, the government cites and relies upon *United States v. The Pictonian*, 3 F. (2d) 145, recently decided in the Eastern district of New York, where it was held that the American–British Treaty did, as to ships of British registry, extend the operation of the criminal laws of the United States to the shifting line designated in the treaty. I have carefully read Judge Campbell's opinion and find myself unable to agree with its reasoning. The learned judge speaks of the treaty as self-executing. The significance of the phrase in this connection is somewhat obscure. As a treaty, there was no need of congressional legislation to make it effective, and in this sense all treaties are self-executing. But if it was the intent of the government to make it a crime for a ship of British registry to unlade liquor within a sea zone on our coast, traversable in one hour, then that intent was not effectuated by the mere execution of the treaty. It is not the function of treaties to enact the fiscal or criminal law of a nation. For this purpose no treaty is self-executing. Congress may be under a duty to enact that which has been agreed upon by treaty, but duty and its performance are two separate and distinct things. Nor is there any doubt that the treaty making power has its limitations. What these are has never been defined, perhaps never need by defined. Certain it is that no part of the criminal law of this country has ever been enacted by treaty.

EDWARDS v. CARTER

580 F.2d 1055, 1057–58 (D.C.Cir.1978), *cert. denied*, 436 U.S. 907 (1978).

Per Curiam

The grant of authority to Congress under the property clause states that "The Congress shall have Power . . . ," *not* that only the Congress shall have power, or that Congress shall have *exclusive* power. In this respect the property clause is parallel to Article I, sec. 8, which also states that "The Congress shall have power. . . ."

Many of the powers thereafter enumerated in sec. 8 involve matters that were at the time the Constitution was adopted, and that are at the present time, also commonly the subject of treaties. The most prominent example of this is the regulation of commerce with foreign nations, Art. 1, sec. 8, cl. 3, and appellants do not go so far as to contend that the treaty process is not a constitutionally allowable means for regulating foreign commerce. It thus seems to us that, on its face, the property clause is intended not to restrict the scope of the treaty clause, but, rather, is intended to permit Congress to accomplish through legislation what may *concurrently* be accomplished through other means provided in the Constitution [*e.g.*, the treaty power].

Notes and Questions

1. How does the *Edwards* rationale add to inquiry whether Article I, § 8, cl. 10 is an exclusive or concurrent congressional power? If it is merely concurrent, and "the treaty process is . . . a constitutionally allowable means for regulating" international crime, what can follow? Recall *Henfield's Case*.

2. In the 1865 opinion of the Attorney General on the laws of war, *supra*, a difference was recognized between congressional power with respect to international crimes (*i.e.*, Congress has the power to "define" and not "to make") and ordinary federal crimes (*i.e.*, the power is "to make"). Does the nature of such powers provide guidance as to whether a treaty defining an international crime could be self-executing?

3. *See also* United States v. Kelly, 2 Extrater. Cases, 665, 669–70 (U.S.C. China 1923) (a treaty prohibiting contraband trade can be self-executing for criminal sanction purposes); Morris v. United States, 161 F. 672 (8th Cir. 1908), *supra*; United States v. Tiede (U.S. Ct. for Berlin 1979), *infra* in Section 2 C 1 d; United States v. Worrall, 2 U.S. (2 Dall.) 384, 391 (Chase, J.), 395 (Peters, J.) (C.C.D. Pa. 1798); *Henfield's Case, supra* (on direct incorporation of treaties); 1 Op. Att'y Gen. 57, 58 (1795) (violation of treaty).

4. Further references concerning this controversy include: Myres S. McDougal & Richard Arens, *The Genocide Convention and the Constitution*, 3 VAND. L. REV. 683, 690–91 (1950) (adding: "No good reason has been, or can be, given to justify treating this one particular power of the Congress, the power 'to define and punish ... offenses against the law of nations,' as exclusive...."); Jordan J. Paust, *Self-Executing Treaties*, 82 AM. J. INT'L L. 760 (1988), revised in JORDAN J. PAUST, INTERNATIONAL LAW AS LAW OF THE UNITED STATES chpt. 2 (2 ed. 2003) (the rediscovered predominant view of the Founders was that all treaties are self-executing (except those which, by their terms considered in context, are not) and such is the express language of Article VI, clause 2 of the Constitution. "Merely because the full Congress has an express power to make a law should not be relevant to inquiry whether a treaty is 'self-executing,' since the Senate and President also have an express power to make treaty law and each treaty is supreme law of the land. The mere existence of a concurrent power does not obviate either the existence or the exercise of another." One exception seems to be the congressional power to declare war.); Carlos M. Vásquez, *The Four Doctrines of Self-Executing Treaties*, 89 AM. J. INT'L L. 695 (1995).

5. If treaties are not inherently (constitutionally) non-self-executing for criminal sanction purposes because relevant congressional powers are not exclusive, the next question becomes whether or not a particular treaty is self-executing according to acceptable criteria (*e.g.*, using language of the treaty and intent of the signatories' tests). See also Jordan J. Paust, *Self-Executing Treaties, supra*; and RESTATEMENT § 111; this chapter, Section 2 C 1 c.

3. *Indirect Incorporation*

RODRIGUEZ–FERNANDEZ v. WILKINSON

654 F.2d 1382 (10th Cir.1981).

LOGAN, J.

This is an appeal from a decision of the district court granting a writ of habeas corpus, ordering immediate release of Pedro Rodriguez–Fernandez to the custody of an American citizen upon such conditions as the Attorney General of the United States may impose. Rodriguez–Fernandez is a Cuban national who arrived in the United States aboard the so-called Freedom Flotilla which carried approximately 125,000 people from Cuba to Key West, Florida. Petitioner arrived at Key West on June 2, 1980, seeking admission to this country as a refugee....

... Upon Cuba's refusal to accept petitioner, the Attorney General ordered his continued detention in the federal penitentiary at Leavenworth. He was incarcerated there in September 1980, when he filed the instant petition for a writ of habeas corpus. Thereafter, he was transferred to the United States Penitentiary in Atlanta, Georgia, where he is currently held with approximately 1,700 other excludable Cubans similarly situated.

By an order dated December 31, 1980, the district court held that Rodriguez–Fernandez has no rights to avoid detention under either the Fifth or Eighth Amendments to the United States Constitution. However, it held that the Attorney General's actions under the circumstances were arbitrary and an abuse of his discretion. It found that although the Attorney General's actions did not offend any statute, they violated principles of customary international law which create a right to be free from such detention. The order gave the government ninety days to release Rodriguez–Fernandez. The court later denied a government motion to reopen based upon the transfer of petitioner to Atlanta. On April 22, 1981, a compliance hearing was held with respect to its earlier order. The government reported that, exercising the discretionary parole power, representatives of the Attorney General determined Rodriguez–Fernandez to be releasable pursuant to 8 U.S.C. § 1182(d)(5). He had not been released, however, because of a suspension imposed by the new national administration of President Reagan to permit a reconsideration of government policies. The court was informed that the President had appointed a special task force due to file a report May 4, 1981, discussing, *inter alia*, what should be done with the excluded Cubans still being detained. It requested an additional sixty days to effect either the deportation or parole of Rodriguez–Fernandez. On April 23, 1981, the district court denied the government's request and ordered petitioner's release within twenty-four hours to the sponsorship of an American citizen living in Kansas City. From these orders the government has appealed....

Rodriguez–Fernandez has committed no offense against the United States; he has merely appeared on our shores as a member of the Freedom Flotilla seeking permission to immigrate. Yet, he has been confined in a maximum security federal prison, some of the time in solitary confinement, for more than a year.

The case presents unusual difficulties. The applicable statutes are vague with regard to the problem facing this Court. Also, the case law generally recognizes almost absolute power in Congress concerning immigration matters, holding that aliens in petitioner's position cannot invoke the Constitution to avoid exclusion and that detention pending deportation is only a continuation of exclusion rather than "punishment" in the constitutional sense.

In the instant case the detention is imprisonment under conditions as severe as we apply to our worst criminals. It is prolonged; perhaps it is permanent....

We dispose of the appeal by construing the applicable statutes to require Rodriguez–Fernandez' release at this time. Nevertheless, it seems important to discuss the serious constitutional questions involved if the statute were construed differently.

It is clear Rodriguez–Fernandez can invoke no constitutional protection against his exclusion from the United States. He may be excluded for considerations of race, politics, activities, or associations that would be constitutionally prohibited if he were a citizen. See Kleindienst v. Mandel, 408 U.S. 753 ... (1972); United States *ex rel.* Turner v. Williams, 194 U.S. 279 ... (1904); The Chinese Exclusion Case, 130 U.S. 581 ... (1889). He would fare no better if he were an alien resident in the United States. Harisiades v. Shaughnessy, 342 U.S. 580 ... (1952); Fong Yue Ting v. United States, 149 U.S. 698 ... (1893)....

Under the theory that Congress' power in this area is plenary and that, in any case, a deportation is not penal in nature, it has been held that normal criminal rights are inapplicable. Thus, aliens may be arrested by administrative warrant issued without the order of a magistrate, Abel v. United States, 362 U.S. 217 ... (1960), and may thereafter be held without bail. Carlson v. Landon, 342 U.S. 524 ... (1952). Nevertheless, if an alien in Rodriguez–Fernandez' position should be accused of committing a crime against the laws of this country, he would be entitled to the constitutional protections of the Fifth and Fourteenth Amendments. Yick Wo v. Hopkins, 118 U.S. 356 ... (1886), stated,

> "The Fourteenth Amendment to the Constitution is not confined to the protection of citizens. It says: 'Nor shall any State deprive any person of life, liberty or property without due process of law; nor deny to any person within its jurisdiction the equal protection of the laws.' These provisions are universal in their application, to all persons within the territorial jurisdiction, without regard to any difference of race, of color, or of nationality; and the equal protection of the laws is a pledge of the protection of equal laws."

118 U.S. at 369.... In Wong Wing v. United States, 163 U.S. 228 ... (1896), the Court extended this concept.

> "Applying this reasoning to the 5th and 6th Amendments, it must be concluded that all persons within the territory of the United States are entitled to the protection guaranteed by those amendments, and that even aliens shall not be held to answer for a capital or other infamous crime, unless on a presentment or indictment of a grand jury, nor be deprived of life, liberty, or property without due process of law."

163 U.S. at 238 ... The Court there struck down as unconstitutional a statute allowing administrative officials to arrest and imprison for up to one year Chinese found to be illegally within the country. The opinion quoted with apparent approval language from Fong Yue Ting v. United States, 149 U.S. 698 ... (1893), which declared orders of deportation are not punishment for crime, but distinguished "those provisions of the statute which contemplate only the exclusion or expulsion of Chinese persons and those which provide for their imprisonment at hard labor, pending which their deportation is suspended." 163 U.S. at 236....

Thus, it would appear that an excluded alien in physical custody within the United States may not be "punished" without being accorded the substantive and procedural due process guarantees of the Fifth Amendment. Surely Congress could not order the killing of Rodriguez–Fernandez and others in his status on the ground that Cuba would not take them back and this country does not want them. Even petitioner's property cannot be taken without just compensation, absent the existence of a state of war between the United States and his country. Russian Volunteer Fleet v. United States, 282 U.S. 481 ... (1931). Certainly imprisonment in a federal prison of one who has been neither charged nor convicted of a criminal offense is a deprivation of liberty in violation of the Fifth Amendment, except for the fiction applied to these cases that detention is only a continuation of the exclusion. This euphemistic fiction was created to accommodate the necessary detention of excludable and deportable aliens while their cases are considered and arrangements for expulsion are made....

... Due process is not a static concept, it undergoes evolutionary change to take into account accepted current notions of fairness. Finally, we note that in upholding the plenary power of Congress over exclusion and deportation of aliens, the Supreme Court has sought support in international law principles. *E.g.*, Fong Yue Ting v. United States, 149 U.S. 698 ... (1893). It seems proper then to consider international law principles for notions of fairness as to propriety of holding aliens in detention. No principle of international law is more fundamental than the concept that human beings should be free from arbitrary imprisonment. See Universal Declaration of Human Rights, Arts. 3 and 9, U.N. Doc. A/801 (1948); The American Convention on Human Rights, Part I, ch. II, Art. 7, 77 Dept. of State Bull. 28 (July 4, 1977). For these several reasons, we believe *Mezei* does not compel the conclusion that no constitutional problems inhere in petitioner's detention status....

... This construction [of the statute] is consistent with accepted international law principles that individuals are entitled to be free of arbitrary imprisonment. It is also consistent with the statutory treatment of deportable resident aliens and with the constitutional principles outlined above....

RESTATEMENT OF THE FOREIGN RELATIONS LAW OF THE UNITED STATES § 114 (3 ed. 1987).

Where fairly possible, a United States statute is to be construed so as not to conflict with international law or with an international agreement of the United States.

Notes and Questions

1. It was understood quite early that statutes must be interpreted so as to be consistent with international law. *See, e.g.*, The Charming Betsy, 6 U.S. (2 Cranch) 64, 117–18 (1804) ("An Act of Congress ought never to be construed to violate the law of nations if any other possible construction remains, and, consequently, can never be construed to violate ... rights ...

further than is warranted by the law of nations....''); Talbot v. Seeman, 5 U.S. (1 Cranch) 1, 43 (1801); 1 Op. Att'y Gen. 26, 27 (1792); *see also id.* at 53 (stating that the municipal law is strengthened by the law of nations); Ross v. Rittenhouse, 2 U.S. (2 Dall.) 160, 162 (Pa.1792); The Resolution, 2 U.S. (2 Dall.) 1, 4 (1781); 11 Op. Att'y Gen. 297, 299–300 (1865); 9 Op. Att'y Gen. 356, 362–63 (1859); The Ship Rose, 36 Ct.Cl. 290, 301 (1901); The Schooner Nancy, 27 Ct.Cl. 99, 109 (1892); Rutgers v. Waddington, Mayor's Court of the City of New York (1784) (cited in 2 AMERICAN LEGAL RECORDS, SELECT CASES OF THE MAYOR'S COURT OF NEW YORK CITY 1674–1784, at 302 (R. Morris ed. 1935)) (construing the 1783 N.Y. Trespass Act consistently with the Treaty of Peace), discussed in 1 THE LAW PRACTICE OF ALEXANDER HAMILTON 413–14 (J. Goebel ed. 1964); G. WOOD, THE CREATION OF THE AMERICAN REPUBLIC 1776–1787, at 457–58 (1969); United States v. Flores, 289 U.S. 137, 159 (1933) (''it is the duty of the courts of the United States to apply to offenses committed by its citizens on vessels flying its flag, its own statutes, interpreted in light of recognized principles of international law.''); *but see* Mississippi Poultry Ass'n, Inc. v. Madigan, 992 F.2d 1359, 1367 (5th Cir.1993) (''loath ... to extend this maxim to multi-lateral trade agreements.''); United States v. Yunis, 924 F.2d 1086, 1091 (D.C.Cir.1991) (dictum: duty of courts merely to enforce statutes, ''not to conform'' them ''to norms of customary international law'').

2. Today, this rule of construction has been retained by the Supreme Court. Additionally, there has been built into such a rule a stronger primacy for international treaty law, since an unavoidable clash between a treaty and an act of Congress will not even arise unless there is a clear and unequivocal evidence of congressional intent to supersede the treaty. *See, e.g.*, Spector v. Norwegian Cruise Line, Ltd., 125 S.Ct. 2169, 2185 (2005) (Ginsburg, J., concurring); Trans World Airlines, Inc. v. Franklin Mint Corp., 466 U.S. 243, 252 (1984); McCulloch v. Sociedad Nacional de Marineros de Honduras, 372 U.S. 10, 21–22 (1963); Cook v. United States, 288 U.S. 102, 120 (1933); United States v. Payne, 264 U.S. 446, 448 (1924); Chew Heong v. United States, 112 U.S. 536, 539–40, 549–50 (1884); Roeder v. Islamic Republic of Iran, 195 F.Supp.2d 140, 166, 168–70 (D.D.C. 2002) (Executive Agreement formed in the Algiers Accords governs despite subsequent amendment of the FSIA where there is no clear unequivocal intent of Congress to override the Executive Agreement); Beharry v. Reno, 183 F. Supp.2d 584, 593–602 (E.D.N.Y. 2002) (regarding statutory construction consistent with the ICCPR and other international law); United States v. The Palestine Liberation Organization, 695 F.Supp. 1456, 1465, 1468 (S.D.N.Y.1988); JORDAN J. PAUST, INTERNATIONAL LAW AS LAW OF THE UNITED STATES 43–44, 99, 120, 124–25, 127 (2 ed. 2003). Weinberger v. Rossi, 456 U.S. 25, 32 (1982), applied the same approach with respect to an Executive Agreement.

The U.S. Constitution has also been interpreted consistently with international law, especially with regard to basic human rights. *See, e.g., id.* at 34, 83, 99, 105, 108, 193–95, 198, 212–13, 242–45, 248–56, 310, 314, 369–72, 377, 418, 478. In Finzer v. Barry, 798 F.2d 1450, 1463 (D.C.Cir.1986), *rev'd in part and aff'd in part sub nom.*, Boos v. Barry, 485 U.S. 312 (1988), it was stated that it has never ''been suggested that the First Amendment is incompatible with the United States' most basic obligations under the law of nations. The two must be accommodated....'' [see also extract below in

Section 2 B 4 a] In 1814, the Supreme Court recognized that "[i]n expounding ... [the U.S.] constitution, a construction ought not lightly to be admitted which would" produce an effect contrary to or "which would fetter" results under customary international law. Brown v. United States, 12 U.S. (8 Cranch) 110, 125 (1814). *See also* United States v. Caicedo, 47 F.3d 370 (9th Cir. 1995), *infra*; and Section 2 B 5 on enhancement of congressional and executive powers; and recall materials on limitations and enhancement of judicial power.

3. When an unavoidable clash occurs between international law and a federal statute, see Section 2 E, below.

4. Advisory opinions and decisions in cases by the International Court of Justice have had an influence domestically within the United States, especially as relevant evidence of the content of international law. Since the creation of the I.C.J. in 1945, more than forty-two cases in federal courts have applied more than fifteen advisory opinions or decisions to identify or clarify international legal norms–most in the 1980s. This influence has occurred despite the fact that there is no formal *stare decisis* with respect to I.C.J. decisions and they are technically binding only on the parties to a case before the I.C.J. *See* Statute of the I.C.J. arts. 38 (1) (d), 59. Also of interest is the fact that the precursor to the I.C.J., the Permanent Court of International Justice under the League of Nations, has been cited similarly in eighteen federal cases from the 1930s through the 1990s, mostly in the 1980s. Such indirect incorporation of opinions and decisions of the international courts has occurred with respect to a wide array of normative subjects. For actual trends and patterns of use, *see, e.g.*, Jordan J. Paust, *Domestic Influence of the International Court of Justice*, 26 DENV. J. INT'L L. & POL. 787 (1998).

5. Concerning trends and patterns of use by U.S. courts of human rights precepts throughout U.S. history, *see, e.g.*, Jordan J. Paust, *On Human Rights: The Use of Human Rights Precepts in U.S. History and the Right to an Effective Remedy in Domestic Courts*, 10 MICH. J. INT'L L. 543 (1989), revised in JORDAN J. PAUST, INTERNATIONAL LAW AS LAW OF THE UNITED STATES chpt. 5 (2 ed. 2003).

4. *Incorporation by Reference*

a. *General Issues*

If a statute refers to "treaties" or to the "law of nations," would such a terse reference be a constitutionally sufficient exercise of congressional power to "define and punish"—or a vague and improper attempt at incorporation of international law for criminal sanction purposes?

UNITED STATES v. SMITH

18 U.S. (5 Wheat.) 153, 158–62 (1820).

[Editors' note: Smith was being prosecuted for acts of piracy under federal legislation that simply incorporated piracy by reference. Then, as now, relevant U.S. federal legislation simply refers to piracy "under the law of nations." See 18 U.S.C. § 1651. Smith challenged the constitutionality of the statute. Interestingly, Canadian legislation also refers to "any act that, by the law of nations, is piracy." See Criminal Code of Canada, Sec. 74. (1).]

STORY, J.

The first point made at the bar is, whether this enactment be a constitutional exercise of the authority delegated to Congress upon the subject of piracies. The constitution declares that Congress shall have power "to define and punish piracies and felonies committed on the high seas, and offenses against the law of nations." The argument which has been urged in behalf of the prisoner is, that Congress is bound to define, in terms, the offense of piracy, and is not at liberty to leave it to be ascertained by judicial interpretation. If the argument be well founded, it seems admitted by the counsel that it equally applies to the 8th section of the act of Congress of 1790, ch. 9, which declares, that robbery and murder committed on the high seas shall be deemed piracy; and yet, notwithstanding a series of contested adjudications on this section, no doubt has hitherto been breathed of its conformity to the constitution.

In our judgment, the construction contended for proceeds upon too narrow a view of the language of the constitution. The power given to Congress is not merely "to define and punish piracy;" if it were, the words "to define" would seem almost superfluous, since the power to punish piracies would be held to include the power of ascertaining and fixing the definition of the crime. And it has been very justly observed, in a celebrated commentary, that the definition of piracies might have been left without inconvenience to the law of nations, though a legislative definition of them is to be found in most municipal codes. But the power is also given "to define and punish felonies on the high seas, and offenses against the law of nations." The term "felonies" has been supposed, in the same work, not to have a very exact and determinate meaning in relation to offenses at the common law committed within the body of a county. However this may be, in relation to offenses on the high seas, it is necessarily somewhat indeterminate, since the term is not used in the criminal jurisprudence of the admiralty in the technical sense of the common law. Offenses, too, against the law of nations, cannot, with any accuracy, be said to be completely ascertained and defined in any public code recognized by the common consent of nations. In respect, therefore, as well to felonies on the high seas as to offenses against the law of nations, there is a peculiar fitness in giving the power to define as well as to punish; and there is not the slightest reason to doubt that this consideration had very great weight in producing the phraseology in question.

But supposing Congress were bound in all the cases included in the clause under consideration to define the offense, still there is nothing which restricts it to a mere logical enumeration in detail of all the facts constituting the offense. Congress may as well define by using a term of a known and determinate meaning as by an express enumeration of all the particulars included in that term. That is certain which is by necessary reference made certain. When the act of 1790 declares, that any person who shall commit the crime of robbery, or murder, on the high seas, shall be deemed a pirate, the crime is not less clearly ascertained than it would be by using the definitions of these terms as they are found in our treatises of the common law. In fact, by such a reference, the definitions are necessarily included, as much as if they stood in the text of the act. In respect to murder, where "malice aforethought" is of the essence of the offense, even if the common law definition were quoted in express terms, we should still be driven to deny that the definition was perfect, since the meaning of "malice aforethought" would remain to be gathered from the common law. There would then be no end to our difficulties, or our definitions, for each would involve some terms which might still require some new explanation. Such a construction of the constitution is, therefore, wholly inadmissible. To define piracies, in the sense of the constitution, is merely to enumerate the crimes which shall constitute piracy; and this may be done either by a reference to crimes having a technical name, and determinate extent, or by enumerating the acts in detail, upon which the punishment is inflicted.

It is next to be considered, whether the crime of piracy is defined by the law of nations with reasonable certainty. What the law of nations on this subject is, may be ascertained by consulting the works of jurists, writing professedly on public law; or by the general usage and practice of nations; or by judicial decisions recognizing and enforcing that law. There is scarcely a writer on the law of nations who does not allude to piracy as a crime of a settled and determinate nature; and whatever may be the diversity of definitions, in other respects, all writers concur in holding that robbery, or forcible depredations upon the sea, *animo furandi*, is piracy. The same doctrine is held by all the great writers on maritime law, in terms that admit of no reasonable doubt. The common law, too, recognizes and punishes piracy as an offense, not against its own municipal code, but as an offense against the law of nations (which is part of the common law), as an offense against the universal law of society, a pirate being deemed an enemy of the human race.... And it is manifest from the language of Sir William Blackstone, in his comments on piracy, that he considered the common law definition as distinguishable in no essential respect from that of the law of nations. So that, whether we advert to writers on the common law, or the maritime law, or the law of nations, we shall find that they universally treat of piracy as an offense against the law of nations, and that its true definition by that law is robbery upon the sea. And the general practice of all nations in punishing all persons, whether natives or foreigners, who have committed this offense against any persons whatsoever, with whom they are in amity, is a conclusive proof that the offense is supposed to depend, not upon the particular provisions of any municipal code, but upon the law of nations, both for its definition and punishment. We have, therefore, no hesitation in declaring that piracy, by the law of nations, is robbery upon the sea, and that it is sufficiently and constitutionally defined by the fifth section of the act of 1819.

EX PARTE QUIRIN

317 U.S. 1, 27–30 (1942).

STONE, C.J.

[Editors' note: Habeas petitioners were individuals born in Germany who had lived in the U.S. and returned to Germany by 1933, one of whom claimed U.S. citizenship by virtue of naturalization of his parents when he was five years old. They had been trained in a "sabotage school near Berlin" and were members of one of two teams that had been transported by submarine to the U.S., had landed during darkness "with explosives, fuses, and incendiary and timing devices," had worn German military uniforms or parts thereof upon landing but immediately proceeded "in civilian dress" from landing sites at Amagansett Beach on Long Island, New York, and Ponte Verde Beach, Florida; and had traveled either to New York City or through Jacksonville, Florida to other points within the U.S., and who were captured by the F.B.I. in New York or Chicago. The President of the U.S. created a Military Commission by Order of July 2, 1942, to try them for violations of the laws of war (including efforts to engage in combat acts of sabotage out of uniform), violation of Article 81 of the 1916 Articles of War (concerning provision of intelligence to the enemy), violation of Article 82 of the Articles of War (concerning spying out of uniform), and conspiracy with respect to the above. Petitioners claimed "that the President is without statutory or constitutional authority to order the petitioners to be tried by military tribunal for offenses ... charged; that in consequence they are entitled to be tried in the civil courts," with a jury trial, and that the procedure and method for review of the military tribunal conflict with the Articles of War as adopted by Congress "and are illegal and void." The Supreme Court denied each claim.]

From the very beginning of its history this Court has recognized and applied the law of war as including that part of the law of nations which prescribes, for the conduct of war, the status, rights and duties of enemy nations as well as of enemy individuals. By the [1916] Articles of War, and especially Article 15, Congress has explicitly provided, so far as it may constitutionally do so, that military tribunals shall have jurisdiction to try offenders or offenses against the law of war in appropriate cases. Congress, in addition to making rules for the government of our Armed Forces, has thus exercised its authority to define and punish offenses against the law of nations by sanctioning, within constitutional limitations, the jurisdiction of military commissions to try persons for offenses which, according to the rules and precepts of the law of nations, and more particularly the law of war, are cognizable by such tribunals. And the President, as Commander in Chief, by his Proclamation in time of war has invoked that law. By his Order creating the present Commission he has undertaken to exercise the authority conferred upon him by

Congress, and also such authority as the Constitution itself gives the Commander in Chief, to direct the performance of those functions which may constitutionally be performed by the military arm of the nation in time of war.

An important incident to the conduct of war is the adoption of measures by the military command not only to repel and defeat the enemy, but to seize and subject to disciplinary measures those enemies who in their attempt to thwart or impede our military effort have violated the law of war. It is unnecessary for present purposes to determine to what extent the President as Commander in Chief has constitutional power to create military commissions without the support of congressional legislation. For here Congress has authorized trial of offenses against the law of war before such commissions. We are concerned only with the question whether it is within the constitutional power of the national government to place petitioners upon trial before a military commission for the offenses with which they are charged. We must therefore first inquire whether any of the acts charged is an offense against the law of war cognizable before a military tribunal, and if so whether the Constitution prohibits the trial. We may assume that there are acts regarded in other countries, or by some writers on international law, as offenses against the law of war which would not be triable by military tribunal here, either because they are not recognized by our courts as violations of the law of war or because they are of that class of offenses constitutionally triable only by a jury. It was upon such grounds that the Court denied the right to proceed by military tribunal in *Ex parte Milligan, supra.* But as we shall show, these petitioners were charged with an offense against the law of war which the Constitution does not require to be tried by jury.

It is no objection that Congress in providing for the trial of such offenses has not itself undertaken to codify that branch of international law or to mark its precise boundaries, or to enumerate or define by statute all the acts which that law condemns. An Act of Congress punishing "the crime of piracy as defined by the law of nations" is an appropriate exercise of this constitutional authority, Art. I, sec. 8, cl. 10, "to define and punish" the offense since it has adopted by reference the sufficiently precise definition of international law. United States v. Smith, 5 Wheat. 153 ...; see The Marianna Flora, 11 Wheat. 1, 40, 41 ...; United States v. The Malek Adhel, 2 How. 210, 232 ...; The Ambrose Light, D.C., 25 F. 408, 423, 428; 18 U.S.C. § 481, 18 U.S.C.A. § 481. Similarly by the reference in the 15th Article of War to "offenders or offenses that ... by the law of war may be triable by such military commissions", Congress has incorporated by reference, as within the jurisdiction of military commissions, all offenses which are defined as such by the law of war (compare Dynes v. Hoover, 20 How. 65, 82 ...), and which may constitutionally be included within that jurisdiction. Congress had the choice of crystallizing in permanent form and in minute detail every offense against the law of war, or of adopting the system of common law applied by military tribunals so far as it should be recognized and deemed applicable by the courts. It chose the latter course.

Notes and Questions

1. Chapter 9 of the Act of Congress of 1790 also made it a crime to "assault, strike, wound, imprison, or in any other manner infract the law of nations, by offering violence to the person of an ambassador or other public minister." Ch. 9, § 28, 1 Stat. 112, 118. In 1782, Connecticut had criminalized certain specific violations of the law of nations as well as "any other Infractions or Violations of or Offences against the known received and established Laws of Civilized Nations." See William R. Casto, Correspondence, 83 Am. J. Int'l L. 901, 903 (1989).

Incorporation by reference is also evident with respect to civil sanctions. Consider the Alien Tort Claims Act (ATCA), 28 U.S.C. § 1350. Cases using this statute also appear in Section 2 D 2 and 3.

2. There had been no statute incorporating the laws of war until the 1916 Articles of War addressed in *Ex parte Quirin*. Nonetheless, as the Court recognized, the laws of war formed the basis for criminal sanctions, as well as for other legal matters, since the beginning of the United States. *See also* Jordan J. Paust, M. Cherif Bassiouni, *et al.*, International Criminal Law 261–66, 278–83, 286–87 (2 ed. 2000). Today, 10 U.S.C. §§ 818, 821 perform the same incorporating role as the older Articles of War. § 818 states: "General courts-martial also have jurisdiction to try any person who by the law of war is subject to trial by a military tribunal and may adjudge any punishment permitted by the law of war. . . ."

Does the incorporation of the laws of war as domestic U.S. criminal offenses also implicate federal district court jurisdiction under 18 U.S.C. § 3231, which states: "The district courts of the United States shall have original jurisdiction, exclusive of the courts of the States, of all offenses against the laws of the United States"? See Paust, Bassiouni, *et al.*, *supra* at 253–61; Jordan J. Paust, *After My Lai: The Case for War Crime Jurisdiction Over Civilians in Federal District Courts*, 50 Tex. L. Rev. 6 (1971). If so, the United States can prosecute civilians who are not otherwise subject to the jurisdiction of U.S. military tribunals in the federal district courts.

3. When Congress has exercised its power "to define and punish" under Article I, sec. 8, cl. 10 of the Constitution, how have relevant offenses been described or categorized, as offenses "against the United States," as offenses "against the Laws of the United States," or as offenses against the law of nations or law of war? *See, e.g.,* United States v. Arjona, 120 U.S. 479, 488 (1887); *Ex parte* Quirin, 317 U.S. 1, 27–30 (1942); United States v. Smith, 18 U.S. (5 Wheat.) 153, 158–62 (1820); *see also* United States v. Haun, 26 F. Cas. 227 (C.C.S.D.Ala.1860) (No. 15,329); 11 Op. Att'y Gen. 297, 299–300 (1865) [*supra*]; *cf.* An Act for the Punishment of Certain Crimes Against the United States, sec. 28, 1 Stat. 112, 118 (1790) (making it a crime to "assault, strike, wound, imprison, or in any manner infract the law of nations, by offering violence to the person of an ambassador or other public minister").

4. What should be included within the phrase "offenses against the laws of the United States" in 18 U.S.C. § 3231? Should the statute operate

like that considered in *Ex parte Quirin* so as to incorporate offenses under international law more generally?

THE WAR CRIMES ACT

18 U.S.C. § 2441 (2003).

(a) Offense. Whoever, whether inside or outside the United States, commits a war crime, in any of the circumstances described in subsection (b), shall be fined under this title or imprisoned for life or any term of years, or both, and if death results to the victim, shall also be subject to the penalty of death.

(b) Circumstances. The circumstances referred to in subsection (a) are that the person committing such war crime or the victim of such war crime is a member of the Armed Forces of the United States or a national of the United States (as defined in section 101 of the Immigration and Nationality Act [8 U.S.C. § 1101].

(c) Definition. As used in this section the term "war crime" means any conduct–

(1) defined as a grave breach in any of the international conventions signed at Geneva 12 August 1949, or any protocol to such convention to which the United States is a party;

(2) prohibited by Article 23, 25, 27, or 28 of the Annex to the Hague Convention IV, Respecting the Laws and Customs of War on Land, signed 18 October 1907;

(3) which constitutes a violation of common Article 3 of the international conventions signed at Geneva, 12 August 1949, or any protocol to such convention to which the United States is a party and deals with non-international armed conflict; or

(4) of a person who, in relation to an armed conflict and contrary to the provisions of the Protocol on Prohibitions or Restrictions on the Use of Mines, Booby–Traps and Other Devices as amended at Geneva on 3 May 1996 (Protocol II as amended on 3 May 1996), when the United States is a party to such Protocol, willfully kills or causes serious injury to civilians.

Notes and Questions

1. There are four 1949 Geneva Conventions: Geneva Convention for the Amelioration of the Condition of the Wounded and Sick in Armed Forces in the Field, 12 August 1949, 75 U.N.T.S. 31; Geneva Convention for the Amelioration of the Condition of Wounded, Sick and Shipwrecked Members of Armed Forces at Sea, 12 August 1949, 75 U.N.T.S. 85; Geneva Convention Relative to the Treatment of Prisoners of War, 12 August 1949, 75 U.N.T.S. 135 [hereinafter GPW]; Geneva Convention Relative to the Protection of Civilian Persons in Time of War, 12 August 1949, 75 U.N.T.S. 287 [hereinafter GC and Geneva Civilian Convention]. Each convention has an article

identifying "grave breaches" of that convention. Those concerning GPW and GC follow:

GPW, art. 130: Grave breaches to which the preceding Article relates shall be those involving any of the following acts, if committed against persons or property protected by the Convention: wilful killing, torture or inhuman treatment, including biological experiments, wilfully causing great suffering or serious injury to body or health, compelling a prisoner of war to serve in the forces of the hostile power or wilfully depriving a prisoner of war of the rights of fair and regular trial prescribed in this Convention.

GC, art. 147: Grave breaches to which the preceding Article relates shall be those involving any of the following acts, if committed against persons or property protected by the present Convention: wilful killing, torture or inhuman treatment, including biological experiments, wilfully causing great suffering or serious injury to body or health, unlawful deportation or transfer or unlawful confinement of a protected person, compelling a protected person to serve in the forces of a hostile Power or wilfully depriving a protected person of the rights of fair and regular trial prescribed in the present Convention, taking of hostages and extensive destruction and appropriation of property, not justified by military necessity and carried out unlawfully and wantonly.

2. Note that the new legislation generally incorporates Geneva provisions by reference. Many other states also incorporate the laws of war, crimes against humanity, and genocide by reference. *See, e.g.,* Jordan J. Paust, *It's No Defense:* Nullum Crimen, *International Crime and the Gingerbread Man,* 60 ALBANY L. REV. 657 (1997) (addressing legislation in Australia, Bangladesh, Belgium, Canada, Ethiopia, Finland, France, Germany, Great Britain, Israel, Mexico, the Netherlands, Sweden, Yugoslavia); *cf.* Christopher Blakesley, Report, *reprinted in* 25 DENV. J. INT'L L. & POL. 233 (1997); Edward Wise, Report, *id.* at 313. What are some of the customary types of crimes against humanity that exist in the Charters of the International Military Tribunals at Nuremberg and at Tokyo, in the Documents Supplement? Would al Qaeda attacks on the World Trade Center in New York in 2001 fit within the definitions? Would they fit within Article 7 of the Rome Statute of the ICC?

3. Under the new legislation, is it possible to prosecute former Nazis accused of war crimes? Is it possible to prosecute Bosnian–Serbs accused of war crimes committed against other Bosnians?

4. Article 146 of the 1949 Geneva Convention Relative to the Protection of Civilian Persons in Time of War, 75 U.N.T.S. 287, creates an obligation "to enact any legislation necessary to provide effective penal sanctions for persons committing . . . any . . . grave breaches"? Has the new legislation met that obligation? How might those accused not covered by the new legislation be prosecuted for violations of the laws of war in the United States?

5. Is it possible under the new legislation for the U.S. to comply with another obligation in Article 146 of the Geneva Civilian Convention to "take measures necessary for the suppression of all acts contrary to the . . . Convention other than grave breaches"? How can these be prosecuted?

b. Judicial Review of Executive Detention of "Terrorists" Without Trial

Recall the recognition of the U.S. Supreme Court in *Ex parte Quirin* of judicial power from the very beginning of U.S. history to determine the status, rights, and duties of individuals under the laws of war. After the attacks by members of al Qaeda on the World Trade Center in New York and the Pentagon on September 11, 2001, the Bush Administration made claims that the Executive has an unreviewable power to detain persons without trial in a so-called "war" against "terrorism." Numerous decisions of the Supreme Court and other federal courts demonstrate that this is not correct. *See, e.g.*, Jordan J. Paust, *Judicial Power To Determine the Status and Rights of Persons Detained Without Trial*, 44 HARV. INT'L L.J. 503, 518–25 (2003). Nonetheless, does the Executive have power to detain persons without trial under the laws of war when such laws are relevant to a war in Afghanistan and Iraq? Does the Executive have a relevant delegated power from Congress? If either type of power to detain exists, under what sort of standards is such detention reviewable by the judiciary? Consider the following two Supreme Court cases.

HAMDI v. RUMSFELD

542 U.S. 507 (2004).

O'CONNOR, J.

At this difficult time in our Nation's history, we are called upon to consider the legality of the Government's detention of a United States citizen on United States soil as an "enemy combatant" and to address the process that is constitutionally owed to one who seeks to challenge his classification as such. The United States Court of Appeals for the Fourth Circuit held that petitioner's detention was legally authorized and that he was entitled to no further opportunity to challenge his enemy-combatant label. We now vacate and remand. We hold that although Congress authorized the detention of combatants in the narrow circumstances alleged here, due process demands that a citizen held in the United States as an enemy combatant be given a meaningful opportunity to contest the factual basis for that detention before a neutral decisionmaker.

I

On September 11, 2001, the al Qaeda terrorist network used hijacked commercial airliners to attack prominent targets in the United States. Approximately 3,000 people were killed in those attacks. One week later, in response to these "acts of treacherous violence," Congress passed a resolution authorizing the President to "use all necessary and appropriate force against those nations, organizations, or persons he determines planned, authorized, committed, or aided the terrorist attacks" or "harbored such organizations or persons, in order to prevent any future acts of international terrorism against the United States by such nations, organizations or persons." Authorization for Use of Military Force ("the AUMF"), 115 Stat. 224 [Editors' note: the authorization is reproduced here in Chapter 8, Section B] Soon thereafter, the President ordered United States Armed Forces to Afghanistan, with a mission to subdue al Qaeda and quell the Taliban regime that was known to support it.

This case arises out of the detention of a man whom the Government alleges took up arms with the Taliban during this conflict. His name is Yaser Esam Hamdi. Born an American citizen in Louisiana in 1980, Hamdi moved with his family to Saudi Arabia as a child. By 2001, the parties agree, he resided in Afghanistan. At some point that year, he was seized by members of the Northern Alliance, a coalition of military groups opposed to the Taliban government, and eventually was turned over to the United States military. The Government asserts that it initially detained and interrogated Hamdi in Afghanistan before transferring him to the United States Naval Base in Guantanamo Bay in January 2002. In April 2002, upon learning that Hamdi is an American citizen, authorities transferred him to a naval brig in Norfolk, Virginia, where he remained until a recent transfer to a brig in Charleston, South Carolina. The Government contends that Hamdi is an "enemy combatant," and that this status justifies holding him in the United States indefinitely–without formal charges or proceedings–unless and until it makes the determination that access to counsel or further process is warranted....

On the more global question of whether legal authorization exists for the detention of citizen enemy combatants at all, the Fourth Circuit rejected Hamdi's arguments that 18 U.S.C. § 4001(a) and Article 5 of the Geneva Convention rendered any such detentions unlawful. The court expressed doubt as to Hamdi's argument that § 4001(a), which provides that "[n]o citizen shall be imprisoned or otherwise detained by the United States except pursuant to an Act of Congress," required express congressional authorization of detentions of this sort. But it held that, in any event, such authorization was found in the post-September 11 Authorization for Use of Military Force. 316 F.3d, at 467. Because "capturing and detaining enemy combatants is an inherent part of warfare," the court held, "the 'necessary and appropriate force' referenced in the congressional resolution necessarily includes the capture and detention of any and all hostile forces arrayed against our troops." *Ibid.*; see also *id.*, at 467–468 (noting that Congress, in 10 U.S.C. § 956(5), had specifically authorized the expenditure of funds for keeping prisoners of war and persons whose status was determined "to be similar to prisoners of war," and concluding that this appropriation measure also demonstrated that Congress had "authorized [these individuals'] detention in the first instance"). The court likewise rejected Hamdi's Geneva Convention claim, concluding that the convention is not self-executing and that, even if it were, it would not preclude the Executive from detaining Hamdi until the cessation of hostilities. 316 F.3d, at 468–469.

Finally, the Fourth Circuit rejected Hamdi's contention that its legal analyses with regard to the authorization for the detention scheme and the process to which he was constitutionally entitled should be altered by the fact that he is an American citizen detained on American soil. Relying on *Ex parte* Quirin, 317 U.S. 1 . . . (1942), the court emphasized that "[o]ne who takes up arms against the United States in a foreign theater of war, regardless of his citizenship, may properly be designated an enemy combatant and treated as such." 316 F.3d, at 475. "The privilege of citizenship," the court held, "entitles Hamdi to a limited judicial inquiry into his detention, but only to determine its legality under the war powers of the political branches. At least where it is undisputed that he was present in a zone of active combat operations, we are satisfied that the Constitution does not entitle him to a searching review of the factual determinations underlying his seizure there." *Ibid.*

The Fourth Circuit denied rehearing en banc, 337 F.3d 335 (C.A.4 2003), and we granted certiorari. 540 U.S. 1099 . . . (2004). We now vacate the judgment below and remand.

II

The threshold question before us is whether the Executive has the authority to detain citizens who qualify as "enemy combatants." There is some debate as to the proper scope of this term, and the Government has never provided any court with the full criteria that it uses in classifying individuals as such. It has made clear, however, that, for purposes of this case, the "enemy combatant" that it is seeking to detain is an individual who, it alleges, was " 'part of or supporting forces hostile to the United States or coalition partners' "in Afghanistan and who " 'engaged in an armed conflict against the United States' "there. Brief for Respondents 3. We therefore answer only the narrow question before us: whether the detention of citizens falling within that definition is authorized.

The Government maintains that no explicit congressional authorization is required, because the Executive possesses plenary authority to detain pursuant to Article II of the Constitution. We do not reach the question whether Article II provides such authority, however, because we agree with the Government's alternative position, that Congress has in fact authorized Hamdi's detention, through the AUMF.

Our analysis on that point, set forth below, substantially overlaps with our analysis of Hamdi's principal argument for the illegality of his detention. He posits that his detention is forbidden by 18 U.S.C. § 4001(a). Section 4001(a) states that "[n]o citizen shall be imprisoned or otherwise detained by the United States except pursuant to an Act of Congress." Congress passed § 4001(a) in 1971 as part of a bill to repeal the Emergency Detention Act of 1950, 50 U.S.C. § 811 *et seq.*, which provided procedures for executive detention, during times of emergency, of individuals deemed likely to engage in espionage or sabotage. Congress was particularly concerned about the possibility that the Act could be used to reprise the Japanese internment camps of World War II. H.R.Rep. No. 92–116 (1971); *id.,* at 4, U.S.Code Cong. & Admin.News 1971, 1435, 1438 ("The concentration camp implications of the legislation render it abhorrent"). The Government again presses two alternative positions. First, it argues that § 4001(a), in light of its legislative history and its location in Title 18, applies only to "the control of civilian prisons and related detentions," not to military detentions. Brief for Respondents 21. Second, it maintains that § 4001(a) is satisfied, because Hamdi is being detained "pursuant to an Act of Congress"—the AUMF. *Id.,* at 21–22. Again, because we conclude that the Government's second assertion is correct, we do not address the first. In other words, for the reasons that follow, we conclude that the AUMF is explicit congressional authorization for the detention of individuals in the narrow category we describe (assuming, without deciding, that such authorization is required), and that the AUMF satisfied § 4001(a)'s requirement that a detention be "pursuant to an Act of Congress" (assuming, without deciding, that § 4001(a) applies to military detentions).

The AUMF authorizes the President to use "all necessary and appropriate force" against "nations, organizations, or persons" associated with the September 11, 2001, terrorist attacks. 115 Stat. 224. There can be no doubt that individuals who fought against the United States in Afghanistan as part of the Taliban, an organization known to have supported the al Qaeda terrorist network responsible for those attacks, are individuals Congress sought to target in passing the AUMF. We conclude that detention of individuals falling into the limited category we are considering, for the duration of the particular conflict in which they were captured, is so fundamental and accepted an incident to war as to be an exercise of the "necessary and appropriate force" Congress has authorized the President to use.

The capture and detention of lawful combatants and the capture, detention, and trial of unlawful combatants, by "universal agreement and practice," are "important incident[s] of war." *Ex parte* Quirin, 317 U.S., at 28. The purpose of detention is to prevent captured individuals from returning to the field of battle and taking up arms once again. . . .

There is no bar to this Nation's holding one of its own citizens as an enemy combatant. In *Quirin,* one of the detainees, Haupt, alleged that he was a naturalized United States citizen. 317 U.S., at 20. We held that "[c]itizens who associate themselves with the military arm of the enemy government, and with its aid, guidance and direction enter this country bent on hostile acts, are enemy belligerents within the meaning of ... the law of war." *Id.,* at 37–38. . . . A citizen, no less than an alien, can be "part of or supporting forces hostile to the United States or coalition partners" and "engaged in an armed conflict against the United States," Brief for Respondents 3; such a citizen, if released, would pose the same threat of returning to the front during the ongoing conflict.

In light of these principles, it is of no moment that the AUMF does not use specific language of detention. Because detention to prevent a combatant's return to the battlefield is a fundamental incident of waging war, in permitting the use of "necessary and appropriate force," Congress has clearly and unmistakably authorized detention in the narrow circumstances considered here.

Hamdi objects, nevertheless, that Congress has not authorized the *indefinite* detention to which he is now subject.... The prospect Hamdi raises is therefore not far-fetched. If the Government does not consider this unconventional war won for two generations, and if it maintains during that time that Hamdi might, if released, rejoin forces fighting against the United States, then the position it has taken throughout the litigation of this case suggests that Hamdi's detention could last for the rest of his life.

It is a clearly established principle of the law of war that detention may last no longer than active hostilities. See Article 118 of the Geneva Convention (III) Relative to the Treatment of Prisoners of War, Aug. 12, 1949, [1955] 6 U.S.T. 3316, 3406, T.I.A.S. No. 3364 ("Prisoners of war shall be released and repatriated without delay after the cessation of active hostilities"). See also Article 20 of the Hague Convention (II) on Laws and Customs of War on Land, July 29, 1899, 32 Stat. 1817 (as soon as possible after "conclusion of peace"); Hague Convention (IV), *supra,* Oct. 18, 1907, 36 Stat. 2301("conclusion of peace" (Art. 20)); Geneva Convention, *supra,* July 27, 1929, 47 Stat.2055 (repatriation should be accomplished with the least possible delay after conclusion of peace (Art. 75)); Paust, *Judicial Power to Determine the Status and Rights of Persons Detained without Trial*, 44 HARV. INT'L L.J. 503, 510–511 (2003) (prisoners of war "can be detained during an armed conflict, but the detaining country must release and repatriate them 'without delay after the cessation of active hostilities,' unless they are being lawfully prosecuted or have been lawfully convicted of crimes and are serving sentences" (citing Arts. 118, 85, 99, 119, 129, Geneva Convention (III) ... [GPW])).

Hamdi contends that the AUMF does not authorize indefinite or perpetual detention. Certainly, we agree that indefinite detention for the purpose of interrogation is not authorized. Further, we understand Congress' grant of authority for the use of "necessary and appropriate force" to include the authority to detain for the duration of the relevant conflict, and our understanding is based on longstanding law-of-war principles. If the practical circumstances of a given conflict are entirely unlike those of the conflicts that informed the development of the law of war, that understanding may unravel. But that is not the situation we face as of this date. Active combat operations against Taliban fighters apparently are ongoing in Afghanistan. *See, e.g.,* Constable, U.S. Launches New Operation in Afghanistan, Washington Post, Mar. 14, 2004, p. A22 (reporting that 13,500 United States troops remain in Afghanistan, including several thousand new arrivals); J. Abizaid, Dept. of Defense, Gen. Abizaid Central Command Operations Update Briefing, Apr. 30, 2004, http:// www.defenselink.mil/transcripts/2004/tr20040430–1402.html (as visited June 8, 2004, and available in the Clerk of Court's case file) (media briefing describing ongoing operations in Afghanistan involving 20,000 United States troops). The United States may detain, for the duration of these hostilities, individuals legitimately determined to be Taliban combatants who "engaged in an armed conflict against the United States." If the record establishes that United States troops are still involved in active combat in Afghanistan, those detentions are part of the exercise of "necessary and appropriate force," and therefore are authorized by the AUMF.

Ex parte Milligan, 4 Wall. 2, 125 . . . (1866), does not undermine our holding about the Government's authority to seize enemy combatants, as we define that term today. In that case, the Court made repeated reference to the fact that its inquiry into whether the military tribunal had jurisdiction to try and punish Milligan turned in large part on the fact that Milligan was not a prisoner of war, but a resident of Indiana arrested while at home there. *Id.,* at 118, 131, 71 U.S. 2. That fact was central to its conclusion. Had Milligan been captured while he was assisting Confederate soldiers by carrying a rifle against Union troops on a Confederate battlefield, the holding of the Court might well have been different. The Court's repeated explanations that Milligan was not a prisoner of war suggest that had these different circumstances been present he could have been detained under military authority for the duration of the conflict, whether or not he was a citizen. [court's fn.1: Here the basis asserted for detention by the military is that Hamdi was carrying a weapon against American troops on a foreign battlefield; that is, that he was an enemy combatant. The legal category of enemy combatant has not been elaborated upon in great detail. The permissible bounds of the category will be defined by the lower courts as subsequent cases are presented to them.] . . . .

III

Even in cases in which the detention of enemy combatants is legally authorized, there remains the question of what process is constitutionally due to a citizen who disputes his enemy-combatant status. Hamdi argues that he is owed a meaningful and timely hearing and that "extra-judicial detention [that] begins and ends with the submission of an affidavit based on third-hand hearsay" does not comport with the Fifth and Fourteenth Amendments. Brief for Petitioners 16. The Government counters that any more process than was provided below would be both unworkable and "constitutionally intolerable." Brief for Respondents 46. Our resolution of this dispute requires a careful examination both of the writ of habeas corpus, which Hamdi now seeks to employ as a mechanism of judicial review, and of the Due Process Clause, which informs the procedural contours of that mechanism in this instance.

A

Though they reach radically different conclusions on the process that ought to attend the present proceeding, the parties begin on common ground. All agree that, absent suspension, the writ of habeas corpus remains available to every individual detained within the United States. U.S. Const., Art. I, § 9, cl. 2 ("The Privilege of the Writ of Habeas Corpus shall not be suspended, unless when in Cases of Rebellion or Invasion the public Safety may require it"). Only in the rarest of circumstances has Congress seen fit to suspend the writ. *See, e.g.,* Act of Mar. 3, 1863, ch. 81, § 1, 12 Stat. 755; Act of April 20, 1871, ch. 22, § 4, 17 Stat. 14. At all other times, it has remained a critical check on the Executive, ensuring that it does not detain individuals except in accordance with law. See INS v. St. Cyr, 533 U.S. 289, 301 ... (2001). All agree suspension of the writ has not occurred here. Thus, it is undisputed that Hamdi was properly before an Article III court to challenge his detention under 28 U.S.C. § 2241. Brief for Respondents 12. Further, all agree that § 2241 and its companion provisions provide at least a skeletal outline of the procedures to be afforded a petitioner in federal habeas review. Most notably, § 2243 provides that "the person detained may, under oath, deny any of the facts set forth in the return or allege any other material facts," and § 2246 allows the taking of evidence in habeas proceedings by deposition, affidavit, or interrogatories.

The simple outline of § 2241 makes clear both that Congress envisioned that habeas petitioners would have some opportunity to present and rebut facts and that courts in cases like this retain some ability to vary the ways in which they do so as mandated by due process. The Government recognizes the basic procedural protections required by the habeas statute, *Id.,* at 37–38, but asks us to hold that, given both the flexibility of the habeas mechanism and the circumstances presented in this case, the presentation of the Mobbs Declaration to the habeas court completed the required factual development. It suggests two separate reasons for its position that no further process is due.

B

First, the Government urges the adoption of the Fourth Circuit's holding below–that because it is "undisputed" that Hamdi's seizure took place in a combat zone, the habeas determination can be made purely as a matter of law, with no further hearing or factfinding necessary. This argument is easily rejected....

C

The Government's second argument requires closer consideration. This is the argument that further factual exploration is unwarranted and inappropriate in light of the extraordinary constitutional interests at stake. Under the Government's most extreme rendition of this argument, "[r]espect for separation of powers and the limited institutional capabilities of courts in matters of military decision-making in connection with an ongoing conflict" ought to eliminate entirely any individual process, restricting the courts to investigating only whether legal authorization exists for the broader detention scheme. Brief for Respondents 26. At most, the Government argues, courts should review its determination that a citizen is an enemy combatant under a very deferential "some evidence" standard. *Id.*, at 34 ("Under the some evidence standard, the focus is exclusively on the factual basis supplied by the Executive to support its own determination") (citing Superintendent, Mass. Correctional Institution at Walpole v. Hill, 472 U.S. 445, 455–457 ... (1985) (explaining that the some evidence standard "does not require" a "weighing of the evidence," but rather calls for assessing "whether there is any evidence in the record that could support the conclusion")). Under this review, a court would assume the accuracy of the Government's articulated basis for Hamdi's detention, as set forth in the Mobbs Declaration, and assess only whether that articulated basis was a legitimate one. Brief for Respondents 36; see also 316 F.3d, at 473–474 (declining to address whether the "some evidence" standard should govern the adjudication of such claims, but noting that "[t]he factual averments in the [Mobbs] affidavit, if accurate, are sufficient to confirm" the legality of Hamdi's detention).

In response, Hamdi emphasizes that this Court consistently has recognized that an individual challenging his detention may not be held at the will of the Executive without recourse to some proceeding before a neutral tribunal to determine whether the Executive's asserted justifications for that detention have [a] basis in fact and warrant in law. *See, e.g.*, Zadvydas v. Davis, 533 U.S. 678, 690 ... (2001); Addington v. Texas, 441 U.S. 418, 425–427 ... (1979). He argues that the Fourth Circuit inappropriately "ceded power to the Executive during wartime to define the conduct for which a citizen may be detained, judge whether that citizen has engaged in the proscribed conduct, and imprison that citizen indefinitely," Brief for Petitioners 21, and that due process demands that he receive a hearing in which he may challenge the Mobbs Declaration and adduce his own counter evidence. The District Court, agreeing with Hamdi, apparently believed that the appropriate process would approach the process that accompanies a criminal trial. It therefore disapproved of the hearsay nature of the Mobbs Declaration and anticipated quite extensive discovery of various military affairs. Anything less, it concluded, would not be "meaningful judicial review." App. 291.

Both of these positions highlight legitimate concerns. And both emphasize the tension that often exists between the autonomy that the Government asserts is necessary in order to pursue effectively a particular goal and the process that a citizen contends he is due before he is deprived of a constitutional right. The ordinary mechanism that we use for balancing such serious competing interests, and for determining the procedures that are necessary to ensure that a citizen is not "deprived of life, liberty, or property, without due process of law," U.S. Const., Amdt. 5, is the test that we articulated in Mathews v. Eldridge, 424 U.S. 319 ... (1976). *See, e.g.*, Heller v. Doe, 509 U.S. 312, 330–331 ... (1993); Zinermon v. Burch, 494 U.S. 113, 127–28 ... (1990); United States v. Salerno, 481 U.S. 739, 746 ... (1987); Schall v. Martin, 467 U.S. 253, 274–275 ... (1984)*; Addington v. Texas, supra,* at 425. *Mathews* dictates that the process due in any given instance is determined by weighing "the private interest that will be affected by the official action" against the Government's asserted interest, "including the function involved" and the burdens the Government would face in providing greater process. 424 U.S., at 335. The *Mathews* calculus then contemplates a judicious balancing of these concerns, through an analysis of "the risk of an erroneous deprivation" of the private interest if the process were reduced and the "probable value, if any, of additional or substitute safeguards." *Ibid.* We take each of these steps in turn....

Striking the proper constitutional balance here is of great importance to the Nation during this period of ongoing combat. But it is equally vital that our calculus not give short shrift to the values that this country holds dear or to the privilege that is American citizenship. It is during our most challenging and uncertain moments that our Nation's commitment to due process is most severely tested; and it is in those times that we must preserve our commitment at home to the principles for which we fight abroad. See Kennedy v. Mendoza–Martinez, 372 U.S. 144, 164–165 ... (1963) ("The imperative necessity for safeguarding these rights to procedural due process under the gravest of emergencies has existed throughout our constitutional history, for it is then, under the pressing exigencies of crisis, that there is the greatest temptation to dispense with guarantees which, it is feared, will inhibit government action"); see also United States v. Robel, 389 U.S. 258, 264 ... (1967) ("It would indeed be ironic if, in the name of national defense, we would sanction the subversion of one of those liberties ... which makes the defense of the Nation worthwhile").

With due recognition of these competing concerns, we believe that neither the process proposed by the Government nor the process apparently envisioned by the District Court below strikes the proper constitutional balance when a United States citizen is detained in the United States as an enemy combatant. That is, "the risk of erroneous deprivation" of a detainee's liberty interest is unacceptably high under the Government's proposed rule, while some of the "additional or substitute procedural safeguards" suggested by the District Court are unwarranted in light of their limited "probable value" and the burdens they may impose on the military in such cases. *Mathews,* 424 U.S., at 335.

We therefore hold that a citizen-detainee seeking to challenge his classification as an enemy combatant must receive notice of the factual basis for his classification, and a fair opportunity to rebut the Government's factual assertions before a neutral decisionmaker. See Cleveland Bd. of Ed. v. Loudermill, 470 U.S. 532, 542 ... (1985) ("An essential principle of due process is that a deprivation of life, liberty, or property 'be preceded by notice and opportunity for hearing appropriate to the nature of the case' ") (quoting Mullane v. Central Hanover Bank & Trust Co., 339 U.S. 306, 313 ... (1950)); Concrete Pipe & Products of Cal., Inc. v. Construction Laborers Pension Trust for Southern Cal., 508 U.S. 602, 617 ... (1993) ("due process requires a 'neutral and detached judge in the first instance' ") (quoting Ward v. Monroeville, 409 U.S. 57, 61–62 ... (1972)). "For more than a century the central meaning of procedural due process has been clear: 'Parties whose rights are to be affected are entitled to be heard; and in order that they may enjoy that right they must first be notified.' It is equally fundamental that the right to notice and an opportunity to be heard 'must be granted at a meaningful time and in a meaningful manner.' " Fuentes v. Shevin, 407 U.S. 67, 80 ... (1972) (quoting Baldwin v. Hale, 1 Wall. 223, 233 ... (1864); Armstrong v. Manzo, 380 U.S. 545, 552 ... (1965) (other citations omitted)). These essential constitutional promises may not be eroded.

At the same time, the exigencies of the circumstances may demand that, aside from these core elements, enemy combatant proceedings may be tailored to alleviate their uncommon potential to burden the Executive at a time of ongoing military conflict. Hearsay, for example, may need to be accepted as the most reliable available evidence from the Government in such a proceeding. Likewise, the Constitution would not be offended by a presumption in favor of the Government's evidence, so long as that presumption remained a rebuttable one and fair opportunity for rebuttal were provided. Thus, once the Government puts forth credible evidence that the habeas petitioner meets the enemy-combatant criteria, the onus could shift to the petitioner to rebut that evidence with more persuasive evidence that he falls outside the criteria. A burden-shifting scheme of this sort would meet the goal of ensuring that the errant tourist, embedded journalist, or local aid worker has a chance to prove military error while giving due regard to the Executive once it has put forth meaningful support for its conclusion that the detainee is in fact an enemy combatant. In the words of *Mathews,* process of this sort would sufficiently address the "risk of erroneous deprivation" of a detainee's liberty interest while eliminating certain procedures that have questionable additional value in light of the burden on the Government. 424 U.S., at 335. [court's fn.2: Because we hold that Hamdi is constitutionally entitled to the process described above, we need not address at this time whether any treaty guarantees him similar access to a tribunal for a determination of his status.]

We think it unlikely that this basic process will have the dire impact on the central functions of warmaking that the Government forecasts. The parties agree that initial captures on the battlefield need not receive the process we have discussed here; that process is due only when the determination is made to *continue* to hold those who have been seized. The Government has made clear in its briefing that documentation regarding battlefield detainees already is kept in the ordinary course of military affairs. Brief for Respondents 3–4. Any factfinding imposition created by requiring a knowledgeable affiant to summarize these records to an independent tribunal is a minimal one. Likewise, arguments that military officers ought not have to wage war under the threat of litigation lose much of their steam when factual disputes at enemy-combatant hearings are limited to the alleged combatant's acts. This focus meddles little, if at all, in the strategy or conduct of war, inquiring only into the appropriateness of continuing to detain an individual claimed to have taken up arms against the United States. While we accord the greatest respect and consideration to the judgments of military authorities in matters relating to the actual prosecution of a war, and recognize that the scope of that discretion necessarily is wide, it does not infringe on the core role of the military for the courts to exercise their own time-honored and constitutionally mandated roles of reviewing and resolving claims like those presented here. *Cf.* Korematsu v. United States, 323 U.S. 214, 233–234 ... (1944) (Murphy, J., dissenting) ("[L]ike other claims conflicting with the asserted constitutional rights of the individual, the military claim must subject itself to the judicial process of having its reasonableness determined and its conflicts with other interests reconciled"); Sterling v. Constantin, 287 U.S. 378, 401 ... (1932) ("What are the allowable limits of military discretion, and whether or not they have been overstepped in a particular case, are judicial questions").

In sum, while the full protections that accompany challenges to detentions in other settings may prove unworkable and inappropriate in the enemy-combatant setting, the threats to military operations posed by a basic system of independent review are not so weighty as to trump a citizen's core rights to challenge meaningfully the Government's case and to be heard by an impartial adjudicator.

D

In so holding, we necessarily reject the Government's assertion that separation of powers principles mandate a heavily circumscribed role for the courts in such circumstances. Indeed, the position that the courts must forgo any examination of the individual case and focus exclusively on the legality of the broader detention scheme cannot be mandated by any reasonable view of separation of powers, as this approach serves only to *condense* power into a single branch of government. We have long since made clear that a state of war is not a blank check for the President when it comes to the rights of the Nation's citizens. *Youngstown Sheet & Tube,* 343 U.S., at 587. Whatever power the United States Constitution envisions for the Executive in its exchanges with other nations or with enemy organizations in times of conflict, it most assuredly envisions a role for all three branches when individual liberties are at stake.... [I]t would turn our system of checks and balances on its head to suggest that a citizen could not make his way to court with a challenge to the factual basis for his detention by his government, simply because the Executive opposes making available such a challenge. Absent suspension of the writ by Congress, a citizen detained as an enemy combatant is entitled to this process.

Because we conclude that due process demands some system for a citizen detainee to refute his classification, the proposed "some evidence" standard is inadequate. Any process in which the Executive's factual assertions go wholly unchallenged or are simply presumed correct without any opportunity for the alleged combatant to demonstrate otherwise falls constitutionally short. As the Government itself has recognized, we have utilized the "some evidence" standard in the past as a standard of review, not as a standard of proof. Brief for Respondents

35. That is, it primarily has been employed by courts in examining an administrative record developed after an adversarial proceeding–one with process at least of the sort that we today hold is constitutionally mandated in the citizen enemy-combatant setting. *See, e.g., St. Cyr, supra*; *Hill,* 472 U.S., at 455–457. This standard therefore is ill suited to the situation in which a habeas petitioner has received no prior proceedings before any tribunal and had no prior opportunity to rebut the Executive's factual assertions before a neutral decisionmaker.

Today we are faced only with such a case. Aside from unspecified "screening" processes, Brief for Respondents 3–4, and military interrogations in which the Government suggests Hamdi could have contested his classification, Tr. of Oral Arg. 40, 42, Hamdi has received no process. An interrogation by one's captor, however effective an intelligence-gathering tool, hardly constitutes a constitutionally adequate factfinding before a neutral decisionmaker.... Plainly, the "process" Hamdi has received is not that to which he is entitled under the Due Process Clause.

There remains the possibility that the standards we have articulated could be met by an appropriately authorized and properly constituted military tribunal. Indeed, it is notable that military regulations already provide for such process in related instances, dictating that tribunals be made available to determine the status of enemy detainees who assert prisoner-of-war status under the Geneva Convention. See Enemy Prisoners of War, Retained Personnel, Civilian Internees and Other Detainees, Army Regulation 190–8, § 1–6 (1997). In the absence of such process, however, a court that receives a petition for a writ of habeas corpus from an alleged enemy combatant must itself ensure that the minimum requirements of due process are achieved. Both courts below recognized as much, focusing their energies on the question of whether Hamdi was due an opportunity to rebut the Government's case against him. The Government, too, proceeded on this assumption, presenting its affidavit and then seeking that it be evaluated under a deferential standard of review based on burdens that it alleged would accompany any greater process. As we have discussed, a habeas court in a case such as this may accept affidavit evidence like that contained in the Mobbs Declaration, so long as it also permits the alleged combatant to present his own factual case to rebut the Government's return. We anticipate that a District Court would proceed with the caution that we have indicated is necessary in this setting, engaging in a factfinding process that is both prudent and incremental. We have no reason to doubt that courts faced with these sensitive matters will pay proper heed both to the matters of national security that might arise in an individual case and to the constitutional limitations safeguarding essential liberties that remain vibrant even in times of security concerns.

IV

Hamdi asks us to hold that the Fourth Circuit also erred by denying him immediate access to counsel upon his detention and by disposing of the case without permitting him to meet with an attorney. Brief for Petitioners 19. Since our grant of certiorari in this case, Hamdi has been appointed counsel, with whom he has met for consultation purposes on several occasions, and with whom he is now being granted unmonitored meetings. He unquestionably has the right to access to counsel in connection with the proceedings on remand. No further consideration of this issue is necessary at this stage of the case.

The judgment of the United States Court of Appeals for the Fourth Circuit is vacated, and the case is remanded for further proceedings. It is so ordered.

SOUTER, J., with whom GINSBURG, J. joins, concurring in part, dissenting in part, and concurring in the judgment.

... The Government asserts a right to hold Hamdi under these conditions indefinitely, that is, until the Government determines that the United States is no longer threatened by the terrorism exemplified in the attacks of September 11, 2001.

In these proceedings on Hamdi's petition, he seeks to challenge the facts claimed by the Government as the basis for holding him as an enemy combatant. And in this Court he presses the distinct argument that the Government's claim, even if true, would not implicate any authority for holding him that would satisfy 18 U.S.C. § 4001(a) (Non–Detention Act), which bars imprisonment or detention of a citizen "except pursuant to an Act of Congress."

The Government responds that Hamdi's incommunicado imprisonment as an enemy combatant seized on the field of battle falls within the President's power as Commander in Chief under the laws and usages of war, and is in any event authorized by two statutes. Accordingly, the Government contends that Hamdi has no basis for any challenge by petition for habeas except to his own status as an enemy combatant; and even that challenge may go no further than to enquire whether "some evidence" supports Hamdi's designation, see Brief for Respondents 34–36; if there is "some evidence," Hamdi should remain locked up at the discretion of the Executive. At the argument of this case, in fact, the Government went further and suggested that as long as a prisoner could challenge his enemy combatant designation when responding to interrogation during incommunicado detention he was accorded sufficient process to support his designation as an enemy combatant. See Tr. of Oral Arg. 40; *id.,* at 42 ("[H]e has an opportunity to explain it in his own words" "[d]uring interrogation"). Since on either view judicial enquiry so limited would be virtually worthless as a way to contest detention, the Government's concession of jurisdiction to hear Hamdi's habeas claim is more theoretical than practical, leaving the assertion of Executive authority close to unconditional.

The plurality rejects any such limit on the exercise of habeas jurisdiction and so far I agree with its opinion. The plurality does, however, accept the Government's position that if Hamdi's designation as an enemy combatant is correct, his detention (at least as to some period) is authorized by an Act of Congress as required by § 4001(a), that is, by the Authorization for Use of Military Force, 115 Stat. 224 (hereinafter Force Resolution). *Ante,* at 2639–2642. Here, I disagree and respectfully dissent. The Government has failed to demonstrate that the Force Resolution authorizes the detention complained of here even on the facts the Government claims. If the Government raises nothing further than the record now shows, the Non–Detention Act entitles Hamdi to be released.

I

The Government's first response to Hamdi's claim that holding him violates § 4001(a), prohibiting detention of citizens "except pursuant to an Act of Congress," is that the statute does not even apply to military wartime detentions, being beyond the sphere of domestic criminal law. Next, the Government says that even if that statute does apply, two Acts of Congress provide the authority § 4001(a) demands: a general authorization to the Department of Defense to pay for detaining "prisoners of war" and "similar" persons, 10 U.S.C. § 956(5), and the Force Resolution, passed after the attacks of 2001. At the same time, the Government argues that in detaining Hamdi in the manner described, the President is in any event acting as Commander in Chief under Article II of the Constitution, which brings with it the right to invoke authority under the accepted customary rules for waging war. On the record in front of us, the Government has not made out a case on any theory.

II

The threshold issue is how broadly or narrowly to read the Non–Detention Act, the tone of which is severe: "No citizen shall be imprisoned or otherwise detained by the United States except pursuant to an Act of Congress." Should the severity of the Act be relieved when the Government's stated factual justification for incommunicado detention is a war on terrorism, so that the Government may be said to act "pursuant" to congressional terms that fall short of explicit authority to imprison individuals? With one possible though important qualification, ... the answer has to be no. For a number of reasons, the prohibition within § 4001(a) has to be read broadly to accord the statute a long reach and to impose a burden of justification on the Government.

First, the circumstances in which the Act was adopted point the way to this interpretation. The provision superseded a cold-war statute, the Emergency Detention Act of 1950 (formerly 50 U.S.C. § 811 *et seq.* (1970 ed.)), which had authorized the Attorney General, in time of emergency, to detain anyone reasonably thought likely to engage in espionage or sabotage. That statute was repealed in 1971 out of fear that it could authorize a repetition of the World War II internment of citizens of Japanese ancestry; Congress meant to preclude another episode like the one described in Korematsu v. United States, 323 U.S. 214 ... (1944)....

Second, when Congress passed § 4001(a) it was acting in light of an interpretive regime that subjected enactments limiting liberty in wartime to the requirement of a clear statement and it presumably intended § 4001(a) to be read accordingly. This need for clarity was unmistakably expressed in *Ex parte* Endo, [323 U.S. 283 (1944)] decided the same day as *Korematsu. Endo* began with a petition for habeas corpus by an interned citizen claiming to be loyal and law-abiding and thus "unlawfully detained." 323 U.S., at 294. The petitioner was held entitled to habeas relief in an opinion that set out this principle for scrutinizing wartime statutes in derogation of customary liberty....

Finally, even if history had spared us the cautionary example of the internments in World War II, even if there had been no *Korematsu,* and *Endo* had set out no principle of statutory interpretation, there would be a compelling reason to read § 4001(a) to demand manifest authority to detain before detention is authorized. The defining character of American constitutional government is its constant tension between security and liberty, serving both by partial helpings of each. In a government of separated powers, deciding finally on what is a reasonable degree of guaranteed liberty whether in peace or war (or some condition in between) is not well entrusted to the Executive Branch of Government, whose particular responsibility is to maintain security....

III

Under this principle of reading § 4001(a) robustly to require a clear statement of authorization to detain, none of the Government's arguments suffices to justify Hamdi's detention....

Even so, there is one argument for treating the Force Resolution as sufficiently clear to authorize detention of a citizen consistently with § 4001(a). Assuming the argument to be sound, however, the Government is in no position to claim its advantage.

Because the Force Resolution authorizes the use of military force in acts of war by the United States, the argument goes, it is reasonably clear that the military and its Commander in Chief are authorized to deal with enemy belligerents according to the treaties and customs known collectively as the laws of war. Brief for Respondents 20–22; see *ante,* at 2639–2642 (accepting this argument). Accordingly, the United States may detain captured enemies, and *Ex parte* Quirin, 317 U.S. 1 ... (1942), may perhaps be claimed for the proposition that the American citizenship of such a captive does not as such limit the Government's power to deal with him under the usages of war. *Id.,* at 31, 37–38. Thus, the Government here repeatedly argues that Hamdi's detention amounts to nothing more than customary detention of a captive taken on the field of battle: if the usages of war are fairly authorized by the Force Resolution, Hamdi's detention is authorized for purposes of § 4001(a).

There is no need, however, to address the merits of such an argument in all possible circumstances. For now it is enough to recognize that the Government's stated legal position in its campaign against the Taliban (among whom Hamdi was allegedly captured) is apparently at odds with its claim here to be acting in accordance with customary law of war and hence to be within the terms of the Force Resolution in its detention of Hamdi. In a statement of its legal position cited in its brief, the Government says that "the Geneva Convention applies to the Taliban detainees." Office of the White House Press Secretary, Fact Sheet, Status of Detainees at Guantanamo (Feb. 7, 2002), www.whitehouse.gov/news/releases/2002/ 02/20020207–13.html (as visited June 18, 2004, and available in Clerk of Court's case file) (hereinafter White House Press Release) (cited in Brief for Respondents 24, n. 9). Hamdi presumably is such a detainee, since according to the Government's own account, he was taken bearing arms on the Taliban side of a field of battle in Afghanistan. He would therefore seem to qualify for treatment as a prisoner of war under the Third Geneva Convention, to which the United States is a party. Article 4 of the Geneva Convention (III) Relative to the Treatment of Prisoners of War, Aug. 12, 1949, [1955] 6 U.S. T. 3316, 3320, T. I. A. S. No. 3364.

By holding him incommunicado, however, the Government obviously has not been treating him as a prisoner of war, and in fact the Government claims that no Taliban detainee is entitled to prisoner of war status. See Brief for Respondents 24; White House Press Release. This treatment appears to be a violation of the Geneva Convention provision that even in cases of doubt, captives are entitled to be treated as prisoners of war "until such time as their status has been determined by a competent tribunal." Art. 5, 6 U.S. T., at 3324. The Government answers that the President's determination that Taliban detainees do not qualify as prisoners of war is conclusive as to Hamdi's status and removes any doubt that would trigger application of the Convention's tribunal requirement. See Brief for Respondents 24. But reliance on this categorical pronouncement to settle doubt is apparently at odds with the military regulation, Enemy Prisoners of War, Retained Personnel, Civilian Internees and Other Detainees, Army Reg. 190–8, §§ 1–5, 1–6 (1997), adopted to implement the Geneva Convention, and setting out a detailed procedure for a military tribunal to determine an individual's status. See, *e.g., id.*, § 1–6 ("A competent tribunal shall be composed of three commissioned officers"; a "written record shall be made of proceedings"; "[p]roceedings shall be open" with certain exceptions; "[p]ersons whose status is to be determined shall be advised of their rights at the beginning of their hearings," "allowed to attend all open sessions," "allowed to call witnesses if reasonably available, and to question those witnesses called by the Tribunal," and to "have a right to testify"; and a tribunal shall determine status by a "[p]reponderance of evidence"). One of the types of doubt these tribunals are meant to settle is whether a given individual may be, as Hamdi says he is, an "[i]nnocent civilian who should be immediately returned to his home or released." *Id.*, 1–6*e* (10)(*c*). The regulation, jointly promulgated by the Headquarters of the Departments of the Army, Navy, Air Force, and Marine Corps, provides that "[p]ersons who have been determined by a competent tribunal not to be entitled to prisoner of war status may not be executed, imprisoned, or otherwise penalized without further proceedings to determine what acts they have committed and what penalty should be imposed." *Id.*, § 1–6*g*. The regulation also incorporates the Geneva Convention's presumption that in cases of doubt, "persons shall enjoy the protection of the ... Convention until such time as their status has been determined by a competent tribunal." *Id.*, § 1–6*a*. Thus, there is reason to question whether the United States is acting in accordance with the laws of war it claims as authority.

Whether, or to what degree, the Government is in fact violating the Geneva Convention and is thus acting outside the customary usages of war are not matters I can resolve at this point. What I can say, though, is that the Government has not made out its claim that in detaining Hamdi in the manner described, it is acting in accord with the laws of war authorized to be applied against citizens by the Force Resolution. I conclude accordingly that the Government has failed to support the position that the Force Resolution authorizes the described detention of Hamdi for purposes of § 4001(a)....

IV

Because I find Hamdi's detention forbidden by § 4001(a) and unauthorized by the Force Resolution, I would not reach any questions of what process he may be due in litigating disputed issues in a proceeding under the habeas statute or prior to the habeas enquiry itself. For me, it suffices that the Government has failed to justify holding him in the absence of a further Act of Congress, criminal charges, a showing that the detention conforms to the laws of war, or a demonstration that § 4001(a) is unconstitutional. I would therefore vacate the judgment of the Court of Appeals and remand for proceedings consistent with this view.

Since this disposition does not command a majority of the Court, however, the need to give practical effect to the conclusions of eight members of the Court rejecting the Government's position calls for me to join with the plurality in ordering remand on terms closest to those I would impose. See Screws v. United States, 325 U.S. 91, 134 ... (1945) (Rutledge, J., concurring in result). Although I think litigation of Hamdi's status as an enemy combatant is unnecessary, the terms of the plurality's remand will allow Hamdi to offer evidence that he is not an enemy combatant, and he should at the least have the benefit of that opportunity.

It should go without saying that in joining with the plurality to produce a judgment, I do not adopt the plurality's resolution of constitutional issues that I would not reach. It is not that I could disagree with the plurality's determinations (given the plurality's view of the Force Resolution) that someone in Hamdi's position is entitled at a minimum to notice of the Government's claimed factual basis for holding him, and to a fair chance to rebut it before a neutral decision maker, ... nor, of course, could I disagree with the plurality's affirmation of Hamdi's right to counsel.... On the other hand, I do not mean to imply agreement that the Government could claim an evidentiary presumption casting the burden of rebuttal on Hamdi, ... or that an opportunity to litigate before a military tribunal might obviate or truncate enquiry by a court on habeas....

Subject to these qualifications, I join with the plurality in a judgment of the Court vacating the Fourth Circuit's judgment and remanding the case.

SCALIA, J. with whom STEVENS, J. joins, dissenting.

... Where the Government accuses a citizen of waging war against it, our constitutional tradition has been to prosecute him in federal court for treason or some other crime. Where the exigencies of war prevent that, the Constitution's Suspension Clause, Art. I, § 9, cl. 2, allows Congress to relax the usual protections temporarily. Absent suspension, however, the Executive's assertion of military exigency has not been thought sufficient to permit detention without charge. No one contends that the congressional Authorization for Use of Military Force, on which the Government relies to justify its actions here, is an implementation of the Suspension Clause. Accordingly, I would reverse the decision below.

I

The very core of liberty secured by our Anglo–Saxon system of separated powers has been freedom from indefinite imprisonment at the will of the Executive....

Justice O'Connor, writing for a plurality of this Court, asserts that captured enemy combatants (other than those suspected of war crimes) have traditionally been detained until the cessation of hostilities and then released.... That is probably an accurate description of wartime practice with respect to enemy *aliens*. The tradition with respect to American citizens, however, has been quite different. Citizens aiding the enemy have been treated as traitors subject to the criminal process....

The proposition that the Executive lacks indefinite wartime detention authority over citizens is consistent with the Founders' general mistrust of military power permanently at the Executive's disposal. In the Founders' view, the "blessings of liberty" were threatened by "those military establishments which must gradually poison its very fountain." THE FEDERALIST NO. 45, p. 238 (J. Madison). No fewer than 10 issues of the Federalist were devoted in whole or part to allaying fears of oppression from the proposed Constitution's authorization of standing armies in peacetime. Many safeguards in the Constitution reflect these concerns....

The plurality finds justification for Hamdi's imprisonment in the Authorization for Use of Military Force, 115 Stat. 224, which provides:

"That the President is authorized to use all necessary and appropriate force against those nations, organizations, or persons he determines planned, authorized, committed, or aided the terrorist attacks that occurred on September 11, 2001, or harbored such organizations or persons, in order to prevent any future acts of international terrorism against the United States by such nations, organizations or persons." § 2(a).

This is not remotely a congressional suspension of the writ, and no one claims that it is. Contrary to the plurality's view, I do not think this statute even authorizes detention of a citizen with the clarity necessary to satisfy the interpretive canon that statutes should be construed so as to avoid grave constitutional concerns, see Edward J. DeBartolo Corp. v. Florida Gulf Coast Building & Constr. Trades Council, 485 U.S. 568, 575 ... (1988); with the clarity necessary to comport with cases such as *Ex parte* Endo, 323 U.S. 283, 300 ... (1944), and Duncan v. Kahanamoku, 327 U.S. 304, 314–316, 324 ... (1946); or with the clarity necessary to overcome the statutory prescription that "[n]o citizen shall be imprisoned or otherwise detained by the United States except pursuant to an Act of Congress." 18 U.S.C. § 4001(a). But even if it did, I would not permit it to overcome Hamdi's entitlement to habeas corpus relief....

Notes and Questions

1. Note that Justice Souter, with whom Justice Ginsburg joined, disagreed with the majority's conclusion that a competence that exists for all countries under the laws of war to detain certain persons (*e.g.*, prisoners of war) without trial was implicitly infused within the congressional use of force authorization or within the President's power as Commander in Chief, especially when a prior federal statute prohibited detention of any citizen "except pursuant to an Act of Congress" (The Non–Detention Act, 18 U.S.C. § 4001(a) (2000)). Do you agree, given that international law is normally available as an aid for statutory interpretation (see materials on indirect incorporation)? Justice Souter also made the valid point that an implied congressional authorization to detain in accordance with the laws of war would bring with it other limitations under the laws of war, such as the obligation under GPW Article 5 to treat Hamdi and members of the Taliban as prisoners of war until a competent tribunal determines their status. 124 S.Ct. at 2657–58. For numerous cases and opinions of Attorneys General recognizing that the President and every member of the Executive branch is bound by the laws of war, see *infra* Section 2 D 1.

2. If a person is not a prisoner of war, do the Geneva Conventions permit detention of such a person without trial? See Geneva Civilian Convention (GC), arts. 5, 42–43, 78.

3. Concerning congressional power to set limits on presidential war powers, *see, e.g.*, McCulloch v. Maryland, 17 U.S. (4 Wheat.) 316, 407 (1819); Gelston v. Hoyt, 16 U.S. (3 Wheat.) 246, 330–38 (1818); Brown v. United States, 12 U.S. (8 Cranch) 110 (1814); Little v. Barreme (The Flying Fish), 6 U.S. (2 Cranch) 170, 177–78 (1804); Talbot v. Seeman, 5 U.S. (1 Cranch) 1, 28, 41 (1801); Bas v. Tingy, 4 U.S. (4 Dall.) 37, 40–42 (1800); Hamdan v. Rumsfeld, 344 F.Supp.2d 152 (D.D.C. 2004); 9 Op. Att'y Gen. 517, 518–19 (1860); JORDAN J. PAUST, INTERNATIONAL LAW AS LAW OF THE UNITED STATES 461–62, 474–75 n.54, 478 n.58 (2 ed. 2003)

4. Would the congressional use of force authorization (Authorization for Use of Military Force, 115 Stat. 224, § 2(a) (Sept. 18, 2001)) reach a person found in Canada who had been "associated" with al Qaeda but was not directly involved in the September 11, 2001 attacks within the United States or the harboring of persons participating in such attacks? The congressional authorization is limited, but how limited? Consider the following: [In *Hamdi*,] Justice O'Connor argued that those "associated with the September 11, 2001 terrorist attacks" included those "who fought against the United States in Afghanistan as part of the Taliban, an organization known to have supported the al Qaeda terrorist network responsible for those attacks." 124 S.Ct. at 2640; *see also id.* at 2642 (stating that "individuals legitimately determined to be Taliban combatants who 'engaged in armed conflict against the United States' " are also covered). However, the congressional authorization ... appears to be far more restrictive. With respect to persons, Congress merely authorized "necessary and appropriate force" against those "nations, organizations, or persons" that "planned, authorized, committed, or aided" the 9/11 terrorist attacks as such or that "harbored such ... persons." *Id.* It does not authorize "force" against persons who were merely "associated" with the 9/11 attacks, much less those persons who were merely fighting with a defacto government that had "supported" al Qaeda more generally. In particular, there was no clear proof that Mr. Hamdi had "aided" the 9/11 attacks or "harbored" those who planned, authorized, committed, or aided the 9/11 attacks as such. If the Taliban "organization" had "harbored" al Qaeda, it is not clear that an authorization to use force against the Taliban "organization" as such extends to persons who are merely members of the Taliban, and it would not extend to a person who merely "took up arms with the Taliban." These points are relevant to inquiry whether others detained at Guantanamo actually fit within the language of the congressional authorization. It can be noted, for example, that the statement in Khalid v. Bush, 355 F.Supp.2d 311 (D.D.C. 2005), that the authorization reaches anyone who "posed a threat of future terrorist attacks" (355 F.Supp.2d at 315) is clearly incorrect. Moreover, Justice O'Connor stated that the majority's interpretation of the congressional grant of authority to detain was "based on longstanding law-of-war principles." 124 S.Ct. at 2641. Thus, when persons have been captured and detained outside the theater of war or a war-related occupation in Afghanistan or Iraq in circumstances where the laws of war do not apply, the expanded interpretation of the congressional authorization might be doubly doubtful and the laws of war would not provide executive authority to detain a person to whom the laws of war do not apply. Professor Paust notes: the U.S. cannot be at "war" with al Qaeda as such because it is not an insurgent, belligerent, nation, or state. *See, e.g.*, Jordan J. Paust, *Judicial Power to Determine the Status and Rights of Persons Detained Without Trial*, 44 HARV. INT'L L.J. 503, 513 n.30 (2003). Similarly, the laws of war do not protect them or authorize their detention outside an actual theater of war or war-related occupied territory, unless a particular person is engaged in belligerent acts in direct support of a party to an armed conflict in, for example, Afghanistan. The ICCPR prohibits "arbitrary" detention (International Covenant on Civil and Political Rights, art. 9(1), 999 U.N.T.S. 171 (Dec. 9, 1966) [hereinafter ICCPR]), but it does not grant a power to detain persons when such detention is not "arbitrary." Moreover, the ICCPR

requires that detention be "on ... grounds and in accordance with procedures ... established by law." *Id.*" Jordan J. Paust, *International Law Before the Supreme Court: A Mixed Record of Recognition*, 45 SANTA CLARA L. REV. _ (2005).

5. Because *Hamdi* rested primarily on due process rights under the Constitution, Justice O'Connor did not reach the point that law of war and human rights treaties guarantee "similar access to a tribunal for a determination of his status." 124 S.Ct. at 2649 n.2. Concerning such requirements under international law, *see, e.g.*, ICCPR, art. 9(4); Geneva Civilian Convention, arts. 43, 78; Paust, *Judicial Power*, *supra* at 507–10, 514.

RASUL v. BUSH

542 U.S. 466 (2004).

STEVENS, J.

These two cases present the narrow but important question whether United States courts lack jurisdiction to consider challenges to the legality of the detention of foreign nationals captured abroad in connection with hostilities and incarcerated at the Guantanamo Bay Naval Base, Cuba.

I

On September 11, 2001, agents of the al Qaeda terrorist network hijacked four commercial airliners and used them as missiles to attack American targets. While one of the four attacks was foiled by the heroism of the plane's passengers, the other three killed approximately 3,000 innocent civilians, destroyed hundreds of millions of dollars of property, and severely damaged the U.S. economy. In response to the attacks, Congress passed a joint resolution authorizing the President to use "all necessary and appropriate force against those nations, organizations, or persons he determines planned, authorized, committed, or aided the terrorist attacks ... or harbored such organizations or persons." Authorization for Use of Military Force, Pub.L. 107–40, §§ 1–2, 115 Stat. 224. Acting pursuant to that authorization, the President sent U.S. Armed Forces into Afghanistan to wage a military campaign against al Qaeda and the Taliban regime that had supported it.

Petitioners in these cases are 2 Australian citizens and 12 Kuwaiti citizens who were captured abroad during hostilities between the United States and the Taliban. Since early 2002, the U.S. military has held them–along with, according to the Government's estimate, approximately 640 other non-Americans captured abroad–at the Naval Base at Guantanamo Bay. Brief for United States 6. The United States occupies the Base, which comprises 45 square miles of land and water along the southeast coast of Cuba, pursuant to a 1903 Lease Agreement executed with the newly independent Republic of Cuba in the aftermath of the Spanish–American War. Under the Agreement, "the United States recognizes the continuance of the ultimate sovereignty of the Republic of Cuba over the [leased areas]," while "the Republic of Cuba consents that during the period of the occupation by the United States ... the United States shall exercise complete jurisdiction and control over and within said areas." [Lease of Lands for Coaling and Naval Stations, Feb. 23, 1903, U.S.-Cuba, Art. III, T.S. No. 418 (hereinafter 1903 Lease Agreement). A supplemental lease agreement, executed in July 1903, obligates the United States to pay an annual rent in the amount of "two thousand dollars, in gold coin of the United States" and to maintain "permanent fences" around the base. Lease of Certain Areas for Naval or Coaling Stations, July 2, 1903, U.S.-Cuba, Arts. I–II, T.S. No. 426.] In 1934, the parties entered into a treaty providing that, absent an agreement to modify or abrogate the lease, the lease would remain in effect "[s]o long as the United States of America shall not abandon the ... naval station of Guantanamo." [Treaty Defining Relations with Cuba, May 29, 1934, U.S.-Cuba, Art. III, 48 Stat. 1683, T.S. No. 866 (hereinafter 1934 Treaty)]

In 2002, petitioners, through relatives acting as their next friends, filed various actions in the U.S. District Court for the District of Columbia challenging the legality of their detention at the Base. All alleged that none of the petitioners has ever been a combatant against the United States or has ever engaged in any terrorist acts. They also alleged that none has been charged with any wrongdoing, permitted to consult with counsel, or provided access to the courts or any other tribunal. App. 29, 77, 108.

The two Australians, Mamdouh Habib and David Hicks, each filed a petition for writ of habeas corpus, seeking release from custody, access to counsel, freedom from interrogations, and other relief. *Id.,* at 98–99, 124–126. Fawzi Khalid Abdullah Fahad Al Odah and the 11 other Kuwaiti detainees filed a complaint seeking to be informed of the charges against them, to be allowed to meet with their families and with counsel, and to have access to the courts or some other impartial tribunal. *Id.,* at 34. They claimed that denial of these rights violates the Constitution, international law, and treaties of the United States. Invoking the court's jurisdiction under 28 U.S.C. §§ 1331 and 1350, among other statutory bases, they asserted causes of action under the Administrative Procedure Act, 5 U.S.C. §§ 555, 702, 706; the Alien Tort Statute, 28 U.S.C. § 1350; and the general federal habeas corpus statute, §§ 2241–2243. App. 19.

Construing all three actions as petitions for writs of habeas corpus, the District Court dismissed them for want of jurisdiction. The court held, in reliance on our opinion in Johnson v. Eisentrager, 339 U.S. 763 ... (1950), that "aliens detained outside the sovereign territory of the United States [may not] invok[e] a petition for a writ of habeas corpus." 215 F.Supp.2d 55, 68 (D.D.C.2002). The Court of Appeals affirmed. Reading *Eisentrager* to hold that " 'the privilege of litigation' does not extend to aliens in military custody who have no presence in 'any territory over which the United States is sovereign,' " 321 F.3d 1134, 1144 (C.A.D.C.2003) (quoting *Eisentrager,* 339 U.S. at 777–778), it held that the District Court lacked jurisdiction over petitioners' habeas actions, as well as their remaining federal statutory claims that do not sound in habeas. We granted certiorari, 540 U.S. 1003 ... (2003), and now reverse.

II

Congress has granted federal district courts, "within their respective jurisdictions," the authority to hear applications for habeas corpus by any person who claims to be held "in custody in violation of the Constitution or laws or treaties of the United States." 28 U.S.C. §§ 2241(a), (c)(3). The statute traces its ancestry to the first grant of federal court jurisdiction: Section 14 of the Judiciary Act of 1789 authorized federal courts to issue the writ of habeas corpus to prisoners "in custody, under or by colour of the authority of the United States, or committed for trial before some court of the same." Act of Sept. 24, 1789, ch. 20, § 14, 1 Stat. 82. In 1867, Congress extended the protections of the writ to "all cases where any person may be restrained of his or her liberty in violation of the constitution, or of any treaty or law of the United States." Act of Feb. 5, 1867, ch. 28, 14 Stat. 385. See Felker v. Turpin, 518 U.S. 651, 659–660 ... (1996).

Habeas corpus is, however, "a writ antecedent to statute, ... throwing its root deep into the genius of our common law." Williams v. Kaiser, 323 U.S. 471, 484, n.2 ... (1945)....

As it has evolved over the past two centuries, the habeas statute clearly has expanded habeas corpus "beyond the limits that obtained during the 17th and 18th centuries." Swain v. Pressley, 430 U.S. 372, 380, n.13 ... (1977). But "[a]t its historical core, the writ of habeas corpus has served as a means of reviewing the legality of Executive detention, and it is in that context that its protections have been strongest." INS v. St. Cyr, 533 U.S. 289, 301 ... (2001)....

Consistent with the historic purpose of the writ, this Court has recognized the federal courts' power to review applications for habeas relief in a wide variety of cases involving Executive detention, in wartime as well as in times of peace. The Court has, for example, entertained the habeas petitions of an American citizen who plotted an attack on military installations during the Civil War, *Ex parte* Milligan, 4 Wall. 2 ... (1866), and of admitted enemy aliens convicted of war crimes during a declared war and held in the United States, *Ex parte* Quirin, 317 U.S. 1 ... (1942), and its insular possessions, *In re* Yamashita, 327 U.S. 1 ... (1946)

The question now before us is whether the habeas statute confers a right to judicial review of the legality of Executive detention of aliens in a territory of which the United States exercises plenary and exclusive jurisdiction, but not "ultimate sovereignty."

III

Respondents' primary submission is that the answer to the jurisdictional question is controlled by our decision in *Eisentrager*. In that case, we held that a Federal District Court lacked authority to issue a writ of habeas corpus to 21 German citizens who had been captured by U.S. forces in China, tried and convicted of war crimes by an American military commission headquartered in Nanking, and incarcerated in the Landsberg Prison in occupied Germany....

Petitioners in these cases differ from the *Eisentrager* detainees in important respects: They are not nationals of countries at war with the United States, and they deny that they have engaged in or plotted acts of aggression against the United States; they have never been afforded access to any tribunal, much less charged with and convicted of wrongdoing; and for more than two years they have been imprisoned in territory over which the United States exercises exclusive jurisdiction and control.

Not only are petitioners differently situated from the *Eisentrager* detainees, but the Court in *Eisentrager* made quite clear that all six of the facts critical to its disposition were relevant only to the question of the prisoners' *constitutional* entitlement to habeas corpus. *Id.,* at 777.... The Court had far less to say on the question of the petitioners' *statutory* entitlement to habeas review. Its only statement on the subject was a passing reference to the absence of statutory authorization: "Nothing in the text of the Constitution extends such a right, nor does anything in our statutes." *Id.*, at 768....

Because subsequent decisions of this Court have filled the statutory gap that had occasioned *Eisentrager's* resort to "fundamentals," persons detained outside the territorial jurisdiction of any federal district court no longer need rely on the Constitution as the source of their right to federal habeas review. In Braden v. 30th Judicial Circuit Court of Ky., 410 U.S. 484, 495 ... (1973), this Court held, contrary to *Ahrens* [335 U.S. 188 (1948)], that the prisoner's presence within the territorial jurisdiction of the district court is not "an invariable prerequisite" to the exercise of district court jurisdiction under the federal habeas statute. Rather, because "the writ of habeas corpus does not act upon the prisoner who seeks relief, but upon the person who holds him in what is alleged to be unlawful custody," a district court acts "within [its] respective jurisdiction" within the meaning of § 2241 as long as "the custodian can be reached by service of process." 410 U.S., at 494–495....

Because *Braden* overruled the statutory predicate to *Eisentrager*'s holding, *Eisentrager* plainly does not preclude the exercise of § 2241 jurisdiction over petitioners' claims.

IV

Putting *Eisentrager* and *Ahrens* to one side, respondents contend that we can discern a limit on § 2241 through application of the "longstanding principle of American law" that congressional legislation is presumed not to have extraterritorial application unless such intent is clearly manifested. EEOC v. Arabian American Oil Co., 499 U.S. 244, 248 ... (1991). Whatever traction the presumption against extraterritoriality might have in other contexts, it certainly has no application to the operation of the habeas statute with respect to persons detained within "the territorial jurisdiction" of the United States. Foley Bros., Inc. v. Filardo, 336 U.S. 281, 285 ... (1985). By the express terms of its agreements with Cuba, the United States exercises "complete jurisdiction and control" over the Guantanamo Bay Naval Base, and may continue to exercise such control permanently if it so chooses. 1903 Lease Agreement, Art. III; 1934 Treaty, Art. III. Respondents themselves concede that the habeas statute would create federal-court jurisdiction over the claims of an American citizen held at the base. Tr. of Oral Arg. 27. Considering that the statute draws no distinction between Americans and aliens held in federal custody, there is little reason to think that Congress intended the geographical coverage of the statute to vary depending on the detainee's citizenship. Aliens held at the base, no less than American citizens, are entitled to invoke the federal courts' authority under § 2241.

Application of the habeas statute to persons detained at the base is consistent with the historical reach of the writ of habeas corpus....

In the end, the answer to the question presented is clear. Petitioners contend that they are being held in federal custody in violation of the laws of the United States. [fn. 15: Petitioners' allegations–that, although they have engaged neither in combat nor in acts of terrorism against the United States, they have been held in Executive detention for more than two years in territory subject to the long-term, exclusive jurisdiction and control of the United States, without access to counsel and without being charged with any wrongdoing–unquestionably describe "custody in violation of the Constitution or laws or treaties of the United States." 28 U.S.C. § 2241(c)(3). *Cf.* United States v. Verdugo–Urquidez, 494 U.S. 259, 277–278 ... (1990) (Kennedy, J., concurring), and cases cited therein.] No party questions the District Court's jurisdiction over petitioners' custodians. *Cf. Braden,* 410 U.S., at 495. Section 2241, by its terms, requires nothing more. We therefore hold that § 2241 confers on the District Court jurisdiction to hear petitioners' habeas corpus challenges to the legality of their detention at the Guantanamo Bay Naval Base.

V

In addition to invoking the District Court's jurisdiction under § 2241, the *Al Odah* petitioners' complaint invoked the court's jurisdiction under 28 U.S.C. § 1331, the federal question statute, as well as § 1350, the Alien Tort Statute. The Court of Appeals, again relying on *Eisentrager,* held that the District Court correctly dismissed the claims founded on § 1331 and § 1350 for lack of jurisdiction, even to the extent that these claims "deal only with conditions of confinement and do not sound in habeas," because petitioners lack the "privilege of litigation" in U.S. courts. 321 F.3d, at 1144 (internal quotation marks omitted). Specifically, the court held that because petitioners' § 1331 and § 1350 claims "necessarily rest on alleged violations of the same category of laws listed in the habeas corpus statute," they, like claims founded on the habeas statute itself, must be "beyond the jurisdiction of the federal courts." *Id.,* at 1144–1145.

As explained above, *Eisentrager* itself erects no bar to the exercise of federal court jurisdiction over the petitioners' habeas corpus claims. It therefore certainly does not bar the exercise of federal-court jurisdiction over claims that merely implicate the "same category of laws listed in the habeas corpus statute." But in any event, nothing in *Eisentrager* or in any of our other cases categorically excludes aliens detained in military custody outside the United States from the " 'privilege of litigation' "in U.S. courts. 321 F.3d, at 1139. The courts of the United States have traditionally been open to nonresident aliens. *Cf.* Disconto Gesellschaft v. Umbreit, 208 U.S. 570, 578 . . . (1908) ("Alien citizens, by the policy and practice of the courts of this country, are ordinarily permitted to resort to the courts for the redress of wrongs and the protection of their rights"). And indeed, 28 U.S.C. § 1350 explicitly confers the privilege of suing for an actionable "tort . . . committed in violation of the law of nations or a treaty of the United States" on aliens alone. The fact that petitioners in these cases are being held in military custody is immaterial to the question of the District Court's jurisdiction over their nonhabeas statutory claims.

VI

Whether and what further proceedings may become necessary after respondents make their response to the merits of petitioners' claims are matters that we need not address now. What is presently at stake is only whether the federal courts have jurisdiction to determine the legality of the Executive's potentially indefinite detention of individuals who claim to be wholly innocent of wrongdoing. Answering that question in the affirmative, we reverse the judgment of the Court of Appeals and remand for the District Court to consider in the first instance the merits of petitioners' claims.

It is so ordered.

KENNEDY, J., concurring

The Court is correct, in my view, to conclude that federal courts have jurisdiction to consider challenges to the legality of the detention of foreign nationals held at the Guantanamo Bay Naval Base in Cuba. While I reach the same conclusion, my analysis follows a different course. . . . In my view, the correct course is to follow the framework of *Eisentrager.*

The facts here are distinguishable from those in *Eisentrager* in two critical ways, leading to the conclusion that a federal court may entertain the petitions. First, Guantanamo Bay is in every practical respect a United States territory, and it is one far removed from any hostilities. The opinion of the Court well explains the history of its possession by the United States. In a formal sense, the United States leases the Bay; the 1903 lease agreement states that Cuba retains "ultimate sovereignty'' over it. Lease of Lands for Coaling and Naval Stations, Feb. 23, 1903, U.S.-Cuba, Art. III, T.S. No. 418. At the same time, this lease is no ordinary lease. Its term is indefinite and at the discretion of the United States. What matters is the unchallenged and indefinite control that the United States has long exercised over Guantanamo Bay. From a practical perspective, the indefinite lease of Guantanamo Bay has produced a place that belongs to the United States, extending the "implied protection" of the United States to it. *Eisentrager, supra,* at 777–778....

The second critical set of facts is that the detainees at Guantanamo Bay are being held indefinitely, and without benefit of any legal proceeding to determine their status. In *Eisentrager,* the prisoners were tried and convicted by a military commission of violating the laws of war and were sentenced to prison terms. Having already been subject to procedures establishing their status, they could not justify "a limited opening of our courts" to show that they were "of friendly personal disposition" and not enemy aliens. 339 U.S., at 778.... Indefinite detention without trial or other proceeding presents altogether different considerations. It allows friends and foes alike to remain in detention. It suggests a weaker case of military necessity and much greater alignment with the traditional function of habeas corpus. Perhaps, where detainees are taken from a zone of hostilities, detention without proceedings or trial would be justified by military necessity for a matter of weeks; but as the period of detention stretches from months to years, the case for continued detention to meet military exigencies becomes weaker.

In light of the status of Guantanamo Bay and the indefinite pretrial detention of the detainees, I would hold that federal-court jurisdiction is permitted in these cases. This approach would avoid creating automatic statutory authority to adjudicate the claims of persons located outside the United States, and remains true to the reasoning of *Eisentrager*. For these reasons, I concur in the judgment of the Court.

Notes and Questions

1. What Justice Stevens recognized as U.S. "territorial jurisdiction" at Guantanamo has similar meaning under customary international law, because territorial jurisdictional competencies and responsibilities can reach beyond formal U.S. territory as such to include territory at Guantanamo. Professor Paust notes: the focus of the habeas statute is on "jurisdiction," despite selectively activist judges who had preferred to legislate by adding limiting words such as "sovereign borders," "sovereign territory," or "sovereignty" that Congress has not chosen. See 28 U.S.C. § 2241 (a), (c)(3).

2. Additionally, the word "treaties" that is found in the habeas statute obviously implicates international law, and various Founders, Supreme Court Justices and other federal judges have long recognized more generally that the phrase "laws of the United States" encompasses the law of nations or what we term customary international law. The habeas statute incorporates international law for habeas purposes by reference in two ways: (1) expressly with respect to treaties of the United States, and (2) impliedly with respect to customary international law through the phrase "law ... of the

United States." *See* 28 U.S.C. § 2441 (a), (c)(3). Under treaty-based international law and customary international law that are both directly incorporable and executed by and incorporated by reference through the habeas statute, the United States has a clearly relevant obligation to assure meaningful and effective judicial review of Executive decisions to detain persons without trial wherever it exercises control over a detained person. *See, e.g.*, ICCPR, arts. 2(1), 9(4); Jordan J. Paust, *Judicial Power To Determine the Status and Rights of Persons Detained Without Trial*, 44 HARV. INT'L L.J. 503, 507–10, 514 (2003). *Rasul v. Bush* allows the United States to comply with international duties and fundamental rights of persons detained at Guantanamo through a statute that permits habeas review with respect to persons who claim to be detained in violation of the Constitution, laws, or treaties of the United States.

3. In *Rasul*, Justice Stevens also recognized that "[a]liens held at the base, no less than American citizens, are entitled to invoke the federal courts' authority" under the habeas statutes. Since customary and treaty-based human rights law prohibits the "denial of justice" to aliens and requires freedom from discrimination on the basis of national or social origin, equal protection, and equal access to courts, the *Rasul* outcome also allows the United States to comply with such international obligations.

IN RE GUANTANAMO DETAINEE CASES

355 F.Supp.2d 443 (D.D.C. 2005).

GREEN, J.

These eleven coordinated *habeas* cases were filed by detainees held as "enemy combatants" at the United States Naval Base at Guantanamo Bay, Cuba. Presently pending is the government's motion to dismiss or for judgment as a matter of law regarding all claims filed by all petitioners, including claims based on the United States Constitution, treaties, statutes, regulations, the common law, and customary international law. Counsel filed numerous briefs addressing issues raised in the motion and argued their positions at a hearing in early December 2004. Upon consideration of all filings submitted in these cases and the arguments made at the hearing, and for the reasons stated below, the Court concludes that the petitioners have stated valid claims under the Fifth Amendment to the United States Constitution and that the procedures implemented by the government to confirm that the petitioners are "enemy combatants" subject to indefinite detention violate the petitioners' rights to due process of law. The Court also holds that at least some of the petitioners have stated valid claims under the Third Geneva Convention [GPW]. Finally, the Court holds that the government is entitled to the dismissal of the petitioners' remaining claims. . . .

In response to the horrific and unprecedented terrorist attacks by al Qaeda against the United States of America on September 11, 2001, Congress passed a joint resolution authorizing the President "to use all necessary and appropriate force against those nations, organizations, or persons he determines planned, authorized, committed, or aided the terrorist attacks ... , or harbored such organizations or persons, in order to prevent any future acts of international terrorism against the United States by such nations, organizations or persons." Authorization for Use of Military Force, Pub.L. No. 107–40, § 2(a), 115 Stat. 224 (2001) (hereinafter "AUMF"). In accordance with the AUMF, President George W. Bush ordered the commencement of military operations in Afghanistan against al Qaeda and the Taliban regime, which harbored the terrorist organization. During the course of the military campaign, United States forces took custody of numerous individuals who were actively fighting against allied forces on Afghan soil. Many of these individuals were deemed by military authorities to be "enemy combatants" and, beginning in early 2002, were transferred to facilities at the United States Naval Base at Guantanamo Bay, Cuba, where they continue to be detained by U.S. authorities.

In addition to belligerents captured during the heat of war in Afghanistan, the U.S. authorities are also detaining at Guantanamo Bay pursuant to the AUMF numerous individuals who were captured hundreds or thousands of miles from a battle zone in the traditional sense of that term. For example, detainees at Guantanamo Bay who are presently seeking *habeas* relief in the United States District Court for the District of Columbia include men who were taken into custody as far away from Afghanistan as Gambia, Zambia, Bosnia, and Thailand. Some have already been detained as long as three years while others have been captured as recently as September 2004. Although many of these individuals may never have been close to an actual battlefield and may never have raised conventional arms against the United States or its allies, the military nonetheless has deemed them detainable as "enemy combatants" based on conclusions that they have ties to al Qaeda or other terrorist organizations.

... It is the government's position that once someone has been properly designated as such, that person can be held indefinitely until the end of America's war on terrorism or until the military determines on a case by case basis that the particular detainee no longer poses a threat to the United States or its allies. Within the general set of "enemy combatants" is a subset of individuals whom the administration decided to prosecute for war crimes before a military commission established pursuant to a Military Order issued by President Bush on November 13, 2001.... Should individuals be prosecuted and convicted in accordance with the Military Order, they would be subject to sentences with fixed terms of incarceration or other specific penalties.

... Although detainees at Guantanamo Bay not subject to prosecution could suffer the same fate as those convicted of war crimes–potentially life in prison, depending on how long America's war on terrorism lasts–they were not given any significant procedural rights to challenge their status as alleged "enemy combatants," at least until relatively recently. From the beginning of 2002 through at least June 2004, the substantial majority of detainees not charged with war crimes were not informed of the bases upon which they were detained, were not permitted access to counsel, were not given a formal opportunity to challenge their "enemy combatant" status, and were alleged to be held virtually *incommunicado* from the outside world. Whether those individuals deemed "enemy combatants" are entitled under the United States Constitution and other laws to any rights and, if so, the scope of those rights is the focus of the government's motion to dismiss and this Memorandum Opinion.

[In *Rasul*,] [t]he Supreme Court expressly acknowledged that the allegations contained in the petitions for writs of *habeas corpus* "unquestionably describe 'custody in violation of the Constitution or laws or treaties of the United States' " as required by the *habeas* statute, 124 S.Ct. at 2698 n.15 (*quoting* 28 U.S.C. § 2241(c)(3)). . . .

On July 7, 2004, nine days after the issuance of the *Rasul* decision, Deputy Secretary of Defense Paul Wolfowitz issued an Order creating a military tribunal called the Combatant Status Review Tribunal (hereinafter "CSRT") to review the status of each detainee at Guantanamo Bay as an "enemy combatant." [court's note 9: The document . . . can be found at http:// www.defenselink.mil/news/Jul2004/d20040707review.pdf.] It appears that this is the first formal document to officially define the term "enemy combatant" as used by the respondents. That definition is as follows:

> [T]he term "enemy combatant" shall mean an individual who was part of or supporting Taliban or al Qaeda forces, or associated forces that are engaged in hostilities against the United States or its coalition partners. This includes any person who has committed a belligerent act or has directly supported hostilities in aid of enemy armed forces.

The Deputy Secretary's Order notes that all Guantanamo detainees were previously determined to be "enemy combatants" through what the Order describes without additional specificity as "multiple levels of review by officers of the Department of Defense." Order at 1. The Order sets forth procedures by which detainees can contest this status before a panel of three commissioned military officers.

The CSRT procedures will be described in more detail below, but in brief, under the terms of the July 7 Order and a July 29, 2004 Memorandum issued by Secretary of the Navy Gordon England implementing the Order, [court's n.10: The Implementing Memorandum . . . can be found at http://www.defenselink.mil/news/Jul2004/d20040730comb.pdf.] detainees for the first time have the right to hear the factual bases for their detention, at least to the extent that those facts do not involve information deemed classified by the administration. Detainees also have the right to testify why they contend they should not be considered "enemy combatants" and may present additional evidence they believe might exculpate them, at least to the extent the tribunal finds such evidence relevant and "reasonably available." The detainees do not have a right to counsel in the proceedings, although each is assigned a military officer who serves as a "Personal Representative" to assist the detainee in understanding the process and presenting his case. Formal rules of evidence do not apply, and there is a presumption in favor of the government's conclusion that a detainee is in fact an "enemy combatant." Although the tribunal is free to consider classified evidence supporting a contention that an individual is an "enemy combatant," that individual is not entitled to have access to or know the details of that classified evidence.

The record of the CSRT proceedings, including the tribunal's decision regarding "enemy combatant" status, is reviewed for legal sufficiency by the Staff Judge Advocate for the Convening Authority, the body designated by the Secretary of the Navy to appoint tribunal members and Personal Representatives. After that review, the Staff Judge Advocate makes a recommendation to the Convening Authority, which is then required either to approve the panel's decision or to send the decision back to the panel for further proceedings. It is the government's position that in the event a conclusion by the tribunal that a detainee is an "enemy combatant" is affirmed, it is legal to hold the detainee in custody until the war on terrorism has been declared by the President to have concluded or until the President or his designees have determined that the detainee is no longer a threat to national security. If the tribunal finally determines that a detainee should no longer be deemed an "enemy combatant," a written report of the decision is forwarded to the Secretary of Defense or his designee, who is then obligated to contact the Secretary of State for coordination of the transfer of the detainee either to his country of citizenship or elsewhere in accordance with law and U.S. foreign policy....

The petitioners in these eleven cases allege that the detention at Guantanamo Bay and the conditions thereof violate a variety of laws. All petitions assert violations of the Fifth Amendment, and a majority claim violations of the Alien Tort Claims Act, the Administrative Procedure Act, [5 U.S.C. §§ 555, 702, 706 (1996)] and the Geneva Conventions. In addition, certain petitions allege violations of the Sixth, Eighth, and Fourteenth Amendments; the War Powers Clause; the Suspension Clause; Army Regulation 190–8, entitled "Enemy Prisoners of War, Retained Personnel, Civilian Internees and Other Detainees;" the International Covenant on Civil and Political Rights ("ICCPR"); the American Declaration on the Rights and Duties of Man ("ADRDM"); the Optional Protocol to the Convention on the Rights of the Child on the Involvement of Children in Armed Conflict; the International Labour Organization's Convention 182, Concerning the Prohibition and Immediate Action for the Elimination of the Worst Forms of Child Labour; and customary international law. The respondents contend that none of these provisions constitutes a valid basis for any of the petitioners' claims and seek dismissal of all counts as a matter of law under Fed.R.Civ.P. 12(b)(6) for failing to state a claim upon which relief can be granted. In the alternative, the respondents seek a judgment based on the pleadings pursuant to Fed.R.Civ.P. 12(c). The respondents have not requested entry of summary judgment pursuant to Fed.R.Civ.P. 56, and they have opposed requests for discovery made by counsel for the petitioners on the ground that those requests are premature at this stage of the proceedings....

Notwithstanding the Supreme Court's decision in *Rasul* that the District Court's dismissal of the petitioners' claims was incorrect as a matter of law, the respondents argue in their October 2004 motion that the *Rasul* decision resolved only whether individuals detained at Guantanamo Bay had the right merely to *allege* in a United States District Court under the *habeas* statute that they are being detained in violation of the Constitution and other laws. Respondents argue that the decision was silent on the issue of whether the detainees actually *possess* any underlying substantive rights, and they further contend that earlier Supreme Court precedent and the law of this Circuit make clear that the detainees do not hold any such substantive rights. Accordingly, it is the respondents' position that although *Rasul* clarified that a detainee has every right to file papers in the Clerk's Office alleging violations of the Constitution, statutes, treaties and other laws, and although the Court has jurisdiction to accept the filing and to consider those papers, the Court must not permit the case to proceed beyond a declaration that no underlying substantive rights exist. While the Court would have welcomed a clearer declaration in the *Rasul* opinion regarding the specific constitutional and other substantive rights of the petitioners, it does not interpret the Supreme Court's decision as narrowly as the respondents suggest it should. To the contrary, the Court interprets *Rasul,* in conjunction with other precedent, to require the recognition that the detainees at Guantanamo Bay possess enforceable constitutional rights....

[After addressing the opinions of Justices Stevens and Kennedy in *Rasul*, the district court stated:] These passages alone would be sufficient for this Court to recognize the special nature of Guantanamo Bay and, in accordance with *Ralpho v. Bell,* to treat it as the equivalent of sovereign U.S. territory where fundamental constitutional rights exist. But perhaps the strongest basis for recognizing that the detainees have fundamental rights to due process rests at the conclusion of the *Rasul* majority opinion. In summarizing the nature of these actions, the Court recognized [that Petitioners' allegations ... unquestionably describe "custody in violation of the Constitution or laws or treaties of the United States." 28 U.S.C. § 2241(c)(3)] ...

There would be nothing impracticable and anomalous in recognizing that the detainees at Guantanamo Bay have the fundamental right to due process of law under the Fifth Amendment. Recognizing the existence of that right at the Naval Base would not cause the United States government any more hardship than would recognizing the existence of constitutional rights of the detainees had they been held within the continental United States. American authorities are in full control at Guantanamo Bay, their activities are immune from Cuban law, and there are few or no significant remnants of native Cuban culture or tradition remaining that can interfere with the implementation of an American system of justice....

Of course, it would be far easier for the government to prosecute the war on terrorism if it could imprison all suspected "enemy combatants" at Guantanamo Bay without having to acknowledge and respect any constitutional rights of detainees. That, however, is not the relevant legal test. By definition, constitutional limitations often, if not always, burden the abilities of government officials to serve their constituencies. Although this nation unquestionably must take strong action under the leadership of the Commander in Chief to protect itself against enormous and unprecedented threats, that necessity cannot negate the existence of the most basic fundamental rights for which the people of this country have fought and died for well over two hundred years. As articulated by the Supreme Court after the conclusion of the Civil War:

> The Constitution of the United States is a law for rulers and people, equally in war and in peace, and covers with the shield of its protection all classes of men, at all times, and under all circumstances. No doctrine, involving more pernicious consequences, was ever invented by the wit of man than that any of its provisions can be suspended during any of the great exigencies of government. Such a doctrine leads directly to anarchy or despotism, but the theory of necessity on which it is based is false; for the government, within the Constitution, has all the powers granted to it, which are necessary to preserve its existence; as has been happily proved by the result of the great effort to throw off its just authority.

Ex Parte Milligan, 71 U.S. (4 Wall.) 2, 120–21 ... (1866). *See also* United States v. Robel, 389 U.S. 258, 264 ... (1967) ("It would indeed be ironic if, in the name of national defense, we would sanction the subversion of one of those liberties ... which makes the defense of the Nation worthwhile.").

In sum, there can be no question that the Fifth Amendment right asserted by the Guantanamo detainees in this litigation—the right not to be deprived of liberty without due process of law–is one of the most fundamental rights recognized by the U.S. Constitution. In light of the Supreme Court's decision in *Rasul,* it is clear that Guantanamo Bay must be considered the equivalent of a U.S. territory in which fundamental constitutional rights apply....

Having found that the Guantanamo detainees are entitled to due process under the Fifth Amendment to the United States Constitution, the Court must now address the exact contours of that right as it applies to the government's determinations that they are "enemy combatants." Due process is an inherently flexible concept, and the specific process due in a particular circumstance depends upon the context in which the right is asserted. Morrissey v. Brewer, 408 U.S. 471, 481 ... (1972). Resolution of a due process challenge requires the consideration and weighing of three factors: the private interest of the person asserting the lack of due process; the risk of erroneous deprivation of that interest through use of existing procedures and the probable value of additional or substitute procedural safeguards; and the competing interests of the government, including the financial, administrative, and other burdens that would be incurred were additional safeguards to be provided. Mathews v. Eldridge, 424 U.S. 319, 335 . . . (1976).

The Supreme Court applied a *Mathews v. Eldridge* analysis in Hamdi v. Rumsfeld, 542 U.S. 507, 124 S.Ct. 2633 (2004), a decision issued the same day as *Rasul* which considered an American citizen's due process challenge to the U.S. military's designation of him as an "enemy combatant." Although none of the detainees in the cases before this Court is an American citizen, the facts under *Hamdi* are otherwise identical in all material respects to those in *Rasul*. Accordingly, *Hamdi* forms both the starting point and core of this Court's consideration of what process is due to the Guantanamo detainees in these cases. . . .

It must be added that the liberty interests of the detainees cannot be minimized for purposes of applying the *Mathews v. Eldridge* balancing test by the government's allegations that they are in fact terrorists or are affiliated with terrorist organizations. The purpose of imposing a due process requirement is to prevent mistaken characterizations and erroneous detentions, and the government is not entitled to short circuit this inquiry by claiming *ab initio* that the individuals are alleged to have committed bad acts. *See Hamdi*, 124 S.Ct. at 2647 ("our starting point for the *Mathews v. Eldridge* analysis is unaltered by the allegations surrounding the particular detainee or the organizations with which he is alleged to have associated"). Moreover, all petitioners in these cases have asserted that they are not terrorists and have not been involved in terrorist activities, and under the standards provided by the applicable rules of procedure, those allegations must be accepted as true for purposes of resolving the government's motion to dismiss. . . .

According to the plurality in *Hamdi*, an individual detained by the government on the ground that he is an "enemy combatant" "must receive notice of the factual basis for his classification, and a fair opportunity to rebut the Government's factual assertions before a neutral decisionmaker." *Id.* at 2648. Noting the potential burden these requirements might cause the government at a time of ongoing military conflict, the plurality stated that it would not violate due process for the decision maker to consider hearsay as the most reliable available evidence. *Id.* at 2649. In addition, the plurality declared it permissible to adopt a presumption in favor of "enemy combatant" status, "so long as that presumption remained a rebuttable one and fair opportunity for rebuttal were provided." *Id.* For that presumption to apply and for the onus to shift to the detainee, however, the plurality clarified that the government first would have to "put[ ] forth credible evidence that the [detainee] meets the enemy-combatant criteria." *Id.*

After setting forth these standards, the plurality suggested the "possibility" that constitutional requirements of due process could be met by an "appropriately authorized and properly constituted military tribunal" and referenced the military tribunals used to determine whether an individual is entitled to prisoner of war status under the Geneva Convention. *Id.* at 2651 (*citing* Enemy Prisoners of War, Retained Personnel, Civilian Internees and Other Detainees, Army Regulation 190–8, § 1–6 (1997)).... The plurality concluded by affirming that the detainee "unquestionably [had] the right to access to counsel in connection with the proceedings on remand." *Id.*

Hamdi was decided before the creation of the Combatant Status Review Tribunal, and the respondents contend in their motion to dismiss that were this Court to conclude that the detainees are entitled to due process under the Fifth Amendment, the CSRT proceedings would fully comply with all constitutional requirements. More specifically, the respondents claim that the CSRT regulations were modeled after Army Regulation 190–8 governing the determination of prisoner of war status, referenced in *Hamdi*, and actually exceed the requirements set forth by the *Hamdi* plurality. For example, respondents cite the facts that under CSRT rules, tribunal members must certify that they have not been involved in the "apprehension, detention, interrogation, or previous determination of status of the detainee[s]," that detainees are provided a "Personal Representative" to assist in the preparation of their cases, that the "Recorder"–that is, the person who presents evidence in support of "enemy combatant" status–must search for exculpatory evidence, that the detainee is entitled to an unclassified summary of the evidence against him, and that the tribunal's decisions are reviewed by a higher authority. Motion to Dismiss at 34–35. Notwithstanding the procedures cited by the respondents, the Court finds that the procedures provided in the CSRT regulations fail to satisfy constitutional due process requirements in several respects.

The constitutional defects in the CSRT procedures can be separated into two categories. The first category consists of defects which apply across the board to all detainees in the cases before this Judge. Specifically, those deficiencies are the CSRT's failure to provide the detainees with access to material evidence upon which the tribunal affirmed their "enemy combatant" status and the failure to permit the assistance of counsel to compensate for the government's refusal to disclose classified information directly to the detainees. The second category of defects involves those which are detainee specific and may or may not apply to every petitioner in this litigation. Those defects include the manner in which the CSRT handled accusations of torture and the vague and potentially overbroad definition of "enemy combatant" in the CSRT regulations. While additional specific defects may or may not exist, further inquiry is unnecessary at this stage of the litigation given the fundamental deficiencies [that the court thereafter addressed in detail]....

Additional defects in the CSRT procedures support the denial of the respondents' motion to dismiss at least some of the petitions, though these grounds may or may not exist in every case before the Court and though the respondents might ultimately prevail on these issues once the petitioners have been given an opportunity to litigate them fully in the *habeas* proceedings.

a. Reliance on Statements Possibly Obtained Through Torture or Other Coercion

The first of these specific grounds involves the CSRT's reliance on statements allegedly obtained through torture or otherwise alleged to have been provided by some detainees involuntarily. The Supreme Court has long held that due process prohibits the government's use of involuntary statements obtained through torture or other mistreatment....

b. Vague and Overly Broad Definition of "Enemy Combatant"

Although the government has been detaining individuals as "enemy combatants" since the issuance of the AUMF in 2001, it apparently did not formally define the term until the July 7, 2004 Order creating the CSRT. The lack of a formal definition seemed to have troubled at least the plurality of the Supreme Court in *Hamdi*, but for purposes of resolving the issues in that case, the plurality considered the government's definition to be an individual who was " 'part of or supporting forces hostile to the United States or coalition partners' in Afghanistan *and* who 'engaged in an armed conflict against the United States' there." 124 S.Ct. 2633, 2639 (*quoting* Brief for the Respondents) (emphasis added). The Court agreed with the government that the AUMF authorizes the Executive to detain individuals falling within that limited definition, *id.*, with the plurality explaining that "[b]ecause detention to prevent a combatant's return to the battlefield is a fundamental incident of waging war, in permitting the use of 'necessary and appropriate force,' Congress has clearly and unmistakably authorized detention in the narrow circumstances considered here." *Id.* at 2641. The plurality cautioned, however, "that indefinite detention for the purpose of interrogation is not authorized" by the AUMF, and added that a congressional grant of authority to the President to use "necessary and appropriate force" might not be properly interpreted to include the authority to detain individuals for the duration of a particular conflict if that conflict does not take a form that is based on "longstanding law-of-war principles." *Id.*

The definition of "enemy combatant" contained in the Order creating the CSRT is significantly broader than the definition considered in *Hamdi*. According to the definition currently applied by the government, an "enemy combatant" "shall mean an individual who was part of or supporting Taliban or al Qaeda forces, or associated forces that are engaged in hostilities against the United States or its coalition partners. This *includes* any person who has committed a belligerent act or has directly supported hostilities in aid of enemy armed forces." July 7, 2004 Order at 1 (emphasis added). Use of the word "includes" indicates that the government interprets the AUMF to permit the indefinite detention of individuals who never committed a belligerent act or who never directly supported hostilities against the U.S. or its allies. This Court explored the government's position on the matter by posing a series of hypothetical questions to counsel at the December 1, 2004 hearing on the motion to dismiss. In response to the hypotheticals, counsel for the respondents argued that the Executive has the authority to detain the following individuals until the conclusion of the war on terrorism: "[a] little old lady in Switzerland who writes checks to what she thinks is a charity that helps orphans in Afghanistan but [what] really is a front to finance al-Qaeda activities," Transcript at 25, a person who teaches English to the son of an al Qaeda member, *id.* at 27, and a journalist who knows the location of Osama Bin Laden but refuses to disclose it to protect her source. *Id.* at 29.

... The petitioners have argued in opposition to the respondents' motion to dismiss, however, that at least with respect to some detainees, the expansive definition of "enemy combatant" currently in use in the CSRT proceedings violates long standing principles of due process by permitting the detention of individuals based solely on their membership in anti-American organizations rather than on actual activities supporting the use of violence or harm against the United States....

Whether the detention of each individual petitioner is authorized by the AUMF and satisfies the mandates of due process must ultimately be determined on a detainee by detainee basis. At this stage of the litigation, however, sufficient allegations have been made by at least some of the petitioners and certain evidence exists in some CSRT factual returns to warrant the denial of the respondents' motion to dismiss on the ground that the respondents have employed an overly broad definition of "enemy combatant." ...

D. Claims Based on the Geneva Conventions

The petitioners in all of the above captioned cases except *Al Odah v. United States,* 02–CV–0828, have also asserted claims based on the Geneva Conventions, which regulate the treatment of certain prisoners of war and civilians. The respondents contend that all Geneva Convention claims filed by the petitioners must be dismissed because Congress has not enacted any separate legislation specifically granting individuals the right to file private lawsuits based on the Conventions and because the Conventions are not "self-executing," meaning they do not by themselves create such a private right of action. Motion to Dismiss at 68–71. In the alternative, the respondents argue that even if the Geneva Conventions are self-executing, they do not apply to members of al Qaeda because that international terrorist organization is not a state party to the Conventions. *Id.* at 70 n.80. Finally, although respondents concede that Afghanistan is a state party to the Conventions and admit that the Geneva Conventions apply to Taliban detainees, they emphasize that President Bush has determined that Taliban fighters are not entitled to prisoner of war status under the Third Geneva Convention and contend that this decision is the final word on the matter. *Id.*

The Constitution provides that "all Treaties made ... under the Authority of the United States, shall be the supreme Law of the Land." U.S. Const. art. VI, cl. 2 .....

The Third and Fourth Geneva Conventions do not expressly grant private rights of action, and whether they impliedly create such rights has never been definitively resolved by the D.C. Circuit. The Court of Appeals is currently reviewing the matter in the appeal of Hamdan v. Rumsfeld, 344 F.Supp.2d 152 (D.D.C.2004), but until that court issues a definitive ruling, this Court must make its own determination. After reviewing *Hamdan* and the briefs filed by petitioners and respondents in the instant cases, the Court concludes that the Conventions are self-executing and adopts the following reasoning provided by Judge Robertson:

> Because the Geneva Conventions were written to protect individuals, because the Executive Branch of our government has implemented the Geneva Conventions for fifty years without questioning the absence of implementing legislation, because Congress clearly understood that the Conventions did not require implementing legislation except in a few specific areas, and because nothing in the Third Geneva Convention itself manifests the contracting parties' intention that it not become effective as domestic law without the enactment of implementing legislation, I conclude that, insofar as it is pertinent here, the Third Geneva Convention is a self-executing treaty. *Id.* at 165.

Although the Court rejects the primary basis argued by the respondents for dismissal of claims based on the Geneva Conventions, it does accept one of the alternative grounds put forth in their motion, namely that the Geneva Conventions do not apply to al Qaeda. Article 2 of the Third and Fourth Geneva Conventions provides, "In addition to the provisions which shall be implemented in peacetime, the present Convention shall apply to all cases of declared war or of any other armed conflict which may arise between two or more of the High Contracting Parties, even if the state of war is not recognized by one of them." Clearly, al Qaeda is not a "High Contracting Party" to the Conventions, and thus individuals detained on the ground that they are members of that terrorist organization are not entitled to the protections of the treaties.

This does not end the analysis for purposes of resolving the respondents' motion to dismiss, however, because some of the petitioners in the above-captioned cases are being detained either solely because they were Taliban fighters or because they were associated with both the Taliban and al Qaeda. Significantly, the respondents concede that the Geneva Conventions apply to the Taliban detainees in light of the fact that Afghanistan is a High Contracting Party to the Conventions.... They argue in their motion to dismiss, however, that notwithstanding the *application* of the Third Geneva Convention to Taliban detainees, the treaty does not *protect* Taliban detainees because the President has declared that no Taliban fighter is a "prisoner of war" as defined by the Convention. *Id.* The respondents' argument in this regard must be rejected, however, for the Third Geneva Convention does not permit the determination of prisoner of war status in such a conclusory fashion.

Article 4 of the Third Geneva Convention [GPW] defines who is considered a "prisoner of war" under the treaty [see the various tests for pw status under GPW art. 4, in the Documents Supplement]. . . . If there is any doubt as to whether individuals satisfy the Article 4 prerequisites, Article 5 entitles them to be treated as prisoners of war "until such time as their "status has been determined by a competent tribunal." Army Regulation 190–8 created the rules for the "competent tribunal" referenced in Article 5 of the Third Geneva Convention, and the CSRT was established in accordance with that provision. *See* Army Regulation 190–8 § 1–1.b. . . .

Nothing in the Convention itself or in Army Regulation 190–8 authorizes the President of the United States to rule by fiat that an entire group of fighters covered by the Third Geneva Convention falls outside of the Article 4 definitions of "prisoners of war." To the contrary, and as Judge Robertson ruled in *Hamdan,* the President's broad characterization of how the Taliban generally fought the war in Afghanistan cannot substitute for an Article 5 tribunal's determination on an individualized basis of whether a particular fighter complied with the laws of war or otherwise falls within an exception denying him prisoner of war status. 344 F.Supp.2d at 161–62. Clearly, had an appropriate determination been properly made by an Article 5 tribunal that a petitioner was not a prisoner of war, that petitioner's claims based on the Third Geneva Convention could not survive the respondents' motion to dismiss. But although numerous petitioners in the above-captioned cases were found by the CSRT to have been Taliban fighters, nowhere do the CSRT records for many of those petitioners reveal specific findings that they committed some particular act or failed to satisfy some defined prerequisite entitling the respondents to deprive them of prisoner of war status. Accordingly, the Court denies that portion of the respondents' motion to dismiss addressing the Geneva Convention claims of those petitioners who were found to be Taliban fighters but who were not specifically determined to be excluded from prisoner of war status by a competent Article 5 tribunal.

. . . Finally, having found that all detainees possess Fifth Amendment due process rights and that some detainees possibly possess rights under the Geneva Conventions, it is unnecessary to look to customary international law to resolve the petitioners' claims. *See* The Paquete Habana, 175 U.S. 677, 699 . . . (1900) ("where there is no treaty and no controlling executive or legislative act or judicial decision, resort must be had to the customs and usages of civilized nations"). . . .

Notes and Questions

1. Judge Green's statement in *In re Guantanamo Detainee Cases* that members of al Qaeda could not be protected by Geneva law since al Qaeda is not a signatory to the 1949 Geneva Conventions is in error since whenever the Conventions apply to certain armed conflicts (such as those in Afghanistan and Iraq) persons are protected under various articles in the Conventions. *See, e.g.,* Jordan J. Paust, *Executive Plans and Authorizations to*

Violate International Law Concerning Treatment and Interrogation of Detainees, 43 COLUM. J. TRANSNAT'L L. 811, 816–21, 830 (2005). Further, members of al Qaeda are most likely nationals of various signatories to the Conventions, because nearly every state is a contracting party. Additionally, the Conventions reflect customary international law that is universally applicable and protects all human beings according to the terms of various articles. Moreover, any person who is not a prisoner of war is protected by common Article 3 of the Conventions and various articles in the Geneva Convention Relative to the Protection of Civilian Persons in Time of War [Geneva Civilian Convention]. There are no gaps in coverage because of the status of a person detained. *See, e.g., id.* at 816–17 & n.20.

2. In Rumsfeld v. Padilla, 542 U.S. 426 (2004), Justice Stevens had stressed the importance of "the constraints imposed on the Executive by the rule of law," rightly condemned torture of the mind imposed through incommunicado detention, and offered a prescient warning: "Whether the information so procured is more or less reliable than that acquired by more extreme forms of torture is of no consequence. For if this Nation is to remain true to the ideals symbolized in its flag, it must not wield the tools of tyrants even to resist an assault by the forces of tyranny." *Id.* at 546–47 (Stevens, J., dissenting).

c. *Military Commissions at Guantanamo*

On November 13, 2001, President George W. Bush issued a Military Order for the purpose of creating military commissions with allegedly exclusive jurisdiction to try certain designated foreign persons "for violations of the laws of war and other applicable laws" relevant to any prior or future "acts of international terrorism." Military Order of Nov. 13, 2001, 66 Fed. Reg. 57,833 §§ 1(e), 2(a)(1)(ii)-(iii) (Nov. 16, 2001). The Order would create military commissions with a structure and procedures that are inconsistent with the requirements of international law and raise serious constitutional issues, some of which are explored below. In particular, the military commissions would prosecute only aliens (thus, resulting in national origin discrimination and denials of equality required, for example, in Articles 2, 14, and 26 of the ICCPR) and would utilize procedures violative of human rights law and the laws of war.

HAMDAN v. RUMSFELD

344 F.Supp.2d 152 (D.D.C. 2004).

ROBERTSON, J.

Salim Ahmed Hamdan petitions for a writ of habeas corpus, challenging the lawfulness of the Secretary of Defense's plan to try him for alleged war crimes before a military commission convened under special orders issued by the President of the United States, rather than before a court-martial convened under the Uniform Code of Military Justice. The government moves to dismiss. Because Hamdan has not been determined by a competent tribunal to be an offender triable under the law of war, 10 U.S.C. § 821, and because in any event the procedures established for the Military Commission by the President's order are "contrary to or inconsistent" with those applicable to courts-martial, 10 U.S.C. § 836, Hamdan's petition will be granted in part. The government's motion will be denied. The reasons for these rulings are set forth below.

Hamdan was captured in Afghanistan in late 2001, during a time of hostilities in that country that followed the terrorist attacks in the United States on September 11, 2001 mounted by al Qaeda, a terrorist group harbored in Afghanistan. He was detained by American military forces and transferred sometime in 2002 to the detention facility set up by the Defense Department at Guantanamo Bay Naval Base, Cuba. On July 3, 2003, acting pursuant to the Military Order he had issued on November 13, 2001, [court's fn.1: Detention, Treatment, and Trial of Certain Non–Citizens in the War Against Terrorism, 66 Fed.Reg. 57,833 (Nov. 13, 2001)] and finding "that there is reason to believe that [Hamdan] was a member of al Qaida or was otherwise involved in terrorism directed against the United States," the President designated Hamdan for trial by military commission. Press Release, Dep't of Defense, President Determines Enemy Combatants Subject to His Military Order (July 3, 2003), http://www.defenselink.mil/releases/2003/nr20030703–0173.html. In December 2003, Hamdan was placed in a part of the Guantanamo Bay facility known as Camp Echo, where he was held in isolation. On December 18, 2003, military counsel was appointed for him. On February 12, 2004, Hamdan's counsel filed a demand for charges and speedy trial under Article 10 of the Uniform Code of Military Justice. On February 23, 2004, the legal advisor to the Appointing Authority [court's fn.2: The Department of Defense has implemented the President's Military Order of November 3, 2001 with a series of Military Commission Orders, Instructions, and other documents. *See generally* Dep't of Defense, Military Commissions (providing extensive links to background materials on the Military Commissions), *at* http:// www.defenselink.mil/news/commissions.html. The Secretary of Defense may designate an "Appointing Authority" to issue orders establishing and regulating military commissions. Military Commission Order No. 1 (March 21, 2002), 32 C.F.R. § 9.2, http:// www.defenselink.mil/news/Mar2002/d20020321ord.pdf. Secretary Rumsfeld designated John D. Altenburg, Jr. as Appointing Authority. Press Release, Dep't of Defense, Appointing Authority Decision Made (December 30, 2003), http:// www.defenselink.mil/releases/2003/nr20031230–0820.html.] ruled that the UCMJ did not apply to Hamdan's detention. On April 6, 2004, in the United States District Court for the Western District of Washington, Hamdan's counsel filed the petition for mandamus or habeas corpus that is now before this court. On July 9, 2004, Hamdan was formally charged with conspiracy to commit the following offenses: "attacking civilians; attacking civilian objects; murder by an unprivileged belligerent; destruction of property by an unprivileged belligerent; and terrorism." Dep't of Defense, Military Commission List of Charges for Salim Ahmed Hamdan, http://www.defenselink.mil/news/Jul2004/d20040714hcc.pdf. Following the Supreme Court's decision on June 28, 2004, that federal district courts have jurisdiction of habeas petitions filed by Guantanamo Bay detainees, Rasul v. Bush, 542 U.S. 466, 124 S.Ct. 2686 ... (2004), and the Ninth Circuit's decision on July 8, 2004, that all such cases should be heard in the District of the District of Columbia, Gherebi v. Bush, 374 F.3d 727 (9th Cir.2004), the case was transferred here, where it was docketed on September 2, 2004. Oral argument was held on October 25, 2004.

Hamdan's petition is stated in eight counts. It alleges the denial of Hamdan's speedy trial rights in violation of Article 10 of the Uniform Code of Military Justice, 10 U.S.C. § 810 (count 1); challenges the nature and length of Hamdan's pretrial detention as a violation of the Third Geneva Convention (count 2) and of Common Article 3 of the Geneva Conventions (count 3); challenges the order establishing the Military Commission as a violation of the separation of powers doctrine (count 4) and as purporting to invest the Military Commission with authority that exceeds the law of war (count 7); challenges the creation of the Military Commission as a violation of the equal protection guarantees of the Fifth Amendment (count 5) and of 42 U.S.C. § 1981 (count 6); and argues that the Military Order does not, on its face, apply to Hamdan (count 8).

Although Judge Lasnik (W.D.Wash.) ordered the respondents to file a "return," Order Granting Motion to Hold Petition in Abeyance (W.D.Wash. No. 04–0777) (May 11, 2004), and although the motion to dismiss now before this court is styled a "consolidated return to petition and memorandum of law in support of cross-motion to dismiss," no formal show cause order has issued, nor have the respondents ever filed a factual response to Hamdan's allegations. An order issued October 4, 2004 [Dkt #26] by Judge Joyce Hens Green, who is coordinating and managing all of the Guantanamo Bay cases in this court, provided that "[r]espondents are not required ... to file a response addressing enemy combatant status issues ... or a factual return providing the factual basis for petitioner's detention as an enemy combatant, pending further order of the Court." The absence of a factual return is of no moment, however. The issues before me will be resolved as a matter of law. The only three facts that are necessary to my disposition of the petition for habeas corpus and of the cross-motion to dismiss are that Hamdan was captured in Afghanistan during hostilities after the 9/11 attacks, that he has asserted his entitlement to prisoner-of-war status under the Third Geneva Convention, and that the government has not convened a competent tribunal to determine whether Hamdan is entitled to such status. All of those propositions appear to be undisputed.

1. Abstention is neither required nor appropriate.

The well-established doctrine that federal courts will "normally not entertain habeas

petitions by military prisoners unless all available military remedies have been exhausted," Schlesinger v. Councilman, 420 U.S. 738 ...

(1975), is not applicable here. *Councilman* involved a court-martial, not a military commission. . . .

2. No proper determination has been made that Hamdan is an offender triable by military tribunal under the law of war.

a. The President may establish military commissions only for offenders or offenses triable by military tribunal under the law of war.

The major premise of the government's argument that the President has untrammeled power to establish military tribunals is that his authority emanates from Article II of the Constitution and is inherent in his role as commander-in-chief. None of the principal cases on which the government relies, *Ex parte* Quirin, 317 U.S. 1 . . . (1942); Application of Yamashita, 327 U.S. 1 . . . (1946); and Madsen v. Kinsella, 343 U.S. 341 . . . (1952), has so held. In *Quirin* the Supreme Court located the power in Article I, § 8, emphasizing the President's *executive* power as commander-in-chief "to wage war which *Congress* has declared, and to carry into effect all laws passed by *Congress* for the conduct of war and for the government and regulation of the Armed Forces, and all laws defining and punishing offences against the law of nations, including those which pertain to the conduct of war." *Quirin,* 317 U.S. at 26 . . . (emphasis added). *Quirin* stands for the proposition that the authority to appoint military commissions is found, not in the inherent power of the presidency, but in the Articles of War (a predecessor of the Uniform Code of Military Justice) by which *Congress* provided rules for the government of the army. *Id.* Thus, *Congress* provided for the trial by courts-martial of members of the armed forces and specific classes of persons associated with or serving with the army, *id.,* and "the *Articles* [*of War*] also recognize the 'military commission' appointed by military command as an appropriate tribunal for the trial and punishment of offenses against the law of war not ordinarily tried by court martial." *Id.* The President's authority to prescribe procedures for military commissions was conferred by Articles 38 and 46 of the Articles of War. *Id.* The *Quirin* Court sustained the President's order creating a military commission, because "[b]y his Order creating the . . . Commission [the President] has undertaken to exercise the authority conferred upon him by *Congress* . . . ." *Id.* at 28.

This sentence continues with the words ". . . and also such authority as the Constitution itself gives the Commander in Chief, to direct the performance of those functions which may constitutionally be performed by the military arm of the nation in time of war." *Id.* at 28. That dangling idea is not explained–in *Quirin* or in later cases. The Court expressly found it unnecessary in *Quirin* "to determine to what extent the President as Commander in Chief has constitutional power to create military commissions without the support of Congressional legislation. For here Congress has authorized trial of offenses against the law of war before such commissions." *Id.*

In *Yamashita,* the Supreme Court noted that it had "had occasion [in *Quirin*] to consider at length the sources and nature of the authority to create military commissions for the trial of enemy combatants for offenses against the law of war," *Yamashita,* at 327 U.S. at 7, and noted:

> [W]e there pointed out that *Congress,* in the exercise of the power conferred upon it by Article I, § 8 Cl. 10 of the Constitution to 'define and punish ... Offenses against the Law of Nations ... ,' of which the law of war is a part, had by the Articles of War [citation omitted] recognized the 'military commission' appointed by military command as it had previously existed in United States Army practice, as an appropriate tribunal for the trial and punishment of offenses against the law of war.

Id. at 7, 66 S.Ct. 340 (emphasis added). Further on, the Court noted:

> We further pointed out that *Congress,* by sanctioning trial of enemy combatants for violations of the law of war by military commission, had not attempted to codify the law of war or to mark its precise boundaries. Instead, by Article 15 it had incorporated, by reference, as within the preexisting jurisdiction of military commissions created by appropriate military command, all offenses which are defined as such by the law of war, and which may constitutionally be included within that jurisdiction. It thus adopted the system of military common law applied by military tribunals so far as it should be recognized and deemed applicable by the courts, and as further defined and supplemented by the Hague Convention, to which the United States and the Axis powers were parties."

Id. at 7–8 (emphasis added). And again:

> *Congress,* in the exercise of its constitutional power to define and punish offenses against the law of nations, of which the law of war is a part, has recognized the 'military commission' appointed by military command, as it had previously existed in United States Army practice, as an appropriate tribunal for the trial and punishment of offenses against the law of war.

Id. at 16 (emphasis added). *Yamashita* concluded that, by giving "sanction ... to any use of the military commission contemplated by the common law of war," *Congress* "preserve[d] their traditional jurisdiction over enemy combatants unimpaired by the Articles [of War]...." *Id.* at 20.

What was then Article 15 of the Articles of War is now Article 21 of the Uniform Code of Military Justice, 10 U.S.C. § 821. It provides:

> The provisions of this chapter conferring jurisdiction upon courts-martial do not deprive military commissions, provost courts, or other military tribunals of concurrent jurisdiction with respect to offenders or offenses that by statute or by the law of war may be tried by military commissions, provost courts, or other military tribunals.

Quirin and *Yamashita* make it clear that Article 21 represents Congressional approval of the historical, traditional, non-statutory military commission. The language of that approval, however, does not extend past "offenders or offenses that by statute or by the law of war may be tried by military commissions...." 10 U.S.C. § 821.

Any additional jurisdiction for military commissions would have to come from some inherent executive authority that *Quirin, Yamashita,* and *Madsen* neither define nor directly support. If the President does have inherent power in this area, it is quite limited. Congress has the power to amend those limits and could do so tomorrow. Were the President to act outside the limits now set for military commissions by Article 21, however, his actions would fall into the most restricted category of cases identified by Justice Jackson in his concurring opinion in Youngstown Sheet & Tube Co. v. Sawyer, 343 U.S. 579, 637 ... (1952), in which "the President takes measures incompatible with the expressed or implied will of Congress," and in which the President's power is "at its lowest ebb."

b. The law of war includes the Third Geneva Convention, which requires trial by court-martial as long as Hamdan's POW status is in doubt.

"From the very beginning of its history this Court has recognized and applied the law of war as including that part of the law of nations which prescribes, for the conduct of war, the status, rights and duties of enemy nations as well as of enemy individuals."

This language is from *Quirin,* 317 U.S. at 27–28. The United States has ratified the Geneva Convention Relative to the Treatment of Prisoners of War of August 12, 1949, 6 U.S.T. 3316, 74 U.N.T.S. 135 (the Third Geneva Convention). Afghanistan is a party to the Geneva Conventions. The Third Geneva Convention is acknowledged to be part of the law of war, 10/25/04 Tr. at 55; Military Commission Instruction No. 2, § (5)(G) (Apr. 30, 2003); 32 C.F.R. § 11.5(g), http://www.defenselink.mil/news/May2003/d20030430milcominstno2.pdf. It is applicable by its terms in "all cases of declared war or of any other armed conflict which may arise between two or more of the High Contracting Parties, even if the state of war is not recognized by one of them." Third Geneva Convention, art. 2. That language covers the hostilities in Afghanistan that were ongoing in late 2001, when Hamdan was captured there. If Hamdan is entitled to the protections accorded prisoners of war under the Third Geneva Convention, one need look no farther than Article 102 for the rule that requires his habeas petition to be granted:

> A prisoner of war can be validly sentenced only if the sentence has been pronounced by the same courts according to the same procedure as in the case of members of the armed forces of the Detaining Power, and if, furthermore, the provisions of the present Chapter have been observed.

The Military Commission is not such a court. Its procedures are not such procedures.

The government does not dispute the proposition that prisoners of war may not be tried by military tribunal. Its position is that Hamdan is not entitled to the protections of the Third Geneva Convention at all, and certainly not to prisoner-of-war status, and that in any event the protections of the Third Geneva Convention are not enforceable by way of habeas corpus.

(1) The government's first argument that the Third Geneva Convention does not protect Hamdan asserts that Hamdan was captured, not in the course of a conflict between the United States and Afghanistan, but in the course of a "separate" conflict with al Qaeda. That argument is rejected. The government apparently bases the argument on a Presidential "finding" that it claims is "not reviewable." *See* Motion to Dismiss at 33, Hicks v. Bush (D.D.C. No. 02–00299) (October 14, 2004). The finding is set forth in Memorandum from the President, to the Vice President *et al.,* Humane Treatment of al Qaeda and Taliban Detainees (February 7, 2002), http://www.library.law.pace.edu/research/020207_bushmemo.pdf, stating that the Third Geneva Convention applies to the Taliban detainees, but not to the al Qaeda detainees captured in Afghanistan, because al Qaeda is not a state party to the Geneva Conventions. Notwithstanding the President's view that the United States was engaged in two separate conflicts in Afghanistan (the common public understanding is to the contrary, *see* Joan Fitzpatrick, *Jurisdiction of Military Commissions and the Ambiguous War on Terrorism*, 96 AM. J. INT'L. L. 345, 349 (2002) (conflict in Afghanistan was international armed conflict in which Taliban and al Qaeda joined forces against U.S. and its Afghan allies)), the government's attempt to separate the Taliban from al Qaeda for Geneva Convention purposes finds no support in the structure of the Conventions themselves, which are triggered by the place of the conflict, and not by what particular faction a fighter is associated with. *See* Amicus Brief of General David M. Brahms (ret.), Admiral Lee F. Gunn (ret.), Admiral John D. Hutson (ret.), General Richard O'Meara (ret.) (Generals and Admirals Amicus Brief) at 17 (citing Memorandum from William H. Taft IV, Legal Adviser, Dep't of State, to Counsel to the President ¶ 3 (Feb. 2, 2002), http:// www.fas.org/sgp/othergov/taft.pdf). Thus at some level—whether as a prisoner-of-war entitled to the full panoply of Convention protections or only under the more limited protections afforded by Common Article 3 . . . –the Third Geneva Convention applies to all persons detained in Afghanistan during the hostilities there.

(2) The government next argues that, even if the Third Geneva Convention might theoretically apply to anyone captured in the Afghanistan theater, members of al Qaeda such as Hamdan are not entitled to POW status because they do not satisfy the test established by Article 4(2) of the Third Geneva Convention–they do not carry arms openly and operate under the laws and customs of war. Gov't Resp. at 35. *See also* The White House, Statement by the Press Secretary on the Geneva Convention (May 7, 2003), http:// www.whitehouse.gov/news/releases/2003/05/20030507–18.html. We know this, the government argues,

because the President himself has determined that Hamdan was a member of al Qaeda or otherwise involved in terrorism against the United States. *Id.* Presidential determinations in this area, the government argues, are due "extraordinary deference." 10/25/04 Tr. at 38. Moreover (as the court was advised for the first time at oral argument on October 25, 2004) a Combatant Status Review Tribunal (CSRT) found, after a hearing on October 3, 2004, that Hamdan has the status of an enemy combatant "as either a member of or affiliated with Al Qaeda." 10/25/04 Tr. at 12.

Article 5 of the Third Geneva Convention provides:

> Should any doubt arise as to whether persons, having committed a belligerent act and having fallen into the hands of the enemy, belong to any of the categories enumerated in Article 4 such persons shall enjoy the protection of the present Convention until such time as their status has been determined by a competent tribunal.

This provision has been implemented and confirmed by Army Regulation 190–8, Enemy Prisoners of War, Retained Personnel, Civilian Internees and Other Detainees, http://www.army.mil/usapa/epubs/pdf/r190_8.pdf., Hamdan has asserted his entitlement to POW status, and the Army's regulations provide that whenever a detainee makes such a claim his status is "in doubt." Army Regulation 190–8, § 1–6(a); *Hamdi*, 542 U.S. at _, 124 S.Ct. at 2658 (Souter, J., concurring). The Army's regulation is in keeping with general international understandings of the meaning of Article 5. *See generally* Generals and Admirals Amicus Brief at 18–22.

Thus the government's position that no doubt has arisen as to Hamdan's status does not withstand scrutiny, and neither does the government's position that, if a hearing is required by Army regulations, "it was provided," 10/25/04 Tr. at 40. There is nothing in this record to suggest that a competent tribunal has determined that Hamdan is not a prisoner-of-war under the Geneva Conventions. Hamdan has appeared before the Combatant Status Review Tribunal, but the CSRT was not established to address detainees' status under the Geneva Conventions. It was established to comply with the Supreme Court's mandate in *Hamdi*, *supra*, to decide "whether the detainee is properly detained as an enemy combatant" for purposes of continued detention. Memorandum From Deputy Secretary of Defense, to Secretary of the Navy, Order Establishing Combatant Status Review Tribunal 3 (July 7, 2003), http://www.defenselink.mil/news/Jul2004/d20040707review.pdf; *see also* Memorandum From Secretary of the Navy, Implementation of Combatant Status Review Tribunal Procedures for Enemy Combatants Detained at Guantanamo Bay Naval Base, Cuba (July 29, 2004), http://www.defenselink.mil/news/Jul2004/d20040730comb.pdf.

The government's legal position is that the CSRT determination that Hamdan was a member of or affiliated with al Qaeda is also determinative of Hamdan's prisoner-of-war status, since the President has already determined that detained al Qaeda members are not prisoners-of-war under the Geneva Conventions, *see* 10/25/04 Tr. at 37. The President is not a "tribunal," however. The government must convene a competent tribunal (or address a competent tribunal already convened) and seek a specific determination as to Hamdan's status under the Geneva Conventions. Until or unless such a tribunal decides otherwise, Hamdan has, and must be accorded, the full protections of a prisoner-of-war.

(3) The government's next argument, that Common Article 3 does not apply because it was meant to cover local and not international conflicts, is also rejected. It is universally agreed, and is demonstrable in the Convention language itself, in the context in which it was adopted, and by the generally accepted law of nations, that Common Article 3 embodies "international human norms," Mehinovic v. Vuckovic, 198 F.Supp.2d 1322, 1351 (N.D.Ga.2002), and that it sets forth the "most fundamental requirements of the law of war." Kadic v. Karadzic, 70 F.3d at 232, 243 (2d Cir.1995). The International Court of Justice has stated it plainly: "There is no doubt that, in the event of international armed conflicts . . . [the rules articulated in Common Article 3] . . . constitute a minimum yardstick, in addition to the more elaborate rules which are also to apply to international conflicts; and they are rules which, in the Court's opinion, reflect what the court in 1949 called 'elementary considerations of humanity.' " Nicaragua v. United States, 1986 I.C.J. 14, 114 (Judgment of June 27). The court went on to say that, "[b]ecause the minimum rules applicable to international and non-international conflicts are identical, there is no need to address the question whether . . . [the actions alleged to be violative of Common Article 3] must be looked at in the context of the rules which operate for one or the other category of conflict." *Id.*

The government has asserted a position starkly different from the positions and behavior of the United States in previous conflicts, one that can only weaken the United States' own ability to demand application of the Geneva Conventions to Americans captured during armed conflicts abroad. *Amici* remind us of the capture of U.S. Warrant Officer Michael Durant in 1993 by forces loyal to a Somali warlord. The United States demanded assurances that Durant would be treated consistently with protections afforded by the Convention, even though, if the Convention were applied as narrowly as the government now seeks to apply it to Hamdan, "Durant's captors would not be bound to follow the convention because they were not a 'state' ". Neil McDonald & Scott Sullivan, *Rational Interpretation in Irrational Times: The Third Geneva Convention and "War On Terror"*, 44 Harv. Int'l. L.J. 301, 310 (2003). Examples of the way other governments have already begun to cite the United States' Guantanamo policy to justify their own repressive policies are set forth in Lawyers Committee for Human Rights, Assessing the New Normal: Liberty and Security for the Post–September 11 United States, at 77–80 (2003).

(4) The government's putative trump card is that Hamdan's rights under the Geneva Conventions, if any, and whatever they are, are not

enforceable by this Court–that, in effect, Hamdan has failed to state a claim upon which relief can be granted–because the Third Geneva Convention is not "self-executing" and does not give rise to a private cause of action.

As an initial matter, it should be noted Hamdan has not asserted a "private right of action" under the Third Geneva Convention. The Convention is implicated in this case by operation of the statute that limits trials by military tribunal to "offenders ... triable under the law of war." 10 U.S.C. § 821. The government's argument thus amounts to the assertion that no federal court has the authority to determine whether the Third Geneva Convention has been violated, or, if it has, to grant relief from the violation.

Treaties made under the authority of the United States are the supreme law of the land. U.S. Const. art. VI, cl. 2. United States courts are bound to give effect to international law and to international agreements of the United States unless such agreements are "non-self-executing." The Paquete Habana, 175 U.S. 677, 708 ... (1900); Restatement (Third) of the Foreign Relations Law of the United States § 111. A treaty is "non-self-executing" if it manifests an intention that it not become effective as domestic law without enactment of implementing legislation; or if the Senate in consenting to the treaty requires implementing legislation; or if implementing legislation is constitutionally required. *Id.* at § 111(4). The controlling law in this Circuit on the subject of whether or not treaties are self-executing is Diggs v. Richardson, 555 F.2d 848 (D.C.Cir.1976), a suit to prohibit the importation of seal furs from Namibia, brought by a citizen plaintiff who sought to compel United States government compliance with a United Nations Security Council resolution calling on member states to have no dealings with South Africa. The decision in that case instructs a court interpreting a treaty to look to the intent of the signatory parties as manifested by the language of the treaty and, if the language is uncertain, then to look to the circumstances surrounding execution of the treaty. *Id.* at 851. *Diggs* relies on the *In re* Head Money Cases, 112 U.S. 580 ... (1884), which established the proposition that a "treaty is a law of the land as an act of congress is, whenever its provisions prescribe a rule by which the rights of the private citizen or subject may be determined." *Id.* at 598. The Court in *Diggs* concluded that the provisions of the Security Council resolution were not addressed to the judicial branch of government, that they did not by their terms confer rights on individuals, and that instead the resolution clearly called upon governments to take action. *Diggs,* 555 F.2d at 851.

The Geneva Conventions, of course, are all about prescribing rules by which the rights of individuals may be determined. Moreover, as petitioner and several of the *amici* have pointed out, *see, e.g.,* Pet'r's Mem. Supp. of Pet. at 39 n.11, it is quite clear from the legislative history of the ratification of the Geneva Conventions that Congress carefully considered what further legislation, if any, was deemed "required to give effect to the provisions contained in the four conventions,"

S.Rep. No. 84–9, at 30 (1955), and found that only four provisions required implementing legislation. Articles 5 and 102, which are dispositive of Hamdan's case, *supra,* were not among them. What did require implementing legislation were Articles 129 and 130, providing for additional criminal penalties to be imposed upon those who engaged in "grave" violations of the Conventions, such as torture, medical experiments, or "wilful" denial of Convention protections, none of which is involved here. Third Geneva Convention, art. 130. Judge Bork must have had those provisions in mind, together with Congress' response in enacting the War Crimes Act, 18 U.S.C. § 2441, when he found that the Third Geneva Convention was not self-executing because it required "implementing legislation." Tel–Oren v. Libyan Arab Republic, *et al.,* 726 F.2d 774, 809 (D.C.Cir.1984) (Bork, J., concurring). That opinion is one of three written by a three-judge panel, none of which was joined by any other member of the panel. It is not Circuit precedent and it is, I respectfully suggest, erroneous. "Some provisions of an international agreement may be self-executing and others non-self-executing." RESTATEMENT (THIRD) OF FOREIGN RELATIONS LAW OF THE UNITED STATES § 111 cmt. h.

Because the Geneva Conventions were written to protect individuals, because the Executive Branch of our government has implemented the Geneva Conventions for fifty years without questioning the absence of implementing legislation, because Congress clearly understood that the Conventions did not require implementing legislation except in a few specific areas, and because nothing in the Third Geneva Convention itself manifests the contracting parties' intention that it not become effective as domestic law without the enactment of implementing legislation, I conclude that, insofar as it is pertinent here, the Third Geneva Convention is a self-executing treaty. I further conclude that it is at least a matter of some doubt as to whether or not Hamdan is entitled to the protections of the Third Geneva Convention as a prisoner of war and that accordingly he must be given those protections unless and until the "competent tribunal" referred to in Article 5 concludes otherwise. It follows from those conclusions that Hamdan may not be tried for the war crimes he is charged with except by a court-martial duly convened under the Uniform Code of Military Justice.

c. Abstention is appropriate with respect to Hamdan's rights under Common Article 3.

There is an argument that, even if Hamdan does not have prisoner-of-war status, Common Article 3 would be violated by trying him for his alleged war crimes in this Military Commission. Abstention is appropriate, and perhaps required, on that question, because, unlike Article 102, which unmistakably mandates trial of POW's only by general court-martial and thus implicates the jurisdiction of the Military Commission, the Common Article 3 requirement of trial before a "regularly constituted court affording all the judicial guarantees which are recognized as indispensable by civilized peoples" has no fixed, term-of-art meaning. A substantial number of rights and procedures conferred by the UCMJ are missing from the Military Commission's rules. *See infra* note 12; Generals and Admirals Amicus Brief at 24. I am aware of no authority that defines the word "guarantees" in Common Article 3 to mean that all of these rights must be guaranteed in advance of trial. Only Hamdan's right to be present at every phase of his trial and to see all the evidence admitted against him is of immediate pretrial concern. That right is addressed in the next section of this opinion.

3. In at least one critical respect, the procedures of the Military Commission are fatally contrary to or inconsistent with those of the Uniform Code of Military Justice.

In most respects, the procedures established for the Military Commission at Guantanamo under the President's order define a trial forum that looks appropriate and even reassuring when seen through the lens of American jurisprudence. The rules laid down by Military Commission Order No. 1, 32 C.F.R. § 9.3, provide that the defendant shall have appointed military counsel, that he may within reason choose to replace "detailed" counsel with another military officer who is a judge advocate if such officer is available, that he may retain a civilian attorney if he can afford it, that he must receive a copy of the charges in a language that he understands, that he will be presumed innocent until proven guilty, that proof of guilt must be beyond a reasonable doubt, that he must be provided with the evidence the prosecution intends to introduce at trial and with any exculpatory evidence known to the prosecution, with important exceptions discussed below, that he is not required to testify at trial and that the Commission may not draw an adverse inference from his silence, that he may obtain witnesses and documents for his defense to the extent necessary and reasonably available, that he may present evidence at trial and cross-examine prosecution witnesses, and that he may not be placed in jeopardy twice for any charge as to which a finding has become final. *Id.* at §§ 9.4 and 9.5.

The Military Commission is remarkably different from a court-martial, however, in two important respects. The first has to do with the structure of the reviewing authority after trial; the second, with the power of the appointing authority or the presiding officer to exclude the accused from hearings and deny him access to evidence presented against him.

Petitioner's challenge to the first difference is unsuccessful. It is true that the President has made himself, or the Secretary of Defense acting at his direction, the final reviewing authority, whereas under the Uniform Code of Military Justice there would be two levels of independent review by members of the Third Branch of government—an appeal to the Court of Appeals for the Armed Forces, whose active bench consists of five civilian judges, and possible review by the Supreme Court on writ of *certiorari*. The President has, however, established a Review Panel that will review the trial record and make a recommendation to the Secretary of Defense, or, if the panel finds an error of law, return the case for further proceedings. . . .

The second difference between the procedures adopted for the Military Commission and those applicable in a court-martial convened under the Uniform Code of Military Justice is far more troubling. That difference lies in the treatment of information that is classified; information that is otherwise "protected"; or information that might implicate the physical safety of participants, including witnesses, or the integrity of intelligence and law enforcement sources and methods, or "other national security interests." *See* Military Commission Order No. 1(6)(B)(3); 32 C.F.R. § 9.6(b). Under the Secretary of Defense's regulations, the Military Commission must "[h]old open proceedings except where otherwise decided by the Appointing Authority or the Presiding Officer." *Id.* Detailed military defense counsel may not be excluded from proceedings, nor may evidence be received that has not been presented to detailed defense counsel, Military Commission Order No. 1 (6)(B)(3), (6)(D)(5); 32 C.F.R. §§ 9.6(b)(3), (d)(5). *The accused himself may be excluded from proceedings,* however, and evidence may be adduced that he will never see (because his lawyer will be forbidden to disclose it to him). *See id.*

Thus, for example, testimony may be received from a confidential informant, and Hamdan will not be permitted to hear the testimony, see the witness's face, or learn his name. If the government has information developed by interrogation of witnesses in Afghanistan or elsewhere, it can offer such evidence in transcript form, or even as summaries of transcripts. *See* Military Commission Order No. 1(6)(D); 32 C.F.R. § 9.6(d). The Presiding Officer or the Appointing Authority may receive it in evidence if it meets the "reasonably probative" standard but forbid it to be shown to Hamdan. *See id.* As counsel for Hamdan put it at oral argument, portions of Mr. Hamdan's trial can be conducted "outside his presence. He can be excluded, not for his conduct, [but] because the government doesn't want him to know what's in it. They make a great big deal out of I can be there, but anybody who's practiced trial law, especially criminal law, knows that where you get your cross examination questions from is turning to your client and saying, 'Did that really happen? Is that what happened?' I'm not permitted to do that." 10/25/04 Tr. at 97.

It is obvious beyond the need for citation that such a dramatic deviation from the confrontation clause could not be countenanced in any American court, particularly after Justice Scalia's extensive opinion in his decision this year in Crawford v. Washington, 541 U.S. 36 ... (2004). It is also apparent that the right to trial "in one's presence" is established as a matter of international humanitarian and human rights law. [court's note 14: International Covenant on Civil and Political Rights, Dec. 19, 1966, 999 U.N.T.S. 171, art. 14(d)(3); Protocol Additional to the Geneva Conventions of 12 August 1949, and relating to the Protection of Victims of International Armed Conflicts, June 8, 1977, 1125 U.N.T.S. 3, art. 75.4(e). "This includes, at a minimum, all hearings in which the prosecutor participates. *E.g.,* Eur.Ct.H.Rts., Belziuk v. Poland, App. No. 00023103/93, Judgment of 25 March 1998, para. 39."

Brief Amici Curiae of Louise Doswald–Beck *et al.* at 32–33 n.137. In this country, as Justice Scalia noted in Crawford v. Washington, 541 U.S. at _ , 124 S.Ct. at 1363, the right to be present was held three years after the adoption of the Sixth Amendment to be a rule of common law "founded on natural justice" (quoting from *State v. Webb,* 2 N.C. 103, 1794 WL 98 (1794)).] But it is unnecessary to consider whether Hamdan can rely on any American constitutional notions of fairness, or whether the nature of these proceedings really is, as counsel asserts, akin to the Star Chamber, 10/25/04 Tr. at 97 (and violative of Common Article 3), because–at least in this critical respect–the rules of the Military Commission are fatally "contrary to or inconsistent with" the statutory requirements for courts-martial convened under the Uniform Code of Military Justice, and thus unlawful....

Conclusion

It is now clear, by virtue of the Supreme Court's decision in *Hamdi,* that the detentions of enemy combatants at Guantanamo Bay are not unlawful per se. The granting (in part) of Hamdan's petition for habeas corpus accordingly brings only limited relief. The order that accompanies this opinion provides: (1) that, unless and until a competent tribunal determines that Hamdan is not entitled to POW status, he may be tried for the offenses with which he is charged only by court-martial under the Uniform Code of Military Justice; (2) that, unless and until the Military Commission's rule permitting Hamdan's exclusion from commission sessions and the withholding of evidence from him is amended so that it is consistent with and not contrary to UCMJ Article 39, Hamdan's trial before the Military Commission would be unlawful; and (3) that Hamdan must be released from the pre-Commission detention wing of Camp Delta and returned to the general population of detainees, unless some reason other than the pending charges against him requires different treatment. Hamdan's remaining claims are in abeyance....

Notes and Questions

1. *Hamdan* was reversed on appeal before the D.C. Circuit (see 415 F.3d 33 (D.C.Cir.2005)) after this casebook went to the publishers. There had also been a petition for *certiorari* and briefs filed before the Supreme Court. Concerning some of the errors in the Government's arguments before the district court, see also Jordan J. Paust, *Executive Plans and Authorizations to Violate International Law Concerning Treatment and Interrogation of Detainees,* 43 Columbia J. Trananat'l L. 811 (2005).

2. The district court in *Hamdan* did not consider a number of other points involving international law that is directly incorporable, incorporated by reference in certain federal statutes or authorizations, and is a necessary background for interpretive purposes or indirect incorporation. *See, e.g.,* Jordan J. Paust, *Post–9/11 Overreaction and Fallacies Regarding War and Defense, Guantanamo, The Status of Persons, Treatment, Judicial Review of Detention, and Due Process in Military Commissions,* 79 Notre Dame L. Rev. 1335, 1361–63 (2004), adding: Since 9/11, we have witnessed the deliberate creation of rules of procedure for U.S. military commissions that would

violate human rights and Geneva law guarantees.... Present Department of Defense rules for military commissions would assure denial of the human rights to trial before a regularly constituted, competent, independent, and impartial court; to counsel of one's choice and to effective representation; to fair procedure and fair rules of evidence [for example, by allowing use of unsworn written statements, declassified summaries of evidence, testimony from prior trials or proceedings, certain forms of hearsay, other testimony from witnesses who do not appear before the military commission, and reports]; to review by a competent, independent, and impartial court of law; and to various other human rights (including impermissible discrimination on the basis of national origin, denial of equal access to courts and to equality of treatment and equal protection of the law, "denials of justice" in violation of customary international law, and denial of the human right to fair, meaningful and effective judicial review of the propriety of detention)....

Moreover, a serious violation of the separation of powers exists with respect to the total lack of judicial review of military commission decisions concerning offenses against the laws of war (which have been incorporated by Congress as offenses against the laws of the United States–*e.g.*, in 10 U.S.C. § 818) and other international crimes over which there is concurrent jurisdictional competence in federal district courts. Under Article I, Section 8, clause 9 of the Constitution, Congress merely has power "[t]o constitute Tribunals inferior to the supreme Court" and, thus, tribunals subject to ultimate control by the Supreme Court. For this reason, the congressional authorization for creation of ad hoc military commissions in 10 U.S.C. § 821 is subject to the constitutional restraint contained in Article I, Section 8, clause 9. See also Paust, *Antiterrorism Military Commissions: The Ad Hoc DOD Rules of Procedure*, 23 MICH. J. INT'L L. 677 (2002) (providing detailed attention to DOD Rules of Procedure that run afoul of human rights law and the laws of war). Of significant importance are the refusals of the Executive Military Order and the DOD Rules to provide for fair and meaningful review by a competent, independent, and impartial court of law, as required, for example, by Article 14(5) of the ICCPR. *See, e.g., id.* at 685–87.

3. An additional problem with respect to military commissions at Guantanamo involves the limitations of presidential power to set up a military commission. The President's power to set up a military commission and the jurisdictional competence of a military commission are limited in terms of time to a circumstance of actual war until peace is finalized. *See, e.g.*, Madsen v. Kinsella, 343 U.S. 341, 346–48 (1952) ("related to war," "war courts"); *In re* Yamashita, 327 U.S. 1, 11–13 (such power exists after cessation of hostilities "at least until peace has been officially recognized by treaty or proclamation of the political branch of the Government."), 20 n.7 (a military commission is a "war court") (1946); *Ex parte* Quirin, 317 U.S. 1, 28 (1942); The Grapeshot, 76 U.S. (9 Wall.) 129, 132–33 (1869) (permitting jurisdiction "so long as the war continued" and "during war"); Cross v. Harrison, 57 U.S. (16 How.) 164, 190 (1853) (permitting jurisdiction until a "treaty of peace"); 24 Op. Att'y Gen. 570, 571 (1903); 11 Op. Att'y Gen. 297, 298 (1865) (quoted in the following Note); JORDAN J. PAUST, M. CHERIF BASSIOUNI, *ET AL.*, INTERNATIONAL CRIMINAL LAW 309–10 (2 ed. 2000); WILLIAM WINTHROP, MILITARY LAW AND PRECEDENTS 86 (jurisdiction of military commis-

sions "is determined by the existence and continuance of war"), 831 (jurisdiction is tied to the war powers, "exclusively war-court"), 837 ("An offence ... must have been committed within the period of the war or of the exercise of military government.... jurisdiction ... cannot be maintained after the date of a peace....") (2 ed. 1920); DIGEST OF OPINIONS OF THE JUDGE ADVOCATE GENERAL 1067 (1912); Major General Henry W. Halleck, *Military Tribunals and Their Jurisdiction*, 5 AM. J. INT'L L. 958, 965–66 (1911) (military commissions "are established by the President, by virtue of his war power as commander-in-chief, and have jurisdiction of cases arising under the laws of war," adding: "[they] are war courts and can exist only in time of war"), *reprinted in* MIL. L. REV. BICENTENNIAL ISSUE 15, 21 (1975); Michael A. Newton, *Continuum Crimes: Military Jurisdiction Over Foreign Nationals Who Commit International Crimes*, 153 MIL. L. REV. 1, 15 (1996); Jordan J. Paust, *Antiterrorism Military Commissions: Courting Illegality*, 23 MICH. J. INT'L L. 1, 5 & n.14, 9, 25 n.70 (2001), and references cited.

The President's power is also limited in terms of the place for a military commission's direct functioning to a theater of war or a war-related occupied territory. *See, e.g.*, The Grapeshot, 76 U.S. (9 Wall.) at 132–33 ("wherever the insurgent power was overthrown"); WINTHROP, *supra* at 836 ("A military commission ... can legally assume jurisdiction only of offences committed within the field of command of the convening commander," and regarding military occupation, "cannot take cognizance of an offence committed without such territory.... The place must be the theatre of war or a place where military government or martial law may be legally exercised; otherwise a military commission ... will have no jurisdiction...."); Paust, *supra*, at 5 & n.14, 25 n.70, 26–27; see also Madsen v. Kinsella, 343 U.S. 341, 348 (1952) (a military commission is proper in a war-related occupied enemy territory "in time of war"); Duncan v. Kahanamoku, 327 U.S. 304, 324 ("occupied enemy territory"), 326 ("[o]nly when a foreign invasion or civil war") (1946); Coleman v. Tennessee, 97 U.S. 509, 515 ("when ... in the enemy's country"), 517 (when occupation of enemy territory) (1878). The military commission set up within the United States during World War II and recognized in *Ex parte Quirin* had been created during war for prosecution of enemy belligerents for violations of the laws of war that occurred within the United States and within the convening authority's field of command–which in that case was within the Eastern Defense Command of the United States Army. See 317 U.S. at 22 n.1. The U.S. military base at Guantanamo is neither in a theater of actual war nor in a war-related occupied territory, and, thus, a military commission at Guantanamo would not be properly constituted and would be without lawful jurisdiction.

4. The 1865 Opinion of the Attorney General cited in the preceding note affirmed: "A military tribunal exists under and according to the Constitution in time of war. Congress may prescribe how all such tribunals are to be constituted, what shall be their jurisdiction, and mode of procedure. Should Congress fail to create such tribunals, then, under the Constitution, they must be constituted according to the laws and usages of civilized warfare. They may take cognizance of such offences as the laws of war permit.... In time of peace neither Congress nor the military can create any military tribunals, except such as are made in pursuance of that clause of the Constitution which gives to Congress the power 'to make rules for the

government of the land and naval forces.' " 11 Op. Att'y Gen. 297, 298 (1865). Clearly, Congress can regulate the jurisdiction and procedure of military commissions, but must do so consistently with international law and the requirements of international law "are of binding force upon the departments and citizens of the Government, though not defined by any law of Congress" and neither Congress nor the Executive can "abrogate them or authorize their infraction." *See, e.g., id.* at 298–300; Madsen v. Kinsella, 343 U.S. at 348–49; *see also* U.S. Const., art. II, § 3; Dooley v. United States, 182 U.S. 222, 231 (1901) (Executive military powers are " 'regulated and limited . . . directly from the laws of war' "), *quoting* 2 Henry W. Halleck, International Law 444 (1st ed. 1861); Paust, International Law as Law of the United States 7–9, 169–92, 488, 493–94 (2 ed. 2003).

d. New Statutes and New Fora

If a statute incorporates customary international law by reference, can a prosecution properly occur with respect to crimes committed before enactment of the statute? Is there an "*ex post facto*" problem or "*nullum crimen sine lege*" defense?

DEMJANJUK v. PETROVSKY

776 F.2d 571, 582–83 (6th Cir. 1985), *cert. denied*, 475 U.S. 1016 (1986).

Lively, J.

Israel is seeking to enforce its criminal law for the punishment of Nazis and Nazi collaborators for crimes universally recognized and condemned by the community of nations. The fact that Demjanjuk is charged with committing these acts in Poland does not deprive Israel of authority to bring him to trial.

Further, the fact that the State of Israel was not in existence when Demjanjuk allegedly committed the offenses is no bar to Israel's exercising jurisdiction under the universality principle. When proceeding on that jurisdictional premise, neither the nationality of the accused or the victim(s), nor the location of the crime is significant. The underlying assumption is that the crimes are offenses against the law of nations or against humanity and that the prosecuting nation is acting for all nations. This being so, Israel or any other nation, regardless of its status in 1942 or 1943, may undertake to vindicate the interest of all nations by seeking to punish the perpetrators of such crimes.

Notes and Questions

1. Other portions of the *Demjanjuk* opinion appear in Chapter 3. Demjanjuk was deported to Israel, convicted there and sentenced to death on April 25, 1988. Later, his conviction was overturned, he was released and, in 1993, returned to the United States where he faces deportation.

2. *See also* Edward Sherman, *Songmy 2: Some Knotty Legal Questions*, N.Y. Times, Feb. 21, 1970 (new "legislation to provide for trial in federal court of servicemen who have been discharged . . . would merely give the Federal court jurisdiction to try crimes already on the books"); 11 Op. Att'y

Gen. 297, 299–300 (extract reprinted *supra*), 306; statements of Duponceau & Representative Marshall, *supra*; Triquet v. Bath, 3 Burrow 1478 (K.B. 1764) (act only created new punishment).

3. After the Civil War, it was noted that: "Where an accused is charged with a violation of the laws of war, as laid down in paragraph 86 of General Orders No. 100, of War Department, of April 24, 1863 [the Lieber Code], it is no defence that the actual offence for which he was tried was committed before the date of the order; the latter being merely a publication and affirmance of the law as it had previously existed." DIGEST OF OPINIONS OF JAG, ARMY 244 (1866).

4. The U.S. does not have legislation criminalizing crimes against humanity as such. Is it possible to incorporate crimes against humanity by reference in new legislation and for such legislation to be applied retroactively?

5. *Enhancement of Congressional and Executive Powers*

a. *Congressional Power*

UNITED STATES v. HAUN

26 F. Cas. 227 (C.C.S.D. Ala. 1860) (No. 15,329).

CAMPBELL, J. (on circuit)

This indictment contains three counts, and charges that the defendant held, sold and disposed of, in this district, negroes, as slaves, illegally imported into the United States in 1859, from a foreign place, by some person unknown....

The indictment must be supported under the sixth section of the act of April 20, 1818, for the suppression of the African slave trade. The section is: "If any person or persons whatsoever shall, from and after the passage of this act, bring within the jurisdiction of the United States, in any manner whatsoever, from any foreign kingdom, place, or country, or from sea, or shall hold, sell, or otherwise dispose of any such negro, mulatto, or person of color so brought in, as a slave, or to be held to service or labor, or be in anywise aiding or abetting therein, every person so offending shall, on conviction thereof by the due course of law, forfeit and pay a sum not exceeding ten thousand dollars, nor less than one thousand dollars, one moiety to the use of the United States and the other to the person or persons who shall sue for such forfeiture and prosecute the same to effect; and, moreover, shall suffer imprisonment for a term not exceeding seven years, nor less than three years." The object of this section of the act was to prevent the introduction of persons who, for the purpose of this discussion I will denominate Africans, and their employment, sale, or other disposition as slaves within the United States. This introduction or use is made penal, however, or by whomsoever made. By the language of the section, the act of importation and the acts of holding, selling, or disposing of the African, the subject of importation, are distinct offences. It is, "if any person," "shall bring," "in any manner" from abroad, "or shall hold, sell, or dispose of any negro so brought in" as a slave. Neither is it necessary that the offenders under the one clause shall be in any relation of accessories or accomplices under the other clauses of the act. "Every person aiding or abetting" in either of the criminal acts, is denounced as criminal in the degree of his principal, by its plain language. The manifest import of this section of the act is, that if any person shall import an African, as a slave, into the United States from abroad, (*i.e.* foreign kingdom, place, or country, or by sea,) or be in anywise concerned therewith, or shall hold, sell, or otherwise dispose of as a slave, an African, being illegally imported, be shall suffer the penalties prescribed. Now, upon this construction of this section of the act there is charged against this defendant acts that are criminal, and which subject him properly to a presentment of the grand jury. But it is said that the act must be limited to such as were concerned with the importation, and that a proprietor by purchase ex post facto, is not embraced within the terms of this section of the act. An analysis of the section shows that "if any person or persons whatsoever" "shall bring within the jurisdiction of the United States" any African as a slave, "or be in anywise aiding or abetting therein," "or shall hold, sell, or dispose of such African as a slave, or be in anywise aiding or abetting therein, every person so offending shall forfeit and pay," & c. To justify the argument relied on, the word "and" should be substituted for the word "or," and the act should read: "If any person shall bring within the jurisdiction of the United States, 'and' shall hold, sell, or dispose of any African as a slave." But the exigency must be imperious which will justify this court to take such a license with an act of congress as to substitute the one word for the other....

But another rule is invoked which is entitled to consideration. It is said that the power of congress is limited to a cognizance of the acts of the importer, and those concerned with him. That Africans, whether considered as persons or as property, after they come within the jurisdiction and limits of a state, cease to be under the dominion of the federal authority. They are no longer subject to the commercial power of congress which alone applies to the subject, and the crime of holding them as slaves is a state, not a federal crime. The cases of Brown v. Maryland, 12 Wheat. [25 U.S. 419,] 438; Norris v. City of Boston, 7 How. [48 U.S.] 283, and the popular opinion and judgment on the alien law of 1798, are supposed to confirm this opinion. It may be admitted that property or persons introduced or entering the United States by their consent; and mingling with property and persons in the states, in some manner and to some extent, fall under state authority, and in some manner and to some extent, are not subject to federal control. The decision of *Brown v. Maryland* was a case of property legally introduced through the customhouse of the United States. The supreme court of the United States held that it was not subject to state taxation until it had ceased to exist as in the condition of an import, and had not become confused or mingled with the common property of the state. The case of

Norris v. City of Boston recognized a similar limitation on state authority as to persons, and that passengers on a foreign ship could not be taxed by state authority until they were fairly separated from the ship and voyage. But these cases only prove when state authority may begin to operate, and not when the federal authority terminates, upon property or persons legally introduced into the country. . . .

. . . The case before the court is one in which the power of congress to pass laws to prohibit the importation of Africans, or slaves, cannot be denied. The subject entered into the debates of the continental congress, and forms one of the compromises on which the constitution rests. Under the constitution the "migration or importation of such persons as any of the states now existing shall think proper to admit, shall not be prohibited (by congress) prior to the year 1808." On the first day of the year 1808, by an act of congress made to meet the approach of their plenary authority, the importation of Africans as slaves, or the purchasing of them from the importer, became illegal. In 1814 [8 Stat. 218], in the treaty of peace negotiated at Ghent with Great Britain, the trade was declared to be "contrary to humanity and justice," and an obligation was then entered into to discourage it. The act of 1818 was subsequently passed, and the more severe act of May, 1820, completed their penal legislation on the subject. No system of measures exists in our legislation that has been more carefully considered, or which obtained more completely the deliberate, impartial and conscientious approbation of states and statesmen. It requires no small measure of moral and intellectual intrepidity to impugn them. A few have expressed the opinion that the power of congress was derived only from their control over foreign commerce. But in early debates in congress this was denied, and it was said "that a reference to the constitution would expose the fallacy." Among the powers delegated by that instrument to congress, was the power to define and punish offences against the law of nations. It was afterwards added that the migration or importation of such persons as any of the states now existing shall think proper to admit, shall not be prohibited prior to 1808, but a tax or duty may be imposed on such importation, not exceeding ten dollars for each person. Before 1808 this last provision would expire, and the first provision would be reinstated in full efficacy, which unquestionably gave congress a full power over the subject, independently of that derived from their right to regulate commerce.

Unquestionably, President Jefferson, when he congratulated congress at the approach of the period at which they might interpose their authority constitutionally to withdraw the citizens of the United States from all further violations of human rights which have been so long continued on the unoffending inhabitants of Africa, and which the morality, the reputation and the best interests of our country, have been long eager to proscribe, supposed that something beyond a regulation of commerce was concerned in the action to be taken. President Madison in accepting, and the senate of the United States in unanimously ratifying, the treaty of Ghent, before mentioned, probably agreed with the argument I have quoted. The act of May, 1820, declaring the slave trade by American citizens to be piracy, and the treaty of Washington of 1842, in which the United States agreed with Great Britain to unite in all becoming representations and remonstrances with any and all powers within whose dominions such markets (markets for Africans) are allowed to exist, and that they will urge upon all such powers the propriety and duty of closing such markets effectually, at once and forever evidently imply that the suppression of the slave trade has become a part of the domain of international law, and belongs to the jurisdiction of congress as a part of that foreign intercourse of the Union which is submitted to its exclusive control. I do not consider this question of any importance in the solution of the present inquiry, for, considered merely as a commerce that the congress may suppress or prevent, they are clothed with powers adequate to the accomplishment of their policy. They are not dependent upon the state governments for ancillary legislation, nor can they be obstructed by their inaction or opposition. . . .

The expectations of the states which framed the constitution, and stipulated that after 1808 congress might abolish the trade at once and forever: the solemn treaties, binding the nation to employ moral and material force to effect throughout the world the closing of slave markets for Africans forever: the acts of congress prohibiting the trade, and confiscating the implements and machines employed in it, as if they were accomplices in the guilt—acts passed with unanimity, and sanctioned by an approving people, might be frustrated and defeated if the African could be held, sold, or otherwise disposed of, without responsibility to those in whom the constitution has conferred the power of making these laws and treaties. No such consequences can follow. The constitution . . . confers upon congress the power "to make all laws which shall be necessary and proper for carrying into execution the foregoing powers, and all other powers vested by the constitution in the government of the United States, or in any department or officer thereof." The power to inflict punishment for the infraction of laws incidental to the power of making laws. This is the usual as it is the appropriate means, by which a government secures obedience, and upon this foundation the criminal jurisdiction of the United States reposes. Before the enactments under consideration had been made, philosophic and practical statesmen had discovered "that the true origin of the slave trade was not in the place it was begun at, but at the place of its final destination." If there were not men who held, sold, or otherwise disposed of Africans, after the termination of the slave voyage, and the act of importation completed, there would be no building, equipping and manning of ships, no voyages to the African coast for slaves, no barracoons to supply American vessels, no piratical seizures, no confinements or detentions of Africans as slaves, no mortuary lists of the victims of such acts to startle and shock humanity, no need of African squadrons, or slave trade treaties, no illegal entries or importations. A complete preventive of the holding, selling or disposing of Africans within the limits of the United States, or by the citizens thereof, would remove the stain which has fallen upon our country by the abuse of its flag. This legislation of congress, then strikes at the root of this evil. If enforced it would extirpate a large share of the mischief. Such being the case, I am unable to bring myself to the conclusion that the means congress have selected by imposing penalties upon an offender against their laws are not necessary and proper to the end. I cannot assent to the conclusion, that they cannot execute their obligations to suppress a trade which they have declared to be contrary to humanity and justice, by punishing the citizens who hold and dispose of the subjects of that trade anywhere within their jurisdiction. . . .

UNITED STATES v. ARJONA

120 U.S. 479 (1887).

WAITE, C.J.

This is an indictment containing three counts against Ramon Arjona, for violations of §§ 3 and 6, of the act of May 16, 1884, c. 52, 23 Stat. 22, "to prevent and punish the counterfeiting within the United States of notes, bonds, and other securities of foreign Governments." The first and second counts were found under § 6 of the statute, and the third under § 3. . . .

The first count of the indictment charges Arjona with having "in his control and custody a certain metallic plate from which there might then and there be printed in part a counterfeit note in the likeness and similitude in part of the notes theretofore issued by a foreign bank, to wit, the bank known as El Banco del Estado de Bolivar, which said bank was then and there a bank authorized by the laws of a foreign state, to wit, the state of Bolivar, said state being then and there one of the states of the United States of Columbia."

In the second count, he is charged with having caused and procured "to be engraved a certain metallic plate in the likeness and similitude of a plate designated for the printing of the genuine issues of the obligations of a foreign bank, that is to say, of the bank notes of the bank known as El Banco del Estado de Bolivar, the same being then and there a bank authorized by the laws of a foreign state, to wit, the state of Bolivar, said state being then and there one of the states of the United States of Columbia."

In the third count, the charge is that he, "unlawfully and with intent to defraud, did cause and procure to be falsely made a certain note in the similitude and resemblance of the notes theretofore issued by a bank of a foreign country, to wit, the bank known as El Banco del Estado de Bolivar, the same being then and there a bank authorized by laws of one of the states of the United States or Columbia, that is to say, the state of Bolivar, and the notes issued by the said bank being then and by the usage of the said state of Bolivar intended to circulate as money."

To this indictment a demurrer was filed, and the judges holding the court have certified that at the hearing the following questions arose, upon which their opinions were opposed:

1. Whether the third section of the statute is constitutional.

2. Whether the sixth section is constitutional so far as it relates to "foreign banks and corporations."

3. Whether the counterfeiting within the United States of the notes of a foreign bank or corporation can be constitutionally made by Congress an offence against the law of nations.

4. Whether the obligations of the law of nations, as referred to in the Constitution of the United States, include the punishment of counterfeiting the notes of a foreign bank or corporation, or of having in possession a plate from which may be printed counterfeits of the notes of foreign banks or corporations, as mentioned in the third and sixth sections, "unless it appear or is alleged in the indictment that the notes of said foreign bank or corporation are the notes or money of issue of a foreign Government, prince, potentate, state, or power."

5. Whether, if there is power to "so define the law of nations" as to include the offences mentioned in the third and sixth sections, it is not necessary, in order "to define" the offence, that it be declared in the statute itself "to be an offence against the law of nations."

6. Whether the indictment is sufficient in law.

The fourth of the questions thus stated embraces the 4th, 5th, 6th, 7th, and 8th of those certified, and the fifth embraces the 9th and 10th.

Congress has power to make all laws which shall be necessary and proper to carry into execution the powers vested by the Constitution in the Government of the United States, Art. I, sec. 8, clause 18; and the Government of the United States has been vested exclusively with the power of representing the nation in all its intercourse with foreign countries. It alone can "regulate commerce with foreign nations," Art, I, sec. 8, clause 3; make treaties and appoint ambassadors and other public ministers and consuls. Art. II, sec. 2, clause 2. A state is expressly prohibited from entering into any "treaty, alliance, or confederation." Art. I, sec. 10, clause 1. Thus all official intercourse between a state and foreign nations is prevented, and exclusive authority for that purpose given to the United States. The national government is in this way made responsible to foreign nations for all violations by the United States of their international obligations, and because of this, Congress is expressly authorized "to define and punish . . . offences against the law of nations." Art. I, sec. 8, clause 10.

The law of nations requires every national government to use "due diligence" to prevent a wrong being done within its own dominion to another nation with which it is at peace, or to the people thereof; and because of this the obligation of one nation to punish those who within its own jurisdiction counterfeit the money of another nation has long been recognized. Vattel, in his LAW OF NATIONS, which was first printed at Neuchatel in 1758, and was translated into English and published in England in 1760, uses this language: "From the principles thus laid down, it is easy to conclude, that if one nation counterfeits the money of another, or if she allows and protects false coiners who presume to do it, she does that nation an injury." ... In a note by Mr. Chitty in his London edition of 1834 it is said: "This is a sound principle, which ought to be extended so as to deny effect to any fraud upon a foreign nation or its subjects." *Id.* 47, note 50.

This rule was established for the protection of nations in their intercourse with each other....

In the time of Vattel certificates of the public debt of a nation, government bonds, and other government securities, were rarely seen in any other country than that in which they were put out.... Now, however, the amount of national and corporate debt and of corporate property represented by bonds, certificates, notes, bills, and other forms of commercial securities, which are bought and sold in all the money markets of the world, both in and out of the country under whose authority they were created, is something enormous....

No nation can be more interested in this question than the United States. Their money is practically composed of treasury notes or certificates issued by themselves, or of bank bills issued by banks created under their authority and subject to their control. Their own securities, and those of the states, the cities, and the public corporations, whose interests abroad they alone have the power to guard against foreign national neglect, are found on sale in the principal money markets of Europe. If these securities, whether national, municipal, or corporate, are forged and counterfeited with impunity at the places where they are sold, it is easy to see that a great wrong will be done to the United States and their people. Any uncertainty about the genuineness of the security necessarily depreciates its value as a merchantable commodity, and against this international comity requires that national protection shall, as far as possible, be afforded. If there is neglect in that, the United States may, with propriety, call on the proper government to provide for the punishment of such an offence, and thus secure the restraining influences of a fear of the consequences of wrong doing. A refusal may not, perhaps, furnish sufficient cause for war, but it would certainly give just ground of complaint, and thus disturb that harmony between the governments which each is bound to cultivate and promote.

But if the United States can require this of another, that other may require it of them, because international obligations are of necessity reciprocal in their nature. The right, if it exists at all, is given by the law of nations, and what is law for one is, under the same circumstances, law for the other. A right secured by the law of nations to a nation, or its people, is one the United States as the representatives of this nation are bound to protect. Consequently, a law which is necessary and proper to afford this protection is one that Congress may enact, because it is one that is needed to carry into execution a power conferred by the Constitution on the Government of the United States exclusively. There is no authority in the United States to require the passage and enforcement of such a law by the states. Therefore the United States must have the power to pass it and enforce it themselves, or be unable to perform a duty which they may owe to another nation, and which the law of nations has imposed on them as part of their international obligations. This, however, does not prevent a state from providing for the punishment of the same thing; for here, as in the case of counterfeiting the coin of the United States, the act may be an offence against the authority of a state as well as that of the United States.

Again, our own people may be dealers at home in the public or quasi public securities of a foreign government, or of foreign banks or corporations, brought here in the course of our commerce with foreign nations, or sent here from abroad for sale in the money markets of this country. As such they enter into and form part of the foreign commerce of the country. If such securities can be counterfeited here with impunity, our own people may be made to suffer by a wrong done which affects a business that has been expressly placed by the Constitution under the protection of the government of the United States.

It remains only to consider those questions which present the point whether, in enacting a statute to define and punish an offence against the law of nations, it is necessary, in order "to define" the offence, that it be declared in the statute itself to be "an offence against the law of nations." This statute defines the offence, and if the thing made punishable is one which the United States are required by their international obligations to use due diligence to prevent, it is an offence against the law of nations. Such being the case, there is no more need of declaring in the statute that it is such an offence than there would be in any other criminal statute to declare that it was enacted to carry into execution any other particular power vested by the Constitution in the Government of the United States. Whether the offence as defined is an offence against the law of nations depends on the thing done, not on any declaration to that effect by Congress. As has already been seen, it was incumbent on the United States as a nation to use due diligence to prevent any injury to another nation or its people by counterfeiting its money, or its public or quasi public securities. This statute was enacted as a means to that end, that is to say, as a means of performing a duty which had been cast on the United States by the law of nations, and it was clearly appropriate legislation for that purpose. Upon its face, therefore, it defines an offence against the law of nations as clearly as if Congress had in express terms so declared. Criminal statutes passed for enforcing and preserving the neutral relations of the United States with other nations were passed by Congress at a very early date; June 5, 1794, c. 50, 1 Stat. 381; June 14, 1797, c. 1, 1 Stat. 520; March 3, 1817, c. 58, 3 Stat. 370; April 20, 1818, c. 88, 3 Stat. 447: and those now in force are found in Title LXVII of the Revised Statutes. These all rest on the same power of Congress that is here invoked, and it has never been supposed they were invalid because they did not expressly declare that the offences there defined were offences against the law of nations....

MISSOURI v. HOLLAND

252 U.S. 416 (1920).

HOLMES, J.

This is a bill in equity brought by the State of Missouri to prevent a game warden of the United States from attempting to enforce the Migratory Bird Treaty Act of July 3, 1918, c. 128, 40 Stat. 755, and the regulations made by the Secretary of Agriculture in pursuance of the same. The ground of the bill is that the statute is an unconstitutional interference with the rights reserved to the States by the Tenth Amendment, and that the acts of the defendant done and threatened under that authority invade the sovereign right of the State and contravene its will manifested in statutes. The State also alleges a pecuniary interest, as owner of the wild birds within its borders and otherwise, admitted by the Government to be sufficient, but it is enough that the bill is a reasonable and proper means to assert the alleged quasi sovereign rights of a State....

On December 8, 1916, a treaty between the United States and Great Britain was proclaimed by the President. It recited that many species of birds in their annual migrations traversed certain parts of the United States and of Canada, that they were of great value as a source of food and in destroying insects injurious to vegetation, but were in danger of extermination through lack of adequate protection. It therefore provided for specified close seasons and protection in other forms, and agreed that the two powers would take or propose to their law-making bodies the necessary measures for carrying the treaty out. 39 Stat. 1702. The above mentioned Act of July 3, 1918, entitled an act to give effect to the convention, prohibited the killing, capturing or selling any of the migratory birds included in the terms of the treaty except as permitted by regulations compatible with those terms, to be made by the Secretary of Agriculture. Regulations were proclaimed on July 31, and October 25, 1918. 40 Stat. 1812; 1863. It is unnecessary to go into any details, because, as we have said, the question raised is the general one whether the treaty and statute are void as an interference with the rights reserved to the States.

To answer this question it is not enough to refer to the Tenth Amendment, reserving the powers not delegated to the United States, because by Article II, § 2, the power to make treaties is delegated expressly, and by Article VI treaties made under the authority of the United States, along with the Constitution and laws of the United States made in pursuance thereof, are declared the supreme law of the land. If the treaty is valid there can be no dispute about the validity of the statute under Article I, § 8, as a necessary and proper means to execute the powers of the Government. The language of the Constitution as to the supremacy of treaties being general, the question before us is narrowed to an inquiry into the ground upon which the present supposed exception is placed.

It is said that a treaty cannot be valid if it infringes the Constitution, that there are limits, therefore, to the treaty-making power, and that one such limit is that what an act of Congress could not do unaided, in derogation of the powers reserved to the States, a treaty cannot do. An earlier act of Congress that attempted by itself and not in pursuance of a treaty to regulate the killing of migratory birds within the States had been held bad in the District Court. United States v. Shauver, 214 Fed. Rep. 154. United States v. McCullagh, 221 Fed. Rep. 288. Those decisions were supported by arguments that migratory birds were owned by the States in their sovereign capacity for the benefit of their people, and that under cases like Geer v. Connecticut, 161 U.S. 519, this control was one that Congress had no power to displace. The same argument is supposed to apply now with equal force.

Whether the two cases cited were decided rightly or not they cannot be accepted as a test of the treaty power. Acts of Congress are the supreme law of the land only when made in pursuance of the Constitution, while treaties are declared to be so when made under the authority of the United States. It is open to question whether the authority of the United States means more than the formal acts prescribed to make the convention. We do not mean to imply that there are no qualifications to the treaty-making power; but they must be ascertained in a different way. It is obvious that there may be matters of the sharpest exigency for the national well being that an act of Congress could not deal with but that a treaty followed by such an act could, and it is not lightly to be assumed that, in matters requiring national action, "a power which must belong to and somewhere reside in every civilized government" is not to be found. Andrews v. Andrews, 188 U.S. 14, 33. What was said in that case with regard to the powers of the States applies with equal force to the powers of the nation in cases where the States individually are incompetent to act. We are not yet discussing the particular case before us but only are considering the validity of the test proposed. With regard to that we may add that when we are dealing with words that also are a constituent act, like the Constitution of the United States, we must realize that they have called into life a being the development of which could not have been foreseen completely by the most gifted of its begetters. It was enough for them to realize or to hope that they had created an organism; it has taken a century and has cost their successors much sweat and blood to prove that they created a nation. The case before us must be considered in the light of our whole experience and not merely in that of what was said a hundred years ago. The treaty in question does not contravene any prohibitory words to be found in the Constitution. The only question is whether it is forbidden by some invisible radiation from the general terms of the Tenth Amendment. We must consider what this country has become in deciding what that Amendment has reserved.

The State as we have intimated founds its claim of exclusive authority upon an assertion of title to migratory birds, an assertion that is embodied in statute. No doubt it is true that as between a State and its inhabitants the State may regulate the killing and sale of such birds, but it does not follow that its authority is exclusive of paramount powers. To put the claim of the State upon title is to lean upon a slender reed. Wild birds are not in the possession of anyone; and possession is the beginning of ownership. The whole foundation of the State's rights is the presence within their jurisdiction of birds that yesterday had not arrived, tomorrow may be in another State and in a week a thousand miles away. If we are to be accurate we cannot put the case of the State upon higher ground than that the treaty deals with creatures that for the moment are within the state borders, that it must be carried out by officers of the United States within the same territory, and that but for the treaty the State would be free to regulate this subject itself.

As most of the laws of the United States are carried out within the States and as many of them deal with matters which in the silence of such laws the State might regulate, such general grounds are not enough to support Missouri's claim. Valid treaties of course "are as binding within the territorial limits of the States as they are elsewhere throughout the dominion of the United States." Baldwin v. Franks, 120 U.S. 678, 683. No doubt the great body of private relations usually fall within the control of the State, but a treaty may override its power. We do not have to invoke the later developments of constitution law for this proposition; it was recognized as early as Hopkirk v. Bell, 3 Cranch, 454, with regard to statutes of limitation, and even earlier, as to confiscation, in Ware v. Hylton, 3 Dall. 199. It was assumed by Chief Justice Marshall with regard to the escheat of land to the State in Chirac v. Chirac, 2 Wheat. 259, 275. Hauenstein v. Lynham, 100 U.S. 483. Geofroy v. Riggs, 133 U.S. 258. Blythe v. Hinckley, 180 U.S. 333, 340. So as to a limited jurisdiction of foreign consuls within a State. Wildenhus's Case, 120 U.S. 1. See Ross v. McIntyre, 140 U.S. 453. Further illustration seems unnecessary, and it only remains to consider the application of established rules to the present case.

Here a national interest of very nearly the first magnitude is involved. It can be protected only by national action in concert with that of another power. The subject-matter is only transitorily within the State and has no permanent habitat therein. But for the treaty and the statute there soon might be no birds for any powers to deal with. We see nothing in the Constitution that compels the Government to sit by while a food supply is cut off and the protectors of our forests and our crops are destroyed. It is not sufficient to rely upon the States. The reliance is vain, and were it otherwise, the question is whether the United States is forbidden to act. We are of opinion that the treaty and statute must be upheld....

FINZER v. BARRY

798 F.2d 1450 (D.C.Cir.1986).

BORK, J.

[Editor's note: Individuals who sought to demonstrate and protest near the Soviet and Nicaraguan Embassies in Washington, D.C. challenged the constitutionality of § 22–1115 of the District of Columbia Code, which prohibited the display within 500 feet of any foreign embassy of "any flag, banner, placard, or device designed or adapted to intimidate, coerce, or bring into public odium any foreign government, party, or organization, or any officer or officers thereof."]

The appellants in Frend v. United States [100 F.2d 691 (D.C.Cir. 1938)] had been convicted of violating section 22–1115 by demonstrating in front of the Austrian and German embassies. Finding that there was no question that their activities ran afoul of the statute, the *Frend* court proceeded to examine the statute's constitutionality.

The court noted that section 22–1115 was enacted as an exercise of Congress' constitutionally vested authority to "define and punish ... Offenses against the Law of Nations," U.S. Const. art 1, § 8, cl. 10, its purpose being to fulfill the United States' duty under international law "of protecting the residence of an ambassador or minister against invasion as well as against any other act tending to disturb the peace or dignity of the mission or of the member of a mission." 100 F.2d at 692, 693. Limited as the statute was to "public demonstrations calculated to arouse passions and resentments in those governments with which we have official relations," this court held that section 22–1115 was a legitimate and constitutional exercise of congressional authority. *Id.* at 693.

Although *Frend* is persuasive precedent, we cannot decide this case simply by citing it as the binding law of the circuit. The case was decided almost a half century ago and in the interval the Supreme Court has developed constitutional law in ways that must be taken into account. Appellants challenge section 22–1115 in part on the basis of a hybrid of equal protection and first amendment law that became part of the doctrinal landscape several decades after *Frend*. Indeed, much of modern first amendment law took shape after *Frend* was decided. We are compelled, therefore, to reexamine *Frend* in light of intervening precedent. Upon review, we find much of its analysis still convincing, and the basic holding fully consistent with the constitutional standards that have evolved.

... [T]he core of this case lies in the relationship between the United States' national interests and international obligations and the first amendment's guarantee of free speech. The question to be determined is whether section 22–1115 achieves a permissible accommodation between the competing claims of these profound constitutional values.

Section 22–1115 was enacted pursuant to Congress' power, under article I, section 8 of the Constitution, "To define and punish ... Offences against the Law of Nations." The need for such authority was, of course, one of the reasons a new constitution was desired, and the power was placed among the great powers granted the new government. Implementation of the law of nations by the American government was seen as crucial to the conduct of our foreign relations, a subject of pervasive concern in the Constitution. For that reason, the statute before us, though rooted in Congress' power to define and punish offenses against the law of nations, also draws sustenance from all those provisions of articles I and II that empower the national government, as a whole, to manage American intercourse with other nations.

In vesting Congress with the power to define, as well as to punish, offenses against the Law of Nations, article I, section 8 of the Constitution authorized Congress to derive from the often broadly phrased principles of international law a more precise code, as it determined that to be necessary to bring the United States into compliance with rules governing the international community. In enacting section 22–1115, Congress sought to guarantee to foreign diplomats, long understood as "objects of especial respect and protection," the security to which they have always been entitled under legal doctrines accepted and enforced throughout the world. Since the days of Blackstone, "infringement of the rights of ambassadors" have been regarded as one of "the principal offenses against the law of nations." 4 W. BLACKSTONE, COMMENTARIES 68, and for as long as the United States has been a nation, those rights have been recognized to include those that are implicated here—protection from intimidation and the potential of violence, and from assaults on the dignity and peace of the embassy as well.

The principle that host states have a special responsibility to ensure that foreign embassies and the personnel inside them are free from threats of violence and intimidation is "solidly entrenched in the Law of Nations." 2 C. HYDE, INTERNATIONAL LAW 1249 (1945). Vattel, one of the first to attempt to codify the Law of Nations, wrote in the eighteenth century that embassies:

> being of such great importance in the universal society of nations, and so necessary to their common well-being, the persons of ministers charged with those embassies are to be held sacred and inviolable among all nations.... This safety is particularly due to the minister, from the sovereign to whom he is sent. To admit a minister, to acknowledge him in such character, is engaging to grant him the most particular protection, and that he shall enjoy all possible safety. It is true, indeed, that the sovereign is bound to protect every person within his dominions, whether native or foreign, and to shelter him from violence: but this attention is in a higher degree due to a foreign minister.

VATTEL, THE LAW OF NATIONS 464–65 (1863)....

... Thus, the tearing down in Philadelphia in 1802 of the flag of the Spanish minister, "with the most aggravating insults," was considered actionable in the Pennsylvania courts as a violation of the law of nations. 4 J. MOORE, DIGEST OF INTERNATIONAL LAW 627 (1906) (quoting letter from Secretary of State Madison to Governor McKean (May 11, 1802)). A complaint by the British government in 1794 concerning a "riot committed by a number of persons tumultuously assembled before the house of a foreign consul, require him to deliver up certain persons supposed to be resident with him, and insulting him with improper language," was determined not to be subject to prosecution in the United States only because a consul was not considered a public minister. 1 Op. Att'y Gen. 41–42 (1794). Indeed, Attorney General William Bradford, in 1794, published an opinion in which he noted that the law of libel, when applied "in the case of a foreign public minister, ... is strengthened by the law of nations, which secures the minister a peculiar protection, not only from violence, but also from insult." 1 Op. Att'y Gen. 52 (1794). *Accord* 1 Op. Att'y Gen. 73 (1794) ("it is usual [for foreign nations] to complain of insults to their ambassadors, and to require the parties to be brought to punishment"). The longstanding principle of diplomatic immunity reflects the same concern. One of the statutes enacted by the First Congress protected ambassadors from arrest and from suit. Any person who sought to prosecute or serve a writ upon an ambassador was subject to up to three years' imprisonment, as were his attorney and any official who sought to execute the writ. Act of Apr. 30, 1790, ch. 9, §§ 25–26, 1 Stat. 112, 117–18.

It was assumed by the framers and ratifiers of the Constitution that our obligations under international law would be honored. In the course of their rebellion, the American colonies were quick to assure the world that the "law of nations [would be] strictly observed." 14 J. CONT. CONG. 635 (1779). The Continental Congress, lacking meaningful authority, had to content itself with passing a resolution urging the states to provide judicial remedies for infringements of the rights of ambassadors. 21 J. CONT. CONG. 1136–37 (1781). This resolution was apparently ineffective, for Edmund Randolph was later, at the constitutional convention, to identify as one of the defects of the Articles of Confederation that "they could not cause infractions of treaties or of the law of nations, to be punished," and to note as an example that "if the rights of an ambassador are invaded by any citizen it is only in a few states that any laws exist to punish the offender." 1 M. FARRAND, THE RECORDS OF THE FEDERAL CONVENTION OF 1787, at 19, 25 (1911). In arguing for ratification, John Jay subsequently characterized it as "of high importance to the peace of America that she observe the law of nations." THE FEDERALIST NO. 3, at 13 (P. Ford ed. 1898). Accord Dickinson, *The Law of Nations as Part of the National Law of the United States*, 101 U. PA. L. REV. 26, 55–56 (1952) ("the Constitution was framed in firm reliance upon the premise, frequently articulated, that ... the Law of Nations in all its aspects familiar to men of learning in the eighteenth century was accepted by the framers, expressly or implicitly, as a constituent part of the national law of the United States").

... As the Supreme Court has shown, it is often instructive to examine the practices at the time of the Constitution's framing as a guide to understanding the meaning of its provisions. See Marsh v. Chambers, 463 U.S. 783 ... (1983).

These were among the considerations that motivated the Congress that enacted section 22–1115. These principles were repeatedly invoked during the debate on the Senate floor....

The requirements imposed by international law have changed somewhat since the days of Vattel, since the founding of the Republic, and even since the era in which section 22–1115 was enacted. The legal principles embodied in section 22–1115, however, have gained rather than lost force in the intervening years. Article 22 of the 1961 Vienna Convention on Diplomatic Relations, to which the United States is a signatory, sets out duties expected of a host state in regard to the mission premises of foreign nations.... [see Documents Supplement] The principles embodied in the Vienna Convention were for the most part already established under customary international law....

We think it clear beyond quibble that since the founding of our nation adherence to the law of nations, and most particularly that branch of the law that demands security for the persons and respect for the dignity and peace of foreign emissaries, has been regarded as a fundamental and compelling national interest. It is also clear that the founders, who explicitly gave Congress the power to enforce adherence to the standards of the law of nations, which they understood well, saw no incompatibility between this national interest and any guaranteed individual freedom....

We have here an unusually strong case for judicial deference, over and above the traditional and general requirement of restraint in the area of foreign relations, for we asked to review a statute which both Congress and successive Presidents have declared to be necessary to fulfill our obligations under both customary international law and a treaty which we have signed. It has long been understood that the interpretation given by the executive branch of the country's responsibilities under the treaties to which it is a signatory are entitled to "great weight." See Sumitomo Shoji America, Inc. v. Avagliano, 457 U.S. 176, 184–85 ... (1982); Kolovrat v. Oregon, 366 U.S. 187, 194 ... (1961). This necessarily shapes the nature of the scrutiny to which we subject the justifications offered for section 22–1115, for in this context a court cannot lightly dispute a determination by the political branches that the statute meets important international obligations, that the interests at stake are compelling, or that those interests cannot be met by a statute with a more narrow reach. When a provision is enacted in order to bring the United States into compliance with international law, and when those obligations are reaffirmed by treaty, a court must give careful consideration before it sets aside that which the legislative and executive branches have deemed necessary to fulfill the nation's international responsibilities. It would be quite improper for the judiciary to disregard international obligations that are inseparable from our nationhood....

The obligations of the United States under international law, reaffirmed by treaty, do not, of course, supersede the first amendment. Neither, however, has it ever been suggested that the first amendment is incompatible with the United States' most basic obligations under the law of nations. The two must be accommodated and section 22–1115 accomplishes an accommodation well within the range of the permissible....

If international law were ... just another code of rules, like the common law of negligence or statutory law governing commercial transactions, it would of course offer little that need be weighed against a constitutional provision. As a matter of formal description, leaving aside the real interests in play, it is true that in the American legal hierarchy, the Constitution trumps all other law. But it is also true ... that other law sometimes expresses values and concerns that are of legitimate constitutional dimension.... As we have tried to make clear, international law in the aspect dealt with here is important not in the merely formal sense just described but because it embodies American interests that are themselves given weight in the Constitution and that must, for that reason, find accommodation with the first amendment. Those interests have to do with the place of the United States among nations, with the respect it is accorded, with the raising or lowering of tensions between our country and others, with the conduct of our foreign policy, primarily by the President but also in some measure by Congress in ways specified by the Constitution, and, in extreme cases, with war and peace. When, in the considered judgment of the branches charged by the Constitution with the responsibility for these matters, a minor regulation of picketing is necessary to preserve the peace and dignity of foreign emissaries, it is preposterous to say that no interest is present that courts need to respect and weigh....

Notes and Questions

1. The general approach utilized in *Finzer v. Barry* was basically the approach of the Supreme Court in the same case on appeal, although the decision was reversed in part and affirmed in part. *See* Boos v. Barry, 485 U.S. 312, 322–29 (1988). Justice O'Connor added: "the fact that an interest is recognized in international law does not automatically render the interest 'compelling' for purposes of First Amendment analysis. We need not decide today whether, or to what extent, the dictates of international law could ever require that First Amendment analysis be adjusted to accommodate the interests of foreign officials." *Id.* at 324.

2. Note Vattel's recognition of a broad duty to protect and shelter from violence one's own nationals and aliens. The duty to protect aliens became part of customary international law concerning "denial of justice." *See, e.g.*, RESTATEMENT § 711; MYRES S. MCDOUGAL, HAROLD D. LASSWELL, LUNG-CHU CHEN, HUMAN RIGHTS AND WORLD PUBLIC ORDER 739–40 (1980).

3. In Brown v. United States, 12 U.S. (8 Cranch) 110, 122–29 (1814), it was recognized that war gives to the sovereign full right to confiscate enemy property and held that such a sovereign right was not that of the President, but of Congress, that the legislature has that power derived from the law of nations, and it is "not of the executive or judiciary." Justice Story disagreed with the Court: "I ... admit that a declaration of war does not, of itself, import a confiscation of enemies' property.... All that I contend for is, that a declaration of war gives [the U.S.] a right to confiscate enemies' property [under the laws of war], and enables the power to whom execution of the laws and the prosecution of the war are confided, to enforce that right. If, indeed, there be a limit imposed as to the extent to which hostilities may be

carried by the executive, I admit, that the executive cannot lawfully transcend that limit; but if no such limit exist, the war may be carried on according to the principles of the modern law of nations, and enforced when, and where, and on what property, the executive chooses.... He has a discretion vested in him, as to the manner and extent; but he cannot lawfully transcend the rules of warfare...." A longer extract of *Brown v. United States* appears in Chapter 8, Section 2 B.

Later, in Miller v. United States, 78 U.S. (11 Wall.) 268 (1871), Justice Field stated: "Whatever any independent civilized nation may do in the prosecution of war, according to the law of nations, Congress, under the Constitution, may authorize to be done...." *Id.* at 316 (Field, J., dissenting). Concerning other cases relevant to the enhancement of congressional power, *see, e.g.*, United States v. Lara, 541 U.S. 193, 201 (2004), quoting *Missouri v. Holland*, 252 U.S. at 433 ("treaties ... can authorize Congress to deal with 'matters' with which otherwise 'Congress could not deal.' "); Frend v. United States, 100 F.2d 691, 692–93 (D.C.Cir.1938), *cert. denied*, 306 U.S. 640 (1939); Jordan J. Paust, International Law as Law of the United States 9, 11–12, 49–50 ns.58–60, 153, 424 n.2 (2 ed. 2003); Beth Stephens, *Federalism and Foreign Affairs: Congress's Power to "Define and Punish ... Offenses Against the Law of Nations,"* 42 W & M L. Rev. 447 (2000); *see also In re* Yamashita, 327 U.S. 1, 7 (1946); *Ex parte* Quirin, *supra*.

4. Prior to *Missouri v. Holland* and after Holmes' opinion (despite his question about limits of the treaty power and treaties made under the "authority" of the U.S.) it was recognized that domestically the U.S. Constitution prevails over a treaty in case of an unavoidable clash (even though at the international level the United States remains liable to fulfill the treaty). *See, e.g.*, Asakura v. City of Seattle, 265 U.S. 332, 341 (1924); Downes v. Bidwell, 182 U.S. 244, 370 (1901) (Fuller, J., dissenting); De Geofroy v. Riggs, 133 U.S. 258, 267 (1890); The Cherokee Tobacco, 78 U.S. (11 Wall.) 616, 620–21 (1870); Doe v. Braden, 57 U.S. (16 How.) 635, 657 (1853); Pollard v. Hagan, 44 U.S. (3 How.) 212, 225 (1845); New Orleans v. United States, 35 U.S. (10 Pet.) 662, 736–37 (1836); *Ex parte* Dos Santos, 7 F.Cas. 949, 955 (C.C.D.Va.1835) (No. 4,016); Paust, *supra* at 81, 102. Especially cited today concerning the primacy of the Constitution is Reid v. Covert, 354 U.S. 1, 16–17 (1957). Justice Black's plurality opinion in *Reid* also noted that "[t]he United States is entirely a creature of the Constitution. Its power and authority have no other source." *Id. See also* Section 2 C 1, below.

5. If Congress has power to implement a treaty to protect ducks, does Congress also have power to implement human rights law to protect women? Consider the Violence Against Women Act, 42 U.S.C. § 13981 *et seq.* (1994) (VAWA). What treaty-based and/or customary human rights are at stake? Do they reach private perpetrators? Recall Chapter 1; *United States v. Haun*, *supra*. In it first report to the Human Rights Committee under the International Covenant, the United States stated that the VAWA was enacted to meet human rights requirements under the Covenant. See Summary Record of the 1401st Meeting: United States of America, at para. 29, CCPR/C/SR. 140 (17/04/95). What cases would you cite in support of the enhancement of congressional power to enact the VAWA by customary international law, by treaty law? Portions of the VAWA providing civil rights remedies were

struck down as not being within congressional powers under the commerce clause (I, § 8, cl. 3) or the Fourteenth Amendment. Congressional powers to implement treaty law and the treaty power as such were not addressed. See United States v. Morrison, 529 U.S. 598 (2000).

When exercising a power to implement treaty-based or customary international law, must Congress refer to international law in the legislation or legislative history? Recall *United States v. Arjona*. More generally, *see also* E.E.O.C. v. Wyoming, 460 U.S. 226, 243–44 n. 18 (1983) (courts can "discern some legislative purpose or factual predicate that supports the exercise of ... power."); Woods v. Miller, 333 U.S. 138, 144 (1948). For congressional recognition of the purpose of the VAWA partly to protect human rights, *see e.g.*, Hearing of the Senate Judiciary Committee, Federal News Service, July 21, 1993 (Judge Ginsburg and Senator Biden); Pam Maples, *Bringing Fear Home: U.S. Women Face Pervasive Threat of Violence, Often at the Hands of Husbands, Boyfriends*, THE DALLAS MORNING NEWS 1A, June 6, 1993; Paust, *Human Rights Purposes of the Violence Against Women Act and International Law's Enhancement of Congressional Power*, 22 HOUS. J. INT'L L. 209 (2000).

6. We will also consider *Missouri v. Holland* and related cases on another point in Section 2 F. 1. Note the subjects of early treaty law that were addressed in early cases cited in *Missouri*. Early treaties also addressed rights of alien persons concerning title to land, inheritance, and debts (*see, e.g.*, Carneal v. Banks, 23 U.S. (10 Wheat.) 181, 189 (1825); Hughes v. Edwards, 22 U.S. (9 Wheat.) 489 (1824); Orr v. Hodgson, 17 U.S. (4 Wheat.) 453 (1819); Chirac v. Chirac, 15 U.S. (2 Wheat.) 259, 262 (1817); Martin v. Hunter's Lessee, 14 U.S. (1 Wheat.) 304, 340–41, 370–71 (1816); Harden v. Fisher, 14 U.S. (1 Wheat.) 300 (1816); Fairfax's Devisee v. Hunter's Lessee, 11 U.S. (7 Cranch) 603, 627 (1813); Georgia v. Brailsford, 3 U.S. (3 Dall.) 1, 4 (1794); Gordon v. Kerr, 10 F. Cas. 801, 802 (C.C.D.Pa.1806) (No. 5,611); Hamilton v. Eaton, 11 F. Cas. 336, 337–38, 340 (C.C.D.N.C.1792) (No. 5,980) (regarding an action on debt owed to former residents of North Carolina who had refused an oath at the time of the U.S. Revolution and left the state, the treaty of peace "became obligatory on the people of the United States when made and duly ratified," and a treaty "must necessarily control all acts issuing from the inferior authority which might contravene it," *i.e.*, that of the state)); other rights (*see, e.g.*, Owings v. Norwood's Lessee, 9 U.S. (5 Cranch) 344, 348–49 (1809); Ware v. Hylton, 3 U.S. (3 Dall.) 199 (1796)); human rights or rights of man (*see, e.g.*, Chew Heong v. United States, 112 U.S. 536, 541 (1884); *In re* Parrott, 1 F. 481, 503, 506–07 (C.C.D.Cal.1880); Baker v. City of Portland, 2 F. Cas. 472, 473 (C.C.D. Ore. 1879) (No. 777); *In re* Ah Fong, 1 F. Cas. 213, 217 n. 3, 218 (C.C.D.Cal.1874); United States v. Haun, 26 F. Cas. 227, 230–32 (C.C.S.D.Ala.1860) (No. 15, 329); *see also* Fletcher v. Peck, 10 U.S. (6 Cranch) 87, 133 (1810) (our federal courts "are established ... to decide on human rights")); slavery (*see, e.g.*, The Schooner Amistad, 40 U.S. (15 Pet.) 518 (1841); The Antelope, 23 U.S. (10 Wheat.) 66 (1825)); acquisition of territory, control of persons within it, and creation of rights and immunities of the inhabitants equal to those of citizens of the U.S., including property rights (*see, e.g.*, United States v. Percheman, 32 U.S. (7 Pet.) 51, 89 (1833); American Insurance Co. v. 356 Bales of Cotton, 26 U.S. (1 Pet.) 511, 542 (1828); Green v. Biddle, 21 U.S. (8 Wheat.) 1, 100

(1823)); conferral of title to land (*see, e.g.*, Holden v. Joy, 84 U.S. (17 Wall.) 211, 247 (1872); Crews v. Burcham, 66 U.S. (1 Black) 352, 356 (1861); Doe v. Wilson, 64 U.S. (23 How.) 457, 463 (1859); Mitchel v. United States, 34 U.S. (9 Pet.) 711, 748 (1835); Godfrey v. Beardsley, 10 F. Cas. 520, 522 (C.C.D.Ind.1841) (No. 5,497)); international criminal law (*see, e.g.*, Talbot v. Janson, 3 U.S. (3 Dall.) 133, 159–61 (1795); Henfield's Case, 11 F. Cas. 1099 (C.C.D.Pa.1793) (No. 6,360); 1 Op. Att'y Gen. 57, 58 (1795)); ship seizures (*see, e.g.*, The Schooner Peggy, 5 U.S. (1 Cranch) 103, 110 (1801)); and extradition (*see, e.g.*, United States v. Cooper, 25 F. Cas. 631, 641–42 (C.C.D.Pa.1800) (No. 14,865)); Martin S. Flaherty, *Are We to Be a Nation? Federal Power vs. "States' Rights" in Foreign Affairs*, 70 U. Col. L. Rev. 1277, 1313–14 (1999).

7. Soon after *Missouri*, another 10th Amendment police power or interest of the states fell in the face of inconsistent treaty law. See Asakura v. City of Seattle, 265 U.S. 332 (1924), considered below. After *Missouri* and *Asakura*, what untouchable powers of the states remain under the Tenth Amendment? In National League of Cities v. Usery, 426 U.S. 833 (1976), the Court declared that the commerce clause does not confer power on Congress to "directly displace the States' freedom to structure integral operations in areas of traditional governmental functions." The case was overruled in Garcia v. San Antonio Metro. Transit Authority, 469 U.S. 528 (1985), and in neither case was there attention to international law. A reinvigorated Tenth Amendment appears also in other cases not involving international law. *See, e.g.*, Printz v. United States, 521 U.S. 898 (1997) (weapons background-check provisions of federal legislation resting on commerce power invalidated); United States v. Lopez, 514 U.S. 549 (1995) (gun controls in schools adopted in federal legislation invalidated). Do you think that cases like *Printz* and *Lopez* will pose a threat to *Missouri* and *Asakura*? Do the powers of our national political branches to effectuate international law provide an overriding constitutional propriety, especially in view of the Supremacy Clause? See also U.S. Const., arts. I, § 10, VI, cl. 2, and Amend. X.

For a Bricker-type "federalism" critique of treaty supremacy with respect to nearly any subject matter, *see, e.g.*, Curtis A. Bradley, *The Treaty Power and American Federalism*, 97 Mich. L. Rev. 390 (1998), assuming incorrectly that human rights or rights of man would not have been a proper subject matter (*id.* at 451); *but see* David M. Golove, *Treaty-Making and the Nation: The Historical Foundations of the Nationalist Conception of the Treaty Power*, 98 Mich. L. Rev. 1075 (2000); Martin S. Flaherty, *Are We to be a Nation? Federal Power vs. "States' Rights" in Foreign Affairs*, 70 U. Colo. L. Rev. 1277 (1999). Human rights were of fundamental importance to the Founders, especially civil and political rights against one's own government, state or federal. They were partly what our nation and much of the Bill of Rights, including particularly the Ninth Amendment, were founded upon. *See, e.g.*, Paust, *supra* at 5, 8, 44, 95, 142, 169–75, 192–94, 198–203, 209–10, 216–23, 248, 256–70, 288–91, 323–25, 329–33, 339–40, 356–57 (also listing many other types of rights). More generally, what is the purpose of the Supremacy Clause?

8. If the United States and Canada entered into a treaty prohibiting or otherwise controlling the use of weapons in schools because of stated international interests in protecting children and young adults from gun-

related violence and death, would the treaty prevail against a Tenth Amendment claim?

b. Executive Power

Alexander Hamilton, *Pacificus No. 1* (June 29, 1793)

[The President] is charged with the execution of all laws, [has a] duty to enforce the laws [including treaties and] the laws of Nations, as well.... It is consequently bound.... [and since] Our Treaties and the laws of Nations form a part of the law of the land, [the President has both] a right, and ... duty, as Executor of the laws ... [to execute them].

Representative John Marshall, 10 ANNALS OF CONGRESS 614 (1800)

He is charged to execute the laws. A treaty is declared to be a law. He must then execute a treaty, where he, ... possesses the means of executing it ... [and the President] is accountable to the nation for the violation of its engagements with foreign nations, and for the consequences resulting from such violation....

1 **OP. ATT'Y GEN.** 566, 569–71 (1822)

The President is the executive officer of the laws of the country; these laws are not merely the constitution, statutes, and treaties of the United States, but those general laws of nations which ... impose on them, in common with other nations, the strict observance of a respect for their natural rights and sovereignties.... This obligation becomes one of the laws of the country; to the enforcement of which, the President, charged by his office with the execution of all our laws ... is bound to look.

Notes and Questions

1. Concerning other recognitions of the enhancement of Executive power by international law, *see, e.g.*, Francis v. Francis, 203 U.S. 233, 240, 242 (1906) ("The location of the lands became a duty devolving on the President by the treaty. This duty he could execute without an act of Congress; the treaty, when ratified, being the supreme law of the land, which the President was bound to see executed...."); Dooley v. United States, 182 U.S. 222, 231 (1901) ("powers of such government [by military occupation under control of the Executive] are regulated and limited. Such authority and such rules are derived directly from the laws of war ... the law of nations"); Cunningham v. Neagle, 135 U.S. 1, 64 (1890) ("The constitution ... declares that the president 'shall take care that the laws be faithfully executed.... Is this duty limited to the enforcement of acts of congress or of treaties of the United States according to their express terms; or does it include the rights, duties, and obligations growing out of the constitution itself, our international relations ... ?"); *In re* The Nuestra Senora de Regla, 108 U.S. 92, 102 (1882) ("It is objected, however, that the executive department of the Government had no power.... It was the duty of the United States, under the law of nations.... The executive department

had the right. . . ."); JORDAN J. PAUST, INTERNATIONAL LAW AS LAW OF THE UNITED STATES 9, 12–13, 16, 45–47 n.55, 82 n.14, 180, 185, 457, 468–69, 480–81 (2 ed. 2003); Chapter 8.

2. Can international law also enhance presidential use of the peace power? See Chapter 8, Section 2 B 5; PAUST, *supra* at 439–68. Normally, peace has been finalized by use of the treaty process. *See, e.g., id.* at 444, 463–64.

C. *International Agreements in the U.S. Domestic Process*

1. *Treaties*

a. *Formation*

In the United States, treaties as such are ratified by the President after the President has obtained the advice and consent of the Senate. Recall U.S. Constitution, Article II, Section 2. The President is also ultimately responsible for negotiation of international agreements on behalf of the United States.

b. *Interpretation and Amendment*

Concerning interpretation of treaties generally, recall Chapter 1, Section 2 A 2.

SALE v. HAITIAN CENTERS COUNCIL, INC., *ET AL.*

509 U.S. 155 (1993).

[recall the Court's approach to interpretation in *Sale*, in Chapter 1, Section 2 A 2, pp. 72–79]

Notes and Questions

1. Is the President bound by prior Senate understandings concerning the meaning of a treaty? Should the President be bound by prior domestic interpretations if the meaning of a treaty at the international level has changed? Should the courts? See also Vienna Convention on the Law of Treaties, Article 31. Should the President be required to obtain new advice and consent of the Senate each time the meaning of part of a treaty changes? Would that be realistic?

2. If a formal amendment to a treaty is attempted at the international level, should the President seek advice and consent of the Senate concerning the amendment? Is there a difference between a formal amendment to and a new meaning of a treaty?

3. Of course, a federal statute does not "amend" a treaty of the United States. *See, e.g.*, Gouveia v. Vokes, 800 F.Supp. 241, 259 (E.D.Pa.1992).

4. The judiciary attempts to identify and clarify the evolved or new meaning of treaty law when applying such in a case. *See, e.g.*, Kadic v. Karadzic, 70 F.3d 232, 238 (2d Cir.1995), *cert. denied*, 518 U.S. 1005 (1996); Amerada Hess Shipping Corp. v. Argentine Republic, 830 F.2d 421, 425 (2d Cir.1987), *rev'd on other gds.*, 488 U.S. 428 (1989). This is, of course, consistent with Article 31 of the Vienna Convention on the Law of Treaties.

5. Treaties are to be construed liberally to protect express and implied rights. *See, e.g.*, Factor v. Laubenheimer, 290 U.S. 276, 293–94 (1933); Nielsen v. Johnson, 279 U.S. 47, 51 (1929); Jordan v. Tashiro, 278 U.S. 123, 127 (1928); Asakura v. City of Seattle, 265 U.S. 332, 342 (1924) ("Treaties are to be construed in a broad and liberal spirit, and, when two constructions are possible, one restrictive of rights that may be claimed under it and the other favorable to them, the latter is to be preferred."); United States v. Payne, 264 U.S. 446, 448 (1924) ("Construing the treaty liberally in favor of the rights claimed under it, as we are bound to do...."); De Geofroy v. Riggs, 133 U.S. 258, 271 (1890) ("where a treaty admits of two constructions, one restrictive of rights that may be claimed under it and the other favorable to them, the latter is to be preferred."); Hauenstein v. Lynham, 100 U.S. 483, 487 (1879) ("Where a treaty admits of two constructions, one restrictive as to the rights, that may be claimed under it, and the other liberal, the latter is to be preferred."), *citing* Shanks v. Dupont, 28 U.S. (3 Pet.) 242, 249 (1830) ("If the treaty admits of two interpretations, and one is limited, and the other liberal; one which will further, and the other exclude private rights; why should not the most liberal exposition be adopted?"). Also see Owings v. Norwood's Lessee, below.

6. The judiciary often gives "particular weight" to the views of the Executive branch when interpreting a treaty, although the identification and clarification of law are ultimately judicial tasks. *See, e.g.*, RESTATEMENT § 112, cmt. c; see also *id.* § 113(1), § 326 (2) and RN 2; INS v. Aguirre–Aguirre, 526 U.S. 415 (1999); El Al Israel Airlines v. Tseng, 525 U.S. 155 (1999) (excerpts in Chapter 7, Section 1 B 4); Japan Whaling Association v. American Cetacean Society, 478 U.S. 221, 230 (1986). If the content or meaning of a treaty presents a legal question within the competence of the judiciary, should courts give "particular" or "substantial" weight to views of the Executive branch? *See also* The Paquete Habana, 175 U.S. 677 (1900) (Executive view of content of customary international law was in error); Section 2 D 1 of this Chapter.

c. *Self–Executing Treaties*

Some commentators and judicial opinions have recently argued that most treaties should be non-self-executing in the sense that they would not create rights of individuals that are directly enforceable in U.S. courts. Although some treaties clearly do not create rights of individuals, it has historically been presumed that most treaties creating individual rights or duties are self-executing, or, for example, that treaties creating individual rights are directly enforceable in U.S. courts without implementing legislation or executive acts that have the force of law. Consider whether the recent claims to avoid such a presumption are consistent with the views of the Founders, Framers, and early judiciary (documented in the following excerpt). Moreover, what is the general test concerning self-execution?

JORDAN J. PAUST, INTERNATIONAL LAW AS LAW OF THE UNITED STATES 51–63, 97–98 (1996), 67–80, 118–19 (2 ed. 2003)

The distinction found in certain cases between "self-executing" and "non-self-executing" treaties is a judicially invented notion that is patently inconsistent with express language in the Constitution affirming that "*all* Treaties ... shall be the supreme Law of the Land." Indeed, such a distinction may involve the most glaring of attempts to deviate from the specific text of the Constitution. For some 40 years after the formation of the Constitution, President George Washington's recognition in 1796 that "every Treaty [properly ratified] ... thenceforward becomes the law of the land" was widely shared. Yet today not all treaties are thought to be capable of operating as supreme federal law of their own effect....

The year before the Constitutional Convention, on October 13, 1786, John Jay, as Secretary of Foreign Affairs of the Confederation, reported to Congress that a treaty "made, ratified and published by Congress, ... immediately [became] binding on the whole nation, and superadded to the laws of the land.... Hence [it was to be] ... received and observed by every member of the nation...." By unanimously adopting Jay's historic report, Congress affirmed this early expectation that all treaties would be self-executing and superadded immediately to the laws of the land.

Jay's report also reflected the expectation that treaties would be national acts creating a supreme law of the land "independent of the will and power of" state legislatures and that they were to be applied in all courts hearing causes or questions arising from or touching on such law. With respect to the concept of national preemption, now termed federal preemption, Jay added: "the legislatures of the several states cannot of right pass any act or acts for interpreting, explaining or construing a national treaty, or any part or clause of it; nor for restraining, limiting or counteracting the operation or execution of the same." Yet, as noted above, judicial power certainly applied, and "[a]ll doubts, in cases between private individuals, respecting the meaning of a treaty, like all doubts respecting the meaning of a law," were to be resolved by the judiciary.

Soon afterward, Jay's report was referred to by Judge James Iredell of North Carolina (who later joined the U.S. Supreme Court), Iredell recognizing, much like the Secretary, " 'that a treaty when once made pursuant to the sovereign authority, *ex vi termini* became immediately the law of the land' "and was " 'binding upon those who delegated authority for that purpose,' " *i.e.*, the people. Indeed, recommendations during the 1787 Convention that treaties be ratified or sanctioned by congressional legislation, since they "are to have the operation of laws," were defeated. Draft phrases such as "enforce treaties" were also considered "superfluous, since treaties were to be 'laws' "and thus were directly enforceable. A proposal by James Madison that there be two types of treaties (*i.e.*, those requiring only action by the Senate and the President, and those also requiring House action before they could take effect as law) was also rejected—further evidence that there was to be one type of treaty law, that which is immediately operative as supreme federal law when approved by the Senate and ratified by the President.

That this expectation predominated among the Framers can be seen as well in the *Federalist* papers and in the various debates on ratification of the Constitution in the states....

These historic patterns of expectation demonstrate that most of the Framers intended *all* treaties *immediately* to become binding on the whole nation, superadded to the laws of the land; to be observed by every member of the nation; to be applied by the courts whenever a cause or question arose from or touched on them; and to prevail over and preempt any inconsistent state action. In these ways at least, all treaties (to the extent of their grants, guarantees or obligations) were to be self-executing. Additionally, it would have made no sense to argue that a particular treaty was not self-executing unless one agreed that whether or not a treaty was self-executing was to be tested by the language of the treaty considered in context (with the possible exception posed by some exclusive congressional power expressly documented as such in the new Constitution).

These recaptured views of the Founders are certainly consistent with the actual text of the Constitution and would require acknowledgment, in modern parlance, that all treaties are self-executing except those (or the portions of them) which, by their very terms, require domestic implementing legislation. According to the predominant expectations of the Founders, as the words of the Constitution affirm, each treaty is supreme law of the land, especially for use by the judiciary and for supremacy purposes. Each treaty is law; but if a treaty provision expressly requires domestic implementing legislation before it becomes directly operative, that is merely a condition of such law. Further, as explained below, merely because the full Congress (*i.e.*, the House and Senate) has an express power to make a law should not be relevant to whether a treaty is self-executing, since the President and Senate also have an express power to make treaty law and each treaty is supreme law of the land.

Early Cases

The earliest federal cases addressing the domestic effect of treaties made no mention of any distinction between self-executing and non-self-executing treaties. Not surprisingly, the language in early judicial opinions mirrored the predominant expectations of the Framers noted above. In 1792, for example, Judge Oliver Ellsworth, who would join the U.S. Supreme Court four years later, wrote that a treaty, "being ratified and made ... became a complete national act and law of every state." Judge Sitgreaves, writing in the same case, declared that "the treaty consequently became obligatory on the people ... when made and duly ratified," which "was alone sufficient" for its "validity and legality" within the United States with respect to judicial decisionmaking.

In 1801 Chief Justice Marshall declared broadly: "If the law [there, a treaty] be constitutional, ... I know of no court which can contest its obligation." And in 1809 the Chief Justice wrote: "*Whenever* a right grows out of, or is protected by, a treaty, ... it is to be protected." In fact, in several federal cases decided up until 1829, treaty law was accepted as operating directly as supreme federal law in the face of inconsistent state law, or more generally for other purposes. Moreover, it was early recognized that statutes should be interpreted so as to be consistent with international law, a recognition that was not hinged upon whether or not a treaty was self-executing or directly operative. And it was recognized, at least since 1796, that federal judges, as state judges under the Supremacy Clause, are equally "bound by duty and oath" to apply treaty law. Indeed, in 1809 Chief Justice Marshall affirmed: "The reason for inserting that clause [Art. III, § 2, cl. 1] ... was, that all persons who have real claims under a treaty should have their causes decided...."

Ever since these cases, the supremacy of international law over state law has been complete and in no Supreme Court decision has that supremacy had to depend upon the status of a treaty as self-executing law. Of course, nothing in the written Constitution requires that a treaty be self-executing in order to be supreme law of the land. By express terms, "all" treaties made under the authority of the United States "shall" have that status. Indeed, it is difficult to imagine that something shall be supreme federal "law of the land" but not operate directly as "law" except by believing in one of the most transparent of judicial delusions. That sort of vision has been applied by the Supreme Court only with regard to competing congressional power (*i.e.*, of the full Congress, including the House), for example, when a constitutionally required power of Congress was thought to be at stake. It first occurred, moreover, nearly 40 years after the formation of the Constitution, without any evident precedent and in seeming contrast to the predominant expectations of the Framers and early judicial opinions noted above.

The Judicial Invention

The first Supreme Court opinion that actually used the phrase "self-executing" did not appear until 1887. Yet Chief Justice Marshall had invented the concept in 1829 when opining that a treaty "is carried into execution ... whenever it operates of itself," the notion being that some treaties do not operate of themselves but require domestic legislation to carry them "into execution." [Foster v. Neilson, 27 U.S. (2 Pet.) 253 (1829)] This judicial invention, considered in historical context and with reference to other words in Marshall's 1829 opinion, was relatively proper. Later commentators, however, have distorted his meaning and created tests concerning self-executing and non-self-executing treaties that are patently inconsistent with the text of the Constitution, the predominant expectations of the Framers and early judicial opinions. What Marshall actually declared and his evident criterion are worth examining.

Marshall knew that in some countries a treaty is "not a legislative act" and "does not generally effect, of itself, the object to be accomplished . . . but is carried into execution by'' legislation or other exercises of "sovereign power." He added, however, that "[i]n the United States a different principle is established. Our constitution declares a treaty to be the law of the land. It is, consequently, to be regarded in courts of justice as equivalent to an act of the legislature, whenever it operates of itself. . . ." Therefore, even though Marshall still maintained that every treaty was "the law of the land," his suggestion that some treaties did not operate of themselves represented a new twist, perhaps, with respect to precedent—but, in context, a minor new twist. After all, *the* criterion as to whether or not a treaty, as law, was to be "carried into execution" was to be the treaty itself. It was to be carried into execution "*whenever* it operates *of itself*," and it was not to be self-executory if its terms so indicated. Thus, it was the language of such supreme federal law, considered in context, that was to be determinative . . . . .

. . . Applying this general test [of language considered in context] (hereinafter termed the language of the treaty criterion), Marshall found that a specific portion of a treaty between the United States and Spain protecting private land titles (couched in the terms "shall be ratified and confirmed") was not directly operative. Four years later, however, he reversed himself after construing the terms of the same treaty differently: "*They* may import that they 'shall be ratified and confirmed' *by* force of *the instrument itself*." [United States v. Percheman, 32 U.S. (7 Pet.) 51, 89 (1833)] In effect, Marshall had retained and reapplied a language of the treaty test. It was not a "political question" test, and it was not a test that was hinged upon the existence of some concurrent congressional power. Thus, under Marshall's test, no particular subject matter would render a treaty inherently non-self-operative. . . .

Before other postulated tests or criteria are addressed, it is worth noting that other writers have rightly recognized that Chief Justice Marshall's related criterion of "contract . . . to perform a particular act" does "not itself provide a workable test to determine whether a provision in a treaty requires legislative action." "In almost all treaties one of the 'parties engages to perform a particular act,' "and such a test has not generally been applied. Similarly, "to take 'futurity of language' as the test makes little sense since the future tense is often used in treaties . . . and it in no way indicates that legislation is necessary." Moreover, as the signatories rarely concern themselves with the details of domestic implementation, treaties are hardly ever addressed "to the political, not the judicial department," or to any domestic governmental apparatus.

Marshall, it may be recalled, had great difficulty applying these criteria to the particular treaty at stake, and they seem to be no more useful today. Significantly, some of his earlier opinions lend support to Marshall's language of the treaty criterion. More importantly, he might well have expected, even after 1829, that treaties were to be self-operative, in his words, "[w]henever a right grows out of, or is protected by, a treaty" or persons "have real claims under a treaty." These latter tests (herein termed the rights under a treaty test) would certainly guarantee that human rights treaties were self-operative, unless a treaty expressly required domestic legislation implementing such rights before they could become directly operative.

Post–1829 Criteria and Separate Lines of Cases

After 1829, Marshall retained both the language of the treaty criterion and the rights under a treaty test. As mentioned, he used those criteria in 1833 in reinterpreting the treaty involved in *Foster*. In 1835 he applied them again in holding that language in a treaty reading "they shall be maintained and protected in the free enjoyment of their liberty, property, and ... religion" protected the right to property and meant, "then, [that it] is protected and secured by the treaty" in a direct or self-operative manner. Justice Story, in his 1833 *Commentaries*, seemed to accept Marshall's language of the treaty criterion, but he stressed that, in most cases, "treaties ... should be held, when made, to be the supreme law of the land" and that it is "indispensable, that they should have the obligation and force of a law, that they may be executed by the judicial power, and obeyed like other laws." For Justice Story, treaties "ought to have a positive binding efficacy, as laws," and he emphasized that the "difference between considering them as laws, and considering them as executory, or executed contracts, is exceedingly important.... If they are supreme laws, courts of justice will enforce them directly in all cases, to which they can be judicially applied...."

Very few courts, however, paid attention to Marshall's invented distinction between self-and non-self-operative treaties until the end of the 19th century. Rather, two lines of cases at the Supreme Court level began to emerge: one line (hereinafter termed the invented distinction cases) accepted the general distinction between self-and non-self-operative treaties, while the other (hereinafter termed the law of the land cases) seems simply to have ignored it....

The *Restatement (Third) of Foreign Relations Law of the United States* seeks to explain away this separate line of cases, but it still remains. Interestingly, however, the new *Restatement* also seems to have used these and other cases as support for the general presumption that treaties are self-executing.... Furthermore, the *Restatement* basically adopts Marshall's criterion of the language of the treaty considered in context, as to self-executing status, but adds that in some rare cases implementing legislation may be "constitutionally required." In practice, the language of the treaty test has found significant acceptance, and some cases have sought to elucidate other aspects of context that might be considered while focusing on language and probable intent.

From the above, it is evident that Marshall's approach and the *Restatement*'s presumption and general test can be compatible with the text of the Constitution and the predominant views of the Framers. Again, all treaties, to the extent of their grants, guarantees or obligations, are self-executing. Those that are not are those which, by their terms, require domestic implementing legislation or otherwise express an intention that they not be self-operative. Thus, non-self-execution is to be tested by the language of the treaty considered in context and, according to the *Restatement*, against a strong presumption of self-execution.

THE ROLE OF CONGRESSIONAL POWER

Need one stress that this rediscovered view rejects completely the current insistence that certain treaties are inherently non-self-executing because legislative power exists, for example, to regulate commerce, to define and punish crimes, and to appropriate money? The Senate and President also have an express power to make a treaty, which is supreme law of the land, and the mere existence of a concurrent power does not obviate either the existence or the exercise of another. Indeed, to claim that certain treaties should be inherently non-self-executing merely because Congress has a relevant concurrent power is to ignore or subvert the separation of powers between the legislative and judicial branches, to rewrite the Constitution at the expense of the treaty power. It is the judiciary, not Congress, that has been granted the power (indeed, the textual commitment) under Article III of the Constitution to apply treaty law in cases or controversies otherwise properly before the courts.

For these or related reasons, commentators and others have recognized that treaty provisions can be directly applicable despite the existence of a relevant congressional power, and the same recognition has appeared in recent cases. Nonetheless, the *Restatement (Third)* seeks to retain the possibility that a treaty may not be self-executing in a case where "implementing legislation is constitutionally required." One can agree, but this test does not answer the question at stake, *i.e.*, whether legislation is "constitutionally required." Thus, this test, as the new *Restatement* recognizes, might only apply where Congress is thought to have an exclusive power (*i.e.*, not merely a concurrent power with respect to matters that can also be effectuated by treaty). The *Restatement* even adds: "That a subject is within the legislative power of Congress does not preclude a treaty on the same subject."

Yet the *Restatement* assumes that agreements involving the appropriation of funds do require congressional action. More cautiously, the *Restatement* states that it has been "assumed" that agreements creating a state of war or a crime or calling for punishment of certain conduct require congressional implementing legislation, adding that "[i]t has also been suggested" that treaties cannot "raise revenue" by imposing taxes or tariffs. A Reporters' Note remarks more openly:

> There is no definitive authority for the rule set forth . . . that agreements on some subjects cannot be self-executing. . . . No particular clause of the Constitution conferring power on Congress states or clearly implies that the power can be exercised only by Congress and not by treaty. . . . The principle declared . . . is nevertheless generally assumed for the cases given.

What the Reporters' Note nearly admits is that powers conferred on Congress by Article I, section 8 of the Constitution are merely concurrent powers, not exclusive powers. This recognition was even more evident in *Edwards v. Carter* [580 F.2d 1055 (D.C.Cir.), *cert. denied*, 436 U.S. 907, 98 S.Ct. 2240 (1978)], although there the circuit court was uncomfortable with the notion that none of the section 8 powers (especially the war power) were exclusive.... [The treatise then argues that the power to involve the U.S. in war is not an exclusive congressional power, although the power to declare war is (because of, among other things, what *Edwards* recognized as the "*sui generis* nature of a declaration of war and ... unique history," plus a consistent recognition by the courts of its exclusive nature); and that the power to appropriate money is not exclusive in Congress and can be exercised per terms of the Constitution "by Law," which arguably can include law other than a federal statute.]

... Using the *Edwards* rationale (but not all of the conclusory dicta), one can see that, with the exception of the power to declare war, no seemingly relevant congressional power is exclusive....

LEGAL EFFECTS OF NON-SELF-EXECUTING TREATIES

It is important to note that even generally non-self-executing treaties can produce legal effects. Although such treaties cannot operate directly without implementing legislation or some other law or legal act (such as another self-executing treaty, an Executive agreement, or an Executive order that has the force of law), non-self-executing treaties can be used indirectly as a means of interpreting relevant constitutional, statutory, common law or other legal provisions. Indirect incorporation of international law, moreover, is the most prevalent form of judicial incorporation. Further, the fact that a treaty is not self-executing domestically should not inhibit any effect it may have abroad.... Additionally ..., even generally non-self-executing treaties can operate through the Supremacy Clause of the Constitution to obviate inconsistent state law and/or be utilized more generally to demonstrate federal preemption.

As noted, the President also has an executing power. Execute is nearly the very name of the Executive, and the Constitution confirms that the President has the power (Article II § 1) and duty (Article II § 3) to execute law. Thus, unless a matter lies directly within the exclusive prerogative of Congress, it is otherwise constitutionally precluded, or legislation is required by the international instrument, the President must faithfully execute an otherwise non-self-executing treaty. [*See, e.g.*, Francis v. Francis, 203 U.S. 233, 240, 242 (1906); The Lessee of Pollard's Heirs v. Kibbe, 39 U.S. (14 Pet.) 353, 415 (1840)].... Also, Comment h of Section 111 of the *Restatement* recognizes that a non-self-executing agreement can be executed by "appropriate executive or administrative action."

An early draft of the new *Restatement* had mirrored an incorrect and overly broad statement in an opinion of the Court of Appeals for the Fifth Circuit that "treaties affect" domestic law only when they "are given effect by congressional legislation or are, by their nature, self-executing." . . . [H]owever, such assertions are clearly out of line with predominant trends in judicial decision and are fallacious for at least three reasons. First, the self-executing treaty doctrine does not apply to customary international law. The doctrine therefore poses no obstacle to the direct incorporation of customary norms for use in domestic litigation. Because non-self-executing treaties often are evidence of customary international law, these treaties can affect the municipal law of the United States. Second, although some decisions pay great attention to the self-executing treaty doctrine, usually so as to deny claims of incorporation, in another line of cases treaty provisions have been incorporated directly for judicial use without any mention of the doctrine. Third, non-self-executing treaties are available for interpretive purposes and, thus, can at least affect domestic law indirectly. . . .

Notes and Questions

1. Read, for example, Articles 6–19 in the International Covenant on Civil and Political Rights (ICCPR). Would these be self-executing under Chief Justice Marshall's test focusing on the language of the treaty considered in context? Under the tests noted in the following cases?

2. During formation of the Constitution, Jefferson and a few others had argued for a system whereby no treaty could operate directly as law of the United States unless it had been implemented by congressional legislation, but this rare viewpoint failed to gain support. As the extract from Professor Paust's treatise demonstrates, the Founders and Framers understood that the treaty power was freed from such attempted limitations. Treaties would be made by the President with the advice and consent merely of the U.S. Senate, not the House of Representatives. In the 1950s, there were other attempts to amend the Constitution so that treaties had to have approval by the House and be implemented by legislation, but those attempts also failed to gain much support.

3. Such attempts to change the constitutional text, structure and history emerged again when a so-called "revisionist" view argued that treaties, especially those that are multilateral, should be presumed to be non-self-executing in order to protect an alleged "right" of Congress to determine how and to what extent the United States should adhere to its international obligations. Such a viewpoint is frequently associated with the statement made by Judge Robert Bork in Tel–Oren v. Libyan Arab Republic, 726 F.2d 774, 808 (D.C. Cir. 1984) (Bork, J., concurring), that "[t]reaties of the United States, though the law of the land, do not generally create rights that are privately enforceable in courts." This position is supported by a few textwriters. *See, e.g.*, John C. Yoo, *Globalism and the Constitution: Treaties, Non–Self–Execution, and the Original Understanding*, 99 COLUM. L. REV. 1955 (1999); John C. Yoo, *Treaties and Public Lawmaking: A Textual and Structural Defense of Non–Self–Execution*, 99 COLUM. L. REV. 2218 (1999); Curtis A. Bradley, *International Delegations, the Structural Constitution, and Non–Self–Execution*, 55 STAN. L. REV. 1557, 1587–95 (2003); *but see* Martin S. Flaherty, *History Right?: Historical Scholarship, Original Understanding, and Treaties as "Supreme Law of the Land"*, 99 COLUM. L. REV. 2095 (1999) (demonstrating that the historical evidence is contrary to that

presented in Professor Yoo's articles); Jordan J. Paust, *Customary International Law and Human Rights Treaties* Are *Law of the United States*, 20 MICH. J. INT'L L. 301, 321–31 (1999); extract from Professor Paust's treatise, above. Others have characterized the revisionist view as "implausible," inconsistent with the language of the Supremacy Clause, and "mistaken." *See, e.g.*, Carlos Manuel Vazquez, *Laughing at Treaties*, 99 COLUM. L. REV. 2154, 2156, 2169–73, 2216 (1999).

Moreover, the "revisionist" view is sharply inconsistent with the approach taken by the early judges and almost all of today's judges. Today, judges do not automatically assume that treaties are non-self-executing, but resolve that issue by examining the language of the treaty considered in context, the normal test. As others explain, the traditional view has been that "there should be a strong presumption that a treaty is self-executing unless the contrary is clearly indicated," because if the treaty has been in effect and has not been implemented by legislation "a finding that it is not self-executing in effect puts the United States in default on its international obligations." LOUIS HENKIN, RICHARD CRAWFORD PUGH, OSCAR SCHACHTER & HANS SMIT, INTERNATIONAL LAW 215 (3d ed. 1993) (*citing, inter alia*, RESTATEMENT § 111, Reporters' Note 5 (1987)). Many courts have also cited non-self-executing treaties as part of the "potpourri" of evidence that courts examine to determine the content of customary international law, and these treaties have also been used indirectly to interpret relevant constitutional and statutory provisions. One recent example is Justice Ginsburg's citation to the International Convention on the Elimination of All Forms of Racial Discrimination (see the Documents Supplement) for guidance on the question whether affirmative action programs should have a termination point. Grutter v. Bollinger, 539 U.S. 306, 342 (2003) (Ginsburg, J., concurring). The provisions of this treaty were deemed to be non-self-executing when the Senate gave its advice and consent to the treaty in 1994. See 140 Cong. Rec. S7634 (daily ed. June 24, 1994).

3. For inquiry into racial and racist aspects and consequences of the creation and continued application of the doctrine of non-self-execution, *see, e.g.*, Henry J. Richardson, III, *Excluding Race Strategies from International Legal History: The Self-Executing Treaty Doctrine and the South Africa Tripartite Agreement*, 45 VILL. L. REV. 1091, 1099–1117 (2000).

4. Should the power of Congress, not merely to declare war, but to involve the United States in a "state of war" be exclusive? *See also* Chapter 8 regarding U.S. use of armed force pursuant to authorizations by the U.N. Security Council and/or NATO, *e.g.*, in Korea (1950s), The Gulf War (1990, before nonretroactive congressional authorization in 1991), Bosnia–Herzegovina (1994 and subsequent years), and Kosovo (1999); and Section 8 of the War Powers Resolution. In fact, given these examples of Executive use of force pursuant to treaties, is the Restatement correct when stating that it is widely assumed that treaties cannot be self-executing in this regard or authorize use of force without congressional approval?

For other tests or approaches to self-execution, consider:

OWINGS v. NORWOOD'S LESSEE

9 U.S. (5 Cranch) 344, 348–49 (1809).

MARSHALL, C.J.

The reason for inserting that clause in the constitution [Art. III, Section 2, clause 1] was, that all persons who have real claims under a treaty should have their causes decided by the national tribunals.... Each treaty stipulates something respecting the citizens of the two nations, and gives them rights. Whenever a right grows out of, or is protected by, a treaty, it is sanctioned against all the laws and judicial decisions of the states; and whoever may have this right, it is to be protected.

THE LESSEE OF POLLARD'S HEIRS v. KIBBE

39 U.S. (14 Pet.) 353, 415 (1840).

BALDWIN, J., concurring.

All treaties, compacts, and articles of agreement in the nature of treaties to which the United States are parties, have ever been held to be the supreme law of the land, executing themselves by their own fiat, having the same effect as an act of Congress, and of equal force with the Constitution; and if any act is required on the part of the United States, it is to be performed by the executive, and not the legislative power, as declared in the case of *The Peggy* in 1801, and since affirmed with the exception of only *Foster and Elam*. Whether that case, standing solitary and alone, shall stand in its glory or its ruins, a judicial monument or a warning beacon, is not dependent on my opinion; my duty is performed by the preceding review of the law of this case in all its various branches....

EDYE v. ROBERTSON

112 U.S. 580, 598–99 (1884).

MILLER, J.

[Certain rights are] capable of enforcement as between private parties in the courts of the country.... A treaty, then, is a law of the land as an Act of Congress is, whenever its provisions prescribe a rule by which the rights of the private citizen or subject may be determined. And when such rights are of a nature to be enforced in a court of justice, that court resorts to the treaty for a rule of decision for the case before it, as it would to a statute.

BALDWIN v. FRANKS

120 U.S. 678, 703–04 (1887).

FIELD, J., dissenting.

... But in many instances a treaty operates by its own force, that is, without the aid of any legislative enactment; and such is generally the case when it declares the rights and privileges which the citizens or subjects of each nation may enjoy in the country of the other. This was so with the cause in some of our early treaties with European nations, declaring that their subjects might dispose of lands held by them in the United States, and that their heirs might inherit such property, or the proceeds thereof, notwithstanding their alienage. Thus the treaty with Great Britain of 1794 provided....

PEOPLE OF SAIPAN v. UNITED STATES DEP'T OF INTERIOR

502 F.2d 90 (9th Cir.1974).

GOODWIN, J.

Plaintiffs, citizens of the Trust Territory of the Pacific Islands (known also as Micronesia), sued in the district court to challenge the execution by the High Commissioner of the Trust Territory of a lease permitting Continental Airlines to construct and operate a hotel on public land adjacent to Micro Beach, Saipan. Plaintiffs appeal a judgment of dismissal.

The district court held that the Trust Territory government is not a federal agency subject to judicial review under the Administrative Procedure Act (APA), 5 U.S.C. §§ 701–706, or the National Environmental Policy Act (NEPA), 42 U.S.C. § 4321 *et seq.*, and that the Trusteeship Agreement does not vest plaintiffs with individual legal rights which they can assert in a federal court.... We affirm the judgment, but, for the reasons set out below, we do so without prejudice to the right of the plaintiffs to refile in the district court should the High Court of the Trust Territory deny that it has jurisdiction to review the legality of the actions of the High Commissioner.

... In brief, Continental applied in 1970 to the Trust Territory government for permission to build a hotel on public land adjacent to Micro Beach, Saipan, an important historical, cultural, and recreational site for the people of the islands. Pursuant to the requirements of the Trust Territory Code, 67 T.T.C.§ 53, Continental's application was submitted to the Mariana Islands District Land Advisory Board for its consideration. In spite of the Board's unanimous recommendation that the area be reserved for public park purposes, the District Administrator of the Marianas District recommended approval of a lease. The High Commissioner himself executed the lease on behalf of the Trust Territory government. An officer appointed by the President of the United States with the advice and consent of the Senate (48 U.S.C. § 1681a), the High Commissioner is the highest official in the executive branch of the Trust Territory government.

Following its execution in 1972, the lease was opposed by virtually every official body elected by the people of Saipan. Indeed, the record in this case shows that the High Commissioner's decision was officially supported only by the United States Department of the Interior, the

Trust Territory Attorney General (a United States citizen), and the District Administrator of the Marianas District (appointed by the High Commissioner, serving directly under him, and subject to removal by him).

Later in 1972, an action against some of the parties here was commenced before the High Court of the Trust Territory to enjoin construction of the hotel. The High Court, while denying defendants' motions to dismiss on certain nonfederal causes of action, held that NEPA did not apply to actions of the Trust Territory government, as plaintiffs had contended. Soon afterward, the plaintiffs filed this action in the United States District Court for the District of Hawaii, and the High Court thereupon stayed proceedings before it pending the outcome of this action....

Plaintiffs also asserted below and assert here that the action of the governmental defendants in leasing public land to an American corporation against the expressed opposition of the elected representatives of the people of Saipan and without compliance with NEPA is a violation of their duties under the Trusteeship Agreement. The district court rejected this argument, holding that the Trusteeship Agreement did not vest the citizens of the Trust Territory with rights which they can assert in a district court.

We cannot accept the full implications of this holding. We do not dispute the district court's conclusion that compliance with NEPA was not required by the Trusteeship Agreement. We do, however, disagree with the holding insofar as it can be read to say that the Trusteeship Agreement does not create for the islanders substantive rights that are judicially enforceable.

The district court relied for its conclusion on language in Pauling v. McElroy, 164 F. Supp. 390, 393 (D.D.C.1958), *aff'd on other grounds*, 107 U.S. App. D.C. 372, 278 F.2d 252, *cert. denied*, 364 U.S. 835 ... (1960). *Pauling* concerned an attempt to enjoin United States officials from proceeding with nuclear tests in the Marshall Islands, an area within the trusteeship. The controversy there, unlike the one here, involved the Trusteeship Agreement's grant of broad discretion to use the area for military purposes. See Trusteeship Agreement arts. 1, 5, 13, 61 Stat. 3301, 3302, 3304. We do not find *Pauling* to support the defendants' contention here that the plaintiffs cannot invoke the provisions of the Trusteeship Agreement to challenge the High Commissioner's power to lease local public land for commercial exploitation by private developers.

The right of Rhodesian and American citizens to maintain an action in the courts of the United States seeking enforcement of the United Nations embargo against Rhodesia was recently recognized in Diggs v. Shultz, 152 U.S. App. D.C. 313, 470 F.2d 461 (1972), *cert. denied*, 411 U.S. 931 ... (1973). On the merits, the court denied specific relief because of Congressional action which was held to have abrogated the United Nations Security Council Resolution, but the right to seek enforcement in federal court was firmly established. That decision, if correct, suggests that the islanders here can enforce their treaty rights, if need be in federal court.

... Although the plaintiffs have argued that articles [73 and 76] of the United Nations Charter, standing alone, create affirmative and judicially enforceable obligations, we assume without deciding that they do not.

However, pursuant to Article 79 of the Charter, the general principles governing the administration of trust territories were covered in more detail in a specific trusteeship agreement for the Trust Territory of the Pacific Islands.... Specifically, Article 6 of the Trusteeship Agreement requires the United States to "promote the economic advancement and self-sufficiency of the inhabitants, and to this end ... regulate the use of natural resources" and to "protect the inhabitants against the loss of their lands and resources...."

The extent to which an international agreement establishes affirmative and judicially enforceable obligations without implementing legislation must be determined in each case by reference to many contextual factors: the purposes of the treaty and the objectives of its creators, the existence of domestic procedures and institutions appropriate for direct implementation, the availability and feasibility of alternative enforcement methods, and the immediate and long-range social consequences of self-or non-self-execution. *See generally* M. McDougal, H. Lasswell, & J. Miller, The Interpretation of Agreements and World Public Order; Principles of Content and Procedure *passim* (1967).

The preponderance of features in this Trusteeship Agreement suggests the intention to establish direct, affirmative, and judicially enforceable rights. The issue involves the local economy and environment, not security; the concern with natural resources and the concern with political development are explicit in the agreement and are general international concerns as well; the enforcement of these rights requires little legal or administrative innovation in the domestic fora; and the alternative forum, the Security Council, would present to the plaintiffs obstacles so great as to make their rights virtually unenforceable.

Moreover, the Trusteeship Agreement constitutes the plaintiffs' basic constitutional document.... For all these reasons, we believe that the rights asserted by the plaintiffs are judicially enforceable. However, we see no reason why they could not and should not have been enforced in the High Court of the Trust Territory....

Admittedly, the substantive rights guaranteed through the Trusteeship Agreement are not precisely defined. However, we do not believe that the agreement is too vague for judicial enforcement. Its language is no more general than such terms as "due process of law," "seaworthiness," "equal protection of the law," "good faith," or "restraint of trade," which courts interpret every day. Moreover, the High Court can look for guidance to its own recently enacted environmental quality and protection act, T.T. Pub. L. No. 4C–78 of Apr. 14, 1972, codified at 63 T.T.C. §§ 501–509, to the relevant principles of international law and resource use which have achieved a substantial degree of codification and consensus (see Banco Nacional de Cuba v. Sabbatino, 376 U.S. 398, 428 ... (1964)), and to the general direction, although not necessarily the specific provisions, of NEPA. *Cf.* Pyramid Lake Paiute Tribe of Indians v. Morton, 354 F. Supp. 252 (D.D.C.1972). These sources should provide a sufficiently definite standard against which to test the High Commissioner's approval of a 50–year lease of unique public lands to an American corporation, allegedly in disregard of the protests of the islands' elected officials and without a showing of consideration of cultural and environmental factors....

TRASK, J., concurring.

... [I]t appears clear to me that the Charter of the United Nations is not self-executing and does not in and of itself create rights which are justiciable between individual litigants. Although under Article VI of the Constitution treaties are part of the supreme law of the land, it was early held that to be immediately binding upon our courts a treaty must be self-executing. Chief Justice Marshall enunciated this principle in *Foster v. Neilson*.... Unless a treaty is self-executing, in order to be cognizable before the courts it must be implemented by legislation. Otherwise it constitutes a compact between sovereign and independent nations dependent for its recognition and enforcement upon the honor and the continuing self-interest of the parties to it. If, however, the treaty contains language which confers rights or obligations on the citizenry of the compacting nations then, upon ratification, it becomes a part of the law of the land under Article VI. In Head Money Cases, 112 U.S. 580 ... (1884), the Court said:

> "A treaty, then, is the law of the land as an act of Congress is, whenever its provisions prescribe a rule by which the rights of the private citizen or subject may be determined. And when such rights are of a nature to be enforced in a court of justice, that court resorts to the treaty for a rule of decision for the case before it as it would to a statute." 112 U.S. at 598–99.

I find nothing in a reading of the Charter and nothing has been called to my attention which would persuade me to believe that the Charter itself creates individual rights which may be enforced in the courts. There is little definitive case law elucidating the issue of self-implementation vel non....

I agree with the federal appellees and with the court in *Pauling v. McElroy*, *supra*, that the Trusteeship Agreement is not self-executing. Yet, a series of actions all ultimately founded upon congressional authority have so executed the Agreement that its provisions may now properly be regarded as judicially enforceable. Thus, the Agreement was approved by the President pursuant to a joint resolution of Congress ... and implemented by Executive orders promulgated pursuant to congressional authority, 48 U.S.C. § 1681. Finally, the Trust Territory Government, created by the Department of the Interior, has declared the Agreement "to be in full force and to have the effect of law in the Trust Territory." 1 T.T.C. § 101(1)....

Notes and Questions

1. FCN [Friendship, Commerce and Navigation] treaties are often found to be self-executing. *See, e.g.*, Spiess v. Itoh, 643 F.2d 353, 356 (5th Cir.1981).

2. In *In re* Sheazle, 21 F. Cas. 1214, 1217 (C.C.D.Mass.1845) (No. 12,734), it was declared that the President can exercise "ministerial acts" to implement a treaty by surrendering an individual requested by the United Kingdom pursuant to an extradition treaty even though no congressional implementing legislation existed. *See also* United States v. Robins, 27 F. Cas. 825, 867 (D.C.D. So. Car. 1799) (President bound to execute a treaty by delivering an individual); 1 Op. Att'y Gen. 509, 521 (1821). In *In re* Metzger, 17 F. Cas. 232, 233–35 (D.C.S.D.N.Y. 1847) (No. 9,511), it was declared: "apprehension and commitment of persons charged with crimes cannot be carried into effect in this country, but by aid of judicial authority.... But in the United States the provisions in a treaty addressed to the judicial power become a rule of law of themselves, and are carried into execution by that department without other direction or authority ... the same as if they were incorporated into a statute.... The like provision in Jay's treaty was so accepted and acted upon. A judge of the United States took cognizance of the matter under authority of the treaty law alone. Soult v. L'Africaine [Case No. 13,179]; 1 Hall, Journ. Jur. 13; 5 Wheat. [18 U.S.] Append. 19.... And no where, in the severe scrutiny the subject underwent, does it appear an objection was raised to the competency of the judge to arrest and commit by virtue of that law.... So other eminent judges have recognized a treaty as supplying all the law necessary to compel them to interfere and cause the apprehension of fugitives from justice. U.S. v. Davis and *Ex parte* Dos Santos...."

Enhancement of presidential power and the competence of the President to execute a treaty was also recognized in Francis v. Francis, 203 U.S. 233, 240, 242 (1906), *quoting* Stockton v. Williams, Walk. Ch. (Mich.) 120, 129 (1843): " 'The location of the lands became a duty devolving on the President by treaty. This duty he could execute without an act of Congress; the treaty, when ratified, being the supreme law of the land, which the President was bound to see executed....' "; and The Lessee of Pollard's Heirs v. Kibbe, extract set forth, *supra*.

3. It has also been recognized that a treaty is self-executing if it "inhibits the doing of a certain thing" or provides "that certain acts shall not be done, or that certain limitations or restrictions shall not be disregarded or exceeded." Commonwealth v. Hawes, 76 Ky. 697, 702 (1878), cited in Blandford v. State, 10 Tex.App. 627, 639–40 (1881); RESTATEMENT § 111, RN 5. How would such a test apply with respect to various human rights? *See, e.g.*, the 1966 International Covenant on Civil and Political Rights, Articles 1–27, in the Documents Supplement.

4. More generally, should the human rights provisions of the U.N. Charter be considered "self-executing" within the United States? Should other human rights treaties? What tests are noted above? Could certain

provisions in the 1966 International Covenant on Civil and Political Rights be self-executing, while others are not, in view of language employed in the treaty?

SEI FUJII v. STATE

38 Cal.2d 718, 242 P.2d 617 (1952).

[Editors' note: Mr. Sei Fujii had challenged a racist California Alien Property Initiative Act of 1920, which had denied aliens ineligible for U.S. citizenship (then primarily Japanese and Chinese aliens, a status changed for Chinese persons by federal law in 1940) the right to own land. He lost in the state district court and won on appeal in the District Court of Appeal, 97 A.C.A. 154, 217 P.2d 481 (1950). The intermediate appellate court found that the California legislation conflicted with the U.N. Charter (Articles 55(c) and 56), as supplemented by the Universal Declaration of Human Rights (Articles 2 and 17), adding: "Clearly such a discrimination against a people of one race is contrary both to the letter and to the spirit of the Charter, which, as a treaty, is paramount to every law of every state in conflict with it." The Supreme Court of California affirmed on the basis of the Fourteenth Amendment to the U.S. Constitution, but considered Articles 55(c) and 56 of the Charter to be not self-executing.]

GIBSON, C.J.

It is first contended that the land law has been invalidated and superseded by the provisions of the United Nations Charter pledging the member nations to promote the observance of human rights and fundamental freedoms without distinction as to race. Plaintiff relies on statements in the preamble and in articles 1, 55 and 56 of the charter.

It is not disputed that the charter is a treaty, and our federal Constitution provides that treaties made under the authority of the United States are part of the supreme law of the land and that the judges in every state are bound thereby. (U.S. Const., art. VI) A treaty, however, does not automatically supersede local laws which are inconsistent with it unless the treaty provisions are self-executing. In the words of Chief Justice Marshall: A treaty is "to be regarded in courts of justice as equivalent to an act of the Legislature, whenever it operates of itself, without the aid of any legislative provision. But when the terms of the stipulation import a contract—when either of the parties engages to perform a particular act, the treaty addresses itself to the political, not the judicial department; and the Legislature must execute the contract, before it can become a rule for the court." (Foster v. Neilson (1829), 2 Pet. (U.S.) 253, 314....)

In determining whether a treaty is self-executing courts look to the intent of the signatory parties as manifested by the language of the instrument, and, if the instrument is uncertain, recourse may be had to the circumstances surrounding its execution. (See Foster v. Neilson, 2 Pet. (U.S.) 253, 310–316 ... [citing other cases]) In order for a treaty provision to be operative without the aid of implementing legislation and to have the force and effect of a statute, it must appear that the framers of the treaty intended to prescribe a rule that, standing alone, would be enforceable in the courts. (See Head Money Cases [Edye v. Robertson], 112 U.S. 580, 598 ... ; Whitney v. Robertson, 124 U.S. 190, 194 ... ; Cook v. United States, 288 U.S. 102, 118–119 ... ; Valentine v. United States, 299 U.S. 5, 10 ... ; Bacardi Corp. v. Domenech, 311 U.S. 150, 161....)

It is clear that the provisions of the preamble and of article 1 of the charter which are claimed to be in conflict with the alien land law are not self-executing. They state general purposes and objectives of the United Nations Organization and do not purport to impose legal obligations on the individual member nations or to create rights in private persons. It is equally clear that none of the other provisions relied on by plaintiff is self-executing. Article 55 declares that the United Nations "shall promote ... universal respect for, and observance of, human rights and fundamental freedoms for all without distinction as to race, sex, language, or religion," and in article 56, the member nations "pledge themselves to take joint and separate action in cooperation with the Organization for the achievement of the purposes set forth in Article 55." Although the member nations have obligated themselves to cooperate with the international organization in promoting respect for, and observance of, human rights, it is plain that it was contemplated that future legislative action by the several nations would be required to accomplish the declared objectives, and there is nothing to indicate that these provisions were intended to become rules of law for the courts of this country upon the ratification of the charter.

The language used in articles 55 and 56 is not the type customarily employed in treaties which have been held to be self-executing and to create rights and duties in individuals. For example, the treaty involved in Clark v. Allen, 331 U.S. 503, 507–508 ... , relating to the rights of a national of one country to inherit real property located in another country, specifically provided that "such national shall be allowed a term of three years in which to sell the property ... and withdraw the proceeds ..." free from any discriminatory taxation. (See, also, Hauenstein v. Lynham, 100 U.S. 483, 488–490.... In Nielsen v. Johnson, 279 U.S. 47, 50 ... , the provision treated as being self-executing was equally definite. There each of the signatory parties agreed that "no higher or other duties, charges, or taxes of any kind, shall be levied" by one country on removal of property therefrom by citizens of the other country "than are or shall be payable in each State, upon the same, when removed by a citizen or subject of such state respectively." In other instances treaty provisions were enforced without implementing legislation where they prescribed in detail the rules governing rights and obligations of individuals or specifically provided that citizens of one nation shall have the same rights while in the other country as are enjoyed by that country's own citizens....

It is significant to note that when the framers of the charter intended to make certain provisions effective without the aid of implementing legislation they employed language which is clear and definite and manifests that intention. For example, article 104 provides: "The Organization shall enjoy in the territory of each of its Members such legal capacity as may be necessary for the exercise of its functions and the fulfillment of its purposes." Article 105 provides: "1. The Organization shall enjoy in the territory of each of its Members such privileges and immunities as are necessary for the fulfillment of its purposes. 2. Representatives of the Members of the United Nations and officials of the Organization shall similarly enjoy such privileges and immunities as are necessary for the independent exercise of their functions in connection with the Organization." In Curran v. City of New York, 77 N.Y.S.2d 206, 212, these articles were treated as being self-executory. (See, also, Balfour, Guthrie & Co. v. United States, 90 F.Supp. 831, 832.)

The provisions in the charter pledging cooperation in promoting observance of fundamental freedoms lack the mandatory quality and definiteness which would indicate an intent to create justiciable rights in private persons immediately upon ratification. Instead, they are framed as a promise of future action by the member nations. . . .

Notes and Questions

1. *Sei Fujii* is one of the few cases asserting that non-self-executing treaties are not supreme law of the land under the Supremacy Clause of the U.S. Constitution. Another case is *In re* Alien Children Education Litigation, 501 F.Supp. 544, 590 (S.D.Tex.1980) (Texas legislation had denied children of undocumented aliens in Texas a right to free elementary school education, as required by several international instruments. *See, e.g.*, American Declaration of the Rights and Duties of Man, art. XII; Universal Declaration of Human Rights, art. 26; U.N. Charter, arts. 55 (c), 56; *see also* American Convention on Human Rights, preamble and arts. 1, 3, 19, 24, 26, 29 (c) and (d) [signed but not yet ratified by the U.S.]; all in the Documents Supplement. The district court would not apply human rights treaties, such as the U.N. and O.A.S. Charters, that it found to be non-self-executing, but did guarantee the rights of the children under the Fourteenth Amendment). In Beharry v. Reno, 183 F.Supp.2d 584 (E.D.N.Y. 2002), a district court took a different approach with respect to rights of children that are addressed a treaty that has not been ratified by the U.S., the Convention on the Rights of the Child. In *Beharry* the district court stated that the treaty "has been adopted by every organized government in the world except the United States. This overwhelming acceptance is strong reason to hold that some CRC provisions have attained the status of customary international law." *Id.* at 600.

In view of the word "all" in the Supremacy Clause, does the approach taken in *Sei Fujii* and *In re Alien Children Education Litigation* make sense? What was the view of the Founders? *See, e.g.*, PAUST, *supra*. As noted, in no Supreme Court case has supremacy been denied when a treaty was non-self-executing. *See, e.g., id.* at 55, 68 n.42, 92, 97–98, 133–35; also see Gordon v. Kerr, 10 F. Cas. 801, 802 (C.C.D.Pa.1806) (No. 5,611) (stating that a seemingly non-self-executing treaty "is supreme" over a state constitution); 6 Op. Att'y Gen. 291, 293 (1854) (declaring that all treaties are supreme law over that of the states—even treaties requiring "enactment of a statute to regulate the details"); Jordan J. Paust, *Race-Based Affirmative Action and International Law*, 18 Mich. J. Int'l L. 659, 671–72 (1997), and references cited.

2. Subsequent legal developments have undercut the two prongs of the *Sei Fujii* rationale related to its conclusion about the non-self-executing character of human rights obligations under the U.N. Charter. *See, e.g.*, Paust, *supra* at 74, 282 (today at least, U.N. Charter arts. 55 (c) and 56 set forth legal duties and the needed specificity with respect to human rights content can be derived from the Universal Declaration and other human rights instruments, as in *Filartiga* [see extract in Chapter 1, Section 1 C of this book]).

d. Reservations, Understandings, Declarations

Concerning reservations, understandings and declarations generally, recall Chapter 1, Section 2 A 3.

U.S. RESERVATIONS, UNDERSTANDINGS, AND DECLARATIONS CONCERNING THE 1966 COVENANT ON CIVIL AND POLITICAL RIGHTS

U.S. Senate Executive Report 102–23, 102d Cong. 2d Sess. (1992).

Understandings

1. Article 2(1), 4(1) and 26 (non-discrimination)

The very broad anti-discrimination provisions contained in the above articles do not precisely comport with long-standing Supreme Court doctrine in the equal protection field. In particular, Articles 2(1) and 26 prohibit discrimination not only on the basis of "race, colour, sex, language, religion, political or other opinion, national or social origin, property, birth" but also on any "other status." Current U.S. civil rights law is not so open-ended; discrimination is only prohibited for specific statuses, and there are exceptions which allow for discrimination. For example, under the Age Discrimination Act of 1975, age may be taken into account in certain circumstances. In addition, U.S. laws permit additional distinctions, for example between citizens and non-citizens and between different categories of non-citizens, especially in the context of the immigration laws.

In interpreting the relevant Covenant provisions, the Human Rights Committee has observed that not all differentiation of treatment constitutes discrimination, if the criteria for such differentiation are reasonable and objective and if the aim is to achieve a purpose which is legitimate under the Covenant. In its General Comment on non-discrimination, for example, the Committee noted that the enjoyment of rights and freedoms on an equal footing does not mean identical treatment in every instance.

Notwithstanding the very extensive protections already provided under U.S. law and the Committee's interpretive approach to the issue, we recommend ... [an] understanding....

4. Article 14 (right to counsel, compelled witness, and double jeopardy)

In a few particular aspects, this Article could be read as going beyond existing U.S. domestic law. In particular, current Federal law does not entitle a defendant to counsel of his own choice when he is either indigent or financially able to retain counsel in some form; nor does federal law recognize a right to counsel with respect to offenses for which imprisonment is not imposed. With respect to the compelled attendance and examination of witnesses, a criminal defendant must show that the requested witness is necessary to his defense. Under the Constitution, double jeopardy attaches only to multiple prosecutions by the same sovereign and does not prohibit trial of the same defendant for the same crime in, for example, state and federal courts or in the courts of two states. See Benton v. Maryland, 395 U.S. 784 (1969).

To clarify our reading of the Covenant with respect to these issues, we recommend ... [an] understanding....

5. Article 50 (federalism)

In light of Article 50 ("The provisions of the present Covenant shall extend to all parts of federal States without any limitations or exceptions"), it is appropriate to clarify that, even though the Covenant will apply to state and local authorities, it will be implemented consistent with U.S. concepts of federalism....

The proposed understanding serves to emphasize domestically that there is no intent to alter the constitutional balance of authority between the State and Federal governments or to use the provisions of the Covenant to "federalize" matters now within the competence of the States. (During the negotiation of the Covenant, the "federal-state" issue assumed some importance because there were legally justified practices, at the State and local level, which were both manifestly inconsistent with the Covenant and beyond the reach of Federal authority under the law in force at that time; that is no longer the case.)

A reservation is not necessary with respect to Article 50 since the intent is not to modify or limit U.S. undertakings under the Covenant but rather to put our future treaty partners on notice with regard to the implications of our federal system concerning implementation. Moreover, an attempt to reserve to this article would likely prove contentious. For example, in the face of objections from other States Parties, Australia recently withdrew its initial reservation to Article 50 (to the effect that implementation of the Covenant would be a matter for the authorities of its constituent States where the subject-matter was within the States' legislative, executive and judicial jurisdiction), replacing it with a declaration that, since it has a federal system, the Covenant will be implemented by Commonwealth, State and Territorial authorities having regard to their respective constitutional powers and arrangements concerning their exercise. The proposed understanding is similarly intended to signal to our treaty partners that the U.S. will implement its obligations under the Covenant by appropriate legislative, executive and judicial means, federal or state as appropriate, and that the Federal Government will remove any federal inhibition to the States' abilities to meet their obligations.

Declarations

1. Non-self-executing treaty

For reasons of prudence, we recommend including a declaration that the substantive provisions of the Covenant are not self-executing. The intent is to clarify that the Covenant will not create a private cause of action in U.S. courts. As was the case with the Torture Convention, existing U.S. law generally complies with the Covenant; hence, implementing legislation is not contemplated....

2. Restrictions on rights

In a number of respects the Covenant recognizes the possibility that States Party may in exceptional circumstances limit or circumscribe certain rights otherwise protected. For example, Article 12(3) permits States Party by law to impose restrictions on the rights to liberty of movement and freedom to choose residence when "necessary to protect national security, public order (*ordre public*), public health or morals or the rights and freedoms of others," when consistent with the other rights recognized in the Covenant. Similar restrictions are permissible with regard to the right of peaceful assembly (Article 21) and freedom of association (Article 22(2)); somewhat narrower restrictions are authorized with respect to the right to a fair and public hearing (Article 14(1)), freedom of religion (Article 18(3)), and the right to freedom of expression (Article 19(3)). Certain limited derogations from recognized rights are also permitted during times of public emergency threatening the life of the nation under Article 4.

Since such limitations are permissible rather than required, it is not necessary to condition U.S. ratification on a reservation. However, because of concerns raised in particular by representatives of the U.S. media over restrictions placed by foreign governments on the free flow of information and ideas, we believe it would be beneficial to include in our instrument of ratification a declaration....

The Covenant is designed to guarantee civil and political rights to persons within each country that ratifies it. In many instances, the rights parallel those provided to U.S. citizens in the Bill of Rights. Ratification would permit the United States to participate in the work of the Human Rights Committee, which monitors compliance of nations that have ratified the Covenant. Funding for the Human Rights Committee is currently provided by the United Nations, and ratification would not obligate the United States to provide any additional funding....

Resolved, (two-thirds of the Senators present concurring therein), that the Senate advice and consent to the ratification of the International-al Covenant on Civil and Political Rights, adopted by the United Nations General Assembly on December 16, 1966, and signed on behalf of the United States on October 5, 1977, (Executive E, 95–2), [is given] subject to the following reservations, understandings, declarations and proviso:

I. The Senate's advice and consent is subject to the following reservations:

(1) That Article 20 does not authorize or require legislation or other action by the United States that would restrict the right of free speech and association protected by the Constitution and laws of the United States.

(2) That the United States reserves the right, subject to its Constitutional constraints, to impose capital punishment on any person (other than a pregnant woman) duly convicted under existing or future laws permitting the imposition of capital punishment, including such punishment for crimes committed by persons below 18 years of age.

(3) That the United States considers itself bound by Article 7 to the extent that "cruel, inhuman or degrading treatment or punishment" means the cruel and unusual treatment or punishment prohibited by the Fifth, Eighth and/or Fourteenth Amendments to the Constitution of the United States.

(4) That because U.S. law generally applies to an offender the penalty in force at the time the offense was committed, the United States does not adhere to the third clause of paragraph 1 of Article 15.

(5) That the policy and practice of the United States are generally in compliance with and supportive of the Covenant's provisions regarding treatment of juveniles in the criminal justice system. Nevertheless, the United States reserves the right, in exceptional circumstances, to treat juveniles as adults, notwithstanding paragraphs 2(b) and 3 of Article 10 and paragraph 4 of Article 14. The United States further reserves to these provisions with respect to individuals who volunteer for military service prior to age 18.

II. The Senate's advice and consent is subject to the following understandings, which shall apply to the obligations of the United States under this Covenant:

(1) That the Constitution and laws of the United States guarantee all persons equal protection of the law and provide extensive protections against discrimination. The United States understands distinctions based upon race, colour, sex, language, religion, political or other opinion, national or social origin, property, birth or any other status—as those terms are used in Article 2, paragraph 1 and Article 26—to be permitted when such distinctions are, at minimum, rationally related to a legitimate governmental objective. The United States further understands the prohibition in paragraph 1 of Article 4 upon discrimination, in time of public emergency, based "solely" on the status of race, colour, sex, language, religion or social origin not to bar distinctions that may have a disproportionate effect upon persons of a particular status.

(2) That the United States understands the right to compensation referred to in Articles 9(5) and 14(6) to require the provision of effective and enforceable mechanisms by which a victim of an unlawful arrest or detention or a miscarriage of justice may seek and, where justified, obtain compensation from either the responsible individual or the appropriate governmental entity. Entitlement to compensation may be subject to the reasonable requirements of domestic law.

(3) That the United States understand the reference to "exceptional circumstances" in paragraph 2(a) of Article 10 to permit the imprisonment of an accused person with convicted persons where appropriate in light of an individual's overall dangerousness, and to permit accused persons to waive their right to segregation from convicted persons. The United States further understands that paragraph 3 of Article 10 does not diminish the goals of punishment, deterrence, and incapacitation as additional legitimate purposes for a penitentiary system.

(4) That the United States understands that subparagraphs 3(b) and (d) of Article 14 do not require the provision of a criminal defendant's counsel of choice when the defendant is provided with court-appointed counsel on grounds of indigence, when the defendant is financially able to retain alternative counsel, or when imprisonment is not imposed. The United States further understands that paragraph 3(e) does not prohibit a requirement that the defendant make a showing that any witness whose attendance he seeks to compel is necessary for his defense. The United States understands the prohibition upon double jeopardy in paragraph 7 to apply only when the judgment of acquittal has been rendered by a court of the same governmental unit, whether the Federal Government or a constituent unit, as is seeking a new trial for the same cause.

(5) That the United States understands that this Convention shall be implemented by the Federal Government to the extent that it exercises legislative and judicial jurisdiction over the matters covered therein, and otherwise by the state and local governments; to the extent that state and local governments exercise jurisdiction over such matters, the Federal Government shall take measures appropriate to the Federal system to the end that the competent authorities of the state or local governments may take appropriate measures for the fulfillment of the Convention.

III. The Senate's advice and consent is subject to the following declarations:

(1) That the United States declares that the provisions of Articles 1 through 27 of the Covenant are not self-executing.

(2) That it is the view of the United States that States Party to the Covenant should wherever possible refrain from imposing any restrictions or limitations on the exercise of the rights recognized and protected by the Covenant, even when such restrictions and limitations are permissible under the terms of the Covenant. For the United States, Article 5, paragraph 2, which provides that fundamental human rights existing

in any State Party may not be diminished on the pretext that the Covenant recognizes them to a lesser extent, has particular relevance to Article 19, paragraph 3, which would permit certain restrictions on the freedom of expression. The United States declares that it will continue to adhere to the requirements and constraints of its Constitution in respect to all such restrictions and limitations.

(3) That the United States declares that it accepts the competence of the Human Rights Committee to receive and consider communications under Article 41 in which a State Party claims that another State Party is not fulfilling its obligations under the Covenant.

(4) That the United States declares that the right referred to in Article 47 may be exercised only in accordance with international law. . . .

Notes and Questions

1. Concerning the status and special meaning of the U.S. declaration of partial non-self-execution (which expressly does not apply to Article 50), recall Chapter 1, Section 2 A 3, especially the Committee's General Comment No. 24 (1994). Recall that, particularly in view of Article 50 and the Executive Explanations, the declaration is not a general declaration of non-self-execution. See pp. 85–87.

Since the Supremacy Clause of the U.S. Constitution mandates that all treaties are supreme law of the land, would not a general declaration of non-self-execution have been unavoidably unconstitutional and void? at least for supremacy purposes? See Paust, *supra* at 51, 55, 59, 63–64, 370–71; Malvina Halberstam, *United States Ratification of the Convention on the Elimination of All Forms of Discrimination Against Women*, 31 G.W. J. Int'l L. & Econ. 49, 64, 67–69 (1997). Certainly a mere declaration of the President, even with full consent of the Senate, cannot alter a constitutional command.

2. As noted above, even generally non-self-executing treaties can be used indirectly as aids for interpretation of other laws, defensively in civil or criminal contexts, for supremacy or preemptive purposes. *See, e.g.*, United States v. Duarte-Acero, 208 F.3d 1282, 1284 (11th Cir. 2000); *id.*, 132 F.Supp.2d 1036, 1040 n.8 (S.D. Fla. 2001); Paust, *supra* at 62–64, 68, 97–98, 134–35, 370, 384; Connie de la Vega, *Civil Rights During the 1990s: New Treaty Law Could Help Immensely*, 65 U. Cinn. L. Rev.423, 457 n.206, 460, 467, 470 (1997); Joan Fitzpatrick, *The Preemptive and Interpretive Force of International Human Rights Law in State Courts*, 90 Proc., Am. Soc. Int'l L. 262, 264 (1996); David Sloss, *Ex parte Young and Federal Remedies for Human Rights Treaty Violations*, 75 Wash. L. Rev. 1103, 1108 & n.19, 1121 & n.79, 1123 & n.85, 1129–30, 1141–42, 1199 (2000). For example, human rights precepts have been used to inform the meaning of the Eighth Amendment to the U.S. Constitution. *See, e.g.*, Roper v. Simmons, 125 S.Ct. 1183, 1194, 1199 (2005) (ICCPR); Paust, *supra* at 192–93, 196, 248 n.392, 253 n.449, 371. Human rights in the Covenant have also been used by federal courts to clarify or provide content of other federal law. *See, e.g., id.* at 369–70, 383–84 ns.54–66, 74. Thus, such treaties can be invoked by individuals seeking relief under treaty-enhanced interpretations of federal statutes such as civil rights legislation and that concerning habeas corpus

(28 U.S.C. § 2254 (a)), especially since federal statutes must be interpreted consistently with treaties. *See, e.g.,* Murray v. The Charming Betsy, 6 U.S. (2 Cranch) 64, 118 (1804); PAUST, *supra* at 107–08 n.9. Additionally, such federal statutes can serve an 'executing' function whether or not the Covenant is partly self-executing, especially since the primary purpose of non-self-execution is to assure that there is some statutory or other legal base for bringing a relevant claim. See PAUST, *supra* at 179, 192–93, 226 n.163, 246–47 ns. 380–81 and 383–84, 371–72, 385 n.88; RESTATEMENT, *supra* § 111, cmt. h ("There can, of course, be instances in which the United States Constitution, or previously enacted legislation, will be fully adequate to give effect to an apparently non-self-executing international agreement...."). For example, even if the Covenant cannot be used directly to create a cause of action, other federal law may provide a cause of action and allow implementation or "execution" of treaty-based human rights. 42 U.S.C. § 1983, with a human rights purpose, is such a statute. *See, e.g.,* PAUST, *supra* at 179, 192–93, 226 n.163 and cases cited, 246–47 n.382. As cases in this chapter demonstrate, so is the Torture Victim Protection Act (TVPA). Also see *id.* at 207, 282 n.571, 371–72. 28 U.S.C. §§ 2241, 2254 (a) have a similar effect since the statute provides what is equivalent to a "cause of action" when mandating that a relevant federal court "shall entertain an application for a writ of habeas corpus in behalf of a person in custody pursuant to the judgement of a State court ... on the ground that he is in custody in violation of ... treaties of the United States." *Id.* For that purpose, the statute expressly "incorporates by reference" treaties of the United States. A federal statute need not even refer to international law in order to function as implementary legislation. *See, e.g.,* United States v. Arjona, 120 U.S. 479, 488 (1887). Statutes that do all the more clearly perform such a function.

3. As the U.S. Senate Executive Report, Understanding 1, and the approved Understanding II (1) recognize, certain forms of "differentiation" may not be impermissible "discrimination" within the meaning of the International Covenant. For example, authoritative General Comments of the Human Rights Committee created by the Covenant have recognized the permissibility of race-based and sex-based affirmative action. See Human Rights Committee, General Comment No. 18, para. 10 (Thirty-seventh session 1989), *reprinted in* U.N. Doc. HRI/GEN/1 (4 Sept. 1992) (race-based affirmative action); Human Rights Committee, General Comment No. 4, para. 2 (Thirteenth session 1981) (sex-based affirmative action). Concerning the permissibility of race-based and sex-based affirmative action under human rights law, also see International Convention on the Elimination of All Forms of Racial Discrimination, arts. 1–2; Convention on the Elimination of All Forms of Discrimination Against Women, art. 4 (both in the Documents Supplement); Ruth Bader Ginsburg, Deborah Jones Merritt, *Affirmative Action: An International Human Rights Dialogue*, 21 CARDOZO L. REV. 253, 260–61 (1999); Paust, *Race-Based Affirmative Action and International Law*, 18 MICH. J. INT'L L. 659 (1997).

As treaty law of the United States, how might the International Covenant, coupled with the U.S. Understanding and authoritative General Comments, be used to support federal or state measures of affirmative action?

4. How might one challenge the U.S. reservation concerning imposition of capital punishment on persons below 18 years of age? *See generally* articles of textwriters cited in note 7 in Chapter 1, Section 2 A 3. If the reservation is not void, can customary international law inform the meaning of the U.S. Constitution or relevant federal statutes? What should prevail domestically if there is an unavoidable clash between a treaty reservation as such and customary international law? or customary norms *jus cogens*? In view of the Court's decision in *Roper v. Simmons*, the matter is functionally moot where the U.S. Constitution applies.

5. Concerning the "federal clause" contained in Understanding No. 5 and Executive Explanations, also see Section 2 F 2 of this chapter, *infra*.

6. The Senate's advice and consent concerning the Covenant was also given "subject to the following proviso, which shall not be included in the instrument of ratification to be deposited by the President:

> Nothing in the covenant requires or authorizes legislation, or other action, by the United States of America prohibited by the Constitution of the United States as interpreted by the United States."

As requested, the constitutional proviso was not included in the instrument of ratification and did not operate as a reservation to the treaty. Should it have been added as a reservation? With respect to the domestic primacy of the Constitution, consider *Reid v. Covert*, below. Is this sufficient to protect the United States if it follows its constitution? What would you recommend? Consider also Advisory Opinion, Treatment of Polish Nationals in Danzig, P.C.I.J., Ser. A/B, No. 44, at 24 (1932) ("a State cannot adduce ... its own Constitution with a view to evading obligations incumbent upon it under international law or treaties in force.").

7. Declaration No. 3 accepts the competence of the Human Rights Committee to address state-to-state claims, but does not accept its competence to receive individual claims. Individual claims are covered by an Optional Protocol to the International Covenant, one that the U.S. has not ratified.

REID v. COVERT

354 U.S. 1 (1957).

BLACK, J. [plurality opinion, joined by WARREN, C.J. and DOUGLAS, J. and BRENNAN, J.]

These cases raise basic constitutional issues of the utmost concern. They call into question the role of the military under our system of government. They involve the power of Congress to expose civilians to trial by military tribunals, under military regulations and procedures, for offenses against the United States thereby depriving them of trial in civilian courts, under civilian laws and procedures and with all the safeguards of the Bill of Rights. These cases are particularly significant because for the first time since the adoption of the Constitution wives of soldiers have been denied trial by jury in a court of law and forced to trial before courts-martial.

In No. 701 Mrs. Clarice Covert killed her husband, a sergeant in the United States Air Force, at an airbase in England. Mrs. Covert, who was not a member of the armed services, was residing on the base with her husband at the time. She was tried by a court-martial for murder under Article 118 of the Uniform Code of Military Justice (UCMJ). The trial was on charges preferred by Air Force personnel and the court-martial was composed of Air Force officers. The court-martial asserted jurisdiction over Mrs. Covert under Article 2 (11) of the UCMJ, which provides:

> "The following persons are subject to this code: . . .
>
> "(11) Subject to the provisions of any treaty or agreement to which the United States is or may be a party or to any accepted rule of international law, all persons serving with, employed by, or accompanying the armed forces without the continental limits of the United States. . . ."

Counsel for Mrs. Covert contended that she was insane at the time she killed her husband, but the military tribunal found her guilty of murder and sentenced her to life imprisonment. The judgment was affirmed by the Air Force Board of Review, 16 CMR 465, but was reversed by the Court of Military Appeals, 6 USCMA 48, because of prejudicial errors concerning the defense of insanity. While Mrs. Covert was being held in this country pending a proposed retrial by court-martial in the District of Columbia, her counsel petitioned the District Court for a writ of habeas corpus to set her free on the ground that the Constitution forbade her trial by military authorities. Construing this Court's decision in United States *ex rel.* Toth v. Quarles, 350 U.S. 11, as holding that "a civilian is entitled to a civilian trial" the District Court held that Mrs. Covert could not be tried by court-martial and ordered her released from custody. The Government appealed directly to this Court. . . .

In No. 713 Mrs. Dorothy Smith killed her husband, an Army officer, at a post in Japan where she was living with him. She was tried for murder by a court-martial and despite considerable evidence that she was insane was found guilty and sentenced to life imprisonment. The judgment was approved by the Army Board of Review, 10 CMR 350, 13 CMR 307, and the Court of Military Appeals, 5 USCMA 314. Mrs. Smith was then confined in a federal penitentiary in West Virginia. Her father, respondent here, filed a petition for habeas corpus in a District Court for West Virginia. The petition charged that the court-martial was without jurisdiction because Article 2 (11) of the UCMJ was unconstitutional insofar as it authorized the trial of civilian dependents accompanying servicemen overseas. The District Court refused to issue the writ, 137 F. Supp. 806, and while an appeal was pending in the Court of Appeals for the Fourth Circuit we granted certiorari at the request of the Government, 350 U.S. 986. . . .

. . . We hold that Mrs. Smith and Mrs. Covert could not constitutionally be tried by military authorities.

At the beginning we reject the idea that when the United States acts against citizens abroad it can do so free of the Bill of Rights. The United States is entirely a creature of the Constitution. Its power and authority have no other source. It can only act in accordance with all the limitations imposed by the Constitution. When the Government reaches out to punish a citizen who is abroad, the shield which the Bill of Rights and other parts of the Constitution provide to protect his life and liberty should not be stripped away just because he happens to be in another land....

The language of Art. III, § 2 manifests that constitutional protections for the individual were designed to restrict the United States Government when it acts outside of this country, as well as here at home. After declaring that all criminal trials must be by jury, the section states that when a crime is "not committed within any State, the Trial shall be at such Place or Places as the Congress may by Law have directed." If this language is permitted to have its obvious meaning, § 2 is applicable to criminal trials outside of the States as a group without regard to where the offense is committed or the trial held. From the very first Congress, federal statutes have implemented the provisions of § 2 by providing for trial of murder and other crimes committed outside the jurisdiction of any State "in the district where the offender is apprehended, or into which he may first be brought." The Fifth and Sixth Amendments, like Art. III, § 2, are also all inclusive with their sweeping references to "no person" and to "all criminal prosecutions."

This Court and other federal courts have held or asserted that various constitutional limitations apply to the Government when it acts outside the continental United States. While it has been suggested that only those constitutional rights which are "fundamental" protect Americans abroad, we can find no warrant, in logic or otherwise, for picking and choosing among the remarkable collection of "Thou shalt nots" which were explicitly fastened on all departments and agencies of the Federal Government by the Constitution and its Amendments. Moreover, in view of our heritage and the history of the adoption of the Constitution and the Bill of Rights, it seems peculiarly anomalous to say that trial before a civilian judge and by an independent jury picked from the common citizenry is not a fundamental right.... Trial by jury in a court of law and in accordance with traditional modes of procedure after an indictment by grand jury has served and remains one of our most vital barriers to governmental arbitrariness. These elemental procedural safeguards were embedded in our Constitution to secure their inviolateness and sanctity against the passing demands of expediency or convenience....

At the time of Mrs. Covert's alleged offense, an executive agreement was in effect between the United States and Great Britain which permitted United States' military courts to exercise exclusive jurisdiction over offenses committed in Great Britain by American servicemen or their dependents. [The Executive agreement was a NATO Status of Forces Agreement (SOFA), that was connected to the NATO treaty.] For its part, the United States agreed that these military courts would be willing and able to try and to punish all offenses against the laws of Great Britain by such persons. In all material respects, the same situation existed in Japan when Mrs. Smith killed her husband. Even though a court-martial does not give an accused trial by jury and other Bill of Rights protections, the Government contends that Art. 2 (11) of the UCMJ, insofar as it provides for the military trial of dependents accompanying the armed forces in Great Britain and Japan, can be sustained as legislation which is necessary and proper to carry out the United States' obligations under the international agreements made with those countries. The obvious and decisive answer to this, of course, is that no agreement with a foreign nation can confer power on the Congress, or on any other branch of Government, which is free from the restraints of the Constitution.

Article VI, the Supremacy Clause of the Constitution, declares:

> "This Constitution, and the Laws of the United States which shall be made in Pursuance thereof; and all Treaties made, or which shall be made, under the Authority of the United States, shall be the supreme Law of the Land;. . . . "

There is nothing in this language which intimates that treaties and laws enacted pursuant to them do not have to comply with the provisions of the Constitution. Nor is there anything in the debates which accompanied the drafting and ratification of the Constitution which even suggests such a result. These debates as well as the history that surrounds the adoption of the treaty provision in Article VI make it clear that the reason treaties were not limited to those made in "pursuance" of the Constitution was so that agreements made by the United States under the Articles of Confederation, including the important peace treaties which concluded the Revolutionary War, would remain in effect. It would be manifestly contrary to the objectives of those who created the Constitution, as well as those who were responsible for the Bill of Rights—let alone alien to our entire constitutional history and tradition—to construe Article VI as permitting the United States to exercise power under an international agreement without observing constitutional prohibitions. In effect, such construction would permit amendment of that document in a manner not sanctioned by Article V. The prohibitions of the Constitution were designed to apply to all branches of the National Government and they cannot be nullified by the Executive or by the Executive and the Senate combined.

There is nothing new or unique about what we say here. This Court has regularly and uniformly recognized the supremacy of the Constitution over a treaty. For example, in Geofroy v. Riggs, 133 U.S. 258, 267, [it was declared that the treaty power is subject to constitutional restraints.] . . . .

There is nothing in Missouri v. Holland, 252 U.S. 416, which is contrary to the position taken here. There the Court carefully noted that the treaty involved was not inconsistent with any specific provision of the Constitution. The Court was concerned with the Tenth Amendment which reserves to the States or the people all power not delegated to the National Government. To the extent that the United States can validly make treaties, the people and the States have delegated their power to the National Government and the Tenth Amendment is no barrier.

In summary, we conclude that the Constitution in its entirety applied to the trials of Mrs. Smith and Mrs. Covert. Since their court-martial did not meet the requirements of Art. III, § 2 or the Fifth and Sixth Amendments we are compelled to determine if there is anything within the Constitution which authorizes the military trial of dependents accompanying the armed forces overseas....

... Even during time of war the Constitution must be observed. *Ex parte* Milligan, 4 Wall. 2 [1866], at 120, declares:

> "The Constitution of the United States is a law for rulers and people, equally in war and in peace, and covers with the shield of its protection all classes of men, at all times, and under all circumstances. No doctrine, involving more pernicious consequences, was ever invented by the wit of man than that any of its provisions can be suspended during any of the great exigencies of government."

...

HARLAN, J., concurring

We return, therefore, to the *Ross* [140 U.S. 453 (1891)] question: to what extent do these provisions of the Constitution apply outside the United States?

As I have already stated, I do not think that it can be said that these safeguards of the Constitution are never operative without the United States, regardless of the particular circumstances. On the other hand, I cannot agree with the suggestion that every provision of the Constitution must always be deemed automatically applicable to American citizens in every part of the world. For *Ross* and the *Insular Cases* do stand for an important proposition, one which seems to me a wise and necessary gloss on our Constitution. The proposition is, of course, not that the Constitution "does not apply" overseas, but that there are provisions in the Constitution which do not necessarily apply in all circumstances in every foreign place.... To take but one example: Balzac v. Porto Rico, 258 U.S. 298, is not good authority for the proposition that jury trials need never be provided for American citizens tried by the United States abroad; but the case is good authority for the proposition that there is no rigid rule that jury trial must always be provided in the trial of an American overseas, if the circumstances are such that trial by jury would be impractical and anomalous. In other words, what *Ross* and the *Insular Cases* hold is that the particular local setting, the practical necessities, and the possible alternatives are relevant to a question of judgment, namely, whether jury trial should be deemed a necessary condition of the exercise of Congress' power to provide for the trial of Americans overseas.

. . . [F]or me, the question is which guarantees of the Constitution should apply in view of the particular circumstances, the practical necessities, and the possible alternatives which Congress had before it. The question is one of judgment, not of compulsion . . . [O]ne can say, in fact, that the question of which specific safeguards of the Constitution are appropriately to be applied in a particular context overseas can be reduced to the issue of what process is "due" a defendant in the particular circumstances of a particular case. . . .

Notes and Questions

1. Justice Black's opinion in *Reid* became a landmark approach to issues addressed in the excerpt. However, it was a plurality opinion, with Chief Justice Warren and Justices Douglas and Brennan joining. Separate concurring opinions were filed by Justices Harlan and Frankfurter. Justices Clark and Burton dissented, and Justice Whittaker did not participate.

2. Cases prior to *Reid v. Covert*, and several subsequent cases, recognized that in case of an unavoidable clash between provisions of a treaty and the U.S. Constitution, the Constitution will prevail domestically. *See, e.g.*, JORDAN J. PAUST, INTERNATIONAL LAW AS LAW OF THE UNITED STATES 99, 123 (2 ed. 2003).

3. After reading *Reid*, of what value is a constitutional proviso that has not been included in the instrument of ratification? Should the provisos concerning the 1966 Covenant and the Convention on the Elimination of Race Discrimination have been reservations? Why?

4. Does *Reid* add to *Missouri* when recognizing that "the Tenth Amendment is no barrier" to the treaty power? Also see U.S. Const., amend. X; United States v. Lue, 134 F.3d 79, 84–85 (2d Cir. 1998) ("Since the Treaty Power was delegated to the federal government, whatever is within its scope is not reserved to the states: the Tenth Amendment is not material"); Commonwealth v. Blodgett, 53 Mass. 56, 81 (1846) ("the states are expressly prohibited from entering into any treaty. . . . [T]he power of making . . . treaties . . . is vested absolutely and exclusively in the general government, with their incidents.").

UNITED STATES v. TOSCANINO

500 F.2d 267 (2d Cir.1974).

[see extract in Chapter 3, Section 3 B, concerning applicability of the Fifth Amendment to the U.S. Constitution abroad to aliens.]

UNITED STATES v. TIEDE

86 F.R.D. 227 (U.S. Ct. for Berlin, 1979).

STERN, J.

This is a criminal proceeding arising out of the alleged diversion of a Polish aircraft by the defendants from its scheduled landing in East Berlin to a forced landing in West Berlin.

United States authorities exercised jurisdiction over this matter and convened this Court. Court-appointed defense counsel have now moved for a trial by jury. The Prosecution objects, contending that these proceedings are not governed by the United States Constitution, but by the requirements of foreign policy and that the Secretary of State, as interpreter of that policy, has determined that these defendants do not have the right to a jury trial.

The special nature of this Court and the unusual position taken by the United States Attorney for Berlin require an extensive account and analysis of the history of the occupation of Berlin, the jurisdictional basis of this Court, and the limitations, if any, on the Secretary of State and the American authorities who govern the 1.2 million people who reside in the American sector of Berlin. The Court holds that the United States Constitution applies to these proceedings and that defendants charged with criminal offenses before the United States Court for Berlin have constitutional rights, including the right to a trial by jury. . . .

On August 30, 1978, a Polish civilian aircraft on a scheduled flight from Gdansk, Poland, to Schoenefeld Airport in East Berlin, was diverted and forced to land at Tempelhof Airport in the United States sector of West Berlin. Following the landing, defendants Hans Detlef Alexander Tiede and Ingrid Ruske, together with Mrs. Ruske's twelve-year-old daughter, were detained by United States military authorities at a U.S. Air Force installation located at Tempelhof. On November 1, 1978, the United States Mission in Berlin advised the German authorities in West Berlin that it would exercise jurisdiction over the investigation and prosecution of any crimes committed in connection with the diversion of the Polish airliner. Mrs. Ruske was released from detention on November 3; her daughter had been released several weeks earlier.

The United States authorities, acting under the authority of Law No. 46, a law promulgated in 1955 by the former United States High Commissioner for Germany, then convened this Court. . . . [the court then addressed the military occupation of Germany, including Berlin, and certain agreements among the Allies and, later, between the Western Allies (not including the USSR) concerning, among other matters, the creation of an Allied High Commission.]

On April 28, 1955, only a few days before the occupation regime terminated in the rest of Germany, the U.S. High Commissioner promulgated Law No. 46 establishing the "United States Court for Berlin." The Law defines the jurisdiction of the Court, sets forth the applicable substantive law and provides for the appointment of judges and other principal court personnel by the United States Ambassador to the Federal Republic of Germany. Despite the fact that this Court was established in 1955, this is the first time in its 24–year history that the Court has been convened.

As previously noted, the President has delegated to the United States Ambassador to the Federal Republic of Germany his "supreme authority . . . with respect to all responsibilities, duties, and governmental functions of the United States in all Germany [including Berlin] under the supervision of the Secretary of State and subject to the ultimate direction of the President." Thus, this court sits in Berlin as an instrumentality of the United States, executing the sovereign powers of the United States. As a matter of United States law, it is a court established pursuant to the powers granted to the President by Article II of the United States Constitution.

Article 3(1) of Law No. 46 provides that "the Court shall have original jurisdiction to hear and decide any criminal cases arising under any legislation in effect in the United States Sector for Berlin if the offense was committed within the area of Greater Berlin." The criminal jurisdiction of the Court is concurrent with that of the Berlin courts, except to the extent that the American Sector Commandant withdraws jurisdiction from the German courts in a given case. Thus, the Court exercises jurisdiction which is territorial in nature. If the American authorities choose to do so, they can arraign before this Court any person physically present in the American Sector of Berlin, regardless of such person's nationality, including—when authorized by the American Sector Commandant—members of the United States Armed Forces stationed in West Berlin. Pursuant to Article 5, convictions or sentences pronounced by the Court may be reviewed by the American Ambassador to the Federal Republic.

Article 3(5) confers broad powers upon the judges appointed to this Court, including the power "to establish consistently with the applicable legislation rules of practice and proceedings" for the Court. Pursuant to that authority, on November 30, 1978, Judge Bonsal promulgated as Rules of Criminal Procedure for the United States Court for Berlin a set of rules which, with one exception, adopted almost verbatim the Federal Rules of Criminal Procedure and the Federal Rules of Evidence; the exception related to jury trials. Thus, under the Rules of Criminal Procedure of this Court, the defendants here are not entitled to a trial by jury.

We now turn to the question of whether the Constitution of the United States, which might require a jury trial under these circumstances, applies to the proceedings in this court.

III. Application of the United States Constitution to These Proceedings

The Prosecution's basic position is that the United States Constitution does not apply to these proceedings because Berlin is a territory governed by military conquest. The Prosecution maintains that the question whether constitutional rights must be afforded in territories governed by United States authorities outside the United States depends on the nature and degree of association between such territories and the United States, and that the relationship between the United States and Berlin is such that the Constitution does not apply to proceedings in Berlin....

The Prosecution further argues that this Court is not an independent tribunal established to adjudicate the rights of the defendants and lacks the power to make a ruling contrary to the foreign policy interests of the United States. This, it contends follows from the fact that "United States occupation courts in Germany have been instruments of the United States occupation policy." According to the Prosecution, this political aspect was expressed by General Lucius D. Clay, the former United States Military Governor for Germany, who described his aspirations for the administration of justice in the United States area of occupation as follows:

> We are trying to make our own judicial procedures an example of democratic justice and concern for the individual.

From the earliest point of the occupation of Germany, the Prosecution contends, the United States occupation courts functioned as an extension of American foreign policy. . . .

Thus, the Prosecution maintains that any rights to which the defendants are entitled must be granted by Secretary of State. . . .

Pursuing its thesis that this Court is nothing more than an implementing arm of the United States' foreign policy, the Prosecution instructs the Court that the Secretary of State has determined, as a matter of foreign policy, that the right to a jury trial should not be afforded to the defendants. . . .

The Court finds the Prosecution's argument to be entirely without merit. First, there has never been a time when United States authorities exercised governmental powers in any geographical area—whether at war or in times of peace—without regard for their own Constitution. *Ex parte Milligan*, 71 U.S. (4 Wall.) 2 (1866). Nor has there ever been a case in which constitutional officers, such as the Secretary of State, have exercised the powers of their office without constitutional limitations. Even in the long-discredited case of *In re Ross*, 140 U.S. 453 (1891), in which American consular officers were permitted to try United States citizens in certain "non-Christian" countries, the Court made its decision under the Constitution—not in total disregard of it. The distinction is subtle but real: The applicability of any provision of the Constitution is itself a point of constitutional law, to be decided in the last instance by the judiciary, not by the Executive Branch.

This fundamental principle was forcefully and clearly announced by the Supreme Court more than a century ago in *Ex parte Milligan*, 71 U.S. (4 Wall.) 2, 120–21 (1866):

> [The Framers of the American Constitution] foresaw that troublous times would arise, when rulers and people would become restive under restraint, and seek by sharp and decisive measures to accomplish ends deemed just and proper; and that the principles of constitutional liberty would be in peril, unless established by irrepealable law. The history of the world had taught them that what was done in the past might be attempted in the future. *The Constitution of the United States is a law for rulers and people, equally in war and in peace, and covers with the shield of its*

> *protection all classes of men, at all times, and under all circumstances.* No doctrine, involving more pernicious consequences, was ever invented by the wit of man than that any of its provisions can be suspended during any of the great exigencies of government. Such a doctrine leads directly to anarchy or despotism, but the theory of necessity on which it is based is false; for the government, within the Constitution, has all the powers granted to it, which are necessary to preserve its existence; as has been happily proved by the result of the great effort to throw off its just authority. [emphasis added]

Although the Supreme Court was reviewing the power of military commissions organized by military authorities in the United States during the Civil War, the wisdom of the principle set forth above is nowhere better demonstrated than in this city, during this occupation, and before this Court.

The Prosecution's position, if accepted by this Court, would have dramatic consequences not only for the two defendants whom the United States has chosen to arraign before the Court, but for every person within the territorial limits of the United States Sector of Berlin.... If there are no constitutional protections, there is no First Amendment, no Fifth Amendment or Sixth Amendment; even the Thirteenth Amendment's prohibition of involuntary servitude would be inapplicable. The American authorities, if the Secretary of State so decreed, would have the power, in time of peace and with respect to German and American citizens alike, to arrest any person without cause, to hold a person incommunicado, to deny an accused the benefit of counsel, to try a person summarily and to impose sentence—all as a part of the unreviewable exercise of foreign policy.

... It is a first principle of American life—not only life at home but life abroad—that everything American public officials do is governed by, measured against, and must be authorized by the United States Constitution.

As the Supreme Court made clear in *Ex parte Milligan*, *supra*, the Constitution is a living document to be applied under changing circumstances, in changing conditions and even in different places. The Court finds devoid of merit the suggestion that the Prosecution has no constitutional obligations or that this Court lacks the competence to inquire into those obligations. The Constitution of the United States manifestly applies to these proceedings.

Second, the Court rejects the Prosecution's contention that, even if the Constitution applies to these proceedings, it is the State Department rather than the Court which interprets the Constitution....

IV. The Requirements of the Constitution in These Proceedings

A. *The Question Presented*

The sole but novel question before the Court is whether friendly aliens, charged with civil offenses in a United States court in Berlin, under the unique circumstances of the continuing United States Occupation of Berlin, have a right to a jury trial. This Court is not concerned with the procedures to be used by a United States military commission trying a case in wartime or during the belligerent occupation of enemy territory before the termination of war. This case does not involve the theft or destruction of military property. Nor does in involve spying, an offense against Allied military authority or a violation of the laws of war. Further, this Court does not sit as an international tribunal, but only an American court.

The defendants are German citizens. It is of no moment whether they be deemed citizens of the Federal Republic or of the German Democratic Republic because the United States is at peace with, and maintains diplomatic relations with, both states. Thus, in law, the defendants are friendly aliens. They are not enemy nationals, enemy belligerents or prisoners of war. The defendants are charged with non-military offenses under German law which would have been fully cognizable in the open and functioning German courts in West Berlin, but for the withdrawal of the German courts' jurisdiction by the United States Commander....

... The logic of Mr. Justice Black's opinion [in *Reid v. Covert*] with respect to the question whether the Constitution applies abroad—or in the vernacular of the time, "whether the Constitution follows the flag"—is, in this Court's view, irrefutable and deserves to be cited at length.... [Judge Stern then quoted several portions of the opinion.]

As regards the continued vitality of the doctrine enunciated in *In re Ross, supra*, Mr. Justice Black said:

> The *Ross* case is one of those cases that cannot be understood except in its peculiar setting; even then, it seems highly unlikely that a similar result would be reached today....
>
> The *Ross* approach that the Constitution has no applicability abroad has long since been directly repudiated by numerous cases. That approach is obviously erroneous if the United States Government, which has no power except that granted by the Constitution, can and does try citizens for crimes committed abroad. Thus the *Ross* case rested, at least in substantial part, on a fundamental misconception and the most that can be said is support of the result reached there is that the consular court jurisdiction had a long history antedating the adoption of the Constitution.... At best, the *Ross* case should be left as a relic from a different era.

354 U.S. at 10–12....

D. THE SIGNIFICANCE OF THE NATURE OF THE TRIBUNAL

The Prosecution argues, however, that *Duncan* is inapplicable here because this Court is a type of Military commission and it claims defendants tried by a military commission have no right to a jury trial. In support of this contention, the Prosecution relies principally on *Ex parte Quirin*, 317 U.S. 1 (1942), and *Madsen v. Kinsella*, 343 U.S. 341

(1952). Although both cases are unquestionably relevant to these proceedings, an examination of them reveals that they do not support the Prosecution's contention.

In *Ex parte Quirin*, 317 U.S. 1 (1942), the Supreme Court ... decided only the questions "whether it is within the constitutional power of the National Government to place petitioners upon trial before a military commission *for the offenses with which they are charged.*" *Id.* at 29 (emphasis supplied). The Court extensively reviewed the history of trials of violations of the laws of war, including trials held before the Constitution was enacted, and found that "these petitioners were charged with *an offense against the law of war which the Constitution does not require to be tried by jury.*" *Id.* at 29 (emphasis supplied). The Court held that:

> [T]he Fifth and Sixth Amendments did not restrict whatever authority was conferred by the Constitution to try *offenses against the law of war* by military commission, and that *petitioners, charged with such an offense* not required to be tried by jury at common law, were lawfully placed on trial by the Commission without a jury.

317 U.S. at 45 (emphasis supplied)....

... *Quirin* does *not* stand for the proposition that the nature of the tribunal dictates whether defendants must be accorded a trial by jury or that individuals tried before a military commission are never entitled to a jury. *Quirin* holds that whether an individual is entitled to a jury trial is determined by the nature of the crime with which he is charged.

The defendants here are not charged with violations of the laws of war. They are neither enemy aliens nor associated with the armed forces of an enemy....

In *Madsen v. Kinsella*, 343 U.S. 341 (1952), the Supreme Court addressed a petition for a writ of habeas corpus filed by the wife of an air force lieutenant stationed in Germany who, in 1949, had been convicted of murdering her husband by the United States Court of the Allied High Commission for Germany, a predecessor of this Court. Mrs. Madsen challenged the jurisdiction of the court which convicted her, contending that she could only be tried by a regularly convened United States general court-martial. The issue before the Supreme Court was:

> whether a United States Court of the Allied High Commission for Germany had jurisdiction, in 1950, to try a civilian citizen of the United States, who was the dependent wife of a member of the United States Armed Forces, on a charge of murdering her husband in violation of § 211 of the German Criminal Code. The homicide occurred in October, 1949, within the United States Area of Control in Germany.

343 U.S. 342–43. The Court concluded that the military commission had jurisdiction over Mrs. Madsen.

The Court traced the history of United States military commissions and other United States tribunals in the nature of such commissions. Its discussion of the United States Military Government Courts for Germany, which became the United States Courts for the Allied High Commission for Germany, referred to the procedures used [which did not provide for juries]. . . .

In this Court's view, however, *Madsen v. Kinsella* does not support the Prosecution's thesis that a jury trial is never required in an occupation court. First, the statement of the issue in *Madsen*, as formulated by the Supreme Court, clearly indicates that the question of Mrs. Madsen's right to a trial by jury was neither presented nor considered. She never claimed the right to trial by jury. Indeed, Mrs. Madsen's claim was that she should have been tried by a general court-martial, pursuant to the Articles of War, which did *not* provide for trial by jury.

Second, the Court's reference to the absence of jury trials before occupation courts in Germany in 1949 is hardly dispositive of the issue here. Because *Madsen* was decided long before *Duncan v. Louisiana* declared the right to trial by jury to be a "fundamental" right under the Constitution, *Madsen* certainly cannot be considered conclusive authority that the Constitution does not require a jury trial in this Court in 1979.

Finally, when Mrs. Madsen was tried, the United States and Germany were technically still at war. The Constitution does not require that the "enemy" be accorded self-government or be taken into the bosom of the occupation authority. Occupation courts need not share their jurisdiction with "enemy" aliens, nor are "enemy" aliens to be permitted to nullify the provisions or proceedings of any arm of the occupation government.

However, "occupations" which survive not merely hostilities but also belligerency, and which are maintained to "protect" the occupied and to preserve their democratic institutions, are of an altogether different kind. Such occupations are asserted not *against* but *on behalf of* the "occupied." Such occupation authorities are not viewed as military representatives of a hostile power bivouacked in the Town Square; rather, they are benign forces of protection—like the police or military of the occupied country itself. Their role as protectors gives them no license to abuse the inhabitants. The Constitution of the United States does not permit an American policeman or an American soldier to disregard the rights of those on whose behalf they stand watch. . . .

F. Constitutional Rights Afforded to Aliens

Finally, the Prosecution seeks to distinguish most prior decisions dealing with the rights of accused in occupation courts and the instant proceeding on the ground that the prior adjudications concerned the rights to be afforded to American citizens, whereas the defendants here are aliens.

Although it is true that most of the cases discussed concerned prosecutions of American citizens abroad, the Court finds the purported distinction unpersuasive in the context of a trial of friendly aliens, accused of non-military offenses, in Berlin in 1979. The Prosecution conceded in oral argument that in its view aliens, as well as citizens, enjoyed the same "non-rights" in this Court; that is, neither need be afforded a trial by jury. More importantly, whatever distinction may still be permissible between citizens and friendly aliens in civil cases, the Fifth Amendment to the Constitution requires, in terms admitting of no ambiguity, that "no *person*" shall be deprived of life or liberty without due process of law; similarly, the Sixth Amendment protects all who are "*accused*", without qualification. Finally, it appears to the Court that the United States is precluded from treating these defendants less favorably than United States citizens, not only by its own Constitution, but also by an international agreement to which the United States is a party.

Article 15, paragraph 2, of the Convention on Offenses and Certain Other Acts Committed on Board Aircraft (The Tokyo Convention) provides in part that—

> [A] Contracting State in whose territory a person has been disembarked ... , or delivered [by the aircraft commander], or has disembarked and is suspected of having committed an act [of hijacking], shall accord to such person treatment which is no less favorable for his protection and security than that accorded to nationals of such Contracting State in like circumstances.

[The court then addressed Executive views concerning the meaning of such phrases, which provide treatment and protection equal to that on nationals.]

Therefore, this Court believes that these defendants should be afforded the same constitutional rights that the United States would have to afford its own nationals when brought before this Court.

In sum, this Court does not hold that jury trials must be afforded in occupation courts *everywhere* and under *all* circumstances; the Court holds only that if the United States convenes a United States court in Berlin, under the present circumstances, and charges civilians with non-military offenses, the United States must provide the defendants with the same constitutional safeguards that it must provide to civilian defendants in any other United States court....

Notes and Questions

1. After receiving a jury trial in accordance with U.S. constitutional guarantees, Tiede was convicted of some offenses but was sentenced by Judge Stern "to time served" while awaiting trial. See Herbert J. Stern, Judgment in Berlin 350–351, 367–72 (1984). Judge Stern made it clear that he was not about to turn over persons for incarceration to a government that had demonstrated its unwillingness to follow law and had argued that judges, in, of all places, Berlin, should merely follow orders.

For additional background, see Ed Gordon, *American Courts, International Law and "Political Questions" which Touch Foreign Relations*, 14 Int'l Law. 297 (1980); Jordan J. Paust, *Is the President Bound by the*

Supreme Law of the Land?—Foreign Affairs and National Security Reexamined, 9 HASTINGS CONST. L.Q. 719, 723–25, 729–30 (1982); RESTATEMENT OF THE FOREIGN RELATIONS LAW OF THE UNITED STATES § 722, RNs 15–16 (3 ed. 1987).

2. As *Tiede* declares, the Constitution applies abroad to restrain Executive conduct. Do you agree that the restraints on Executive power thereby protect aliens? *Compare* Paul B. Stephan, *Constitutional Limits on the Struggle Against International Terrorism: Revisiting the Rights of Overseas Aliens*, 19 CONN. L. REV. 831 (1987) *with* United States v. Toscanino, 500 F.2d 267, 276–80 (2d Cir.1974); United States v. Yunis, 681 F.Supp. 896, 916–18 (D.D.C.1988); RESTATEMENT §§ 433, RNs 3–4, and 722, RNs 15–16; Jordan J. Paust, *An Introduction to and Commentary on Terrorism and the Law*, 19 CONN. L. REV. 697, 721–35 (1987). Did the *Reid* rationale (focusing on the lack of U.S. power to act anywhere inconsistently with the Constitution, as opposed to the reach of "rights" as such) change the sweep of *Eisentrager*? Also see Jordan J. Paust, *Antiterrorism Military Commissions: Courting Illegality*, 23 MICH. J. INT'L L. 1, 18–20 (2001).

3. Has *United States v. Verdugo–Urquidez*, 494 U.S. 259 (1990) (which ruled that evidence seized without a U.S. judicial warrant by U.S. officials from a home in Mexico of a Mexican national who had no ties with the U.S. could be introduced into evidence in a U.S. court even though such evidence would have been excluded under the Fourth Amendment if it had been seized similarly in the U.S.) changed the *Tiede, Toscanino* and *Yunis* approach? Does the decision apply only to the Fourth Amendment? Is the majority opinion in *Verdugo-Urquidez* correct? Consider the following extract from the majority opinion per Chief Justice Rehnquist concerning U.S. searches abroad and claimed rights of aliens under the Fourth Amendment:

" ... [Regarding] the Fourth Amendment, we think it significant to note that it operates in a different manner than the Fifth Amendment....

" ... [The text of the Fourth Amendment], by contrast with the Fifth and Sixth Amendments, extends its reach only to 'the people.' Contrary to the suggestion of *amici curiae* that the Framers used this phrase 'simply to avoid [an] awkward rhetorical redundancy,' Brief for American Civil Liberties Union *et al.* as *Amici Curiae* 12, n.4, 'the people' seems to have been a term of art employed in select parts of the Constitution. The Preamble declares that the Constitution is ordained and established by 'the People of the United States.' The Second Amendment protects 'the right of the people to keep and bear Arms,' and the Ninth and Tenth Amendments provide that certain rights and powers are retained by and reserved to 'the people.' See also U.S. Const., Amdt. 1 ('Congress shall make no law ... abridging ... *the right of the people* peaceably to assemble') (emphasis added); Art. I, § 2, cl. 1 ('The House of Representatives shall be composed of Members chosen every second Year *by the People of the several States*') (emphasis added). While this textual exegesis is by no means conclusive, it suggests that 'the people' protected by the Fourth Amendment, and by the First and Second Amendments, and to whom rights and power are reserved in the Ninth and Tenth Amendments, refers to a class of persons who are part of a national community or who have otherwise developed sufficient connection with this country to be considered part of that community ... The language of these

Amendments contrasts with the words 'person' and 'accused' used in the Fifth and Sixth Amendments regulating procedure in criminal cases....

"[Yet,] ... we have rejected the claim that aliens are entitled to Fifth Amendment rights outside the sovereign territory of the United States. In Johnson v. Eisentrager, 339 U.S. 763 (1950), the Court held that enemy aliens arrested in China and imprisoned in Germany after World War II could not obtain writs of habeas corpus in our federal courts on the ground that their convictions for war crimes had violated the Fifth Amendment....

"Respondent urges that we interpret ... [*Reid*] to mean that federal officials are constrained by the Fourth Amendment wherever and against whomever they act. But the holding of *Reid* stands for no such sweeping proposition: it decided that United States citizens stationed abroad could invoke the protection of the Fifth and Sixth Amendments...."

Can United States officials ever act lawfully in contravention of the Constitution? Also *see generally* United States v. Curtiss–Wright Export Corp., 299 U.S. 304, 320 (1936); United States v. Lee, 106 U.S. 196, 220 (1882); JORDAN J. PAUST, INTERNATIONAL LAW AS LAW OF THE UNITED STATES 487–95, *passim* (2 ed. 2003).

4. Application of the Fifth Amendment abroad to protect U.S. citizen property interests was recognized at least as early as the 1860s. *See, e.g.*, William S. Grant v. United States, 1 Ct.Cl. 41 (1863) (in Nicaragua); James S. Wiggins v. United States, 3 Ct.Cl. 412 (1867) (in Tucson, then outside the U.S., in what is now in Arizona within the U.S.). More recently, *see, e.g.*, Ramirez de Arellano v. Weinberger, 745 F.2d 1500 (D.C.Cir.1984).

5. In addition to any constitutional guarantees as such, human rights treaties create certain minimum due process guarantees. In addition to the general norm of nondiscrimination, consider Articles 2, 9–10, 14–15 of the International Covenant on Civil and Political Rights, 999 U.N.T.S. 171; and Articles 8–11 of the Universal Declaration of Human Rights. With respect to aliens, *see also* RESTATEMENT, *supra* § 711 (re: "denial of justice"). Also see Note 2 on the previous page.

6. In Hirota v. MacArthur, 338 U.S. 197, 198 (1948), it was stated that the international tribunal in occupied Japan was one of the Allied powers under the Joint Command and was "not a tribunal of the United States" and that "courts of the United States have no power or authority to review, to affirm, set aside or annul the judgments and sentences" of such international tribunals. In a concurring opinion (*id.* at 205), Justice Douglas suggested that a U.S. citizen would, however, have recourse via habeas corpus to U.S. courts with respect to U.S. action carrying out the decision of an international tribunal. Have *Reid* and *Tiede* expanded upon Justice Douglas's suggestion? Would the decision in *Rasul v. Bush* that the habeas statute applies in Guantanamo Bay, Cuba (where the U.S. has significant jurisdiction and control) supplement Justice Douglas's suggestion?

7. With respect to *Tiede*, if hostilities had ended and peace was formally declared by 1951, constitutionally was the war power thereafter inoperative? *See also In re* Yamashita, 327 U.S. 1 (1946); Cross v. Harrison, 57 U.S. (16 How.) 164, 190 (1853); and 24 Op. Att'y Gen. 570, 571 (1903). The "occupation regime" terminated in 1955; but see the court's label

("protective occupation"). If not, with whom was the U.S. still at "war"? If so, can Berlin be "occupied" territory?

If the war power was inoperative in Berlin, what constitutional power exists to authorize U.S. "governmental functions" in Berlin, including the retention of a U.S. Court for Berlin described as an Article II court? In *Tiede*, the court noted that "[i]n 1952 a series of agreements among the Three Powers and the Federal Republic of Germany, known collectively as the 'Bonn Convention,' were signed. These agreements, however, did not enter into force until May 5, 1955. On that date, the occupation regime in the Federal Republic of Germany was terminated . . . The Bonn Convention however, did not provide for the termination of the occupation in Berlin. There, the occupation continued." Was the occupation in Berlin one that continued by Executive Agreement? If so, can the President, by Executive Agreement, set up a court on foreign territory? Does the agreement enhance presidential power because the President under the U.S. Constitution, Article II, section 3, must faithfully execute the law (*e.g.*, an Executive agreement)?

8. What criminal law formed the basis for prosecution in *Tiede*? How was that law created? Was it necessary that U.S. federal legislation create a federally prosecutable crime in *Tiede* or *Madsen v. Kinsella*? In *Tiede*, did Executive Law No. 46 execute an Executive agreement?

9. Article 43 in the Annex to the Hague Convention No. IV Respecting the Laws and Customs of War on Land (1907), which is itself customary international law, recognizes the competence and the duty of occupying powers "to restore, and ensure, as far as possible, public order and safety, while respecting, unless absolutely prevented, the laws in force in the country." Article 64 of the Geneva Civilian Convention (1949) also affirms: "The penal laws of the occupied shall remain in force, with the exception that they may be repealed or suspended by the Occupying Power in cases where they constitute a threat to its security or an obstacle to the application of the present Convention." Could such treaties and customary international law also form a basis for Executive Law No. 46 addressed in *Tiede*? If so, could the Executive execute treaty and/or customary international law for criminal sanction purposes when creating Law No. 46? Also recall United States v. Kelly, 2 Extrater. Cases 665 (U.S.C. China 1923), in Section 2 B 2 b 2. See also GC arts. 2, 6.

e. Suspension and Termination

Within the U.S., what branch(es) should have the competence to recognize that a breach of a treaty has occurred? In response to a foreign breach, what branch(es) should choose suspension of performance or termination of a treaty?

WARE v. HYLTON

3 U.S. (3 Dall.) 199, 258–62 (1796).

[Editors' note: British creditors of U.S. debtors were protected under the Treaty of Peace with Great Britain following the Revolution. A question arose whether inconsistent state laws should prevail over the rights of British creditors under the treaty. The Supreme Court ruled in this case that the treaty prevails under the Supremacy Clause of the U.S. Constitution. See this chapter, Section 2 F 1, where relevant extracts of *Ware* appear. Another issue arose concerning whether and how such a treaty obligation could be suspended or terminated as a matter of international and U.S. law.]

IREDELL, J.

The 4th plea alleges a non-compliance with the treaty on the part of Great Britain, and, therefore, that the British creditor cannot now recover a benefit under the same treaty. It also alleges acts of hostility by Great Britain since the peace, as likewise forming a bar to the recovery of the Plaintiff, who is a British creditor....

I am clearly of the opinion, that the fourth plea is not maintainable.

It is grounded on two allegations.

1st. The breach of the treaty by Great Britain, as alleged in the plea.

2d. New acts of hostility on the part of that kingdom.

1. In regard to the first, I consider the law of nations to be decided as to the following position, viz:

"That if a treaty be broken by one of the contracting parties it becomes (in the expressive language of the law) not absolutely void, but voidable; and voidable, not at the option of any individual of the contracting country injured, however much he may be affected by it, but at the option of the sovereign power of that country, of which such individual is a member". The authorities, I think, are full and decisive to that effect. Grotius, b. 2 c. 15. s. 15. ib. b. 3. c. 20. s. 35, 36, 37, 38. 2 Burl. p. 355. part. 4. c. 14. in s. 8. Vattel, b. 4. c. 4. s. 54. [Justice Iredell next addressed the writings of Grotius, Vattel, and Burlamaqui on the need for the nation to recognize that a treaty was breached and whether to terminate the treaty or take other action.]....

When any individual, therefore, of any nation, has cause of complaint against another nation, or any individual of it, not immediately amenable to the authority of his own, he may complain to that power in his own nation, which is entrusted with the sovereignty of it as to foreign negociations, and he will be entitled to all the redress which the nature of his case requires, and the situation of his own country will enable him to obtain.

The people of the United States, in their present Constitution, have devolved on the President and Senate, the power of making treaties; and upon Congress, the power of declaring war.

To one or other of these powers, in case of an infraction of a treaty that has been entered into with the United States, I apprehend application is to be made.

Upon such an application various important considerations would necessarily occur.

1. Whether the treaty was first violated on the part of the United States, or on that of the other contracting power?

2. Whether, if first violated by the latter, it was a violation in an important or an inconsiderable article; whether the violation was by design or accident, or owing to unforeseen obstacles; whether, in short, it was wholly or partially without excuse?

3. Whether, admitting it was either, it was a matter for which compensation could be made, or otherwise?

4. Whether the injury was of such a nature as to admit of negociation, or to require immediate satisfaction, peremptorily and without delay?

5. Whether, if the circumstances in all other cases justified it, it was adviseable, upon an extensive view and wise estimation of all the relative circumstances of the United States, to declare the treaty broken, and of course void: for though the party first breaking the treaty cannot make it absolutely void, but it is only voidable at the election of the injured party, yet when that election is made, by declaring the treaty void, I conceive it is totally so as to both parties, and that all rights enjoyed under the treaty are absolutely annulled, as if no stipulation had been made for them?

These are considerations of policy, considerations of extreme magnitude, and certainly entirely incompetent to the examination and definition of a Court of Justice.

Miserable and disgraceful indeed, would be the situation of the citizens of the United States, if they were obliged to comply with a treaty on their part, and had no means of redress for a non-compliance by the other contracting power.

But they have, and the law of nations points out the remedy. The remedy depends on the discretion and sense of duty of their own government.

This plea is therefore defective, so far as concerns the breach of the treaty, not because this court hath no cognizance of a breach of treaty, but because by the law of nations, we have no authority upon any information or concessions of any individuals, to consider or declare it broken; but our judgment must be grounded on the solemn declaration of Congress alone, (to whom, I conceive, the authority is entrusted) given for the very purpose of vacating the treaty on the principles I have stated. . . .

[The U.S. defendant next argued that it is not a congressional but judicial power to declare that a treaty is breached.] The judiciary is undoubtedly to determine in all cases in law and equity, coming before them concerning treaties.

The subject of treaties, Gentlemen truly say, is to be determined by the law of nations.

It is a part of the law of nations, that if a treaty be violated by one party, it is at the option of the other party, if innocent, to declare, in consequence of the breach, that the treaty is void.

If Congress, therefore, (who, I conceive, alone have such authority under our Government) shall make such a declaration, in any case like the present, I shall deem it my duty to regard the treaty as void, and then to forbear any share in executing it as a Judge.

But the same law of nations tells me, that until that declaration be made, I must regard it (in the language of the law) valid and obligatory. . . .

2. In regard to the second branch of this plea, new acts of hostility, if meant as constituting a breach, (which I don't understand it to be) the observations I have already made will equally apply to this part of the plea. If meant as a proof, that a war in fact, tho' not in name subsists, and therefore that the plaintiff is an alien enemy, the same observations will apply still more forcibly. We must receive a declaration, that we are in a state of war, from that part of the sovereignty of the union to which that important subject is entrusted. We certainly want some better information of the fact than we have at present.—However, this point seems so clear, that the defendant's counsel very faintly attempted to maintain this idea of the case.

I conclude, therefore, for these reasons, that there is nothing in the 4th plea which is a bar to the plaintiff's action.

TERLINDEN v. AMES

184 U.S. 270, 285 (1902).

FULLER, C.J.

This brings us to the real question, namely, the denial of the existence of a [1852] treaty of extradition between the United States and the Kingdom of Prussia, or the German Empire. In these proceedings the application was made by the official representative of both the Empire and the Kingdom of Prussia, but was based on the extradition treaty of 1852. The contention is that, as the result of the formation of the German Empire [in 1866], this treaty had been terminated by operation of law.

Treaties are of different kinds and terminable in different ways. The fifth article of this treaty provided, in substance, that it should continue in force until 1858, and thereafter until the end of a twelve months' notice by one of the parties of the intention to terminate it. No such notice has ever been given, and extradition has been frequently awarded under it during the entire intervening time.

Undoubtedly treaties may be terminated by the absorption of Powers into other Nationalities and the loss of separate existence, as in the case of Hanover and Nassau, which became by conquest incorporated into the Kingdom of Prussia in 1866. Cessation of independent existence rendered the execution of treaties impossible. But where sovereignty in that respect is not extinguished, and the power to execute remains unimpaired, outstanding treaties cannot be regarded as avoided because of impossibility of performance.

This treaty was entered into by His Majesty the King of Prussia in his own name and in the names of eighteen other States of the Germanic Confederation, including the Kingdom of Saxony and the free city of Frankfort, and was acceded to by six other States, including the Kingdom of Wurtemburg, and the free Hanseatic city of Bremen, but not including the Hanseatic free cities of Hamburg and Lubeck. The war between Prussia and Austria in 1866 resulted in the extinction of the Germanic Confederation and the absorption of Hanover, Hesse Cassel, Nassau and the free city of Frankfort, by Prussia.

The North German Union was then created under the praesidium of the Crown of Prussia, and our minister to Berlin, George Bancroft, thereupon recognized officially not only the Prussian Parliament, but also the Parliament of the North German United States, and the collective German Customs and Commerce Union, upon the ground that by the paramount constitution of the North German United States, the King of Prussia, to whom he was accredited, was at the head of those several organizations or institutions; and his action was entirely approved by this Government. Messages and Documents, Dep. of State, 1867–8, Part I, p. 601; Dip. Correspondence, Secretary Seward to Mr. Bancroft, Dec. 9, 1867.

February 22, 1868, a treaty relative to naturalization was concluded between the United States and His Majesty, the King of Prussia, on behalf of the North German Confederation, the third article of which read as follows: "The convention for the mutual delivery of criminals, fugitives from justice, in certain cases, concluded between the United States on the one part and Prussia and other States of Germany on the other part, the sixteenth day of June, one thousand eight hundred and fifty-two, is hereby extended to all the States of the North German Confederation." 15 Stat. 615. This recognized the treaty as still in force, and brought the Republics of Lubeck and Hamburg within its scope. Treaties were also made in that year between the United States and the Kingdoms of Bavaria and Wurtemburg, concerning naturalization, which contained the provision that the previous conventions between them and the United States in respect of fugitives from justice should remain in force without change. . . .

And without considering whether extinguished treaties can be renewed by tacit consent under our Constitution, we think that on the question whether this treaty has ever been terminated, governmental action in respect to it must be regarded as of controlling importance. During the period from 1871 to the present day, extradition from this country to Germany, and from Germany to this country, has been frequently granted under the treaty, which has thus been repeatedly recognized by both governments as force. Moore's Report on Extradition with Returns of all Cases, 1890. . . .

[In another case, referred to in notes accompanying the State Department's compilation of Treaties and Conventions between the United States and other Powers, published in 1889,] . . . *In re* Thomas, 12 Blatch. 370, in which the continuance of the extradition treaty with Bavaria was called in question, and Mr. Justice Blatchford, then District Judge, said:

. . . "Where a treaty is violated by one of the contracting parties, it rests alone with the injured party to pronounce it broken, the treaty being, in such case, not absolutely void, but voidable, at the election of the injured party, who may waive or remit the infraction committed, or may demand a just satisfaction, the treaty remaining obligatory if he chooses not to come to a rupture. 1 Kent's Com. 174. In the present case the mandate issued by the Government of the United States shows that the convention in question is regarded as in force both by the United States and by the German Empire, represented by its envoys, and by Bavaria, represented by the same envoy. The application of the foreign government was made through the proper diplomatic representative of the German Empire and of Bavaria, and the complaint before the commissioner was made by the proper consular authority representing the German Empire and also representing Bavaria."

We concur in the view that the question whether power remains in a foreign State to carry out its treaty obligations is in its nature political and not judicial, and that the courts ought not to interfere with the conclusions of the political department in that regard.

CHARLTON v. KELLY

229 U.S. 447, 469, 472–76 (1913).

[Editors' note: A U.S. citizen who was being extradited to Italy complained that the U.S.–Italy extradition treaty had been breached by Italy, that it was therefore no longer operative, and that therefore the accused could not be extradited to Italy pursuant to the treaty. Concerning extradition more generally, see Chapter 3, Section 4.]

LURTON, J.

We come now to the contention that by the refusal of Italy to deliver up fugitives of Italian nationality, the treaty has thereby ceased to be of obligation on the United States. The attitude of Italy is indicated by its Penal Code of 1900 which forbids the extradition of citizens, and by the denial in two or more instances to recognize this obligation of the treaty as extending to its citizens. . . .

This [Italian] adherence to a view of the obligation of the treaty as not requiring one country to surrender its nationals while it did the other, presented a situation in which the United States might do either of two things, namely: abandon its own interpretation of the word "persons" as including citizens, or adhere to its own interpretation and surrender the appellant, although the obligation had, as to nationals, ceased to be reciprocal. The United States could not yield its own interpretation of the treaty, since that would have had the most serious consequence on five other treaties in which the word "persons" had been used in its ordinary meaning, as including all persons, and, therefore, not exempting citizens. If the attitude of Italy was, as contended, a violation of the obligation of the treaty, which, in international law, would have justified the United States in denouncing the treaty as no longer obligatory, it did not automatically have that effect. If the United States elected not to declare its abrogation, or come to a rupture, the treaty would remain in force. It was only voidable, not void; and if the United States should prefer, it might waive any breach which in its judgment had occurred and conform to its own obligation as if there had been no such breach. 1 KENT'S COMM., p. 175.... [The Court then quoted Vattel and Grotius in a manner similar to Justice Iredell in *Ware.*]

That the political branch of the Government recognizes the treaty obligation as still existing is evidenced by its action in this case. In the memorandum giving the reasons of the Department of State for determining to surrender the appellant, after stating the difference between the two governments as to the interpretation of this clause of the treaty, Mr. Secretary Knox said:

"The question is now for the first time presented as to whether or not the United States is under obligation under treaty to surrender to Italy for trial and punishment citizens of the United States fugitive from the justice of Italy, notwithstanding the interpretation placed upon the treaty by Italy with reference to Italian subjects. In this connection it should be observed that the United States, although, as stated above, consistently contending that the Italian interpretation was not the proper one, has not treated the Italian practice as a breach of the treaty obligation necessarily requiring abrogation, has not abrogated the treaty or taken any step looking thereto, and has, on the contrary, constantly regarded the treaty as in full force and effect and has answered the obligations imposed thereby and has invoked the rights therein granted. It should, moreover, be observed that even though the action of the Italian Government be regarded as a breach of the treaty, the treaty is binding until abrogated, and therefore the treaty not having been abrogated, its provisions are operative against us.

"The question would, therefore, appear to reduce itself to one of interpretation of the meaning of the treaty, the Government of the United States being now for the first time called upon to declare whether it regards the treaty as obliging it to surrender its citizens to Italy, notwithstanding Italy has not and insists it can not surrender its citizens to us. It should be observed, in the first place, that we have always insisted not only with reference to the Italian extradition treaty, but when reference to the other extradition treaties similarly phrased that the word 'persons' includes citizens. We are, therefore, committed to that interpretation. The fact that we have for reasons already given ceased generally to make requisition upon the Government of Italy for the surrender of Italian subjects under the treaty, would not require of necessity that we should, as a matter of logic or law, regard ourselves as free from the obligation of surrendering our citizens, we laboring under no such legal inhibition regarding surrender as operates against the government of Italy. Therefore, since extradition treaties need not be reciprocal, even in the matter of the surrendering of citizens, it would seem entirely sound to consider ourselves as bound to surrender our citizens to Italy even though Italy should not, by reason of the provisions of her municipal law be able to surrender its citizens to us."

The executive department having thus elected to waive any right to free itself from the obligation to deliver up its own citizens, it is the plain duty of this court to recognize the obligation to surrender the appellant as one imposed by the treaty as the supreme law of the land and as affording authority for the warrant of extradition.

GOLDWATER v. CARTER

444 U.S. 996 (1979).

[Editors' note: The decision of the court of appeals below, 617 F2d. 697 (D.C.Cir.1979), had recognized the power of the President to terminate a treaty with Taiwan, noting the President's broad "foreign affairs" powers and the need, at times, to respond to changing conditions and to respond quickly. At the Supreme Court, the Justices split, but reversed and remanded with directions to dismiss. Then Justice Rehnquist concurred primarily on the ground that the matter raised a political question. Rehnquist was joined by Chief Justice Burger, Justice Stewart, and Justice Stevens.]

POWELL, J., concurring.

Although I agree with the result reached by the Court, I would dismiss the complaint as not ripe for judicial review....

In this case, a few Members of Congress claim that the President's action in terminating the treaty with Taiwan has deprived them of their constitutional role with respect to a change in the supreme law of the land. Congress has taken no official action. In the present posture of this case, we do not know whether there ever will be an actual confrontation between the Legislative and Executive Branches. Although the Senate has considered a resolution declaring that Senate approval is necessary for the termination of any mutual defense treaty ... no final vote has been taken on the resolution.... Moreover, it is unclear whether the resolution would have retroactive effect.... It cannot be said that either the Senate or the House has rejected the President's claim. If the Congress chooses not to confront the President, it is not our task to do so. I therefore concur in the dismissal of this case.

Mr. Justice Rehnquist suggests, however, that the issue presented by this case is a nonjusticiable political question which can never be considered by this Court. I cannot agree....

BRENNAN, J., dissenting.

... In stating that this case presents a nonjusticiable "political question," Mr. Justice Rehnquist, in my view, profoundly misapprehends the political-question principle as it applies to matters of foreign relations. Properly understood, the political-question doctrine restrains courts from reviewing an exercise of foreign policy judgment by the coordinate political branch to which authority to make that judgment has been "constitutional[ly] commit[ted]." Baker v. Carr, 369 U.S. 186, 211–213, 217 (1962). But the doctrine does not pertain when a court is faced with the antecedent question whether a particular branch has been constitutionally designated as the repository of political decision making power. *Cf.* Powell v. McCormack, 395 U.S. 486, 519–521 (1969). The issue of decision making authority must be resolved as a matter of constitutional law, not political discretion; accordingly, it falls within the competence of the courts.

The constitutional question raised here is prudently answered in narrow terms. Abrogation of the defense treaty with Taiwan was a necessary incident to Executive recognition of the Peking Government, because the defense treaty was predicated upon the now-abandoned view that the Taiwan Government was the only legitimate political authority in China. Our cases firmly establish that the Constitution commits to the President alone the power to recognize, and withdraw recognition from, foreign regimes. See Banco Nacional de Cuba v. Sabbatino, 376 U.S. 398, 410 (1964); Baker v. Carr, *supra*, at 212; United States v. Pink, 315 U.S. 203, 228–230 (1942). That mandate being clear, our judicial inquiry into the treaty rupture can go no further. See Baker v. Carr, *supra*, at 212; United States v. Pink, *supra*, at 229.

Notes and Questions

1. Justice Washington noted in Bas v. Tingy, 4 U.S. (4 Dall.) 37 (1800), that Congress had "dissolved our treaty" with France during the limited war with France. Does such dictum indicate an expectation that Congress can dissolve treaties? that only Congress can do so? Does that fact that a limited war existed enhance or limit relevant powers? The Restatement prefers an absolute right of the President to terminate. RESTATEMENT § 339(a) ("the President has the power ... to suspend or terminate an agreement in accordance with its terms").

2. Who should decide on behalf of the United States whether there is a material breach of a treaty? Nonetheless, is such a question a legal question? If there is a material breach, who should decide what sanctions, if any, should be applied on behalf of the United States, *e.g.*, suspension of performance or termination of the treaty?

2. *Executive Agreements*

a. *Types and Trends in Use*

U.S. DEP'T OF STATE CIRCULAR 175 (revised 1974)

... An international agreement [other than a treaty] may be concluded pursuant to one or more of ... [three] constitutional bases:

(1) Agreements Pursuant to Treaty

The President may conclude an international agreement pursuant to a treaty brought into force with the advice and consent of the Senate, whose provisions constitute authorization for the agreement by the Executive without subsequent action by the Congress;

(2) Agreements Pursuant to Legislation

The President may conclude an international agreement on the basis of existing legislation or subject to legislation to be enacted by the Congress; and

(3) Agreements Pursuant to the Constitutional Authority of the President

The President may conclude an international agreement on any subject within his constitutional authority so long as the agreement is not inconsistent with legislation enacted by the Congress in the exercise of its constitutional authority. The constitutional authority for the President to conclude international agreements includes:

(a) The President's authority as Chief Executive to represent the nation in foreign affairs;

(b) The President's authority to receive ambassadors and other public ministers;

(c) The President's authority as "Commander-in-Chief"; and

(d) The President's authority to "take care that the laws be faithfully executed."

11 Foreign Affairs Manual 720 (1985)

721.3 Considerations for Selecting Among Constitutionally Authorized Procedures

In determining a question as to the procedure which should be followed for any particular international agreement, due consideration is given to the following factors . . . :

a. The extent to which the agreement involves commitments or risks affecting the nation as a whole;

b. Whether the agreement is intended to affect State laws;

c. Whether the agreement can be given effect without the enactment of subsequent legislation by the Congress;

d. Past United States practice with respect to similar agreements;

e. The preference for the Congress with respect to a particular type of agreement;

f. The degree of formality desired for an agreement;

g. The proposed duration of the agreement, the need for prompt conclusion of an agreement, and the desirability of concluding a routine or short-term agreement; and

h. The general international practice with respect to similar agreements.

In determining whether any international agreement should be brought into force as a treaty or as an international agreement other than a treaty, the utmost care is to be exercised to avoid any invasion or compromise of the constitutional powers of the Senate, the Congress as a whole, or the President.

Notes and Questions

1. Today, the United States is a party or signatory to over 14,000 international agreements. Studies indicate that most of these agreements are not treaties but executive agreements. Moreover, most are executive agreements pursuant to legislation or what are termed congressional-executive agreements. *See, e.g.,* Louis Henkin, Foreign Affairs and the US Constitution 492 (2 ed. 1996) (a congressional study indicated: "Between 1930 and 1992 the United States made 891 treaties and 13,178 other international agreements. Since 1939, more than 90% of international agreements of the United States were executive agreements."); Loch K. Johnson, The Making of International Agreements 12 (1986) ("almost 87 percent ... between 1946 and 1973 have been statutory [based agreements]. By contrast, [sole] executive agreements and treaties account for only 7 percent and 6 percent, respectively...."); L. Margolis, Executive Agreements and Presidential Power in Foreign Policy 108 (1985) (from 1789–1979, treaties comprised some 13 percent of U.S. international agreements and most executive agreements were congressional-executive). The use of congressional-executive agreement was sanctified as early as the 1890s. See Field v. Clark, 143 U.S. 649 (1892).

2. Why would a President find it politically convenient to use a congressional-executive agreement rather than a treaty? Why not simply use a sole executive agreement?

3. Would a "topical" analysis (relating the topic or subject of an agreement either to legislative or executive powers) be appropriate concerning choice whether to enter into a sole executive agreement as opposed to a congressional-executive agreement or treaty? See Kenneth C. Randall, *The Treaty Power*, 51 Ohio St. L.J. 1089 (1990). Is a "topical" approach potentially improperly attentive to Circular No. 175's factors, practice, and broad legal policies at stake?

4. Should congressional-executive agreements be interchangeable with treaties? Should sole executive agreements? What consequences would follow? *See generally* Bruce Ackerman & David Golove, *Is NAFTA Constitutional?*, 108 Harv. L. Rev. 801 (1995); Edwin Borchard, *Shall the Executive Agreement Replace the Treaty?*, 53 Yale L.J. 664 (1944); *Treaties and Executive Agreements—A Reply, id.* at 616 (1945); Myres S. McDougal & Asher Lans, *Treaties and Congressional–Executive or Presidential Agreements: Interchangeable Instruments of National Policy*, 54 Yale L.J. (pts. 1 & 2) 181, 534 (1945); John F. Murphy, *Treaties and International Agreements Other Than Treaties: Constitutional Allocation of Power and Responsibility Among the President, the House of Representatives, and the Senate*, 23 Kan. L. Rev. 221 (1975).

5. Are most congressional-executive agreements inherently "self-executing"? *See, e.g.*, Henkin, *supra* at 217.

6. Cases addressing the validity of congressional-executive agreements include: B. Altman & Co. v. United States, 224 U.S. 583 (1912); Field v. Clark, 143 U.S. 649 (1892); Von Cotzhausen v. Nazro, 107 U.S. 215 (1882); Star–Kist Foods v. United States, 275 F.2d 472 (Cust. & Pat. App.1959) (trade agreement with Iceland executed by the President pursuant to a Trade Agreements Act).

b. Trends in Judicial Decision

UNITED STATES v. CURTISS-WRIGHT EXPORT CORP.

299 U.S. 304 (1936).

Sutherland, J.

On January 27, 1936, an indictment was returned in the court below, the first count of which charges that appellees, beginning with the 29th day of May, 1934, conspired to sell in the United States certain arms of war, namely fifteen machine guns, to Bolivia, a country then engaged in armed conflict in the Chaco, in violation of the Joint Resolution of Congress approved May 28, 1934, and the provisions of a proclamation issued on the same day by the President of the United States pursuant to authority conferred by § 1 of the resolution. In pursuance of the conspiracy, the commission of certain overt acts was alleged, details of which need not be stated. The Joint Resolution (c. 365, 48 Stat. 811) follows:

> "Resolved by the Senate and House of Representatives of the United States of America in Congress assembled, That if the President finds that the prohibition of the sale of arms and munitions of war in the United States to those countries now engaged in armed conflict in the Chaco may contribute to the reestablishment of peace between those countries, and if after consultation with the governments of other American Republics and with their cooperation, as well as that of such other governments as he may deem necessary, he makes proclamation to that effect, it shall be unlawful to sell, except under such limitations and exceptions as the President prescribes, any arms or munitions of war in any place in the United States to the countries now engaged in that armed conflict, or to any person, company, or association acting in the interest of either country, until otherwise ordered by the President or by Congress.
>
> "Sec. 2. Whoever sells any arms or munitions of war in violation of section 1 shall, on conviction, be punished by a fine not exceeding $10,000 or by imprisonment not exceeding two years, or both."

The President's proclamation (48 Stat. 1744), after reciting the terms of the Joint Resolution, declares:

> "Now, therefore, I, Franklin D. Roosevelt, President of the United States of America, acting under and by virtue of the authority conferred in me by the said joint resolution of Congress, do hereby declare and proclaim that I have found that the prohibition of the sale of arms and munitions of war in the United States to those countries now engaged in armed conflict in the Chaco may contribute to the reestablishment of peace between those countries, and that I have consulted with the governments of other American Republics and have been assured of the cooperation of such governments as I have deemed necessary as contemplated by the said joint resolution; and I do hereby admonish all citizens of the United States and every person to abstain from every violation of the provisions of the joint resolution above set forth, hereby made applicable to Bolivia and Paraguay, and I do hereby warn them that all violations of such provisions will be rigorously prosecuted.
>
> "And I do hereby enjoin upon all officers of the United States charged with the execution of the laws thereof, the utmost diligence in preventing violations of the said joint resolution and this my proclamation issued thereunder, and in bringing to trial and punishment any offenders against the same.
>
> "And I do hereby delegate to the Secretary of State the power of prescribing exceptions and limitations to the application of the said joint resolution of May 28, 1934, as made effective by this my proclamation issued thereunder." . . .

. . . It is contended that by the Joint Resolution, the going into effect and continued operation of the resolution was conditioned (a) upon the President's judgment as to its beneficial effect upon the reestablishment of peace between the countries engaged in armed conflict in the Chaco; (b) upon the making of a proclamation, which was left to his unfettered discretion, thus constituting an attempted substitution of the President's will for that of Congress; (c) upon the making of a proclamation putting an end to the operation of the resolution, which again was left to the President's unfettered discretion; and (d) further, that the extent of its operation in particular cases was subject to limitation and exception by the President, controlled by no standard. In each of these particulars, appellees urge that Congress abdicated its essential functions and delegated them to the Executive. [Editors' note: Thus, defendant-appellees raised issues concerning the delegation doctrine, which precludes the delegation of legislative power by Congress to the Executive without adequate standards.]

Whether, if the Joint Resolution had related solely to internal affairs it would be open to the challenge that it constituted an unlawful delegation of legislative power to the Executive, we find it unnecessary to determine. The whole aim of the resolution is to affect a situation entirely external to the United States, and falling within the category of foreign affairs. The determination which we are called to make, therefore, is whether the Joint Resolution, as applied to that situation, is vulnerable to attack under the rule that forbids a delegation of the law-making power. In other words, assuming (but not deciding) that the challenged delegation, if it were confined to internal affairs, would be invalid, may it nevertheless be sustained on the ground that its exclusive aim is to afford a remedy for a hurtful condition within foreign territory?

It will contribute to the elucidation of the question if we first consider the differences between the powers of the federal government in respect of foreign or external affairs and those in respect of domestic or internal affairs. That there are differences between them, and that these differences are fundamental, may not be doubted.

The two classes of powers are different, both in respect of their origin and their nature. The broad statement that the federal government can exercise no powers except those specifically enumerated in the Constitution, and such implied powers as are necessary and proper to carry into effect the enumerated powers, is categorically true only in respect of our internal affairs. In that field, the primary purpose of the Constitution was to carve from the general mass of legislative powers then possessed by the states such portions as it was thought desirable to vest in the federal government, leaving those not included in the enumeration still in the states. Carter v. Carter Coal Co., 298 U.S. 238, 294. That this doctrine applies only to powers which the states had, is self evident. And since the states severally never possessed international powers, such powers could not have been carved from the mass of state powers but obviously were transmitted to the United States from some other source. During the colonial period, those powers were possessed exclusively by and were entirely under the control of the Crown. By the Declaration of Independence, "the Representatives of the United States of America" declared the United [not the several] Colonies to be free and independent states, and as such to have "full Power to levy War, conclude Peace, contract Alliances, establish Commerce and to do all other Acts and Things which Independent States may of right do."

As a result of the separation from Great Britain by the colonies acting as a unit, the powers of external sovereignty passed from the Crown not to the colonies severally, but to the colonies in their collective and corporate capacity as the United States of America. Even before the Declaration, the colonies were a unit in foreign affairs, acting through a common agency—namely the Continental Congress, composed of delegates from the thirteen colonies. That agency exercised the powers of war and peace, raised an army, created a navy, and finally adopted the Declaration of Independence. Rulers come and go; governments end and forms of government change; but sovereignty survives. A political society cannot endure without a supreme will somewhere. Sovereignty is never held in suspense. When, therefore, the external sovereignty of Great Britain in respect of the colonies ceased, it immediately passed to the Union. See Penhallow v. Doane, 3 Dall. 54, 80–81. That fact was given practical application almost at once. The treaty of peace, made on September 23, 1783, was concluded between his Britannic Majesty and the "United States of America." . . .

It results that the investment of the federal government with the powers of external sovereignty did not depend upon the affirmative grants of the Constitution. The powers to declare and wage war, to conclude peace, to make treaties, to maintain diplomatic relations with other sovereignties, if they had never been mentioned in the Constitution, would have vested in the federal government as necessary concomitants of nationality. Neither the Constitution nor the laws passed in pursuance of it have any force in foreign territory unless in respect of our own citizens (see American Banana Co. v. United Fruit Co., 213 U.S. 347, 356); and operations of the nation in such territory must be governed by treaties, international understandings and compacts, and the principles of international law. As a member of the family of nations, the right and power of the United States in that field are equal to the right and power of the other members of the international family. Otherwise, the United States is not completely sovereign. The power to acquire territory by discovery and occupation (Jones v. United States, 137 U.S. 202, 212), the power to expel undesirable aliens (Fong Yue Ting v. United States, 149 U.S. 698, 705 *et seq.*), the power to make such international agreements as do not constitute treaties in the constitutional sense (Altman & Co. v. United States, 224 U.S. 583, 600–601 . . .), none of which is expressly affirmed by the Constitution, nevertheless exist as inherently inseparable from the conception of nationality. This the court recognized, and in each of the cases cited found the warrant for its conclusions not in the provisions of the Constitution, but in the law of nations.

In Burnet v. Brooks, 288 U.S. 378, 396, we said, "As a nation with all the attributes of sovereignty, the United States is vested with all the powers of government necessary to maintain an effective control of international relations." *Cf. Carter v. Carter Coal Co., supra*, p. 295.

Not only, as we have shown, is the federal power over external affairs in origin and essential character different from that over internal affairs, but participation in the exercise of the power is significantly limited. In this vast external realm, with its important, complicated, delicate and manifold problems, the President alone has the power to speak or listen as a representative of the nation. He makes treaties with the advice and consent of the Senate; but he alone negotiates. Into the field of negotiation the Senate cannot intrude; and Congress itself is powerless to invade it. As Marshall said in his great argument of March 7, 1800, in the House of Representatives, "The President is the sole organ of the nation in its external relations, and its sole representative with foreign nations." . . .

It is important to bear in mind that we are here dealing not alone with an authority vested in the President by an exertion of legislative power, but with such an authority plus the very delicate, plenary and exclusive power of the President as the sole organ of the federal government in the field of international relations—a power which does not require as a basis for its exercise an act of Congress, but which, of course, like every other governmental power, must be exercised in subordination to the applicable provisions of the Constitution. It is quite apparent that if, in the maintenance of our international relations, embarrassment—perhaps serious embarrassment—is to be avoided and success for our aims achieved, congressional legislation which is to be made effective through negotiation and inquiry within the international field must often accord to the President a degree of discretion and freedom from statutory restriction which would not be admissible were domestic affairs alone involved. Moreover, he, not Congress, has the better opportunity of knowing the conditions which prevail in foreign countries, and especially is this true in time of war. He has his confidential sources of information. He has his agents in the form of diplomatic, consular and other officials. Secrecy in respect of information gathered by them may be highly necessary, and the premature disclosure of it productive of harmful results. Indeed, so clearly is this true that the first President refused to accede to a request to lay before the House of Representatives the instructions, correspondence and documents relating to the negotiation of the Jay Treaty—a refusal the wisdom of which was recognized by the House itself and has never since been doubted. In his reply to the request, President Washington said:

> "The nature of foreign negotiations requires caution, and their success must often depend on secrecy; and even when brought to a conclusion a full disclosure of all the measures, demands, or eventual concessions which may have been proposed or contemplated would be extremely impolitic; for this might have a pernicious influence on future negotiations, or produce immediate inconveniences, perhaps danger and mischief, in relation to other powers. The necessity of such caution and secrecy was one cogent reason for vesting the power of making treaties in the President, with the advice and consent of the Senate, the principle on which that body was formed confining it to a small number of members. To admit, then, a right in the House of Representatives to demand and to have as a matter of course all the papers respecting a negotiation with a foreign power would be to establish a dangerous precedent." . . .

We deem it unnecessary to consider, seriatim, the several clauses which are said to evidence the unconstitutionality of the Joint Resolution as involving an unlawful delegation of legislative power. It is enough to summarize by saying that, both upon principle and in accordance with precedent, we conclude there is sufficient warrant for the broad discretion vested in the President to determine whether the enforcement of the statute will have a beneficial effect upon the reestablishment of peace in the affected countries; whether he shall make proclamation to bring the resolution into operation; whether and when the resolution shall cease to operate and to make proclamation accordingly; and to prescribe limitations and exceptions to which the enforcement of the resolution shall be subject. . . .

Notes and Questions

1. Justice Sutherland asserted that "the states severally never possessed international powers. . . ." Was that correct? Concerning the result in

Curtiss-Wright, would it matter? Some states had treaties with Indian nations. The scheme adopted under the Articles of Confederation required each state to vote for war. There are also retained war powers of states under the U.S. Constitution. See Article I, § 10, cl. 3.

2. Was Justice Sutherland's notion of "sovereignty" consistent with the view of the Founders that the federal government is one of limited powers delegated from the people, with ultimate "sovereignty" remaining in the people? *See also* U.S. Const., preamble and Amend. X; JORDAN J. PAUST, INTERNATIONAL LAW AS LAW OF THE UNITED STATES 54, 84, 145, 186, 209, 254, 257–58, 261, 286, 305–08, 328–31, 334, 340, 347, 380, 403, 487–88, 502 (2 ed. 2003).

3. Can the following powers be implied from the Constitution: the power to acquire territory (see U.S. Const., Art. IV (the property clause)); the power to expel undesirable aliens (see *id.* Art. I, § 8, cls. 4, 18); the power to make international agreements that are not treaties (see *id.* Art. II, § 2, cl. 1, § 3)? If there are doubts about the meaning of some of Justice Sutherland's remarks concerning the existence of "such implied powers as are necessary and proper to carry into effect the enumerated powers" and, perhaps, to carry into effect other implied powers (implied even partly from "the law of nations") as opposed to whether powers exist outside the Constitution, newer cases affirm older notions of authority and sovereignty shared by the Founders. *See, e.g.*, Reid v. Covert, 354 U.S. 1 (1957); Youngstown Sheet & Tube Co. v. Sawyer, 343 U.S. 579 (1952) (especially concerning the fact that there are no powers *ex necessitate*); and other cases *supra*, Section 2 C 1 d.

4. What broad "standards" set forth by Congress in the Joint Resolution limited presidential discretion concerning the creation of aspects of federal crime such as "limitations and exceptions"?

UNITED STATES v. PINK

315 U.S. 203 (1942).

DOUGLAS, J.

This action was brought by the United States to recover the assets of the New York branch of the First Russian Insurance Co. which remained in the hands of respondent after the payment of all domestic creditors. The material allegations of the complaint were, in brief, as follows:

The First Russian Insurance Co., organized under the laws of the former Empire of Russia, established a New York branch in 1907. It deposited with the Superintendent of Insurance, pursuant to the laws of New York, certain assets to secure payment of claims resulting from transactions of its New York branch. By certain laws, decrees, enactments and orders, in 1918 and 1919, the Russian Government nationalized the business of insurance and all of the property, wherever situated, of all Russian insurance companies (including the First Russian Insurance Co.), and discharged and canceled all the debts of such companies and the rights of all shareholders in all such property. The New York branch of the First Russian Insurance Co. continued to do business in New York until 1925. At that time, respondent, pursuant to an order of the Supreme Court of New York, took possession of its assets for a determination and report upon the claims of the policyholders and creditors in the United States. Thereafter, all claims of domestic creditors, *i.e.*, all claims arising out of the business of the New York branch, were paid by respondent, leaving a balance in his hands of more than $1,000,000.... On November 16, 1933, the United States recognized the Union of Soviet Socialist Republics as the *de jure* Government of Russia and as an incident to that recognition accepted an assignment (known as the Litvinov Assignment) of certain claims. The Litvinov Assignment was in the form of a letter, dated November 16, 1933, to the President of the United States from Maxim Litvinov, People's Commissar for Foreign Affairs....

This was acknowledged by the President on the same date. The acknowledgment, after setting forth the terms of the assignment, concluded:

> "I am glad to have these undertakings by your Government and I shall be pleased to notify your Government in each case of any amount realized by the Government of the United States from the release and assignment to it of the amounts admitted to be due, or that may be found to be due, the Government of the Union of Soviet Socialist Republics, and of the amount that may be found to be due on the claim of the Russian Volunteer Fleet." ...

[T]he present suit was instituted in the Supreme Court of New York. The defendants, other than respondent, were certain designated policyholders and other creditors who had presented in the liquidation proceedings claims against the corporation. The complaint prayed, *inter alia*, that the United States be adjudged to be the sole and exclusive owner entitled to immediate possession of the entire surplus fund in the hands of the respondent.

Respondent's answer denied the allegations of the complaint that title to the funds in question passed to the United States and that the Russian decrees had the effect claimed. It also set forth various affirmative defenses—that the order of distribution pursuant to the decree ..., could not be affected by the Litvinov Assignment; that the Litvinov Assignment was unenforceable because it was conditioned upon a final settlement of claims and counterclaims which had not been accomplished; that under Russian law the nationalization decrees in question had no effect on property not factually taken into possession by the Russian Government prior to May 22, 1922; that the Russian decrees had no extraterritorial effect, according to Russian law; that if the decrees were given extraterritorial effect, they were confiscatory and their recognition would be unconstitutional and contrary to the public policy of the United States and of the State of New York; and that the United States, under the Litvinov Assignment, acted merely as a collection agency for the Russian Government and hence was foreclosed from asserting any title to the property in question....

The New York Court of Appeals held in the Moscow case that the Russian decrees in question had no extraterritorial effect. If that is true, it is decisive of the present controversy. For the United States acquired, under the Litvinov Assignment, only such rights as Russia had. Guaranty Trust Co. v. United States, 304 U.S. 126, 143. If the Russian decrees left the New York assets of the Russian insurance companies unaffected, then Russia had nothing here to assign. But that question of foreign law is not to be determined exclusively by the state court. The claim of the United States based on the Litvinov Assignment raises a federal question. United States v. Belmont, 301 U.S. 324 [1937]....

We hold that, so far as its intended effect is concerned, the Russian decree embraced the New York assets of the First Russian Insurance Co.

... The question of whether the decree should be given extraterritorial effect is, of course, a distinct matter. One primary issue raised in that connection is whether, under our constitutional system, New York law can be allowed to stand in the way....

... [The] power of New York to deny enforcement of a claim under the Litvinov Assignment because of an overriding policy of the State which denies validity in New York of the Russian decrees on which the assigned claims rest ... was denied New York in *United States v. Belmont*, *supra*, 301 U.S. 324. With one qualification, to be noted, the *Belmont* case is determinative of the present controversy.

That case involved the right of the United States under the Litvinov Assignment to recover, from a custodian or stakeholder in New York, funds which had been nationalized and appropriated by the Russian decrees.

This Court, speaking through Mr. Justice Sutherland, held that the conduct of foreign relations is committed by the Constitution to the political departments of the Federal Government; that the propriety of the exercise of that power is not open to judicial inquiry; and that recognition of a foreign sovereign conclusively binds the courts and "is retroactive and validates all actions and conduct of the government so recognized from the commencement of its existence." 301 U.S. at p. 328. It further held (p. 330) that recognition of the Soviet Government, the establishment of diplomatic relations with it, and the Litvinov Assignment were "all parts of one transaction, resulting in an international compact between the two governments." After stating that, "in respect of what was done here, the Executive had authority to speak as the sole organ" of the national government, it added (p. 330): "The assignment and the agreements in connection therewith did not, as in the case of treaties, as that term is used in the treaty making clause of the Constitution (Art. II, § 2), require the advice and consent of the Senate." It held (p. 331) that the "external powers of the United States are to be exercised without regard to state laws or policies. The supremacy of a treaty in this respect has been recognized from the beginning." And it added that "all international compacts and agreements" are to be treated with similar dignity for the reason that "complete power over international affairs is in the national government and is not and cannot be subject to any curtailment or interference on the part of the several states." p. 331. This Court did not stop to inquire whether in fact there was any policy of New York which enforcement of the Litvinov Assignment would infringe since "no state policy can prevail against the international compact here involved." p. 327....

... The purpose of the discussions leading to the policy of recognition was to resolve "all questions outstanding" between the two nations. Establishment of Diplomatic Relations with the Union of Soviet Socialist Republics, Dept. of State, Eastern European Series, No. 1 (1933), p. 1. Settlement of all American claims against Russia was one method of removing some of the prior objections to recognition based on the Soviet policy of nationalization. The Litvinov Assignment was not only part and parcel of the new policy of recognition (*id.*, p. 13), it was also the method adopted by the Executive Department for alleviating in this country the rigors of nationalization. Congress tacitly recognized that policy. Acting in anticipation of the realization of funds under the Litvinov Assignment (H. Rep. No. 865, 76th Cong., 1st Sess.), it authorized the appointment of a Commissioner to determine the claims of American nationals against the Soviet Government. Joint Resolution of August 4, 1939, 53 Stat. 1199.

If the President had the power to determine the policy which was to govern the question of recognition, then the Fifth Amendment does not stand in the way of giving full force and effect to the Litvinov Assignment. To be sure, aliens as well as citizens are entitled to the protection of the Fifth Amendment. Russian Volunteer Fleet v. United States, 282 U.S. 481. A State is not precluded, however, by the Fourteenth Amendment from according priority to local creditors as against creditors who are nationals of foreign countries and whose claims arose abroad. Disconto Gesellschaft v. Umbreit, 208 U.S. 570. By the same token, the Federal Government is not barred by the Fifth Amendment from securing for itself and our nationals priority against such creditors....

... The powers of the President in the conduct of foreign relations included the power, without consent of the Senate, to determine the public policy of the United States with respect to the Russian nationalization decrees. "What government is to be regarded here as representative of a foreign sovereign state is a political rather than a judicial question, and is to be determined by the political department of the government." Guaranty Trust Co. v. United States, *supra*, 304 U.S. at p. 137. That authority is not limited to a determination of the government to be recognized. It includes the power to determine the policy which is to govern the question of recognition. Objections to the underlying policy as well as objections to recognition are to be addressed to the political department and not to the courts. See Guaranty Trust Co. v. United States, *supra*, p. 138; Kennett v. Chambers, 14 How. 38, 50–51. As we have noted, this Court in the *Belmont* case recognized that the Litvinov

Assignment was an international compact which did not require the participation of the Senate. It stated (301 U.S. pp. 330–331): "There are many such compacts, of which a protocol, a modus vivendi, a postal convention, and agreements like that now under consideration are illustrations." And see Monaco v. Mississippi, 292 U.S. 313, 331; United States v. Curtiss–Wright Corp., 299 U.S. 304, 318. Recognition is not always absolute; it is sometimes conditional. 1 MOORE, INTERNATIONAL LAW DIGEST (1906), pp. 73–74; 1 HACKWORTH, DIGEST OF INTERNATIONAL LAW (1940), pp. 192–195. Power to remove such obstacles to full recognition as settlement of claims of our nationals (Levitan, *Executive Agreements*, 35 ILL. L. REV. 365, 382–385) certainly is a modest implied power of the President who is the "sole organ of the federal government in the field of international relations." *United States v. Curtiss–Wright Corp., supra*, p. 320. Effectiveness in handling the delicate problems of foreign relations requires no less. Unless such a power exists, the power of recognition might be thwarted or seriously diluted. No such obstacle can be placed in the way of rehabilitation of relations between this country and another nation, unless the historic conception of the powers and responsibilities of the President in the conduct of foreign affairs . . . is to be drastically revised. It was the judgment of the political department that full recognition of the Soviet Government required the settlement of all outstanding problems including the claims of our nationals. Recognition and the Litvinov Assignment were interdependent. We would usurp the executive function if we held that that decision was not final and conclusive in the courts.

"All constitutional acts of power, whether in the executive or in the judicial department, have as much legal validity and obligation as if they proceeded from the legislature, . . ." THE FEDERALIST, NO. 64. A treaty is a "Law of the Land" under the supremacy clause (Art. VI, Cl. 2) of the Constitution. Such international compacts and agreements as the Litvinov Assignment have a similar dignity. *United States v. Belmont, supra*, 301 U.S. at p. 331. See CORWIN, THE PRESIDENT, OFFICE & POWERS (1940), pp. 228–240.

It is, of course, true that even treaties with foreign nations will be carefully construed so as not to derogate from the authority and jurisdiction of the States of this nation unless clearly necessary to effectuate the national policy. Guaranty Trust Co. v. United States, *supra*, p. 143 and cases cited. For example, in Todok v. Union State Bank, 281 U.S. 449, this Court took pains in its construction of a treaty, relating to the power of an alien to dispose of property in this country, not to invalidate the provisions of state law governing such dispositions. Frequently the obligation of a treaty will be dependent on state law. Prevost v. Greneaux, 19 How. 1. But state law must yield when it is inconsistent with, or impairs the policy or provisions of, a treaty or of an international compact or agreement. See Nielsen v. Johnson, 279 U.S. 47. Then, the power of a State to refuse enforcement of rights based on foreign law which runs counter to the public policy of the forum (Griffin v. McCoach, 313 U.S. 498, 506) must give way before the superior Federal policy evidenced by a treaty or international compact or agreement. *Santovincenzo v. Egan, supra*, 284 U.S. 30; *United States v. Belmont, supra*.

Enforcement of New York's policy as formulated by the Moscow case would collide with and subtract from the Federal policy, whether it was premised on the absence of extraterritorial effect of the Russian decrees, the conception of the New York branch as a distinct juristic personality, or disapproval by New York of the Russian program of nationalization. For the Moscow case refuses to give effect or recognition in New York to acts of the Soviet Government which the United States by its policy of recognition agreed no longer to question. Enforcement of such state policies would indeed tend to restore some of the precise impediments to friendly relations which the President intended to remove on inauguration of the policy of recognition of the Soviet Government. In the first place, such action by New York, no matter what gloss be given it, amounts to official disapproval or non-recognition of the nationalization program of the Soviet Government. That disapproval or non-recognition is in the face of a disavowal by the United States of any official concern with that program. It is in the face of the underlying policy adopted by the United States when it recognized the Soviet Government. In the second place, to the extent that the action of the State in refusing enforcement of the Litvinov Assignment results in reduction or non-payment of claims of our nationals, it helps keep alive one source of friction which the policy of recognition intended to remove. Thus the action of New York tends to restore some of the precise irritants which had long affected the relations between these two great nations and which the policy of recognition was designed to eliminate....

We repeat that there are limitations on the sovereignty of the States. No State can rewrite our foreign policy to conform to its own domestic policies. Power over external affairs is not shared by the States; it is vested in the national government exclusively. It need not be so exercised as to conform to state laws or state policies, whether they be expressed in constitutions, statutes, or judicial decrees. And the policies of the States become wholly irrelevant to judicial inquiry when the United States, acting within its constitutional sphere, seeks enforcement of its foreign policy in the courts. For such reasons, Mr. Justice Sutherland stated in *United States v. Belmont, supra*, 301 U.S. at p. 331, "In respect of all international negotiations and compacts, and in respect of our foreign relations generally, state lines disappear.... As to such purposes the State of New York does not exist."

We hold that the right to the funds or property in question became vested in the Soviet Government as the successor to the First Russian Insurance Co.; that this right has passed to the United States under the Litvinov Assignment; and that the United States is entitled to the property as against the corporation and the foreign creditors....

STONE, C.J., dissenting

I think the judgment should be affirmed....

... The only questions before us are whether New York has constitutional authority to adopt its own rules of law defining rights in property located in the state, and, if so, whether that authority has been curtailed by the exercise of a superior federal power by recognition of the Soviet Government and acceptance of its assignment to the United States of claims against American nationals, including the New York property.

I shall state my grounds for thinking that the pronouncements in the *Belmont* case, on which the Court relies for the answer to these questions, are without the support of reason or accepted principles of law. No one doubts that the Soviet decrees are the acts of the government of the Russian state, which is sovereign in its own territory, and that in consequence of our recognition of that government they will be so treated by our State Department. As such, when they affect property which was located in Russia at the time of their promulgation, they are subject to inquiry, if at all, only through our State Department and not in our courts. Underhill v. Hernandez, 168 U.S. 250; Oetjen v. Central Leather Co., 246 U.S. 297; Ricaud v. American Metal Co., 246 U.S. 304, 308–10; Salimoff & Co. v. Standard Oil Co., 262 N.Y. 220, 186 N.E. 679. But the property to which the New York judgment relates has at all relevant times been in New York....

At least since 1797, Barclay v. Russell, 3 Vesey, Jr., 424, 428, 433, the English courts have consistently held that foreign confiscatory decrees do not operate to transfer title to property located in England, even if the decrees were so intended, whether the foreign government has or has not been recognized by the British Government.... Never has the forum's refusal to follow foreign transfers of title to such property been considered inconsistent with the most friendly relations with the recognized foreign government, or even with an active military alliance at the time of the transfer....

I assume for present purposes that these sweeping alterations of the rights of states and of persons could be achieved by treaty or even executive agreement, although we are referred to no authority which would sustain such an exercise of power as is said to have been exerted here by mere assignment unratified by the Senate....

Recognition, like treaty making, is a political act, and both may be upon terms and conditions. But that fact no more forecloses this Court, where it is called upon to adjudicate private rights, from inquiry as to what those terms and conditions are than it precludes, in like circumstances, a court's ascertaining the true scope and meaning of a treaty....

We are not pointed to anything on the face of the documents or in the diplomatic correspondence which even suggests that the United States was to be placed in a better position, with respect to the claim which it now asserts, than was the Soviet Government and nationals. Nor is there any intimation in them that recognition was to give to prior public acts of the Soviet Government any greater extraterritorial effect than attaches to such acts occurring after recognition—acts which, by the common understanding of English and American courts, are ordinarily deemed to be without extraterritorial force, and which, in any event, have never before been considered to restrict the power of the states to apply their own rules of law to foreign-owned property within their territory. . . .

Notes and Questions

1. Reconsider the text of the U.S. Constitution. Is there recognition of the power of the President alone to create an executive agreement? If an executive agreement power can be implied (*e.g.*, from the power to recognize foreign governments, which is implied from the receipt of Ambassadors clause), does it follow that the agreement should be more than a political agreement at the international level or that it should have the force of law domestically? If power over foreign affairs is in the national government, does it follow that the President can exercise that power without Congress? During debates concerning the lawmaking function of treaties, the Framers where emphatic that the President should not create law alone, but could with the advice and consent of two thirds of the Senate.

2. Does the executive agreement in *Pink* function to cause a "taking" of property within the meaning of the Fifth Amendment? If so, who pays? Why didn't the assignment to the U.S. merely assign a claim, as opposed to title, to the property?

In *Belmont*, Justice Sutherland had stated that "the answer" to a Fifth Amendment claim concerning the taking of property "is that our Constitution, laws, and policies have no extraterritorial operation, unless in respect of our own citizens," adding: "[w]hat another country has done in the way of taking over property of its nationals, and especially of its corporations, is not a matter for judicial consideration here." 301 U.S. 324 (1937). Is that an answer? Concerning extraterritorial application, see Chapter 3. Was the Soviet "taking" "done"?

Note that the executive agreement in *Pink* reached private rights in property located within the United States and that it functionally executed an otherwise illegal confiscation of property. Confiscation (*i.e.*, a taking without payment of any amount, as opposed to expropriation) is unlawful under international and domestic U.S. law, whether attempted unilaterally by the Soviet Union (*see, e.g.*, Banco Nacional de Cuba v. Sabbatino, 376 U.S. 398 (1964); Banco Nacional de Cuba v. Farr, Whitlock & Co., 383 F.2d 166 (2d Cir.1967), *cert. denied*, 390 U.S. 956 (1968); Republic of Iraq v. First National City Bank, 353 F.2d 47 (2d Cir.1965), *cert. denied*, 382 U.S. 1027 (1966); Bandes v. Harlow & Jones, Inc., 826 F.Supp. 700 (S.D.N.Y. 1993) (when property is located within the U.S., foreign confiscatory decree will not be followed if taking violates U.S. laws or policy); *but see* Banco Nacional de Cuba v. Chemical Bank New York Trust Co., 658 F.2d 903 (2d Cir.1981)) or by the U.S. Executive (*see, e.g.*, United States v. Lee, 106 U.S. 196 (1882); Brown v. United States, 12 U.S. (8 Cranch) 110 (1814)). In any event, the Soviet confiscatory decree, by itself, could not reach property in the U.S. If one "thief" cannot confiscate property and another "thief" cannot confiscate property, should the agreement of the two to do so be lawful? Isn't such an agreement normally the basis for a conspiracy?

3. Reconsider the extract from *Brown v. United States* in Section 2 B 5 a. The sole executive agreement in *Pink* was directly operative domestically, or self-executing, functionally to change title to private property within the United States. Should the President have the power to seize or confiscate property within the U.S. by a sole executive agreement? *Brown* considered this to be an exclusive congressional power. Does *Pink* change *Brown*? Did Congress acquiesce with respect to the Litvinov Assignment in *Pink*?

4. Earlier, claims settlement had occurred by treaty, *i.e.*, with Senate involvement. *See, e.g.*, United States v. The Schooner Peggy, 5 U.S. (1 Cranch) 103 (1801). There, Chief Justice Marshall addressed another issue when stating that if a treaty gives up vested rights of individuals, it is for the government, not the courts, to decide whether proper compensation exists through such a claims settlement process. *Id.* at 110. A contrary view was expressed in Ware v. Hylton, 3 U.S. (3 Dall.) 199 (1796), by Justice Chase: "compensation ought to be made to all the debtors who have been injured by the treaty for the benefit of the public. This principle is recognized by the constitution.... That Congress had the power to sacrifice the rights and interests of private citizens to secure the safety or prosperity of the public, I have no doubt," but the government must pay. *Id.* at 245; see also *id.* at 279 (Iredell, J.). If the Executive has the power to settle claims of U.S. nationals against a foreign government by an executive agreement which operates at the international level to settle such claims by their waiver (*i.e.*, for zero cents on the dollar), presumably as a trade-off for some other benefit obtained for the United States, should the U.S. pay for a taking of property (*e.g.*, a chose in action or claim) or should the agreement also wipe out the claim for all domestic purposes? What happened to the Fifth Amendment issue in *Pink* or *Belmont*?

Concerning settlement of claims by executive agreement, apparently with implied approval by Congress of the general process of Executive settlement of claims, also see Dames and Moore v. Regan, 453 U.S. 654, 660–61, 674 n. 6, 688–89 (1981), extract addressed *infra* in Section 2 C 2 b; *id.* at 690–91 (Powell, J., concurring) (settlement by executive agreement, but unaddressed Fifth Amendment issues might arise); Gray v. United States, 12 Ct. Cl. 340, 346–47 (1886) (adding: "where a treaty is the law of the land, and as such affects the rights of parties litigating in court, that treaty as much binds those rights, and is as much to be regarded by the court, as an act of congress...."); *cf.* Shanghai Power Co. v. United States, 4 Cl.Ct. 237 (1983). Should "rights of parties litigating in court" be wiped out domestically by a sole executive agreement? Should judgments already obtained against a foreign state but which are being appealed be wiped out? Do these questions also raise concerns about independent judicial powers at stake and issues concerning the separation of powers? *See, e.g.*, Barbara Budros, Comment, *The Former American Hostages' Human Rights Claims Against Iran: Can They Be Waived?*, 4 HOUS. J. INT'L L. 101 (1981).

DAMES AND MOORE v. REGAN

453 U.S. 654 (1981).

REHNQUIST, J.

... On November 4, 1979, the American Embassy in Tehran was seized and our diplomatic personnel were captured and held hostage. In response to that crisis, President Carter, acting pursuant to the International Emergency Economic Powers Act, 91 Stat. 1626, 50 U.S.C. §§ 1701–1706 (1976 ed., Supp. III) (hereinafter IEEPA), declared a national emergency on November 14, 1979, and blocked the removal or transfer of "all property and interests in property of the Government of Iran, its instrumentalities and controlled entities and the Central Bank of Iran which are or become subject to the jurisdiction of the United States...." Exec. Order No. 12170, 3 CFR 457 (1980), note following 50 U.S.C. § 1701 (1976 ed., Supp. III). President Carter authorized the Secretary of the Treasury to promulgate regulations carrying out the blocking order. On November 15, 1979, the Treasury Department's Office of Foreign Assets Control issued a regulation providing that "[unless] licensed or authorized ... any attachment, judgment, decree, lien, execution, garnishment, or other judicial process is null and void with respect to any property in which on or since [November 14, 1979,] there existed an interest of Iran." 31 CFR § 535.203 (e) (1980). The regulations also made clear that any licenses or authorizations granted could be "amended, modified, or revoked at any time." § 535.805.

On November 26, 1979, the President granted a general license authorizing certain judicial proceedings against Iran but which did not allow the "entry of any judgment or of any decree or order of similar or analogous effect...." § 535.504 (a). On December 19, 1979, a clarifying regulation was issued stating that "the general authorization for judicial proceedings contained in § 535.504 (a) includes pre-judgment attachment." § 535.418.

On December 19, 1979, petitioner Dames & Moore filed suit in the United States District Court for the Central District of California against the Government of Iran, the Atomic Energy Organization of Iran, and a number of Iranian banks. In its complaint, petitioner alleged that its wholly owned subsidiary, Dames & Moore International, S.R.L., was a party to a written contract with the Atomic Energy Organization, and that the subsidiary's entire interest in the contract had been assigned to petitioner. Under the contract, the subsidiary was to conduct site studies for a proposed nuclear power plant in Iran. As provided in the terms of the contract, the Atomic Energy Organization terminated the agreement for its own convenience on June 30, 1979. Petitioner contended, however, that it was owed $3,436,694.30 plus interest for services performed under the contract prior to the date of termination. The District Court issued orders of attachment directed against property of the defendants, and the property of certain Iranian banks was then attached to secure any judgment that might be entered against them.

On January 20, 1981, the Americans held hostage were released by Iran pursuant to an Agreement entered into the day before and embodied in two Declarations of the Democratic and Popular Republic of Algeria. Declaration of the Government of the Democratic and Popular Republic of Algeria (App. to Pet. for Cert. 21–29), and Declaration of the Government of the Democratic and Popular Republic of Algeria Concerning the Settlement of Claims by the Government of the United States of America and the Government of the Islamic Republic of Iran (*id.*, at 30–35). The Agreement stated that "[it] is the purpose of [the United States and Iran] . . . to terminate all litigation as between the Government of each party and the nationals of the other, and to bring about the settlement and termination of all such claims through binding arbitration." *Id.*, at 21–22. In furtherance of this goal, the Agreement called for the establishment of an Iran–United States Claims Tribunal which would arbitrate any claims not settled within six months. Awards of the Claims Tribunal are to be "final and binding" and "enforceable . . . in the courts of any nation in accordance with its laws." *Id.*, at 32. Under the Agreement, the United States is obligated:

> "to terminate all legal proceedings in United States courts involving claims of United States persons and institutions against Iran and its state enterprises, to nullify all attachments and judgments obtained therein, to prohibit all further litigation based on such claims, and to bring about the termination of such claims through binding arbitration." *Id.*, at 22.

In addition, the United States must "act to bring about the transfer" by July 19, 1981, of all Iranian assets held in this country by American banks. *Id.*, at 24–25. One billion dollars of these assets will be deposited in a security account in the Bank of England, to the account of the Algerian Central Bank, and used to satisfy awards rendered against Iran by the Claims Tribunal. *Ibid.*

On January 19, 1981, President Carter issued a series of Executive Orders implementing the terms of the agreement. Exec. Orders Nos. 12276–12285, 46 Fed. Reg. 7913–7932. These Orders revoked all licenses permitting the exercise of "any right, power, or privilege" with regard to Iranian funds, securities, or deposits; "nullified" all non-Iranian interests in such assets acquired subsequent to the blocking order of November 14, 1979; and required those banks holding Iranian assets to transfer them "to the Federal Reserve Bank of New York, to be held or transferred as directed by the Secretary of the Treasury." Exec. Order No. 12279, 46 Fed. Reg. 7919.

On February 24, 1981, President Reagan issued an Executive Order in which he "ratified" the January 19th Executive Orders. Exec. Order No. 12294, 46 Fed. Reg. 14111. Moreover, he "suspended" all "claims which may be presented to the . . . Tribunal" and provided that such claims "shall have no legal effect in any action now pending in any court of the United States." *Ibid.* The suspension of any particular claim terminates if the Claims Tribunal determines that it has no jurisdiction over that claim; claims are discharged for all purposes when the Claims Tribunal either awards some recovery and that amount is paid, or determines that no recovery is due....

... In its complaint, petitioner alleged that the actions of the President and the Secretary of the Treasury implementing the Agreement with Iran were beyond their statutory and constitutional powers and, in any event, were unconstitutional to the extent they adversely affect petitioner's final judgment against the Government of Iran and the Atomic Energy Organization, its execution of that judgment in the State of Washington, its prejudgment attachments, and its ability to continue to litigate against the Iranian banks. *Id.*, at 1–12. On May 28, 1981, the District Court denied petitioner's motion for a preliminary injunction and dismissed petitioner's complaint for failure to state a claim upon which relief could be granted. *Id.*, at 106–107....

In nullifying post-November 14, 1979, attachments and directing those persons holding blocked Iranian funds and securities to transfer them to the Federal Reserve Bank of New York for ultimate transfer to Iran, President Carter cited five sources of express or inherent power. The Government, however, has principally relied on § 203 of the IEEPA, 91 Stat. 1626, 50 U.S.C. § 1702 (a)(1) (1976 ed., Supp. III), as authorization for these actions....

The Government contends that the acts of "nullifying" the attachments and ordering the "transfer" of the frozen assets are specifically authorized by the plain language of the above statute. The two Courts of Appeals that have considered the issue agreed with this contention....

Although we have concluded that the IEEPA constitutes specific congressional authorization to the President to nullify the attachments and order the transfer of Iranian assets, there remains the question of the President's authority to suspend claims pending in American courts. Such claims have, of course, an existence apart from the attachments which accompanied them. In terminating these claims through Executive Order No. 12294, the President purported to act under authority of both the IEEPA and 22 U.S.C. § 1732, the so-called "Hostage Act." 46 Fed. Reg. 14111 (1981).

We conclude that although the IEEPA authorized the nullification of the attachments, it cannot be read to authorize the suspension of the claims. The claims of American citizens against Iran are not in themselves transactions involving Iranian property or efforts to exercise any rights with respect to such property. An in personam lawsuit, although it might eventually be reduced to judgment and that judgment might be executed upon, is an effort to establish liability and fix damages and does not focus on any particular property within the jurisdiction. The terms of the IEEPA therefore do not authorize the President to suspend claims in American courts. This is the view of all the courts which have considered the question....

The Hostage Act, passed in 1868, provides:

> "Whenever it is made known to the President that any citizen of the United States has been unjustly deprived of his liberty by or under the authority of any foreign government, it shall be the duty of the President forthwith to demand of that government the reasons of such imprisonment; and if it appears to be wrongful and in violation of the rights of American citizenship, the President shall forthwith demand the release of such citizen, and if the release so demanded is unreasonably delayed or refused, the President shall use such means, not amounting to acts of war, as he may think necessary and proper to obtain or effectuate the release; and all the facts and proceedings relative thereto shall as soon as practicable be communicated by the President to Congress." Rev. Stat. § 2001, 22 U.S.C. § 1732.

We are reluctant to conclude that this provision constitutes specific authorization to the President to suspend claims in American courts. Although the broad language of the Hostage Act suggests it may cover this case, there are several difficulties with such a view. The legislative history indicates that the Act was passed in response to a situation unlike the recent Iranian crisis. Congress in 1868 was concerned with the activity of certain countries refusing to recognize the citizenship of naturalized Americans traveling abroad, and repatriating such citizens against their will. *See, e.g.*, Cong. Globe, 40th Cong., 2d Sess., 4331 (1868) (Sen. Fessenden); *id.*, at 4354 (Sen. Conness); see also 22 U.S.C. § 1731. These countries were not interested in returning the citizens in exchange for any sort of ransom. This also explains the reference in the Act to imprisonment "in violation of the rights of American citizenship." Although the Iranian hostage-taking violated international law and common decency, the hostages were not seized out of any refusal to recognize their American citizenship—they were seized precisely because of their American citizenship. The legislative history is also somewhat ambiguous on the question whether Congress contemplated Presidential action such as that involved here or rather simply reprisals directed against the offending foreign country and its citizens. *See, e.g.*, Cong. Globe, 40th Cong., 2d Sess., 4205 (1868); American Int'l Group, Inc. v. Islamic Republic of Iran, ... 657 F.2d, at 452–453 (opinion of Mikva, J.).

Concluding that neither the IEEPA nor the Hostage Act constitutes specific authorization of the President's action suspending claims, however, is not to say that these statutory provisions are entirely irrelevant to the question of the validity of the President's action. We think both statutes highly relevant in the looser sense of indicating congressional acceptance of a broad scope for executive action in circumstances such as those presented in this case. As noted ... the IEEPA delegates broad authority to the President to act in times of national emergency with respect to property of a foreign country. The Hostage Act similarly indicates congressional willingness that the President have broad discretion when responding to the hostile acts of foreign sovereigns....

Although we have declined to conclude that the IEEPA or the Hostage Act directly authorizes the President's suspension of claims for the reasons noted, we cannot ignore the general tenor of Congress' legislation in this area in trying to determine whether the President is acting alone or at least with the acceptance of Congress. As we have noted, Congress cannot anticipate and legislate with regard to every possible action the President may find it necessary to take or every possible situation in which he might act. Such failure of Congress specifically to delegate authority does not, "especially ... in the areas of foreign policy and national security," imply "congressional disapproval" of action taken by the Executive.... On the contrary, the enactment of legislation closely related to the question of the President's authority in a particular case which evinces legislative intent to accord the President broad discretion may be considered to "invite" "measures on independent presidential responsibility," *Youngstown*, 343 U.S., at 637 (Jackson, J., concurring). At least this is so where there is no contrary indication of legislative intent and when, as here, there is a history of congressional acquiescence in conduct of the sort engaged in by the President. It is to that history which we now turn.

Not infrequently in affairs between nations, outstanding claims by nationals of one country against the government of another country are "sources of friction" between the two sovereigns. United States v. Pink, 315 U.S. 203, 225 (1942). To resolve these difficulties, nations have often entered into agreements settling the claims of their respective nationals. As one treatise writer puts it, international agreements settling claims by nationals of one state against the government of another "are established international practice reflecting traditional international theory." L. HENKIN, FOREIGN AFFAIRS AND THE CONSTITUTION 262 (1972). Consistent with that principle, the United States has repeatedly exercised its sovereign authority to settle the claims of its nationals against foreign countries. Though those settlements have sometimes been made by treaty, there has also been a longstanding practice of settling such claims by executive agreement without the advice and consent of the Senate. Under such agreements, the President has agreed to renounce or extinguish claims of United States nationals against foreign governments in return for lump-sum payments or the establishment of arbitration procedures. To be sure, many of these settlements were encouraged by the United States claimants themselves, since a claimant's only hope of obtaining any payment at all might lie in having his Government negotiate a diplomatic settlement on his behalf. But it is also undisputed that the "United States has sometimes disposed of the claims of its citizens without their consent, or even without consultation with them, usually without exclusive regard for their interests, as distinguished from those of the nation as a whole." HENKIN, *supra*, at 262–263. *Accord*, RESTATEMENT (SECOND) OF FOREIGN RELATIONS LAW OF THE UNITED STATES § 213 (1965) (President "may waive or settle a claim against a foreign state ... [even] without the consent of the [injured] national"). It is clear that the practice of settling claims continues today. Since 1952, the President has entered into at least 10 binding settlements with foreign nations, including an $80 million settlement with the People's Republic of China.

Crucial to our decision today is the conclusion that Congress has implicitly approved the practice of claim settlement by executive agreement. This is best demonstrated by Congress' enactment of the International Claims Settlement Act of 1949, 64 Stat. 13, as amended, 22 U.S.C. § 1621 *et seq.* (1976 ed. and Supp. IV). The Act had two purposes: (1) to allocate to United States nationals funds received in the course of an executive claims settlement with Yugoslavia, and (2) to provide a procedure whereby funds resulting from future settlements could be distributed. To achieve these ends Congress created the International Claims Commission, now the Foreign Claims Settlement Commission, and gave it jurisdiction to make final and binding decisions with respect to claims by United States nationals against settlement funds. 22 U.S.C. § 1623 (a). By creating a procedure to implement future settlement agreements, Congress placed its stamp of approval on such agreements. Indeed, the legislative history of the Act observed that the United States was seeking settlements with countries other than Yugoslavia and that the bill contemplated settlements of a similar nature in the future....

Over the years Congress has frequently amended the International Claims Settlement Act to provide for particular problems arising out of settlement agreements, thus demonstrating Congress' continuing acceptance of the President's claim settlement authority....

... Petitioner thus insists that the President, by suspending its claims, has circumscribed the jurisdiction of the United States courts in violation of Art. III of the Constitution.

We disagree. In the first place, we do not believe that the President has attempted to divest the federal courts of jurisdiction. Executive Order No. 12294 purports only to "suspend" the claims, not divest the federal court of "jurisdiction." As we read the Executive Order, those claims not within the jurisdiction of the Claims Tribunal will "revive" and become judicially enforceable in United States courts. This case, in short, illustrates the difference between modifying federal-court jurisdiction and directing the courts to apply a different rule of law. See United States v. Schooner Peggy, 1 Cranch 103 (1801). The President has exercised the power, acquiesced in by Congress, to settle claims and, as such, has simply effected a change in the substantive law governing the lawsuit....

Just as importantly, Congress has not disapproved of the action taken here. Though Congress has held hearings on the Iranian Agreement itself, Congress has not enacted legislation, or even passed a resolution, indicating its displeasure with the Agreement. Quite the contrary, the relevant Senate Committee has stated that the establishment of the Tribunal is "of vital importance to the United States." S. Rep. No. 97–71, p. 5 (1981). We are thus clearly not confronted with a situation in which Congress has in some way resisted the exercise of Presidential authority.

Finally, we re-emphasize the narrowness of our decision. We do not decide that the President possesses plenary power to settle claims, even as against foreign governmental entities. As the Court of Appeals for the First Circuit stressed, "[the] sheer magnitude of such a power, considered against the background of the diversity and complexity of modern international trade, cautions against any broader construction of authority than is necessary." Chas. T. Main Int'l, Inc. v. Khuzestan Water & Power Authority, 651 F.2d, at 814. But where, as here, the settlement of claims has been determined to be a necessary incident to the resolution of a major foreign policy dispute between our country and another, and where, as here, we can conclude that Congress acquiesced in the President's action, we are not prepared to say that the President lacks the power to settle such claims.

We do not think it appropriate at the present time to address petitioner's contention that the suspension of claims, if authorized, would constitute a taking of property in violation of the Fifth Amendment to the United States Constitution in the absence of just compensation. Both petitioner and the Government concede that the question whether the suspension of the claims constitutes a taking is not ripe for review. However, this contention, and the possibility that the President's actions may effect a taking of petitioner's property, make ripe for adjudication the question whether petitioner will have a remedy at law in the Court of Claims under the Tucker Act, 28 U.S.C. § 1491 (1976 ed., Supp. III), in such an event. That the fact and extent of the taking in this case is yet speculative is inconsequential because "there must be at the time of taking 'reasonable, certain and adequate provision for obtaining compensation.' " ...

... Accordingly, to the extent petitioner believes it has suffered an unconstitutional taking by the suspension of the claims, we see no jurisdictional obstacle to an appropriate action in the United States Court of Claims under the Tucker Act....

Notes and Questions

1. Concerning the "taking" issue and due compensation, recall Section 2 B 4 b, note 3.

2. Was the executive agreement in *Dames & Moore* a "sole" executive agreement? What impact might the implied will of Congress have on your conclusion? Should the executive agreement prevail against prior federal statutes (*e.g.*, authorizing lawsuits in federal courts)? *See also* Section 2 E 1 b.

3. Was the executive agreement in *Dames & Moore* partly an unconstitutional invasion of judicial power because it had also voided claims of the U.S. hostages against Iran, some of which were pending in U.S. courts and/or had reached a judgment against Iran? *See, e.g.*, Budros, *The Former American Hostages' Human Rights Claims, supra*.

In Plaut v. Spendthrift Farm, Inc., 514 U.S. 211 (1995), the Supreme Court invalidated an Act of Congress mandating the reopening of certain final judgments in security fraud cases, on grounds that the Act invaded the core Article III powers of the federal judiciary. Should an executive agreement concerning claims settlements be treated differently than a statute concerning securities fraud litigation?

4. With respect to Executive control of claims of U.S. nationals at the international level, *see also* Neely v. Henkel, 180 U.S. 109 (1901); Briehl v. Dulles, 248 F.2d 561 (D.C.Cir.1957); Ware v. Hylton, 3 U.S. (3 Dall.) 199, 260 (1796) (Iredell, J.) (pursuit of individuals' claims at the international level "depends on the discretion and sense of duty of their own government"); *In re* World War II Era Japanese Forced Labor Litigation, 114 F.Supp.2d 939, 948–49 (N.D. Cal. 2000) (Treaty of Peace with Japan settled private claims even against private companies).

D. Customary International Law in the U.S. Domestic Process

1. Restraining Executive Abuse

Concerning the incorporation of customary international law and its impact on presidential powers, duties, and responsibilities, also recall Section 2 B 4 b, at pp. 240–241.

9 **OP. ATT'Y GEN.** 356, 357, 362–63 (1859)

. . . [A] law which operates on the interests and rights of other States or peoples must be made and executed according to the law of nations. A sovereign who tramples upon the public law of the world cannot excuse himself by pointing to a provision of his own municipal code. The municipal code of each country is the offspring of its own sovereign will; and public law must be paramount to local law in every question where local laws are in conflict. . . . [and what you, the President,] will do must of course depend upon the law of our own country, as controlled and modified by the law of nations.

UNITED STATES v. SMITH

27 F. Cas. 1192, 1220–21 (argument of counsel
and questions of Paterson, J.), 1228–31.
(C.C.D.N.Y. 1806) (No. 16,342) (Paterson, J.).

[Editors' note: Col. William S. Smith, son-in-law of former President John Adams, was indicted for violating the Neutrality Act of 1794. He claimed that he had authority to act from President Thomas Jefferson and Secretary of State James Madison in support of an expedition to liberate Venezuela that was interrupted in Caracas. Smith had been raising money, outfitting a merchant ship with weapons, and enlisting recruits for the expedition. See Christopher Stone, " 'Original Intent' and Following Orders," L.A. Times, Jul. 22, 1987, pt. II, at 5.]

[Counsel for Smith] . . . [A]s to the acts charged in the indictment, they are only preparatory, and independent of any actual hostility. As to them, the state of the country forms an irresistible justification both of

Colonel Smith and of the president. The constitution indeed does not allow the latter to declare war, but does it forbid his providing and preparing the means of carrying it on, while congress are in actual and secret deliberation whether they shall declare war against a nation that is committing and provoking hostilities? Spain, indeed, was technically at peace by the treaty of San Lorenzo, but she was actually at war by the law of nations; she had broken that treaty, plundered our ships, invaded our territories, and carried our citizens from thence as prisoners by military force....

The circumstances of the times, we have shown, justified the president in giving his approbation, and my client, under that approbation, in providing and preparing the means of a military enterprise against Spain. And surely no enterprise could be more useful or effectual for drawing the enemy from our southern and western frontiers; none more worthy of the exalted and philosophic mind of our chief magistrate; none more consonant to the enlightened and philosophic views of society and politics, which he has exhibited to the world, than an expedition to liberate South America; to destroy at once Spanish tyranny and power on our own continent; to enfranchise, by one effort, millions of our fellow creatures from the most frightful bondage; and to lay the foundations, in so large a portion of the globe, for the freedom and the happiness of man!

PATERSON, CIRCUIT JUSTICE. You state in the affidavit that it was done with the knowledge and approbation of the president, but it is stated in the affidavit that he authorized the fitting out of the expedition?

[Counsel for Smith] I conceive it was not necessary; for though I have argued upon the effects of an authorization, it was only to show that the argument of the adverse counsel went much too far, when they contended that the president could not authorize any such measure. For our defence, it will be only necessary to shown that the president was, under the circumstances of the times, warranted to provide and prepare the means for a military expedition; and that, in what he might do, we acted with his knowledge and approbation.... The knowledge and approbation of the chief magistrate and heads of departments, if we shall prove them to have been sufficiently express and positive, will amount to justification; but even if we shall fail in establishing them to that extent, they will still afford very powerful inducements for mitigating the punishment.... In this case we do not rely upon mere general and vague approbation of the measure; we will show that approbation was given to this very defendant's being concerned in it....

PATERSON, CIRCUIT JUSTICE. It appears to the court, that James Madison, secretary of state, Robert Smith, secretary of the navy, and Jacob Wagner and William Thornton, who are officers under the department of the secretary of state, have been duly served with subpoenas to attend as witnesses on the part of the defendant, and that they do not attend pursuant to the process of the court.... [T]he defendant has come forward with an affidavit stating the material facts, which he conceives he will be able to prove by the evidence of Mr. Madison, Mr. Smith, Mr. Wagner and Mr. Thornton....

... The evidence must be pertinent to the issue. The witnesses must be material. If the evidence be not pertinent, nor the witnesses material, the court ought not to receive either. Let us test the affidavit of the defendant by this principle or rule. The defendant is indicted for providing the means, to wit, men and money, for a military enterprise against the dominions of the king of Spain with whom the United States are at peace, against the form of a statute in such case made and provided. He has pleaded not guilty; and to evince his innocence, to justify his infraction of the act of congress, or to purge his guilt, he offers evidence to prove, that this military enterprise was begun, prepared, and set on foot with the knowledge and approbation of the executive department of our government. Sitting here in our judicial capacities, we should listen with caution to a suggestion of this kind, because the president of the United States is bound by the constitution to "take care that the laws be faithfully executed." These are the words of the instrument; and, therefore, it is to be presumed that he would not countenance the violation of any statute, and particularly if such violation consisted in expeditions of a warlike nature against friendly powers. The law, indeed, presumes, that every officer faithfully executes his duties, until the contrary be proved....

... Are the contents of the affidavit pertinent—are they material—are they relevant? The fifth section of the statute, on which the indictment is founded, is expressed in general, unqualified terms; it contains no condition, no exception; it invests no dispensing power in any officer or person whatever. Thus it reads: "And be it further enacted and declared, that if any person shall, within the territory or jurisdiction of the United States, begin or set on foot, or provide or prepare the means for, any military expedition or enterprise to be carried on from thence against the territory or dominion of any foreign prince or state with whom the United States are at peace, every such person so offending shall, upon conviction, be adjudged guilty of a high misdemeanor, and shall suffer fine and imprisonment at the discretion of the court, in which the conviction shall be had, so as that such fine shall not exceed three thousand dollars, nor the term of imprisonment be more than three years." The section [of the Neutrality Act] which I have read is declaratory of the law of nations.... This fifth section, which prohibits military enterprises against nations with which the United States are at peace, imparts no dispensing power to the president. Does the constitution give it? Far from it, for it explicitly directs that he shall "take care that the laws be faithfully executed." This instrument, which measures out the powers and defines the duties of the president, does not vest in him any authority to set on foot a military expedition against a nation with which the United States are at peace. And if a private individual, even with the knowledge and approbation of this high and preeminent officer of our government, should set on foot such a military expedition, how can he expect to be exonerated from the obligation of the law? Who holds the power of dispensation? True, a nolle prosequi may be entered, a pardon may be granted; but these presume criminality, presume guilt, presume amenability to judicial investigation and punishment, which are very different from a power to dispense with the law.

Supposing then that every syllable of the affidavit is true, of what avail can it be on the present occasion? Of what use or benefit can it be to the defendant in a court of law? Does it speak by way of justification? The president of the United States cannot control the statute, nor dispense with its execution, and still less can he authorize a person to do what the law forbids. If he could, he would render the execution of the laws dependent on his will and pleasure; which is a doctrine that has not been set up, and will not meet with any supporters in our government. In this particular, the law is paramount. Who has dominion over it? None but the legislature; and even they are not without their limitation in our republic. Will it be pretended that the president could rightfully grant a dispensation and license to any of our citizens to carry on a war against a nation with whom the United States are at peace? Ingenious and learned counsel may imagine, and put a number of cases in the wide field of conjecture; but we are to take facts as we find them, and to argue from the existing state of things at the time. If we were at war with Spain, there is an end to the indictment; but, if at peace, what individual could lawfully make war or carry on a military expedition against the dominions of his Catholic majesty? The indictment is founded on a state of peace, and such state is presumed to continue until the contrary appears. A state of war is not set up in the affidavit. If, then, the president knew and approved of the military expedition set forth in the indictment against a prince with whom we are at peace, it would not justify the defendant in a court of law, nor discharge him from the binding force of the act of congress; because the president does not possess a dispensing power. Does he possess the power of making war? That power is exclusively vested in congress; for, by the eighth section of the 1st article of the constitution, it is ordained, that congress shall have power to declare war, grant letters of marque and reprisal, raise and support armies, provide and maintain a navy, and to provide for calling forth the militia to execute the laws of the Union, suppress insurrections, and repel invasions. And we accordingly find, that congress have been so circumspect and provident in regard to the last three particulars, that they have from time to time vested the president of the United States with ample powers....

JORDAN J. PAUST, INTERNATIONAL LAW AS LAW OF THE UNITED STATES

143–46 (1996), revised in 169–73 (2 ed. 2003).

Perhaps the earliest judicial recognition of the fact that the Executive is bound by international law [treaty-based or customary] is that of Justice Iredell in *Ware v. Hylton* [3 U.S. (3 Dall.) 199 (1796)–extract in this chapter, Section 2 F 1], in which the Justice affirmed in a clear and trenchant manner: a treaty is obligatory "on all, as well on the Legislative, Executive, and Judicial Departments . . . as on every individual of the nation." Later, following a lower federal court decision in 1799, Representative Marshall (the year before he became Chief Justice) also recognized that the President is bound to execute a treaty because it is supreme federal law; and in 1800, Justice Chase, while sitting on circuit, added:

> If the president, . . . by this treaty, was bound to give this Nash up to justice, he was so bound by the law; for the treaty is the law of the land. . . . His delivery was the necessary act of the president, which he was by the treaty and the law of the land, bound to perform; . . . [the] president . . . [has a] duty . . . [of] carrying a solemn treaty into effect. [United States v. Cooper, 25 F. Cas. 631, 641–42 (C.C.D.Pa.1800)]

Justice Chase also affirmed in 1800 that war's "extent and operations are . . . restricted by the *jus belli*, forming a part of the law of nations." [Bas v. Tingy, 4 U.S. (4 Dall.) 37, 43 (1800)]

In 1801, Chief Justice Marshall recognized that if the President were to condemn a vessel in violation of a treaty, which is supreme law of the land, it "would be a direct infraction of that law, and, of consequence, improper"; and in 1804, he affirmed that if the President were to order a violation of international law to occur, such an executive order would not be an excuse or defense for lower officials. By 1806, Justice Paterson, sitting on circuit, had affirmed similarly: "the law is paramount," and the President, in exercising the war power, cannot "authorize a person to do what the law [either domestic or international] forbids." And in 1813, Justice Story, sitting on circuit, addressed a claim that the President might be able to violate the law of nations, stating: although it was "argued, on behalf of the United States, in some of the causes before the court, that the authority of the president" delegated by Congress included "a power to abridge the general rights of capture" under the law of nations, "I cannot yield to this construction." The constitutional duty of the President, law and authority, as well as prior judicial precedent, had been saved. Indeed, precedent relative to an adequate reading of *Brown v. United States* [12 U.S. (8 Cranch) 110 (1814)] had been set.

Brown, the reader may recall, is one of the cases referred to in *The Paquete Habana* (two of the very few judicial opinions addressed by writers on this question). Professor Charney has argued that *Brown* provides "the clearest case" in which the President recognizably has discretion to engage in a "violation of international law" because Chief Justice Marshall stated that mere " 'usage is a guide which the sovereign follows or abandons at his will.' "As noted in other writings, however, mere usage is certainly not the equivalent of international law but is merely a long-term practice, which, of course, is not per se binding on the United States. As the quoted language actually recognizes, it is merely "a guide which the sovereign" can follow or abandon. Further, in

Brown, it was also recognized that mere "usage . . . is not an immutable rule of law," but "is a question rather of policy than of law." Indeed, as documented in other writings, the various opinions of the Justices in *Brown* and the holding actually affirm that the President is bound by international law. Moreover, no other reading of Chief Justice Marshall's opinion in *Brown* could be consistent even with the prior recognitions of the Chief Justice noted above, much less the thrust of relevant judicial decisionmaking up to 1814. *Brown* also recognized that the President is not the "sovereign" in the United States and that the legislature was delegated such a sovereign power—it is a power "not of the executive or judiciary"—an important point in this sort of debate that seems conveniently to have been forgotten.

What also seems to have been forgotten is the fact that the majority opinion in *The Paquete Habana*, however ambiguous elsewhere, openly affirmed that although Congress may authorize an infraction of, merely, the "usage" of nations, such an infraction cannot be made "even by direction of the Executive, without express authority from Congress." Since the President cannot order a violation even of "usage," it seems obvious that *The Paquete Habana* affirms that the President is bound by international law.

After the decision in *Brown*, an opinion of an attorney general rightly declared that the President has a duty to enforce and to obey "not merely . . . treaties of the United States, but those general laws of nations," laws which are "the laws of the country; to the enforcement of which, the President, charged by his office with the execution of all our laws, . . . is bound to look." [1 Op. Att'y Gen. 566, 571–72 (1822)] Two years later, the Court's opinion in *The Apollon* [22 U.S. (9 Wheat.) 362 (1824)] recognized:

> It would be monstrous to suppose that our revenue officers were authorized to enter into foreign ports and territories, for the purpose of seizing vessels which had offended against our laws. It cannot be presumed that Congress would voluntarily justify such a clear violation of the law of nations.

In 1841, counsel had successfully argued for individual claimants that neither the "federal executive" nor our judicial tribunals have "the power of making our nation accessories to . . . atrocious violations of human right." Even a Michigan court in 1843 recognized that a "duty" is imposed upon the President by treaties, and that with regard to a particular treaty, "he could execute [such duty] without an act of Congress; the treaty, when ratified, being the supreme law of the land, which the President was bound to see executed." In 1855, Justice Curtis, while sitting on circuit, emphatically affirmed that "treaties must continue to operate as part of our municipal law, and be obeyed by the people, applied by the judiciary and executed by the President, while they remain unrepealed," adding: "no body other than Congress possesses" the power to "refuse to execute a treaty." And in 1859, another opinion of an attorney general recognized that the public law of nations "must be paramount to local law in every question where local laws are in conflict" and that what the President "will do *must* of course depend upon the law of our country, *as controlled* and modified by the law of nations."

In 1862, the U.S. Supreme Court recognized once again that the President "is bound to take care that the laws be faithfully executed," including, in context, the customary laws of war. And in 1865, an opinion of the attorney general acknowledged that "the law of nations ... [is] a part of the law of the land," adding: "laws of nations ... are of binding force upon the departments and citizens of the Government.... Congress cannot abrogate them or authorize their infraction. The Constitution does not permit this Government [to do so either]." Importantly also, in 1884, the Supreme Court reaffirmed earlier language that " 'treaties must continue to operate as part of our municipal law, and be obeyed by the people, applied by the judiciary and executed by the President, while they continue unrepealed.' "In 1890, the Court noted in addition that the duty faithfully to execute treaties implicitly includes all "obligations growing out of ... our international relations." Five years later, a federal district court reaffirmed that "the duty and obligation rests upon the executive branch" to comply with a treaty.

Thus, by 1900, the date of Justice Gray's opinion in *The Paquete Habana*, all relevant trends in legal opinion from the time of the Framers to the 20th century clearly supported the expectation that the President is bound by supreme federal law whether that law is customary or treaty-based. Indeed, by 1900, the point was simply beyond responsible debate. Importantly, nothing in the text of the Constitution would allow the President to violate the law, including international law; no Founder is known to have declared or to have even suggested that the President could violate the law of nations or treaties; and no opinion of the judiciary or the Attorneys General in the Eighteenth or Nineteenth centuries had expressed the view that the President could violate the law of nations, treaties or customary international law. All relevant patterns of expectation affirmed just the opposite. Moreover, Justice Gray's opinion in 1900, however abused, recognizably affirmed that the President is bound by international law. In two other Supreme Court opinions, in 1906 and 1936, the Court also affirmed that the President has no authority or power lawfully to act inconsistently with a treaty obligation. Also in 1936, Justice Sutherland, in a famous opinion otherwise articulating significant and far-reaching powers of the President in foreign relations, affirmed two profoundly compelling limits to such powers: "operations of the nation in ... ["foreign"] territory *must* be governed by treaties ... and the principles of international law." In 1984, Justice O'Connor also recognized that although the political branches may terminate a treaty, power "delegated by Congress to the Executive Branch" as well as a relevant congressional-executive "arrangement" must not be "exercised in a manner inconsistent with ... international law."

Note

1. Other cases and opinions recognize that the President and other members of the executive branch, including the military, are bound by the laws of war. *See, e.g.*, U.S. Const., art. II, § 3 (the President is constitutionally bound faithfully to execute the "Laws"); Dooley v. United States, 182 U.S. 222, 231 (1901); The Paquete Habana, 189 U.S. 453, 464 (1903); *id.*, 175 U.S. 677, 698 ("law of war"), 700, 708, 711, 714 (1900); New Orleans v. The Steamship Co., 87 U.S. (20 Wall.) 387, 394 (1874) (limits exist "in the laws and usages of war"); Miller v. United States, 78 U.S. (11 Wall.) 268, 314–16 (1870) (Field, J., dissenting); The Prize Cases, 67 U.S. (2 Black) 635, 667–68, 671 (1863) (the President is bound to see that the laws are executed, including in context the "laws of war," "*jure belli*"); Brown v. United States, 12 U.S. (8 Cranch) 110, 149, 153 (1814) (Story, J., dissenting); Talbot v. Seeman, 5 U.S. (1 Cranch) 1, 28 (1801) (Marshall, C.J.); Bas v. Tingy, 4 U.S. (4 Dall.) 37, 43 (1800) (Chase, J.) (war's "extent and operations are ... restricted by the *jus belli*, forming part of the law of nations"); Vietnam Ass'n for Victims of Agent Orange/Dioxin v. Dow Chemical Co. (*In re* Agent Orange Prod. Liab. Litig.), 373 F.Supp.2d 7, 99 (E.D.N.Y. 2005); 11 Op. Att'y Gen. 297, 299–300 (1865); JORDAN J. PAUST, INTERNATIONAL LAW AS LAW OF THE UNITED STATES 7–9, 67–70, 169–73, 175, 488–89, 493–94 (2 ed. 2003), and numerous cases, Attorney General opinions, and unanimous views of Founders and Framers cited; Paust, *Judicial Power To Determine the Status and Rights of Persons Detained Without Trial*, 44 HARV. INT'L L.J. 503, 514, 517–22 (2003); Jordan J. Paust, Paquete *and the President: Rediscovering the Brief for the United States*, 34 VA. J. INT'L L. 981 (1994); *see also* United States v. Curtiss–Wright Export Co., 299 U.S. 304, 318 (1936) ("operations of the nation in ... ["foreign"] territory must be governed by treaties ... [as well as] the principles of international law"); Herrera v. United States, 222 U.S. 558, 572 (1912), quoting Planters' Bank v. Union Bank, 83 U.S. (16 Wall.) 483, 495 (1873) ("it was there decided that the military commander at New Orleans 'had power to do all that the laws of war permitted,' " adding: "if it was done in violation of the laws of war ... , it was done in wrong." *Id.* at 573.); United States v. Adams, 74 U.S. 463 (1869) (argument of counsel: "The war powers of Congress, and of the President, as commander-in-chief ... , and (as a necessary consequence) of his subordinate commanding generals ... , are unlimited in time of war, except by the law of war itself."); Mitchell v. Harmony, 54 U.S. (13 How.) 115, 134–35, 137 (1852) (illegal orders provide no defense); *Ex parte* Duncan, 153 F.2d 943, 956 (9th Cir. 1946) (Stephens, J., dissenting) (occupation commander's "will is law subject only to the application of the laws of war"); United States v. American Gold Coin, 24 F. Cas. 780, 782 (C.C.D. Mo. 1868) (No. 14,439) (it became necessary for the national government to take every possible measure against an enemy "and at the same time [to use measures] consistent with the laws of war"); Elgee's Adm'r v. Lovell, 8 F. Cas. 449, 454 (C.C.D. Mo. 1865) (No. 4,344) (Miller, J., on circuit) (concerning the "law of nations, ... no proclamation of the president can change or modify this law"); United States *ex rel.* Henderson v. Wright, 28 F. Cas. 796, 798 (C.C.W.D. Pa. 1863) (No. 16,777) (war cartel is like a treaty and "[u]nder the law of nations the president could not [do a particular act], and what the president of the United States cannot do, will not be assumed by the judiciary"); Johnson v.

Twenty–One Bales, 13 F. Cas. 855, 863 (C.C.D.N.Y. 1814) (No. 7,417) (courts cannot construe Executive orders so as to abrogate a right under the law of war); Dias v. The Revenge, 7 F. Cas. 637, 639 (C.C.D. Pa. 1814) (No. 3,877) (Washington, J., on circuit) (concerning improper conduct under the laws of war, the owner of a privateer cannot "shield himself, by saying that the privateer . . . acts under the president's instructions"); 8 Op. Att'y Gen. 365 (1857) (re: *jus belli*, "[t]he commander of the invading, occupying, or conquering army, rules . . . with supreme power, limited only by international law, and the orders of the sovereign or government"); State *ex rel.* Tod v. Court of Common Please, 15 Ohio St. 377, 389–91 (1864) ("There is no limitation placed upon this grant of the power to carry on war, except those contained in the laws of war. . . . If a party bring a suit against the president, or any one of his subordinates, . . . do not questions at once arise, of the extent and lawfulness of the power exercised, and of the right to shield the subaltern acting under orders, and hold his superior alone responsible? And are not these constitutional questions? If so, then, the case is one 'arising under the constitution' [for federal courts]. . . . The controversy is merely as to the occasions and manner of its exercise, and as to the parties who should be held responsible for its abuse. In time of war, . . . he possesses and exercises such powers, not in spite of the constitution and laws of the United States, or in derogation from their authority, but in virtue thereof and in strict subordination thereto. . . . And in time of war, without any special legislation, not the commander-in-chief only, but every commander . . . is lawfully empowered by the constitution and laws of the United States to do whatever is necessary, and is sanctioned by the laws of war. . . . The president is responsible for the abuse of this power. He is responsible civilly and criminally. . . ."); *In re* Kemp, 16 Wis. 359, 392 ("His duty is still only to execute the laws, by the modes which the laws themselves prescribe; to wage the war by employing the military power according to the laws of war."), 395 ("Within those limits let the war power rage, controlled by nothing but the laws of war.") (1863); Ward v. Broadwell, 1 N.M. 75, 79 (1854) (quoting President Polk: " 'The power to declare war against a foreign country, and to prosecute it according to the laws of war, . . . exists under our constitution. When congress has declared that war exists with a foreign nation, the laws of war apply . . . and it becomes the duty of the president . . . to prosecute it' "; citing Message of the President of July 24, 1848, Exec. Doc. No. 70). That the President is also bound by other forms of international law, *see, e.g.*, PAUST, *supra* at 169–73. Moreover, judicial power clearly exists to review the legality of Executive decisions and actions in time of war in the face of Executive views to the contrary, and the laws of war are clearly judicially enforceable. *See, e.g.*, cases cited above; PAUST, *supra* at 170–73, 175, 488–90, 493–94; Paust, *Judicial Power*, *supra* at 514, 518–24, and cases cited.

THE PAQUETE HABANA

175 U.S. 677 (1900).

[recall the portion of Justice Gray's opinion in Chapter 1]

International law is part of our law, and must be ascertained and administered by the courts of justice of appropriate jurisdiction, as often as questions of right depending upon it are duly presented for their determination. For this purpose, where there is no treaty, and no controlling executive or legislative act or judicial decision, resort must be had to the customs and usages of civilized nations; and, as evidence of these, to the works of jurists and commentators, who by years of labor, research and experience, have made themselves peculiarly well acquainted with the subjects of which they treat. Such works are resorted to by judicial tribunals, not for the speculations of their authors concerning what the law ought to be, but for trustworthy evidence of what the law really is. Hilton v. Guyot, 159 U.S. 113, 163, 164, 214, 215....

This review of the precedents and authorities on the subject appears to us abundantly to demonstrate that at the present day, by the general consent of the civilized nations of the world, and independently of any express treaty or other public act, it is an established rule of international law, founded on considerations of humanity to a poor and industrious order of men, and of the mutual convenience of belligerent States, that coast fishing vessels, with their implements and supplies, cargoes and crews, unarmed, and honestly pursuing their peaceful calling of catching and bringing in fresh fish, are exempt from capture as prize of war.

The exemption, of course, does not apply to coast fishermen or their vessels, if employed for a warlike purpose, or in such a way as to give aid or information to the enemy; nor when military or naval operations create a necessity to which all private interests must give way.

Nor has the exemption been extended to ships or vessels employed on the high sea in taking whales or seals, or cod or other fish which are not brought fresh to market, but are salted or otherwise cured and made a regular article of commerce.

This rule of international law is one which prize courts, administering the law of nations, are bound to take judicial notice of, and to give effect to, in the absence of any treaty or other public act of their own government in relation to the matter....

On April 21, 1898, the Secretary of the Navy gave instructions to Admiral Sampson, commanding the North Atlantic Squadron, to "immediately institute a blockade of the north coast of Cuba, extending from Cardenas on the east to Bahia Honda on the west." Bureau of Navigation Report of 1898, appx. 175. The blockade was immediately instituted accordingly. On April 22, the President issued a proclamation, declaring that the United States had instituted and would maintain that blockade, "in pursuance of the laws of the United States, and the law of nations applicable to such cases." 30 Stat. 1769. And by the act of Congress of April 25, 1898, c. 189, it was declared that the war between the United States and Spain existed on that day, and had existed since and including April 21. 30 Stat. 364.

On April 26, 1898, the President issued another proclamation, which, after reciting the existence of the war, as declared by Congress, contained this further recital: "It being desirable that such war should be conducted upon principles in harmony with the present views of nations and sanctioned by their recent practice." This recital was followed by specific declarations of certain rules for the conduct of the war by sea, making no mention of fishing vessels. 30 Stat. 1770. But the proclamation clearly manifests the general policy of the Government to conduct the war in accordance with the principles of international law sanctioned by the recent practice of nations.

On April 28, 1898, (after the capture of the two fishing vessels now in question,) Admiral Sampson telegraphed to the Secretary of the Navy as follows: "I find that a large number of fishing schooners are attempting to get into Havana from their fishing grounds near the Florida reefs and coasts. They are generally manned by excellent seamen, belonging to the maritime inscription of Spain, who have already served in the Spanish navy, and who are liable to further service. As these trained men are naval reserves, have a semi-military character, and would be most valuable to the Spaniards as artillerymen, either afloat or ashore, I recommend that they should be detained prisoners of war, and that I should be authorized to deliver them to the commanding officer of the army at Key West." To that communication the Secretary of the Navy, on April 30, 1898, guardedly answered: "Spanish fishing vessels attempting to violate blockade are subject, with crew, to capture, and any such vessel or crew considered likely to aid enemy may be detained." Bureau of Navigation Report of 1898, appx. 178. The Admiral's despatch assumed that he was not authorized, without express order, to arrest coast fishermen peaceably pursuing their calling; and the necessary implication and evident intent of the response of the Navy Department were that Spanish coast fishing vessels and their crews should not be interfered with, so long as they neither attempted to violate the blockade, nor were considered likely to aid the enemy....

The two vessels and their cargoes were condemned by the District Court as prize of war; the vessels were sold under its decrees; and it does not appear what became of the fresh fish of which their cargoes consisted.

Upon the facts proved in either case, it is the duty of this court, sitting as the highest prize court of the United States, and administering the law of nations, to declare and adjudge that the capture was unlawful, and without probable cause; and it is therefore, in each case,

Ordered, that the decree of the District Court be reversed, and the proceeds of the sale of the vessel, together with the proceeds of any sale of her cargo, be restored to the claimant, with damages and costs....

FULLER, C.J., dissenting.

The District Court held these vessels and their cargoes liable [to capture] because not "satisfied that as a matter of law, without any ordinance, treaty or proclamation, fishing vessels of this class are exempt from seizure."

This court holds otherwise, not because such exemption is to be found in any treaty, legislation, proclamation or instruction, granting it, but on the ground that the vessels were exempt by reason of an established rule of international law applicable to them, which it is the duty of the court to enforce.

I am unable to conclude that there is any such established international rule, or that this court can properly revise action which must be treated as having been taken in the ordinary exercise of discretion in the conduct of war.

It cannot be maintained "that modern usage constitutes a rule which acts directly upon the thing itself by its own force, and not through the sovereign power." That position was disallowed in Brown v. The United States, 8 Cranch, 110, 128....

It is impossible to concede that the Admiral ratified these captures in disregard of established international law and the proclamation, or that the President, if he had been of opinion that there was any infraction of law or proclamation, would not have intervened prior to condemnation.

The correspondence of April 28, 30, between the Admiral and the Secretary of the Navy, quoted from in the principal opinion, was entirely consistent with the validity of the captures.

The question put by the Admiral related to the detention as prisoners of war of the persons manning the fishing schooners "attempting to get into Havana." Non-combatants are not so detained except for special reasons. Sailors on board enemy's trading vessels are made prisoners because of their fitness for immediate use on ships of war. Therefore the Admiral pointed out the value of these fishing seamen to the enemy, and advised their detention. The Secretary replied that if the vessels referred to were "attempting to violate blockade" they were subject "with crew" to capture, and also that they might be detained if "considered likely to aid enemy." The point was whether these crews should be made prisoners of war. Of course they would be liable to be if involved in the guilt of blockade running, and the Secretary agreed that they might be on the other ground in the Admiral's discretion.

All this was in accordance with the rules and usages of international law, with which, whether in peace or war, the naval service has always been necessarily familiar....

In truth, the exemption of fishing craft is essentially an act of grace, and not a matter of right, and it is extended or denied as the exigency is believed to demand.

It is, said Sir William Scott, "a rule of comity only, and not of legal decision." ...

Being of opinion that these vessels were not exempt as matter of law, I am constrained to dissent from the opinion and judgment of the court; and my brothers Harlan and McKenna concur in this dissent.

RODRIGUEZ FERNANDEZ v. WILKINSON

505 F.Supp. 787 (D.Kan.1980).

ROGERS, J.

Pedro Rodriguez, currently detained at the United States Penitentiary, Leavenworth, Kansas, having paid the necessary fee, has filed with the Clerk of the Court, this petition for writ of habeas corpus pursuant to 28 U.S.C. § 2241. A rule to show cause issued, respondent has filed an answer and return, and petitioner has filed his traverse. Kansas Legal Services, Inc., submitted an *Amicus Curiae* brief in behalf of petitioner. An evidentiary hearing was conducted and oral argument was heard by the Court from counsel for both parties and the Amicus attorney. Having heard the evidence, examined the pleadings and considered all legal arguments and authorities offered, the Court makes the following factual and legal findings.

The material facts are found by the Court to be as follows:

1. Petitioner is a native and a citizen of Cuba who was incarcerated in a Cuban prison at the time he was given the opportunity to come to the United States.

2. He was transported to this country by boat along with approximately 130,000 Cuban nationals who arrived at Key West, Florida, on or about June 2, 1980, seeking admission to this country....

11. The INS and the Department of State are attempting to make necessary arrangements to return petitioner and the other excluded aliens to Cuba; however, Cuba has either not responded or responded negatively to six diplomatic notes transmitted by the United States. Thus, the Government has been unable to expeditiously carry out the order of deportation and cannot even speculate as to a date of departure. No other country has been contacted about possibly accepting petitioner.

Attorneys for petitioner assert that his continued confinement at Leavenworth without bail and without having been charged with or convicted of a crime in this country is cruel and unusual punishment in contravention of the Eighth Amendment to the United States Constitution, and a violation of the Fifth Amendment Due Process Clause.

The claim that excludable aliens who have not gained entry are entitled to the protection afforded by either the Fifth or Eighth Amendments to the United States Constitution was explicitly rejected by this Court in Mir, *et al.* v. Wilkinson, 80–3139 (D. Kan., Sept. 2, 1980, unpublished) *accord*: Knauff v. Shaughnessy, 338 U.S. 537 ... (1950); Petition of Cahill, 447 F.2d 1343 (2d Cir.1971). As has been observed by the United States Supreme Court, "... [t]he Bill of Rights is a futile authority for the alien seeking admission for the first time to these shores." Kwong Hai Chew v. Colding, 344 U.S. 590, 596 n. 5 ... (1953) *citing* Bridges v. Wixon, 326 U.S. 135, 161 ... (1945 concurring opinion). In *Kwong Hai Chew v. Colding*, the Court referred to "excludable aliens'' as not within the protection of the Fifth Amendment, 344 U.S. at 600. . . . While we have never disagreed with petitioner's counsel that alien entrants to this country are extended certain rights under the United States Constitution, we have repeatedly emphasized the distinctiveness of the Cuban aliens detained pending exclusion. This case concerns a member of the relatively small subset of excludable and excluded aliens who, due to a time-honored legal fiction, are not recognized under the law as having entered our borders. Consequently, these nonentrants customarily have not enjoyed the panoply of rights guaranteed to citizens and alien entrants by our Constitution. . . .

. . . Nevertheless, it has also long been established that the discretionary judgment of a political branch of government is judicially reviewable in federal court on a writ of habeas corpus for abuse of discretion. . . .

. . . We find that extended, indefinite confinement in a federal prison is deleterious to the personal integrity of petitioner and can only be viewed as arbitrary detention. Moreover, it appears that had petitioner remained in the Cuban prison, he might now be eligible for release. It is the further finding of this Court that indeterminate detention of petitioner in the maximum security facility at Leavenworth is not authorized by law and is an abuse of discretion on the part of the Attorney General and his delegates. . . .

We have declared that indeterminate detention of petitioner in a maximum security prison pending unforeseeable deportation constitutes arbitrary detention. Due to the unique legal status of excluded aliens in this country, it is an evil from which our Constitution and statutory laws afford no protection. Our domestic laws are designed to deter private individuals from harming one another and to protect individuals from abuse by the State. But in the case of unadmitted aliens detained on our soil, but legally deemed to be outside our borders, the machinery of domestic law utterly fails to operate to assure protection.

The *Amicus Curiae* in this case contends, and counsel for petitioner urges, that the continued detention of petitioner is in contravention of fundamental human justice as embodied in established principles of international law. Cited as legal authority are *The Universal Declaration of Human Rights*, U.N. Doc. A/801 (1948) and *The American Convention of Human Rights*, 77 Dept. of State Bulletin 28 (July 4, 1977), signed by President Carter on July 1, 1977. We agree that international law secures to petitioner the right to be free of arbitrary detention and that his right is being violated. . . .

The most important source of international law is international treaties. At present, the United States has ratified and is a party to only a few human rights treaties. Petitioner does not assert that his detention is in direct violation of any treaty to which the United States is a party. . . .

The difficulty with international agreements as a legal source is that the courts are simply not bound by these documents unless they have been ratified by the United States. And we are signatory to very few international human rights agreements and ratifying state to even fewer such agreements.

One important document by which the United States is bound is the United Nations Charter.... This document "stands as the symbol of human rights on an international scale." Stotzky, at 237. The Charter entered into force on October 24, 1945, and resolves to reaffirm faith in fundamental human rights and in the dignity of the human person. Almost all nations in the world are now parties to the U.N. Charter.

There are a great number of other international declarations, resolutions, and recommendations. While not technically binding, these documents establish broadly recognized standards. The most important of these is the *Universal Declaration of Human Rights*, adopted by the U.N. General Assembly in 1948. Mrs. Franklin D. Roosevelt, as Chairman of the Commission on Human Rights and a representative of the United States, explained the force and effect of the *Declaration* before the General Assembly of the U.N. preceding its final vote:

> In giving our approval to the declaration today, it is of primary importance that we keep clearly in mind the basic character of the document. It is not a treaty; it is not an international agreement. It is not and does not purport to be a statement of law or of legal obligation. It is a declaration of basic principles of human rights and freedoms, to be stamped with the approval of the General Assembly by formal vote of its members, and to serve as a common standard of achievement for all peoples of all nations.

5 WHITEMAN, DIGEST OF INTERNATIONAL LAW 623 (1965).

Richard Bilder, an international legal scholar, has suggested it may currently be argued that:

> standards set by the Universal Declaration of Human Rights, although initially only declaratory and non-binding, have by now, through wide acceptance and recitation by nations as having normative effect, become binding customary law. Whatever may be the weight of this argument, it is certainly true that the Declaration is in practice frequently invoked as if it were legally binding, both by nations and by private individuals and groups.

Bilder, R., *The Status of International Human Rights Law: An Overview*, 1978 INTERNATIONAL LAW AND PRACTICE 1, 8.

It is a jurist's opinion that:

"although the affirmations of the *Declaration* are not binding *qua* international convention within the meaning of Article 38, paragraph 1(a) of the Statute of the Court, they can bind states on the basis of custom within the meaning of the same Article, whether because they constitute a codification of customary law as was said in respect of Article 6 of the Vienna Convention on the Law of Treaties, or because they have acquired the force of custom through a general practice accepted as law, in the words of Article 38, paragraph 1(b), of the Statute."

Separate Opinion of Vice–President Ammoun in Advisory Opinion on the continued presence of South Africa in Namibia (S.W. Africa) 1971 I.C.J. Reports 16, 76. Thus, it appears that the *Declaration* has evolved into an important source of international human rights law.

Articles 3 and 9 of the *Declaration* provide that "everyone has the right to life, liberty, and the security of person," and that "no one shall be subjected to arbitrary arrest, detention or exile."

The *American Convention on Human Rights*, cited by the Amicus Curiae, pertinently declares in Article 5 that "punishment shall not be extended to any person other than the criminal," and "all persons deprived of their liberty shall be treated with respect for the inherent dignity of the human person." In Article 7 of the Convention it is agreed:

1. Every person has the right to personal liberty and security.

2. No one shall be deprived of his physical liberty except for the reasons and under the conditions established beforehand by the Constitution of the State Party concerned or by a law established pursuant thereto.

3. No one shall be subject to arbitrary arrest or imprisonment.

Two other principle sources of fundamental human rights are the *European Convention for the Protection of Human Rights and Fundamental Freedoms* (Rome 1950), and the *International Covenant on Civil and Political Rights*, G. A. Res. 2200A(XXI) Dec. 16, 1966, U.N. Gen.Ass. Off.Rec., 21st Sess., Supp. No. 16(A/6316) p. 52. Although the United States is not bound by either of these documents, they are indicative of the customs and usages of civilized nations.

The *European Convention*, brought into force in 1953 (213 U.N.T.S. 221) provides that everyone has the right to liberty and security of person and may not be deprived of liberty except in the specified cases and in accordance with a procedure prescribed by law. Section 4 further provides:

> Everyone who is deprived of his liberty by arrest or detention shall be entitled to take proceedings by which the lawfulness of his detention shall be decided speedily by a court and his release ordered if the detention is not lawful.

The *International Covenant on Civil and Political Rights* contains several apposite paragraphs.... [The opinion quoted Articles 14 (7), 9 (1) and (4), 10 (1), and 12 (1).]

Members of our Congress and executive department have also recognized an international legal right to freedom from arbitrary detention. Congressman Donald M. Frasier as Chairman of the Subcommittee on International Organizations and the Commission on International Relations, House of Representatives, described prolonged detention without charges or trial as a gross violation of human rights:

> Congress has sought to write some general laws establishing standards for the granting or withholding of military and economic aid to nations in relation to the human rights issue. Generally we have said the military aid should be reduced or terminated to a country guilty of a consistent pattern of gross violations of internationally recognized human rights. We define gross violations as those involving the integrity of the person: torture, prolonged detention without charges or trial, and other cruel and inhuman treatment.

Frasier, D., *Human Rights and U.S. Foreign Policy—The Congressional Perspective*, 1978 INTERNATIONAL HUMAN RIGHTS LAW AND PRACTICE, 171, 178. Patricia M. Derian, Assistant Secretary of State for Human Rights and Humanitarian Affairs, in discussing President Carter's policy on human rights stated:

> Our human rights concerns embrace those internationally recognized rights found in the United Nations Declaration of Human Rights. The specific focus of our policy is to seek greater observance by all governments of the rights of the person including freedom from torture and cruel and inhuman treatment, freedom from the fear of security forces breaking down doors and kidnapping citizens from their homes, and freedom from arbitrary detention.

Derian, P., *Human Rights in U.S. Foreign Policy—The Executive Perspective*, 1978 INTERNATIONAL HUMAN RIGHTS LAW AND PRACTICE 183.

Tribunals enforcing international law have also recognized arbitrary detention as giving rise to a legal claim. The arbitrator in *France ex rel. Madame Julien Chevreau*, opined that the arbitrary arrest, detention or deportation of a foreigner may give rise to a claim under international law and that if detention is unnecessarily prolonged, a claim is justified. The arbitrator further stated that a claim is justified if the rule is not observed that the prisoner should be treated in a manner appropriate to his situation, and corresponding to the standard customarily accepted among civilized nations. M.S. Dept. of State, file no. 500. AIA/1197, *cited in* WHITEMAN, M., DAMAGES IN INTERNATIONAL LAW (Washington 1937).

The cases cited earlier in this opinion which condemned protracted detention and detention beyond a reasonable time for deportation display our own judiciary's abhorrence of arbitrary detention.

Principles of customary international law may be discerned from an overview of express international conventions, the teachings of legal scholars, the general custom and practice of nations and relevant judicial decisions. Filartiga v. Pena–Irala, 630 F.2d 876 (2d Cir.1980). When, from this overview a wrong is found to be of mutual, and not merely several, concern among nations, it may be termed an international law violation. *Id.*

International law is a part of the laws of the United States which federal courts are bound to ascertain and administer in an appropriate case. The Nereide, 13 U.S. (9 Cranch) 388, 422 . . . (1815); The Paquete Habana, 175 U.S. 677 . . . (1900); *Filartiga v. Pena–Irala, supra.* Our review of the sources from which customary international law is derived clearly demonstrates that arbitrary detention is prohibited by customary international law. Therefore, even though the indeterminate detention of an excluded alien cannot be said to violate the United States Constitution or our statutory laws, it is judicially remedial as a violation of international law. Petitioner's continued, indeterminate detention on restrictive status in a maximum security prison, without having been convicted of a crime in this country or a determination having been made that he is a risk to security or likely to abscond, is unlawful; and as such amounts to an abuse of discretion on the part of the Attorney General and his delegates....

This Court has absolutely no desire to intrude upon matters of national security or executive decision-making and is not so arrogant as to feign expertise in the area of immigration law and policy....

These rationalizations do not, however, assuage the extant violation of petitioner's fundamental human rights. Perpetuating a state of affairs which results in the violation of an alien's fundamental human rights is clearly an abuse of discretion on the part of the responsible agency officials. This Court is bound to declare such an abuse and to order its cessation. When Congress and the executive department decided to exclude certain aliens from entry into this country and thereafter allowed thousands to arrive upon our shores at once, it was their corollary responsibility to develop methods for processing this large influx of admissible and excludable aliens without offending any of their fundamental human rights. If, due solely to the morass created by these official decisions, some aliens who may not seem desirable have been caused to remain in the United States for attenuated periods of time, the courts cannot deny them protection from arbitrary governmental action....

In sum, we hold that the indeterminate detention of petitioner in a maximum security federal prison under conditions providing less freedom than that granted to ordinary inmates constitutes arbitrary detention and is a violation of customary international law; and that the continuation of such detention is an abuse of discretion on the part of the Attorney General and his delegates.

It is therefore ordered that respondent be granted ninety (90) days from the date hereof in which to lawfully terminate the arbitrary detention of petitioner, and that if such detention is not terminated at the end of said period, the writ shall be granted and petitioner released on parole....

GARCIA-MIR v. MEESE

788 F.2d 1446 (11th Cir.1986).

JOHNSON, J.

These cases pose the question whether unadmitted aliens properly may claim the protection of the Due Process Clause of the United States

Constitution to secure parole revocation hearings. We earlier determined that, for unadmitted aliens, the right to such hearings is not resident in the core values of the Due Process Clause per se. We are today asked to determine whether some actionable liberty interest exists, not based on a core value, which is nonetheless protected by the Fifth Amendment's guarantee of due process of law. For the reasons explained herein, we find it unnecessary to reach that question within the confines of this controversy. It is our opinion that, assuming that undocumented aliens may have actionable nonconstitutionally-based liberty interests, these particular aliens have not stated a viable claim for relief under the Due Process Clause. We also determine that customary international law does not afford these aliens a remedy in American courts.

This is an appeal and cross-appeal from the final decision of the trial court ordering the government to prepare and implement a plan to provide individual parole revocation hearings for unadmitted aliens. The appellees-cross appellants ["appellees" or "aliens" or "Mariels"] are a certified class of Mariel Cuban refugees who were accorded a special immigration parole status by the Refugee Education Assistance Act of 1980, Pub.L.No. 96–422, § 501(e), 94 Stat. 1799 (1980), reprinted at 8 U.S.C.A. § 1522 note (1985). The district court has broken the class into two sub-classes. The "First Group" includes those who are guilty of crimes committed in Cuba before the boatlift or who are mentally incompetent. They have never been paroled into this country. The "Second Group" consists of all other Mariels—those who, because there was no evidence of criminal or mental defect, were paroled under the provisions of the general alien parole statute, 8 U.S.C.A. § 1182(d)(5) (1985), but whose parole was subsequently revoked. All are currently detained in the Atlanta Penitentiary....

The public law of nations was long ago incorporated into the common law of the United States. The Paquete Habana, 175 U.S. 677, 700 ... (1900); The Nereide, 13 U.S. (9 Cranch) 388, 423 ... (1815); Restatement of the Law of Foreign Relations Law of the United States (Revised) § 131 cmt. d (Tent. Draft No. 6, 1985) [hereinafter "Restatement 6"]. To the extent possible, courts must construe American Law so as to avoid violating principles of public international law. Murray v. The Schooner Charming Betsy, 6 U.S. (2 Cranch) 64, 102, 118 ... (1804); Lauritzen v. Larsen, 345 U.S. 571, 578 ... (1953). But public international law is controlling only "where there is no treaty and no controlling executive or legislative act or judicial decision...." 175 U.S. at 700. Appellees argue that, because general principles of international law forbid prolonged arbitrary detention, we should hold that their current detention is unlawful.

We have previously determined that the general deportation statute, 8 U.S.C.A. § 1227(a) (1985), does not restrict the power of the Attorney General to detain aliens indefinitely. Fernandez–Roque II, 734 F.2d at 580 n.6. But this does not resolve the question whether there has been an affirmative legislative grant of authority to detain. As to the First Group there is sufficiently express evidence of congressional intent as to interdict the application of international law: Pub.L.No. 96–533, Title VII, § 716, 94 Stat. 3162 (1980), reprinted at 8 U.S.C.A. § 1522 note.

The trial court found, correctly, that there has been no affirmative legislative grant to the Justice Department to detain the Second Group without hearings because 8 U.S.C.A. § 1227(c) does not expressly authorize indefinite detention. Fernandez–Roque v. Smith, 622 F. Supp. 887, 902 (N.D.Ga.1985). Thus we must look for a controlling executive act. The trial court found that there was such a controlling act in the Attorney General's termination of the status review plan and in his decision to incarcerate indefinitely pending efforts to deport. *Id.* at 903. The appellees and the *amicus* challenge this by arguing that a controlling executive act can only come from an act by or expressly sanctioned by the President himself, not one of his subordinates. Amicus Brief at 12. They rely for that proposition upon *The Paquete Habana* and upon the RESTATEMENT OF THE LAW OF FOREIGN RELATIONS LAW OF THE UNITED STATES (REVISED) § 131 cmt. c (Tent. Draft No. 1, 1980) [hereinafter "Restatement 1"].

As to *The Paquete Habana*, that case involved the capture and sale as war prize of several fishing boats during the Spanish–American War. The Supreme Court found this contrary to the dictates of international law. The *amicus* characterizes the facts of the case such that the Secretary of the Navy authorized the capture and that the Supreme Court held that this did not constitute a controlling executive act because it was not ordered by the President himself. This is a mischaracterization. After the capture of the two vessels at issue, an admiral telegraphed the Secretary for permission to seize fishing ships, to which the Secretary responded that only those vessels " 'likely to aid enemy may be detained.' "175 U.S. at 713. Seizing fishing boats aiding the enemy would be in obvious accord with international law. But the facts of *The Paquete Habana* showed the boats in question to be innocent of aiding the Spanish. The Court held that the ships were seized in violation of international law because they were used solely for fishing. It was the admiral who acted in excess of the clearly delimited authority granted by the Secretary, who instructed him to act only consistent with international law. Thus *The Paquete Habana* does not support the proposition that the acts of cabinet officers cannot constitute controlling executive acts. At best it suggests that lower level officials cannot by their acts render international law inapplicable. That is not an issue in this case, where the challenge is to the acts of the Attorney General.

As to the Restatement 1, the provision upon which amicus relies has been removed in subsequent drafts. The most recent version of that provision notes that the President, "acting within his constitutional authority, may have the power under the Constitution to act in ways that constitute violations of international law by the United States." The Constitution provides for the creation of executive departments, U.S. Const. art. 2, § 2, and the power of the President to delegate his authority to those department to act on his behalf is unquestioned. *See, e.g.*, Jean v. Nelson, 472 U.S. 846.... Likewise, in Restatement 6, § 135

Reporter's Note 3, the power of the President to disregard international law in service of domestic needs is reaffirmed. Thus we hold that the executive acts here evident constitute a sufficient basis for affirming the trial court's finding that international law does not control.

Even if we were to accept, arguendo, the appellees' interpretation of "controlling executive act," *The Paquete Habana* also provides that the reach of international law will be interdicted by a controlling judicial decision. In *Jean v. Nelson*, we interpreted the Supreme Court's decision in *Mezei* to hold that even an indefinitely incarcerated alien "could not challenge his continued detention without a hearing." 727 F.2d at 974–75. This reflects the obligation of the courts to avoid any ruling that would "inhibit the flexibility of the political branches of government to respond to changing world conditions...." Mathews v. Diaz, 426 U.S. 67, 81 ... (1976). We find this decision sufficient to meet the test of *The Paquete Habana*....

Notes and Questions

1. Did the court in *Garcia-Mir* read the U.S. Constitution, history, trends in judicial opinions, and *The Paquete Habana* correctly? *See, e.g.*, Louis Henkin, *The President and International Law*, 80 Am. J. Int'l L. 930, 936 (1986) ("[T]he president has no power ... to violate international law.... *Garcia-Mir* misinterpreted and misapplied *The Paquete Habana*."); Jordan J. Paust, International Law as Law of the United States 172–79, 183–84 n.24, 189–90 n.67 (also noting that the President did not order a release of the vessels, cargo or subsequent proceeds for two years after the seizure when the Executive was still arguing before the Supreme Court that the seizures were valid executive seizures by the naval officers and "the discretion lodged in the Executive has been exercised, and, we contend, under the circumstances, soundly exercised by the commanders of the capturing vessels." Three years after the decision in *Paquete Habana*, the Executive was back before the Court still arguing that the U.S. made the captures "its own.") (2 ed. 2003), partially extracted:

> Moreover, not only does *The Paquete Habana* not affirm that an executive-created "law" that is inconsistent with international law is a "controlling" executive act (much less an authoritative or constitutionally permissible act), but it also clearly affirms that the President cannot lawfully order a violation even of "usage" and, thus necessarily, that an executive order to violate (or that would violate) international law would be impermissible and certainly not a "controlling" executive order. As Professor Henkin admits, *The Paquete Habana* "did not explain ... which legislative or executive acts were controlling," or, it must be emphasized here, whether any such acts are "controlling" in the face of identifiable norms of customary international law. The word "controlling" provides no further guidance. Significantly, such an ambiguous criterion has never been adopted by any Justice other than Justice Gray, either before or after his 1900 opinion.
>
> Indeed, it is far more likely that the word "controlling" was used merely with regard to proper ascertainment of the *content* of international law. The phrase "[f]or this purpose" at the start of the second sentence conditions the rest of that sentence, and it necessarily directs attention back to a purpose

articulated in the preceding sentence. Justice Gray had just declared that such law "is part of our law" and that it "must be ascertained" by the courts. The Justice seems merely to have said that for that purpose (of ascertaining international law), "resort must be had" to practice and text-writers if there is no controlling executive or legislative act or judicial decision concerning the content of international law. Justice Gray then cites *Hilton*, which is quite informing since it mirrors his language in *The Paquete Habana*. The mirror of his second sentence is built around the judicial task or purpose of ascertaining the content of international law: "The most certain guide ... is ... a treaty or a statute ... [b]ut when ... there is no written law upon the subject, the duty still rests upon the judicial tribunals of ascertaining and declaring what the law is...." If the two forms of dictum are placed together (as the citation to *Hilton* suggests) and this interpretation is correct, then, at most, Justice Gray opined that some (but not all) executive or legislative acts or judicial decisions might be "controlling" concerning ascertainment of the content of international law. For example, even using Justice Gray's dictum it does not follow that every executive interpretation is to be a "controlling" interpretation of the law, and it certainly does not follow that the Executive could violate the law. This, of course, is actually what the Court ruled when it not only voided the executive seizure of certain vessels, but also decided against claims of the Solicitor General and an Assistant Attorney General, still being made, that the vessels were not exempt from seizure under an executive view of international law. Certainly, neither the executive acts nor the executive interpretations were controlling.

Indeed, in its brief before the Supreme Court, the Executive had argued that an English approach (considering an exemption of enemy fishing vessels to be "discretionary" under customary international law), and not a continental European approach (considering that an exemption is "fixed into a rule"), should be followed. Thus, the Executive argued that an exemption from seizure should not automatically be found in custom but should only exist where there is "some treaty obligation which requires it, or some specific ordinance or proclamation by which the executive shows an exercise of discretion in favor of the property claimed to be exempted." The Supreme Court obviously disagreed and found the vessels to be exempt under customary international law—thus also conforming its approach to decision to that in *Hilton* whereby even in the absence of some treaty, specific legislation or executive proclamation, the Court must still identify, clarify and apply customary international law as often as questions of right depending upon it are duly presented. If anything, the ambiguous phrase in *The Paquete Habana*, which is close to the language of the executive claim, seems to have been used precisely in order to defeat such a claim. Further, the executive had argued that not only did no such exemption appear in written law but also,"on the contrary, the discretion lodged in the Executive has been exercised" and actually should control. Similarly, the Supreme Court disagreed, thereby affirming that executive discretion and executive acts did not control either the content or application of law.

Further, the word "must," which appears in the following quote from *The Paquete Habana* in both the first and the second sentence, is used to demonstrate those situations where custom "must" be applied.... Importantly, Justice Gray's opinion did not address those situations where custom "may" or "can" also be applied (or could "only" be applied). The point is all the more important when one realizes that historic use of customary law was both direct and indirect (*i.e.*, as a direct basis for decision and as an indirect basis—for example, as an aid in interpreting a relevant statutory or constitutional provision). Indeed, it has been "applied" and "referred to" when there was also "a treaty," and it has been used even as an aid in interpreting a relevant treaty or federal statute. Thus, an attempt to limit the use of custom to situations where there is no other domestic law would be completely unrealistic in terms of the actual patterns of use by the judiciary both before and after the *Paquete Habana* decision. The Court did not ignore such historic use by stating, falsely, that customary international law can "only" be applied where there is "no treaty, and no controlling executive or legislative act." Nor did Judge McWilliams, in his dissenting opinion in *Rodriguez Fernandez*, say that custom "can" be used "only" when there is no treaty or controlling domestic law. [Such an improper and ahistorical limitation of the use of customary international law is termed the "only 'where' "error, since Justice Gray did not use the word "only" before the word "where" and it is erroneous to claim that customary international law can be used, for example, "only 'where' " there is no treaty.]

Despite these facts, the related points made here about the actual statement of Justice Gray in *The Paquete Habana*, and the rich history of use of custom by federal courts, the Justice Department misled a district court judge. In *Fernandez-Roque v. Smith*, Judge Shoob stated per dicta, and incorrectly: "according to *The Paquete Habana*, plaintiffs can rely on customary international law *only if* 'there is no treaty and no controlling executive or legislative act or judicial decision.' "["only if" involves the same error as "only 'where' "] . . .

In view of the claims of the Executive before the Supreme Court, there is only one other possible explanation of the meaning of "controlling" executive acts. In its brief, the point that the Executive argued was not that it could act in violation of law and that such an act should be controlling, but that a constitutionally-based power of the Executive was at stake and that the exercise of executive political discretion within the law and under such a power should be controlling (at least when supported by Congress). What the Executive seemed to stress was that presidential power to recognize foreign governments and the related political power to recognize the existence of a foreign belligerency (and thus a foreign "belligerent" or "insurgent" status) is a power of the President and that choice exercised directly within such a power should control what sort of international rules should be administered. *See* Brief for the United States, at 5–6, 25–32 (stressing, *id.* at 27, that such a status "is a political question not committed to the decision of the courts"; but, curiously in view of what we consider to be an exclusive presidential and particularly sensitive political power of recognition, adding: "the political question was determined by the resolution of Congress in light of what preceded that resolution...." An evident reason for this latter statement is that Congress, by joint resolution, had declared war and we were engaged in a war against Spain (making Spanish vessels "enemy" vessels) and the Executive had not chosen to recognize the Cuban people as belligerents against Spain and possibly, therefore, neutrals or friends of the

United States. Thus, the status had been "enemy" by resolution of Congress and such a status was not changed by exercise of a presidential recognition power). It followed that international law concerning "enemy" vessels, cargoes and crews was to be administered. Certain current lower court misinterpretations, then, have gone entirely too far and are fraught with dangerous consequences. Again, the Executive did not argue, and the Court did not state, that the President could violate the law. On the contrary, it argued the content of applicable law and lost (having achieved the other points that a war between Spain and the U.S. existed and not an unrecognized "belligerency" between Spanish and Cuban contenders, and that these were enemy (Spanish) and not neutral (Cuban belligerent) vessels. See 175 U.S. at 678–79, but not addressing the dispute as such). See also Jordan J. Paust, Paquete *and the President: Rediscovering the Brief for the United States*, 34 VA. J. INT'L L. 981 (1994).

2. Lower federal courts have been merely copying language from *Garcia-Mir* without independent inquiry or reasoning, or have merely cited the case while permitting illegal controls over certain aliens. Lawyers in the Department of Justice had pressed for recognition of a new Executive power to violate customary international law when cases involve mistreatment of aliens. *See, e.g.*, Galo–Garcia v. INS, 86 F.3d 916, 918 (9th Cir.1996) ("where a controlling executive or legislative act does exist, customary international law is inapplicable"); Barrera–Echavarria v. Rison, 44 F.3d 1441, 1450–51 (9th Cir.1995) (using the "only 'where' " error); Gisbert v. United States Attorney General, 988 F.2d 1437, 1447–48, amended, 997 F.2d 1122 (5th Cir.1993) ("other circuits have held in the context of immigration detention that international law is not controlling because federal executive, legislative, and judicial actions supersede the application of these principles of international law."); Echeverria–Hernandez v. United States INS, 923 F.2d 688, 692 (9th Cir.1991) (using the "only 'where' " error); Cruz–Elias v. United States Attorney General, 870 F.Supp. 692, 698 (E.D.Va.1994); Rodriguez v. Thornburgh, 831 F.Supp. 810, 814 (D.Kan.1993); Barrios v. Thornburgh, 754 F.Supp. 1536 (W.D.Okla.1990); Sanchez v. Kindt, 752 F.Supp. 1419 (S.D.Ind.1990). Concerning the "only 'where' " error, see PAUST, *supra*, at 44, 137, 150, 161–62. Because there is little, if any, reasoning in these cases and inadequate attention to the Founders, the text of the Constitution, history and the actual ruling in *Paquete Habana*, the decisions seem result-oriented. *See also* Jordan J. Paust, *Customary International Law in the United States: Clean and Dirty Laundry*, 40 GERMAN Y.B. INT'L L. 78 (1998).

3. Other 20th Century cases addressing Executive responsibility to comply with international law include: Trans World Airlines v. Franklin Mint Corp., 466 U.S. 243, 261 (1984); United States v. Verdugo–Urquidez, 494 U.S. 259, 275 (1990) (treaty restrictions); United States v. Curtiss-Wright Export Corp., 299 U.S. 304, 318 (1936) (treaties and customary international law); Valentine v. Neidecker, 299 U.S. 5, 14 & n. 12, 18 (1936) (treaty); Ford v. United States, 273 U.S. 593, 606 (1927) (treaty); Francis v. Francis, 203 U.S. 233, 240, 242 (1906) (treaty); Dooley v. United States, 182 U.S. 222, 231 (1901); United States v. Toscanino, 500 F.2d 267, 276–79 (2d Cir.1974); Shapiro v. Ferrandina, 478 F.2d 894, 906 n. 10 (2d Cir.1973); United States v. Ferris, 19 F.2d 925, 926 (N.D.Cal.1927); United States v. Yunis, 681 F.Supp. 896, 906 (D.D.C.1988); Fernandez v. Wilkinson, 505

F.Supp. 787, 799–800 (D.Kan.1980). See also the extensive list of cases addressing the duty to comply with the laws of war that is set forth in a note just before the extract of *Paquete Habana*, above. In previously secret DOJ memos during the Bush Administration in 2002 written by John Yoo, Robert J. Delahunty, and Jay S. Bybee one finds argument that the President is not bound by the laws of war. *See, e.g.*, John Yoo, Robert J. Delahunty, Memorandum for William J. Haynes II, General Counsel, Department of Defense, Application of Treaties and Laws to al Qaeda and Taliban Detainees (Jan. 9, 2002), available at http://www.msnbc.msn.com/id/5025040/site/newsweek; Jay S. Bybee, Memorandum for Alberto R. Gonzales, Counsel to the President, Re: Standards of Conduct for Interrogation under 18 U.S.C. §§ 2340–2340A (Aug. 1, 2002), available at http://news.findlaw.com/wp/docs/doj/bybee80102mem.pdf; Jordan J. Paust, *Executive Plans and Authorizations to Violate International Law Concerning Treatment and Interrogation of Detainees*, 43 Columbia J. Transnat'l L. 801, 830–36, 856–61 (2005). What do you think of such arguments?

4. As *Paquete Habana* and other cases have affirmed, courts can take judicial notice of customary international law since it is law of the United States. Nonetheless, attorneys often brief judges on the nature, evidences, and content of customary international law during litigation.

2. *Litigating Human Rights and Related Claims*

Concerning the customary human rights of access to courts and to an effective remedy, read Article 8 of the Universal Declaration of Human Rights and the following materials regarding the International Covenant. One should also consider General Comment No. 24 of the Human Rights Committee established by the International Covenant, in Chapter 1, Section 2 A 3, as well as the customary law of "denial of justice" noted, for example, in § 711 of the Restatement.

INTERNATIONAL COVENANT ON CIVIL AND POLITICAL RIGHTS

999 U.N.T.S. 171.

Article 14

1. All persons shall be equal before the courts and tribunals. In the determination of any . . . of his rights and obligations in a suit at law, everyone shall be entitled to a fair and public hearing by a competent, independent and impartial tribunal established by law. . . .

GENERAL COMMENT NO. 13, REPORT OF THE HUMAN RIGHTS COMMITTEE

39 U.N. GAOR, Supp. (No. 40), at 143, U.N. Doc. A/39/40 (Twenty-first session 1984), *reprinted at* International Human Rights Instruments, U.N. Doc. HRI/GEN/1 (4 September 1992), at 13.

1. . . . All of [Article 14's] provisions are aimed at ensuring the proper administration of justice and to this end uphold a series of

individual rights to equality before the courts and tribunals and the right to a fair and public hearing by a competent, independent and impartial tribunal established by law....

2. ... article 14 applies not only to procedures for the determination of criminal charges against individuals but also to procedures to determine their rights and obligations in a suit at law....

3. ... ensure that equality before the courts, including equal access to courts, fair and public hearings and competence, impartiality and independence of the judiciary are established by law and guaranteed in practice....

4. The provisions of article 14 apply to all courts and tribunals within the scope of that article whether ordinary or specialized....

GENERAL COMMENT NO. 15

41 U.N. GAOR, Supp. No. 40, Annex VI, at 117, U.N. Doc. A/41/40 (Twenty-third session 1986), *reprinted at* International Human Rights Instruments, U.N. Doc. HRI/GEN/1 (4 September 1992), at 17–19.

The position of aliens under the Covenant

1. ... each State party must ensure the rights in the Covenant to "all individuals within its territory and subject to its jurisdiction" (art. 2, para. 1). In general, the rights set forth in the Covenant apply to everyone, irrespective of reciprocity, and irrespective of his or her nationality or statelessness.

2. Thus, the general rule is that each one of the rights of the Covenant must be guaranteed without discrimination between citizens and aliens....

7. ... Aliens shall be equal before the courts and tribunals, and shall be entitled to a fair and public hearing by a competent, independent and impartial tribunal established by law in the determination of any ... rights or obligations in a suit at law.... Aliens are entitled to equal protection of the law. There shall be no discrimination between aliens and citizens in the application of these rights....

Notes and Questions

1. Concerning the customary right of access to courts and to an effective remedy, *see, e.g.*, JORDAN J. PAUST, INTERNATIONAL LAW AS LAW OF THE UNITED STATES 224–38, 284–322 ns.468–623 (2 ed. 2003); Beth Stephens, *Translating* Filartiga*: A Comparative and International Law Analysis of Domestic Remedies for International Human Rights Violations*, 27 YALE J. INT'L L. 1, 20–21, 46–48 (2002); Jon M. Van Dyke, *The Fundamental Human Right to Prosecution and Compensation*, 29 DENV. J. INT'L L. & POL'Y 77 (2001); General Comment No. 20 (1992), para. 15 ("right to an effective remedy, including compensation...."). For recognition of such rights under the 1966 Covenant, also see Dubai Petroleum Co., *et al.* v. Kazi, 12 S.W.3d 71, 82 (Tex. 2000) ("Article 14(1) requires all signatory countries to confer

the right of equality before the courts to citizens of all other signatories.... The Covenant not only guarantees foreign citizens equal treatment in the signatorie's courts, but also guarantees them equal access to these courts"), also citing General Comment No. 13 (1984).

2. With respect to the more extensive elaboration of human rights to due process in criminal proceedings, *see, e.g.*, International Covenant on Civil and Political Rights, arts. 9–10, 14; Rome Statute of the ICC, arts. 21(3), 63–69; Jordan J. Paust, M. Cherif Bassiouni, *et al.*, International Criminal Law 641–50, 663–64, 667–68, 670–71 (2 ed. 2000); Jordan J. Paust, *Antiterrorism Military Commissions: Courting Illegality*, 23 Mich. J. Int'l L. 1, 10–18 (2001); *Antiterrorism Military Commissions: The Ad Hoc DOD Rules of Procedure*, 23 Mich. J. Int'l L. 677 (2002).

ALIEN TORT CLAIMS ACT (ATCA)

28 U.S.C. § 1350.

The district courts shall have original jurisdiction of any civil action by an alien for a tort only, committed in violation of the law of nations or a treaty of the United States.

TORTURE VICTIM PROTECTION ACT (TVPA)

Public Law 102–256; 106 Stat. 73 (1992).

To carry out obligations of the United States under the United Nations Charter and other international agreements pertaining to the protection of human rights by establishing a civil action for recovery of damages from an individual who engages in torture or extrajudicial killing.

Be it enacted by the Senate and House of Representatives of the United States of America in Congress assembled,

Sec. 2. Establishment of Civil Action.

(a) Liability. An individual who, under actual or apparent authority, or color of law, of any foreign nation—

(1) subjects an individual to torture shall, in a civil action, be liable for damages to that individual; or

(2) subjects an individual to extrajudicial killing shall, in a civil action, be liable for damages to the individual's legal representative, or to any person who may be a claimant in an action for wrongful death.

(b) Exhaustion of Remedies. A court shall decline to hear a claim under this section if the claimant has not exhausted adequate and available remedies in the place in which the conduct giving rise to the claim occurred.

(c) Statute of Limitations. No action shall be maintained under this section unless it is commenced within 10 years after the cause of action arose.

Sec. 3. Definitions.

(a) Extrajudicial Killing. For the purpose of this Act, the term "extrajudicial killing" means a deliberated killing not authorized by a previous judgment pronounced by a regularly constituted court affording all the judicial guarantees which are recognized as indispensable by civilized peoples. Such term, however, does not include any such killing that, under international law, is lawfully carried out under the authority of a foreign nation.

(b) Torture. For the purposes of this Act—

(1) the term "torture" means any act, directed against an individual in the offender's custody or physical control, by which severe pain or suffering (other than pain or suffering arising only from or inherent in, or incidental to, lawful sanctions), whether physical or mental, is intentionally inflicted on that individual for such purposes as obtaining from that individual or a third person information or a confession, punishing that individual for an act that individual or a third person has committed or is suspected of having committed, intimidating or coercing that individual or a third person, or for any reason based on discrimination of any kind; and

(2) mental pain or suffering refers to prolonged mental harm caused by or resulting from—

(A) the intentional infliction or threatened infliction of severe physical pain or suffering;

(B) the administration or application, or threatened administration or application, of mind altering substances or other procedures calculated to disrupt profoundly the senses or the personality;

(C) the threat of imminent death; or

(D) the threat that another individual will imminently be subjected to death, severe physical pain or suffering, or the administration or application of mind altering substances or other procedures calculated to disrupt profoundly the senses or personality.

THE ANTITERRORISM ACT OF 1990

18 U.S.C.

§ 2331. Definitions

As used in this chapter [18 USCS §§ 2331 *et seq.*]—

(1) the term "international terrorism" means activities that—

(A) involve violent acts or acts dangerous to human life that are a violation of the criminal laws of the United States or of any State, or that would be a criminal violation if committed within the jurisdiction of the United States or of any State;

(B) appear to be intended—

(i) to intimidate or coerce a civilian population;

(ii) to influence the policy of a government by intimidation or coercion; or

(iii) to affect the conduct of a government by assassination or kidnapping; and

(C) occur primarily outside the territorial jurisdiction of the United States, or transcend national boundaries in terms of the means by which they are accomplished, the persons they appear intended to intimidate or coerce, or the locale in which their perpetrators operate or seek asylum;

(2) the term "national of the United States" has the meaning given such term in section 101(a)(22) of the Immigration and Nationality Act [8 USCS § 1101(a)(22)];

(3) the term "person" means any individual or entity capable of holding a legal or beneficial interest in property; and

(4) the term "act of war" means any act occurring in the course of—

(A) declared war;

(B) armed conflict, whether or not war has been declared, between two or more nations; or

(C) armed conflict between military forces of any origin.

§ 2332. Criminal penalties

(a) Homicide. Whoever kills a national of the United States, while such national is outside the United States, shall,—

(1) if the killing is murder (as defined in section 1111(a)), be fined under this title, punished by death or imprisonment for any term of years or for life, or both;

(2) if the killing is a voluntary manslaughter as defined in section 1112(a) of this title, be fined under this title or imprisoned not more than ten years, or both; and

(3) if the killing is an involuntary manslaughter as defined in section 1112(a) of this title, be fined under this title or imprisoned not more than three years, or both.

(b) Attempt or conspiracy with respect to homicide. Whoever outside the United States attempts to kill, or engages in a conspiracy to kill, a national of the United States shall—

(1) in the case of an attempt to commit a killing that is a murder as defined in this chapter [18 USCS §§ 2331 *et seq.*], be fined under this title or imprisoned not more than 20 years, or both; and

(2) in the case of a conspiracy by two or more persons to commit a killing that is a murder as defined in section 1111(a) of this title, if one or more of such persons do any overt act to effect

the object of the conspiracy, be fined under this title or imprisoned for any term of years or for life, or both so fined and so imprisoned.

(c) Other conduct. Whoever outside the United States engages in physical violence—

(1) with intent to cause serious bodily injury to a national of the United States; or

(2) with the result that serious bodily injury is caused to a national of the United States;

shall be fined under this title or imprisoned not more that ten years, or both.

(d) Limitation on prosecution. No prosecution for any offense described in this section shall be undertaken by the United States except on written certification of the Attorney General or the highest ranking subordinate of the Attorney General with responsibility for criminal prosecutions that, in the judgment of the certifying official, such offense was intended to coerce, intimidate, or retaliate against a government or a civilian population.

§ 2332a. Use of weapons of mass destruction

(a) Offense. A person who uses, or attempts or conspires to use, a weapon of mass destruction—

(1) against a national of the United States while such national is outside of the United States;

(2) against any person within the United States; or

(3) against any property that is owned, leased or used by the United States or by any department or agency of the United States, whether the property is within or outside the United States,

shall be imprisoned for any term of years or for life, and if death results, shall be punished by death or imprisoned for any term of years or for life. . . .

§ 2332b. Acts of terrorism transcending national boundaries

(a) Prohibited acts.

(1) Offenses. Whoever, involving conduct transcending national boundaries and in a circumstance described in subsection (b)—

(A) kills, kidnaps, maims, commits an assault resulting in serious bodily injury, or assaults with a dangerous weapon any person within the United States; or

(B) creates a substantial risk of serious bodily injury to any other person by destroying or damaging any structure, conveyance, or other real or personal property within the United States or by attempting or conspiring to destroy or damage any structure, conveyance, or other real or personal property within the United States;

in violation of the laws of any State, or the United States, shall be punished as prescribed in subsection (c).

(2) Treatment of threats, attempts and conspiracies. Whoever threatens to commit an offense under paragraph (1), or attempts or conspires to do so, shall be punished under subsection (c).

(b) Jurisdictional bases.

(1) Circumstances. The circumstances referred to in subsection (a) are–

(A) the mail or any facility of interstate or foreign commerce is used in furtherance of the offense;

(B) the offense obstructs, delays, or affects interstate or foreign commerce, or would have so obstructed, delayed, or affected interstate or foreign commerce if the offense had been consummated;

(C) the victim, or intended victim, is the United States Government, a member of the uniformed services, or any official, officer, employee, or agent of the legislative, executive, or judicial branches, or of any department or agency, of the United States;

(D) the structure, conveyance, or other real or personal property is, in whole or in part, owned, possessed, or leased to the United States, or any department or agency of the United States;

(E) the offense is committed in the territorial sea (including the airspace above and the seabed or subsoil below, and artificial islands and fixed structures erected thereon) of the United States; or

(F) the offense is committed within the special maritime and territorial jurisdiction of the United States.

(2) Co-conspirators and accessories after the fact. Jurisdiction shall exist over all principals and co-conspirators of an offense under this section, and accessories after the fact to any offense under this section, if at least one of the circumstances described in subparagraphs (A) through (F) of paragraph (1) is applicable to at least one offender....

§ 2333. Civil remedies

(a) Action and jurisdiction. Any national of the United States injured in his or her person, property, or business by reason of an act of international terrorism, or his or her estate, survivors, or heirs, may sue therefor in any appropriate district court of the United States and shall recover threefold the damages he or she sustains and the cost of the suit, including attorney's fees....

§ 2334. Jurisdiction and venue....

(d) Convenience of the forum. The district courts shall not dismiss . . . unless—

(1) the action may be maintained in a foreign court that has jurisdiction over the subject matter and over all the defendants;

(2) that foreign court is significantly more convenient and appropriate; and

(3) that foreign court offers a remedy which is substantially the same as the one available in the courts of the United States. . . .

§ 2335. Limitations of actions

(a) In general. Subject to subsection (b), a suit for recovery of damages under section 2333 of this title shall not be maintained unless commenced within 4 years after the date the cause of action accrued.

(b) Calculation of period. The time of the absence of the defendant from the United States or from any jurisdiction in which the same or a similar action arising from the same facts may be maintained by the plaintiff, or of any concealment of the defendant's whereabouts, shall not be included in the 4–year period set forth in subsection (a).

§ 2336. Other limitations.

(a) Acts of war. No action shall be maintained under section 2333 of this title for injury or loss by reason of an act of war. . . .

§ 2337. Suits against Government officials

No action shall be maintained under section 2333 of this title against—

(1) the United States, an agency of the United States, or an officer or employee of the United States or any agency thereof acting within his or her official capacity or under color of legal authority; or

(2) a foreign state, an agency of a foreign state, or an officer or employee of a foreign state or an agency thereof acting within his or her official capacity or under color of legal authority.

Notes and Questions

1. What customary international law is reflected in the Torture Victim Protection Act (TVPA) and the Antiterrorism Act? Under each form of legislation, who can sue whom for what? Are private perpetrators outside the reach of the TVPA? Are public perpetrators immune under the TVPA? Are they immune under § 2337 of the Antiterrorism Act? Are foreign states or foreign state entities suable under the TVPA? How are such lawsuits different from lawsuits under the Alien Tort Claims Act (ATCA), 28 U.S.C. § 1350 [see Section 2 B 4 a and *Filartiga* below]? *See generally*, Joan Fitzpatrick, *The Future of the Alien Tort Claims Act of 1789: Lessons from* In re Marcos Human Rights Litigation, 67 St. John's L. Rev. 491 (1993); Jordan J. Paust, *Suing Karadzic*, 10 Leiden J. Int'l L. 91 (1997). Does the word "individual" in the TVPA reach corporations? *See, e.g.*, Estate of Rodriquez v. Drummond Co., 256 F.Supp.2d 1250, 1268 (N.D. Ala. 2003).

Under § 2333 of the Antiterrorism Act, can Holocaust survivors who subsequently became U.S. nationals sue an alleged Nazi perpetrator of "terrorism" within the meaning of § 2331, as "[a]ny national" within the meaning of the statute, or must the plaintiffs be nationals at the time of the wrongful conduct?

2. Does the TVPA, which reaches an individual acting, for example, under "actual authority" of a foreign nation, override judicially-created or "common law" doctrines of immunity? Does every federal statute trump mere common law? *See also* references in the preceding note; Chapter 4 (re: the common law "act of state" doctrine and so-called "head-of-state" immunity).

3. Is "nation" the same as "state" under international law? within the meaning of the TVPA?

4. Can a U.S. national ever be a proper defendant under the TVPA?

5. Why would an alien sue under the TVPA if suit is possible under the ATCA? Consider this question also after the Supreme Court's 2004 decision in *Sosa v. Alvarez–Machain, infra*. A recent Seventh Circuit panel ruled that the TVPA "preempts" that ATCA and, thus, requires exhaustion of remedies pursuant to the TVPA. See Enahoro v. Abubakar, 408 F.3d 877 (7th Cir. 2005). Does this seem correct? *But see* Sarei v. Rio Tinto PLC, 221 F.Supp.2d 1116, 1132–39, 1162 (C.D. Cal. 2002) ("the ATCA does not require the exhaustion of national remedies").

6. Precedential use of the ATCA prior to *Filartiga* included attention to claims against private violators of international law, U.S. and foreign. *See, e.g.*, Adra v. Clift, 195 F.Supp. 857, 865 (D.Md.1961); Moxon v. The Fanny, 17 F. Cas. 942, 943 (D.C.D. Pa. 1793) (No. 9,895) (federal courts are "particularly by law vested with authority where an alien sues for a tort only in violation of the laws of nations, & c."); M'Grath v. Candalero, 16 F. Cas. 128 (D.C.D. S.C. 1794) (No. 6,810) ("tort" remedy, ATCA addressed by analogy: "If an alien sue here for a tort under the law of nations or a treaty . . . the suit will be sustained"); Bolchos v. Darrel, 3 F. Cas. 810 (D.S.C.1795) (No. 1,607); 26 Op. Att'y Gen. 250 (1907); 1 Op. Att'y Gen. 57, 58–59 (1795) ("there can be no doubt that the company or individuals who have been injured by these acts of hostility have a remedy by civil suit in the courts of the United States; jurisdiction being expressly given to these courts in all cases where an alien sues for a tort only, in violation of the law of nations, or a treaty of the United States."); see also symposium, 4 Hous. J. Int'l L. no. 1 (1981). As it does today, the ATCA applied to conduct and/or injuries or other harm here or abroad.

Under the ATCA, must a plaintiff be an alien at the time of filing? Can plaintiffs be U.S. citizens who, at the time their causes of action arose, were aliens?

7. The language of the ATCA expressly applies to a violation of any treaty of the U.S. and prior to *Sosa* in 2004 the ATCA provides a cause of action (see cases *infra*). In fact, the ATCA is congressional legislation that executes, implements or incorporates by reference treaties of the United States. The ATCA performs the very role that implementing legislation plays with respect to a partly or wholly non-self-executing treaty and it also

provides a cause of action and a remedy. Thus, treaties that are not self-executing are executed or implemented by the ATCA. *See, e.g.*, Estate of Cabello v. Fernandez–Larios, 157 F.Supp.2d 1345, 1359–60 (S.D. Fla. 2001); Ralk v. Lincoln County, 81 F.Supp.2d 1372, 1380 (S.D. Ga. 2000) ("because the ICCPR is not self-executing, Ralk can advance no private right of action under the" treaty, but "could bring a claim under the Alien Tort Claims Act for violations of the ICCPR"); PAUST, *supra*, at 207, 282 n.571, 371–72. An opinion missing this point is Iwanowa v. Ford Motor Co., 67 F.Supp.2d at 439 n.16 (stating in false dictum that two law of war treaties do not "confer rights enforceable by private parties" [*but see* Weisshaus v. Swiss Bankers Ass'n *(In re* Holocaust Victim Assets Litigation), 225 F.3d 191 (2d Cir. 2000); *Kadic*, 70 F.3d at 242–43; *In re* World War II Era Japanese Forced Labor Litigation, 114 F.Supp.2d 939 (N.D. Cal. 2000) (private claims under HC IV settled by peace treaty); Paust, *Suing Saddam: Private Remedies for War Crimes and Hostage–Taking*, 31 VA. J. INT'L L. 351, 360–69 (1991); Paust, *Judicial Power To Determine the Status and Rights of Persons Detained Without Trial*, 44 HARV. INT'L L.J. 503 (2003)] and are entirely non-self-executing–then falsely concluding, in terse, unreasoned and unsupported dictum beyond what plaintiff had argued or briefed (*see id.* at 439), that "[s]ince neither . . . provide a private action, they cannot provide a basis for suit under the ATCA." Of course, human rights treaties are clearly distinguishable in any event since they provide rights enforceable by private parties, access to domestic courts, and the right to an effective remedy).

Must treaties confer private rights expressly? The treaty addressed in 26 Op. Att'y Gen. 250 (1907) did not mention any right of action or "private action," individuals, or private rights, but the Attorney General found that a violation of the treaty by a U.S. company (also recognized as a treaty violation by an International Water Boundary Commission) was actionable in view of the fact that the ATCA provides a right of action. See Convention between the United States of America and the United States of Mexico touching the international boundary line where it follows the bed of the Rio Grande and the Rio Colorado, Nov. 12, 1884, 24 Stat. 1011. Article III of the treaty stated in pertinent part: "No artificial change in the navigable course of the river . . . or by dredging to deepen . . . shall be permitted to affect or alter the dividing line. . . ." *Id.* art. III. This was also the approach at the time of formation of the ATCA. *See, e.g.*, Bolchos v. Darrel, 3 F.Cas. at 811 (Article 14 of the U.S.-France Treaty of Amity and Commerce, 17 July 1778, 8 Stat. 12, T.S. 83, required forfeiture of property interest of Darrel's principal, treaty did not mention any "right of action" or "private action," but claimant Bolchos had an actionable claim under the ATCA to restitution of property wrongfully seized by Darrel); M'Grath v. Candalero, 16 F.Cas. at 128 (1778 U.S.-French Treaty of Amity and Commerce, *supra*, did not mention any "right of action" or "private action," but was used to support a U.S. plaintiff's "tort" remedy, and the ATCA was addressed by analogy and per dictum; *cf* arts. 17, 22 of the treaty, recognizing that some individuals shall be "bound to make Satisfaction for all Matter of Damage, and the Interest thereof, by reparation, under the Pain and obligation of their Person and Goods," "full Satisfaction shall be made"); 1 Op. Att'y Gen. 57 (1795) (apparently U.S.-British Treaty of Peace, 3 Sept. 1783, 8 Stat. 80, T.S. 104, was "a" treaty violated, and the ATCA provided a right of action even though the Treaty of Peace did not mention a relevant "right of action"; *cf* Treaty of Amity, Commerce and Navigation, 19 Nov. 1794, arts. 19, 21, 8 Stat. 116, not mentioning any "right of action" or "private action," but re: injuries by Men of War or Privateers, individuals "shall be bound in their persons and Estates to make satisfaction and reparation for all Damages, and the interest thereof, of whatever nature the said Damages may be." Injuries addressed in the Opinion occurred September 28, 1794, before ratification of the Treaty of Amity. The Opinion also emphasizes a warning to U.S. citizens by the President issued April 22, 1793–when only the Treaty of Peace was operative). More generally, the ATCA expressly incorporates all treaties of the United States by reference and it is the ATCA that provides the direct basis for a lawsuit, not the treaties as such.

8. Is the ten-year limitation in the TVPA tolled when a defendant is outside the territory of the United States? *See also* Hilao v. Estate of Marcos, 103 F.3d 767, 773 (9th Cir.1996) (the Senate Report on the TVPA states that the ten-year statute of limitation is subject to equitable tolling, including for periods in which the defendant is absent from the jurisdiction or immune from lawsuits and for periods in which the plaintiff is imprisoned or incapacitated.); Barrueto, *et al.* v. Larios, 205 F.Supp.2d 1325 (S.D. Fla. 2002); Estate of Cabello, *et al.* v. Fernandez–Larios, 157 F.Supp.2d 1345 (S.D. Fla. 2001).

9. There are no statutes of limitation under international law, and there are none expressed by Congress with respect to the ATCA. *See also* Vietnam Ass'n for Victims of Agent Orange/Dioxin v. Dow Chemical Co. (*In re* Agent Orange Prod. Liab. Litig.), 373 F.Supp.2d 7, 63 (E.D.N.Y. 2005). When courts "legislate" by "borrowing" limitations in other federal statutes, the matter can become complex.

Addressing claims under the ATCA, the district court in Forti v. Suarez–Mason, 672 F.Supp. 1531 (N.D.Cal.1987) noted that there is no statute of limitation under international law regarding such claims, but addressed causes of action with "closest analogies" in state and ordinary federal law and statutes of limitation relating to such. The district court did so arguing that "[w]hile international law provides the substantive standard . . . , the cause of action itself is created by the federal statute," *i.e.*, the ATCA. *Id.* at 1547 n.10. Nonetheless, the court recognized that "because the claim itself is a federal claim, federal equitable tolling doctrines apply" and that such occurs: "(1) where defendant's wrongful conduct prevented plaintiff from timely asserting his claim, or (2) where extraordinary circumstances outside plaintiff's control make it impossible for plaintiff to timely assert his claim." *Id.* at 1549. Plaintiffs had claimed that international law's lack of a statute of limitation, which is itself part of the law of the U.S., is the most analogous federal law. *Id.* at 147 n.10. Which approach is preferable in view of the legal policies at stake with respect to serious violations of international law over which there is universal jurisdiction (see Chapter 3)? Is it relevant that human rights law guarantees a right to an effective remedy in domestic tribunals? *See, e.g.*, Universal Declaration of Human Rights, art. 8; International Covenant on Civil and Political Rights, arts. 2, 14; Paust, *supra* at 198–203. Is it relevant that Congress used a statute of limitations in the TVPA but did not amend the ATCA? *See also* Kadic v. Karadzic, 70 F.3d at 241 (Congress chose not to diminish the reach of the ATCA). Is it relevant that a purpose of the ATCA was to avoid a "denial of justice" to aliens under international law?

10. Are acts of terrorism proscribed under international law regardless of motive, the status of the perpetrator, and the method used? *See, e.g.*, the 1991, 1994, and 2004 U.N. General Assembly resolutions in the Documents Supplement). Are acts of terrorism contrary to human rights law? *See, e.g.*, the 2004 U.N. G.A. resolutions. Are some acts of terrorism crimes against humanity? *See, e.g.*, Charters of the International Military Tribunals at Nuremberg and for the Far East; Control Council Law No. 10.

What would be an objective and descriptive definition of terrorism? Should it include elements of (1) intent (as opposed to mere negligence), (2) to produce terror, (3) a terror outcome, and (4) by methods of violence or weapons (broadly defined to include chemical, biological, or bacteriological agents) or a threat thereof? *See* the 1994 General Assembly resolution, para. 3. Should "terrorism" involve a political, religious, or ideologic motive? Under § 2331 of the Antiterrorism Act, must all acts of "terrorism" involve acts of violence, political motives, or terror outcomes? Is the definitional orientation adequate or too broad? What would you recommend?

11. Are terroristic tactics used against civilians in time of war violations of the laws of war? *See, e.g.*, Geneva Civilian Convention (GC), art. 33; Geneva Protocol I, art. 51(2); 1919 List of War Crimes, in the Documents Supplement.

12. Under § 2336 (a) of the Antiterrorism Act, are only lawful acts of war impliedly covered? Recall that Supreme Court cases recognize that judges must try to interpret legislation consistently with international law if at all possible. Further, war crimes are nonimmune.

13. Under § 2337, with respect to states and agencies thereof, are they not immune when acting outside official capacity or color of legal authority? Was use of the phrase "his or her" sloppy (*e.g.*, should it have read: "its, his or her"?) or intentionally restrictive? Should § 2337 be interpreted consistently with U.S. treaty law on nonimmunity with respect to persons "acting in an official capacity," such as Article 2 (3) (a) of the ICCPR? See also Article 25(1) of the American Convention on Human Rights; Article 13 of the European Convention for the Protection of Human Rights and Fundamental Freedoms. Concerning suits against foreign states and foreign state entities for certain terrorist acts, see also the Foreign Sovereign Immunities Act, 28 U.S.C. § 1605 (a) (7), in the Documents Supplement.

14. Consider § 2332 again when addressing jurisdiction to prescribe under international law (in Chapter 3). What basis(es) exist for prescription regarding murder and serious bodily injury to U.S. nationals? Is there universal jurisdiction with respect to human rights violations?

15. Cases utilizing § 2333 include: Smith v. Islamic Emirate of Afghanistan, *et al.*, 262 F.Supp.2d 217 (S.D.N.Y. 2003) (suit arising out of 9/11 attacks by al Qaeda, *et al.*); Estate of Ungar v. Palestinian Authority, 304 F.Supp.2d 232 (D.R.I. 2004) and 153 F.Supp.2d 76, 85 (D.R.I. 2001) (complicity in killing of U.S. national in Israel); Boim v. Quranic Literary Institute, 127 F.Supp.2d 1002 (N.D.Ill. 2001) (claim of parents of U.S. national in

Israel against an entity that allegedly funded terrorism), *aff'd*, 291 F.3d 1000 (7th Cir. 2002).

16. Recall the War Crimes Act of 2003, 18 U.S.C. § 2441, in Section 2 B 3 a. Are "grave breach" violations of the Geneva Conventions thereby tortious per se? If so, can U.S. nationals sue under 28 U.S.C. § 1331, using the tortious per se approach (without some other statute providing subject matter jurisdiction)? Aliens can sue for such infractions of the laws of war under the Alien Tort Claims Act (ATCA). What other statutes incorporate such customary international law for U.S. plaintiffs (and with respect to what sort of violations)? *See also* Jordan J. Paust, *Suing Saddam: Private Remedies for War Crimes and Hostage–Taking*, 31 VA. J. INT'L L. 351 (1991).

FILARTIGA v. PENA–IRALA

630 F.2d 876 (2d Cir.1980).

KAUFMAN, J.

Upon ratification of the Constitution, the thirteen former colonies were fused into a single nation, one which, in its relations with foreign states, is bound both to observe and construe the accepted norms of international law, formerly known as the law of nations. Under the Articles of Confederation, the several states had interpreted and applied this body of doctrine as a part of their common law, but with the founding of the "more perfect Union" of 1789, the law of nations became preeminently a federal concern.

Implementing the constitutional mandate for national control over foreign relations, the First Congress established original district court jurisdiction over "all causes where an alien sues for a tort only (committed) in violation of the law of nations." Judiciary Act of 1789, ch. 20, § 9(b), 1 Stat. 73, 77 (1789), codified at 28 U.S.C. § 1350 [the ATCA]. Construing this rarely-invoked provision, we hold that deliberate torture perpetrated under color of official authority violates universally accepted norms of the international law of human rights, regardless of the nationality of the parties. Thus, whenever an alleged torturer is found and served with process by an alien within our borders, § 1350 provides federal jurisdiction. Accordingly, we reverse the judgment of the district court dismissing the complaint for want of federal jurisdiction.

I

The appellants, plaintiffs below, are citizens of the Republic of Paraguay. Dr. Joel Filartiga, a physician, describes himself as a long-standing opponent of the government of President Alfredo Stroessner, which has held power in Paraguay since 1954. His daughter, Dolly Filartiga, arrived in the United States in 1978 under a visitor's visa, and has since applied for permanent political asylum. The Filartigas brought this action in the Eastern District of New York against Americo Norberto Pena–Irala (Pena), also a citizen of Paraguay, for wrongfully causing the death of Dr. Filartiga's seventeen-year old son, Joelito. Because the district court dismissed the action for want of subject matter jurisdiction, we must accept as true the allegations contained in the Filartigas' complaint and affidavits for purposes of this appeal.

The appellants contend that on March 29, 1976, Joelito Filartiga was kidnapped and tortured to death by Pena, who was then Inspector General of Police in Asuncion, Paraguay. Later that day, the police brought Dolly Filartiga to Pena's home where she was confronted with the body of her brother, which evidenced marks of severe torture. As she fled, horrified, from the house, Pena followed after her shouting, "Here you have what you have been looking for for so long and what you deserve. Now shut up." The Filartigas claim that Joelito was tortured and killed in retaliation for his father's political activities and beliefs.

Shortly thereafter, Dr. Filartiga commenced a criminal action in the Paraguayan courts against Pena and the police for the murder of his son. As a result, Dr. Filartiga's attorney was arrested and brought to police headquarters where, shackled to a wall, Pena threatened him with death. This attorney, it is alleged, has since been disbarred without just cause.

During the course of the Paraguayan criminal proceeding, which is apparently still pending after four years, another man, Hugo Duarte, confessed to the murder. Duarte, who was a member of the Pena household, claimed that he had discovered his wife and Joelito in flagrante delicto, and that the crime was one of passion. The Filartigas have submitted a photograph of Joelito's corpse showing injuries they believe refute this claim. Dolly Filartiga, moreover, has stated that she will offer evidence of three independent autopsies demonstrating that her brother's death "was the result of professional methods of torture." Despite his confession, Duarte, we are told, has never been convicted or sentenced in connection with the crime.

In July of 1978, Pena sold his house in Paraguay and entered the United States under a visitor's visa. He was accompanied by Juana Bautista Fernandez Villalba, who had lived with him in Paraguay. The couple remained in the United States beyond the term of their visas, and were living in Brooklyn, New York, when Dolly Filartiga, who was then living in Washington, D. C., learned of their presence. Acting on information provided by Dolly the Immigration and Naturalization Service arrested Pena and his companion, both of whom were subsequently ordered deported on April 5, 1979 following a hearing. They had then resided in the United States for more than nine months.

Almost immediately, Dolly caused Pena to be served with a summons and civil complaint at the Brooklyn Navy Yard, where he was being held pending deportation. The complaint alleged that Pena had wrongfully caused Joelito's death by torture and sought compensatory and punitive damages of $10,000,000. The Filartigas also sought to enjoin Pena's deportation to ensure his availability for testimony at trial. The cause of action is stated as arising under "wrongful death statutes; the U. N. Charter; the Universal Declaration on Human Rights; the U. N. Declaration Against Torture; the American Declaration of the Rights and Duties of Man; and other pertinent declarations, documents and practices constituting the customary international law of human rights and the law of nations," as well as 28 U.S.C. § 1350, Article II, sec. 2 and the Supremacy Clause of the U.S. Constitution. Jurisdiction is claimed under the general federal question provision, 28 U.S.C. § 1331 and, principally on this appeal, under the Alien Tort Statute, 28 U.S.C. § 1350.

Judge Nickerson stayed the order of deportation, and Pena immediately moved to dismiss the complaint on the grounds that subject matter jurisdiction was absent and for forum non conveniens. On the jurisdictional issue, there has been no suggestion that Pena claims diplomatic immunity from suit. The Filartigas submitted the affidavits of a number of distinguished international legal scholars, who stated unanimously that the law of nations prohibits absolutely the use of torture as alleged in the complaint.[Profs. Falk, Franck, Lillich, and McDougal] Pena, in support of his motion to dismiss on the ground of forum non conveniens, submitted the affidavit of his Paraguayan counsel, Jose Emilio Gorostiaga, who averred that Paraguayan law provides a full and adequate civil remedy for the wrong alleged. Dr. Filartiga has not commenced such an action, however, believing that further resort to the courts of his own country would be futile.

Judge Nickerson heard argument on the motion to dismiss on May 14, 1979, and on May 15 dismissed the complaint on jurisdictional grounds. The district judge recognized the strength of appellants' argument that official torture violates an emerging norm of customary international law. Nonetheless, he felt constrained by dicta contained in two recent opinions of this Court, Dreyfus v. von Finck, 534 F.2d 24 (2d Cir.), *cert. denied*, 429 U.S. 835 . . . (1976); IIT v. Vencap, Ltd., 519 F.2d 1001 (2d Cir.1975), to construe narrowly "the law of nations," as employed in § 1350, as excluding that law which governs a state's treatment of its own citizens.

The district court continued the stay of deportation for forty-eight hours while appellants applied for further stays. These applications were denied by a panel of this Court on May 22, 1979, and by the Supreme Court two days later. Shortly thereafter, Pena and his companion returned to Paraguay.

II

Appellants rest their principal argument in support of federal jurisdiction upon the Alien Tort Statute, 28 U.S.C. § 1350, which provides: "The district courts shall have original jurisdiction of any civil action by an alien for a tort only, committed in violation of the law of nations or a treaty of the United States." Since appellants do not contend that their action arises directly under a treaty of the United States,[1] a threshold

1. [Court's note 7] Appellants "associate themselves with" the argument of some of the *amici curiae* that their claim arises directly under a treaty of the United States, Brief for Appellants at 23 n.*, but nonetheless primarily rely upon treaties and other

question on the jurisdictional issue is whether the conduct alleged violates the law of nations. In light of the universal condemnation of torture in numerous international agreements, and the renunciation of torture as an instrument of official policy by virtually all of the nations of the world (in principle if not in practice), we find that an act of torture committed by a state official against one held in detention violates established norms of the international law of human rights, and hence the law of nations.

The Supreme Court has enumerated the appropriate sources of international law. The law of nations "may be ascertained by consulting the works of jurists, writing professedly on public law; or by the general usage and practice of nations; or by judicial decisions recognizing and enforcing that law." United States v. Smith, 18 U.S. (5 Wheat.) 153, 160–61 ... (1820); Lopes v. Reederei Richard Schroder, 225 F. Supp. 292, 295 (E.D.Pa.1963). In *Smith*, a statute proscribing "the crime of piracy (on the high seas) as defined by the law of nations," 3 Stat. 510(a) (1819), was held sufficiently determinate in meaning to afford the basis for a death sentence. The *Smith* Court discovered among the works of Lord Bacon, Grotius, Bochard and other commentators a genuine consensus that rendered the crime "sufficiently and constitutionally defined." *Smith*, *supra*, 18 U.S. (5 Wheat.) at 162....

The Paquete Habana, 175 U.S. 677 ... (1900), reaffirmed that:

> where there is no treaty, and no controlling executive or legislative act or judicial decision, resort must be had to the customs and usages of civilized nations; and, as evidence of these, to the works of jurists and commentators, who by years of labor, research and experience, have made themselves peculiarly well acquainted with the subjects of which they treat. Such works are resorted to by judicial tribunals, not for the speculations of their authors concerning what the law ought to be, but for trustworthy evidence of what the law really is.

Id. at 700.... Modern international sources confirm the propriety of this approach.

Habana is particularly instructive for present purposes, for it held that the traditional prohibition against seizure of an enemy's coastal fishing vessels during wartime, a standard that began as one of comity only, had ripened over the preceding century into "a settled rule of international law" by "the general assent of civilized nations." *Id.* at 694 ... ; *accord*, *id.* at 686.... Thus it is clear that courts must interpret international law not as it was in 1789, but as it has evolved and exists among the nations of the world today. See Ware v. Hylton, 3 U.S. (3 Dall.) 199 ... (1796) (distinguishing between "ancient" and "modern" law of nations).

international instruments as evidence of an emerging norm of customary international law, rather then independent sources of law.

The requirement that a rule command the "general assent of civilized nations" to become binding upon them all is a stringent one. Were this not so, the courts of one nation might feel free to impose idiosyncratic legal rules upon others, in the name of applying international law. Thus, in Banco Nacional de Cuba v. Sabbatino, 376 U.S. 398 ... (1964), the Court declined to pass on the validity of the Cuban government's expropriation of a foreign-owned corporation's assets, noting the sharply conflicting views on the issue propounded by the capital-exporting, capital-importing, socialist and capitalist nations. *Id.* at 428–30....

The case at bar presents us with a situation diametrically opposed to the conflicted state of law that confronted the *Sabbatino* Court. Indeed, to paraphrase that Court's statement, *id.* at 428 ... , there are few, if any, issues in international law today on which opinion seems to be so united as the limitations on a state's power to torture persons held in its custody.

The United Nations Charter ... makes it clear that in this modern age a state's treatment of its own citizens is a matter of international concern. It provides:

> With a view to the creation of conditions of stability and well-being which are necessary for peaceful and friendly relations among nations ... the United Nations shall promote ... universal respect for, and observance of, human rights and fundamental freedoms for all without distinctions as to race, sex, language or religion.

Id. Art. 55. And further:

> All members pledge themselves to take joint and separate action in cooperation with the Organization for the achievement of the purposes set forth in Article 55.

Id. Art. 56.

While this broad mandate has been held not to be wholly self-executing, Hitai v. Immigration and Naturalization Service, 343 F.2d 466, 468 (2d Cir.1965), this observation alone does not end our inquiry. For although there is no universal agreement as to the precise extent of the "human rights and fundamental freedoms" guaranteed to all by the Charter, there is at present no dissent from the view that the guaranties include, at a bare minimum, the right to be free from torture. This prohibition has become part of customary international law, as evidenced and defined by the Universal Declaration of Human Rights, General Assembly Resolution 217 (III)(A) (Dec. 10, 1948) which states, in the plainest of terms, "no one shall be subjected to torture." The General Assembly has declared that the Charter precepts embodied in this Universal Declaration "constitute basic principles of international law." G.A. Res. 2625 (XXV) (Oct. 24, 1970).

Particularly relevant is the Declaration on the Protection of All Persons from Being Subjected to Torture, General Assembly Resolution 3452, 30 U.N. GAOR Supp. (No. 34) 91, U.N.Doc. A/1034 (1975).... The

Declaration expressly prohibits any state from permitting the dastardly and totally inhuman act of torture. Torture, in turn, is defined as "any act by which severe pain and suffering, whether physical or mental, is intentionally inflicted by or at the instigation of a public official on a person for such purposes as . . . intimidating him or other persons." The Declaration goes on to provide that "[w]here it is proved that an act of torture or other cruel, inhuman or degrading treatment or punishment has been committed by or at the instigation of a public official, the victim shall be afforded redress and compensation, in accordance with national law." This Declaration, like the Declaration of Human Rights before it, was adopted without dissent by the General Assembly. Nayar, *"Human Rights: The United Nations and United States Foreign Policy,"* 19 HARV. INT'L L.J. 813, 816 n.18 (1978).

These U.N. declarations are significant because they specify with great precision the obligations of member nations under the Charter. Since their adoption, "[m]embers can no longer contend that they do not know what human rights they promised in the Charter to promote." Sohn, *"A Short History of United Nations Documents on Human Rights,"* in THE UNITED NATIONS AND HUMAN RIGHTS, 18TH REPORT OF THE COMMISSION (Commission to Study the Organization of Peace ed. 1968). Moreover, a U.N. Declaration is, according to one authoritative definition, "a formal and solemn instrument, suitable for rare occasions when principles of great and lasting importance are being enunciated." 34 U.N. ESCOR, Supp. (No. 8) 15, U.N. Doc. E/cn.4/1/610 (1962) (memorandum of Office of Legal Affairs, U.N. Secretariat). Accordingly, it has been observed that the Universal Declaration of Human Rights "no longer fits into the dichotomy of 'binding treaty' against 'non-binding pronouncement,' but is rather an authoritative statement of the international community." E. SCHWELB, HUMAN RIGHTS AND THE INTERNATIONAL COMMUNITY 70 (1964). Thus, a Declaration creates an expectation of adherence, and "insofar as the expectation is gradually justified by State practice, a declaration may by custom become recognized as laying down rules binding upon the States." 34 U.N. ESCOR, *supra.* Indeed, several commentators have concluded that the Universal Declaration has become, in toto, a part of binding, customary international law. Nayar, *supra,* at 816–17; Waldlock, *"Human Rights in Contemporary International Law and the Significance of the European Convention,"* INT'L & COMP. L.Q., SUPP. Publ. No. 11 at 15 (1965).

Turning to the act of torture, we have little difficulty discerning its universal renunciation in the modern usage and practice of nations. *Smith, supra,* 18 U.S. (5 Wheat.) at 160–61. . . . The international consensus surrounding torture has found expression in numerous international treaties and accords. *E.g.,* American Convention on Human Rights, Art. 5, OAS Treaty Series No. 36 at 1, OAS Off. Rec. OEA/Ser 4 v/II 23, Doc. 21, rev. 2 (English ed., 1975) ("No one shall be subjected to torture or to cruel, inhuman or degrading punishment or treatment"); International Covenant on Civil and Political Rights, U.N. General Assembly Res. 2200 (XXI)A, U.N. Doc. A/6316 (Dec. 16, 1966) (identical language); European Convention for the Protection of Human Rights and Fundamental Freedoms, Art. 3, Council of Europe, European Treaty Series No. 5 (1968), 213 U.N.T.S. 211 (semble). The substance of these international agreements is reflected in modern municipal, *i.e.*, national law as well. Although torture was once a routine concomitant of criminal interrogations in many nations, during the modern and hopefully more enlightened era it has been universally renounced. According to one survey, torture is prohibited, expressly or implicitly, by the constitutions of over fifty-five nations, including both the United States and Paraguay. Our State Department reports a general recognition of this principle:

> There now exists an international consensus that recognizes basic human rights and obligations owed by all governments to their citizens.... There is no doubt that these rights are often violated; but virtually all governments acknowledge their validity.

Department of State, COUNTRY REPORTS ON HUMAN RIGHTS FOR 1979, published as Joint Comm. Print, House Comm. on Foreign Affairs, and Senate Comm. on Foreign Relations, 96th Cong. 2d Sess. (Feb. 4, 1980), Introduction at 1. We have been directed to no assertion by any contemporary state of a right to torture its own or another nation's citizens. Indeed, United States diplomatic contacts confirm the universal abhorrence with which torture is viewed:

> In exchanges between United States embassies and all foreign states with which the United States maintains relations, it has been the Department of State's general experience that no government has asserted a right to torture its own nationals. Where reports of torture elicit some credence, a state usually responds by denial or, less frequently, by asserting that the conduct was unauthorized or constituted rough treatment short of torture.[2]

Memorandum of the United States as *Amicus Curiae* at 16 n.34.

Having examined the sources from which customary international law is derived the usage of nations, judicial opinions and the works of jurists we conclude that official torture is now prohibited by the law of nations. The prohibition is clear and unambiguous, and admits of no distinction between treatment of aliens and citizens. Accordingly, we must conclude that the dictum in *Dreyfus v. von Finck*, *supra*, 534 F.2d at 31, to the effect that "violations of international law do not occur when the aggrieved parties are nationals of the acting state," is clearly out of tune with the current usage and practice of international law. The treaties and accords cited above, as well as the express foreign policy of our own government, all make it clear that international law confers

2. [Court's note 15] The fact that the prohibition of torture is often honored in the breach does not diminish its binding effect as a norm of international law. As one commentator has put it, "The best evidence for the existence of international law is that every actual State recognizes that it does exist and that it is itself under an obligation to observe it. States often violate international law, just as individuals often violate municipal law; but no more than individuals do States defend their violations by claiming that they are above the law." J. BRIERLY, THE OUTLOOK FOR INTERNATIONAL LAW 4–5 (Oxford 1944).

fundamental rights upon all people vis-a-vis their own governments. While the ultimate scope of those rights will be a subject for continuing refinement and elaboration, we hold that the right to be free from torture is now among them. We therefore turn to the question whether the other requirements for jurisdiction are met.

III

Appellee submits that even if the tort alleged is a violation of modern international law, federal jurisdiction may not be exercised consistent with the dictates of Article III of the Constitution. The claim is without merit. Common law courts of general jurisdiction regularly adjudicate transitory tort claims between individuals over whom they exercise personal jurisdiction, wherever the tort occurred. Moreover, as part of an articulated scheme of federal control over external affairs, Congress provided, in the first Judiciary Act, § 9(b), 1 Stat. 73, 77 (1789), for federal jurisdiction over suits by aliens where principles of international law are in issue. The constitutional basis for the Alien Tort Statute is the law of nations, which has always been part of the federal common law.

It is not extraordinary for a court to adjudicate a tort claim arising outside of its territorial jurisdiction. A state or nation has a legitimate interest in the orderly resolution of disputes among those within its borders, and where the *lex loci delicti commissi* is applied, it is an expression of comity to give effect to the laws of the state where the wrong occurred. Thus, Lord Mansfield in Mostyn v. Fabrigas, 1 Cowp. 161 (1774), *quoted in* McKenna v. Fisk, 42 U.S. (1 How.) 241, 248 ... (1843) said:

> If A becomes indebted to B, or commits a tort upon his person or upon his personal property in Paris, an action in either case may be maintained against A in England, if he is there found.... As to transitory actions, there is not a colour of doubt but that any action which is transitory may be laid in any county in England, though the matter arises beyond the seas.

Mostyn came into our law as the original basis for state court jurisdiction over out-of-state torts, McKenna v. Fisk, *supra*, 42 U.S. (1 How.) 241 ... (personal injury suits held transitory); Dennick v. Railroad Co., 103 U.S. 11 ... (1880) (wrongful death action held transitory), and it has not lost its force in suits to recover for a wrongful death occurring upon foreign soil, Slater v. Mexican National Railroad Co., 194 U.S. 120 ... (1904), as long as the conduct complained of was unlawful where performed. Restatement (Second) of Foreign Relations Law of the United States § 19 (1965). Here, where *in personam* jurisdiction has been obtained over the defendant, the parties agree that the acts alleged would violate Paraguayan law, and the policies of the forum are consistent with the foreign law, state court jurisdiction would be proper. Indeed, appellees conceded as much at oral argument.

Recalling that *Mostyn* was freshly decided at the time the Constitution was ratified, we proceed to consider whether the First Congress acted constitutionally in vesting jurisdiction over "foreign suits," *Slater*, *supra*, 194 U.S. at 124 . . . , alleging torts committed in violation of the law of nations. A case properly "aris(es) under the . . . laws of the United States" for Article III purposes if grounded upon statutes enacted by Congress or upon the common law of the United States. See Illinois v. City of Milwaukee, 406 U.S. 91, 99–100 . . . (1972); Ivy Broadcasting Co., Inc. v. American Tel. & Tel. Co., 391 F.2d 486, 492 (2d Cir.1968). The law of nations forms an integral part of the common law, and a review of the history surrounding the adoption of the Constitution demonstrates that it became a part of the common law of the United States upon the adoption of the Constitution. Therefore, the enactment of the Alien Tort Statute was authorized by Article III.

During the eighteenth century, it was taken for granted on both sides of the Atlantic that the law of nations forms a part of the common law. 1 BLACKSTONE, COMMENTARIES 263–64 (1st Ed. 1765–69); 4 *id.* at 67. Under the Articles of Confederation, the Pennsylvania Court of Oyer and Terminer at Philadelphia, per McKean, Chief Justice, applied the law of nations to the criminal prosecution of the Chevalier de Longchamps for his assault upon the person of the French Consul–General to the United States, noting that "[t]his law, in its full extent, is a part of the law of this state . . ." Respublica v. DeLongchamps, 1 U.S. (1 Dall.) 111, 119 (1784). Thus, a leading commentator has written:

> It is an ancient and a salutary feature of the Anglo–American legal tradition that the Law of Nations is a part of the law of the land to be ascertained and administered, like any other, in the appropriate case. This doctrine was originally conceived and formulated in England in response to the demands of an expanding commerce and under the influence of theories widely accepted in the late sixteenth, the seventeenth and the eighteenth centuries. It was brought to America in the colonial years as part of the legal heritage from England. It was well understood by men of legal learning in America in the eighteenth century when the United Colonies broke away from England to unite effectively, a little later, in the United States of America.

Dickinson, *The Law of Nations as Part of the National Law of the United States*, 101 U. PA. L. REV. 26, 27 (1952).

Indeed, Dickinson goes on to demonstrate, *id.* at 34–41, that one of the principal defects of the Confederation that our Constitution was intended to remedy was the central government's inability to "cause infractions of treaties or of the law of nations, to be punished." 1 FARRAND, RECORDS OF THE FEDERAL CONVENTION 19 (Rev. ed. 1937) (Notes of James Madison). And, in Jefferson's words, the very purpose of the proposed Union was "to make us one nation as to foreign concerns, and keep us distinct in domestic ones." Dickinson, *supra*, at 36 n. 28.

As ratified, the judiciary article contained no express reference to cases arising under the law of nations. Indeed, the only express reference to that body of law is contained in Article I, sec. 8, cl. 10, which grants to the Congress the power to "define and punish ... offenses against the law of nations." Appellees seize upon this circumstance and advance the proposition that the law of nations forms a part of the laws of the United States only to the extent that Congress has acted to define it. This extravagant claim is amply refuted by the numerous decisions applying rules of international law uncodified in any act of Congress. *E.g.*, Ware v. Hylton, 3 U.S. (3 Dall.) 199 ... (1796); *The Paquete Habana, supra*, 175 U.S. 677 ... ; *Sabbatino, supra*, 376 U.S. 398 ... (1964). A similar argument was offered to and rejected by the Supreme Court in United States v. Smith, *supra*, 18 U.S. (5 Wheat.) 153, 158–60 ... and we reject it today. As John Jay wrote in THE FEDERALIST NO. 3, at 22 (1 Bourne ed. 1901), "Under the national government, treaties and articles of treaties, as well as the laws of nations, will always be expounded in one sense and executed in the same manner, whereas adjudications on the same points and questions in the thirteen states will not always accord or be consistent." Federal jurisdiction over cases involving international law is clear.

Thus, it was hardly a radical initiative for Chief Justice Marshall to state in The Nereide, 13 U.S. (9 Cranch) 388, 422 ... (1815), that in the absence of a congressional enactment,[3] United States courts are "bound by the law of nations, which is a part of the law of the land." These words were echoed in The Paquete Habana, *supra*, 175 U.S. at 700 ... : "international law is part of our law, and must be ascertained and administered by the courts of justice of appropriate jurisdiction, as often as questions of right depending upon it are duly presented for their determination."

The Filartigas urge that 28 U.S.C. § 1350 be treated as an exercise of Congress's power to define offenses against the law of nations. While such a reading is possible, see Lincoln Mills v. Textile Workers, 353 U.S. 448 ... (1957) (jurisdictional statute authorizes judicial explication of federal common law), we believe it is sufficient here to construe the Alien Tort Statute, not as granting new rights to aliens, but simply as opening the federal courts for adjudication of the rights already recognized by international law. The statute nonetheless does inform our analysis of Article III, for we recognize that questions of jurisdiction "must be considered part of an organic growth part of an evolutionary process," and that the history of the judiciary article gives meaning to its pithy phrases. Romero v. International Terminal Operating Co., 358 U.S. 354, 360 ... (1959). The Framers' overarching concern that control over international affairs be vested in the new national government to safe-

3. [Court's note 20] The plainest evidence that international law has an existence in the federal courts independent of acts of Congress is the long-standing rule of construction first enunciated by Chief Justice Marshall: "an act of congress ought never to be construed to violate the law of nations, if any other possible construction remains...." The Charming Betsy, 6 U.S. (2 Cranch), 64, 67 ... (1804)....

guard the standing of the United States among the nations of the world therefore reinforces the result we reach today....

Pena also argues that "if the conduct complained of is alleged to be the act of the Paraguayan government, the suit is barred by the Act of State doctrine." This argument was not advanced below, and is therefore not before us on this appeal. We note in passing, however, that we doubt whether action by a state official in violation of the Constitution and laws of the Republic of Paraguay, and wholly unratified by that nation's government, could properly be characterized as an act of state. See Banco Nacionale de Cuba v. Sabbatino, *supra*, 376 U.S. 398 ... ; Underhill v. Hernandez, 168 U.S. 250 ... (1897). Paraguay's renunciation of torture as a legitimate instrument of state policy, however, does not strip the tort of its character as an international law violation, if it in fact occurred under color of government authority. See Declaration on the Protection of All Persons from Being Subjected to Torture, *supra* note 11; *cf.* Ex parte Young, 209 U.S. 123 ... (1908) (state official subject to suit for constitutional violations despite immunity of state)....

... In the modern age, humanitarian and practical considerations have combined to lead the nations of the world to recognize that respect for fundamental human rights is in their individual and collective interest. Among the rights universally proclaimed by all nations, as we have noted, is the right to be free of physical torture. Indeed, for purposes of civil liability, the torturer has become like the pirate and slave trader before him *hostis humani generis*, an enemy of all mankind. Our holding today, giving effect to a jurisdictional provision enacted by our First Congress, is a small but important step in the fulfillment of the ageless dream to free all people from brutal violence.

FILARTIGA v. PENA–IRALA

577 F.Supp. 860 (E.D.N.Y.1984).

NICKERSON, J.

The Court of Appeals decided only that Section 1350 gave jurisdiction. We must now face the issue left open by the Court of Appeals, namely, the nature of the "action" over which the section affords jurisdiction. Does the "tort" to which the statute refers mean a wrong "in violation of the law of nations" or merely a wrong actionable under the law of the appropriate sovereign state?....

The word "tort" has historically meant simply "wrong" or "the opposite of right," so-called, according to Lord Coke, because it is "wrested" or "crooked," being contrary to that which is "right" and "straight". SIR EDWARD COKE ON LITTLETON 158b; see also W. PROSSER, LAW OF TORTS 2 (1971). There was nothing about the contemporary usage of the word in 1789, when Section 1350 was adopted, to suggest that it should be read to encompass wrongs defined as such by a national state but not by international law. Even before the adoption of the Constitution piracy was defined as a crime by the law of nations. United States v. Smith, 18 U.S. (5 Wheat.) 153, 157 ... (1820). As late as 1819 Congress passed legislation, now 18 U.S.C. § 1651, providing for punishment of "the crime of piracy, as defined by the law of nations." 3 Stat. 510 (1819). Congress would hardly have supposed when it enacted Section 1350 that a "crime," but not the comparable "tort," was definable by the law of nations. Nor is there any legislative history of the section to suggest such a limitation.

Accordingly, there is no basis for adopting a narrow interpretation of Section 1350 inviting frustration of the purposes of international law by individual states that enact immunities for government personnel or other such exemptions or limitations. The court concludes that it should determine the substantive principles to be applied by looking to international law....

The international law described by the Court of Appeals does not ordain detailed remedies but sets forth norms. But plainly international "law" does not consist of mere benevolent yearnings never to be given effect. Indeed, the Declaration on the Protection of All Persons from Being Subjected to Torture, General Assembly Resolution 3452, 30 U.N. GAOR Supp. (No.34) 91, U.N. Doc. A/1034 (1975), adopted without dissent by the General Assembly, recites that where an act of torture has been committed by or at the instigation of a public official, the victim shall be afforded redress and compensation "in accordance with national law," art. 11, and that "each state" shall ensure that all acts of torture are offenses under its criminal law, art. 7.

The international law prohibiting torture established the standard and referred to the national states the task of enforcing it. By enacting Section 1350 Congress entrusted that task to the federal courts and gave them power to choose and develop federal remedies to effectuate the purposes of the international law incorporated into United States common law.

In order to take the international condemnation of torture seriously this court must adopt a remedy appropriate to the ends and reflective of the nature of the condemnation. Torture is viewed with universal abhorrence.... If the courts of the United States are to adhere to the consensus of the community of humankind, any remedy they fashion must recognize that this case concerns an act so monstrous as to make its perpetrator an outlaw around the globe....

Plaintiffs claim punitive damages, and the Magistrate recommended they be denied on the ground that they are not recoverable under the Paraguayan Civil Code....

Yet because, as the record establishes, Paraguay will not undertake to prosecute Pena for his acts, the objective of the international law making torture punishable as a crime can only be vindicated by imposing punitive damages....

Moreover, there is some precedent for the award of punitive damages in tort even against a national government. In *I'm Alone* (Canada v. United States), U.N. Rep. Int. Arb. Awards, vol. 3, at 1609, the American and Canadian claims Commissioners recommended, in addition to compensatory damages, payment of $25,000 by the United States to Canada for intentionally sinking a Canadian ship. In de Letelier v. Republic of Chile, 502 F. Supp. 259, 266, 267 (D.D.C.1980), the court awarded $2,000,000 in punitive damages against the Republic of Chile and various of its employees to the survivors and personal representatives of the former Chilean Ambassador to the United States and a passenger in his car, both killed by the explosion of a bomb. While the court imposed the damages under domestic laws, it mentioned that the "tortious actions" proven were "in violation of international law." *Id.* at 266.

Where the defendant is an individual, the same diplomatic considerations that prompt reluctance to impose punitive damages are not present. The Supreme Court in dicta has recognized that punishment is an appropriate objective under the law of nations, saying in The Marianna Flora, 24 U.S. (11 Wheat.) 1, 41 ... (1826), that "an attack from revenge and malignity, from gross abuse of power, and a settled purpose of mischief ... may be punished by all the penalties which the law of nations can properly administer." ...

This court concludes that it is essential and proper to grant the remedy of punitive damages in order to give effect to the manifest objectives of the international prohibition against torture.

In concluding that the plaintiffs were entitled only to damages recoverable under Paraguayan law, the Magistrate recommended they be awarded $150,000 each as compensation for emotional pain and suffering, loss of companionship and disruption of family life. He also suggested that Dolly Filartiga receive $25,000 for her future medical expenses for treatment of her psychiatric impairment and that Dr. Filartiga receive $50,000 for past expenses related to funeral and medical expenses and to lost income. The Magistrate recommended against an award of punitive damages and of $10,364 in expenses incurred in connection with this action. Plaintiffs object only to these last recommendations....

The record in this case shows that torture and death are bound to recur unless deterred. This court concludes that an award of punitive damages of no less than $5,000,000 to each plaintiff is appropriate to reflect adherence to the world community's proscription of torture and to attempt to deter its practice.

Judgment may be entered for plaintiff Dolly M. E. Filartiga in the amount of $5,175,000 and for plaintiff Joel Filartiga in the amount of $5,210,364, a total judgment of $10,385,364. So ordered.

Notes and Questions

1. In *Filartiga*, both the Second Circuit and the district court paid some attention to Paraguayan law. In view of the fact that the substantive

legal standards incorporated by reference under the ATCA are those under international law, should a court look to foreign domestic law? Near the time of formation of the ATCA, violations of international law were also the focus of attention. *See, e.g.*, Bolchos v. Darrel, 3 F.Cas. 810 (D.S.C. 1795); 1 Op. Att'y Gen. 57 (1795); *see also* Moxon v. The Fanny, 17 F.Cas. 942, 943 (D.C.D. Pa. 1793) (No. 9,895); M'Grath v. Candalero, 16 F.Cas. 128 (D.C.D.S.C. 1794) (No. 6,810). What dangers might occur if courts looked to foreign law and the foreign state allowed torture, cruel treatment, disappearances of individuals?

2. How was the United Nations Charter utilized in *Filartiga*? How was the Universal Declaration of Human Rights?

When identifying and clarifying actionable human rights, one need only identify rights that are "sufficiently determinable." *See, e.g.*, Alvarez–Machain v. United States, *et al.*, 331 F.3d 604, 612 (9th Cir. 2003) ("sufficient consensus," " 'sufficiently ... defined,' " *quoting* United States v. Smith, 18 U.S. (5 Wheat.) 153, 162 (1820)); *id.*, 266 F.3d 1045 (9th Cir. 2001) (norm need not be specific in human rights instruments); Hilao v. Estate of Marcos (*In re* Estate of Ferdinand Marcos Human Rights Litig.), 25 F.3d at 1475 (" 'definable' "); Tel–Oren v. Libyan Arab Republic, 726 F.2d at 781 (Edwards, J.) ("definable"); Filartiga v. Pena–Irala, 630 F.2d at 880–82 (above); Xuncax v. Gramajo, 886 F.Supp. at 185 ("adequately defined"), 187 ("not necessary that every aspect ... be fully defined"); Forti v. Suarez–Mason, 672 F.Supp. at 1540–42 (below: "definable," "sufficient consensus to evince"); *id.*, 694 F.Supp. at 710–11 (below: "sufficient to establish"); *see also* Kadic v. Karadzic, 70 F.3d at 238 (courts ascertain the evolving content of the law of nations); *cf id.* at 239 ("well-established" norms). *See also* Sosa v. Alvarez–Machain, 542 U.S. 692 (2004) ("courts should require any claim based on the present day law of nations to rest on a norm of international character accepted by the civilized world and defined with a specificity comparable to the features of the 18th-century paradigms" recognized by the Court, which included piracy, acts of hostility or breaches of neutrality, infringements of rights of ambassadors, violations of safe conduct, and war crimes [and how were these defined?], also addressing *United States v. Smith* as a case "illustrating the specificity with which the law of nations defined piracy" and *In re Estate of Marcos*, and stating that the issue is "whether a norm is sufficiently definite to support a cause of action."

Further, as noted in *Filartiga*, 630 F.2d at 881, courts must use international law as it has evolved. *See, e.g.*, Kadic v. Karadzic, 70 F.3d at 238, 241; Amerada Hess Shipping Corp. v. Argentine Republic, 830 F.2d at 425; Tel–Oren v. Libyan Arab Republic, 726 F.2d at 777 (Edwards, J.); Estate of Rodriquez v. Drummond Co., Inc., 256 F.Supp.2d at 1263; Presbyterian Church of Sudan v. Talisman Energy, Inc., 374 F.Supp.2d 331 (S.D.N.Y. 2005), *id.*, 244 F.Supp.2d at 304; Maria v. McElroy, 68 F.Supp. 2d 206, 233 (E.D.N.Y. 1999); Iwanowa v. Ford Motor Co., 67 F.Supp.2d at 445; Jama v. U.S. I.N.S., 22 F.Supp.2d at 362; Doe v. Islamic Salvation Front, 993 F.Supp. at 8; Xuncax v. Gramajo, 886 F.Supp. at 179 n.18; Forti v. Suarez–Mason, 672 F.Supp. at 1539; Paust, *supra*, at 206, 281–82 n.562; H.R. Rep. No. 102–367, at 3–4 (1991), *reprinted in* 4 U.S.C.C.A.N. 86 (1992) ("norms ... may ripen in the future into rules of customary international law").

3. The U.S. and all states in the Americas are bound by the American Declaration of the Rights and Duties of Man, which is now a legally authoritative indicia of human rights protected through Article 3 (k) of the O.A.S. Charter, done April 30, 1948, 119 U.N.T.S. 3, 2 U.S.T. 2394, T.I.A.S. No. 2631, amended by the Protocol of Buenos Aires, done 27 Feb. 1967, 21 U.S.T. 607, T.I.A.S. No. 6847 [*see also id.* arts. 44, 111]. *See, e.g.*, Advisory Opinion OC–10/89, Inter–Am. Court H.R., Ser. A, No. 10, para. 45 (1989); Inter–American Comm. on Human Rights, Report on the Situation of the Inhabitants of the Interior of Ecuador Affected by Development Activities, Chapter VII (1996), O.A.S. Doc. OEA/Ser.L/V/II.96, doc. 10, rev. 1 (April 24, 1997) ("The American Declaration ... continues to serve as a source of international obligation for all member states...."); *see also* American Convention on Human Rights, preamble and art. 29 (d). The U.S. has signed but has not yet ratified the American Convention. In view of Article 18(a) of the Vienna Convention on the Law of Treaties, what is the U.S. obligation with respect to rights protected by the American Convention?

4. Another case not mentioned in *Filartiga* concerning punitive or aggravated damages is The Apollon, 22 U.S. (9 Wheat.) 362, 374, 377 (1824) (foreign private plaintiff has standing and can sue the U.S. for a violation of the law of nations by unlawfully seizing a foreign ship in foreign territorial waters and can obtain damages, travel expenses concerning the suit, attorney fees, and "vindictive" or "aggravated" damages).

5. Several of the post-*Filartiga* cases (*infra*) recognized jurisdictional competence in U.S. courts even though there was no nexus with the forum. Under customary international law, all states have jurisdictional competence to provide civil or criminal proceedings with respect to violations of customary international law, if not other violations by treaty. Recall the excerpts from Talbot v. Janson, 3 U.S. (3 Dall.) 133 (1795); Demjanjuk v. Petrovsky, 776 F.2d 571 (6th Cir. 1985). See Chapter 3 (a competence termed universal jurisdiction to prescribe). Also under international law, litigation or prosecution of such claims can occur once the defendant is on U.S. territory. In domestic U.S. law, court's would recognize the existence of "personal jurisdiction" at that point. See Chapter 3 (exercise of a competence termed enforcement jurisdiction). Personal jurisdiction is possible, for example, if an individual is served process, or arrested, while the person is temporarily within the U.S.

Would universal jurisdiction be a basis for U.S. application of the ATCA in *Filartiga*? Note that the customary international law that provides universal jurisdictional competence is part of the law of the United States. Is such a jurisdictional competence relevant to general federal judicial jurisdiction (under the U.S. Const., Art. III) and federal question jurisdiction (under 28 U.S.C. § 1331)? Recall Section 2 B 1 of this chapter. Several of the cases in this section address additional jurisdictional issues under domestic law (*e.g.*, federal question jurisdiction and subject matter jurisdiction).

6. Concerning universal jurisdiction over customary human rights violations, *see, e.g.*, Beth Stephens, *Translating* Filartiga*: A Comparative and International Law Analysis of Domestic Remedies for International Human Rights Violations*, 27 Yale J. Int'l L. 1, 35, 42, 49–50 (2002); Jordan J. Paust, *Suing Karadzic*, 10 Leiden J. Int'l L. 91, 95–96 (1997); Paust, *Suing*

Saddam: Private Remedies for War Crimes and Hostage–Taking, 31 VA. J. INT'L L. 351, 371–74 (1991); and cases that follow.

7. Are leaders liable for more than direct participation in, complicity in, or giving orders to violate international law? What if a leader merely tolerates torture, cruel treatment, or other war crimes or human rights violations by those under the leader's effective control? Consider the extract from Kadic v. Karadzic in Chapter 1 and the international legal precept of leader or command responsibility or dereliction of duty mirrored partly in several cases that follow.

Concerning leader or command responsibility under the knew or should have known test, *see, e.g.*, PAUST, BASSIOUNI, *ET AL.*, *supra* at 27–33, 46–79, 86–99, 621–22, 660, 702–03, 717, 741–47; Ilias Bantekas, *The Contemporary Law of Superior Responsibility*, 93 AM. J. INT'L L. 573 (1999); William Hays Parks, *Command Responsibility for War Crimes*, 62 MIL. L. REV. 1 (1973); Jordan J. Paust, *My Lai and Vietnam: Norms, Myths and Leader Responsibility*, 57 MIL. L. REV. 99, 175–85 (1972). The general test includes responsibility for negligence or dereliction of duty if a leader, under the circumstances, (1) should have known that persons under his or her authority or control had committed, were committing or were about to commit relevant infractions; (2) the leader had an opportunity to act; and (3) the leader took no reasonable corrective action. Article 28(1)(a) of the Rome Statute for the ICC generally reflects this customary test with respect to military leaders, but paragraph (b) sets forth a far more limiting test for civilian leaders prosecutable before the ICC. It changes "should have known" to "or consciously disregarded information which clearly indicated," and thus does not reflect a long and rich history of leader responsibility under the "knew or should have known" test that has been applied to nonmilitary officials, leaders, and persons with actual control.

FORTI v. SUAREZ–MASON

672 F.Supp. 1531 (N.D.Cal.1987).

JENSEN, J.

This is a civil action brought against a former Argentine general by two Argentine citizens currently residing in the United States. Plaintiffs Forti and Benchoam sue on their own behalf and on behalf of family members, seeking damages from defendant Suarez–Mason for actions which include, *inter alia*, torture, murder, and prolonged arbitrary detention, allegedly committed by military and police personnel under defendant's authority and control. As will be discussed more fully below, plaintiffs predicate federal jurisdiction on 28 U.S.C. §§ 1350 (the "Alien Tort Statute") and 1331. They claim jurisdiction for their various state-law claims under the doctrine of pendent and ancillary jurisdiction....

Plaintiffs' action arises out of events alleged to have occurred in the mid-to late 1970s during Argentina's so-called "dirty war" against suspected subversives. In 1975 the activities of terrorists representing the extremes of both ends of the political spectrum induced the constitutional government of President Peron to declare a "state of siege" under

Article 23 of the Argentine Constitution. President Peron also decreed that the Argentine Armed Forces should assume responsibility for suppressing terrorism. The country was accordingly divided into defense zones, each assigned to an army corps. In each zone the military was authorized to detain suspects and hold them in prison or in military installations pursuant to the terms of the "state of siege." Zone One—which included most of the Province of Buenos Aires and encompassed the national capital—was assigned to the First Army Corps. From January 1976 until January 1979 defendant Suarez–Mason was Commander of the First Army Corps.

On March 24, 1976 the commanding officers of the Armed Forces seized the government from President Peron. The ruling military junta continued the "state of siege" and caused the enactment of legislation providing that civilians accused of crimes of subversion would be judged by military law. *See, e.g.*, Law 21.264. In the period from 1976 to 1979, tens of thousands of persons were detained without charges by the military, and it is estimated that more than 12,000 were "disappeared," never to be seen again. *See generally Nunca Mas*: The Report of the Argentine National Commission on the Disappeared (1986).

In January 1984 the constitutionally elected government of President Raul Alfonsin assumed power. The Alfonsin government commenced investigations of alleged human rights abuses by the military, and the criminal prosecution of certain former military authorities followed. The government vested the Supreme Council of the Armed Forces with jurisdiction over the prosecution of military commanders. Summoned by the Supreme Council in March 1984, defendant failed to appear and in fact fled the country. In January of 1987 Suarez–Mason was arrested in Foster City, California pursuant to a provisional arrest warrant at the request of the Republic of Argentina. While defendant was in custody awaiting an extradition hearing he was served with the Complaint herein....

B. Allegations of the Complaint

The Complaint alleges claims for damages based on acts allegedly committed by personnel within the defense zone under General Suarez–Mason's command. According to the Complaint, police and military officials seized plaintiff Alfredo Forti, along with his mother and four brothers, from an airplane at Buenos Aires' Ezeiza International Airport on February 18, 1977. Compl. paras. 3, 10. The entire family was held at the "Pozo de Quilmes" detention center, located in a suburb of Buenos Aires in Buenos Aires Province.... No charges were ever filed against the Fortis. After six days the five sons were released, dropped blindfolded on a street in the capital. The mother, Nelida Azucena Sosa de Forti, was not released, and remains "disappeared" to this day, despite efforts on behalf of the Forti family by the Interamerican Commission on Human Rights and several members of the United States Congress....

When seizing the six members of the Forti family at Ezeiza Airport, the authorities also allegedly seized all of the family's belongings, which included several thousand dollars in cash. To date, only some personal effects have been returned....

An Argentine court which adjudicated criminal liability of the nine former junta members has attributed direct responsibility for the February 18, 1977 seizure of the Forti family to the First Army Corps....

As to plaintiff Debora Benchoam, the Complaint alleges that Benchoam and her brother were abducted from their Buenos Aires bedroom before dawn on July 25, 1977 by military authorities in plain clothes.... At the time Benchoam was sixteen years old and her brother, seventeen.

Benchoam was blindfolded and taken first to an unidentified house and later to a police station in Buenos Aires, where she was held incommunicado for a month.... For the first week of detention Benchoam was kept blindfolded with her hands handcuffed behind her back, and was provided neither food nor clothing. A guard attempted to rape her....

On August 28, 1977, allegedly at the direction of defendant Suarez–Mason, Benchoam was transferred to Devoto Prison in Buenos Aires. Here she was imprisoned, without charge, for more than four years.... In 1979 or 1980 plaintiff obtained a writ of habeas corpus, but the writ was reversed on appeal. Finally, as a result of international and domestic appeals, plaintiff was granted the "right of option" and allowed to leave the country. She was released from prison on November 5, 1981 and came to the United States as a refugee....

The military personnel also abducted plaintiff's seventeen-year-old brother on July 25, 1977.... The brother's body was returned to the Benchoam family the following day. He had died of internal bleeding from bullet wounds, and his face was "severely disfigured" from blows....

Additionally, plaintiff's abductors allegedly stole jewelry, cash, and clothing valued at $20,000, none of which has ever been returned....

Although the individual acts are alleged to have been committed by military and police officials, plaintiffs allege that these actors were all agents, employees, or representatives of defendant acting pursuant to a "policy, pattern and practice" of the First Army Corps under defendant's command. Plaintiffs assert that defendant "held the highest position of authority" in Buenos Aires Province; that defendant was responsible for maintaining the prisons and detention centers there, as well as the conduct of Army officers and agents; and that he "authorized, approved, directed and ratified" the acts complained of....

Plaintiff Forti filed a criminal complaint against defendant and others in November 1983, shortly after the election of President Alfonsin. That complaint has not yet been adjudicated as against Suarez–Mason.... Plaintiff Benchoam has apparently not filed criminal charges against defendant. Although both plaintiffs retain their Argentine citizenship, both reside currently in Virginia.... Plaintiffs predicate federal jurisdiction principally on the "Alien Tort Statute," 28 U.S.C. § 1350, and alternatively on federal question jurisdiction, 28 U.S.C. § 1331. Additionally, they assert jurisdiction for their common-law tort claims under principles of pendent and ancillary jurisdiction....

Based on these above allegations, plaintiffs seek compensatory and punitive damages for violations of customary international law and laws of the United States, Argentina, and California. They press eleven causes of action. Both allege claims for torture; prolonged arbitrary detention without trial; cruel, inhuman and degrading treatment; false imprisonment; assault and battery; intentional infliction of emotional distress; and conversion. Additionally Forti claims damages for "causing the disappearance of individuals," and Benchoam asserts claims for "murder and summary execution," wrongful death, and a survival action.

In response to these allegations, defendant moves to dismiss the entire Complaint under Federal Rule of Civil Procedure 12(b), subsections (1) and (6). He argues that the Court lacks subject matter jurisdiction under 28 U.S.C. § 1350 to adjudicate tort claims arising out of "politically motivated acts of violence in other countries" and, alternatively, that not all of the torts alleged constitute violations of the law of nations. Defendant also argues that adjudication of plaintiffs' claims is barred by the act of state doctrine, which prohibits United States courts from adjudicating the legality of the actions of a foreign government official acting in his official capacity. Further, he contends that plaintiffs' claims are time-barred under the applicable Argentine statute of limitations; that plaintiffs have failed to join indispensable parties, and that plaintiff Benchoam lacks capacity to sue for her brother's death....

SUBJECT MATTER JURISDICTION

As a threshold matter, defendant argues that the Court lacks subject matter jurisdiction under 28 U.S.C. § 1350, the "Alien Tort Statute." Defendant urges the Court to follow the interpretation of § 1350 as a purely jurisdictional statute which requires that plaintiffs invoking it establish the existence of an independent, private right of action in international law. Defendant argues that the law of nations provides no tort cause of action for the acts of "politically motivated terrorism" challenged by plaintiffs' Complaint. Alternatively, defendant argues that even if § 1350 provides a cause of action for violations of the law of nations, not all of the torts alleged by plaintiffs qualify as violations of the law of nations. For the reasons set out below, the Court rejects defendant's construction of § 1350 and finds that plaintiffs allege sufficient facts to establish subject matter jurisdiction under both the Alien Tort Statute and 28 U.S.C. § 1331. However, the Court agrees with defendant that not all of the alleged claims constitute "international torts" cognizable under 28 U.S.C. § 1350. Accordingly, the Court dismisses with prejudice the claims for "causing disappearance" and "cruel, inhuman, or degrading treatment." Further, the Court orders plaintiffs to amend the Complaint to state more definitely the facts constituting their claim for official torture.

A. The Alien Tort Statute

The Alien Tort Statute provides that federal district courts shall have "original jurisdiction of any civil action by an alien for a tort only, committed in violation of the law of nations or a treaty of the United States." 28 U.S.C. § 1350 (1982). The district courts' jurisdiction is concurrent with that of state courts. See Act of Sept. 24, 1789 (First Judiciary Act), ch. 20, § 9, 1 Stat. 73, 77. As the cases and commentaries recognize, the history of the Alien Tort Statute is obscure. *See, e.g.*, IIT v. Vencap, Ltd., 519 F.2d 1001, 1015 (2d Cir.1975) (§ 1350 a "kind of legal Lohengrin"). Nonetheless, the proper interpretation of the statute has been discussed at some length in the principal decisions upon which the parties rely: the unanimous decision in Filartiga v. Pena–Irala, 630 F.2d 876 (2d Cir.1980) and the three concurring opinions in Tel–Oren v. Libyan Arab Republic, ... 726 F.2d 774 (D.C.Cir.1984), *cert. denied*, 470 U.S. 1003 ... (1985).

Defendant urges the Court to adopt the reasoning of Judges Bork and Robb in *Tel-Oren, supra*, where the court affirmed the dismissal of a § 1350 tort action against various defendants based on a terrorist attack in Israel by members of the Palestine Liberation Organization. While the three judges concurred in the result, they were unable to agree on the rationale. Judge Bork found that § 1350 constitutes no more than a grant of jurisdiction; that plaintiffs seeking to invoke it must establish a private right of action under either a treaty or the law of nations; and that in the latter category the statute can support jurisdiction at most over only three international crimes recognized in 1789—violation of safe-conducts, infringement of ambassadorial rights, and piracy. *Tel-Oren, supra*, 726 F.2d at 798–823 (Bork, J., concurring). Judge Robb, on the other hand, found that the dispute involved international political violence and so was "nonjusticiable" within the meaning of the political question doctrine. *Id.* at 823–27 (Robb, Jr., concurring).

The Court is persuaded, however, that the interpretation of § 1350 forwarded by the Second Circuit in *Filartiga, supra*, and largely adopted by Judge Edwards in *Tel-Oren*, is better reasoned and more consistent with principles of international law. There appears to be a growing consensus that § 1350 provides a cause of action for certain "international common law torts." *See, e.g., Filartiga, supra*; *Tel-Oren, supra* (Edwards, J., concurring); Guinto v. Marcos, 654 F. Supp. 276, 279–80 (S.D.Cal.1986); Von Dardel v. USSR, 623 F. Supp. 246, 256–59 (D.D.C. 1985) (finding violation under any of the three *Tel-Oren* approaches); Siderman v. Republic of Argentina, No. CV 82–1772–RMT(MCx) (C.D. Cal. September 28, 1984), *vacated on other grounds*. (C.D. Cal March 7, 1985) (Lexis, Genfed library, Dist. file). It is unnecessary that plaintiffs establish the existence of an independent, express right of action, since the law of nations clearly does not create or define civil actions, and to require such an explicit grant under international law would effectively nullify that portion of the statute which confers jurisdiction over tort suits involving the law of nations. See Tel–Oren, 726 F.2d at 778 (Edwards, J., concurring). Rather, a plaintiff seeking to predicate jurisdiction on the Alien Tort Statute need only plead a "tort . . . in violation of the law of nations."

The contours of this requirement have been delineated by the *Filartiga* court and by Judge Edwards in *Tel-Oren*. Plaintiffs must plead a violation of the law of nations as it has evolved and exists in its contemporary form. Filartiga, 630 F.2d at 881; Tel–Oren, 726 F.2d at 777 (Edwards, J., concurring); Amerada Hess Shipping Corp. v. Argentine Republic, 830 F.2d 421, [425] (2d Cir.1987).... This "international tort" must be one which is definable, obligatory (rather than hortatory), and universally condemned. Filartiga, 630 F.2d at 881; *Tel-Oren*, 726 F.2d at 781 (Edwards, J., concurring); Guinto, *supra*, 654 F. Supp. at 279–80; *see also* Blum & Steinhardt, *Federal Jurisdiction over International Human Rights Claims: The Alien Tort Claims Act after* Filartiga v. Pena–Irala, 22 Harv. Int'l L.J. 53, 87–90 (1981) ["Blum & Steinhardt"]; Schneebaum, *The Enforceability of Customary Norms of Public International Law*, 8 Brooklyn J. Int'l L. 189, 301–02 (1982). The requirement of international consensus is of paramount importance, for it is that consensus which evinces the willingness of nations to be bound by the particular legal principle, and so can justify the court's exercise of jurisdiction over the international tort claim.

It is appropriate here to dispose of two arguments advanced by defendant. First, defendant's contention that the law of nations extends only to relations between sovereign states is unsupported. Defendant relies on the Second Circuit's statement in Dreyfus v. Von Finck, 534 F.2d 24, 30–31 (2d Cir.), *cert. denied*, 429 U.S. 835 ... (1976), that the law of nations deals "with the relationship among nations rather than individuals." The Second Circuit has expressly disavowed this dictum, at least insofar as it concerns individual injuries under the international law of human rights. Filartiga, 630 F.2d at 884; *see also* de Sanchez v. Banco Central de Nicaragua, 770 F.2d 1385, 1396 & n. 15 (5th Cir.1985). Second, it is evident that plaintiffs need not establish that every tort claim alleged constitutes an international tort within the meaning of § 1350....

The Court thus interprets 28 U.S.C. § 1350 to provide not merely jurisdiction but a cause of action, with the federal cause of action arising by recognition of certain "international torts" through the vehicle of § 1350. These international torts, violations of current customary international law, are characterized by universal consensus in the international community as to their binding status and their content. That is, they are universal, definable, and obligatory international norms. The Court now examines the allegations of the Complaint to determine whether plaintiffs have stated cognizable international torts for purposes of jurisdiction under § 1350.

B. Analysis Under 28 U.S.C. § 1350

In determining whether plaintiffs have stated cognizable claims under Section 1350, the Court has recourse to "the works of jurists, writing professedly on public law; ... the general usage and practice of nations; [and] judicial decisions recognizing and enforcing that law." United States v. Smith, 18 U.S. (5 Wheat.) 153, 160–61 ... (1820). For purposes of defendant's motion to dismiss, the Court must accept as true all of plaintiffs' allegations, construing them in the light most favorable to plaintiffs.... The Court may grant dismissal only if it is clear that plaintiffs can prove no set of facts which would entitle them to relief....

1. Official Torture

In Count One, plaintiffs both allege torture conducted by military and police personnel under defendant's command. The Court has no doubt that official torture constitutes a cognizable violation of the law of nations under § 1350. This was the very question addressed by the Second Circuit in *Filartiga, supra*. There, after examining numerous sources of international law, see Filartiga, 630 F.2d at 880–84 & n.16, the court concluded that the law of nations contains a "clear and unambiguous" prohibition of official torture. This proscription is universal, obligatory, and definable. Of course, purely private torture will not normally implicate the law of nations, since there is currently no international consensus regarding torture practiced by non-state actors. See Tel–Oren, 726 F.2d at 791–95 (Edwards, J., concurring). Here, however, plaintiffs allege torture by military and police personnel under the supervision and control of defendant while he served as Commander of the First Army Corps. The claim would thus allege torture committed by state officials and so fall within the international tort first recognized in *Filartiga*....

2. Prolonged Arbitrary Detention

In Count Four plaintiffs both allege a claim for prolonged arbitrary detention, stating that defendant "arbitrarily and without justification, cause or privilege, forcibly confined both plaintiff Benchoam and Nelida Azucena Sosa de Forti for a prolonged period." ... Elsewhere plaintiffs allege that Benchoam was imprisoned for more than four years without ever being charged, while Forti's mother was arrested in 1977 but was never charged or released.

There is case law finding sufficient consensus to evince a customary international human rights norm against arbitrary detention. Rodriguez Fernandez v. Wilkinson, 505 F. Supp. 787, 795–98 (D.Kan.1980) (citing international treaties, cases, and commentaries), *aff'd*, 654 F.2d 1382 (10th Cir.1981); *see also* De Sanchez, *supra*, 770 F.2d at 1397 (right "not to be arbitrarily detained" incorporated into law of nations); Nguyen Da Yen v. Kissinger, 528 F.2d 1194, 1201 n. 13 (9th Cir.1975) (illegal detention may constitute international tort); *but see* Jean v. Nelson, 727 F.2d 957, 964 & n. 4 (11th Cir.1984) (disagreed with *Rodriguez Fernan-*

dez in holding that detention of uninvited aliens under national sovereign's exclusion power is no violation of customary international law), *aff'd*, 472 U.S. 846 . . . (1985). The consensus is even clearer in the case of a state's prolonged arbitrary detention of its own citizens. *See, e.g.*, RESTATEMENT (REVISED) OF THE FOREIGN RELATIONS LAW OF THE UNITED STATES § 702 (Tent. Draft No. 6, 1985) (prolonged arbitrary detention by state constitutes international law violation). The norm is obligatory, and is readily definable in terms of the arbitrary character of the detention. The Court finds that plaintiffs have alleged international tort claims for prolonged arbitrary detention.

3. SUMMARY EXECUTION

The Second Count alleges plaintiff Benchoam's claim for "murder and summary execution." Benchoam alleges that "defendant's torture, murder, beating and cruel, inhuman and degrading treatment of Ruben Benchoam resulted in and proximately caused his death." . . . In support of this claim, plaintiff cites several international documents which proscribe summary execution. Universal Declaration of Human Rights, art. 3, G.A. Res. 217A, U.N. Doc. A/810 (1948); International Covenant on Civil and Political Rights, art. 6, G.A. Res. 2200, 21 U.N. GAOR Supp. (No. 16), U.N. Doc. A/6316 (1966); American Convention on Human Rights, art. 5, OAS Treaty Series No. 36, OAS Off. Rec. OEA/Ser. 4 v/II 23, Doc. 21, rev. 2 (English ed. 1975). Similarly, murder—where practiced, encouraged, or condoned by a state—is listed among the international law violations to which Judge Edwards looked for guidance in identifying possible violations of the law of nations. See Tel–Oren, 726 F.2d at 781 (*quoting* RESTATEMENT (REVISED) OF THE FOREIGN RELATIONS LAW OF THE UNITED STATES § 702 (Tent. Draft No. 3, 1982)); *see also* Guinto, *supra*, 654 F. Supp. at 280. Further, the Fifth Circuit has acknowledged the right not to be murdered [by the state] as among the "basic rights" which "have been generally accepted—and hence incorporated into the law of nations." De Sanchez, *supra*, 770 F.2d at 1397.

The proscription of summary execution or murder by the state appears to be universal, is readily definable, and is of course obligatory. The Court emphasizes that plaintiff's allegations raise no issue as to whether or not the execution was within the lawful exercise of state power; rather, she alleges murder by state officials with neither authorization nor recourse to any process of law. Under these circumstances, the Court finds that plaintiff Benchoam has stated a cognizable claim under § 1350 for the 1977 murder/summary execution of her brother by Argentine military personnel.

4. CAUSING DISAPPEARANCE

In Count Three plaintiff Forti alleges a claim for "causing the disappearance" of his mother, in that defendant "arbitrarily and without justification, cause or privilege, abducted Nelida Azucena Sosa de Forti, held her in secret captivity and caused her 'disappearance' to this day." . . .

Sadly, the practice of "disappearing" individuals—*i.e.*, abduction, secret detention, and torture, followed generally by either secret execution or release—during Argentina's "dirty war" is now well documented in the official report of the Argentine National Commission on the Disappeared, *Nunca Mas*. Nor are such practices necessarily restricted to Argentina. With mounting publicity over the years, such conduct has begun to draw censure as a violation of the basic right to life. Plaintiff cites a 1978 United Nations resolution and a 1980 congressional resolution to this effect. U.N. G.A. Res. /173 (1978); H.R. Con. Res. 285, 96th Cong., 2d Sess. The Court notes, too, that the proposed Restatement of the Law of Foreign Relations lists "the murder or causing the disappearance of individuals," where practiced, encouraged, or condoned by the state, as a violation of international law. RESTATEMENT (REVISED) OF THE FOREIGN RELATIONS LAW OF THE UNITED STATES, § 702 (Tent. Draft No. 6, 1985). However, plaintiffs do not cite the Court to any case finding that causing the disappearance of an individual constitutes a violation of the law of nations.

Before this Court may adjudicate a tort claim under § 1350, it must be satisfied that the legal standard it is to apply is one with universal acceptance and definition; on no other basis may the Court exercise jurisdiction over a claimed violation of the law of nations. Unfortunately, the Court cannot say, on the basis of the evidence submitted, that there yet exists the requisite degree of international consensus which demonstrates a customary international norm. Even if there were greater evidence of universality, there remain definitional problems. It is not clear precisely what conduct falls within the proposed norm, or how this proscription would differ from that of summary execution. The other torts condemned by the international community and discussed above—official torture, prolonged arbitrary detention, and summary execution—involve two types of conduct by the official actor: (1) taking the individual into custody; and (2) committing a wrongful, tortious act in excess of his authority over that person. In the case of "causing disappearance," only the first of these two actions can be proven—the taking into custody. However, the sole act of taking an individual into custody does not suffice to prove conduct which the international community proscribes. The Court recognizes the very real problems of proof presented by the disappearance of an individual following such custody. Yet there is no apparent international consensus as to the additional elements needed to make out a claim for causing the disappearance of an individual. For instance, plaintiffs have not shown that customary international law creates a presumption of causing disappearance upon a showing of prolonged absence after initial custody.

For these reasons the Court must dismiss Count Four for failure to state a claim upon which relief may be grounded....

5. CRUEL, INHUMAN AND DEGRADING TREATMENT

Finally, in Count Five plaintiffs both allege a claim for "cruel, inhuman and degrading treatment" based on the general allegations of the Complaint and consisting specifically of the alleged torture, murder, forcible disappearance and prolonged arbitrary detention....

This claim suffers the same defects as Count Four. Plaintiffs do not cite, and the Court is not aware of, such evidence of universal consensus regarding the right to be free from "cruel, inhuman and degrading treatment as exists, for example, with respect to official torture." Further, any such right poses problems of definability. The difficulties for a district court in adjudicating such a claim are manifest. Because this right lacks readily ascertainable parameters, it is unclear what behavior falls within the proscription—beyond such obvious torts as are already encompassed by the proscriptions of torture, summary execution and prolonged arbitrary detention. Lacking the requisite elements of universality and definability, this proposed tort cannot qualify as a violation of the law of nations. Accordingly, the Court dismisses Count Five of the Complaint for failure to state a claim upon which relief may be granted.

In sum, the Court finds that plaintiffs have stated claims for prolonged arbitrary detention and summary execution. On the other hand, the Court dismisses with prejudice Counts Three ("causing disappearance") and Five ("cruel, inhuman and degrading treatment") for failure to state a claim—*i.e.*, failure to allege a violation of the law of nations cognizable under the Alien Tort Statute. The Court orders plaintiffs to amend Count One; to make a more definite statement of the acts upon which they allege the claim for official torture. It follows from the above statements that this Court has federal subject matter jurisdiction, with respect to both plaintiffs, under 28 U.S.C. § 1350.

C. Federal Question Jurisdiction

Alternatively, plaintiffs predicate jurisdiction on 28 U.S.C. § 1331, the federal question statute. Section 1331 provides that "the district courts shall have jurisdiction of all civil actions arising under the Constitution, laws, or treaties of the United States." This statute provides jurisdiction over claims founded on federal common law....

It has long been settled that federal common law incorporates international law. The Nereide, 13 U.S. (9 Cranch) 388, 423 ... (1815); The Paquete Habana, 175 U.S. 677, 700 ... (1900). More recently, the Supreme Court has held that the interpretation of international law is a federal question. *Sabbatino, supra*, 376 U.S. at 415. Thus, a case presenting claims arising under customary international law arises under the laws of the United States for purposes of federal question jurisdiction. See 13B C. Wright, A. Miller & E. Cooper, Federal Practice and Procedure § 3563, at 60–63 (2d ed. 1984)....

Defendant next argues that the act of state doctrine bars adjudication of plaintiffs' claims....

Here, ... plaintiffs allege acts by a subordinate government official in violation not of economic rights, but of fundamental human rights lying at the very heart of the individual's existence. These are not the public official acts of a head of government, nor is it clear at this stage of the proceedings to what extent defendant's acts were "ratified" by the *de facto* military government. Further, plaintiffs have submitted evidence that the acts, if committed, were illegal even under Argentine law at all relevant times....

Congress did not provide a statute of limitations for claims brought pursuant to 28 U.S.C. § 1350. When a federal statute provides a civil cause of action but includes no express limitations period, courts must generally borrow the most analogous state statute.... However, state statutes of limitations are not to be borrowed blindly....

... Since the Alien Tort Statute is a highly remedial statute, the limitations rule adopted should promote the policy of providing a forum for claims of violations of internationally recognized human rights....

Plaintiffs rely upon principles of equitable tolling of the statute of limitations to raise an issue of fact as to timeliness. Although the limitations period of a claim under the Alien Tort Statute is governed by state law, because the claim itself is a federal claim, federal equitable tolling doctrines apply....

FORTI v. SUAREZ–MASON

694 F.Supp. 707 (N.D.Cal.1988).

JENSEN, J.

Plaintiffs subsequently filed this Motion, supported by numerous international legal authorities, as well as affidavits from eight renowned international law scholars. The Court has reviewed these materials and concludes that plaintiffs have met their burden of showing an international consensus as to the status and content of the international tort of "causing disappearance." Accordingly, the motion to reconsider is in this regard and the claim is reinstated. The Court also concludes that plaintiffs have again failed to establish that there is any international consensus as to what conduct falls within the category of "cruel, inhuman or degrading treatment." Absent such consensus as to the content of this alleged tort, it is not cognizable under the Alien Tort Statute. Therefore, the Motion to Reconsider dismissal of this claim is denied.

... The plaintiff's burden in stating a claim is to establish the existence of a "universal, definable, and obligatory international norm[]." ... To meet this burden plaintiffs need not establish unanimity among nations. Rather, they must show a general recognition among states that a specific practice is prohibited. It is with this standard in mind that the Court examines the evidence presented by plaintiffs....

The legal scholars whose declarations have been submitted in connection with this Motion are in agreement that there is universal consensus as to the two essential elements of a claim for "disappearance." In Professor Franck's words:

> The international community has also reached a consensus on the definition of a "disappearance." It has two essential elements: (a)

> abduction by a state official or by persons acting under state approval or authority; and (b) refusal by the state to acknowledge the abduction and detention.

Franck Declaration, para. 7. See also Falk Declaration, at 3; Henkin Declaration, para. 9; Steiner Declaration, para. 3, 5; Weissbrodt Declaration, para. 8(b); Weston Declaration, para. 5.

Plaintiffs cite numerous international legal authorities which support the assertion that "disappearance" is a universally recognized wrong under the law of nations. For example, United Nations General Assembly Resolution 33/173 recognizes "disappearance" as violative of many of the rights recognized in the Universal Declaration of Human Rights, G.A. Res. 217 A (III), adopted by the United Nations General Assembly, Dec. 10, 1948, U.N. Doc. A/810 (1948) [hereinafter Universal Declaration of Human Rights]. These rights include: (1) the right to life; (2) the right to liberty and security of the person; (3) the right to freedom from torture; (4) the right to freedom from arbitrary arrest and detention; and (5) the right to a fair and public trial. *Id.*, articles 3, 5, 9, 10, 11. See also International Covenant on Political and Civil Rights, G.A. Res. 2200 (XXI), adopted by the United Nations General Assembly, December 16, 1966, U.N. Doc. A/6316 (1966), articles 6, 7, 9, 10, 14, 15, 17.

Other documents support this characterization of "disappearance" as violative of universally recognized human rights. The United States Congress has denounced "prolonged detention without charges and trial" along with other "flagrant denial[s] of the right to life, liberty, or the security of person." 22 U.S.C. § 2304(d)(1). The recently published RESTATEMENT (THIRD) OF THE FOREIGN RELATIONS LAW OF THE UNITED STATES § 702 includes "disappearance" as a violation of the international law of human rights. The Organization of American States has also denounced "disappearance" as "an affront to the conscience of the hemisphere and . . . a crime against humanity." Organization of American States, Inter–American Commission on Human Rights, General Assembly Resolution 666 (November 18, 1983).

Of equal importance, plaintiffs' submissions support their assertion that there is a universally recognized legal definition of what constitutes the tort of "causing disappearance." The Court's earlier order expressed concern that "the sole act of taking an individual into custody does not suffice to prove conduct which the international community proscribes." 672 F. Supp. at 1543. Plaintiffs' submissions on this Motion, however, establish recognition of a second essential element—official refusal to acknowledge that the individual has been taken into custody. For example, the United Nations General Assembly has expressed concern at the:

> difficulties in obtaining reliable information from competent authorities as to the circumstances of such persons, including reports of the persistent refusal of such authorities or organizations to acknowledge that they hold such persons in custody or otherwise to account for them.

U.N. General Assembly Resolution 33/173 (December 20, 1978).

Likewise, the Organization of American States has recognized the importance of this element, commenting on the:

> numerous cases wherein the government systematically denies the detention of individuals, despite the convincing evidence that the claimants provide to verify their allegations that such persons have been detained by police or military authorities and, in some cases, that those persons are, or have been, confined in specified detention centers.

Organization of American States, Inter–American Commission on Human Rights, 1977 ANNUAL REPORT, at 26. See also M. Berman & R. Clark, *State Terrorism: Disappearances*, 13 RUTGERS L.J. 531, 533 (1982) ("The denial of accountability is the factor which makes disappearance unique among human rights violations.").

In the Court's view, the submitted materials are sufficient to establish the existence of a universal and obligatory international proscription of the tort of "causing disappearance." This tort is characterized by the following two essential elements: (1) abduction by state officials or their agents; followed by (2) official refusals to acknowledge the abduction or to disclose the detainee's fate....

In dismissing plaintiffs' earlier "cruel, inhuman or degrading treatment" claim this Court found that the proposed tort lacked "the requisite elements of universality and definability." 672 F. Supp. at 1543. Plaintiffs now submit the aforementioned declarations ... and several international legal authorities in support of their argument that "the definition of cruel, inhuman or degrading treatment or punishment is inextricably related to that for torture." ... Specifically, plaintiffs argue that the two are properly viewed on a continuum, and that "torture and cruel, inhuman or degrading treatment differ essentially in the degree of ill treatment suffered." *Id.* Thus while the latter treatment is not torture it is an analytically distinct tort which, in plaintiffs' view, is actionable under the Alien Tort Statute.

Plaintiffs emphasize that virtually all international legal authorities which prohibit torture also prohibit cruel, inhuman or degrading treatment. For example, § 702 of the RESTATEMENT (THIRD) OF THE FOREIGN RELATIONS LAW OF THE UNITED STATES: "A state violates international law if, as a matter of state policy, it practices, encourages, or condones ... torture or other cruel, inhuman or degrading treatment or punishment." Likewise, 22 U.S.C. § 2304(d)(1) lists "torture or cruel, inhuman or degrading treatment or punishment," among "gross violations of internationally recognized human rights." Article 5 of the Universal Declaration of Human Rights, *supra*, states that "no one shall be subjected to torture or to cruel, inhuman or degrading treatment." See also de Sanchez v. Banco Central De Nicaragua, 770 F.2d 1385, 1397 (5th Cir.1985) (recognizing "right not to be ... tortured, or otherwise subjected to cruel, inhuman or degrading treatment").

While these and other materials establish a recognized proscription of "cruel, inhuman or degrading treatment," they offer no guidance as to what constitutes such treatment. The RESTATEMENT does not define the term. The cited statute (22 U.S.C. § 2304) and the Universal Declaration of Human Rights also both fail to offer a definition. The scholars whose declarations have been submitted likewise decline to offer any definition of the proposed tort. In fact, one of the declarations appears to concede the lack of a universally recognized definition. See Lillich Declaration, at 8 ("only the contours of the prohibition, not its existence as a norm of customary international law, are the subject of legitimate debate.").

... Absent some definition of what constitutes "cruel, inhuman or degrading treatment" this Court has no way of determining what alleged treatment is actionable, and what is not.

Plaintiffs cite The Greek Case, 12 T.B. Eur. Conv. on Human Rights 186 (1969), for a definition of "degrading treatment" as that which "grossly humiliates [the victim] before others or drives him to act against his will or conscience." ... But this definitional gloss is of no help. From our necessarily global perspective, conduct, particularly verbal conduct, which is humiliating or even grossly humiliating in one cultural context is of no moment in another. An international tort which appears and disappears as one travels around the world is clearly lacking in that level of common understanding necessary to create universal consensus. Likewise, the term "against his will or conscience" is too abstract to be of help. For example, a pacifist who is conscripted to serve in his country's military has arguably been forced to act "against his will or conscience." Would he thus have a claim for degrading treatment?

To be actionable under the Alien Tort Statute the proposed tort must be characterized by universal consensus in the international community as to its binding status *and its content*. In short, it must be a "universal, *definable*, and obligatory international norm[]." Forti, 672 F. Supp. at 1541 (emphasis added)....

Notes and Questions

1. Concerning lists of *jus cogens* norms, *see, e.g.*, Chapter 1, Section 1 F 3. *Compare*, for example, Section 702 of the U.S. Restatement and the Human Rights Committee's General Comment No. 24 *with* the opinions in *Forti I* and *Forti II*. Why was the Restatement not persuasive to the district judge? What was quite persuasive with respect to a definition of "disappearance"?

In its Memorial before the International Court of Justice in Case Concerning United States Diplomatic and Consular Staff in Tehran (United States v. Iran), 1980 I.C.J. Pleadings, the Executive Branch recognized that the following articles, among others, in the Universal Declaration of Human Rights reflect human rights guaranteed under customary international law: Articles 3, 5, 7, 9, 12, 13. Should these human rights be considered to provide needed specificity for judicial protection? What other rights recognized in the Universal Declaration provide sufficient normative content? Congress has also recognized that gross violations of human rights include:

"torture or cruel, inhumane, or degrading treatment or punishment, prolonged arbitrary detention without charges, or other flagrant denial to life, liberty, and the security of person." 22 U.S.C. § 262 d(a).

2. Violations of international law actionable under the ATCA have not been limited to norms *jus cogens* and such a limit would be contrary to the clear language of the ATCA. For cases and Executive opinions addressing non-*jus cogens* violations, *see, e.g.*, Alvarez–Machain v. United States, 331 F.3d 604 (9th Cir. 2003) (not limited to *jus cogens*, "guided by the language of the statute, not an imported restriction"); *id.*, 266 F.3d 1045 (9th Cir. 2001) ("never held that a *jus cogens* violation is required"); Wiwa v. Royal Dutch Petroleum Co., 226 F.3d 88 (2d Cir. 2000), *cert. denied*, 532 U.S. 941 (2001) (imprisonment, among other violations); Weisshaus v. Swiss Bankers Ass'n, 225 F.3d 191 (2d Cir. 2000) (re: war crimes, among other violations); Kadic v. Karadzic, 70 F.3d at 242–43 (war crimes); Nguyen da Yen v. Kissinger, 528 F.2d 1194, 1201–02 n.13 (9th Cir. 1975); Doe v. Islamic Salvation Front, 993 F.Supp. 3, 5, 7–8 (D.D.C. 1998) (claims re: war crimes, hijacking, mutilation, among others); Adra v. Clift, 195 F.Supp. 857 (D. Md. 1961); Bolchos v. Darrel, 3 F.Cas. 810 (D.S.C. 1795); 26 Op. Att'y Gen. 250 (1907); 1 Op. Att'y Gen. 57 (1795); *see also* M'Grath v. Candalero, 16 F.Cas. at 128; *but see* Doe v. Unocal, 110 F.Supp.2d 1294, 1304 (C.D. Cal. 2000), settled (2005). The ATCA contains no list or limitations of applicable customary international law or treaties of the U.S. and expressly applies to "any" civil action for a tort in violation of such international law. For the judiciary to add limits that Congress has not chosen would be to rewrite the clear language of a long-standing federal statute and to violate the separation of powers. Further, at the time of formation of the ATCA the notion of a complete enumeration or short list of human rights would have been anathema to the Founders. *See, e.g.*, Paust, *supra* at 174–75, 221 n.90, 330–32, 349–50 ns.45, 50. The same would have been true more generally with respect to the law of nations. *See, e.g.*, *id.* at 8, 48–50 ns.60–88; Resolution of the Continental Congress (1781), *supra*. Still today, the general statute incorporating the laws of war by reference as offenses against the law of the United States does not attempt to list the numerous war crimes proscribed by international law. See 10 U.S.C. §§ 818, 821. These points are of importance after the Court's 2004 decision in *Sosa v. Alvarez–Machain*, addressed *infra*, since the majority opinion is clearly interested in what actionable violations of international law would have been evident to the Founders and early judiciary and the Court will also allow certain more modern claims.

3. Concerning recognized crimes against humanity, see also those listed in various instruments in the Documents Supplement (*e.g.*, The Charters of the I.M.T. at Nuremberg and the I.M.T. for the Far East) and the 1919 Report of the Responsibilities Commission, in Chapter 8 (regarding offenses against the laws of humanity). Are "inhumane acts" covered? Are "persecution," torture, and rape covered? The crimes against humanity within the jurisdiction of the International Criminal Court (ICC) are quite limited, especially by phrases such as "widespread or systematic," "with knowledge of the attack," and "persecution against any identifiable group or collectivity." *See* Statute of the ICC, art. 7, in the Documents Supplement. *See also* Paust, Bassiouni, *et al.*, *supra*, at 861, 864–65, 889–90, 905–07, 909.

Concerning secret detentions or disappearances as a crime against humanity, see also the Inter–American Convention on the Forced Disappearance of Persons, preamble; Jordan J. Paust, *Post–9/11 Overreaction and Fallacies Regarding War and Defense, Guantanamo, the Status of Persons, Treatment, Judicial Review of Detention, and Due Process in Military Commissions*, 79 Notre Dame L. Rev. 1335, 1352–56 (2004).

4. Is "universal consensus" required with respect to the content of customary international law? or treaty-based international law? See Chapter 1.

5. As stated in *Forti I*, is it true that "the law of nations clearly does not create or define civil actions"? *See, e.g.*, the Universal Declaration of Human Rights, art. 8; International Covenant on Civil and Political Rights, arts. 2, 14, and General Comments Nos. 13, 15; Paust, International Law as Law of the United States 224–29 (2 ed. 2003); note 14 at the end of Section 2 D 3.

PAUL v. AVRIL

812 F.Supp. 207 (S.D.Fla.1993).

Palermo, Magistrate J.

This case involves an action by six (6) Haitians, Evans Paul, Jean–Auguste Mesyeux, Marino Etienne, Gerald Emile "Aby" Brun, Serge Gilles and Fernand Gerard Laforest. All six (6) Plaintiffs were citizens and residents of Haiti when this action was filed. The Plaintiffs seek compensatory and punitive damages against Defendant, Lieutenant General Prosper Avril (Avril), the former head of the Haitian military, for alleged "torture[,] cruel, inhuman or degrading treatment; arbitrary arrest and detention without trial; and other violations of customary international law." ... Since March 12, 1990, and at the time the Complaint was filed, Avril resided within the jurisdiction of the United States District Court for the Southern District of Florida. These acts allegedly all took place in Haiti.

The Complaint spans some twenty (20) pages delineating the acts committed upon Plaintiffs by soldiers and individuals allegedly acting under and with the "order, approval, instigation, and knowledge of Defendant Avril." ... These include acts such as severe beatings, being dragged up flights of stairs, having lit cigarettes inserted in the nostrils, being put in contortionistic positions while beaten with particular attention being paid to the skull and groin, refusal to administer medical treatment, being paraded on national television and falsely accused of being involved in an assassination plot, deliberate starvation and other equally indescribable acts of unmerciful treatment.... None of the acts enunciated are alleged to have been committed by Avril himself. The brutality of the acts committed is uncontroverted and undisputed.

The Complaint contains six (6) claims for relief: Torture; Arbitrary Detention; Cruel, Inhuman and Degrading Treatment; False Imprisonment; Assault and Battery; and Intentional Infliction of Emotional Distress. The Complaint prays for damages in excess of three million

(3,000,000) dollars for each Plaintiff individually, and at least ten million (10,000,000) in punitive damages collectively....

The Defendant now moves to dismiss the complaint primarily relying on five (5) theories. First, that the Foreign Sovereign Immunities Act, 28 U.S.C. § 1602 *et seq.*, prohibits judicial consideration of the suit against Avril. Second, that Avril is immune from the jurisdiction of this court under the doctrine of Head of State Immunity. Third, Defendant argues there is no subject matter jurisdiction under 28 U.S.C. § 1350 as predicated by Plaintiffs. Fourth, Plaintiffs have not stated a justiciable cause of action under 28 U.S.C. §§ 1350–1351, and fifth, under the Act of State and Political Question doctrine this suit is nonjusticiable....

As stated, Defendant first contends that Avril is covered by the Foreign Sovereign Immunities Act ... and therefore this suit cannot be maintained. This argument is unconvincing for several reasons....

Plaintiffs do not argue the application of the FSIA exceptions, instead they argue the FSIA itself does not apply in three ways. First, they argue the FSIA offers no protection to individuals. Second, they claim that even if it does, Avril is not provided with immunity under the Act for acts that are outside of the scope of his authority. Last, Plaintiffs argue that any possible immunity has bean waived by the Haitian government.

The Government of Haiti, on April 9, 1991, waived any and all immunity enjoyed by Prosper Avril....

Defendant next argues that he is immune from the jurisdictional arm of this court under the Head of State doctrine. This argument must also fail....

... The waiver of immunity by the Haitian government is complete and also affects his residual head of state immunity. See *In Re* Doe, 860 F.2d at 46.

Defendant's third argument asserts there is no subject matter jurisdiction under the Alien Tort Statute, 28 U.S.C. § 1350, the statute Plaintiffs bring this action under. Defendant reasons that § 1350 is not applicable "to suits between aliens for actions arising outside the United States." ... The undersigned finds that contrary to Defendant's conclusions, there is subject matter under the statute.

Specifically, 28 U.S.C. § 1350 ... requires that jurisdiction be limited to cases: 1) involving aliens; 2) with a tort only; and 3) committed in violation of the law of nations or a treaty of the United States.... [the court addressed several cases] Additionally, these cases all involved torts, in violation of the laws of nations which occurred outside of the U.S.

Defendant's fourth argument centers around the theory that 28 U.S.C. § 1350 does not provide a cause of action, but merely provides a jurisdictional gateway to the court. The plain language of the statute and the use of the words "committed in violation" strongly implies that a well pled tort if committed in violation of the law of nations, would be sufficient. There are cases that hold 28 U.S.C. § 1350 as providing both a jurisdictional basis and a right of action. See Forti, 672 F. Supp. at 1540; Filartiga, 630 F. Supp. at 887; Handel v. Artukovic, 601 F. Supp. 1421, 1426–27 (C.D.Cal.1985) ("thus, while the 'violation' language of section 1350 may be interpreted as explicitly granting a cause of action, the 'arising under' language of section 1351 cannot be so interpreted"); Tel–Oren v. Libyan Arab Republic, 233 U.S. App. D.C. 384, 726 F.2d 774, 777–780 (D.C.Cir.1984) (Edwards, J., concurring) (plaintiffs, mostly Israeli citizens brought action against defendants, various Arab organizations under the law of nations and treaties of the United States for deaths occurring in a bus in Israel), *cert. denied*, 470 U.S. 1003 ... (1985).

Moreover, even if this were not the case, it is clear 28 U.S.C. § 1350 authorizes remedies for aliens suing for torts committed in violation of the law of nations. See Filartiga, 630 F.2d at 888; Jaffe v. Boyles, 616 F. Supp. 1371, 1379 (W.D.N.Y.1985) (recognized premise of Filartiga); Jones v. Petty Ray Geophysical Geosource, Inc., 722 F. Supp. 343, 348 (S.D.Tex.1989) (dismissed where plaintiff did not allege either alien status or tort committed in violation of the law of nations).

Last in this regard, Plaintiffs' causes of action sounding in False Imprisonment, Assault and Battery and Intentional Infliction of Emotional Distress under Florida law are cognizable at this stage of the proceedings under principles of pendant and ancillary jurisdiction. See Forti, 672 F. Supp. at 1540.

Defendant's fifth and final argument, that this suit is foreclosed because of the act of state and political question doctrines is completely devoid of merit. The acts as alleged in the complaint, if true would hardly qualify as official public acts. W.S. Kirkpatrick & Co. v. Environmental Tectonics Corp., 493 U.S. 400, 403 ... (1990); Banco Nacional de Cuba v. Sabbatino, 376 U.S. 398, 428 ... (1964). Further, if the argument asserted by Defendant were true, and the federal courts would refuse to handle cases such as this one because the standards would be difficult to discern, discovery would be arduous to acquire, and the witnesses would have to travel substantial distances, cases such as *Forti*, *Siderman*, *Filartiga*, and Jimenez v. Aristeguieta, 311 F.2d 547, 557 (5th Cir.1962) (act of state doctrine applicable only where acts involved are official acts of state), would never have been adjudicated. Defendant has not distinguished this case from those precedents. The same is true with regard to Defendants' assertion of the political question doctrine. This case presents clearly justiciable legal issues as illustrated herein.

Notes and Questions

1. Was the district court opinion in *Paul v. Avril* correct concerning the nature of defendants that are suable under the ATCA?

2. In a subsequent proceeding, the following damages were awarded. Paul v. Avril, 901 F.Supp. 330 (S.D.Fla.1994), explaining:

"As a result of the torture and detention, plaintiffs suffered extensive physical, psychological, and consequential damages. Both compensatory and punitive damages are recoverable for violations of international law. *See, e.g.*, Filartiga v. Pena–Irala, 577 F.Supp. 860 (E.D.N.Y.1984). The Court awards compensatory damages for the pain and suffering, medical expenses, and lost income suffered by the plaintiffs in the following amounts:

Evans Paul	$2,500,000.00
Jean August Mesyeux	$2,500,000.00
Marino Etienne	$3,500,000.00
Gerald Emile Brun	$2,500,000.00
Serge Gilles	$3,000,000.00
Fernand Gerard Laforest	$3,000,000.00

"The Court finds that punitive damages are appropriate in this case as the acts committed by the defendant were malicious, wanton, and oppressive. An award of punitive damages must reflect the egregiousness of the defendant's conduct, the central role he played in the abuses, and the international condemnation with which these abuses are viewed. Filartiga, 577 F.Supp. at 866.

"... The Court concludes that an award of punitive damages in the amount of $4,000,000.00 to each plaintiff is appropriate considering the extreme brutality of the defendant's acts, which such damages are designed to punish.

"Final Judgement is hereby entered against the defendant, in favor of the plaintiffs individually for damages as found herein, in the total amount of $41,000,000.00...."

XUNCAX v. GRAMAJO

886 F.Supp. 162 (D.Mass.1995).

WOODLOCK, J.

The plaintiffs allege that the defendant Gramajo, as Vice Chief of Staff and director of the Army General Staff [of Guatamala] from March of 1982 through 1983, as commander from July through December of 1982 of the military zone in which the plaintiffs resided, and as Minister of Defense from 1987 through 1990, was personally responsible for ordering and directing the implementation of the program of persecution and oppression that resulted in the terrors visited upon the plaintiffs and their families.... I find their allegations supported by the record. I also find that Gramajo may be held liable for the acts of members of the military forces under his command.

In Application of Yamashita, 327 U.S. 1 ... (1946), the commander of Japanese armed forces in the Philippine Islands during World War II was held responsible for numerous acts of atrocity committed by servicemembers under his command. The allegations contained in the prosecution's Bill of Particulars against Yamashita are eerily parallel to those made here:

> "a deliberate plan and purpose to massacre and exterminate a large part of the civilian population of Batangas Province, and to devastate and destroy public, private and religious property therein, as a result of which more than 25,000 men, women and children, all unarmed noncombatant civilians, were brutally mistreated and killed, without cause or trial, and entire settlements were devastated and destroyed wantonly and without military necessity."

372 U.S. at 14. The Court upheld Yamashita's conviction by a United States military tribunal, explaining:

> It is not denied that such acts directed against the civilian population of an occupied country and against prisoners of war are recognized in international law as violations of the law of war. But it is argued that the charge does not allege that petitioner has either committed or directed the commission of such acts, and consequently that no violation is charged as against him. But this overlooks the fact that the gist of the charge is an unlawful breach of duty by petitioner as an army commander to control the operations of the members of his command by "permitting them to commit" the extensive and widespread atrocities specified....
>
> It is evident that the conduct of military operations by troops whose excesses are unrestrained by the orders or efforts of their commander would almost certainly result in violations which it is the purpose of the law of war to prevent.... Hence the law of war presupposes that its violation is to be avoided through the control of the operations of war by commanders who are to some extent responsible for their subordinates.

327 U.S. at 14–15 (citation to [1907] Hague Convention omitted).

In Forti v. Suarez–Mason, 672 F. Supp. 1531 (N.D.Cal.1987), the court held an Argentine General responsible for acts of brutality committed by military personnel in the defense zone under his command. The court explained:

> Although the individual acts are alleged to have been committed by military and police officials, plaintiffs allege that these actors were all agents, employees, or representatives of defendant acting pursuant to a "policy, pattern and practice" of the First Army Corps under defendant's command. Plaintiffs assert that the defendant "held the highest position of authority" in Buenos Aires Province; that defendant was responsible for maintaining the prisons and detention centers there, as well as the conduct of Army officers and agents; and that he "authorized, approved, directed and ratified" the acts complained of.

672 F. Supp. at 1537–38 (citation omitted).

In enacting the Torture Victim Protection Act of 1991, Congress apparently endorsed this approach. As the Senate Committee Report explained:

> The legislation is limited to lawsuits against persons who ordered, abetted, or assisted in the torture. It will not permit a lawsuit against a former leader of a country merely because an isolated act of torture occurred somewhere in that country. However, a higher official need not have personally performed or ordered the abuses in order to be held liable. Under international law, responsibility for torture, summary execution, or disappearances extends beyond the person or persons who actually committed those acts—anyone with higher authority who authorized, tolerated or knowingly ignored those acts is liable for them.

S. Rep. No. 249, 102d Cong., 1st Sess. 9 (1991) (footnote omitted). The Senate Committee Report used *Yamashita* and *Forti I* to illustrate this principal of "command responsibility:"

> ... although Suarez Mason was not accused of directly torturing or murdering anyone, he was found civilly liable for those acts which were committed by officers under his command about which he was aware and which he did nothing to prevent.
>
> Similarly, in *In re Yamashita*, the Supreme Court held a general of the Imperial Japanese Army responsible for a pervasive pattern of war crimes committed by his officers when he knew or should have known that they were going on but failed to prevent or punish them. Such "command responsibility" is shown by evidence of a pervasive pattern and practice of torture, summary execution or disappearances. n3.

Id. (citation and one footnote omitted) (footnote in original).

In this case, plaintiffs have convincingly demonstrated that, at a minimum, Gramajo was aware of and supported widespread acts of brutality committed by personnel under his command resulting in thousands of civilian deaths.... Gramajo refused to act to prevent such atrocities. When publicly confronted with the murder of innocent civilians by soldiers under his command, Gramajo "did not deny the stated facts. He instead replied that he saw his actions as appropriate and involving the use of 'flexible' and 'humanitarian' tactics." ... In the face of public outcry, "the massacres continued and indeed got worse." ...

Indeed, the evidence suggests that Gramajo devised and directed the implementation of an indiscriminate campaign of terror against civilians such as plaintiffs and their relatives....

Upon review of the evidence adduced in support of default judgment, I find that the acts which form the basis of these actions exceed anything that might be considered to have been lawfully within the scope of Gramajo's official authority. Accordingly, I conclude that the defendant is not entitled to immunity under the FSIA, even if that statute were construed to apply to individuals acting in their official capacity. *Cf.* Letelier v. Republic of Chile, 488 F. Supp. 665, 673 (D.D.C.1980) (assassination is "clearly contrary to the precepts of humanity as recognized in both national and international law" and so cannot be part of official's "discretionary" authority), *cert. denied*, 471 U.S. 1125 ... (1985)....

... I conclude that retroactive application of the TVPA as the law in effect at the time of decision is entirely proper in this case.

Given retroactive application of the TVPA, federal statutory law clearly creates the cause of action upon which plaintiff Ortiz's lawsuit is founded. The case thus "arises under" the laws of the United States for purposes of federal question jurisdiction under 28 U.S.C. § 1331. *See, e.g.*, Merrell Dow Pharmaceuticals Inc. v. Thompson, 478 U.S. 804, 808 ... (1986) (*quoting* Franchise Tax Board v. Construction Laborers Vacation Trust, 463 U.S. 1, 8–9 ... (1983)). This Court therefore has subject matter jurisdiction to hear plaintiff Ortiz's TVPA claims....

Judicial opinions that have had occasion to impart meaning to § 1350 have not reached a consensus regarding the statute's import. A majority of courts, interpreting the statute broadly, have held that if an alien plaintiff can establish that the abuses allegedly inflicted upon her constitute violations of international law, § 1350 grants both a federal private cause of action as well as a federal forum in which to assert the claim. *See, e.g.*, Marcos Estate II, 25 F.3d at 1475 (9th Cir. 1994) (§ 1350 "creates a cause of action for violations of specific, universal and obligatory human rights standards,"); Amerada Hess Shipping Corp. v. Argentine Republic, 830 F.2d 421, 424–25 (2d Cir.1987), *rev'd on other grounds*, 488 U.S. 428 ... (1989); Filartiga v. Pena–Irala, 630 F.2d 876, 887 (2d Cir.1980); Paul v. Avril, 812 F. Supp. 207, 212 (S.D.Fla.1993); Forti v. Suarez–Mason, 672 F. Supp. 1531, 1539 (N.D.Cal.1987), on reconsideration on other grounds, 694 F. Supp. 707 (N.D.Cal.1988). The Ninth Circuit has concluded that § 1350 plaintiffs may look to municipal law as a source of substantive law. See Marcos Estate I, 978 F.2d at 503 (9th Cir. 1992), *cert. denied*, 113 S.Ct. 2960 (1993). See also Marcos Estate II, 25 F.3d at 1476 n.10. Judges of the District of Columbia Circuit, meanwhile, via separate concurrences, have at length and in a considered fashion propounded alternative views. See Tel–Oren v. Libyan Arab Republic, ... 726 F.2d 774 (D.C.Cir.1984); *id.* at 798 *et seq.* (Bork, J., concurring) (independent cause of action must be created by federal statute or international law itself, § 1350 inadequate to do so), *cert. denied*, 470 U.S. 1003 ... (1985), *id.* at 775, *et seq.* (Edwards, J., concurring) (suggesting domestic tort law may provide substantive cause of action under § 1350). After extended reflection, I find that § 1350 yields both a jurisdictional grant and a private right to sue for tortious violations of international law (or a treaty of the United States), without recourse to other law as a source of the cause of action.

a. The *Filartiga* Approach

In *Filartiga*, the wellspring of modern § 1350 case law, the Second Circuit first determined that the acts of torture there at issue violated international law. *Id.* at 882–84 n.18. The court then concluded that international law forms an integral part of the common law of the

United States and that, accordingly, "federal jurisdiction over cases involving international law is clear." *Id.* at 887. In reaching this point, the Filartiga court flatly rejected the argument that, under the Constitution's grant of power to Congress to "define and punish ... offenses against the law of nations," Art. I, sec. 8, cl. 10, international law fell within federal common law "only to the extent that Congress has acted to define it," citing "numerous decisions applying rules of international law uncodified in any act of Congress." *Id.* at 886 (citations omitted). The court similarly rejected the notion that § 1350 itself was but a grant by Congress to the federal judiciary to define what constitutes a violation of international law....

2. *Xuncax Plaintiffs' Claims of Violations of International Law*

a. Peremptory Norms of International Law

As the Ninth Circuit has noted, "for a court to determine whether a plaintiff has a claim for a tort committed in violation of international law, it must [first] decide whether there is an applicable norm of international law ... and [then] whether it was violated in the particular case." Marcos Estate I, 978 F.2d at 502. In reaching such a decision, courts are guided by "the usage of nations, judicial opinions and the works of jurists" as "the sources from which customary international law is derived." Filartiga, 630 F.2d at 884. For further guidance regarding the "norms" of international law, courts and international law scholars look to whether the standard can be said to be "universal, definable and obligatory." Forti I, 672 F. Supp. at 1540. These qualifications essentially require that 1) no state condone the act in question and there is a recognizable "universal" consensus of prohibition against it; 2) there are sufficient criteria to determine whether a given action amounts to the prohibited act and thus violates the norm; 3) the prohibition against it is non-derogable and therefore binding at all times upon all actors. *See generally* Forti I, 672 F. Supp. at 1539–40; Aff. of Int'l Law Scholars, Ortiz Ex. M; RESTATEMENT (THIRD) OF FOREIGN RELATIONS LAW §§ 701–02.

The Xuncax plaintiffs allege five violations of international law:

(1) Summary execution: Xuncax, for her husband's death, Doe, for his father's death, and Pedro–Pascual, for her sister's death;

(2) Disappearance: Callejas, based on his father's disappearance;

(3) Torture: Xuncax, for her husband, Doe, for his father, and Diego–Francisco, for himself and his wife;

(4) Arbitrary detention: Xuncax, for her husband, Doe, for his father, and Diego–Francisco, for himself and his wife;

(5) Cruel, inhuman and degrading treatment: Xuncax, Diego–Francisco, Doe, Pedro–Pascual, Francisco–Marcos, Manuel–Mendez, the Ruiz–Gomez brothers, and Callejas.

I am satisfied that four of these claims—torture, summary execution, disappearance, and arbitrary detention—constitute fully recognized violations of international law....

It is not necessary that every aspect of what might comprise a standard such as "cruel, inhuman or degrading treatment" be fully defined and universally agreed upon before a given action meriting the label is clearly proscribed under international law, any more than it is necessary to define all acts that may constitute "torture" or "arbitrary detention" in order to recognize certain conduct as actionable misconduct under that rubric. Accordingly, any act by the defendant which is proscribed by the Constitution of the United States and by a cognizable principle of international law plainly falls within the rubric of "cruel, inhuman or degrading treatment" and is actionable before this Court under § 1350.

Plaintiffs' contend that defendant is responsible for "cruel, inhuman or degrading treatment" because the actions taken at his direction "had the intent and the effect of grossly humiliating and debasing the plaintiffs, forcing them to act against their will and conscience, inciting fear and anguish, breaking physical or moral resistance, and/or forcing them to leave their homes and country and flee into exile[.]" (Xuncax Complaint p. 76.) This general allegation may be divided into two categories.

The first category includes acts by soldiers under defendant's command that caused a plaintiff to: (1) witness the torture (Xuncax and Doe) or severe mistreatment (Diego–Francisco) of an immediate relative; (2) watch soldiers ransack their home and threaten their family (Xuncax and Francisco–Marcos); (3) be bombed from the air (the Ruiz–Gomez brothers); or (4) have a grenade thrown at them (Callejas). I have no difficulty concluding that acts in this category constitute "cruel, inhuman or degrading treatment" in violation of international law. *See generally* The Greek Case, Y.B. EUR. CONV. ON H.R. 186, 461–65 (1969) (describing cases where political detainees were subjected to acts of intimidation, humiliation, threats of reprisal against relatives, presence at torture of another, and interference with family life in violation of Article 3 of the European Convention on the Protection of Human Rights and Fundamental Freedom).

The second category consists of the claim that, as a consequence of Gramajo's acts, plaintiffs "were placed in great fear for their lives ... and were forced to leave their homes and country and flee into exile." Although I find that all plaintiffs have made such a showing, I do not agree that this showing independently constitutes "cruel, inhuman and degrading treatment" in violation of the law of nations and actionable under § 1350....

[the court awarded significant compensatory and punitive damages]

Notes and Questions

1. There were several errors in the full opinion in *Xuncax*. Can you spot any in the extract above? For a norm to be established under customary

international law, is it necessary that "no state condone the act in question and there is a recognizable 'universal' consensus of prohibition against it"? Further, must every violation of customary international law, or treaty-based international law, implicate a "non-derogable" prohibition "binding at all times upon all actors"? Does even the Restatement require this?

2. Should U.S. standards as to what is "cruel" determine the content of applicable international law incorporated by reference in the ATCA? What exactly did the district court state in *Xuncax*?

KADIC v. KARADZIC

70 F.3d 232 (2d Cir.1995), *cert. denied*, 518 U.S. 1005 (1996).

[reread the first portions of the opinion of Judge Newman, in Chapter 1, Section 1 A, pp. 21–27]

Appellants' allegations entitle them to prove that Karadzic's regime satisfies the criteria for a state, for purposes of those international law violations requiring state action. Srpska is alleged to control defined territory, control populations within its power, and to have entered into agreements with other governments. It has a president, a legislature, and its own currency. These circumstances readily appear to satisfy the criteria for a state in all aspects of international law. Moreover, it is likely that the state action concept, where applicable for some violations like "official" torture, requires merely the semblance of official authority. The inquiry, after all, is whether a person purporting to wield official power has exceeded internationally recognized standards of civilized conduct, not whether statehood in all its formal aspects exists.

(b) Acting in concert with a foreign state. Appellants also sufficiently alleged that Karadzic acted under color of law insofar as they claimed that he acted in concert with the former Yugoslavia, the statehood of which is not disputed. The "color of law" jurisprudence of 42 U.S.C. § 1983 is a relevant guide to whether a defendant has engaged in official action for purposes of jurisdiction under the Alien Tort Act. See Forti v. Suarez–Mason, 672 F. Supp. 1531, 1546 (N.D.Cal.1987), reconsideration granted in part on other grounds, 694 F. Supp. 707 (N.D.Cal.1988). A private individual acts under color of law within the meaning of section 1983 when he acts together with state officials or with significant state aid. See Lugar v. Edmondson Oil Co., 457 U.S. 922, 937 . . . (1982). The appellants are entitled to prove their allegations that Karadzic acted under color of law of Yugoslavia by acting in concert with Yugoslav officials or with significant Yugoslavian aid.

The Torture Victim Act, enacted in 1992, provides a cause of action for official torture and extrajudicial killing. . . .

By its plain language, the Torture Victim Act renders liable only those individuals who have committed torture or extrajudicial killing "under actual or apparent authority, or color of law, of any foreign nation." Legislative history confirms that this language was intended to "make[] clear that the plaintiff must establish some governmental involvement in the torture or killing to prove a claim," and that the statute "does not attempt to deal with torture or killing by purely private groups." H.R. Rep. No. 367, 102d Cong., 2d Sess., at 5 (1991).... In construing the terms "actual or apparent authority" and "color of law," courts are instructed to look to principles of agency law and to jurisprudence under 42 U.S.C. § 1983, respectively. *Id.*

Though the Torture Victim Act creates a cause of action for official torture, this statute, unlike the Alien Tort Act, is not itself a jurisdictional statute. The Torture Victim Act permits the appellants to pursue their claims of official torture under the jurisdiction conferred by the Alien Tort Act and also under the general federal question jurisdiction of section 1331, see Xuncax v. Gramajo, 886 F. Supp. 162, 178 (D.Mass. 1995), to which we now turn.

The appellants contend that section 1331 provides an independent basis for subject-matter jurisdiction over all claims alleging violations of international law. Relying on the settled proposition that federal common law incorporates international law, see The Paquete Habana, 175 U.S. 677, 700 ... (1900); *In re* Estate of Ferdinand E. Marcos Human Rights Litigation (Marcos I), 978 F.2d 493, 502 (9th Cir. 1992), *cert. denied*, 125 L. Ed. 2d 661 ... (1993); Filartiga, 630 F.2d at 886, they reason that causes of action for violations of international law "arise under" the laws of the United States for purposes of jurisdiction under section 1331. Whether that is so is an issue of some uncertainty that need not be decided in this case.

In *Tel-Oren* Judge Edwards expressed the view that section 1331 did not supply jurisdiction for claimed violations of international law unless the plaintiffs could point to a remedy granted by the law of nations or argue successfully that such a remedy is implied. Tel–Oren, 726 F.2d at 779–80 n.4. The law of nations generally does not create private causes of action to remedy its violations, but leaves to each nation the task of defining the remedies that are available for international law violations. *Id.* at 778 (Edwards, J., concurring). Some district courts, however, have upheld section 1331 jurisdiction for international law violations. See Abebe–Jiri v. Negewo, No. 90–2010 (N.D. Ga. Aug. 20, 1993), appeal argued, No. 93–9133 (11th Cir. Jan. 10, 1995); Martinez–Baca v. Suarez–Mason, No. 87–2057, slip op. at 4–5 (N.D. Cal. Apr. 22, 1988); Forti v. Suarez–Mason, 672 F. Supp. 1531, 1544 (N.D.Cal.1987).

We recognized the possibility of section 1331 jurisdiction in Filartiga, 630 F.2d at 887 n.22, but rested jurisdiction solely on the applicable Alien Tort Act. Since that Act appears to provide a remedy for the appellants' allegations of violations related to genocide, war crimes, and official torture, and the Torture Victim Act also appears to provide a remedy for their allegations of official torture, their causes of action are statutorily authorized, and, as in *Filartiga*, we need not rule definitively on whether any causes of action not specifically authorized by statute may be implied by international law standards as incorporated into United States law and grounded on section 1331 jurisdiction....

Two nonjurisdictional, prudential doctrines reflect the judiciary's concerns regarding separation of powers: the political question doctrine and the act of state doctrine. It is the " 'constitutional' underpinnings" of these doctrines that influenced the concurring opinions of Judge Robb and Judge Bork in *Tel-Oren*. Although we too recognize the potentially detrimental effects of judicial action in cases of this nature, we do not embrace the rather categorical views as to the inappropriateness of judicial action urged by Judges Robb and Bork. Not every case "touching foreign relations" is nonjusticiable, see Baker v. Carr, 369 U.S. 186, 211 ... (1962); Lamont v. Woods, 948 F.2d 825, 831–32 (2d Cir.1991), and judges should not reflexively invoke these doctrines to avoid difficult and somewhat sensitive decisions in the context of human rights. We believe a preferable approach is to weigh carefully the relevant considerations on a case-by-case basis. This will permit the judiciary to act where appropriate in light of the express legislative mandate of the Congress in section 1350, without compromising the primacy of the political branches in foreign affairs.

Karadzic maintains that these suits were properly dismissed because they present nonjusticiable political questions. We disagree. Although these cases present issues that arise in a politically charged context, that does not transform them into cases involving nonjusticiable political questions. "The doctrine 'is one of "political questions," not one of "political cases." ' " Klinghoffer, 937 F.2d at 49 (*quoting Baker*, 369 U.S. at 217).

... With respect to the first three factors, we have noted in a similar context involving a tort suit against the PLO that "the department to whom this issue has been 'constitutionally committed' is none other than our own—the Judiciary." Klinghoffer, 937 F.2d at 49. Although the present actions are not based on the common law of torts, as was *Klinghoffer*, our decision in *Filartiga* established that universally recognized norms of international law provide judicially discoverable and manageable standards for adjudicating suits brought under the Alien Tort Act, which obviates any need to make initial policy decisions of the kind normally reserved for nonjudicial discretion. Moreover, the existence of judicially discoverable and manageable standards further undermines the claim that such suits relate to matters that are constitutionally committed to another branch. See Nixon v. United States, 506 U.S. 224 ... (1993)....

The act of state doctrine, under which courts generally refrain from judging the acts of a foreign state within its territory, see Banco Nacional de Cuba v. Sabbatino, 376 U.S. at 428 ... ; Underhill v. Hernandez, 168 U.S. 250, 252 ... (1897), might be implicated in some cases arising under section 1350. However, as in Filartiga, 630 F.2d at 889, we doubt that the acts of even a state official, taken in violation of a nation's fundamental law and wholly unratified by that nation's government, could properly be characterized as an act of state.

In the pending appeal, we need have no concern that interference with important governmental interests warrants rejection of appellants' claims. After commencing their action against Karadzic, attorneys for the plaintiffs in Doe wrote to the Secretary of State to oppose reported attempts by Karadzic to be granted immunity from suit in the United States; a copy of plaintiffs' complaint was attached to the letter. Far from intervening in the case to urge rejection of the suit on the ground that it presented political questions, the Department responded with a letter indicating that Karadzic was not immune from suit as an invitee of the United Nations. See Habib Letter, *supra*. After oral argument in the pending appeals, this Court wrote to the Attorney General to inquire whether the United States wished to offer any further views concerning any of the issues raised. In a "Statement of Interest," signed by the Solicitor General and the State Department's Legal Adviser, the United States has expressly disclaimed any concern that the political question doctrine should be invoked to prevent the litigation of these lawsuits: "Although there might be instances in which federal courts are asked to issue rulings under the Alien Tort Statute or the Torture Victim Protection Act that might raise a political question, this is not one of them." Statement of Interest of the United States at 3. Though even an assertion of the political question doctrine by the Executive Branch, entitled to respectful consideration, would not necessarily preclude adjudication, the Government's reply to our inquiry reinforces our view that adjudication may properly proceed.

As to the act of state doctrine, the doctrine was not asserted in the District Court and is not before us on this appeal. See Filartiga, 630 F.2d at 889. Moreover, the appellee has not had the temerity to assert in this Court that the acts he allegedly committed are the officially approved policy of a state. Finally, as noted, we think it would be a rare case in which the act of state doctrine precluded suit under section 1350. *Banco Nacional* was careful to recognize the doctrine "in the absence of ... unambiguous agreement regarding controlling legal principles," 376 U.S. at 428, such as exist in the pending litigation, and applied the doctrine only in a context—expropriation of an alien's property—in which world opinion was sharply divided, see *id.* at 428–30....

ABEBE–JIRA v. NEGEWO

72 F.3d 844 (11th Cir.1996).

HATCHETT, J.

Appellant, Kelbessa Negewo, appeals a judgment of the District Court for the Northern District of Georgia awarding compensatory and punitive damages to appellees, Hirute Abebe–Jira, Edge Gayehu Taye, and Elizabeth Demissie, for torture and cruel, inhuman, and degrading treatment, pursuant to the Alien Tort Claims Act, 28 U.S.C. § 1350. We affirm.

In the mid–1970s, a military dictatorship, known as "the Dergue," ruled Ethiopia and employed a campaign of torture, arbitrary imprisonment, and summary executions against perceived enemies of the government. Leaders of local governing units carried out the terror campaign, called "the Red Terror," at the local level. The dictatorship divided Ethiopia's capital, Addis Ababa, into twenty-five governing units called Higher Zones. During the relevant period, Negewo served as chairman of Higher Zone 9.

In December 1977, guards from Higher Zone 9 arrested Abebe–Jira and took her to a prison where she met Negewo. She remained imprisoned for two weeks without any charges being filed against her. In January 1978, Higher Zone 9 guards arrested Abebe–Jira and her sixteen-year-old sister and took them to the prison where Abebe–Jira had been previously detained. Negewo and other men tortured and interrogated Abebe–Jira for several hours. They ordered her to undress, bound her arms and legs, and whipped her on her legs and back with a wire. Abebe–Jira's torturers also repeatedly threatened her with death. The district court found that Negewo personally supervised at least some of the interrogation and torture of Abebe–Jira and also personally interrogated and participated directly in some of the acts of torture. Following her interrogation and torture, Abebe–Jira remained imprisoned for three months.

Higher Zone 9 guards arrested Taye in February 1978. Shortly after her arrest, Negewo and guards interrogated and tortured her for a period of several hours. Negewo and several guards instructed Taye to remove her clothes, bound her arms and legs together, hung her from a pole, and severely beat her. They then poured water onto her wounds to increase her pain. Taye received no medical care for the wounds and, as a result of the torture, bears permanent physical scars. Taye remained incarcerated for a period of ten months, and during that time she endured frequent interrogations and several incidents of torture. The district court found that Negewo personally supervised and participated in some of the interrogation and torture of Taye.

In April 1977, Negewo and several guards arrested Demissie, a seventeen-year-old student, three of her sisters, and her father. Demissie and her family remained imprisoned for two weeks without charges. In October 1977, Higher Zone 9 guards again arrested Demissie and her fifteen-year-old sister, Haimanot. After being detained at two different prisons, guards took Demissie and her sister to the jail in Higher Zone 9 that Negewo controlled, where guards interrogated and tortured them. The guards ordered Demissie to undress, bound her arms and feet, and placed a wooden pole under her legs and lifted her into the air; then, they beat her severely. After torturing her, the guards returned Demissie to her cell with her sister. Several days later, guards took Demissie's sister from the cell. Demissie and her family have not heard from nor seen Haimanot since that day. Demissie remained in custody until June 1978. The district court found that Negewo personally supervised some of the interrogation and torture of Demissie.

Following their release, the appellees fled Ethiopia and sought exile in the United States and Canada. In 1989, Taye encountered Negewo in an Atlanta, Georgia, hotel where they both worked.

In September 1990, the appellees filed this lawsuit against Negewo charging him with responsibility for their torture and other cruel acts in violation of the Alien Tort Claims Act, 28 U.S.C. § 1350. Prior to trial, Negewo made three requests for the appointment of counsel. The district court denied the first two requests on the ground that Negewo had not made a showing sufficient to authorize or justify the appointment. The district court apparently did not enter a written order on Negewo's third request. Following a two-day bench trial, the court found Negewo liable for the torture and cruel, inhuman, and degrading treatment of the appellees and awarded each appellee $200,000 in compensatory damages and $300,000 in punitive damages. Negewo appeals.

Negewo argues that the district court lacked subject matter jurisdiction because the Alien Tort Claims Act neither provides a private right of action nor incorporates a right of action through reference to a treaty or federal law. He also contends that this suit is barred because it involves a nonjusticiable political question.

The appellees contend that a literal reading of the Alien Tort Claims Act demonstrates that the district court had subject matter jurisdiction. They also contend that the political question doctrine does not bar this action.

... The leading case interpreting the Alien Tort Claims Act was decided by the Second Circuit Court of Appeals in Filartiga v. Pena–Irala, 630 F.2d 876 (2d Cir.1980).... The court of appeals emphasized that federal courts considering whether to assume jurisdiction under section 1350 should interpret international law as it has evolved and exists at the time of the case. Filartiga, 630 F.2d at 881. The court then concluded that official torture is now prohibited by the law of nations. Filartiga, 630 F.2d at 884.

The *Filartiga* court was not squarely presented with the question of whether the Alien Tort Claims Act provided a private right of action. The Second Circuit, however, in dicta, "construed the Alien Tort Statute, not as granting new rights to aliens, but simply as opening the federal courts for adjudication of the rights already recognized by international law." Filartiga, 630 F.2d at 887. Since *Filartiga*, a majority of courts have interpreted section 1350 as providing both a private cause of action and a federal forum where aliens may seek redress for violations of international law. *See, e.g.*, Kadic v. Karadzic, 70 F.3d 232, 236 (2d Cir.1995) ("[The] Act appears to provide a remedy for the appellants' allegations of violations related to genocide, war crimes, and official torture...."); Hilao v. Estate of Marcos (*In re* Estate of Ferdinand Marcos, Human Rights Litigation), 25 F.3d 1467, 1474–75 (9th Cir.1994) ("Marcos") (rejecting the assertion that section 1350 is a jurisdictional provision that does not grant a cause of action and concluding that the section "creates a cause of action for violations of specific, universal and obligatory international human rights standards"), *cert. denied*, ... U.S ... , 115 S.Ct. 934 ... (1995); Xuncax v. Gramajo, 886 F. Supp. 162, 179 (D.Mass.1995) ("§ 1350 yields both a jurisdictional grant and a private right to sue for tortious violations of international law ... without recourse to other law as a source of the cause of action."); Paul v. Avril, 812 F. Supp. 207, 212 (S.D.Fla.1993) ("The plain language of the statute and the use of the words "committed in violation' strongly implies that a well pled tort[,] if committed in violation of the law of nations, would be sufficient [to give rise to a cause of action]."); Forti v. Suarez–Mason, 672 F. Supp. 1531, 1539 (N.D.Cal.1987) (same), on reconsideration on other grounds, 694 F. Supp. 707 (N.D.Cal.1988). *But see* Tel–Oren v. Libyan Arab Republic, ... 726 F.2d 774, 798 (D.C.Cir.1984) (Bork, J., concurring) (concluding that neither federal common law, federal statute, nor international law affords an alien plaintiff a cause of action), *cert. denied*, 470 U.S. 1003 ... (1985).

We reject Negewo's assertion that the district court lacked subject matter jurisdiction because the Alien Tort Claims Act does not provide a private right of action. On its face, section 1350 requires the district courts to hear claims "by an alien for a tort only, committed in violation of the law of nations." ... We read the statute as requiring no more than an allegation of a violation of the law of nations in order to invoke section 1350. *See, e.g.*, *Kadic*, 70 F.3d at ... ("[The] statute confers federal subject-matter jurisdiction when the following three conditions are satisfied: (1) an alien sues (2) for a tort (3) committed in violation of the law of nations (*i.e.*, international law)."); *Marcos*, 25 F.3d at 1475 (" 'Nothing more than a *violation* of the law of nations is required to invoke section 1350.' ") (*quoting Tel–Oren*, 726 F.2d at 779 (Edwards, J., concurring)); *Xuncax*, 886 F. Supp. at 180 ("All that the statute requires is that an alien plaintiff allege that a 'tort' was committed 'in violation' of international law or treaty of the United States."). Moreover, the "committed in violation" language of the statute suggests that Congress did not intend to require an alien plaintiff to invoke a separate enabling statute as a precondition to relief under the Alien Tort Claims Act. *See, e.g.*, Handel v. Artukovic, 601 F. Supp. 1421, 1427 (C.D.Cal.1985) ("The 'violation' language of section 1350 may be interpreted as explicitly granting a cause of action...."); *Paul*, 812 F. Supp. at 212 (same); *Forti*, 672 F. Supp. at 1539 (same). Lastly, we find support for our holding in the recently enacted Torture Victim Protection Act of 1991 (TVPA).... In enacting the TVPA, Congress endorsed the *Filartiga* line of cases:

> The TVPA would establish an unambiguous and modern basis for a cause of action *that has been successfully maintained under an existing law*, section 1350 of the Judiciary Act of 1789 (the Alien Tort Claims Act), *which permits Federal district courts to hear claims by aliens for torts committed "in violation of the law of nations."*

H.R.Rep. No. 367, 102d Cong., 2d Sess. 3, *reprinted in* 1992 U.S.C.C.A.N. 84, 86 (emphasis added). Congress, therefore, has recognized that the

Alien Tort Claims Act confers both a forum and a private right of action to aliens alleging a violation of international law.

Accordingly, we conclude that the Alien Tort Claims Act establishes a federal forum where courts may fashion domestic common law remedies to give effect to violations of customary international law. *See, e.g.*, *Kadic*, 70 F.3d at 236; *Filartiga*, 630 F.2d at 887; *Xuncax*, 886 F. Supp. at 179–83. Congress, of course, may enact a statute that confers on the federal courts jurisdiction over a particular class of cases while delegating to the courts the task of fashioning remedies that give effect to the federal policies underlying the statute. *See, e.g.*, Textile Workers of America v. Lincoln Mills, 353 U.S. 448 . . . (1957).

APPLICABILITY OF THE POLITICAL QUESTION DOCTRINE

Negewo also contends that this case should have been dismissed because it presents a nonjusticiable political question. The political question doctrine prevents the judicial branch from deciding issues textually committed to the legislative or executive branches. Baker v. Carr, 369 U.S. 186, 211 . . . (1962). However, "it is error to suppose that every case or controversy which touches foreign relations lies beyond judicial cognizance." *Baker*, 369 U.S. at 211. . . . In Linder v. Portocarrero, 963 F.2d 332, 337 (11th Cir.1992), we held that the political question doctrine did not bar a tort action instituted against Nicaraguan Contra leaders. Consequently, we reject Negewo's contention in light of *Linder*.

Notes and Questions

1. *Compare* the test for "color of law" responsibility in *Kadic* (*i.e.*, when a private actor acts "together with" or "in concert with" a state or "with significant state aid") *with* Iwanowa v. Ford Motor Co., 67 F.Supp.2d at 445–46 & n.27 (when defendant was "in close cooperation with" or had "worked closely with" a state). In Doe v. Unocal Corp., 110 F.Supp.2d 1294 (C.D. Cal. 2000), the district court dismissed claims against Unocal, "finding no evidence that Unocal 'participated in or influenced' the military's unlawful conduct," that Unocal conspired with the military, or that Unocal's conduct amounted to "participation or cooperation in the forced labor practices" beyond mere knowledge of and benefits from the unlawful military practices. 110 F.Supp.2d at 1306–07, 1310. Is this consistent with the tests in *Kadic* and *Iwanowa*? Apparently the district court did not realize that various human rights prohibitions other than those relating to slavery or forced labor, genocide, other crimes against humanity, or war crimes can form the basis for private actor liability in the absence of conspiratorial state involvement, complicity with a state actor, or "color of law," and that U.S. tests for "color of law" or "state action" responsibility are not part of international law and are inappropriate and too limiting with respect to private actor liability for various other human rights violations. *Compare id.* at 1304–05, 1307–08 (apparently unaware of judicial recognitions and opinions of Attorneys General not cited therein, the Executive's Amicus brief in *Filartiga*, and other recognitions of private actor liability noted in this book). The district court also seemed to be unaware of the full range of complicity standards under international law. Concerning standards regarding criminal

complicity that can include both action and inaction amounting to participation, assistance, aiding, encouragement, reinforcement, or inducement (each with some minimally demonstrated criminal intent), *see, e.g.*, Paust, Bassiouni, *et al.*, International Criminal Law 39–43 (2 ed. 2000). However, civil liability should require a lower standard than criminal intent, *e.g.*, negligence or fault. *See* the Soering Case, 161 Eur. Ct. H.R. (Ser. A), paras. 80–92 (1989) (conduct in the context of a foreseeable "real risk" of a human rights violation by another actor leading to an independent violation, an "associated" violation, or a form of complicitous violation of human rights)); Chahal v. United Kingdom, Eur. Ct. H.R. (15 Nov. 1996)); Cicippio v. Islamic Republic of Iran, 18 F.Supp.2d 62 (D.D.C. 1998) (regarding complicity of Iran in hostage-taking). Civil liability for fault is normal in international law. *See, e.g.*, Restatement § 601.

Clearly, if the military had acted as a de facto agent of Unocal, liability also could have been based on negligence under the "knew or should have known" standard. Concerning such a standard under international criminal law, *see, e.g.*, Paust, Bassiouni, *et al.*, *supra*, at 29–30, 46–76, 99, *passim*. Plaintiffs had argued that Unocal knew that the Burmese military violated human rights in furtherance and for the benefit of a joint venture with Unocal. 110 F.Supp.2d at 1295–96, 1306. The court should have considered whether Unocal was liable as a *private* actor during a joint venture with another actor that, with the knowledge of Unocal, committed violations in furtherance and to the benefit of the joint venture (perhaps implicating vicarious liability); whether Unocal thus acquiesced in and is responsible for such violations; whether, in context, its knowledge and failure to object or its acquiescence amounted to some form of encouragement, reinforcement, influence, or participation; and whether Unocal is otherwise liable under the circumstances instead of shifting to a more limiting test of responsibility developed for "color of law" or "state action" labels and responsibility or looking merely at criminal complicity under international law. *See id.* at 1309–10. Additionally, the panel in *Kadic v. Karadzic* did not state that all or any other human rights violations required state actors or "color of law," which would have been incorrect. *See also* Kadic v. Karadzic, 70 F.3d at 241 (no state-action requirement applies to actions under the ATCA), 245 ("the state action concept, *where applicable for some* violations like 'official' torture. . . ." (emphasis added)). Indeed, the phrase "color of law" is not one used in international law or in the ATCA, and courts should not amend federal statutes by adding words that Congress has not chosen. That phrase appears only in the Torture Victim Protection Act and Congress chose not to amend the ATCA to limit claims to those involving state action or in any other way. *See* Kadic v. Karadzic, 70 F.3d at 241, 245. The *Unocal* case was settled out of court in 2005 with an undisclosed large amount to be paid to plaintiffs.

In Doe v. Saravia, 348 F.Supp.2d 1112 (E.D. Cal. 2004), plaintiffs obtained a judgment for compensatory and punitive damages and costs against defendant Saravia, a civilian (former Captain in the Salvadoran Air Force) and co-conspirator in the assassination of Archbishop Romero in El Salvador in 1980. The district court used the *Kadic* test of " 'acts together with' " or "acts with 'significant state aid' " to find that Saravia acted with both apparent authority and under color of law in connection with a death squad assassination carried out " 'with the financial and logistical support of the Salvadoran armed forces and far right Salvadoran civilians inside and outside El Salvador.' " *Id.* at 1149–50. In particular, the court noted that "Saravia's role in coordinating and planning the assassination ... is sufficient to establish liability against him under the TVPA and ATCA as a direct participant, conspirator, accomplice, and aider and abettor," adding that our courts "have recognized that principles of accomplice liability apply under the ATCA to those who assist others in the commission of torts that violate customary international law" and "[p]rinciples of accomplice liability are well-established under international law." *Id.* at 1148–49. Addressing the Supreme Court's decision in *Sosa v. Alvarez–Machain* [*infra*], the district court in *Saravia* found that both extrajudicial killing and crimes against humanity are modern violations of international law that are well-defined and actionable under the ATCA (and that extrajudicial killing is also actionable under the TVPA). *Id.* at 1154–57, also specifically citing Justice Breyer's concurring opinion in *Sosa*, *id.* at 1157.

Far more cautious was the decision in Aldana v. Del Monte Fresh Produce, N.A., Inc., 416 F.3d 1242 (11th Cir. July 8, 2005). *Aldana* assumed plaintiffs' allegations of involvement of defendant, its subsidiary, and defendant's hired private security forces with a local mayor in connection with the abduction and acts and threats of violence against plaintiffs to be true. *Aldana* noted plaintiffs' allegations of "three state acts or acts by state officials," but considered involvement by the mayor and allegations of government assistance to the security force " 'at the urging of Defendants and/or their agents' " to be sufficient regarding "state action" and upheld plaintiffs' claims under the ATCA and TVPA concerning alleged torture. The court cited *Kadic* for a "state action" test and also noted that "[a] claim for state-sponsored torture ... may be based on indirect liability as well as direct liability. *Cabello* [v. Fernandez–Larios], 402 F.3d [1148] at 1157 [11th Cir. 2005]. The Alien Tort Act 'reaches conspiracies and accomplice liability,' and the Torture Victim Protection Act reaches those who ordered, abetted, or assisted in the wrongful act. *Id.*" With respect to claims concerning cruel, inhuman, and degrading treatment, the opinion noted that two district court cases within the Circuit, *Mehinovic v. Vuckovic* and *Cabello v. Fernandez–Larios*, had recognized that such claims are actionable under the ATCA, but the Eleventh Circuit panel dismissed these claims based on its questionable conclusion that *Sosa* had stated that claims resting on the ICCPR do not create obligations enforceable in federal courts. *But see* ICCPR, arts. 2(3), 14(1), 50; Note 7, *infra*. With respect to claims of arbitrary detention, the panel quoted *Sosa*'s decision that " 'a single illegal detention of less than a day ... violates no norm of customary international law so well defined as to support the creation of a federal remedy' " (quoting *Sosa*, 124 S.Ct. at 2769) and noted that "detention alleged here was more frightening," but thought "the short time of the detention here causes the legal principle announced by the Court in *Sosa* to guide us." Consider this conclusion after reading *Sosa* and noting the actual holding in the case with respect to alleged "illegal" detention.

In Sarei v. Rio Tinto PLC, 221 F.Supp.2d 1116, 1148, 1151 n.146, 1153 (C.D.Cal. 2002), the District Court drew upon tests used by the *Kadic* and *Unocal* courts to determine that plaintiffs' allegations were sufficient to charge the corporate defendants with war crimes, crimes against humanity, and racial discrimination because the acts of the Papua New Guinea (PNG) Government were "fairly attributable" to Rio Tinto, the PNG Government acted as Rio Tinto's agent, Rio Tinto "controlled" its own actions, and Rio Tinto was a "willful participant" and "conspirator" in these actions. Was the District Court imposing too high a standard on the plaintiffs? Private individuals can commit "crimes against humanity" without any linkage with a government; can private corporations?

2. What test is generally adopted in the post-*Filartiga* line of cases concerning the "act of state" and "political question" claims of defense? *See also* Chapter 4; Paust, *infra*, next note.

3. With respect to Judge Newman's dictum in *Kadic v. Karadzic*, should the judiciary ever rightly conclude that if one brings a lawsuit pursuant to a legislatively approved scheme (*e.g.*, under the ATCA or the TVPA), claims made pursuant to such a scheme raise nonjusticiable "political" questions? *See also* Jordan J. Paust, *Suing Karadzic*, 10 LEIDEN J. INT'L L. 91 (1997). Some courts have subsequently refused to decide legal questions before them when the State Department has filed a suggestion of interest indicating that foreign affairs would be serious. Consider the next note. Nonetheless, note that the Supreme Court stated in United States v. Alvarez–Machain, 504 U.S. 655, 667 (1992), that the U.S.—Mexico extradition treaty "has the force of law, and if, as respondent asserts, it is self-executing, it would appear that a court must enforce it on behalf of an individual regardless of the offensiveness of the practice of one nation to the other nation." Earlier, the Supreme Court had affirmed: "we administer the public law of nations, and are not at liberty to inquire what is for the particular ... disadvantage of our own or another country." The Peterhoff, 72 U.S. (5 Wall.) 28, 57 (1866).

4. In Sarei v. Rio Tinto PLC, 221 F.Supp.2d 1116 (C.D. Cal. 2002), residents of Papua New Guinea brought claims for war crimes, crimes against humanity, racial discrimination, and environmental harm under the Alien Tort Claims Act (ATCA) against British and Australian corporations for their conduct in operating a massive mine on the island of Bougainville in Papua New Guinea, which had led to a "ten-year civil war, during which thousands of civilians died or were injured." After the U.S. executive branch submitted a "Statement of Interest" to the court indicating that this "lawsuit could negatively impact the peace process, and that the success of that process is an important United States foreign policy objective," the District Court dismissed the entire case, ruling that it was "thus quintessentially one that calls for invocation of the political question doctrine as to each of plaintiffs' causes of action." In view of prior cases noted here that addressed a political question claim, is such a choice preferable?

Before reaching that ultimate conclusion, however, the District Court ruled that plaintiffs' pleadings were sufficient to allege claims based on war crimes, concluding that blocking medical supplies needed by civilians violated the 1949 Geneva Conventions, and thereby rejecting the views of Professor Barry Carter, submitted on behalf of the corporations, who had contended (without citations) that a government's blockade of its own territory is permitted by customary international law, which, according to Professor

Carter, "recognizes and respects the political independence and territorial sovereignty of a state[,] including the inherent right to police its own territory." Similarly, the Court concluded that plaintiffs' allegations were sufficient to charge a crimes against humanity under the ATCA , based on the medical blockade, which allegedly " 'constitute[d] genocide because it foreseeably resulted in the killing of natives, caused serious bodily harm, was deliberately calculated to destroy plaintiffs and their way of life,' and constituted an 'act[] of official torture.' " With regard to both the allegations of war crimes and crimes against humanity, the District Court also concluded that the acts of the corporations were sufficiently linked to those of the government of Papua New Guinea (PNG) so that "the acts of PNG are 'fairly attributable' to Rio Tinto, that it was a 'willful participant' in those acts, and/or that it exercised 'control' over them."

With regard to the racial discrimination claims, the Court agreed that "[m]any courts ... have held that practicing racial discrimination violates a *jus cogens* norm," and that plaintiffs had alleged sufficient linkage between the private corporations and the government of Papua New Guinea to meet the "state action" required to establish that acts of racial discrimination constituted violations of international law. The District Court dismissed the claims based on environmental harm, ruling that they had failed to articulate a " 'specific, universal, and obligatory' norm of the type that will support a claim for violation of the law of nations," but upheld a claim based on pollution in violation of the 1982 Law of the Sea Convention, concluding that because the Convention "reflects customary international law, plaintiffs may base an ATCA claim upon it."

5. In August, 2000, the jury awarded the plaintiffs in *Kadic* $745 million ($265 million compensatory, $480 million punitive), and in October, 2000, a jury awarded plaintiffs in *Doe v. Karadzic* $4.207 billion ($407 million compensatory, $3.8 billion punitive). The district court opinion in *Negewo* awarded $1.5 million to three plaintiffs (an Ethiopian and two Canadians) for prolonged arbitrary detention, torture, and cruel, inhuman, and degrading treatment. Abebe–Jiri v. Negewo, 1993 WL 814304 (N.D. Ga. 1993). What other cases approved claims of cruel, inhuman, and degrading treatment?

Also see Mehinovic v. Vuckovic, 198 F.Supp.2d 1322, 1347–49 (N.D. Ga. 2002) ("Cruel, inhuman, or degrading treatment is a discrete and well-recognized violation of customary international law and is, therefore, a separate ground for liability under the ATCA."); Estate of Cabello v. Fernandez–Larios, 157 F.Supp.2d at 1360–61; Xuncax v. Gramajo, 886 F.Supp. at 187.

6. Other recent cases addressing private duties under international law include: Wiwa v. Royal Dutch Petroleum Co., 226 F.3d 88 (2d Cir. 2000); Weisshaus v. Swiss Bankers Ass'n, 225 F.3d 191 (2d Cir. 2000); Vietnam Ass'n for Victims of Agent Orange/Dioxin v. Dow Chemical Co. (*In re* Agent Orange Prod. Liab. Litig.), 373 F.Supp.2d 7 (E.D.N.Y. 2005); Presbyterian Church of Sudan v. Talisman Energy, Inc., 374 F.Supp.2d 331 (S.D.N.Y. 2005), *id.*, 244 F.Supp.2d 289, 305, 308–20, 328, 333 (S.D.N.Y. 2003); Bodner v. Banque Paribas, 114 F.Supp.2d 117 (E.D.N.Y. 2000); Iwanowa v. Ford Motor Co., 57 F.Supp.2d 41, 60–62 (D.N.J.1999); Jama v. Immigration and

Naturalization Service, 22 F.Supp.2d 353, 362–63 (D.N.J.1998); Doe I v. Islamic Salvation Front, 993 F.Supp. 3, 8 (D.D.C.1998); Eastman Kodak Co. v. Kavlin, 978 F.Supp. 1078, 1090–95 (S.D. Fla. 1997); Doe I v. Unocal Corp., 963 F.Supp. 880 (C.D. Cal. 1997).

7. Prior to the Supreme Court's decision in *Sosa v. Alveraz–Machain* [the next case extract] in 2004, a long line of decisions had recognized that the ATCA creates a domestic cause of action concerning violations of international law. *See, e.g.*, Alvarez–Machain v. United States, 331 F.3d 604 (9th Cir. 2003); Papa v. United States, 281 F.3d 1004, 1013 (9th Cir. 2002); Alvarez–Machain v. United States, 266 F.3d 1045, 1050 (9th Cir. 2001); Martinez v. City of Los Angeles, 141 F.3d 1373, 1383 (9th Cir. 1998); Abebe–Jira v. Negewo, 72 F.3d at 847–48; Kadic v. Karadzic, 70 F.3d at 236, 238; Hilao v. Estate of Marcos, 25 F.3d at 1474–75; Amerada Hess Shipping Corp. v. Argentine Republic, 830 F.2d at 424–25; Tel–Oren v. Libyan Arab Republic, 726 F.2d 774, 777–80 (D.C. Cir. 1984) (Edwards, J., concurring); Filartiga v. Pena–Irala, 630 F.2d at 880–82, 884–85, 887; Presbyterian Church of Sudan v. Talisman Energy, Inc., 244 F.Supp.2d at 320; Estate of Cabello v. Fernandez–Larios, 157 F.Supp.2d 1345, 1359–60 (S.D. Fla. 2001); Iwanowa v. Ford Motor Co., 67 F.Supp.2d at 441–43; Jama v. U.S. I.N.S., 22 F.Supp.2d at 362–63; Xuncax v. Gramajo, 886 F.Supp. at 179; Paul v. Avril, 812 F.Supp. at 212; Forti v. Suarez–Mason, 672 F.Supp. at 1539–40; Guinto v. Marcos, 654 F.Supp. 276, 279–80 (S.D. Cal. 1986); Handel v. Artukovic, 601 F.Supp. 1421, 1426–27 (C.D. Cal. 1985); 26 Op. Att'y Gen. 250, 252–53 (1907); 1 Op. Att'y Gen. 57, 58 (1795); PAUST, INTERNATIONAL LAW AS LAW OF THE UNITED STATES 14, 65, 229, 232–34, 311 (2 ed. 2003); *but see* Tel–Oren v. Libyan Arab Republic, 726 F.2d at 798 (Bork, J., concurring). Judge Bork's view to the contrary in *Tel-Oren* was recognized as being in error, opposed by Judge Edwards, and had not been followed until *Sosa*. *See, e.g.*, Iwanowa v. Ford Motor Co., 67 F.Supp.2d at 442 n.20 (Bork's "highly criticized opinion," "reasoning is flawed"); *Kadic*, 70 F.3d at 238; *Forti*, 672 F.Supp. at 1539.

The right of access to domestic courts and to an effective remedy concerning human rights violations also happens to be part of human rights law. *See, e.g.*, General Comment No. 24, U.N. GAOR, Hum. Rts. Comm., U.N. Doc. CCPR/C/Rev.1/add.6, paras. 8–9, 11–12 (2 Nov. 1994); Dubai Petroleum Co., *et al.* v. Kazi, 12 S.W.3d 71, 82 (Tex. 2000) ("The Covenant [ICCPR] not only guarantees foreign citizens equal treatment in the signatorie's courts, but also guarantees them equal access to these courts."); PAUST, *supra*, at 224–29; Jon M. VanDyke, *The Fundamental Right to Prosecution and Compensation*, 29 DEN. J. INT'L & POL'Y 77 (2001). This should be important regarding litigation of human rights clams after the decision in *Sosa*.

8. For cases addressing war crime liability under the Geneva Conventions and other laws of war, *see, e.g.*, Weisshaus v. Swiss Bankers Ass'n, 225 F.3d 191 (2d Cir. 2000); Hilao v. Estate of Marcos, 103 F.3d 767, 777 (9th Cir. 1996) (re: leader responsibility); Kadic v. Karadzic, 70 F.3d 232, 242–43 (2d Cir. 1995), *cert. denied*, 518 U.S. 1005 (1996); Linder v. Portocarrero, 963 F.2d 332, 336–37 (11th Cir. 1992); Estate of Rodriquez v. Drummond Co., Inc., 256 F.Supp.2d 1250 (N.D. Ala. 2003); Presbyterian Church of Sudan v. Talisman Energy, Inc., 244 F.Supp.2d at 310–11; Barrueto v. Larios, 205

F.Supp.2d 1325, 1333 (S.D. Fla. 2002) (re: individual responsibility); Mehinovic v. Vuckovic, 198 F.Supp.2d 1322, 1350–54, 1358 (N.D. Ga. 2002); *In re* World War II Era Japanese Forced Labor Litigation, 114 F.Supp.2d 939 (N.D. Cal. 2000) (private claims were settled by international agreement); Doe v. Islamic Salvation Front, 993 F.Supp. 3, 8 (D.D.C. 1998); Xuncax v. Gramajo, 886 F.Supp. 162, 171–72 (D. Mass. 1995) (re: leader liability).

Since the beginning of the United States, private remedies have been available in courts for violations of the laws of war. *See, e.g.*, *Ex parte* Quirin, 317 U.S. 1, 27 (1942) ("From the very beginning of its history this Court has recognized and applied the law of war as including that part of the law of nations which prescribes ... the status, right and duties of enemy ... individuals"); The Paquete Habana, 175 U.S. 677, 698 ("law of war"), 714 (1900); Freeland v. Williams, 131 U.S. 405, 416–17 (1889) ("no civil liability attached" when no war crime occurred); Ford v. Surget, 97 U.S. 594, 605–06 (1878) (individuals "relieved from civil liability" where no war crime occurred); Mitchell v. Harmony, 54 U.S. (13 How.) 115, 137 (1851) (suit could be brought in "any district in which the defendant might be found"); Bas v. Tingy, 4 U.S. (4 Dall.) 37, 43 (1800) (Chase, J.); Ware v. Hylton, 3 U.S. (3 Dall.) 199, 279 (1796) (Iredell, J.) "rights ... derived from the laws of war ... and in that case the individual might have been entitled to compensation"); Paust, *supra*, at 64 n.130, 226–27, 291–92 nn.489–95.

SOSA v. ALVAREZ–MACHAIN

542 U.S. 692 (2004).

Souter, J.

The two issues are whether respondent Alvarez–Machain's allegation that the Drug Enforcement Administration instigated his abduction from Mexico for criminal trial in the United States supports a claim against the Government under the Federal Tort Claims Act (FTCA or Act), 28 U.S.C. § 1346(b)(1), §§ 2671–2680, and whether he may recover under the Alien Tort Statute (ATS) [ATCA], 28 U.S.C. § 1350. We hold that he is not entitled to a remedy under either statute. [Editors' note: the Court ruled that an exception to the FTCA's waiver of immunity for claims "arising in a foreign country" applied. 28 U.S.C. § 2680(k)]

We have considered the underlying facts before, United States v. Alvarez–Machain, 504 U.S. 655 ... (1992) [Editors' note: addressed in Chapter 3, Section 3 B. The case was decided on the narrow ground that the abduction was not expressly a violation of a bilateral extradition treaty between the U.S. and Mexico]. In 1985, an agent of the Drug Enforcement Administration (DEA), Enrique Camarena–Salazar, was captured on assignment in Mexico and taken to a house in Guadalajara, where he was tortured over the course of a 2–day interrogation, then murdered. Based in part on eyewitness testimony, DEA officials in the United States came to believe that respondent Humberto Alvarez–Machain (Alvarez), a Mexican physician, was present at the house and acted to prolong the agent's life in order to extend the interrogation and torture. *Id.* at 657.

In 1990, a federal grand jury indicted Alvarez for the torture and murder of Camarena–Salazar, and the United States District Court for the Central District of California issued a warrant for his arrest. 331 F.3d 604, 609 (C.A.9 2003) (en banc). The DEA asked the Mexican Government for help in getting Alvarez into the United States, but when the requests and negotiations proved fruitless, the DEA approved a plan to hire Mexican nationals to seize Alvarez and bring him to the United States for trial. As so planned, a group of Mexicans, including petitioner Jose Francisco Sosa, abducted Alvarez from his house, held him overnight in a motel, and brought him by private plane to El Paso, Texas, where he was arrested by federal officers. *Ibid.*

Once in American custody, Alvarez moved to dismiss the indictment on the ground that his seizure was "outrageous governmental conduct," *Alvarez-Machain*, 504 U.S. at 568, and violated the extradition treaty between the United States and Mexico. The District Court agreed, the Ninth Circuit affirmed, and we reversed, *id.* at 670, holding that the fact of Alvarez's forcible seizure did not affect the jurisdiction of a federal court. The case was tried in 1992, and ended at the close of the Government's case, when the District Court granted Alvarez's motion for a judgment of acquittal.

In 1993, after returning to Mexico, Alvarez began the civil action before us here. He sued Sosa, Mexican citizen and DEA operative Antonio Garate–Bustamante, five unnamed Mexican civilians, the United States, and four DEA agents. 331 F.3d at 610. So far as it matters here, Alvarez sought damages from the United States under the FTCA, alleging false arrest, and from Sosa under the ATS, for a violation of the law of nations. The former statute authorizes suit "for ... personal injury ... caused by the negligent or wrongful act or omission of any employee of the Government while acting within the scope of his office or employment." 28 U.S.C. § 1346(b)(1). The latter provides in its entirety that "[t]he district courts shall have original jurisdiction of any civil action by an alien for a tort only, committed in violation of the law of nations or a treaty of the United States." § 1350....

Alvarez has also brought an action under the ATS against petitioner, Sosa, who argues (as does the United States supporting him) that there is no relief under the ATS because the statute does no more than vest federal courts with jurisdiction, neither creating nor authorizing the courts to recognize any particular right of action without further congressional action. Although we agree the statute is in terms only jurisdictional, we think that at the time of enactment the jurisdiction enabled federal courts to hear claims in a very limited category defined by the law of nations and recognized at common law. We do not believe, however, that the limited, implicit sanction to entertain the handful of international law *cum* common law claims understood in 1789 should be taken as authority to recognize the right of action asserted by Alvarez here....

The parties and *amici* here advance radically different historical interpretations of this terse provision. Alvarez says that the ATS was intended not simply as a jurisdictional grant, but as authority for the creation of a new cause of action for torts in violation of international law. We think that reading is implausible. As enacted in 1789, the ATS gave the district courts "cognizance" of certain causes of action, and the term bespoke a grant of jurisdiction, not power to mold substantive law. *See, e.g.*, THE FEDERALIST NO. 81, pp. 447, 451 (J. Cooke ed. 1961) (A. Hamilton) (using "jurisdiction" interchangeably with "cognizance"). The fact that the ATS was placed in § 9 of the Judiciary Act, a statute otherwise exclusively concerned with federal-court jurisdiction, is itself support for its strictly jurisdictional nature. Nor would the distinction between jurisdiction and cause of action have been elided by the drafters of the Act or those who voted on it. As Fisher Ames put it, "there is a substantial difference between the jurisdiction of courts and rules of decision." 1 ANNALS OF CONG. 807 (Gales ed. 1834). It is unsurprising, then, that an authority on the historical origins of the ATS has written that "section 1350 clearly does not create a statutory cause of action," and that the contrary suggestion is "simply frivolous." Casto, *The Federal Courts' Protective Jurisdiction Over Torts Committed in Violation of the Law of Nations*, 18 CONN. L. REV. 467, 479, 480 (1986) (hereinafter Casto, *Law of Nations*); *Cf.* Dodge, *The Constitutionality of the Alien Tort Statute: Some Observations on Text and Context*, 42 VA. J. INT'L L. 687, 689 (2002). In sum, we think the statute was intended as jurisdictional in the sense of addressing the power of the courts to entertain cases concerned with a certain subject.

But holding the ATS jurisdictional raises a new question, this one about the interaction between the ATS at the time of its enactment and the ambient law of the era. Sosa would have it that the ATS was stillborn because there could be no claim for relief without a further statute expressly authorizing adoption of causes of action. *Amici* professors of federal jurisdiction and legal history take a different tack, that federal courts could entertain claims once the jurisdictional grant was on the books, because torts in violation of the law of nations would have been recognized within the common law of the time. Brief for Vikram Amar *et al.* as *Amici Curiae*. We think history and practice give the edge to this latter position.

"When the *United States* declared their independence, they were bound to receive the law of nations, in its modern state of purity and refinement." Ware v. Hylton, 3 Dall. 199, 281 . . . (1796) (Wilson, J.). In the years of the early Republic, this law of nations comprised two principal elements, the first covering the general norms governing the behavior of national states with each other: *"the science which teaches the rights subsisting between nations or states, and the obligations correspondent to those rights,"* E. DE VATTEL, THE LAW OF NATIONS, PRELIMINARIES § 3 (J. Chitty *et al.* transl. and ed. 1883) (hereinafter Vattel) (footnote omitted), or "that code of public instruction which defines the rights and prescribes the duties of nations, in their intercourse with each other," 1

James Kent Commentaries *1. This aspect of the law of nations thus occupied the executive and legislative domains, not the judicial. See 4 W. Blackstone, Commentaries on the Laws of England 68 (1769) (hereinafter Commentaries) ("[O]ffenses against" the law of nations are "principally incident to whole states or nations").

The law of nations included a second, more pedestrian element, however, that did fall within the judicial sphere, as a body of judge-made law regulating the conduct of individuals situated outside domestic boundaries and consequently carrying an international savor. To Blackstone, the law of nations in this sense was implicated "in mercantile questions, such as bills of exchange and the like; in all marine causes, relating to freight, average, demurrage, insurances, bottomry . . . ; [and] in all disputes relating to prizes, to shipwrecks, to hostages, and ransom bills." *Id.*, at 67. The law merchant emerged from the customary practices of international traders and admiralty required its own transnational regulation. And it was the law of nations in this sense that our precursors spoke about when the Court explained the status of coast fishing vessels in wartime grew from "ancient usage among civilized nations, beginning centuries ago, and gradually ripening into a rule of international law. . . ." The Paquete Habana, 175 U.S. 677, 686 . . . (1900).

There was, finally, a sphere in which these rules binding individuals for the benefit of other individuals overlapped with the norms of state relationships. Blackstone referred to it when he mentioned three specific offenses against the law of nations addressed by the criminal law of England: violation of safe conducts, infringement of the rights of ambassadors, and piracy. 4 Commentaries 68. An assault against an ambassador, for example, impinged upon the sovereignty of the foreign nation and if not adequately redressed could rise to an issue of war. See Vattel 463–464. It was this narrow set of violations of the law of nations, admitting of a judicial remedy and at the same time threatening serious consequences in international affairs, that was probably on minds of the men who drafted the ATS with its reference to tort.

Before there was any ATS, a distinctly American preoccupation with these hybrid international norms had taken shape owing to the distribution of political power from independence through the period of confederation. The Continental Congress was hamstrung by its inability to "cause infractions of treaties, or of the law of nations to be punished," J. Madison, Journal of the Constitutional Convention 60 (E. Scott ed. 1893), and in 1781 the Congress implored the States to vindicate rights under the law of nations. In words that echo Blackstone, the congressional resolution called upon state legislatures to "provide expeditious, exemplary, and adequate punishment" for "the violation of safe conducts or passports, . . . of hostility against such as are in amity, . . . with the United States, . . . infractions of the immunities of ambassadors and other public ministers . . . [and] "infractions of treaties and conventions to which the United States are a party." 21 Journals of the Continental Congress 1136–1137 (G. Hunt ed.1912) (hereinafter Journals of the

Continental Congress). The resolution recommended that the States "authorise suits . . . for damages by the party injured, and for compensation to the United States for damage sustained by them from an injury done to a foreign power by a citizen." *Id.*, at 1137; *cf.* VATTEL 463–464 ("Whoever offends . . . a public minister . . . should be punished . . . , and . . . the state should, at the expense of the delinquent, give full satisfaction to the sovereign who has been offended in the person of his minister"). Apparently only one State acted upon the recommendation, see FIRST LAWS OF THE STATE OF CONNECTICUT 82, 83 (J. Cushing ed. 1982) (1784 compilation; exact date of Act unknown), but Congress had done what it could to signal a commitment to enforce the law of nations.

Appreciation of the Continental Congress's incapacity to deal with this class of cases was intensified by the so-called Marbois incident of May 1784, in which a French adventurer, Longchamps, verbally and physically assaulted the Secretary of the French Legion in Philadelphia. See Respublica v. De Longchamps, 1 Dall. 111 . . . (O.T. Phila. 1784). Congress called again for state legislation addressing such matters, and concern over the inadequate vindication of the law of nations persisted through the time of the constitutional convention. See 1 RECORDS OF THE FEDERAL CONVENTION OF 1787, p. 25 (M. Farrand ed. 1911) (speech of J. Randolph). During the Convention itself, in fact, a New York City constable produced a reprise of the Marbois affair and Secretary Jay reported to Congress on the Dutch Ambassador's protest, with the explanation that "the federal government does not appear . . . to be vested with any judicial Powers competent to the Cognizance and Judgment of such Cases." Casto, *Law of Nations* 494, and n.152.

The Framers responded by vesting the Supreme Court with original jurisdiction over "all Cases affecting Ambassadors, other public ministers and Consuls." U.S. Const., Art. III, § 2, and the First Congress followed through. The Judiciary Act reinforced this Court's original jurisdiction over suits brought by diplomats, see 1 Stat. 80, ch. 20, § 13, created alienage jurisdiction, § 11 and, of course, included the ATS, § 9. . . .

Although Congress modified the draft of what became the Judiciary Act, *see generally* Warren, *New Light on the History of the Federal Judiciary Act of 1789*, 37 HARV. L. REV. 49 (1923), it made hardly any changes to the provisions on aliens, including what became the ATS, see Casto, *Law of Nations* 498. There is no record of congressional discussion about private actions that might be subject to the jurisdictional provision, or about any need for further legislation to create private remedies; there is no record even of debate on the section. . . .

Still, the history does tend to support two propositions. First, there is every reason to suppose that the First Congress did not pass the ATS as a jurisdictional convenience to be placed on the shelf for use by a future Congress or state legislature that might, some day, authorize the creation of causes of action or itself decide to make some element of the law of nations actionable for the benefit of foreigners. The anxieties of the preconstitutional period cannot be ignored easily enough to think that the statute was not meant to have a practical effect. Consider that the principal draftsman of the ATS was apparently Oliver Ellsworth, previously a member of the Continental Congress that had passed the 1781 resolution and a member of the Connecticut Legislature that made good on that congressional request. *See generally* W. BROWN, THE LIFE OF OLIVER ELLSWORTH (1905). Consider, too, that the First Congress was attentive enough to the law of nations to recognize certain offenses expressly as criminal, including the three mentioned by Blackstone. See An Act for the Punishment of Certain Crimes Against the United States, § 8, 1 Stat. 113–114 (murder or robbery, or other capital crimes, punishable as piracy if committed on the high seas), and § 28, *id.*, at 118 (violation of safe conducts and assaults against ambassadors punished by imprisonment and fines described as "infract[ions of] the law of nations"). It would have been passing strange for Ellsworth and this very Congress to vest federal courts expressly with jurisdiction to entertain civil causes brought by aliens alleging violations of the law of nations, but to no effect whatever until the Congress should take further action. There is too much in the historical record to believe that Congress would have enacted the ATS only to leave it lying fallow indefinitely.

The second inference to be drawn from the history is that Congress intended the ATS to furnish jurisdiction for a relatively modest set of actions alleging violations of the law of nations. Uppermost in the legislative mind appears to have been offenses against ambassadors, see *id.*, at 118; violations of safe conduct were probably understood to be actionable, *ibid.*, and individual actions arising out of prize captures and piracy may well have also been contemplated. *Id.*, at 113–114. But the common law appears to have understood only those three of the hybrid variety as definite and actionable, or at any rate, to have assumed only a very limited set of claims. As Blackstone had put it, "offences against this law [of nations] are principally incident to whole states or nations," and not individuals seeking relief in court. 4 COMMENTARIES 68.

The sparse contemporaneous cases and legal materials referring to the ATS tend to confirm both inferences, that some, but few, torts in violation of the law of nations were understood to be within the common law. In Bolchos v. Darrel, 3 F.Cas. 810 (No. 1,607) (D.S.C. 1795), the District Court's doubt about admiralty jurisdiction over a suit for damages brought by a French privateer against the mortgagee of a British slave ship was assuaged by assuming that the ATS was a jurisdictional basis for the court's action. Nor is Moxon v. The Fanny, 17 F.Cas. 942 (No. 9,895) (D. Pa. 1793), to the contrary, a case in which the owners of a British ship sought damages for its seizure in United States waters by a French privateer. The District Court said in dictum that the ATS was not the proper vehicle for suit because "[i]t cannot be called a suit for a tort only, when the property, as well as damages for the supposed trespass, are sought for." *Id.* at 948. But the judge gave no intimation that further legislation would have been needed to give the District Court jurisdiction over a suit limited to damages.

Then there was the 1795 opinion of Attorney General William Bradford, who was asked whether criminal prosecution was available against Americans who had taken part in the French plunder of a British slave colony in Sierra Leone. 1 Op. Atty. Gen. 57. Bradford was uncertain, but he made it clear that a federal court was open for the prosecution of a tort action growing out of the episode:

> "But there can be no doubt that the company or individuals who have been injured by these acts of hostility have a remedy by a *civil* suit in the courts of the United States; jurisdiction being expressly given to these courts in all cases where an alien sues for a tort only, in violation of the laws of nations, or a treaty of the United States...." *Id.*, at 59.

Although it is conceivable that Bradford (who had prosecuted in the Marbois incident, see Casto, *Law of Nations* 503, n.201) assumed that there had been a violation of a treaty, 1 Op. Atty. Gen., at 58, that is certainly not obvious, and it appears likely that Bradford understood the ATS to provide jurisdiction over what must have amounted to common law causes of action....

In sum, although the ATS is a jurisdictional statute creating no new causes of action, the reasonable inference from the historical materials is that the statute was intended to have practical effect the moment it became law. The jurisdictional grant is best read as having been enacted on the understanding that the common law would provide a cause of action for the modest number of international law violations with a potential for personal liability at the time.

We think it is correct, then, to assume that the First Congress understood that the district courts would recognize private causes of action for certain torts in violation of the law of nations, though we have found no basis to suspect Congress had any examples in mind beyond those torts corresponding to Blackstone's three primary offenses: violation of safe conducts, infringement of the rights of ambassadors, and piracy. We assume, too, that no development in the two centuries from the enactment of § 1350 to the birth of the modern line of cases beginning with Filartiga v. Pena–Irala, 630 F.2d 876 (C.A.2 1980), has categorically precluded federal courts from recognizing a claim under the law of nations as an element of common law; Congress has not in any relevant way amended § 1350 or limited civil common law power by another statute. Still, there are good reasons for a restrained conception of the discretion a federal court should exercise in considering a new cause of action of this kind. Accordingly, we think courts should require any claim based on the present-day law of nations to rest on a norm of international character accepted by the civilized world and defined with a specificity comparable to the features of the 18th-century paradigms we have recognized. This requirement is fatal to Alvarez's claim.

A series of reasons argue for judicial caution when considering the kinds of individual claims that might implement the jurisdiction conferred by the early statute. First, the prevailing conception of the common law has changed since 1789 in a way that counsels restraint in judicially applying internationally generated norms. When § 1350 was enacted, the accepted conception was of the common law as "a transcendental body of law outside of any particular State but obligatory within it unless and until changed by statute." Black and White Taxicab & Transfer Co. v. Brown and Yellow Taxicab & Transfer Co., 276 U.S. 518, 533 ... (1928) (Holmes, J., dissenting). Now, however, in most cases where a court is asked to state or formulate a common law principle in a new context, there is a general understanding that the law is not so much found or discovered as it is either made or created....

... [A] judge deciding in reliance on an international norm will find a substantial element of discretionary judgment in the decision.

Second, along with, and in part driven by, that conceptual development in understanding common law has come an equally significant rethinking of the role of the federal courts in making it. Erie R. Co. v. Tompkins, 304 U.S. 64 ... (1938), was the watershed in which we denied the existence of any federal "general" common law, *id.*, at 78, which largely withdrew to havens of specialty, some of them defined by express congressional authorization to devise a body of law directly, *e.g.*, Textile Workers v. Lincoln Mills of Ala., 353 U.S. 448 ... (1957) (interpretation of collective-bargaining agreements); Fed. Rule Evid. 501 (evidentiary privileges in federal-question cases). Elsewhere, this Court has thought it was in order to create federal common law rules in interstitial areas of particular federal interest. *E.g.*, United States v. Kimbell Foods, Inc., 440 U.S. 715, 726–727 ... (1979). And although we have even assumed competence to make judicial rules of decision of particular importance to foreign relations, such as the act of state doctrine, see Banco Nacional de Cuba v. Sabbatino, 376 U.S. 398, 427 ... (1964), the general practice has been to look for legislative guidance before exercising innovative authority over substantive law. It would be remarkable to take a more aggressive role in exercising a jurisdiction that remained largely in shadow for much of the prior two centuries.

Third, this Court has recently and repeatedly said that a decision to create a private right of action is one better left to legislative judgment in the great majority of cases.... [E]ven when Congress has made it clear by statute that a rule applies to purely domestic conduct, we are reluctant to infer intent to provide a private cause of action where the statute does not supply one expressly. While the absence of congressional action addressing private rights of action under an international norm is more equivocal than its failure to provide such a right when it creates a statute, the possible collateral consequences of making international rules privately actionable argue for judicial caution.

Fourth, the subject of those collateral consequences is itself a reason for a high bar to new private causes of action for violating international law, for the potential implications for the foreign relations of the United States of recognizing such causes should make courts particularly wary of impinging on the discretion of the Legislative and Executive Branches in managing foreign affairs. It is one thing for American courts to enforce constitutional limits on our own State and Federal Governments' power, but quite another to consider suits under rules that would go so far as to claim a limit on the power of foreign governments over their own citizens, and to hold that a foreign government or its agent has transgressed those limits. *Cf. Sabbatino, supra,* at 431–432. Yet modern international law is very much concerned with just such questions, and apt to stimulate calls for vindicating private interests in § 1350 cases. Since many attempts by federal courts to craft remedies for the violation of new norms of international law would raise risks of adverse foreign policy consequences, they should be undertaken, if at all, with great caution. *Cf.* Tel–Oren v. Libyan Arab Republic, 726 F.2d 774, 813 (C.A.D.C. 1984) (Bork, J., concurring) (expressing doubt that § 1350 should be read to require "our courts [to] sit in judgment of the conduct of foreign officials in their own countries with respect to their own citizens").

The fifth reason is particularly important in light of the first four. We have no congressional mandate to seek out and define new and debatable violations of the law of nations, and modern indications of congressional understanding of the judicial role in the field have not affirmatively encouraged greater judicial creativity....

These reasons argue for great caution in adapting the law of nations to private rights. Justice Scalia (opinion concurring in part and concurring in judgment) concludes that caution is too hospitable, and a word is in order to summarize where we have come so far and to focus our difference with him on whether some norms of today's law of nations may ever be recognized legitimately by federal courts in the absence of congressional action beyond § 1350. All Members of the Court agree that § 1350 is only jurisdictional. We also agree, or at least Justice Scalia does not dispute, that the jurisdiction was originally understood to be available to enforce a small number of international norms that a federal court could properly recognize as within the common law enforceable without further statutory authority. Justice Scalia concludes, however, that two subsequent developments should be understood to preclude federal courts from recognizing any further international norms as judicially enforceable today, absent further congressional action. As described before, we now tend to understand common law not as a discoverable reflection of universal reason but, in a positivistic way, as a product of human choice. And we now adhere to a conception of limited judicial power first expressed in reorienting federal diversity jurisdiction, see Erie v. Tompkins, 304 U.S. 64 ... (1938), that federal courts have no authority to derive "general" common law.

Whereas Justice Scalia sees these developments as sufficient to close the door to further independent judicial recognition of actionable international norms, other considerations persuade us that the judicial power should be exercised on the understanding that the door is still ajar subject to vigilant doorkeeping, and thus open to a narrow class of international norms today. *Erie* did not in terms bar any judicial recognition of new substantive rules, no matter what the circumstances, and post-*Erie* understanding has identified limited enclaves in which federal courts may derive some substantive law in a common law way. For two centuries we have affirmed that the domestic law of the United States recognizes the law of nations. *See, e.g., Sabbatino*, 376 U.S. at 423 ("[I]t is, of course, true that United States courts apply international law as a part of our own in appropriate circumstances"); *The Paquete Habana*, 175 U.S. at 700 ("International law is part of our law, and must be ascertained and administered by the courts of justice of appropriate jurisdiction, as often as questions of right depending upon it are duly presented for their determination"); The Nereide, 9 Cranch 388, 423 ... (1815) (Marshall, C.J.) ("[T]he Court is bound by the law of nations which is a part of the law of the land"); see also Texas Industries, Inc. v. Radcliff Materials, Inc., 451 U.S. 630, 641 ... (1981) (recognizing that "international disputes implicating ... our relations with foreign nations" are one of the "narrow areas" in which "federal common law" continues to exist). It would take some explaining to say now that federal courts must avert their gaze entirely from any international norm intended to protect individuals.

We think an attempt to justify such a position would be particularly unconvincing in light of what we know about congressional understanding bearing on this issue lying at the intersection of the judicial and legislative powers. The First Congress, which reflected the understanding of the framing generation and included some of the Framers, assumed that federal courts could properly identify some international norms as enforceable in the exercise of § 1350 jurisdiction. We think it would be unreasonable to assume that the First Congress would have expected federal courts to lose all capacity to recognize enforceable international norms simply because the common law might lose some metaphysical cachet on the road to modern realism. Later Congresses seem to have shared our view. The position we take today has been assumed by some federal courts for 24 years, ever since the Second Circuit decided Filartiga v. Pena–Irala, 630 F.2d 876 (C.A.2 1980), and for practical purposes the point of today's disagreement has been focused since the exchange between Judge Edwards and Judge Bork in Tel–Oren v. Libyan Arab Republic, 726 F.2d 774 (C.A.D.C. 1984). Congress, however, has not only expressed no disagreement with our view of the proper exercise of the judicial power, but has responded to its most notable instance by enacting legislation supplementing the judicial determination in some detail....

We must still, however, derive a standard or set of standards for assessing the particular claim Alvarez raises, and for this case it suffices to look to the historical antecedents. Whatever the ultimate criteria for accepting a cause of action subject to jurisdiction under § 1350, we are persuaded that federal courts should not recognize private claims under federal common law for violations of any international law norm with less definite content and acceptance among civilized nations than the historical paradigms familiar when § 1350 was enacted. *See, e.g.*, United

States v. Smith, 5 Wheat. 153, 163–180 n.a ... (1820) (illustrating the specificity with which the law of nations defined piracy). This limit upon judicial recognition is generally consistent with the reasoning of many of the courts and judges who faced the issue before it reached this Court. See *Filartiga, supra,* at 890 ("[F]or purposes of civil liability, the torturer has become–like the pirate and slave trader before him–*hostis humani generis,* an enemy of all mankind"); *Tel-Oren, supra,* at 781 (Edwards, J., concurring) (suggesting that the "limits of section 1350's reach" be defined by "a handful of heinous actions–each of which violates definable, universal and obligatory norms"); see also *In re* Estate of Marcos Human Rights Litigation, 25 F.3d 1467, 1475 (C.A.9 1994) ("Actionable violations of international law must be of a norm that is specific, universal, and obligatory"). And the determination whether a norm is sufficiently definite to support a cause of action should (and, indeed, inevitably must) involve an element of judgment about the practical consequences of making that cause available to litigants in the federal courts. [Court's note 21, in part: This requirement of clear definition is not meant to be the only principle limiting the availability of relief in the federal courts for violations of customary international law, though it disposes of this case....]

Thus, Alvarez's detention claim must be gauged against the current state of international law, looking to those sources we have long, albeit cautiously, recognized.... [the Court quoted *The Paquete Habana,* 175 U.S. at 700.]

To begin with, Alvarez cites two well-known international agreements that, despite their moral authority, have little utility under the standard set out in this opinion. He says that his abduction by Sosa was an "arbitrary arrest" within the meaning of the Universal Declaration of Human Rights (Declaration), G.A. Res. 217A (III), U.N. Doc. A/810 (1948). And he traces the rule against arbitrary arrest not only to the Declaration, but also to article nine of the International Covenant on Civil and Political Rights (Covenant), Dec. 19, 1996, 999 U.N.T.S. 171, to which the United States is a party, and to various other conventions to which it is not. But the Declaration does not of its own force impose obligations as a matter of international law. See Humphrey, *The UN Charter and the Universal Declaration of Human Rights,* in THE INTERNATIONAL PROTECTION OF HUMAN RIGHTS 39, 50 (E. Luard ed.1967) (quoting Eleanor Roosevelt calling the Declaration " 'a statement of principles ... setting up a common standard of achievement for all peoples and all nations' " and " 'not a treaty or international agreement ... impos[ing] legal obligations' "). [Court's note 23, in part: It has nevertheless had substantial indirect effect on international law....] And, although the Covenant does bind the United States as a matter of international law, the United States ratified the Covenant on the express understanding that it was not self-executing and so did not itself create obligations enforceable in the federal courts. Accordingly, Alvarez cannot say that the Declaration and Covenant themselves establish the relevant and applicable rule of international law. He instead attempts to show that prohibition of arbitrary arrest has attained the status of binding customary international law.

Here, it is useful to examine Alvarez's complaint in greater detail. As he presently argues it, the claim does not rest on the cross-border feature of his abduction. [Court's note 24: Alvarez's brief contains one footnote seeking to incorporate by reference his arguments on cross-border abductions before the Court of Appeals. Brief for Respondent Alvarez–Machain 47, n.46. That is not enough to raise the question fairly, and we do not consider it.] Although the District Court granted relief in part on finding a violation of international law in taking Alvarez across the border from Mexico to the United States, the Court of Appeals rejected that ground of liability for failure to identify a norm of requisite force prohibiting a forcible abduction across a border. Instead, it relied on the conclusion that the law of the United States did not authorize Alvarez's arrest, because the DEA lacked extraterritorial authority under 21 U.S.C. § 878, and because Federal Rule of Criminal Procedure 4(d)(2) limited the warrant for Alvarez's arrest to "the jurisdiction of the United States." It is this position that Alvarez takes now: that his arrest was arbitrary and as such forbidden by international law not because it infringed the prerogatives of Mexico, but because no applicable law authorized it.

Alvarez thus invokes a general prohibition of "arbitrary" detention defined as officially sanctioned action exceeding positive authorization to detain under the domestic law of some government, regardless of the circumstances. Whether or not this is an accurate reading of the Covenant, Alvarez cites little authority that a rule so broad has the status of a binding customary norm today. He certainly cites nothing to justify the federal courts in taking his broad rule as the predicate for a federal lawsuit, for its implications would be breathtaking. His rule would support a cause of action in federal court for any arrest, anywhere in the world, unauthorized by the law of the jurisdiction in which it took place, and would create a cause of action for any seizure of an alien in violation of the Fourth Amendment, supplanting the actions under Rev. Stat. § 1979, 42 U.S.C. § 1983 and Bivens. v. Six Unknown Fed. Narcotics Agents, 403 U.S. 388 . . . (1971), that now provide damages remedies for such violations. It would create an action in federal court for arrests by state officers who simply exceed their authority; and for the violation of any limit that the law of any country might place on the authority of its own officers to arrest. And all of this assumes that Alvarez could establish that Sosa was acting on behalf of a government when he made the arrest, for otherwise he would need a rule broader still.

Alvarez's failure to marshal support for his proposed rule is underscored by the RESTATEMENT (THIRD) OF FOREIGN RELATIONS LAW OF THE UNITED STATES (1987), which says in its discussion of customary international human rights law that a "state violates international law if, as a matter of state policy, it practices, encourages, or condones . . . prolonged arbitrary detention." *Id.* § 702. Although the Restatement does not explain its requirements of a "state policy" and of "prolonged" detention, the implication is clear. Any credible invocation of a principle against arbitrary detention that the civilized world accepts as binding customary international law requires a factual basis beyond relatively brief detention in excess of positive authority....

Whatever may be said for the broad principle Alvarez advances, in the present, imperfect world, it expresses an aspiration that exceeds any binding customary rule having the specificity we require. Creating a private cause of action to further that aspiration would go beyond any residual common law discretion we think it appropriate to exercise. It is enough to hold that a single illegal detention of less than a day, followed by the transfer of custody to lawful authorities and a prompt arraignment, violates no norm of customary international law so well defined as to support the creation of a federal remedy.

BREYER, J., concurring in part and concurring in the judgment

I join Justice Ginsburg's concurrence and join the Court's opinion in respect to the Alien Tort Statute (ATS) claim. The Court says that to qualify for recognition under the ATS a norm of international law must have a content as definite as, and an acceptance as widespread as, those that characterized 18th-century international norms prohibiting piracy.... The norm must extend liability to the type of perpetrator (*e.g.*, a private actor) the plaintiff seeks to sue.... And Congress can make clear that courts should not recognize any such norm, through a direct or indirect command or by occupying the field.... The Court also suggests that principles of exhaustion might apply, and that courts should give "serious weight" to the Executive Branch's view of the impact on foreign policy that permitting an ATS suit will likely have in a given case or type of case.... I believe all of these conditions are important.

I would add one further consideration. Since enforcement of an international norm by one nation's courts implies that other nations' courts may do the same, I would ask whether the exercise of jurisdiction under the ATS is consistent with those notions of comity that lead each nation to respect the sovereign rights of other nations by limiting the reach of its laws and their enforcement. In applying those principles, courts help assure that "the potentially conflicting laws of different nations" will "work together in harmony," a matter of increasing importance in an ever more interdependent world. F. Hoffman–La Roche Ltd. v. Empagram S.A., 542 U.S. 155 (2004); *cf.* Murray v. Schooner Charming Betsy, 2 Cranch 64, 118 ... (1804). Such consideration is necessary to ensure that ATS litigation does not undermine the very harmony that it was intended to promote....

These comity concerns normally do not arise (or at least are mitigated) if the conduct in question takes place in the country that provides the cause of action or if that conduct involves that country's own national–where, say, an American assaults a foreign diplomat and the diplomat brings suit in an American court. See RESTATEMENT (THIRD) OF FOREIGN RELATIONS LAW OF THE UNITED STATES §§ 402(1), (2) (1987) (hereinafter Restatement) (describing traditional bases of territorial and nationality jurisdiction). They do arise, however, when foreign persons injured abroad bring suit in the United States under the ATS, asking the courts to recognize a claim that a certain kind of foreign conduct violates an international norm.

Since different courts in different nations will not necessarily apply even similar substantive laws similarly, workable harmony, in practice, depends upon more than substantive uniformity among the laws of those nations. That is to say, substantive uniformity does not *automatically* mean that universal jurisdiction is appropriate. Thus, in the 18th century, nations reached consensus not only on the substantive principle that acts of piracy were universally wrong but also on the jurisdictional principle that any nation that found a pirate could prosecute him. *See, e.g.*, United States v. Smith, 5 Wheat. 153, 162 ... (1820) (referring to "the general practice of all nations in punishing all persons, whether natives or foreigners, who have committed [piracy] against any persons whatsoever, with whom they are in amity").

Today international law will sometimes similarly reflect not only substantive agreement as to certain universally condemned behavior but also procedural agreement that universal jurisdiction exists to prosecute a subset of that behavior. See RESTATEMENT § 404, and Comment *a*; International Law Association, Final Report on the Exercise of Universal Jurisdiction in Respect of Gross Human Rights Offences 2 (2000). That subset includes torture, genocide, crimes against humanity, and war crimes. See *id.* at 5–8; see also, *e.g.,* Prosecutor v. Furundzija, Case No. IT–95–17/1–T, paras. 155–156 (International Tribunal for Prosecution of Persons Responsible for Serious Violations of International Humanitarian Law Committed in Territory of Former Yugoslavia since 1991 [ICTY], Dec. 10, 1998); Attorney Gen. of Israel v. Eichmann, 36 I.L.R. 277 (Sup.Ct. Israel 1962).

The fact that this procedural consensus exists suggests that recognition of universal jurisdiction in respect to a limited set of norms is consistent with principles of international comity. That is, allowing every nation's courts to adjudicate foreign conduct involving foreign parties in such cases will not significantly threaten the practical harmony that comity principles seek to protect. That consensus concerns criminal jurisdiction, but consensus as to universal criminal jurisdiction itself suggests that universal tort jurisdiction would be no more threatening. *Cf.* RESTATEMENT § 404, Comment *b*. That is because the criminal courts of many nations combine civil and criminal proceedings, allowing those injured by criminal conduct to be represented, and to recover damages, in the criminal proceeding itself. Brief for European Commission as *Amicus Curiae* 21, n.48 (citing 3 Y. Donzallaz, La Convention de Lugano du 16 septembre 1998 concernant la competence judiciaire et l'execution des decisions en matiere civile et commerciale, paras. 5203–5272 (1998); EC Council Regulation Art. 5, § 4, 44/2001, 2001 O.J. (L 12/1) (Jan. 16, 2001)). Thus, universal criminal jurisdiction necessarily contemplates a significant degree of civil tort recovery as well.

Taking these matters into account, as I believe courts should, I can find no similar procedural consensus supporting the exercise of jurisdiction in this case. That lack of consensus provides additional support for the Court's conclusion that the ATS does not recognize the claim at issue here–where the underlying substantive claim concerns arbitrary arrest, outside the United States, of a citizen of one foreign country by another.

Notes and Questions

1. The majority opinion in *Sosa* concluded that the ATCA does not create a cause of action. It is unlikely that the Court will revisit its conclusion. Nevertheless, if it entertains the issue in the future it is of interest that no other judicial opinion had concluded that the ATCA does not create a cause of action other than the highly criticized concurring opinion of former Judge Bork in *Tel-Oren*. For early cases and opinions of the Attorneys General, recall 1 Op. Att'y Gen. 57, 58 (1795) ("the company or individuals who have been injured by these acts of hostility have a remedy by a civil suit in the courts of the United States."); *see also* United States v. Greene, 26 F. Cas. 33, 33 (C.C.D. Maine 1827) (No. 15,258) (Story, J: "gives . . . right . . . to sue"); M'Grath v. Candalero, 16 F. Cas. 128 (D.S.C. 1794) (No. 6,810) ("sue here for a tort . . . the suit will be sustained"); Jansen v. The Vrow Christina Magdalena, 13 F. Cas. 356, 358 (D.S.C. 1794) (No. 7,216) ("the powers of the district courts are expressed . . . as to civil causes . . . where an alien sues for a tort only"); Bolchos v. Darrel, 3 F. Cas. 810, 810 (D.S.C. 1795) (No. 1,607) ("the original cause arose at sea . . . [and ATCA allows the court] to take cognizance of the cause"); 26 Op. Att'y Gen. 250, 252–53 (1907) (ATCA provides "a forum and a right of action"); Jordan J. Paust, *The History, Nature, and Reach of the Alien Tort Claims Act*, 16 FLA. J. INT'L L. 249, 250–52 n.3, 254 & n.11 (2004).

2. What is now of great significance after *Sosa* is the question concerning what types of violations of customary international law that the majority on the Court will recognize as actionable under the ATCA. Professor Paust notes that the Court in *Sosa* was not fully briefed on the types of infractions of both treaties and the customary law of nations known to the Founders, Framers, and early judiciary and, in view of the majority opinion in *Sosa*, such a history should be revisited. In particular, Justice Souter cited portions of the 1781 Resolution of the Continental Congress [set forth here in Chapter 1], but he did not mention the point expressed in the Resolution that some of the listed infractions of the customary law of nations were only those what are most obvious. Additionally, it is curious why Justice Souter stated that "[i]t was . . . [a] narrow set of" three violations of the law of nations mentioned by Blackstone "that was probably on minds of the men who drafted the ATS" when Justice Souter had also recognized that the 1781 Resolution addressed two others: (1) acts of hostility against such as are in amity with the U.S. (also addressed in the 1795 Opinion of the Attorney General), and (2) all "infractions of treaties and conventions to which the United States are a party"—and having neglected a third: other less obvious customary "offences against the law of nations." These should also be considered if what was "on the minds of the men who drafted the" statute is important.

Justice Breyer recognized that torture, war crimes, genocide, and crimes against humanity are actionable under the ATCA (124 S.Ct. at 2783 (Breyer, J., concurring)). It is also worth emphasizing that the Supreme Court recognized early in our history in Talbot v. Janson, 3 U.S. (3 Dall.) 133, 159–61 (1795) (Iredell, J.) that "all . . . trespasses committed against the general law of nations, are enquirable, and may be proceeded against"). In Fletcher v. Peck, 10 U.S. (6 Cranch) 87, 133 (1810), Chief Justice Marshall also affirmed that our judicial tribunals "are established . . . to decide on human rights." *See also* The Julia, 12 U.S. (8 Cranch) 181, 193 (1814) (Story, J., dissenting) ("rights of humanity" in time of war); Chisholm v. Georgia, 2 U.S. (2 Dall.) 419, 421 (counsel referring to "human rights"), 478 ("rights of men") (1793) (Jay, C.J.); Vanhorne's Lessee v. Dorrance, 2 U.S. (2 Dall.) 304, 310 (1795) (Paterson, J.) ("rights of man"); Henfield's Case, 11 F. Cas. 1099, 1120 (C.C.D. Pa. 1793) (No. 6,360) (Wilson, J., with Iredell, J., on circuit, and Judge Peters) ("rights of man"). Concerning later attention to human rights precepts in thousands of federal and state cases, *see, e.g.*, Jordan J. Paust, International Law as Law of the United States 210–23 (2 ed. 2003), and cases cited. Concerning other types of infractions known early in our history, *see, e.g.*, *id.* at 11–12.

3. How might other actionable modern violations of customary international law be discovered? Recall the majority opinion's recognition that "courts should require any claim based on the present day law of nations to rest on a norm of international character accepted by the civilized world and defined with a specificity comparable to the features of the 18th-century paradigms" recognized by the Court, which included piracy, acts of hostility or breaches of neutrality, infringements of rights of ambassadors, violations of safe conduct, and war crimes [and how were these defined?]. The majority opinion also addressed *United States v. Smith* as a case "illustrating the specificity with which the law of nations defined piracy" and *In re Estate of Marcos*, and stated that the issue is "whether a norm is sufficiently definite to support a cause of action."

4. Despite the statement about *The Paquete Habana* in the majority opinion, students should note that *The Paquete Habana* did not rest on the "law merchant" or "admiralty" law as such. The Court in *Paquete* expressly referred to "international law," the "law of war," and the "law of nations" as the bases for its decision that the Executive seizures abroad of enemy alien vessels and enemy aliens in time of war were illegal. The law merchant and admiralty law as such had long been separated from the law of nations by 1900. In *Paquete Habana*, what the Court had considered with respect to the proof of the content of international law were various forms of state practice and patterns of *opinio juris*.

5. The majority of the Court clearly rejected a radical ahistorical claim of a few textwriters that customary international law was mere common law, that such was law of the United States only insofar as Congress incorporated it, and that *Erie* had obviated its use in federal courts. Justice Scalia made that argument in dissent when claiming that the law of nations was mere "general common law" and that *Erie* (which did not address international law) precludes its use. 124 S.Ct. at 2770, also citing Young, *Sorting out the Debate Over Customary International Law*, 42 Va. J. Int'l L. 365, 374 (2002); Bradley & Goldsmith, *Customary International Law as Federal Common*

Law: A Critique of the Modern Position, 110 HARV. L. REV. 815, 824 (1997); Brief for Vikram Amar *et al.*, as *Amici Curiae* 12–13. *But see* Jordan J. Paust, *International Law Before the Supreme Court: A Mixed Record of Recognition*, 45 SANTA CLARA L. REV. & n.118 (2005); *Customary International Law and Human Rights Treaties* Are *Law of the United States*, 20 MICH. J. INT'L L. 301, 301–21 (1999); Jon Van Dyke, *The Role of Customary International Law in Federal and State Court Litigation*, 26 U. HAWAII L. REV. 361 (2004).

6. Article 9(1) of the ICCPR prohibits "arbitrary" detention. Is arbitrary detention of less than a day covered by the prohibition? Under the circumstances, was the detention of Alvarez–Machain "arbitrary"? Was this the issue actually addressed by the *Sosa* majority? See the next note.

7. The Human Rights Committee created pursuant to and operating under the ICCPR and the European Court of Human Rights, among other international institutions, have concluded that abductions from other countries violate the human rights to liberty and personal security that are directly related to the prohibition of arbitrary detention. Moreover, the U.N. Security Council has previously affirmed that "abductions are offenses of grave concern to the international community, having severe adverse consequences for the rights of the victims" and it has condemned "unequivocally all acts of . . . abduction." U.N. S.C. Res. 579 (1985). See Chapter 3, Section 3 B. Was this the issue addressed in *Sosa*?

Footnote 24 and the accompanying and nearby text of the majority opinion in *Sosa* noted that Alvarez's attorney did not adequately raise the issue of "cross-border abductions," that the Court did "not consider it," and "[a]s he presently argues it, the claim does not rest on the cross-border feature of his abduction" but only on a claim that "his arrest was arbitrary . . . because no applicable [federal] law authorized it" and because it was "officially sanctioned action exceeding positive authorization to detain under the domestic law of some government, regardless of the circumstances." If so, was this the best argument for his counsel to make? Furthermore, what exactly was the ruling in *Sosa* with respect to detentions? Was it that detention must be "beyond relatively brief detention in excess of positive authority," that "a single illegal detention of less than a day" is not proscribed under customary international law or merely that such was not proven to be a violation of domestic law? Would either be consistent with recognitions in *Fernandez-Rodriguez v. Wilkinson*, *Forti v. Suarez–Mason*, and *Xuncax v. Gramajo*? See also Kim Ho Ma v. Ashcroft, 257 F.3d 1095, 1114 (9th Cir. 2001); Ma v. Reno, 208 F.3d 815, 830 (9th Cir. 2000); Martinez v. City of Los Angeles, 141 F.3d 1373, 1384 (9th Cir. 1998); De Sanchez v. Banco Central de Nicaragua, 770 F.2d 1385, 1397 (5th Cir. 1985); Chiminya Tachiona v. Mugabe, 216 F.Supp.2d 262, 279–80 (S.D.N.Y. 2002); Mehinovic v. Vuckovic, 198 F.Supp.2d 1322, 1328–29, 1344, 1349–50, 1352, 1357–58, 1360 (N.D. Ga. 2002); Wiwa v. Royal Dutch Petroleum Co., No. 96 CIV. 8386, 2002 WL 319887, at *6 (S.D.N.Y. 2002)? Might the majority have assumed that if "detention of less than a day" occurred in Mexico, "the transfer of custody to lawful authorities . . . [coupled with] a prompt arraignment" in the U.S. was not a continuation of a "detention" that started in Mexico? Would this be a proper characterization of an unlawful and continued "detention" or "abduction"?

8. The Court in *Sosa* was also not adequately briefed on the fact that the International Covenant on Civil and Political Rights (ICCPR) is at the very least partly self-executing. As noted in Chapter 1, Section 2 A 3, the U.S. declaration of partial non-self-execution is expressly inapplicable to Article 50 of the ICCPR, which mandates in clear, unavoidable, and self-executing terms that all of "[t]he provisions of the ... Covenant shall extend to all parts of federal States without any limitations or exceptions" whatsoever. Moreover, the U.S. understanding upon ratification and the Executive Explanation concerning Article 50 demonstrate the clear intent that the U.S. Executive and judiciary, among others, will comply with Article 50's mandate. Recall Chapter 1, Section 2 A 3.

ALPERIN v. VATICAN BANK

410 F.3d 532 (9th Cir. 2005).

McKeown, Circuit Judge.

A group of twenty-four individuals and four organizations (the "Holocaust Survivors") claim that the Vatican Bank ... , the Order of Friars Minor and the Croatian Liberation Movement ... , profited from the genocidal acts of the Croatian Ustasha political regime ... which was supported throughout World War II by Nazi forces. That profit allegedly passed through the Vatican Bank in the form of proceeds from looted assets and slave labor. The Holocaust Survivors brought suit in federal court claiming conversion, unjust enrichment, restitution, the right to an accounting, and human rights violations and violations of international law arising out of the defendants' alleged involvement with the Ustasha during and following World War II.

The Vatican Bank and the Order of Friars Minor moved to dismiss ... on multiple grounds; by agreement of the parties the district court limited its discussion to the issue of whether the Holocaust Survivors' claims should be dismissed under the political question doctrine. The district court reasoned that the political question doctrine bars consideration of the merits of the claims in their entirety.... We reverse in part because certain of the Holocaust Survivors' claims–those with respect to lost and looted property ... –are no barred by this doctrine. In contrast, the broad human rights allegations tied to the Vatican Bank's alleged assistance to the war objectives of the Ustasha present nonjusticiable controversies....

... [A]s many as 700,000 victims, most of them Serbs, had been killed at the Ustasha death camps.... [A 1998 U.S. Department of State report] describes the Vatican's role in less [than] generous terms: "The Vatican, which maintained an 'Apostolic visitor' in Zagreb from June 1941 until the end of the War, was aware of the killing campaign.... Croatian Catholic authorities condemned the atrocities committed by the Ustashi, but remained otherwise supportive of the regime." ...

The late 1990s saw a flurry of legal activity over Holocaust-era claims after years of quietude. See Michael J. Bazyler, Nuremberg in America: Litigating the Holocaust in United States Courts, 34 U. Rich.

L. Rev. 1, 19 (2000) ("A total of ten cases involving Holocaust-era claims were filed in the United States between the end of World War II and October 1996, the start of the new era of Holocaust-claim litigation). The cases break down into several categories: finding of justiciability, finding of no justiciability, and skirting the political question doctrine or not reaching the doctrine.

The Eleventh Circuit's recent decision involving claims against banks fall into the first category. The court held that claims against two German banks that profited from the practice of Aryanization during World War II were not political questions. See Ungaro–Benages v. Dresdner Bank AG, 379 F.3d 1227, 1235–37 (11th Cir. 2004).

In contrast, the district court in this case relied heavily of litigation in federal district courts in New Jersey in which the courts determined that various Holocaust claims raised non-justiciable political questions. See Burger–Fischer v. DeGussa AG, 65 F. Supp.2d 248 (D.N.J. 1999); Iwanowa v. Ford Motor Co., 67 F.Supp.2d 424 (D.N.J. 1999)....

We conclude that the claims for conversion, unjust enrichment, restitution, and an accounting with respect to lost and looted property are not committed to the political branches (the "Property Claims"). Recovery for lost and looted property, however, stands in stark contrast to the broad allegations tied to the Vatican Bank's alleged assistance to the war objectives of the Ustasha, including the slave labor claims, which essentially call on us to make a retroactive political judgment as to the conduct of war (the "War Objectives Claims"). Such judgment calls are, by nature, political questions. With this bifurcation as a framework, we first address the Property Claims.

None of the *Baker* [Baker v. Carr, 369 U.S. 186 (1962)] formulations are inextricable from the Property Claims. Simply because a foreign bank is involved and the case arises out of a "politically charged" context does not transform the Property Claims into political questions. See Kadic v. Karadzic, 70 F.3d 232, 249 (2d Cir. 1995) (holding that political question doctrine did not bar adjudication of claims brought under the ATS against a Bosnian–Serb leader for committing genocide and other atrocities).

As ... excerpts from the Complaint demonstrate, the Property Claims consist of garden-variety legal and equitable claims for the recovery of property....

Our inquiry is further based on the premise that, unlike some World War II-era claims, the Holocaust Survivors' claims are not expressly barred by treaty. U.S. Const. art. II, § 2, cl. 1 (granting the President the power to make treaties); *see, e.g., In re* World War II Era Japanese Forced Labor Litig., 114 F. Supp.2d 939, 945 (N.D. Cal. 2000), *aff'd*, Deutsch v. Turner Corp., 324 F.3d 692 (9th Cir. 2003) (determining that the 1951 Peace Treaty with Japan essentially precludes all claims arising out of actions taken by Japan and its nationals during World War II).

Nor are the Holocaust Survivors' claims against the Vatican Bank the subject of an executive-agreement. See [Am. Ins. Ass'n v.] Garamendi, 539 U.S. at 415–16 [2003] ... ("Historically, wartime claims against even nominally private entities have become issues is international diplomacy, and three of the postwar settlements dealing with reparations implicating private parties were made by the Executive alone.'); Dames & Moore v. Regan, 453 U.S. 654, 680 ... (1981) ("Crucial to our decision today is the conclusion that Congress has implicitly approved the practice of claim settlement by executive agreement.").

In other circumstances, the Executive Branch has taken formal steps to intervene in certain claims arising out of the Holocaust. Most notably, the United States and Germany signed an executive agreement in July 2000 in which Germany agreed to enact legislation establishing a foundation (the "Foundation") to oversee the compensation of those "who suffered at the hands of German companies during the National Socialist era and World War II." Agreement Concerning the Foundation "Remembrance, Responsibility and the Future," July 17, 2000, U.S.—F.R.G., 39 I.L.M. 1298, 1298 ("Foundation Agreement"); see also *Garamnedi*, 539 U.S. at 405–08 ... (describing the Foundation Agreement and similar agreements concluded with Austria and France).

The Holocaust Survivors' case is distinguishable from those involving the Foundation in that there is no analogous executive agreement covering claims to the Ustasha treasury.... At bottom, the Property Claims simply seek restitution for looted assets belonging to purported class members. Reparation for stealing, even during wartime, is not a claim that finds textual commitment in the Constitution....

... [T]he claims here bear more similarities to the property claims considered by the Supreme Court last year in *Altmann* [v. Republic of Austria]. See 124 S.Ct. at 2243. Altmann brought suit against Austria and its national art gallery seeking to recover six Klimt paintings that were allegedly wrongfully obtained by the gallery after Nazi forces seized them during World War II. *Id.* The Court granted certiorari on the limited question of whether the FSIA applies retrospectively, *id.*, and did not address the political question doctrine. Nonetheless, that the Court allowed the case to proceed underscores that courts have a place in deciding Holocaust-era claims concerning looted assets....

... [T]he Property Claims ultimately boil down to whether the Vatican Bank is wrongfully holding assets. Deciding this sort of controversy is exactly what courts do.... the underlying property issues are not "political questions" that are constitutionally committed to the political branches....

The Holocaust Survivors' most straightforward claims involve identifiable personal property for which federal statutes, common law, state law, and well-established case law provide concrete legal bases for courts to reach a reasoned decision....

... As evidenced by the Vatican's protest to the State Department, this case implicates foreign relations. Whether the court's involvement would inevitably express a lack of respect for the Executive Branch's handling of U.S.—Vatican relations, as well as relations with other foreign states, is a separate matter. We conclude that judicial handling of the Property Claims will not run afoul of this fourth test [from *Baker*].

More than four years have passed since the Vatican sent its protest to the State Department. The Holocaust Survivors represented to the court that the State Department has been apprised of this appeal but has said that its decision not to intervene is not reflective of its view on the merits of this case.

Had the State Department expressed a view, that fact would certainly weigh in evaluating the fourth *Baker* formulation. In *Altmann*, the Court explained that "should the State Department choose to express its opinion on the implications of exercising jurisdiction over *particular* petitioners in connection with *their* alleged conduct, that opinion might well be entitled to deference as the considered judgment of the Executive on a particular question of foreign policy." 124 S.Ct. at 2255.... [W]e cannot discern whether the State Department's decision not to intervene is an implicit endorsement, an objection, or simple indifference. At best, this silence is a neutral factor....

In contrast to the Property Claims, the Holocaust Survivors' allegations that "[t]he actions and conduct of Defendants, in addition to being profitable, actively assisted the war objectives of the Ustasha Regime" strike at the hear of the Ustasha's wartime conduct....

Simply because the Nuremberg Charter does not expressly preclude national courts from trying war criminals ... does not mean that it is our place to step in a half-century later and condemn the Vatican Bank and related parties for "participat[ing] in the activities of the Ustasha Regime in furtherance of the commission of war crimes, crimes against humanity, [and] crimes against peace." We are not a war crimes tribunal. To act as such would require use to "intrud[e] unduly on certain policy choices and value judgments that are constitutionally committed to [the political branches.]" *Koohi*, 976 F.2d at 1331, for we do not and cannot know why the Allies made the policy choice not to prosecute the Ustasha and the Vatican Bank....

Indeed, the Holocaust Survivors' allegations that the Vatican Bank violated international law by "creat[ing] a 'ratline' or 'pipeline' to help the war criminals flee from prosecution" could also be levied against the United States, which provided similar aid driven by the sudden shift in priorities from fighting the Nazis to driving back Communism....

It is not our role to sit in judgment as to whether the perceived Communist threat justified assisting alleged war criminals....

... Although the Complaint maintains that many of the Ustasha officials were Roman Catholic clergy, it does not indicate that the Vatican Bank itself directly exploited the slave labor. Unlike cases in which the defendants were enslaving entities, the slave labor claims against the Vatican Bank are, in effect, derivative claims: The Ustasha profited from slave labor, these profits benefitted the Ustasha treasury, and portions of those tainted funds were transferred to the Vatican Bank....

Determining whether the Vatican Bank was unjustly enriched by profits derived from slave labor would therefore necessitate that we look behind the Vatican Bank and indict the Ustasha regime for its wartime conduct. We are not willing to take this leap....

It is not our place to speak for the U.S. Government by declaring that a foreign government is at fault for using forced labor during Word War II. Any such policy condemning the Ustasha regime must first emanate from the political branches....

Nor does our decision conflict with the Second Circuit's reasoning in *Kadic*, a case which, in addition to geographic parallels, involved claims tied to similar genocidal acts. See 70 F.3d at 236–37. In *Kadic*, Croats and Muslims brought suit against Radovan Karadzic under the ATS alleging that he oversaw the genocidal campaign conducted by Bosnian–Serb military forces. *Id.* In holding that the claims were not barred by the political question doctrine, the court cautioned that "judges should not reflexively invoke the ... doctrine ... to avoid difficult and somewhat sensitive decisions in the context of human rights." *Id.* at 249. We agree. [In] *Kadic*, however, ... the State Department "expressly disclaime[d] any concern that the political question doctrine should be invoked" ... [and] the claims in *Kadic* focused on the acts of a single individual during a localized conflict rather than asking the court to undertake the complex calculus of assigning fault for actions taken by a foreign regime during the morass of a world war....

Notes and Questions

1. Do you agree with the decision to bar claims allegedly involving genocide, war crimes, and other violations of international law under the political question doctrine? Would this be consistent with the fact that international crimes implicate universal jurisdiction and responsibility regardless of "war objectives," political motives or implications and that no state or entity has authority to violate international law (and, *e.g.*, such conduct would be *ultra vires*)? Since war crimes cannot lawfully be committed during the "conduct of war" and questions whether war crimes have occurred are legal questions involving judicially manageable legal standards, should the political question doctrine ever apply to war crimes?

2. Under international law and the Charter of the I.M.T. at Nuremberg, can a government or a bank be "prosecuted" for international crimes?

3. Would the failure to prosecute alleged international crimes under a standard of proof beyond reasonable doubt necessarily obviate the possibility of civil sanctions? Would a politically motivated failure of the Executive to prosecute necessarily bar civil sanctions by private plaintiffs? What judicial power and responsibility identified in § 111 of the Restatement is at stake?

4. Does a federal district court have competence to handle prosecutions of war crimes? *See, e.g.*, 10 U.S.C. §§ 818, 821; 18 U.S.C. § 3231; *Ex parte*

Quirin, 317 U.S. 1, 27–30 (1942); Section 2 B 4 pp. 162–164. What do you think of the Ninth Circuit panel's claim that for courts to act as war crimes tribunals would require undue intrusion into policy choices committed to the political branches? Is this conclusion consistent with the broad recognition in *Ex parte Quirin* concerning judicial competence to apply the laws of war with respect to the status, rights and duties of nations and individuals–much less the rich history of judicial application of the laws of war?

5. Should the lack of an international agreement for settlement of claims concerning genocide, war crimes, and other violations of international law be as relevant as the lack of a settlement agreement concerning the property claims?

3. *Case Study: The Marcos Human Rights Litigation*

Ferdinand E. Marcos served as President of the Republic of the Philippines from 1965 to 1972, when he declared martial law and proceeded thereafter to rule by decree, effectively suppressing all dissent. He fled the Philippines in March 1986, after a series of "People Power" demonstrations filled the streets of Manila to protest a rigged election, and came to Honolulu, Hawai'i. Almost immediately thereafter, complaints were filed against him under the Alien Tort Claims Act, 28 U.S.C. § 1350, by victims of human rights abuses. This litigation was vigorously contested by Marcos's attorneys, and required more than half a dozen appeals to the U.S. Court of Appeals for the Ninth Circuit during the decade that it took to reach a final judgment and the continuing and unfinished efforts to collect the judgment. The factual issues were presented to a jury in a trifurcated format—first to determine liability, then to determine exemplary damages, and finally to determine compensatory damages.

Facts regarding the human rights abuses during the Marcos martial-law period are presented in the following decision issued by the U.S. district court:

IN RE ESTATE OF FERDINAND E. MARCOS HUMAN RIGHTS LITIGATION

910 F.Supp. 1460, 1462–63 (D.Haw.1995).

REAL, J.

At the time martial law was declared, a Constitutional Convention, elected by the people, had been meeting and was near completion of proposed revisions to the 1935 Constitution. On orders from Marcos, some delegates to the Convention were arrested and placed under detention while others went into hiding or left the country leaving the revisions uncompleted.

Without allowing for ratification of the new Constitution by a plebiscite, on January 17, 1973, Marcos ordered ratification of a revised Constitution, tailor-made for his maintenance of power. With those actions Marcos planted the seeds for what grew into a virtual dictatorship in the Philippines. . . .

Proclamation 1081 not only declared martial law, but also set the stage for what plaintiffs alleged, and the jury found, to be acts of torture, summary execution, disappearance, arbitrary detention, and numerous other atrocities for which the jury found Marcos personally responsible.

Marcos gradually increased his own power to such an extent that there were no limits to his orders of the human rights violations suffered by plaintiffs in this action. Marcos promulgated General Order No. 1 which stated he was the Commander-in-Chief of the Armed Forces of the Philippines. The order also stated that Marcos was to govern the nation and direct the operation of the entire Government, including all its agencies and instrumentalities. By General Orders 2 and 2–A, signed by Marcos immediately after proclaiming martial law, Marcos authorized the arrest, by the military, of a long list of dissidents. By General Order 3, Marcos maintained, as captive, the executive and judicial branches of all political entities in the Philippines until otherwise ordered by himself personally.

Immediately after the declaration of martial law the issuance of General Orders 1, 2, 2A, 3 and 3A caused arrests of persons accused of subversion, apparently because of their real or apparent opposition to the Marcos government. These arrests were made pursuant to orders issued by the Secretary of Defense Juan Ponce Enrile ... , or Marcos himself.

The arrest orders were means for detention of each of the representatives of the plaintiff class as well as each of the individual plaintiffs. During those detentions the plaintiffs experienced human rights violations including, but not limited to the following:

1. Beatings while blindfolded by punching, kicking and hitting with the butts of rifles;

2. The "telephone" where a detainee's ears were clapped simultaneously, producing a ringing sound in the head;

3. Insertion of bullets between the fingers of a detainee and squeezing the hand;

4. The "wet submarine", where a detainee's head was submerged in a toilet bowl full of excrement;

5. The "water cure", where a cloth was placed over the detainee's mouth and nose, and water poured over it producing a drowning sensation;

6. The "dry submarine", where a plastic bag was placed over the detainee's head producing suffocation;

7. Use of a detainee's hands for putting out lighted cigarettes;

8. Use of flat-irons on the soles of a detainee's feet;

9. Forcing a detainee while wet and naked to sit before an air conditioner often while sitting on a block of ice;

10. Injection of a clear substance into the body a detainee believed to be truth serum;

11. Stripping, sexually molesting and raping female detainees; one male plaintiff testified he was threatened with rape;

12. Electric shock where one electrode is attached to the genitals of males or the breast of females and another electrode to some other part of the body, usually a finger, and electrical energy produced from a military field telephone is sent through the body;

13. Russian roulette; and

14. Solitary confinement while hand-cuffed or tied to a bed.

All of these forms of torture were used during "tactical interrogation," attempting to elicit information from detainees concerning opposition to the Marcos government. The more the detainees resisted, whether purposefully or out of lack of knowledge, the more serious the torture used.

Eventually, Marcos, his family and others loyal to him fled to Hawaii in February of 1986. One month later, a number of lawsuits were filed, including those that are the subject of this case.... [Editors' note: The lawsuits against Marcos were initially dismissed in 1986 by the District Court based on the act of state doctrine, but this ruling was overturned in 1989 by the U.S. Court of Appeals for the Ninth Circuit. Hilao v. Marcos, 878 F.2d 1438 (9th Cir. 1989) (table decision). The class action then went to trial, and after jury verdicts finding liability and awarding the 9,531 plaintiffs $1.2 billion in exemplary damages and $776 million in compensatory damages, the following decisions affirmed the judgment.]

IN RE ESTATE OF FERDINAND MARCOS, HUMAN RIGHTS LITIGATION HILAO v. ESTATE OF FERDINAND MARCOS ("ESTATE II")

25 F.3d 1467 (9th Cir. 1994).

TANG, J.

Defendant Estate of Ferdinand Marcos ("the Estate") appeals from the district court's order preliminarily enjoining the Estate from transferring, secreting or dissipating the Estate's assets pendente lite. On this interlocutory appeal, the Estate also challenges the district court's subject matter jurisdiction under the Foreign Sovereign Immunities Act and Alien Tort Act, claims that the plaintiffs do not state a cause of action, and contends that any cause of action abated upon Marcos' death. We have jurisdiction and affirm.

During Ferdinand Marcos' tenure as President of the Philippines, up to 10,000 people in the Philippines were allegedly tortured, summarily executed or disappeared at the hands of military intelligence personnel acting pursuant to martial law declared by Marcos in 1971. Military intelligence allegedly operated under the authority of Marcos, General Fabian Ver, and Imee Marcos–Manotoc (Ferdinand Marcos' daughter).

Marcos, his family, Ver and others loyal to Marcos fled to Hawaii in February, 1986. One month later, a number of lawsuits were filed against Marcos, Ver, and/or Imee Marcos–Manotoc, claiming that the plaintiffs had been arrested and tortured, or were the families of people arrested, tortured, and executed between 1971 and 1986.

All actions were dismissed by district courts on the "act of state" defense; we reversed and remanded in an unpublished decision. Hilao v. Marcos, 878 F.2d 1438 (9th Cir.1989); Trajano v. Marcos, 878 F.2d 1439 (9th Cir.1989) (table decisions). The Judicial Panel on Multi–District Litigation then consolidated all cases in the District of Hawaii on September 5, 1990. The case was certified as a class action on April 8, 1991, and a consolidated amended complaint naming the Estate as a defendant was filed on behalf of the class.

Default was entered against Imee Marcos–Manotoc in 1986 in *Trajano v. Marcos*, one of the individual cases consolidated in this action. In 1991, Marcos–Manotoc moved to set aside the default and moved to dismiss for lack of subject matter jurisdiction under the Alien Tort Act and immunity under the Foreign Sovereign Immunities Act. The motions were denied, and judgment was entered against Marcos–Manotoc. We affirmed on appeal. *See* Trajano v. Marcos (*In re*: Estate of Ferdinand E. Marcos Litigation), 978 F.2d 493 (9th Cir.1992) ("Estate I"), *cert. denied*, 508 U.S. 972 . . . (1993).

On November 1, 1991, the plaintiffs moved for a preliminary injunction to prevent the Estate from transferring or secreting any assets in order to preserve the possibility of collecting a judgment. The Estate had earlier been enjoined from transferring or secreting assets in an action brought by the Republic of the Philippines against Ferdinand Marcos. That preliminary injunction had been appealed, and was affirmed. *See* Republic of Philippines v. Marcos, 862 F.2d 1355 (9th Cir.1988) (*en banc*), *cert. denied*, 490 U.S. 1035 (1989). When the preliminary injunction in that case was dissolved due to a settlement, the plaintiffs in this action immediately sought the continuation of that injunction. The district court granted the motion.

Pending this interlocutory appeal of the preliminary injunction, trial on liability proceeded. On September 24, 1992, the jury rendered a verdict in favor of the class and the individually-named plaintiffs (except for plaintiff Wilson Madayag). The Estate's motion for JNOV was denied, and judgment was entered in favor of the prevailing plaintiffs. The preliminary injunction was modified on November 16, 1993, to set forth the jury verdict on liability, to compel the legal representatives of the Estate to fully and completely answer plaintiffs' interrogatories regarding the assets of the estate, to name the Swiss banks at which the Marcoses had deposited monies as representatives of the Estate, and to permit the plaintiffs to take discovery regarding these assets.

On February 23, 1994, the jury awarded the plaintiffs $1.2 billion in exemplary damages. The jury will reconvene to determine compensatory damages.

I. THE FOREIGN SOVEREIGN IMMUNITIES ACT

The Foreign Sovereign Immunities Act ("FSIA"), 28 U.S.C. §§ 1330, 1602–11, is the sole basis for obtaining jurisdiction over a foreign state and its agencies or instrumentalities. Argentine Republic v. Amerada Hess Shipping Corp., 488 U.S. 428, 434 (1989)....

However, we have previously rejected the Estate's argument that FSIA immunizes alleged acts of torture and execution by a foreign official. On appeal from entry of default judgment against Imee Marcos–Manotoc, we rejected Marcos–Manotoc's assertion that she was entitled to sovereign immunity because her challenged actions were premised on her authority as a government agent. *Estate I*, 978 F.2d at 497. In Chuidian v. Philippine Nat'l Bank, 912 F.2d 1095 (9th Cir.1990), we had held that FSIA does not immunize a foreign official engaged in acts beyond the scope of his authority:

> Where the officer's powers are limited by statute, his actions beyond those limitations are considered individual and not sovereign actions. The officer is not doing the business which the sovereign has empowered him to do.

Id. at 1106 (quotation omitted). We held that upon default, Marcos–Manotoc admitted that she acted on her own authority, not that of the Republic of the Philippines. Her acts were not taken within any official mandate and were therefore not the acts of an agency or instrumentality of a foreign state within the meaning of FSIA. *Estate I*, 978 F.2d at 498.

Like Marcos–Manotoc, the Estate argues that Marcos' acts were premised on his official authority, and thus fall within FSIA. However, because the allegations of the complaint are taken as true for purposes of determining whether an action should be dismissed,[4] ... Marcos' actions should be treated as taken without official mandate pursuant to his own authority.

Further, we rejected the argument that Marcos' actions were "official" or "public" acts when we reversed the dismissal of the actions against Ferdinand Marcos on the "act of state doctrine." In *Estate I*, we explained:

> This [conclusion that Marcos–Manotoc's acts were not taken pursuant to an official mandate] is consistent with our earlier decision that the same allegations against former President Marcos are not nonjusticiable "acts of state." *See* Trajano v. Marcos, 878 F.2d 1439

4. The complaint alleges, *inter alia*, that "Marcos under color of law, ordered, orchestrated, directed, sanctioned and tolerated the continuous and systematic violation of human rights of plaintiffs and the class through the military, para-military and intelligence forces he controlled"; that at "the direction or with the approval of Marcos, plaintiffs and about 10,000 class members were arrested without cause, held incommunicado and routinely subjected to 'tactical interrogation,' a euphemism for torture during interrogation"; that following tactical interrogation "many class members were arbitrarily detained for a year or more with Marcos' authorization and approval"; and that over 2,000 class members were summarily executed. [CR 3 at 13–14]. Further, the complaint alleges that these actions were violations of international law and the constitution and law of the Philippines.

> (9th Cir.1989) [table decision]. In so holding, we implicitly rejected the possibility that the acts set out in Trajano's complaint were public acts of the sovereign.

Id. at 498 n.10.

Moreover, in *Republic of the Philippines*, we held that Marcos' alleged illegal acts were not official acts pursuant to his authority as President of the Philippines. We rejected the contention that the Republic's RICO suit against Marcos involved a nonjusticiable political question:

> Although sometimes criticized as a ruler and at times invested with extraordinary powers, Ferdinand Marcos does not appear to have had the authority of an absolute autocrat. He was not the state, but the head of the state, bound by the laws that applied to him. Our courts have had no difficulty in distinguishing the legal acts of a deposed ruler from his acts for personal profit that lack a basis in law. As in the case of the deposed Venezuelan ruler, Marcos Perez Jimenez, the latter acts are as adjudicable and redressable as would be a dictator's act of rape.

Republic of the Philippines, 862 F.2d at 1361, *citing* Jimenez v. Aristeguieta, 311 F.2d 547 (5th Cir.1962), *cert. denied*, 373 U.S. 914 (1963).

In *Jimenez*, the former dictator of Venezuela was charged in the United States with murder and various financial crimes committed for personal gain in Venezuela. *Jimenez*, 311 F.2d at 552. The Fifth Circuit rejected Jimenez' argument that his acts were those of the sovereign because he was dictator, and therefore immunized under the "act of state" doctrine. The court stated:

> Even though characterized as a dictator, appellant was not himself the sovereign—government—of Venezuela within the Act of State Doctrine. He was chief executive, a public officer, of the sovereign nation of Venezuela. It is only when officials having sovereign authority act in an official capacity that the Act of State Doctrine applies.
>
> Appellant's acts ... were not acts of Venezuelan sovereignty.... They constituted common crimes committed by the Chief of State done in violation of his position and not in pursuance of it. They are as far from being an act of state as rape which appellant concedes would not be an "Act of State."

Id. at 557–58 (citations omitted). In citing *Jimenez* with approval, we adopted its conclusion that the illegal acts of a dictator are not "official acts" unreviewable by federal courts.

Siderman does not dictate a contrary result. In that case, we held that Argentina's official acts of torture, though clearly constituting *jus cogens* violations of international law, were immunized under FSIA. *Siderman,* 965 F.2d at 718. We noted that the Supreme Court in *Amerada Hess* had been "emphatic in its pronouncement 'that immunity is granted in those cases involving alleged violations of international law that do not come within one of the FSIA's exceptions,' "and concluded that "if violations of *jus cogens* committed outside the United States are to be exceptions to immunity, Congress must make them so." *Id.* at 719. However, *Siderman* was an action against the Republic of Argentina, which clearly fell within the "foreign state" scope of FSIA. In this case, the action is against the estate of an individual official who is accused of engaging in activities outside the scope of his authority. FSIA thus does not apply to this case.

This interpretation is consistent with FSIA's codification of the "restrictive" principle of sovereign immunity in international law, which limits the immunity of a foreign state to its "inherently governmental or 'public' acts," but does not extend to suits based on its commercial or private acts. *Chuidian,* 912 F.2d at 1099–1100. *See also Siderman*, 965 F.2d at 705–06 (reviewing history of foreign state immunity and the enactment of FSIA); *McKeel*, 722 F.2d at 587 n.6. Immunity is extended to an individual only when acting on behalf of the state because actions against those individuals are "the practical equivalent of a suit against the sovereign directly." *Chuidian,* 912 F.2d at 1101. A lawsuit against a foreign official acting outside the scope of his authority does not implicate any of the foreign diplomatic concerns involved in bringing suit against another government in United States courts.

This is evidenced by the Philippine government's agreement that the suit against Marcos proceed. The Minister of Justice of the Republic of the Philippines, Neptali A. Gonzales, prepared a letter to the Deputy Minister of Foreign Affairs, Leticia R. Shahani, concluding that "Marcos may be held liable for acts done as President during his incumbency, when such acts, like torture, inhuman treatment of detainees, etc. are clearly in violation of existing law ... the government or its officials may not validly claim state immunity for acts committed against a private party in violation of existing law." The Republic also filed an amicus curiae brief in the appeal from the dismissals on "act of state" grounds which urged the Ninth Circuit to reverse the district courts. The Republic stated that "foreign relations with the United States will not be adversely affected if these human rights claims against Ferdinand Marcos are heard in U.S. courts."[5]

In conclusion, Marcos' acts of torture, execution, and disappearance were clearly acts outside of his authority as President. Like those of Marcos–Manotoc, Marcos' acts were not taken within any official mandate and were therefore not the acts of an agency or instrumentality of a

5. The plaintiffs argue that these submissions constitute a waiver of sovereign immunity under FSIA by the Republic of the Philippines, and that Marcos' derivative immunity is thus also waived. The Estate objects that neither of these documents contain an explicit "waiver" of immunity, and that there is no authority allowing one government official to waive the immunity of another official. *See Chuidian*, 912 F.2d at 1103–05 (waiver by one Philippine governmental entity does not extend to a different entity). It is unnecessary to reach this issue, in view of the conclusion that FSIA does not immunize the illegal conduct of government officials. *See Estate I*, 978 F.2d at 498 n.11 (finding it unnecessary to reach the waiver of immunity issue).

foreign state within the meaning of FSIA.[6] *Estate I*, 978 F.2d at 498; *Chuidian*, 912 F.2d at 1106. No exception to FSIA thus need be demonstrated.

II. Subject Matter Jurisdiction Under the Alien Tort Act

... In upholding the default judgment against Marcos–Manotoc [under the ATCA], we held that a "suit as an alien for the tort of wrongful death, committed by military intelligence officials through torture prohibited by the law of nations, is within the jurisdictional grant of § 1350." *Estate I,* 978 F.2d at 499. In so holding, we rejected all of the Estate's arguments now asserted on appeal.

The Estate contends that there is no jurisdiction pursuant to the "Arising Under" Clause of Art. III because 28 U.S.C. § 1350 is purely a jurisdictional statute. In *Estate I*, we agreed that a jurisdictional statute could "not alone confer jurisdiction on the federal courts, and that the rights of the parties must stand or fall on federal substantive law to pass constitutional muster." *Estate I*, 978 F.2d at 501, *citing* Mesa v. California, 489 U.S. 121, 136–37 (1989) and *Verlinden*, 461 U.S. at 495–97. However, we disagreed that there was no federal substantive law governing the dispute.

First, we concluded that even where FSIA was held inapplicable, there was federal subject matter jurisdiction by virtue of the required analysis of whether immunity would be granted under FSIA. *Estate I*, 978 F.2d at 501. This court stated:

> [W]e have concluded that [Marcos–Manotoc's] actions were not those of the Republic of the Philippines for purposes of sovereign immunity under Chuidian. Nevertheless, when questions of sovereign immunity under the FSIA are raised, as they have been here, ... [u]nder *Verlinden*, subject-matter jurisdiction over this action satisfies Article III.

Id. at 502 (footnote omitted).

We also rejected the Estate's argument that international law does not provide a basis for federal court jurisdiction under § 1350:

> [T]he prohibition against official torture carries with it the force of a *jus cogens* norm, which enjoys the highest status within international law.... We therefore conclude that the district court did not err in founding jurisdiction on a violation of the *jus cogens* norm prohibiting official torture.

6. We also reject the Estate's argument that because "only individuals who have acted under official authority or under color of such authority may violate international law," *Estate I*, 978 F.2d at 501–02, a finding that Marcos' alleged actions were outside the scope of his official authority necessarily leads to the conclusion that there was no violation of international law. An official acting under color of authority, but not within an official mandate, can violate international law and not be entitled to immunity under FSIA. *See* Filartiga v. Pena–Irala, 630 F.2d 876, 890 (2d Cir.1980) ("Paraguay's renunciation of torture as a legitimate instrument of state policy, however, does not strip the tort of its character as an international law violation, if it in fact occurred under color of government authority.").

Estate I, 978 F.2d at 500 (internal quotations omitted), *citing Siderman,* 965 F.2d at 717. "It is ... well settled that the law of nations is part of federal common law." *Id.* at 502, *citing* The Paquete Habana, 175 U.S. 677 (1900) ("International law is part of our law, and must be ascertained and administered by the courts of justice of appropriate jurisdiction")....

The Estate also argues that the assertion of federal jurisdiction over an action between aliens regarding injuries occurring in a foreign nation violates Article III of the Constitution. We held in *Estate I* that there is "ample indication" that the "Arising Under" Clause was meant to apply to "all cases involving foreigners." *Estate I,* 978 F.2d at 502 (discussing papers of James Madison and Alexander Hamilton). The Estate nonetheless argues that early decisions regarding the interpretation of section 11 of the First Judiciary Act (the Diversity Clause), should control the interpretation of section 9 of the Act (the "Arising Under" Clause). In Mossman v. Higginson, 4 Dall. 12, 13 (1800), for instance, the Court stated:

> [The] 11th section of the judiciary act can and must receive a construction consistent with the constitution. It says, it is true, in general terms, that the circuit court shall have cognisance of suits "where an alien is a party;" but ... the legislative power of conferring jurisdiction on the federal courts, is, in this respect, confined to suits between citizens and foreigners.

The Estate's argument that section 9 requires one of the parties to be a citizen was explicitly rejected by the Supreme Court in *Verlinden.* The Supreme Court held that "the 'Arising Under' Clause of Art. III provides an appropriate basis for the statutory grant of subject-matter jurisdiction to actions by foreign plaintiffs under the Act." *Verlinden,* 461 U.S. at 492. The Court reviewed the "controlling decision on the scope of Art. III 'arising under' jurisdiction," Osborn v. Bank of United States, 9 Wheat. 738 (1824), and concluded that it reflected

> a broad conception of "arising under" jurisdiction, according to which Congress may confer on the federal courts jurisdiction over any case or controversy that might call for the application of federal law.... [A] suit against a foreign state under [FSIA] necessarily raises questions of substantive federal law at the very outset, and hence clearly "arises under" federal law, as that term is used in Art. III.

Verlinden, 461 U.S. at 492–93. *See also Chuidian,* 912 F.2d at 1098 ("Federal courts have jurisdiction over suits against foreign sovereigns under [FSIA], even where the parties are not diverse and the underlying claims do not present a federal question") (citation to *Verlinden* omitted); Filartiga v. Pena–Irala, 630 F.2d 876, 878 (2d Cir.1980). In conclusion, this action brought for torts "committed by military intelligence officials through torture prohibited by the law of nations, is within the jurisdictional grant of § 1350." *Estate I,* 978 F.2d at 499. This exercise of jurisdiction does not violate Article III.

III. Cause of Action Under the Alien Tort Act

The Estate argues that the Alien Tort Act is a purely jurisdictional statute which does not provide the plaintiffs a cause of action. The Estate contends that § 1350, like the § 1331 "arising under" jurisdictional provision, does not grant a cause of action. *See* Montana–Dakota Util. Co. v. Northwestern Pub. Serv. Co., 341 U.S. 246, 249 (1951) (the "Judicial Code, in vesting jurisdiction in the District Courts, does not create causes of action, but only confers jurisdiction to adjudicate those arising from other sources which satisfy its limiting provisions").

However, in contrast to section 1331, "which requires that an action 'arise under' the laws of the United States, section 1350 does not require that the action 'arise under' the law of nations, but only mandates a 'violation of the law of nations' in order to create a cause of action." Tel–Oren v. Libyan Arab Republic, 726 F.2d 774, 779 (D.C.Cir.1984) (Edwards, J., concurring), *cert. denied*, 470 U.S. 1003 (1985). It is unnecessary that international law provide a specific right to sue. International law "does not require any particular reaction to violations of law.... Whether and how the United States wished to react to such violations are domestic questions." *Id.*, at 777–78 (*quoting* L. Henkin, Foreign Affairs and the Constitution 224 (1972)). "[N]othing more than a violation of the law of nations is required to invoke section 1350." *Id.* at 779.

Actionable violations of international law must be of a norm that is specific, universal, and obligatory. *See Filartiga*, 630 F.2d at 881; *Tel–Oren,* 726 F.2d at 781; *cf. Guinto v. Marcos*, 654 F. Supp. 276, 280 (S.D.Cal.1986) ("violation of the First Amendment right of free speech does not rise to the level of such universally recognized rights and so does not constitute a 'law of nations' "); *see also* Forti v. Suarez–Mason, 672 F. Supp. 1531, 1539–40 (N.D.Cal.1987) ("This 'international tort' must be one which is definable, obligatory (rather than hortatory), and universally condemned"), amended in part, 694 F. Supp. 707 (N.D.Cal. 1988).

Our reading of the plain text of § 1350 is confirmed by the Torture Victim Protection Act.... See S. Rep. No. 249, 102d Cong., 1st Sess. 4–5 (1991); H.R. Rep. No. 367, 102d Cong., 1st Sess. pt. 1, *reprinted in* 1992 U.S.C.C.A.N. 84, 86.

The allegations in this case satisfy the specific, universal and obligatory standard. "Under international law, ... official torture violates *jus cogens*." *Siderman*, 965 F.2d at 717.

> [T]he right to be free from official torture is fundamental and universal, a right deserving of the highest stature under international law, a norm of *jus cogens*. The crack of the whip, the clamp of the thumb screw, the crush of the iron maiden, and, in these more efficient modern times, the shock of the electric cattle prod are forms of torture that the international order will not tolerate. To subject a person to such horrors is to commit one of the most

> egregious violations of the personal security and dignity of a human being.

Id. See also Tel–Oren, 726 F.2d at 781 (Edwards, J., concurring) (torture is violation of customary international law); *Tel-Oren,* 726 F.2d at 819–20 (Bork, J., concurring) ("the proscription of official torture [is] a principle that is embodied in numerous international conventions and declarations, that is 'clear and unambiguous' ... and about which there is universal agreement 'in the modern usage and practice of nations' "); *Filartiga,* 630 F.2d at 880–84 (discussing declarations of the United Nations General Assembly, human rights conventions prohibiting torture, modern municipal law, and the works of jurists); *Forti,* 672 F. Supp. at 1541 (prohibition against official torture is "universal, obligatory, and definable"). The United States signed the Convention Against Torture and Other Cruel, Inhuman or Degrading Treatment or Punishment, 39 U.N. GAOR Supp. (No. 51), 23 I.L.M. 1027 (1987), to which the United States Senate gave its advice and consent. *Siderman,* 965 F.2d at 716. The prohibition against summary execution or causing "disappearance" is similarly universal, definable, and obligatory. *Forti,* 672 F. Supp. at 1542, amended, 694 F. Supp. at 710–11.

We thus join the Second Circuit in concluding that the Alien Tort Act, 28 U.S.C. § 1350, creates a cause of action for violations of specific, universal and obligatory international human rights standards which "confer [ ] fundamental rights upon all people vis-a-vis their own governments." *Filartiga,* 630 F.2d at 885–87. The plaintiffs state a cause of action.

HILAO v. ESTATE OF FERDINAND MARCOS ("ESTATE III")

103 F.3d 767 (9th Cir. 1996).

FLETCHER, J.

The Estate of Ferdinand E. Marcos appeals from a final judgment entered against it in a class-action suit after a trifurcated jury trial on the damage claims brought by a class of Philippine nationals (hereinafter collectively referred to as "Hilao") who were victims of torture, "disappearance", or summary execution under the regime of Ferdinand E. Marcos. We have jurisdiction over the appeal pursuant to 28 U.S.C. sec.1291 and we affirm.

This case arises from human-rights abuses—specifically, torture, summary execution, and "disappearance"—committed by the Philippine military and paramilitary forces under the command of Ferdinand E. Marcos during his nearly 14–year rule of the Philippines. The details of Marcos' regime and the human-rights abuses have been set forth by the district court at 910 F. Supp. 1460, 1462–63 (D.Haw.1995).

... The district court ordered issues of liability and damages tried separately. In September 1992, a jury trial was held on liability; after three days of deliberation, the jury reached verdicts against the Estate and for the class and for 22 direct plaintiffs and a verdict for the Estate and against one direct plaintiff. Judgment was entered and the preliminary injunction modified to take account of the verdict.

The district court then ordered the damage trial bifurcated into one trial on exemplary damages and one on compensatory damages. The court ordered that notice be given to the class members that they must file a proof-of-claim form in order to opt into the class. Notice was provided by mail to known claimants and by publication in the Philippines and the U.S.; over 10,000 forms were filed.

In February 1994, the same jury that had heard the liability phase of the trial considered whether to award exemplary damages. After two days of evidence and deliberations, the jury returned a verdict against the Estate in the amount of $1.2 billion. The court appointed a special master to supervise proceedings related to the compensatory-damage phase of the trial in connection with the class. In January 1995, the jury reconvened a third time to consider compensatory damages. The compensatory-damage phase of the trial is explained in greater detail below. After seven days of trial and deliberation, the jury returned a compensatory-damage award for the class of over $766 million; after two further days of trial and deliberation, the jury returned compensatory-damage awards in favor of the direct plaintiffs. On February 3, 1995, the district court entered final judgment in the class action suit. The Estate appeals from this judgment.

The district court exercised jurisdiction under the Alien Tort Claims Act, 28 U.S.C. § 1350. The existence of subject-matter jurisdiction is a question of law reviewed *de novo*. Valdez v. United States, 56 F.3d 1177, 1179 (9th Cir.1995).

The Estate argues that this case does not "arise under" federal law for Article III purposes and therefore the federal courts cannot constitutionally exercise jurisdiction. This court has twice rejected these arguments in *Estate I* and *Estate II*. See 978 F.2d at 501–503, 25 F.3d at 1472–74. The published decisions in those cases are both the controlling law of the circuit and the law of this case. The Estate has presented no compelling arguments that the law has changed in the interim or that the two previous decisions of this court were "clearly erroneous and would work a manifest injustice". Leslie Salt Co. v. United States, 55 F.3d 1388, 1393 (9th Cir.), *cert. denied*, 516 U.S. 955 (1995). We therefore decline to reconsider the Estate's arguments and instead follow the court's prior decisions as the law of the circuit and of the case.

The Estate also argues that the Alien Tort Claims Act does not apply to conduct that occurs abroad and that all of the acts on which Hilao's judgment is based occurred within the Philippines. Again, however, this court rejected the argument when the Estate made it in a prior appeal. See *Estate I*, 978 F.2d at 499–501 ("[S]ubject-matter jurisdiction was not inappropriately exercised under sec. 1350 even though the actions of Marcos–Manotoc which caused a fellow citizen to be the victim of official torture and murder occurred outside of the United States.").

The Estate has offered no arguments for why we should not follow that decision as the law of the circuit and of the case, and we therefore decline to reconsider that decision.

I. Statute of Limitations

The Estate argues that the district court erred in not subjecting Hilao's claims to a two-year statute of limitations. The question of the appropriate statute of limitations is a question of law that we review de novo. Mendez v. Ishikawajima–Harima Heavy Indus. Co., 52 F.3d 799, 800 (9th Cir.1995). The Alien Tort Claims Act does not contain a statute of limitations. The Estate argues, therefore, that the courts should follow the general practice of adopting an analogous state statute of limitations if such adoption would not be inconsistent with federal law or policy. Because the Alien Tort Claims Act involves, as its title suggests, torts, and because the case was heard in the District of Hawai'i', the Estate argues that Hawai'i's two-year statute of limitations for tort claims should apply. The Estate argues alternatively that the appropriate statute of limitations might be that imposed by Philippine law, which appears to require that claims for personal injury arising out the exercise by a public officer of authority arising from martial law be brought within one year. Philippine Civil Code, Art. 1146. Hilao argues that the ten-year statute of limitations in the Torture Victim Protection Act, 28 U.S.C. § 1350 (note, § 2 (c)) (the TVPA), is the most closely analogous federal statute of limitations, and cites to a recent district court case applying that limit to claims under both the Alien Tort Claims Act and the TVPA. *See* Xuncax v. Gramajo, 886 F. Supp. 162, 192 (D.Mass.1995). Alternatively, Hilao points to the conclusion in *Estate II* that a claim under the Alien Tort Claims Act is closely analogous to a violation of 42 U.S.C. § 1983, 25 F.3d at 1476 (*citing* Forti v. Suarez–Mason, 672 F. Supp. 1531, 1548–50 (N.D.Cal.1987)), and argues that the jurisprudence on statutes of limitations under sec. 1983 should govern.

We need not decide which statute of limitations applies because Hilao's suit was timely under any of the proposed statutes when equitable tolling principles are applied. The Senate Report on the TVPA states that the ten-year statute is subject to equitable tolling, including for periods in which the defendant is absent from the jurisdiction or immune from lawsuits and for periods in which the plaintiff is imprisoned or incapacitated. S. Rep. No. 249, 102d Cong., 1st Sess., at 11 (1991). Section 1983 generally borrows its statute of limitations from state laws, Johnson v. Railway Express Agency, Inc., 421 U.S. 454, 462 (1975), and incorporates equitable-tolling principles of either state or federal law in cases where a defendant's wrongful conduct, or extraordinary circumstances outside a plaintiff's control, prevented a plaintiff from timely asserting a claim. *See, e.g.*, Hardin v. Straub, 490 U.S. 536 (1989); Bianchi v. Bellingham Police Dept., 909 F.2d 1316 (9th Cir.1990); Williams v. Walsh, 558 F.2d 667 (2d Cir.1977). Hawai'i courts have allowed equitable tolling in similar situations. *See, e.g.*, Cleghorn v. Bishop, 3 Haw. 483, 483–84 (1873) (statute of limitations tolled during lifetime of King Kamehameha V because he was immune from suit; after his death, claim could be brought against estate).

Any action against Marcos for torture, "disappearance", or summary execution was tolled during the time Marcos was president. A Philippine attorney who testified as an expert witness at trial stated that in 1981 Marcos engineered the passage of a constitutional amendment granting him, and others acting at his direction, immunity from suit during his tenure in office. Another expert witness testified that many victims of torture in the Philippines did not report the human-rights abuses they suffered out of intimidation and fear of reprisals; this fear seems particularly understandable in light of testimony on the suspension of habeas corpus between 1972 and 1981, and on the effective dependence of the judiciary on Marcos. Given these extraordinary conditions, any claims against Marcos for injury from torture, "disappearance", or summary execution were tolled until he left office in February 1986. The Estate appears to concede that the claims in this suit were asserted in March 1986. Thus, the filing of this action was timely under any of the asserted statutes of limitations.

II. Abatement

The Estate argues that Hilao's cause of action abated upon the death of Marcos because the federal common-law rule is that an action for an intentional tort abates upon the death of either party. *See* Heikkila v. Barber, 308 F.2d 558, 560–61 (9th Cir.1962). This court has previously rejected this argument in *Estate II,* analogizing Hilao's cause of action to claims for violation of the Eighth Amendment right to freedom from cruel and unusual punishment or of 42 U.S.C. § 1983, neither of which abates upon the death of the defendant. 25 F.3d at 1476. We reject the Estate's argument that that decision was clearly erroneous and simply follow *Estate II* as the law of the circuit and of the case on the issue of abatement. . . .

V. Instructions on Liability of the Estate

A claim that the trial court misstated the elements that must be proven at trial is a question of law to be reviewed de novo. Oglesby v. Southern Pacific Transportation Co., 6 F.3d 603, 606 (9th Cir.1993).

The district court instructed the jury that it could find the Estate liable if it found either that (1) Marcos directed, ordered, conspired with, or aided the military in torture, summary execution, and "disappearance" or (2) if Marcos knew of such conduct by the military and failed to use his power to prevent it. The Estate challenges the latter basis for liability, arguing that liability is not imposed under such conditions in analogous U.S. law claims, that "no international law decision . . . has ever imposed liability upon a foreign official" on those grounds, and that the district court essentially made the Estate liable on a respondeat superior theory that is inapplicable in intentional torts.

The principle of "command responsibility" that holds a superior responsible for the actions of subordinates appears to be well accepted in U.S. and international law in connection with acts committed in wartime, as the Supreme Court's opinion in *In Re Yamashita* indicates:

> [T]he gist of the charge is an unlawful breach of duty by petitioner as an army commander to control the operations of the members of his command by 'permitting them to commit' the extensive and widespread atrocities specified.... [T]he law of war presupposes that its violation is to be avoided through the control of the operations of war by commanders who are to some extent responsible for their subordinates.... [P]rovisions [of international law] plainly imposed on petitioner, who at the time specified was military governor of the Philippines, as well as commander of the Japanese forces, an affirmative duty to take such measures as were within his power and appropriate in the circumstances to protect prisoners of war and the civilian population. This duty of a commanding officer has heretofore been recognized, and its breach penalized[,] by our own military tribunals.

In re Yamashita, 327 U.S. 1, 14–16 (1946). *See also* Art. 86 (2), Protocol to the Geneva Conventions of August 12, 1949, opened for signature December 12, 1977, reprinted in 16 I.L.M. 1391, 1429 (1977) ("The fact that a breach of the Conventions or of this Protocol was committed by a subordinate does not absolve his superiors from penal [or] disciplinary responsibility ... if they knew, or had information which should have enabled them to conclude in the circumstances at the time, that he was committing or was going to commit such a breach and if they did not take all feasible measures within their power to prevent or repress the breach."); Art. 7 (3), Statute of the International Tribunal for the Prosecution of Persons Responsible for Serious Violations of International Humanitarian Law Committed in the Territory of the Former Yugoslavia, 32 I.L.M. 1159, 1192–94 (1993) ("The fact that any [act of genocide, crime against humanity, or violation of the Geneva Conventions or of the laws or customs of war] was committed by a subordinate does not relieve his superior of criminal responsibility if he knew or had reason to know that the subordinate was about to commit such acts or had done so and the superior failed to take the necessary and reasonable measures to prevent such acts or to punish the perpetrators thereof."); *see generally* Lt. Cmdr. Weston D. Burnett, *Command Responsibility and a Case Study of the Criminal Responsibility of Israeli Military Commanders for the Pogrom at Shatila and Sabra,* 107 Mil. L.J. 71 (1985).

The United States has moved toward recognizing similar "command responsibility" for torture that occurs in peacetime, perhaps because the goal of international law regarding the treatment of noncombatants in wartime—"to protect civilian populations and prisoners ... from brutality", *In re Yamashita*, 327 U.S. at 15—is similar to the goal of international human-rights law. This move is evidenced in the legislative history of the TVPA:

> [A] higher official need not have personally performed or ordered the abuses in order to be held liable. Under international law, responsibility for torture, summary execution, or disappearances extends beyond the person or persons who actually committed those acts—anyone with higher authority who authorized, tolerated or knowingly ignored those acts is liable for them.

S. Rep. No. 249, 102d Cong., 1st Sess. at 9 (1991) (footnote omitted) (*citing Forti* and *In re Yamashita*). At least one district court has recognized such liability. *Xuncax*, 886 F. Supp. at 171–73, 174–75 ("Gramajo was aware of and supported widespread acts of brutality committed by personnel under his command resulting in thousands of civilian deaths.... Gramajo refused to act to prevent such atrocities." "... Gramajo may be held liable for the acts of members of the military forces under his command."). *See also* Paul v. Avril, 901 F. Supp. 330, 335 (S.D.Fla.1994) ("Defendant Avril [former military ruler of Haiti] bears personal responsibility for a systematic pattern of egregious human rights abuses in Haiti during his military rule.... He also bears personal responsibility for the interrogation and torture of each of the plaintiffs.... All of the soldiers and officers in the Haitian military responsible for the arbitrary detention and torture of plaintiffs were employees, representatives, or agents of defendant Avril, acting under his instructions, authority, and control and acting within the scope of authority granted by him."). The conduct at issue in this case involved violations by members of military or paramilitary forces of a *jus cogens* norm of international law parallel to the types of war crimes for which international law imposes command responsibility. Siderman de Blake v. Republic of Argentina, 965 F.2d 699, 714–717 (9th Cir.1992) (prohibition against torture has attained status of *jus cogens* norm from which no derogation is permitted). In these circumstances, the district court's instruction on the second category of liability was proper under international law....

IX. Methodology of Determining Compensatory Damages

The Estate challenges the method used by the district court in awarding compensatory damages to the class members.

A. *District Court Methodology*

The district court allowed the use of a statistical sample of the class claims in determining compensatory damages. In all, 10,059 claims were received. The district court ruled 518 of these claims to be facially invalid, leaving 9,541 claims. From these, a list of 137 claims was randomly selected by computer. This number of randomly selected claims was chosen on the basis of the testimony of James Dannemiller, an expert on statistics, who testified that the examination of a random sample of 137 claims would achieve "a 95 percent statistical probability that the same percentage determined to be valid among the examined claims would be applicable to the totality of claims filed". Of the claims selected, 67 were for torture, 52 were for summary execution, and 18 were for "disappearance".

1. Special Master's Recommendations

The district court then appointed Sol Schreiber as a special master (and a court-appointed expert under Rule 706 of the Federal Rules of Evidence). Schreiber supervised the taking of depositions in the Philippines of the 137 randomly selected claimants (and their witnesses) in October and November 1994. These depositions were noticed and conducted in accordance with the Federal Rules of Civil Procedure; the Estate chose not to participate and did not appear at any of the depositions. [The Estate also did not depose any of the remaining class members.]

Schreiber then reviewed the claim forms (which had been completed under penalty of perjury) and depositions of the class members in the sample. On the instructions of the district court, he evaluated

> (1) whether the abuse claimed came within one of the definitions, with which the Court charged the jury at the trial . . . , of torture, summary execution, or disappearance; (2) whether the Philippine military or paramilitary was . . . involved in such abuse; and (3) whether the abuse occurred during the period September 1972 through February 1986.

He recommended that 6 claims of the 137 in the sample be found not valid [for insufficient evidence].

Schreiber then recommended the amount of damages to be awarded to the 131 claimants. Following the decision in Filartiga v. Pena–Irala, 577 F. Supp. 860, 863 (E.D.N.Y.1984), he applied Philippine, international, and American law on damages. In the cases of torture victims, Schreiber considered:

> (1) physical torture, including what methods were used and/or abuses were suffered; (2) mental abuse, including fright and anguish; (3) amount of time torture lasted; (4) length of detention, if any; (5) physical and/or mental injuries; (6) victim's age; and (7) actual losses, including medical bills.

In the cases of summary execution and "disappearance", the master considered

> (1) [the presence or absence of] torture prior to death or disappearance; (2) the actual killing or disappearance; . . . (3) the victim's family's mental anguish[;] and (4) lost earnings [computed according to a formula established by the Philippine Supreme Court and converted into U.S. dollars].

The recommended damages for the 131 valid claims in the random sample totalled $3,310,000 for the 64 torture claims (an average of $51,719), $6,425,767 for the 50 summary-execution claims (an average of $128,515), and $1,833,515 for the 17 "disappearance" claims (an average of $107,853).

Schreiber then made recommendations on damage awards to the remaining class members. Based on his recommendation that 6 of the 137 claims in the random sample (4.37%) be rejected as invalid, he recommended the application of a five-per-cent invalidity rate to the remaining claims. He then performed the following calculations to determine the number of valid class claims remaining:

Summary

	Torture	Execution	Disappearance
Claims Filed	5,372	3,677	1,010
Facially Invalid Claims	– 179	– 273	– 66
Remaining Claims	5,193	3,404	944
Less 5% Invalidity Rate	– 260	– 170	– 47
Valid Claims	4,933	3,234	897
Valid Sample Claims	– 64	– 50	– 17
Valid Remaining Claims	4,869	3,184	880

He recommended that the award to the class be determined by multiplying the number of valid remaining claims in each subclass by the average award recommended for the randomly sampled claims in that subclass:

Summary

	Torture	Execution	Disappearance
Valid Remaining Claims	4,869	3,184	880
x Average Awards	$ 51,719	$ 128,515	$ 107,853
Class Awards	$251,819,811	$409,191,760	$94,910,640

By adding the recommended awards in the randomly sampled cases, Schreiber arrived at a recommendation for a total compensatory damage award in each subclass:

Summary

	Torture	Execution	Disappearance
Class Awards	$251,819,811	$409,191,760	$94,910,640
Sample Awards	$ 3,310,000	$ 6,425,767	$ 1,833,515
Totals	$255,129,811	$415,617,527	$96,744,155

Adding together the subclass awards, Schreiber recommended a total compensatory damage award of $767,491,493.

2. Jury Proceedings

A jury trial on compensatory damages was held in January 1995. Dannemiller testified that the selection of the random sample met the standards of inferential statistics, that the successful efforts to locate and obtain testimony from the claimants in the random sample "were of the highest standards" in his profession, that the procedures followed conformed to the standards of inferential statistics, and that the injuries of the random-sample claimants were representative of the class as a whole. Testimony from the 137 random-sample claimants and their witnesses was introduced. Schreiber testified as to his recommendations, and his report was supplied to the jury. The jury was instructed that it could accept, modify or reject Schreiber's recommendations and that it could independently, on the basis of the evidence of the random-sample claimants, reach its own judgment as to the actual damages of those claimants and of the aggregate damages suffered by the class as a whole.

The jury deliberated for five days before reaching a verdict. Contrary to the master's recommendations, the jury found against only two of the 137 claimants in the random sample. As to the sample claims, the jury generally adopted the master's recommendations, although it did not follow his recommendations in 46 instances. As to the claims of the remaining class members, the jury adopted the awards recommended by the master. The district court subsequently entered judgment for 135 of the 137 claimants in the sample in the amounts awarded by the jury, and for the remaining plaintiffs in each of the three subclasses in the amounts awarded by the jury, to be divided pro rata.

B. *Estate's Challenge*

The Estate's challenge to the procedure used by the district court is very narrow. It challenges specifically only "the method by which [the district court] allowed the validity of the class claims to be determined": the master's use of a representative sample to determine what percentage of the total claims were invalid.

The grounds on which the Estate challenges this method are unclear. It states that to its knowledge this method "has not previously been employed in a class action". This alone, of course, would not be grounds for reversal, and in any case the method has been used before in an asbestos class-action case, the opinion in which apparently helped persuade the district court to use this method. *See* Cimino v. Raymark Indus., Inc., 751 F. Supp. 649, 659–667 (E.D.Tex.1990).

The Estate also argues that the method was "inappropriate" because the class consists of various members with numerous subsets of claims based on whether the plaintiff or his or her decedent was subjected to torture, "disappearance", or summary execution. The district court's methodology, however, took account of those differences by grouping the class members' claims into three subclasses.

Finally, the Estate appears to assert that the method violated its rights to due process because "individual questions apply to each subset of claims, *i.e.*, whether the action was justified, the degree of injury, proximate cause, etc.". It does not, however, provide any argument or case citation to explain how the methodology violated its due-process rights. Indeed, the "individual questions" it identifies—justification, degree of injury, proximate cause—are irrelevant to the challenge it makes: the method of determining the validity of the class members' claims. The jury had already determined that Philippine military or paramilitary forces on Marcos' orders—or with his conspiracy or assistance or with his knowledge and failure to act—had tortured, summarily executed, or "disappeared" untold numbers of victims and that the Estate was liable to them or their survivors. The only questions involved in determining the validity of the class members' claims were whether or not the human-rights abuses they claim to have suffered were proven by sufficient evidence.

Although poorly presented, the Estate's due-process claim does raise serious questions. Indeed, at least one circuit court has expressed "profound disquiet" in somewhat similar circumstances. *In re* Fibreboard Corp., 893 F.2d 706, 710 (5th Cir.1990). The *Fibreboard* court was reviewing a petition for a writ of mandamus to vacate trial procedures ordered in over 3,000 asbestos cases. The district court had consolidated the cases for certain purposes and certified a class for the issue of actual damages. The district court ordered a trial first on liability and punitive damages, and then a trial (Phase II) on actual damages. In the Phase II trial, the jury was "to determine actual damages in a lump sum for each [of 5] disease categor[ies] for all plaintiffs in the class" on the basis of "a full trial of liability and damages for 11 class representatives and such evidence as the parties wish to offer from 30 illustrative plaintiffs" (half chosen by each side), as well as "opinions of experts ... regarding the total damage award". 893 F.2d at 708–09. The Fifth Circuit noted that the parties agreed that "there will inevitably be individual class members whose recovery will be greater or lesser than it would have been if tried alone" and that "persons who would have had their claims rejected may recover". *Id.* at 709. The court said that

> [t]he inescapable fact is that the individual claims of 2,990 persons will not be presented. Rather, the claim of a unit of 2,990 persons will be presented. Given the unevenness of the individual claims, this Phase II process inevitably restates the dimensions of tort liability. Under the proposed procedure, manufacturers and suppliers are exposed to liability not only in 41 cases actually tried with success to the jury, but in 2,990 additional cases whose claims are indexed to those tried.

Id. at 711. The court granted the petitions for mandamus and vacated the trial court's order, but it did so not on due-process grounds but because the proposed procedure worked a change in the parties' substantive rights under Texas law that was barred by the *Erie* doctrine.

On the other hand, the time and judicial resources required to try the nearly 10,000 claims in this case would alone make resolution of Hilao's claims impossible. *See Cimino*, 751 F. Supp. at 652–53 ("If the Court could somehow close thirty cases a month, it would take six and one-half years to try these [2,298] cases...."). The similarity in the injuries suffered by many of the class members would make such an effort, even if it could be undertaken, especially wasteful, as would the fact that the district court found early on that the damages suffered by the class members likely exceed the total known assets of the Estate.

While the district court's methodology in determining valid claims is unorthodox, it can be justified by the extraordinarily unusual nature of this case. " 'Due process,' unlike some legal rules, is not a technical conception with a fixed content unrelated to time, place and circumstances". Cafeteria and Restaurant Workers Union, Local 473 v. McElroy, 367 U.S. 886, 895 (1961). In Connecticut v. Doehr, 501 U.S. 1, 10 (1991), a case involving prejudgment attachment, the Supreme Court set forth a test, based on the test of Mathews v. Eldridge, 424 U.S. 319 (1976), for determining whether a procedure by which a private party invokes state power to deprive another person of property satisfies due process:

> [F]irst, consideration of the private interest that will be affected by the [procedure]; second, an examination of the risk of erroneous deprivation through the procedures under attack and the probable value of additional or alternative safeguards; and third, . . . principal attention to the interest of the party seeking the [procedure], with, nonetheless, due regard for any ancillary interest the government may have in providing the procedure or forgoing the added burden of providing greater protections.

501 U.S. at 11. The interest of the Estate that is affected is at best an interest in not paying damages for any invalid claims. If the Estate had a legitimate concern in the identities of those receiving damage awards, the district court's procedure could affect this interest. In fact, however, the Estate's interest is only in the total amount of damages for which it will be liable: if damages were awarded for invalid claims, the Estate would have to pay more. The statistical method used by the district court obviously presents a somewhat greater risk of error in comparison to an adversarial adjudication of each claim, since the former method requires a probabilistic prediction (albeit an extremely accurate one) of how many of the total claims are invalid. The risk in this case was reduced, though, by the fact that the proof-of-claim form that the district court required each class member to submit in order to opt into the class required the claimant to certify under penalty of perjury that the information provided was true and correct. Hilao's interest in the use of the statistical method, on the other hand, is enormous, since adversarial resolution of each class member's claim would pose insurmountable practical hurdles. The "ancillary" interest of the judiciary in the procedure is obviously also substantial, since 9,541 individual adversarial determinations of claim validity would clog the docket of the district court for years. Under the balancing test set forth in *Mathews* and *Doehr*, the procedure used by the district court did not violate due process.

Conclusion

The district court had jurisdiction over Hilao's cause of action. Hilao's claims were neither barred by the statute of limitations nor abated by Marcos' death. The district court did not abuse its discretion in certifying the class. The challenged evidentiary rulings of the district court were not in error. The district court properly held Marcos liable for human rights abuses which occurred and which he knew about and failed to use his power to prevent. The jury instructions on the Torture Victim Protection Act and on proximate cause were not erroneous. The award of exemplary damages against the Estate was allowed under Philippine law and the Estate's due-process rights were not violated in either the determination of those damages or of compensatory damages. The judgment of the district court is therefore affirmed.

RYMER, J., concurring in part and dissenting in part

Because I believe that determining causation as well as damages by inferential statistics instead of individualized proof raises more than "serious questions" of due process, I must dissent from Part IX of the majority opinion. Otherwise, I concur.

Here's what happened: Hilao's statistical expert, James Dannemiller, created a computer database of the abuse of each of the 10,059 victims based on what they said in a claim form that assumed the victim's torture. Although Dannemiller would have said that 384 claims should be examined to achieve generalizability to the larger population of 10,059 victims within 5 percentage points at a 95% confidence level, he decided that only 136 randomly selected claims would be required in light of the "anticipated validity" of the claim forms and testimony at the trial on liability that the number of abuses was about 10,000.

He selected three independent sample sets of 242 (by random selection but eliminating duplicates). Hilao's counsel then tried to contact and hold hearings or depositions with each of the claimants on the first list, but when attempts to contact a particular claimant proved fruitless, the same number in the next list was used. When the sample results for the first 137 victims proved insufficient to produce the level of sampling precision desired for the project, Hilao's counsel continued from case 138 to case 145. Eventually, 124 were completed from list A, 11 from list B, and 2 from list C.

The persons culled through this process went to Manila to testify at a deposition (which Dannemiller thought was "remarkable"). Dannemiller Narrative Statement, p. 6. He opined that "this random selection method in determining the percentage of valid claims was fair to the Defendant" as "[a] random selection method of a group of 9541 individuals is more accurate than where each individual is contacted." *Id.* Further, the statistician observed that "[t]he cost and time required to do 9541 would be overwhelming and not justified when greater precision can and was achieved through sampling." *Id.* at 7. Finally, he concluded that "the procedures followed conformed to the standards of inferential statistics and therefore ... the injuries of the 137 claimants examined are representative of the 9541 victims." *Id.*

In accordance with the "computer-generated plan developed by James Dannemiller," the Special Master oversaw the taking of the 137 depositions in the Philippines. In accordance with the district court's order, the Special Master was to determine "(1) whether the abuse claimed came within one of the definitions, with which the Court charged the jury at the trial held in Hawaii, of torture, summary execution, or disappearance; (2) whether the Philippine military or para-military was or were involved in such abuse; and (3) whether the abuse occurred during the period September 1972 through February 1986." Special Master and Court Appointed Expert's Recommendations, p. 1. Based on a review of the deposition transcripts of the 137 randomly selected victim claims, and a review of the claims, the Special Master found that 131 were valid within the definitions which the court gave to the jury; the Philippine military or para-military were involved in the abuse of the valid claims; and the abuse occurred during the period 1972 through February 1986. As a result, he recommended the amount of compensatory damages to be awarded to the valid 131 claimants, and for the entire class based on the average awards for torture, for summary execution (including lost earnings, which the Special Master determined should be capped at $120,000 per claimant, and which would be determined by the average for the occupation when a witness did not state the amount of income earned), and disappearance (including lost earnings similarly calculated). His report indicates that "for all three categories, moral damages as a proximate result of defendants' wrongful acts or omissions, Phil.Civ.Code secs. 2216, 2217 were weighed into the compensation." *Id.* at 7.

Thus, causation and $766 million compensatory damages for nearly 10,000 claimants rested on the opinion of a statistical expert that the selection method in determining valid claims was fair to the Estate and more accurate than individual testimony; Hilao's counsel's contact with the randomly selected victims until they got 137 to be deposed; and the Special Master's review of transcripts and finding that the selected victims had been tortured, summarily executed or disappeared, that the Philippine military was "involved," that the abuse occurred during the relevant period, and that moral damages occurred as a proximate result of the Estate's wrongful acts. This leaves me "with a profound disquiet," as Judge Higginbotham put it in *In re* Fibreboard Corp., 893 F.2d 706, 710 (5th Cir.1990). Although I cannot point to any authority that says so, I cannot believe that a summary review of transcripts of a selected sample of victims who were able to be deposed for the purpose of inferring the type of abuse, by whom it was inflicted, and the amount of damages proximately caused thereby, comports with fundamental notions of due process.

Even in the context of a class action, individual causation and individual damages must still be proved individually. As my colleagues on the Sixth Circuit explained in contrasting generic causation—that the defendant was responsible for a tort which had the capacity to cause the harm alleged—with individual proximate cause and individual damage:

> Although such generic causation and individual causation may appear to be inextricably intertwined, the procedural device of the class action permitted the court initially to assess the defendant's

> potential liability for its conduct without regard to the individual components of each plaintiff's injuries. However, from this point forward, it became the responsibility of each individual plaintiff to show that his or her specific injuries or damages were proximately caused by [the defendant's conduct]. We cannot emphasize this point strongly enough because generalized proofs will not suffice to prove individual damages. The main problem on review stems from a failure to differentiate between the general and the particular. This is an understandably easy trap to fall into in mass tort litigation. Although many common issues of fact and law will be capable of resolution on a group basis, individual particularized damages still must be proved on an individual basis.

Sterling v. Velsicol Chem. Corp., 855 F.2d 1188, 1200 (6th Cir.1988).

There is little question that Marcos caused tremendous harm to many people, but the question is which people, and how much. That, I think, is a question on which the defendant has a right to due process. If due process in the form of a real prove-up of causation and damages cannot be accomplished because the class is too big or to do so would take too long, then (as the Estate contends) the class is unmanageable and should not have been certified in the first place. As Judge Becker recently wrote for the Third Circuit in declining to certify a 250,000–member class in an asbestos action: "Every decade presents a few great cases that force the judicial system to choose between forging a solution to a major social problem on the one hand, and preserving its institutional values on the other. This is such a case." Georgine v. Amchem Prod., Inc., 83 F.3d 610, 617 (3d Cir.1996).

So is this. I think that due process dictates the choice: a real trial. I therefore dissent.

Notes and Questions

1. Were the procedures used by the Philippine military and described in the 1995 district court opinion "torture" as defined in Article 1 of the Convention Against Torture and Other Cruel, Inhuman, or Degrading Treatment or Punishment (in the Documents Supplement)? If so, did these actions also violate other human rights treaties? Did they also violate customary international law? Did these actions violate a *jus cogens* norm of customary international law?

2. What level of responsibility and involvement by Ferdinand E. Marcos with regard to these human rights violations did the jury have to find in order to determine that he was personally liable for the suffering of the victims? Was the standard of "command responsibility" approved by the Ninth Circuit in *Estate III* appropriate and fair? Did it fit within the "knew or should have known" test, including dereliction of duty, identified previously in connection with *Xuncax* (at pp. 385–387) and p. 367?

3. Did Marcos authorize and supervise the human rights abuses discussed in these cases as part of his official responsibilities as President of the Republic of the Philippines? Were they lawful under domestic law? Should

he (and later his Estate) have been able to claim sovereign immunity for these actions? See Chapter 4.

4. Were Marcos's acts of ordering torture, summary execution, and disappearances lawful public acts that should have triggered the act of state doctrine? See Chapter 4.

5. If the acts of torturing and murdering Marcos's opponents were not undertaken pursuant to Marcos's responsibilities as President of the Republic of the Philippines, can they nonetheless be considered to be violations of international law, or were they merely domestic crimes and torts?

6. How did the district court gain personal jurisdiction over Marcos?

7. What was the statutory basis for the subject-matter jurisdiction exercised by the federal courts in these cases? Was a "cause of action" enacted by the U.S. Congress, or did international law provide the cause of action? Other decisions since *Estate II* that have agreed that a cause of action can be determined from customary international law include Alvarez–Machain v. United States, 107 F.3d 696, 703 (9th Cir. 1996); Abebe–Jira v. Negewo, 72 F.3d 844, 848 (11th Cir. 1996) ("we read the [ATCA] as requiring no more than an allegation of a violation of the law of nations in order to invoke section 1350"); White v. Paulsen, 997 F.Supp. 1380, 1382–83 (E.D.Wash.1998) (recognizing that "federal courts have the authority to imply the existence of a private right of action [under § 1331] for violations of *jus cogens* norms of international law," but declining to find such a cause of action in a case involving nonconsensual medical experimentation because ample adequate domestic remedies existed for the plaintiffs); Iwanowa v. Ford Motor Co., 67 F.Supp.2d 424, 442 (D.N.J.1999) (adding that "it is well-established that [customary] international law is 'self-executing' and is applied by courts in the United States without any need for it to be enacted or implemented by Congress."); cases in the last subsection.

8. In *Estate III,* how did the court determine what the applicable statute of limitations should be? Was this approach correct?

9. How were the compensatory damages owed to members of the class of victims determined? Was this system fair to both sides?

10. How much money was awarded on behalf of each victim of torture, summary execution, and disappearance? Was this amount appropriate?

11. The Class of Human Rights Victims have spent the past decade in search of assets. One source was in Swiss banks. After extensive negotiation and litigation, the Swiss Federal Supreme Court ruled that deposits in Marcos accounts of about $570 million in Swiss banks should be transferred to the Philippines. *Federal Office for Police Matters v. District Attorney's Office IV for the Canton of Zurich*, 1A.87/1994/err (Swiss Federal Supreme Court, Dec. 10, 1997); *see also* Associated Press, *Swiss Court Approves Return of Marcos Funds*, N.Y. TIMES, June 16, 1998, at A12. But this transfer was conditional, and the Swiss Court stated explicitly in its ruling that the Philippine Government had a responsibility to ensure that the human rights victims receive adequate compensation for their injuries, that the Philippine government had a duty to keep the Swiss Government informed about the steps it took to provide compensation to the human rights victims, and that the Swiss Government should monitor the situation to ensure that such

compensation was forthcoming. The Swiss Court explained that both the Philippines and Switzerland had duties international law to "safeguard[] human rights" and that this duty is "incumbent upon ... the courts as executors of the international law regime." The Court recognized that all parties to the International Covenant of Civil and Political Rights and the Torture Convention have a duty to ensure that victims of human rights abuse have a right to establish their right to compensation through competent judicial tribunals. The Swiss Court also recognized that the Philippine judiciary has "shortcomings" and that it is "reputed to be ponderous and susceptible to corruption and political influence." For this reason, the Swiss Court included as a condition of transferring the money to the Philippines the requirement that the Philippine government "regularly update" the Swiss authorities on the procedures established "to compensate the victims of human rights violations under the Marcos regime." The Philippine government has not fulfilled these conditions, however, and on July 15, 2003, the Philippine Supreme Court exacerbated the problem by ruling—in a case from which the Human Rights Victims were excluded—that all these assets should go to the Philippine government.

More recently, a Merrill Lynch securities account valued at about $35,000,000 has been identified, and after extensive discovery and a trial, the District Court ruled in 2004 that these funds should be awarded to the Class of Human Rights Victims. Merrill Lynch, Pierce, Fenner & Smith Incorporated v. Arelma, Inc., Civil No. CV00–595MLR (D.Hawai'i 2004). As this second edition is being prepared for publication, this decision is now on appeal before the U.S. Court of Appeals for the Ninth Circuit. The Human Rights Victims are also pursuing claims involving land linked to the Marcos Estate in Colorado and Texas and are involved in an interpleader action in Singapore.

12. The position of the Philippine Government opposing the efforts of the human rights victims to collect their hard-earned judgment is hard to understand or accept. After the end of the Marcos era in 1986, the Philippine Government established the Presidential Commission on Good Government (PCGG) to pursue assets plundered by the Marcoses, but it has taken no affirmative steps to compensate the victims of human rights abuses during the Marcos Regime, even though international law has recognized the unambiguous duty of the government to do so. The Inter–American Court of Human Rights explained, for instance, that the duty to investigate human rights abuses and compensate the victims of these abuses continues despite "changes of government" even if the "the attitude of the new government may be much more respectful of those rights than that of the government in power when the violations occurred." *Velasquez Rodriguez Case* (1988), para. 184, 28 I.L.M. 291, 327–28 (1989). In 2004, the Class of Human Rights Victims filed a petition with the Human Rights Committee created by the International Covenant of Civil and Political Rights complaining that the government of the Philippines has failed to meet its obligation to provide an effective remedy for the Class of Human Rights Victims.

13. The human rights plaintiffs in the *Siderman* and *UNOCAL* cases received undisclosed but substantial out-of-court settlements in 1996 and 2004. *See, e.g.*, Tim Golden, *Argentina Settles Lawsuit By a Victim of Torture*, N.Y. TIMES, Sept. 14, 1996, at 6. The U.S. citizens of Japanese

ancestry who were wrongfully interred during World War II received an apology from the U.S. Congress and $20,000 each in the late 1980s. Was this amount sufficient? How much money would be needed to reach an adequate settlement for the Class of Human Rights Victims in the *Marcos* case?

14. Recall that international human rights law includes the right to an effective remedy in domestic tribunals. Does international law permit countries to grant civil immunities to perpetrators of human rights abuses? Decisions that confirm that the right to an effective remedy is a continuing one that cannot be waived include: *The Velasquez Rodriguez Case*, Judgment of 29 July 1988, Inter–American Court of Human Rights, Ser. C/4, para. 174, *reprinted in* 28 I.L.M. 291 (1989) (holding that the American Convention on Human Rights imposes on each state party a "legal duty to ... ensure the victim adequate compensation"); Chumbipuma Aguirre, *et al.* v. Peru (Barrios Altos Case), Inter–American Court of Human Rights (March 14, 2001), para. 41 (amnesty laws cannot eliminate responsibility "for serious human rights violations such as torture, extrajudicial, summary or arbitrary execution and forced disappearance"); IACHR *Report No. 61/01, Case No. 11.771* (Catalán Lincoleo v. Chile), Inter–American Commission on Human Rights, April 16, 2001 (ruling that Chile's amnesty law preventing criminal investigation and prosecution of those involved in disappearance, torture, and extrajudicial killing impermissibly interfered with right of claimants to obtain reparations through civil courts); *Chanfeau Orayce and Others v. Chile*, Cases 11.505 *et al.*, Inter–American Commission on Human Rights 512, OEA/ser.L/V/II.98, doc. 7 rev. (1997) (stating that Chile's amnesty law violated Articles 1 (1), 2, and 25 of the American Convention on Human Rights, that countries have a duty to "investigate the violations committed within its jurisdiction, identify those responsible and impose the pertinent sanctions on them, as well as ensure the adequate reparation of the consequences suffered by the victim"); IACHR *Report No. 36/96, Case No. 10.843*, paras. 68, 105, 112, Inter–American Commission on Human Rights, October 15, 1996 (ruling that Chile's 1978 Amnesty Decree Law violated Article 25 of the American Convention on Human Rights because "the [human rights] victims and their families were deprived of their right to effective recourse against the violations of their rights"); *Mentes v. Turkey*, European Court of Human Rights, para. 89, *reprinted in* 37 I.L.M. 858, 882 (1998) (ruling that Turkey violated the rights of its citizens who were prevented from bringing a claim for the deliberate destruction of their houses and possessions, and noting that "the notion of an 'effective remedy' entails, in addition to the payment of compensation where appropriate, a thorough and effective investigation capable of leading to the identification and punishment of those responsible and including effective access for the complainant to the investigative procedure"); *Rodriguez v. Uruguay*, U.N. Doc. CCPR/C/51/D/322/1988, Annex (Human Rights Committee 1994) (stating that "amnesties for gross violations of human rights ... are incompatible with the obligations of the State party" under the International Covenant on Civil and Political Rights and that each country has a "responsibility to provide effective remedies to the victims of those abuses" to allow the victims to gain appropriate compensation for their injuries).

15. Sovereign immunity issues concerning the Marcos cases also appear in Chapter 4, Section 2 B.

E. Conflicts With Federal Statutes

When there is an unavoidable clash between an international treaty and the United States Constitution, U.S. courts will apply the Constitution domestically even though such action places the United States in violation of international law at the international level. Although supportive dictum appears in merely one case, the same pertains with respect to customary international law. Regarding treaties, recall *Reid v. Covert*, in Section 2 C 1. See JORDAN J. PAUST, INTERNATIONAL LAW AS LAW OF THE UNITED STATES 99, 123–24 n.1 (2 ed. 2003).

1. International Agreements

a. Treaties Conflicting With Statutes

COOK v. UNITED STATES

288 U.S. 102, 118–22 (1933).

BRANDEIS, J.

The main question for decision is whether § 581 of the Tariff Act of 1930, c. 497, 46 Stat. 590, 747, is modified, as applied to British vessels suspected of being engaged in smuggling liquors into the United States, by the Treaty between this country and Great Britain proclaimed May 22, 1924. (43 Stat. 1761.) That section—which is a reenactment in identical language of § 581 of the Tariff Act of 1922, c. 356, 42 Stat. 858, 979—declares that officers of the Coast Guard are authorized to stop and board any vessel at any place within four leagues (12 miles) of the coast of the United States "to examine the manifest and to inspect, search and examine" the vessel and any merchandise therein; and if it shall appear that any violation of any law of the United States has been committed by reason of which the vessel or merchandise is liable to forfeiture, it shall be the duty of such officers to seize the same.

On the evening of November 1, 1930, the British motor screw *Mazel Tov*—a vessel of speed not exceeding 10 miles an hour—was discovered by officers of the Coast Guard within four leagues of the coast of Massachusetts and was boarded by them at a point 11 ½ miles from the nearest land. The manifest was demanded and exhibited. Search followed, which disclosed that the only cargo on board, other than ship stores, was unmanifested intoxicating liquor which had been cleared from St. Pierre, a French possession. The vessel ostensibly bound for Nassau, a British possession, had, when boarded, been cruising off our coast with the intent that ultimately the liquor should be taken to the United States by other boats. But the evidence indicated that she did not intend to approach nearer than four leagues to our coast; and, so far as appeared, she had not been in communication with our shores and had not unladen any part of her cargo. The boarding officers seized the *Mazel Tov* at a point more than 10 miles from our coast; took her to the Port of Providence; and there delivered the vessel and cargo to the customs officials.

The Collector of Customs, acting pursuant to § 584 of the Tariff Act of 1930, assessed against Frank Cook, as master of the *Mazel Tov*, a penalty of $14,286.18 for failure to include the liquor in the manifest. By § 584, if merchandise not described in the manifest is found on board a vessel "bound to the United States," the master is subject to a penalty equal to its value, and the merchandise belonging or consigned to him is subject to forfeiture. By § 594, whenever a master becomes subject to a penalty, the vessel may be seized and proceeded against summarily by libel to recover the penalty. The Government proceeded, in the federal court for Rhode Island, to collect the assessed penalty by means of libels against both the cargo and the vessel. The cases were consolidated.

Cook, claiming as master and bailee of the vessel and as consignee and claimant of the cargo, alleged that the *Mazel Tov* was of British registry and owned by a Nova Scotia corporation. He answered to the merits; and excepted to the jurisdiction on the ground that the "vessel was not seized within the territorial limits of any jurisdiction of the United States, but, on the contrary, was captured and boarded at a point more than four (4) leagues from the coast," and that "it was not the intention at any time to enter any of the territorial limits of the United States."

The District Court, having found the facts above stated, dismissed the libels. 51 F.2d 292. The Government appealed to the Circuit Court of Appeals, which held that the Treaty did not "effect a change in the customs-revenue laws of the United States wherein Congress had fixed a four league protective zone"; reversed the judgments; and remanded the cases to the District Court for further proceedings. 56 F.2d 921. This Court granted certiorari.

Cook contends, among other things, that by reason of the Treaty between the United States and Great Britain proclaimed May 22, 1924 (43 Stat. 1761), the seizure was unlawful under the laws of the United States; that the authority conferred by § 581 of the Tariff Act of 1922 to board, search and seize within the four league limit, was, as respects British vessels, modified by the Treaty so as to substitute for four leagues from our coast, the distance which "can be traversed in one hour by the vessel suspected of endeavoring to commit the offense"; that Congress by re-enacting § 581 in the Tariff Act of 1930 intended to continue in force the modification effected by the Treaty; and, hence, that the *Mazel Tov*, being a British vessel of a speed not exceeding 10 miles an hour, could not be lawfully boarded, searched and seized at a distance of 11 ½ miles from the coast because suspected of "endeavoring to import or have imported alcoholic beverages into the United States in violation of the laws there in force."

The Government insists that the Treaty did not have the effect of so modifying § 581 of the Act of 1922; and that, if it did, the re-enactment of § 581 without change, by the Act of 1930, removed the alleged modification. It contends further that the validity of the seizure was not material; and if ever material had been waived.

The Treaty provides, among other things, as follows:

"Article I. The High Contracting Parties declare that it is their firm intention to uphold the principle that 3 marine miles extending from the coast line outwards and measured from low-water mark constitute the proper limits of territorial waters.

"Article II. (1) His Britannic Majesty agrees that he will raise no objection to the boarding of private vessels under the British flag outside the limits of territorial waters by the authorities of the United States, its territories or possessions in order that enquiries may be addressed to those on board and an examination be made of the ship's papers for the purpose of ascertaining whether the vessel or those on board are endeavoring to import or have imported alcoholic beverages into the United States, its territories or possessions in violation of the laws there in force. When such enquiries and examination show a reasonable ground for suspicion, a search of the vessel may be instituted.

"(2) If there is reasonable cause for belief that the vessel has committed or is committing or attempting to commit an offense against the laws of the United States, its territories or possessions prohibiting the importation of alcoholic beverages, the vessel may be seized and taken into a port of the United States, its territories or possessions for adjudication in accordance with such laws.

"(3) The rights conferred by this article shall not be exercised at a greater distance from the coast of the United States, its territories or possessions than can be traversed in one hour by the vessel suspected of endeavoring to commit the offense. In cases, however, in which the liquor is intended to be conveyed to the United States, its territories or possessions by a vessel other than the one boarded and searched, it shall be the speed of such other vessel and not the speed of the vessel boarded, which shall determine the distance from the coast at which the right under this article can be exercised."

We are of opinion that the decrees entered by the District Court should have been affirmed....

Second. The Treaty, being later in date than the Act of 1922, superseded, so far as inconsistent with the terms of the Act, the authority which had been conferred by § 581 upon officers of the Coast Guard to board, search and seize beyond our territorial waters. Whitney v. Robertson, 124 U.S. 190, 194. For in a strict sense the Treaty was self-executing, in that no legislation was necessary to authorize executive action pursuant to its provisions.

The purpose of the provisions for seizure in § 581, and their practical operation, as an aid in the enforcement of the laws prohibiting alcoholic liquors, leave no doubt that the territorial limitations there established were modified by the Treaty. This conclusion is supported by the course of administrative practice. Shortly after the Treaty took effect, the Treasury Department issued amended instructions for the

Coast Guard which pointed out, after reciting the provisions of § 581, that "in cases of special treaties, the provisions of those treaties shall be complied with"; and called attention particularly to the recent treaties dealing with the smuggling of intoxicating liquors. The Commandant of the Coast Guard, moreover, was informed in 1927, as the Solicitor General states, that all seizures of British vessels captured in the rum-smuggling trade should be within the terms of the Treaty and that seizing officers should be instructed to produce evidence, not that the vessel was found within the four-league limit, but that she was apprehended within one hour's sailing distance from the coast.

Third. The Treaty was not abrogated by re-enacting § 581 in the Tariff Act of 1930 in the identical terms of the Act of 1922. A treaty will not be deemed to have been abrogated or modified by a later statute unless such purpose on the part of Congress has been clearly expressed. Chew Heong v. United States, 112 U.S. 536; United States v. Payne, 264 U.S. 446, 448. Here, the contrary appears. The committee reports and the debates upon the Act of 1930, like the re-enacted section itself, make no reference to the Treaty of 1924. Any doubt as to the construction of the section should be deemed resolved by the consistent departmental practice existing before its reenactment. *Compare* United States v. G. Falk & Brother, 204 U.S. 143; Nagle v. Loi Hoa, 275 U.S. 475, 481; Brewster v. Gage, 280 U.S. 327, 337; McCaughn v. Hershey Chocolate Co., 283 U.S. 488, 492; United States v. Ryan, 284 U.S. 167, 175. No change, in this respect, was made either by the Department of the Treasury or the Department of Justice after the Tariff Act of 1930.

Searches and seizures in the enforcement of the laws prohibiting alcoholic liquors are governed, since the 1930 Act, as they were before, by the provisions of the Treaty. Section 581, with its scope narrowed by the Treaty, remained in force after its re-enactment in the Act of 1930. The section continued to apply to the boarding, search and seizure of all vessels of all countries with which we had no relevant treaties. It continued also, in the enforcement of our customs laws not related to the prohibition of alcoholic liquors, to govern the boarding of vessels of those countries with which we had entered into treaties like that with Great Britain.

Fourth. As the *Mazel Tov* was seized without warrant of law, the libels were properly dismissed. The Government contends that the alleged illegality of the seizure is immaterial. It argues that the facts proved show a violation of our law for which the penalty of forfeiture is prescribed; that the United States may, by filing a libel for forfeiture, ratify what otherwise would have been an illegal seizure; that the seized vessel having been brought into the Port of Providence, the federal court for Rhode Island acquired jurisdiction; and that, moreover, the claimant by answering to the merits waived any right to object to enforcement of the penalties. The argument rests upon misconceptions.

It is true that where the United States, having possession of property, files a libel to enforce a forfeiture resulting from a violation of its laws, the fact that the possession was acquired by a wrongful act is immaterial. Dodge v. United States, 272 U.S. 530, 532. *Compare* Ker v. Illinois, 119 U.S. 436, 444. The doctrine rests primarily upon the common-law rules that any person may, at his peril, seize property which has become forfeited to, or forfeitable by, the Government; and that proceedings by the Government to enforce a forfeiture ratify a seizure made by one without authority, since ratification is equivalent to antecedent delegation of authority to seize. Gelston v. Hoyt, 3 Wheat. 246, 310; Taylor v. United States, 3 How. 197, 205–206. The doctrine is not applicable here. The objection to the seizure is not that it was wrongful merely because made by one upon whom the Government had not conferred authority to seize at the place where the seizure was made. The objection is that the Government itself lacked power to seize, since by the Treaty it had imposed a territorial limitation upon its own authority. The Treaty fixes the conditions under which a "vessel may be seized and taken into a port of the United States, its territories or possessions for adjudication in accordance with" the applicable laws. Thereby, Great Britain agreed that adjudication may follow a rightful seizure. Our Government, lacking power to seize, lacked power, because of the Treaty, to subject the vessel to our laws. To hold that adjudication may follow a wrongful seizure would go far to nullify the purpose and effect of the Treaty. *Compare* United States v. Rauscher, 119 U.S. 407....

UNITED STATES v. THE PALESTINE LIBERATION ORGANIZATION

695 F.Supp. 1456 (S.D.N.Y.1988).

PALMIERI, J.

The Anti-terrorism Act of 1987 (the "ATA"), is the focal point of this lawsuit. At the center of controversy is the right of the Palestine Liberation Organization (the "PLO") to maintain its office in conjunction with its work as a Permanent Observer to the United Nations. The case comes before the court on the government's motion for an injunction closing this office and on the defendants' motions to dismiss.

The United Nations' Headquarters in New York were established as an international enclave by the Agreement Between the United States and the United Nations Regarding the Headquarters of the United Nations (the "Headquarters Agreement"). This agreement followed an invitation extended to the United Nations by the United States, one of its principal founders, to establish its seat within the United States....

The PLO ... [with a Permanent Observer Mission] ... is present at the United Nations as its invitee. See Headquarters Agreement, § 11, 61 Stat. at 761 (22 U.S.C. § 287 note). The PLO has none of the usual attributes of sovereignty. It is not accredited to the United States and does not have the benefits of diplomatic immunity. There is no recognized state it claims to govern. It purports to serve as the sole political representative of the Palestinian people. *See generally* Kassim, *The*

Palestine Liberation Organization Claim to Status: A Juridical Analysis Under International Law, 9 DEN. J. INT'L L. & POL. 1 (1980). The PLO nevertheless considers itself to be the representative of a state, entitled to recognition in its relations with other governments, and is said to have diplomatic relations with approximately one hundred countries throughout the world. *Id.* at 19.

In 1974, the United Nations invited the PLO to become an observer at the U.N., to "participate in the sessions and the work of the General Assembly in the capacity of observer." The right of its representatives to admission to the United States as well as access to the U.N. was immediately challenged under American law. Judge Costantino rejected that challenge in *Anti-Defamation League of B'nai B'rith v. Kissinger*, Civil Action No. 74 C 1545 (E.D.N.Y. November 1, 1974). The court upheld the presence of a PLO representative in New York with access to the United Nations, albeit under certain entrance visa restrictions which limited PLO personnel movements to a radius of 25 miles from Columbus Circle in Manhattan....

Since 1974, the PLO has continued to function without interruption as a permanent observer and has maintained its Mission to the United Nations without trammel, largely because of the Headquarters Agreement, which we discuss below....

[In 1987, Congress enacted] ... the ATA, 22 U.S.C. § 5201–5203. It is of a unique nature. We have been unable to find any comparable statute in the long history of Congressional enactments. The PLO is stated to be "a terrorist organization and a threat to the interests of the United States, its allies, and to international law and should not benefit from operating in the United States." 22 U.S.C. § 5201(b)....

The ATA, which became effective on March 21, 1988, forbids the establishment or maintenance of "an office, headquarters, premises, or other facilities or establishments within the jurisdiction of the United States at the behest or direction of, or with funds provided by" the PLO, if the purpose is to further the PLO's interests. 22 U.S.C. § 5202(3). The ATA also forbids spending the PLO's funds or receiving anything of value except informational material from the PLO, with the same mens rea requirement. *Id.* §§ 5202(1) and (2)....

The United States commenced this lawsuit the day the ATA took effect, seeking injunctive relief to accomplish the closure of the Mission. The United States Attorney for this District has personally represented that no action would be taken to enforce the ATA pending resolution of the litigation in this court....

If the ATA were construed as the government suggests, it would be tantamount to a direction to the PLO Observer Mission at the United Nations that it close its doors and cease its operations *instanter*. Such an interpretation would fly in the face of the Headquarters Agreement, a prior treaty between the United Nations and the United States, and would abruptly terminate the functions the Mission has performed for many years. This conflict requires the court to seek out a reconciliation between the two.

Under our constitutional system, statutes and treaties are both the supreme law of the land, and the Constitution sets forth no order of precedence to differentiate between them. U.S. Const. art. VI, cl. 2. Wherever possible, both are to be given effect. *E.g.*, Trans World Airlines, Inc. v. Franklin Mint Corp., 466 U.S. 243, 252 ... (1984); Weinberger v. Rossi, 456 U.S. 25, 32 ... (1982); Washington v. Washington State Commercial Passenger Fishing Vessel Association, 443 U.S. 658, 690 ... , *modified*, 444 U.S. 816 ... (1979); McCulloch v. Sociedad Nacional de Marineros de Honduras, 372 U.S. 10, 21–22 ... (1963); Clark v. Allen, *supra*, 331 U.S. at 510–11; Chew Heong v. United States, 112 U.S. 536, 550 ... (1884). Only where a treaty is irreconcilable with a later enacted statute and Congress has clearly evinced an intent to supersede a treaty by enacting a statute does the later enacted statute take precedence. *E.g.* The Chinese Exclusion Case, *supra*, 130 U.S. at 599–602 (finding clear intent to supersede); Edye v. Robertson (The Head Money Cases), 112 U.S. 580, 597–99 ... (1884) (same, decided on the same day as *Chew Heong*, *supra*, which found no such intent); South African Airways v. Dole, ... 817 F.2d 119, 121, 125–26 (D.C.Cir.) (Anti-Apartheid Act of 1986, directing the Secretary of State to "terminate the Agreement Between the United States of America and the Government of the Union of South Africa" irreconcilable with that treaty), *cert. denied*, 484 U.S. 896 ... (1987); Diggs v. Shultz, ... 470 F.2d 461, 466 (D.C.Cir.1972), *cert. denied*, 411 U.S. 931 ... (1973). *Compare* Menominee Tribe of Indians v. United States, 391 U.S. 404, 413 ... (1968) (finding no clear intent to abrogate treaty); McCulloch v. Sociedad de Marineros, *supra*, 372 U.S. at 21–22 (same); Cook v. United States, 288 U.S. 102, 119–20 ... (1933) (same).

... [U]nless ... [congressional power to override a treaty] is clearly and unequivocally exercised, this court is under a duty to interpret statutes in a manner consonant with existing treaty obligations. This is a rule of statutory construction sustained by an unbroken line of authority for over a century and a half.... [The then court cited most of the previously cited cases and quoted § 115 (1) (a) of the Restatement.]

We believe the ATA and the Headquarters Agreement cannot be reconciled except by finding the ATA inapplicable to the PLO Observer Mission....

The principles enunciated and applied in *Chew Heong* and its progeny.... require the clearest of expressions on the part of Congress. We are constrained by these decisions to stress the lack of clarity in Congress' action in this instance. Congress' failure to speak with one clear voice on this subject requires us to interpret the ATA as inapplicable to the Headquarters Agreement. This is so, in short, for the reasons which follow.

First, neither the Mission nor the Headquarters Agreement is mentioned in the ATA itself. Such an inclusion would have left no doubt as to Congress' intent on a matter which had been raised repeatedly with respect to this act, and its absence here reflects equivocation and avoidance, leaving the court without clear interpretive guidance in the language of the act. Second, ... the ATA ... does not purport to apply notwithstanding any treaty. The absence of that interpretive instruction is especially relevant because elsewhere in the same legislation Congress expressly referred to "United States law (including any treaty)." 101 Stat. at 1343.... Third, no member of Congress expressed a clear and unequivocal intent to supersede the Headquarters Agreement by passage of the ATA. In contrast, most who addressed the subject of conflict denied that there would be a conflict: in their view, the Headquarters Agreement did not provide the PLO with any right to maintain an office. Here again, Congress provided no guidance for the interpretation of the ATA in the event of a conflict which was clearly foreseeable....

The Permanent Observer Mission to the United Nations is nowhere mentioned in haec verba in this act, as we have already observed. It is nevertheless contended by the United States that the foregoing provision requires the closing of the Mission, and this in spite of possibly inconsistent international obligations. According to the government, the act is so clear that this possibility is nonexistent. The government argues that its position is supported by the provision that the ATA would take effect "notwithstanding any provision of law to the contrary," 22 U.S.C. § 5202(3), suggesting that Congress thereby swept away any inconsistent international obligations of the United States. In effect, the government urges literal application of the maxim that in the event of conflict between two laws, the one of later date will prevail: *leges posteriores priores contrarias abrogant.*

We cannot agree.... There were conflicting voices both in Congress and in the executive branch before the enactment of the ATA. Indeed, there is only one matter with respect to which there was unanimity—the condemnation of terrorism. This, however, is extraneous to the legal issues involved here. At oral argument, the United States Attorney conceded that there was no evidence before the court that the Mission had misused its position at the United Nations or engaged in any covert actions in furtherance of terrorism....

Jordan J. Paust, International Law as Law of the United States 82–88, 99 (1996), 100–107 (2 ed. 2003)

The Supremacy Clause of the U.S. Constitution is generally silent on these matters [of conflict], declaring merely: "This Constitution, and the Laws of the United States which shall be made in Pursuance thereof; and all Treaties made, or which shall be made, under the Authority of the United States, shall be the supreme Law of the land...." In 1788, one of our Founders declared that treaties are "paramount to an ordinary act of legislation," and John Jay stated in *The Federalist* that treaties are "just as far beyond the lawful reach of legislative acts now, as they will be at any future period...." However, the notion that all treaties always prevail domestically over federal legislation has not been accepted by the judiciary. Indeed, nearly one hundred years later the U.S. Supreme Court declared that a treaty is not "irrepealable or unchangeable" and added:

> The constitution gives it no superiority over an act of Congress in this respect, which may be repealed or modified by an act of a later date. Nor is there anything in its essential character, or in the branches of the government by which the treaty is made, which gives it this superior sanctity. [Edye v. Robertson, 112 U.S. 580, 599 (1884)]

This latter view generally prevails and the courts now accept the approach as extended and set forth four years later by the Supreme Court in *Whitney v. Robertson* [124 U.S. 190 (1888)]:

> Congress may modify such provisions, so far as they bind the United States, or supersede them altogether. By the Constitution a treaty is placed on the same footing, and made of like obligation, with an act of legislation. Both are declared by that instrument to be the supreme law of the land, and no superior efficacy is given to either over the other. When the two relate to the same subject, the courts will always endeavor to construe them so as to give effect to both, if that can be done without violating the language of either; but if the two are inconsistent, the one last in date will control the other. . . .

The opinion of the Court, per Justice Field, added a requirement that the relevant provision of a treaty be self-executing for such a direct effect on federal law to occur. Although there was some precedent for such a qualification of the last in time rule, the notion that a treaty must be self-executing in order to supersede U.S. federal law appears in only eight Supreme Court cases, none of which were decided after 1913. Moreover, it is absent from thirty-five other Supreme Court cases addressing the last in time rule, and it is patently inconsistent with the text of the Constitution and the evident intent of the Framers. With such a severely limited articulation of the requirement that treaties not directly supplant congressional legislation unless they are self-executing, one might question whether such a requirement has been accepted by the majority of Supreme Court justices in the twentieth century. In any event, it is sufficient to note that treaties can affect domestic law, at least indirectly, whether or not they are self-executing. They may even be used as aids in interpreting the Constitution, and may thereby influence domestic law at the expense of a congressional enactment that is found to be inconsistent with the Constitution. In this sense, one can speak of an exception to the last in time rule (the indirect incorporation exception) that operates primarily on the recognized supremacy of the Constitution. Moreover, there are other exceptions.

B. The Executed or Vested Exception

Although too little known today, within the line of cases affirming the propriety of the last in time rule there are recognitions of possible exceptions to the rule or limits on its full operation. One might refer to these cases as "last in time cases." As a group, they serve to establish what may be called the "executed or vested" exception to the rule and they generally recognize a particular application of such an exception to property rights. In addition, there is arguably a separate line of cases not mentioning the last in time rule, but necessarily posing an exception thereto (the "rights under treaties exception"), an exception that is arguably consistent with the "last in time" cases.

The first of the federal "last in time" cases to recognize an exception seems to have been the case of *In re Ah Ping* [23 F. 329 (C.C.D.Cal. 1885)], a lower federal court case decided in 1885. The court recognized that an alien had a "vested right" under a treaty and construed a subsequent congressional act so as not to interfere with that right or, as the court declared, so as not "to cut off this right ... to work this wrong." The opinion did not pose a clear exception to the last in time rule however, because it next quoted a relevant Supreme Court statement that courts should "refuse to give to statutes a retrospective operation[,] whereby rights previously vested are injuriously affected, unless compelled to do so by ... the legislature." The intimation, then, was that rights previously vested could be injuriously affected.

Three years later, the Supreme Court seemed to recognize what might be a related exception. In *Whitney v. Robertson*, the Court stated that when a subsequent congressional act is clear, "its validity cannot be assailed before the courts for want of conformity to stipulations of a previous treaty not already executed." The intimation was that a treaty provision previously executed could not be injuriously affected. That same year, in the lower federal courts, such an intimation was expressed far more openly. In *In re Chae Chan Ping* [36 F. 431 (C.C.N.D.Cal. 1888)], the circuit court was faced with claims that subsequent legislation (1) could not divest a right indefeasibly vested, and (2) that otherwise the legislation would be impermissible as an *ex post facto* law. In response, the circuit court ruled that the *ex post facto* prohibition did not apply where an alien was merely being excluded and where there was no "offense ... punishment or ... penalty" involved, an approach that is generally accepted but which has been questioned where individual rights are at stake. It also ruled that the right claimed under a treaty was not a "vested" right, adding:

> Some rights *accrue* and become indefeasibly *vested* by covenants or stipulations that have ceased to be executory and have become fully *executed*, as in the case of title to property acquired thereunder. But we do not regard the privilege of going and coming from one country to another as of this class of rights. The being here with a right of remaining is one thing, but voluntarily going away with a right at the time to return is quite another. [*Id.* at 434.]

With this decision, arguably one has the first recognition of what might be termed the "executed or vested" exception to the last in time rule.

While affirming the lower court in *Chae Chan Ping*, the Supreme Court apparently recognized the "executed or vested" exception, declaring:

> Of course, whatever of a permanent character had been *executed* or *vested* under the treaties was not affected by [subsequent legislation]. In that respect the abrogation of the obligations of a treaty operates, like the repeal of a law, only upon the future, leaving transactions executed under it to stand unaffected. [130 U.S. 581, 601–02 (1889)]

Thus, the Court also recognized the prohibition of an "ex post facto" result with respect to "executed or vested" rights; but, of course, what is a recognizably "vested" right might be subject to a certain amount of judicial manipulation.

In the Court's opinion in *Chae Chan Ping*, Justice Field also declared that a distinction exists "[b]etween property rights not affected by the termination or abrogation of a treaty, and expectations of benefits from the continuance of existing legislation," adding:

> The rights and interests created by a treaty, which have become so vested that its expiration or abrogation will not destroy or impair them, are such as are connected with and lie in property, capable of sale and transfer or other disposition, not such as are personal and untransferable in their character. [*Id.* at 609.]

Four years later, in 1893, Justice Field's statements were quoted by Justice Gray in *Fong Yue Ting* [149 U.S. 698, 722–23 (1893)]. "In view of that decision," Justice Gray added, "it appears to be impossible to hold that a Chinese laborer acquired, under any of the [relevant] treaties ... any right ... to be and remain in this country, except by the license, permission, and sufferance of Congress...."

From the "last in time" line of cases, it appears that an exception to the last in time rule exists where rights under a treaty are "executed or vested." Justice Field, however, would not have applied such an exception to rights that "are personal and untransferable," and Justice Gray in *Fong Yue Ting* apparently felt that the Chinese laborer in question had no right under any relevant treaty to be and remain in the United States. In *Fong Yue Ting*, the human right recognized in a treaty with China was merely a right to change one's home and allegiance; it was not a right to live in the United States without congressional approval. It certainly is not clear whether the human right at stake was thought to be "personal," however transferable such right might be. In the sense used, it is arguable that human rights are not "personal" but apply generally to each person and are thus "transferable" to all (or are, in a sense, "intertransferable") and are to be enjoyed by all. Further, in the context of *In re Chae Chan Ping* the word "personal" undoubtedly related to the personal certificate issued to Chae Chan Ping by the collector of customs of the port of San Francisco, a certificate that he thought would guarantee a vested right of reentry but which was found to have been annulled and made void by subsequent legislation and which granted "no rights ... beyond what is secured ... by the treaties" in question. The lower court added:

> Instead of enlarging ... [his] rights, the acts of congress are restrictive in character, and the restrictions were adopted in pursuance of the agreement allowing such restriction in the last treaty. The certificates are mere instruments of evidence, issued to afford convenient proof of the identity of the party entitled to enjoy the privileges secured by the treaties.... The ... certificates provided ... are, simply, sovereign commands and prohibitions, to which the Chinese laborers affected were compelled to submit, willing or unwilling.

C. The Rights Under Treaties Exception

Another line of Supreme Court cases, beginning in 1835, but decided mostly in the latter part of the nineteenth century, presents what one might term the "rights under treaties" exception to the last in time rule. Although the language in several cases is broad, applying to all "rights under treaties," each of these cases involves a right to property located within the United States and guaranteed or conferred by a treaty. In this sense, each case is arguably consistent with the above-noted cases establishing the "executed or vested" exception and recognizing a particular application of such an exception to property rights. It is interesting, however, that although many of these cases were decided in the same general time period, apparently neither set of cases contains cites to the other that are on point. Thus, they are arguably separate lines of cases posing separate exceptions.

The broadest language to be found in this last line of cases is that from Justice Clifford's opinion in *Holden v. Joy*:

> Congress has no constitutional power to settle or interfere with rights under treaties, except in cases purely political. [84 U.S. (17 Wall.) 211, 247 (1872)]

What this language necessarily implies is that a subsequent act of Congress cannot "interfere with rights under treaties, except in cases purely political" and, thus, that such rights remain as rights unaffected by subsequent congressional enactments. Necessarily there is a "rights under treaties" exception to the last in time rule.

Five years earlier, in 1867, Justice Grier made similar statements in two cases involving title to land. In *Reichart v. Felps*, he declared:

> Congress is bound to regard the public treaties, and it had no power to organize a board of revision to nullify titles confirmed many years before.... [73 U.S. (6 Wall.) 160, 165–66 (1867)]

In *Wilson v. Wall*, he stated that the government "cannot affect titles before given" and that "Congress has no constitutional power to settle the rights under treaties except in cases purely political," adding: "[t]he construction of them is the peculiar province of the judiciary."

In the earliest decision of this line of cases, the Supreme Court recognized that treaties with Indians acknowledging rights of property were binding upon the King of Great Britain and that "rights secured by a treaty" could not be annulled by the King's proclamation, adding later:

> When [the United States] acquired and took possession of the Floridas, these treaties remained in force ... and were binding on the United States, by the obligation they had assumed by the Louisiana Treaty, as a supreme law of the land, *which was inviolable by the power of Congress*. [Mitchel v. United States, 34 U.S. (9 Pet.) 711, 749, 755 (1835)]

Most of these cases were cited finally by Justice Gray in 1899 in support of the Court's ruling that with title to a strip of land "having been granted ... by the treaty itself," rights thereunder "could not be divested by any subsequent action of ... Congress, or of the Executive Departments," adding:

> The construction of treaties is the peculiar province of the judiciary; and, except in cases purely political, Congress has no constitutional power to settle the rights under a treaty, or to affect titles already granted by the treaty itself. [Jones v. Meehan, 175 U.S. 1, 32 (1899)]

Subsequent congressional action, the Court ruled, "must therefore be held to be of no effect upon the rights previously acquired...." Importantly for the protection of fundamental human rights, there have been no qualifications of the "rights under a treaty" exception such as those purported by Justice Field with respect to the "executed or vested" exception. Importantly also, human rights guaranteed in a human rights treaty are certainly "rights under a treaty" and Congress should have no power to "interfere with" such rights, "except in cases purely political."

D. Prior Rights and Extinguished Treaties

More generally, where a treaty might have been terminated by war as opposed to an act of Congress, the Supreme Court also noted early in our history that "the termination of a treaty cannot devest rights of property already vested under it," adding:

> If real estate be purchased or secured under a treaty, it would be most mischievous to admit, that the extinguishment of the treaty extinguished the right to such estate. In truth, it no more affects such rights, than the repeal of a municipal law affects rights acquired under it. [The Society for the Propagation of the Gospel in Foreign Parts v. New Haven, 21 U.S. (8 Wheat.) 464, 493 (1823)]

Interestingly, this case was prior to all of the others thus far considered. However, although not mentioned in any case until *Chae Chan Ping*, it might fit easily with the "executed or vested" line of cases even though the words used were "purchased or secured" and "rights acquired." If so, when rights are "secured" or "acquired" under a treaty, one might consider them "vested" and one might speak of a rights "executed, purchased, vested, secured or acquired" exception; but, for convenience, the exceptions will be kept separate.

E. The War Powers Exception

From the above, one can identify three exceptions to the last in time rule: (1) the indirect incorporation exception, (2) the "executed or vested" exception, and (3) the "rights under treaties" exception. A fourth exception was recognized by Justice Field in 1870 and may be termed the war powers exception. While dissenting in *Miller v. United States* [78 U.S. (11 Wall.) 268, 314 (1870)], Justice Field affirmed an expectation that otherwise went unchallenged. He recognized that "legislation founded [on] the war powers" is subject to "limitations ... imposed by the law of nations," adding: "The power to prosecute war ... is a power to prosecute war according to the law of nations, and not in violation of that law. The power to make rules ... is ... subject to the condition that they are within the law of nations. There is a limit ... imposed by the law of nations, and [it] is no less binding upon Congress than if the limitation were written in the Constitution." [*Id.* at 315–16.]

Thus, according to Justice Field, the law of nations would necessarily prevail in case of a clash with inconsistent legislation. Since the law of nations included both treaties and custom, Justice Field's recognition is relevant to questions concerning the primacy of treaties and actually poses another exception to the last in time rule, one where war powers are involved and a treaty is inconsistent with a subsequent statute. In such a circumstance, the treaty should prevail. Further, the war power happens to be among those most obviously related to international law and international relations. If a direct relationship between a congressional power, international law and international relations becomes an important criterion, the Court might follow the lead of Justice Field and recognize that similar limitations exist on congressional powers to regulate foreign commerce, to regulate naturalization and immigration, and to define and punish piracies and felonies committed on the high seas and offenses against the law of nations. The relationship in these instances, at least, is no less obvious. It happens also that most of the laws of war are humanitarian in purpose and effect; and most are of a higher status under international law as *obligatio erga omnes* (*i.e.*, obligations not of an ordinary nature, but owing by and to all humankind regardless of noncompliance by an enemy). Such a higher status under international law might compel recognition of a higher status under domestic law, as noted also at the end of the next section.

The war powers exception also finds support in an opinion of the Attorney General written five years earlier [11 Op. Att'y Gen. 297, 299–300 (1865)], in an 1800 opinion of Justice Chase [Bas v. Tingy, 4 U.S. (4 Dall.) 37, 43 (1800)], as well as in subsequent Supreme Court opinions by Justice Sutherland, who in one such opinion declared, as if to affirm Justice Field's recognized limitation on congressional power: "From its very nature, the war power ... tolerates no qualifications or *limitations*, unless *found in* the Constitution or in *applicable principles of international law*." [283 U.S. 605, 622 (1931); also recall United States v. Curtiss–Wright Export Co., 299 U.S. 304 at 318 (1936) (Sutherland, J.)]

Necessarily then, international law imposes limitations on or creates exceptions to that power. . . .

Appendix

Recommended Restatement of the Restatement (Third)

. . .

§ 115. Inconsistency Between International Law or Agreement and Domestic Law: Law of the United States

(1) (a) An Act of Congress supersedes a preexisting rule of international law or a provision of an international agreement as domestic law of the United States if: (1) the legislation is last in time, (2) the legislation is unavoidably inconsistent, (3) the purpose of the Act to supersede the earlier rule or provision is clear and unequivocal, (4) the legislation is not unconstitutional (for example, as an impermissible infringement on the constitutional separation of powers or an amendment to the Constitution), and (5) none of the following exceptions to the last in time rule apply:

(i) the earlier rule or provision has achieved constitutional status (directly or indirectly),

(ii) the earlier rule or provision has been executed with respect to the matter in issue or has produced a vested right that is in issue,

(iii) the earlier provision has established a "right under a treaty", or

(iv) Congress is acting under the war power [or the laws of war apply].

(b) A new or continuing rule of customary international law has priority domestically over any inconsistent domestic law except the U.S. Constitution. This should especially be so with respect to *obligatio erga omnes* and *jus cogens* norms. . . .

Notes and Questions

1. Prior to *Edye* (1884) and *Whitney* (1888), it was uncertain whether the Chinese Exclusion Acts would prevail over a prior treaty between the United States and China, and two presidents had vetoed some of the Acts on the ground that the treaty must prevail. *See, e.g.*, Veto Message of Pres. Rutherford B. Hayes, Mar. 1, 1879, 8 Cong. Rec. 2275; Veto Message of Pres. Chester A. Arthur, Apr. 2, 1882, 13 Cong. Rec. 2551.

2. In a case addressing a 1924 Immigration Act and the denial of admission to the U.S. of wives and children of resident Chinese merchants who entered for purposes of trade and commerce under the 1880 U.S.—China treaty, the Supreme Court ruled in favor of the wives and children stating: "[t]hat Act must be construed with the view to preserve the treaty rights unless clearly annulled, and we cannot conclude that, considering its history, the general terms therein disclose a congressional intent absolutely

to exclude the petitioners from entry." Cheung Sum Shee v. Nagle, 268 U.S. 336, 345–46 (1925).

3. Consider Article 4(1) of the American Convention on Human Rights (not yet ratified by the U.S.) and Article 4 of the International Convention on the Elimination of All Forms of Racial Discrimination (ratified by the U.S. in 1994). Do they raise issues concerning present interpretations of the U.S. Constitution? Are treaties useful for interpreting and reinterpreting the Constitution?

In case of an unavoidable clash between either convention's Article 4 and a prior federal statute, which prevails domestically? In case of such a clash with a federal statute enacted after ratification of the treaty, which prevails? Would exceptions to the last-in-time rule be applicable? Assuming that both treaties are ratified, is it possible for those opposed to abortion or racist speech and organizations to have their preferences guaranteed through time as a matter of domestic U.S. law?

4. Should a treaty have to be self-executing to supersede a federal statute as law of the United States with respect to conduct, duties, or competencies here and abroad? Can the Executive execute a non-self-executing treaty? See U.S. Const., art. II, § 3.

b. Executive Agreements Conflicting With Statutes

UNITED STATES v. GUY W. CAPPS, INC.

204 F.2d 655 (4th Cir.1953), *aff'd on other gds.*, 348 U.S. 296 (1955).

PARKER, J.

This is an appeal by the United States from a judgment entered on a verdict directed for the defendant, Guy W. Capps, in an action instituted to recover damages alleged to have been sustained by the United States as the result of alleged breach by defendant of a contract with respect to the importation of seed potatoes from Canada. The District Court denied a motion to dismiss the action. United States v. Guy W. Capps, Inc., 100 F. Supp. 30. Upon the subsequent trial, however, the court directed a verdict and entered judgment for defendant on the ground that there was no sufficient showing of breach of contract or damage to the United States.

The contract sued on has relation to the potato price support program of 1948 and the executive agreement entered into between Canada and the United States through the Canadian Ambassador and the Acting Secretary of State of the United States. Pursuant to the Agricultural Act of 1948, Public Law 897, 80th Cong. 2d Sess., 62 Stat. 1247, the United States committed itself to purchase from eligible potato growers, directly or through dealers, all table stock and seed potatoes that could not be sold commercially at a parity price. The purchase and disposal of potatoes under this program was carried out by the Commodity Credit Corporation. In a manifest attempt to protect the American Potato Market in which this price support program was operating from an influx of Canadian grown potatoes, the Acting Secretary of State of the United States, on November 23, 1948, entered into an executive agreement with the Canadian Ambassador, who was acting for the Canadian Government, to the effect that the Canadian Government would place potatoes in the list of commodities for which export permits were required and that export permits would be granted therefor only to Canadian exporters who could give evidence that they had firm orders from legitimate United States users of Canadian seed potatoes and that "Canadian exporters would also be required to have included in any contract into which they might enter with a United States seed potato importer a clause in which the importer would give an assurance that the potatoes would not be diverted or reconsigned for table stock purposes". In consideration of this agreement on the part of the Canadian Government, the United States Government undertook that it would not impose "any quantitative limitations or fees on Canadian potatoes of the 1948 crop exported to the United States" under the system of regulating the movement of potatoes to the United States outlined in the Canadian proposal and would not consider the Canadian Government's guarantee of a floor price with respect to certain potatoes to be the payment of a bounty or grant and would not levy any countervailing duty on such potatoes under the provisions of section 303 of the Tariff Act of 1930. On November 26, 1948, the Canadian Privy Council added potatoes to the list of products under export permit control and exporters of seed potatoes to the United States could not secure an export permit without complying with the condition required by the executive agreement.

Defendant, a corporation engaged in business in Norfolk, Virginia, entered into a contract in December 1948 with H. B. Willis, Inc., a Canadian exporter, to purchase 48,544 sacks of Canadian seed potatoes, containing 100 lbs. each, to be shipped on the S. S. Empire Gangway docking in Jacksonville, Florida, in January 1949. Defendant's officers admittedly knew of the agreement with Canada and stated in a telegram to an official of the United States Department of Agriculture that the potatoes were being brought in for seed purposes. Defendant sent a telegram to the exporter in Canada on the same day that the potatoes were billed stating that they were for planting in Florida and Georgia. Defendant sold the potatoes while in shipment to the Atlantic Commission Company, a wholly owned agency of Great Atlantic & Pacific Tea Company, a retail grocery organization. No attempt was made to restrict their sale so that they would be used for seed and not for food, and there is evidence from which the jury could properly have drawn the conclusion that they were sold on the market as food displacing potatoes grown in this country and causing damage to the United States by requiring greater purchases of American grown potatoes in aid of the price support program than would have been necessary in the absence of their importation.

On these facts we think that judgment was properly entered for the defendant, but for reasons other than those given by the District Court. We have little difficulty in seeing in the evidence breach of contract on the part of defendant and damage resulting to the United States from the breach. We think, however, that the executive agreement was void because it was not authorized by Congress and contravened provisions of a statute dealing with the very matter to which it related and that the contract relied on, which was based on the executive agreement, was unenforceable in the courts of the United States for like reason. We think, also, that no action can be maintained by the government to recover damages on account of what is essentially a breach of a trade regulation, in the absence of express authorization by Congress. The power to regulate foreign commerce is vested in Congress, not in the executive or the courts; and the executive may not exercise the power by entering into executive agreements and suing in the courts for damages resulting from breaches of contracts made on the basis of such agreements.

In the Agricultural Act of 1948, Congress had legislated specifically with respect to the limitations which might be imposed on imports if it was thought that they would render ineffective or materially interfere with any program or operation undertaken pursuant to that act. . . .

There was no pretense of complying with the requirements of this statute. The President did not cause an investigation to be made by the Tariff Commission, the Commission did not conduct an investigation or make findings or recommendations, and the President made no findings of fact and issued no proclamation imposing quantitative limitations and determined no representative period for the application of the 50% limitation contained in the proviso. All that occurred in the making of this executive agreement, the effect of which was to exclude entirely a food product of a foreign country from importation into the United States, was an exchange of correspondence between the Acting Secretary of State and the Canadian Ambassador. Since the purpose of the agreement as well as its effect was to bar imports which would interfere with the Agricultural Adjustment program, it was necessary that the provisions of this statute be complied with and an executive agreement excluding such imports which failed to comply with it was void. Morgan v. United States, 304 U.S. 1 . . . ; Panama Refining Co. v. Ryan, 293 U.S. 388. . . . As was said by Chief Justice Hughes in the case last cited: "We are not dealing with action which, appropriately belonging to the executive province, is not the subject of judicial review or with the presumptions attaching to executive action. . . . we are concerned with the question of the delegation of legislative power. . . ."

It is argued, however, that the validity of the executive agreement was not dependent upon the Act of Congress but was made pursuant to the inherent powers of the President under the Constitution. The answer is that while the President has certain inherent powers under the Constitution such as the power pertaining to his position as Commander in Chief of Army and Navy and the power necessary to see that the laws are faithfully executed, the power to regulate interstate and foreign commerce is not among the powers incident to the Presidential office, but is expressly vested by the Constitution in the Congress. It cannot be upheld as an exercise of the power to see that the laws are faithfully executed, for, as said by Mr. Justice Holmes in his dissenting opinion in Myers v. United States, 272 U.S. 52, 177 . . . , "The duty of the President to see that the laws be executed is a duty that does not go beyond the laws or require him to achieve more than Congress sees fit to leave within his power". . . .

We think that whatever the power of the executive with respect to making executive trade agreements regulating foreign commerce in the absence of action by Congress, it is clear that the executive may not through entering into such an agreement avoid complying with a regulation prescribed by Congress. Imports from a foreign county are foreign commerce subject to regulation, so far as this county is concerned, by Congress alone. The executive may not by-pass congressional limitations regulating such commerce by entering into an agreement with the foreign county that the regulation be exercised by that county through its control over exports. Even though the regulation prescribed by the executive agreement be more desirable than that prescribed by Congressional action, it is the latter which must be accepted as the expression of national policy.

It is argued that irrespective of the validity of the executive agreement, the contract sued on was a valid contract between defendant and the Canadian exporter and that since the contract was made for the benefit of the United States, this country may maintain action upon it. The answer is that the contract was but the carrying out of the executive agreement entered into in contravention of the policy declared by Congress; and the courts of the United States will not lend their aid to enforcing it against the public policy of the country so declared. As stated, the regulation of imports from foreign countries is a matter for Congress and, when Congress has acted, the executive may not enforce different regulations by suing on contracts made with reference thereto. . . .

SOUTH AFRICAN AIRWAYS v. DOLE

817 F.2d 119 (D.C.Cir.1987).

BUCKLEY, J.

Petitioner South African Airways ("SAA") asks this court to set aside an order issued on October 31, 1986 by the Secretary of Transportation revoking its permit to provide air service between the United States and South Africa. The order was issued pursuant to section 306(a) of the Comprehensive Anti–Apartheid Act of 1986, which directed the revocation of the right of any designee of the South African government to provide air service pursuant to the terms of an executive agreement between the United States and South Africa dated May 23, 1947 ("Agreement").

Petitioner challenges the Secretary of Transportation's order on the principal grounds that as the immediate revocation of its permit was neither allowed by the Agreement (which remains in effect at least until October 1987) nor required by the Anti–Apartheid Act, the order violates both a provision of the Federal Aviation Act directing the Secretary of Transportation to observe international agreements and Supreme Court precedent requiring that statutes and executive agreements be interpreted, where possible, so as to give effect to both.

We reject these arguments because we conclude that Congress intended the immediate suspension of the rights enjoyed by SAA pursuant to the Agreement. As Congress has authority to "regulate Commerce with foreign Nations" and to "make all Laws which shall be necessary" for the exercise of that authority, section 306(a) of the Act overrides any provision of the Agreement or of the Federal Aviation Act with which it may be inconsistent.

In October 1986, Congress enacted the Comprehensive Anti–Apartheid Act of 1986, Pub. L. No. 99–440, 100 Stat. 1086 ("Anti–Apartheid Act" or "Act"). Section 306(b)(1) of the Act directs the Secretary of State to "terminate the Agreement Between the Government of the United States of America and the Government of the Union of South Africa Relating to Air Services Between Their Respective Territories, signed May 23, 1947, in accordance with the provisions of that agreement." Article XI of the Agreement provides for its termination upon one year's notice given by either party. Agreement, 61 Stat. at 3061. The Agreement also specifies limited conditions under which permits issued pursuant to the Agreement may be revoked. Agreement, art. VI, 61 Stat. at 3059–60. Section 306(a)(2) of the Act, which was offered in the Senate as a floor amendment [the Sarbanes amendment], provides:

> Ten days after the enactment of this Act, the President shall direct the Secretary of Transportation to revoke the right of any air carrier designated by the Government of South Africa under the Agreement to provide service pursuant to the Agreement.

On October 10, 1986, the Secretary of State delivered the one-year termination notice to the South African Ambassador, and seventeen days later the President issued Executive Order 12,571 directing the Secretary of Transportation ("Secretary") to take the steps specified in section 306(a)(2) of the Act. Exec. Order No. 12,571, 51 Fed. Reg. 39,505 (1986). The Secretary thereupon issued Department of Transportation ("DOT") Final Order 86–11–29 ("Final Order") in which she initiated the steps required to effect an immediate revocation of South African Airways' permit. As required by section 801(a) of the Federal Aviation Act of 1958 ("Aviation Act"), 49 U.S.C. App. § 1461(a) (1982), the Final Order was transmitted to the President for review, at which point he could have exercised his prerogative under that section to disapprove the Final Order on foreign policy or national security grounds. He declined to do so, and SAA's permit was accordingly revoked effective November 16, 1986.

SAA challenges the Secretary's action as not required by the Act, as in violation of the Agreement, and consequently, both in conflict with

Supreme Court precedent and illegal under section 1102(a) of the Aviation Act, which provides:

> In exercising and performing their powers and duties under this chapter, the [Civil Aeronautics] Board and the Secretary of Transportation shall do so consistently with any obligation assumed by the United States in any treaty, convention, or agreement that may be in force between the United States and any foreign country....

49 U.S.C. App. § 1502(a) (1982)....

... "The courts have the authority to construe treaties and executive agreements, and it goes without saying that interpreting congressional legislation is a recurring and accepted task for the federal courts." Japan Whaling Ass'n v. American Cetacean Soc'y, 478 U.S. 221 ... (1986) (construing *Baker v. Carr* [369 U.S. at 211 (1962)]).

It is clear that we have the competence to interpret the meaning of section 306(a)(2) of the Anti–Apartheid Act and to assess its intended impact on the permit granted SAA pursuant to the Agreement....

We now address petitioner's principal argument; namely, that because section 306(a)(2) does not require the immediate revocation of SAA's permit, and because such a revocation violates provisions of the Agreement, the Secretary is required both by Supreme Court precedent, Murray v. The Schooner Charming Betsy, 6 U.S. (2 Cranch) 64, 118 ... (1804) ("An act of congress ought never to be construed to violate the law of nations if any other possible construction remains...."), and by section 1102(a) of the Aviation Act to adopt an interpretation of section 306(a) that does not conflict with the provisions of the Agreement. Petitioner's argument may be broken down into three distinct claims: (1) immediate revocation is not required by the Act; (2) as immediate revocation entails a violation of the Agreement, such a revocation is impermissible under the applicable principle of statutory construction; and (3) the Secretary is bound by section 1102 of the Aviation Act to construe section 306(a)(2) consistently with the permit revocation provisions of the Agreement....

SAA argues that notwithstanding the evident meaning of section 306 and its legislative history, Supreme Court precedent nevertheless requires that it be construed in a manner that will not require the United States to violate its obligations under an executive agreement. SAA points out that Article VI of the Agreement specifies the circumstances under which a permit may be revoked and contends that this court must construe section 306 in a manner consistent with the permit revocation provision of the Agreement....

... [T]here is no indication in the legislative history to suggest that in adopting the Anti–Apartheid Act as amended, Congress intended to abrogate any provision of the Agreement.... Nevertheless, for the narrow purpose of addressing petitioner's reliance on a principle of statutory construction, we will assume, arguendo, that the mandate in section 306(a)(2) does in fact violate the Agreement.

If petitioner's construction of section 306(a)(2) were permissible, the lack of an express congressional intent to abrogate the permit revocation provision of the Agreement would lend support to SAA's position.[2] Since the days of Chief Justice Marshall, the Supreme Court has consistently held that congressional statutes must be construed wherever possible in a manner that will not require the United States "to violate the law of nations." The Schooner Charming Betsy, 6 U.S. (2 Cranch) at 118 (*quoted in* Weinberger v. Rossi, 456 U.S. 25, 32 ... (1982)). The Court's extreme reluctance to find a conflict between an act of Congress and a pre-existing international agreement of the United States finds eloquent expression in Chew Heong v. United States, 112 U.S. 536 ... (1884):

> "There would no longer be any security," says Vattel, "no longer any commerce between mankind, if [nations] did not think themselves obliged to keep faith with each other, and to perform their promises." Vattel, Book 2, ch. 12. And as sovereign nations, acknowledging no superior, cannot be compelled to accept any interpretation, however just and reasonable, "the faith of treaties constitutes in this respect all the security of contracting powers." *Id.* ch. 17.... Aside from the duty imposed by the Constitution to respect treaty stipulations when they become the subject of judicial proceedings, the court cannot be unmindful of the fact, that the honor of the government and people of the United States is involved in every inquiry whether rights secured by such stipulations shall be recognized and protected. *Id.* at 539–40.

The Court in *Chew Heong* compared the abrogation of a treaty through an act of Congress to the repeal of one statute by another, noting that ... repeals by implication are not favored, and are never admitted where the former can stand with the new act. *Id.* at 549. The Court went on to suggest the circumstances that will permit such implied repeal:

> "There must be a positive repugnancy between the provisions of the new laws and those of the old, and even then the old law is repealed by implication only pro tanto, to the extent of the repugnancy." ... "It must appear that the later provision is certainly and clearly in hostility to the former. If, by any reasonable construction, the two statutes can stand together, they must so stand. If harmony is impossible, and only in that event, the former law is repealed in part, [sic] or wholly, as the case may be."

2. Petitioner relies heavily on the Court's reasoning in United States v. Lee Yen Tai, 185 U.S. 213, 221 ... (1902) ("the purpose by statute to abrogate a treaty or any designated part of a treaty ... must not be lightly assumed, but must appear clearly and distinctly from the words used in the statute"), and Weinberger v. Rossi, 456 U.S. 25, 35 ... (1982) ("affirmative congressional expression [is] necessary to evidence an intent to abrogate provisions in 13 international agreements"). Both of these cases can be distinguished; in neither case did the Court face an unambiguous congressional mandate to do something which in turn might abrogate U.S. international obligations. As we mentioned earlier, we do not decide whether the Anti–Apartheid Act does in fact abrogate terms of the Agreement. Furthermore, even if the Act did effect an abrogation, the Court's reasoning in *Lee Yen Tai* and *Weinberger v. Rossi* cannot defeat the unambiguous statutory mandate before us now.

Id. at 549–50 (*quoting* Wood v. United States, 41 U.S. (16 Pet.) 342, 362–63 . . . (1842), and State v. Stoll, 84 U.S. (17 Wall.) 425, 431 . . . (1873)).

As we have noted, however, the purpose of Congress in adopting the Sarbanes amendment was unambiguous. Therefore, if there is in fact "a positive repugnancy" between section 306(a) of the Anti–Apartheid Act and Article VI of the Agreement, the latter must yield. "So far as the provisions of [an] act [of Congress are] in conflict with any treaty, they must prevail in all courts of this country. . . ." Whitney v. Robertson, 124 U.S. at 195. Furthermore, "it is wholly immaterial to inquire whether by the act . . . [Congress] has departed from the [Agreement] or not, or whether such departure was by accident or design. . . ." *Id*. . . .

As we conclude that section 306(a)(2) supersedes whatever provisions of the Agreement may be in conflict with that section, so must it supersede, to the degree required, the Secretary's general duty under section 1102 of the Aviation Act, 49 U.S.C. § 1502(a) (1982), to exercise her powers "consistently with any obligations assumed by the United States in any treaty, convention, or agreement that may be in force between the United States and any foreign country." Section 306(a)(2) of the Anti–Apartheid Act is a very specific congressional directive. "Where there is no clear intention otherwise, a specific statute will not be controlled or nullified by a general one, regardless of the priority of enactment." Morton v. Mancari, 417 U.S. 535, 550–551 . . . (1974). . . . Petitioner's argument that the Secretary was bound by section 1102 of the Aviation Act to construe section 306(a)(2) consistently with the permit revocation provisions of the Agreement is therefore without merit. . . .

Restatement of Foreign Relations Law of the United States § 115 (3 ed. 1987)

Comment c. *International agreement inconsistent with prior federal statute*. . . . [A]n executive agreement pursuant to a treaty . . . derives its authority from that treaty and has the same effect as the treaty to supersede an earlier inconsistent federal statute (or an earlier United States agreement) in United States law. A Congressional–Executive agreement . . . draws its authority from the joint powers of the President and Congress and supersedes any prior inconsistent federal legislation (or United States agreement). . . . The effect in domestic law of an executive agreement made by the President under his own constitutional authority . . . in respect of an earlier treaty or federal statute has not been established. However, a sole executive agreement on a matter within the express constitutional authority of Congress, such as a trade embargo or other regulation of commerce with foreign nations, will not be given effect in the face of an inconsistent statute. . . .

Reporters' Note 5. *Sole executive agreement inconsistent with State or federal law.* A sole executive agreement made by the President on his own constitutional authority is the law of the land and supreme to State law. United States v. Belmont, 301 U.S. 324 . . . (1937); United States v.

Pink, 315 U.S. 203 ... (1942). It has been held, however, that an executive agreement made by the President on a matter expressly within the constitutional authority of Congress, such as the regulation of commerce with foreign nations, is subject to the controlling authority of Congress and will not be given effect in the face of an inconsistent Congressional act. United States v. Guy W. Capps, Inc., 204 F.2d 655 (4th Cir.1953) ... ; Swearingen v. United States, 565 F. Supp. 1019 (D.Col.1983) (executive agreement inconsistent with Internal Revenue Code); *cf.* American Cetacean Society v. Baldrige, 768 F.2d 426 (D.C.Cir. 1985) ... (Supreme Court interpreted statute so as to render subsequent executive agreement not in conflict with statute).... A different principle might govern an executive agreement on a matter within the President's primary constitutional authority such as recognition of governments.... even if a sole executive agreement were held to supersede a statute, Congress could reenact the statute and thereby supersede the intervening executive agreement as domestic law.

Notes and Questions

1. In view of the U.S. Constitution, Article I, § 8, cl. 18, what matter is not "expressly within the constitutional authority of Congress"? Would such a matter only involve an exclusive Executive power (such as recognition of foreign states or foreign governments and creation of armistice agreements)? If Congress passed a statute interfering with an exclusive Executive power, wouldn't the statute be unconstitutional as a violation of the separation of powers? See JORDAN J. PAUST, INTERNATIONAL LAW AS LAW OF THE UNITED STATES 107–08, 121–22 (2 ed. 2003) ("Only a sole executive agreement within an exclusive Executive power ... should prevail over legislation, but it would be the separation of powers and not the last-in-time rule that compels such a result. The same result follows even more logically with respect to a clash between a mere executive regulation (not within an exclusive Executive power) and an act of Congress...."). Concerning presidential recognition of foreign governments, *see, e.g.*, United States v. Palmer, 16 U.S. (3 Wheat.) 610, 634 (1818); The Elwine Kreplin, 8 F. Cas. 588, 589 (C.C.E.D.N.Y.1872) (No. 4,426).

2. What type of executive agreement was involved in *Guy Capps*? in *South African Airways*? In *Guy Capps*, the court stated that a sole executive agreement was void for two reasons—the first being that it was void because "it was not authorized by Congress," it dealt with an area of power "vested in Congress" (*i.e.*, the commerce power), and that such power is not incident to the President alone. Since the commerce power is not an exclusive congressional power but a shared power vis a vis the treaty power, does *Guy Capps* suggest that, unlike a treaty, no sole executive agreement can be constitutionally valid if it addresses a matter that lies within a shared power of Congress? If so, the only valid sole executive agreements would be those that lie within an exclusive Executive power (such as recognition of a foreign government). Is this preferable? Again, was the agreement in *Dames & Moore* a sole executive agreement or an implied-congressional-executive agreement?

3. In Swearingen v. United States, 565 F.Supp. 1019 (D.Col.1983), the district court ruled that an executive agreement was a sole executive agreement, that executive agreements "are not directly authorized by or described in the Constitution," and "executive agreements do not supersede prior inconsistent acts of Congress because, unlike treaties, they are not the 'supreme Law of the Land.' See United States v. Guy W. Capps, Inc. . . ." In Coplin v. United States, 6 Cl.Ct. 115 (1984), *rev'd on other gds.*, 761 F.2d 688 (Fed.Cir.1985), the Court of Claims found that the same executive agreement "formed an integral part" of the same treaty addressed in *Swearingen*; stated that "[t]reaties, like other laws, can form the basis of the President's authority to enter into executive agreements . . . ," *citing* Wilson v. Girard, 354 U.S. 524, 526–29 (1957); and stated that "[s]uch agreements supersede prior United States law to the extent it is inconsistent" and that this treaty-executive agreement "implicitly repeals prior conflicting laws." Which approach seems appropriate, if any?

4. Does a treaty-executive agreement or a congressional executive agreement at least have the status of its coordinate legal base (*i.e.*, a treaty or a statute)? Should an executive agreement pursuant to the United Nations Charter carry the date of the agreement or the Charter for purposes of the last in time rule?

2. *Customary International Law*

THE PAQUETE HABANA

175 U.S. 677 (1900).

[see extract in Section 2 D]

Jordan J. Paust, International Law as Law of the United States
89–92, 94–95, 100 (1996), 108–15, 120–21 (2 ed. 2003)

The Field–Sutherland–Chase limitations are also relevant to a fifth circumstance, that involving an unavoidable clash between customary international law and a federal statute. The war powers exception [to the last in time rule] noted above was not limited to treaties, but was expressed in terms of the law of nations or international law and must therefore include the primacy of customary international law. The exception was only expressly operative, however, when the war powers were involved. For this reason, one might question whether customary international law should always prevail in the case of an unavoidable clash with congressional power exercised in the form of a federal statute (*i.e.*, whether customary international law should prevail more generally when the war powers are not involved).

Addressing this question one should note initially that if the last in time rule were applied to any circumstance involving an unavoidable clash between customary international law and a federal statute, the application of customary international law would not pose an exception to the last in time rule but would represent actually its logical extension. This is so because customary international law would necessarily be "last in time," since custom is either constantly re-enacted through a process of recognition and behavior involving patterns of expectation and practice or it loses its validity and force as law. Thus, custom would always prevail.

Interestingly, there is additional precedent for the primacy of customary international law. In 1865, an opinion of the Attorney General recognized that "the law of nations ... [is] a part of the law of the land," adding:

> Hence Congress may define those laws, but cannot abrogate them ... laws of nations ... are of binding force upon the departments and citizens of the Government, though not defined by any law of Congress.... Congress cannot abrogate them or authorize their infraction. The Constitution does not permit this Government [to do so either]. [11 Op. Att'y Gen. 297 (1865)]

One of the earliest opinions of an Attorney General also recognized that the law of nations is part of the law of the land, "subject to modifications on some points of indifference," [1 Op. Att'y Gen. 26 (1792)] but, of course, the "modifications" would have to be "of indifference."

There is only an implication from dictum in one Supreme Court decision that might lead one to conclude that Congress could authorize an infraction of, merely, the "usage of nations," but the Court was quick to point out that such an infraction could not be made, "even by direction of the Executive, without express authority from Congress." Importantly, the Supreme Court also recognized in *Chew Heong v. United States* that "treaties must continue to operate as part of our municipal law, and be obeyed by the people, applied by the judiciary and executed by the President, while they continue unrepealed." The *Chew Heong* opinion was quoting *Taylor v. Morton*, which also declared that "no body other than Congress possesses" the power to refuse to execute a treaty.

These recognitions are consistent, moreover, with the many cases which affirm that the President, at least, is bound by international law. Indeed, they confirm that point emphatically.

There is also dictum in a district court opinion written sixty years ago that "Congress may, in disregard of the law of nations, prohibit acts by foreign nationals not committed within our domain," adding: "but unless such intent clearly appears from the language of the statute such intent is not to be presumed." This unreasoned conclusion of a district court, without any citations, is clearly inconsistent with relevant opinions of the Attorneys General and other sources noted above and was completely unnecessary since relevant legislation was found to be consistent with a relevant treaty and customary international law, although it may have been somewhat consistent with the dictum noted above in *The Paquete Habana*. The district court opinion also lacks authority because it demonstrates confusion with respect to the difference, well-understood elsewhere, between practice, comity, usage, and law. To say that Congress may disregard mere "practice" or "comity" is hardly new or relevant.

Dicta in a 1959 opinion of a federal appeals court has also been cited by the few who argue that acts of Congress should prevail over customary international law. In *Tag v. Rogers*, it was said that "it has long been settled ... that the federal courts are bound to recognize ... [a "treaty, statute, or constitutional provision"] as superior to canons of international law," adding:

> There is no power in this Court to declare null and void a statute adopted by Congress or a declaration included in a treaty merely on the ground that such provision violates a principle of international law.

That these statements were mere dicta is clear from the opinion, the court noting that the only issue it addressed was whether a 1923 treaty was superseded by subsequent legislative action. No customary law was shown to have been involved and none was addressed as such. Arguably, however, the court framed even this issue incorrectly, for it noted that a newer international agreement, in 1952, "gave support" to a law which "provided that the right, title and interest of German nationals in German external assets were extinguished as of the time of their vesting" and that under the agreement Germany would raise no objections and would even compensate "the former owners of the property so seized." In this sense, a subsequent international agreement (in 1952) was not inconsistent with prior congressional action, although the legislative measures might have been inconsistent with an agreement prior to both (in 1923), and the subsequent international agreement effectively amended a prior international agreement. The last in time, therefore, was an agreement that was actually consistent with prior congressional action.

Still, dicta about custom aside, one might question whether the case was decided correctly in view of the many Supreme Court decisions, now rediscovered and seemingly unknown to the 1959 court, which set forth the "executed or vested" exception to the last in time rule. If subsequent congressional legislation cannot interfere with property rights vested by or pursuant to a treaty, it would seem to follow that a subsequent treaty could not divest such rights and that they could not lawfully be divested by subsequent legislative action, sanctified by a subsequent international agreement. Yet in the actual case this point may have been recognized by the U.S. executive and Germany, for Germany, it was agreed, would assume the burden of compensating "the former owners of property so seized." In this sense, there might have been a taking of vested property interests pursuant to governmental power but, by international agreement, the duty to compensate for such a taking would shift to a foreign entity.

What is more disturbing than the phrasing of the issue, however, is the fact that the dicta about customary law, purportedly "long ... settled," was completely without support. The second portion of the statement quoted above was made without supporting reasoning or citations, and the first portion was similarly unreasoned but made with allegedly supporting case citations. Nonetheless, not one of the cases cited actually declares that courts are bound to recognize statutes over custom or that courts have no power to declare as void a statute that contravenes customary international law. The unreasoned dicta, therefore, is untrue and, at best, it stands alone. Importantly also, the court seemed to be unaware of the contrary opinions of Attorneys General and the implications from certain judicial opinions noted above and the three federal cases noted below which support the view that customary international law prevails over an inconsistent statute. . . .

More importantly, at least three federal cases support a rule that custom must prevail over inconsistent federal statutes. As expressly recognized in one of the three cases, when there is "any conflict between the municipal law of the United States, as exemplified in the statute, and the well-recognized principles of international law [there, custom], the latter must prevail in the determination of the rights of the parties." Also of interest is the fact that the Draft Restatement supported the view that customary international law supersedes any "preexisting" statute, a view which necessarily supports the primacy of customary international law, as opposed to a treaty of a particular date, because custom must necessarily be "last in time" since it is constantly "re-enacted" or, if it is not, it will lose its validity and efficacy as law.

To conclude inquiry into the problem posed by customary international law, one can identify at least three federal cases, three opinions of the Attorneys General and the Restatement in support of the superiority of customary international law. Also partly supportive of the primacy of custom are Chief Justice Marshall's statement in *The Charming Betsy*, which impliedly affirms the primacy of rights under customary international law but not necessarily the primacy of other customary law; implications from other early judicial opinions, including those of Justices Marshall, Wilson, and Story; Justice Field's dissent in *Miller*, Justice Chase's opinion in *Bas*, and Justice Sutherland's opinion in *Macintosh,* which support the superiority of the law of nations whenever the war powers are involved—a viewpoint that is quite similar to that expressed in the 1865 opinion of the Attorney General which affirmed that Congress has no power to abrogate the law of nations or to authorize its infraction since its power is merely to define and punish and the law of nations is binding on all branches of our government and on our citizens. Unreasoned dicta in *The Paquete Habana* is clear in both directions, although other dicta there and in a few lower court opinions arguably lend support to a minority view that statutes should always prevail. Additionally, if one wishes to abandon what arguably is the more widely shared and authoritative set of preferences for customary international law and propose some new rule that is more flexible, one should ask: what custom or what legislation, in view of what other legal policies at stake, in what social context, with what probable social consequences, is to be preferred and why? This more flexible approach may also allow a distinction to be made between peremptory customary prohibitions or protections (such as those concerning genocide, war crimes, and fundamental human rights) and more ordinary customary law.

In any event, it is important to note that with respect to fundamental human rights supported by customary international law the critical focus is not on the question whether or not customary international law as such should prevail over an inconsistent statute. The significant question is whether fundamental human rights are protected under the Constitution and, if so, whether relevant constitutional guarantees are to prevail over an inconsistent statute. As documented elsewhere, the answer to the first part of the question is yes. As noted here, the answer to the second part of the question also is yes. For this reason, in the case on an unavoidable clash between fundamental human rights supported by customary international law and a federal statute, the human rights (which have a constitutional status) must prevail. Further, when customary human rights in times of armed conflict are at stake, there is already precedential recognition by Justice Field and others of the primacy of such rights and of the constitutional basis for such a restraint on congressional power....

Appendix

Recommended Restatement of the Restatement (Third)

§ 115. Comment d.... Whether a rule of customary international law that developed after, and is inconsistent with, an earlier statute or international agreement of the United States should be given effect as the law of the United States has also not been authoritatively and clearly determined by the Supreme Court, although several lower federal court opinions and opinions of the Attorneys General affirm the primacy of customary international law and Supreme Court justices have recognized the primacy of customary international law in time of war. See also Murray v. The Charming Betsy, 6 U.S. (2 Cranch) 64, 118 (1804) (impliedly affirming the primacy of rights under customary law). Additionally, fundamental human rights appear to have a uniquely important status throughout U.S. history, and some are clearly peremptory *jus cogens*. See sec. 702. Customary human rights should prevail under various amendments, including the ninth amendment, to the U.S. Constitution.

Notes

1. More recently, outside the context of war and laws of war some courts have ruled that federal statutes prevail. *See, e.g.*, Munoz v. Ashcroft, 339 F.3d 950, 958 (9th Cir. 2003); United States v. Yousef, 327 F.3d 56, 93 (2d Cir. 2003); *In re* Cuban, 822 F.Supp. 192, 197–98 (M.D. Pa. 1993).

2. Since customary international law derives from a complex process involving many types of actors and their legal expectations or *opinio juris*, it cannot rightly be considered to be like mere U.S. judge-made general common law or mere common law as such, but is of a higher, transnational

status. *See also* Sosa v. Alvarez–Machain, 542 U.S. 692, & n.19 (2004) ("federal courts have no authority to derive 'general' common law," but can apply customary international law as "actionable international norms" "derived from the law of nations"). Moreover, in view of its nature and status, customary international law should trump inconsistent common law in case of a clash. *See* PAUST, *supra* at 5–8, 30 n.34, 36 n.39, 42–43 n.47, 92, 120–22 n.55, 244 n.363; RESTATEMENT, *supra* §§ 111, 115, cmt. e; cases cited in Section 2 F. 1 (Notes and Questions).

F. *Supremacy and Federalism*

1. *Supremacy and Preemption*

WARE v. HYLTON

3 U.S. (3 Dall.) 199 (1796).

[Editors' note: The treaty involved in this case protected the rights of British creditors against debtors within the United States. Virginia had passed legislation obviating the legal effect of any debts owed to British creditors. Among the issues presented were whether the treaty prevails over state law and whether the law of nations was relevant law.]

CHASE, J.

. . . It is the declared will of the people of the United States that any treaty made by the authority of the United States shall be superior to the constitution and laws of any individual State; and their will alone is to decide. . . . Four things are apparent on a view of the sixth article of the National Constitution. First, that it is retrospective, and is to be considered in the same light as if the Constitution had been established before the making of the treaty [of peace with Great Britain] of 1783; second, that the constitution or laws of any of the States so far as either of them shall be found contrary to the treaty are by force of said article, prostrated before the treaty; third, that consequently the treaty of 1783 has superior power to the legislature of any State, because no legislature of any State has any kind of power over the Constitution, which was its creator; fourth, that it is the declared duty of the State judges to determine any constitution or laws of any State contrary to that treaty (or any other) made under the authority of the United States, null and void. National and federal judges are bound by duty and oath to the same conduct.

WILSON, J.

There are two points involved in the discussion of this power of confiscation [by Virginia of British creditors' rights]. The first arising from the rule prescribed by the law of nations; and the second arising from the construction of the treaty of peace.

When the United States declared their independence, they were bound to receive the law of nations, in its modern state of purity and refinement. By every nation, whatever is its form of government, the confiscation of debts has long been considered disreputable. . . .

But even if Virginia had the power to confiscate; the treaty annuls the confiscation....

OWINGS v. NORWOOD'S LESSEE

9 U.S. (5 Cranch) 344, 348–49 (1809).

The reason for inserting that clause [U.S. Const., Art. III, § 2, cl. 1] in the constitution was, that all persons who have real claims under a treaty should have their causes decided by the national tribunals.... Each treaty stipulates something respecting the citizens of the two nations, and gives them rights. Whenever a right grows out of, or is protected by, a treaty, it is sanctioned against all the laws and judicial decisions of the states; and whoever may have this right, it is to be protected.

BAKER v. CITY OF PORTLAND

2 F. Cas. 472, 472 (C.C.D. Ore. 1879).

This treaty [with China, recognizing "the inherent and inalienable right of man to change his home and allegiance"] ... is the supreme law of the land, and the courts are bound to enforce it fully and fairly....

The state cannot legislate so as to interfere with the operation of this treaty or limit or deny the privileges or immunities granted by it to the Chinese residents in this country.

MAIORANO v. BALTIMORE & OHIO R.R.

213 U.S. 268, 272–73 (1909).

A treaty ... by the express words of the Constitution, is the supreme law of the land, binding alike National and state Courts, and is capable of enforcement, and must be enforced by them in the litigation of private rights.

MISSOURI v. HOLLAND

[see Section 2 B 5 a, p. 229]

ASAKURA v. CITY OF SEATTLE

265 U.S. 332 (1924).

BUTLER, J.

Plaintiff in error is a subject of the Emperor of Japan, and, since 1904, has resided in Seattle, Washington. Since July, 1915, he has been engaged in business there as a pawnbroker. The city passed an ordinance, which took effect July 2, 1921, regulating the business of pawnbroker and repealing former ordinances on the same subject. It makes it unlawful for any person to engage in the business unless he shall have a license, and the ordinance provides "that no such license shall be granted unless the applicant be a citizen of the United States." Violations of the ordinance are punishable by fine or imprisonment or both. Plaintiff in error brought this suit in the Superior Court of King County, Washington, against the city, its Comptroller and its Chief of Police to restrain them from enforcing the ordinance against him. He attacked the ordinance on the ground that it violates the treaty between the United States and the Empire of Japan, proclaimed April 5, 1911, 37 Stat. 1504; violates the constitution of the State of Washington, and also the due process and equal protection clauses of the Fourteenth Amendment of the Constitution of the United States. He declared his willingness to comply with any valid ordinance relating to the business of pawnbroker. It was shown that he had about $5,000 invested in his business, which would be broken up and destroyed by the enforcement of the ordinance. The Superior Court granted the relief prayed. On appeal, the Supreme Court of the State held the ordinance valid and reversed the decree....

Does the ordinance violate the treaty? Plaintiff in error invokes and relies upon the following provisions: "The citizens or subjects of each of the High Contracting Parties shall have liberty to enter, travel and reside in the territories of the other to carry on trade, wholesale and retail, to own or lease and occupy houses, manufactories, warehouses and shops, to employ agents of their choice, to lease land for residential and commercial purposes, and generally to do anything incident to or necessary for trade upon the same terms as native citizens or subjects, submitting themselves to the laws and regulations there established.... The citizens or subjects of each ... shall receive, in the territories of the other, the most constant protection and security for their persons and property,...."

A treaty made under the authority of the United States "shall be the supreme law of the land; and the judges in every State shall be bound thereby, any thing in the constitution or laws of any State to the contrary notwithstanding." Constitution, Art. VI, § 2.

The treaty-making power of the United States is not limited by any express provision of the Constitution, and, though it does not extend "so far as to authorize what the Constitution forbids," it does extend to all proper subjects of negotiation between our government and other nations. Geofroy v. Riggs, 133 U.S. 258, 266, 267; *In re* Ross, 140 U.S. 453, 463; Missouri v. Holland, 252 U.S. 416. The treaty was made to strengthen friendly relations between the two nations. As to the things covered by it, the provision quoted establishes the rule of equality between Japanese subjects while in this country and native citizens. Treaties for the protection of citizens of one country residing in the territory of another are numerous, and make for good understanding between nations. The treaty is binding within the State of Washington. Baldwin v. Franks, 120 U.S. 678, 682–683. The rule of equality established by it cannot be rendered nugatory in any part of the United States by municipal ordinances or state laws. It stands on the same footing of supremacy as do the provisions of the Constitution and laws of the United States. It operates of itself without the aid of any legislation, state or national; and it will be applied and given authoritative effect by the courts. Foster v. Neilson, 2 Pet. 253, 314; Head Money Cases, 112 U.S. 580, 598; Chew Heong v. United States, 112 U.S. 536, 540; Whitney v. Robertson, 124 U.S. 190, 194; Maiorano v. Baltimore & Ohio R.R. Co., 213 U.S. 268, 272.

The purpose of the ordinance complained of is to regulate, not to prohibit, the business of pawnbroker. But it makes it impossible for aliens to carry on the business. It need not be considered whether the State, if it sees fit, may forbid and destroy the business generally. Such a law would apply equally to aliens and citizens, and no question of conflict with the treaty would arise. The grievance here alleged is that plaintiff in error, in violation of the treaty, is denied equal opportunity.

It remains to be considered whether the business of pawnbroker is "trade" within the meaning of the treaty. Treaties are to be construed in a broad and liberal spirit, and, when two constructions are possible, one restrictive of rights that may be claimed under it and the other favorable to them, the latter is to be preferred. Hauenstein v. Lynham, 100 U.S. 483, 487; Geofroy v. Riggs, *supra*, 271; Tucker v. Alexandroff, 183 U.S. 424, 437.... The language of the treaty is comprehensive. The phrase "to carry on trade" is broad. That it is not to be given a restricted meaning is plain. The clauses "to own or lease ... shops, ... to lease land for ... commercial purposes, and generally to do anything incident to or necessary for trade," and "shall receive ... the most constant protection and security for their ... property ..." all go to show the intention of the parties that the citizens or subjects to either shall have liberty in the territory of the other to engage in all kinds and classes of business that are or reasonably may be embraced within the meaning of the word "trade" as used in the treaty....

UNITED STATES v. PINK

[see Section 2 B 4 b, p. 300]

OYAMA v. CALIFORNIA

332 U.S. 633, 672–73 (1948).

[Editors' note: In this case, the Court struck down a portion of a 1920 California statute denying aliens who were not eligible for U.S. citizenship the right to own land in California. The portion addressed involved a presumption concerning an attempt to violate the statute when one alien purchased land with funds provided by another alien, and that portion was struck down on the basis of the equal protection clause of the Fourteenth Amendment. The inequality with respect to categories of aliens who could own land under the statute was later struck down under the same equal protection clause in Sei Fujii v. State, 38 Cal.2d 718 (1952). In *Oyama*, Justice Black, joined by Justice Douglas, concurred but added: "How can this nation be faithful to this international pledge [in the U.N. Charter, art. 56] if state laws which bar land ownership and occupancy by aliens on account of race are permitted to be enforced?" 332 U.S. at 649–50. Justice Murphy filed a separate concurring opinion, with whom Justice Rutledge joined.]

MURPHY, J., concurring.

... [T]he basic vice, the constitutional infirmity, of the [California] Alien Land Law is that its discrimination rest upon an unreal racial foundation. It assumes that there is some racial characteristic, common to all Japanese aliens, that makes them unfit to own or use agricultural land in California....

Added to this constitutional defect, or course, is the fact that the Alien Land Law from its inception has proved an embarrassment to the United States Government. This statute has been more than a local regulation of internal affairs. It has overflowed into the realm of foreign policy; it has had direct and unfortunate consequences on this country's relations with Japan. Drawn on a background of racial animosity, the law was so patent in its discrimination against Japanese aliens as to cause serious antagonism in Japan, even to the point of demands for war against the United States. The situation was so fraught with danger that three Presidents of the United States were forced to intervene in an effort to prevent the Alien Land Law from coming into existence. A Secretary of State made a personal plea that the passage of the law might turn Japan into an unfriendly nation....

Moreover, this nation has recently pledged itself, through the United Nations Charter, to promote respect for, and observance of, human rights and fundamental freedoms for all without distinction as to race, sex, language and religion. The Alien Land Law stands as a barrier to the fulfillment of that national pledge. Its inconsistency with the Charter, which has been duly ratified and adopted by the United States, is but one more reason why the statute must be condemned.

And so in origin, purpose, administration and effect, the Alien Land Law does violence to the high ideals of the Constitution of the United States and the Charter of the United Nations. It is an unhappy facsimile, a disheartening reminder, of the racial policy pursued by those forces of evil whose destruction recently necessitated a devastating war. It is racism in one of its most malignant forms....

ZSCHERNIG v. MILLER

389 U.S. 429 (1968).

DOUGLAS, J.

This case concerns the disposition of the estate of a resident of Oregon who died there intestate in 1962. Appellants are decedent's sole heirs and they are residents of East Germany. Appellees include members of the State Land Board that petitioned the Oregon probate court for the escheat of the net proceeds of the estate under the provisions of Ore. Rev. Stat. § 111.070 (1957), which provides for escheat in cases where a nonresident alien claims real or personal property unless three requirements are satisfied:

(1) the existence of a reciprocal right of a United States citizen to take property on the same terms as a citizen or inhabitant of the foreign country;

(2) the right of United States citizens to receive payment here of funds from estates in the foreign country; and

(3) the right of the foreign heirs to receive the proceeds of Oregon estates "without confiscation."

The Oregon Supreme Court held that the appellants could take the Oregon realty involved in the present case by reason of Article IV of the 1923 Treaty of Friendship, Commerce and Consular Rights with Germany (44 Stat. 2135) but that by reason of the same Article, as construed in Clark v. Allen, 331 U.S. 503, they could not take the personalty. 243 Ore. 567, 592, 412 P.2d 781, 415 P.2d 15....

... We conclude that the history and operation of this Oregon statute make clear that § 111.070 is an intrusion by the State into the field of foreign affairs which the Constitution entrusts to the President and the Congress. See Hines v. Davidowitz, 312 U.S. 52, 63....

We held in *Clark v. Allen* that a general reciprocity clause did not on its face intrude on the federal domain. 331 U.S., at 516–517. We noted that the California statute, then a recent enactment, would have only "some incidental or indirect effect in foreign countries." *Id.*, at 517.

Had that case appeared in the posture of the present one, a different result would have obtained. We were there concerned with the words of a statute on its face, not the manner of its application. State courts, of course, must frequently read, construe, and apply laws of foreign nations. It has never been seriously suggested that state courts are precluded from performing that function, albeit there is a remote possibility that any holding may disturb a foreign nation—whether the matter involves commercial cases, tort cases, or some other type of controversy. At the time *Clark v. Allen* was decided, the case seemed to involve no more than a routine reading of foreign laws. It now appears that in this reciprocity area under inheritance statutes, the probate courts of various States have launched inquiries into the type of governments that obtain in particular foreign nations—whether aliens under their law have enforceable rights, whether the so-called "rights" are merely dispensations turning upon the whim or caprice of government officials, whether the representation of consuls, ambassadors, and other representatives of foreign nations is credible or made in good faith, whether there is in the actual administration in the particular foreign system of law any element of confiscation....

In its brief amicus curiae, the Department of Justice states that: "The government does not ... contend that the application of the Oregon escheat statute in the circumstances of this case unduly interferes with the United States' conduct of foreign relations."

The Government's acquiescence in the ruling of *Clark v. Allen* certainly does not justify extending the principle of that case, as we would be required to do here to uphold the Oregon statute as applied; for it has more than "some incidental or indirect effect in foreign countries," and its great potential for disruption or embarrassment makes us hesitate to place it in the category of a diplomatic bagatelle.

As we read the decisions that followed in the wake of *Clark v. Allen*, we find that they radiate some of the attitudes of the "cold war," where the search is for the "democracy quotient" of a foreign regime as opposed to the Marxist theory. The Oregon statute introduces the concept of "confiscation," which is of course opposed to the Just Compensation Clause of the Fifth Amendment. And this has led into minute inquiries concerning the actual administration of foreign law, into the credibility of foreign diplomatic statements, and into speculation whether the fact that some received delivery of funds should "not preclude wonderment as to how many may have been denied 'the right to receive' ..." See State Land Board v. Kolovrat, 220 Ore. 448, 461–462, 349 P.2d 255, 262, *rev'd sub nom.*, Kolovrat v. Oregon, 366 U.S. 187, on other grounds.

That kind of state involvement in foreign affairs and international relations—matters which the Constitution entrusts solely to the Federal Government—is not sanctioned by *Clark v. Allen*. Yet such forbidden state activity has infected each of the three provisions of § 111.070, as applied by Oregon....

As one reads the Oregon decisions, it seems that foreign policy attitudes, the freezing or thawing of the "cold war," and the like are the real desiderata....

It seems inescapable that the type of probate law that Oregon enforces affects international relations in a persistent and subtle way. The practice of state courts in withholding remittances to legatees residing in Communist countries or in preventing them from assigning them is notorious. The several States, of course, have traditionally regulated the descent and distribution of estates. But those regulations must give way if they impair the effective exercise of the Nation's foreign policy.... Where those laws conflict with a treaty, they must bow to the superior federal policy. See Kolovrat v. Oregon, 366 U.S. 187. Yet, even in absence of a treaty, a State's policy may disturb foreign relations.

As we stated in *Hines v. Davidowitz, supra*, at 64: "Experience has shown that international controversies of the gravest moment, sometimes even leading to war, may arise from real or imagined wrongs to another's subjects inflicted, or permitted, by a government." Certainly a State could not deny admission to a traveler from East Germany nor bar its citizens from going there. Passenger Cases, 7 How. 283; *cf.* Crandall v. Nevada, 6 Wall. 35; Kent v. Dulles, 357 U.S. 116. If there are to be such restraints, they must be provided by the Federal Government. The present Oregon law is not as gross an intrusion in the federal domain as those others might be. Yet, as we have said, it has a direct impact upon foreign relations and may well adversely affect the power of the central government to deal with those problems.

The Oregon law does, indeed, illustrate the dangers which are involved if each State, speaking through its probate courts, is permitted to establish its own foreign policy.

STEWART, J., concurring.

... In my view, each of the three provisions of the Oregon law suffers from the same fatal infirmity. All three launch the State upon a prohibited voyage into a domain of exclusively federal competence. Any realistic attempt to apply any of the three criteria would necessarily involve the Oregon courts in an evaluation, either expressed or implied, of the administration of foreign law, the credibility of foreign diplomatic statements, and the policies of foreign governments. Of course state courts must routinely construe foreign law in the resolution of controversies properly before them, but here the courts of Oregon are thrust into these inquiries only because the Oregon Legislature has framed its inheritance laws to the prejudice of nations whose policies it disapproves and thus has trespassed upon an area where the Constitution contemplates that only the National Government shall operate. "For local interests the several States of the Union exist, but for national purposes, embracing our relations with foreign nations, we are but one people, one nation, one power." Chinese Exclusion Case, 130 U.S. 581, 606. "Our system of government is such that the interest of the cities, counties and states, no less than the interest of the people of the whole nation, imperatively requires that federal power in the field affecting foreign relations be left entirely free from local interference." Hines v. Davidowitz, 312 U.S. 52, 63.

The Solicitor General, as amicus curiae, says that the Government does not "contend that the application of the Oregon escheat statute in the circumstances of this case unduly interferes with the United States' conduct of foreign relations." But that is not the point. We deal here with the basic allocation of power between the States and the Nation. Resolution of so fundamental a constitutional issue cannot vary from day to day with the shifting winds at the State Department. Today, we are told, Oregon's statute does not conflict with the national interest. Tomorrow it may. But, however that may be, the fact remains that the conduct of our foreign affairs is entrusted under the Constitution to the National Government, not to the probate courts of the several States. To the extent that Clark v. Allen, 331 U.S. 503, is inconsistent with these views, I would overrule that decision.

HARLAN, J., concurring.

... My Brother Douglas does cite a few unfortunate remarks made by state court judges in applying statutes resembling the one before us. However, the Court does not mention, nor does the record reveal, any instance in which such an occurrence has been the occasion for a diplomatic protest, or, indeed, has had any foreign relations consequence whatsoever. The United States says in its brief as amicus curiae that it "does not ... contend that the application of the Oregon escheat statute in the circumstances of this case unduly interferes with the United States' conduct of foreign relations." . . .

Essentially, the Court's basis for decision appears to be that alien inheritance laws afford state court judges an opportunity to criticize in dictum the policies of foreign governments, and that these dicta may adversely affect our foreign relations. In addition to finding no evidence of adverse effect in the record, I believe this rationale to be untenable because logically it would apply to many other types of litigation which come before the state courts. It is true that, in addition to the many state court judges who have applied alien inheritance statutes with proper judicial decorum, some judges have seized the opportunity to make derogatory remarks about foreign governments. However, judges have been known to utter dicta critical of foreign governmental policies even in purely domestic cases, so that the mere possibility of offensive utterances can hardly be the test. . . .

AMERICAN INSURANCE ASSOC. v. GARAMENDI

539 U.S. 396 (2003).

Souter, J.

[Editors' note: California created a Holocaust Victim Insurance Relief Act (HVIRA) of 1999 compelling insurers and any "related company" (including "any parent, subsidiary, reinsurer, successor in interest, managing general agent, or affiliate company of the insurer," whether or not they were related when policies were sold) doing business in California to disclose information concerning any policies sold in Europe between 1920 and 1945 and providing a cause of action for Holocaust survivors. Similar laws were passed in Florida, Maryland, Minnesota, New York, Texas, and Washington.]

The principal argument for preemption made by petitioners and the United States as amicus curiae is that HVIRA interferes with foreign policy of the Executive branch, as expressed principally in the executive agreements with Germany, Austria, and France. The major premises of the argument, at least, are beyond dispute. There is, of course, no question that at some point an exercise of state power that touches on foreign relations must yield to the National Government's policy, given the "concern for uniformity in this country's dealings with foreign nations" that animated the Constitution's allocation of the foreign relations power to the National Government in the first place. Banco Nacional de Cuba v. Sabbatino, 376 U.S. 398, 427 n.25 . . . (1964); see Crosby v. National Foreign Trade Council, 530 U.S. 363, 381–82 n.16 . . . (2000) (" 'The peace of the whole ought not to be left at the disposal of a part' " (quoting The Federalist No. 80, pp 535–36 (J. Cooke ed. 1961) (A. Hamilton)); The Federalist No. 44, p 299 (J. Madison) (emphasizing "the advantage of uniformity in all points which relate to foreign powers"); The Federalist no. 42, p 279 (J. Madison) ("If we are to be one nation in any respect, it clearly ought to be in respect to other nations"); see also First Nat. City Bank v. Banco Nacional de Cuba, 406 U.S. 759, 769 . . .

(1972) (act of state doctrine was "fashioned because of fear that adjudication would interfere with the conduct of foreign relations"); Japan Line, Ltd. v. County of Los Angeles, 441 U.S. 434, 449 ... (1979) (negative Commerce Clause protects the National Government's ability to speak with "one voice" in regulating commerce with foreign countries).

Nor is there any question generally that there is executive authority to decide what that policy should be. Although the source of the President's power to act in foreign affairs does not enjoy any textual detail, the historical gloss on the "executive Power" vested in Article II of the Constitution has recognized the President's "vast share of responsibility for the conduct of our foreign relations." Youngstown Sheet & Tube Co. v. Sawyer, 343 U.S. 579, 610–11 ... (1952) (Frankfurter, J., concurring). While Congress holds express authority to regulate public and private dealings with other nations in its war and foreign commerce powers, in foreign affairs the President has a degree of independent authority to act. *See, e.g.*, Chicago & Southern Air Lines, Inc. v. Waterman S.S. Corp., 333 U.S. 103, 109 ... (1948) ("The President ... possesses in his own right certain powers conferred by the Constitution on him as Commander-in-Chief and as the Nation's organ in foreign affairs"); *Youngstown*, *supra*, at 635–36....

At a more specific level, our cases have recognized that the President has authority to make "executive agreements" with other countries, requiring no ratification by the Senate or approval by Congress, this power having been exercised since the early years of the Republic. See Dames & Moore v. Regan, 453 U.S. 654, 679, 682–83 ... (1981); United States v. Pink, 315 U.S. 203, 223, 230 ... (1942) ... ; see also L. Henkin, Foreign Affairs and the United States Constitution 219, 496 n.163 (2 ed. 1996) ("Presidents from Washington to Clinton have made many thousands of agreements ... on matters running the gamut of U.S. foreign relations"). Making executive agreements to settle claims of American nationals against foreign governments is a particularly longstanding practice, the first example being as early as 1799, when the Washington administration settled demands against the Dutch Government by American citizens who lost their cargo when Dutch privateers over-took the schooner Washington Packet. See *Dames & Moore*, *supra*, at 679–80 and n.8; 5 Dep't of State, Treaties and Other International Acts of the United States 1075, 1078–79 (H. Miller ed. 1937). Given the fact that the practice goes back over 200 years to the first presidential administration, and has received congressional acquiescence throughout its history, the conclusion "that the President's control of foreign relations includes the settlement of claims is indisputable." *Pink*, *supra*, at 240 (Frankfurter, J., concurring)....

The executive agreements at issue here do differ in one respect from those just mentioned insofar as they address claims associated with formerly belligerent states, but against corporations, not the foreign governments. But the distinction does not matter. Historically, wartime claims against even nominally private entities have become issues in international diplomacy, and three of the postwar settlements dealing with reparations implicating private parties were made by the Executive alone. Acceptance of this historical practice is supported by a good pragmatic reason for depending on executive agreements to settle claims against foreign corporations associated with wartime experience. As shown by the history of insurance confiscation mentioned earlier, untangling government policy from private initiative during war time is often so hard that diplomatic action settling claims against private parties may be just as essential in the aftermath of hostilities as diplomacy to settle claims against foreign governments. . . .

Generally, then, valid executive agreements are fit to preempt state law, just as treaties are, and if the agreements here had expressly preempted laws like HVIRA, the issue would be straightforward. . . . But petitioners and the United States as amicus curiae both have to acknowledge that the agreements include no preemption clause, and so leave their claim of preemption to rest on asserted interference with the foreign policy those agreements embody. Reliance is place on our decision in Zschernig v. Miller, 399 U.S. 429. . . . (1968). . . . [Regardless of which tests are appropriate from *Zschernig*], we think petitioners and the Government have demonstrated a sufficiently clear conflict to require finding preemption here. . . .

. . . [R]esolving Holocaust-era insurance claims that may be held by residents of this country is a matter well within the Executive's responsibility for foreign affairs. Since claims remaining in the aftermath of hostilities may be "sources of friction" acting as an "impediment to resumption of friendly relations" between the countries involved, *Pink*, *supra*, at 225, there is a "longstanding practice" of the national Executive to settle them in discharging its responsibility to maintain the Nation's relationships with other countries, *Dames & Moore*, 453 U.S. at 679. The issue of restitution for Nazi crimes has in fact been addressed in Executive Branch diplomacy and formalized in treaties and executive agreements over the last half century, and although resolution of private claims was postponed by the Cold War, securing private interests is an express object of diplomacy today, just as it was addressed in agreements soon after the Second World War. Vindicating victims injured by acts and omissions of enemy corporations in wartime is thus within the traditional subject matter of foreign policy in which national, not state, interests are overriding, and which the National Government has addressed.

The exercise of the federal executive authority means that state law must give way where, as here, there is evidence of clear conflict between the policies adopted by the two. . . . [Here,] negotiations toward the three settlement agreements . . . illustrate[s] that the consistent presidential foreign policy has been to encourage European governments and companies to volunteer settlement funds in preference to litigation or coercive sanctions. . . .

... The situation created by the California legislation calls to mind the impact of the Massachusetts Burma law on the effective exercise of the President's power, as recounted in the statutory preemption case, Crosby v. National Foreign Trade Council, 530 U.S. 363 ... (2000). HVIRA's economic compulsion to make public disclosure, of far more information about far more policies than [federal] rules require, employs "a different, state system of economic pressure," and in doing so undercuts the President's diplomatic discretion and the choice he has made exercising it. *Id.* at 376. Whereas the President's authority to provide for settling claims in winding up international hostilities requires flexibility in wielding "the coercive power of the national economy" as a tool of diplomacy, *id.* at 377, HVIRA denies this, by making exclusion from a large sector of the American insurance market the automatic sanction for noncompliance with the State's own policies on disclosure. "Quite simply, if the [California] law is enforceable the President has less to offer and less economic and diplomatic leverage as a consequence." *Ibid*, citing Dames & Moore, 453 U.S. at 673. The law thus "compromise[s] the very capacity of the President to speak for the Nation with one voice in dealing with other governments" to resolve claims against European companies arising out of World War II. 530 U.S. at 381 n.14.

Notes and Questions

1. In Tayyari v. New Mexico State University, 495 F.Supp. 1365 (D.N.M. 1980), the district court ruled that action taken by the Regents of New Mexico State University to deny admission or readmission to "any student whose home government holds, or permits the holding of U.S. citizens hostage" during the Iranian Hostage Crisis was obviated by federal preemption because of "its potential effect on this nation's management of immigration and foreign affairs," adding: "[t]he treatment of aliens has consistently been viewed as a national concern," and "[r]egardless of the effect" the Regents' action "frustrates the exercise of the federal government's authority to conduct foreign relations" and "imposes an impermissible burden on the federal government power to regulate immigration and conduct foreign affairs."

Subsequently, the Supreme Court has recognized that claims concerning selective enforcement by the Executive are unavailable to aliens in the context of deportation. *See, e.g.*, Reno v. American–Arab Anti–Discrimination Committee, 525 U.S. 471 (1999).

2. During the Apartheid regime in South Africa and U.N. and U.S. sanction efforts, the City of San Antonio, Texas, banned the sale of Krugerrands. Should states within the U.S. have any flexibility to positively supplement federal sanction efforts against a foreign state? Consider also In the Matter of New York Times v. City of New York Commission on Human Rights, 41 N.Y.2d 345, 352, 361 N.E.2d 963, 969 (Ct. of App. of N.Y. 1977).

Should cities or states be permitted to declare that they are a "nuclear free" zone (regarding nuclear weapons or environmental effects)?

3. In 1996, Massachusetts adopted a statute that prohibits the state's agencies and authorities from purchasing goods or services from individuals or companies that do business in Burma. Companies on the restricted purchase list may enter into contracts with the state only if the procurement is essential and there is no other bidder, if the contract concerns certain medical supplies, or if the offer is at least ten percent below the next lowest offer. Exempted from the restrictions are companies reporting the news from Burma, providing telecommunications or providing medical supplies. Of the 346 companies on the restricted list, 44 were U.S. companies and the rest were foreign. Massachusetts' aim is to place pressure on the Burmese military regime to moderate its violations of human rights and to restore democracy. Japan, the European Union (EU) and the Association of Southeast Asian Nations (ASEAN) protested the law, and the EU lodged a complaint with the WTO. Massachusetts purchases approximately $2 billion of goods and services per year. Some companies have withdrawn from doing business in Burma, a few citing the Massachusetts law and similar restrictions adopted by local governments.

In 1997, Congress passed a different set of sanctions against Burma to pressure it to improve human rights. These sanctions do not limit trade. Instead, they authorize the President to prohibit "new investment" by U.S. entities in the development of resources (but not other types of investment). The statute also prohibits most direct foreign assistance by the United States to Burma, instructs the U.S. Government to oppose international financial assistance for the Burmese regime, excludes many Burmese officials from admission to the United States, and instructs the President to cooperate with ASEAN and other states to develop a multilateral strategy to improve human rights conditions in Burma.

A trade association challenged the Massachusetts law, alleging that it impermissibly infringes upon the foreign affairs power, under the precedent of *Zschernig*; that it violates the dormant foreign commerce power of Congress; and that it is preempted by the congressional sanctions law. Massachusetts defended the law on the grounds that its impact on foreign affairs is indirect; that, unlike the Oregon law in *Zschernig,* Massachusetts does not undertake an ongoing critical review of a foreign state's application of its own laws; and that *Zschernig* permits the courts to balance the weightiness of Massachusetts' aims against the impact on foreign affairs. With respect to the foreign commerce clause of Article I § 8 cl. 3, Massachusetts argued that it should enjoy a "market participant" exception, analogous to that recognized in several Supreme Court opinions concerning the domestic commerce clause; that its law treats foreign and U.S. companies doing business in Burma identically; and that to force it to purchase goods and services from companies doing business in Burma would invade its reserved powers under the Tenth Amendment. Massachusetts argued that its law is not preempted by the congressional sanctions because Congress was aware of the Massachusetts law at the time it adopted sanctions and consciously refrained from preempting it and similar local ordinances; that Congress has not occupied the field; that it is not impossible to comply with both laws; and that, although different techniques are adopted, both federal law and the Massachusetts law have an identical aim, to pressure Burma to improve its respect for human rights.

The First Circuit found the Massachusetts law to be invalid on all three grounds (foreign affairs power, foreign commerce clause, and preemption under the Supremacy Clause). In particular, the First Circuit held that no balancing of the importance of the state's interests against the impact on foreign affairs is permissible, with respect to state laws that have more than an incidental effect; that no "market participant" exception exists under the foreign commerce clause and in any case Massachusetts was acting as a regulator rather than a market participant; that the law discriminates against foreign commerce even though U.S. and foreign companies are treated alike, since the statute is aimed at a particular foreign government and its trading partners; that state laws that impinge upon the conduct of foreign affairs are especially liable to preemption; and that Massachusetts' unilateral approach interfered with Congress' choice to seek multilateral approaches to Burma that do not involve restrictions on trade. The First Circuit examined two lines of Supreme Court preemption precedent: Hines v. Davidowitz, 312 U.S. 52 (1941), which struck down a Pennsylvania alien registration law; and DeCanas v. Bica, 424 U.S. 351 (1976), which upheld a California law penalizing employers who hire non-citizens forbidden to work under federal immigration laws. The First Circuit distinguished the Massachusetts Burma law from the California statute in *DeCanas* on grounds that the employment criminalized by California was already forbidden by federal law; the court noted that the federal Burma sanctions do not penalize companies that sell goods or services in Burma. National Foreign Trade Council v. Natsios and Anderson, 181 F.3d 38 (1st Cir.1999).

Do you agree with the First Circuit's reasoning? How exclusive is the foreign affairs power, and how incidental must the effects of state regulation be on foreign affairs in order to survive this type of constitutional challenge? Massachusetts noted that it has twenty-three agreements with "sister states" and other sub-national foreign governments and foreign trade promotion organizations.

The Supreme Court affirmed the First Circuit decision in Crosby v. National Foreign Trade Council, 530 U.S. 363 (2000) (finding implicit preemption in the 1997 federal sanctions statute and noting that the effect of the state law undermined the intended purpose and natural effect of a delegation of discretion to the President to control economic sanctions against Burma).

3. What is the test in *Pink* with respect to the supremacy of international law? Is it different than those found in *Zschernig*? In view of the recognitions in *Missouri v. Holland* and *Reid v. Covert* that treaties are supreme law of the land, that the treaty power is expressly delegated to the federal government and expressly denied to the states, and that the Tenth Amendment is no barrier, should federal preemption tests even be considered in the context of a clash between state legislation and a treaty? Is preemption more relevant when state law is not inconsistent with a relevant treaty?

4. For another Supreme Court case on the preemption by treaties when no intent is expressed in the treaty concerning its domestic primacy, see El Al Israel Airlines, Ltd. v. Tseng, 525 U.S. 155 (1999), extract in Chapter 7.

5. Are non-self-executing treaties supreme law of the land for supremacy purposes? for purposes of federal preemption? Recall Sei Fujii v. California, 38 Cal.2d 718 (1952), in Section 2 C 1. That case was not appealed to the U.S. Supreme Court. Further, in no U.S. Supreme Court decision has a treaty had to be self-executing for such purposes. *See, e.g.*, JORDAN J. PAUST, INTERNATIONAL LAW AS LAW OF THE UNITED STATES 111 ("Ever since *Ware v. Hylton*, the supremacy of international law (treaty-based, customary, or that based on executive agreement) over state law has been complete."), 112, 115–16, 156–58, 361–62, 389 n.86 (2 ed. 2003); *see also* United States v. Duarte–Acero, 208 F.3d 1282, 1284 (11th Cir. 2000); Gordon v. Kerr, 10 F. Cas. 801, 802 (C.C.D.Pa.1806) (No. 5,611) (seemingly non-self-executing treaty "is supreme" over a state constitution); 6 Op. Att'y Gen. 291, 293 (1854) (all treaties are supreme law over the states—even treaties requiring "enactment of a statute to regulate the details"); BURNS H. WESTON, *ET AL.*, INTERNATIONAL LAW AND WORLD ORDER 192 (1980); Quincy Wright, *National Courts and Human Rights—The Fujii Case*, 45 AM. J. INT'L L. 62, 69 (1951) ("the distinction between self-executing and non-self-executing treaties has been used in American constitutional law only with reference to the agency of the Federal Government competent to execute the treaty and has had no reference to the relations between the Federal Government and the States. . . ."); RESTATEMENT § 115, cmt. e ("Since any treaty . . . is federal law . . . , it supersedes inconsistent State law or policy. . . . Even a non-self-executing agreement . . . may sometimes be held to be federal policy superseding State law or policy . . . [and] may also be held to occupy a field and preempt a subject, and supersede State law or policy. . . ."); *but see In re* Alien Children Education Litigation, 501 F.Supp. 544, 590 (S.D.Tex.1980).

What does the word "all" in Article VI, clause 2, of the U.S. Constitution mean when it mandates: "all Treaties made, or which shall be made, under the Authority of the United States, shall be supreme Law of the Land. . . ."? What did Justice Chase mean in *Ware* by the word "any"? Since the human rights provisions of the U.N. Charter have not yet been found to be self-executing, what did Justice Murphy mean in *Oyama*? Also recall Justice Douglas in *Zschernig* ("even in absence of a treaty"). See also Jordan J. Paust, *Race-Based Affirmative Action and International Law*, 18 MICH. J. INT'L L. 659, 671–72 & n.45 (1997) (also noting the special meaning of the U.S. declaration on non-self-execution concerning the Covenant); *Customary International Law and Human Rights Treaties* Are *Law of the United States*, 20 MICH. J. INT'L L. 301, 322–27 (1999).

6. Is customary international law also supreme law of the land? *See, e.g.*, Chisholm v. Georgia, 2 U.S. (2 Dall.) 419, 474 (1793) (Jay, C.J.); United States v. Ravara, 2 U.S. (2 Dall.) 297, 298 (Wilson, J.), 299 n.* (C.C.D. Pa. 1793); Page v. Pendleton, 1 Va. Rep. (Wythe) 211 (Ch. 1793); RESTATEMENT § 111 (1) and cmt. d, § 115, cmt. e; LOUIS HENKIN, FOREIGN AFFAIRS AND THE UNITED STATES CONSTITUTION 234, 510 n.20 (2 ed. 1996); PAUST, *supra* at 7–8, 10–11, 38, 53–54, 56–59, 111, 116, 118, 121, 165–67, 205, 208–09, 213, 255–56, 275, 333–34; Harold Hongju Koh, *Is International Law Really State Law?*, 111 HARV. L. REV. 1824 (1998); Jordan J. Paust, *Customary International Law in the United States: Clean and Dirty Laundry*, 40 GERMAN Y.B. INT'L L. 78 (1998); *Customary International Law and Human Rights Treaties* Are *Law of the United States*, 20 MICH. J. INT'L L. 301 (1999); *but see* Curtis

A. Bradley, Jack L. Goldsmith, *Customary International Law as Federal Common Law: A Critique of the Modern Position*, 110 Harv. L. Rev. 815, 821, 824–25, 851 (1997); *Federal Courts and the Incorporation of International Law*, 111 Harv. L. Rev. 2260 (1998).

For additional recognition that states are bound by the law of nations and that customary international law is supreme law for supremacy and preemptive purposes, *see, e.g.*, Skiriotes v. Florida, 313 U.S. 69, 72–73 (1941) ("International law ... is the law of all States of the Union."); Manchester v. Massachusetts, 139 U.S. 240, 264 (1891) (states are bound by law of nations in defining their boundaries); Dred Scott v. Sandford, 60 U.S. (19 How.) 393, 560 (1857) (McLean, J., dissenting) ("our States ... are independent, ... subject only to international laws...."); Murray v. Chicago & N.W. Railway Co., 62 F. 24, 42 (N.D. Iowa 1894) ("no more subject to abrogation or modification by state legislation than are the principles of the law of nations...."); United States *ex rel.* Wheeler v. Williamson, 28 F. Cas. 686, 692 (D.C.E.D. Pa. 1855) (No. 16,726) (each state "is bound by ... , because of its universal obligation, ... the 'law of nations.' What it could not do if freed from federative restrictions, it cannot do now; every restraint upon its policy ... binds it still.... "); Thompson v. Doaksum, 68 Cal. 593, 596, 10 P. 199, 201 (1886) (the obligation to protect private rights under the law of nations "passed to the new government"); Teschemacher v. Thompson, 18 Cal. 11, 22–23 (1861) (inviolability of property rights exists under the law of nations); Riddell v. Fuhrman, 233 Mass. 69, 73, 123 N.E. 237, 239 (1919) (" 'International law is a part of our law' and must be administered whenever involved in causes presented for determination."); Territory *ex rel.* Wade v. Ashenfelter, 4 N.M. 93, 148, 12 P. 879 (1887) (New Mexico judicial duty is "to maintain only those principles of law ... proper for the protection of human rights...."); People v. Liebowitz, 140 Misc.2d 820, 822, 531 N.Y.S.2d 719, 721 (1988) ("Even in the absence of a treaty, it is a court's obligation to enforce recognized principles of international law where questions of right depending on such principles are presented for the court's determination."); Republic of Argentina v. City of New York, 25 N.Y.2d 252, 259, 250 N.E.2d 698, 700, 303 N.Y.S.2d 644, 647 (Ct. of App. N.Y. 1969) (action "in this case is mandated by the rules of international law. It is settled that ... all domestic courts must give effect to customary international law."); De Simone v. Transportes Maritimos do Estado, 200 A.D. 82, 89, 192 N.Y.S. 815 (S.Ct. N.Y., App. Div., 1st Dep't. 1922) ("... the court has no jurisdiction and could not disregard the protest and overrule the objection by a claim ... [under] the municipal law of this State ... , for by the law of nations an adjudication ... could not be made...."); Stanley v. Ohio, 24 Ohio St. 166, 174 (1873) (state has concern "to discharge such duties as are imposed upon it by the law of nations"); Peters v. McKay, 195 Ore. 412, 424, 426, 238 P.2d 225, 230–31 (1951) ("... the rule is firmly established and uniformly recognized that 'International law is part of our law and as such is the law of all States of the Union.... The rule has been briefly stated as follows: ... the law of nations is to be treated as part of the law of the land. The courts of all nations judicially notice this law, and it must be ascertained and administered by the courts of appropriate jurisdiction as often as questions of right depending upon it are duly presented for their determination....' 30 Am. Jur., International Law, p. 178 § 7.... In essence, the rule appears to be that international law is part of the law of every state which is enforced by its courts without any constitutional or statutory act of incorporation by reference, and ... relevant provisions of the law of nations are legally paramount whenever international rights and duties are involved before a court having jurisdiction to enforce them."); Cheriot v. Foussat, 3 Binn. 220, 257 (Pa. 1810) ("The United States have always considered themselves bound by the law of nations.... The nation which makes a penal municipal law, has a right to direct the proceedings under it, in what manner it pleases, provided it does not violate the law of nations."); Banks v. Greenleaf, 10 Va. 271, 277 (1799) ("Admiralty causes bind all the world; because decided, upon the laws of nations...."); *Ex parte* Holmes, 12 Vt. 631, 636 (1840) ("The law of nations is binding upon us, not as a part of the common law"); State v. Pang, 132 Wash.2d 852, 908, 940 P.2d 1293, 1322 (1997) ("International law is incorporated into our domestic law."); *see also* Woodworth v. Fulton, 1 Cal. 295, 306 (1850) ("the law of nations ... , as it is a part of the laws of all civilized countries, forms also a branch of American jurisprudence."); People *ex rel.* Attorney–General v. Naglee, 1 Cal. 232, 234 (1850) (state has "power to do a given act, which, without a transgression of international law, falls within the scope of powers of any independent nation," unless transferred to federal government); Maryland v. Turner, 75 Misc. 9, 11, 132 N.Y.S. 173, 174 (1911) ("however inclined courts may be to follow the interpretation of such statutes by the courts of the State which has enacted the statute, their interpretation is not conclusive, and ... the Supreme Court distinctly lays down the rule that the question of international law as to whether the action is to enforce a penalty or not 'must be determined by the court, State or National, in which the suit is brought.' The test is not by what name the statute is called by the Legislature or by the courts of the State in which it was passed...."); Lehman v. McBride, 15 Ohio St. 573, 607 (1863) (in face of argument that state legislation violates international law and is therefore void, state legislation was construed so as not to be extraterritorial in violation of international law); *Ex parte* Bushnell, 9 Ohio St. 77, 189 (1859) ("The constitution of the United States was framed, and the union perfected, subordinate to, and without violating the fundamental laws of nations.... "); McArthur v. Kelly, 5 Ohio 139, 143 (1831) ("The law of nations require it."); Siplyak v. Davis, 276 Pa. 49, 52, 119 A. 745, 746 (S.Ct. Pa. 1923) ("'... where the general law of nations and those of foreign commerce say the contrary ... I very much question the power or authority of any state or nation ... to pass such a law ... ,'" *quoting* Hanger v. Abbott, 73 U.S. (6 Wall.) 532, 536 (1867)); Manhattan Life Ins. Co. v. Warwick, 61 Va. 614, 651 (1871) ("can it be maintained that this statute ... shall override the public and universal law of nations ... ? ... The refutation of such a proposition is found in its simple statement. It would be a solecism in law and reason....").

7. In 1997, Alberto Gonzales, General Counsel for Governor George W. Bush of Texas, wrote to Michael J. Matheson, Acting Legal Adviser of the U.S. Dep't of State: "Since the State of Texas is not a signatory to the Vienna Convention on Consular Relations [ratified by the United States], we believe it is inappropriate to ask Texas to determine whether a breach of Article 36 of the Vienna Convention ... occurred in connection with the arrest and conviction of Mr. Montoya [a Mexican national].... Additionally,

... I felt it would be inappropriate for the Governor's Office to give an opinion regarding the consequences and materiality of any breach of the treaty.... Such legal matters are best left to our courts...." Letter of June 16, 1997 regarding "Death Penalty Case of Mexican National, Irineo Tristan Montoya. Does the letter make sense?

8. In Breard v. Greene, 523 U.S. 371 (1998) (6–3 vote), the Supreme Court denied a petition for habeas corpus of Angel Francisco Breard, who was later executed by the State of Virginia. Breard had claimed that he was denied the right to consult with a consul from his native country, Paraguay, as required by the Vienna Convention on Consular Relations, 21 U.S.T. 77, 596 U.N.T.S. 261 (in the Documents Supplement). The Supreme Court found that Breard had "procedurally defaulted his claim, if any, under the Vienna Convention by failing to raise that claim in the state courts." 523 U.S. at 375. Portions of the per curiam opinion follow. Read relevant provisions of the Convention on Consular Relations in connection with the Court's opinion. Read especially Articles 5 and 36 of the Vienna Convention.

BREARD v. GREENE

523 U.S. 371 (1998).

Per Curiam.

In September 1996, the Republic of Paraguay, the Ambassador of Paraguay to the United States, and the Consul General of Paraguay to the United States (collectively Paraguay) brought suit in Federal District Court against certain Virginia officials, alleging that their separate rights under the Vienna Convention had been violated by the Commonwealth's failure to inform Breard of his rights under the treaty and to inform the Paraguayan consulate of Breard's arrest, conviction, and sentence. In addition, the Consul General asserted a parallel claim under 42 U.S.C. § 1983, alleging a denial of his rights under the Vienna Convention. The District Court concluded that it lacked subject-matter jurisdiction over these suits because Paraguay was not alleging a "continuing violation of federal law" and therefore could not bring its claims within the exception to Eleventh Amendment immunity established in Ex parte Young, 209 U.S. 123 ... (1908). Republic of Paraguay v. Allen, 949 F. Supp. 1269, 1272–1273 (E.D.Va.1996). The Fourth Circuit affirmed on Eleventh Amendment grounds. Republic of Paraguay v. Allen, 134 F.3d 622 (1998). Paraguay has also petitioned this Court for a writ of certiorari.

On April 3, 1998, nearly five years after Breard's conviction became final, the Republic of Paraguay instituted proceedings against the United States in the International Court of Justice (ICJ), alleging that the United States violated the Vienna Convention at the time of Breard's arrest. On April 9, the ICJ noted jurisdiction and issued an order requesting that the United States "take all measures at its disposal to ensure that Angel Francisco Breard is not executed pending the final decision in these proceedings...." The ICJ set a briefing schedule for this matter, with oral argument likely to be held this November. Breard then filed a petition for an original writ of habeas corpus and a stay application in this Court in order to "enforce" the ICJ's order. Paraguay filed a motion for leave to file a bill of complaint in this Court, citing this Court's original jurisdiction over cases "affecting Ambassadors ... and Consuls." U.S. Const., Art. III, § 2.

It is clear that Breard procedurally defaulted his claim, if any, under the Vienna Convention by failing to raise that claim in the state courts. Nevertheless, in their petitions for certiorari, both Breard and Paraguay contend that Breard's Vienna Convention claim may be heard in federal court because the Convention is the "supreme law of the land" and thus trumps the procedural default doctrine.... This argument is plainly incorrect for two reasons.

First, while we should give respectful consideration to the interpretation of an international treaty rendered by an international court with jurisdiction to interpret such, it has been recognized in international law that, absent a clear and express statement to the contrary, the procedural rules of the forum State govern the implementation of the treaty in that State.... This proposition is embodied in the Vienna Convention itself, which provides that the rights expressed in the Convention "shall be exercised in conformity with the laws and regulations of the receiving State," provided that "said laws and regulations must enable full effect to be given to the purposes for which the rights accorded under this Article are intended." Article 36(2), [1970] 21 U.S. T., at 101. It is the rule in this country that assertions of error in criminal proceedings must first be raised in state court in order to form the basis for relief in habeas. Wainwright v. Sykes, 433 U.S. 72 ... (1977). Claims not so raised are considered defaulted. *Ibid.* By not asserting his Vienna Convention claim in state court, Breard failed to exercise his rights under the Vienna Convention in conformity with the laws of the United States and the Commonwealth of Virginia. Having failed to do so, he cannot raise a claim of violation of those rights now on federal habeas review.

Second, although treaties are recognized by our Constitution as the supreme law of the land, that status is no less true of provisions of the Constitution itself, to which rules of procedural default apply. We have held "that an Act of Congress ... is on a full parity with a treaty, and that when a statute which is subsequent in time is inconsistent with a treaty, the statute to the extent of conflict renders the treaty null." ... The Vienna Convention—which arguably confers on an individual the right to consular assistance following arrest—has continuously been in effect since 1969. But in 1996, before Breard filed his habeas petition raising claims under the Vienna Convention, Congress enacted the Antiterrorism and Effective Death Penalty Act (AEDPA), which provides that a habeas petitioner alleging that he is held in violation of "treaties of the United States" will, as a general rule, not be afforded an evidentiary hearing if he "has failed to develop the factual basis of [the] claim in State court proceedings." 28 U.S.C. A §§ 2254(a), (e)(2) (Supp. 1998). Breard's ability to obtain relief based on violations of the Vienna Convention is subject to this subsequently-enacted rule, just as any claim arising under the United States Constitution would be. This rule prevents Breard from establishing that the violation of his Vienna Convention rights prejudiced him. Without a hearing, Breard cannot establish how the Consul would have advised him, how the advice of his attorneys differed from the advice the Consul could have provided, and what factors he considered in electing to reject the plea bargain that the State offered him. That limitation, Breard also argues, is not justified because his Vienna Convention claims were so novel that he could not have discovered them any earlier. Assuming that were true, such novel claims would be barred on habeas review under Teague v. Lane, 489 U.S. 288 ... (1989). Even were Breard's Vienna Convention claim properly raised and proven, it is extremely doubtful that the violation should result in the overturning of a final judgment of conviction without some showing that the violation had an effect on the trial. Arizona v. Fulminante, 499 U.S. 279 ... (1991). In this case no such showing could even arguably be made. Breard decided not to plead guilty and to testify at his own trial contrary to the advice of his attorneys, who were likely far better able to explain the United States legal system to him than any consular official would have been. Breard's asserted prejudice—that had the Vienna Convention been followed, he would have accepted the State's offer to forgo the death penalty in return for a plea of guilty—is far more speculative than the claims of prejudice courts routinely reject in those cases were an inmate alleges that his plea of guilty was infected by attorney error.... As for Paraguay's suits (both the original action and the case coming to us on petition for certiorari), neither the text nor the history of the Vienna Convention clearly provides a foreign nation a private right of action in United States' courts to set aside a criminal conviction and sentence for violation of consular notification provisions. The Eleventh Amendment provides a separate reason why Paraguay's suit might not succeed. That Amendment's "fundamental principle" that "the States, in the absence of consent, are immune from suits brought against them ... by a foreign State" was enunciated in Principality of Monaco v. Mississippi, 292 U.S. 313, 329–330 ... (1934). Though Paraguay claims that its suit is within an exemption dealing with continuing consequences of past violations of federal rights, see Milliken v. Bradley, 433 U.S. 267 ... (1977), we do not agree. The failure to notify the Paraguayan Consul occurred long ago and has no continuing effect. The causal link present in *Milliken* is absent in this case. Insofar as the Consul General seeks to base his claims on § 1983, his suit is not cognizable. Section 1983 provides a cause of action to any "person within the jurisdiction" of the United States for the deprivation "of any rights, privileges, or immunities secured by the Constitution and laws." As an initial matter, it is clear that Paraguay is not authorized to bring suit under § 1983. Paraguay is not a "person" as that term is used in § 1983.... Nor is Paraguay "within the jurisdiction" of the United States. And since the Consul General is acting only in his official capacity, he has no greater ability to proceed under § 1983 than does the country he represents. Any rights that the Consul General might have by virtue of the Vienna Convention exist for the benefit of Paraguay, not for him as an individual. It is unfortunate that this matter comes before us while proceedings are pending before the ICJ that might have been brought to that court earlier. Nonetheless, this Court must decide questions presented to it on the basis of law. The Executive Branch, on the other hand, in exercising its authority over foreign relations may, and in this case did, utilize diplomatic discussion with Paraguay. Last night the Secretary of State sent a letter to the Governor of Virginia requesting that he stay Breard's execution. If the Governor wishes to wait for the decision of the ICJ, that is his prerogative. But nothing in our existing case law allows us to make that choice for him. For the foregoing reasons, we deny the petition for an original writ of habeas corpus, the motion for leave to file a bill of complaint, the petitions for certiorari, and the accompanying stay applications filed by Breard and Paraguay.

Statement of Justice SOUTER

I agree with the Court that the lack of any reasonably arguable causal connection between the alleged treaty violations and Breard's conviction and sentence disentitle him to relief on any theory offered....

[Dissents by Justices STEVENS, BREYER and GINSBURG omitted]

Notes and Questions

1. Do you agree with the per curiam opinion?

2. There have been varied but mostly critical responses to the Court's ruling. *See, e.g., Agora:* Breard, 92 AM. J. INT'L L. 666–712 (1998) (remarks of Professors Charney, Reisman, Bradley and Goldsmith, Henkin, Vasquez, Paust, Damrosch, Kirgis, Slaughter); Henry J. Richardson, *The Execution of Angel Breard by the United States: Violating an Order of the International Court of Justice*, 12 TEMPLE INT'L & COMP. L.J. 121 (1998); *see also* S. Adele Shank & John Quigley, *Foreigners on Texas's Death Row and the Right of Access to a Consul*, 26 ST. MARY'S L.J. 719 (1995); Victor M. Uribe, *Consuls at Work: Universal Instruments of Human Rights and Consular Protection in the Context of Criminal Justice*, 19 HOUS. J. INT'L L. 375 (1997); *but see* Curtis A. Bradley, *Breard, Our Dualist Constitution and the Internationalist Conception*, 51 STAN. L. REV. 529 (1999). One of our editors stresses that the decision was incorrect for, among others, the following reasons:

Article 36 (1) (a) of the Vienna Convention on Consular Relations provides that (a) "[n]ationals ... shall have the same freedom with respect to communication and access to consular officers," and that (b) "... [t]he said authorities shall inform the person concerned without delay of his rights under this subparagraph". In *Breard v. Greene*, the Supreme Court nearly recognized that, under the Convention, the individual petitioner had actionable rights under the Convention that were violated. The Court concluded, however, that the rights were "defaulted" when not pursued in the state courts, that the errors would not be prejudicial, and that the subsequently enacted federal Antiterrorism and Effective Death Penalty Act limited the petitioner's "ability to obtain relief based on violations of the Vienna Convention."

In my opinion, application of both the procedural "default" doctrine and the subsequent statute to defeat the treaty-based rights of the individual was inappropriate. In view of *The Charming Betsy* rule, the procedural doctrine should be interpreted consistently with international law. In this case, Article 36 (2) of the treaty mandates that domestic "laws and regulations must enable full effect to be given to the purposes for which the rights accorded ... are intended." Applied to the Consular Convention claims, the "default" doctrine would be inconsistent with such a mandate, since "full effect" would not be given to the purposes at stake, which concern the rights to be notified, to communicate and to have consular assistance. As supreme federal law under the Constitution, the admittedly self-executing treaty should have trumped inconsistent judicially created federal procedural doctrines. As the Court has recognized at least since 1796, federal judges are bound to apply treaty law. If they were not, they could fashion procedural rules to subvert the domestic effect of a treaty. Such a result would be contrary to the views of the Founders, the constitutional design and predominant trends in judicial decision....

The per curiam opinion stated that international law requires "a clear and express statement to the contrary" or else "procedural rules of the forum state [will] govern implementation of" a treaty. This statement reflects several misunderstandings: (1) evident confusion of conflicts principles with international law; (2) a miserly misstatement of the law of treaties (especially the obligation to perform in good faith and the rule that internal law may not be invoked as justification for a failure to perform); (3) inattention to the role of customary law as interpretive background; and (4) inattention to the rule that treaties are to be construed liberally to protect express and implied rights. Procedural guarantees under international law, including rights of access to courts, to communicate with and assistance of consuls, and of an effective judicial remedy, can certainly be implied. Express or implied, they must govern good faith implementation of a relevant treaty. Moreover, in this case a clear and express mandate contained in Article 36 (2) of the treaty requires that domestic "laws and regulations must enable full effect to be given to the purposes" of the rights accorded in the treaty. Especially in view of such a mandate, it would be disingenuous to argue that domestic procedural rules can deny full effect to such treaty-based rights....

The exception addressed by the Court [regarding foreign state suits against a U.S. state and the Eleventh Amendment], concerning "continuing consequences of past violations of federal rights," seems applicable despite the per curiam's terse dismissal of its relevance. First, the individual who is incarcerated after conviction without having had contact with and timely advice and assistance from a consular officer because of the local state's failure to notify suffers a continuing violation of a treaty-based federal right and seeks relief from the continuing wrong. To declare that the violation has ended because communication with a consular officer is permitted much later during appeal, but that the conviction remains, is bizarre. Second, to say that a past failure to notify "has no continuing effect" seems unreal in view of the outcry from several foreign states and Paraguay's efforts within the United States and before the International Court of Justice. The failure to notify the consulate effectively precluded the foreign consul and the foreign state from meaningfully assisting their national. A conviction without notice to the consulate and opportunity for consultation and assistance and a resulting incarceration are "continuing consequences." Moreover, an unregulated violation might have a continuing effect by spawning additional violations in other cases.

Another exception should be recognized in view of the text and structure of the Constitution. Article VI, clause 2 assures that "all Treaties ... shall be the supreme law of the Land...." The mandate of Article VI is absolute, whereas immunity from foreign state suits provided by the Eleventh Amendment is implied and has exceptions designed to assure the primacy of rights under federal law. Although treaty-based rights fit within such an exception, the absolute supremacy and reach of treaties to the states under Article VI should condition the meaning of the Eleventh Amendment. Hence, courts should recognize that treaty-based rights form an exception to local state immunities. Clearly, the constitutional plan was that states are not to be immune from the reach of treaties. Jordan J. Paust, *Breard and Treaty–Based Rights under the Consular Convention*, 92 Am. J. Int'l L. 691 (1998).

3. After Breard was executed, Paraguay withdrew its case against the U.S. in the I.C.J. Thereafter, Germany brought a similar case against the U.S. in the I.C.J. concerning denial of the right of German nationals to communicate with consular officials and their subsequent execution by the state of Arizona.

In the LaGrand Case (Germany v. United States), 2001 I.C.J. 466, the I.C.J. found the United States to be in breach of the Vienna Convention on Consular Relations and declared that the U.S. must provide "by means of its own choosing ... review and reconsideration" of such matters in the future and that a domestic rule regarding procedural default cannot be used to deny judicial consideration of violations of the treaty. The I.C.J. also recognized that Article 36(1) creates individual rights and that Article 36(2) prevents use of a procedural default rule to bar challenges to convictions and sentences. See 2001 I.C.J. 466. The I.C.J. reiterated that Article 36(1) creates individual rights in Avena and Other Mexican Nationals (Mexico v. United States), 2004 I.C.J. 1, para. 106. The *Avena* opinion also found the U.S. to be in violation of Articles 36(1)(a) and (c) by not enabling Mexican consular officials to communicate with and have access to their nationals and to arrange for their legal representation. *Id.* paras. 106(3)-(4), 153(6)-(7). As a required remedy, the I.C.J. held that the U.S. must permit "review and reconsideration" of the convictions and sentences of relevant Mexican nationals. *Id.* paras. 14, 121–22, 153(9).

While a case involving one of the Mexican nationals in *Avena* was before the U.S. Supreme Court in *Medellin v. Dretke* (see Note 5 below) and was scheduled for oral argument in a few weeks, President Bush notified the U.S. Attorney General that he had determined "that the United States will discharge its international obligations under the decision of the International Court of Justice" and stated that he has constitutional authority to order state courts to comply. Does the President have such an authority? See also U.N. Charter, art. 94(1); U.S. Const., arts. II, VI, cl. 2. In an amicus brief, the U.S. Government claimed that rights of the Mexican nationals recognized in the I.C.J. decision pertain only under the presidential determination (a type of treaty-executive order), which, "like an executive agreement, has independent legal force and effect, and contrary state rules must give way under the Supremacy Clause." Do you agree?

4. In United States v. Lombera–Camorlinga, 170 F.3d 1241 (9th Cir. 1999), the Ninth Circuit recognized, contrary to the argument of the government, that rights under Article 36 belong to the detainee and that the detainee has standing to raise a claim under the treaty. The case was remanded to determine whether post-arrest statements can be suppressed because the detainee was not advised of his rights under the Vienna Convention and whether he was prejudiced thereby.

In United States *ex rel.* Madej v. Schomig, 2002 WL 31386480 (N.D. Ill. 2002), the district court stated: "After *LaGrand* . . . , no court can credibly hold that the Vienna Convention does not create individually enforceable rights. The International Court of Justice was quite clear on this point, announcing that 'Article 36, paragraph 1, creates individual rights.' " The Inter–American Commission on Human Rights agrees. In its Report No. 52/02 on Case No. 11,753, Ramon Martinez Villareal (10 Oct. 2002), the Commission found that a U.S. violation of the Convention led to violations of due process of law and rights to a fair trial under Articles XVIII and XXVI of the American Declaration on the Rights and Duties of Man. Similarly, the Inter–American Court of Human Rights recognized that the Vienna Convention creates individual rights that must be effectuated to serve due process. Advisory Op. OC–16/99, Inter–Am. Ct. H.R., Ser. A, No. 16, paras. 78–80, 82–84 (individual rights), 121–24 (due process) (1999).

5. In 2005, the Supreme Court had a chance to revisit these issues. In a five-to-four decision in *Medellin v. Dretke*, the Court decided to dismiss the writ of certiorari as improvidently granted. The majority gave five factors as determining their decision: violations of the Vienna Convention's provisions may not be cognizable in a federal habeas proceeding, federal habeas relief is only available when adjudication is contrary to or an unreasonable application of federal law, a new rule of law cannot be enforced in a habeas corpus claim for relief, Medellin had to have a certificate of appealability to appeal his claim on its merits, and federal habeas relief may only be sought after exhausting all remedies in state courts. The dismissal of certiorari ended the federal proceedings, but the Court indicated that either Texas or Medellin could seek certiorari based on the Texas court's ruling on his petition.

The dissent asserted that rather than dismissing the writ, the case should have been remanded to the Court of Appeals for the Fifth Circuit in order to make initial rulings on the difficult issues involved in the case. These issues included whether I.C.J. decisions are binding on U.S. courts, whether Article 36(1)(b) of the Vienna Convention created an individual right to obtain judicial enforcement, and whether Article 36(2) of the Convention requires state courts to set aside procedural rules in order to satisfy treaty requirements. The dissent also indicated that if the case had been remanded it would be possible to delay the federal decision until the state court had resolved Medellin's petition in state court. Medellin v. Dretke, 73 U.S.L.W. 4381 (May 24, 2005) (No. 04–5928).

2. Shared Powers

CHRISTIAN COUNTY COURT v. RANKIN AND THARP

63 Ky. 502, 505–06 (1866).

[After noting that the burning of a courthouse by Confederate soldiers was an unlawful act of war in violation of "the laws of nations," the Supreme Court of Kentucky declared:]

There must be a remedy, and of that remedy the State judiciary has jurisdiction. There is nothing in the Federal Constitution which deprives a State court of power to decide a question of international law incidentally involved in a case over which it has jurisdiction; and for every wrong the common law ... provides an adequate remedy. To sustain this action, therefore, it is not necessary to invoke any statutory aid....

Wherefore, on international and common law principles, we adjudge that the petition in this case sets forth a good cause of action....

Notes and Questions

1. With respect to state competence to identify and apply customary international law, by necessary implication the very fact that under the Supremacy Clause state courts are bound to apply international law enhances their power to do so. The Restatement notes:

> Questions under international law or international agreements of the United States often arise in State courts. As law of the United States, international law is also the law of every State, is a basis for the exercise of judicial authority by State courts, and is cognizable in cases in State courts.

RESTATEMENT § 111, cmt. d. It adds: "State courts take judicial notice of federal law and will therefore take judicial notice of international law as law of the United States." *Id.* § 113, cmt. b. Today, 28 U.S.C. § 1441 (b) allows removal of an action from a state to a federal court, but per terms of the statute only if jurisdiction is actually "founded on a claim or right arising under" international law. The same follows if international law is only incidentally involved. *See, e.g.,* Marathon Oil Co. v. Ruhrgas, 115 F.3d 315 (5th Cir.1997) (under "the well-pleaded complaint rule," if the complaint alleges only state law causes of action, removal to a federal court will not obtain unless there is "a cause of action necessarily requiring 'the resolution of a substantial question of federal law' "and mere intervention by Germany does not meet the test); Torres v. Southern Peru Copper Corp., 113 F.3d 540 (5th Cir.1997); Baker v. Bell Helicopter/Textron, Inc., 907 F.Supp. 1007, 1011–12 (N.D.Tex.1995); *see also* Delgado v. Shell Oil Co., 890 F.Supp. 1324, 1348–49 (S.D.Tex.1995).

2. U.S. instruments of ratification for both the 1966 Covenant on Civil and Political Rights and the 1965 International Convention on the Elimination of All Forms of Racial Discrimination have an Understanding that contains a federal clause. The Race Discrimination Convention's clause is typical. It reads:

> this Convention shall be implemented by the Federal Government to the extent that it exercises jurisdiction over the matters therein, and otherwise by the state and local governments. To the extent that state and local governments exercise jurisdiction ... , the Federal Government shall, as necessary, take appropriate measures to ensure the fulfillment of this Convention.

Instead of the phrase "shall, as necessary, take appropriate measures to ensure fulfillment of this Convention," the Understanding with respect to the Covenant provides: "shall take measures appropriate to the federal system to the end that the competent authorities of the state or local governments may take appropriate measures for the fulfillment of the Covenant." What does such an understanding mean in terms of federal responsibility and state competence? In connection with treaty-based permissibility of affirmative action, Professor Paust has written: "Such a clause does not change the fact that permissibility of affirmative action is assured under the treaty, nor that the Convention's obligations are to be fulfilled.

"Yet, whether or not various entities within the federal government or the states are to proceed affirmatively to mandate affirmative action may be a relevant question for consideration. For example, although Article 2 (2) of the Race Discrimination Convention requires the United States, 'when the circumstances so warrant,' to take 'special and concrete measures,' it may be left to the discretion of the United States to exercise its jurisdictional competence to implement the treaty or to allow states to proceed. If the states do not proceed, the United States is bound by Article 2 of the treaty to take action (*i.e.,* there is no gap in the U.S. duty under Article 2 merely because neither the states nor federal governmental entities have yet proceeded to adopt special measures).

"That the federal government has jurisdictional competence to implement treaty law is well understood. Moreover, at a minimum, the states cannot deny the permissibility of affirmative action assured under the treaties. Indeed, the federal clauses require that the treaties 'shall be implemented ... otherwise by the state and local governments,' thus making duties under the treaties concurrent." Jordan J. Paust, *Race-Based Affirmative Action and International Law*, 18 MICH. J. INT'L L. 659, 673 (1997). Do you agree? Do the "federal clauses" recognize that federal and state competencies to effectuate the Covenant's guarantees are concurrent?

3. Article 50 of the 1966 Covenant on Civil and Political Rights requires: "The provisions of the present Covenant shall extend to all parts of federal States without any limitations or exceptions." In view of Article 50, is the U.S. Understanding wrong? Is the Understanding void? How should it be interpreted? Is it compatible with Article VI, cl. 2, of the U.S. Constitution? *See also* David P. Stewart, *United States Ratification of the Covenant on Civil and Political Rights: The Significance of the Reservations, Understandings, and Declarations*, 42 DEPAUL L. REV. 1183, 1201 (1993) ("Article 50 ... was included precisely to prevent federal states from limiting their obligations to areas within the federal government's authority), a reservation exempting constituent units might readily be characterized as contrary to the object and purpose of the Article, if not the Covenant as a whole."); Executive Explanation of Proposed Reservations, Understandings and Decla-

rations, U.S. Senate Executive Report of the Bush Administration 102–23, 102d Cong., 2d Sess., *reprinted in* 31 I.L.M. 645, 656–57 (1992) ("In light of Article 50 . . . , it is appropriate to clarify that, even though the Covenant will apply to state and local authorities, it will be implemented consistent with U.S. concepts of federalism.... A reservation is not necessary with respect to Article 50 since the intent is not to modify or limit U.S. undertakings under the Covenant.... the U.S. will implement its obligations under the Covenant by appropriate legislative, executive and judicial means, federal or state as appropriate...."). Recall Chapter 1, Section 2 A.

4. Does the "federal clause" in the Understanding concerning the Covenant (see Section 2 C 1 d) assure that states and subentities within the U.S. can choose to execute a non-self-executing treaty or to further implement rights under the Covenant as long as there is no denial of such rights? Consider especially the last phrase of the Understanding concerning the Covenant. Would that be compatible with the Supremacy Clause of the Constitution? Can fifty states implement the Covenant fifty different ways as long as all rights under the Covenant are effective? Is there some room for flexibility in implementation because of the nature of certain rights, the circumstances pertaining in certain states, and/or a flexibility among affirmative options permitted by the U.S. Understanding?

Does the "federal clause," coupled with Article 50 of the Covenant and the Supremacy Clause of the U.S. Constitution, do more—*e.g.*, does it mean that states are bound to execute and effectuate the treaty but can choose among affirmative and permissible options while not denying rights under the Covenant?

Do the federalism understandings preclude Congress from further implementing relevant treaties by federal legislation? Do they preclude the federal judiciary from implementing treaties by the exercise of "judicial jurisdiction"? How should one interpret the federalism understanding concerning the Covenant in view of Article 50 of the treaty?

Chapter Three

JURISDICTION AND EXTRADITION

SECTION 1. GENERAL PRESCRIPTIVE COMPETENCE

Introductory Problem

Ms. Ginger Breadmann, a naturalized U.S. citizen, was arrested in Toronto, Canada, while visiting her family. She is accused of serious terroristic crimes against the state of Canada under new legislation containing an extremely broad definition of terrorism and seeking to reach extraterritorial acts of "any person who intends to harm Canada or its citizens by engaging in terroristic acts."

Prior to her arrest, Ms. Breadmann had created a letter bomb at her residence in Akron, Ohio. She had intended to mail it to her former boyfriend at his office in a government building in Ottawa, Canada in order to kill or seriously injure him because he had been unfaithful to her. Ms. Breadmann mistakenly addressed and mailed the letter bomb to Ottumwa, which is a city in Iowa, where it was intercepted by U.S. postal authorities, who found her name along with a virulent note inside the package and notified Canadian authorities.

Does Canada have jurisdiction over this matter under international law?

Restatement of the Foreign Relations Law of the United States (3 ed. 1987)

§ 431. Jurisdiction to Enforce

(1) A state may employ judicial or nonjudicial measures to induce or compel compliance or punish noncompliance with its laws or regulations, provided it has jurisdiction to prescribe in accordance with §§ 402 and 403. [§ 403 appears near the end of Section 1 of this chapter.]

Comment *a*. *Relation of jurisdiction to enforce to jurisdiction to prescribe and to adjudicate*. Under international law, a state may not exercise authority to enforce law that it has no jurisdiction to prescribe. Such assertion of jurisdiction, whether carried out through the courts or by nonjudicial means, may be objected to by both the affected person directly and by the other state concerned.

§ 402. Bases of Jurisdiction to Prescribe

. . . a state has jurisdiction to prescribe law with respect to

(1)(a) conduct that, wholly or in substantial part, takes place within its territory;

(b) the status of persons, or interests in things, present within its territory;

(c) conduct outside its territory that has or is intended to have substantial effect within its territory;

(2) the activities, interests, status, or relations of its nationals outside as well as within it territory; and

(3) certain conduct outside its territory by persons not its nationals that is directed against the security of the state or against a limited class of other state interests.

[Editors' note: § 404 concerns universal jurisdiction with respect to violations of international law, whether or not there is any nexus with the forum, and appears in Section 2 of this chapter.]

Notes and Questions

1. As the Restatement notes, a state does not have jurisdiction to enforce its laws if, under international law, it did not have competence under international law to prescribe domestic law attempting to reach relevant acts or omissions. Customary international law recognizes four bases of prescriptive jurisdiction: (1) territorial (subjective and objective), (2) nationality, (3) protective, and (4) universal. In general, §§ 402 and 404 of the Restatement nearly reflect these customary principles. Because customary international law is law of the United States also for jurisdictional purposes and relevant to the exercise of judicial power under Articles III and VI of the U.S. Constitution (recall Chapter 2), before proceeding to enforce domestic laws, a U.S. court should be assured that the United States has prescriptive competence under one or more of these four principles. *See, e.g.*, United States v. Darnaud, 25 F. Cas. 754, 759–60 (C.C.E.D.Pa.1855) (No. 14, 918) ("if the Congress . . . were to call upon the courts of justice to extend the jurisdiction of the United States beyond the limits . . . [set by the 'law of nations'], it would be the duty of courts of justice to decline. . . ."); JORDAN J. PAUST, INTERNATIONAL LAW AS LAW OF THE UNITED STATES 6–6, 38, 44–46 (1996).

Application of one or more of these principles merely satisfies a requirement that jurisdiction pertain under international law. Whether or not a state like Canada or the United States has enacted legislation to take advantage of such competence and whether domestic requirements or elements set forth in the legislation are met are separate issues.

Additionally, not every element of an offense or civil wrong under domestic law has to occur within the forum state as far as international law is concerned. Some states require that each element of certain offenses takes place within their territory (or its equivalent). As long as prescriptive jurisdiction exists under international law, such self-limitations are a matter of domestic preference, provided the state has no conflicting duty under treaty-based or customary international law (*e.g.*, to enact laws proscribing certain international crimes even if there is no nexus with the forum).

2. One general preference in the United States involves a principle of statutory construction. Legislation is presumed to be territorial, not extra-territorial, in its reach. *See, e.g.*, Hartford Fire Insurance Co. v. California, 509 U.S. 764, 814 (1993) (Scalia, J., dissenting) (referring to the "longstanding principle of American law 'that legislation of Congress, unless a contrary intent appears, is meant to apply only within the territorial jurisdiction of the United States' "); EEOC v. Arabian American Oil Co., 499 U.S. 244, 248 (1991); Argentine Republic v. Amerada Hess Shipping, 488 U.S. 428, 440 (1989); Foley Bros., Inc. v. Filardo, 336 U.S. 281, 285 (1949); United States v. Bowman, 260 U.S. 94, 97–98 (1922), adding: in some cases "Congress has not thought it necessary to make specific provision in the law that the locus shall include the high seas and foreign countries, but allows it to be inferred from the nature of the offense." *Cf.* United States v. Layton, 855 F.2d 1388, 1395 (9th Cir.1988). Canada also uses a similar approach. *See, e.g.,* Libman v. The Queen, (1985), 21 C.C.C. (3d) 206 (S.C. Canada).

In United States v. Usama bin Laden, *et al.*, 92 F.Supp.2d 189 (S.D.N.Y. 2000), the district court stated that "the Supreme Court has established a limited exception to this standard approach for 'criminal statutes which are, as a class, not logically dependent on their locality for the Government's jurisdiction, but are enacted because of the right of the government to defend itself against obstruction, or fraud wherever perpetrated....' United States v. Bowman, 260 U.S. 94, 98 ... (1922). As regards statutes of this type, courts may infer the requisite intent 'from the nature of the offense' described in the statute, and need not examine its legislative history." *Id.* at 193. The opinion then noted that "*Bowman* rests on two factors: (1) the right of the United States to protect itself from harmful conduct–irrespective of the locus of this conduct, and (2) the presumption that Congress would not both (a) enact a statute designed to serve this protective function, and ... (b) undermine this protective intention by limiting the statute's application to United States territory." *Id.* at 194. The court added: "the underlying *Bowman* rationale ... depends on the right of the United States to defend itself from harmful conduct regardless of its locus, and a presumption that Congress would not undercut the effectiveness of statutes intended to serve this protective purpose by limiting them to United States territory and United States nationals." *Id.* at 197, adding, *id.* at 196, "[t]he *Bowman* rule would appear to be most directly related to the protective principle" of prescriptive jurisdiction under international law.

As the court explained, *bin Laden* involved an indictment charging "fifteen defendants with conspiracy to murder United States nationals, to use weapons of mass destruction against United States nationals, to destroy United States buildings and property, and to destroy United States defense utilities. The Indictment also charges defendants Mohamed Sadeek Odeh, Mohamed Rashed Daoud al-'Owhali, and Khalfan Khamis Mohamed, among others, with numerous crimes in connection with the August 1998 bombings of the United States Embassies in Nairobi, Kenya, and Dar es Salaam, Tanzania, including 223 counts of murder. The Indictment also charges defendant Wadih el Hage with numerous perjury and false statement counts. Six of the Defendants are presently in the custody of the Bureau of Prisons:

Mamdouh Mahmud Salim, Ali Mohamed, Wadih El Hage, Mohamed Rashed Daoud Al-Owhali, Khalfan Khamis Mohamed, and Mohamed Sadeek Odeh ("Odeh")." *Id.* at 192.

Applying the *Bowman* rationale and using other indicia of congressional intent, the court concluded that "Congress intended each of the following statutory provisions to reach conduct by foreign nationals on foreign soil: 18 U.S.C. § 844(f)(1), (f)(3), (h) and (n); 18 U.S.C. § 924(c); 18 U.S.C. § 930(c); 18 U.S.C. § 1114; and 18 U.S.C. § 2155." *Id.* at 198. With respect to U.S. jurisdiction to prescribe under international law, supporting various congressional enactments used as bases for numerous counts in the indictments, the district court concluded that § 844 (f)(3) "is justified by the protective principle—to reach all of the deaths caused by the two embassy bombings"; § 2332a(a)(1) and (a)(3) "are justified, respectively, by the passive personality principle and the protective principle—to reach all of the deaths caused by the two embassy bombings"; § 930 (c) "is based on the protective principle"; § 1114 "is based on the protective principle"; and § 1116 "is based on the universality principle, see United States v. Layton, 509 F.Supp. 212, 221–24 (N.D. Cal. 1981)—to reach the murders of Internationally Protected Persons in connection with the two embassy bombings." *Id.* at 215 n.42. Addressing the Antiterrorism Act (18 U.S.C. § 2331, *et seq.*; see Chapter 2, Section 2D2), the court also noted: "In penalizing extraterritorial conspiracies to kill nationals of the United States, Section 2332(b) is clearly designed to protect a vital United States interest. And, indeed, Congress expressly identified this protective function as the chief purpose of Section 2332." *Id.* at 221. Are each of the enactments also justified under the universal principle in view of customary human rights at stake and the international community's condemnation of all acts of terrorism as criminal (*e.g.*, in U.N. G.A. Res. 40/61, 40 U.N. GAOR, Supp. No. 53, at 301 (1985) ("[u]nequivocally condemns as criminal, all acts, methods and practices of terrorism wherever and by whomever committed"))? Later, on another motion, the district court noted that two of the named defendants "as well as some unindicted co-conspirators, are also said to have committed acts in furtherance of the conspiracy while inside the United States." *Id.*, 93 F.Supp.2d 484 (S.D.N.Y. 2000). What additional principle of jurisdiction therefore applies?

When faced with a claim that due process requires a sufficient nexus or minimum contacts with the U.S., especially in view of United States v. Davis, 905 F.2d 245, 248–49 (9th Cir. 1990), *cert. denied*, 498 U.S. 1047 (1991), and United States v. Caicedo, 47 F.3d 370, 372 (9th Cir. 1995), the district court in *bin Laden* stated that they agreed with another Ninth Circuit case, United States v. Peterson, 812 F.2d 486, 493–94 (9th Cir. 1987), "that if the extraterritorial application of a statute is justified by the protective principle, such application accords with due process." 92 F.Supp.2d at 220. Other cases state that if the protective principle applies due process requirements are met. *See, e.g.*, United States v. Tinoco, 304 F.3d 1088, 1110 n.21 (11th Cir. 2002), *citing*, United States v. Gonzalez, 776 F.2d 931, 938–41 (11th Cir. 1985).

3. A fifth basis of prescriptive jurisdiction is claimed directly as a general customary basis by only a few states (*e.g.*, Brazil, France, Germany,

Israel, Italy, Japan, Mexico, Turkey). The principle is known as the "passive personality," "passive nationality," or "victim" theory. Comment g of the Restatement states: "The passive personality principle asserts that a state may apply law—particularly criminal law—to an act committed outside its territory by a person not its national where the victim of the act was its national. The principle has not been generally accepted for ordinary torts or crimes, but it is increasingly accepted as applied to terrorist and other organized attacks on a state's nationals by reason of their nationality, or to assassination of a state's diplomatic representatives or other officials."

4. Recall *Filartiga v. Pena–Irala* (in Chapter 2) and the discussion of the transitory tort doctrine. With respect to civil suits against individuals, customary international law also permits jurisdiction over "the settlement of claims between persons . . . present in the territory" under the well-recognized fiction that civil claims follow the person. *See, e.g.*, Joseph M. Sweeney, Covey T. Oliver, Noyes E. Leech, The International Legal System 128 (2 ed. 1981); Jordan J. Paust, International Law as Law of the United States 393, 403 (1996). When universal jurisdiction is not implicated, the fiction best relates to territorial theory. It is similar to in rem jurisdiction whereby claims with respect to property follow the property. *See* Restatement § 402(1)(b).

5. When reading cases and materials that follow, consider whether the U.S. Restatement actually reflects trends in judicial decision or is too self-limiting when claiming that subjective territorial jurisdiction requires at least "substantial" conduct within the forum (§ 402(1)(a)) or that objective territorial jurisdiction requires a "substantial effect" or an intent to produce a "substantial effect" within the forum (§ 402(1)(c)). Indeed, what is a "substantial" effect? If a defendant in Canada used radio advertising primarily in Canada but also received in Michigan to defraud people by having them send money to a bank account in Canada as part of a fraudulent scheme and a few persons from the U.S. were thereby defrauded, would objective territorial jurisdiction apply with respect to lawsuits in the U.S.?

Moreover, is it enough that there is merely a substantial effect, but no acts or intent to produce such an effect within the forum? Is it enough that there is merely an intent to produce a substantial effect, but no act or effect within the forum?

6. Contrary to the Restatement, can protective jurisdiction also pertain with respect to conduct of a forum state's nationals abroad?

7. Consider the following hypothetical in connection with principles of jurisdiction to prescribe and the law review extract that follows: Under international law, does the United States have jurisdiction to prescribe laws attempting to reach an Italian national and a U.S. citizen who, acting together in Italy, kidnapped a U.S. General stationed in Italy and made demands of the U.S. government as a precondition for the General's release, also threatening to kill the General if their demands are not met?

JORDAN J. PAUST, *FEDERAL JURISDICTION OVER EXTRATERRITORIAL ACTS OF TERRORISM AND NONIMMUNITY FOR VIOLATORS OF INTERNATIONAL LAW UNDER THE FSIA AND THE ACT OF STATE DOCTRINE*

Revised from the original, 23 VA. J. INT'L L. 191, 201–13 (1983).*

When federal courts have addressed the issue of jurisdictional competence, they have referred to five bases of jurisdiction under international law. These are the (1) territorial, (2) nationality, (3) protective, (4) universality, and (5) passive personality principles of jurisdiction. Although each of these principles could be relevant to extraterritorial acts, two of them, the passive personality and the nationality principles, require only brief attention in this study.

Under the passive personality (or victim) theory, a State has prescriptive jurisdiction over anyone anywhere who injures one of its nationals. Jurisdiction is based on the nationality of the victim. The United States, however, does not generally recognize this theory—despite its recitation in certain case opinions—and there is doubt whether more than a handful of other States actually accept it as a valid principle of customary international law. For this reason, U.S. federal courts should decline jurisdiction where it would rest solely on supposedly customary bases of the passive personality principle.

The nationality principle provides that a State has competence under international law to prescribe laws regulating the conduct of its nationals wherever they are. If, for example, the United States chose to proscribe terrorist acts of U.S. nationals both here and abroad, the extraterritorial reach of such a law would not be in doubt as a matter of international law. It may therefore be useful to point out that where there are gaps in the extraterritorial reach of U.S. domestic law, one method of filling them, at least partly, would be to enact legislation based on the nationality principle.

THE TERRITORIAL PRINCIPLE OF JURISDICTION

Two types of jurisdiction based on territorial principles have been recognized: (1) ordinary or subjective territorial jurisdiction, and (2) objective or "impact" territorial jurisdiction. Subjective territorial jurisdiction exists where acts are initiated in or, as is often the case, nearly all the events relevant to a particular case occur within the territorial confines of a State or on vessels, aircraft, spacecraft, or space stations subject to its "flag" jurisdiction.[2] In contrast, objective territorial juris-

2. . . . For recognition that a flag vessel is the equivalent of flag territory, *see, e.g.*, Lauritzen v. Larsen, 345 U.S. 571 (1953); United States v. Flores, 289 U.S. 137, 155–59 (1933); United States v. Crews, 605 F. Supp. 730, 736 (S.D.Fla.1985); United States v. Cooper, 25 F. Cas. 631 (C.C.D.Pa. 1800)(No. 14,865); S.S. Lotus (France v. Turkey), P.C.I.J. (ser. A) No. 10 (1927). *See also* United States v. Davis, 25 F. Cas. 786,

diction usually involves extraterritorial acts occurring totally outside the reach of ordinary or subjective territorial jurisdiction. Since the first type rarely involves external acts, it is not relevant to a consideration of extraterritorial activity. Moreover, the first type of territorial jurisdiction poses no real problem, since acts occurring within a State's territory are clearly subject to its jurisdiction absent some immunity. However, the objective or "impact" principle is worthy of more detailed attention.

Objective Territorial Jurisdiction

Under the principle of objective territorial jurisdiction it is possible to obtain jurisdiction over a foreign person, entity, or State based on certain types of conduct abroad.

The clearest case for jurisdiction is where acts occur partly outside and partly inside the United States. Where the case is less clear, the three factors most often considered by U.S. courts are: (1) acts, (2) intent, and (3) effects within the United States. But even if all the relevant acts occur outside the United States, it is still possible to obtain objective territorial jurisdiction. Thus, it is not always necessary that all three factors point in some way to the United States in a given case, nor do principles of international law or relevant factors have anything to do with domestic notions of "contact" with the forum. What is recognizably necessary for objective territorial jurisdiction is that at least two of the three factors identified above (or substitutes therefore) exist.

One example where jurisdiction would be recognized even though all the defendant's acts occurred outside the United States is where an agency relationship could be implied. Under this rationale a U.S. court would have jurisdiction if the defendant knowingly used an agent to consummate some plan or activity within the United States. " 'The general rule of the law is that what one does through another's agency is to be regarded as done by himself.' "[3]

In establishing jurisdiction over the defendant it does not even matter whether the "agent" is a knowing or unknowing agent, or, using different categories, a "conscious or unconscious agent" or an "innocent agent." What matters is that the defendant used the agent to further a plan or activity. Thus, a defendant standing outside the United States can be subject to U.S. jurisdiction if the defendant knowingly uses the U.S. mail service to carry out a plan or activity within this country. The same would follow from the use of other "innocent agents" to further criminal designs, for example, the use of telephone or wire services. With respect to a hypothetical problem of a kidnapped U.S. General, if an

787 (C.C.D.Mass.1837)(No. 14,932) (also recognizing that where a shot fired is from a ship, jurisdiction also exists where the effects occurred, given an intent to produce plus the existence of relevant effects). Concerning aircraft, *see, e.g.*, Chumney v. Nixon, 615 F.2d 389, 391 (6th Cir.1980); United States v. Cordova, 89 F. Supp. 298, 302–03 (E.D.N.Y.1950).

3. Ford v. United States, 273 U.S. 593, 623 (1927). In a situation of this kind, where both intent and effect exist, the "act" factor will be supplied by the agency rationale. See Strassheim v. Daily, 221 U.S. 280, 284–85 (1911); Rivard v. United States, 375 F.2d 882, 885 (5th Cir.1967).

Italian terrorist used the U.S. mail service to send a communiqué to several U.S. newspapers while ordering them to reprint it in the United States, the mail service could be viewed as an "innocent agent" acting within the country. The same would follow if the terrorist used the telephone or some other electronic medium, or even a government official, to communicate such a demand to the President and other government officials in the United States.

A slightly different rationale makes jurisdiction possible even though the defendant acts abroad and has not used an agent within the United States. This second rationale, known as the continuing act theory, allows jurisdiction where the defendant engages in an act or activity that the law views as continuing into the territory of another country. Thus, where a person stands in Mexico and shoots a person standing in the United States, the Mexican defendant cannot successfully argue that the United States does not have jurisdiction over him.[4] Jurisdiction exists in that case because there is an intent to produce an effect within the United States, an actual effect within the United States, and an "act" set in motion abroad that "continues" into the United States. Conceptually this is similar to the agency rationale.

The Supreme Court recognized the continuing act rationale in *Ford v. United States*,[5] where it quoted Judge John Bassett Moore of the Permanent Court of International Justice:

> The principle that a man, who outside of a country wilfully puts in motion a force to take effect in it, is answerable at the place where the evil is done, is recognized in the criminal jurisprudence of all countries....
>
> Its logical soundness and necessity received early recognition in the common law. Thus, it was held that a man who erected a nuisance in one county which took effect in another was criminally liable in the county in which the injury was done.

Other courts have recognized objective territorial jurisdiction where acts outside the United States were intended to produce (intent) and actually did produce effects (effects) within the United States. Courts have also recognized jurisdiction under an "effects" theory,[6] a "constructive pres-

4. See Burton v. United States, 202 U.S. 344, 388 (1906); *In re* Palliser, 136 U.S. 257, 265–66 (1890); Simpson v. State, 92 Ga. 41, 17 S.E. 984 (1893) (Georgia had jurisdiction over accused standing in South Carolina who fired a bullet across the state line in an attempt to shoot a person standing in Georgia—an intent to produce effect in Georgia and effect in Georgia were clearly present; the "act" in Georgia is supplied by the continuing act fiction); United States v. Davis, 25 F. Cas. at 787 (addressed *supra* note 1).... For a case involving a claim to enjoin a shooting establishment that endangered adjoining territory, see Judgment of Nov. 1, 1900, Bundesgerichtes, Switz., 26 Entscheidungen des Schweizerischen Bundesgerichts, Antliche Sammlung [BG] I 444 [hereinafter cited as Swiss Case], cited in the Trail Smelter Case (U.S. v. Can.), 3 R. INT'L ARB. AWARDS 1905, 1963 (1949). For a reverse shooting situation involving Mexican claimants and U.S. government actors, see the Garcia Case (Mex. v. U.S.), 4 R. INT'L ARB. AWARDS 119 (1926), *reprinted in* H. STEINER & D. VAGTS, TRANSNATIONAL LEGAL PROBLEMS 283 (1968).

5. 273 U.S. 593 (1927).

6. See Hammond v. Sittel, 59 F.2d 683, 686 (9th Cir.1932) (recognizing both the effects theory and the continuing act theory

ence" theory, and a continuing act theory.[7] Courts have even recognized jurisdiction when the intent amounted to negligence, provided it was reasonably foreseeable that the effects would be felt within the United States.[8] Thus, foreseeability can be a substitute for the intent element.

This negligence based version of the objective territorial principle formed the basis for both the U.S. competence to complain and Canada's responsibility for the damage in the famous *Trail Smelter Case*.[9] In *Trail Smelter*, the tribunal implicitly recognized the test earlier proposed by Judge Moore when it found that Canada owed a duty to protect the United States " 'against injurious acts by individuals from within its jurisdiction.' "The tribunal recognized that the United States was competent to complain about acts engaged in by Canadians within Canada that caused injury "in or to the territory" of the United States "or the properties or persons therein, when the case is of serious consequence and injury is established by clear and convincing evidence." What was involved in *Trail Smelter* was a continuing act—the activity that set the pollutant particles in motion—and injurious effects that were of "serious consequence." It did not matter that the particles were not "willfully" put in motion since it was clear there were pollutants and it was reasonably foreseeable that they would produce transnational effects.

Based on *Trail Smelter*, therefore, the three factors of act, intent, and effects can be met where (1) acts do not really occur as such in U.S. territory but the continuing act rationale applies, (2) willful intent does not exist but reasonable foreseeability does, and (3) effects—seemingly necessary—actually are felt within the territory. And if it was intentional that the effects should be felt, the case is even stronger, since intent

as bases for jurisdiction).... Foreign states are rightly critical of a *mere* "effects" theory. *See, e.g.*, Barry E. Carter & Phillip R. Trimble, International Law 733, 738 (2 ed. 1995); *but see* Restatement, § 402(1)(c) (conduct outside that "has *or* is intended to have ... effect"), cmt. d and RN 2 (emphasis added). For purposes of international law, it should not matter whether a court recognized that more than mere effects occurred if in fact jurisdiction can be justified on the basis of act plus effect or intent plus effect.

7. See United States v. Freeman, 239 U.S. 117, 120 (1915); Brown v. Elliott, 225 U.S. 392, 400, 402 (1912); Reass v. United States, 99 F.2d 752, 754 (4th Cir.1938); Moran v. United States, 264 F. 768, 770 (6th Cir. 1920); *see also* 1 Op. Att'y Gen. 123, 123 (1802) (Lincoln, Att'y Gen.) (theft of ship and goods can constitute a continuous act for jurisdictional purposes, and jurisdiction could exist "in every successive place to which the vessel was carried"). With regard to jurisdiction over those who broadcast from outside a territory and thus set radio waves in motion to take effect within the territory, see J. Sweeney, C. Oliver & N. Leech, The International Legal System 190 (2 ed. 1981). Radio transmissions are arguably similar to pollutant particles for purposes of the continuing act fiction.

8. See Duple Motor Bodies, Ltd. v. Hollingsworth, 417 F.2d 231, 233–35 (9th Cir. 1969).... For a relevant case at the international level, see The S.S. Lotus, (Fr. v. Turk.), 1927 P.C.I.J., Ser. A, No. 10. The *Lotus* involved the unique circumstances of two territorial bases for jurisdiction (two vessels) crashing into each other or, as rephrased in terms of the continuing act theory, the placing in motion of a force (one vessel) to take effect within another "territory" (on the other vessel). The element of intent was satisfied by the existence of negligence or foreseeability. For additional foreign cases see Restatement (Second), *supra*, at 55–56.

9. (U.S. v. Can.), 3 R. Int'l Arb. Awards 1905 (1949). [Editors' note: *Trail Smelter* involved an arbitration between the U.S. and Canada and Canadian responsibility for pollution of U.S. air by a private Canadian smelter.]

plus effects can override the need for either an agency or continuing act circumstance.[10]

It should be clear from the preceding discussion that the objective territorial principle can be quite important to any effort to control extraterritorial civil or criminal acts. In the case of the kidnapped U.S. General, objective territorial jurisdiction would allow prosecution of the Italian national whose terroristic conduct took place outside the United States: the acts of the postal service, telephone company, or other electronic media would be attributable to the accused, and they, as "agents," produced effects within the United States. In such a case, the critical elements of intent and effects would be met, as well as the third factor of acts partly within the United States. If the Italian national had sent a letter-bomb to another U.S. General that exploded within the United States, objective territorial jurisdiction under both the agency

10. *See, e.g.*, Steele v. Bulova Watch Co., Inc., 344 U.S. 280, 288 (1952); Ford v. United States, 273 U.S. 593, 620–21 (1926); Strassheim v. Daily, 221 U.S. 280, 284–85 (1911) (a case involving all three elements: acts, intent, and effects); United States v. Pizzarusso, 388 F.2d 8, 10 (2d Cir.1968), *cert. denied*, 392 U.S. 936 (1968); Rivard v. United States, 375 F.2d 882, 886–88 (5th Cir.1967); United States v. Aluminum Co. of America, 148 F.2d 416, 443 (2d Cir.1945) (despite dictum elsewhere in the opinion, a case emphasizing both the intent and effects elements); United States v. Layton, 509 F. Supp. 212, 215–16 (N.D.Cal. 1981)....

The Restatement avers that if there exists an intent to produce effects and some "activity" abroad demonstrates such an intent, "the fact that a plan or conspiracy was thwarted" and effects did not actually occur within a state "does not deprive the target state of jurisdiction...." See RESTATEMENT § 402, cmt. d. Use of this approach with respect to interrupted drug smuggling has been seemingly approved. *See, e.g.*, United States v. Columba–Colella, 604, F.2d 356, 358–59 (5th Cir. 1979) (dictum: "might be sufficient"). Those wishing to gain recognition of jurisdiction to prescribe in such cases, however, should inquire further whether there were some acts occurring within the target state under the agency (and conspiracy) rationale or whether acts or effects occurred in the past as part of a continuing pattern or process of smuggling. Presumably most smugglers have contacts within the target state either for sale or distribution of items attempted to be smuggled into the target country. Such contacts might be coconspirators, actual agents, and/or those communicated with from abroad through use of innocent agents in furtherance of a plan or conspiracy. Otherwise, the interruption of smuggling by an arrest outside U.S. territorial bases for jurisdiction negates both a continuing act of smuggling and effects within the U.S., leaving only the intent factor. Yet, must the state stand by and suffer a continuing act or predictable consequences in all such cases? In some circumstances it would be relatively easy to wait until acts in furtherance begin within areas under the state's control, but in others avoidance of serious consequences may require interruption outside such areas of control. In another context, if nuclear missiles are headed for its territory, the U.S. does not need consent of the government of "registry" to target the missiles.

The following chart identifies the general factors to be used and their substitutes (*e.g.*, the continuing act as substitute for an act within, foreseeability as a substitute for an intent to produce and act within):

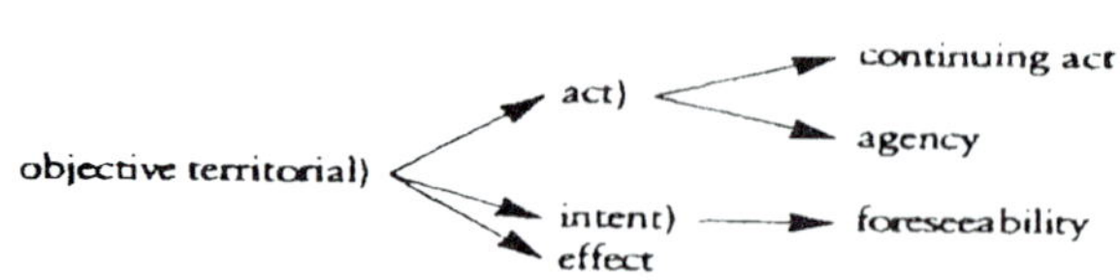

rationale (use of the mails) and the continuing act theory (accused set in motion a force to take effect within the United States and "serious consequences" were thereby produced) would clearly be permissible. Actually, all that would be required would be the existence of two out of three of the primary factors.

THE PROTECTIVE PRINCIPLE OF JURISDICTION

The protective principle is another useful basis for jurisdiction over extraterritorial civil or criminal acts. Even though all relevant acts occur outside the ordinary territorial jurisdiction of the United States, jurisdiction is possible under the protective principle if a significant national interest is at stake and it is not otherwise impermissible under international law to exercise jurisdiction.[11]

As recognized in an early study, relevant protective interests can involve threats to national security, territorial integrity, or political independence. Other authors have also related the protective principle to self-defense. Thus, it would not be unreasonable to recognize the application of the protective principle to any violation of article 2(4) of the U.N. Charter directed against the United States. Moreover, in light of the increase in the number of terroristic threats against U.S. citizens abroad, there can be no doubt that the United States has significant security and protective interests at stake, at least when demands are made upon the U.S. government or the security of the United States is threatened. With respect the hypothetical problem about the kidnapped U.S. General, the national security interests might be of even greater magnitude. The fact that a U.S. General was involved as an instrumental target, and that the President and other U.S. government officials were being coerced as primary targets (no doubt with regard to important matters of national security and foreign affairs) would heighten the national security interests at stake.

There is a danger in pushing the protective theory too far, however, and I suspect that the better view is that actual effects should be felt, or be likely to be felt, before the protective principle could properly be seen

11. *See, e.g.*, United States v. Pizzarusso, 388 F.2d 8, 10 (2d Cir.1968), *cert. denied,* 392 U.S. 936 (1968); Rivard v. United States, 375 F.2d 882, 885–87 (5th Cir.1967), *cert. denied, sub nom.*, Groleau v. United States, 389 U.S. 884 (1967); Rocha v. United States, 288 F.2d 545, 549 (9th Cir.), *cert. denied*, 366 U.S. 948 (1961); United States v. Zehe, 601 F. Supp. 196, 196–98 (D.Mass. 1985); United States v. Layton, 509 F. Supp. 212, 215–16 (N.D.Cal.1981); United States v. Keller, 451 F. Supp. 631, 635 (D.P.R.1978); United States v. Archer, 51 F. Supp. 708, 711 (S.D.Cal.1943)....

As several of the U.S. cases noted above demonstrate, the protective principle has been applied to protect national interests concerning the sanctity of government documents despite the fact that these interests are not as clearly significant as security and self-defense interests.... Most all of the government documents cases are actually justifiable under the objective territorial principle because there is (1) an intent—at least in part—to produce an effect in the United States (or the foreseeability of such), (2) an effect in the United States (or the potential for an effect), and (3) the use of an "innocent agent" to further the intended plan or effect. It is also possible to use the continuing act rationale in government document cases, because they always involve an alien who "sets in motion" abroad a document to take effect—at least in part—in the United States....

to apply. The national interests at stake, when viewed in context, should be of real significance; but these are matters best left to the courts for refinement. It is worth noting, however, that where both the objective territorial and the protective principles point to jurisdiction, the choice concerning application of the protective principle may be easier. An interesting example of such a case is *Schoenbaum v. Firstbrook* [405 F.2d 200 (2d Cir.1968)]. There, both protection from detrimental effects and use of the mails were mentioned, but jurisdiction seemed to rest on the so-called effects doctrine alone.

Notes and Questions

1. As noted, theft, by fiction, can constitute a continuing act. If an item is stolen in the United States by Ima Thief and then transported into Canada, the thievery continues into Canada. Ima intends to retain control over the stolen item and the effect of the thievery also occurs in Canada. See also 1 Op. Att'y Gen. 123 (1802) ("a person charged with barratry on private property . . . being here, it appears to me clear he would be amenable to our courts. The tortious act must have originated on the high seas, or, at least, must have been so continued as to have existed on the high seas, and constituted a new act of barratry in every successive place to which the vessel was carried. If, therefore, it was a criminal offence, I conceive he would be triable in our courts. . . .").

There is a split internationally and within the United States as to whether fraud as such involves the same fiction of continuing act or continuing offense. *See, e.g.*, 2 MOORE'S DIGEST OF INTERNATIONAL LAW 244 *ff.* (1906).

2. Alberto Bueno makes bogus "Bulova" watches in Mexico to sell to touristas from the U.S. and Canada in Mexico, who subsequently bring them home. Does the U.S. or Canada have prescriptive jurisdiction with respect to Alberto's activities? In Steele v. Bulova Watch Co., 344 U.S. 280 (1952), the defendant was a U.S. national. The Court nonetheless spoke of trade practices which radiate unlawful consequences in the U.S. *Id.* at 288. Is that sufficient?

3. Will Horwitz and Manuel Guerra operated a lottery in Mexico and solicited business in Texas by radio located in Reynosa, Mexico. As part of the lottery business, deposits and withdrawals of money were made with a bank in McAllen, Texas. Money was sent in by mail either to Mexico (which was thereafter transferred to the U.S. bank) or to the bank located in the U.S. Assuming that neither defendant is a U.S. national, does the U.S. have jurisdiction to prescribe? See Horwitz *et al.* v. United States, 63 F.2d 706 (5th Cir.1933).

4. Some argue that the standard concerning the "state responsibility" of Canada for pollution caused by acts and/or omissions of the private company in *Trail Smelter* may not have been based on negligence as such but on "nuisance" theory (thus arguing also that there is a necessary difference in these standards). Is there a significant difference? *See, e.g.,* BLACK'S LAW DICTIONARY, "nuisance," 1214–15 (4 ed. 1968) (stressing, if relevant acts or omissions are not "unlawful," standards concerning "unreasonable" effects, "reasonable men," and discomfort to "persons of ordinary

sensibility and ordinary tastes and habits"); JESSE DUKEMINIER, JAMES E. KRIER, PROPERTY 956–57, 959 (3 ed. 1993), adding: "Regarding the question of unreasonableness [within inquiry under 'nuisance' theory], the case of unintentional nuisance seems clear enough. Liability here is based on traditional tort categories—negligence, recklessness, abnormally dangerous activities—all of which 'embody in some degree the concept of unreasonableness.' ". Canada's responsibility was not based on strict liability.

The Tribunal, in language admittedly not perfectly clear, concluded that "under principles of international law ... no State has the right to ... permit the use of its territory in such a manner as to cause injury by fumes in or to the territory of another or the properties or persons therein, when the case is of serious consequence and the injury is established by clear and convincing evidence." What standard(s) are implicated by the word "permit" and the phrase "in such a manner as to cause" when one also is interested in the "consequence" of acts or omissions? *See generally* RESTATEMENT § 601 cmt. d ("... a state is responsible for injury due to the state's own defaults.... In general, the applicable international rules and standards do not hold a state responsible when it has taken the necessary and practicable measures; some international agreements provide also for responsibility regardless of fault...."); Günther Handl, *The Case for Mexican Liability for Transnational Pollution Damage Resulting from the Ixtoc I Oilspill*, 2 HOUS. J. INT'L L. 229, 232–33 (1979) ("strong opposition ... to ... absolute or strict liability [has existed] ... negligence was a prerequisite.... in general, the additional element of negligence is, indeed, more appropriate."); *see also* Sanford E. Gaines, *Taking Responsibility for Transboundary Environmental Effects*, 14 HAST. INT'L & COMP. L. REV. 781, 784–86 (general "fault" standard exists, with some strict liability for ultrahazardous activity), 795 (flexible "risk" aspect), 799–800 & n.77 ("unreasonable," "acceptable" qualifiers are connected with the term "risk") (1991); *International Principles for Transnational Environmental Liability: Can Developments in Municipal Law Help Break the Impasse?*, 30 HARV. INT'L L.J. 311, 330 ("fault-based concepts like foreseeability or the opportunity to prevent harm"), 333–35 (1989). Regardless of the standard for liability as such, factors utilized for analysis of objective territorial jurisdictional competence include foreseeability as a substitute for actual intent to produce deleterious effects.

UNITED STATES v. YUNIS

681 F.Supp. 896, 899–900, 901–03 (D.D.C.1988).

[Editors' note: The accused, Yunis, was treated as a national of Lebanon. The incident involved the hijacking of a Jordanian airliner on the ground in Beirut, Lebanon, and holding of crew and passengers, including three U.S. nationals, hostage during flights to Tunis, Tunisia (which would not allow the plane to land), Cyprus, Sicily, and Syria (which refused landing) and in Lebanon. Lebanon had ratified a relevant aircraft hijacking convention, but had not ratified the Hostage Taking Convention discussed below.]

PARKER, J.

The parties agree that there are five traditional bases of jurisdiction over extraterritorial crimes under international law:

Territorial, wherein jurisdiction is based on the place where the offense is committed;

National, wherein jurisdiction is based on the nationality of the offender;

Protective, wherein jurisdiction is based on whether the national interest is injured;

Universal, wherein jurisdiction is conferred in any forum that obtains physical custody of the perpetrator of certain offenses considered particularly heinous and harmful to humanity.

Passive personal, wherein jurisdiction is based on the nationality of the victim.

These general principles were developed in 1935 by a Harvard Research Project in an effort to codify principles of jurisdiction under international law. *See Harvard Research in International Law, Jurisdiction with Respect to Crime*, 29 AM. J. INT'L L. 435, 445 (Supp. 1935). Most courts, including our Court of Appeals, have adopted the Harvard Research designations on jurisdiction. *See, e.g.,* Tel–Oren v. Libyan Arab Republic, 726 F.2d 774, 781, n. 7 (D.C.Cir.1984), *cert. denied*, 470 U.S. 1003 ... (1985); Chua Han Mow. v. United States, 730 F.2d 1308, 1311 (9th Cir.1984), *cert. denied*, 470 U.S. 1031 ... (1985); Rivard v. United States, 375 F.2d 882, 885 (5th Cir.), *cert. denied*, 389 U.S. 884 ... (1967)....

PASSIVE PERSONAL PRINCIPLE

This principle authorizes states to assert jurisdiction over offenses committed against their citizens abroad. It recognizes that each state has a legitimate interest in protecting the safety of its citizens when they journey outside national boundaries. Because American nationals were on board the Jordanian aircraft, the government contends that the Court may exercise jurisdiction over Yunis under this principle. Defendant argues that this theory of jurisdiction is neither recognized by the international community nor the United States and is an insufficient basis for sustaining jurisdiction over Yunis.

Although many international legal scholars agree that the principle is the most controversial of the five sources of jurisdiction, they also agree that the international community recognizes its legitimacy. Most accept that "the extraterritorial reach of a law premised upon the ... principle would not be in doubt as a matter of international law." Paust, *Jurisdiction and Nonimmunity*, 23 VA. J. INT'L LAW 191, 203 (1983). More importantly, the international community explicitly approved of the principle as a basis for asserting jurisdiction over hostage takers. As noted above, the Hostage Taking Convention set forth certain mandatory sources of jurisdiction. But it also gave each signatory country discretion to exercise extraterritorial jurisdiction when the offense was committed "with respect to a hostage who is a national of that state if that state considers it appropriate." Art. 5(a)(d). Therefore, even if there are doubts regarding the international community's acceptance, there can be no doubt concerning the application of this principle to the offense of hostage taking, an offense for which Yunis is charged. See M. BASSIOUNI, II INTERNATIONAL CRIMINAL LAW ch. 4 at 120.

Defendant's counsel correctly notes that the Passive Personal principle traditionally has been an anathema to United States lawmakers. But his reliance on the Restatement (Revised) of Foreign Relations Laws for the claim that the United States can never invoke the principle is misplaced. In the past, the United States has protested any assertion of such jurisdiction for fear that it could lead to indefinite criminal liability for its own citizens. This objection was based on the belief that foreigners visiting the United States should comply with our laws and should not be permitted to carry their laws with them. Otherwise Americans would face criminal prosecutions for actions unknown to them as illegal. However, in the most recent draft of the Restatement, the authors noted that the theory "has been increasingly accepted when applied to terrorist and other organized attacks on a state's nationals by reason of their nationality, or to assassinations of a state's ambassadors, or government officials." Restatement (Revised) § 402, cmt. g (Tent. Draft No. 6). *See also* McGinley, *The* Achille Lauro *Affair-Implications for International Law*, 52 TENN. L. REV. 691, 713 (1985). The authors retreated from their wholesale rejection of the principle, recognizing that perpetrators of crimes unanimously condemned by members of the international community, should be aware of the illegality of their actions. Therefore, qualified application of the doctrine to serious and universally condemned crimes will not raise the specter of unlimited and unexpected criminal liability.

Finally, this case does not present the first time that the United States has invoked the principle to assert jurisdiction over a hijacker who seized an American hostage on foreign soil.[12] The government relied on this very principle when it sought extradition of Muhammed Abbas Zaiden, the leader of the terrorists who hijacked the Achille Lauro vessel in Egyptian waters and subsequently killed Leon Klinghoffer, an American citizen. As here, the only connection to the United States was Klinghoffer's American citizenship. Based on that link, an arrest warrant was issued charging Abbas with hostage taking, conspiracy and piracy. *Id.* at 719; See also N.Y. Times, Oct. 16, 1985, at 1 col. 6.

[Additional footnotes from *Yunis*]

13. Only recently, the Justice Department announced it had withdrawn the arrest warrant issued against Abbas after reviewing the outstanding indictment and weighing the fact that the defendant had been convicted

12. At least one Court has explicitly relied on the passive personality principle to assert jurisdiction over foreigners committing crimes against U.S. nationals overseas. United States v. Benitez, 741 F.2d 1312, 1316 (11th Cir.1984) (Colombian charged with conspiracy to murder DEA agent) ("The nationality of the victims, who are United States Government agents, clearly supports jurisdiction.").

and sentenced in absentia in an Italian Court. *See* Wash. Post, Jan. 17, 1988.

14. The government also argues that a third doctrine, the Protective principle, offers grounds for asserting jurisdiction over Yunis. Because this principle gives states wide latitude in defining the parameters of their jurisdiction, the international community has strictly construed the reach of this doctrine to those offenses posing a direct, specific threat to national security. *See* Blakesley, *United States Jurisdiction over Extraterritorial Crime*, 73 J. Crim. L. & Criminology at 1136, Bassiouni, II International Criminal Law ch. 2 at 21. Recently, some academicians have urged a more liberal interpretation of the protective principle when applied to terroristic activities. Given "the increase in the number of terroristic threats against United States nationals abroad, there can be no doubt that the United States has significant security and protective interests at stake." Paust, *Federal Jurisdiction Over Extraterritorial Acts of Terrorism*, 23 Va. J. Int'l Law 191, 210 (1983).

In this case, the hijackers never made any demands upon the United States government nor directly threatened its security. Indeed, it was almost happenstance that three American nationals were on board the aircraft. Given the regional focus of the hijacking, a court would have to adopt an expansive view of the principle to assert jurisdiction over Yunis. Since jurisdiction is available under the universality and passive personality principle, there is no reason to reach out and rely on the protective principle as well.

Notes and Questions

1. We will revisit this case in Section 2 concerning universal jurisdiction at p. 570.

2. The district court misquoted Professor Paust, who had addressed, not the passive personality, but the nationality principle.

3. Does it result from the court's qualification of the victim theory that it is swallowed by another principle? Without such a limitation, are the fears of potentially indefinite liability under the victim theory for actions unknown to be illegal in the country of nationality still valid?

4. A recent case accepting the victim theory as valid in the context of an airplane hijacking in the Mediterranean during which a U.S. citizen was killed is United States v. Rezaq, 134 F.3d 1121 (D.C.Cir.1998) (the opinion quoted from the Restatement § 402, cmt. g (1987): "The principle has not been generally accepted for ordinary torts or crimes, but it is increasingly accepted as applied to terrorist and other organized attacks on a state's nationals by reason of their nationality...."). *Rezaq* also used the principle of universal jurisdiction.

5. Which principles of prescriptive jurisdiction that you are aware of would support which sections of Article 5 of the International Convention Against the Taking of Hostages, 1316 U.N.T.S. 205, not then ratified by Lebanon, which states:

1. Each State Party shall take such measures as may be necessary to establish its jurisdiction over any of the offences set forth in Article 1 which are committed:

(a) in its territory or on board a ship or aircraft registered in that State;

(b) by any of its nationals or, if that State considers it appropriate, by those stateless persons who have their habitual residence in its territory;

(c) in order to compel that State to do or abstain from doing any act; or

(d) with respect to a hostage who is a national of that State, if that State considers it appropriate.

2. Each State Party shall likewise take such measures as may be necessary to establish its jurisdiction over the offences set forth in Article 1 in cases where the alleged offender is present in its territory and it does not extradite him to any of the States mentioned in paragraph 1 of this article.

3. This Convention does not exclude any criminal jurisdiction exercised in accordance with internal law.

JOYCE v. DIRECTOR OF PUBLIC PROSECUTIONS

[1946] A.C. 347 (England, House of Lords).

LORD JOWITT, L.C.

. . . The appellant [William Joyce] was born in the U.S.A., in 1906, the son of a naturalised American citizen who had previously been a British subject by birth. He thereby became himself a natural-born American citizen. At about three years of age he was brought to Ireland, where he stayed until 1921, when he came to England. He stayed in England until 1939. . . . On July 4, 1933, he applied for a British passport, describing himself as a British subject by birth, born in Galway. He asked for the passport for the purpose of holiday touring in [Europe, and the passport was renewed in 1938 and 1939.] . . . .

On some day after Aug. 24, 1939, the appellant left the realm. . . . Upon his arrest in 1945 there was found upon his person a "work book" issued by the German State on Oct. 4, 1939, from which it appeared that he had been employed by the German Radio Company of Berlin, as an announcer of English news from Sept. 18, 1939. . . . It was proved to the satisfaction of the jury that he had at the dates alleged in the indictment broadcast propaganda on behalf of the enemy. He was found guilty accordingly.

. . . [T]he question for consideration is bound up with the question of allegiance. Allegiance is owed to their Sovereign Lord the King by his natural born subjects; so it is by those who, being aliens, become his subjects by denisation or naturalisation (I will call them all 'naturalized subject'); so it is by those who, being aliens, resident within the King's realm.... [and] an alien owes allegiance so long as he is within the realm ... [, but does he, concerning treason,] during absence[?]

... It is said in Foster's Crown Cases (3rd ed.), p. 183—"Local allegiance is founded in the protection a foreigner enjoyeth for his person, his family or effects, during his residence here; and it ceaseth, whenever he withdraweth with his family and effects".... And if such alien, seeking the protection of the Crown, and having a family and effects here, should during a war with his native country, go thither, and there adhere to the King's enemies for purposes of hostility, he might be dealt with as a traitor. For he came and settled here under the protection of the Crown; and, though his person was removed for a time, his effects and family continued still under the same protection. This rule was laid down by all the judges assembled at the Queen's command January 12, 1707....

The question then is how is this principle to be applied to the circumstances of the present case.... [T]he appellant had long resided here and appears to have had many ties with this country, but I make no assumption one way or another about his intention to return and I do not attach any importance to the fact that the original passport application and, therefore, presumably the renewals also were for "holiday touring".... It does not matter that he made false representations as to his status, asserting that he was a British subject by birth.... It is thus described by Lord Alverstone, C.J., in *R.* v. *Brailsford*, [1905] 2 K.B. 730: "It is a document issued in the name of the sovereign on the responsibility of a minister of the Crown to a named individual, intended to be presented to the governments of foreign nations and to be used for that individual's protection as a British subject in foreign countries". By its terms it requests and requires in the name of His Majesty all those whom it may concern to allow the bearer to pass freely without let or hindrance and to afford him every assistance and protection of which he may stand in need.... [T]he possession of a passport by one who is not a British subject gives him rights and imposes upon the sovereign obligations which would otherwise not be given or imposed. It is immaterial that he has obtained it by misrepresentation and that he is not in law a British subject. By the possession of that document he is enabled to obtain in a foreign country the protection extended to British subjects. By his own act he has maintained the bond which while he was within the realm bound him to his sovereign.... [H]e sought and obtained protection ... while abroad.

... Armed with that document the holder may demand from the State's representatives abroad and from the officials of foreign governments that he be treated as a British subject, and even in the territory of a hostile state may claim the intervention of the protecting power.... Here there was no suggestion that the appellant had surrendered his passport or taken any other overt step to withdraw from his allegiance, unless indeed reliance is placed on the act of treason itself as a withdrawal. That in my opinion he cannot do. For such an act is not inconsistent with his still availing himself of the passport in other countries than Germany and possibly even in Germany itself.... Moreover the special value to the enemy of the appellant's services as a broadcaster was that he could be represented as speaking as a British subject and his German work book showed that it was in this character that he was employed, for which his passport was doubtless accepted as the voucher....

Notes and Questions

1. Was it a defense that Joyce was following German law?

2. Does the nationality principle justify British jurisdiction in the *Joyce* case? For a U.S. case involving a U.S. citizen convicted of treason "by working as a radio speaker, announcer, script writer and broadcaster for the Imperial Japanese Government" from 1943–1945, see D'Aquino v. United States, 192 F.2d 338 (9th Cir.1951).

3. Would the objective territorial principle justify British jurisdiction in the *Joyce* case?

4. Would the protective principle apply in this case? The protective principle generally reaches crimes against the state that are known as "pure" political offenses in the context of extradition—offenses such as espionage, subversion, and sedition, treason—since they involve threats to significant national security interests. Yet, could any alien abroad (*e.g.*, including those with no connection with the forum) rightly be prosecuted for treason? Why would treason be treated differently than espionage with respect to aliens having no connection with the forum? For an Italian case involving a resident alien convicted of treason with respect to conduct in Italy, see *Re* Penati, Court of Cassation, 1946, [1946] Ann. Dig. 74 (No. 30). The Inter–American Court of Human Rights found that Peru could prosecute foreign nationals under a law proscribing "treason" when the crimes alleged were actually forms of terrorism and, thus, there was no violation of the "right to nationality" under Article 20 of the American Convention on Human Rights. See Castillo Petruzzi, Merits, Judgment, para. 102, Inter–Am. Ct. H.R. (30 May 1999). Prosecution before a military tribunal, however, had involved several human rights violations. *Id.*

Are some forms of subversion and sedition protected under international law? Recall the 1984 General Assembly resolution concerning the Apartheid regime in South Africa, in Chapter 1. What about subversive speech? See also note 5, below.

5. Assume that during the "Cold War" a U.S. national working in West Germany for Radio Free Europe had participated in broadcasts into Eastern Europe that Czechoslovakia had thought were subversive and criminally sanctionable. The U.S. national was later arrested in Czechoslovakia. Is there jurisdiction to prescribe? Some states have argued that if an activity is a basic "freedom" engaged in in the territory of origin, that subsequent prosecution is impermissible. *See, e.g.*, 1935 Harvard Research in International Law, art. 7, in 29 AM. J. INT'L L. 435 (Supp. 1935). Was that what was involved in the *Joyce* case? in *D'Aquino*, in note 2 above?

Can you make a similar argument based on human rights law? *See, e.g.*, Universal Declaration of Human Rights, Article 19 (*but see id.*, art. 29(2));

1966 Covenant on Civil and Political Rights, Article 19. Does it matter that the right to participate in transnational speech is a derogable human right? What test pertains with respect to claims to derogate? In the *Joyce* case, what state could rightly claim power to derogate from a right of transnational free speech? Where was the speech?

When comparing general principles of jurisdiction under customary international law and customary human rights law, are there any priorities to consider? See also U.N. Charter, art. 103; Chapter 1.

6. International law provides competence for states to claim nationality status over individuals on the bases of place of birth (*jus soli*) and blood of the parent(s) (*jus sanguinis*). Section 211 of the Restatement notes that "other states need not accept ... [a state's claim of nationality] when it is not based on a genuine link between the state and the individual," but adding that place of birth and blood are considered to be "genuine links." *See also* The Nottebohm Case (Liechtenstein v. Guatemala), 1955 I.C.J. 4 (addressing "real and effective nationality" and genuine links based on several factors).

If Ina Crunch was born in the U.S. and one of her parents was a French national and the other a Canadian national, which states have claims based on the nationality principle? Can the U.S., France, and Canada attempt to tax Ina's income earned in Germany, where she now resides? Can they if Ina becomes a German citizen? Do you need more information? *See also* RESTATEMENT § 211, cmt. c; Universal Declaration of Human Rights, art. 15; 1966 Covenant on Civil and Political Rights, arts. 12, 24 (3); American Convention on Human Rights, art. 20; MYRES S. MCDOUGAL, HAROLD D. LASSWELL, LUNG-CHU CHEN, HUMAN RIGHTS AND WORLD PUBLIC ORDER 861–958 (1980). Treaties regarding "double taxation" and domestic tax credits may provide some relief.

7. The U.S. attempts to tax resident aliens with respect to income earned in the U.S. and abroad. Is such permissible under international law?

8. Under customary international law, the nationality of a corporation is determined by a simple but easily applied rule, the place of incorporation. See The Barcelona Traction, Light and Power Co., Ltd. (Belgium v. Spain), 1970 I.C.J. 3; RESTATEMENT § 213. Factors such as nationality of the owners, nationality of corporate directors or board members, or the primary place of management or business are not considered.

9. If a U.S. parent corporation (incorporated in Delaware) orders its Canadian subsidiary (incorporated in Toronto) to perform acts in Canada in violation of Canadian law and such acts take place, does Canada have prescriptive jurisdiction over the U.S. parent on the basis of nationality jurisdiction? objective territorial jurisdiction? Can the U.S. prescribe laws directly regulating the Canadian subsidiary's acts in Canada? Can the U.S. reach the U.S. parent corporation?

10. Should corporate elites with no contact with the forum be subject to foreign prosecution for economic damage to a foreign state's economy? if there is an intent to do so (or foreseeability) and actual effects? Application of the protective principle when merely economic interests of the state are

threatened is problematic. Might economic coercion in some contexts become as threatening as an armed attack?

11. For other cases using the protective principle, *see, e.g.*, United States v. Yousef, 327 F.3d 56, 93–94 (2d Cir. 2003) (terroristic aircraft sabotage and threats to U.S. national security, also using universal jurisdiction).

12. Should drug smuggling implicate the protective principle or is the extension too dangerous? In making such a choice, should it be relevant whether the particular defendant has engaged in such conduct before and whether the amount of drugs the defendant has been involved with is substantial? *See also* United States v. Tinoco, 304 F.3d 1088, 1110 (11th Cir. 2002); United States v. Gonzalez, 311 F.3d 440, 446 (1st Cir. 2002) (Torruella, J., concurring); United States v. Suerte, 291 F.3d 366, 370 (5th Cir. 2002); United States v. Romero–Galue, 757 F.2d 1147 (11th Cir.1985) (dictum); United States v. Mosquera, 192 F.Supp.2d 1334, 1339 (M.D. Fla. 2002); United States v. Keller, 451 F.Supp. 631 (D.P.R.1978). United States v. Cardales, 168 F.3d 548 (1st Cir.1999), relied on the protective principle to justify U.S. prescriptive jurisdiction over a drug-smuggling Venezuelan-flag vessel apprehended 150 miles south of Puerto Rico.

UNITED STATES v. GEORGESCU

723 F.Supp. 912 (E.D.N.Y.1989).

WEINSTEIN, J.

Over the mid-Atlantic on a Scandinavian Airlines flight from Copenhagen, Denmark to John F. Kennedy International Airport in Queens, the defendant, a Romanian national, allegedly accosted a nine year old girl who is a national of Norway by placing his hand on her genitals. He was indicted for committing a criminal sexual act while in the special aircraft jurisdiction of the United States. 18 U.S.C. § 2241(c) (Supp. V 1987), 49 U.S.C. § 1472(k)(1) (Supp. V 1987). In this case of first impression, he moves to dismiss, claiming lack of jurisdiction in United States courts. His motion must be denied for the reasons stated below.

STATUTORY LANGUAGE

Section 2241 of chapter 109A of title 18 of the United States Code deals with sexual abuse of a child under the age of twelve, making it a crime punishable by up to life imprisonment. It provides in part:

> Whoever in the special maritime and territorial jurisdiction of the United States ... knowingly engages in a sexual act with another person who has not attained the age of 12 years, or attempts to do so, shall be fined ... , imprisoned for any term of years or life, or both.

18 U.S.C. § 2241(c) (Supp. V 1987).

The special maritime and territorial jurisdiction of the United States is defined in section 7 of title 18. Insofar as relevant, it covers only American owned aircraft, 18 U.S.C. § 7(5) (1982), and offenses "against a national of the United States." 18 U.S.C. § 7(7) (Supp. V 1987). Neither applies here. Title 18 deals with crimes and criminal procedure generally. Many crimes are defined in the substantive titles of the Code.

Subsequent legislation, incorporated in the transportation title of the United States Code, title 49, established a new "special aircraft jurisdiction." Congress authorized the exercise of this jurisdiction over specified crimes, including sexual abuse crimes defined under chapter 109A of title 18. This provision reads:

> Whoever, while aboard an aircraft *within the special aircraft jurisdiction* of the United States, *commits an act which, if committed within the special maritime and territorial jurisdiction of the United States*, as defined in section 7 of Title 18, would be in violation of ... chapter 109A ... of such Title 18 shall be punished as provided therein.

49 U.S.C. App. § 1472(k)(1) (Supp. V 1987) (emphasis added).

The broad definition of "special aircraft jurisdiction of the United States" includes a foreign aircraft scheduled to stop in the United States if it actually lands here. The statute states:

> (38) The term "special aircraft jurisdiction of the United States includes—
>
> (d) any other aircraft outside the United States—
>
> (i) that has its next scheduled destination ... in the United States, if that aircraft next actually lands in the United States....
>
> while that aircraft is in flight, which is from the moment when all external doors are closed following embarkation until the moment when one such door is opened for disembarkation.... "

49 U.S.C. App. § 1301(38)(d) (Supp. V 1987). This definition covers the aircraft of the foreign airline aboard which the defendant and his alleged victim were traveling; Kennedy Airport was the next scheduled destination and the aircraft actually landed there....

LEGISLATIVE HISTORY

The statutory language is clear enough so as to need no buttressing from legislative history. In fact, language and history are in accord. The history of the statutes regarding crimes committed aboard aircraft makes plain the congressional design to criminalize and create jurisdiction over specified acts committed in non-United States airspace aboard foreign carriers bound for and landing in the United States, including aggravated sexual abuse as defined in section 2241 of title 18....

In 1969, the Senate consented to the ratification of the multilateral Convention on Offences and Certain other Acts Committed on Board Aircraft, [hereinafter Tokyo Convention].... The purpose of the Tokyo Convention was in part to encourage countries to punish crimes and certain non-criminal acts committed aboard aircraft. The Tokyo Convention allows parties to exercise jurisdiction over crimes committed aboard foreign aircraft in foreign or international airspace....

When the Senate consented to ratification, it was aware of the Tokyo Convention's broad jurisdictional provisions. The President's message of transmittal of the Tokyo Convention to the Senate pointed out the concurrent jurisdiction provision. S. Exec. Doc. L, 90th Cong., 2d Sess. 3 & 6 (1968). In its report, the Senate reprinted testimony of the deputy legal advisor to the Department of State, who noted that the Tokyo Convention "would permit the United States to continue to exercise jurisdiction over acts aboard foreign aircraft flying to, in, or from the United States." S. Exec. Rep. No. 3, 91st Sess. 7 (1969).

In 1970, Congress enacted legislation regarding crimes committed aboard aircraft, in part to implement the Tokyo Convention. The 1970 legislation supplanted the vague notion of "in flight in air commerce" with a new jurisdictional definition, "special aircraft jurisdiction." The statute defined special aircraft jurisdiction to include:

> (c) any other aircraft (i) within the United States or (ii) outside the United States which has its next scheduled destination or last point of departure in the United States provided that in either case it next actually lands in the United States....

The special aircraft jurisdiction was amended in 1974 to comply with the Convention for the Suppression of Unlawful Seizure of Aircraft (Hijacking), Dec. 16, 1970 ... [hereinafter Hague Convention]. See Pub.L. No. 93–366, 88 Stat. 409, 409–10 (1974). The amended definition added clause (ii) (italicized below) to the existing clause (i), to include, in relevant part, any aircraft outside the United States:

> (i) that has its next scheduled destination ... in the United States, if that aircraft next actually lands in the United States; or *(ii) having "an offense" as defined in the [Hague Convention] committed aboard, if that aircraft lands in the United States with the alleged offender still aboard....*

Pub.L. No. 93–366, 88 Stat. 409, 410 (1974) (emphasis added). The amended definition added Hague Convention offenses committed aboard foreign aircraft not scheduled to land in the United States, but that do in fact land there. The purpose of the amendment was to implement the Hague Convention by "extend[ing] the definition to include ... categories of aircraft not now covered by existing law." H.R. Rep. No. 93–885, 93rd Cong., 2d Sess. 11; H.R. Conf. Rep. No. 93–1194, 93d Cong., 2d Sess. 14. Jurisdiction over foreign aircraft that are scheduled to and do in fact land in the United States was retained unchanged from the original statute.

The definition of special aircraft jurisdiction reached its present form in 1984, when Congress amended the statute to cover certain offenses defined in the Convention for the Suppression of Unlawful Acts Against the Safety of Civil Aviation (Sabotage) art. 1, §§ 1(d), 1(e), (1971) [Montreal Convention]. See Pub.L. No. 98–473, 98 Stat. 1837,

2189 (1984). Clause (iii) (italicized below) was added to the existing clauses (I) and (ii) so that the special aircraft jurisdiction now includes, in relevant part:

> (d) any other aircraft outside the United States
>
> (i) that has its next scheduled destination or last point of departure in the United States, if that aircraft actually lands in the United States;
>
> (ii) having "an offense" as defined in the [Hague Convention] committed aboard, if that aircraft lands in the United States with the alleged offender still aboard; or
>
> *(iii) regarding which an offense as defined in [certain parts of the Montreal Convention] is committed if the aircraft lands in the United States with an alleged offender still on board;*

49 U.S.C. App. § 1472(k)(1) (Supp. V 1987) (emphasis added). This amendment is analogous to the 1974 amendment in that it adds to the ambit of jurisdiction certain Montreal Convention offenses committed aboard foreign aircraft not scheduled to land in the United States, but actually landing there. The amendment "expands the protection accorded to aircraft ... by establishing criminal jurisdiction over certain aircraft-related offenses." S. Rep. No. 98–619, 98th Cong., 2d Sess. 1. And, like the 1974 amendment, it leaves intact jurisdiction over specified crimes committed on foreign aircraft scheduled to land and actually landing in the United States.

Defendant insists that the special aircraft jurisdiction should be read to cover foreign aircraft only when Hague or Montreal Convention offenses are committed on board. In other words, he contends, subsection (d)(i) does not stand on its own, but requires in addition the occurrence of (d)(ii) or (d)(iii). There is nothing in the legislative history to indicate that Congress meant to qualify the broad jurisdiction over crimes aboard foreign aircraft that it conferred in the 1961 and 1970 criminal provisions. Rather, the 1974 and 1984 amendments left the earlier provision intact while it expanded jurisdiction to include Hague or Montreal offenses committed aboard foreign aircraft that make *unscheduled* landings in the United States.

In 1986, Congress added chapter 109A of title 18 to the list of crimes punishable under 49 U.S.C. § 1472(k)(1). See Pub.L. No. 99–646, 100 Stat. 3592, 3624 (1986). The statute now reads:

> Whoever, while aboard an aircraft within the special aircraft jurisdiction of the United States, commits an act which, if committed within the special maritime and territorial jurisdiction of the United States, as defined in section 7 of Title 18, would be in violation of section 113, 114, 661, 662, 1111, 1112, 1113, chapter 109A, or 2111 of such Title 18 shall be punished as provided therein.

49 U.S.C. App. § 1472(k)(1) (Supp. V 1987). Adding a reference to chapter 109A—and thus to section 2241 of title 18 under which defendant is charged—did not change the pattern of the underlying jurisdic-

tional statute. Thus, the knowing engagement or attempted engagement in a sexual act with a child under the age of 12, aboard a foreign aircraft in non-United States airspace that is next scheduled to land and actually lands in the United States, is a federal crime punishable in a United States court....

The special aircraft jurisdiction statute was originally created to comply with treaty obligations under the Tokyo Convention. While the Tokyo Convention was intended primarily to deal with the punishment of air piracy, it was also designed to cover any other criminal offense. Article 1 defines the Tokyo Convention's scope as covering:

a) offences against penal law;

b) acts which, whether or not they are offences, may or do jeopardize the safety of the aircraft or of persons or property therein or which jeopardize good order and discipline on board.

The record of the drafting conference reports that the secretary general of the conference stated that the Convention was intended to apply to all penal offences "irrespective of whether or not they affected the safety of the aircraft." 1 International Civil Aviation Organization, International Conference on Air Law, Tokyo, August–September 1963 16 (1966). *See* 1 P. Keenan, A. Lester, P. Martin & J. McMahon, Shawcross and Beaumont on Air Law 702–03 (3d ed. 1966); Mendelsohn, *In-Flight Crime: The International and Domestic Picture Under the Tokyo Convention*, 53 Va. L. Rev. 509, 521 (1967). While the United States delegate expressed misgivings about article 1 (a), he strongly supported article 1 (b), 1 International Civil Aviation Organization, *supra*, at 17. The United States signed and ratified the Convention, including article 1(a), without reservations. 20 U.S.T. at 2958.

The Tokyo Convention's primary goal was to encourage nations to exercise jurisdiction over crimes committed aboard aircraft registered in that nation. Nevertheless, the Tokyo Convention explicitly provides for jurisdiction over crimes committed aboard aircraft of foreign registry. Article 3(3) provides, "This Convention does not exclude any criminal jurisdiction exercised in accordance with national law." ...

POWER OF COURTS TO REFUSE JURISDICTION

Despite this court's reservations about the wisdom of further prosecution in this country, it lacks the power to refuse jurisdiction on equitable grounds. The court is empowered to dismiss a criminal case only for unnecessary delay, Fed.R.Crim.P. 48(b), failure to comply with the time limits set by the Speedy Trial Act, 18 U.S.C. § 3161 (1982) or lack of jurisdiction or the failure of the indictment to charge an offense, Fed.R.Crim.P. 12(b)(2). See 1 C. Wright, Federal Practice and Procedure § 3, at 12 (1982) (Rule 48(b) and Speedy Trial Act); United States v. Weinstein, 511 F.2d 622, 627 (2d Cir.), *cert. denied*, 422 U.S. 1042, (1975) (Rule 12(b)(2), and generally noting the limited power of the court to act *sua sponte*); United States v. Dooling, 406 F.2d 192 (2d Cir.), *cert. denied*, 395 U.S. 911 (1969) (Rule 48(b), and generally noting that "inherent power of a district court 'to do justice' "is limited). In this case, where jurisdiction exists, the indictment properly charges an offense, and the prosecution is timely, the court must allow the case to proceed. The decision on whether to prosecute or refrain and leave prosecution to another country is entirely one for the prosecutor, guided by the Departments of Justice and State.

Questions

1. In *Georgescu*, what basis for jurisdiction in the United States existed in international law? Was there territorial jurisdiction? Did the offense continue into the U.S. or was it completed abroad?

2. Was the criminal sexual act a violation of international law? Human rights law? *See, e.g.*, Universal Declaration of Human Rights, arts. 1, 3, 5. Whether or not there was a universal jurisdictional basis for enforcement of the U.S. statute, was there consent to jurisdiction by treaty or a competence under "universal by treaty"? See Section 2 of this chapter at p. 560. What role did the Tokyo Convention play in this regard?

3. Could the United States regulate the "airworthiness" or safety of the SAS aircraft? require security standards on board the aircraft? require special protections for unaccompanied children?

UNITED STATES v. CAICEDO

47 F.3d 370 (9th Cir.1995).

We must decide whether the Maritime Drug Law Enforcement Act, 46 U.S.C. app. §§ 1901–1903, can be applied, consistent with due process, to defendants apprehended aboard a "stateless" vessel on the high seas when there is no nexus between the defendants and the United States. . . .

This is an appeal from the district court's order granting a defense motion to dismiss. We accept the facts alleged by the government as true. United States v. Buckley, 689 F.2d 893, 897 (9th Cir.1982), *cert. denied,* 460 U.S. 1086 (1983).

On November 15, 1993, the United States Coast Guard apprehended the six defendants, all foreign nationals, on a thirty-five foot power boat floating dead in the water approximately 200 miles off the coast of Nicaragua and 2,000 miles from San Diego. The defendants' boat was not registered to any nation, and it flew no nation's flag. Before being boarded by the Coast Guard, the defendants jettisoned 2,567 pounds of cocaine into the ocean. The Coast Guard recovered the cocaine. The government acknowledges "[t]here was no evidence that the vessel, its cargo or its crew were destined for the United States, or that any part of the criminal venture occurred in the United States."

Each of the defendants was charged with possession of cocaine with intent to distribute and conspiracy in violation of 46 U.S.C. app. § 1903(a), (j). The district judge dismissed the complaint, concluding that because the government failed to demonstrate any nexus with the

United States, prosecution was "arbitrary and fundamentally unfair under the Fifth Amendment." We have jurisdiction, 18 U.S.C. § 3731, and reverse....

We review de novo the dismissal of an indictment on due process grounds. United States v. Barrera–Moreno, 951 F.2d 1089, 1091 (9th Cir.1991), *cert. denied,* 113 S.Ct. 417 (1992).

Section 1903(a) makes it "unlawful for any person on board a vessel ... subject to the jurisdiction of the United States, ... to knowingly or intentionally ... possess with intent to ... distribute, a controlled substance." A "vessel subject to the jurisdiction of the United States" is defined to include "a vessel without nationality." 46 U.S.C. app. § 1903(c)(1)(A). The act explicitly provides for extraterritorial effect. § 1903(h). Moreover, it extends the United States' jurisdiction over stateless vessels on the high seas without enumerating any further requirements, and particularly without requiring that there be a nexus between a defendant's conduct aboard a stateless vessel and the United States. *See* § 1903(c)(1)(A); United States v. Alvarez–Mena, 765 F.2d 1259, 1264 (5th Cir.1985) (discussing similar provision in predecessor statute). On its face, the act applies to the defendants' conduct.

The defendants' due process argument is premised primarily on our recent statement that "[i]n order to apply extraterritorially a federal criminal statute to a defendant consistently with due process, there must be a sufficient nexus between the defendant and the United States." United States v. Davis, 905 F.2d 245, 248–49 (9th Cir.1990), *cert. denied,* 498 U.S. 1047 (1991). *Davis* examined the application of § 1903 to a defendant apprehended on the high seas aboard a ship of British registry. We found the nexus requirement satisfied by facts indicating that the defendant intended to smuggle drugs into the United States. 905 F.2d at 249. *Davis's* nexus requirement has been reiterated in United States v. Aikins, 946 F.2d 608, 613 (9th Cir.1990) and United States v. Khan, 35 F.3d 426, 429–30 (9th Cir.1994).

Davis, *Aikins* and *Khan* do not control the result in this case. Those cases all involved defendants apprehended on foreign flagged vessels. The radically different treatment afforded to stateless vessels as a matter of international law convinces us that there is nothing arbitrary or fundamentally unfair about prosecuting the defendants in the United States. We decline the defendants' invitation to extend *Davis* and its progeny to a stateless vessel on the high seas.

Principles of international law are "useful as a rough guide" in determining whether application of the statute would violate due process. *Davis,* 905 F.2d at 249 n.2. The First, Second, Fourth, Fifth and Eleventh Circuits agree that the United States may exercise jurisdiction consistent with international law over drug offenders apprehended aboard stateless vessels on the high seas without demonstrating any nexus to the United States. United States v. Victoria, 876 F.2d 1009, 1010–11 (1st Cir.1989); United States v. Alvarez–Mena, 765 F.2d 1259, 1265 (5th Cir.1985); United States v. Pinto–Mejia, 720 F.2d 248, 261 (2d

Cir.1983), modified, 728 F.2d 142 (2d Cir.1984); United States v. Marino–Garcia, 679 F.2d 1373, 1383 (11th Cir.1982), *cert. denied,* 459 U.S. 1114 (1983); United States v. Howard–Arias, 679 F.2d 363, 371–72 (4th Cir.), *cert. denied,* 459 U.S. 874 (1982). We have recognized the substantial protections forfeited by stateless vessels on the high seas. United States v. Rubies, 612 F.2d 397, 403 (9th Cir.1979), *cert. denied,* 446 U.S. 940 (1980).

There is much discussion in the briefs and the district court opinion regarding objective territorial, protective and universal jurisdiction. These are each principles of international law that provide a basis for one nation to apply its law extraterritorially. United States v. Vasquez–Velasco, 15 F.3d 833, 840 (9th Cir.1994). Under appropriate circumstances, these principles would allow the United States to exercise jurisdiction over another nation's vessel operating on the high seas. However, international law "restrictions on the right to assert jurisdiction over foreign vessels on the high seas and the concomitant exceptions have no applicability in connection with stateless vessels." *Marino–Garcia,* 679 F.2d at 1382. Such vessels are "international pariahs." *Id.* By attempting to shrug the yoke of any nation's authority, they subject themselves to the jurisdiction of all nations "solely as a consequence of the vessel's status as stateless." *Id.* at 1383....

The nexus requirement in *Davis* is grounded on the international law principles applicable to foreign flag vessels....

A nexus requirement, imposed as a matter of due process, makes sense when the "rough guide" of international law also requires a nexus.... But where a defendant attempts to avoid the law of all nations by travelling on a stateless vessel, he has forfeited these protections of international law and can be charged with the knowledge that he has done so. *Marino–Garcia,* 679 F.2d at 1384 n.19. Because stateless vessels do not fall within the veil of another sovereign's territorial protection, all nations can treat them as their own territory and subject them to their laws. *Id.* at 1382–83.

The result we reach is consistent with all other federal circuits that have addressed the question. The Third Circuit has held directly that § 1903 can be applied consistently with due process to punish conduct aboard a foreign flag vessel even when there is no nexus with the United States. United States v. Martinez–Hidalgo, 993 F.2d 1052, 1056 (3d Cir.1993), *cert. denied,* 114 S.Ct. 699 (1994). Although many of the other circuit court decisions cited above focused primarily on the international law question, opinions from the Fourth, Fifth and Eleventh Circuits explicitly acknowledge and reject any due process problem. *Alvarez–Mena,* 765 F.2d at 1266 (5th Cir.) (elimination of a nexus requirement permissible "at least where, as here, there is no basis for any claim of due process violation"); *Howard–Arias,* 679 F.2d at 371–72 (4th Cir.) (affirming as consistent with due process jurisdiction over defendants apprehended on stateless vessels with "intent to distribute [narcotics] anywhere"); *Marino–Garcia,* 679 F.2d at 1384 (11th Cir.) ("[F]ailure to unmistakably accede to the authority of a single sovereign while traversing the high seas will render [ship's occupants] subject to the criminal jurisdiction of the United States. The Constitution does not require more.'').

The defendants do not point to any jurisdiction where the conduct they are alleged to have been engaged in was legal, nor are we aware of any. See 46 U.S.C. app. § 1902 (''trafficking in controlled substances aboard vessels is a serious international problem and is universally condemned''). These defendants ''should therefore have been on notice that the United States or any other nation concerned with drug trafficking'' could subject their vessel to its jurisdiction. *Marino–Garcia,* 679 F.2d at 1384 n. 19. Reversed and Remanded.

Notes and Questions

1. Do you agree with the court's reasoning in *Caicedo* that a ''stateless vessel'' is an ''international pariah'' and should therefore be subject to the ''jurisdiction'' of any nation, even in the absence of any nexus between the defendant and the asserting nation? *See also* Section 2, below; 1982 U.N. Convention on the Law of the Sea, art. 110(1)(d) and (2), in the Documents Supplement; note 6 below. Is it international law that provides a stateless vessel with no protection and also allows any state to prescribe? Was there possibly some confusion between issues involving prescriptive and enforcement jurisdiction under international law?

2. In terms of prescriptive jurisdiction, if there is no proven intent to smuggle drugs into the U.S. and no other contacts with the U.S. exist, is it quite likely that jurisdiction cannot be based on objective territorial, protective, or victim (passive nationality) principles? If the accused are not U.S. nationals, what would you like to demonstrate as a U.S. prosecutor faced with defense claims that there is no prescriptive jurisdiction (recall Restatement § 431(1) and cmt. a)?

3. If you are advising an official directing U.S. or Canadian drug interdiction efforts, when would enforcement more easily comply with prescriptive jurisdictional requirements? Why not wait?

4. Is it ''reasonable'' to permit a country to assert prescriptive jurisdiction over crimes committed on board a stateless vessel (or a foreign flag vessel) absent any nexus? Does international law concerning protective or universal prescriptive jurisdiction require a ''nexus''? If not (and more generally), is the exercise of protective or universal (or even nationality) jurisdiction an impermissible ''intrusion into the sovereign territory of another nation''?

5. Should the ''due process'' clause of the Fifth Amendment to the U.S. Constitution require a greater ''nexus'' to the United States than international law allows concerning nationality, protective, or universal jurisdiction? In view of the trends in judicial decision noted thus far, what process do you think is ''due''?

6. See Article 110 of the 1982 U.N. Law of the Sea Convention (in the Documents Supplement). If a vessel is flying no flag, is the exercise of enforcement jurisdiction all the more permissible? *See also id.* Art. 92(2);

Louis B. Sohn, Kristen Gustafson, The Law of the Sea 22–23 (1984). Article 108 of the Convention also provides:

Illicit Traffic in Narcotic Drugs or Psychotropic Substances

1. All States shall co-operate in the suppression of illicit traffic in narcotic drugs and psychotropic substances by ships on the high seas contrary to international conventions.

2. Any State which has reasonable grounds for believing that a vessel flying its flag is engaged in illicit traffic in narcotic drugs or psychotropic substances may request the co-operation of other States to suppress such traffic.

Does this Convention provide an implied consent in advance to board suspect vessels? Does paragraph 1 cover all vessels, including those flying no flag or "stateless" vessels, whereas any implied limits in paragraph 2 relate to "flag" State consent? Does paragraph 1 provide implied consent to board and "suppress" whereas paragraph 2 provides an additional opportunity for the "flag" State to request other efforts in cooperation with the flag State? *Cf.* Louis B. Sohn, Kristen Gustafson, The Law of the Sea 21 (1984) (neither Article 108 of the LOS nor Article 35 of the 1961 Single Convention on Narcotic Drugs "authorizes the boarding, searching or seizure of a foreign flag vessel suspected of engaging in illicit drug trade."). Do you agree?

7. For examples of U.S. practice in obtaining ad hoc foreign flag consent to board and search, *see, e.g.,* United States v. Crews, 605 F.Supp. 730 (S.D.Fla.1985), and apparently United States v. Romero–Galue, 757 F.2d 1147 (11th Cir.1985).

8. Do states within the United States have extraterritorial criminal jurisdictional competencies? In Florida v. Stepansky, 761 So.2d 1027 (Fla. 2000), the Florida Supreme Court upheld the reach of a Florida statute to an alleged burglary and attempted sexual battery of a 13 year old U.S. national on a foreign cruise vessel some 100 miles off the Florida coast, finding an "interest" of Florida as a "major center for international travel and trade by sea" in assuring protection of persons traveling to and from Florida and noting that "Florida's tourism industry could be significantly affected." Does this meet tests for prescriptive jurisdictional competence under international law? If the foreign vessels leave from and return to Florida?

UNITED STATES v. NORIEGA

746 F.Supp. 1506, 1509–10, 1512–19, 1525–28 (S.D.Fla.1990).

Hoeveler, J.

This Cause comes before the Court on the several motions of Defendants General Manuel Antonio Noriega and Lt. Col. Luis Del Cid to dismiss for lack of jurisdiction the indictment which charges them with various narcotics-related offenses.

The case at bar presents the Court with a drama of international proportions, considering the status of the principal defendant and the difficult circumstances under which he was brought before this Court. The pertinent facts are as follows:

On February 14, 1988, a federal grand jury sitting in Miami, Florida returned a twelve-count indictment charging General Manuel Antonio Noriega with participating in an international conspiracy to import cocaine and materials used in producing cocaine into and out of the United States. Noriega is alleged to have exploited his official position as head of the intelligence branch of the Panamanian National Guard, and then as Commander-in-Chief of the Panamanian Defense Forces, to receive payoffs in return for assisting and protecting international drug traffickers, including various members of the Medellin Cartel, in conducting narcotics and money laundering operations in Panama.

Specifically, the indictment charges that General Noriega protected cocaine shipments from Colombia through Panama to the United States; arranged for the transshipment and sale to the Medellin Cartel of ether and acetone, including such chemicals previously seized by the Panamanian Defense Forces; provided refuge and a base for continued operations for the members of the Medellin Cartel after the Colombian government's crackdown on drug traffickers following the murder of the Colombian Minister of Justice, Rodrigo Lara–Bonilla; agreed to protect a cocaine laboratory in Darien Province, Panama; and assured the safe passage of millions of dollars of narcotic proceeds from the United States into Panamanian banks. Noriega also allegedly traveled to Havana, Cuba and met with Cuban president Fidel Castro, who, according to the indictment, mediated a dispute between Noriega and the Cartel caused by the Panamanian troops' seizure of a drug laboratory that Noriega was paid to protect. All of these activities were allegedly undertaken for General Noriega's own personal profit. Defendant Del Cid, in addition to being an officer in the Panamanian Defense Forces, was General Noriega's personal secretary. He is charged with acting as liaison, courier, and emissary for Noriega in his transactions with Cartel members and other drug traffickers.

Because of the activities alleged, Defendants are charged with engaging in a pattern of racketeering activity, in violation of the RICO statutes, 18 U.S.C. §§ 1962(c) and 1962(d); conspiracy to distribute and import cocaine into the United States, in violation of 21 U.S.C. § 963; and distributing and aiding and abetting the distribution of cocaine, intending that it be imported into the United States, in violation of 21 U.S.C. § 959 and 18 U.S.C. § 2. Defendant Noriega is further charged with aiding and abetting the manufacture of cocaine destined for the United States, in violation of 21 U.S.C. § 959 and 18 U.S.C. § 2; conspiring to manufacture cocaine intending that it be imported into the United States, in violation of 21 U.S.C. § 963; and causing interstate travel and use of facilities in interstate commerce to promote an unlawful activity, in violation of 18 U.S.C. § 1952(a)(3) and 18 U.S.C. § 2. Subsequent to the indictment, the Court granted General Noriega's motion to allow special appearance of counsel, despite the fact that Noriega was a fugitive and not before the Court at that time. Noriega's counsel then moved to dismiss the indictment on the ground that United States laws could not be applied to a foreign leader whose alleged illegal activities all occurred outside the territorial bounds of the United States. Counsel further argued that Noriega was immune from prosecution as a head of state and diplomat, and that his alleged narcotics offenses constituted acts of state not properly reviewable by this Court.

Upon hearing arguments of counsel, and after due consideration of the memoranda filed, the Court denied Defendant's motion, for reasons fully set forth below. At that time, the Court noted that this case was fraught with political overtones, but that it was nonetheless unlikely that General Noriega would ever be brought to the United States to answer the charges against him....

Jurisdiction Over The Offense

The first issue confronting the Court is whether the United States may exercise jurisdiction over Noriega's alleged criminal activities. Noriega maintains that "the extraterritorial application of the criminal law is unreasonable under the unique facts of this case, and cannot be relied upon to secure jurisdiction over a leader of a sovereign nation who has personally performed no illegal acts within the borders of the United States." Although the defendant attempts to weave his asserted status as a foreign leader into his challenge to the extraterritorial application of this country's criminal laws, the question of whether the United States may proscribe conduct which occurs beyond its borders is separate from the question of whether Noriega is immune from prosecution as a head of state. This distinction is made clear in the defendant's own discussion of the applicable international law on extraterritorial jurisdiction, which does not look to a foreign defendant's official status but rather to the nature and effect of the conduct at issue. The Court therefore reserves analysis of Noriega's claim to head of state immunity and confines its discussion here to the ability of the United States to reach and prosecute acts committed by aliens outside its territorial borders. While the indictment cites specific instances of conduct occurring within the United States, including the shipment of cocaine from Panama to Miami and several flights to and from Miami by Noriega's alleged co-conspirators, the activity ascribed to Noriega occurred solely in Panama with the exception of the one trip to Cuba. Noriega is charged with providing safe haven to international narcotic traffickers by allowing Panama to be used as a location for the manufacture and shipment of cocaine destined for this country's shores.

Where a court is faced with the issue of extraterritorial jurisdiction, the analysis to be applied is 1) whether the United States has the power to reach the conduct in question under traditional principles of international law; and 2) whether the statutes under which the defendant is charged are intended to have extraterritorial effect. As Noriega concedes, the United States has long possessed the ability to attach criminal consequences to acts occurring outside this country which produce effects within the United States. Strassheim v. Daily, 221 U.S. 280, 285 (1911); Restatement (Third) of the Foreign Relations Law of the United States [hereinafter Restatement (Third)] § 402(1)(c). For example, the

United States would unquestionably have authority to prosecute a person standing in Canada who fires a bullet across the border which strikes a second person standing in the United States. See *Restatement (Third)* § 402, cmt. d. "All the nations of the world recognize 'the principle that a man who outside of a country willfully puts in motion a force to take effect in it is answerable at the place where the evil is done ...'" Rivard v. United States, 375 F.2d 882, 887 (5th Cir.) (citations omitted), *cert. denied*, 389 U.S. 884 (1967). The objective territorial theory of jurisdiction, which focuses on the effects or intended effects of conduct, can be traced to Justice Holmes' statement that "[a]cts done outside a jurisdiction, but intended to produce or producing effects within it, justify a State in punishing the cause of the harm as if he had been present at the effect, if the State should succeed in getting him within its power." Strassheim v. Daily, 221 U.S. at 285. See also Church v. Hubbart, 6 U.S. (2 Cranch) 187, 234 (1804) ("[a nation's] power to secure itself from injury may certainly be exercised beyond the limits of its territory."). Even if the extraterritorial conduct produces no effect within the United States, a defendant may still be reached if he was part of a conspiracy in which some co-conspirator's activities took place within United States territory. United States v. Baker, 609 F.2d 134, 138 (5th Cir.1980). The former Fifth Circuit, whose decisions establish precedent for this Court, has on numerous occasions upheld jurisdiction over foreigners who conspired to import narcotics into the United States but never entered this country nor personally performed any acts within its territorial limits, as long as there was proof of an overt act committed within the United States by a co-conspirator. *See* United States v. Postal, 589 F.2d 862 (5th Cir.), *cert. denied*, 444 U.S. 832 (1979); United States v. Cadena, 585 F.2d 1252 (5th Cir.1978); United States v. Winter, 509 F.2d 975 (5th Cir.), *cert. denied*, 423 U.S. 825 (1975); *Rivard v. United States, supra*.

More recently, international law principles have expanded to permit jurisdiction upon a mere showing of intent to produce effects in this country, without requiring proof of an overt act or effect within the United States. See United States v. Wright–Barker, 784 F.2d 161, 168 (3d Cir. 1986); United States v. Postal, 589 F.2d at 886, n.39; United States v. Columba–Colella, 604 F.2d at 358, 360. According to the *Restatement (Third)*:

> Cases involving intended but unrealized effect are rare, but international law does not preclude jurisdiction in such instances, subject to the principle of reasonableness. When the intent to commit the proscribed act is clear and demonstrated by some activity, and the effect to be produced by the activity is substantial and foreseeable, the fact that a plan or conspiracy was thwarted does not deprive the target state of jurisdiction to make its law applicable. § 402, cmt. d.

In the drug smuggling context, the "intent doctrine" has resulted in jurisdiction over persons who attempted to import narcotics into the United States but never actually succeeded in entering the United States or delivering drugs within its borders. The fact that no act was committed and no repercussions were felt within the United States did not preclude jurisdiction over conduct that was clearly directed at the United States. *United States v. Wright–Barker, supra* ("The purpose of these [narcotics laws] is to halt smugglers *before* they introduce their dangerous wares into and distribute them in this country.") (emphasis in original); United States v. Quemener, 789 F.2d 145, 156 (2d Cir.), *cert. denied*, 479 U.S. 829 (1986); United States v. Loalza–Vasquez, 735 F.2d 153, 156 (5th Cir.1984); United States v. Baker, 609 F.2d at 138–39.

These principles unequivocally support jurisdiction in this case. The indictment charges Noriega with conspiracy to import cocaine into the United States and alleges several overt acts performed within the United States in furtherance of the conspiracy. Specifically, the indictment alleges that co-conspirators of Noriega purchased a Lear jet in Miami, which was then used to transport drug proceeds from Miami to Panama. Moreover, Noriega's activities in Panama, if true, undoubtedly produced effects within this country as deleterious as the hypothetical bullet fired across the border. The indictment alleges that, as a result of Noriega's facilitation of narcotics activity in Panama, 2,141 pounds of cocaine were illegally brought into Miami from Panama. While the ability of the United States to reach and proscribe extraterritorial conduct having effects in this country does not depend on the amount of narcotics imported into the United States or the magnitude of the consequences, the importation of over 2,000 pounds of cocaine clearly has a harmful impact and merits jurisdiction. Finally, even if no overt acts or effects occurred within the territorial borders, the object of the alleged conspiracy was to import cocaine into the United States and therefore an intent to produce effects is present.

The defendant's argument that the exercise of jurisdiction over his alleged activities in Panama is unreasonable is simply unsupportable in light of established principles of international law and the overwhelming case law in this Circuit upholding jurisdiction under similar circumstances.[1] Other than asserting his status as a foreign leader, which presents a different question from the one posed here, Noriega does not

1. Defendant's citation to *United States v. Bank of Nova Scotia* for the proposition that extraterritorial jurisdiction must be exercised delicately does not balance in his favor. In that case, which involved a grand jury subpoena served upon a Canadian-chartered bank located in the Bahamas, the Eleventh Circuit acknowledged that enforcing the subpoena might provoke international friction but nonetheless held that it "simply cannot acquiesce in the proposition that United States criminal investigations must be thwarted whenever there is a conflict with the interest of other states." 691 F.2d 1384, 1391 (11th Cir.1982) (quoting *In re* Grand Jury Proceedings (Field), 532 F.2d 404, 410 (5th Cir.), *cert. denied*, 429 U.S. 940 (1976)), *cert. denied*, 462 U.S. 1119 (1983). *Bank of Nova Scotia* is therefore in accord with the cases cited above.

Similarly unpersuasive in Defendant's reference to a legal treatise arguing that the effects doctrine should not be applied to extraterritorial conduct resulting in "more or less remote repercussions." *See* Jennings, *Extraterritorial Jurisdiction and the United States Antitrust Laws*, 33 Brit. Y.B.C.L. 146, 159 (1957). Since Noriega is alleged to have conspired to import narcotics *into* the United States, the delivery of over 2,000 pounds of cocaine into Miami—far from being a 'remote repercussion' of the conspiracy—is in fact a direct and intended result of his alleged activities in Panama.

distinguish this case from those cited above. He cites the principle of reasonableness recently articulated in the *Restatement (Third)* § 403, but fails to say how extending jurisdiction over his conduct would be unreasonable. In fact, the defendant's invocation of a reasonableness requirement supports rather than undermines the application of jurisdiction in the present case. Thus, for example, Noriega quotes the following language from the *Restatement*:

> In applying the principle of reasonableness, the exercise of criminal (as distinguished from civil) jurisdiction in relation to acts committed in another state may be perceived as particularly intrusive....
>
> It is generally accepted by enforcement agencies of the United States government that criminal jurisdiction over activity with substantial foreign elements should be exercised more sparingly than civil jurisdiction over the same activity, and only upon strong justification.

Restatement (Third) § 403, RN 8. However, the same section of the *Restatement* establishes that narcotics offenses provide the strong justification meriting criminal jurisdiction: "Prosecution for activities committed in a foreign state have generally been limited to serious and universally condemned offenses, such as treason or traffic in narcotics, and to offenses by and against military forces. In such cases the state in whose territory the act occurs is not likely to object to regulation by the state concerned." *Id.* (citations omitted). The *Restatement* therefore explicitly recognizes the reasonableness of extending jurisdiction to narcotics activity such as that alleged here. See also United States v. Wright–Barker, 784 F.2d at 168 (construing § 403 to permit jurisdiction over extraterritorial narcotics trafficking). Even if another state were likely to object to jurisdiction here, the United States has a strong interest in halting the flow of illicit drugs across its borders. In assessing the reasonableness of extraterritorial jurisdiction, one of the factors to be considered is the character of the activity to be regulated, including the importance of regulation to the regulating state and the degree to which the desire to regulate is generally accepted. *Restatement (Third)* § 403(1)(c). The consensus of the American public on the need to stem the flow of drugs into this country is well publicized and need not be elaborated upon in detail. Further, the Court notes that the United States has an affirmative duty to enact and enforce legislation to curb illicit drug trafficking under the Single Convention on Narcotics Drugs, 18 U.S.T. 1409, T.I.A.S. No. 6298, New York, March 30, 1961, ratified by the United States, 1967, amended 26 U.S.T. 1441, T.I.A.S. No. 8118. See *In re* Grand Jury Proceedings Bank of Nova Scotia, 740 F.2d 817, 830–31 (11th Cir.1984), *cert. denied*, 469 U.S. 1106 (1985) (discussing the Single Convention on Narcotics Drugs)....

This conclusion does not end the Court's analysis, however, since a further requirement is that the criminal statutes under which the defendant is charged be intended to apply to conduct outside the United States....

Section 959, prohibiting the distribution of narcotics intending that they be imported into the United States, is clearly meant to apply extraterritorially. The statute expressly states that it is "intended to reach acts of manufacture or distribution committed outside the territorial jurisdiction of the United States." 21 U.S.C. § 959(c). The remaining statutes, by contrast, do not on their face indicate an express intention that they be given extraterritorial effect. Where a statute is silent as to its extraterritorial reach, a presumption against such application normally applies. United States v. Benitez, 741 F.2d 1312, 1316–17 (11th Cir.1984), *cert. denied*, 471 U.S. 1137 (1985). However, "such statutes may be given extraterritorial effect if the nature of the law permits it and Congress intends it. Absent an express intention on the face of the statutes to do so, the exercise of that power may be inferred from the nature of the offenses and Congress' other legislative efforts to eliminate the type of crime involved." United States v. Baker, 609 F.2d at 136. (*citing* United States v. Bowman, 260 U.S. 94, 97–98 (1922)).

With respect to 21 U.S.C. § 952, it is apparent from the very nature of the offense that the statute was intended to reach extraterritorial acts. Section 952 makes it unlawful to import narcotics "into the United States from *any place outside* thereof ..." (emphasis added). Because importation by definition involves acts originating outside of the territorial limits of the United States, the Court can only infer that § 952 applies to conduct which begins abroad; any interpretation to the contrary would render the statute virtually meaningless. United States v. Cadena, 585 F.2d at 1259. With jurisdiction over the substantive violations of §§ 959 and 952 established, jurisdiction over the conspiracy and aiding and abetting counts likewise follows. Since a conspiracy to commit an offense is closely related to the offense itself, courts have regularly inferred the extraterritorial reach of the § 963 conspiracy statute on the basis of a finding that the substantive statutes apply abroad. *See, e.g.,* Chua Han Mow v. United States, 730 F.2d 1308, 1311 (9th Cir.1984), *cert. denied*, 470 U.S. 1031 (1985); United States v. Baker, 609 F.2d at 139. The same must be said for an aiding and abetting charge; if anything, the act of aiding and abetting is even more intimately connected to the underlying crime. In short, the Court perceives no sound jurisdictional reason for distinguishing the conspiracy and aiding and abetting charges from the substantive offense for purposes of extraterritorial application. Section 963 and 18 U.S.C. § 2 must therefore be given extraterritorial effect as well.

Whether the RICO and Travel Act statutes reach conduct abroad is a more difficult question. None of the cases cited by the parties address this point and the Court is unaware of any case reaching the issue.[2] The

2. In *Republic of Philippines v. Marcos (Marcos II)*, the Philippine government brought a RICO action against deposed president Ferdinand Marcos and his wife Imelda for allegedly converting funds belonging to the Philippine people for their own personal use. The indictment charged that some of the funds were invested in properties in the United States and that other monies and valuables were transported to Hawaii upon the Marcos' arrival there. On the question of RICO's applicabil-

question of these statutes' extraterritorial effect is therefore a matter of apparent first impression. For the reasons stated below, the Court finds that RICO, 18 U.S.C. §§ 1962(c) and (d), and the Travel Act, 18 U.S.C. § 1952(a)(3), apply to conduct outside the United States.

Section 1962(c) makes it unlawful for "any person associated with any enterprise engaged in, or the activities of which affect, interstate or foreign commerce, to conduct or participate ... in the conduct of such enterprise's affairs through a pattern of racketeering activity...." 18 U.S.C. § 1962(c).... Section 1962(d) similarly makes it illegal for "any person to conspire to violate" Section 1962(c). 18 U.S.C. § 1962(d).... These prohibitions are on their face all-inclusive and do not suggest parochial application. Indeed, if any statute reaches far and wide, it is RICO.... [The court also addressed "the overall purpose of the Act" and found it to be extraterritorial. With respect to the Travel Act, it was recognized that it was enacted as "an attempt to reach criminal activities uniquely broad and transitory ... beyond state and national borders," and that "the Act itself indicates no ... territorial limitation...."]

Jurisdiction over Defendant's extraterritorial conduct is therefore appropriate both as a matter of international law and statutory construction....

Notes and Questions

1. In *Noriega*, could objective territorial jurisdiction have been better explained or supported? Were acts within the United States attributable to Noriega? Was there an intent to produce effects and, over the years, were there effects in the United States?

2. Were there arguably other bases of prescriptive jurisdiction? Explain. The court noted that when Congress enacted RICO, it was concerned partly with efforts "to subvert and corrupt our democratic processes" and with "domestic security."

3. Professor Christopher Blakesley has been highly critical of application of the objective territorial principle to justify jurisdiction in narcotics conspiracy cases where no overt act was committed within the territory of the forum state (and no actual effects occur):

> [A] conspiracy outside the sovereign territory, by definition, cannot have any effect within the territory as it is an inchoate offense; it has no effect at all, until the substantive offense to which the parties are conspiring has occurred within the sovereign territory (or has occurred outside the territory with its own effects impacting within the territory).

ity, the court in dicta suggested that the Marcos' alleged conduct in the Philippines could not be reached but did not ultimately decide the issue since it upheld jurisdiction based upon the Marcos' alleged transportation of stolen property into the United States. The holding in that case thus provides little, if any, guidance on the issue. 818 F.2d 1473, 1478–79 (9th Cir.1987), *op. withdrawn, reh. gr., rev'd on other grounds on reh. en banc,* Republic of Philippines v. Marcos (Marcos III), 862 F.2d 1355 (9th Cir. 1988), *cert. denied,* 490 U.S. 1035 (1989).

Christopher L. Blakesley, *United States Jurisdiction Over Extraterritorial Crime,* 73 J. CRIM. & CRIMINOLOGY 1109, 1131 (1982). *But see* RESTATEMENT § 402, cmt. d.

Do you agree with either Professor Blakesley or the Restatement?

4. Despite the Restatement, "intent" alone is not sufficient under international law. Can you make a more sophisticated claim for jurisdiction in interrupted smuggling cases? Look for other factors like the agency circumstance or a process of smuggling involving also prior acts and effects.

5. On the legality of Noriega's capture in Panama with consent of the lawfully elected President of Panama, consider RESTATEMENT § 433, in Section 3, below; *The Panamanian Revolution: Diplomacy, War and Self-Determination in Panama: Self-Determination and Intervention in Panama,* and *Extraterritorial Law Enforcement and the "Receipt" and Trial of Noriega,* 84 PROC., AM. SOC. INT'L L. 182–202, 236–56 (1990); Jordan J. Paust, *After* Alvarez–Machain*: Abduction, Standing, Denials of Justice, and Unaddressed Human Rights Claims,* 67 ST. JOHN'S L. REV. 551, 566–67 & n.57 (1993).

6. 18 U.S.C.A. § 7(3) reads: "The term 'special maritime and territorial jurisdiction of the United States,' as used in this title includes: . . . (3) Any lands reserved or acquired for the use of the United States, and under the exclusive or concurrent jurisdiction thereof, or any place purchased or otherwise acquired by the United States by consent of the legislature of the State in which the same shall be, for the erection of a fort, magazine, arsenal, dockyard, or other needful building." In 1996, Congress recognized that the 12 mile territorial sea of the United States, "for purposes of Federal criminal jurisdiction is part of the United States . . . , and is within the special maritime and territorial jurisdiction of the United States. . . ." Act of April 24, 1996, P.L. 104–132, Title IX, § 901(a), 110 Stat. 1317.

In view of the presumption against extraterritoriality, should § 7(3) be construed to be extraterritorial? to reach acts within a U.S. embassy in foreign territory? to reach acts within an apartment in foreign territory that happens to be rented by the Government of the United States as private living areas for embassy or consular staff and their family members? Under international law, utilizable as an interpretive background, would the U.S. have territorial jurisdiction over acts occurring in a U.S. embassy in foreign territory? in an apartment in foreign territory? One case held that § 7(3) reaches acts in a U.S. embassy abroad. United States v. Erdos, 474 F.2d 157 (4th Cir.1973) (Erdos killed a person in the U.S. embassy in the new Republic of Equatorial Guinea. Both were U.S. nationals, Erdos was the senior diplomat and his victim was also an embassy employee.). Was the court correct? *See also* RESTATEMENT § 466, cmts. a (re: diplomatic or consular premises: "That premises are inviolable does not mean that they are extraterritorial. Acts committed on those premises are within the territorial jurisdiction of the receiving state. . . .") and c ("Applying general principles, this section declares that premises and related property are subject to the host state's jurisdiction to prescribe, adjudicate, or enforce law except by means or in circumstances where an exercise of jurisdiction would violate the premises or interfere with their use for the designated purposes. . . ."). Legislative history demonstrates that the constant concern in the House and Senate debates involved inquiry into concurrent and exclusive jurisdictional competencies of the federal government and various States within the United States as well as potential clashes and gaps between them. See 42 Cong. Rec. 586–89 (Jan. 10, 1908), 1184–95 (Jan. 28, 1908). The title of the new legislation openly demonstrates a limitation to the "Territorial Jurisdiction of the United States" when admiralty or maritime jurisdiction does not pertain. *Id.* at 1184. Indeed, legislative history speaks clearly against extraterritoriality. See *id.* at 1185–86 (remarks of Senator Heyburn regarding then Section 269(3), while introducing Senate Bill S. 2982); Jordan J. Paust, *Non-Extraterritoriality of "Special Territorial Jurisdiction" of the United States: Forgotten History and the Errors of* Erdos, 24 Yale J. Int'l L. 305 (1999).

Addressing each of the above in great detail, the district court in *United Sates v. bin Laden* agreed that *Erdos* was incorrect and ruled that counts in the indictment under 18 U.S.C. § 1111, addressing murders committed "within the special maritime and territorial jurisdiction of the United States," as defined in 18 U.S.C. § 7, must be dismissed, since the killing of persons at the U.S. embassy compounds in Nairobi, Kenya and Dar es Salaam, Tanzania would not be covered by § 7(3). 92 F.Supp.2d at 204–15. Reasoning similarly and citing similar and some of the same sources, the Second Circuit held that § 7 (3) does not apply extraterritorially to conduct occurring on a U.S. military installation in Germany. See United States v. Gatlin, 216 F.3d 207 (2d Cir. 2000). However, a panel from the Ninth Circuit split on the issue, the majority considering that § 7(3) is extraterritorial. See United States v. Corey, 232 F.3d 1166 (9th Cir. 2000). What is the better conclusion?

7. If Saudi Arabia required U.S. corporations doing work within Saudi Arabia to not employ Jewish persons, should the U.S. corporations follow Saudi legal requirements? In 1991, employment discrimination regulated under Title VII of the 1964 Civil Rights Act was expressly made extraterritorial, applying to U.S. employers and U.S. controlled corporations. The 1991 amendment, however, built in a foreign-law-sovereign-compulsion exception to the extraterritorial reach of Title VII.

In 1976, the Arab League had published blacklists of firms doing business with Israel. Saudi Arabia, like all Arab League members, was required to assure that companies it contracted with did not purchase supplies from or make subcontracts with blacklisted companies. The U.S. based Bechtel Corporation refused to deal with blacklisted companies with respect to construction work in Saudi Arabia. An amendment to the U.S. Export Administration Act, 50 U.S.C.A. §§ 2402(5)(A) and (b), 2407, made compliance with the boycott illegal within the U.S. Did Bechtel have a defense to any exercise of U.S. prescriptive jurisdiction within the U.S. or abroad? *See* Restatement § 441, RN 5.

8. Section 441 of the Restatement claims that "(1) [i]n general, a state may not require a person (a) to do an act in another state that is prohibited by the law of that state or by the law of the state of which he is a national.... [But (2) i]n general, a state may require a person of foreign nationality (a) to do an act in that state even if it is prohibited by the law of the state of which he is a national...." The Restatement thereby prefers what it terms a "territorial preference" in the case of clashing concurrent

jurisdictional competencies. It also suggests thereby that, in general, there is a defense of "foreign state compulsion". Nonetheless, foreign state compulsion is generally ignored as a defense. *See, e.g., Aerospatiale, supra*; Doe v. United States, 487 U.S. 201 (1988); Marc Rich & Co. v. United States, 707 F.2d 663 (2d Cir.), *cert. denied*, 463 U.S. 1215 (1983); *In re* Grand Jury (United States v. Bank of Nova Scotia), 691 F.2d 1384 (11th Cir.1982); Berta Esperanza Hernandez, *supra*; see also Hartford Fire Insurance Co. v. California, following:

HARTFORD FIRE INSURANCE CO. v. CALIFORNIA

509 U.S. 764 (1993).

SOUTER, J.

The Sherman Act makes every contract, combination, or conspiracy in unreasonable restraint of interstate or foreign commerce illegal. 26 Stat. 209, as amended, 15 U.S.C. § 1. These consolidated cases present questions about the application of that Act to the insurance industry, both here and abroad. The plaintiffs (respondents here) allege that both domestic and foreign defendants (petitioners here) violated the Sherman Act by engaging in various conspiracies to affect the American insurance market. A group of domestic defendants argues that the McCarran–Ferguson Act, 59 Stat. 33, as amended, 15 U.S.C. § 1011 *et seq.*, precludes application of the Sherman Act to the conduct alleged; a group of foreign defendants argues that the principle of international comity requires the District Court to refrain from exercising jurisdiction over certain claims against it. We hold that most of the domestic defendants' alleged conduct is not immunized from antitrust liability by the McCarran–Ferguson Act, and that, even assuming it applies, the principle of international comity does not preclude District Court jurisdiction over the foreign conduct alleged....

Finally, we take up the question ... whether certain claims against the London reinsurers should have been dismissed as improper applications of the Sherman Act to foreign conduct. The Fifth Claim for Relief of the California Complaint alleges a violation of § 1 of the Sherman Act by certain London reinsurers who conspired to coerce primary insurers in the United States to offer CGL coverage on a claims-made basis, thereby making "occurrence CGL coverage ... unavailable in the State of California for many risks." ... The Sixth Claim for Relief of the California Complaint alleges that the London reinsurers violated § 1 by a conspiracy to limit coverage of pollution risks in North America, thereby rendering "pollution liability coverage ... almost entirely unavailable for the vast majority of casualty insurance purchasers in the State of California." ... The Eighth Claim for Relief of the California Complaint alleges a further § 1 violation by the London reinsurers who, along with domestic retrocessional reinsurers, conspired to limit coverage of seepage, pollution, and property contamination risks in North America, thereby eliminating such coverage in the State of California....

At the outset, we note that the District Court undoubtedly had jurisdiction of these Sherman Act claims, as the London reinsurers apparently concede.... [I]t is well established by now that the Sherman Act [with the 1982 amendment] applies to foreign conduct that was meant to produce and did in fact produce some substantial effect in the United States. See Matsushita Elec. Industrial Co. v. Zenith Radio Corp., 475 U.S. 574, 582 ... n. 6 (1986); United States v. Aluminum Co. of America, 148 F.2d 416, 444 (C.A.2 1945) (L. Hand, J.); RESTATEMENT (THIRD) OF FOREIGN RELATIONS LAW OF THE UNITED STATES § 415, and RN 3 (1987) (hereinafter RESTATEMENT (THIRD) FOREIGN RELATIONS LAW); 1 P. AREEDA & D. TURNER, ANTITRUST LAW 236 (1978); *cf.* Continental Ore Co. v. Union Carbide & Carbon Corp., 370 U.S. 690, 704 ... (1962); Steele v. Bulova Watch Co., 344 U.S. 280, 288 ... (1952); United States v. Sisal Sales Corp., 274 U.S. 268, 275–276 ... (1927). Such is the conduct alleged here: that the London reinsurers engaged in unlawful conspiracies to affect the market for insurance in the United States and that their conduct in fact produced substantial effect. See 938 F.2d at 933.

According to the London reinsurers, the District Court should have declined to exercise such jurisdiction under the principle of international comity. The Court of Appeals agreed that courts should look to that principle in deciding whether to exercise jurisdiction under the Sherman Act. *Id.*, at 932. This availed the London reinsurers nothing, however. To be sure, the Court of Appeals believed that "application of [American] antitrust laws to the London reinsurance market 'would lead to significant conflict with English law and policy,'" and that "such a conflict, unless outweighed by other factors, would by itself be reason to decline exercise of jurisdiction." *Id.*, at 933 (citation omitted). But other factors, in the court's view, including the London reinsurers' express purpose to affect United States commerce and the substantial nature of the effect produced, outweighed the supposed conflict and required the exercise of jurisdiction in this case. *Id.*, at 934.

When it enacted the Foreign Trade Antitrust Improvements Act of 1982 (FTAIA), 96 Stat. 1246, 15 U.S.C. § 6a, Congress expressed no view on the question whether a court with Sherman Act jurisdiction should ever decline to exercise such jurisdiction on grounds of international comity. See H. R. Rep. No. 97–686, p. 13 (1982) ("If a court determines that the requirements for subject matter jurisdiction are met, [the FTAIA] would have no effect on the court['s] ability to employ notions of comity ... or otherwise to take account of the international character of the transaction") (*citing Timberlane*). We need not decide that question here, however, for even assuming that in a proper case a court may decline to exercise Sherman Act jurisdiction over foreign conduct (or, as Justice Scalia would put it, may conclude by the employment of comity analysis in the first instance that there is no jurisdiction), international comity would not counsel against exercising jurisdiction in the circumstances alleged here.

The only substantial question in this case is whether "there is in fact a true conflict between domestic and foreign law." Societe Nationale

Industrielle Aerospatiale v. United States District Court, 482 U.S. 522, 555 . . . (1987) (Blackmun, J., concurring in part and dissenting in part). The London reinsurers contend that applying the Act to their conduct would conflict significantly with British law, and the British Government, appearing before us as amicus curiae, concurs. See Brief for Petitioners in No. 91–1128, pp. 22–27; Brief for Government of United Kingdom of Great Britain and Northern Ireland as Amicus Curiae 10–14. They assert that Parliament has established a comprehensive regulatory regime over the London reinsurance market and that the conduct alleged here was perfectly consistent with British law and policy. But this is not to state a conflict "The fact that conduct is lawful in the state in which it took place will not, of itself, bar application of the United States antitrust laws," even where the foreign state has a strong policy to permit or encourage such conduct. RESTATEMENT (THIRD) FOREIGN RELATIONS LAW § 415, cmt. j; see *Continental Ore Co., supra*, at 706–707. No conflict exists, for these purposes, "where a person subject to regulation by two states can comply with the laws of both." RESTATEMENT (THIRD) FOREIGN RELATIONS LAW § 403, cmt. e. Since the London reinsurers do not argue that British law requires them to act in some fashion prohibited by the law of the United States, see Reply Brief for Petitioners in No. 91–1128, pp. 7–8, or claim that their compliance with the laws of both countries is otherwise impossible, we see no conflict with British law. See RESTATEMENT (THIRD) FOREIGN RELATIONS LAW § 403, cmt. e, § 415, cmt. j. We have no need in this case to address other considerations that might inform a decision to refrain from the exercise of jurisdiction on grounds of international comity. . . .

SCALIA, J., dissenting

There is, however, a type of "jurisdiction" relevant to determining the extraterritorial reach of a statute; it is known as "legislative jurisdiction," *Aramco* [EEOC v. Arabian American Oil Co., 499 U.S. 244] at (slip op., at 8), RESTATEMENT (FIRST) CONFLICT OF LAWS § 60 (1934), or "jurisdiction to prescribe," 1 RESTATEMENT (THIRD) OF FOREIGN RELATIONS LAW OF THE UNITED STATES 235 (1987) (hereinafter RESTATEMENT (THIRD)). This refers to "the authority of a state to make its law applicable to persons or activities," and is quite a separate matter from "jurisdiction to adjudicate," see *id.*, at 231. There is no doubt, of course, that Congress possesses legislative jurisdiction over the acts alleged in this complaint: Congress has broad power under Article I, § 8, cl. 3 "to regulate Commerce with foreign Nations," and this Court has repeatedly upheld its power to make laws applicable to persons or activities beyond our territorial boundaries where United States interests are affected. See Ford v. United States, 273 U.S. 593, 621–623 . . . (1927); United States v. Bowman, 260 U.S. 94, 98–99 . . . (1922); *American Banana, supra*, at 356. But the question in this case is whether, and to what extent, Congress has exercised that undoubted legislative jurisdiction in enacting the Sherman Act.

Two canons of statutory construction are relevant in this inquiry. The first is the "long-standing principle of American law 'that legislation of Congress, unless a contrary intent appears, is meant to apply only within the territorial jurisdiction of the United States.' " *Aramco*, supra, at (slip op., at 3) (*quoting* Foley Bros., Inc. v. Filardo, 336 U.S. 281, 285 . . . (1949)). Applying that canon in *Aramco*, we held that the version of Title VII of the Civil Rights Act of 1964 then in force, 42 U.S.C. §§ 2000e–2000e–17 (1988 ed.), did not extend outside the territory of the United States even though the statute contained broad provisions extending its prohibitions to, for example, " 'any activity, business, or industry in commerce.' " *Id.*, at (slip op., at 4) (*quoting* 42 U.S.C. § 2000e(h)). We held such "boilerplate language" to be an insufficient indication to override the presumption against extraterritoriality. *Id.*, at (slip op., at 5); see also *id.*, at (slip op., at 6–8). The Sherman Act contains similar "boilerplate language," and if the question were not governed by precedent, it would be worth considering whether that presumption controls the outcome here. We have, however, found the presumption to be overcome with respect to our antitrust laws; it is now well established that the Sherman Act applies extraterritorially. See Matsushita Elec. Industrial Co. v. Zenith Radio Corp., 475 U.S. 574, 582 . . . n. 6 (1986); Continental Ore Co. v. Union Carbide & Carbon Corp., 370 U.S. 690, 704 . . . (1962); see also United States v. Aluminum Co. of America, 148 F.2d 416 (C.A.2 1945).

But if the presumption against extraterritoriality has been overcome or is otherwise inapplicable, a second canon of statutory construction becomes relevant: "An act of congress ought never to be construed to violate the law of nations if any other possible construction remains." Murray v. The Charming Betsy, 6 U.S. 64, 2 Cranch 64, 118 . . . (1804) (Marshall, C. J.). This canon is "wholly independent" of the presumption against extraterritoriality. *Aramco*, 499 U.S., at (Marshall, J., dissenting) (slip op., at 4). It is relevant to determining the substantive reach of a statute because "the law of nations," or customary international law, includes limitations on a nation's exercise of its jurisdiction to prescribe. See RESTATEMENT (THIRD) §§ 401–416. Though it clearly has constitutional authority to do so, Congress is generally presumed not to have exceeded those customary international-law limits on jurisdiction to prescribe. . . .

More recent lower court precedent has also tempered the extraterritorial application of the Sherman Act with considerations of "international comity." See Timberlane Lumber Co. v. Bank of America, N.T & S.A., 549 F.2d 597, 608–615 (C.A.9 1976); Mannington Mills, Inc. v. Congoleum Corp., 595 F.2d 1287, 1294–1298 (C.A.3 1979); Montreal Trading Ltd. v. Amax Inc., 661 F.2d 864, 869–871 (C.A.10 1981); Laker Airways v. Sabena, Belgian World Airlines, 235 U.S. App. D.C. 207, 236, 731 F.2d 909, and n. 109, 731 F.2d 909, 938, and n. 109 (1984); see also Pacific Seafarers, Inc. v. Pacific Far East Line, Inc., 131 U.S. App. D.C. 226, 236, 404 F.2d 804, and n. 31, 404 F.2d 804, 814, and n. 31 (1968). The "comity" they refer to is not the comity of courts, whereby judges decline to exercise jurisdiction over matters more appropriately adjudged elsewhere, but rather what might be termed "prescriptive comity": the respect sovereign nations afford each other by limiting the reach of their laws. That comity is exercised by legislatures when they enact laws, and courts assume it has been exercised when they come to interpreting the scope of laws their legislatures have enacted. It is a traditional component of choice-of-law theory. See J. STORY, COMMENTARIES ON THE CONFLICT OF LAWS § 38 (1834) (distinguishing between the "comity of the courts" and the "comity of nations," and defining the latter as "the true foundation and extent of the obligation of the laws of one nation within the territories of another"). Comity in this sense includes the choice-of-law principles that, "in the absence of contrary congressional direction," are assumed to be incorporated into our substantive laws having extra-territorial reach. *Romero, supra*, at 382–383; see also *Lauritzen, supra*, at 578–579; Hilton v. Guyot, 159 U.S. 113, 162–166 . . . (1895). Considering comity in this way is just part of determining whether the Sherman Act prohibits the conduct at issue.

In sum, the practice of using international law to limit the extraterritorial reach of statutes is firmly established in our jurisprudence. In proceeding to apply that practice to the present case, I shall rely on the RESTATEMENT (THIRD) OF FOREIGN RELATIONS LAW for the relevant principles of international law. Its standards appear fairly supported in the decisions of this Court construing international choice-of-law principles (*Lauritzen*, *Romero*, and *McCulloch*) and in the decisions of other federal courts, especially *Timberlane*. Whether the Restatement precisely reflects international law in every detail matters little here, as I believe this case would be resolved the same way under virtually any conceivable test that takes account of foreign regulatory interests.

Under the Restatement, a nation having some "basis" for jurisdiction to prescribe law should nonetheless refrain from exercising that jurisdiction "with respect to a person or activity having connections with another state when the exercise of such jurisdiction is unreasonable." RESTATEMENT (THIRD) § 403(1). The "reasonableness" inquiry turns on a number of factors.... Rarely would these factors point more clearly against application of United States law. The activity relevant to the counts at issue here took place primarily in the United Kingdom, and the defendants in these counts are British corporations and British subjects having their principal place of business or residence outside the United States. Great Britain has established a comprehensive regulatory scheme governing the London reinsurance markets, and clearly has a heavy "interest in regulating the activity," *id.*, § 403(2)(g). See 935 F.2d, at 932–933; *In re* Insurance Antitrust Litigation, 723 F. Supp. 464, 487–488 (N.D.Cal.1989); see also J. BUTLER & R. MERKIN, REINSURANCE LAW A.1.1–02 (1992). Finally, § 2(b) of the McCarran–Ferguson Act allows state regulatory statutes to override the Sherman Act in the insurance field, subject only to the narrow "boycott" exception set forth in § 3(b)—suggesting that "the importance of regulation to the [United States]," *id.*, § 403(2)(c), is slight. Considering these factors, I think it unimaginable that an assertion of legislative jurisdiction by the United States would be considered reasonable, and therefore it is inappropriate to assume, in the absence of statutory indication to the contrary, that Congress has made such an assertion....

RESTATEMENT OF THE FOREIGN RELATIONS LAW OF THE UNITED STATES § 403 (3 ed. 1987)

(1) Even when one of the bases for jurisdiction under § 402 is present, a state may not exercise jurisdiction to prescribe law with respect to a person or activity having connections with another state when the exercise of such jurisdiction is unreasonable.

(2) Whether exercise of jurisdiction over a person or activity is unreasonable is determined by evaluating all relevant factors, including, where appropriate:

(a) the link of the activity to the territory of the regulating state, *i.e.*, the extent to which the activity takes place within the territory, or has substantial, direct, and foreseeable effect upon or in the territory;

(b) the connections, such as nationality, residence, or economic activity, between the regulating state and the person principally responsible for the activity to be regulated, or between that state and those whom the regulation is designed to protect;

(c) the character of the activity to be regulated, the importance of regulation to the regulating state, the extent to which other states regulate such activities, and the degree to which the desirability of such regulation is generally accepted;

(d) the existence of justified expectations that might be protected or hurt by the regulation;

(e) the importance of the regulation to the international political, legal, or economic system;

(f) the extent to which the regulation is consistent with the traditions of the international system;

(g) the extent to which another state may have an interest in regulating the activity; and

(h) the likelihood of conflict with regulation by another state.

(3) When it would not be unreasonable for each of two states to exercise jurisdiction ... a state should defer to the other state if that state's interest is clearly greater.

Notes and Questions

1. The Restatement's alleged rule of "reasonableness," preferring an ad hoc "balancing" of factors or contacts approach that might function to limit federal jurisdiction, has not generally been followed by U.S. courts, especially if jurisdiction is possible under the protective or nationality principles. In fact, the alleged "rule" is not a requirement of international law, nor is it a reflection of general practice in the U.S. or abroad. It is a controversial assertion based on "comity" or "choice of law" theory (which

is not customary international law or treaty law) and would operate as a self-denying limit on jurisdictional competencies that pertain under international law. In addition to *United States v. Georgescu, supra, see, e.g.*, Hartford Fire Ins. Co. v. California, 509 U.S. 764 (1993); Laker Airways v. Sabena, 731 F.2d 909, 949–51 (D.C.Cir.1984) (adding: "there is no evidence that interest balancing represents a rule of international law"); *see also* Adra v. Clift, 195 F.Supp. 857, 864 (D.Md.1961) (*quoting* 1 Hyde, International Law § 11A, at 33–34 (2 ed. 1945): even though " 'no connection therewith' "); Barry E. Carter & Phillip R. Trimble, International Law 738, 759, 760 (re: nationality) (2 ed. 1995); Jordan J. Paust, International Law as Law of the United States 403–04 (1996); David J. Gerber, *Beyond Balancing: International Law Restraints on the Reach of National Laws*, 10 Yale J. Int'l L. 185, 205–06, 208–09 (1984); Berta Esperanza Hernandez, *RIP to IRP—Money Laundering and Drug Trafficking Controls Score a Knockout Victory over Bank Secrecy*, 18 N.C. J. Int'l L. & Comm. Reg. 235, 254 (1993) (when addressed, U.S. courts generally find U.S. interests outweigh foreign interests); Phillip R. Trimble, *The Supreme Court and International Law: The Demise of Restatement Section 403*, 89 Am. J. Int'l L. 53, 55–57 (1995) (adding: "there is no such general practice and hence no customary international law like that advanced in section 403" and "[t]he Souter majority [in *Hartford Fire Insurance Co.*] did not refuse to apply international law. It simply declined to apply section 403 ... the decision itself ... rejects section 403."); *cf.* Andreas F. Lowenfeld, *Conflict, Balancing of Interests, and the Exercise of Jurisdiction to Prescribe: Reflections on the Insurance Antitrust Case, id.* at 48.

The U.S. Supreme Court offered criticism of such an approach in McCulloch v. Sociedad Nacional de Marineros de Honduras, 372 U.S. 10, 19 (1963) ("Application of the sanctions of the Act ... on a purely *ad hoc* weighing of contacts basis ... would inevitably lead to embarrassment in foreign affairs and be entirely infeasible in actual practice"); *cf.* Justice Scalia's dissent in *Hartford Fire Ins. Co., supra*. If used, what weight should be given to what factors? What if there are combinations of prescriptive jurisdictional competence for the forum state? Wouldn't such an approach be haphazard, inflexible and "unreasonable" concerning policies at stake, and unpredictable, leaving others without adequate guidance or notice whether jurisdiction might be exercised? See also Michael Scharf, *Beyond the Rhetoric of Comparative Interest Balancing*, 50 L. & Contemp. Probs. 95 (1987):

The Deficiencies of Comparative Interest Balancing

Vagueness is but one of the many deficiencies inherent in comparative interest balancing which render it an impractical approach to the problem of extraterritorial discovery conflicts. A second major problem with comparative interest balancing is that courts are simply unable to ascertain and to evaluate accurately the interests of the foreign states that are to be weighed against those of the United States. The Restatement (second) required an assessment of the "vital national interest" of the foreign state, and the Restatement (Revised) calls for an inquiry as to "the extent to which compliance with an order to produce the requested information would affect important substantive policies or interests of the state." Yet, unlike the United States Department of State, the judiciary possesses neither the special training nor the resources necessary to analyze the economic, political, and social interests that underlie a foreign state's policies of nondisclosure. Several courts have acknowledged that the judiciary lacks the "institutional resources," the expertise, and perhaps even the authority to "adequately chart the competing problems and priorities that inevitably define the scope of any nation's interest in a legislated remedy."

The Act of State doctrine presents a further barrier to the evaluation of the foreign interests underlying blocking legislation. The doctrine, which prevents an American court from sitting in judgment of the public acts of another country, directly conflicts with the position taken by the Restatement (Revised) that foreign "statutes that frustrate [discovery] need not be given the same deference by courts of the United States as substantive rules of law at variance with the law of the United States." One court has recently rejected this assertion by the Restatement (Revised), noting that it is "somewhat presumptuous, to gauge the importance of the Blocking Statute to France." This view was also highlighted in recent litigation in which the United Kingdom stated that it is as politically intolerable for leaders of foreign democracies to have their official policies evaluated, balanced, and coerced by U.S. courts as it would be for American leaders to have important U.S. policies and interests evaluated, judged, and coerced in foreign courts.

Even assuming domestic courts have the ability and authority to gauge vital foreign interests, they cannot reliably and impartially balance the foreign interests against those of the United States. In *Laker Airways v. Sabena, Belgian World Airlines*, Judge Malcolm Wilkey of the D.C. Circuit Court of Appeals argued that domestic courts are incapable of sitting as international tribunals and evenhandedly balancing national interests. He concluded that "courts inherently find it difficult neutrally to balance competing foreign interests." Given the vagueness of existing comparative interest balancing approaches, it is small wonder that a court might be encouraged to assert the primacy of U.S. interests. A court is likely to have difficulty, especially in a case involving U.S. nationals, in denying jurisdiction, unless it can base its decision on a concrete legal principle that clearly prohibits the exercise of such jurisdiction. Comparative interest balancing provides no such concrete principle.

Finally, judicial use of comparative interest balancing is contrary to the political question doctrine which removes certain issues from the scope of judicial review. In *Baker v. Carr*, the Supreme court extensively reviewed the history and evolution of the political question doctrine and explained that when the resolution of questions touching foreign relations turns on standards that defy judicial application, or involves the exercise of discretion demonstrably committed to the executive or legislature, such questions are nonjusticiable political questions. The preceding discussion has illustrated that comparative interest balancing incorporates "purely political factors" which the court is neither qualified to evaluate comparatively nor capable of properly balancing. In his address to the American Bar Association in August 1981, the Attorney General of Australia, Senator Peter Durack, explained:

> In my view, however, it is not feasible for a court of law applying judicial techniques to balance the disparate interests of two States which they claim to be of national importance....
>
> ... [I]t is not merely that the courts lack the expertise. It is rather that it is not part of the judicial function to decide whether a law or policy is justified by what a court conceives to be in the national interest. That is a political function.

Appraisal of the national interests of a foreign state is therefore more appropriately a political rather than a judicial judgment. In accordance with the political question doctrine, a court should refrain from subscribing to a formulation whose standards are neither judicially discoverable nor manageable.

2. In Societe Nationale Industrielle Aerospatiale v. United States District Court for the Southern District of Iowa, 482 U.S. 522 (1987) [extract in Chapter 5, Section 1], the Court suggested use of a "comity" factors approach concerning compulsion of evidence from abroad. Nonetheless, it noted that U.S. courts can order a foreign party (in that case, two corporations owned by a foreign state) to produce evidence located abroad (in that state), and this even in the face of a foreign state "blocking statute" or a claim of "foreign sovereign compulsion" and a foreign state *amicus* brief.

3. Some courts have devised domestic limits with respect to special forms of economic legislation. *See, e.g.*, Grunenthal GmbH v. Hotz, 712 F.2d 421 (9th Cir.1983) (conduct within the U.S. should be "significant" and further a fraudulent scheme in violation of U.S. securities laws); Continental Grain (Australia) Pty. Ltd. v. Pacific Oilseeds, Inc., 592 F.2d 409 (8th Cir.1979). Attempts to control economic processes abroad seem to have generated the most controversies between states.

4. Are attempts to resolve conflicts concerning concurrent jurisdictional competencies best left to resolutions through international agreements and those favored under customary international law? *See also* Wilson v. Girard, 354 U.S. 524 (1957); Wildenhus's Case, 120 U.S. 1 (1886). Who could obtain tradeoffs for the United States, the courts or the Executive? Should the Executive agree to limits of U.S. jurisdictional competence by sole executive agreement in Congress has enacted extraterritorial legislation or should such limitations be achieved by treaty or congressional-executive agreement? Should subject matter be important, *e.g.*, foreign commerce or jurisdiction over U.S. military personnel? Recall *Guy Capps*.

5. Congress has also generally ignored a comity-factors approach to jurisdiction, especially with respect to international crimes. Consider the Torture Victim Protection Act, P.L. 256, 106 Stat. 73 (1992); 18 U.S.C. § 2340A (torture); the Antiterrorism Act, 18 U.S.C.A. §§ 2331–2337; the Hostage Taking Act, 18 U.S.C.A. § 1203; the Protection of Internationally Protected Persons Act, 18 U.S.C.A. § 112(a), (b) and (e); the Destruction of Aircraft Act, 18 U.S.C.A. § 32. See also the Internal Revenue Code; the 1991 Civil Rights Act, 105 Stat. 1077, 1078 (amending the 1964 Civil Rights Act (42 U.S.C.A. 2000e(f), 2000e–1) and the Americans with Disabilities Act of 1990 (42 U.S.C.A. 12111(4), 121112), to reach employment discrimination abroad but generally to exempt employers from discrimination with respect to employees in a foreign country if compliance with U.S. law would cause

the employer to violate the law of the foreign country in which the workplace is located. A 1982 amendment to the Sherman Act requires that foreign conduct have "a direct, substantial, and reasonably foreseeable effect" with respect to antitrust matters. 15 U.S.C.A. § 6a. Nevertheless, when the new test is met, an extraterritorial reach is preferred. *See also* United States v. Nippon Paper Industries Co., 109 F.3d 1 (1st Cir. 1997) (Sherman Act's criminal application extraterritorially is not restricted by a comity-factors approach, which is merely "voluntary forbearance ... more a matter of grace," and applicable in antitrust "only in those few cases in which the law of the foreign sovereign required a defendant to act in a manner incompatible with the Sherman Act or in which full compliance with both statutory schemes was impossible. *See Hartford Fire*" at 798–99.).

6. The alleged rule of reasonableness would only apply to jurisdictional competencies under § 402. It does *not* apply to universal jurisdiction under § 404. Should such a limiting approach, developed from the field of conflict of laws, have anything to do with international crimes over which there is universal jurisdictional competence and responsibility? With respect to international crimes, what law is ultimately being enforced? Cases in the U.S. addressing violations of international law have ruled that no nexus with the U.S. is required. *See, e.g.*, United States v. Yousef, 327 F.3d 56, 79 (2d Cir. 2003); *In re* Estate of Marcos Litigation, 978 F.2d 493, 499–500 (9th Cir.1992)("no nexus to this country" is required, "no limitation"); United States v. Yunis, 924 F.2d 1086, 1091–92 (D.C.Cir.1991) (may prosecute international crimes "even absent any special connection between the state and the offense"); Filartiga v. Pena–Irala, 630 F.2d 876, 878, 885 (2d Cir.1980); Forti v. Suarez–Mason, 672 F.Supp. 1531 (N.D.Cal.1987); see also Demjanjuk v. Petrovsky, 776 F.2d 571, 581–83 (6th Cir.1985); RESTATEMENT § 404, cmt. a ("international law permits any state to apply its laws to punish certain offenses although the state has no links of territory with the offense, or of nationality with the offender (or even the victim)."); Daliberti v. Republic of Iraq, 97 F. Supp.2d 38, 52–54 (D.D.C. 2000) (re: terrorism and international law); Jordan J. Paust, *An Introduction to and Commentary on Terrorism and the Law*, 19 CONN. L. REV. 697, 718–20 (1987); *but see* Christopher L. Blakesley, *Jurisdiction as Legal Protection Against Terrorism*, 19 CONN. L. REV 895, 909–11, 922, *passim* (1987). For early views, see Talbot v. Janson, 3 U.S. (3 Dall.) 133, 159–61 (1795), quoted in The Divina Pastora, 17 U.S. (4 Wheat.) 52, 65 (1819) (Marshall, C.J.). With respect to conflict of laws as such, see Louise Weinberg, *Against Comity*, 80 GEO. L.J. 53 (1991).

If a U.S. court uses an ad hoc approach and does not permit prosecution, how can the United States live up to its international obligations with respect to international crimes? Should such international law, as law of the United States, condition the court's approach to jurisdiction?

In Daliberti v. Republic of Iraq, 97 F.Supp.2d 38 (D.D.C. 2000), the district court rejected a due process—minimum contacts claim by Iraq with respect to alleged state sponsored terrorism, since " 'states are on notice that state sponsorship of terrorism is condemned by the international community' " (quoting Flatow v. Islamic Republic of Iran, 999 F.Supp. 1, 23 (D.D.C. 1998)), "nations that operate in a manner inconsistent with international norms should not expect to be granted the privilege of immunity from suit," states that sponsor terrorism have "adequate warning" of possible U.S. sanctions, including lawsuits in U.S. courts, and it is "reasonable that foreign states be held accountable in the courts of the United States for terrorist actions perpetrated against U.S. citizens anywhere." 97 F.Supp.2d at 52–54.

7. In some cases where jurisdiction is otherwise proper in courts of the United States, a defendant may seek dismissal of a lawsuit on the basis of *forum non conveniens*, which is a common law doctrine involving inquiry into whether a foreign forum is available, adequate, and more convenient. "In all cases in which the doctrine of forum non conveniens comes into play, it presupposes at least two forums in which the defendant is amenable to process." Gulf Oil Corp. v. Gilbert, 330 U.S. 501, 506–07 (1947). Should dismissal of a lawsuit against an official of a foreign country occur if both the U.S. and the foreign country have jurisdictional competence under international law to prescribe if the complaint rests on alleged acts of persecution on grounds political opinion, arbitrary detention, and torture, all occurring in the foreign country? What else might you want to know?

The Second Circuit recognized in *Wiwa v. Royal Dutch Petroleum Co.* that the U.S. has a "policy interest implicit in our federal statutory law in providing a forum for adjudication of claims of violations of the law of nations" under the TVPA and has interests, in particular, "in furnishing a forum to litigate claims of violations of the international standards of the law of human rights." 226 F.3d 88, 100–01 (2d Cir. 2000); *see also id.* at 105–06, 108. Is such a policy interest also at stake with respect to ATCA suits? The very purpose of the ATCA was in part to serve such interests and to avoid "denial of justice" to aliens.

A defendant has the burden of proving that both a foreign forum is available and adequate. *See, e.g., In re* Air Crash Disaster Near New Orleans, La., 821 F.2d 1147, 1164–65 (5th Cir.1987). Moreover, "the court starts with a presumption in favor of the plaintiff's choice of forum" and "unless the balance is strongly in favor of the defendant, the plaintiff's choice of forum should rarely be disturbed." Peregrine Myanmar, Ltd. v. Segal, 89 F.3d 41, 46 (2d Cir.1996); Gulf Oil Corp. v. Gilbert, 330 U.S. 501, 508 (1947) ("unless the balance is strongly in favor of the defendant, the plaintiff's choice of forum should rarely be disturbed"); Mendes Junior Int'l Co. v. Banco do Brasil, S.A., 15 F. Supp.2d 332, 337 (S.D.N.Y.1998) ("It is well settled under forum non conveniens doctrine, that the plaintiff's choice of forum should rarely be disturbed," *citing* Piper Aircraft Co. v. Reyno, 454 U.S. 235, 241 (1981)). Also, "greater deference [exists] when the plaintiff has chosen the home forum. . . . When the home forum has been chosen, it is reasonable to assume that this choice is convenient." Piper Aircraft Co. v. Reyno, 454 U.S. at 255–56. *See also* the discussion of Article 28 of the Warsaw Convention in Chapter 7.

Additionally, justice is a necessary element of a forum non conveniens inquiry. *See, e.g.,* Mendes Junior Int'l Co. v. Banco do Brasil, S.A., 15 F. Supp.2d at 337 ("The 'central purpose' of a forum non conveniens analysis is to determine where trial will be convenient and will serve the interests of justice."), *citing* R. Maganlal & Co. v. M.G. Chemical Co., Inc., 942 F.2d 164, 167 (2d Cir.1991), which cited Koster v. Lumbermens Mut. Casualty Co., 330

U.S. 518, 527 (1947). The Court has also noted that a mere change in applicable law does not preclude dismissal. Yet, "[o]f course, if the remedy provided by the alternative forum is so clearly inadequate or unsatisfactory that it is no remedy at all, the unfavorable change in law may be given substantial weight...." Piper Aircraft Co. v. Reyno, 454 U.S. at 254.

In Lubbe and others v. Cape PLC, 4 All ER 268 (U.K. House of Lords 2000), Lord Bingham recognized that suit by over 3,000 plaintiffs for asbestos injuries should not be stayed or relegated to South Africa where claimants would effectively be denied "a fair trial on terms of litigious equality with the defendant" corporation because of lack of adequate funding and legal representation in South Africa, that such "would lead to a denial of justice ... in the foreign forum," and that Article 6 of the European Convention for the Protection of Human Rights (claimed by plaintiffs to be violated if proceedings are stayed) does not support "any conclusion which is not already reached ... [on the basis of denial of justice]."

Where *forum non conveniens* is followed, should a plaintiff seek a conditional dismissal, so that the U.S. forum retains jurisdiction in case the foreign forum actually is unavailable or inadequate?

8. In Hosaka v. United Airlines, Inc., 305 F.3d 989 (9th Cir. 2002), *cert. denied*, 537 U.S. 1227 (2003), the Ninth Circuit panel ruled that Article 28(1) of the Warsaw Convention, recognizing types of fora where plaintiffs must be allowed to bring an action, precludes use of the common law doctrine of forum non conveniens. *Id.* at 993–95, also citing the English case Milor v. British Airways, Plc., [1996] Q.B. 702, 706 (Eng. C.A.), which ruled similarly ("'[t]he procedural power to stay on the ground of *forum non conveniens* is ... inconsistent with the right conferred on the plaintiff to choose which of the competent jurisdictions his action will be tried.... [in]'"). Does the fact that the International Covenant on Civil and Political Rights provides a right of equal access to courts mean that the treaty-based right to bring an action has primacy over the common law doctrine of *forum non conveniens*? or is one merely entitled to access and then also to equality of treatment during judicial processes which might consider *forum non conveniens*?

SECTION 2. UNIVERSAL JURISDICTION

Introductory Note

The universality principle authorizes any state jurisdiction under international law to provide criminal or civil prescriptions in an effort to impose sanctions for violations of international law. Universal jurisdiction allows nation-state competence to enforce such laws whenever an alleged offender is found within the state's territory or equivalent jurisdictional bases for enforcement of law (*e.g.*, on its vessels, aircraft, space craft, or space stations, or in occupied territory or territory subject to international regimes or competencies (such as U.N. Security Council powers)). It does not matter where the alleged acts took place, who the alleged victims were, or whether there were any contacts with the forum state. Universal jurisdictional competence is just that—universal. A state's utilization of this competence to prosecute those reasonably accused of international crime will allow such state to fulfill its obligation under international law to initiate prosecution or to extradite. Moreover, if universal jurisdiction pertains, it does not matter whether a criminal charge, cause of action, or statute is expressly related to international law.

There is a new type of related jurisdictional competence termed "universal by treaty" (or "jurisdiction by consent"). Such competence exists only among signatories to a multilateral treaty establishing a new international offense, and it reaches merely their nationals (or possibly others with a significant nexus to a signatory), at least until the offense becomes a part of customary international law (at which time there will exist universal jurisdiction among all nation-states). Universal by treaty is actually a form of consensual jurisdiction among the signatories. Examples of such new treaties are considered below in connection with particular offenses, *e.g.*, aircraft sabotage and the taking of hostages in time of peace.

JORDAN J. PAUST, *FEDERAL JURISDICTION OVER EXTRATERRITORIAL ACTS OF TERRORISM AND NONIMMUNITY FOR FOREIGN VIOLATORS OF INTERNATIONAL LAW UNDER THE FSIA AND THE ACT OF STATE DOCTRINE*

23 VA. J. INT'L L. 191, 211–14 (1983).

The universality principle provides for jurisdiction [both to prescribe domestic laws and] to enforce sanctions against crimes that have an independent basis in international law. In other words, the principle applies "to crimes that affect the international community and are against international law." Universal jurisdiction is thus technically jurisdiction to enforce [international law], and the enforcement is actually made on behalf of the international community.

From the dawn of our own constitutional history, universal enforcement jurisdiction has been recognized over "crimes against mankind and the enemies of the whole human family," or those persons who are "*hostes humani generis*." It was also recognized more generally that violations of international law were subject to criminal sanction, and that civil or criminal sanctions for private violations of international law were often interchangeable, depending on whether an individual or government was seeking enforcement. The government has been successful in numerous instances in enforcing criminal sanctions against individuals for violations of international law. While prosecutions have occurred even in the absence of a domestic statute, it is now generally assumed that a federal statute is needed to impose domestic criminal sanctions on violators of international law. Thus, the same should be true with respect to universal jurisdiction to apply criminal sanctions against persons who have engaged in acts of terrorism in violation of international law.

A different question is whether or not a specific statutory offense prosecutable in federal court is also recognizably related to an international crime. If so, universal jurisdiction to enforce is possible whether or not the domestic statute expressly refers to an offense under international law. In the case of U.S. military prosecutions, for example, violations of international law have been prosecuted as offenses against the law of nations or, alternatively, as "ordinary" offenses under the Uniform Code of Military Justice. Similarly, there have been prosecutions in connection with acts of terrorism under federal law in which the court has explicitly referred to the universality principle despite the fact that relevant congressional legislation was silent or nearly silent on the question.

Whether or not the conduct involved would constitute an offense under international law depends, of course, on international law. A number of terrorist offenses violate customary international law, although several violations relevant to international terrorism are based on treaty law of a relatively recent nature. It is useful to recall further that numerous types of conduct related to terrorism also violate international law. Thus, there are several international norms that are potentially relevant, and new efforts to enact U.S. legislation designed to control terrorism should expressly refer to violations of "international law" in order to cover all potential bases of illegality.

Note

1. The types of international crimes or criminals recognized early in U.S. history and as implicating universal jurisdiction included: violence against ambassadors; piracy; poisoners, assassins, incendiaries by profession; banditti; brigands; violation of passports; slave trading; breaches of neutrality; and war crimes. See *id.* at ns. 76–80, and references cited; JORDAN J. PAUST, INTERNATIONAL LAW AS LAW OF THE UNITED STATES 8, 48–50 (1996).

Concerning piracy, consider also United States v. Furlong, 18 U.S. (5 Wheat.) 184, 197 (1820) ("Robbery on the seas is considered as an offence within the criminal jurisdiction of all nations. It is against all, and punished by all ... within this universal jurisdiction.").

DEMJANJUK v. PETROVSKY

776 F.2d 571, 575–76, 581–83 (6th Cir. 1985).

LIVELY, J.

[Editors' note: an extract of this case appeared in Chapter 2 merely on the point that new domestic laws, courts, and procedures can be created to reach what were crimes under international law at the time of commission without violating an *ex post facto* or *nullum crimen sine lege* prohibition found, for example, in human rights law.]

This international extradition case is before the court on appeal from the denial of a petition for a writ of habeas corpus, 612 F. Supp. 571.

The petitioner, John Demjanjuk, is a native of the Ukraine, one of the republics of the Soviet Union. Demjanjuk was admitted to the United

States in 1952 under the Displaced Persons Act of 1948 and became a naturalized United States citizen in 1958. He has resided in the Cleveland, Ohio area since his arrival in this country.

In 1981 the United States District Court for the Northern District of Ohio revoked Demjanjuk's certificate of naturalization and vacated the order admitting him to United States citizenship. See United States v. Demjanjuk, 518 F. Supp. 1362 (N.D.Ohio 1981), *aff'd per curiam,* 680 F.2d 32 (1982), *cert. denied,* 459 U.S. 1036 ... (1982). Chief Judge Battisti of the district court entered extensive findings of fact from which he concluded that the certificate and order "were illegally procured and were procured by willful misrepresentation of material facts under 8 U.S.C. § 1451(a)." 518 F. Supp. at 1386.

The district court found that Demjanjuk was conscripted into the Soviet Army in 1940 and was captured by the Germans in 1942. After short stays in several German POW camps and a probable tour at the Trawniki SS training camp in Poland, Demjanjuk became a guard at the Treblinka concentration camp, also in Poland, late in 1942. In his various applications for immigration to the United States the petitioner misstated his place of residence during the period 1938–1948 and did not reveal that he had worked for the SS at Treblinka or served in a German military unit later in the war. In the denaturalization proceedings Demjanjuk admitted that his statements concerning residence were false and that he had in fact served in a German military unit. He steadfastly denied that he had been at Trawniki or Treblinka, though documentary evidence placed him at Trawniki and five Treblinka survivors and one former German guard at the camp identified Demjanjuk as a Ukrainian guard who was known as "Ivan or Iwan Grozny," that is, "Ivan the Terrible."

Following the denaturalization order the government began deportation proceedings against Demjanjuk. While these proceedings were underway the State of Israel filed with the United States Department of State a request for the extradition of Demjanjuk. The United States Attorney for the Northern District of Ohio, acting on behalf of the State of Israel, filed a complaint in the District court seeking the arrest of Demjanjuk and a hearing on the extradition request. Following a hearing the district court entered an order certifying to the Secretary of State that Demjanjuk was subject to extradition at the request of the State of Israel pursuant to a treaty on extradition between the United States and Israel signed December 10, 1962, effective December 5, 1963. Bond previously granted Demjanjuk was revoked and he was committed to the custody of the Attorney General of the United States pending the issuance of a warrant of surrender by the Secretary of State....

Before reaching the more technical arguments related to jurisdiction of the district court and the question of whether the crimes charged were within the treaty provisions, we deal with the sufficiency of the evidence. As noted, there are sworn testimony by affidavits from six witnesses who were at Treblinka in 1942 and 1943 who identified Demjanjuk. These witnesses stated that Demjanjuk was a guard who herded prisoners into the gas chambers and then actually operated the mechanism which filled the chambers with gas. In addition, several of the witnesses testified that they saw Demjanjuk beat and maim prisoners, some of whom died. Justice Holmes wrote in *Fernandez* that our task is to determine "whether there was *any* evidence warranting the finding that there was reasonable ground to believe the accused guilty." Surely the evidence in this case satisfied this lenient standard. . . .

The Israeli statute under which Demjanjuk was charged deals with "crimes against the Jewish people," "crimes against humanity" and "war crimes" committed during the Nazi years. It is clear from the language defining the crimes, and other references to acts directed at persecuted persons and committed in places of confinement, that Israel intended to punish under this law those involved in carrying out Hitler's "final solution." This was made explicit in the prosecution of Adolph Eichmann in 1961. *Attorney General v. Eichmann*, 36 I.L.R. 277 (Sup. Ct. Israel 1962). . . . Such a claim of extraterritorial jurisdiction over criminal offenses is not unique to Israel. For example, statutes of the United States provide for punishment in domestic district courts for murder or manslaughter committed within the maritime jurisdiction (18 U.S.C. § 1111) and murder or manslaughter of internationally protected persons wherever they are killed (18 U.S.C. § 1116(c)). We conclude that the reference in 18 U.S.C. § 3184 [concerning extradition, see *infra* Section 4 A] to crimes committed within the jurisdiction of the requesting government does not refer solely to territorial jurisdiction. Rather, it refers to the authority of a nation to apply its laws to particular conduct. In international law this is referred to as "jurisdiction to prescribe." Restatement § 401(1).

The law of the United States includes international law. *The Paquete Habana*, 175 U.S. 677, 712 (1900). International law recognizes a "universal jurisdiction" over certain offenses. Section 404 of the Restatement defines universal jurisdiction:

§ 404. Universal Jurisdiction to Define and Punish Selected Offenses

> A state may exercise jurisdiction to define and punish certain offenses recognized by the community of nations as of universal concern, such as piracy, slave trade, attacks on or hijacking of aircraft, genocide, war crimes, and perhaps terrorism, even where none of the bases of jurisdiction indicated in § 402 is present.

This "universality principle" is based on the assumption that some crimes are so universally condemned that the perpetrators are the enemies of all people. Therefore, any nation which has custody of the perpetrators may punish them according to its law applicable to such offenses. . . .

The wartime allies created the International Military Tribunal which tried major Nazi officials at Nuremberg and courts within the four occupation zones of post-war Germany which tried lesser Nazis. All were tried for committing war crimes, and it is generally agreed that the establishment of these tribunals and their proceedings were based on universal jurisdiction. *E.g.*, Sponsler, *The Universality Principle of Jurisdiction and the Threatened Trials of American Airmen*, 15 LOY. L. REV. 43, 48–51 (1968–69).

Demjanjuk argues that the post-war trials were all based on the military defeat of Germany and that with the disestablishment of the special tribunals there are no courts with jurisdiction over alleged war crimes. This argument overlooks the fact that the post-war tribunals were not military courts, though their presence in Germany was made possible by the military defeat of that country. These tribunals did not operate within the limits of traditional military courts. They claimed and exercised a much broader jurisdiction which necessarily derived from the universality principle. Whatever doubts existed prior to 1945 have been erased by the general recognition since that time that there is a jurisdiction over some types of crimes which extend beyond the territorial limits of any nation.

Turning again to the Restatement, § 443 appears to apply to the present case:

§ 443. Jurisdiction to Adjudicate in Aid of Universal and Other Non–Territorial Crimes.

> A state's courts may exercise jurisdiction to enforce the state's criminal laws which punish universal crimes (§ 404) or other non-territorial offenses within the state's jurisdiction to prescribe (§§ 402–403).

Israel is seeking to enforce its criminal law for the punishment of Nazis and Nazi collaborators for crimes universally recognized and condemned by the community of nations. The fact that Demjanjuk is charged with committing these acts in Poland does not deprive Israel of authority to bring him to trial....

Though it was not explicitly argued, we have considered whether recognition of the power of Israeli courts to punish for war crimes committed outside of its national territory violates any right of Demjanjuk under the Constitution of the United States. Demjanjuk had notice before he applied for residence or citizenship in the United States that this country, by participating in post-war trials of German and Japanese war criminals recognized the universality principle. Israel has chosen to proceed under that principle, and we do not supervise the conduct of another judicial system. To do so "would directly conflict with the principle upon which extradition is based." Jhirad v. Ferrandina, 536 F.2d 478, 485 (2d Cir.) *cert. denied,* 429 U.S. 833 ... (1976). In the absence of any showing that Demjanjuk will be subjected to procedures "antipathetic to a federal court's sense of decency," Gallina v. Fraser, 278 F.2d 77, 79 (2d Cir.), *cert. denied,* 364 U.S. 851 ... (1960), this court will not inquire into the procedures which will apply after he is surrendered to Israel. There is absolutely no showing in this record that Israel will follow procedures which would shock this court's "sense of decency." United States *ex rel.* Bloomfield v. Gengler, 507 F.2d 925, 928 (2d Cir.1974).... [Editors' note: Demjanjuk was deported to Israel, tried and sentenced to death in 1988, but his conviction was overturned later because it was not proven that he was "Ivan the Terrible" or responsible for crimes charged. He was released and returned to the U.S. in 1993, but in 1999 the U.S. sought to revoke his reinstated citizenship and deport him because of accusations that he was otherwise involved as a camp guard and did not disclose this to the U.S. An immigration judge ruled in June 2005 that he can be deported.]

Question

1. What should the standard be with respect to probable process that an extraditee will face? *See, e.g.*, International Covenant on Civil and Political Rights, art. 14; Chapter 4, Section 4.

THE PROSECUTOR v. DUSKO TADIC

International Criminal Tribunal for the Former Yugoslavia, IT–94–1–AR72, Decision on the Defence Motion for Interlocutory Appeal on Jurisdiction (Appeals Chamber 2 Oct. 1995).

[Editors' note: The International Criminal Tribunal for the Former Yugoslavia (ICTY) was created ad hoc by a U.N. Security Council resolution in 1993, and has jurisdiction over certain international crimes committed in the former Yugoslavia from January 1, 1991. For further background, see PAUST, BASSIOUNI, *ET AL.*, INTERNATIONAL CRIMINAL LAW 654–98 (2 ed. 2000). In 1997, Tadic was convicted in a Trial Chamber of the ICTY of crimes against humanity and war crimes concerning mistreatment of persons within a detention camp—with a number of concurrent sentences imposed, including one twenty-year sentence for a crime against humanity. On appeal, while addressing the principle of universal jurisdiction, Judge Cassese declared:]

57. This is all the more so in view of the nature of the offences alleged against Appellant, offences which, if proven, do not affect the interests of one State alone but shock the conscience of mankind.

As early as 1950, in the case of *General Wagener,* the Supreme Military Tribunal of Italy held:

> "These norms [concerning crimes against laws and customs of war], due to their highly ethical and moral content, have a universal character, not a territorial one....
>
> The solidarity among nations, aimed at alleviating in the best possible way the horrors of war, gave rise to the need to dictate rules which do not recognise borders, punishing criminals wherever they may be....
>
> Crimes against the laws and customs of war cannot be considered political offences, as they do not harm a political interest of a particular State, nor a political right of a particular citizen. They are, instead, crimes of *lese-humanite (reati di lesa umanita)* and, as

previously demonstrated, the norms prohibiting them have a universal character, not simply a territorial one. Such crimes, therefore, due to their very subject matter and particular nature are precisely of a different and opposite kind from political offences. The latter generally, concern only the States against whom they are committed; the former concern all civilised States, and are to be opposed and punished, in the same way as the crimes of piracy, trade of women and minors, and enslavement are to be opposed and punished, wherever they may have been committed (articles 537 and 604 of the penal code)." (13 March 1950) in *Rivista Penale* 753, 757 (Sup. Mil. Trib., Italy 1950; unofficial translation.)

Twelve years later the Supreme Court of Israel in the *Eichmann* case could draw a similar picture:

> "[T]hese crimes constitute acts which damage vital international interests; they impair the foundations and security of the international community; they violate the universal moral values and humanitarian principles that lie hidden in the criminal law systems adopted by civilised nations. The underlying principle in international law regarding such crimes is that the individual who has committed any of them and who, when doing so, may be presumed to have fully comprehended the heinous nature of his act, must account for his conduct....
>
> Those crimes entail individual criminal responsibility because they challenge the foundations of international society and affront the conscience of civilised nations....
>
> [T]hey involve the perpetration of an international crime which all the nations of the world are interested in preventing." (Israel v. Eichmann, 36 *International Law Reports* 277, 291–93 (Isr. S. Ct. 1962).)

58. The public revulsion against similar offences in the 1990s brought about a reaction on the part of the community of nations: hence, among other remedies, the establishment of an international judicial body by an organ of an organization representing the community of nations: the Security Council. This organ is empowered and mandated, by definition, to deal with trans-boundary matters or matters which, though domestic in nature, may affect "international peace and security" (United Nations Charter, art 2(1), 2(7), 24, & 37). It would be a travesty of law and a betrayal of the universal need for justice, should the concept of state sovereignty be allowed to be raised successfully against human rights. Borders should not be considered as a shield against the reach of the law and as a protection for those who trample underfoot the most elementary rights of humanity. In the *Barbie* case, the Court of Cassation of France has quoted with approval the following statement of the Court of Appeal:

> "[...] by reason of their nature, the crimes against humanity ... do not simply fall within the scope of French municipal law but are subject to an international criminal order to which the notions of

frontiers and extradition rules arising therefrom are completely foreign." *(Federation Nationale de Deportes et Internes Resistants et Patriotes And Others v. Barbie,* 78 *International Law Reports* 125, 130 (Cass. crim. 1983).)

Indeed, when an international tribunal such as the present one is created, it *must* be endowed with primacy over national courts. Otherwise, human nature being what it is, there would be a perennial danger of international crimes being characterised as "ordinary crimes" (Statute of the International Tribunal, art. 10, para. 2(a)), or proceedings being "designed to shield the accused", or cases not being diligently prosecuted (Statute of the International Tribunal, art. 10, para. 2(b)). . . .

Restatement of the Foreign Relations Law of the United States § 404 (3 ed. 1987)

Comment:

a. Expanding class of universal offenses. This section, and the corresponding section concerning jurisdiction to adjudicate, § 423, recognize that international law permits any state to apply its laws to punish certain offenses although the state has no links of territory with the offense, or of nationality with the offender (or even the victim). Universal jurisdiction over the specified offenses is a result of universal condemnation of those activities and general interest in cooperating to suppress them, as reflected in widely-accepted international agreements and resolutions of international organizations. These offenses are subject to universal jurisdiction as a matter of customary law. Universal jurisdiction for additional offenses is provided by international agreements, but it remains to be determined whether universal jurisdiction over a particular offense has become customary law for states not party to such an agreement. See § 102, Comment f. A universal offense is generally not subject to limitations of time.

There has been wide condemnation of terrorism but international agreements to punish it have not, as of 1987, been widely adhered to, principally because of inability to agree on a definition of the offense. The United States and six states (all in Latin America) have adopted a Convention to Prevent and Punish the Acts of Terrorism Taking the Form of Crimes against Persons and Related Extortion that are of International Significance, 27 U.S.T. 3949, T.I.A.S. No. 8413 (1976). Universal jurisdiction is increasingly accepted for certain acts of terrorism, such as assaults on the life or physical integrity of diplomatic personnel, kidnapping, and indiscriminate violent assaults on people at large. See also § 477, Reporters' Note 6.

b. Universal jurisdiction not limited to criminal law. In general, jurisdiction on the basis of universal interests has been exercised in the form of criminal law, but international law does not preclude the application of non-criminal law on this basis, for example, by providing a remedy in tort or restitution for victims of piracy.

Reporters' Notes

1. *Offenses subject to universal jurisdiction.* Piracy has sometimes been described as "an offense against the law of nations," an international crime. Since there is no international penal tribunal, the punishment of piracy is left to any state that seizes the offender. *See, e.g., United States v. Smith,* 18 U.S. (5 Wheat.) 153, 161–62 (1820); 2 Moore, International Law §§ 951–68 (1906). Compare the power of Congress under Article I, Section 8 of the United States Constitution "to define and punish Piracies and Felonies committed on the high Seas, and Offences against the Law of Nations." Whether piracy is an international crime, or is rather a matter of international concern as to which international law accepts the jurisdiction of all states, may not make any important difference.

Although international law is the law of the United States (§ 111), a person cannot be tried in the federal courts for an international crime unless Congress adopts a statute to define and punish the offense. See *United States v. Hudson and Goodwin,* 11 U.S. (7 Cranch) 32, 34 (1812); *United States v. Coolidge,* 14 U.S. (1 Wheat.) 415, 417 (1816) (no federal common law crimes in U.S.). See § 422, Comment a. The act of Congress may, however, define the offense by reference to international law. *United States v. Smith,* 18 U.S. (5 Wheat.) 153, 160 (1820); *Ex parte Quirin,* 317 U.S. 1, 28, 33 (1942); *In re Yamashita,* 327 U.S. 1 (1946). [see our Chapter 2]

That genocide and war crimes are subject to universal jurisdiction was accepted after the Second World War, although apparently no state has exercised such jurisdiction in circumstances where no other basis for jurisdiction under § 402 was present. In the *Eichmann* case, involving the principal executioner of Hitler's "final solution" during World War II, Israel relied on universal jurisdiction as well as other bases. See Attorney General of Israel v. Eichmann, 36 Int'l L. Rep. 277 (Sup. Ct. Israel 1962).... The principles of the Nuremberg Charter and Judgment were unanimously adopted by the United Nations General Assembly in 1946. G.A. Res. 95(1), 1(2) GAOR Resolutions, at 188. Genocide has also been unanimously condemned by resolution of the General Assembly, G.A. Res. 96(1), *ibid.* The Convention on the Prevention and Punishment of the Crime of Genocide, 1948, 78 U.N.T.S. 277 (1951), had, as of 1986, been adhered to be 100 states.... The Convention provides for trial by the territorial state or by an international penal tribunal to be established.... Universal jurisdiction to punish genocide is widely accepted as a principle of customary law. For genocide as a violation of customary law by a state, see § 702(a).

International agreements have provided for general jurisdiction for additional offenses, *e.g.,* the Hague Convention for the Suppression of Unlawful Seizure of Aircraft, 22 U.S.T. 1641, T.I.A.S. 7192 (1971); the Montreal Convention for the Suppression of Unlawful Acts against the Safety of Civil Aviation, 24 U.S.T. 564, T.I.A.S. 7570 (1973); the Convention on the Prevention and Punishment of Crimes against Internationally Protected Persons including Diplomatic Agents, 28 U.S.T. 1975, T.I.A.S. 8532, 1035 U.N.T.S. 167 (1977); and the International Convention against the Taking of Hostages.... These agreements include an obligation on the parties to punish or extradite offenders, even when the offense was not committed within their territory or by a national. As of 1986, 121 states had become parties to the Hague Convention, 127 states to the Montreal Convention, 69 to the Convention of the Prevention of Crimes against Internationally Protected Persons, and 29 to the Convention against the Taking of Hostages. The United States is party to each of these agreements. The International Convention on the Suppression and Punishment of the Crime of Apartheid, which came into force in 1976, declares that apartheid is a crime against humanity and subject to universal jurisdiction. As of January 1, 1987, 86 states were parties to the Convention ... [The] Convention Against Torture and Other Cruel, Inhuman and Degrading Treatment or Punishment ... in effect provides for universal jurisdiction.... Such agreements are effective only among the parties, unless customary law comes to accept these offenses as subject to universal jurisdiction. See Comment *a*. Articles on State Responsibility, prepared for the International Law Commission, would include a provision that an international crime may result from "a serious breach on a widespread scale of an international obligation of essential importance for safeguarding the human being, such as those prohibiting slavery, genocide and apartheid." Report of the International Law Commission, 33 U.N. GAOR, Supp. No. 10, at 193 (1978). An international crime is presumably subject to universal jurisdiction.

Notes and Questions

1. Must there be "universal" condemnation for a prohibition to become customary international law?

2. Has the U.S. Supreme Court ever ruled that Congress must adopt a relevant statute before those accused of an international crime can be prosecuted in federal courts? See Chapter 2. The Restatement notes that is otherwise assumed that a statute is needed, but the cases cited in the Restatement are not relevant to prosecution of customary international crimes as such, much less treaty-based laws.

3. Must states either "punish" or extradite? Consider also *United States v. Yunis*, below.

4. U.S. legislation implementing the Convention Against Torture by providing criminal sanctions against torture is 18 U.S.C. § 2340A. The legislation is extraterritorial, applying to "[w]hoever outside the United States commits or attempts to commit torture" (subsection (a)), and jurisdiction includes the circumstance where "the alleged offender is present in the United States, irrespective of the nationality of the victim or alleged offender" (subsection (b) (2)). Would this legislation apply to U.S. nationals accused of torture at Guantanamo Bay, Cuba?

5. In view of what you have read so far, what are two false tests offered in the following case concerning applicability of the universality principle to customary international crimes?

UNITED STATES v. YUNIS

681 F.Supp. 896, 900–901 (D.D.C.1988).

[Editors' note: portions of this opinion appear earlier at p. 521; the accused, Yunis, was treated as a national of Lebanon.]

The Universal and Passive Personal principle appear to offer potential bases for asserting jurisdiction over the hostage-taking and aircraft piracy charges against Yunis. However, his counsel argues that the Universal principle is not applicable because neither hostage-taking nor aircraft piracy are heinous crimes encompassed by the doctrine....

UNIVERSAL PRINCIPLE

The Universal principle recognizes that certain offenses are so heinous and so widely condemned that "any state if it captures the offender may prosecute and punish that person on behalf of the world community regardless of the nationality of the offender or victim or where the crime was committed." M. BASSIOUNI, II INTERNATIONAL CRIMINAL LAW, Ch. 6 at 298 (ed. 1986). The crucial question for purposes of defendant's motion is how crimes are classified as "heinous" and whether aircraft piracy and hostage taking fit into this category.

Those crimes that are condemned by the world community and subject to prosecution under the Universal principle are often a matter of international conventions or treaties. *See* Demjanjuk v. Petrovsky, 776 F.2d 571, 582 (6th Cir.1985) (Treaty against genocide signed by a significant number of states made that crime heinous; therefore, Israel had proper jurisdiction over nazi war criminal under the Universal principle).

Both offenses are the subject of international agreements. A majority of states in the world community including Lebanon, have signed three treaties condemning aircraft piracy: The Tokyo Convention, The Hague Convention, and The Montreal Convention. The Hague and Montreal Conventions explicitly rely on the principle of Universal jurisdiction in mandating that all states "take such measures as may be necessary to establish its jurisdiction over the offences ... where the alleged offender is present in its territory." Hague Convention Art. 4 § 2; Montreal Convention Art. 5 § 2. Further, those treaties direct that all "contracting states ... of which the alleged offender is found, ... shall, be obliged *without exception whatsoever and whether or not the offense was committed in its territory*, to submit the case to its competent authorities for the purpose of prosecution." Hague Convention Art. 7; Montreal Convention Art. 7. (emphasis added) These two provisions together demonstrate the international community's strong commitment to punish aircraft hijackers irrespective of where the hijacking occurred.

The global community has also joined together and adopted the International Convention for [sic] the Taking of Hostages, an agreement which condemns and criminalizes the offense of hostage taking. Like the conventions denouncing aircraft piracy, this treaty requires signatory states to prosecute any alleged offenders "present in its territory."

In light of the global efforts to punish aircraft piracy and hostage taking, international legal scholars unanimously agree that these crimes fit within the category of heinous crimes for purposes of asserting universal jurisdiction. *See* M. BASSIOUNI, II INTERNATIONAL CRIMINAL LAW Ch. 2 at 31–32; McCredie, *Contemporary Uses of Force Against Terrorism*, 1986 GA. J. INT'L & COMP. L. 435, 439 (1986); Bazyler, *Capturing the*

Terrorist in the Wild Blue Yonder, 8 WHITTIER L. REV. 685, 687 (1986); Blakesley, *United States Jurisdiction over Extraterritorial Crime*, 73 J. OF CRIM. L. & CRIMINOLOGY 1109, 1140 (1982). In the RESTATEMENT (REVISED) OF FOREIGN RELATIONS LAW OF THE UNITED STATES, a source heavily relied upon by the defendant, aircraft hijacking is specifically identified as a universal crime over which all states should exercise jurisdiction.

Our Circuit has cited the Restatement with approval and determined that the Universal principle, standing alone, provides sufficient basis for asserting jurisdiction over an alleged offender. *See* Tel–Oren v. Libyan Arab Republic, 726 F.2d at 781 n.7 ("The premise of universal jurisdiction is that a state 'may exercise jurisdiction to define and punish certain offenses recognized by the community of nations as of universal concern,' ... even where no other recognized basis of jurisdiction is present.") Therefore, under recognized principles of international law, and the law of this Circuit, there is clear authority to assert jurisdiction over Yunis for the offenses of aircraft piracy and hostage taking.

Notes and Questions

1. Note the universal competence and responsibility recognized in *Yunis* that is reflected in Articles 7 of the Hague and Montreal Conventions.

2. Concerning application of a new treaty creating a new offense to an offender who is not a national of a signatory to the treaty, consider Malvina Halberstam, *Terrorism on the High Seas: The Achille Lauro, Piracy and the IMO Convention on Maritime Safety*, 82 AM. J. INT'L L. 269, 271–72 & n.10 (1988). Yet, if widespread ratification of a new treaty that creates a new offense creates a new *opinio juris* (a least among the signatories) that it is not improper to exercise enforcement jurisdiction over an accused once such person enters the territory of a signatory, has customary international law changed? Does mere ratification of a treaty consenting to such competence among signatory states and their nationals constitute an *opinio juris* concerning the prosecution of nonsignatory nationals? If one can demonstrate an *opinio juris* that even prosecution of nonsignatory nationals is appropriate, is this enough to form new customary international law? What about practice? And is the prosecution of signatory nationals over time (and the absence of prosecution of nonsignatory nationals) sufficient practice? What if no such treaty had ever existed—how is customary international law created?

3. Note that if a new international tribunal is created to prosecute crimes that were already crimes under customary international law universal jurisdiction obtains with respect to such crimes and can be conferred by states creating the tribunal to the new tribunal. Recall *Demjanjuk* regarding formation of the I.M.T. at Nuremberg. In its Opinion and Judgment, the I.M.T. declared with respect to the creation of the international tribunal by the parties to the 1945 London Agreement creating the Charter, "[i]n doing so, they have done together what any one of them might have done singly.... " Exercise of such a universal competence by the tribunal could not rightly be complained of by some other state. For these reasons, if the U.S. prefers not to ratify the new "Rome" Statute creating a permanent International Criminal Court (ICC), the U.S. cannot rightly complain about

the exercise of any universal jurisdictional competence the ICC has under its constitutive treaty even if the U.S. is not a signatory to the treaty.

4. Recall Section 702 of the Restatement, addressing various customary human rights. Under Section 404, customary human rights infractions are subject to universal jurisdiction. Recall the human rights cases in Chapter 2 (esp. Kadic v. Karadzic, 70 F.3d at 236, 240; Xuncax v. Gramajo, 886 F.Supp. at 183 n.25) and international norms concerning the human rights of access to courts and to an effective remedy as well as the customary law of "denial of justice."

Are human rights violations as such also subject to criminal sanctions? See Section 702, RN 12; Jordan J. Paust, M. Cherif Bassiouni, *et al.*, International Criminal Law 167–69, 959–67, *passim* (2 ed. 2000). Could customary human rights law form a basis for prescriptive jurisdiction for hostage-taking?

5. Recall the U.S. Antiterrorism legislation in Chapter 2. What prescriptive bases exist for criminal sanctions under 18 U.S.C.A. § 2332, or civil sanctions under 18 U.S.C.A. § 2333 *et seq.*? Do similar bases exist for civil sanctions under the Torture Victim Protection Act (TVPA), addressed in Chapter 2?

6. The U.S. Hostage Taking Act, 18 U.S.C.A. § 1203, proscribes:

(a) Whoever, whether inside or outside the United States, seizes or detains and threatens to kill, or to injure, or to continue to detain another person in order to compel a third person or a governmental organization to do or to abstain from any act ... shall be punished by imprisonment by any term of years or for life.

(b)(1) It is not an offense under this section if the conduct required for the offense occurred outside the United States unless—

(A) the offender or the person seized or detained is a national of the United States;

(B) the offender is found in the United States; or

(C) the governmental organization sought to be compelled is the Government of the United States.

7. Rape during an armed conflict can constitute a war crime over which there is universal jurisdiction. *See, e.g., Kadic v. Karadzic*, in Chapters 1 and 2; Jordan J. Paust, M. Cherif Bassiouni, *et al.*, International Criminal Law 32, 54, 91, 282, 646, 654–55, 660, 674, 683, 848–49, 913–15, *passim* (2 ed. 2000). Is rape also a violation of human rights law? *See, e.g.*, Universal Declaration of Human Rights, arts. 1, 2, 3, 5; 1966 International Covenant on Civil and Political Rights, arts. 2, 3, 7, 26; Convention Against Torture and Other Cruel, Inhuman or Degrading Treatment or Punishment, arts. 1, 16.

8. Justice Iredell recognized in 1795 that "all ... trespasses committed against the general law of nations, are enquirable, and may be proceeded against, in any nation where no special exemption can be maintained, either by the general law of nations, or by some treaty which forbids or restrains it." Talbot v. Janson, 3 U.S. (3 Dall.) 133, 159–60 (1795), quoted in The Divina Pastora, 17 U.S. (4 Wheat.) 52, 65 (1819) (Marshall, C.J.). Consider

also the following earlier evidence of expectation concerning types of offenses universally sanctionable:

As early as the 1600s, Grotius recognized that crimes against the law of nations are "offenses which affect human society at large ... and which other states or their rulers have a right to deal with." Grotius had also recognized the propriety of a "war" against a ruler who engages in a "manifest oppression" of his or her people, noting that such a military response was "undertaken to protect the subjects of another ruler from oppression" and to assure that they are not further denied "the right of all human society" to freedom from oppression. In that sense, "war" against the oppressor-ruler was a form of sanction strategy in response to acts of oppression. See 2 HUGO GROTIUS, ON THE LAW OF WAR AND PEACE, chpts. 18 (sec. 6), 21 (sec. 3), 25 (sec. 8) (F. Kelsey trans. 1925).

In United States v. Klintock, 18 U.S. (5 Wheat.) 144, 147–48 (1820), it was recognized that piracy "is an offense against all. It is punishable in the Courts of all.... [Our courts] are authorized and bound to punish". The Court also recognized in United States v. Furlong, 18 U.S. (5 Wheat.) 184, 197 (1820) that piracy "is against all, and punished by all ... within this universal jurisdiction." *See also* United States v. Smith, 18 U.S. (5 Wheat.) 153, 161, 163 (1820) (piracy is "an offense against the universal law of society"). More recently, the Second Circuit in Kadic v. Karadzic, 70 F.3d 232, 236, 240 (2d Cir. 1995), *cert. denied*, 518 U.S. 1005 (1996), was quite clear that universal jurisdiction pertains with respect to claims under the ATCA and TVPA concerning war crimes, genocide, and other crimes against humanity, as well as human rights prohibitions of torture and summary execution. Other cases recognizing universal jurisdiction over customary human rights violations (including torture, forced disappearance, summary execution, arbitrary detention, and cruel and inhumane treatment) include: Linder v. Portocarrero, 963 F.2d 332, 336–37 (11th Cir. 1992); Peterson v. Islamic Republic of Iran, 264 F.Supp.2d 46, 60 (D.D.C. 2003) ("international terrorism is subject to universal jurisdiction," extrajudicial killing at Marine barracks in Beirut and FSIA § 1605(a)(7)); Presbyterian Church of Sudan v. Talisman Energy, Inc., 244 F.Supp.2d 289, 306 (S.D.N.Y. 2003); Flatow v. Islamic Republic of Iran, 999 F.Supp. 1, 14 (D.D.C. 1998); Xuncax v. Gramajo, 886 F.Supp. 162, 183 n.25, 193 (D. Mass. 1995); *see also* Abebe–Jira v. Negewo, 72 F.3d 844 (11th Cir. 1996), *cert. denied*, 519 U.S. 830 (1996); *In re* Estate of Ferdinand Marcos, 25 F.3d 1467 (9th Cir. 1994); Filartiga v. Pena–Irala, 630 F.2d 876 (2d Cir. 1980); Iwanowa v. Ford Motor Co., 67 F.Supp.2d 424 (D.N.J. 1999); Doe v. Islamic Salvation Front (FIS), 993 F.Supp. 3 (D.D.C. 1998); Hirsh v. State of Israel, 962 F.Supp. 377, 381 (S.D.N.Y. 1997); Paul v. Avril, 812 F.Supp. 207, 211–12 (S.D. Fla. 1993); Forti v. Suarez–Mason, 672 F.Supp. 1531 (N.D. Cal. 1987), 694 F.Supp. 707 (N.D. Cal. 1988).

Other cases recognizing universal jurisdiction for criminal sanctions or extradition include: United States v. Yousef, 327 F.3d 56, 88–89, 96 (2d Cir. 2003) (universal by treaty, Montreal Sabotage Convention; but "the indefinite category of 'terrorism' is not subject to universal jurisdiction." *Id.* at 79, see also *id.* at 86–87); United States v. Rezaq, 134 F.3d 1121, 1131, 1133 (D.C. Cir. 1998), *cert. denied*, 525 U.S. 834 (1998); United States v. Yunis, 924 F.2d 1086, 1092 (D.C. Cir. 1991); Demjanjuk v. Petrovsky, 776 F.2d 571,

581–83 (6th Cir. 1985), *cert. denied*, 475 U.S. 1016 (1986); United States v. bin Laden, *et al.*, 92 F.Supp.2d 189, 215 n.42, 221–22 (S.D.N.Y. 2000); United States v. Yousef, 927 F.Supp. 673, 681–82 (S.D.N.Y. 1996), *aff'd in part*, 327 F.3d 56 (above); United States v. Yunis, 681 F.Supp. at 900–01, *aff'd*, 924 F.2d 1086 (above); 1 Op. Att'y Gen. 68, 69 (1797) ("violation of territorial rights ... [is] an offence against the law of nations ... [and] it is the interest as well as the duty of every government to punish....").

SECTION 3. ENFORCEMENT JURISDICTION

A. *Enforcement Abroad*

RESTATEMENT OF THE FOREIGN RELATIONS LAW OF THE UNITED STATES (3 ed. 1987)

Section 432. Measures in Aid of Enforcement of Criminal Law

(1) A state may enforce its criminal law within its own territory through the use of police, investigative agencies, public prosecutors, courts, and custodial facilities, provided

(a) the law being enforced is within the state's jurisdiction to prescribe [recall § 431]; ...

(c) the procedures of investigation, arrest, adjudication, and punishment are consistent with the state's obligations under the law of international human rights.

(2) A state's law enforcement officers may exercise their functions in the territory of another state only with the consent of the other state, given by duly authorized officials of that state.

Comment *b. Territoriality and law enforcement.* It is universally recognized, as a corollary of state sovereignty, that officials of one state may not exercise their functions in the territory of another state without the latter's consent....

Reporters' Note 1 ... None of the international human rights conventions ... provides that forcible abduction or irregular extradition is a violation of international human rights law. However, Articles 3, 5, and 9 of the Universal Declaration of Human rights, as well as Articles 7, 9 and 10 of the International Covenant on Civil and Political Rights might be invoked.... In 1981 the Human Rights Committee established pursuant to Article 28 of the Covenant decided that the abduction of a Uruguayan refugee from Argentina by Uruguayan security officers constituted arbitrary arrest and detention in violation of Article 9(1)....

2. *Rule of* "male captus, bene detentus." Nearly all states have followed the rule that, absent protest from other states, they will try persons brought before their courts through irregular means, even through an abduction from another state in violation of international law.... The decisions were based in part on the principle that only states, and not individuals, may raise objections to violations of international law, and in part on the ground that the international law was merely customary. Both of these propositions have been largely abandoned as general principles....

Section 433. External Measures in Aid of Enforcement of Criminal Law: Law of the United States

(1) Law enforcement officers of the United States may exercise their functions in the territory of another state only

(a) with the consent of the other state and if duly authorized by the United States; and

(b) in compliance with the laws both of the United States and of the other state.

(2) A person apprehended ... may be prosecuted in the United States unless his apprehension or delivery was carried out in such reprehensible manner as to shock the conscience of civilized society....

Comment *c. Exception to* Ker–Frisbie *rule.* In the *Toscanino* case [considered below in subsection B], ... the Court of Appeals for the Second Circuit held that allegations of brutal treatment in the course of an abduction from abroad, coupled with active participation by United States government officials in the abduction and torture, if proved to have occurred, would support discharge of the prisoner....

Notes and Questions

1. Consent of a foreign state can come in at least three forms: consent in advance by treaty or customary international law and ad hoc consent.

2. Does a violation of the general prohibition of the use of sovereign, police, or enforcement power in a foreign state without foreign state consent involve merely a territorial infraction, creating a claim for the foreign state that is waivable by the foreign state? Does it depend on what type of enforcement action is involved?

3. In view of the Human Rights Committee decision and the *Toscanino* case, does an individual have standing to raise some claims involving impermissible enforcement actions abroad? See Rest. § 432, RN 1, § 433, cmt. c. *Toscanino* also involved application of the Fifth Amendment to restrain Executive conduct abroad with respect to an alien. Clearly, an individual has standing to raise Fifth Amendment claims. Consider also the materials in subsection B.

4. Given that a U.S. embassy compound in a foreign state is foreign state territory (subject to some immunities with respect to foreign state enforcement jurisdiction and subject to some competencies of the U.S. per treaty and customary international law), can the U.S. arrest someone in the embassy compound? See Restatement § 466, cmt. a ("That premises are inviolable does not mean that they are extraterritorial. Acts committed on those premises are within the territorial jurisdiction of the receiving state, and the mission is required to observe local law....").

Can U.S. officials grant temporary asylum to asylum seekers in U.S. embassy compounds? The Restatement states that grants of asylum on diplomatic or consular premises "is accepted practice," especially with respect to political and other refugees or more general humanitarian concerns. See *id.* § 466, cmt. b and RN 3; *cf.* The Asylum Case (Columbia v. Peru), 1950 I.C.J. 266. Does it also matter that all persons have a general human right "to seek and to enjoy in other countries asylum"? *E.g.*, Universal Declaration of Human Rights, art. 14(1). If this human right is protected through the U.N. Charter (arts. 55(c) and 56)? If so, what would the import be of U.N. Charter Article 103?

5. If the United States is an occupying power in foreign state territory, does the United States have some forms of enforcement competence within occupied territory? *See, e.g.*, Geneva Convention Relative to the Protection of Civilian Persons in Time of War, arts. 5, 49, 78, 147. Can the United States lawfully transfer non-prisoners of war out of occupied territory? See *id.* arts. 49, 147.

COMMODITY FUTURES TRADING COMMISSION v. NAHAS

738 F.2d 487 (D.C.Cir.1984).

TAMM, J.

This appeal concerns a federal district court's jurisdiction under 7 U.S.C. § 15 (1982) to enforce an investigative subpoena served by the Commodity Futures Trading Commission (Commission) on a foreign citizen in a foreign nation. Naji Robert Nahas, a citizen and resident of Brazil, was served in Brazil with a subpoena duces tecum issued by the Commission. The subpoena required Nahas to appear and produce documents at the Commission's offices in Washington, D.C. Nahas did not comply with the subpoena, nor did he comply when the district court, exercising jurisdiction pursuant to 7 U.S.C. § 15, enforced the subpoena. The district court then froze pendente lite Nahas' assets in the United States and, after a full hearing, found Nahas in contempt for his failure to comply with the enforcement order. On appeal, Nahas contends that the enforcement order is void and that he should not be held in contempt for noncompliance with a void enforcement order.

Because we find that the district court lacks jurisdiction under 7 U.S.C. § 15 to enforce an investigative subpoena served on a foreign citizen in a foreign nation, the court's enforcement order, freeze order, and contempt order are void. Accordingly, we vacate all three orders....

On November 14, 1983, Nahas formally responded for the first time in this proceeding. He filed a cross-motion to quash the Commission's subpoena, vacate the freeze order, deny the Commission's motion for contempt, and dismiss the proceedings in their entirety.... Nahas contended that the Commission had exceeded its statutory authority in issuing an investigative subpoena to a foreign citizen in a foreign nation, and that the Commission's method of serving the subpoena was illegal.... In support of his contentions, Nahas submitted an affidavit prepared by Professor Irineu Strenger, a Brazilian attorney and a professor of law at the University of Sao Paulo, stating that the service of the Commission's subpoena violated Brazilian and international law.... Nahas also submitted a document signed by thirty-five members of the Congress of Brazil protesting the administrative and judicial proceedings taken against Nahas as violative of Brazilian and international law....

Nahas challenges the subject-matter jurisdiction of the district court to enforce the Commission's subpoena under 7 U.S.C. § 15. He contends that 7 U.S.C. § 15 does not empower a district court to enforce an administrative subpoena served on a foreign citizen in a foreign country. He claims the court therefore erred at the contempt proceeding in finding him in contempt and in imposing civil sanctions to compel his compliance. We agree....

In the instant case, the jurisdiction of the district court to enforce Commission subpoenas arises from 7 U.S.C. § 15:

> For the purpose of securing effective enforcement ... and for the purpose of any investigation or proceeding ... , any member of the Commission ... may ... subpena [sic] witnesses ... and require the production of any ... records that the Commission deems relevant.... The attendance of witnesses and the production of any such records may be required from any place in the United States or any State at any designated place of hearing. In case of ... refusal to obey a subpena [sic] ... , the Commission may invoke the aid of any court of the United States within the jurisdiction in which the investigation or proceeding is conducted.... Such court may issue an order requiring such person to appear before the Commission ... to produce records ... or to give testimony.... Any failure to obey such order of the court may be punished by the court as a contempt thereof.

7 U.S.C. § 15.... The district court thus has jurisdiction to enforce only those subpoenas issued to "such person[s]" as defined in section 15. The plain language of the statute limits "such person[s]" to "witnesses ... from any place in the United States or any State...." *Id.*

Although courts, in some instances, have construed similar language as authorizing enforcement of administrative subpoenas requiring the production of records from outside the United States, those subpoenas were served on individuals within the United States.... No court has expressly considered whether Congress intended 7 U.S.C. § 15 to authorize judicial enforcement of an investigative subpoena served upon a foreign citizen in a foreign nation. Although the plain language of the statute does not confer such power, the district court in this case nevertheless inferred jurisdiction. Because this inference is not supported by legislative history or analogous precedent, we believe that sound rules of statutory construction compel a different conclusion.

An important canon of statutory construction teaches that "legislation of Congress, unless a contrary intent appears, is meant to apply only within the territorial jurisdiction of the United States...." Foley Bros., Inc. v. Filardo, 336 U.S. 281, 285 ... (1949). See Steele v. Bulova Watch Co., 344 U.S. 280, 285 ... (1952); United States v. Mitchell, 553 F.2d 996, 1001–03 (5th Cir.1977). The text of 7 U.S.C. § 15 does not empower the Commission to serve subpoenas on foreign nationals in foreign countries. Similarly, the legislative history does not indicate that Congress intended to clothe the Commission with the power to serve investigative subpoenas extraterritorially. We are not prepared, in the face of a silent statute and an uninstructive legislative history, to infer the existence of this power:

> The service of an investigative subpoena on a foreign national in a foreign country ... [is] a sufficiently significant act as to require that Congress should speak to it clearly. FTC v. Compagnie de Saint–Gobain–Pont–A–Mousson, 205 U.S. App. D.C. 172, 636 F.2d 1300, 1327 (D.C.Cir.1980) (McGowan, J., concurring).

We are influenced as well by another canon of statutory construction that requires courts, wherever possible, to construe federal statutes to ensure their application will not violate international law. Murray v. The Schooner Charming Betsy, 6 U.S. (2 Cranch) 64, 118 ... (1804); Saint–Gobain, 636 F.2d at 1323 & n.130. To construe 7 U.S.C. § 15 as empowering the district court to enforce an investigative subpoena served on a foreign citizen in a foreign nation would seriously impinge on principles of international law. "When compulsory process is served [on a foreign citizen on foreign soil in the form of an investigative subpoena n.14], ... the act of service itself constitutes an exercise of one nation's sovereignty within the territory of another sovereign. Such an exercise [absent consent by the foreign nation] constitutes a violation of international law." *Id.* at 1313 (footnote omitted). See also *id.*, at 1313–14, 1317; Restatement (Second) of the Foreign Relations Law of the United States §§ 7, 8, 32 & cmt. b, 44 (1965).

The extent of the intrusion on Brazil's sovereignty in this case is reflected in a letter of protest sent by the Brazilian government to the United States Secretary of State. Brazilian law requires that service of process by foreign nations be made pursuant to a letter rogatory or a letter of request transmitted through diplomatic channels.... In its letter of protest, Brazil remonstrated that the Commission's method of serving the subpoena "[did] not conform to the [Brazilian laws] governing the handling ... material [at the international level]...." Letter from Brazilian Ministry of Foreign Affairs to United States Embassy (Mar. 2, 1984).... Brazil therefore admonished the United States to "ensure compliance, in future cases, with the formalities prescribed by Brazilian law for the execution of legal instruments required by foreign courts." *Id.* ... In light of this apparently significant intrusion on Brazilian sovereignty, inferring enforcement jurisdiction under 7 U.S.C. § 15 would seriously impact on principles of international law. Because "an act of Congress ought never to be construed to violate the law of nations, if any other possible construction remains," The Schooner Charming Betsy, 6 U.S. (2 Cranch) at 118, we are unwilling to infer enforcement jurisdiction absent a clearer indication of congressional intent.

We emphasize that this case does not pose a question about the authority of Congress; rather, it poses a question about the congressional intent embodied in 7 U.S.C. § 15. Federal courts must give effect to a valid, unambiguous congressional mandate, even if such effect would conflict with another nation's laws or violate international law. Saint–Gobain, 636 F.2d at 1323. A clear congressional mandate authorizing the Commission to serve investigative subpoenas on foreign citizens in foreign nations is lacking in 7 U.S.C. § 15, and inferring such a mandate would run contrary to established canons of statutory construction. In short, construing enforcement jurisdiction in the instant case would be, we believe, tantamount to enacting, rather than explicating, a law.

Finally, our conclusion that Congress did not intend in 7 U.S.C. § 15 to empower federal courts to enforce investigative subpoenas served on foreign citizens in foreign nations comports with analogous cases in which courts have construed similar language. For example, in SEC v. Minas De Artemisa, S.A., 150 F.2d 215 (9th Cir.1945), the agency was statutorily authorized to subpoena witnesses and documents "from any place in the United States or any Territory...." *Id.* at 218. "The Ninth Circuit construed the agency's authority broadly to require the production of documents outside the United States, provided only that the service of the subpoena is made within the territorial limits of the United States." *Id.* ... In Ludlow Corp. v. DeSmedt, 249 F. Supp. 496 (S.D.N.Y.), *aff'd sub nom.*, FMC v. DeSmedt, 366 F.2d 464 (2d Cir.), *cert. denied*, 385 U.S. 974 ... (1966), the agency was authorized to subpoena documents "from any place in the United States...." 249 F. Supp. at 498 n.2. The court there also construed broadly the agency's power to require the production of documents located outside the country, but it was careful to acknowledge "that the service of the subpoena [was] made within the territorial limits of the United States...." *Id.* at 500 (emphasis added); see *id.* at 501. Finally, in SEC v. Zanganeh, 470 F. Supp. 1307 (D.D.C.1978), the agency was authorized to subpoena witnesses "from any place in the United States or any State...." *Id.* The court stated that where no individual service occurred and respondent was not in the United States, "the [agency] has no power to subpoena an alien nonresident to appear before it from a foreign land." *Id.*...

Our construction of 7 U.S.C. § 15 is further strengthened by the existence of statutes in which Congress explicitly has authorized the extraterritorial service of investigative subpoenas on aliens. For example, Congress has authorized the Department of Justice in its antitrust investigations to serve civil investigative demands on foreign nationals "in such manner as the Federal Rules of Civil Procedure prescribe for service in a foreign country." 15 U.S.C. § 1312(d)(2) (1982). Congress also has empowered the Federal Trade Commission to serve its subpoenas on foreign nationals "in such manner as the Federal Rules of Civil Procedure prescribe for service in a foreign nation." *Id.* § 57b–1(c)(6)(B). The existence of these statutes "indicates that when Congress intends to authorize extraterritorial service of investigative subpoenas, it will express that intent explicitly." Saint–Gobain, 636 F.2d at 1325 n.140. An explicit grant of power is conspicuously absent from 7 U.S.C. § 15. Sound rules of statutory construction as well as analogous precedent therefore compel a construction of 7 U.S.C. § 15 that does not authorize enforcement jurisdiction in the instant case.

For the foregoing reasons, we find that the district court lacked jurisdiction under 7 U.S.C. § 15 to enforce the investigative subpoena served on Nahas in Brazil. The enforcement order, freeze order, and contempt order are therefore void. Accordingly, all three orders are vacated....

[court's n.14: The distinction between service of compulsory process and service of notice is critical under principles of international law due to the difference in judicial enforcement power that accompanies each. When process in the form of a complaint is served extraterritorially, the informational nature of the process renders the act of service relatively benign in terms of infringement on the foreign nation's sovereignty. FTC v. Compagnie de Saint–Gobain–Pont–A–Mousson, 205 U.S. App. D.C. 172, 636 F.2d 1300, 1313 (D.C.Cir.1980).... For example, when an agency serves a formal complaint on a foreign citizen in a foreign nation, the recipient simply receives information upon which he may decide whether to negotiate a consent order or proceed to litigation. The result of the litigation may always be appealed before a cease-and-desist order will issue. Not until the cease-and-desist order becomes final can the enforcement power of the courts be invoked.

By contrast, when an agency serves compulsory process in the form of an investigative subpoena, it compels the recipient to act. Should the recipient refuse to comply with the subpoena, the enforcement power of the federal courts can be invoked immediately. See Saint–Gobain, 636 F.2d at 1311–13. In the instant case, service of the Commission's subpoena on Nahas in Brazil constituted an act of American sovereignty within Brazil, because the subpoena carried with it the full array of American judicial power. See *id.* at 1312, 1313 & n.67. Such an intrusion on the sovereignty of another nation impinges on principles of international law and should be avoided unless expressly mandated by Congress.]

Notes and Questions

1. In Blackmer v. United States, 284 U.S. 421 (1932), the Court stated that service of notice to a U.S. national to return to the U.S. is not a sovereignty violation. Is the service of notice in a foreign country also a sovereign, police, or enforcement effort? Switzerland has objected to the mailing of a notice of suit. See 23 ANN. SUISSE DE DROIT INT'L 203 (1977). *See also* Article 271, Penal Code of Switzerland.

2. The Restatement notes that "[u]nder international law, a state may determine the conditions for service of process in its territory...." RESTATEMENT § 471(1). Rule 4(f) of the 1993 Federal Rules of Civil Procedure generally requires that service in a foreign country be effectuated "in the manner prescribed by the law of the foreign country" if not done by an "internationally agreed means" (*e.g.*, by applicable treaty). Several states have become parties to the Hague Convention on the Service Abroad of Judicial and Extrajudicial Documents in Civil or Commercial Matters, in-

cluding the United States and Canada (with declarations), 658 U.N.T.S. 163, 20 U.S.T. 361. Service within States Parties to the Hague Service Convention is thus service based on consent in advance by treaty, but service must conform to procedures set forth in the Convention, *i.e.*, they are mandatory. *See, e.g.*, Societe Nationale Industrielle Aerospatiale v. United States District Court for the Southern District of Iowa, 482 U.S. 522 (1987). Under the Hague Convention, a request for service and relevant documents will be transmitted to a Central Authority designated by the requested state. In the case of the U.S., the Central Authority is the Office of International Judicial Assistance within the Department of Justice. Service in non-Parties is usually done through a letter rogatory or request from one court to a foreign court or designated entity (usually involving a more formal, timely, and costly process). See Restatement § 471, cmts. b, d, and RN 1. There is also an Inter–American Letters Rogatory Convention, 14 I.L.M. 339 (1975), with Protocol, 18 I.L.M. 1238 (1979). Service under the Inter–American Convention is not mandatory, so service under the Federal Rules of Civil Procedure may be an alternative.

3. Service upon a foreign state or foreign state agency or instrumentality must comply with the FSIA, 28 U.S.C. § 1608. See Chapter 4.

UNITED STATES v. BENT–SANTANA

774 F.2d 1545 (11th Cir.1985).

Johnson, J.

We are here asked to determine what constitutes a "treaty or other arrangement" between the United States and other governments, for purposes of 19 U.S.C.A. § 1401(j) (1985), sufficient to support a conviction under 21 U.S.C.A. § 955a(c) (1985). We hold that assent to board and search a foreign flag vessel by a duly authorized official of that foreign government, communicated verbally or in writing to appropriate United States Department of State personnel, is adequate to meet the terms of Section 1401(j). From that holding, it follows that the judgment of the United States District Court for the Southern District of Florida must be affirmed.

At 10:30 p.m. on January 24, 1984, a United States Coast Guard spotter plane observed the ship *Adventura*, a Panamanian flag vessel, engaged in off-loading 10 miles from the coast of Great Abaco Island, Bahamas. The Coast Guard observed bales of marijuana being moved from the *Adventura* to several smaller boats. When one of the smaller boats headed toward the Florida coast, it was kept in constant surveillance by the spotter plane and was intercepted by the Coast Guard cutter *Seahawk* 35 miles east of Florida. The *Seahawk* crew observed the hands on the small boat dumping bales of marijuana into the water. Upon boarding the boat, an American flag vessel, the Coast Guard found 14 to 17 bales of marijuana, arrested the crew and seized the boat.

The cutter then intercepted the *Adventura*, which was headed in an easterly direction and in international waters approximately 100 miles from the United States coast, at 8:00 a.m. on January 25. The commander of the cutter, Lieutenant Bernard, radioed the captain of the *Adventura*, the appellant Oscar Bent–Santana, and received permission to board. Bernard also radioed United States Coast Guard Command requesting that it contact the Panamanian government for permission to seize the vessel if investigation found some violation of United States law.

There is no dispute that Bent–Santana gave permission to board and inspect documents showing that the *Adventura* was cleared by the Colombian government to travel between Baranquilla, Colombia, and Freeport, Bahamas. There is dispute as to whether the appellant also gave permission for Bernard to search the vessel, the appellant saying he authorized Bernard only to board to inspect papers, Bernard claiming the appellant twice gave him permission to "look at whatever you like." During his look around Bernard determined that a portion of the fuel tank was hollow, detected the strong odor of marijuana coming from the ventilation system, and found a marijuana stem on the deck. He thereupon ordered his crew to begin digging with pickaxes an area of "freshly painted cement" deck near the crew members' bunks; he there found a hidden hatch leading to the hollowed out portion of the fuel tank. This niche contained marijuana residue. Bernard apparently did not ask permission to dig up the deck. Upon further investigation the other fuel tank was discovered to contain several tons of marijuana.

At this point, around 9:00 a.m., the crew of the *Adventura* were read their rights by Bernard. At 1:00 p.m. the Government of Panama communicated to United States officials its assent to the search and seizure of the boat. Bernard was notified of the consent at 5:00 p.m., at which point formal arrests were made. When the boat was one mile off the Florida coast the crew were handcuffed.

The appellant was indicted on two counts by a Grand Jury in the Southern District of Florida on February 7, 1984. The first count was conspiracy to possess marijuana with intent to distribute in violation of 21 U.S.C.A. § 955a(c). The second count was for possession with intent to distribute marijuana in violation of Section 955a(c) and 18 U.S.C.A. § 2. Upon appellant's motion, the magistrate dismissed the second count, though not the first, for lack of jurisdiction. The government appealed the dismissal to the district judge, claiming that the appellant did not give them notice....

The appellant contends first that an American court is not properly seized of jurisdiction over a flag vessel of another nation in international waters under Section 955a(a)....

The statute, in subsection (a), extends jurisdiction to persons "on board a vessel of the United States, or on board a vessel subject to the jurisdiction of the United States on the high seas [if such persons] knowingly or intentionally manufacture or distribute, or ... possess with intent to manufacture or distribute a controlled substance." Subsection (b) extends this proscription to all United States citizens on board any vessel. Subsection (c) covers persons on board "any vessel within the customs waters of the United States...." "Customs waters" is defined by 19 U.S.C.A. § 1401(j) and includes any "foreign vessel subject to a treaty or other arrangement between a foreign government and the United States enabling or permitting the authorities of the United States to board, examine, search, seize, or otherwise to enforce upon such vessel upon the high seas the laws of the United States. . . ."

Bent–Santana argues that this case should be reviewed under subsection (a) rather than subsection (c), claiming that he was charged under the former, rather than the latter. From this he argues that under the terms of subsection (a) an American court would not have jurisdiction over the appellant because the statute by its terms and well-settled principles of international law does not permit jurisdiction by one nation over the flag vessels of other nations on the high seas absent consent. Whatever the merits of this contention, it is clear from the record that Bent–Santana was tried and convicted of violating Section 955a(c). Accordingly, this argument is completely misplaced.

Appellant contends that the search and seizure of the *Adventura* was improper because it was not within the customs waters of the United States. He premises this on the claim that the consent given by the Panamanian government does not come within that contemplated by the "other arrangement" language of Section 1401(j). . . .

This Circuit has not yet definitively construed the language of Section 1401(j) as to the meaning of "treaty or other arrangement." The only discussion of customs waters in our jurisprudence appears to be United States v. Romero–Galue, 757 F.2d 1147 (11th Cir.1985). There this Court reversed and remanded on the "mixed question of law and fact" whether Panamanian approval conveyed through the United States State Department was sufficient to support seizure of a Panamanian ship used to smuggle marijuana. The Court reserved judgment as to whether this relayed consent was consistent with the terms of Section 1401(j). 757 F.2d at 1154.

At least four other circuits have considered this question, or one analogous to it, and all have held that verbal or written consent conveyed by the country of the vessel's flag constitutes an agreement sufficient to place the vessel in the customs waters of the United States. In U.S. v. Loalza–Vasquez, 735 F.2d 153, 157–58 (5th Cir.1984), the court held that a series of teletype messages, from the American Embassy in Panama to a Coast Guard cutter, of Panamanian assent to American boarding and searching of a Panamanian shrimper 250 miles off the United States coast (that was found to be carrying 36,000 pounds of marijuana) was sufficient to bring the seizure under the terms of Section 955a(c).

In United States v. Streifel, 665 F.2d 414 (2d Cir.1981), the Second Circuit considered the case of a Panamanian ship intercepted off the United States coast in international waters. The boat was boarded with the verbal permission of the Panamanian government, and marijuana was discovered in the hold. The court of appeals affirmed the defendant's conviction, *inter alia*, under Section 955(a). 655 F.2d at 417–19. While this is dictum, since the defendants did not appeal on the question of the validity of the search, the court did state that ad hoc assent would be sufficient to sustain a conviction and hence would constitute an "other agreement" for purposes of the statute.

In United States v. Green, 671 F.2d 46, 51 (1st Cir.), *cert. denied*, 457 U.S. 1135 ... (1982), the court held that a similar communication, conveyed by the American Embassy in Britain, of consent to board and search a ship later found to be carrying marijuana was sufficient to constitute a "special arrangement" under the terms of Section 1581(h). That statute prohibits an American officer from boarding a foreign vessel on the high seas to enforce United States law in contravention of a treaty absent "special arrangement" with the foreign government involved. The Fourth Circuit reached a similar result under Section 1581(h) in United States v. Dominguez, 604 F.2d 304, 308 (4th Cir.1979), *cert. denied*, 444 U.S. 1014 ... (1980), involving a Bahamian boat 200 miles off the United States coast where the Bahamian government sent the American Embassy a written confirmation of permission to seize the ship.

In this case the Panamanian government gave its assent through means similar to that deemed adequate in the cases *supra*. Appellant objects that no Panamanian official was on board the ship, as agreed to in the understanding set forth in Exhibit 2 [which set forth a letter from a Panamanian Consul in New York concerning what was "not a formal agreement" between the U.S. and Panama, but which addressed the need for a Panamanian consular official to be on board during any boarding], and that in any event assent can only come through Executive Agreement. This fails for two reasons. First, we find it clear from the past instances of American seizure of Panamanian vessels that agreements of the type at issue here are intended to appoint American Coast Guard officers as agents of the Panamanian government. To that extent, the understanding is respected. Moreover, even if this were not enough to meet the terms of the agreement, and assuming arguendo that there was some binding force to the points in Exhibit 2, it is a settled principle of both public international law and American constitutional law that unless a treaty or intergovernmental agreement is "self-executing"—that is, unless it expressly creates privately enforceable rights—an individual citizen does not have standing to protest when one nation does not follow the terms of such agreement. Foster v. Neilson, 2 Pet. (27 U.S.) 253, 313–14 ... (1829); Dreyfus v. Von Finck, 534 F.2d 24, at 29–30 (2d Cir. 1976). Only Panama could invoke Point 2 and it evinces no such inclination. Bent–Santana lacks standing to complain under the terms of this understanding.

More importantly, it is clear from the language of Exhibit 2, and from the statements of American diplomatic personnel contacted by appellant's counsel, that the points set forth in that document do not function as a formal, binding agreement. Nor is there any authority to suggest that only a formal intergovernmental agreement would be adequate to meet the terms of Section 955a(c). Past and consistent practice suggests that arrangements are made on an ad hoc basis by the two governments.

Accordingly, we follow the holdings of the other four circuits that have had occasion to consider this question and hold that the ad hoc grant of permission to search a foreign flag vessel, issued by the government of that flag to the appropriate officials of the United States State Department, is sufficient to place a foreign flag vessel within American customs waters under Section 1401(j) and hence subject to search for and seizure of contraband under American law....

For the reasons set forth above, we find no merit in appellant's contentions. The consent relayed from the Government of Panama to American officials was sufficient to bring this case under the terms of Section 1401(j) and thus under Section 955a(c). Further, we find that the Coast Guard in this case acted in accordance with the constitutional requisites for search and seizure under the Fourth Amendment....

Note

1. In United States v. Romero–Galue, 757 F.2d 1147 (11th Cir.1985), the court noted: the "goal ... of section 955a(c) of the Marijuana on the High Seas Act was not unlike the one Congress had in mind when it passed the Anti–Smuggling Act; both statutes authorize the prosecution of smugglers hovering on the high seas beyond the twelve mile limit [then, beyond our contiguous zone for enforcement purposes—see Chapter 6]. Under section 955a(c), the government can now reach narcotics smugglers aboard vessels of nontreaty nations within twelve miles of our coast and those aboard vessels of treaty nations within the area on the high seas designated by treaty or other arrangement.... Nothing in international law prohibits two nations from entering into a treaty ... to extend the customs waters and the reach of the domestic law of one of the nations into the high seas." The court was addressing jurisdiction to prescribe and consent in advance by treaty or "other arrangement" for prescriptive competence with respect to vessels hovering outside our contiguous zone on the high seas. Enforcement is still subject to ad hoc consent of a foreign flag when its vessel is on the high seas unless customary international law, the 1982 U.N. Law of the Sea Convention, or some other international agreement also provides enforcement authorization.

B. Abductions

The general approach of the judiciary in the United States, Canada and the United Kingdom has been that a fugitive should not succeed in escaping trial merely because he or she was brought illegally into the jurisdiction of the prosecuting state. This practice is evidenced in the Latin maxim, *mala captus bene detentus*, which means that the court once in possession of the accused has jurisdiction over the person. A notable exception in U.S. cases has involved violations of treaty law. *See, e.g.,* Cook v. United States, 288 U.S. 102 (1933); United States v. Ferris, 19 F.2d 925, 926 (N.D. Cal. 1927); *see also* (all re: customary international law) *The Apollon,* 22 U.S. (9 Wheat.) 362, 370–71, 376–79 (1824); Motherwell v. United States *ex rel.* Alexandroff, 107 F. 437, 446 (3d

Cir.1901) (Gray, J., concurring), *rev'd*, 183 U.S. 424 (1902). Although the U.S. Second Circuit Court of Appeals in *United States v. Toscanino*, below, also declared that there exists an exception in cases when the manner in which the fugitive is apprehended "shocks the conscience of the Court," and this general exception is recognized in the Restatement, the exception has not actually been applied.

UNITED STATES v. TOSCANINO

500 F.2d 267 (2d Cir.1974).

MANSFIELD, J.

Francisco Toscanino appeals from a narcotics conviction entered against him in the Eastern District of New York by Chief Judge Jacob Mishler after a jury trial. Toscanino was sentenced to 20 years in prison and fined $20,000. He contends that the court acquired jurisdiction over him unlawfully through the conduct of American agents who kidnapped him in Uruguay, used illegal electronic surveillance, tortured him and abducted him to the United States for the purpose of prosecuting him here. We remand the case to the district court for further proceedings in which the government will be required to respond to his allegations concerning the methods by which he was brought into the Eastern District and the use of electronic surveillance to gather evidence against him.

Toscanino, who is a citizen of Italy, and four others were charged with conspiracy to import narcotics into the United States in violation of 21 U.S.C. §§ 173 and 174 in a one count indictment returned by a grand jury sitting in the Eastern District on February 22, 1973. The other defendants were S. Nicolay, Segundo Coronel, Roberto Arenas and Umberto Coronel. Also named as a conspirator but not as a defendant was one Hosvep Caramian. At a joint trial of all the defendants (except for Nicolay who had fled to Argentina), which began on May 22, 1973, the only government witness against Toscanino was Caramian who testified that he met with Toscanino in Montevideo, Uruguay, during the summer of 1970 and agreed to find buyers for a shipment of heroin into the United States, which would be delivered by Nicolay. Caramian testified further that in November, 1970, he left Uruguay and came to the United States where he met with Arenas and the Coronel brothers who agreed to buy the heroin. On November 30, 1970, Caramian received part of Toscanino's shipment delivered by Nicolay in Miami, Florida, but ultimate distribution of the narcotics was intercepted by government agents who posed as buyers from Arenas and the Coronel brothers. Toscanino, testifying in his own behalf, denied any knowledge of these transactions. On June 5, 1973, the jury returned a verdict of guilty against him and all the other defendants.

Toscanino does not question the sufficiency of the evidence or claim any error with respect to the conduct of the trial itself. His principal argument, which he voiced prior to trial and again after the jury verdict was returned, is that the entire proceedings in the district court against him were void because his presence within the territorial jurisdiction of the court had been illegally obtained. He alleged that he had been kidnapped from his home in Montevideo, Uruguay, and brought into the Eastern District only after he had been detained for three weeks of interrogation accompanied by physical torture in Brazil....

The government prosecutor neither affirmed nor denied these allegations but claimed they were immaterial to the district court's power to proceed.

Toscanino alleged further that, prior to his forcible abduction from Montevideo, American officials bribed an employee of the public telephone company to conduct electronic surveillance of him and that the results of the surveillance were given to American agents and forwarded to government prosecutors in New York. According to Toscanino the telephone company employee was eventually arrested in Uruguay for illegal eavesdropping and was indicted and imprisoned. In connection with these later allegations Toscanino moved, pursuant to 18 U.S.C. § 3594, to compel the government to affirm or deny whether in fact there had been any electronic surveillance of him in Uruguay.

Toscanino's motion for an order vacating the verdict, dismissing the indictment and ordering his return to Uruguay was denied by the district court on November 2, 1973, without a hearing. Relying principally on the decisions of the Supreme Court in Ker v. Illinois, 119 U.S. 436 ... (1886), and Frisbie v. Collins, 342 U.S. 519 ... (1952), the court held that the manner in which Toscanino was brought into the territory of the United States was immaterial to the court's power to proceed, provided he was physically present at the time of trial....

In an era marked by a sharp increase in kidnapping activities, both here and abroad, ... we face the question, as we must in the state of the pleadings, of whether a federal court must assume jurisdiction over the person of a defendant who is illegally apprehended abroad and forcibly abducted by government agents to the United States for the purpose of facing criminal charges here. The answer necessitates a review and appraisal of two Supreme Court decisions, heavily relied upon by the government and by the district court, Ker v. Illinois, 119 U.S. 436 ... (1886), and Frisbie v. Collins, 342 U.S. 519 ... (1952). For years these two cases have been the mainstay of a doctrine to the effect that the government's power to prosecute a defendant is not impaired by the illegality of the method by which it acquires control over him. This teaching originated almost 90 years ago in *Ker*. While residing in Peru, Ker was indicted by an Illinois grand jury for larceny and embezzlement. At the request of the Governor of Illinois the President, invoking the current treaty of extradition between the United States and Peru, issued a warrant authorizing a Pinkerton agent to take custody of Ker from the authorities of Peru. The warrant, however was never served, probably for the reason that by the time the agent arrived there, armed forces of Chile, then at war with Peru, were in control of Lima. See *Ker v. Illinois Revisited*, 47 Am. J. Int'l L. 678 (1953). Instead Ker was forcibly abducted by the agent, placed aboard an American vessel and eventually taken to the United States, where he was tried and convicted in Illinois. The Supreme Court rejected Ker's argument that he was entitled by virtue of the treaty with Peru to a right of asylum there and held that the abduction of Ker did not violate the Due Process Clause of the Fourteenth Amendment (then less than 20 years old), which was construed as merely requiring that the party be regularly indicted and brought to trial "according to the forms and modes prescribed for such trials." The Court accordingly held that Ker might be tried by Illinois, regardless of the method by which it acquired control over him....

... [U]nder the so-called "Ker–Frisbie" rule, due process was limited to the guarantee of a constitutionally fair trial, regardless of the method by which jurisdiction was obtained over the defendant. Jurisdiction gained through an indisputably illegal act might still be exercised, even though the effect could be to reward police brutality and lawlessness in some cases....

In light of ... [post-*Frisbie*] developments we are satisfied that the "Ker–Frisbie" rule cannot be reconciled with the Supreme Court's expansion of the concept of due process, which now protects the accused against pretrial illegality by denying to the government the fruits of its exploitation of any deliberate and unnecessary lawlessness on its part. Although the issue in most of the cases forming part of this evolutionary process was whether evidence should have been excluded (*e.g., Mapp, Miranda, Wong Sun, Silverman*), it was unnecessary in those cases to invoke any other sanction to insure that an ultimate conviction would not rest on governmental illegality. Where suppression of evidence will not suffice, however, we must be guided by the underlying principle that the government should be denied the right to exploit its own illegal conduct, Wong Sun v. United States, 371 U.S. 471, 488 ... (1963), and when an accused is kidnapped and forcibly brought within the jurisdiction, the court's acquisition of power over his person represents the fruits of the government's exploitation of its own misconduct. Having unlawfully seized the defendant in violation of the Fourth Amendment, which guarantees "the right of the people to be secure in their persons ... against unreasonable ... seizures," the government should as a matter of fundamental fairness be obligated to return him to his *status quo ante*.

Faced with a conflict between the two concepts of due process, the one being the restricted version found in *Ker-Frisbie* and the other the expanded and enlightened interpretation expressed in more recent decisions of the Supreme Court, we are persuaded that to the extent that the two are in conflict, the *Ker-Frisbie* version must yield. Accordingly we view due process as now requiring a court to divest itself of jurisdiction over the person of a defendant where it has been acquired as the result of the government's deliberate, unnecessary and unreasonable invasion of the accused's constitutional rights. This conclusion represents but an extension of the well-recognized power of federal courts in the civil context to decline to exercise jurisdiction over a defendant whose presence has been secured by force or fraud. See *In re* Johnson, 167 U.S. 120, 126 ... (1896); Fitzgerald Construction Co. v. Fitzgerald, 137 U.S. 98 ... (1890).

If the charges of government misconduct in kidnapping Toscanino and forcibly bringing him to the United States should be sustained, the foregoing principles would, as a matter of due process, entitle him to some relief. The allegations include corruption and bribery of a foreign official as well as kidnapping, accompanied by violence and brutality to the person. Deliberate misconduct on the part of United States agents, in violation not only of constitutional prohibitions but also of the federal Kidnapping Act, *supra*, and of two international treaties obligating the United States Government to respect the territorial sovereignty of Uruguay, is charged. See U.N. Charter, art. 2; O.A.S. Charter, art. 17.... Here, ... not only were several laws allegedly broken and crimes committed at the behest of government agents but the conduct was apparently unnecessary, as the extradition treaty between the United States and Uruguay, see 35 Stat. 2028, does not specifically exclude narcotics violations so that a representative of our government might have been able to conclude with Uruguay a special arrangement for Toscanino's extradition....

... In this case we may rely simply upon our supervisory power over the administration of criminal justice in the district courts within our jurisdiction.... Clearly this power may legitimately be used to prevent district courts from themselves becoming "accomplices in wilful disobedience of law." See *McNabb, supra* at 345. Moreover the supervisory power is not limited to the admission or exclusion of evidence, but may be exercised in any manner necessary to remedy abuses of a district court's process. *Cf.* Rea v. United States, 350 U.S. 214 ... (1956). Drawing again from the field of civil procedure, we think a federal court's criminal process is abused or degraded where it is executed against a defendant who has been brought into the territory of the United States by the methods alleged here. *Cf.* Commercial Mutual Accident Co. v. Davis, 213 U.S. 245 ... (1909); *Fitzgerald Construction Co.* v. *Fitzgerald, supra.* We could not tolerate such an abuse without debasing "the processes of justice".

If distinctions are necessary, *Ker* and *Frisbie* are clearly distinguishable on other legally significant grounds which render neither of them controlling here. Neither case, unlike that here, involved the abduction of a defendant in violation of international treaties of the United States. *Frisbie* presented an alleged interstate abduction in which the appellant was clearly extraditable and an order returning him to his asylum state, Illinois, would have been an exercise in futility since Illinois would have been obligated to return him to Michigan for trial. U.S. Const. Art. IV, § 2, cl. 2; 18 U.S.C. § 3182. Although the appellant in *Ker* argued that his forcible abduction by the Pinkerton agent violated the extradition treaty between the United States and Peru, the Supreme Court disagreed, holding that the extradition treaty did not apply and that it would have been violated by the demanding state only if, after receiving a fugitive, it tried him for a crime other than that for which he was surrendered. See United States v. Rauscher, 119 U.S. 407 ... (1886). Here, in contrast, Toscanino alleges that he was forcibly abducted from Uruguay, whose territorial sovereignty this country has agreed in two international treaties to respect. The Charter of the United Nations, the members of which include the United States and Uruguay, see Department of State, Treaties in Force 402–03 (1973), obligates "All Members" to "refrain ... from the threat or use of force against the territorial integrity or political independence of any state...." See U.N. Charter, art. 2 para. 4. Additionally, the Charter of the Organization of American States, whose members also include the United States and Uruguay, see Department of State, Treaties in Force 359 (1973), provides that the "territory of a state is inviolable; it may not be the object, even temporarily, ... of ... measures of force taken by another state, directly or indirectly, on any grounds whatever...." See O.A.S. Charter, art. 17.

That international kidnappings such as the one alleged here violate the U.N. Charter was settled as a result of the Security Council debates following the illegal kidnapping in 1960 of Adolf Eichmann from Argentina by Israeli "volunteer groups." In response to a formal complaint filed by the U.N. representative from Argentina pursuant to article 35 of the U.N. Charter the Security Council, by eight votes to none (with two abstentions and one member—Argentina—not participating in the vote), adopted a resolution condemning the kidnapping and requesting "the Government of Israel to make appropriate reparation in accordance with the Charter of the United Nations and rules of international law...." U.N. Doc. S/4349 (June 23, 1960), quoted in W. FRIEDMANN, O. LISSITZYN & R. PUGH, INTERNATIONAL LAW: CASES AND MATERIALS 497 (1969). The resolution merely recognized a long standing principle of international law that abductions by one state of persons located within the territory of another violate the territorial sovereignty of the second state and are redressable usually by the return of the person kidnapped. See *The Vincenti Affair*, 1 HACKWORTH, DIGEST OF INTERNATIONAL LAW 624 (1920); *The Cantu Case*, 2 HACKWORTH 310 (1914); *The Case of Blatt and Converse*, 2 HACKWORTH 309 (1911).

Since the United States thus agreed not to seize persons residing within the territorial limits of Uruguay, appellant's allegations in this case are governed not by *Ker* but by the Supreme Court's later decision in Cook v. United States, 288 U.S. 102 ... (1933). In *Cook* officers of the United States Coast Guard boarded and seized a British vessel, the Mazel Tov, in violation of territorial limits fixed by a treaty then in force between the United States and Great Britain. The Supreme Court held that the government's subsequent libel for forfeiture of the vessel in the federal district court was properly dismissed, since under the treaty the forcible seizure was incapable of giving the district court power to adjudicate title to the vessel regardless of the vessel's physical presence within the court's jurisdiction.... Thus *Ker* does not apply where a defendant has been brought into the district court's jurisdiction by forcible abduction in violation of a treaty.... It derives directly from the

Court's earlier decision in *United States* v. *Rauscher*, 119 U.S. 407 ... (1886), decided the same day as *Ker* and written by the same Justice. In *Rauscher*, the Court held that United States courts were barred from trying a fugitive, surrendered by Great Britain pursuant to a treaty of extradition, for a crime other than that for which he had been extradited, at least until he had been afforded an opportunity to return to the country from which he had been brought. In reaching this result the Court rejected the argument that even where a trial might be in violation of a treaty obligation, the defendant's exclusive remedy was an "appeal to the executive branches of the treaty governments for redress." See 119 U.S. at 430–432. See also Johnson v. Browne, 205 U.S. 309 ... (1907)....

The case is remanded to the district court for further proceedings not inconsistent with this opinion. Our remand should be construed as requiring an evidentiary hearing with respect to Toscanino's allegations of forcible abduction only if, in response to the government's denial, he offers some credible supporting evidence including specifically evidence that the action was taken by or at the direction of United States officials. Upon his failure to make such an offer the district court may, in its discretion, decline to hold an evidentiary hearing.

Notes and Questions

1. The RESTATEMENT has adopted the *Toscanino* exception. See RESTATEMENT § 433(2), cmt. c and RN 3. The majority of textwriters are also opposed to *mala captus* practices. *See, e.g.,* M.C. BASSIOUNI, INTERNATIONAL EXTRADITION IN UNITED STATES LAW AND PRACTICE § 2–9 (1983). In later cases such as United States v. Herrera, 504 F.2d 859 (5th Cir.1974); United States *ex rel.* Lujan v. Gengler, 510 F.2d 62 (2d Cir.1975); United States v. Lira, 515 F.2d 68 (2d Cir.1975); and Marschner v. United States, 470 F.Supp. 201 (D.Conn.1979), the *Toscanino* decision was distinguished. It was distinguished in *Gengler* on the ground that although government agents do not have a *carte blanche* to bring defendants from abroad to the United States by the use of torture, brutality and similar outrageous conduct, not every violation of law by the government or irregularity in the circumstances of a defendant's arrival in the jurisdiction is sufficient to vitiate the proceedings in a criminal court. Here the conduct of the U.S. government agents was not outrageous and furthermore the offended state did not object to that conduct. In fact, the "*Toscanino* exception" failed as a basis for requiring the court to divest itself of jurisdiction in every case but that of United States v. Caro–Quintero, 745 F.Supp. 599 (C.D.Cal.1990). That decision was later reversed by the U.S. Supreme Court in United States v. Alvarez–Machain, 504 U.S. 655 (1992), below.

2. Canadian courts in R. v. Walton, (1905), 10 C.C.C. 269, and *Re* Hartnett and the Queen: *Re* Hudson and the Queen, (1973), 1 O.R. (2d) 206, have applied the *mala captus bene detentus* maxim although, as indicated in the Brief submitted by Canada in *Alvarez-Machain*, it seems unlikely that they will address the question in future.

3. What policies underlie the *Ker-Frisbie* doctrine (the U.S. version of the *mala captus bene detentus* maxim)? What policies underlie the *Cook, Rauscher,* and *Toscanino* exceptions to the doctrine?

4. In Kear v. Hilton, U.S. Marshal, 699 F.2d 181 (4th Cir.1983), a writ of habeas corpus seeking to prevent extradition to Canada of two U.S. bounty hunters (Kear and Johnson) for the kidnapping from Canada of Jaffe, a Florida "bail jumper," was denied. The court quoted Reese v. United States, 76 U.S. (9 Wall.) 13 (1869) to confirm that the bondsmen's " 'power of arrest can only be exercised within the territory of the United States.' " Kear and Johnson were extradited to Canada and later convicted of kidnapping. Jaffe was later returned to Canada and Canada refused to extradite him upon a request for extradition.

If a person in the U.S. offers a reward to anyone who captures and returns to the U.S. a person accused of violating U.S. law, is the person offering the reward a complicitor in a subsequent kidnapping in violation of foreign law?

5. In 1985, the U.N. Security Council recognized that "abductions are offenses of grave concern to the international community, having severe adverse consequences for the rights of the victims and for the promotion of friendly relations and co-operation among States," condemned "unequivocally all acts of . . . abduction," and recognized the "obligation of all States in whose territory hostages or abducted persons are held urgently to take all appropriate measures to secure their safe release and to prevent the commission of acts of hostage-taking and abduction in the future." U.N. S.C. Res. 579 (1985), reprinted in 25 I.L.M. 243 (1986).

6. The Human Rights Committee established under the International Covenant on Civil and Political Rights has also recognized that forcible abductions can violate the human rights of the abductee. Views of the Human Rights Committee on the Complaint of Lopez, 36 U.N. GAOR, Supp. No. 40, at 176–84, U.N. Doc. A/36/40 (1981); *see also id.* at 185–89; RESTATEMENT § 432, RN 1; *id.* § 702 (c). The Human Rights Committee, in Canon Garcia v. Ecuador (Decision of May 11, 1991, U.N. Doc. CCPR/C/43/319/1988), has also found that Ecuador violated article 9 of the Covenant by participating in an abduction of a person to the U.S. accused of drug trafficking. In Europe, abductions are also considered to violate human rights protecting the individual from arbitrary deprivation of liberty. *See, e.g.,* Bozano v. France, Ser. A, No. 111 (18 Dec. 1986), 9 EHRR 297 (1987), *id.* (2 Dec. 1991), 13 EHRR 428 (1991). In *Bozano,* the European Court found a violation of Article 5(1) of the European Convention on Human Rights in a context where the individual had been found to be not extraditable from France (to Italy, the requesting state) and the French Government nonetheless issued a deportation order and French police took him against his will to Switzerland where he was extradited to Italy to serve sentence after conviction in Italy in absentia. The Court noted that " 'lawfulness' " "implies absence of any arbitrariness," that the deportation was a disguised form of extradition contrary to French judicial rulings, and that the individual's "deprivation of liberty . . . was neither 'lawful' . . . , nor compatible with the 'right to security of person' " within the meaning of the Convention. *Id.* at paras. 58–60. In Bennett v. Horseferry Road Magistrates Court, [1993] All

ER 138 (House of Lords), jurisdiction was refused where a person had been deported from South Africa and deportation was used as disguised extradition. *See also* International Law Association, REPORT OF THE SIXTY-SIXTH CONFERENCE—BUENOS AIRES, ARGENTINA 142, 162–65 (1994) (noting several of the above as well as cases in New Zealand, Zimbabwe, South Africa and Switzerland). *But see* Sosa v. Alvarez–Machain, 542 U.S. 692 (2004), extract and Notes and Questions in Chapter 2, pp. 404–421.

For a discussion of relevant human rights and "denial of justice" claims, *see, e.g.,* Paust, *After* Alvarez–Machain*: Abduction, Standing, Denials of Justice, and Unaddressed Human Rights Claims,* 67 ST. JOHN'S L. REV. 551, 560–67, 577–78 (1993), also recognizing exceptions under international law. *Id.* at 563–66, 574–80, and authorities cited. The exceptions include: (1) reasonably necessary international criminal-napping (when, on balance, not arbitrary, cruel, inhumane, degrading, unjust, or otherwise unlawful), (2) capture of a dictator, (3) acts of self-defense under the U.N. Charter, and (4) permissible actions under Chapters VII and VIII of the U.N. Charter. Clearly, the last two exceptions are based directly in the U.N. Charter. The first two are probably still a minority viewpoint, especially given the Eichmann and abductions resolutions of the Security Council in 1960 and 1985.

7. Is dismissing the case against the defendant an appropriate remedy for abuses committed by arresting agents? *Compare* RESTATEMENT § 432, cmt. c and RN 3 *with* Paust, *supra,* at 567–68, and authorities cited. What other remedies would be available to a defendant so apprehended? In this regard, note that Dr. Alvarez–Machain, who was abducted from Mexico, has sued DEA officials and the Department of Justice in U.S. federal court for $20 million in damages relating to his abduction. *See* Alvarez–Machain v. United States, 107 F.3d 696 (9th Cir.1996) (allowing an action under the Federal Tort Claims Act and the TVPA), *rev'd,* Sosa v. Alvarez–Machain, 542 U.S. 692 (2004).

8. The Brief of the Government of Canada as Amicus Curiae in Support of the Respondent in the case of *United States* v. *Alvarez-Machain* is reprinted in 31 I.L.M. 919 (1992). For the Brief of Mexico, see *id.* at 934.

UNITED STATES v. ALVAREZ–MACHAIN

504 U.S. 655 (1992).

REHNQUIST, C.J.

The issue in this case is whether a criminal defendant, abducted to the United States from a nation with which it has an extradition treaty, thereby acquires a defense to the jurisdiction of this country's courts. We hold that he does not, and that he may be tried in federal district court for violations of the criminal law of the United States.

Respondent, Humberto Alvarez–Machain, is a citizen and resident of Mexico. He was indicted for participating in the kidnap and murder of United States Drug Enforcement Administration (DEA) special agent Enrique Camarena–Salazar and a Mexican pilot working with Camarena, Alfredo Zavala–Avelar. The DEA believes that respondent, a medical doctor, participated in the murder by prolonging agent Camarena's life so that others could further torture and interrogate him. On April 2, 1990, respondent was forcibly kidnapped from his medical office in Guadalajara, Mexico, to be flown by private plane to El Paso, Texas, where he was arrested by DEA officials. The District Court concluded that DEA agents were responsible for respondent's abduction, although they were not personally involved in it. United States v. Caro–Quintero, 745 F. Supp. 599, 602–604, 609 (C.D.Cal.1990).

Respondent moved to dismiss the indictment, claiming that his abduction constituted outrageous governmental conduct, and that the District Court lacked jurisdiction to try him because he was abducted in violation of the extradition treaty between the United States and Mexico. *Extradition Treaty, May 4, 1978, [1979] United States–United Mexican States*, 31 U.S.T. 5059, T.I.A.S. No. 9656 (*Extradition Treaty* or *Treaty*). The District Court rejected the outrageous governmental conduct claim, but held that it lacked jurisdiction to try respondent because his abduction violated the *Extradition Treaty*. The district court discharged respondent and ordered that he be repatriated to Mexico. *Caro-Quintero, supra*, at 614.

The Court of Appeals affirmed the dismissal of the indictment and the repatriation of respondent, relying on its decision in United States v. Verdugo–Urquidez, 939 F.2d 1341 (9th Cir.1991), *cert. pending*, No. 91–670. 946 F.2d 1466 (1991). In *Verdugo*, the Court of Appeals held that the forcible abduction of a Mexican national with the authorization or participation of the United States violated the *Extradition Treaty* between the United States and Mexico. Although the *Treaty* does not expressly prohibit such abductions, the Court of Appeals held that the "purpose" of the *Treaty* was violated by a forcible abduction, 939 F.2d, at 1350, which, along with a formal protest by the offended nation, would give a defendant the right to invoke the *Treaty* violation to defeat jurisdiction of the district court to try him. The Court of Appeals further held that the proper remedy for such a violation would be dismissal of the indictment and repatriation of the defendant to Mexico.

In the instant case, the Court of Appeals affirmed the district court's finding that the United States had authorized the abduction of respondent, and that letters from the Mexican government to the United States government served as an official protest of the *Treaty* violation. Therefore, the Court of Appeals ordered that the indictment against respondent be dismissed and that respondent be repatriated to Mexico. 946 F.2d, at 1467. We granted *certiorari* . . . and now reverse.

. . . In construing a treaty, as in construing a statute, we first look to its terms to determine its meaning. . . . The *Treaty* says nothing about the obligations of the United States and Mexico to refrain from forcible abductions of people from the territory of the other nation, or the consequences under the Treaty if such an abduction occurs. Respondent submits that Article 22(1) of the *Treaty* which states that it "shall apply to offenses specified in Article 2 [including murder] committed before and after this *Treaty* enters into force," 31 U.S.T., at 5073–5074, evidences an intent to make application of the Treaty mandatory for those offenses. However, the more natural conclusion is that Article 22 was included to ensure that the Treaty was applied to extraditions requested after the *Treaty* went into force, regardless of when the crime of extradition occurred.

More critical to respondent's argument is Article 9 of the *Treaty* which provides:

"1. Neither Contracting Party shall be bound to deliver up its own nationals, but the executive authority of the requested Party shall, if not prevented by the laws of that Party, have the power to deliver them up if, in its discretion, it be deemed proper to do so.

"2. If extradition is not granted pursuant to paragraph 1 of this Article, the requested Party shall submit the case to its competent authorities for the purpose of prosecution, provided that Party has jurisdiction over the offense." *Id.*, at 5065.

According to respondent, Article 9 embodies the terms of the bargain which the United States struck: if the United States wishes to prosecute a Mexican national, it may request that individual's extradition. Upon a request from the United States, Mexico may either extradite the individual, or submit the case to the proper authorities for prosecution in Mexico. In this way, respondent reasons, each nation preserved its right to choose whether its nationals would be tried in its own courts or by the courts of the other nation. This preservation of rights would be frustrated if either nation were free to abduct nationals of the other nation for the purposes of prosecution. More broadly, respondent reasons, as did the Court of Appeals, that all the processes and restrictions on the obligation to extradite established by the *Treaty* would make no sense if either nation were free to resort to forcible kidnapping to gain the presence of an individual for prosecution in a manner not contemplated by the *Treaty*. *Verdugo, supra*, at 1350.

We do not read the *Treaty* in such a fashion. Article 9 does not purport to specify the only way in which one country may gain custody of a national of the other country for the purposes of prosecution. In the absence of an extradition treaty, nations are under no obligation to surrender those in their country to foreign authorities for prosecution. . . .(United States may not extradite a citizen in the absence of a statute or treaty obligation). Extradition treaties exist so as to impose mutual obligations to surrender individuals in certain defined sets of circumstances, following established procedures. See 1 J. Moore, A Treatise on Extradition and Interstate Rendition, § 72 (1891). The *Treaty* thus provides a mechanism which would not otherwise exist, requiring, under certain circumstances, the United States and Mexico to extradite individuals to the other country, and establishing the procedures to be followed when the *Treaty* is invoked.

The history of negotiation and practice under the *Treaty* also fails to show that abductions outside of the *Treaty* constitute a violation of the *Treaty*. As the Solicitor General notes, the Mexican government was made aware, as early as 1906, of the *Ker* doctrine, and the United States' position that it applied to forcible abductions made outside of the terms of the United States–Mexico extradition treaty. Nonetheless, the current version of the *Treaty*, signed in 1978, does not attempt to establish a rule that would in any way curtail the effect of *Ker*. Moreover, although language which would grant individuals exactly the right sought by respondent had been considered and drafted as early as 1935 by a prominent group of legal scholars sponsored by the faculty of Harvard Law School, no such clause appears in the current treaty.

Thus, the language of the *Treaty*, in the context of its history, does not support the proposition that the *Treaty* prohibits abductions outside of its terms. The remaining question, therefore, is whether the Treaty should be interpreted so as to include an implied term prohibiting prosecution where the defendant's presence is obtained by means other than those established by the *Treaty*. See *Valentine*, 299 U.S., at 17 ... ("Strictly the question is not whether there had been a uniform practical construction denying the power, but whether the power had been so clearly recognized that the grant should be implied").

Respondent contends that the *Treaty* must be interpreted against the backdrop of customary international law, and that international abductions are "so clearly prohibited in international law" that there was no reason to include such a clause in the *Treaty* itself. Brief for Respondent 11. The international censure of international abductions is further evidenced, according to respondent, by the *United Nations Charter* and the *Charter of the Organization of American States*. *Id*., at 17, 57 S.Ct., at 106. Respondent does not argue that these sources of international law provide an independent basis for the right respondent asserts not to be tried in the United States, but rather that they should inform the interpretation of the *Treaty* terms.

The Court of Appeals deemed it essential, in order for the individual defendant to assert a right under the *Treaty*, that the affected foreign government had registered a protest. *Verdugo*, 939 F.2d, at 1357 ("in the kidnapping case there must be a formal protest from the offended government after the kidnapping"). Respondent agrees that the right exercised by the individual is derivative of the nation's right under the *Treaty*, since nations are authorized, notwithstanding the terms of an extradition treaty, to voluntarily render an individual to the other country on terms completely outside of those provided in the *Treaty*. The formal protest, therefore, ensures that the "offended" nation actually objects to the abduction and has not in some way voluntarily rendered the individual for prosecution. Thus the *Extradition Treaty* only prohibits gaining the defendant's presence by means other than those set forth in the *Treaty* when the nation from which the defendant was abducted objects.

This argument seems to us inconsistent with the remainder of respondent's argument. The *Extradition Treaty* has the force of law, and if, as respondent asserts, it is self-executing, it would appear that a court must enforce it on behalf of an individual regardless of the offensiveness of the practice of one nation to the other nation....

More fundamentally, the difficulty with the support respondent garners from international law is that none of it relates to the practice of nations in relation to extradition treaties. In *Rauscher*, we implied a term in the *Webster-Ashburton Treaty* because of the practice of nations with regard to extradition treaties. In the instant case, respondent would imply terms in the extradition treaty from the practice of nations with regards to international law more generally. Respondent would have us find that the *Treaty* acts as a prohibition against a violation of the general principle of international law that one government may not "exercise its police power in the territory of another state." Brief for Respondent 16. There are many actions which could be taken by a nation that would violate this principle, including waging war, but it cannot seriously be contended an invasion of the United States by Mexico would violate the terms of the extradition treaty between the two nations.

In sum, to infer from this *Treaty* and its terms that it prohibits all means of gaining the presence of an individual outside of its terms goes beyond established precedent and practice. In *Rauscher*, the implication of a doctrine of specialty into the terms of the Webster–Ashburton *Treaty* which, by its terms, required the presentation of evidence establishing probable cause of the crime of extradition before extradition was required, was a small step to take. By contrast, to imply from the terms of this *Treaty* that it prohibits obtaining the presence of an individual by means outside of the procedures the *Treaty* establishes requires a much larger inferential leap, with only the most general of international law principles to support it. The general principles cited by respondent simply fail to persuade us that we should imply in the *United States–Mexico Extradition Treaty* a term prohibiting international abductions.

Respondent and his amici may be correct that respondent's abduction was "shocking," Tr. of Oral Arg. 40, and that it may be in violation of general international law principles. Mexico has protested the abduction of respondent through diplomatic notes, App. 33–38, and the decision of whether respondent should be returned to Mexico, as a matter outside of the *Treaty*, is a matter for the Executive Branch. We conclude, however, that respondent's abduction was not in violation of the *Extradition Treaty between the United States and Mexico*, and therefore the rule of *Ker* v. *Illinois* is fully applicable to this case. The fact of respondent's forcible abduction does not therefore prohibit his trial in a court in the United States for violations of the criminal laws of the United States.

The judgment of the Court of Appeals is therefore reversed, and the case is remanded for further proceedings consistent with this opinion. So ordered.

STEVENS, J., dissenting

The Court correctly observes that this case raises a question of first impression.... The case is unique for several reasons. It does not involve an ordinary abduction by a private kidnaper, or bounty hunter, as in Ker v. Illinois, 119 U.S. 436 ... (1886); nor does it involve the apprehension of an American fugitive who committed a crime in one State and sought asylum in another, as in Frisbie v. Collins, 342 U.S. 519 ... (1952). Rather, it involves this country's abduction of another country's citizen; it also involves a violation of the territorial integrity of that other country, with which this country has signed an extradition treaty.

... The *Extradition Treaty* with Mexico is a comprehensive document containing 23 articles and an appendix listing the extraditable offenses covered by the agreement. The parties announced their purpose in the preamble: The two Governments desire "to cooperate more closely in the fight against crime and, to this end, to mutually render better assistance in matters of extradition." From the preamble, through the description of the parties' obligations with respect to offenses committed within as well as beyond the territory of a requesting party, the delineation of the procedures and evidentiary requirements for extradition, the special provisions for political offenses and capital punishment, and other details, the *Treaty* appears to have been designed to cover the entire subject of extradition. Thus, Article 22, entitled "Scope of Application" states that the "*Treaty* shall apply to offenses specified in Article 2 committed before and after this *Treaty* enters into force," and Article 2 directs that "[e]xtradition shall take place, subject to this *Treaty*, for wilful acts which fall within any of [the extraditable offenses listed in] the clauses of the Appendix." Moreover, as noted by the Court, ... Article 9 expressly provides that neither Contracting Party is bound to deliver up its own nationals, although it may do so in its discretion, but if it does not do so, it "shall submit the case to its competent authorities for purposes of prosecution."

Petitioner's claim that the *Treaty* is not exclusive, but permits forcible governmental kidnaping, would transform these, and other, provisions into little more than verbiage. For example, provisions requiring "sufficient" evidence to grant extradition (Art. 3), withholding extradition for political or military offenses (Art. 5), withholding extradition when the person sought has already been tried (Art. 6), withholding extradition when the statute of limitations for the crime has lapsed (Art. 7), and granting the requested State discretion to refuse to extradite an individual who would face the death penalty in the requesting country (Art. 8), would serve little purpose if the requesting country could simply kidnap the person. As the Court of Appeals for the Ninth Circuit recognized in a related case, "[e]ach of these provisions would be utterly frustrated if a kidnapping were held to be a permissible course of governmental conduct." United States v. Verdugo–Urquidez, 939 F.2d 1341, 1349 (1991). In addition, all of these provisions "only make sense if they are understood as requiring each treaty signatory to comply with those procedures whenever it wishes to obtain jurisdiction over an individual who is located in another treaty nation." *Id.*, at 1351.

It is true, as the Court notes, that there is no express promise by either party to refrain from forcible abductions in the territory of the other Nation.... Relying on that omission, the Court, in effect, concludes that the *Treaty* merely creates an optional method of obtaining jurisdiction over alleged offenders, and that the parties silently reserved the right to resort to self help whenever they deem force more expeditious than legal process. If the United States, for example, thought it more expedient to torture or simply to execute a person rather than to attempt extradition, these options would be equally available because they, too, were not explicitly prohibited by the *Treaty*. That, however, is a highly improbable interpretation of a consensual agreement, which on its face appears to have been intended to set forth comprehensive and exclusive rules concerning the subject of extradition. In my opinion, "the manifest scope and object of the treaty itself," *Rauscher,* 119 U.S. at 422 ... , plainly imply a mutual undertaking to respect the territorial integrity of the other contracting party....

... It is shocking that a party to an extradition treaty might believe that it has secretly reserved the right to make seizures of citizens in the other party's territory. Justice Story found it shocking enough that the United States would attempt to justify an American seizure of a foreign vessel in a Spanish port:

> "But, even supposing, for a moment, that our laws had required an entry of the Apollon, in her transit, does it follow, that the power to arrest her was meant to be given, after she had passed into the exclusive territory of a foreign nation? We think not. It would be monstrous to suppose that our revenue officers were authorized to enter into foreign ports and territories, for the purpose of seizing vessels which had offended against our laws. It cannot be presumed that Congress would voluntarily justify such a clear violation of the laws of nations." *The Apollon*, 9 Wheat. 362, 370–371 ... (1824) (emphasis added).

The law of nations, as understood by Justice Story in 1824, has not changed. Thus, a leading treatise explains: "A State must not perform acts of sovereignty in the territory of another State....

> "It is ... a breach of International Law for a State to send its agents to the territory of another State to apprehend persons accused of having committed a crime. Apart from other satisfaction, the first duty of the offending State is to hand over the person in question to the State in whose territory he was apprehended." 1 OPPENHEIM'S INTERNATIONAL LAW 295, and n.1 (H. Lauterpacht 8th ed. 1955).

Commenting on the precise issue raised by this case, the chief reporter for the American Law Institute's RESTATEMENT OF FOREIGN RELATIONS used language reminiscent of Justice Story's characterization of an official seizure in a foreign jurisdiction as "monstrous:"

"When done without consent of the foreign government, abducting a person from a foreign country is a gross violation of international law and gross disrespect for a norm high in the opinion of mankind. It is a blatant violation of the territorial integrity of another state; it eviscerates the extradition system (established by a comprehensive network of treaties involving virtually all states)."

... A critical flaw pervades the Court's entire opinion. It fails to differentiate between the conduct of private citizens, which does not violate any treaty obligation, and conduct expressly authorized by the Executive Branch of the Government, which unquestionably constitutes a flagrant violation of international law, and in my opinion, also constitutes a breach of our treaty obligations. Thus, at the outset of its opinion, the Court states the issue as "whether a criminal defendant, abducted to the United States from a nation with which it has an extradition treaty, thereby acquires a defense to the jurisdiction of this country's courts.".... That, of course, is the question decided in Ker v. Illinois, 119 U.S. 436 ... (1886); it is not, however, the question presented for decision today.

The importance of the distinction between a court's exercise of jurisdiction over either a person or property that has been wrongfully seized by a private citizen, or even by a state law enforcement agent, on the one hand, and the attempted exercise of jurisdiction predicated on a seizure by federal officers acting beyond the authority conferred by treaty, on the other hand, is explained by Justice Brandeis in his opinion for the Court in Cook v. United States, 288 U.S. 102 ... (1933). That case involved a construction of a prohibition era treaty with Great Britain that authorized American agents to board certain British vessels to ascertain whether they were engaged in importing alcoholic beverages. A British vessel was boarded 11 ½ miles off the coast of Massachusetts, found to be carrying unmanifested alcoholic beverages, and taken into port. The Collector of Customs assessed a penalty which he attempted to collect by means of libels against both the cargo and the seized vessel. The Court held that the seizure was not authorized by the treaty because it occurred more than 10 miles off shore. The Government argued that the illegality of the seizure was immaterial because, as in *Ker*, the Court's jurisdiction was supported by possession even if the seizure was wrongful. Justice Brandeis acknowledged that the argument would succeed if the seizure had been made by a private party without authority to act for the Government, but that a different rule prevails when the Government itself lacks the power to seize....

The same reasoning was employed by Justice Miller to explain why the holding in *Rauscher* did not apply to the *Ker* case. The arresting officer in *Ker* did not pretend to be acting in any official capacity when he kidnaped Ker. As Justice Miller noted, "the facts show that it was a clear case of kidnapping within the dominions of Peru, without any pretence of authority under the treaty or from the government of the United States." *Ker* v. *Illinois*, 119 U.S., at 443.... The exact opposite is true in this case, as it was in *Cook*.

The Court's failure to differentiate between private abductions and official invasions of another sovereign's territory also accounts for its misplaced reliance on the 1935 proposal made by the Advisory Committee on Research in International Law.... As the text of that proposal plainly states, it would have rejected the rule of the *Ker* case. The failure to adopt that recommendation does not speak to the issue the Court decides today. The Court's admittedly "shocking" disdain for customary and conventional international law principles ... , is thus entirely unsupported by case law and commentary....

The significance of this Court's precedents is illustrated by a recent decision of the Court of Appeal of the Republic of South Africa. Based largely on its understanding of the import of this Court's cases—including our decision in *Ker* v. *Illinois*—that court held that the prosecution of a defendant kidnaped by agents of South Africa in another country must be dismissed. *S* v. *Ebrahim*, S.Afr.L.Rep. (Apr.-June 1991). The Court of Appeal of South Africa—indeed, I suspect most courts throughout the civilized world—will be deeply disturbed by the "monstrous" decision the Court announces today. For every Nation that has an interest in preserving the Rule of Law is affected, directly or indirectly, by a decision of this character. As Thomas Paine warned, an "avidity to punish is always dangerous to liberty" because it leads a Nation "to stretch, to misinterpret, and to misapply even the best of laws." To counter that tendency, he reminds us:

> "He that would make his own liberty secure must guard even his enemy from oppression; for if he violates this duty he establishes a precedent that will reach to himself."....

Notes and Questions

1. Do you agree with the majority's opinion or the dissent, or with portions thereof? Which arguments do you find most persuasive? The majority opinion stated that it was deciding on a narrow ground. Did that ground include attention to treaties other than the bilateral extradition treaty, customary international law, or the Fifth Amendment to the U.S. Constitution?

2. Using the majority's approach to interpretation of the bilateral extradition treaty and recalling the point of Justice Stevens concerning silence or omitted language, do you think that assassination is also permissible? If so, why? If not, why, and do you agree with the majority's interpretive approach? *See also* citations in note 4 below and articles 31 and 32 of the Vienna Convention on the Law of Treaties (1969) (utilizing especially "the ordinary meaning to be given to the terms of the treaty in their context and in light of its object and purpose" and "any relevant rules of international law").

3. Upon remand, the defendant argued that, the extradition treaty aside, the abduction nevertheless was a violation of other international laws and that *Ker*, therefore, did not control. *See* United States v. Alvarez–Machain, 971 F.2d 310 (9th Cir.1992). The Court of Appeals, however, ruled that the Supreme Court's decision and its reliance on *Ker* were nevertheless

controlling. Ironically, after the question of jurisdiction in the case had been considered by the Supreme Court and twice by the Court of Appeals, the District Court ultimately dismissed the charges against Alvarez–Machain on the ground that the prosecution had failed to produce adequate proof of its charges. *See* Seth Mydons, *Judge Clears Mexican in Agent's Killing*, N.Y. Times, Dec. 15, 1992, at A20. Recall the earlier note that Alvarez–Machain also sued relevant U.S. officials.

4. For differing views on the Supreme Court's holding in this case or related issues, *see, e.g.*, Secretaria de Relaciones Exteriores, Limits to National Jurisdiction vols. 1 and 2 (Mexico 1992 and 1993); Abraham Abramovsky, *Extraterritorial Abductions: America's Catch and Snatch Policy Run Amok,* 31 Va. J. Int'l L. 151 (1991); Richard Bilder, remarks, 86 Proc., Am. Soc. Int'l L. 451, 454 (1992); Valerie Epps, *Forcible Abduction, Jurisdiction And Treaty Interpretation,* Int'l Pract. Notebook No. 55, at 6 (1992); Joan Fitzpatrick, remarks, 86 Proc., Am. Soc. Int'l L. 451–52 (1992); Michael Glennon, *State-Sponsored Abduction: A Comment on* United States v. Alvarez–Machain, 86 Am. J. Int'l L. 746 (1992); Jimmy Gurulé, *Terrorism, Territorial Sovereignty, and the Forcible Apprehension of International Criminals Abroad,* 17 Hast. Int'l & Comp. L. Rev. 457 (1994); Malvina Halberstam, *In Defense of the Supreme Court Decision in* Alvarez–Machain, 86 *id.* at 736; correspondence, *id.* vol. 87 at 256; remarks, 86 Proc., Am. Soc. Int'l L. 453–54 (1992); Alan Kreczko, remarks, *id.* at 451–52, 454; Monroe Leigh, *Is the President Above Customary International Law?, id.* vol. 86 at 757; Jordan J. Paust, correspondence, *id.* vol. 87 at 252; Paust, *After* Alvarez–Machain, *supra*; John Quigley, *Government Vigilantes at Large: The Danger to Human Rights from Kidnapping of Suspected Terrorists,* 10 Hum. R.Q. 193 (1988); Hernan Ruiz–Bravo, *Monstrous Decision: Kidnapping Is Legal,* 24 Hast. Const. L.Q. 833 (1993); Ruth Wedgwood, remarks, 84 Proc., Am. Soc. Int'l L. 241 (1990).

5. Does *Alvarez-Machain* recognize a general right to abduct abroad, or was the matter framed much more narrowly? Refer to the specific jurisdictional issue outlined by the Chief Justice and his conclusion. Note that the Court stated that the abduction might be "shocking" but that, as a matter outside the treaty, it was a matter for the Executive to decide whether the respondent should be returned to Mexico. *See also* references in note 4 above.

6. Has the Supreme Court's holding in *Alvarez-Machain* foreclosed application of the *Toscanino* exception to nonconsensual extraterritorial abductions? Recall that the court in *Toscanino* based its holding on two separate and independent grounds: (1) the due process clause of the Constitution; and (2) the supervisory power of federal courts over the administration of the federal criminal justice system. With respect to this second ground, the Court stated: "[c]learly this power may legitimately be used to prevent district courts from themselves becoming 'accomplices in wilful disobedience of law.' " *Toscanino*, like *Cook* and *Rauscher*, also focused on the fact that relevant treaties were violated.

The District Court in *Alvarez-Machain* held that there was no evidence that the defendant had been tortured by his abductors, and the issue was not considered by the Supreme Court.

7. For other U.S. cases, *see, e.g.*, Cook v. United States, 288 U.S. 102, 120–21 (1933) (illegal seizure voided); Tucker v. Alexandroff, 183 U.S. 424, 433 (1902); The Paquete Habana, 175 U.S. 677 (1900) (illegal seizure of vessels voided); The Apollon, 22 U.S. (9 Wheat) 362, 370–71 (1824); United States v. Ferris, 19 F.2d 925, 926 (N.D.Cal.1927); United States v. Steinberg, 478 F.Supp. 29, 31, 33 (N.D.Ill.1979) (duty "to observe with good faith and scrupulous care" the U.N. Charter and relevant Security Council resolutions during process of extradition).

8. United States v. Best, 304 F.3d 308 (3rd Cir. 2002), involved a prosecution for attempting to smuggle 33 Chinese nationals into the U.S. Virgin Islands. Defendant Robert Best was arrested on a Brazilian-flag vessel, the *Cordeiro de Deus,* apprehended by the U.S. Coast Guard beyond the 12–nautical-mile U.S. territorial sea. The District Court dismissed the indictment because the United States had not obtained the consent of Brazil before stopping the ship and seizing Best, citing to the 1958 High Seas and Territorial Seas Convention and the 1982 Law of the Sea Convention. The Third Circuit reversed, relying on Frisbie v. Collins, 342 U.S. 519 (1952) and Ker v. Illinois, 119 U.S. 436 (1886), for the proposition that "it is well established that a court's power to try a defendant is ordinarily not affected by the manner in which the defendant is brought to trial."

In the course of its opinion, the Third Circuit noted that the Coast Guard's seizure of Best did "not come close to resembling the 'shocking governmental conduct' that the Second Circuit equated with a violation of due process" in United States v. Toscanino, 500 F.2d 267 (2d Cir. 1974), and added that "the exception described in *Toscanino* rests on shaky ground" because subsequent Supreme Court decisions "indicate that there is reason to doubt the soundness of the *Toscanino* exception." The Third Circuit relied in particular on United States v. Alvarez–Machain, 504 U.S. 655 (1992), which, it said, "held that the rule of *Ker-Frisbie* was fully applicable to a case in which a Mexican national had been forcibly abducted, even though the abduction may have been 'shocking' and in violation of general international law principles."

The Third Circuit also concluded that the exception to the *Ker-Frisbie* rule when a treaty is violated, which was recognized in Ford v. United States, 273 U.S. 593 (1927) and Cook v. United States, 288 U.S. 102 (1933), did not apply because Brazil had not ratified the 1958 High Seas and Territorial Sea Conventions and the United States had not ratified the 1982 Law of the Sea Convention, and hence "[b]ecause none of these are treaties to which both Brazil and the United States are parties, the seizure of Best from the *Cordeiro de Deus* could not have been in violation of any of them,": because the United States has not yet ratified the 1982 Law of the Sea Convention, it "does not have the force of law."

Was the Third Circuit correct in concluding that *Toscanino* now "rests on shaky ground" and that it is inconsistent with the narrow holding in *United States v. Alvarez–Machain*?

9. Alan J. Kreczko, the Deputy Legal Adviser of the Department of State, testified before a House Judiciary Subcommittee about the international reaction to the Supreme Court's opinion in *Alvarez-Machain*:

The Supreme Court's decision has caused considerable concern among a wide range of governments, particularly in the Americans, but elsewhere as well. Many governments have expressed outrage that the United States believes it has the right to decide unilaterally to enter their territory and abduct one of their nationals. Governments have informed us that they would regard such action as a breach of international law. They have also informed us that they would protect their nationals from such action, that such action would violate their domestic law, and that they would vigorously prosecute such violations. Some countries, as well, have told us that they believe that such actions would violate our extradition treaties with them. Some have also suggested that they will challenge the lawfulness of such abductions in international forums. Some have indicated that the decision could affect their parliaments' review of pending law enforcement agreements with the United States....

- The Presidents of Argentina, Bolivia, Brazil, Chile, Paraguay, and Uruguay issued a declaration on June 26 expressing their concern with the U.S. Supreme Court decision and requesting that the Inter–American Juridical Committee of the Organization of American States (OAS) issue an opinion on the "international juridical validity" of the *Alvarez-Machain* decision. That request was made formally to the Permanent Council of the OAS on July 15, which adopted a resolution referring this matter to the Juridical Committee.
- The lower house of the parliament of Uruguay voted on June 30 that the decision shows "a lack of understanding of the most elemental norms of international law, and in particular an absolute perversion of the function of extradition treaties."
- On June 15, the Government of Columbia stated that it "energetically rejects the judgment issued by the United States Supreme Court.... "Although recognizing that the decision dealt only with a treaty between the United States and Mexico, the government felt that "its substance threatens the legal stability of all public treaties."
- The reaction has not been confined, of course, to official government statements. Political leaders in and out of government, and commentaries in the media, have generally criticized the decision and the attitude of the U.S. Government that the decision is supposed to represent....

The Supreme Court's decision led to a rigorous debate in the Canadian Parliament. The Canadian Minister of External Affairs told the Canadian Parliament that any attempt by the United States to kidnap someone in Canada would be regarded as a criminal act and a violation of the U.S. Canada Extradition Treaty. Spain's President publicly criticized the decision as "erroneous." And the media in Europe generally has been critical of the decision.

These negative reactions reflect a concern that the *Alvarez-Machain* decision constitutes a "green light" for international abductions. The reactions are grounded in the desire of countries to preserve their sovereignty and territorial integrity and to reassure their nationals. We expect that countries will continue to press this concern with us, bilaterally and multilaterally. As noted above, this matter has already been brought before the OAS.

The U.S. Government has moved actively to isolate the question of whether domestic legal authority exists from the separate question of whether the President will, in fact, exercise that authority. We have reassured other countries that the United States has not changed its policies toward cooperation in international law enforcement, and that the *Alvarez-Machain* case does not represent a "green light" for the United States to conduct operations on foreign territory.

Specifically, immediately following the Supreme Court's decision, the White House issued a public statement reaffirming that:

> . . . The United States strongly believes in fostering respect for international rules of law, including, in particular, the principles of respect for territorial integrity and sovereign equality of states. U.S. policy is to cooperate with foreign states in achieving law enforcement objectives. Neither the arrest of Alvarez–Machain, nor the . . . Supreme Court decision reflects any change in this policy. . . .

At the same time, we are not prepared categorically to rule out unilateral action. It is not inconceivable that in certain extreme cases, such as the harboring by a hostile foreign country of a terrorist who has attacked U.S. nationals and is likely to do so again, the President might decide that such an abduction is necessary and appropriate as a matter of the exercise of our right of self-defense. This necessary reservation of right for extreme cases does not, however, detract from our strong support for the principles of sovereignty and territorial integrity generally. To reinforce this point, the White House statement also noted the Administration has in place procedures designed to ensure that U.S. law enforcement activities overseas fully take into account foreign relations and international law. These procedures require that decisions as to extraordinary renditions from foreign territory be subject to full inter-agency coordination and that they be considered at the highest levels of the government. . . .

In the aftermath of the *Alvarez-Machain* decision, the Mexican foreign Minister gave a press conference with the following highlights:

- Mexico repudiates as invalid and illegal the decision of the Supreme Court;
- Mexico will consider as a criminal act any attempt by foreign persons or governments to apprehend in Mexican territory any person suspected of a crime;
- Mexico demands the return of Alvarez–Machain;
- Mexico declares that the only legal means for moving persons from one nation to face trial in another are treaties and mechanisms of extradition established under international law;
- Foreign law enforcement officials of any country who operate in Mexican territory will be asked to observe updated rules that the Government of Mexico will establish.

Mexico sought assurances that further abductions will not take place on Mexican territory and stated that collaboration by Mexicans with foreign governments in criminal acts that violate Mexican sovereignty would be classified as acts of treason against Mexico.

The United States has responded to these Mexican concerns as follows:

- President Bush sent a letter to President Salinas containing unequivocal assurances that his Administration will "neither conduct, encourage nor condone" such trans-border abductions from Mexico.
- The two governments agreed to review the U.S.-Mexico Extradition Treaty within the framework of the next U.S.-Mexico Binational Commission meeting this fall, in order to analyze the implications of the recent Supreme Court decision and to avoid any possible repetitions of events such as the abduction of Alvarez–Machain.
- There was an exchange of letters between Secretary Baker and Foreign Secretary Solana of Mexico recognizing that trans-border abductions by so-called "bounty hunters" and other private individuals will be considered extraditable offenses by both nations. Both nations also stated their commitment to continue their efforts to discourage trans-border abductions by state and local officials.
- The two governments are also reviewing the rules governing the conduct of DEA and other U.S. law enforcement officials to ensure full respect for Mexican sovereignty.

3 U.S. Dept. of State Dispatch 614 (1992).

10. In the case of Eichmann, the U.N. Security Council condemned the use of self-help to capture Eichmann. See U.N. S.C. Res. 138, 15 U.N. SCOR, U.N. Doc. S/4349 (1960), cited in United States v. Toscanino, 500 F.2d 267, 276–79 (2d Cir.1974). *See also* U.N. S.C. Res. 579, U.N. Doc. S/Res/579 (1985) (condemns "unequivocally ... all acts of abduction"). Israel expressed regret without admitting direct involvement, Argentina accepted the near apology, and Israel went on with the trial of Eichmann.

11. What powers does the Security Council have to authorize the capture of alleged international criminals in the territory of a state? See U.N. Charter, arts. 25, 39–45, 48–49, 103. Can the Security Council lawfully order such a state to hand over the accused to another state or to an international tribunal? Do these powers override other international agreements? See also Article 29 (2)(e) of the Statute of the International Tribunal for the Former Yugoslavia, adopted by U.N. S.C. Res. 827 (25 May 1993) ("States shall comply without undue delay with any request for assistance or an order issued by a Trial Chamber, including ... the surrender or the transfer of the accused to the International Tribunal.").

12. With respect to judicial power and responsibilities, Professor Paust adds: "Certain extraordinary circumstances ... [noted above] pose reasonable exceptions to a flat prohibition of the use of force to arrest persons in foreign territory without foreign state consent. Nonetheless, absent such extraordinary circumstances, transnational abductions recognizably constitute violations of several international norms, including those providing relevant rights of the individual victim of an abduction.... [A]ll of this assumes an executive branch willing to abide by customary and treaty-based international law, and thus the mandate of Article II, Section 3 of the United States Constitution, and an executive branch capable of making fine point

distinctions with respect to the context and relevant legal policies at stake. When it becomes evident that this is not the case, when the executive claims to be above the law and able to act in lawless disregard of its duty under the Constitution, the need for judicial review, indeed judicial supervisory power, becomes all the more necessary in a free society.... Ultimately, this quest for unbounded power threatens much more than law and justice or our own rights and liberties. Ultimately, this quest for power uncontrolled by law is subversive of constitutional democracy." Paust, *After* Alvarez–Machain, *supra*, at 577–78.

13. In United States v. Yunis, 681 F.Supp. 909, 914–5 (D.D.C.1988) [addressed above in connection with principles of jurisdiction], the accused was lured from Lebanon to Cyprus by a friend who had been co-opted by the United States Drug Enforcement Administration and the CIA. He was arrested on a boat in international waters off the coast of Cyprus by an FBI agent who was posing as a drug dealer, for whom Yunis thought he would be working. Yunis was transferred to a U.S. Navy communications vessel, from there to the U.S. aircraft carrier "Saratoga" and finally by non-stop Navy jet to Andrews Air Force Base outside of Washington, D.C. Yunis' arrest had been authorized by a United States magistrate. He had, with others, hijacked a Royal Jordanian Airlines aircraft in Beirut, Lebanon which was eventually blown up. The prosecution in the United States was founded on legislation contained in 18 U.S.C.A. § 2331 entitled "Terrorist Acts Against U.S. Nationals." Yunis was found guilty and sentenced to 30 years in prison. How is the *Yunis* case different from *Toscanino* and *Alvarez-Machain*? Should luring or trickery be treated like abduction? See JORDAN J. PAUST, M. CHERIF BASSIOUNI, *ET AL.*, INTERNATIONAL CRIMINAL LAW 436–53 (2 ed. 2000). Would the flag or registry of the vessel that Yunis was lured onto be important for enforcement jurisdiction? Recall RESTATEMENT §§ 432–433; and see Paust, *After* Alvarez–Machain, *supra* at 568–69 n.65. Does it make a difference that Yunis was wanted for aircraft hijacking, sabotage, and hostage-taking?

SECTION 4. EXTRADITION

Introductory Problem

Willie Makeit, a U.S. businessman, escaped from an Iraqi prison in December of 1998 during the regime of Saddam Hussein while U.S. and British warplanes bombed military targets inside Iraq. Willie had been convicted in a military tribunal for "crimes against the state and the Iraqi people" allegedly involving espionage. The U.S. had officially protested his trial and imprisonment as "a sham prosecution" involving "serious human rights violations during trial and his incarceration."

The new Iraqi government now has an extradition treaty with the U.S. similar to the U.S.-Canadian agreements reproduced in this chapter. The new government has requested the U.S. to extradite Willie to Iraq to stand trial for illegal business practices leading to the "reaping of grossly excessive profits" and for the killing of an Iraqi prison guard during his escape (the charge is involuntary manslaughter). Is Willie "extraditable"? Should the U.S. extradite him to Iraq?

A. *U.S. Extradition Law*

18 U.S.C.

§ 3181. Scope and limitation of chapter

The provisions of this chapter relating to the surrender of persons who have committed crimes in foreign countries shall continue in force only during the existence of any treaty of extradition with such foreign government. . . .

§ 3184. Fugitives from foreign country to United States

Whenever there is a treaty or convention for extradition between the United States and any foreign government, any justice or judge of the United States, or any magistrate authorized so to do by a court of the United States, or any judge of a court of record of general jurisdiction of any Sate, may, upon complaint made under oath, charging any person found within his jurisdiction, with having committed within the jurisdiction of any such foreign government any of the crimes provided for by such treaty or convention, issue his warrant for the apprehension of the person so charged, that he may be brought before such justice, judge, or magistrate, to the end that the evidence of criminality may be heard and considered. Such complaint may be filed before and such warrant may be issued by a judge or magistrate of the United States District court for the District of Columbia if the whereabouts within the United States of the person charged are not known. If, on such hearing, he deems the evidence sufficient to sustain the charge under the provisions of the proper treaty or convention, he shall certify the same, together with a copy of all the testimony taken before him, to the Secretary of State, that a warrant may issue upon the requisition of the proper authorities of such foreign government, for the surrender of such person, according to the stipulations of the treaty or convention; and he shall issue his warrant for the commitment of the person so charged to the proper jail, there to remain until such surrender shall be made. . . .

§ 3189. Place and character of hearing

Hearings in cases of extradition under treaty stipulation or convention shall be held on land, publicly, and in a room or office easily accessible to the public.

§ 3190. Evidence on hearing

Depositions, warrants, or other papers or copies thereof offered in evidence upon the hearing of any extradition case shall be received and admitted as evidence on such hearing for all the purposes of such hearing if they shall be properly and legally authenticated so as to entitle them to be received for similar purposes by the tribunals of the foreign country from which the accused party shall have escaped, and the certificate of the principal diplomatic or consular officer of the United States resident in such foreign country shall be proof that the same, so offered, are authenticated in the manner required. . . .

§ 3195. Payment of fees and costs

All costs or expenses incurred in any extradition proceeding in apprehending, securing, and transmitting a fugitive shall be paid by the demanding authority.

All witness fees and costs of every nature in cases of international extradition, including the fees of the magistrate, shall be certified by the judge or magistrate before whom the hearing shall take place to the Secretary of State of the United States, and the same shall be paid out of appropriations to defray the expenses of the judiciary or the Department of Justice as the case may be.

The Attorney General shall certify to the Secretary of State the amounts to be paid to the United States on account of said fees and costs in extradition cases by the foreign government requesting the extradition, and the Secretary of State shall cause said amounts to be collected and transmitted to the Attorney General for deposit in the Treasury of the United States.

Notes and Questions

1. As indicated in the statute, the U.S. may extradite only pursuant to an extradition treaty. *See also* Valentine v. United States *ex rel.* Neidecker, 299 U.S. 5 (1936); Restatement § 475, cmt. b and RN 3. Nonetheless, it is permissible for the U.S. to receive an accused without a treaty-based extradition (if no international norms are violated). Restatement § 475, RN 3. Some countries do not need a treaty to extradite. Restatement § 475, cmt. b.

2. Can an executive agreement constitute a "treaty" for purposes of extradition from the U.S., *e.g.*, for purposes of §§ 3181 and 3184 of the U.S. legislation? The word "treaty" in some U.S. statutes has been interpreted to include executive agreements. *See, e.g.*, Restatement §§ 111, RN 4, 303, RN 1. The United States entered into two treaty-executive agreements with the International Criminal Tribunals for Former Yugoslavia and for Rwanda for the purpose of rendering accused to the Tribunals. The executive agreements are based ultimately on the authority of the U.N. Charter and Security Council resolutions setting up the Tribunals and their competencies. *See generally*, Robert Kushen, Kenneth J. Harris, *Surrender of Fugitives by the United States to the War Crimes Tribunals for Yugoslavia and Rwanda*, 90 Am. J. Int'l L. 510 (1996); correspondence, *id.* vol. 91, at 90 (1997).

In Ntakirutimana v. Reno, 184 F.3d 419 (5th Cir. 1999), *cert. denied*, 528 U.S. 1135 (2000), Circuit Judge Garza ruled that the 1995 executive agreement with the ICTR, coupled with a 1996 statute "to implement the Agreement" (National Defense Authorization Act, Pub. L. 104–106, § 1342, 110 Stat. 486 (1996)), provided a constitutional basis for extradition of Ntakirutimana, a former President of the Seventh Day Adventist Church for Rwanda, to the ICTR to stand trial on charges of genocide, complicity in genocide, conspiracy to commit genocide, crimes against humanity, and serious violations of Article 3 common to the Geneva Conventions and of Additional Protocol II thereto. The opinion noted that *Valentine* had stated that " '[t]here is no executive discretion to surrender ... unless that discretion is granted by law ... by an act of Congress or by the terms of a treaty' "; that *Valentine* concluded that the President's " 'power, in the absence of [a] statute conferring an independent power, must be found in the terms of the treaty ...' "; and that *Valentine* "supports the constitutionality of using the Congressional–Executive Agreement to extradite...." *Id.* at 425. Was the agreement a congressional-treaty-executive agreement?

3. Since there is no duty under customary international law to extradite (RESTATEMENT § 475 cmt. a), there is a need for consent of the requested state—either ad hoc (for countries that do not need a treaty-base) or by a bilateral or multilateral agreement. *See also Ex parte* dos Santos, 7 F.Cas. 949, 953–56 (C.C.D. Va. 1835) (No. 4,016) (no duty to extradite without a treaty); 1 Op. Att'y Gen. 521 (1821). Normally, there is a bilateral extradition treaty forming the basis of consent.

4. Bilateral treaties to which the United States is a party typically contain a list of extraditable offenses. When the treaty contains a list, the listed offenses are liberally construed to support extradition. Yet, under the customary "speciality" doctrine (read into any extradition treaty), the accused can be extradited, and then prosecuted, only for a listed offense (and one for which the accused has been extradited, unless there is a subsequent waiver by the requested or extraditing state). *See, e.g.,* United States v. Rauscher, 119 U.S. 407, 411–12 (1886); RESTATEMENT § 477. Other doctrines or requirements that are a part of customary international law (and thus background with respect to any extradition treaty), include the requirement of dual or double criminality (explored below), the political offense exception to extradition (explored below), and the extraditability of nationals of the requested state (changed by bilateral treaty exceptions, if applicable). Concerning their customary nature, *see, e.g.,* RESTATEMENT § 475, cmt. f (nationals), § 476 & cmts. a, d, g (re: dual criminality and the political offense exception).

Recall, however, that Judge Cassese in the *Tadic* case before the Appeals Chamber of the ICTY quoted the Court of Cassation of France in the *Barbie* case for the proposition that "extradition rules" arising from municipal law are "completely foreign" to "an international criminal order." This chapter, Section 2. Should the doctrines of dual criminality or speciality preclude extradition or prosecution of persons accused of international crimes when states have a duty under customary international law or a particular treaty to initiate prosecution of or extradite persons reasonably accused of such crimes? If the requested state has failed to enact needed domestic legislation as required by another treaty for prosecution of the international crime (as in Articles I and V of the Genocide Convention), can the requested state rightly insist that it cannot extradite because the crime is not a domestic crime within the requested state? If the accused is extradited for some other crime, can the requested state rightly insist that the receiving state cannot prosecute the international crime even though such state also has a duty to initiate prosecution of or extradite persons accused of such international crime and has enacted legislation to prosecute such crime? If so, would this provide a functional immunity for international crime? Should the requested state be able to impose the consequences of its own breach of international law on other states? More generally, recall that a state party to a treaty cannot set up its own breach of that treaty or some other international obligation as an excuse for nonperformance or a claimed impossibility. *See, e.g.*, Vienna Convention on the Law of Treaties, arts. 26, 61(2), in Chapter 1. Further, "[a] party may not invoke the provisions of its internal law as justification for its failure to perform the treaty." *Id.* art. 27.

5. The United States is a party to the Multilateral Convention on Extradition signed at Montevideo on Dec. 26, 1933, entered into force for the U.S. on Jan. 25, 1935. 49 Stat. 3111. Other state signatories include: Argentina, Chile, Colombia, Dominican Republic, Ecuador, El Salvador, Guatemala, Honduras, Mexico, Nicaragua, Panama.

6. Several other multilateral treaties exist which allow states to treat such an agreement as an extradition treaty. These are especially relevant to international criminal law. *See, e.g.,* Article 10(2) of the 1979 International Convention Against the Taking of Hostages. Article 10(1) adds that the offenses therein "shall be deemed to be included as extraditable offences in any extradition treaty existing between States Parties." *See also* RESTATEMENT § 475, RN 5.

7. An offense committed prior to the existence of an extradition treaty can be covered by the new treaty or new amendment (and without violating ex post facto prohibitions). *See, e.g.,* Factor v. Laubenheimer, 290 U.S. 276, 304 (1933); *In re* Giacomo, 7 F. Cas. 366, 369–70 (C.C.S.D.N.Y.1874) (No. 3,747); Demjanjuk v. Petrovsky, in this chapter; RESTATEMENT § 476, cmt. b; Jordan J. Paust, *Extradition and United States Prosecution of the* Achille Lauro *Hostage-Takers: Navigating the Hazards,* 20 VAND. J. TRANSNAT'L. L. 235, 238 n.9 (1987).

8. In United States v. Duarte–Acero, 208 F.3d 1282 (11th Cir. 2000), the Eleventh Circuit recognized that although the International Covenant on Civil and Political Rights guarantees the human right to freedom from double jeopardy, such does not apply to prosecutions by two different sovereigns, adding that the Rome Statute for the ICC creates a different form of *non bis in idem* and noting the ICCPR Human Rights Committee's view in A.P. v. Italy (2 Nov. 1987) (no double jeopardy for Italy to prosecute a person convicted in Switzerland for acts arising from the same conduct). Colombia had refused to extradite the defendant to the U.S. "apparently citing the *non bis in idem* clause of the extradition treaty then in effect between the United States and Colombia" when he had already been prosecuted in Colombia. The defendant had been lured into Equador, where he was arrested.

UNITED STATES v. PUENTES

50 F.3D 1567 (11TH CIR.1995).

HATCHETT, J.

The government correctly points out that this circuit has not squarely addressed the issue of whether a defendant has standing to assert a violation of an extradition treaty. When faced with appellants' challenges to extradition, this court has assumed, without deciding, that the appellants had standing to bring the claim. *See, e.g.,* United States v. Herbage, 850 F.2d 1463, 1466 (11th Cir.1988), *cert. denied,* 489 U.S. 1027 (1989); United States v. Lehder–Rivas, 955 F.2d 1510, 1520 n. 7 (11th Cir.), *cert. denied,* Reed v. United States, 113 S.Ct. 347 (1992)....

Under the doctrine of speciality, a nation that receives a criminal defendant pursuant to an extradition treaty may try the defendant only for those offenses for which the other nation granted extradition. *Herbage,* 850 F.2d at 1465; M. BASSIOUNI, INTERNATIONAL EXTRADITION: UNITED STATES LAW AND PRACTICE, vol. 1, ch. 7, p. 359–60 (2d rev. ed. 1987)....

Extradition is "the surrender by one nation to another of an individual accused or convicted of an offense outside of its own territory, and within the territorial jurisdiction of the other, which, being competent to try and to punish him, demands the surrender." Terlinden v. Ames, 184 U.S. 270, 289 (1902). As a matter of international law, however, nations are under no legal obligation to surrender a fugitive from justice in the absence of a treaty. BASSIOUNI, at 319; Factor v. Laubenheimer, 290 U.S. 276, 287 (1933). An extradition treaty is, therefore, a cooperative agreement between two governments for the prosecution and punishment of criminal offenders. *See* BASSIOUNI, at 319. Extradition treaties typically specify certain offenses for which extradition will be granted as between the two respective nations. Upon receipt of an extradition request, the surrendering nation may examine the substance of each of the charges specified in the request, and may choose to grant extradition for only the extraditable offenses listed in the treaty....

In United States v. Rauscher, 119 U.S. 407 (1886), the Court drew a distinction between this country's treatment of a treaty and other countries in which a treaty is essentially a contract between two nations. Under our Constitution, the Court explained, a treaty is the law of the land and the equivalent of an act of the legislature. *Rauscher,* 119 U.S. at 418. The Court's opinion suggests that the rights described in the treaty are conferred on both the extradited individual and the respective governments. The Court stated:

> *[A] treaty may also contain provisions which confer certain rights upon the citizens* or subjects of one of the nations residing in the territorial limits of the other, which partake of the nature of municipal law, and *which are capable of enforcement as between private parties in the courts of the country*.... The Constitution of the United States places such provisions as these in the same category as other laws of Congress, by its declaration that "This Constitution and the laws made in pursuance thereof, and all treaties made or which shall be made under authority of the United States, shall be the supreme law of the land." A treaty, then, is a law of the land, as an Act of Congress is, whenever its provisions prescribe a rule by which the *rights of the private citizen or subject may be determined.* And when such rights are of a nature to be enforced in a court of justice, that court resorts to the treaty for a rule of decision for the case before it as it would to a statute.

Rauscher, 119 U.S. at 418–19 (*quoting* Chew Heong v. United States, 112 U.S. 536 (1884)) (emphasis added)....

All of the circuit courts of appeals have not embraced the holding we announce today. Other courts have held that an extradited individual lacks standing to assert the doctrine of specialty in the absence of an express objection on the part of the requested nation. Invariably, the courts that adhere to this rule consider the principle of specialty to be a matter of international law that inures solely to the benefit of the requested nation, protects its dignity and interests, and confers no rights on the accused. *Cf.* Shapiro v. Ferrandina, 478 F.2d 894, 906 (2d Cir.), *cert. dismissed,* 414 U.S. 884 (1973). These courts have taken the international law rule of construction that only nations may enforce treaty obligations, and inferred that an individual cannot, therefore, assert any rights under a treaty in our national courts. This analysis is flawed, we submit, because it ignores both the history of the concept of extradition and *Rauscher*.

As we stated earlier, extradition is not a part of customary international law. Therefore, in order to broaden the reach of their criminal justice systems, two nations may enter into a cooperative agreement for the exchange of criminal suspects: an extradition contract. *See* Geofroy v. Riggs, 133 U.S. 258, 271 . . . (1890) (characterizing treaties as contracts between nations). The doctrine of specialty is but one of the provisions of this contract. Of course, the rights conferred under the contract ultimately belong to the contracting parties, the signatory nations. This does not mean, however, that provisions of the contract may not confer certain rights under the contract on a non-party who is the object of the contract. We believe that *Rauscher* clearly confers such a right on the extradited defendant. The extradited individual's rights, however, need not be cast in stone; rather, the individual may enjoy these protections only at the sufferance of the requested nation. The individual's rights are derivative of the rights of the requested nation. We believe that *Rauscher* demonstrates that even in the absence of a protest from the requested state, an individual extradited pursuant to a treaty has standing to challenge the court's personal jurisdiction under the rule of specialty. The courts which have adopted the contrary holding, in effect, consider the requested state's objection to be a condition precedent to the individual's ability to raise the claim. We believe the Supreme Court's recent opinion in United States v. Alvarez–Machain, 504 U.S. 655 (1992) seriously undermines any vitality that approach may have once possessed.

A grand jury indicted Humberto Alvarez–Machain, a citizen and resident of Mexico, for participating in the kidnap and murder of United States Drug Enforcement Administration (DEA) special agent Enrique Camarena–Salazar. Following unsuccessful informal negotiations between the United States and Mexico to obtain Alvarez–Machain's presence in this country, DEA successfully contracted with certain individuals for Alvarez–Machain's forcible kidnap and delivery to the United States. Alvarez–Machain contested the district court's personal jurisdiction over him on the grounds that his abduction violated the extradition treaty between the United States and Mexico. The district court granted his request and ordered his return to Mexico. The court of appeals affirmed the district court. The Supreme Court reversed.

The actual holding of the case is that Alvarez–Machain could not contest the court's jurisdiction over him under the extradition treaty because he was not extradited pursuant to treaty proceedings. The Court's analysis, however, rejects the premise underlying the cases that require the requested nation to object as a condition precedent to the individual's ability to claim the benefits of the rule of specialty.

In *Alvarez-Machain,* the Court rejected the Court of Appeals's reasoning that found that the extradition treaty prohibited forcible abduction, but that the abducted individual could only raise the issue if the offended government had formally protested. In rejecting the notion of conditionally self-executing treaty provisions, the Court explained that "if the [e]xtradition [t]reaty has the force of law ... it would appear that a court must enforce it on behalf of an individual *regardless of the offensiveness of the practice of one nation to the other nation.*" *Alvarez-Machain,* 504 U.S. at 667 (emphasis added). Importantly, the Court cited *Rauscher* in support of this proposition:

> In *Rauscher,* the Court noted that Great Britain had taken the position in other cases that the Webster–Ashburton Treaty included the doctrine of specialty, *but no importance was attached to whether or not Great Britain had protested the prosecution of Rauscher for the crime of cruel and unusual punishment as opposed to murder.*

Alvarez-Machain, 504 U.S. at 667 ... (emphasis added). *Alvarez-Machain* demonstrates the infirmity in the reasoning of those cases which require an affirmative protest by the requested nation in order for the extradited individual to contest personal jurisdiction under the rule of specialty.

We, therefore, hold that an individual extradited pursuant to an extradition treaty has standing under the doctrine of specialty to raise any objections which the requested nation might have asserted. The extradited individual, however, enjoys this right at the sufferance of the requested nation. As a sovereign, the requested nation may waive its right to object to a treaty violation and thereby deny the defendant standing to object to such an action.

Notes and Questions

1. Is the court correct in its criticism of those circuits that hold that a defendant lacks standing to challenge his extradition on doctrine of specialty grounds absent a protest by the asylum nation (*i.e.*, that individual rights are merely derivative)? The *Puentes* court stated:

> These courts have taken the international law rule of construction that only nations may enforce treaty obligations, and inferred that an individual cannot, therefore, assert any rights under a treaty in our national courts. This analysis is flawed, we submit, because it ignores both the history of the concept of extradition and *Rauscher*. 50 F.3d at 1574.

Do you agree with the court's statement? See RESTATEMENT § 477, cmt. b; Jordan J. Paust, *After* Alvarez–Machain*: Abduction, Standing, Denials of Justice, and Unaddressed Human Rights Claims,* 67 ST. JOHN'S L. REV. 551, 555–58, 568–74 (1993). Is there a general "rule of construction" that treaties are agreements between contracting nations which confer no rights on private parties? *See generally* Chapters 1 and 2; J. PAUST, INTERNATIONAL LAW AS LAW OF THE UNITED STATES chpts. 2, 3, 5–7 (2ed. 2003). Do extradition treaties confer rights on third parties, who are non-signatories (or their nationals) to the treaty? Professor Bassiouni adds: "only the Second and Seventh Circuits currently require a protest by the requesting state before allowing the relator to raise the issue of speciality. The broader question concerns standing of individuals to raise other extradition treaty-related issues." *Id.* at 285; *see also id.* at 351–52.

2. In contrast to the Second (see *Shapiro*), Fifth (see United States v. Kaufman, 874 F.2d 242, 242 (5th Cir. 1989)), and Seventh Circuits, the Eighth, Ninth, Tenth, and Eleventh Circuits hold that the defendant may raise whatever objections the extraditing country is entitled to raise even absent an objection by the extraditing nation. *See* United States v. Thirion, 813 F.2d 146, 150 (8th Cir.1987) (defendant may raise whatever objections to his prosecution that the surrendering country might have); United States v. Andonian, 29 F.3d 1432, 1435 (9th Cir.1994) ("An extradited person may raise whatever objections the extraditing country is entitled to raise."); *accord* United States v. Cuevas, 847 F.2d 1417, 1426 (9th Cir.1988), *cert. denied*, 489 U.S. 1012 (1989); United States v. Najohn, *supra*; Abello–Silva, 948 F.2d at 1172; United States v. Levy, 905 F.2d 326, 328 n. 1 (10th Cir.1990) (same), *cert. denied*, 498 U.S. 1049 (1991); United States v. Puentes, 50 F.3d 1567, 1573 (11th Cir.1995); United States v. Herbage, 850 F.2d 1463, 1466 (11th Cir.1988) ("For purposes of this case, we assume, without deciding, that an individual has standing to allege a violation of the specialty principle."), *cert. denied*, 489 U.S. 1027 (1989).

3. Should silence or failure to object constitute a waiver by a state of any of its interests concerning a violation under the extradition treaty?

B. The Canada–U.S. Treaties

Treaty on Extradition Between the Government of Canada and the Government of the United States of America

[read the Treaty and Protocol thereto in the Documents Supplement]

Notes and Questions

1. The most important provisions of the 1971 Canada–U.S. Extradition Treaty can be summarized as follows: Article 2 of the treaty (together with the annexed Schedule) specifies what is to be considered an extraditable offense. Article 3 provides that the treaty shall apply to extraterritorial offenses as well as offenses committed within the territory of the requesting state. Article 4 sets forth the following exceptions to the treaty: double jeopardy (known internationally as "non bis in idem"); statute of limitations; and the political offense exception. Article 5 grants the requested state the option of denying extradition of its residents who are under 18 years of age. Article 6 grants the requested state the option of denying extradition

when the charge is punishable by death, unless the requesting state provides an assurance that the death penalty shall not be imposed. Article 9 specifies the documentation that is required for an extradition request and Article 10 sets forth the standard of proof applicable to the extradition proceedings. Article 11 governs provisional arrest. Article 12 codifies the "specialty doctrine."

2. Note that the 1971 Canada–U.S. Extradition Treaty contained a schedule of extraditable offenses. Pursuant to Article 2 of the Treaty, only crimes that were specifically listed in the Schedule were considered extraditable offenses. What serious crimes are missing from this list?

3. In 1988, the United States and Canada signed a Protocol to the treaty, which among other things substitutes a dual criminality clause for the schedule of offenses. A dual criminality clause permits extradition for any crime that is punishable in both countries by imprisonment or other detention for at least one year. This obviates the need to renegotiate or supplement the treaty as new offenses become punishable under the laws of both states. In addition, Article I of the Protocol allows the United States to request extradition of offenses including interstate mail fraud or interstate transportation in aid of racketeering enterprises even though the Canadian laws do not include analogous jurisdictional elements for similar underlying criminal behavior.

4. While the dual criminality principle employed in Article 2 of the Protocol Amending the Canada–U.S. Extradition Treaty requires that the offense charged be punishable as a serious crime in both countries, the requesting and requested countries need not have identical penal statutes. *See generally* RESTATEMENT § 476, cmt. d and RNs 1 & 2. In *Collins v. Loisel*, 259 U.S. 309 (1922), the Supreme Court stated:

> The law does not require that the name by which the crime is described in the two countries shall be the same; nor that the scope of the liability shall be coextensive, or, in other respects, the same in the two countries. It is enough if the particular act charged is criminal in both jurisdictions.

Id. at 312. The primary focus is on the "acts of the defendant, not on the legal doctrines of the country requesting extradition." United States v. Sensi, 879 F.2d 888, 893 (D.C.Cir.1989). "If the acts upon which the charges of the requesting country are based are also proscribed by a law of the requested nation, the requirement of double criminality is satisfied." Demjanjuk v. Petrovsky, 776 F.2d 571, 579–80 (6th Cir.1985), *cert. denied*, 475 U.S. 1016 (1986). The mere fact that the crime charged in the requesting state is not a crime under the laws of the asylum country does not defeat extradition, so long as the alleged acts are prohibited under foreign law. "The fact that a particular act is classified differently in the criminal law of the two states does not prevent extradition under the double criminality rule." *Sensi*, 879 F.2d at 893.

5. Note that Article III of the Protocol Amending the Canada–U.S. extradition treaty reproduced above allows the requested State to grant extradition for an offense committed outside the requesting State even if the requested State's laws do not have a similar extraterritorial reach. What is

the importance of this provision? Consider the following excerpt from the 1975 Digest of United States Practice in International Law 177:

> The Department of State informed the Embassy of the Federal Republic of Germany, in a note dated November 11, 1975, that it was not possible to comply with the Embassy's request for the provisional arrest for extradition to Germany of four foreign crewmen for the alleged murder on October 10, 1975, of four German officers on board the vessel *Mimi* on the high seas. The Department's note stated, in part:
>
> The Department of State has carefully studied the facts of the case as developed by investigation, and the extradition treaty in force between the United States and the Federal Republic of Germany, and has determined that extradition is not possible in this case because of lack of dual criminality as required by Article I of the treaty. Although it appears that the Federal Republic of Germany would have jurisdiction by its internal law to prosecute fugitives for offenses committed against German citizens outside the territory of the Federal Republic of Germany, the United States under its law may prosecute for offenses committed outside its territory only if the offenses occurred within the special maritime and territorial jurisdiction of the United States as defined in section 7 of Title 18 of the *United States Code*. The United States has no jurisdiction to prosecute fugitives based upon United States citizenship of the victim of the offense.

Dep't. of State File No. P75 0175–0032. The extradition treaty in force between the United States and the Federal Republic of Germany was signed July 12, 1930 (T.S. No. 836; 47 Stat. 1862; 8 Bevans 214; entered into force Apr. 26, 1931).

6. Article 6 of the Canada–U.S. extradition treaty provides that the requested State may deny extradition if the offense is punishable by death unless the requesting State provides such assurances as the requested party considers sufficient that the death penalty will not be imposed or executed. Article IX of the 1983 extradition treaty between the U.S. and Italy is the same except for the fact that "State" (in the Canada–U.S. treaty) is "Party" and "may be refused" (in the Canada–U.S. treaty) is "shall be refused". Oct. 13, 1983, T.I.A.S. 10837. Should the language in the U.S.-Italy treaty make a difference? If so, for which state? What if the death penalty was not mentioned in either treaty, but becomes a recognized violation of customary international law? See also subsection E on Non–Inquiry and Human Rights, *infra*. An assurance by the United States, oral or in writing, that the death penalty would not be sought or imposed is an Executive Agreement. Are such agreements binding on states within the U.S. Recall generally United States v. Pink, 315 U.S. 203 (1942).

The European Court of Human Rights examined the requirements of a "death penalty assurance" and related issues in the 1989 *Soering Case*, 161 Eur. Ct. Hum. Rts. (Series A) (1989), 11 Eur. Hum. Rts. Rep. 439 (1989).

SOERING CASE

161 Eur. Ct. H.R. (Ser. A) (1989).

Procedure

1. The case was brought before the Court ... by the European Commission of Human Rights ("the Commission"), ... by the Government of the United Kingdom ... within ... the Convention for the Protection of Human Rights and Fundamental Freedoms ("the Convention"). It originated in an application ... against the United Kingdom lodged with the Commission under Article 25 by a German national, Mr. Jens Soering....

The object of the request ... was to obtain a decision from the Court as to whether or not the facts of the case disclosed a breach by the respondent State of its obligations under Articles 3, 6 and 13 of the Convention....

11. The applicant, Mr. Jens Soering, was born on August 1966 and is a German national. He is currently detained in prison in England pending extradition to the United States of America to face charges of murder in the Commonwealth of Virginia.

12. The homicides in question were committed in Bedford County, Virginia, in March 1985. The victims, William Reginald Haysom (aged 72) and Nancy Astor Haysom (aged 53) were the parents of the applicant's girlfriend, ... a Canadian national.... At the time the applicant ..., aged 18 ..., [was a student] at the University of Virginia. [He] disappeared ... from Virginia in October 1985, but [was] arrested in England in April 1986 in connection with cheque fraud.

13. The applicant was interviewed in England between 5 and 8 June 1986 by a police investigator from the Sheriff's Department of Bedford County. In a sworn affidavit dated 24 July 1986 the investigator recorded the applicant as having admitted the killings....

14. [T]he government of the United States of America requested the applicant's ... extradition under the terms of the Extradition Treaty of 1972 between the United States and the United Kingdom....

15. [T]he British Embassy in Washington addressed a request to the United States' authorities in the following terms:

> "Because the death penalty has been abolished in Great Britain, the Embassy has been instructed to seek an assurance, in accordance with the terms of ... the Extradition Treaty, that, in the event of Mr. Soering being surrendered and being convicted of the crimes for which he has been indicted ..., the death penalty, if imposed, will not be carried out.
>
> Should it not be possible on constitutional grounds for the United States Government to give such assurance, the United Kingdom authorities ask that the United States Government undertake

to recommend to the appropriate authorities that the death penalty should not be imposed or, if imposed, should not be executed."

20. Mr. Updike swore an affidavit in his capacity as Attorney for Bedford County, in which he certified as follows:

> "I hereby certify that should Jens Soering be convicted of the offence of capital murder as charged in Bedford County, Virginia ... a representation will be made in the name of the United Kingdom to the judge at the time of sentencing that it is the wish of the United Kingdom that the death penalty should not be imposed or carried out." ...

During the course of the present proceedings the Virginia authorities have informed the United Kingdom Government that Mr. Updike was not planning to provide any further assurances and intended to seek the death penalty in Mr. Soering's case because the evidence, in his determination, supported such action....

24. ... [T]he Secretary of State signed a warrant ordering the applicant's surrender to the United States' authorities. However, the applicant has not been transferred to the United States by virtue of the interim measures indicated in the present proceedings firstly by the European Court....

25. On 5 August 1988 the applicant was transferred to a prison hospital where he remained until early November 1988 under the special regime applied to suicide-risk prisoners.

According to psychiatric evidence adduced on behalf of the applicant ... , the applicant's dread of extreme physical violence and homosexual abuse from other inmates in death row in Virginia is in particular having a profound psychiatric effect on him. The psychiatrist's report records a mounting desperation in the applicant, together with objective fears that he may seek to take his own life.

36. There is no provision in the Extradition Acts relating to the death penalty, but Article IV of the United Kingdom–United States Treaty provides:

> "If the offence for which extradition is requested is punishable by death under the relevant law of the requesting Party, but the relevant law of the requested Party does not provide for the death penalty in a similar case, extradition may be refused unless the requesting Party gives assurances satisfactory to the requested Party that the death penalty will not be carried out."

37. In the case of a fugitive requested by the United State who faces a charge carrying the death penalty, it is the Secretary of State's practice, pursuant to Article IV of the United Kingdom–United States Extradition Treaty, to accept an assurance from the prosecuting authorities of the relevant State that a representation will be made to the judge at the time of sentencing that it is the wish of the United Kingdom that the death penalty should be neither imposed nor carried out....

44. The imposition of the death penalty on a young person who has reached the age of majority—which is 18 years ... —is not precluded under Virginia law. Age is a fact to be weighed by the jury....

56. ... The average time between trial and execution in Virginia, calculated on the basis of the seven executions which have taken place since 1977, is six to eight years. The delays are primarily due to a strategy by convicted prisoners to prolong the appeal proceedings as much as possible. The United States Supreme Court has not as yet considered or ruled on the "death row phenomenon" and in particular whether it falls foul of the prohibition of "cruel and unusual punishment" under the Eighth Amendment to the Constitution of the United States....

61. There are currently 40 people under sentence of death in Virginia. The majority are detained in Mecklenburg Correctional Center, which is a modern maximum security institution with a total capacity of 335 inmates....

63. The size of a death row inmate's cell is 3m by 2.2m. Prisoners have an opportunity for approximately 7½ hours' recreation per week n summer and approximately 6 hours' per week, weather permitting, in winter. The death row area has two recreation yards, both of which are equipped with basketball courts and one of which is equipped with weights and weight benches. Inmates are also permitted to leave their cells on other occasions, such as to receive visits, to visit the law library or to attend the prison infirmary. In addition, death row inmates are given one hour out-of-cell time in the morning in a common area. Each death row inmate is eligible for work assignments, such as cleaning duties. When prisoners move around the prison they are handcuffed with special shackles around the waist.

When not in their cells, death row inmates are housed in a common area called "the pod." The guards are not within this area and remain in a box outside. In the event of disturbance or inter-inmate assault, the guards are not allowed to intervene until instructed to do so by the ranking officer present.

64. The applicant adduced much evidence of extreme stress, psychological deterioration and risk of homosexual abuse and physical attack undergone by prisoners on death row, including Mecklenburg Correctional Center. This evidence was strongly contested by the United Kingdom Government on the basis of affidavits sworn by administrators from the Virginia Department of Corrections....

68. A death row prisoner is moved to the death house 15 days before he is due to be executed. The death house is next to the death chamber where the electric chair is situated. Whilst the prisoner is in the death house he is watched 24 hours a day. He is isolated and has no light in his cell. The lights outside are permanently lit. A prisoner who utilizes the appeals process can be placed in the death house several times....

69. Relations between the United Kingdom and the United States of America on matters concerning extradition are conducted by and with the Federal and not the State authorities. However, in respect of offenses against State laws the Federal authorities have no legally binding power to provide, in an appropriate extradition case, an assurance that the death penalty will not be imposed or carried out. In such cases the power rests with the State. If a State does decide to give a promise in relation to the death penalty, the United States Government would have the power to give assurance to the extraditing Government that the State's promise will be honoured....

PROCEEDINGS BEFORE THE COMMISSION

76. Mr. Soering's application ... was lodged with the Commission on 8 July 1988. In his application Mr. Soering stated his belief that, notwithstanding the assurance given to the United Kingdom Government, there was a serious likelihood that he would be sentenced to death if extradited to the United States of America. He maintained that in the circumstances and, in particular, having regard to the "death row phenomenon" he would thereby be subjected to inhuman and degrading treatment and punishment contrary to Article 3 of the Convention. In his further submission his extradition to the United States would constitute a violation of Article 6 § 3(c) because of the absence of legal aid in the State of Virginia to pursue various appeals. Finally, he claimed that, in breach of Article 13, he had no effective remedy under United Kingdom law in respect of his complaint under Article 3....

78. The Commission declared the application admissible on 10 November 1988.

In its report adopted on 19 January 1989 (Article 31) the Commission expressed the opinion that there had been a breach of Article 13 (seven votes to four) but no breach of either Article 3 (six votes to five) or Article 6 § 3(c) (unanimously)....

AS TO THE LAW

I. Alleged Breach of Article 3

80. The applicant alleged that the decision by the Secretary of State for the Home Department to surrender him to the authorities of the United States of America would, if implemented, give rise to a breach by the United Kingdom of Article 3 of the Convention, which provides:

> "No one shall be subjected to torture or to inhuman or degrading treatment or punishment."

A. *Applicability of Article 3 in cases of extradition*

81. The alleged breach derives from the applicant's exposure to the so-called "death row phenomenon." This phenomenon may be described as consisting in a combination of circumstances to which the applicant would be exposed if, after having been extradited to Virginia to face a capital murder charge, he were sentenced to death....

82. In its report ... the Commission reaffirmed "its case-law that a person's deportation or extradition may give rise to an issue under Article 3 of the Convention where there are serious reasons to believe that the individual will be subjected, in the receiving State, to treatment contrary to that Article."

The Government of the Federal Republic of Germany supported the approach of the Commission, pointing to a similar approach in the case-law of the German courts.

The applicant likewise submitted that Article 3 ... also embodies an associated obligation not to put a person in a position where he will or may suffer such treatment or punishment at the hands of other States.

83. The United Kingdom Government, on the other hand, contended that Article 3 should not be interpreted so as to impose responsibility ... for acts which occur outside its jurisdiction ... In the alternative, the United Kingdom Government submitted that the application of Article 3 in extradition cases should be limited to those occasions in which the treatment or punishment is certain, imminent and serious ...

86. ... These considerations cannot, however, absolve the Contracting Parties from responsibility under Article 3 for all and any foreseeable consequences of extradition suffered outside their jurisdiction.

87. In interpreting the Convention regard must be had to its special character as a treaty for the collective enforcement of human rights and fundamental freedoms ... Thus, the object and purpose of the Convention as an instrument for the protection of individual human beings require that its provisions be interpreted and applied so as to make its safeguards practical and effective....

88. ... The question remains whether the extradition of a fugitive to another State where he would be subjected or be likely to be subjected to torture or to inhuman or degrading treatment or punishment would itself engage the responsibility of a Contracting State under Article 3. The abhorrence of torture has such implications is recognized in Article 3 of the United Nations Convention Against Torture and Other Cruel, Inhuman or Degrading Treatment or Punishment, which provides that "no State Party shall ... extradite a person where there are substantial grounds for believing that he would be in danger of being subjected to torture". The fact that a specialized treaty should spell out in detail a specific obligation attaching to the prohibition of torture does not mean that an essentially similar obligation is not already inherent in the general terms of Article 3 of the European Convention. It would hardly be compatible with the underlying values of the Convention, the "common heritage of political traditions, ideals, freedoms and the rule of law" to which the Preamble refers, were a Contracting State knowingly to surrender a fugitive to another State where there were substantial grounds for believing that he would be in danger of being subjected to torture, however heinous the crime allegedly committed. Extradition in

such circumstances, while not explicitly referred to in the brief and general wording of Article 3, would plainly be contrary to the spirit and intendment of the Article, and in the Court's view this inherent obligation not to extradite also extends to cases in which the fugitive would be faced in the receiving State by a real risk of exposure to inhuman or degrading treatment or punishment proscribed by that Article....

91. In sum, the decision by a Contracting State to extradite a fugitive may give rise to an issue under Article 3, and hence engage the responsibility of that State under the Convention, where substantial grounds have been shown for believing that the person concerned, if extradited, faces a real risk of being subjected to torture or to inhuman or degrading treatment or punishment in the requesting country. The establishment of such responsibility inevitably involves an assessment of conditions in the requesting country against the standards of Article 3 of the Convention. Nonetheless, there is no question of adjudicating on or establishing the responsibility of the receiving country, whether under general international law, under the Convention or otherwise. In so far as any liability under the Convention is or may be incurred, it is liability incurred by the extraditing Contracting State by reason of its having taken action which has a direct consequence the exposure of an individual to proscribed ill-treatment....

92. ... It therefore has to be determined on the above principles whether the foreseeable consequences of Mr. Soering's return to the United States are such as to attract the application of Article 3. This inquiry must concentrate firstly on whether Mr. Soering runs a real risk of being sentenced to death in Virginia, since the source of the alleged "death row phenomenon," lies in the imposition of the death penalty. Only in the event of an affirmative answer to this question need the Court examine whether exposure to the "death row phenomenon" in the circumstances of the applicant's case would involve treatment or punishment incompatible with Article 3.

1. Whether the applicant runs a real risk of a death sentence and hence of exposure to the "death row phenomenon"

98. ... Whatever the position under Virginia law and practice ... , and notwithstanding the diplomatic context of the extradition relations between the United Kingdom and the United States, objectively it cannot be said that the undertaking to inform the judge at the sentencing stage of the wishes of the United Kingdom eliminates the risk of the death penalty being imposed. In the independent exercise of his discretion the Commonwealth's Attorney has himself decided to seek and to persist in seeking the death penalty because the evidence, in his determination, supports such action.... If the national authority with responsibility for prosecuting the offence takes such a firm stance, it is hardly open to the Court to hold that there are no substantial grounds for believing that the applicant faces a real risk of being sentenced to death and hence experiencing the "death row phenomenon".

99. The Court's conclusion is therefore that the likelihood of the feared exposure to the applicant to the "death row phenomenon" has been shown to be such as to bring Article 3 into play.

2. *Whether in the circumstances the risk of exposure to the "death row phenomenon" would make extradition a breach of Article 3*

(a) *General considerations*

100. As is established in the Court's case-law, ill-treatment, including punishment, must attain a minimum level of severity if it is to fall within the scope of Article 3. The assessment of this minimum is, in the nature of things, relative; it depends on all the circumstances of the case, such as the nature and context of the treatment or punishment, the manner and method of its execution, its duration, its physical or mental effects and, in some instances, the sex, age and state of health of the victim....

Treatment has been held by the Court to be both "inhuman" because it was premeditated, was applied for hours at a stretch and "caused, if not actual bodily injury, at least intense physical and mental suffering", and also "degrading" because it was "such as to arouse in [its] victims feelings of fear, anguish and inferiority capable of humiliating and debasing them and possibly breaking their physical or moral resistance".... In order for a punishment or treatment associated with it to be "inhuman" or "degrading", the suffering or humiliation involved must in any event go beyond that inevitable element of suffering or humiliation connected with a given form of legitimate punishment.... In this connections, account is to be taken not only of the physical pain experienced but also, where there is a considerable delay before execution of the punishment, of the sentenced person's mental anguish of anticipating the violence he is to have inflicted on him.

101. Capital punishment is permitted under certain conditions by Article 2 § 1 of the Convention....

(b) *The particular circumstances ...*

i. *Length of detention prior to execution*

106. The period that a condemned prisoner can expect to spend on death row in Virginia before being executed is on average six to eight years.... This length of time awaiting death is, as the Commission and the United Kingdom noted, in a sense largely of the prisoner's own making in that he takes advantage of all avenues of appeal which are offered to him by Virginia law....

Nevertheless, just as some lapse of time between sentence and execution is inevitable if appeal safeguards are to be provided to the condemned person, so it is equally part of human nature that the person will cling to life by exploiting those safeguards to the full. However well-intentioned and even potentially beneficial is the provision of the complex of post-sentence procedures in Virginia, the consequence is that the condemned prisoner has to endure for many years the conditions on death row and the anguish and mounting tension of living in the ever-present shadow of death.

ii. *Conditions on death row*

107. As to conditions in Mecklenburg Correctional Center, where the applicant could expect to be held if sentenced to death, the Court bases itself on the facts which were uncontested by the United Kingdom Government, without finding it necessary to determine the reliability of the additional evidence adduced by the applicant, notably as to the risk of homosexual abuse and physical attack undergone by prisoners on death row....

... In this connection, the United Kingdom Government drew attention to the necessary requirement of extra security for the safe custody of prisoners condemned to death for murder. Whilst it might thus well be justifiable in principle, the severity of a special regime such as that operated on death row in Mecklenburg is compounded by the fact of inmates being subject to it for a protracted period lasting on average six to eight years.

iii. *The applicant's age and mental state*

108. At the time of the killings, the applicant was only 18 years old and there is some psychiatric evidence, which was not contested as such, that he "was suffering from [such] an abnormality of mind ... as substantially impaired his mental responsibility for his acts"....

Unlike Article 2 of the Convention, Article 6 of the 1966 International Covenant on Civil and Political Rights and Article 4 of the 1969 American Convention on Human Rights expressly prohibit the death penalty from being imposed on persons aged less than 18 at the time of commission of the offence. Whether or not such a prohibition be inherent in the brief and general language of Article 2 of the European Convention, its explicit enunciation in other, later international instruments, the former of which has been ratified by a large number of States Parties to the European Convention, at the very least indicates that as a general principle the youth of the person concerned is a circumstance which is liable, with others, to put in question the compatibility with Article 3 of measures connected with a death sentence.

It is in line with the Court's case-law ... to treat disturbed mental health as having the same effect for the application of Article 3....

Conclusion

111. For any prisoner condemned to death, some element of delay between imposition and execution of the sentence and the experience of severe stress in conditions necessary for strict incarceration are inevitable. The democratic character of the Virginia legal system in general and the positive features of Virginia trial, sentencing and appeal procedures in particular are beyond doubt. The Court agrees with the Commission that the machinery of justice to which the applicant would be subject in the United States is in itself neither arbitrary nor unreason-

able, but, rather, respects the rule of law and affords not inconsiderable procedural safeguards to the defendant in a capital trial. Facilities are available on death row for the assistance of inmates, notably through provision of psychological and psychiatric services....

However, in the Court's view, having regard to the very long period of time spent on death row in such extreme conditions, with the ever present and mounting anguish of awaiting execution of the death penalty, and to the personal circumstances of the applicant, especially his age and mental state at the time of the offence, the applicant's extradition to the United States would expose him to a real risk of treatment going beyond the threshold set by Article 3. A further consideration of relevance is that in the particular instance the legitimate purpose of extradition could be achieved by another means which would not involve suffering of such exceptional intensity or duration.

Accordingly, the Secretary of State's decision to extradite the applicant to the United States would, if implemented, give rise to a breach of Article 3.

For these Reasons, the Court Unanimously

1. *Holds* that, in the event of the Secretary of State's decision to extradite the applicant to the United States of America being implemented, there would be a violation of Article 3....

Notes and Questions

1. After the European Court's decision, the prosecutor of Bedford County, Virginia, amended the charges to remove the offense of capital murder. The United Kingdom then extradited Mr. Soering to Virginia for trial. He was convicted of first-degree murder in June of 1990. See RICHARD B. LILLICH & HURST HANNUM, INTERNATIONAL HUMAN RIGHTS 768 (3 ed. 1995).

2. Would a U.S. assurance to the U.K. (that a death penalty will not be sought or imposed) by the U.S. Secretary of State on behalf of the United States constitute an Executive agreement between the U.K. and U.S.? If so, would it be binding on states within the U.S.?

3. In dissent regarding a denial of certiorari, Justice Breyer cited *Soering*, the Universal Declaration of Human Rights, and a decision of the Human Rights Committee, among others, concerning a death penalty delay of more than 20 years. See Knight v. Florida, 528 U.S. 990, 996 (1999). He also noted that "[a] growing number of courts outside the United States ... have held that lengthy delay ... renders ultimate execution inhuman, degrading, or unusually cruel." *Id.* at 995.

4. The human right to freedom from torture or cruel, inhumane or degrading treatment or punishment exception to extradition has been followed in "a long line of decisions by the [European] Commission and the Court." See *id.* at 759. One related case is Chahal v. United Kingdom, Eur. Ct. H.R., No. 70/1995/576/662 (15 Nov. 1996), *reprinted in* 92 AM. J. INT'L L. 71 (1998). *Chahal* involved a potential deportation of a Sikh activist from the U.K. on grounds of "national security" and an assessment of a real risk of being tortured in India, a complicitous violation of Article 3 by the U.K. The

European Court of Human Rights ruled that the U.K.'s limitation of judicial review of deportation orders failed to provide Mr. Chahal with an effective remedy as mandated by the European Convention on Human Rights. Later, *compare Chahal with* the approach of the U.S. court in *Ahmad v. Wigen*.

On applicability of the European Convention to state acts abroad or the effects abroad of state acts, *see also* Drozd & Janousek v. France and Spain, Case No. 21/1991/273/344, para. 91 (23 & 27 Jan. 1992); Cyprus v. Turkey, Eur. Cm. H.R., 1975 Y.B. EUR. CONV. HUM. RTS. 82, 118 (1976) (state duty to secure human rights protections "to all persons under their actual authority and responsibility, whether that authority is exercised within their own territory or abroad."); Juliane Kokott & Beate Rudolf, note re: *Loizidou v. Turkey*, 310 Eur. Ct. H.R. (Ser. A) (1995), in 90 AM. J. INT'L L. 98 (1996). In 2001, Spain and other countries refused to render detainees to the U.S. for detention at Guantanamo Bay, Cuba because of alleged violations of human rights law that would occur there.

The ICCPR also applies to all persons subject to the jurisdiction of a signatory. *See, e.g.*, ICCPR, art. 2(1); Advisory Opinion, Legal Consequences of the Construction of a Wall in the Occupied Palestinian Territory, 2004 I.C.J. paras. 108–111 (The ICCPR "is applicable in respect of acts done by a State in the exercise of its jurisdiction outside its own territory"), *reprinted in* 43 I.L.M. 1009, 1039–40 (2004); Human Rights Committee, General Comment No. 31, at para. 10 (applies "to all persons subject to their jurisdiction. This means ... anyone within the power or effective control of that State party, even if not situated within the territory of the State.... [The ICCPR applies] to all individuals ... who may find themselves in the territory or subject to the jurisdiction of a State Party.... [It] also applies to those within the power or effective control of the forces of a State Party acting outside its territory, regardless of the circumstances in which such power or effective control was obtained), para. 11 ("the Covenant applies also in the situation of armed conflict to which the rules of international humanitarian law are applicable."), U.N. Doc. CCPR/C/21/Rev.1/Add.13 (2004); General Comment No. 24, *supra*, at paras. 4, 12 ("all those under a State party's jurisdiction"); HENCKAERTS & DOSWALD-BECK, 1 CUSTOMARY INTERNATIONAL HUMANITARIAN LAW 305 (ICRC 2005) ("wherever they have jurisdiction ... [or] effective control.... State practice has interpreted this widely."); Thomas Buergenthal, *To Respect and to Ensure: State Obligations and Permissible Derogations*, in THE INTERNATIONAL BILL OF RIGHTS: THE COVENANT ON CIVIL AND POLITICAL RIGHTS 72, 74 (Louis Henkin ed., 1981); Theodor Meron, *Extraterritoriality of Human Rights Treaties*, 89 AM. J. INT'L L. 78, 78–80 (1995); Alfred de Zayas, *The Status of Guantanamo Bay and the Status of Detainees*, 37 U.B.C. L. REV. 277, 281–82, 310–12 (2004). Clearly, persons detained and being interrogated by the United States at Guantanamo Bay, Cuba and elsewhere are subject to jurisdiction of the United States. Moreover, Guantanamo and U.S. naval vessels are under the complete jurisdiction and control of the United States. *See, e.g.*, Rasul v. Bush, 542 U.S. 466 (2004); Jordan J. Paust, *Post–9/11 Overreaction and Fallacies Regarding War and Defense, Guantanamo, the Status of Persons, Treatment, Judicial Review of Detention, and Due Process in Military Commissions*, 79 NOTRE DAME L. REV. 1335, 1347–49 (2004); Zayas, *supra*, at 282, 311–12. Where the U.S. is an occupying power, it also has jurisdiction and control of detainees. *See, e.g.*, Paust, *supra* at 1347. More generally, U.S. obligations under the U.N. Charter to respect and ensure respect for human rights are applicable universally. See U.N. Charter, arts. 55(c), 56.

5. For a contrary argument with respect to the requirement that an extraditing state seek a so-called "death penalty assurance" (*i.e.*, an assurance that it will not be imposed), consider the 1991 majority opinion of the Supreme Court of Canada in Kindler v. Canada (Minister of Justice), [1991] 2 S.C.R. 779.

C. Speciality

STATE OF WASHINGTON v. PANG

132 Wash.2d 852, 940 P.2d 1293 (1997).

SMITH, J.

Petitioner Martin Shaw Pang seeks review of a King County Superior Court decision which denied his motion to dismiss or sever four counts of murder in the first degree from one count of arson in the first degree based upon his claim that the Federal Supreme Court of Brazil approved his extradition from that country for prosecution in the State of Washington only for the crime of arson in the first degree. We reverse.

The basic question in this case is whether the State of Washington may prosecute Petitioner Martin Shaw Pang for four counts of murder in the first degree and one count of arson in the first degree when the Federal Supreme Court of Brazil, ruling on the State's petition for extradition, granted his extradition for prosecution in the State of Washington "for the crime of arson in the first degree, resulting in four deaths ... without the additional charge of four counts of first degree murder." To answer the basic question, we must answer these additional questions:

(1) Does Petitioner Pang have standing to object to violation by the State of Washington of the terms of the order on extradition issued by the Federal Supreme Court of Brazil?

(2) Did the United States of Brazil explicitly or implicitly waive any objection it could have made to prosecution by the State of Washington of Petitioner Pang for murder in the first degree contrary to the specific terms of the extradition order issued by the Federal Supreme Court of Brazil?

(3) Does the "specialty doctrine" in international extradition law prohibit the State of Washington from prosecuting Petitioner Pang for crimes specifically excluded in the extradition order?

(4) Does the Extradition Treaty between the United States of America and the United States of Brazil prohibit the State of Washington from prosecuting Petitioner Pang for crimes not authorized in the extradition order?

(5) Is the State of Washington obligated to follow the decision of the Federal Supreme Court of Brazil which ruled that, as a condition

for extraditing Petitioner Pang to the State, he can be prosecuted only "for the crime of arson in the first degree resulting in four deaths ... without the additional charge of four counts of first degree murder"?

On January 5, 1995, four firefighters died while fighting a fire at the Mary Pang Products, Inc. warehouse at 811 Seventh Avenue South in Seattle, Washington. Fire investigators later determined the fire had been deliberately set. Martin Shaw Pang became a suspect. A fugitive warrant was issued for his arrest. On March 3, 1995 the King County Prosecuting Attorney by Information charged Petitioner Pang with four counts of murder in the first degree....

(1) Does Petitioner Pang have standing to object to violation by the State of Washington of the terms of the order on extradition issued by the Federal Supreme Court of Brazil?

The State argues that Petitioner Pang does not have standing to assert any post-extradition limitations on his prosecution because the Brazilian Executive, through Minister of Justice Nelson A. Jobim, does not object to King County prosecuting Petitioner on four counts of murder in the first degree. The State correctly recognizes the exception to the doctrine of specialty which allows the requesting state to prosecute an accused for a crime other than that for which the accused was extradited when the asylum state consents. However, in the absence of that consent by the asylum state, an extradited person may raise any objections to post-extradition proceedings which might have been raised by the rendering country.

The rule in at least three United States circuit courts is that an extraditee has standing "to raise any objections which the requested nation might have asserted," subject to the limitation that "the requested nation may waive its right to object to a treaty violation and thereby deny the defendant standing to object to such action." At least four other circuits have left the question of standing unanswered, with some indicating approval of the prevailing rule.

The State also asserts that a minority of United States circuit courts deny standing absent affirmative protest by the surrendering State. However, this purported split in the circuits is illusory. Two of the three cases the State cited for this proposition are not standing cases at all, but were resolved against the extraditees on the merits. The third case merely noted the defendant's standing was questionable before reaching the merits.

The State urges this Court to find that Brazil's Executive, through Minister of Justice Nelson A. Jobim, "implicitly consented" to prosecution of Petitioner Pang by the State of Washington on four counts of murder in the first degree. We agree with the rule expressed in *Najohn* that only express consent to prosecution will be considered a waiver of the doctrine of specialty. The letter from Brazil Minister of Justice Jobim to United States Attorney General Janet Reno cannot logically be interpreted as either an implicit waiver or an explicit waiver. The subsequent letter of February 26, 1997 from Minister Jobim unequivocally explains the meaning and intent of his letter to Attorney General Reno. It completely contradicts the interpretation urged by the State. That letter states in part:

> I'd like to inform you that at no time did I provide any type of interpretation on the content and reach of the decision passed by the Federal Supreme Court. Thus, I ratify all the words used in said correspondence, its only objective being to clarify to Ms. Janett [sic] Reno, Attorney–General of the United States, some aspects of the Brazilian Constitutional system.

While some United States circuit courts have questioned whether an extraditee has standing to assert limitations on post-extradition prosecution, and other courts have declined to address the issue, no court has dismissed such a claim because an extraditee did not have standing. The only firm decisions on this issue agree that an extraditee may raise any objection the surrendering State could make, as long as that country has not waived its right to object. From the entire record in this case, we cannot conclude that the United States of Brazil has said, done or implied by words, action or inaction anything which would require this Court to deny Petitioner Pang the right to make post-extradition objections to his prosecution by the State of Washington in violation of the conditions of his extradition from Brazil. We conclude that Petitioner Pang does have standing to assert limitations on his post-extradition prosecution in King County.

(2) Did the United States of Brazil explicitly or implicitly waive any objection it could have made to prosecution by the State of Washington of Petitioner Pang for murder in the first degree contrary to the specific terms of the extradition order issued by the Federal Supreme Court of Brazil?

The trial court concluded that the United States of Brazil, by not objecting when it had numerous opportunities to do so, "implicitly waived objection," thereby defeating Petitioner Pang's standing. The State urges this Court to adopt that implicit waiver rationale, arguing that Justice Minister Jobim's letter of September 26, 1996 to Attorney General Reno indicates that Brazil does not object to Petitioner Pang being prosecuted for four counts of murder in the first degree. Nothing in the entire record before this Court supports such a conclusion. We reject it as being completely unsound and totally contrary to the record.

The United States of Brazil has from the outset expressed its position that Petitioner Pang should not be charged with murder in the first degree by the State of Washington. The Federal Supreme Court of Brazil fully considered and unequivocally rejected extradition of Petitioner on the murder charges as requested by the State of Washington. That position was reaffirmed when the court uncategorically rejected the appeal filed by the United States and the motion for clarification filed by the State of Washington. Despite repeated requests through diplomatic channels, Brazil has not only affirmatively denied permission to charge

Petitioner with murder, but its President and Minister of Justice affirmatively declined in no uncertain terms the request of President Clinton that Brazil waive its right to object to prosecution of Petitioner Pang by the State of Washington for murder in the first degree following the extradition order.

The State's insistence that Justice Minister Jobim waived objection on behalf of Brazil to the State of Washington charging Petitioner Pang with murder distorts the facts established in this case. The letter from Minister Jobim to Attorney General Reno merely reiterated that Petitioner Pang was extradited to stand trial "for the crime of arson in the first degree, resulting in four deaths and the consequences thereof under U.S. law." This is only a portion of the words used in the extradition order issued by the Federal Supreme Court of Brazil. In that same statement the Federal Supreme Court of Brazil continued its words to specifically exclude "the additional charge of four counts of first-degree murder."

From a reading of the complete series of opinions from the Federal Supreme Court of Brazil it is evident beyond question that the point of disagreement between the majority and the dissenting minority was on the question whether the extradition order would exclude punishment beyond the 30–year maximum under Brazilian law or whether the order would allow the maximum punishment of life imprisonment for arson in the first degree as allowed under Washington law.

We are not convinced an implied waiver, even if made, would overcome the standing of Petitioner Pang to object in this case. The United States Court of Appeals for the Ninth Circuit has held that an express waiver of objection does divest an extraditee of standing. We conclude from the record in this case that Brazil has not expressly consented to nor implicitly or explicitly waived objection to the State of Washington charging Petitioner with murder in the first degree. We therefore conclude that Petitioner Pang does have standing to object.

(3) Does the "specialty doctrine" in international extradition law prohibit the State of Washington from prosecuting Petitioner Pang for crimes specifically excluded in the extradition order?

The United States Court of Appeals for the Ninth Circuit has stated "We review de novo whether extradition of a defendant satisfies the doctrines of 'dual criminality' and 'specialty.' "The specialty doctrine has been explained:

> The requested state retains an interest in the fate of a person whom it has extradited, so that if, for example, he is tried for an offense other than the one for which he was extradited, or is given a punishment more severe than the one applicable at the time of the request for extradition, the rights of the requested state, as well as the person, are violated. [United States v. Khan, 993 F.2d 1368, 1372 (9th Cir.1993)]

Under international law, the "specialty doctrine" generally prohibits a requesting State from prosecuting an extraditee "for an offense other than the one for which surrender was made." This doctrine "is designed to prevent prosecution for an offense for which the person would not have been extradited." . . .

In *United States v. Rauscher* [119 U.S. 407 (1886)], the United States Supreme Court addressed the question whether the extradition treaty between England and the United States prohibited prosecution of the defendant for a crime other than that for which he was extradited. This was the first case in which the Supreme Court recognized the specialty doctrine. In that case an American merchant ship officer had been extradited from Great Britain, under an extradition treaty, to be charged with murder of a crew member. He was subsequently convicted of assault and inflicting cruel and unusual punishment, neither of which were listed as extraditable offenses in the treaty. The Court held the defendant could be tried only for the offense "with which he is charged in the extradition proceedings, and for which he was delivered up." . . .

Under *Rauscher*, for an extradited defendant to be charged with a crime, that crime must be specified in the treaty (the approval of which is within the sole discretion of the asylum state), and be included in the extradition petition (the content of which is within the sole discretion of the requesting state). The defendant has the right to "be tried only for the offence with which he is charged in the extradition proceedings and for which he was delivered up." "It is unreasonable that the country of the asylum should be expected to deliver up such a person to be dealt with by the demanding government without any limitation, implied or otherwise, upon its prosecution of the party." The doctrine of specialty was not explicitly stated in the treaty between the United States and Great Britain. The court in *Rauscher* interpreted the treaty with consideration of the specialty doctrine which had previously been recognized in international law.

The Court examined the treaty and the history of relations between the United States and Great Britain to determine whether the parties, in the absence of express incorporation, nevertheless intended the doctrine of specialty to be part of the treaty. Under *Rauscher* the specialty doctrine may be implied where a treaty is silent on the issue and there is no reason to assume the signatory nations did not abide by the principles of comity.

Petitioner Pang argues that, because the extradition order specifically excluded the charges of murder in the first degree requested by the State of Washington, under the specialty doctrine the State may not prosecute him on these charges. He argues that under *Rauscher* the specialty doctrine is implied in every treaty.

The State argues that any limitations on post-extradition prosecution are defined only by the terms of the treaty and the doctrine of specialty applies only when it is expressly incorporated into the terms of the treaty. In determining whether there has been a violation to the specialty doctrine, courts have consistently examined the terms of the treaty for any limitations on prosecution. The United States Court of Appeals for the Ninth Circuit observed in a recent case that "we look to the language of the applicable treaty to determine the protection an extradited person is afforded under the doctrine of specialty."

In this case, the doctrine of specialty is incorporated into the terms of the Treaty of Extradition Between the United States of America and the United States of Brazil (Treaty) through Article XXI which provides:

> A person extradited by virtue of the present Treaty may not be tried or punished by the requesting State for any crime or offense committed prior to the request for his extradition, other than that which gave rise to the request, nor may he be re-extradited by the requesting State to a third country which claims him, unless the surrendering State also agrees or unless the person extradited, having been set at liberty within the requesting State, remains voluntarily in the requesting State for more than 30 days from the date on which he was released. Upon such release, he shall be informed of the consequences to which his stay in the territory of the requesting State would subject him.

This provision, read in conjunction with Articles I and II, requires that the crime must be enumerated in the treaty and must satisfy the doctrine of dual criminality, thus incorporating the doctrine of specialty into the Treaty. Because the doctrine is codified in federal statute, 18 U.S.C. sec. 3192, federal law requires acceptance of the requirement of Brazil that an offense must be extraditable under its interpretation of applicable domestic and international law. . . .

(4) Does the Extradition Treaty between the United States of America and the United States of Brazil prohibit the State of Washington from prosecuting Petitioner Pang for crimes not authorized in the extradition order?

International law is incorporated into our domestic law. Treaties are the supreme law of the land. They are binding on the states as well as the federal government. Courts must interpret treaties in good faith. In the 1907 case of *Johnson v. Browne* the United States Supreme Court stated:

> While the escape of criminals is, of course, to be very greatly deprecated, it is still most important that a treaty of this nature between sovereignties should be construed in accordance with the highest good faith, and that it should not be sought, by doubtful construction of some of its provisions, to obtain the extradition of a person for one offense and then punish him for another and different offense. Especially should this be the case where the government surrendering the person has refused to make the surrender for the other offense, on the ground that such offense was not one covered by the treaty. [205 U.S. 309, 321 (1907)]. . . .

We agree with the United States Court of Appeals for the Ninth Circuit in its interpretation of international treaty law. From the extensive record in this case, we cannot conclude that the Federal Supreme Court of Brazil misinterpreted its own laws in rendering its decision on extradition of Petitioner Pang under the Treaty. We conclude without question that under the Treaty, Brazil, as the requested state, has sole authority to determine whether a particular offense is extraditable.

The Treaty provides that "[a] person extradited by virtue of the present Treaty may not be tried or punished by the requesting State for any crime or offense committed prior to the request for his extradition, other than that which gave rise to the request."

The State argues it requested Petitioner's extradition on one count of arson in the first degree and four counts of murder in the first degree and reasons there is no violation of the Treaty because Petitioner is only being prosecuted for those offenses. Petitioner Pang argues that the semantic distinction between the Treaty in this case and those limiting prosecution to offenses "for which extradition was granted" is not meaningful. Two courts have affirmed convictions on charges other than those for which extradition was granted because the express language in the treaties in those cases allowed it.

In *Fiocconi v. Attorney General* [462 F.2d 475], the United States Court of Appeals for the Second Circuit denied habeas corpus relief to an extraditee who had been convicted of crimes other than those for which extradition was granted. The court examined the applicable United States–Italy extradition treaty which provided that "the person ... delivered up for the crimes enumerated ... shall in no way be tried for any ... crime, committed previously to that for which his ... surrender is asked." The court observed:

> If the countries had intended that the requesting government could not try the accused for any crime committed before the time of his surrender other than the crime for which he was extradited, they could have accomplished this by adopting one of the standard clauses to that end.

In *United States v. Sensi* [879 F.2d 888] the defendant was convicted of charges other than those for which he was extradited. The United States Court of Appeals for the District of Columbia upheld the convictions for the reason that the United States–United Kingdom Treaty only prohibited prosecution for offenses other than those "established by the facts in respect of which his extradition has been granted." The court reasoned that, although the crimes charged were not those for which extradition was granted, the charges were based upon the same underlying facts and that therefore there was no treaty violation.

The United States Court of Appeals for the Ninth Circuit in *United States v. Khan* ruled to the contrary. The defendant was charged with conspiring to import drugs and with using a communication facility in furtherance of the conspiracy. The United States requested his extradition from Pakistan for trial on both charges. The Pakistani Commissioner directed that the defendant be "surrendered over to the authorities in the U.S.A. for trial under the relevant American Law," but made no direct reference to the underlying charges. Other documents in the case referred to the conspiracy charge, but not to the communication facility charge. The court held that because Pakistan did not unambiguously agree to extradite the defendant on the communication facility charge, his conviction on that charge must be reversed. The court distinguished *Sensi*, pointing out that the treaty language in that case did not limit prosecution to those offenses for which extradition was granted. The court noted by contrast that "the operative treaty in [the] case contained the following language: 'A person surrendered can in no case be [prosecuted] ... for any other crime or offence, or on account of any other matters, than those for which the extradition shall have taken place.' "....

D. The Political Offense Exception

QUINN v. ROBINSON

783 F.2d 776 (9th Cir.1986).

REINHARDT, J.

Pursuant to 18 U.S.C. § 3184 (1982) and the governing treaty between the United States and the United Kingdom of Great Britain and Northern Ireland ("United Kingdom"), Extradition Treaty of June 8, 1972, United States–United Kingdom, 28 U.S.T. 227, T.I.A.S. No. 8468 [hereinafter cited as *Treaty*], the United Kingdom seeks the extradition of William Joseph Quinn, a member of the Irish Republican Army ("IRA"), in order to try him for the commission of a murder in 1975 and for conspiring to cause explosions in London in 1974 and 1975. After a United States magistrate found Quinn extraditable, Quinn filed a petition for a writ of habeas corpus. The district court determined that Quinn cannot be extradited because a long-standing principle of international law which has been incorporated in the extradition treaty at issue—the political offense exception—bars extradition for the charged offenses. The United States government, on behalf of the United Kingdom, appeals.

This case requires us to examine the parameters of a foreign sovereign's right to bring about the extradition of an accused who maintains that the offenses with which he is charged are of a political character. Ultimately we must determine whether the political offense exception is applicable to the type of violent offenses Quinn is alleged to have committed. We undertake this task with the aid of very little helpful precedent. The United States Supreme Court has discussed the political offense exception only once, and then during the nineteenth century. *See* Ornelas v. Ruiz, 161 U.S. 502 ... (1896). The only time we considered the subject, *see* Karadzole v. Artukovic, 247 F.2d 198 (9th Cir. 1957), the Supreme Court vacated our opinion, see ... 355 U.S. 393 ... (1958) (mem.), an opinion which, in any event, has subsequently been roundly and uniformly criticized, *see* Eain v. Wilkes, 641 F.2d 504, 522 (7th Cir.), *cert. denied*, 454 U.S. 894 ... (1981); Garcia–Mora, *The Nature of Political Offenses: Knotty Problem of Extradition Law*, 48 VA. L. REV. 1226, 1246 (1962); Lubet & Czackes, *The Role of the American Judiciary in the Extradition of Political Terrorists*, 71 J. CRIM. L. & CRIMINOLOGY 193, 205 (1980). Only one circuit has previously considered in any detail how or whether the exception applies when the accused person or persons have engaged in conduct involving the use of some of the more violent techniques or tactics that have come to mark the activities of contemporary insurgent or revolutionary movements. Eain v. Wilkes, 641 F.2d 504 (7th Cir.), *cert. denied*, 454 U.S. 894 ... (1981). The few opinions of other circuits that have considered the exception shed no light on the difficult questions we must resolve here. Therefore, we must carefully examine the historic origins of the political offense exception, analyze the various underpinnings of the doctrine, trace its development in the lower courts and elsewhere, and seek to apply whatever principles emerge to the realities of today's political struggles.

In the case before us, we find, for reasons we will explain in full, that the charged offenses are not protected by the political offense exception. We vacate the writ of habeas corpus and remand to the district court. We hold that Quinn may be extradited on the murder charge but that the district court must consider Quinn's remaining defense to the conspiracy charge before extradition is permitting for that offense....

A. ORIGIN OF THE EXCEPTION

The first-known extradition treaty was negotiated between an Egyptian Pharaoh and a Hittite King in the Thirteenth Century B.C. However, the concept of political offenses as an exception to extradition is a rather recent development. In the centuries after the first known extradition treaty, and throughout the Middle Ages, extradition treaties were used primarily to return political offenders, rather than the perpetrators of common crimes, to the nations seeking to try them for criminal acts. *See* I.A. Shearer, *supra* p. 22, at 166; Recent Decisions, *The Political Offense Exception to Extradition: A 19th Century British Standard in 20th Century American Courts*, 59 NOTRE DAME L. REV. 1005, 1008 (1984) [hereinafter *20th Century American Courts*]. It was not until the early nineteenth century that the political offense exception, now almost universally accepted in extradition law, was incorporated into treaties.

The French and American revolutions had a significant impact on the development of the concept of justified political resistance, *see* Declaration des droits de l'homme et du Citoyen du 26 aout 1789, art. 2 (Fr.), *incorporated as* La preamble de la Constitution de 1791 (Fr.), *reprinted in Les Constitutions de la France Depuis 1789*, at 33, 33 (S. Godechot ed. 1970) (declaring as an inalienable right "la resistance a l'opression"); La Constitution de 1793, art. 120 (Fr.), *reprinted in Les Constitutions de la France Depuis 1789, supra*, at 79, 91 (France "done asile aux etrangers bannis de leur patrie pout la cause de la liberte.");

The Declaration of Independence para. 1 (U.S. 1776) ("[W]henever any Form of Government becomes destructive of these ends, it is the Right of the People to alter or to abolish it. . . ."), as did the political philosophers of the time, *see* J. LOCKE, THE SECOND TREATISE OF CIVIL GOVERNMENT ch. XIX (T. Cook ed. 1947); J.S. MILL, ON LIBERTY AND CONSIDERATIONS ON REPRESENTATIVE GOVERNMENT (R. McCallum ed. 1948). In 1834, France introduced the political offense exception into its treaties, *see* I.A. Shearer, *supra* p. 22, at 166–67, and by the 1850's it had become a general principle of international law incorporated in the extradition treaties of Belgium, England, and the United States as well. *See* C. VAN DEN WIJNGAERT, THE POLITICAL OFFENSE EXCEPTION TO EXTRADITION 5–14 (1980); [Valerie] Epps, [*The Validity of the Political Offender Exception in Extradition Treaties in Anglo-American Jurisprudence*, 20 HARV. INT'L L.J. 61,] 62–63 [(1979)].

The political offense exception is premised on a number of justifications. First, its historical development suggests that it is grounded in a belief that individuals have a "right to resort to political activism to foster political change." Note, *American Courts and Modern Terrorism: The Politics of Extradition*, 13 N.Y.U. J. INT'L L. & POL. 617, 622 (1981) [hereinafter cited as *Politics of Extradition*]; *see also In re* Doherty, 599 F. Supp. 270, 275 n. 4 (S.D.N.Y.1984) ("The concept was first enunciated during an era when there was much concern for and sympathy in England for the cause of liberation for subjugated peoples.") (citation omitted). This justification is consistent with the modern consensus that political crimes have greater legitimacy than common crimes. *Politics of Extradition, supra*. 31, at 632. Second, the exception reflects a concern that individuals—particularly unsuccessful rebels—should not be returned to countries where they may be subjected to unfair trials and punishments because of their political opinions. *See* M. BASSIOUNI, INTERNATIONAL EXTRADITION AND WORLD PUBLIC ORDER 425 (1974); C. VAN DEN WIJNGAERT, *supra* p. 22, at 3; Garcia–Mora, *supra* p. 3, at 1226, 1238. Third, the exception comports with the notion that governments—and certainly their nonpolitical branches—should not intervene in the internal political struggles of other nations. *See* C. VAN DEN WIJNGAERT, *supra* p. 22, at 3, 158, 204; *Politics of Extradition, supra* p. 31, at 622.

B. COMPARATIVE LEGAL STANDARDS

None of the political offense provisions in treaties includes a definition of the word "political." I.A. Shearer, *supra* p. 22 at 168. Thus, the term "political offense" has received various interpretations by courts since the mid-nineteenth century. Garcia–Mora, *supra*, p. 3 at 1230–31; Wise, Book Review, 30 AM.J.COMP.L. 362, 363, (1982) (reviewing C. VAN DEN WIJNGAERT, THE POLITICAL OFFENSE EXCEPTION TO EXTRADITION (1980)); *cf.* M. BASSIOUNI, *supra* p. 32, at 371–72 (inability to define precisely the term "political offense" promotes a necessary flexibility of the concept). Not every offense that is politically motivated falls within the exception. Instead, courts have devised various tests to identify those offenses that comport with the justifications for the exception and that, accordingly, are not extraditable.

Within the confusion about definitions it is fairly well accepted that there are two distinct categories of political offenses: "pure political offenses" and "relative political offenses." *See* Karadzole v. Artukovic, 247 F.2d 198, 203 (9th Cir.1957), vacated, 355 U.S. 393 ... (1958) (mem.); *see generally* Garcia–Mora, *supra* p. 3, at 1230; *20th Century American Courts, supra* p. 30, at 1009. Pure political offenses are acts aimed directly at the government, *see* Lubet & Czackes, *supra* p. 3, at 1230. These offenses, which include treason, sedition, and espionage, Garcia–Mora, *supra* p. 3, at 1234; Lubet & Czackes, *supra* p. 3, at 200, do not violate the private rights of individuals, Garcia–Mora, *supra* p. 3, at 1237. Because they are frequently specifically excluded from the list of extraditable crimes given in a treaty, *see 20th Century American Courts, supra* p. 30, at 1009, courts seldom deal with whether these offenses are extraditable, *see id.*, and it is generally agreed that they are not, *see* Lubet & Czackes, *supra* p. 3, at 200 (*citing In re* Ezeta, 62 F. 972 (1894)).

The definitional problems focus around the second category of political offenses—the relative political offenses. These include "otherwise common crimes committed in connection with a political act," Lubet & Czackes, *supra* p. 3, at 200, or "common crimes ... committed for political motives or in political context," *20th Century American Courts, supra* p. 30, at 1009. Courts have developed various tests for ascertaining whether "the nexus between the crime and the political act is sufficiently close ... [for the crime to be deemed] not extraditable." Lubet & Czackes, *supra* p. 3, at 200. The judicial approaches can be grouped into three distinct categories: (1) the French "objective" test; (2) the Swiss "proportionality" or "predominance" test; and (3) the Anglo–American "incidence" test. *See generally* Carbonneau, *The Political Offense Exception to Extradition and Transnational Terrorists: Old Doctrine Reformulated and New Norms Created*, 1 Assoc. of Student Int'l L. Societies Int'l L.J. 1, 11–31 (1977); Garcia–Mora, *supra* p. 3, at 1239–56; *20th Century American Courts, supra* p. 30, at 1009–17. More recent developments allow for further distinctions between the British test and the test employed in the United States. *See generally* Lubet & Czackes, *supra* p. 3, at 201–10.

The early French test, most clearly represented in *In re* Giovanni Gatti, [1947] Ann.Dig. 145 (No. 70) (France, Ct.App. of Grenoble), considered an offense non-extraditable only if it directly injured the rights of the state. *See 20th Century American Courts, supra* p. 30, at 1010. Applying this rigid formula, French courts refused to consider the motives of the accused. Garcia–Mora, *supra* p. 3, at 1249–50. The test primarily protects only pure political offenses, *see id.* at 1235–36 (discussing cases), and is useless in attempts to define whether an otherwise common crime should not be extraditable because it is connected with a political act, motive, or context. *Id.* at 1252. Because politically motivated and directed acts may injure private as well as state rights, the objective test fails to satisfy the various purposes of the political offense exception. Politics of Extradition, *supra* p. 31, at 629–30. Nevertheless, this test has one benefit: because it is so limited, it is not subject to abuse; perpetrators of common crimes will not be protected because of alleged political motivations. *Id.* at 630; Garcia–Mora, *supra* p. 3, at 1251.

In contrast to the traditional French test, Swiss courts apply a test that protects both pure and relative political offenses. The Swiss test examines the political motivation of the offender, *see* Garcia–Mora, *supra* p. 3, at 1251, but also requires (a) a consideration of the circumstances surrounding the commission of the crime, *see* Carbonneau, *supra* p. 34, at 23–26, and (b) either a proportionality between the means and the political ends, *see 20th Century American Courts, supra* p. 30 at 1010–11, or a predominance of the political elements over the common crime elements, *see* Garcia–Mora, *supra* p. 3, at 1254.

At least one commentator has suggested that the first condition of the Swiss test is a requirement of a direct connection between the crime and the political goal—a condition that essentially requires the presence of a political movement. *See* Garcia Mora, *supra* p. 3, at 1253 (*citing* Swiss cases). Others point out that the early Swiss requirement that a crime be incident to a political movement has been explicitly rejected in later cases. *See, e.g.*, Carbonneau, *supra* p. 34, at 26–28 (*citing* Swiss cases). More recent Swiss cases concentrate less on the accused's motive, relying instead almost entirely on an ends-means test under which politically motivated conduct is protected by the exception only if the danger created by the conduct is proportionate to the objectives, *i.e.*, if the means employed are the only means of accomplishing the end and the interests at stake are sufficiently important to justify the danger and harm to others. *See* Carbonneau, *supra* p. 34, at 28–29 (*citing* Swiss cases).

The comprehensiveness and flexibility of the "predominance" or "proportionality" test allows it to be conformed to changing realities of a modern world. *See* Garcia–Mora, *supra* p. 3 at 1255. But because the relative value of the ends and the necessity of using the chosen means must be considered, the criteria applied by Swiss courts incorporate highly subjective and partisan political considerations within the balancing test. *See* C. VAN DEN WIJNGAERT, *supra* p. 22 at 158; Politics of Extradition, *supra* p. 31, at 631.[1] The test explicitly requires an evaluation of the importance of the interests at stake, the desirability of political change, and the acceptability of the means used to achieve the ends. The infusion of ideological factors in the determination of which offenses are non-extraditable threatens both the humanitarian objectives underlying the exception and the concern about foreign non-intervention in domestic political struggles. Moreover, it severely undermines the

1. The Swiss, aware that their test incorporates factors that preclude ideological neutrality, allow only their highest court to determine when the political offense exception applies. *See Politics of Extradition, supra* p. 31 at 631 (*citing* 1 L. OPPENHEIM, INTERNATIONAL LAW 579 (4th ed. 1928)).

notion that such determinations can be made by an apolitical, unbiased judiciary concerned primarily with individual liberty. *See supra* pp. 788–89.[2]

The "incidence" test that is used to define a non-extraditable political offense in the United States and Great Britain was first set forth by the Divisional Court in *In re* Castioni, [1891] 12 Q.B. 149 (1890). In that case, the Swiss government requested that Great Britain extradite a Swiss citizen who, with a group of other angry citizens, had stormed the palace gates and killed a government official in the process. *Id.* at 150–51. Castioni did not know the victim or have a personal grudge against him. The habeas court considered:

> [W]hether, upon the facts, it is clear that the man was acting as one of a number of persons engaged in acts of violence of a political object, and as part of the political movement and [up]rising in which he was taking part.

Id. at 159 (per Denman, J.). The court denied extradition, finding that Castioni's actions were "incidental to and formed a part of political disturbances," *id.* at 166 (per Hawkind, J.), and holding that common crimes committed "in the course" and "in the furtherance" of a political disturbance would be treated as political offenses, *id.* at 156 (per Denman, J.).

Although both the United States and Great Britain rely explicitly on Castioni, each has developed its own version of the incidence test. British courts proceeded first to narrow the exception in 1894. In *In re* Neunier, [1894] 2 Q.B 415, the court extradited a French anarchist charged with bombing a café and military barracks, *id.* at 415, concluding that anarchist action is not incident to a two-party struggle for political power, *id.* at 419 (per Cave, J.). The court held that the political offense exception protects those who seek to substitute one form of government for another, not those whose actions disrupt the social order and whose "efforts are directed primarily against the general body of citizens." *Id.*

2. A number of commentators have suggested that perhaps the most useful test for when the exception should apply can be derived from the theory of "ideological self-preservation." *See, e.g.*, M. Bassiouni, International Extradition: United States Law & Practices ch. VIII, at § 2–74 to § 2–77 (1983); C Van den Wijngaert, *supra* p. 22, at 157–58. The premise of this theory is that a political crime is justified if it is a form of self-defense, in that the means used to attempt to secure a fundamental right were limited to the least harmful means available. The commentators suggest that an objective test could be derived from this theory and would weigh (a) the nature of the rights violated by the state; (b) the nature of the state conduct that violated these rights; and (c) the nature of the individual conduct that violated the law of the state in an attempt to defend these rights. As one commentator has noted, *see* C. Van den Wijngaert, supra p. 22 at 158, this test resembles the Swiss proportionality test but, in addition to the balancing required by that test, it requires an evaluation of the conduct of the requesting nation. Despite the initial appeal of the theory of ideological self-preservation, we believe it is an inappropriate test. It is subject to all the criticisms to which the Swiss test is subject. Moreover, it requires the kind of evaluation of the conduct of another nation that violates the principle of non-intervention in the internal affairs of another state. *See id.* It thus runs counter to one of the primary tenet underlying the political offense exception, *see supra* pp. 792–93, are requires the judiciary to undertake a task for which it is particularly ill-suited, *see supra* pp. 788–89 & note 6.

The rigid "two-party struggle" requirement of the British incidence test has not survived. More recently, British courts have taken other factors into account, noting that political offenses must be considered "according to the circumstances existing at the time." Regina v. Governor of Brixton Prison (*ex parte* Kolczynski), [1955] 1 Q.B. 540, 549 (1954) (per Cassels, J.). In *Kolczynski*, a British court refused to extradite Polish soldiers who were at risk of being punished for treason although the Polish government officially sought their extradition for common crimes. *See id.* at 543, 545. No political uprising existed at the time the crimes were committed. *Id.* at 544. Instead of a distinct uprising, the new British incidence test requires some "political opposition ... between fugitive and requesting State," Schtraks v. Government of Israel, [1964] A.C. 556, 591 (1962) (per Viscount Radcliffe), and incorporates an examination of the motives of the accused and the requesting country in those situations in which the offense is not part of an uprising, *see* Lubet & Czackes, *supra* p. 3, at 202–03.

C. Original Formulation of the United States Incidence Test

The United States, in contrast to Great Britain, has adhered more closely to the Castioni test in determining whether conduct is protected by the political offense exception. The seminal United States case in this area is *In re* Ezeta, 62 F. 972 (N.D.Cal.1894), in which the Salvadoran government requested the extradition of a number of individuals accused of murder and robbery. The fugitives maintained that the crimes had been committed while they unsuccessfully attempted to thwart a revolution. *See id.* at 995. Extradition was denied because the acts were "committed during the progress of actual hostilities between contending forces," *id.* at 997, and were "closely identified" with the uprising "in an unsuccessful effort to suppress it," *id.* at 1002. However, an alleged act that occurred four months prior to the start of armed violence was held not to be protected by the incidence test despite the accused's contention that El Salvador's extradition request was politically motivated. *Id.* at 986.

As we noted at the outset, the Supreme Court has addressed the political offense issue only once. In Ornelas v. Ruiz, 161 U.S. 502 ... (1896), Mexico sought the extradition of an individual for murder, arson, robbery, and kidnapping committed in a Mexican border town, at or about the time revolutionary activity was in progress. *Id.* at 510 ... The Court allowed extradition on the basis that the habeas court had applied an improper, non-deferential standard of review to the extradition court's findings. *Id.* at 511–12 ... It continued by listing four factors pertinent to the political offense inquiry in the case: (1) the character of the foray; (2) the mode of attack; (3) the persons killed or captured: and (4) the kind of property taken or destroyed. *Id.* at 511 ... It found that although the raid (in December 1892) may have been contemporaneous with a revolutionary movement (in 1891), it was not of a political character because it was essentially unrelated to the uprising. The Court noted that the purported political aspects of the crimes were negated "by the fact that immediately after this occurrence, though no superior armed force of the Mexican government was in the vicinity to hinder their advance into the country, the bandits withdrew with their booty across the river into Texas." *Id.*

Since *Ornelas*, lower American courts have continued to apply the incidence test set forth in *Castioni* and *Ezeta* with its two-fold requirement; (1) the occurrence of an uprising or other violent political disturbance[3] at the time of the charged offense, *see, e.g.*, Garcia–Guillern v. United States, 450 F.2d 1189, 1192 (5th Cir.1971), *cert. denied*, 405 U.S. 989 ... (1972); Ramos v. Diaz, 179 F. Supp. 459, 462 (S.D.Fla.1959),[4] and (2) a charged offense that is "incidental to" "in the course of," or "in furtherance of" the uprising, *see, e.g.*, Eain, 641 F.2d at 518; Sindona v. Grant, 619 F.2d 167, 173 (2d Cir.1980); Garcia–Guillern, 450 F.2d at 1192. While the American view that an uprising must exist is more restrictive than the modern British view and while we, unlike the British, remain hesitant to consider the motives of the accused or the requesting state, *see* Lubet & Czackes, *supra* p. 3, at 203, 205, American courts have been rather liberal in their construction of the requirement that the act be "incidental to" an uprising, *see* Garcia–Mora, *supra* p. 3 at 1244.

The American approach has been criticized as being "both underinclusive and overinclusive," *see* Lubet & Czackes, *supra* p. 3, at 203, and as "yield[ing] anomalous ... results," *see 20th Century American Courts, supra* p. 30, at 1013–14. Although these criticisms have some merit, neither flaw in the American incidence test is serious. Some commentators have suggested that the test is underinclusive because it exempts from judicially guaranteed protection all offenses that are not contemporaneous with an uprising even though the acts may represent legitimate political resistance. *See, e.g.*, Lubet & Czackes, *supra* p. 3, at 203–04. For example, the attempted kidnapping of a Cuban consul, allegedly for the purpose of ransoming the consul for political prisoners held in Cuba, was held by a court not to be a political offense because the act was not "committed in the course of and incidental to a violent political distur-

3. Although unnecessary to the resolution of the cases before them, a number of courts have stated that a "war" could qualify as the violent political disturbance for purposes of the incidence test. *See, e.g.*, Eain v. Wilkes, 641 F.2d 504, 518 (7th Cir.), *cert denied*, 454 U.S. 894 ... (1981); Sindona v. Grant, 619 F.2d 167, 173 (2d Cir. 1980). Although the terms "rebellion," "revolution," "uprising," and "civil war" may for our purposes be treated as synonymous, none is for any purpose synonymous with the term "war." As we discuss further below ... we question the propriety of applying the incidence test in the same manner in the case of crimes occurring during wars as in the case of crimes occurring during uprisings.

4. American courts generally will take judicial notice of a state of uprising. *See, e.g.*, Karadzole v. Artukovic, 247 F.2d 198, 204 (9th Cir.1957) (noting that district court properly took judicial notice of struggle for political control in Croatia), *vacated and remanded*, 355 U.S. 393 ... (1958) (mem.); Ramos v. Diaz, 179 F. Supp. 459, 462 (S.D.Fla.1959) (extradition court took judicial notice of revolutionary movement in Cuba); *In re* McMullen, No. 3–78–1099 MG, slip op. at 4 (N.D. Cal. May 11, 1979) (magistrate took judicial notice of uprising in Northern Ireland). *But see In re* Abu Eain, No. 79 M 175, slip op. at 13–14 (N.D.Ill. Dec. 18, 1979) (magistrate refused to take judicial notice of Middle East hostilities), *reprinted in* Abu Eain v. Adams, 529 F. Supp. 685, 688–95 (N.D.Ill.1980).

bance." Escobedo v. United States, 623 F.2d 1098, 1104 (5th Cir.), *cert. denied*, 449 U.S. 1036 . . . (1980).

There are several responses to the charge of underinclusiveness. First, in their critiques, the commentators fail to give sufficient weight to the existence of a number of ameliorative safeguards. For example, review of certifications of extradition by the Secretary of State, *see supra* pp. 789–90, serves partially to remedy any underinclusiveness problem. If a court finds the accused extraditable, the Secretary has, at the very least, broad discretion to review the available record and conduct a de novo examination of the issues and, if necessary, to consider matters outside the record in determining whether to extradite. *See* Lubet & Czackes, *supra* p. 3, at 199. The potential underinclusiveness dangers of the uprising requirement are also mitigated by the fact that purely political offenses are never extraditable. *See id.* at 206; *supra* pp. 793–94. Additionally, because of the rule of dual criminality, *see supra* pp. 782–83, individuals accused of offenses that constitute protected activity under the First Amendment will not be extradited. *See* Lubet & Czackes, *supra* p. 3, at 206. Second, it is questionable whether the incidence test is, in fact, underinclusive. While it does not protect all politically motivated offenses, it protects those acts that are related to a collective attempt to abolish or alter the government—the form of political offense that the exception was initially designed to protect, *see supra* pp. 792–93. Third, any effort to protect all crimes that are in some way politically motivated would either require the abandonment of the objective test for determining which offenses fall within the exception—in our view a most undesirable result—or would result in the protection of innumerable crimes that fall far outside the original purposes underlying the exception.

A number of commentators suggest, on the other hand, that the America test is overbroad because it makes non-extraditable some offenses that are not of a political character merely because the crimes took place contemporaneously with an uprising. *See* Garcia–Mora, *supra* p. 3, at 1246; Lubet & Czackes, *supra* p. 3, at 205; Politics of Extradition, *supra* p. 3, at 628. We think these commentators misunderstand the test. They all cite Karadzole v. Artukovic, 247 F.2d 198 (9th Cir.1957)—"one of the most roundly criticized cases in the history of American extradition jurisprudence," Eain v. Wilkes, 641 F.2d 504, 522 (7th Cir.), *cert. denied*, 454 U.S. 894 . . . (1981)—to support their argument. In *Artukovic*, the Yugoslavian government sought the extradition of a former Minister of the Interior of the puppet Croatian government which took over a portion of Yugoslavia following the German invasion in April 1941. Artukovic was charged with directing the murder of hundreds of thousands of civilians in concentration camps between April 1941 and October 1942. Prior to a hearing by an extradition magistrate, the district court granted habeas relief, concluding that the charged offenses were non-extraditable political offenses. Artukovic v. Boyle, 140 F. Supp. 245, 246 (S.D.Cal.1956). We affirmed, applying the *Castioni* language and noting that the offenses occurred during the German invasion of Yugoslavia and subsequent establishment of Croatia. Karadzole v. Artukovic, 247 F.2d 198, 202–04 (9th Cir.1957). We considered but were unpersuaded by the argument that because war crimes are so barbaric and atrocious they cannot be considered political crimes, *see id.* at 204 and the United Nations resolutions called for the extradition of war criminals, *see id.* at 205.

The Supreme Court vacated our opinion in a one paragraph per curiam opinion and remanded for an extradition hearing pursuant to 18 U.S.C. § 3184. *See* 355 U.S. 393 (1958). The Court did not comment on the substantive issues and may well have based its order solely on the fact that the habeas court considered the legal questions involved in Artukovic's extradition before an extradition court had an opportunity to make the preliminary findings mandated by section 3184. *See* United States v. Artukovic, 170 F. Supp. 383, 393 (S.D.Cal.1959). In his subsequent decision the magistrate denied extradition on the ground that there was insufficient evidence to establish probable cause of Artukovic's guilt, *see id.* at 392, but in dicta he adopted our vacated political offense analysis, *see id.* at 393.

We do not believe that *Artukovic* adequately supports the commentators' suggestion that the incidence test is overinclusive. We think it more likely that the problem lies not in the test itself but in the fact that we erred by applying it in that case.

The offenses with which Artukovic was charged fall within that very limited category of acts which have been labeled "crimes against humanity." In *Artukovic* we erroneously assumed that "crimes against humanity" was synonymous with "war crimes," and then concluded in a somewhat irrelevant fashion that not all war crimes automatically fall outside the ambit of the political offense exception. *See* 247 F.2d at 204. Our analysis was less than persuasive. We did not need then, and do not need now, to reach a conclusion about whether all war crimes fall outside the bounds of the exception. *Cf.* C.VAN DEN WIJNGAERT, *supra* p. 22, at 1143 (suggesting that, under international law, states remain free to consider war crimes as political offenses). The offenses with which Artukovic was charged were crimes against humanity; it matters not whether or not they were also war crimes; either way, crimes of that magnitude are not protected by the exception.

Crimes against humanity, such as genocide, violate international law and constitute an "abuse of sovereignty" because by definition, they are carried out by or with the toleration of authorities of a state. While some of the same offenses that violate the laws and customs of war are also crimes against humanity, crimes of the latter sort most notably include "murder, extermination, enslavement, ... or persecutions on political, racial, ethnic, national or religious grounds ..." of entire racial, ethnic national or religious groups. The Nurnberg (Nuremberg) Trial, 6 F.R.D. 69, 130 (Int'l Military Tribunal 1946). Various "inhumane acts ... committed after the beginning of [World War II] did not constitute war crimes, [but] ... constituted crimes against humanity." *Id.* at 131.

Wholly aside from the *Artukovic* court's confusion of "war crimes" and "crimes against humanity," we do not believe that the political offense exception, even if meant to protect the acts of representatives of a former government, should have been extended to protect those carrying out a governmental policy calling for acts of destruction whose "nature and scope ... exceeded human imagination." Excerpts from Speech by German President, N.Y. Times, May 9, 1985, at 10, col. 1, 3 (excerpts from Speech to Parliament on May 8, 1985 by President Richard von Weizsacker, as translated by the West German Foreign Ministry) (noting that the Nazi genocide is "unparalleled in history"). These crimes are simply treated differently and are generally excluded from the protection of many normally applicable rules. *See, e.g.*, The Nurmberg (Nuremberg) Trial, 6 F.R.D. at 107–11 (individuals accused of these offenses can be tried before international tribunal because offenses violate international law). They are certainly in our view to be excluded from coverage under the political offense exception.

Accordingly, we do not consider the "underinclusiveness" and "overinclusiveness" problems of the incidence test to have been as severe as has been suggested by some of the commentators. Rather, we believe the incidence test, when properly applied, has served the purposes and objectives of the political offense exception well. More recently, a number of courts have begun to question whether, in light of changing political practices and realities, we should continue to use the traditional American version of that test. They have suggested that basic modifications may be required and, specifically, that certain types of conduct engaged in by some contemporary insurgent groups, conduct that we in our society find unacceptable, should be excluded from coverage. For the reasons we explain below, we believe that the American test in its present form remains not only workable but desirable; that the most significant problems that concern those advocating changes in the test can be dealt with without making the changes they propose; and the efforts to modify the test along the lines suggested would plunge our judiciary into a political morass and require the type of subjective judgments we have so wisely avoided until now.

D. The Recent Political Offense Cases

Recently, the American judiciary has split almost evenly over whether the traditional American incidence test should be applied to new methods of political violence in two categories—domestic revolutionary violence and international terrorism—or whether fundamental new restrictions should be imposed on the use of the political offense exception.

In both *In re* McMullen, No. 3–78–1099 MG (N.D.Cal. May 11, 1979), and *In re* Mackin, No. 80 Cr. Misc 1 (S.D.N.Y. Aug. 13, 1981), extradition magistrates applied the traditional United States incidence test despite expressing serious concern over the nature of the charged offenses. In *McMullen*, the United Kingdom sought the extradition of a former PIRA member accused of murder in connection with the bombing of a military barracks in England. Finding that McMullen's acts took place during a state of uprising throughout the United Kingdom and were incidental to the political disturbance, the magistrate denied extradition noting that "[e]ven though the offense be deplorable and heinous, the criminal actor will be excluded from deportation if the crime is committed under these pre-requisites." Slip op. at 3. The magistrate's formulation of the test for the political offense exception in *Mackin* was similar. In that case, the United Kingdom's request for the extradition of an IRA member accused of murdering a British soldier in Northern Ireland was denied.

In contrast, although asserting that the existing incidence test "is sufficiently flexible to avoid [the] abuses [noted by commentators]," 641 F.2d at 519, and while ostensibly applying the traditional test, *see id.* at 515–16, 518, the Seventh Circuit in Eain v. Wilkes, 641 F.2d 504 (7th Cir.), *cert. denied*, 454 U.S. 894 ... (1981), superimposed a number of limitations on the exception that had not previously been a part of United States law. Abu Eain, a resident of the occupied West Bank and a member of the PLO, was accused by the State of Israel of setting a bomb that exploded in the Israeli city of Tierias in 1979, killing two boys and injuring more than thirty other people. A magistrate granted Israel's extradition request, the district court denied habeas corpus relief, and the Seventh Circuit affirmed.

First, the *Eain* court distinguished between conflicts that involved "on-going, organized battles between contending armies," 641 F.2d at 519, and conflicts that involved groups with "the dispersed nature of the PLO," *id.*, noting that in the former case, unlike the latter, a clear distinction can be drawn between the activities of the military forces and individual acts of violence. Second, although acknowledging that motivation is not determinative of the political character of an act, *see id.* at 520 (*citing* Lubet & Czackes, *supra* p. 3, at 203 n. 102), and characterizing its next requirement as that of a "direct link" between the offense and the conflict, *id.* at 521, the court examined the motivation for and political legitimacy of the act. The court appears to have concluded that, according to the evidence presented, the PLO's objectives were not politically legitimate: the PLO sought changes in "the Israeli political structure as an incident of the expulsion of a certain population from the country," *id.* at 520, and its activities were therefore more properly characterized as aimed at Israel's "social structure," *id.* Third, the court held simply that regardless what the political objective is, "the indiscriminate bombing of a civilian population is not recognized as a protected act." *Id.* at 521.

Thus, the Seventh Circuit in *Eain* redefined an "uprising" as a struggle between organized, non-dispersed military forces; made a policy determination regarding the legitimacy of given political objectives; and excluded violent acts against innocent civilians from the protection afforded by the exception. *Cf.* Note, *Terrorist Extradition and Political Offense Exception: An Administrative Solution*, 21 VA. J.INT'L L. 163, 177–78 (1980) (criticizing *Eain* magistrate's test because it invites ideological and foreign policy determinations by extradition courts). As part of its justification for the new limitations it imposed on the applicability of the exception, the *Eain* court expressed concern that, in the absence of these restrictions,

> nothing would prevent a safe haven in America.... Terrorists who have committed barbarous acts elsewhere would be able to flee to the United States and live in our neighborhoods and walk our streets forever free from any accountability for their acts. We do not need them in our society.... [T]he political offense exception ... should be applied with great care lest our country, become a social jungle....

Id. at 520.

The District Court for the Southern District of New York has recently rejected portions of the Eain analysis but accepted some of the new restrictions propounded by the Seventh Circuit. In *In re* Doherty, 599 F. Supp. 270 (S.D.N.Y.1984), the court denied the United Kingdom's request that a PIRA member accused of attacking a convoy of British soldiers in Northern Ireland be extradited. The extradition court rejected the notion that the exception protects only "actual armed insurrections or more traditional and overt military hostilities." *Id.* at 275. Noting that "political struggles have been ... effectively carried out by armed guerrillas," *id.*, the court concluded that a dissident group's likelihood of success and its ability to effect changes by other than violent means were not determinative factors. *Id.* Nevertheless, the court agreed with the Seventh Circuit's tacit conclusion that the traditional incidence test is "hardly consistent with ... the realities of the modern world," *id.* at 274.

The *Doherty* court continued by approving of the *Eain* court's willingness to balance policy considerations so that the exception "does not afford a haven for persons who commit the most heinous atrocities for political ends." *Id.* at 275 n. 4. Although such issues were not raised in *Doherty*, the court stated explicitly that the exception would not protect bombings in public places, *id.* at 275; acts that "transcend the limits of international law," *id.*; acts "inconsistent with international standards of civilized conduct," *id.* at 274; harm to hostages, *id.* at 276; violations of the Geneva convention, *id.*; or the acts of "amorphous" or "fanatic" groups without structure, organization, or clearly defined political objectives, *id.* Thus, the *Doherty* court, like the *Eain* court, concluded that the traditional incidence test is insufficient to determine which offenses are protected by the exception. Both courts felt it necessary and appropriate to judge the political legitimacy of various ends and means and to exclude "illegitimate" acts from protection even if the incidence test were met. While not identifying their new limitations as such, both incorporated significant aspects of the Swiss ends-means or proportionality test into Anglo–American jurisprudence.

THE POLITICAL OFFENSE EXCEPTION AND THE REALITIES OF CONTEMPORARY POLITICAL STRUGGLES

A. *The Political Reality: The Contours of Contemporary Activity*

The recent lack of consensus among United States courts confronted with requests for the extradition of those accused of violent political acts committed outside the context of an organized military conflict reflects some confusion about the purposes underlying the political offense exception. *See supra* pp. 792–93. The premise of the analyses performed by modern courts favoring the adoption of new restrictions on the use of the exception is either that the objectives of revolutionary violence undertaken by dispersed forces and directed at civilians are by definition, not political, *see, e.g.*, *Eain*, 641 F.2d at 519 ("Terrorist activity seeks to promote social chaos."), or that, regardless of the actors' objectives, the conduct is not politically legitimate because it "is inconsistent with international standards of civilized conduct," *Doherty*, 599 F. Supp. at 274. Both assumptions are subject to debate.

A number of courts appear tacitly to accept a suggestion by some commentators that begins with the observation that the political offense exception can be traced to the rise of democratic governments. *See* I.A. Shearer, *supra* p. 22, at 166; C. VAN DEN WIJNGAERT, *supra* p. 22, at 100; Carbonneau, *supra* p. 34, at 5. Because of this origin, these commentators argue, the exception was only designed to protect the right to rebel against tyrannical governments, *see, e.g.*, Epps, *supra* p. 4, at 65, and should not be applied in an ideologically neutral fashion, *see, e.g.*, Carbonneau, *supra* p. 34, at 44; *see also In re* Gonzales, 217 F. Supp. 717, 721 n. 9 (S.D.N.Y.1963) (evaluating whether acts in question "were blows struck in the cause of freedom against a repressive totalitarian regime") *But see* C. VAN DEN WIJNGAERT, *supra* p. 22, at 102 (noting that democratic states may also suppress political conduct in the guise of criminality).

These courts then proceed to apply the exception in a non-neutral fashion but, in doing so, focus on and explicitly reject only the tactics, rather than the true object of their concern, the political objectives. *See* C. VAN DEN WIJNGAERT, *supra* p. 22, at 102. The courts that are narrowing the applicability of the exception in this manner appear to be moving beyond the role of an impartial judiciary by determining tacitly that particular political objectives are not "legitimate."

We strongly believe that courts should not undertake such a task. The political offense test traditionally articulated by American courts, as well as the text of the treaty provisions, *see, e.g.*, Treaty, *supra* p. 781, at art. V(1)(c), is ideologically neutral. We do not believe it appropriate to make qualitative judgments regarding a foreign government or a struggle designed to alter that government. Accord *In re* Doherty, 599 F. Supp. 270, 277 (S.D.N.Y.1984); *see generally supra* note 6. Such judgments themselves cannot be other than political and, as such, involve determinations of the sort that are not within the judicial role. *See supra* Section II.B.

A second premise may underlie the analyses of courts that appear to favor narrowing the exception, namely, that modern revolutionary tactics which include violence directed at civilians are not politically "legitimate." This assumption, which may well constitute an understandable response to the recent rise of international terrorism, skews any political offense analysis because of an inherent conceptual shortcoming. In deciding what tactics are acceptable, we seek to impose on other nations and cultures our own traditional notions of how internal political struggles should be conducted.

The structure of societies and governments, the relationships between nations and their citizens, and the modes of altering political structures have changed dramatically since our courts first adopted the *Castioni* test. Neither wars nor revolutions are conducted in as clear-cut or mannerly a fashion as they once were. Both the nature of the acts committed in struggles for self-determination, *see* M. BASSIOUNI, INTERNATIONAL EXTRADITION: UNITED STATES LAW & PRACTICE, ch VIII, at §§ 2–71 to 2–72, and the geographic location of those struggles have changed considerably since the time of the French and American revolutions. Now challenges by insurgent movements to the existing order take place most frequently in Third World countries rather than in Europe and North America. In contrast to the organized, clearly identifiable, armed forces of past revolutions, today's struggles are often carried out by networks of individuals joined only by a common interest in opposing those in power.

It is understandable that Americans are offended by the tactics used by many of those seeking to change their governments. Often these tactics are employed by persons who do not share our cultural and social values or mores. Sometimes they are employed by those whose views of the nature, importance, or relevance of individual human life differ radically from ours. Nevertheless, it is not our place to impose our notions of civilized strife on people who are seeking to overthrow the regimes in control of their countries in contexts and circumstances that we have not experienced, and with which we can identify only with the greatest difficulty. It is the fact that the insurgents are seeking to change their governments that makes the political offense exception applicable, not their reasons for wishing to do so or the nature of the acts by which they hope to accomplish that goal.

Politically motivated violence, carried out by dispersed forces and directed at private sector institutions, structures, or civilians, is often undertaken—like the more organized, better disciplined violence of preceding revolutions—as part of an effort to gain the right to self-government. *See Politics of Extradition, supra* p. 31, at 632–33. We believe the tactics that are used in such internal political struggles are simply irrelevant to the question whether the political offense exception is applicable.

B. Relationship Between the Justifications for the Exception, the Incidence Test, and Contemporary Political Realities

One of the principal reasons our courts have had difficulty with the concept of affording certain contemporary revolutionary tactics and protection of the political offense exception is our fear and loathing of international terrorism. *See, e.g., Eain*, 641 F.2d at 520. The desire to exclude international terrorists from the coverage of the political offense exception is a legitimate one; the United States unequivocally condemns all international terrorism. However, the restrictions that some courts have adopted in order to remove terrorist activities from coverage under the political offense exception are overbroad. As we have noted, not all politically motivated violence undertaken by dispersed forces and directed at civilians is international terrorism and not all such activity should be exempted from the protection afforded by the exception.

Although it was not accepted as international law, the position of the United States, not only on international terrorism but also on the extradition of international terrorists, was made clear in 1972 when it introduced its Draft Convention on Terrorism in the United Nations. *See* U.N. Draft Convention for the Prevention and Punishment of Certain Acts of International Terrorism: United States Working Paper, U.N. Doc. A/C.6/L.850 (September 25, 1972), *reprinted in* 1 R. FRIEDLANDER, TERRORISM: DOCUMENTS OF INTERNATIONAL AND LOCAL CONTROL 487 (1979). The Draft Convention calls either for trial of international terrorists in the State where found or for their extradition. *See id.* at art. 3; *see also* 1984 Act to Combat International Terrorism § 201, Pub.L. 98–533, 96 Stat. 2706, 2709 (to be codified at 18 U.S.C. § 3077) (reaffirming United States' position on the extradition of international terrorists).

The policy and legal considerations that underlie our responses to acts of international terrorism differ dramatically from those that form the basis for our attitudes toward violent acts committed as part of other nations' internal political struggles. The application of the political offense exception to acts of domestic political violence comports in every respect with both the original justifications for the exception and the traditional requirements of the incidence test. The application of that exception to acts of international terrorism would comport with neither. First, we doubt whether the designers of the exception contemplated the it would protect acts of international violence, regardless of the ultimate objective of the actors. Second, in cases of international terrorism, we are being asked to return the accused to the government in a country where the acts were committed: frequently that is not a government the accused has sought to change. In such cases there is less risk that the accused will be subjected to an unfair trial or punishment because of his political opinion. Third, the exception was designed, in part, to protect against foreign intervention in internal struggles for political self-determination. When we extradite an individual accused on international terrorism, we are not interfering with any internal struggle; rather, it is the international terrorist who has interfered with the rights of others to exist peacefully under their chosen form of government.

There is no need to create a new mechanism for defining "political offenses" in order to ensure that the two important objectives we have been considering are met: (a) that international terrorists will be subject to extradition, and (b) that the exception will continue to cover the type of domestic revolutionary conduct that inspired its creation in the first place. While the precedent that guides us is limited, the applicable principles of law are clear. The incidence test has served us well and requires no significant modification. The growing problem of international terrorism, serious as it is, does not compel us to reconsider or redefine that test. The test we have used since the 1800's simply does not cover acts of international terrorism.

1. The "Incidence" Test

As all of the various tests for determining whether an offense is extraditable make clear, not every offense of a political character is nonextraditable. In the United States, an offense must meet the incidence test which is intended, like the tests designed by other nations, to comport with the justifications for the exception. We now explain the reasons for our conclusion that the traditional United States incidence test by its terms (a) protects acts of domestic violence in connection with a struggle for political self-determination, but (b) was not intended to and does not protect acts of international terrorism.

2. The "Uprising" Component

The incidence test has two components—the "uprising" requirement and the "incidental to" requirement. The first component, the requirement that there be an "uprising," "rebellion," or "revolution," has not been the subject of much discussion in the literature, although it is firmly established in the case law.... Most analyses of whether the exception applies have focused on whether the act in question was in furtherance of or incidental to a given uprising. Nevertheless, it is the "uprising" component that plays the key role in ensuring that the incidence test protects only those activities that the political offense doctrine was designed to protect.

As we have noted, the political offense doctrine developed out of a concern for the welfare of those engaged in a particular form of political activity—an effort to alter or abolish the government that controls their lives—and not out of a desire to protect all politically motivated violence. *See In re* Ezeta, 62 F. 972, 998 (N.D.Cal.1894) (" 'Any offense committed in the course of or furthering of civil war, insurrection, or political commotion.' ") (*quoting* John Stuart Mill); *In re* Castioni, [1981] 1 Q.B. 149, 156 (1890) ("a sort of overt act in the course of acting in a political matter, a political rising, or a dispute between two parties in the State as to which is to have the government in its hands") (per Denman, J.).

The uprising component serves to limit the exception to its historic purposes. It makes the exception applicable only when a certain level of violence exists and when those engaged in that violence are seeking to accomplish a particular objective. The exception does not apply to political acts that involve less fundamental efforts to accomplish change or that do not attract sufficient adherents to create the requisite amount of turmoil. *See* Escobedo v. United States, 623 F.2d 1098 (5th Cir.), *cert. denied*, 449 U.S. 1036 ... (1980). Thus, acts such as skyjacking (an act that never been used by revolutionaries to bring about a change in the composition or structure of the government in their own country) fall outside the scope of the exception.

Equally important, the uprising component serves to exclude from coverage under the exception criminal conduct that occurs outside the country or territory in which the uprising is taking place. The term "uprising" refers to a revolt by indigenous people against their own government or an occupying power. That revolt can occur only within the country or territory in which those rising up reside. By definition acts occurring in other lands are not part of the uprising. The political offense exception was designed to protect those engaged in internal or domestic struggles over the form or composition of their own government, including, of course, struggles to displace an occupying power. It was not designed to protect international political coercion or blackmail, or the exportation of violence and strife to other locations—even to the homeland of an oppressor nation. Thus, an uprising is not only limited temporally, it is limited spatially. *See 20th Century American Courts, supra* p. 30 at 1021 n. 115.

In his concurring opinion, Judge Duniway points out that the limitation to acts occurring within the territory in which there is an uprising means that persons committing acts of piracy, terrorism, or other crimes on the high seas will be unable to invoke the protection of the political offense exception. His observation is correct. Just as skyjackers and other international terrorists are not protected under the exception, neither are persons who commit or threaten to commit violent crimes on the high seas. The political offense exception was never intended to reach such conduct.

While determining the proper geographic boundaries of an "uprising" involves a legal issue that ordinarily will be fairly simple to resolve, there may be some circumstances under which it will be more difficult to do so. We need not formulate a general rule that will be applicable to all situations. It is sufficient in this case to state that for purposes of the political offense exception an "uprising" cannot extend beyond the borders of the country or territory in which a group of citizens or residents is seeking to change their particular government or governmental structure.

It follows from what we have said that an "uprising" can exist only when the turmoil that warrants that characterization is created by nationals of the land in which the disturbances are occurring. Viewed in that light, it comes clear that had the traditional incidence test been applied in *Eain*, discussed *supra* pp. 801–01, the result would have been identical to that reached by the Seventh Circuit. When PLO members enter Israel and commit unlawful acts, there is simply no uprising for the acts to be incidental to. The plain fact is that the Israelis are not engaged in revolutionary activity directed against their own government. They are not seeking to change its form, structure, or composition through violent means. That the PLO members who commit crimes are seeking to destroy Israel as a state does not help bring them within the political offense exception. In the absence of an uprising, the violence engaged in by PLO members in Israel and elsewhere does not meet the incidence test and is not covered by the political offense exception. To the contrary, the PLO's worldwide campaign of violence, including the crimes its members commit in the state of Israel, clearly constitutes "international terrorism."

Moreover, Eain's conduct may have fallen outside the political offense exception for an additional, though related, reason. Not only was there no uprising in Israel, but Eain himself was not a national of that country. It is not clear whether, even when the violence is primarily conducted by nationals and thus an uprising may properly be found to exist, a foreign citizen who voluntarily joins the fray is protected by the exception. The exception was designed to protect those seeking to change their own government or to oust an occupying power that is asserting sovereignty over them. We question whether it should apply when the accused is not a citizen of the country or territory in which the uprising is occurring. In the absence of a tangible demonstration that he or she has more than a transitory connection with that land, the acts of a foreign national may simply not qualify for protection.

Although we find substantial merit to the argument that foreign nationals should be excluded from coverage under the political offense exception, the incidence test has never previously been analyzed in a manner that considers the question in any detail. Because of the conclusion we reach with respect to other issues in the case before us, there is no need for us to answer the question here. Accordingly, we leave its resolution to a subsequent time. It is enough for our purposes merely to note that the fact that Eain was not an Israeli might well have constituted another basis for holding that his conduct was not protected under the incidence test.

In short, the *Eain* and *Doherty* courts' objective that this country not become a haven for international terrorists can readily be met through a proper application of the incidence test. It is met by interpreting the political offense exception in light of its historic origins and goals. Such a construction excludes acts of international terrorism. There is no reason, therefore, to construe the incidence test in a subjective and judgmental manner that excludes all violent political conduct of which we disapprove. Moreover, any such construction would necessarily exclude some forms of internal revolutionary conduct and thus run contrary to the exception's fundamental purpose. For that reasons, we reject the *Eain* test and especially the concept that courts may determine whether particular forms of conduct constitute acceptable means or methods of engaging in an uprising.

3. The "Incidental to" Component

When describing the second requirement of the incidence test, the "incidental to" component, American courts have used the phrases "in the course of," "connected to," and "in furtherance of" interchangeably. We have applied a rather liberal standard when determining whether this part of the test has been met and have been willing to examine all of the circumstances surrounding the commission of the crime. Garcia–Guillern v. United States, 450 F.2d 1189, 1192 (5th Cir.1971), *cert.*

denied, 405 U.S. 989 . . . (1972); Ramos v. Diaz, 179 F. Supp. 459, 463 (S.D.Fla.1959).

Commentators have criticized United States courts for applying the "incidental to" component too loosely or flexibly. *See supra* p. 797. We disagree with this criticism. To put the matter in its proper context, it is necessary to bear in mind that the offense must occur in the context of an "uprising." Acts "incidental to" an uprising are, as we have noted, limited by the geographic confines of the uprising. In addition, the act must be contemporaneous with the uprising. Moreover, the "incidental to" component is not satisfied by "any connection, however feeble, between a common crime and a political disturbance," Garcia–Mora, *supra* p. 3, at 1244. The act must be causally or ideologically related to the uprising. *See, e.g.,* Ornelas v. Ruiz, 161 U.S. 502 . . . (1896) (concluding that rapid withdrawal of bandits after foray, in absence of threatening armed forces, suggested that acts were not incidental to uprising).

We believe the traditional liberal construction of the requirement that there be a nexus between the act and the uprising, *see supra* p. 797, is appropriate. There are various types of acts that, when committed in the course of an uprising, are likely to have been politically motivated. There is little reason, under such circumstances, to impose a strict nexus standard. Moreover, the application of a strict test would in some instances jeopardize the rights of the accused.

Under the liberal nexus standard, neither proof of the potential or actual effectiveness of the actions in achieving the group's political ends, *In re* Castioni, [1891] 1 Q.B. 149, 158–59 (1890) (refusing to consider whether the act was a wise mode of promoting the cause) (per Denman, J.), nor proof of the motive of the accused, *Eain*, 641 F.2d at 519, or the requesting nation, *Garcia-Guillern*, 450 F.2d at 1192; *Ramos v. Diaz*, 179 F. Supp. at 463, is required. Nor is the organization or hierarchy of the uprising group or the accused's membership in any such group determinative. *See Eain,* 641 F.2d at 519.

When extradition is sought, the "offender" at this stage in the proceedings has ordinarily only been accused, not convicted, of the offense. It would be inconsistent with the rights of the accused to require proof of membership in an uprising group. For example, the accused might be able to show that the acts were incidental to the uprising but might be unable to prove membership because he or she did not commit the offense or was not a member of the group. Furthermore, requiring proof of membership might violate the accused's Fifth Amendment rights both because it might force him to supply circumstantial evidence of guilt of the charged offense and because membership in the group itself might be illegal. Also, we question how one proves membership in an uprising group. Uprising groups often do not have formal organizational structures or document membership. In addition, it is entirely possible to sympathize with, aid, assist, or support a group, help further its objectives and its activities, participate in its projects, or carry on parallel activities of one's own, without becoming a member of the organization. Still, one may be acting in furtherance of an uprising.

On the other hand, a number of factors, though not necessary to the nexus determination, may play a part in evaluating the circumstances surrounding the commission of the offense. For example, proof of membership in an uprising group may make it more likely that the act was incidental to the uprising. *See, e.g., Ramos v. Diaz,* 179 F. Supp. at 463; *Castioni,* 1 Q.B. at 157–59 (per Denman, J.). The similarity of the charged offense to other acts committed by the uprising group, and the degree of control over the accused's acts by some hierarchy within the group, may give further credence to the claim that the act was incidental to the uprising. And while evidence of the accused's political motivation is not required and is usually unavailable, evidence that an act was "committed for purely personal reasons such as vengeance or vindictiveness," *In re* Doherty, 599 F. Supp. 270, 277 n. 7 (S.D.N.Y.1984), may serve to rebut any presumption that a nexus exists. The exception is not designed to protect mercenaries or others acting for nonpolitical motives.

Under the liberal nexus test we have traditionally applied, or even under a strict nexus standard, there is no justification for distinguishing, as Doherty suggests, between attacks on military and civilian targets. The "incidental to" component, like the incidence test as a whole, must be applied in an objective, non-judgmental manner. It is for the revolutionaries, not the courts, to determine what tactics may help further their chances of bringing down or changing the government. All that the courts should do is determine whether the conduct is related to or connected with the insurgent activity. It is clear that various "non-military" offenses, including acts as disparate as stealing food to sustain the combatants, killing to avoid disclosure of strategies, or killing simply to avoid capture, may be incidental to or in furtherance of an uprising. To conclude that attacks on the military are protected by the exception, but that attacks on private sector institutions and civilians are not, ignores the nature and purpose of the test we apply, as well as realities of contemporary domestic revolutionary struggles. *See supra* pp. 804–05.

We should add that the spatial limitations imposed under the "uprising" component may not be circumvented by reliance on the "incidental to" component. As we said earlier, for the political offense exception to be applicable at all, the crime must have occurred in the country or territory in which the uprising was taking place, not in a different geographic location. *See supra* pp. 806–07. . . .

. . . In light of the justifications for the political offense exception, the formulation of the incidence test as it has traditionally been articulated, and the cases in which the exception has historically been applied, we do not believe it would be proper to stretch the term "uprising" to include acts that took place in England as a part of a struggle by nationals of Northern Ireland to change the form of government in their own land. Accordingly, we need not decide whether had an uprising occurred, the protection afforded by the exception would have been extended to one who, like Quinn, is a citizen of a different and uninvolved nation. Because the incidence test is not met, neither the bombing conspiracy nor the murder of Police Constable Tibble is a non-extraditable offense under the political offenses exception to the extradition treaty between the United States and the United Kingdom.

Notes and Questions

1. Noting that there are two types of political offenses (*i.e.*, "pure" and "relative"), what are the policies underlying the political offense exception as identified by the court in *Quinn v. Robinson*? What are the relative advantages and disadvantages of the British, French, Swiss, and various U.S. tests for determining what constitutes a political offense. Which test is most consistent with the policies underlying the political offense exception?

Mere crimes against the state such as espionage, treason, or a military offense such as absence without leave, are "pure" political offenses.

2. With respect to political offenses, see also *Ex parte* Kentucky v. Dennison, 65 U.S. (24 How.) 66, 99–100 (1860) ("According to these usages, ... persons who fled on account of political offences were almost always excepted, and the nation ... exercises a discretion.... And the English Government has always refused to deliver up political offenders."); *In re* Metzger, 46 U.S. (5 How.) 176, 188 n.2 (1847) (" 'it is generally admitted that extradition should not be granted in the case of political offenders, but only in the case of individuals who have committed crimes against the Law of Nature, the laws which all nations regard as the foundation of public and private security' "), quoting 1 PHILLIMORE, INTERNATIONAL LAW 413 (1854); *In re* Ezeta, *et al.*, 62 F. 972, 997–1003 (N.D. Cal. 1894); United States v. Watts, 14 F. 130, 135 (D. Cal. 1882) ("It has been urged that the right of asylum for political offenders is so universally recognized as sacred and inviolable that an infringement of it was ... not ... possible, but jurists ... are not always agreed as to what constitutes a political offense"); *In re* Sheazle, 21 F. Cas. 1214, 1215 (C.C.D. Mass. 1845) (No. 12,734) ("in case of mere political offences, it is seldom done"); Oliver v. Kaufman, 18 F. Cas. 657, 659 (C.C.E.D. Pa. 1850) (No. 10,497) ("law of nations which refuse to deliver up persons guilty of mere political offences").

3. Concerning relative political offenses, there are actually significant splits in U.S. circuits (and among foreign states) as to which tests should be applied and how they can be applied in a given circumstance, although political motive is one necessary criterion. See RESTATEMENT § 476, cmt. g and RNs 4 & 5. As the court in *Quinn v. Robinson* notes, several U.S. Courts have recently attempted to limit the application of the political offense exception in cases involving acts of terrorism. In Eain v. Wilkes, 641 F.2d 504, 520–21 (7th Cir.1981), *cert. denied,* 454 U.S. 894 (1981), the court held that "the indiscriminate bombing of a civilian population is not recognized as a protected political act." In *In re* Doherty, 599 F.Supp. 270, 275 (S.D.N.Y.1984), the court stated that the political offense exception would not protect bombings in public places, acts that transcend the limits of international law, acts inconsistent with international standards of civilized conduct, harm to hostages, violations of the Geneva conventions, or the acts of fanatic groups without structure, organization or clearly defined political

objectives, but it did protect the targeting of a military officer. The court in *Quinn v. Robinson*, however, did not believe such judicially imposed limitations on the traditional test for determining whether an act qualifies as a political offense were justified. Do you agree? What are the problems inherent in the tests employed by the Seventh Circuit and Southern District of New York? What are the benefits in applying a violation of international law exception to the political offense exception?

Note also that Article VII of the Genocide Convention precludes use of the political offense exception for listed crimes. The same type of exclusion is found in Article XI(1) of the International Convention on the Suppression and Punishment of the Crime of "Apartheid" and in Article V of the 1994 Inter–American Convention on the Forced Disappearance of Persons. Does U.N. G.A. Res. 59/195, Human Rights and Terrorism, para. 10, support preclusion of the political offense exception for those who planned, facilitated or participated in the commission of acts of terrorism? See the resolution in the Documents Supplement.

4. If police and military personnel can be lawful targets in an armed conflict, does this add to your consideration one way or the other? Consider Jordan J. Paust, *An Introduction to and Commentary on Terrorism and the Law,* 19 CONN. L. REV. 697, 744 (1987).

5. The court in *Quinn v. Robinson* erred when stating that crimes against humanity, such as genocide, "are carried out by or with the toleration of authorities of a state." *See, e.g.*, Convention on the Prevention and Punishment of the Crime of Genocide, 78 U.N.T.S. 277, art. IV; Kadic v. Karadzic, in Chapter 1; JORDAN J. PAUST, M. CHERIF BASSIOUNI, *ET AL.*, INTERNATIONAL CRIMINAL LAW chpts. 10 and 11 (2 ed. 2000).

6. The court in *Quinn v. Robinson* narrowly construed the geographic and temporal scope of the "uprising requirement" of the incidence test. Thus, it held that a bombing in London did not qualify for the political offense exception because it took place a distance from the "uprising," which was occurring in Northern Ireland. Do you agree with this interpretation? What are its implications for other situations? Not all courts apply an incidence or uprising test, especially in cases where persons are fleeing tyranny. Which approach do you prefer? *Compare* Steven Lubet, *Extradition Unbound: A Reply to Professors Blakesley and Bassiouni,* 24 TEX. INT'L L.J. 47, 50 (1989) *with* Jordan Paust, *An Introduction, supra,* at 745–46.

What if Jews had killed a guard at a German concentration camp while escaping in 1940—should they have been extradited back to Nazi Germany? What if a political prisoner in the former U.S.S.R. killed a camp guard while escaping the gulag? Would they have had "political" motives sufficient to label the killing a relative political offense?

7. In its concluding paragraph, the court in *Quinn v. Robinson* suggested that the political offense exception might not be applicable to cases involving persons who are a "citizen of a different and uninvolved nation." What are the justifications for such a limitation? What problems might it create?

8. During the 1980s, the Executive began to negotiate Supplementary Extradition Treaties with its "stable democratic allies" that exclude from

the political offense exception cases involving listed crimes, such as murder, kidnapping, the hijacking of aircraft, aircraft sabotage, crimes against diplomats and other internationally protected persons, the taking of hostages, "maliciously wounding", "false imprisonment", and "possession of a firearm or ammunition by a person who intends either himself or through another person to endanger life," as well as offenses involving explosives. The United States has so far concluded such treaties with Canada, the United Kingdom, Belgium, Germany, and Spain. See Article IV of the Protocol Amending the US–Canada Extradition Treaty, above.

What problems exist with respect to the ad hoc approach of negotiating supplementary treaties with so-called stable democratic allies? Are all of these bilateral treaty-based exclusions preferable? Do they reach too far and are they too inflexible? *Compare* Steven Lubet, *Taking the Terror Out of Political Terrorism: The Supplementary Treaty on Extradition Between the United States and the United Kingdom,* 19 CONN. L. REV. 863 (1987); *International Criminal Law and the "Ice–Nine" Error: A Discourse on the Fallacy of Universal Solutions,* 28 VA. J. INT'L L. 963 (1988) *with* M. Cherif Bassiouni, *The "Political Offense" Exception Revisited: Extradition Between the U.S. and the U.K.—A Choice Between Friendly Cooperation Among Allies and Sound Law and Policy,* 15 DEN. J. INT'L L. & POL. 255 (1987); Christopher Blakesley, *An Essay on Executive Branch Attempts to Eviscerate the Separation of Powers,* 2 UTAH L. REV. 451 (1987); Jordan J. Paust, *"Such a Narrow Approach" Indeed,* 29 VA. J. INT'L L. 413 (1989).

In the United States, can it be lawful for a private citizen to carry a gun with an intent to perform an act that might "endanger life"? If so, should this sort of possession of a firearm be an automatic bar to use of the political offense exception? Should "false imprisonment"?

E. Non–Inquiry and Human Rights

AHMAD v. WIGEN

726 F.Supp. 389 (E.D.N.Y.1989).

WEINSTEIN, J.

This case raises serious questions—some of them novel—about the United States' obligations under an extradition treaty and the court's role in ensuring that those extradited are treated fairly. As indicated below, two changes in law must now be recognized: The "political offense" bar to extradition is narrowed to exclude terrorism and acts of war against civilians. A correlative expansion is required in courts' power to ensure that those extradited are granted due process and are treated humanely. Petitioner has been afforded due process in this country, and adequate guarantees exist that he will be fairly treated in Israel, the country seeking his extradition to stand trial for alleged terrorist acts against its citizens. . . .

Mahmoud El–Abed Ahmad seeks a writ of habeas corpus, 28 U.S.C. § 2241, to prevent his extradition to Israel to stand trial. On April 12, 1986, he allegedly attacked by firebombs and automatic weapons fire a passenger bus en route to Tel Aviv traveling between Israeli settlements in the occupied territory of the West Bank. Death of the bus driver and serious injury to one of the passengers resulted....

... Petitioner claimed that should he be extradited to Israel he would face procedures and treatment "antipathetic to a court's sense of decency." Because this ground had not been raised in any prior proceeding, petitioner requested an evidentiary hearing to demonstrate that the Israeli judicial system would not afford him due process and that he would not afford him due process and that he would be subject to conditions of detention and interrogation in violation of universally accepted principles of human rights.

The government opposed petitioner's request for a hearing. It asserted that the scope of habeas review is extremely narrow and that the rule of non-inquiry prohibited the court from inquiring into the integrity of the requesting state's judicial system. Neither side requested that the issue be referred to Judge Korman. The petition was referred to the present judge by random selection.

On May 16, 1989 this court ruled from the bench that it would consider petitioner's due process claim and permit both parties to submit further evidence on this and any other issue. The government sought a writ of mandamus from the Court of Appeals for the Second Circuit to prohibit the court from holding a hearing and from receiving evidence on the probable nature of the judicial procedures of the requesting nation in an extradition matter. On June 20, 1989 the Court of Appeals denied the writ of mandamus.

This court held evidentiary hearings in July and August of 1989 to supplement the record before Magistrate Caden and Judge Korman. Both parties submitted documentary evidence. Petitioner called four witnesses to testify on the Israeli judicial process and conditions of detention: Professor John Quigley, Abdeen M. Jabara, Heah Tsemel, Esq. and Sami Esmail. Preserving its objection to the proceedings, respondent called two witnesses, Professors Alan Dershowitz and Monroe Freedman, and submitted statements of United States officials who had observed trials in Israel. A representative of the Israeli government certified the protections petitioner would receive in Israel.... The parties then fully briefed and argued the case in September, 1989.

In all, some fourteen days of evidentiary hearings, and extensive oral argument based upon full briefs and the court's own research, were devoted to this case. Petitioner has had a full opportunity to be heard....

Petitioner contends that should he be extradited to Israel, he would be subjected to torture and cruel and unusual punishment during interrogation to coerce him into confessing the acts alleged; he would not receive even "a semblance of due process" in the Israeli criminal justice system, particularly since any conviction would in all likelihood rest on either his or his alleged accomplices' coerced confessions; and, finally, he would be housed in indecent detention and prison facilities. He contends that extradition under these circumstances violates fundamental principles of due process and human rights.

The claim raises the question of whether a federal court may inquire into the fairness of a requesting country's criminal justice system, including its methods of interrogation, rules of evidence regarding confessions and conditions of detention. If so, the court must determine whether petitioner faces treatment and procedures on extradition so offensive to the court's sense of decency that the habeas corpus writ must be granted and extradition prohibited. This court is empowered to hold an evidentiary hearing to determine the nature of treatment probably awaiting petitioner in a requesting nation to determine whether he or she can demonstrate probable exposure to such treatment as would violate universally accepted principles of human rights.

It should be emphasized that by conducting such an inquiry, we do not make it "the business of our courts to assume the responsibility for supervising the integrity of the judicial system of another sovereign nation." Jhirad v. Ferrandina, 536 F.2d 478, 484–85 (2d Cir.), *cert. denied*, 429 U.S. 833 ... (1976). But neither can another nation use the courts of our country to obtain power over a fugitive intending to deny that person due process. We cannot blind ourselves to the foreseeable and probable results of the exercise of our jurisdiction. *Cf. Jhirad*, 536 F.2d at 485 (requiring demanding state to show that petitioner would not be prosecuted for a crime for which the statute of limitations had run); Gallina v. Fraser, 278 F.2d 77, 79 (2d Cir.), *cert. denied*, 364 U.S. 851 ... (1960) ("federal court's sense of decency may limit extradition"); *In re* Extradition of Burt, 737 F.2d 1477, 1486–87 (7th Cir.1984) ("fundamental conceptions of fair play and decency" and "particularly atrocious procedures or punishments" may be considered by the court); Plaster v. United States, 720 F.2d 340, 348, 354 (4th Cir.1983) ("individual constitutional rights" must be weighed to determine if extradition would be "fundamentally unfair"); United States *ex rel.* Bloomfield v. Gengler, 507 F.2d 925, 928 (2d Cir.1974), *cert. denied*, 421 U.S. 1001 ... (1975) (extradition may be "antipathetic to a federal court's sense of decency").

Reflective of our country's concern for the extraditee is the fact that our State Department has insisted that the requesting nation protect those extradited. It requires, for example, that as a condition of surrender a person found guilty in absentia be retried. Gallina v. Fraser, 278 F.2d 77, 78 (2d Cir.), *cert. denied*, 364 U.S. 851 ... (1960). Moreover, this court was informed that the State Department will observe the trial abroad to ensure that its conditions are fulfilled.

A. Due Process Exception to the Rule of Non-Inquiry

1. *Generally*

The theme that treaties and other international obligations should not inhibit fundamental individual rights policies of the United States is a powerful one. *Cf.* Societe Nationale Industrielle Aerospatiale v. United

States District Court, S.D. Iowa, 482 U.S. 522, 554 ... (1987) (treaty interpreted to leave United States rules for discovery in civil cases intact); Henkin, *Rights: American and Human*, 79 COLUM. L. REV. 405, 411 (1979) (American rights are in some sense supreme because they "antecede the Constitution and are above government"). The inherent conflict between national sovereignty and obligations under treaties which appear to limit that sovereignty is well illustrated by the right of extraditing nations to refuse to violate their own sense of individual justice. *See* Barr v. United States Dep't of Justice, 819 F.2d 25, 27 (2d. Cir.1987) (The "treaty may authorize only such governmental action as in conformity with the Constitution."); Reid v. Covert, 354 U.S. 1, 16–18 ... (1957) (supremacy of Constitution over particular treaty); L. HENKIN, R. PUGH, O. SCHACHTER & H. SMIT, INTERNATIONAL LAW: CASES AND MATERIALS 184–85 (2d ed. 1987).

Treaty obligations will sometimes need to be read and interpreted by the courts of a nation in the context of the fundamental law of the nation that entered into them. In the United States that law includes those principles embodied in the due process clauses of the fifth and fourteenth amendments of the Constitution guaranteeing extensive protections to the criminally accused. *Cf.* L. HENKIN, FOREIGN AFFAIRS AND THE CONSTITUTION 255 (1972) ("In regard to foreign relations ... 'due process of law' requires fair procedures for aliens as for citizens ... in civil as in criminal proceedings, before administrative bodies and in courts."). This principle, we emphasize, does not require us to impose the details of our Constitution or procedural system on a requesting country's judicial system. *See* Neely v. Henkel, 180 U.S. 109, 122 ... (1901). It does entail an obligation not to extradite people who face procedures or treatment that "shocks the conscience" of jurists acting under the United States Constitution and within our current legal ethos. *See* Rosado v. Civiletti, 621 F.2d 1179, 1195–96 (2d Cir.), *cert. denied*, 449 U.S. 856 ... (1980) ("Thus, although the Constitution cannot limit the power of a foreign sovereign to prescribe procedures for the trial and punishment of crimes committed within its territory, it does govern the manner in which the United States may join the effort."). *Cf.* Rochin v. California, 342 U.S. 165, 172 ... (1952).

As pointed out in Section III A(1), *supra*, international custom and treaties limiting attacks on civilians are not derogatory to our Constitution. Rather they expand and give substance to a developing enriched concept of rights of the individual that harmonizes with our own constitutional developments.

The introductory note to the subchapter on extradition of the Restatement points out, "The requested state retains an interest in the fate of a person it has extradited" as well as the probable fate of those whose extradition is sought. *Restatement*, *supra*, at 557. Extradition may be refused, for example, where requested nation has a substantial ground for believing that the person sought "would not receive a fair trial or would risk suffering other violations of human rights" in the requesting nation. *Id.* § 475 cmt. g, at 562, § 476 cmt. h. at 571. "Thus, while extradition treaties obligate the parties to extradite according to their terms, nearly all extradition treaties leave some room—at least by implication—for discretion by the requested state not to extradite in certain cases." *Id.* at 558. *See* Sindona v. Grant, 619 F.2d 167, 176 (2d Cir.1980) ("[T]he executive branch ... is empowered to make the final decision on extradition and has assumed the discretion to deny or delay extradition on humanitarian grounds."); S. Treaty Doc. No 100–20, 100th Cong. 2d Sess. 7 (1988) (executive has discretion to refuse to extradite if extraditee is in danger of being subject to torture); Kester, *Some Myths of United States Extradition Law*, 76 GEO.L.J. 1441, 1478 (1988).

Three independent protections are erected against this country's participation in the wrongful deed of surrendering fugitives to likely abuse by the requesting state. First, Congress and the executive branch do not enter in to extradition treaties with countries in whose criminal justice system they lack confidence. *Restatement, supra*, at 558 (noting absence of extradition treaties with the U.S.S.R., People's Republic of China, North Korea and Iran). Second, when conditions change after an extradition treaty is concluded, without formal denunciation or suspension of the treaty, the executive of the requested state—here the Secretary of State—may refuse to extradite. *Id.*; S. Treaty Doc. No. 100–20, 100th Cong., 2d Sess. 7 (1988). Third, the courts in this country, constituting and independent branch of government, charged with defending the due process rights of all those who appear before them, may grant the accused prisoner a writ of habeas corpus blocking extradition.

2. *United States Precedent*

The existence, and ambit, of this third, court imposed, protection is not settled. Under the traditional rule of non-inquiry, claims of probable lack of due process in the requesting nation would fall within "the exclusive purview of the executive branch" and courts would not inquire into the procedures which await the accused upon extradition. Sindona v. Grant, 619 F.2d 167, 174 (2d Cir.1980). *Accord, e.g.,* Garcia–Guillern v. United States, 450 F.2d 1189 (5th Cir.1971), *cert. denied*, 405 U.S. 989 ... (1972); Peroff v. Hylton, 542 F.2d 1247 (4th Cir. 1976), *cert. denied*, 429 U.S. 1062 ... (1977) (S)upervising the integrity of the judicial system of another sovereign nation ... would directly conflict with the principle of comity which extradition is based. Jhirad v. Ferrandina, 536 F.2d 478, 485 (2d Cir.), *cert. denied*, 429 U.S. 833 ... (1976). *Cf.* Glucksman v. Henkel, 221 U.S. 508, 512 ... (1910) ("We are bound by the existence of an extradition treaty to assume that the trial will be fair.").

Despite this limiting line of cases, the courts, as an independent branch of government, have a duty to stand between the executive and the accused where a case of abdication of State Department responsibility for the protection of the accused has been made out. Courts may not compromise "that judicial integrity so necessary in the true administration of justice." Mapp v. Ohio, 367 U.S. 643, 660 ... (1961). The courts may not be parties to abusive judicial practices, even where sensitive foreign relations matters are concerned. *See* Barr v. United States, 819 F.2d 25, 27 n.2 (2d Cir.1987) ("[It is a] recognized principle that, regardless of the degree of American government involvement in the conduct of a foreign sovereign, the federal courts will not allow themselves to be placed in the position of putting their imprimatur on unconscionable conduct.").

Despite the fact that the executive branch has a constitutional duty and right to conduct foreign policy, and the legislative and executive branches together have the duty and right to enter into treaties for extradition, the courts are not, and cannot be, a rubber stamp of the other branches of government in the exercise of extradition jurisdiction. They must, under article III of the Constitution, exercise their independent judgement in a case or controversy to determine the propriety of an individual's extradition. The executive may not foreclose the courts from exercising their responsibility to protect the integrity of the judicial process. A court must ensure that it is not used for purpose which do not comport with our constitution or principles of fundamental fairness....

The Second Circuit has repeatedly acknowledged that it could "imagine situations where the [accused], upon extradition, would be subject to procedures or punishment so antipathetic to a federal court's sense of decency as to require reexamination" of the rule of non-inquiry. Gallina v. Fraser, 278 F.2d 77, 79 (2d Cir.), *cert. denied*, 364 U.S. 851 ... (1960). *Accord* United States *ex. rel.* Bloomfield v. Gengler, 507 F.2d 925, 928 (2d Cir.1974), *cert. denied* 421 U.S. 1001 ... (1975); Rosado v. Civiletti, 621 F.2d 1179, 1195 (2d Cir.) *cert. denied*, 449 U.S. 856 ... (1980). *See also* Demjanjuk v. Petrovsky, 776 F.2d 571, 583 (6th Cir. 1985), *cert. denied*, 475 U.S. 1016 ... (1986); Arnbjornsdottir–Mendler v. United States, 721 F.2d 679, 683 (9th Cir.1983). The *Gallina* exception to the rule of non-inquiry has apparently yet to be invoked to prevent extradition since thus far no petitioner has persuasively demonstrated that extradition would expose him to unconscionable abuse. *see, e.g., Demjanjuk v. Petrovsky*, 776 F.2d at 583 ("There is absolutely no showing in this record that Israel will follow procedures which would shock this court's 'sense of decency.' "); *Arnbjornsdottir-Mendler v. United States*, 721 F.2d at 683 ("In light of Iceland's outstanding human rights' record and appellant's uncorroborated prediction of maltreatment, the district court had no obligation to hold an evidentiary hearing to consider the claim.").

3. *International Precedent*

The present status of international and human rights law on this issue is demonstrated by the *Soering Case*, decided by the European Court of Human Rights of the Council of Europe in Strasbourg on July 7, 1989. slip sheet 1/1989/161/217. There was strong evidence that Soering a West German citizen, had assisted in the commission of a homicide in Virginia. Soering was arrested in Great Britain and ordered extradited to Virginia, pursuant to a treaty between the United States and the United Kingdom. The European Court intervened upon Soering's application charging the United Kingdom with a breach of its obligations under various articles of the European Convention for the Protection of Human Rights and Fundamental Freedoms, Nov. 4, 1950, 213 U.N.T.S. 221, 224 (1955). In particular, Soering claimed that by ordering his extradition to Virginia, the United Kingdom would subject him to the risk of languishing for years on death row—a fate he contended would constitute a violation of article 3 of the Convention which provides: "No one shall be subjected to torture or to inhuman or degrading treatment or punishment." 213 U.N.T.S. at 224.

The European Court adopted the principle that the requested country bears a responsibility to measure the conditions in the requesting country against article 3 of the Convention "where substantial grounds have been shown for believing that the person concerned, if extradited, faces a real risk of being subjected to torture or to inhuman or degrading treatment or punishment in the requesting country." *Soering Case*, slip sheet at 27. The court found that although the Convention is not considered to be part of United Kingdom law, "the English courts can review the 'reasonableness' of an extradition decision in the light of" such factors. *Id.* at 38.

In an unanimous decision, the Court rejected extradition:

> [H]aving regard to the very long period of time spent on death row in such extreme conditions, with the ever present and mounting anguish of awaiting execution of the death penalty, ... [Soering's] extradition to the United States would expose him to a real risk of treatment going beyond the threshold set by Art. 3.

Id. at 35. It based its decision upon evidence demonstrating that it would probably take at least six years to decide the defendant's fate after conviction and that there was a substantial possibility that he would experience the severely damaging psychological and physical conditions of death row for from six to eight years. *Id.* at 17. Apparently, the European Court believed that the protections of article 3 of the Convention are greater than those that would be provided by the courts of Virginia and the Supreme Court of the United States under our due process and cruel and unusual punishment clauses of the United States Constitution.

The *Soering* case arguably went too far in limiting extradition based upon probable conditions in the requesting country. Its decision perhaps can be justified as a matter of equity if not law on the ground that defendant would not go unwhipped of justice even were he not extradited to Virginia. He was a German national who could be tried for the crime in West Germany where the maximum penalty would be life imprisonment. That country was also seeking his extradition. *Id.* at 34 (majority found this possibility of extradition to a third country not "material," but given some weight in obtaining "a fair balance of interests").

In considering *Soering*, it is significant that the European Court of Human Rights recognized that a court's determination of whether to extradite entails a responsibility to consider the interests of the community in its safety from terrorists and other criminals. The Court declared:

> [I]nherent in the whole of the Convention is a search for a fair balance between the demands of the general interest of the community and the requirements of the protection of the individual's fundamental rights. As movement about the world becomes easier and crime takes on a larger international dimension, it is increasingly in the interest of all nations that suspected offenders who flee abroad should be brought to justice. Conversely, the establishment of safe havens for fugitives would not only result in danger for the State obliged to harbour the protected person but also tend to undermine the foundations of extradition. These considerations must also be included among the factors to be taken into account in the interpretation and application of the notions of inhuman and degrading treatment or punishment in extradition cases.

Id. at 27. Thus, just as national policies and international norms are taken into account by American courts ascertaining the scope of the political offense exception, *see* Section IIE(1) *supra*, so too must these considerations enter into the assessment of whether the likelihood of particular treatment in the requesting country constitutes such a violation of due process and fundamental fairness as to prevent extradition.

Soering constitutes an important precedent on the refusal to extradite because of anticipated torture, cruel conditions of incarceration or lack of due process at trial in the requesting country. It reflects a persuasive though non-binding international standard. *Cf.* Demjanjuk v. Petrovsky, 776 F.2d 571, 582 (6th Cir.1985), *cert. denied*, 475 U.S. 1016 ... (1986) ("The law of the United States includes international law," *citing The Paquete Habana*, 175 U.S. 677, 712 ... (1900)). *Cf.* United Nations Convention Against Torture and Other Cruel, Inhuman and Degrading Treatment or Punishment art. 3, GAOR A/39/506 (1984), 23 I.L.M. 1027, 1028 (1984) ("No State Party shall ... extradite a person to another State where there are substantial grounds for believing that he would be in danger of being subjected to torture."); S. Treaty Doc. No. 100–20, 100th Cong. 2d Sess. 7 (1988) (reprinting Convention, together with message of transmittal recommending ratification).

The opinion in *Soering* sets forth factors a court should consider in assessing the severity of ill-treatment, including "all the circumstances of the case, such as the nature and context of the treatment or punishment, the manner and method of its execution, its duration, its physical or mental effects and , in some instances, the sex, age and state of health of the victim." *Soering Case*, slip sheet at 30. The European Court of Human Rights has also given definition to the vague terms "inhuman and degrading treatment and punishment":

> Treatment has been held by the Court to be both "inhuman" because it was premeditated, was applied for hours at a stretch and "caused, if not actual bodily injury, at least intense physical and mental suffering," and also "degrading" because it was "such as to

> arouse in its victims feelings of fear, anguish and inferiority capable of humiliating and debasing them and possibly breaking their physical and moral resistance."

Id.

Torture and cruel and unusual punishment must be defined for our purposes as including threats and other inhuman psychological pressure may be even more painful and more effective than physical pressure in destroying person's dignity or in overcoming the will of the person interrogate, thus inducing false confessions. Even if the probable inhumane act is unauthorized by the requesting nation and is applied by those abusing power it could constitute a basis for non-extradition. *See Altun v. Federal Republic of Germany*, 36 Eur. Comm'n H.R. 209, 233–35 (1983) (in action challenging extradition, torture incidents considered even though Turkish government had discouraged them by prosecuting police officers responsible).

B. Burden of Proof

As a general rule our courts should rely on the State Department's initial approval and forwarding of the extradition request to the appropriate United States Attorney as certification that the requesting state may be relied upon to treat the accused fairly. *See* S. Treaty Doc. No. 100–20, 100th Cong., 2d Sess. 7 (1988) (Secretary of State should use its discretion to ensure that extraditee will not be subject to torture). The Department has better resources than the courts to make appropriate inquiries. Particularly since it is charged by Congress under sections 116(d) and 502B(b) of the Foreign Assistance Act of 1961 with making an annual review of human rights conditions through the world, the State Department may be assumed to be sensitive to the problem. *See, e.g.*, United States Dep't of State, 101st Cong., 1st Sess., *Country Reports on Human Rights Practices for 1988* (S.Prt. 101–3, 1989). There may, however, be instances where immediate political, military or economic needs of the United States induce the State Department to ignore the rights of the accused. Should such cases occur, the courts must be prepared to act.

There is presumption in favor of the State Department's and a foreign nation's good faith exercise of its powers. Nevertheless, "the presumption of fairness routinely accorded the criminal process of a foreign sovereign may require closer scrutiny if a [petitioner] persuasively demonstrates that extradition would expose him to procedures or punishments 'antipathetic to a federal court's sense of decency.'" Rosado v. Civilleti, 621 F.2d 1179, 1195 (2d Cir.), *cert. denied*, 449 U.S. 856 ... (1980). Because foreign policy is involved, the State Department's decision that extradition is proper will be given considerable weight. The burden of proof is on petitioner to come forward with a written submission showing a substantial probability that he or she can rebut the presumption of State Department propriety in assuming the fairness of the judicial process in the requesting country. *Cf.* Fed.R.Evid. 301

(shifting burden of coming forward). If petitioner makes such a threshold showing, the rule of non-inquiry yields and an evidentiary hearing may be conducted on the issue of probable due process to the accused in the requesting country. The Federal Rules of Evidence do not apply to such extradition hearings. Fed.R.Evid. 1101(d)(3).

In previous cases of extradition to Israel, the courts have repeatedly and uniformly found that the State Department properly concluded that Israeli courts would act fairly. *See, e.g.,* Demjanjuk v. Petrovsky, 776 F.2d 571, 583 (6th Cir.1985), *cert. denied*, 475 U.S. 1016 ... (1986); Eain v. Wilkes, 641 F.2d 504, 512 n. 9 (7th Cir.), *cert. denied*, 454 U.S. 894 ... (1981). Nevertheless, in the instant case, petitioner submitted reports of torture of those who were thought guilty of acts of violence against Israelis in the occupied territory, of trial by military rather than civilian courts, and of unacceptable conditions of imprisonment after conviction. These included the State Department's own report on human rights conditions in Israel which acknowledges that "where security concerns predominate, the strictures [against torture, and other cruel, inhuman or degrading treatment or punishment] have been violated." United States Dep't of State, 101st Cong., 1st Sess., *Country Reports on Human Rights Practices for 1988*, at 1367 (S.Prt. 101–3, 1989). The violations petitioner cited suffice to rebut the presumption. *Cf.* Fed.R.Evid. 301.

Notes and Questions

1. Besides Article 3(1) of the Torture Convention, quoted above, Article 3(2) requires "competent authorities" to "take into account all relevant considerations including, where applicable, the existence in the State concerned of a consistent pattern of gross, flagrant or mass violations of human rights." Article 7(3) also requires that "fair treatment at all stages of the proceedings" brought in connection with an offense obtain. Article 9 of the International Convention Against the Taking of Hostages requires that extradition "shall not be granted if the requested State Party has substantial grounds for believing: (a) That the request ... has been made for the purpose of prosecuting or punishing a person on account of his race, religion, nationality, ethnic origin or political opinion; or (b) That the person's position may be prejudiced (i) for any of the reasons mentioned in subparagraph (a) ... , or (ii) for the reason that communication with him by the appropriate authorities of the State entitled to exercise rights of protection [*e.g.*, state of nationality] cannot be effected." In the case of refugees, Articles 1(A)(2) and 33(1) of the Convention Relating to the Status of Refugees provide similar protections and state responsibilities related to the need for inquiry.

In 1793, Thomas Jefferson informed the French Minister: "until a reformation of the criminal codes of most nations, to deliver fugitives from them would be to become their accomplices", quoted in *Ex parte* Kaine, 14 F. Cas. 78, 81 (C.C.S.D.N.Y.1853) (No. 7,597). See also note 5 below.

2. In February 1999, the United States Department of State implemented Article 3 of the Convention Against Torture and Other Cruel, Inhuman and Degrading Treatment or Punishment in extradition cases by

adopting regulations. Implementation of Torture Convention in Extradition Cases, 64 FED. REG. 9435 (Feb. 26, 1999). These regulations provided, in part:

> § 95.3 Procedures.
>
> (a) Decisions on extradition are presented to the Secretary [of State] only after a fugitive has been found extraditable by a United States judicial officer. In each case where allegations relating to torture are made or the issue is otherwise brought to the Department's attention, appropriate policy and legal offices review and analyze information relevant to the case in preparing a recommendation to the Secretary as to whether or not to sign the surrender warrant.
>
> (b) Based on the resulting analysis of relevant information, the Secretary may decide to surrender the fugitive to the requesting State, to deny surrender of the fugitive, or to surrender the fugitive subject to conditions.
>
> § 95.4 Review and construction.
>
> Decisions of the Secretary concerning surrender of fugitives for extradition are matters of executive discretion not subject to judicial review....

Are you satisfied that these regulations adequately implement the obligations of the United States under Article 3 of the Torture Convention in extradition cases? For regulations concerning persons claiming a risk of torture as a basis to resist deportation, *see* Regulations Concerning the Convention Against Torture, 64 FED. REG. 8477 (Feb. 19, 1999); 64 FED. REG. 13881 (Mar. 23, 1999) (in general, providing for consideration of Torture Convention claims by immigration judges and the Board of Immigration Appeals, with judicial review from final orders of removal as authorized in § 242 of the Immigration and Nationality Act, 8 U.S.C.A. § 1252).

The Ninth Circuit held these regulations invalid to the extent that they would preclude judicial review by habeas corpus petitions (contrary to the Administrative Procedure Act (5 U.S.C. §§ 701–707) and the Convention Against Torture). *See* Cornejo–Barreto v. Seifert, 218 F.3d 1004, 1014–15 (9th Cir. 2000).

3. Should there be a rule of non-inquiry? If so, should it have recognized limits or exceptions based in international law and/or constitutional law (which would relate to the competence and responsibility of the judiciary)? Some also prefer that such a rule relate more to political power and Executive discretion. For example, the Seventh Circuit has stated in connection with what some term the motivation prong of the rule:

> Evaluations of the motivation behind a request for extradition so clearly implicate the conduct of this country's foreign relations as to be a matter better left to the Executive's discretion.... Thus, the Judiciary's deference to the Executive on the "subterfuge" question is appropriate since political questions would permeate any judgment on the motivation of a foreign government.

Eain v. Wilkes, 641 F.2d 504, 507 (7th Cir.), *cert. denied*, 454 U.S. 894 (1981). With respect to the fair trial prong of the non-inquiry rule, the Ninth Circuit, in *Quinn v. Robinson,* stated similarly:

> We do not believe it appropriate to make qualitative judgments regarding a foreign government.... Such judgments themselves cannot be other than political and, as such, involve determinations of the sort that are not within the judicial role.

Quinn v. Robinson, 783 F.2d 776, at 804. If the rule of non-inquiry, as some prefer, is the extradition version of the political question doctrine, did Judge Weinstein's decision to conduct an inquiry into the fairness of the Israeli justice and penal system violate constitutional separation of powers principles or do such matters involve legal issues within Article III powers of the judiciary as opposed to questions concerning the general nature of a foreign government or "motivation" of such a government? Should human rights law, as law of the land, also be appropriate for judicial inquiry—indeed, mandatory in view of the customary human right to an effective remedy in domestic tribunals? *See generally* Paust, Achille Lauro *Hostage-Takers, supra* at 247–49; J. Paust, International Law as Law of the United States chpts. 1, 2, 5, *passim* (2 ed. 2003); Restatement §§ 475, cmt. g, 476 cmt. h, 702, 711, RN 7; note 1 above. Didn't the United Kingdom try to argue for application of a non-inquiry rule in the *Soering* case?

4. The Second Circuit reversed Judge Weinstein's ruling in Ahmad v. Wigen, 910 F.2d 1063 (2d Cir. 1990):

> "... We have no problem with the district court's rejection of Ahmad's remaining argument to the effect that, if he is returned to Israel, he probably will be mistreated, denied a fair trial, and deprived of his constitutional and human rights. We do, however, question the district court's decision to explore the merits of this contention in the manner that it did. The Supreme Court's above-cited cases dealing with the scope of habeas corpus review carefully prescribe the limits of such review. Habeas corpus is not a writ of error, and it is not a means of rehearing what the certification judge or magistrate already has decided. *Fernandez v. Phillips, supra*, 268 U.S. [311] at 312 [1925].... A consideration of the procedures that will or may occur in the requesting country is not within the purview of a habeas corpus judge. *Gallina v. Fraser, supra,* 278 F.2d [77] at 79 [2d Cir. 1960]. Indeed, there is substantial authority for the proposition that this is not a proper matter for consideration by the certifying judicial officer. In Sindona v. Grant, 619 F.2d 167, 174 (2d Cir.1980), we said that 'the degree of risk to [appellant's] life from extradition is an issue that properly falls within the exclusive purview of the executive branch.' In *Jhirad v. Ferrandina, supra*, 536 F.2d at 484–85, we said that '[i]t is not the business of our courts to assume the responsibility for supervising the integrity of the judicial system of another sovereign nation.' *See also* Arnbjornsdottir–Mendler v. United States, 721 F.2d 679, 683 (9th Cir.1983); Garcia–Guillern v. United States, 450 F.2d 1189, 1192 (5th Cir.1971), *cert. denied*, 405 U.S. 989 ... (1972); Matter of Extradition of Tang Yee–Chun, 674 F.Supp. 1058, 1068–69 (S.D.N.Y.1987).
>
> "Notwithstanding the above described judicial roadblocks, the district court proceeded to take testimony from both expert and fact witnesses and received extensive reports, affidavits, and other documentation concerning Israel's law enforcement procedures and its treatment

of prisoners. This, we think, was improper. The interests of international comity are ill-served by requiring a foreign nation such as Israel to satisfy a United States district judge concerning the fairness of its laws and the manner in which they are enforced. *Jhirad v. Ferrandina, supra*, 536 F.2d at 484–85. It is the function of the Secretary of State to determine whether extradition should be denied on humanitarian grounds. *Matter of Extradition of Tang Yee–Chun, supra*, 674 F.Supp. at 1068 (*citing Sindona v. Grant, supra*, 619 F.2d at 174). So far as we know, the Secretary never has directed extradition in the face of proof that the extraditee would be subjected to procedures or punishment antipathetic to a federal court's sense of decency. *See Arnbjornsdottir–Mendler v. United States, supra*, 721 F.2d at 683. Indeed, it is difficult to conceive of a situation in which a Secretary of State would do so."

5. Do you agree with the Second Circuit if human rights law (based in treaties and/or customary international law) is at stake as opposed to mere comity or political considerations? *See generally* RESTATEMENT §§ 475, cmt. g, 476, cmt. h, 711, RN 7. Under international law, can the United States knowingly or foreseeably subject a person to human rights violations? Should that person have a right to an effective remedy in U.S. courts, as required by international human rights law? *See, e.g.*, ICCPR, arts. 2(3)(a), 14; Universal Declaration of Human Rights, art. 8. If not, how can the United States comply with human rights provisions of the U.N. Charter (which are evidenced and defined by authoritative human rights instruments such as the Universal Declaration), *see, e.g., Filartiga v. Pena–Irala,* 630 F.2d 876, 882 (2d Cir.1980); J. PAUST, INTERNATIONAL LAW AS LAW OF THE UNITED STATES 224–29 (2 ed. 2003)), or other human rights treaties? In view of Article 103 of the Charter, obligations under the Charter prevail over any other inconsistent international agreements, such as an extradition treaty.

In Gill v. Imundi, 747 F.Supp. 1028 (S.D.N.Y.1990), Judge Sweet stated that he was not confident concerning the ability of the executive to take human rights into consideration. See *id.* at 1050.

6. During the process of giving its advice and consent to ratification of the U.S.-U.K. Supplementary Extradition Treaty, the U.S. Senate offered an addition to the Treaty, Article 3, which in effect avoids non-inquiry in cases dealing with IRA terrorism:

Article 3

(a) Notwithstanding any other provision of this Supplementary Treaty, extradition shall not occur if the person sought establishes to the satisfaction of the competent judicial authority by a preponderance of the evidence that the request for extradition has in fact been made with a view to try or punish him on account of his race, religion, nationality, or political opinions, or that he would, if surrendered, be prejudiced at his trial or punished, detained or restricted in his personal liberty by reason of his race, religion, nationality, or political opinions.

(b) In the United States, the competent judicial authority shall only consider the defense to extradition set forth in paragraph (a) for offenses listed in Article 1 of this Supplementary Treaty. A finding under paragraph (a) shall be immediately appealable by either party to the

United States district court, or court of appeals, as appropriate. The appeal shall receive expedited consideration at every stage. The time for filing a notice of appeal shall be 30 days from the date of the filing of the decision. In all other respects, the applicable provisions of the Federal Rules of Appellate Procedure or Civil Procedure, as appropriate, shall govern the appeals process.

The First Circuit considers Article 3 to be a compromise "placing most violent crimes beyond the political offense exception's reach but adding certain novel safeguards for the protection of potential extraditees." *In re* Extradition of Howard, 996 F.2d 1320, 1324 (1st Cir.1993). Are these "novel" safeguards? Consider the United Nations Charter, arts. 55(c), 56, 103; Universal Declaration of Human Rights, arts. 2, 8–10; 1966 Covenant on Civil and Political Rights, arts. 2, 9, 26; International Convention Against the Taking of Hostages, art. 9; Convention Against Torture and Other Cruel, Inhuman or degrading Treatment or Punishment, art. 3; Convention Relating to the Status of Refugees, arts. 3, 4, 16, 32, 33—*but see id.* art. 1 F (such treaty rights not applicable re: a crime against humanity, war crime, crime against humanity, "serious non-political crime," acts contrary to the purposes and principles of the U.N. Charter); RESTATEMENT §§ 475, cmt. g, 476, cmt. h, 711, RN 7.

In light of the principles underlying the rule of non-inquiry, in United States v. Smyth, 61 F.3d 711 (9th Cir.1995), the Ninth Circuit held that Article 3 must be interpreted with respect to likely treatment of the accused:

> "... the district court erred in relying extensively upon evidence of the general discriminatory effects of the Diplock system upon Catholics and suspected Republican sympathizers. That evidence does not relate to the treatment Smyth is likely to receive as a consequence of extradition, as required under Article 3(a).... Article 3(a) does not permit denial of extradition on the basis of an inquiry into the general political conditions extant in Northern Ireland. The history of the provision shows that it requires an individualized inquiry."

For a discussion of this issue, *see, e.g.,* Valerie Epps, Note, 90 AM. J. INT'L L. 296 (1996) (considering non-inquiry to be traditional and the U.S.-U.K. Supplementary Treaty to alter non-inquiry—but not addressing human rights claims or other treaties); Michael P. Scharf, *Foreign Courts on Trial: Why U.S. Courts Should Avoid Applying the Inquiry Provision of the Supplementary U.S.-U.K. Extradition Treaty*, 25 STAN. J. INT'L L. 257 (1989). Do you agree with the Ninth Circuit?

JORDAN J. PAUST, *CUSTOMARY INTERNATIONAL LAW IN THE UNITED STATES: CLEAN AND DIRTY LAUNDRY*

40 GERMAN Y.B. INT'L L. 78, 111–14 (1998).

Another embarrassment most often involving the treatment of aliens concerns U.S. extradition processes and what some term a rule of non-inquiry. The so-called rule of non-inquiry would require that courts entertaining claims concerning extradition "not inquire into the procedures which await the accused upon extradition." In a 1989 district court opinion in *Ahmad v. Wigen*, involving a naturalized U.S. citizen, the court noted that such a rule was not settled, that courts have a responsibility to intercede where an accused faces "procedures or treatment that 'shocks the conscience,' "and that the *Soering Case* decided by the European Court of Human Rights constituted important and persuasive, "though non-binding," "precedent on the refusal to extradite because of anticipated torture, cruel conditions of incarceration or lack of due process at trial in the requesting country." It then ruled that an accused need not be extradited to Israel if reports of torture and "unacceptable conditions of imprisonment," including a U.S. Department of State Country Report on Israel concerning human rights practices during 1988, and other evidence prove (under a standard that "it is more probable than not") that the extradited individual will suffer such human rights deprivations. The accused, however, failed to meet his burden of proof.

On appeal, the Second Circuit reversed the district court's approach to non-inquiry, arguing that such claims should be left to the discretion of the Executive and, although based in customary human rights law, they are "not a proper matter for consideration by the judiciary." Other courts are also prepared to not inquire. In one such case, the First Circuit noted:

> The United States has maintained, over time, extradition treaties with some of the world's most oppressive and arbitrary regimes ... The rule of non-inquiry expresses no judgment about a foreign nation's ability and willingness to provide justice; it simply defers that assessment to the second part of every extradition proceeding—review of extraditability and determination of the appropriateness of surrender by the Secretary of State. [United States v. Kin–Hong, 110 F.3d 103 (1st Cir.1997)]

Of course, under such an approach, the judiciary would make itself incapable of protecting an accused from a legally inappropriate decision by the Executive. The Circuit Court added, however, that non-inquiry is not absolute and that in an appropriate case an exception can pertain where the individual " 'would be subject to procedures or punishment so antipathetic to a federal court's sense of decency as to require reexamination of the principle.' "

Yet, in a district court within the Second Circuit, such an exception was thought to be foreclosed. The district court noted that there was "evidence of direct danger" to the individual being extradited to India; that in light of such "evidence of systematic violation of the human rights of Sikhs by the Indian government and the likelihood that the respondents in particular would be subject to such abuses if extradited, this is the rare case where judicial inquiry into the conditions in the requesting country would be warranted"; but concluded that "such an examination has been foreclosed by the Second Circuit ... [by *Ahmad*, which] overrules any suggestion in ... [an earlier case] of an exception to the non-inquiry doctrine." [*In re* Sandhu, 1996 WL 469290 (S.D.N.Y.

1996)] Law, the sometime impertinence that dares to threaten power, will not be tolerated in the Second Circuit, at least under non-inquiry.

In my view, such a rule necessarily leads to the abdication of judicial power and responsibility under the U.S. Constitution to apply customary international law. Further, as the *Soering Case* demonstrates and surely every European judge should know, by looking the other way one does not avoid complicitous involvement in human rights violations that constitute a real risk. In 1793, Thomas Jefferson made this very point to France, but I fear that some of our judges have little sense of history or human responsibility, if only aliens are involved.

More encouraging is the decision of the Human Rights Committee under the International Covenant on Civil and Political Rights recognizing that Canada violated Article 7 of the Covenant by extraditing an accused to a state within the United States where he might suffer cruel, inhuman or degrading punishment if executed by gas asphyxiation. [Ng v. Canada, CCPR/C/49/D/469/1991, decision of 7 Jan. 1994] The United States ratified the Covenant in 1992, after the Second Circuit decision in *Ahmad*, and hopefully the Covenant will play a greater role in U.S. courts in the future. If not, the Covenant's international enforcement processes should be directed to U.S. use of the "rule of non-inquiry." . . .

A 1994 Report of the International Law Association's Committee on Extradition and Human Rights notes that non-inquiry is strong in Canada, the U.S. and the U.K., but that it is not followed in Germany and is not inhibiting of certain human rights inquiries by courts in Switzerland, Ireland and Japan. The Committee's important formal recommendations, welcomed by the Conference after approving its Report, included those concerning abductions and evidence obtained in violation of human rights law as well as recommendations that domestic processes "not preclude inquiry into laws and practices or other circumstances in the requesting state involving human rights violations" and, in particular, that extradition "not be granted where there is a real risk that the requested person is likely to be executed, tortured, subjected to cruel, inhuman or degrading treatment or punishment or denied a fair trial in the requesting state." Attention was also paid to the possibility of creating a model multilateral treaty and draft domestic legislation to more adequately assure compliance with human rights norms, efforts that should be supported. Clearly, human rights obligations of the extraditing state still pertain under the Covenant, which mirrors customary international law, and under the United Nations Charter, which, because of Article 103, will necessarily prevail in case of any putative clash with an extradition treaty.

Chapter Four

FOREIGN SOVEREIGN IMMUNITY AND THE ACT OF STATE DOCTRINE

States, state entities and their representatives engage in many types of conduct that potentially expose them to enforcement processes in other states. Because the exercise of jurisdiction by national tribunals over other states and their agents is sometimes perceived as being inconsistent with "sovereignty," a set of norms has developed to delineate when a foreign state, its entities or officials may properly be sued or punished by domestic tribunals, although some of these are partly in flux. This chapter addresses four distinct issues. Section 1 presents materials and problems on foreign sovereign immunity; Section 2 profiles the related doctrine of head of state immunity; Section 3 presents materials and problems on diplomatic immunity; and Section 4 examines the act of state doctrine, under which national courts decline to examine the legality of certain foreign governmental or public acts completed within their own territory. Each of these norms involves a clash of competing values—for example, between the goal of justice for those aggrieved by acts attributable to foreign governments or officials and the objective of respectful and peaceful coexistence in a world of independent but increasingly interdependent nation-states. When addressing these issues, consider whether and how international law might guide resolution of the tension between justice, peace and respect.

Introductory Problem

Assume that Yugoslavian President Slobodan Milosevic was traveling on a foreign civilian airliner over the Atlantic that was forced to land in Atlanta, Georgia, due to mechanical difficulties. While there, U.S. F.B.I. agents arrested Milosevic for prosecution under U.S. law concerning war crimes and crimes against humanity. While awaiting trial, the federal government allowed various plaintiff groups to serve process on Milosevic with respect to civil litigation in federal court involving claims of leader responsibility and complicity regarding war crimes, genocide, and other crimes against humanity. Thereafter, assume that the U.S.

Executive transferred Milosevic to the International Criminal Tribunal for the Former Yugoslavia (ICTY) for prosecution.

In the U.S., attorneys for Milosevic have recently filed a motion to dismiss for lack of jurisdiction under international law and domestic law, as well as claimed immunity from civil suit under doctrines of sovereign immunity and act of state. Defense attorneys also claim that the suits should be dismissed with prejudice under the political question doctrine since, they aver, litigation will necessarily implicate delicate foreign policy concerns.

How should the federal district court rule on the defense motions?

SECTION 1. FOREIGN SOVEREIGN IMMUNITY

Whether foreign sovereign immunity should now be governed by treaty law, rather than, for example, by national law, is open to question. Multilateral treaties have been concluded on the subject, but they have played a relatively minor role in the doctrine's evolution. These treaties include the 1972 European Convention on State Immunity (Council of Europe No. 74) and the International Convention for the Unification of Certain Rules Relating to the Immunity of State–Owned Vessels (signed at Brussels, April 10, 1926, and Additional Protocol, signed at Brussels, Mary 24, 1934, 176 L.N.T.S. 200). The International Law Commission has drafted a set of principles on state immunity.

In the days when the "absolute" theory of foreign sovereign immunity was widely recognized, principles of comity and customary international law informed the decisions of national courts. The absolute theory categorically barred suits against foreign sovereigns. Some view the *The Schooner Exchange v. McFaddon*, below, as an adoption of absolute immunity, but the Court's language focused instead on the absolute jurisdiction of the United States. By the end of the 20th Century, the absolute immunity doctrine was displaced by the "restrictive" theory, which immunizes certain lawful public acts while subjecting foreign states and sovereigns to suit for private, non-sovereign acts. With the transition to the restrictive principle, the doctrine of foreign sovereign immunity has lost some of its cohesiveness. Foreign sovereign immunity is now largely governed by national law, often by statute.

A. Absolute Theory of Foreign Sovereign Immunity

Some disagree whether early in U.S. history there was adoption of absolute or qualified immunity for foreign sovereigns or states. According to many, a classic articulation of the absolute theory of foreign sovereign immunity is mirrored in Chief Justice John Marshall's opinion in the 1812 case concerning *The Schooner Exchange*. On its facts, *The Schooner Exchange* was an easy case, involving an effort by former owners to invoke the processes of a federal court in Philadelphia to recover a schooner that had been converted into a French warship. In his opinion, Chief Justice Marshall painted in broad strokes, suggesting for some that jurisdictional immunity for the agents and instrumentalities of foreign states was compelled by international legal norms defining the nature of sovereignty. Was this actually the case? Another noteworthy aspect of the case was the appearance by the United States Attorney General, urging the courts to dismiss the proceedings in recognition of the French claim to immunity. Difficulties arising from the involvement of the Executive Branch in cases concerning foreign sovereign immunity helped prompt Congress to adopt the Foreign Sovereign Immunities Act (FSIA) in 1976.

THE SCHOONER EXCHANGE v. McFADDON & OTHERS

11 U.S. (7 Cranch) 116 (1812).

MARSHALL, C.J.

[Editors' note: In 1811, John McFaddon and William Greetham, citizens of the State of Maryland, filed a libel in the United States District Court for the District of Pennsylvania, against the Schooner Exchange. They alleged that they were its sole owners in 1810 when it was forcibly taken by persons acting under the orders of the Emperor Napoleon. The ship, which had been converted by the French into a warship, was brought into the port of Philadelphia. McFaddon and Greetham sought to attach the vessel and to have it restored to them. The Attorney General of the United States appeared to argue that the vessel was immune from attachment under the law of nations.]

This case involves the very delicate and important inquiry, whether an American citizen can assert, in an American court, a title to an armed national vessel, found within the waters of the United States....

The jurisdiction of the nation within its own territory is necessarily exclusive and absolute. It is susceptible of no limitation not imposed by itself. Any restriction upon it, deriving validity from an external source, would imply a diminution of its sovereignty to the extent of the restriction, and an investment of that sovereignty to the same extent in that power which could impose such restriction.

All exceptions, therefore, to the full and complete power of a nation within its own territories, must be traced up to the consent of the nation itself. They can flow from no other legitimate source.

This consent may be either express or implied. In the latter case, it is less determinate, exposed more to the uncertainties of construction; but, if understood, not less obligatory.

The world being composed of distinct sovereignties, possessing equal rights and equal independence, whose mutual benefit is promoted by intercourse with each other, and by an interchange of those good offices which humanity dictates and its wants require, all sovereigns have consented to a relaxation in practice, in cases under certain peculiar circumstances, of that absolute and complete jurisdiction within their respective territories which sovereignty confers....

A nation would justly be considered as violating its faith, although that faith might not be expressly plighted, which should suddenly and without previous notice, exercise its territorial powers in a manner not consonant to the usages and received obligations of the civilized world....

This perfect equality and absolute independence of sovereigns, and this common interest impelling them to mutual intercourse, and an interchange of good offices with each other, have given rise to a class of cases in which every sovereign is understood to waive the exercise of a part of that complete exclusive territorial jurisdiction, which has been stated to be the attribute of every nation.

1st. One of these is admitted to be the exemption of the person of the sovereign from arrest or detention within a foreign territory.

Why has the whole civilized world concurred in this construction? The answer cannot be mistaken. A foreign sovereign is not understood as intending to subject himself to a jurisdiction incompatible with his dignity, and the dignity of his nation....

2d. A second case, standing on the same principles with the first, is the immunity which all civilized nations allow to foreign ministers.

Whatever may be the principle on which this immunity is established, whether we consider him as in the place of the sovereign he represents, or by a political fiction suppose him to be extra-territorial, and, therefore, in point of law, not within the jurisdiction of the sovereign at whose Court he resides; still the immunity itself is granted by the governing power of the nation to which the minister is deputed. This fiction of exterritoriality could not be erected and supported against the will of the sovereign of the territory. He is supposed to assent to it....

3d. A third case in which a sovereign is understood to cede a portion of his territorial jurisdiction is, where he allows the troops of a foreign prince to pass through his dominions....

Without doubt, a military force can never gain immunities of any description than those which war gives, by entering a foreign territory against the will of its sovereign. But if his consent, instead of being expressed by a particular license, be expressed by a general declaration that foreign troops may pass through a specified tract of country, a distinction between such general permit and a particular license is not perceived. It would seem reasonable that every immunity which would be conferred by a special license, would be in like manner conferred by such general permit.

We have seen that a license to pass through a territory implies immunities not expressed, and it is material to enquire why the license itself may not be presumed?

It is obvious that the passage of an army through a foreign territory will probably be at all times inconvenient and injurious, and would often be imminently dangerous to the sovereign through whose dominion it passed.... [T]he general license to foreigners to enter the dominions of a friendly power, is never understood to extend to a military force; and an army marching into the dominions of another sovereign, may justly be considered as committing an act of hostility; and, if not opposed by force, acquires no privilege by its irregular and improper conduct....

But the rule which is applicable to armies, does not appear to be equally applicable to ships of war entering the ports of a friendly power. The injury inseparable from the march of an army through an inhabited country, and the dangers often, indeed generally, attending it, do not ensue from admitting a ship of war, without special license, into a friendly port. A different rule therefore with respect to this species of military force has been generally adopted. If, for reasons of state, the ports of a nation generally, or any particular ports be closed against vessels of war generally, or the vessels of any particular nation, notice is usually given of such determination. If there be no prohibition, the ports of a friendly nation are considered as open to the public ships of all powers with whom it is at peace, and they are supposed to enter such ports and to remain in them while allowed to remain, under the protection of the government of the place....

To the Court, it appears, that where, without treaty, the ports of a nation are open to the private and public ships of a friendly power, whose subjects have also liberty without special license, to enter the country for business or amusement, a clear distinction is to be drawn between the rights accorded to private individuals or private trading vessels, and those accorded to public armed ships which constitute a part of the military force of the nation.

When private individuals of one nation spread themselves through another as business or caprice may direct, mingling indiscriminately with the inhabitants of that other, or when merchant vessels enter for the purposes of trade, it would be obviously inconvenient and dangerous to society, and would subject the laws to continual infraction, and the government to degradation, if such individuals or merchants did not owe temporary and local allegiance, and were not amenable to the jurisdiction of the country....

But in all respects different is the situation of a public armed ship. She constitutes a part of the military force of her nation; acts under the immediate and direct command of the sovereign; is employed by him in national objects. He has many and powerful motives for preventing those objects from being defeated by the interference of a foreign state. Such interference cannot take place without affecting his power and his dignity....

Without indicating any opinion on this question, it may safely be affirmed, that there is a manifest distinction between the private property of the person who happens to be a prince, and that military force which supports the sovereign power, and maintains the dignity and the independence of a nation. A prince, by acquiring private property in a foreign country, may possibly be considered as subjecting that property to the territorial jurisdiction; he may be considered as so far laying down the prince, and assuming the character of a private individual; but this he cannot be presumed to do with respect to any portion of that armed force, which upholds his crown, and the nation he is entrusted to govern.

It seems then to the Court, to be a principle of public law, that national ships of war, entering the port of a friendly power open for their reception, are to be considered as exempted by the consent of that power from its jurisdiction.

Without doubt, the sovereign of the place is capable of destroying this implication. He may claim and exercise jurisdiction either by employing force or by subjecting such vessels to the ordinary tribunals. But until such power be exercised in a manner not to be misunderstood, the sovereign cannot be considered as having imparted to the ordinary tribunals a jurisdiction, which it would be a breach of faith to exercise. Those general statutory provisions therefore which are descriptive of the ordinary jurisdiction of the judicial tribunals, which give an individual whose property has been wrested from him, a right to claim that property in the courts of the country, in which it is found, ought not, in the opinion of this Court, to be so construed as to give them jurisdiction in a case, in which the sovereign power has impliedly consented to waive its jurisdiction.

The arguments in favor of this opinion which have been drawn from the general inability of the judicial power to enforce its decisions in cases of this description, from the consideration, that the sovereign power of the nation is alone competent to avenge wrongs committed by a sovereign, that the questions to which such wrongs give birth are rather questions of policy than of law, that they are for diplomatic, rather than legal discussion, are of great weight, and merit serious attention....

If the preceding reasoning be correct, the Exchange, being a public armed ship, in the service of a foreign sovereign, with whom the government of the United States is at peace, and having entered an American port open for her reception, on the terms on which ships of war are generally permitted to enter the ports of a friendly power, must be considered as having come into the American territory, under an implied promise, that while necessarily within it, and demeaning herself in a friendly manner, she should be exempt from the jurisdiction of the country....

I am directed to deliver it, as the opinion of the Court, that the sentence of the Circuit Court, reversing the sentence of the District Court, in the case of the Exchange be reversed, and that of the District Court, dismissing the libel, be affirmed.

Notes and Questions

1. What state's "jurisdiction ... within its own territory" was C.J. Marshall referring to in the second paragraph of the extract of his opinion?

2. Marshall suggests that private merchant vessels entering foreign ports generally subject themselves to the jurisdiction of the territorial state,

assuming "temporary and local allegiance" to its laws; any other rule would be "obviously inconvenient and dangerous to society". In contrast, "public armed ships" engaged in official conduct are ordinarily immune because the territorial state (in this case, the U.S.) presumably waived its authority to regulate them, out of comity or deference to the foreign sovereign. Marshall's theory of foreign sovereign immunity is consent-based, and the consent of the territorial state may be either express (as in a treaty) or implied. Does Marshall identify a customary norm immunizing foreign warships or is this practice a matter of comity?

3. What should occur when the official business of a state-owned ship is trading? The Supreme Court did not address this question until the *Berizzi Bros.* in 1926, *infra*, although Justice Story held, in another context, in The Santissima Trinidad, 20 U.S. (7 Wheat.) 283, 352–53 (1822), that "whatever may be the exemption of the public ship herself, ... the prize property which she brings into our ports is liable to the jurisdiction of our courts, for the purpose of examination and inquiry, and if a proper case be made out, for restitution to those whose possession has been divested by a violation of our neutrality." Moreover, Attorney General William Wirt asserted in 1820 that "if a foreign armed ship, departing voluntarily from her appropriate character, chooses to adopt that of a merchant ship, she must, I think, be subject to all the consequences of such adoption, and be treated by our revenue officers as a merchant ship; there being no principle of national comity known to me which requires a nation to permit a foreign armed ship to trade in her ports, in evasion of her revenue laws." 1 Op. Att'y Gen. 337–38 (1820). *See also* Nathan v. Virginia, 1 U.S. (1 Dall.) 77, 78 (Common Pleas, Phila. 1781) (argument of counsel). Was Attorney General Wirt's opinion a recognition of a commercial activities exception to immunity?

Consider also E DE VATTEL, THE LAW OF NATIONS bk. I, chpt. IV, sec. 54 (1758) ("The Prince ... who would in his transports of fury take away the life of an innocent person, divests himself of his character, and is no longer to be considered in any other light than that of an unjust and outrageous enemy"); *id.* bk. II, sec. 213 ("all the private obligations of the sovereign, are naturally subject to the same rules, as those of private persons"), *quoted in* United States v. Wilder, 28 F. Cas. 601, 604 (C.C.D.Mass.1838) (No. 16,694) (Story, J.) and The Pesaro, 277 F. 473, 477 (S.D.N.Y.1921), reversed in *Berizzi Bros., infra.*

Marshall, in *The Schooner Exchange*, anticipated the developments that emerged later in the nineteenth century and accelerated in the twentieth (resulting in the development of the restrictive theory) by his dictum concerning the prince who, by acquiring property in a foreign state, "may be considered as so far laying down the prince, and assuming the character of a private individual".

4. Marshall gives three examples in which the territorial state presumably yields a portion of its absolute sovereignty. These examples illustrate the links between the principle of foreign sovereign immunity and the doctrines of head of state immunity and diplomatic immunity. Head of state immunity will be examined in Section 2, while diplomatic immunity is addressed in Section 3 A. 3.

5. Does the Constitution confirm judicial power and jurisdictional competence with respect to some suits "against ambassadors," "public ministers," and "foreign States," thereby implicitly recognizing certain forms of nonimmunity exist? See U.S. Const., art. III, § 2; see also Judiciary act of 1789, chpt. 20, § 13, 1 Stat. 73 (1789).

6. Concerning immunity of the sovereign head of state and exceptions to immunity, consider also:

THE SANTISSIMA TRINIDAD

20 U.S. (7 Wheat.) 283, 350–55 (1822).

STORY, J.

[Editors' note: After noting that grounds for immunity of a public ship of war were "not founded upon any notion that a foreign sovereign had an absolute right," that foreign ships of war receive a presumptive exemption as a matter of comity only if they demean "themselves according to law," that property taken in violation of the law of nations (the laws of neutrality) "is liable to the jurisdiction of our Courts," and that "if the goods are landed from the public ship in our ports, by the express permission of our own government, that does not vary the case, since it involves no pledge that if illegally captured they shall be exempted," the Court declared:]

In the case of the *Exchange*, (7 Cranch, 116.) the grounds of the exemption of public ships were fully discussed and expounded. It was there shown that it was not founded upon any notion that a foreign sovereign had an absolute right, in virtue of his sovereignty, to an exemption of his property from the local jurisdiction of another sovereign, when it came within his territory; for that would be to give him sovereign power beyond the limits of his own empire. But it stands upon principles of public comity and convenience, and arises from the presumed consent or license of nations, that foreign public ships coming into their ports, and demeaning themselves according to law, and in a friendly manner, shall be exempt from the local jurisdiction. But as such consent and license is implied only from the general usage of nations, it may be withdrawn upon notice at any time, without just offence, and if afterwards such public ships come into our ports, they are amenable to our laws in the same manner as other vessels. To be sure, a foreign sovereign cannot be compelled to appear in our Courts, or be made liable to their judgment, so long as he remains in his own dominions, for the sovereignty of each is bounded by territorial limits. If, however, he comes personally within our limits, although he generally enjoy a personal immunity, he may become liable to judicial process in the same way, and under the same circumstances, as the public ships of the nation.

9 OP. ATT'Y GEN. 356, 357 (1859)

[A] law which operates on the interests and rights of other States or peoples must be made and executed according to the law of nations. A sovereign who tramples upon the public law of the world cannot excuse himself by pointing to a provision in his own municipal code . . . public law must be paramount to local law in every question where local laws are in conflict. . . .

1 **OP. ATT'Y GEN.** 47 (1794)

[T]he laws of nations invest the commander of a foreign ship of war with no exemption from the jurisdiction of the country into which he comes.

Does *The Santissima Trinidad* cause you to reconsider whether *The Schooner Exchange* can be cited for the proposition that U.S. courts recognized, or continued to recognize, a principle of absolute immunity?

7. In Verlinden B.V. v. Central Bank of Nigeria, 461 U.S. 480 (1983), Chief Justice Burger declared: "For more than a century and a half, the United States generally granted foreign sovereigns complete immunity from suit in the courts of this country.... As *The Schooner Exchange* made clear, however, foreign sovereign immunity is a matter of grace and comity on the part of the United States, and not a restriction imposed by the Constitution." *See also* Republic of Austria v. Altmann, 541 U.S. 677, 688–89 (2004); Jordan J. Paust, *Federal Jurisdiction Over Extraterritorial Acts of Terrorism and Nonimmunity for Foreign Violators of International Law Under the FSIA and the Act of State Doctrine*, 23 VA. J. INT'L L. 191, 239–41 (1983).

8. Presenting nearly the same issues as those raised in *The Santissima Trinidad* was a case arising out of the impermissible action of a German warship of the Imperial German Navy during World War I addressed in Berg v. British and African Steam Navigation Co. (The Prize Ship "Appam"), 243 U.S. 124, 153–56 (1917), *quoting The Santissima Trinidad*, *id.* at 154–55. In that case, alien private plaintiffs were allowed to sue for "restitution ... conformably to the laws of nations and the treaties and laws of the United States" for the German government's violation both of the law of nations and relevant treaties. Importantly, the Supreme Court recognized jurisdiction and the right to a remedy despite the intervention of the German ambassador, the claim that the U.S. court lacked jurisdiction, and the claim that since other proceedings had been instituted in Germany the U.S. court should decline jurisdiction. See *id.* at 147, 152. The Supreme Court also noted that "an illegal capture would be invested with the character of a tort." *Id.* at 154.

Other cases recognized nonimmunity with respect to violations of international law despite that fact that perpetrators were acting under commissions from foreign governments. *See, e.g.*, United States v. Furlong (The Pirates), 18 U.S. (5 Wheat.) 184, 201–02 (1820); The Estrella, 17 U.S. (4 Wheat.) 298, 299–301, 304, 307–09 (1819); L'Invincible, 14 U.S. (1 Wheat.) 238, 257–58 (1816).

9. In the reverse situation, when foreign plaintiffs sued that United States for a violation of the law of nations by seizure of a foreign ship in foreign territory, the private plaintiffs were entitled to damages, including attorney fees, travel expenses to bring suit and litigate in our courts, and punitive damages for an intentional act committed in violation of international law. *See, e.g.*, The Apollon, 22 U.S. (9 Wheat.) 362, 371, 374, 376–79 (1824); *see also* Cook v. United States, 288 U.S. 102, 120–21 (1933); The Paquete Habana, 175 U.S. 677 (1900) (Executive seizure abroad of foreign enemy vessel in time of war in violation of customary international law led to recovery of money damages and costs); Little v. Barreme (The Flying Fish), 6 U.S. (2 Cranch) 170, 178–79 (1804). The British also recognized the liability of their government for related violations of international law. *See,*

e.g., The Felicity, 2 Dodson 381 (1819); *see also* The Acteon, 2 Dodson 48 (1815); The Maria, 1 C. Rob. 341 (1799).

10. Concerning limitations on sovereignty and the view that "sovereignty" is conditioned on obedience to international law, the law upon which sovereignty rests, consider also: Draft Declaration on Rights and Duties of States, art. 14, Report of the International Law Commission, 4 U.N. GAOR, Supp. No. 10, at 7, 10, U.N. Doc. A/925 (1949); L. Wildhaber, *Sovereignty and International Law*, in THE STRUCTURE AND PROCESS OF INTERNATIONAL LAW 425, 426 (William of Ockham, Bracton, Coke on limited sovereignty), 430 (Grotius, bk. I, chpt. 3, § 16 (sovereignty is limited by and all kings are bound to observe the law of nations), Vattel and Locke), 432, 437–38, 440–41 (R. MacDonald & D. Johnston eds. 1983); H. WHEATON, ELEMENTS OF INTERNATIONAL LAW 119–20 (3 ed. 1846) (sovereignty was not absolute and could not be exercised even within a state's own territory in a manner "inconsistent with the equal rights of other States.").

B. Restrictive Theory of Foreign Sovereign Immunity

The distinction between *acta jure imperii* (governmental or sovereign acts) and *acta jure gestionis* (private, non-sovereign acts) can be of central importance in the contemporary resolution of claims to foreign sovereign immunity. *See* Sir Hersch Lauterpacht, *The Problem of Jurisdictional Immunities of Foreign States*, 28 BRIT. Y.B. INT'L L. 220 (1952); SOMPONG SUCHARITKUL, STATE IMMUNITIES AND TRADING ACTIVITIES IN INTERNATIONAL LAW (1959); Oliver J. Lissitzyn, *Sovereign Immunity as a Norm of International Law*, in TRANSNATIONAL LAW IN A CHANGING SOCIETY: ESSAYS IN HONOR OF PHILIP C. JESSUP (Wolfgang Friedman, *et al.*, eds. 1972); GAMAL MOURSI BADR, STATE IMMUNITY: AN ANALYTICAL AND PROGNOSTIC VIEW (1984); CHRISTOPH SCHREUER, STATE IMMUNITY: SOME RECENT DEVELOPMENTS (1988). This section traces the development of this distinction in cases from several jurisdictions and its eventual codification in influential statutes. For surveys of state practice reflecting the emergence of the restrictive principle, *see, e.g.*, ELEANOR WYLLYS ALLEN, THE POSITION OF FOREIGN STATES BEFORE NATIONAL COURTS (1933); JOSEPH SWEENEY, THE INTERNATIONAL LAW OF SOVEREIGN IMMUNITY (1963); and Materials on Jurisdictional Immunities of States and Their Property, United Nations Legislative Series, U.N. Doc. ST/LEG/SER.B/20 (1982). Professor Sweeney noted that immunity was never absolute because there was at least one exception to immunity "when the litigation involved ownership or other interests in immovables in the territory or when it involved an interest in an estate locally administered." *Id.* at 20–21.

1. Later Supreme Court Practice

As the three excerpts below from *Berizzi Bros.*, *Ex parte Peru* and *Mexico v. Hoffman* illustrate, the path toward adoption of the restrictive theory in the United States was a wavering one, and increasingly less informed by principles of public international law. Can you distinguish *Berg v. British and African Steam Navigation Co.*, 243 U.S. at 153–56, which was decided in 1917? While the Supreme Court determined the immunity question in *Berizzi Bros.* without formal instruction from the

Department of State, which had opposed the grant of immunity to a state-owned vessel engaged in ordinary trade (see The Pesaro, 277 F. 473, 479–80 n. 3 (S.D.N.Y.1921), relying partly on the Executive position), the conflicting results in *Ex parte Peru* and *Mexico v. Hoffman* reflect the differing representations made by the United States Attorneys, under instruction from the Department of State. Foreign sovereigns sued in U.S. courts during this period enjoyed the option of requesting that the Department of State file a suggestion of immunity, or of submitting the issue to the courts to resolve.

BERIZZI BROS. CO. v. THE PESARO

271 U.S. 562 (1926).

[Editors' note: This was a libel *in rem* against the steamship Pesaro for damages arising out of a failure to deliver certain artificial silk in New York. The Italian ambassador to the United States appeared to assert that the vessel was owned and possessed by Italy and therefore was immune from process of the courts of the United States. At the hearing it was stipulated that the vessel was owned, possessed, and controlled by the Italian government; was not connected with its naval or military forces; was employed in the carriage of merchandise for hire between Italian ports and ports in other countries; and that the Italian government never had consented that the vessel be seized or proceeded against by judicial process. The District Court sustained the plea of immunity and dismissed the libel for want of jurisdiction.]

VAN DEVANTER, J.

The single question presented for decision by us is whether a ship owned and possessed by a foreign government, and operated by it in the carriage of merchandise for hire, is immune from arrest under process based on a libel *in rem* by a private suitor in a federal District Court exercising admiralty jurisdiction.

This precise question never has been considered by this court before.... The nearest approach to it in this court's decisions is found in *The Exchange* ...

It will be perceived that the opinion, although dealing comprehensively with the general subject, contains no reference to merchant ships owned and operated by a government. But the omission is not of special significance, for in 1812, when the decision was given, merchant ships were operated only by private owners, and there was little thought of governments engaging in such operations. That came much later.

The decision in *The Exchange* therefore cannot be taken as excluding merchant ships held and used by a government from the principles there announced. On the contrary, if such ships come within those principles, they must be held to have the same immunity as war ships, in the absence of a treaty or statute of the United Stated evincing a different purpose. No such treaty or statute has been brought to our attention.

We think the principles are applicable alike to all ships held and used by a government for a public purpose, and that when, for the purpose of advancing the trade of its people or providing revenue for its treasury, a government acquires, mans, and operates ships in the carrying trade, they are public ships in the same sense that war ships are. We know of no international usage which regards the maintenance and advancement of the economic welfare of a people in time of peace of any less a public purpose than the maintenance and training of a naval force.

It results from this that the court below rightly dismissed the libel for want of jurisdiction.

Notes and Questions

1. Did the Court use the nature of the act or a purpose test?

2. *Berizzi Bros.* adheres to the absolute principle of sovereign immunity and extends it broadly to state trading activities. The Supreme Court cited a British decision extending immunity to a mail boat owned by Belgium, *The Parlement Belge* [1880] 5 P.D. 197. The British courts also extended sovereign immunity to state trading vessels during the early twentieth century. *The Porto Alexandre*, [1920] P. 30.

EX PARTE REPUBLIC OF PERU (THE UCAYALI)

318 U.S. 578 (1943).

STONE, C.J.

[Editors' note: The Republic of Peru sought a writ of prohibition or of mandamus from the Supreme Court against the District Court for the Eastern District of Louisiana, to restrain it from further exercise of jurisdiction over a proceeding *in rem* against petitioner's steamship Ucayali. A Cuban corporation had sought to libel the ship for failure to deliver a cargo of sugar to New York. The questions were whether the Supreme Court had jurisdiction to issue the writ and whether petitioner's appearance and defense of the suit in the district court were a waiver of sovereign immunity.]

[The Peruvian Government] sought recognition by the State Department of petitioner's claim of immunity, and asked that the Department advise the Attorney General of the claim of immunity and that the Attorney General instruct the United States Attorney for the Eastern District of Louisiana to file in the district court the appropriate suggestion of immunity of the vessel from suit. These negotiations resulted in formal recognition by the State Department of the claim of immunity.... The district court denied the motion [to dismiss] on the ground that petitioner had waived its immunity by applying for extensions of time within which to answer, and by taking the deposition of the master....

We conclude that we have jurisdiction to issue the writ as prayed.... When the Secretary [of State] elects, as he may and as he appears to have done in this case, to settle claims against the vessel by diplomatic negotiations between the two countries rather than by continued litigation in the courts, it is of public importance that the action of the political arm of the Government taken within its appropriate sphere be promptly recognized, and that the delay and inconvenience of a prolonged litigation be avoided. . . .

[The governing] principle is that courts may not so exercise their jurisdiction, by the seizure and detention of the property of a friendly sovereign, as to embarrass the executive arm of the government in conducting foreign relations. . . . This practice is founded upon the policy, recognized both by the Department of State and the courts, that our national interest will be better served in such cases if the wrongs to suitors, involving our relations with a friendly foreign power, are righted through diplomatic negotiations rather than by the compulsions of judicial proceedings.

We cannot say that the Republic of Peru has waived its immunity. . . . The certification and the request that the vessel be declared immune must be accepted by the courts as a conclusive determination by the political arm of the Government that the continued retention of the vessel interferes with the proper conduct of our foreign relations. . . .

REPUBLIC OF MEXICO v. HOFFMAN (THE BAJA CALIFORNIA)

324 U.S. 30 (1945).

STONE, C.J.

[Editors' note: The owner of an American fishing vessel filed a libel *in rem* in the District Court for Southern California against the Baja California for damage caused by a collision between the two vessels in Mexican waters. The Mexican Ambassador to the United States filed a suggestion of immunity, asserting that the Baja California was owned by the Republic of Mexico and in its possession. The United States Attorney filed a communication from the Secretary of State, calling attention to the claim of the Mexican government. However, the Department took no position with respect to the asserted immunity of the vessel from suit. The district court denied the claim of immunity, finding that the ship had been leased by the Compania Mexicana de Navigacion del Pacifico, S. de R.L., a privately owned and operated Mexican corporation engaged in the commercial carriage of cargoes for hire. The court of appeals affirmed.]

The principal contention of petitioner is that our courts should recognize the title of the Mexican government as a ground for immunity from suit even though the vessel was not in the possession and public service of that government. Ever since *The Exchange* . . . , this Government has recognized such immunity from suit, of a vessel in the possession and service of a friendly foreign government . . . , a practice which seems to have been followed without serious difficulties to the courts or embarrassment to the executive branch of the government. . . .

In the absence of recognition of the claimed immunity by the political branch of the government, the courts may decide for themselves whether all the requisites of immunity exist....

It is therefore not for the courts to deny an immunity which our government has seen fit to allow, or to allow an immunity on new grounds which the government has not seen fit to recognize.... [R]ecognition by the courts of an immunity upon principles which the political department of government has not sanctioned may be equally embarrassing to it in securing the protection of our national interests and their recognition by other nations....

We can only conclude that it is the national policy not to extend the immunity in the manner now suggested, and that it is the duty of the courts, in a matter so intimately associated with our foreign policy and which may profoundly affect it, not to enlarge an immunity to an extent which the government, although often asked, has not seen fit to recognize....

FRANKFURTER, J., concurring.

My difficulty is that "possession" is too tenuous a distinction on the basis of which to differentiate between foreign government-owned vessels engaged merely in trade that are immune from suit and those that are not....

[C]ourts should not disclaim jurisdiction which otherwise belongs to them in relation to vessels owned by foreign governments however operated except when "the department of the government charged with the conduct of our foreign relations", or of course Congress, explicitly asserts that the proper conduct of these relations calls for judicial abstention....

Notes and Questions

1. Concerning the Court's inability to allow an immunity "which the government has not seen fit to recognize," Justice Stone added: "This salutary principle was not followed in Berizzi Bros. Co. v. S.S. Pesaro, 271 U.S. 562, ... where the court allowed the immunity, for the first time, to a merchant vessel owned by a foreign government and in its possession and service, although the State Department had declined to recognize the immunity.... Since the vessel here, although owned by the Mexican Government, was not in its possession and service, we have no occasion to consider the questions presented in the *Berizzi* case. It is enough that we find no persuasive ground for allowing the immunity in this case, an important reason being that the State Department has declined to recognize it."

2. Are the Supreme Court's concerns about judicial intrusion into the sphere of foreign affairs valid? Are peaceful relations advanced when the issue of foreign sovereign immunity is determined by the political branches of government, rather than by an independent judiciary applying legal standards? Recall that the German Federal Constitutional Court rejected the suggestion of immunity made by the Federal Minister of Justice in *X v. Empire of Iran*, in Section 1 B 1. *See also* The Peterhoff, 72 U.S. (5 Wall.) 28,

57 (1866) ("we administer the public law of nations, and are not at liberty to inquire what is for the particular ... disadvantage of our own or another country"). The Committee on the Judiciary of the U.S. House of Representatives noted in its report on the FSIA that "[i]n virtually every country, the United States has found that sovereign immunity is a question of international law to be determined by the courts. The United States cannot take recourse to a foreign affairs agency abroad as other states have done in this country when they seek a suggestion of immunity from the Department of State." H.R. Rep. No. 94–1487, 1976 U.S. Code Cong. & Admin. News 6604, 6608.

3. Is the real difficulty in these cases the lack of clearly articulated standards for distinguishing *acta jure imperii* from *acta jure gestionis*? Why should the lease arrangements between Mexico and the chartering company expose the Baja California to seizure, while Peru's Ucayali is immune?

2. *The Tate Letter*

A significant effort to move the United States toward the restrictive theory, on a principled and predictable basis, was made with the 1952 publication of the "Tate Letter," in which the Department of State's Acting Legal Adviser set out the criteria the Department would apply in advising U.S. courts whether conduct by foreign states and their entities should be granted jurisdictional immunity. Yet, the Tate Letter failed to provide a clear conceptual basis for distinguishing *acta jure imperii* and *acta jure gestionis*. Moreover, the Department of State continued to dominate the determination whether immunity would be granted or denied, perpetuating the pattern of judicial deference reflected in *Republic of Peru* and *Mexico v. Hoffman*.

LETTER OF ACTING LEGAL ADVISER JACK B. TATE TO THE DEPARTMENT OF JUSTICE

May 19, 1952, 26 Dep't of State Bull. 984 (1952).

The Department of State has for some time had under consideration the question whether the practice of the Government in granting immunity from suit to foreign governments made parties defendant in the courts of the United States without their consent should not be changed. The Department has now reached the conclusion that such immunity should no longer be granted in certain types of cases....

A study of the law of sovereign immunity reveals the existence of two conflicting concepts of sovereign immunity, each widely held and firmly established. According to the classical or absolute theory of sovereign immunity, a sovereign cannot, without his consent, be made a respondent in the courts of another sovereign. According to the newer or restrictive theory of sovereign immunity, the immunity of the sovereign is recognized with regard to sovereign or public acts (*jure imperii*) of a state, but not with respect to private acts (*jure gestionis*). There is agreement by proponents of both theories, supported by practice, that sovereign immunity should not be claimed or granted in actions with respect to real property (diplomatic and perhaps consular property excepted) or with respect to the disposition of the property of a deceased person even though a foreign sovereign is the beneficiary....

[T]en of the thirteen countries which have been classified ... as supporters of the classical theory have ratified the Brussels Convention of 1926 under which immunity for government owned merchant vessels is waived. In addition the United States which is not a party to the Convention, some years ago announced and has since followed, a policy of not claiming immunity for its public owned or operated merchant vessels....

It is thus evident that with the possible exception of the United Kingdom little support has been found except on the part of the Soviet Union and its satellites for continued full acceptance of the absolute theory of sovereign immunity.... The reasons which obviously motivate state trading countries in adhering to the theory with perhaps increasing rigidity are most persuasive that the United States should change its policy. Furthermore, the granting of sovereign immunity to foreign governments in the courts of the United States is most inconsistent with the action of the Government of the United States in subjecting itself to suit in these same courts in both contract and tort and with its long established policy of not claiming immunity in foreign jurisdictions for its merchant vessels. Finally, the Department feels that the widespread and increasing practice on the part of governments of engaging in commercial activities makes necessary a practice which will enable persons doing business with them to have their rights determined in the courts. For these reasons it will hereafter be the Department's policy to follow the restrictive theory of sovereign immunity in the consideration of requests of foreign governments for a grant of sovereign immunity.

It is realized that a shift in policy by the executive cannot control the courts but it is felt that the courts are less likely to allow a plea of sovereign immunity where the executive has declined to do so....

In order that [the Justice] Department, which is charged with representing the interests of the Government before the courts, may be adequately informed it will be the Department [of State's] practice to advise you of all requests by foreign governments for the grant of immunity from suit and of the Department's action thereon.

Note

1. The Tate Letter also noted a trend toward the restrictive theory in the Netherlands, Austria, Belgium, Denmark, Egypt, France, Greece, Italy, Peru, and Romania, and possible future application in Argentina and Sweden.

3. *The Foreign Sovereign Immunities Act of 1976*

The Tate Letter did not put an end to controversy over the contours of the restrictive theory as applied in the United States. After many years of drafting, in 1976 Congress finally enacted the FSIA, a comprehensive statute to regulate grants of foreign sovereign immunity. The basic aims of the FSIA are described in the following excerpts from its legislative history and in 28 U.S.C. §§ 1330 and 1602.

HOUSE REPORT NO. 94–1487

Report on H.R. 11315, Sept. 9, 1976, 1976 U.S. Code Cong. & Admin. News 6604.

At the hearings on the bill it was pointed out that American citizens are increasingly coming into contact with foreign states and entities owned by foreign states. These interactions arise in a variety of circumstances, and they call into question whether our citizens will have access to the courts in order to resolve ordinary legal disputes. Instances of such contact occur when U.S. businessmen sell goods to a foreign state trading company, and disputes may arise concerning the purchase price. Another is when an American property owner agrees to sell land to a real estate investor that turns out to be a foreign government entity and conditions in the contract of sale may become a subject of contention. Still another example occurs when a citizen crossing the street may be struck by an automobile owned by a foreign embassy.

At present, there are no comprehensive provisions in our law available to inform parties when they can have recourse to the courts to assert a legal claim against a foreign state. Unlike other legal systems, U.S. law does not afford plaintiffs and their counsel with a means to commence suit that is specifically addressed to foreign state defendants. It does not provide firm standards as to when a foreign state may validly assert the defense of sovereign immunity; and, in the event a plaintiff should obtain a final judgment against a foreign state or one of its trading companies, our law does not provide the plaintiff with any means to obtain satisfaction of that judgment through execution against ordinary commercial assets.

In a modern world where foreign state enterprises are every day participants in commercial activities, [the FSIA] is urgently needed legislation. The bill . . . would accomplish four objectives:

First, the bill would codify the so-called "restrictive" principle of sovereign immunity, as presently recognized in international law. Under this principle, the immunity of a foreign state is "restricted" to suits involving a foreign state's public acts (*jure imperii*) and does not extend to suits based on its commercial or private acts (*jure gestionis*). This principle was adopted by the Department of State in 1952 and has been followed by the courts and by the executive branch ever since. Moreover, it is regularly applied against the United States in suits against the U.S. Government in foreign courts.

Second, the bill would insure that this restrictive principle of immunity is applied in litigation before U.S. courts. At present, this is not always the case. Today, when a foreign state wishes to assert immunity, it will often request the Department of State to make a formal suggestion of immunity to the court. Although the State Department espouses the restrictive principle of immunity, the foreign state may attempt to bring diplomatic influences to bear upon the State Department's determination. A principal purpose of this bill is to transfer the determination of sovereign immunity from the executive branch to the judicial branch, thereby reducing the foreign policy implications of immunity determinations and assuring litigants that these often crucial decisions are made on purely legal grounds and under procedures that insure due process. The Department of State would be freed from pressures from foreign governments to recognize their immunity from suit and from any adverse consequences resulting from an unwillingness of the Department to support that immunity. As was brought out in the hearings on the bill, U.S. immunity practice would conform to the practice in virtually every other country—where sovereign immunity decisions are made exclusively by the courts and not by a foreign affairs agency.

Third, this bill would for the first time in U.S. law, provide a statutory procedure for making service upon, and obtaining in personam jurisdiction over, a foreign state. This would render unnecessary the practice of seizing and attaching the property of a foreign government for the purpose of obtaining jurisdiction.

Fourth, the bill would remedy, in part, the present predicament of a plaintiff who has obtained a judgment against a foreign state. Under existing law, a foreign state in our courts enjoys absolute immunity from execution, even in ordinary commercial litigation where commercial assets are available for the satisfaction of a judgment. [The FSIA] seeks to restrict this broad immunity from execution. It would conform the execution immunity rules more closely to the jurisdiction immunity rules. It would provide the judgment creditor some remedy if, after a reasonable period, a foreign state or its enterprise failed to satisfy a final judgment.

Notes and Questions

1. Concerning coercion of the Executive branch by foreign states, during the happenstance of private litigation, and the need to turn choice over to the courts on the basis of law, see also the testimony of Legal Adviser Monroe Leigh:

"From a diplomatic standpoint, the Tate letter has continued to leave the diplomatic initiative to the foreign state. The foreign state chooses which case it will bring to the State Department and in which case it will try to raise diplomatic considerations.

"Leaving the diplomatic initiative in such cases to the foreign state places the United States at a disadvantage. This is particularly true since the United States cannot itself obtain similar advantages in other countries. In virtually every other country in the world, sovereign immunity is a question of international law decided exclusively by the courts and not by institutions concerned with foreign affairs.

"... [W]hen we ... are sued abroad, we realize that international law principles will be applied by the courts....

"... [W]hen the foreign state enters the marketplace or when it acts as a private party, there is no justification in modern international law for allowing the foreign state to avoid the economic costs of the agreements which it may breach or the accidents which it may cause...."

Hearings on H.R. 11315, 94th Cong., 2d Sess. 24, 26–7 (1976).

2. If the Executive increasingly intervenes in U.S. domestic litigation (*e.g.*, through amicus briefs or letters of suggestion), and foreign governments become more aware of the pattern, will the Executive be subject to foreign pressures once again?

C. *Scope of the FSIA, Procedures, and General Remedies*

Introductory Problem

Spynam Computer Corporation (SCC) and the country of Spynam have been accused of stealing trade secrets from and sabotaging computer files of our client, Think Lab, Inc., headquartered in Hawaii. SCC is a government trading and investigative corporation of Spynam. The president of Think Lab has gone public with such claims and wants to stop SCC from shipping several suspect crates from its warehouse in Hawaii and to obtain regular and punitive damages from both SCC and Spynam. Spynam has brought suit against our client and the president of Think Lab in a state court in Hawaii for defamation and tortious interference with various other contracts of SCC, seeking injunctive relief and money damages. Our client and the corporate president want to defend and file counterclaims with respect to the state lawsuit.

Read 28 U.S.C. §§ 1330(a)-(b), 1391, 1441, 1602–1603, and 1606–1608, in the Documents Supplement.

How can we serve process on SCC and Spynam under the FSIA? Can we litigate these claims in federal court in Hawaii or must we litigate in the District of Columbia? What sort of counterclaims are now permissible under the FSIA? What types of relief and damages can be awarded to our clients?

1. *"Agency or Instrumentality"*

What entities are entitled to immunity under the FSIA? Read 28 U.S.C. §§ 1330(a), 1602, 1603, and 1604, in the Documents Supplement.

State entities are often given the capacity to sue and be sued in order to facilitate their ability to do business. State trading companies of former communist regimes often agreed to subject themselves to suit in foreign states to insure their access to important markets. The national treasury was not necessarily open to claims against state trading companies; conversely, the general debts of the nation may not always be satisfied against the property of state entities. The separate identity of a foreign state and its agencies may be especially important when a judgment against the state or entity is ready to be executed (*see* Section 1 D 2, *infra*).

Read 28 U.S.C. § 1603, in the Documents Supplement.

H.R. REP. NO. 94–1487 (1976)

The first criterion, that the entity be a separate legal person, is intended to include a corporation, association, foundation, or any other entity which, under the law of the foreign state where it was created, can sue or be sued in its own name, contract in its own name or hold property in its own name.

The second criterion requires that the entity be either an organ of a foreign state (or of a foreign state's political subdivision). If such entities are entirely owned by a foreign state, they would of course be included within the definition. Where ownership is divided between a foreign state and private interests, the entity will be deemed to be an agency or instrumentality of a foreign state only if a majority of the ownership interests (shares of stock or otherwise) is owned by a foreign state or by a foreign state's political subdivision.

The third criterion excludes entities which are citizens of a State ... —for example a corporation organized and incorporated under the laws of the State of New York.... Also excluded are entities which are created under the laws of third countries....

[T]he fact that an entity is an "agency or instrumentality of a foreign state" does not in itself establish an entitlement to sovereign immunity. A court would have to consider whether one of the sovereign immunity exceptions contained in the bill (see sections 1605–1607 and 1610–1611) was applicable.

As a general matter, entities which meet the definition of an "agency or instrumentality of a foreign state" could assume a variety of forms, including a state trading corporation, a mining enterprise, a transport organization such as a shipping line or airline, a steel company, a central bank, an export association, a governmental procurement agency or department or ministry which acts or is suable in its own name.

Notes and Questions

1. The courts generally have had little difficulty applying § 1603(b) to entities of the types mentioned in H.R. Rep. No. 94–1487. *See, e.g.*, Atwood Turnkey Drilling, Inc. v. Petroleo Brasileiro, S.A., 875 F.2d 1174 (5th Cir.1989), *cert. denied*, 493 U.S. 1075 (1990) (national oil company); Seetransport Wiking Trader Schiffarhtsgesellschaft MBH & Co., Kommanditgesellschaft v. Navimpex Centrala Navala, 989 F.2d 572 (2d Cir.1993) (state trading company); O'Connell Machinery Co., Inc. v. M.V. Americana, 734 F.2d 115 (2d Cir.), *cert. denied*, 469 U.S. 1086 (1984) (shipping line).

2. § 1603(b)(2) includes local governments, although they do not generally enjoy sovereign immunity under international law. *See* H.R. Report, *supra* at 6613.

3. Are individual foreign officials "agencies and instrumentalities" within the meaning of § 1603(b) or a "state" within the meaning of § 1604? Clearly, individuals are not included in the text of § 1603(b), nor in its legislative history. Nevertheless, a few courts have concluded that individual

state officials may be treated as "agencies and instrumentalities" of foreign states under the FSIA. *See, e.g.*, Chuidian v. Philippine Nat'l Bank, 912 F.2d 1095 (9th Cir.1990); El–Fadl v. Central Bank of Jordan, 75 F.3d 668 (D.C.Cir.1996); *contra* Enahoro v. Abubakar, 408 F.3d 877 (7th Cir. 2005); Ye v. Zemin, 383 F.3d 620 (7th Cir. 2004); Republic of Philippines by Cent. Bank of Philippines v. Marcos, 665 F.Supp. 793 (N.D.Cal.1987). Which view is correct? Does § 1606(b)(2) require that there be an "organ"? Should other courts rewrite a federal statute?

Also, given the general recognition that common law claims of head of state immunity and diplomatic immunity are separate from the FSIA (*see* Sections 2 and 3 A, *infra*), it has been suggested that individual immunities are not governed by the FSIA. *See* Joan Fitzpatrick, *The Claim to Foreign Sovereign Immunity by Individuals Sued for International Human Rights Violations*, 15 Whittier L. Rev. 465 (1994); Jordan J. Paust, *Suing Saddam: Private Remedies for War Crimes and Hostage–Taking*, 31 Va. J. Int'l L.351, 375 n.118 (1991), also quoting *Amerada Hess*, 488 U.S. at 438 (ATCA, 28 U.S.C. § 1350, "does not distinguish among classes of defendants, and it of course has the same effect after the passage of the FSIA as before with respect to defendants other than foreign states."); *It's No Defense:* Nullum Crimen, *International Crime and the Gingerbread Man*, 60 Albany L. Rev. 657, 660 n.11 (1997); H.R. Report, *supra* at 6620, stating that the FSIA "deals only with the immunity of foreign states and not its diplomatic or consular representatives ... only suits against the foreign state...."

4. Would a broad reading of § 1603(b), adding words that Congress did not choose by extending immunity to individuals, seriously impair the viability of litigation under the Alien Tort Claims Act (ATCA) and the Torture Victim Protection Act (TVPA), 28 U.S.C. § 1350? Some argue that it would, at least with respect to extraterritorial torts in violation of international law committed by foreign political elites or requiring proof of action under color of foreign law, although torture and extrajudicial execution can be committed by private actors and the TVPA can reach some private actors with "apparent" authority or who act complicitly with officials. *See, e.g.*, Kadic v. Karadzic, 70 F.3d 232, 244–45 (2d Cir.1995). The Supreme Court noted the distinction between ATCA suits against foreign states and ATCA suits against individual officials in *Amerada Hess*, 488 U.S. at 437 n.5.

According to some, one means to accommodate the FSIA with the ATCA and TVPA is to import an *ultra vires* theory analogous to the *Ex parte Young* doctrine, which permits individual state officials to be sued, even though the state itself is immune from suit under the Eleventh Amendment. *Ex parte Young*, 209 U.S. 123 (1908).[1] Under this approach, foreign officials committing, for example, gross violations of international human rights are regarded as acting outside the scope of their official duties and beyond any proper

1. This case involved a suit against the Attorney General of Minnesota, seeking to enjoin him from enforcing a state law regulating railroad rates. The Supreme Court found that, since the state statute violated the Due Process Clause of the 14th Amendment, the Attorney General could not have the legal capacity to enforce it and his actions were *ultra vires* and actionable, even though the State of Minnesota could not be sued in federal court due to the 11th Amendment. For use of the *Young* approach to human rights litigation, *see, e.g.*, David Sloss, *Ex parte Young and Federal Remedies for Human Rights Treaty Violations*, 75 Wash. L. Rev. 1103 (2000) (noting that the 11th Amendment should be no bar, *id.* at 1194–95).

delegation of authority from the foreign state, and are thus stripped of sovereign immunity. For examples of cases applying an *ultra vires* approach, *see, e.g.*, Chapter 2, Section 2 D 2; *In re* Estate of Ferdinand Marcos, Human Rights Litigation (Hilao v. Marcos), 25 F.3d 1467, 1470–71 (9th Cir. 1994), *cert. denied*, 513 U.S. 1126 (1995); *In re* Estate of Ferdinand Marcos, Human Rights Litigation (Trajano v. Marcos), 978 F.2d 493, 497 (9th Cir. 1992), *cert. denied*, 508 U.S. 972 (1993); Xuncax v. Gramajo, 886 F.Supp. 162, 175 (D.Mass.1995); Cabiri v. Assasie–Gyimah, 921 F.Supp. 1189, 1197–98 (S.D.N.Y.1996); Regina v. Bartle and the Commissioner of Police for the Metropolis and Others, *Ex Parte* Pinochet, House of Lords, 24 March 1999. As formulated in *Trajano*, 978 F.2d at 497, this approach requires the court to examine two factors, official capacity and scope of authority:

> [A foreign official] is not entitled to immunity for acts which are not committed in an official capacity (such as selling personal property), and for acts beyond the scope of her authority (for example, doing something the sovereign has not empowered the official to do).

The *ultra vires* rationale with respect to violations of international law finds support in Letelier v. Republic of Chile, 488 F.Supp. at 673 ("There is no discretion to commit, or to have one's officers or agents commit, an illegal act.... Whatever policy options may exist for a foreign country, it has no 'discretion' to perpetrate conduct designed to result in the assassination of an individual or individuals, action that is clearly contrary to the precepts of humanity as recognized in both national and international law ... [a]s a consequence, the Republic of Chile cannot claim sovereign immunity."); Chapter 2, Section 2 D 2; Xuncax v. Gramajo, 886 F.Supp. 162, 176 (D.Mass.1995); Filartiga v. Pena–Irala, 577 F.Supp. 860, 862 (E.D.N.Y.1984) (where clear violation of international law exists such law is appropriate for judicial application and "there is no ... justifiable offense to" a foreign state); Jordan J. Paust, *It's No Defense:* Nullum Crimen, *International Crime and the Gingerbread Man*, 60 ALBANY L. REV. 657, 660–61 (1997); *Federal Jurisdiction Over Extraterritorial Acts of Terrorism and Nonimmunity for Foreign Violators of International Law Under the FSIA and the Act of State Doctrine*, 23 VA. J. INT'L L. 191, 236–37 (1983); *Draft Brief Concerning Claims to Foreign Sovereign Immunity and Human Rights*, 8 HOUS. J. INT'L L. 49, 59–60 (1985); also see Berg v. British and African Steam Navigation Co. (The Prize Ship "Appam"), 243 U.S. 124, 153–56 (1917); The Santissima Trinidad, 20 U.S. (7 Wheat.) 283, 352–53 (1822); The Opinion and Judgment of the I.M.T. at Nuremberg (1946):"The principle of international law, which under certain circumstances protects the representatives of a state, cannot be applied to acts which are condemned as criminal by international law. The authors of these acts cannot shelter themselves behind their official position," and one "cannot claim immunity while acting in pursuance of the authority of the State if the State in authorizing action moves outside its competence under international law."

Act of state cases have involved similar recognitions. See Section 4. Concerning use of an *ultra vires* theory in an extradition context, not involving civil suit for alleged violations of international law, where a dictator alleged that he had committed no crimes because, as a dictator, everything he did was a lawful act of state, *see also* Jimenez v. Aristeguieta, 311 F.2d 547, 557–58 (5th Cir.1962), *cert. denied sub nom.*, Jimenez v.

Hixon, 373 U.S. 914, *reh'g denied*, 374 U.S. 858 (1963) (even "common crimes" of a dictator "were not acts of . . . sovereignty," acts of state, or acts "in an official capacity" entitled to any sort of immunity, but were "crimes committed by the Chief of State done in violation of his position. . . .").

5. Given that the TVPA recognizes liability of any individual, for example, who, "under actual . . . authority, or color of law, of any foreign nation" subjects and individual to torture or extrajudicial killing, is the TVPA inconsistent with a common law claim of official immunity? If so, should the congressional statute trump inconsistent common law? Is the liability expressly recognized in the TVPA also necessarily inconsistent with a notion of official immunity under the interpretation of § 1603(b) favored by a few cases? If so, as a latter in time statute, should the TVPA trump or change such interpretations of the FSIA?

6. Is nonimmunity of a public actor built into Article 2(3)(a) of the International Covenant on Civil and Political Rights? *See also* Articles 27, 75 of the Statute of the International Criminal Court; Convention Against Torture and Other Cruel, Inhuman or Degrading Treatment or Punishment, arts. 1, 14.

2. *Service of Process and Venue*

Under the FSIA, if the foreign state or state entity does not make special arrangements for service of process and there is no applicable international agreement on service, where does one file appropriate papers? What are the appropriate papers? See § 1608. Section 1330(b) states that personal jurisdiction shall exist "where service has been made under section 1608." In Verlinden B.V. v. Central Bank of Nigeria, 461 U.S. 480, 485 n. 5 (1983), it was recognized that "[u]nder the Act . . . both statutory subject-matter jurisdiction . . . and personal jurisdiction turn on application of the substantive provisions of the Act. . . . § 1330(b) provides personal jurisdiction wherever subject-matter jurisdiction exists under subsection (a) and service of process has been made under . . . § 1608."

Can plaintiffs serve process directly through the mails? Also recall Chapter 3, Section 3 A.

Where might venue pertain? If an action is started in the state courts, where will it be removed to if removed to a federal court? See §§ 1391, 1441.

3. *Burden of Proof Under the FSIA*

Generally, a foreign state (or one of its agencies or instrumentalities) must establish that it is a "foreign state" within the meaning of § 1603. At that point, some courts consider that the foreign state is presumptively immune. *But see* H.R. Report 1487, at 6616: "sovereign immunity is an affirmative defense . . . the burden will remain on the foreign state to produce evidence in support of its claim to immunity. . . . The ultimate burden would rest with the foreign state." *See also* Letelier v. Republic of Chile, 488 F.Supp. 665, 672 (D.D.C.1980). The burden of production then shifts to the plaintiff to make out a *prima facie* showing that the suit falls within one of the exceptions to the FSIA (for example, the "commercial activity" exception of § 1605(a)(2)). If the plaintiff can make such a *prima facie* showing, the burden of proof shifts to the defendant to establish that the claimed exception does not apply, by a preponderance of the evidence. In many instances, this burden-shifting is not problematic and the court has sufficient evidence for an accurate disposition of the immunity issue.

Some difficulties do arise, however. Courts have occasionally ordered limited discovery where the facts are contested as to the availability of a claimed exception, even though immunity is an entitlement to avoidance of the burdens of litigation. *See, e.g.*, Filus v. Lot Polish Airlines, 907 F.2d 1328, 1332 (2d Cir.1990); Gabay v. Mostazafan Foundation of Iran, 151 F.R.D. 250, 256 (S.D.N.Y.1993).

A particular dilemma is presented where the foreign state denies that it authorized the conduct giving rise to the suit. In Phaneuf v. Republic of Indonesia, 106 F.3d 302 (9th Cir.1997), the Ninth Circuit held that Indonesia was not required to establish as part of its *prima facie* showing of presumptive immunity that the issuance of certain promissory notes was a "public act," where this assertion would be logically inconsistent with its claim that the National Security Defense Council and the individual defendants had acted outside the scope of their official duties in issuing the notes, and that there was thus no "commercial activity of the foreign state" under § 1605(a)(2).

4. *General Remedies*

Read §§ 1606 and 1607 of the FSIA, in the Documents Supplement.

Is ordinary injunctive relief available against a foreign state or entity? *Cf.* §§ 1609 and 1610(d). Are ordinary damages available? Punitive damages? Are there limits regarding set offs and counterclaims?

D. Exceptions to Foreign Sovereign Immunity Under the FSIA

The FSIA was enacted during a period when many other commercial nations were also codifying the restrictive principle of foreign sovereign immunity. For example, the United Kingdom adopted its State Immunity Act in 1978; Singapore adopted its State Immunity Act in 1979; and in 1981 Canada adopted its State Immunity Act, Pakistan adopted its State Immunity Ordinance, and South Africa adopted its Foreign Sovereign Immunity Act. The move toward codification in national law during this period was most noticeable in nations with a common law legal tradition. Among civil law countries, the chief development was the drafting of the European Convention on State Immunity by the Council of Europe in 1972, which contains an explicit list of nonimmune activities. For example, Article 5 specifies the employment contracts that are nonimmune; Article 6 concerns joint state participation with business entities in the forum state; Article 7 addresses industrial, commercial or financial activity engaged in by the foreign state "in the same manner as a private person"; Article 8 relates to intellectual property; Article 9 addresses immovable property in the forum state; Article 10 relates to gifts and inheritance; Article 11 concerns injury to persons or damage to tangible property in the forum state; and Article 12 relates to arbitration agreements. The European Convention on State Immunity and Additional Protocol are reprinted at 11 I.L.M. 470 (1972). *See* I.M. Sinclair, *The European Convention on State Immunity*, 22 INT'L & COMP. L.Q. 254 (1973).

Read 28 U.S.C. § 1330 and §§ 1602–1605, in the Documents Supplement.

1. Exclusivity of the FSIA's Exceptions

ARGENTINE REPUBLIC v. AMERADA HESS SHIPPING CORP.

488 U.S. 428 (1989).

REHNQUIST, C.J.

Two Liberian corporations sued the Argentine Republic in a United States District Court to recover damages for a tort allegedly committed by its armed forces on the high seas in violation of international law. We hold that the District Court correctly dismissed the action, because the Foreign Sovereign Immunities Act of 1976 (FSIA), 28 U.S.C. § 1330 *et seq.*, does not authorize jurisdiction over a foreign state in this situation. . . .

[Amerada Hess Shipping Corporation, a Liberian corporation, chartered an oil tanker (the Hercules) from United Carriers, Inc., another Liberian corporation. The contract was executed in New York City. Amerada Hess used the Hercules to transport crude oil from Alaska to the United States Virgin Islands. On the return voyage in June 1982, the Hercules was in international waters outside the "war zones" designated by Great Britain and Argentina in their conflict over the Falkland Islands/Islas Malvinas. The ship's master twice radioed Argentine officials informing them of the ship's location and neutral character. Without provocation, Argentine military planes bombed the Hercules three times over a period of several hours. United Carriers scuttled the ship off the Brazilian Coast after it was determined that an undetonated bomb in its tank was too dangerous to remove.]

Following unsuccessful attempts to obtain relief in Argentina, respondents commenced this action in the United States District Court for the Southern District of New York for the damage that they sustained from the attack. United Carriers sought $10 million in damages for the loss of the ship; Amerada Hess sought $1.9 million in damages for the fuel that went down with the ship. Respondents alleged that petitioner's attack on the neutral Hercules violated international law. They invoked the District Court's jurisdiction under the Alien Tort Statute, 28 U.S.C. § 1350, which provides that "[t]he district courts shall have original jurisdiction of any civil action by an alien for a tort only, committed in violation of the law of nations or a treaty of the United States." Amerada Hess also brought suit under the general admiralty and maritime jurisdiction, 28 U.S.C. § 1333, and "the principle of universal jurisdiction, recognized in customary international law." ... The District Court dismissed both complaints for lack of subject-matter jurisdiction, ... ruling that respondents' suits were barred by the FSIA.

A divided panel of the United States Court of Appeals for the Second Circuit reversed ... [holding] that the District Court had jurisdiction under the Alien Tort Statute.... The Court of Appeals reasoned that Congress' enactment of the FSIA was not meant to eliminate "existing remedies in United States courts for violations of international law" by foreign states.... The dissenting judge took the view that the FSIA precluded respondents' action....

We start from the settled proposition that the subject-matter jurisdiction of the lower federal courts is determined by Congress.... [The FSIA, § 1604,] provides that "[s]ubject to existing international agreements to which the United States [was] a party at the time of the enactment of this Act[,] a foreign state shall be immune from the jurisdiction of the courts of the United States and of the States except as provided in sections 1605 to 1607 of this chapter." The FSIA also added § 1330(a) to Title 28; it provides that "[t]he district courts shall have original jurisdiction without regard to amount in controversy of any nonjury civil action against a foreign state ... as to any claim for relief in personam with respect to which the foreign state is not entitled to immunity under sections 1605–1607 of this title or under any applicable international agreement." § 1330(a).

We think that the text and structure of the FSIA demonstrate Congress' intention that the FSIA be the sole basis for obtaining jurisdiction over a foreign state in our courts. Sections 1604 and 1330(a) work in tandem: § 1604 bars federal and state courts from exercising jurisdiction when a foreign state is entitled to immunity, and § 1330(a) confers jurisdiction on district courts to hear suits brought by United States citizens and by aliens when a foreign state is not entitled to immunity. As we said in [Verlinden B.V. v. Central Bank of Nigeria, 461 U.S. 480, 493 ... (1983)], the FSIA "must be applied by the district courts in every action against a foreign sovereign, since subject-matter jurisdiction in any such action depends on the existence of one of the specified exceptions to foreign sovereign immunity"....

The Court of Appeals acknowledged that the FSIA's language and legislative history support the "general rule" that the Act governs the immunity of foreign states in federal court. 830 F.2d, at 426. The Court of Appeals, however, thought that the FSIA's "focus on commercial concerns" and Congress' failure to "repeal" the Alien Tort Statute indicated Congress' intention that federal courts continue to exercise jurisdiction over foreign states in suits alleging violations of international law outside the confines of the FSIA. *Id.*, at 427. The Court of Appeals also believed that to construe the FSIA to bar the instant suit would "fly in the face" of Congress' intention that the FSIA be interpreted pursuant to " 'standards recognized under international law.' "*Ibid.*, *quoting* H.R.Rep., at 14, U.S.Code Cong. & Admin.News 1976, p. 6613.

Taking the last of these points first, Congress had violations of international law by foreign states in mind when it enacted the FSIA. For example, the FSIA specifically denies foreign states immunity in suits "in which rights in property taken in violation of international law are in issue." 28 U.S.C. § 1605(a)(3). Congress also rested the FSIA in part on its power under Art. I, § 8, cl. 10, of the Constitution "[t]o define and punish Piracies and Felonies committed on the high Seas, and Offenses against the Law of Nations." *See* H.R.Rep., at 12; S.Rep., at 12, U.S.Code Cong. & Admin.News 1976, p. 6611. From Congress' decision to deny immunity to foreign states in the class of cases just mentioned, we draw the plain implication that immunity is granted in those cases involving alleged violations of international law that do not come within one of the FSIA's exceptions.

As to the other point made by the Court of Appeals, Congress' failure to enact a *pro tanto* repealer of the Alien Tort Statute when it passed the FSIA in 1976 may be explained at least in part by the lack of certainty as to whether the Alien Tort Statute conferred jurisdiction in suits against foreign states....

We think that Congress' decision to deal comprehensively with the subject of foreign sovereign immunity in the FSIA, and the express provision in § 1604 that "a foreign state shall be immune from the jurisdiction of the courts of the United States and of the States except as provided in sections 1605–1607," preclude a construction of the Alien Tort Statute that permits the instant suit.... The Alien Tort Statute by its terms does not distinguish among classes of defendants, and it of course has the same effect after the passage of the FSIA as before with respect to defendants other than foreign states....

Having determined that the FSIA provides the sole basis for obtaining jurisdiction over a foreign state in federal court, we turn to whether any of the exceptions enumerated in the Act apply here. These exceptions include cases involving the waiver of immunity, § 1605(a)(1), commercial activities occurring in the United States or causing a direct effect in this country, § 1605(a)(2), property expropriated in violation of international law, § 1605(a)(3), inherited, gift, or immovable property located in the United States, § 1605(a)(4), non-commercial torts occurring in the United States, § 1605(a)(5), and maritime liens, § 1605(b). We agree with the District Court that none of the FSIA's exceptions applies on these facts....

Respondents assert that the FSIA exception for noncommercial torts, § 1605(a)(5), is most in point....

Section 1605(a)(5) is limited by its terms, however, to those cases in which the damage to or loss of property occurs in the United States. Congress' primary purpose in enacting § 1605(a)(5) was to eliminate a foreign state's immunity for traffic accidents and other torts committed in the United States, for which liability is imposed under domestic tort law. *See* H.R.Rep., at 14, 20–21; S.Rep., at 14, 20–21.

In this case, the injury to respondents' ship occurred on the high seas some 5,000 miles off the nearest shores of the United States.... Because respondents' injury unquestionably occurred well outside the 3–mile limit then in effect for the territorial waters of the United States, the exception for noncommercial torts cannot apply.

The result in this case is not altered by the fact that petitioner's alleged tort may have had effects in the United States. Under the commercial activity exception to the FSIA, § 1605(a)(2), a foreign state may be liable for its commercial activities "outside the territory of the United States" having a "direct effect" inside the United States. But the noncommercial tort exception, § 1605(a)(5), upon which respondents rely, makes no mention of "territory outside the United States" or of "direct effects" in the United States. Congress' decision to use explicit language in § 1605(a)(2), and not to do so in § 1605(a)(5), indicates that the exception in § 1605(a)(5) covers only torts occurring within the territorial jurisdiction of the United States....

We also disagree with respondents' claim that certain international agreements entered into by petitioner and by the United States create an exception to the FSIA here.... As noted, the FSIA was adopted "[s]ubject to international agreements to which the United States [was] a party at the time of [its] enactment." § 1604. This exception applies when international agreements "expressly conflic[t]" with the immunity provisions of the FSIA, H.R. Rep., at 17; S. Rep., at 17, U.S. Code Cong. & Admin. News 1976, p. 6616, hardly the circumstances in this case. Respondents point to the Geneva Convention on the High Seas, Apr. 29, 1958, [1962] 13 U.S.T. 2312, T.I.A.S. No. 5200, and the Pan American Maritime Neutrality Convention, Feb. 20, 1928, 47 Stat.1989, 1990–1991, T.S. No. 845. Brief for Respondents 31–34. These conventions, however, only set forth substantive rules of conduct and state that compensation shall be paid for certain wrongs. They do not create private rights of action for foreign corporations to recover compensation from foreign states in United States courts.... Nor do we see how a foreign state can waive its immunity under § 1605(a)(1) by signing an international agreement that contains no mention of a waiver of immunity to suit in United States courts or even the availability of a cause of action in the United States. We find similarly unpersuasive the argument of respondents and Amicus Curiae Republic of Liberia that the Treaty of Friendship, Commerce and Navigation, Aug. 8, 1938, United States–Liberia, 54 Stat. 1739, T.S. No. 956, carves out an exception to the FSIA....

We hold that the FSIA provides the sole basis for obtaining jurisdiction over a foreign state in the courts of this country, and that none of the enumerated exceptions to the Act apply to the facts of this case. The judgment of the Court of Appeals is therefore reversed.

BLACKMUN, J. (with whom MARSHALL, J. joins), concurring in part

I join the Court's opinion insofar as it holds that the FSIA provides the sole basis for obtaining jurisdiction over a foreign state in federal court. . . .

I, however, do not join the latter part of the Court's opinion to the effect that none of the FSIA's exceptions to foreign sovereign immunity apply in this case. [T]he Court of Appeals did not decide this question, . . . and, indeed, specifically reserved it. . . . Moreover, the question was not among those presented to this Court in the Petition for Certiorari, did not receive full briefing, and it is not necessary to the disposition of the case. Accordingly, I believe it inappropriate to decide here, in the first instance, whether any exceptions to the FSIA apply in this case. I would remand the case to the Court of Appeals on this issue.

Notes and Questions

1. The FSIA, like other foreign sovereign immunity statutes adopted to codify the restrictive principle (such as those of the United Kingdom and Canada) opts for a listing of circumstances under which foreign states may be sued, rather than for a general, open-ended statement of the *acta jure imperii—acta jure gestionis* distinction to be applied on a case-by-case basis by the judiciary. This approach has the potential advantages of clarity, specificity, uniformity and predictability. Are the FSIA definitions of nonimmune activities explicit enough?

2. *Amerada Hess* accentuates the exclusivity of the FSIA's exceptions. Moreover, Chief Justice Rehnquist gives a narrow reading to several of those exceptions, including the international agreement exception in 28 U.S.C. § 1604, the waiver exception in 28 U.S.C. § 1605(a)(1), and the tort exception in 28 U.S.C. § 1605(a)(5). Some of the complexities of the commercial activity exception of 28 U.S.C. § 1605(a)(2), the waiver exception of 28 U.S.C. § 1605(a)(1), and the tort exception of 28 U.S.C. § 1605(a)(5) are addressed below.

3. Can the § 1604 exception be used with respect to human rights violations, even to meet the stringent test proffered by Chief Justice Rehnquist? *See, e.g.*, Universal Declaration of Human Rights, art. 8; International Covenant on Civil and Political Rights (ICCPR), arts. 2(3)(a), 14; Convention Against Torture and Other Cruel, Inhuman or Degrading Treatment or Punishment, arts. 1, 14; JORDAN J. PAUST, INTERNATIONAL LAW AS LAW OF THE UNITED STATES 236–37, 321 (2 ed. 2003). Since the ICCPR was ratified in 1992, after passage of the FSIA in 1976, does the treaty-based exception to immunity in Article 2(3)(a) prevail over any inconsistent limitations in the FSIA under the last in time rule? Further, in view of materials addressed in Chapter 2, should the terms of the FSIA be interpreted restrictively or consistently with international law? In connection with § 1604 of the FSIA, the House Report added: "the international agreement would control . . . where a conflict was manifest." H.R. Rep. at 17. Does "manifest" require and "express" conflict even within the views of the House Report? Are the terms of §§ 1330(a) or 1604 restricted by the word "manifest" or "express"?

4. Reread § 1603(c). Under international law, U.S. Embassy grounds in foreign territory are foreign territory, but are subject to general immunity from local jurisdiction and are territory over which the United States has some jurisdictional competence. Should § 1603(c) be interpreted with reference to international law? Should torts occurring in the U.S. Embassy in Teheran, Iran, have been considered to have occurred within the "United States"?

5. Is the FSIA truly a comprehensive codification of the emerging restrictive principle of foreign sovereign immunity in public international law? Are the nonimmune acts (for example, operating an automobile on embassy business in a manner that causes tortious injury in the United States) inherently non-sovereign conduct? *See* § 1603(d). Or is it more accurate to say that the modern codifications of nonimmune state conduct, including the FSIA, reflect an emerging international consensus as to how to strike a just balance between individuals' demands for redress against a state or its agents and foreign states' claim to noninterference by domestic enforcement authorities?

6. A reading of § 1605 suggests that Congress has, in 1976 and subsequently in 1996 (adding § 1605(a)(7)), reacted to pressure from a narrow set of interests in selecting the circumstances under which foreign states may be sued in the United States. As the following sections of this chapter indicate, the guidance Congress has provided to U.S. courts in the FSIA is sometimes murky, even with respect to central issues such as the definition of "commercial activity" in § 1603(d) or "agency or instrumentality of a foreign state" in § 1603(b). Given this lack of clarity and the patchwork nature of the codified exceptions, should the courts and executive branch defer as extensively as they have to the legislative branch in resolving the foreign sovereign immunity issue?

2. *Commercial Activity*

a. *Congressional Definition of Commercial Activity*

House Report No. 94–1487 (1976)

Paragraph d of section 1603 defines the term "commercial activity" as including a broad spectrum of endeavor, from an individual commercial transaction or act to a regular course of commercial conduct [including] the carrying on of a commercial enterprise such as a mineral extraction company, an airline or a state trading corporation. Certainly, if an activity is customarily carried on for profit, its commercial nature could readily be assumed. At the other end of the spectrum, a single contract, if of the same character as a contract which might be made by a private person, could constitute a "particular transaction or act."

As the definition indicates, the fact that goods or services to be procured through a contract are to be used for a public purpose is irrelevant; it is the essentially commercial nature of an activity or transaction that is critical. Thus, a contract by a foreign government to buy provisions or equipment for its armed forces or to construct a government building constitutes a commercial activity. The same would be true of a contract to make repairs on an embassy building. Such contracts should be considered to be commercial contracts, even if their ultimate objective is to further a public function.

By contrast, a foreign state's mere participation in a foreign assistance program administered by the Agency for International Development (AID) is an activity whose essential nature is public or governmental, and it would not itself constitute a commercial activity. By the same token, a foreign state's activities in and "contacts" with the United States resulting from or necessitated by participation in such a program would not in themselves constitute a sufficient nexus with the United States so as to give rise to jurisdiction (see § 1330) or to assets which could be subjected to attachment or execution with respect to unrelated commercial transactions (see § 1610(b)). However, a transaction to obtain goods or services from private parties would not lose its commercial character because it was entered into in connection with an AID program. Also public or governmental and not commercial in nature, would be employment of diplomatic, civil service, or military personnel, but not employment of American citizens or third country nationals by the foreign state in the United States.

The courts would have a great deal of latitude in determining what is a "commercial activity" for purposes of this bill. It has seemed unwise to attempt an excessively precise definition of this term, even if that were practicable. Activities such as a foreign government's sale of a service or product, its leasing of property, its borrowing of money, its employment or engagement of laborers, clerical staff or public relations or marketing agents, or its investment in a security of an American corporation, would be among those included within the definition.

[A] commercial activity carried on in the United States by a foreign state would include not only a commercial transaction performed and executed in its entirety in the United States, but also a commercial transaction having a "substantial contact" with the United States.... It will be for the courts to determine whether a particular commercial activity has been performed in whole or in part in the United States. This definition, however, is intended to reflect a degree of contact beyond that occasioned simply by U.S. citizenship or U.S. residence of the plaintiff.

b. Nature or Purpose of Activity as Touchstone of its Commercial Character

Non–U.S. jurisdictions that have adopted the restrictive principle of foreign sovereign immunity must grapple with the question whether the distinction between immune acts (*acta jure imperii*) and nonimmune acts (*acta jure gestionis*) should be evaluated in light of the act's nature (in particular, whether private individuals are capable of performing similar acts) or in light of the act's immediate or ultimate public purpose. This issue tends to be particularly acute when the question is whether the conduct is "commercial" activity. One classic example, mentioned in H.R. Rep. No. 94–1487, *supra* in Section 1 C 2 i, and cited by Justice Scalia in *Republic of Argentina v. Weltover*, *infra*, is the purchase of supplies for the army. Although the state may intend to use the supplies for a purpose at the core of sovereignty, the nature of the act is non-sovereign, since any private individual or company might engage in the same conduct.

Many cases present far more complicated issues. Applying the nature/purpose distinction requires the anterior step of identifying precisely what conduct of the foreign state has given rise to the lawsuit. How that conduct is characterized by the court may dramatically affect the outcome of the immunities issue. Is the issuance of government bonds commercial? Is the corrupt sale of tax credits commercial? Is the seizure of passenger aircraft during an invasion and their transfer to the invader's state-owned airline a commercial act?

In I.A.M. v. O.P.E.C., 477 F.Supp. 553 (C.D.Cal.1979), the district judge reclassified the facts. Plaintiffs had claimed that OPEC countries had engaged in oil production cuts and price controls in violation of U.S. laws (arguing that such acts were nonimmune under the nature-of-the-acts test because production cuts and price controls are acts that private entities can and do engage in). In the district court's view, production cuts were the result of "sovereign" acts of oil conservation, which may have had an impact on prices.

An immunity based upon the act's nature will generally be much narrower than an immunity based upon the act's purpose. European states following the restrictive principle have generally adopted the "nature" test to identify nonimmune commercial activity, as indicated in the excerpt above from the German Federal Constitutional Court in *X v. Empire of Iran*. Congress specifically directed the U.S. courts in 28 U.S.C. § 1603(d) to focus upon the act's nature and to ignore its purpose in evaluating claims to foreign sovereign immunity. The United States Supreme Court heeded this directive in *Republic of Argentina v. Weltover* and *Saudi Arabia v. Nelson*, *infra*. Is this approach too simplistic or formalistic? Can the nature of an act be discerned without attention to its context, and does that context necessarily involve an understanding of the actor's purpose? Can U.S. courts rightly rewrite § 1603(d)?

The Australian Law Reform Commission observed:

"It is not possible to classify the nature of any human activity without reference to its purpose. The nature of an activity is not some abstract idea (certainly not for legal purposes), but rather the focused, or relevant, or 'central' purpose (according to some criterion). The classifications 'governmental' and 'commercial' are themselves purposive."

Australian Law Reform Commission, Report No. 24, Foreign State Immunity 28 (1984); *see also* James Crawford, *International Law and Foreign Sovereigns: Distinguishing Immune Transactions*, 1983 BRIT. Y.B. INT'L L. 75, 96 (criticizing nature/purpose distinction); Joan Donoghue, *Taking the "Sovereign" Out of the Foreign Sovereign Immunities Act: A Functional Approach to the Commercial Activity Exception*, 17

YALE J. INT'L L. 489 (1992) (suggesting amendment to FSIA to specify nonimmune activities with greater precision, because of the unworkability of nature/purpose distinction in identifying commercial activity that should be nonimmune).

Compare the recognition in Section 1602 of the FSIA of a broad commercial activities exception to immunity under international law with the narrow set of exceptions contained in Section 1605(a)(2). Which should prevail? Should the federal statute be interpreted consistently with international law if at all possible? Recall cases in Chapter 2 such as The Charming Betsy, 6 U.S. (2 Cranch) 64, 117–18 (1804). Was there a clear, unequivocal intent of Congress to override international law concerning a commercial activities exception?

REPUBLIC OF ARGENTINA v. WELTOVER, INC.

504 U.S. 607 (1992).

SCALIA, J.

This case requires us to decide whether the Republic of Argentina's default on certain bonds issued as part of a plan to stabilize its currency was an act taken "in connection with a commercial activity" that had a "direct effect in the United States" so as to subject Argentina to suit in an American court under the Foreign Sovereign Immunities Act of 1976, 28 U.S.C. § 1602 *et seq*.

[Argentine businesses engaging in foreign transactions must pay in United States dollars or some other internationally accepted currency because of the instability of the Argentine currency. The Republic of Argentina and its central bank, Banco Central (both stipulated to be foreign states within the meaning of the FSIA), in 1981 instituted a foreign exchange insurance contract program (FEIC), under which Argentina effectively agreed to assume the risk of currency depreciation. Argentina agreed to sell to domestic borrowers the necessary United States dollars to repay their foreign debts when they matured, irrespective of intervening devaluations. Argentina did not possess sufficient reserves of United States dollars to cover the FEIC contracts as they became due in 1982. The Argentine Government refinanced the FEIC-backed debts by issuing government bonds called "Bonods" payable in United States dollars in London, Frankfurt, Zurich or New York. Under this refinancing program, the foreign creditor had the option of either accepting the Bonods in satisfaction of the initial debt, thereby substituting the Argentine Government for the private debtor, or maintaining the debtor/creditor relationship with the private borrower and accepting the Argentine Government as guarantor.]

When the Bonods began to mature in May 1986, Argentina concluded that it lacked sufficient foreign exchange to retire them. Pursuant to a Presidential Decree, Argentina unilaterally extended the time for payment and offered bondholders substitute instruments as a means of rescheduling the debts. Respondents, two Panamanian corporations and a Swiss bank who hold, collectively, $1.3 million of Bonods, refused to accept the rescheduling and insisted on full payment, specifying New York as the place where payment should be made. Argentina did not pay, and respondents then brought this breach-of-contract action in the United States District Court for the Southern District of New York, relying on the Foreign Sovereign Immunities Act of 1976 as the basis for jurisdiction. Petitioners moved to dismiss for lack of subject-matter jurisdiction, lack of personal jurisdiction, and *forum non conveniens*. [The District Court denied these motions and the Court of Appeals affirmed.]

The Foreign Sovereign Immunities Act of 1976 (FSIA), 28 U.S.C. § 1602 *et seq.*, establishes a comprehensive framework for determining whether a court in this country, state or federal, may exercise jurisdiction over a foreign state.... The most significant of the FSIA's exceptions—and the one at issue in this case—is the "commercial" exception of § 1605(a)(2)....

In the proceedings below, respondents relied only on the third clause of § 1605(a)(2) ... and our analysis is therefore limited to considering whether this lawsuit is (1) "based ... upon an act outside the territory of the United States"; (2) that was taken "in connection with a commercial activity" of Argentina outside this country; and (3) that "cause[d] a direct effect in the United States".... The dispute pertains to whether the unilateral refinancing of the Bonods was taken "in connection with a commercial activity" of Argentina, and whether it had a "direct effect in the United States." [An excerpt discussing the "direct effect" issue is included in Section 1 C 2 iii, *infra*]

Respondents and their *amicus*, the United States, contend that Argentina's issuance of, and continued liability under, the Bonods constitute a "commercial activity" and that the extension of the payment schedules was taken "in connection with" that activity. The latter point is obvious enough, and Argentina does not contest it; the key question is whether the activity is "commercial" under the FSIA....

Th[e] definition [in § 1603(d)] leaves the critical term "commercial" largely undefined: The first sentence simply establishes that the commercial nature of an activity does not depend upon whether it is a single act or a regular course of conduct; and the second sentence merely specifies what element of the conduct determines commerciality (*i.e.*, nature rather than purpose), but still without saying what "commercial" means.

Fortunately, however, the FSIA was not written on a clean slate. As we have noted ..., the Act (and the commercial exception in particular) largely codifies the so-called "restrictive" theory of foreign sovereign immunity first endorsed by the State Department in 1952. The meaning of "commercial" is the meaning generally attached to that term under the restrictive theory at the time the statute was enacted....

This Court did not have occasion to discuss the scope or validity of the restrictive theory of sovereign immunity until our 1976 decision in

Alfred Dunhill of London, Inc. v. Republic of Cuba, 425 U.S. 682. Although the Court there was evenly divided on the question whether the "commercial" exception that applied in the foreign-sovereign-immunity context also limited the availability of an act-of-state defense . . . , there was little disagreement over the general scope of the exception. . . .

The plurality stated that the restrictive theory of foreign sovereign immunity would not bar a suit based upon a foreign state's participation in the marketplace in the manner of a private citizen or corporation. 425 U.S., at 698–705. A foreign state engaging in "commercial" activities "do[es] not exercise powers peculiar to sovereigns"; rather, it "exercise[s] only those powers that can also be exercised by private citizens." *Id.*, at 704. The dissenters did not disagree with this general description. See id., at 725. Given that the FSIA was enacted less than six months after our decision in *Alfred Dunhill* was announced, we think the plurality's contemporaneous description of the then-prevailing restrictive theory of sovereign immunity is of significant assistance in construing the scope of the Act.

In accord with that description, we conclude that when a foreign government acts, not as regulator of a market, but in the manner of a private player within it, the foreign sovereign's actions are "commercial" within the meaning of the FSIA. Moreover, because the Act provides that the commercial character of an act is to be determined by reference to its "nature" rather than its "purpose," 28 U.S.C. § 1603 (d), the question is not whether the foreign government is acting with a profit motive or instead with the aim of fulfilling uniquely sovereign objectives. Rather, the issue is whether the particular actions that the foreign state performs (whatever the motive behind them) are the type of actions by which a private party engages in "trade and traffic or commerce," BLACK'S LAW DICTIONARY 270 (6th ed. 1990). . . . Thus, a foreign government's issuance of regulations limiting foreign currency exchange is a sovereign activity, because such authoritative control of commerce cannot be exercised by a private party; whereas a contract to buy army boots or even bullets is a "commercial" activity, because private companies can similarly use sales contracts to acquire goods. . . .

The commercial character of the Bonods is confirmed by the fact that they are in almost all respects garden-variety debt instruments: They may be held by private parties; they are negotiable and may be traded on the international market (except in Argentina); and they promise a future stream of cash income. We recognize that, prior to the enactment of the FSIA, there was authority suggesting that the issuance of public debt instruments did not constitute a commercial activity. [Victory Transport, Inc. v. Comisaria General de Abastecimientos y Transportes, 336 F.2d 354, 360 (2d Cir. 1964), *cert. denied*, 381 U.S. 934 (1965)] There is, however, nothing distinctive about the state's assumption of debt (other than perhaps its purpose) that would cause it always to be classified as *jure imperii*, and in this regard it is significant that *Victory Transport* expressed confusion as to whether the "nature" or the "purpose" of a transaction was controlling in determining commerciality, id., at 359–360. Because the FSIA has now clearly established that the "nature" governs, we perceive no basis for concluding that the issuance of debt should be treated as categorically different from other activities of foreign states.

Argentina contends that, although the FSIA bars consideration of "purpose," a court must nonetheless fully consider the context of a transaction in order to determine whether it is "commercial." Accordingly, Argentina claims that the Court of Appeals erred by defining the relevant conduct in what Argentina considers an overly generalized, acontextual manner and by essentially adopting a per se rule that all "issuance of debt instruments" is "commercial." . . .

We have no occasion to consider such a *per se* rule, because it seems to us that even in full context, there is nothing about the issuance of these Bonods (except perhaps its purpose) that is not analogous to a private commercial transaction.

Argentina points to the fact that the transactions in which the Bonods were issued did not have the ordinary commercial consequence of raising capital or financing acquisitions. Assuming for the sake of argument that this is not an example of judging the commerciality of a transaction by its purpose, the ready answer is that private parties regularly issue bonds, not just to raise capital or to finance purchases, but also to refinance debt. That is what Argentina did here: By virtue of the earlier FEIC contracts, Argentina was already obligated to supply the United States dollars needed to retire the FEIC-insured debts; the Bonods simply allowed Argentina to restructure its existing obligations. . . .

Argentina argues that the Bonods differ from ordinary debt instruments in that they "were created by the Argentine Government to fulfill its obligations under a foreign exchange program designed to address a domestic credit crisis, and as a component of a program designed to control that nation's critical shortage of foreign exchange". . . . Indeed, Argentina asserts that the line between "nature" and "purpose" rests upon a "formalistic distinction [that] simply is neither useful nor warranted". . . . We think this line of argument is squarely foreclosed by the language of the FSIA. However difficult it may be in some cases to separate "purpose" (*i.e.*, the reason why the foreign state engages in the activity) from "nature" (*i.e.*, the outward form of the conduct that the foreign state performs or agrees to perform) . . . , the statute unmistakably commands that to be done, 28 U.S.C. § 1603(d). We agree with the Court of Appeals, *see* 941 F.2d, at 151, that it is irrelevant why Argentina participated in the bond market in the manner of a private actor; it matters only that it did so. We conclude that Argentina's issuance of the Bonods was a "commercial activity" under the FSIA.

Note

1. *Weltover* was a unanimous decision. Yet, Argentina's argument that the nature/purpose distinction is misleading and formalistic is not without force. Were the Court's hands tied by the text of § 1603(d)?

SAUDI ARABIA v. NELSON

507 U.S. 349 (1993).

SOUTER, J.

[Scott Nelson was hired, in the United States, to be an administrator at the state-owned King Faisal Hospital in Saudi Arabia. Shortly after Nelson reported unsafe conditions in the hospital, he was arrested, allegedly interrogated under torture, and detained for thirty days by members of the Saudi Arabian security forces. After his release had been procured through the intervention of a U.S. Senator, Nelson and his wife returned to the United States and filed suit in federal court in Florida. The Nelsons' suit alleged various torts. No claims of breach of contract were included, presumably because Nelson's employment contract specified that it would be enforceable in Saudi Arabia's courts. The issue was whether Nelson's suit was based upon commercial activity in the United States, so as to fit within the exception to foreign sovereign immunity in 28 U.S.C. § 1605(a) (2). The relevance of 28 U.S.C. § 1603(d) in resolving that issue was also addressed by the Supreme Court.]

Petitioners' tortious conduct itself fails to qualify as "commercial activity" within the meaning of the Act, although the Act is too " 'obtuse' "to be of much help in reaching that conclusion.... [T]he Act defines "commercial activity" as "either a regular course of commercial conduct or a particular commercial transaction or act," and provides that "[t]he commercial character of an activity shall be determined by reference to the nature of the course of conduct or particular transaction or act, rather than by reference to its purpose." 28 U.S.C. § 1603(d). If this is a definition, it is one distinguished only by its diffidence; as we observed in our most recent case on the subject, it "leaves the critical term 'commercial' largely undefined." Republic of Argentina v. Weltover, Inc., 504 U.S. 607, 612.... We do not, however, have the option to throw up our hands. The term has to be given some interpretation, and congressional diffidence necessarily results in judicial responsibility to determine what a "commercial activity" is for purposes of the Act....

Under the restrictive, as opposed to the "absolute," theory of foreign sovereign immunity, a state is immune from the jurisdiction of foreign courts as to its sovereign or public acts (*jure imperii*), but not as to those that are private or commercial in character (*jure gestionis*).... Put differently, a foreign state engages in commercial activity for purposes of the restrictive theory only where it acts "in the manner of a private player within" the market....

We emphasized in *Weltover* that whether a state acts "in the manner of" a private party is a question of behavior, not motivation....

Unlike Argentina's activities that we considered in Weltover, the intentional conduct alleged here (the Saudi Government's wrongful arrest, imprisonment, and torture of Nelson) could not qualify as commercial under the restrictive theory. The conduct boils down to abuse of the power of its police by the Saudi Government, and however monstrous such abuse undoubtedly may be, a foreign state's exercise of the power of its police has long been understood for purposes of the restrictive theory as peculiarly sovereign in nature ... ; K. RANDALL, FEDERAL COURTS AND THE INTERNATIONAL HUMAN RIGHTS PARADIGM 93 (1990) (the Act's commercial-activity exception is irrelevant to cases alleging that a foreign state has violated human rights). Exercise of the powers of police and penal officers is not the sort of action by which private parties can engage in commerce. "[S]uch acts as legislation, or the expulsion of an alien, or a denial of justice, cannot be performed by an individual acting in his own name. They can be performed only by the state acting as such." Lauterpacht, *The Problem of Jurisdictional Immunities of Foreign States*, 28 BRIT. Y.B. INT'L L. 220, 225 (1952); see also *id.*, at 237.

The Nelsons and their *amici* urge us to give significance to their assertion that the Saudi Government subjected Nelson to the abuse alleged as retaliation for his persistence in reporting hospital safety violations, and argue that the character of the mistreatment was consequently commercial. One *amicus*, indeed, goes so far as to suggest that the Saudi Government "often uses detention and torture to resolve commercial disputes." Brief for Human Rights Watch as *Amicus Curiae* 6. But this argument does not alter the fact that the powers allegedly abused were those of police and penal officers. In any event, the argument is off the point, for it goes to purpose, the very fact the Act renders irrelevant to the question of an activity's commercial character. Whatever may have been the Saudi Government's motivation for its allegedly abusive treatment of Nelson, it remains the case that the Nelsons' action is based upon a sovereign activity immune from the subject-matter jurisdiction of United States courts under the Act.

The Nelsons' action is not "based upon a commercial activity" within the meaning of the first clause of § 1605(a)(2) of the Act, and the judgment of the Court of Appeals is accordingly reversed.

WHITE, J. (with whom BLACKMUN, J., joins), concurring

... The majority concludes that petitioners enjoy sovereign immunity because respondents' action is not "based upon a commercial activity." I disagree. I nonetheless concur in the judgment because in my view the commercial conduct upon which respondents base their complaint was not "carried on in the United States."

... The majority [finds] that petitioners' conduct is not commercial because it "is not the sort of action by which private parties can engage in commerce".... If by that the majority means that it is not the manner in which private parties ought to engage in commerce, I wholeheartedly agree. That, however, is not the relevant inquiry. Rather, the question we must ask is whether it is the manner in which private parties at times do engage in commerce.

Indeed, I am somewhat at a loss as to what exactly the majority believes petitioners have done that a private employer could not. As countless cases attest, retaliation for whistle-blowing is not a practice foreign to the marketplace. . . . On occasion, private employers also have been known to retaliate by enlisting the help of police officers to falsely arrest employees. . . .

Therefore, had the hospital retaliated against Nelson by hiring thugs to do the job, I assume the majority—no longer able to describe this conduct as "a foreign state's exercise of the power of its police,"—would consent to calling it "commercial." For, in such circumstances, the state-run hospital would be operating as any private participant in the marketplace and respondents' action would be based on the operation by Saudi Arabia's agents of a commercial business.

At the heart of the majority's conclusion, in other words, is the fact that the hospital in this case chose to call in government security forces. I find this fixation on the intervention of police officers, and the ensuing characterization of the conduct as "peculiarly sovereign in nature," to be misguided. To begin, it fails to capture respondents' complaint in full. Far from being directed solely at the activities of the Saudi police, it alleges that agents of the hospital summoned Nelson to its security office because he reported safety concerns and that the hospital played a part in the subsequent beating and imprisonment. Without more, that type of behavior hardly qualifies as sovereign. Thus, even assuming for the sake of argument that the role of the official police somehow affected the nature of petitioners' conduct, the claim cannot be said to "res[t] entirely upon activities sovereign in character." At the very least it "consists of both commercial and sovereign elements," thereby presenting the specific question the majority chooses to elude. The majority's single-minded focus on the exercise of police power, while certainly simplifying the case, thus hardly does it justice.

. . . That, when the hospital calls in security to get even with a whistle-blower, it comes clothed in police apparel says more about the state-owned nature of the commercial enterprise than about the noncommercial nature of its tortious conduct. . . .

Contrary to the majority's suggestion, this conclusion does not involve inquiring into the purpose of the conduct. Matters would be different, I suppose, if Nelson had been recruited to work in the Saudi police force and, having reported safety violations, suffered retributive punishment, for there the Saudi authorities would be engaged in distinctly sovereign activities. *Cf.* House Report, at 16 ("Also public or governmental and not commercial in nature, would be the employment of diplomatic, civil service, or military personnel"); Senate Report, at 16. The same would be true if Nelson was a mere tourist in Saudi Arabia and had been summarily expelled by order of immigration officials. See Arango v. Guzman Travel Advisors Corp., 621 F.2d 1371 (5th Cir. 1980). . . .

KENNEDY, J., concurring in part and dissenting in part

I agree with the Court's holding that the Nelsons' claims of intentional wrongdoing by the hospital and the Kingdom of Saudi Arabia are based on sovereign, not commercial, activity, and so fall outside the commercial activity exception to the grant of foreign sovereign immunity contained in 28 U.S.C. § 1604. The intentional tort counts of the Nelsons' complaint recite the alleged unlawful arrest, imprisonment, and torture of Mr. Nelson by the Saudi police acting in their official capacities. These are not the sort of activities by which a private party conducts its business affairs; if we classified them as commercial, the commercial activity exception would in large measure swallow the rule of foreign sovereign immunity Congress enacted in the FSIA.

Notes and Questions

1. For criticism of the approach taken in *Nelson* and inquiry into related claims, *see, e.g.*, panel, International Human Rights in American Courts: The Case of *Nelson v. Saudi Arabia*, 86 Proc., Am. Soc. Int'l L. 324–48 (1992).

2. Congress, in its spare if not circular definition of "commercial activity" in 28 U.S.C. § 1603(d), has provided little guidance to U.S. courts on this key issue, although Congress clearly has adopted the nature of the act test. In both *Weltover* and *Nelson*, the majority opinions adopt an abstract, formalistic approach, focusing narrowly on the precise conduct alleged to have injured the plaintiffs. On the commercial activity exception generally, see Michael W. Gordon, Foreign State Immunity in Commercial Transactions (1991).

3. Courts in other countries have been willing to concede that the nature/purpose distinction can be unsatisfying, and have shifted their focus toward the ultimate issue—whether the foreign state should enjoy immunity for the conduct in question. For example, the Supreme Court of Canada noted that, unlike the FSIA, the Canadian 1981 State Immunity Act does not strictly forbid reference to an acts's purpose in discerning its nature. Section 2 of the State Immunity Act defines commercial activity as "any particular transaction, act or conduct or any regular course of conduct that by reason of its nature is of a commercial character." The Court considered the overall context of the employment relationship between the United States military and Canadian civilian employees at a base in Newfoundland, before extending immunity. United States v. Public Service Alliance of Canada, (1992) 91 D.L.R. (4th) 449 (S.C.C.).

4. Characterizing the conduct in issue may be difficult. For example, in I Congresso del Partido, [1983] 1 A.C. 244 (H.L.), the U.K. House of Lords struggled with a dispute between a Chilean corporation and a Cuban state trading enterprise. The Cuban company refused to deliver two shipments of sugar that had been in transit to Chile at the time General Augusto Pinochet overthrew the Allende government, which had close relations with Cuba. Cuba immediately severed diplomatic relations with Chile, announced the cancellation of the contracts and ordered that a portion of the sugar be donated instead to the people of North Vietnam. Noting this highly charged political context, Lord Wilberforce nevertheless decided that the breach of contract was nonimmune, but also observed:

> [T]he court must consider the whole context in which the claim against the state is made, with a view to deciding whether the relevant act(s) upon which the claim is based, should, in that context, be considered as

fairly within an area of activity, trading or commercial, or otherwise of a private law character, in which the state has chosen to engage, or whether the relevant act(s) should be considered as having been done outside that area, and within the sphere of governmental or sovereign activity.

[1983] 1 A.C. 244, 267.

5. Taking a similar contextual approach, the New Zealand Court of Appeal determined that the sale of tax credits by authorities in the Cook Islands to several New Zealand corporations seeking to avoid New Zealand income taxes, though on its surface a classically sovereign act, had sufficient elements of commerciality to be nonimmune under the common law (New Zealand having never codified foreign sovereign immunity). Controller and Auditor–General v. Davison [1996] 2 NZLR 278, 36 I.L.M. 721 (1997).

6. It may be necessary to separate a course of conduct by a state or state entity into distinct components in order to resolve the issue of immunity. *See, e.g.*, Arango v. Guzman Travel Advisors Corp., 621 F.2d 1371 (5th Cir.1980) (distinguishing causes of action relating to nonperformance of contract for vacation services from torts involving actions of immigration officials). Kuwait Airways Corp . v. Iraqi Airways Co., [1995] 1 W.L.R. 1147 (H.L.(E.)), involved Iraq's 1990 invasion and attempted annexation of Kuwait. Iraq's armed forces seized ten passenger airplanes owned by Kuwait Airways Corporation (K.A.C.) and transferred them to the state-owned Iraqi Airways Co. (I.A.C.), with the expectation that the planes would be employed in commercial air transportation. Instead, four were destroyed in the Gulf War and six were flown for safe-keeping to Iran and eventually returned to K.A.C. While the initial seizure was regarded as an immune sovereign act, the later conversion of the planes by I.A.C. to commercial use (by flying some on internal routes and repainting their insignia) was found by a majority of the U.K. House of Lords to be nonimmune.

7. Disagreement over the "nature/purpose" distinction has hampered the transformation of the International Law Commission's 1991 draft articles on state immunity into binding treaty form. Article 2.2 of the draft articles attempts a compromise:

> In determining whether a contract or transaction is a "commercial transaction," ... reference should be made primarily to the nature of the contract or transaction, but its purpose should also be taken into account if, in the practice of the State which is a party to it, that purpose is relevant to determining the noncommercial character of the contract or transaction.

International Law Commission Draft Articles on Jurisdictional Immunities of States and Their Property, U.N. Doc. A/46/405 (1991), *reprinted in* 30 I.L.M. 1554, 1565–66 (1991). *See* Convention on Jurisdictional Immunities of States and Their Property: Report of the Sixth Committee, U.N. Doc. A/49/744 (1994); Summary Records of the Sixth Committee, 49 U.N. GAOR, U.N. Docs. A/C.6/SR.32, A/C.6/SR.33 (1994) (indicating disagreement among states such as China that prefer a "purpose" test, states such as France that find the two concepts to be intertwined, and states such as the United States and the United Kingdom that prefer an unequivocal "nature" test). Hazel Fox, *A "Commercial Transaction" Under the State Immunity Act 1978*, 43

INT'L & COMP. L.Q. 193 (1994), describes the shifting landscape concerning the public international law dimension of foreign sovereign immunity, with particular reference to the ILC's draft articles. She notes that there appears to be a greater chance for a treaty adopting a restrictive theory, but there is still disagreement whether the purpose as well as the nature of commercial activity should be part of a restrictive principle, and a few states, such as the PRC and some South American countries still favor an absolute theory. *Id.* at 193. *See also* Wang Houli, *Sovereign Immunity: Chinese Views and Practices*, 1 J. CHINESE L. 22 (1987); Joseph W. Dellapenna, *Foreign State Immunity in Europe*, 5 N.Y. INT'L L. REV. 51 (1992); Joan Donoghue, *The Public Face of Private International Law: Prospects for a Convention on Foreign State Immunity*, 57 LAW & CONTEMP. PROBS. 305 (1994).

Problems

How should the following claims be resolved under the FSIA?

1. A foreign state sends military trainees to a base in Texas, assuring U.S. officials that it will be responsible for their living expenses. Some trainees make unauthorized long-distance telephone calls during their stay. The long-distance carrier sues the foreign state and its defense ministry, arguing that making telephone calls is by its nature commercial activity and that the exception of § 1605(a)(2) applies. What result? See MCI Telecommunications Corp. v. Alhadhood, 82 F.3d 658 (5th Cir.), *reh'g en banc denied*, 91 F.3d 142, *cert. denied*, MCI Telecommunications Corp. v. United Arab Emirates, 519 U.S. 1007 (1996).

2. A group of American scholars sues the national university of a Pacific state, alleging that it and its officials infringed their copyright by publishing a dictionary of "Austronesian" languages that was pirated from a text they had originally compiled. The government of the Pacific state underwrote the university publication with $800,000 in support. These costs are highly unlikely to be recovered through sales; thus, no profit motive for the activity can be discerned. Is the university nevertheless engaged in "commercial activity" under the FSIA because of the nature of the publishing activity? See Intercontinental Dictionary Series v. De Gruyter, 822 F.Supp. 662 (C.D.Cal.1993).

3. A developing state breaches a licensing agreement with a corporation to export rhesus monkeys for purposes of medical experimentation. The foreign state argues that the agreement did not involve "commercial activity" because control over natural resources is an inherently sovereign act. What result under § 1605(a)(2)? See MOL, Inc. v. Peoples Republic of Bangladesh, 736 F.2d 1326 (9th Cir.), *cert. denied*, 469 U.S. 1037 (1984).

c. *"Nexus" With the Forum State*

With respect to the commercial activities exception, domestic courts exercising jurisdiction over foreign states must be satisfied that a sufficient link exists between the foreign state's conduct and the forum state. Where the entire course of conduct does not take place within the territory of the forum, difficult issues may arise. Under the FSIA exception for commercial activity, § 1605(a)(2), three separate clauses set out alternative tests by which a plaintiff may establish a link between commercial activity and the United States: (1) where the action is "based upon" a commercial activity carried on in the United States by a foreign state; (2) where the action is "based upon" an act performed in the United States "in connection with" a commercial activity of the foreign state elsewhere; or (3) where the action is "based upon" an act outside the territory of the United States, performed "in connection with" commercial activity of the foreign state elsewhere and causing a "direct effect" in the United States. The definition of "commercial activity carried on in the United States," for purposes of § 1605(a)(2) (i), includes a reference in § 1603(e) to "substantial contact with the United States."

Saudi Arabia v. Nelson, *Argentina v. Weltover*, and *Siderman de Blake v. Argentina*, *infra*, explore the complex interactions among these statutory provisions, which have given rise to much litigation.

SAUDI ARABIA, KING FAISAL SPECIALIST HOSPITAL AND ROYSPEC v. NELSON

507 U.S. 349 (1993).

SOUTER, J.

[The facts are set out in the excerpt included in Section 1 at p. 710, *supra*]

The District Court dismissed for lack of subject-matter jurisdiction ... because there was no sufficient "nexus" between Nelson's recruitment and the injuries alleged. "Although [the Nelsons] argu[e] that but for [Scott Nelson's] recruitment in the United States, he would not have taken the job, been arrested, and suffered the personal injuries," the court said, "this 'connection' [is] far too tenuous to support jurisdiction" under the Act.... Likewise, the court concluded that Royspec's commercial activity in the United States, purchasing supplies and equipment for the hospital ... had no nexus with the personal injuries alleged in the complaint....

The Court of Appeals reversed. 923 F.2d 1528 (11th Cir.1991). It concluded that Nelson's recruitment and hiring were commercial activities of Saudi Arabia and the hospital, carried on in the United States for purposes of the Act, *id.*, at 1533, and that the Nelsons' action was "based upon" these activities within the meaning of the statute, *id.*, at 1533–1536. There was, the court reasoned, a sufficient nexus between those commercial activities and the wrongful acts that had allegedly injured the Nelsons: "the detention and torture of Nelson are so intertwined with his employment at the Hospital," the court explained, "that they are 'based upon' his recruitment and hiring" in the United States. *Id.*, at 1535....

II

The first clause of § 1605(a)(2) of the Act provides that a foreign state shall not be immune from the jurisdiction of United States courts in any case "in which the action is based upon a commercial activity carried on in the United States by the foreign state." The Act defines such activity as "commercial activity carried on by such state and having substantial contact with the United States," § 1603(e), and provides that a commercial activity may be "either a regular course of commercial conduct or a particular commercial transaction or act," the "commercial character of [which] shall be determined by reference to" its "nature," rather than its "purpose," § 1603(d).

Although the Act contains no definition of the phrase "based upon," and the relatively sparse legislative history offers no assistance, guidance is hardly necessary. In denoting conduct that forms the "basis," or "foundation," for a claim, see BLACK'S LAW DICTIONARY 151 (6th ed. 1990) (defining "base"); RANDOM HOUSE DICTIONARY 172 (2d ed. 1987) (same); Webster's Third New International Dictionary 180, 181 (1976) (defining "base" and "based"), the phrase is read most naturally to mean those elements of a claim that, if proven, would entitle a plaintiff to relief under his theory of the case....

What the natural meaning of the phrase "based upon" suggests, the context confirms.... § 1605(a)(2) contains two clauses following the one at issue here. The second allows for jurisdiction where a suit "is based ... upon an act performed in the United States in connection with a commercial activity of the foreign state elsewhere," and the third speaks in like terms, allowing for jurisdiction where an action "is based ... upon an act outside the territory of the United States in connection with a commercial activity of the foreign state elsewhere and that act causes a direct effect in the United States"....

In this case, the Nelsons have alleged that petitioners recruited Scott Nelson for work at the hospital, signed an employment contract with him, and subsequently employed him. While these activities led to the conduct that eventually injured the Nelsons, they are not the basis for the Nelsons' suit. Even taking each of the Nelsons' allegations about Scott Nelson's recruitment and employment as true, those facts alone entitle the Nelsons to nothing under their theory of the case. The Nelsons have not, after all, alleged breach of contract ..., but personal injuries caused by petitioners' intentional wrongs and by petitioners' negligent failure to warn Scott Nelson that they might commit those wrongs. Those torts, and not the arguably commercial activities that preceded their commission, form the basis for the Nelsons' suit.

WHITE, J. (with whom BLACKMUN, J., joins), concurring

The majority concludes that petitioners enjoy sovereign immunity because respondents' action is not "based upon a commercial activity." I disagree. I nonetheless concur in the judgment because in my view the commercial conduct upon which respondents base their complaint was not "carried on in the United States."

As the majority notes, the first step in the analysis is to identify the conduct on which the action is based. Respondents have pointed to two distinct possibilities. The first, seemingly pressed at trial and on appeal, consists of the recruiting and hiring activity in the United States.... Although this conduct would undoubtedly qualify as "commercial," I agree with the majority that it is "not the basis for the Nelsons' suit," for it is unrelated to the elements of respondents' complaint.

In a partial change of course, respondents suggest to this Court both in their brief and at oral argument that we focus on the hospital's commercial activity in Saudi Arabia, its employment practices and disciplinary procedures. Under this view, the Court would then work its way back to the recruiting and hiring activity in order to establish that the commercial conduct in fact had "substantial contact" with the United States.... The majority never reaches this second stage, finding instead that petitioners' conduct is not commercial because it "is not the sort of action by which private parties can engage in commerce"....

Nevertheless, I reach the same conclusion as the majority because petitioners' commercial activity was not "carried on in the United States." The Act defines such conduct as "commercial activity ... having substantial contact with the United States." 28 U.S.C. § 1603(e). Respondents point to the hospital's recruitment efforts in the United States, including advertising in the American media, and the signing of the employment contract in Miami.... As I earlier noted, while these may very well qualify as commercial activity in the United States, they do not constitute the commercial activity upon which respondents' action is based. Conversely, petitioners' commercial conduct in Saudi Arabia, though constituting the basis of the Nelsons' suit, lacks a sufficient nexus to the United States. Neither the hospital's employment practices, nor its disciplinary procedures, has any apparent connection to this country. On that basis, I agree that the Act does not grant the Nelsons access to our courts.

KENNEDY, J. (with whom BLACKMUN, J. and STEVENS, J., join as to Parts I–B and II), concurring in part and dissenting in part

I join all of the Court's opinion except the last paragraph of Part II, where, with almost no explanation, the Court rules that, like the intentional tort claim, the claims based on negligent failure to warn are outside the subject-matter jurisdiction of the federal courts. These claims stand on a much different footing from the intentional tort claims for purposes of the Foreign Sovereign Immunities Act (FSIA). In my view, they ought to be remanded to the District Court for further consideration.

I. B

[T]he Nelsons' claims alleging that the hospital, the Kingdom, and Royspec were negligent in failing during their recruitment of Nelson to warn him of foreseeable dangers are based upon commercial activity having substantial contact with the United States. As such, they are within the commercial activity exception and the jurisdiction of the federal courts. Unlike the intentional tort counts of the complaint, the failure to warn counts do not complain of a police beating in Saudi

Arabia; rather, they complain of a negligent omission made during the recruiting of a hospital employee in the United States. To obtain relief, the Nelsons would be obliged to prove that the hospital's recruiting agent did not tell Nelson about the foreseeable hazards of his prospective employment in Saudi Arabia. Under the Court's test, this omission is what the negligence counts are "based upon"....

Omission of important information during employee recruiting is commercial activity.... It seems plain that recruiting employees is an activity undertaken by private hospitals in the normal course of business. Locating and hiring employees implicates no power unique to the sovereign....

The recruiting activity alleged in the failure to warn counts of the complaint also satisfies the final requirement for invoking the commercial activity exception: that the claims be based upon commercial activity "having substantial contact with the United States." 28 U.S.C. § 1603 (e). Nelson's recruitment was performed by Hospital Corporation of America, Ltd. (HCA), a wholly owned subsidiary of a United States corporation, which, for a period of at least 16 years beginning in 1973, acted as the Kingdom of Saudi Arabia's exclusive agent for recruiting employees for the hospital. HCA in the regular course of its business seeks employees for the hospital in the American labor market. HCA advertised in an American magazine, seeking applicants for the position Nelson later filled. Nelson saw the ad in the United States and contacted HCA in Tennessee. After an interview in Saudi Arabia, Nelson returned to Florida, where he signed an employment contract and underwent personnel processing and application procedures. Before leaving to take his job at the hospital, Nelson attended an orientation session conducted by HCA in Tennessee for new employees. These activities have more than substantial contact with the United States; most of them were "carried on in the United States." 28 U.S.C. § 1605(a)(2). In alleging that the petitioners neglected during these activities to tell him what they were bound to under state law, Nelson meets all of the statutory requirements for invoking federal jurisdiction under the commercial activity exception.

Stevens, J., dissenting

In this case, as Justice White has demonstrated, petitioner Kingdom of Saudi Arabia's operation of the hospital and its employment practices and disciplinary procedures are "commercial activities" within the meaning of the statute, and respondent Scott Nelson's claim that he was punished for acts performed in the course of his employment was unquestionably "based upon" those activities.

Unlike Justice White, however, I am also convinced that petitioner's commercial activities—whether defined as the regular course of conduct of operating a hospital or, more specifically, as the commercial transaction of engaging respondent "as an employee with specific responsibilities in that enterprise," Brief for Respondents 25—have sufficient contact with the United States to justify the exercise of federal jurisdiction.

Petitioner Royspec maintains an office in Maryland and purchases hospital supplies and equipment in this country. For nearly two decades the hospital's American agent has maintained an office in the United States and regularly engaged in the recruitment of personnel in this country. Respondent himself was recruited in the United States and entered into his employment contract with the hospital in the United States. Before traveling to Saudi Arabia to assume his position at the hospital, respondent attended an orientation program in Tennessee. The position for which respondent was recruited and ultimately hired was that of a monitoring systems manager, a troubleshooter, and, taking respondent's allegations as true, it was precisely respondent's performance of those responsibilities that led to the hospital's retaliatory actions against him.

Whether the first clause of § 1605(a)(2) broadly authorizes "general" jurisdiction over foreign entities that engage in substantial commercial activity in this country, or, more narrowly, authorizes only "specific" jurisdiction over particular commercial claims that have a substantial contact with the United States, petitioners' contacts with the United States in this case are, in my view, plainly sufficient to subject petitioners to suit in this country on a claim arising out of its nonimmune commercial activity relating to respondent. If the same activities had been performed by a private business, I have no doubt jurisdiction would be upheld. And that, of course, should be a touchstone of our inquiry.... I would therefore affirm the judgment of the Court of Appeals.

REPUBLIC OF ARGENTINA v. WELTOVER, INC.

504 U.S. 607 (1992).

[The facts are summarized in Section 1 C 2 ii, at p. 706 *supra*]

II. B

The remaining question is whether Argentina's unilateral rescheduling of the Bonods had a "direct effect" in the United States, 28 U.S.C. § 1605(a)(2). In addressing this issue, the Court of Appeals rejected the suggestion in the legislative history of the FSIA that an effect is not "direct" unless it is both "substantial" and "foreseeable".... That suggestion is found in the House Report, which states that conduct covered by the third clause of § 1605(a)(2) would be subject to the jurisdiction of American courts "consistent with principles set forth in section 18, RESTATEMENT OF THE LAW, SECOND, FOREIGN RELATIONS LAW OF THE UNITED STATES (1965)." H.R.Rep. No. 94–1487, pp. 1, 19, U.S.Code Cong. & Admin.News 1976, pp. 6604, 6618 (1976). Section 18 states that American laws are not given extraterritorial application except with respect to conduct that has, as a "direct and foreseeable result," a "substantial" effect within the United States. Since this obviously deals with jurisdiction to legislate rather than jurisdiction to adjudicate, this passage of the House Report has been charitably described as "a bit of a non sequitur," Texas Trading & Milling Corp. v. Federal Republic of

Nigeria, 647 F.2d 300, 311 (2d Cir.1981), *cert. denied*, 454 U.S. 1148 (1982).... But we reject the suggestion that § 1605(a)(2) contains any unexpressed requirement of "substantiality" or "foreseeability." As the Court of Appeals recognized, an effect is "direct" if it follows "as an immediate consequence of the defendant's ... activity." 941 F.2d, at 152.

We ... have little difficulty concluding that Argentina's unilateral rescheduling of the maturity dates on the Bonods had a "direct effect" in the United States. Respondents had designated their accounts in New York as the place of payment, and Argentina made some interest payments into those accounts before announcing that it was rescheduling the payments. Because New York was thus the place of performance for Argentina's ultimate contractual obligations, the rescheduling of those obligations necessarily had a "direct effect" in the United States.... We reject Argentina's suggestion that the "direct effect" requirement cannot be satisfied where the plaintiffs are all foreign corporations with no other connections to the United States. We expressly stated in *Verlinden* that the FSIA permits "a foreign plaintiff to sue a foreign sovereign in the courts of the United States, provided the substantive requirements of the Act are satisfied," 461 U.S., at 489.

Notes and Questions

1. Siderman de Blake v. Republic of Argentina, 965 F.2d 699 (9th Cir.1992), *cert. denied*, 507 U.S. 1017 (1993), presents an unusual set of facts in which human rights torts were closely linked with commercial activity as defined in 28 U.S.C. §§ 1605(a)(2) and 1603(e). The facts are set forth at pp. 722–723 *infra*. The Sidermans owned a hotel in Argentina that had been seized and operated by military authorities. Susana Siderman de Blake, who owned a 33% share, was a U.S. citizen. The hotel advertised for customers in the U.S. and accepted payment by U.S. credit card, which the Ninth Circuit found to be "substantial contact" within the meaning of § 1603(e). The Sidermans' claims in part related to the diversion of profits from the hotel, so the action was "based upon" commercial activity carried on in the U.S. within the meaning of clause one of § 1605(a)(2). Further, the Argentine authorities had performed acts in the U.S. in connection with commercial activity elsewhere, satisfying the second clause of § 1605(a)(2). Finally, defendants' commercial activity had a "direct effect" in the U.S., because of the non-payment of profits owed to Susana Siderman de Blake, satisfying the third clause of § 1605(a)(2). The Ninth Circuit relied on precedent indicating that such a "direct effect" must be "substantial and foreseeable". On the eve of trial, Argentina entered into a substantial settlement with the Sidermans. Daniel R. Marcus, *Winning Justice for an Argentinean Refugee*, Am. Lawyer 33 (Nov. 1996). Some lower courts, relying on *Weltover*, dispense with the requirement that a "direct effect" be either substantial or foreseeable. These courts demand only that the effect follow as an immediate consequence of the defendant's activity. *See, e.g.*, Voest–Alpine Trading USA Corp. v. Bank of China, 142 F.3d 887, 893 (5th Cir.), *reh'g en banc denied*, 149 F.3d 1181, *cert. denied*, 525 U.S. 1041, 119 S.Ct. 591 (1998).

2. The three sub-clauses of § 1605(a)(2) and their interrelationship with § 1603(e) have been the subject of much litigation. Cases noting that the "nexus" inquiry consists of two parts—the link between the foreign state's commercial activity and the United States and the link between the commercial activity and the plaintiff's cause of action—include NYSA–ILA Pension Trust Fund By and Through Bowers v. Garuda Indonesia, 7 F.3d 35 (2d Cir.1993), *cert. denied*, 510 U.S. 1116 (1994); Federal Ins. Co. v. Richard I. Rubin & Co., Inc., 12 F.3d 1270 (3d Cir.1993), *cert. denied sub nom.*, Ejay Travel, Inc. v. Algemeen Burgerlijk Pensioenfonds, 511 U.S. 1107 (1994), *appeal after remand*, 74 F.3d 1226 (3d Cir.1995); Tubular Inspectors, Inc. v. Petroleos Mexicanos, 977 F.2d 180 (5th Cir.1992); Santos v. Compagnie Nationale Air France, 934 F.2d 890 (7th Cir.1991); Goodman Holdings v. Rafidain Bank, 26 F.3d 1143 (D.C.Cir.1994), *cert. denied*, 513 U.S. 1079 (1995).

3. Given the ambiguity of the FSIA's terms "based upon," "in connection with," "direct effect" and "substantial contact," are the opinions in *Weltover*, *Nelson*, and *Siderman de Blake* really textual? Or are the opinions based on unstated assumptions (or educated guesses about Congressional attitudes) toward the types of cases against foreign sovereigns best handled by the U.S. judiciary?

3. *Waiver of Sovereign Immunity*

To protect themselves in dealings with foreign states, contracting parties may insist upon an explicit waiver of sovereign immunity. Contracts may contain explicit forum-selection clauses and choice-of-law provisions as well. See Eckert Intern., Inc. v. Government of Sovereign Democratic Republic of Fiji, 32 F.3d 77 (4th Cir.1994). Waiver may also be implicit, as in Joseph v. Office of Consulate General of Nigeria, 830 F.2d 1018 (9th Cir.1987), *cert. denied*, 485 U.S. 905 (1988) (lease between U.S. landlord and foreign consulate). Congress codified an exception based upon explicit or implicit waiver in 28 U.S.C. § 1605(a)(1).

The House Report on the FSIA cited the filing of a responsive pleading, without raising the defense of sovereign immunity, as an example of implied waiver. H.R. Rep. No. 94–1487. Nevertheless, some courts have found no waiver where the defendant's appearance at an early stage of the proceedings did not give "unambiguous" evidence of a conscious decision to take part in litigation. Drexel Burnham Lambert Group Inc. v. Committee of Receivers for Galadari, 12 F.3d 317, 325–28 (2d Cir.1993), *cert. denied*, 511 U.S. 1069 (1994), *citing* Foremost–McKesson, Inc. v. Islamic Republic of Iran, 905 F.2d 438, 443–44 (D.C.Cir.1990); Frolova v. Union of Soviet Socialist Republics, 761 F.2d 370, 378 (7th Cir.1985).

SIDERMAN DE BLAKE v. REPUBLIC OF ARGENTINA

965 F.2d 699 (9th Cir.1992), *cert. denied*, 507 U.S. 1017 (1993).

FLETCHER, J.

Susana Siderman de Blake and Jose, Lea, and Carlos Siderman (collectively, "the Sidermans") appeal the dismissal of their action against the Republic of Argentina and the Argentine Province of Tucuman (collectively, "Argentina"). The Sidermans' complaint alleged eighteen causes of action arising out of the torture of Jose Siderman and the expropriation of the Sidermans' property by Argentine military officials.

The factual record ... tells a horrifying tale of the violent and brutal excesses of an anti-Semitic military junta that ruled Argentina. On March 24, 1976, the Argentine military overthrew the government of President Maria Estela Peron and seized the reins of power for itself, installing military leaders of the central government and the provincial governments of Argentina. That night, ten masked men carrying machine guns [acting under the direction of the military governor of Tucuman] forcibly entered the home of Jose and Lea Siderman, husband and wife, in Tucuman Province, Argentina. [Jose Siderman was detained and tortured for seven days] because of his Jewish faith.

In June 1976, Jose, Lea, and Carlos left Argentina for the United States, where they joined Susana Siderman de Blake, the daughter of Jose and Lea and a United States citizen.... [Jose was forced to raise cash by selling at a steep discount part of his interest in 127,000 acres of land in Tucuman. The Sidermans also granted management powers over their family business, Inmobiliaria del Nor–Oeste, S.A. ("INOSA"), an Argentine corporation, to a certified public accountant. Susana Siderman de Blake, Carlos Siderman and Lea Siderman each owned 33% of INOSA and Jose owned the remaining one percent. Its assets comprised numerous real estate holdings including a large hotel in Tucuman, the Hotel Gran Corona.

[After the Sidermans' flight to the United States, Argentine military officers altered real property records in Tucuman to show that Jose had owned not 127,000, but 127 acres of land. They then initiated a criminal action against him in Argentina, claiming that he had sold land that did not belong to him. Argentina sought the assistance of the Los Angeles Superior Court in obtaining jurisdiction over Jose, requesting via a letter rogatory that it serve him with documents relating to the action. The court complied with the request.

[While he was traveling in Italy, Jose was arrested pursuant to an extradition request from Argentina, detained for 27 days and forbidden to leave Italy for seven months. Eventually, the Italian Appeals Court rejected the extradition request as politically motivated and pretextual.

[In April 1977, INOSA was seized through a sham "judicial intervention." The Sidermans were unable to oppose the intervention because Argentine officials had imprisoned and killed the accountant to whom they had granted management powers. In 1978, the Sidermans retained an attorney in Argentina and brought a derivative action in a Tucuman court in an effort to end the intervention. Though the Tucuman courts ordered that the intervention cease, the order was not enforced. Argentine military officials and INOSA's appointed receivers extracted funds from INOSA, purchased INOSA assets at sharply discounted prices, and diverted INOSA's profits and revenues to themselves.]

II. C. Implied Waiver Exception

The Sidermans contend that Argentina availed itself of our courts in its pursuit of Jose Siderman and, in doing so, implicitly waived its immunity defense with respect to their claims for torture and persecution. They assert that after the elder Siderman fled to this country, Argentina commenced malicious criminal proceedings against him in Argentina, and requested the assistance of the California state courts in obtaining jurisdiction over his person. The California courts, unaware of Argentina's true intentions, complied by effecting service of process.

The FSIA's waiver exception "is narrowly construed." Joseph v. Office of Consulate General of Nigeria, 830 F.2d 1018, 1022 (9th Cir. 1987), *cert. denied*, 485 U.S. 905 . . . (1988). The House Report accompanying the passage of the FSIA gives three examples of an implied waiver:

> With respect to implicit waivers, the courts have found such waivers in cases where a foreign state has agreed to arbitration in another country or where a foreign state has agreed that the law of a particular country should govern a contract. An implicit waiver would also include a situation where a foreign state has filed a responsive pleading in an action without raising the defense of sovereign immunity.

H.R.Rep. No. 1487, 94th Cong., 2d Sess. 18 (1976), *reprinted in* 1976 U.S.C.C.A.N. 6604, 6617. The House Report does not purport to provide an exclusive list of the circumstances giving rise to implied waivers, however, and we have not construed it in this fashion. Thus, while we stated in Joseph that implied waivers will "ordinarily [be] found" only in the three situations mentioned in the legislative history, 830 F.2d at 1022 (*citing* Frolova v. Union of Soviet Socialist Republics, 761 F.2d 370, 377 (7th Cir.1985)), we went beyond those examples to establish the more general proposition that where a written agreement entered into by a foreign sovereign "contemplates adjudication of a dispute by the United States courts," we will find the sovereign to have waived its immunity. *Joseph*, 830 F.2d at 1023.

Thus, the essential inquiry in written agreement cases is whether a sovereign contemplated the involvement of United States courts in the affair in issue. Here, we confront a situation where Argentina apparently not only envisioned United States court participation in its persecution of the Sidermans, but by its actions deliberately implicated our courts in that persecution.... The letter rogatory, dated May 11, 1980, informed the Presiding Judge of the Los Angeles Superior Court that criminal proceedings were pending against Jose Siderman in the Supreme Court of Tucuman. It requested the court's assistance in serving papers on Siderman, who was living in Los Angeles at the time. While the court complied with the request, the record is not clear as to the subsequent course of the lawsuit. In their papers in support of jurisdiction, the Sidermans suggest that the Argentine military authorities sought to obtain Jose's return to Argentina in order to further torture and perhaps even to kill him.

We conclude that the Sidermans have presented evidence sufficient to support a finding that Argentina has implicitly waived its sovereign immunity with respect to their claims for torture. The evidence indicates that Argentina deliberately involved United States courts in its efforts to persecute Jose Siderman. If Argentina has engaged our courts in the very course of activity for which the Sidermans seek redress, it has waived its immunity as to that redress.

Argentina will have an opportunity to rebut the Siderman's evidence on remand. We do not suggest that because Argentina may have implicitly waived its immunity in this suit, any foreign sovereign which takes actions against a private party in our courts necessarily opens the way to all manner of suit by that party. To support a finding of implied waiver, there must exist a direct connection between the sovereign's activities in our courts and the plaintiff's claims for relief. Only because the Sidermans have presented evidence indicating that Argentina's invocation of United States judicial authority was part and parcel of its efforts to torture and persecute Jose Siderman have they advanced a sufficient basis for invoking that same authority with respect to their causes of action for torture. It will be up to the district court on remand to determine whether the requisite direct connection exists. If it does, Argentina will be subject to the court's jurisdiction for the torture claims.

The district court erred in dismissing the Sidermans' torture claims.

4. *Noncommercial Torts*

Congress clearly intended that garden-variety torts such as automobile accidents in the United States would be encompassed within the exception of § 1605(a)(5). Two cases involving assassinations by foreign agents within the territory of the United States established that more politically charged events may also come within § 1605(a)(5). See Letelier v. Republic of Chile, 488 F.Supp. 665 (D.D.C.1980); Liu v. Republic of China, 892 F.2d 1419 (9th Cir.1989), *cert. dismissed*, 497 U.S. 1058 (1990).

There are two important limitations to § 1605(a)(5):

(1) § 1605(a)(5)(A) excludes claims based upon "the exercise or performance or the failure to exercise or perform a discretionary function, regardless of whether the discretion be abused"; and

(2) § 1605(a)(5)(B) excludes actions "arising out of malicious prosecution, abuse of process, libel, slander, misrepresentation, deceit, or interference with contract rights".

These limitations are analogous to similar bars on suits against the United States under the Federal Tort Claims Act, 28 U.S.C. § 2680. See H.R. Rep. No. 94–1487. Courts have struggled with the "exception to the exception" in § 1605(a)(5)(B), in particular with the question whether suits for libel, slander, misrepresentation, deceit, or interference with contractual rights that arise out of "commercial activity" of a foreign state are actionable under § 1605(a)(2), even though they are not actionable under § 1605(a)(5)(B). *Compare* Export Group v. Reef Industries, Inc., 54 F.3d 1466, 1473–77 (9th Cir.1995), *cert. denied sub nom.*, Figueroa v. Mexican Coffee Inst., 525 U.S. 1141, 119 S.Ct. 1033, (1999); United World Trade, Inc. v. Mangyshlakneft Oil Production Ass'n, 33 F.3d 1232, 1236 (10th Cir.1994), *cert. denied*, 513 U.S. 1112 (1995) (suits actionable under § 1605(a)(2) although barred by § 1605(a)(5)(B), since the provisions are intended to operate independently of each other) *with* Gregorian v. Izvestia, 871 F.2d 1515, 1522 (9th Cir.), *cert. denied*, 493 U.S. 891 (1989); Bryks v. Canadian Broadcasting Corp., 906 F.Supp. 204 (S.D.N.Y.1995) (suits cannot be brought under § 1605(a)(2) if they involve types of tortious activity, such as libel or slander, for which suit is barred under § 1605(a)(5)(B)).

The courts have adopted a consistently narrow approach toward § 1605(a) (5) where the tort occurs outside the United States, even though significant harmful effects are felt within the United States. *See, e.g., Amerada Hess, supra*; McKeel v. Islamic Republic of Iran, 722 F.2d 582 (9th Cir.1983), *cert. denied*, 469 U.S. 880 (1984); Upton v. Iran Nat'l Airlines, 450 F.Supp. 176 (S.D.N.Y. 1978). Is it significant that Congress failed to include a "direct effect" concept, analogous to that in the third clause of the commercial activity exception of § 1605(a)(2), in § 1605(a)(5)?

PERSINGER v. ISLAMIC REPUBLIC OF IRAN

729 F.2d 835 (D.C.Cir.), *cert. denied*, 469 U.S. 881 (1984).

BORK, J.

This is an action for damages against the Islamic Republic of Iran for injuries inflicted by the seizure and detention of American hostages. Appellants, plaintiffs below, are a former hostage and his parents. . . .

II. A

[I]f a foreign state's "act[s] or omission[s]" cause tortious injury within the United States, as defined in section c), the foreign state's immunity is abrogated, subject to the exceptions set out in section 1605(a)(5), and there can be both subject matter and personal jurisdiction in United States courts. 28 U.S.C. § 1330(a), (b).

That Congress has the power to exercise jurisdiction over certain activities at U.S. embassies abroad is not disputed. . . . The issue before this court, then, is whether Congress, in enacting the FSIA, intended to exercise its jurisdiction to give courts in this country competence to hear suits against foreign states for torts committed on United States embassy premises abroad. . . . We are persuaded by the language of the statute, its legislative history, and by the consequences of adopting a contrary position that section 1605(a)(5) does not remove Iran's immunity here.

Congress' principal concern was with torts committed in this country. The House Report makes clear that "Section 1605(a)(5) is *directed primarily at the problem of traffic accidents* but is cast in general terms as applying to all tort actions for money damages...."House Report at 20–21, U.S. Code Cong. & Admin. News, 1976 p. 6619 (emphasis added)....

[A]t the 1973 hearings to the predecessor bill ... one of the Act's principal draftsmen, Bruno Ristau, testified that:

> We would like, based on our experience as a litigant abroad to subsume to the jurisdiction of our domestic courts foreign governments and foreign entities who engage in certain activities *on our territory* to the same extent that the U.S. Government is already at the present time subject to the jurisdiction of foreign courts, when it engages in certain activities *on their soil.*
>
> [W]e would like to afford *our local citizens* and entities who deal with foreign governments *in the United States* effective redress through the instrumentality of our courts. If a dispute arises as a result of an activity which a government carries on *in this country*, the most appropriate place to resolve such a dispute would be through the courts....

Immunities of Foreign States: Hearings on H.R. 3493 Before the Subcomm. on Claims and Governmental Relations of the House Comm. on the Judiciary, 93d Cong., 1st Sess. 29 (1973) (testimony of Bruno Ristau) (emphasis added).

Another reason for finding that sovereign immunity exists here is the series of unhappy consequences that would follow if we read section 1603 (c) broadly to cover areas in which the United States had jurisdiction of any sort. These consequences would entail not only serious inconvenience and injustice but also embarrassment to our foreign relations. We offer these considerations not as policies we choose but as throwing light on congressional intent. If Congress had meant to remove sovereign immunity for governments acting on their own territory, with all of the potential for international discord and for foreign government retaliation that involves, it is hardly likely that Congress would have ignored those topics and discussed instead automobile accidents in this country.

II. B

The claims brought by Sergeant Persinger's parents present a variation on the issue just discussed. They seek to recover for mental and emotional distress suffered within the continental United States. Such injuries are said to be actionable because section 1605(a)(5) requires only that the injury be suffered in the United States but does not require that the tortious act or omission occur here.

Section 1605(a)(5) is ambiguous on this point. It states that immunity is removed in actions "for personal injury or death, or damage to or loss of property, occurring in the United States and caused by the tortious act or omission" of a foreign state. It is thus unclear whether both the tort and the injury must occur here or whether the tort may occur abroad and be actionable so long as the injury is suffered here....

We have shown that the proper construction of the statute deprives the district court of jurisdiction to entertain Sergeant Persinger's claim. Iran is immune from tort suits here for actions taken by it on its own territory. It would be anomalous to say that Congress intended to deny a remedy to him—a hostage imprisoned and physically abused for more than a year—and yet also intended to expose Iran to a suit by his parents for their emotional distress....

Moreover, a comparison of the noncommercial tort exception—section 1605(a)(5), under which this suit was brought—with the commercial activity exception, section 1605(a)(2), demonstrates that Congress intended the former to be narrower than the latter. The commercial activity exception expressly provides that a foreign sovereign's commercial activities "outside the territory of the United States" having a "direct effect" inside the United States may vitiate the sovereign's immunity. Any mention of "direct effect[s]" is noticeably lacking from the noncommercial tort exception....

For the reasons stated, we have concluded that the FSIA shields Iran from liability and this court has no jurisdiction over the claims of appellants Jacqueline and Lawrence Persinger, and their son, Sergeant Gregory Persinger. Our prior opinion is therefore vacated, and the judgment of the district court is affirmed.

EDWARDS, J., dissenting in part and concurring in part

I concur in the result in Part II.A, but I dissent from the rationale and holding of Part II.B.

[T]he statute plainly requires that *only the injury*, and not the tortious act or omission, occur in the United States. I see no reason to resort to the legislative history to clarify the plain language of the statute. Congress never enacted the language of the House Report that "the tortious act or omission must occur within the jurisdiction of the United States." H.R. Rep. No. 1487, 94th Cong., 2d Sess. 21, U.S. Code Cong. & Admin. News 1976, p. 6619 (1976).

My main point of dissent is that the clear terms of the statute allow for the parents' claim. I do not think that we are at liberty to decide otherwise on "policy grounds."

Notes and Questions

1. Is Bruno Ristau's quoted testimony as clear in excluding jurisdiction over extraterritorial torts as Judge Bork asserts? Was too much "emphasis added" by Judge Bork to the quoted excerpts from the legislative history? Is Judge Edwards correct in suggesting that the majority is swayed by its perception of adverse foreign policy consequences in rejecting a broad reading of § 1605(a)(5), at least for the parents' claims, rather than by the text of the statute? Should the court have extended jurisdiction to torts committed on the grounds of U.S. embassies and consulates? On U.S.

military bases? Libraries and cultural centers? To any tort whose ill effects are felt in the United States?

2. Jurisdiction under § 1605(a)(5) for torts committed on U.S. airliners flying outside the territorial limits of the United States was rejected in Smith v. Socialist People's Libyan Arab Jamahiriya, 101 F.3d 239 (2d Cir.1996), *cert. denied*, 520 U.S. 1204, *reh'g denied*, 520 U.S. 1259 (1997) (bombing of Pan Am flight 103 over Lockerbie, Scotland). In view of the fact that under international law U.S. flag aircraft and vessels are the equivalent of U.S. territory for jurisdictional purposes and in view of § 1603(c), do you agree with *Smith*? The same claims were found actionable under § 1605(a)(7), *infra* in Section 1 C 5.

Recall *Amerada Hess* and the Chief Justice's treatment of the § 1603 claim concerning vessels on the high seas. Since the dissent in *Amerada Hess* recognized that this and other issues concerning exceptions to immunity were not fully briefed and the dissent stressed that other Justices did not accept all points made in the Rehnquist opinion, does *Amerada Hess* foreclose inquiry into the § 1603 claim?

5. *Acts of State–Sponsored Terrorism*

The scope of the FSIA's exception for tortious conduct was widened selectively in 1996 when Congress enacted the Antiterrorism and Effective Death Penalty Act (AEDPA), Pub. L. 104–132, 110 Stat. 1214 (1996). AEDPA added § 1605(a)(7), which applies to causes of action arising before, on, or after 1996, and related provisions (see also § 1605(e)-(g)). Does AEDPA's amendment to the FSIA provide relief to Scott Nelson? To the Iranian hostages such as Sergeant Persinger? To the victims of the bombing of Pan Am flight 103? The lower courts have already permitted two actions to go forward under § 1605(a)(7) that had been dismissed when brought under § 1605(a)(5). *See, e.g.*, Cicippio v. Islamic Republic of Iran, 18 F.Supp.2d 62 (D.D.C.1998) (action by three hostages held in Lebanon with complicity of Iran); Rein v. Socialist People's Libyan Arab Jamahiriya, 995 F.Supp. 325 (E.D.N.Y.), *aff'd in part and appeal dismissed in part*, 162 F.3d 748 (2d Cir.1998), *cert. denied*, 527 U.S. 1003 (1999) (action brought by representatives and survivors of bombing of Pan Am Flight 103 over Lockerbie, Scotland). Several other sizable judgments have been obtained under § 1605(a)(7). *See, e.g.*, Hill v. Republic of Iraq, 328 F.3d 680 (D.C. Cir. 2003) (U.S. persons held hostage and as "human shields" by Saddam Hussein's regime in Kuwait in 1990); *id.*, 175 F.Supp.2d 36 (D.D.C. 2001); Kilburn v. Republic of Iran, 277 F.Supp.2d 24 (D.D.C. 2003); Smith v. Islamic Emirate of Afghanistan, *et al.*, 262 F.Supp.2d 217 (2003) (suite re: 9/11 attacks on the World Trade Center); Flatow v. Islamic Republic of Iran, 999 F.Supp. 1 (D.D.C.1998); Alejandre v. Republic of Cuba, 996 F.Supp. 1239 (S.D.Fla.1997). For other cases proceeding under § 1605(a)(7), *see, e.g.,* Dammarell v. Islamic Republic of Iran, ___ F.Supp.2d ___, 2005 WL 756090 (D.D.C. Mar. 29, 2005); Simpson v. Socialist People's Libyan Arab Jamahiriya, 362 F.Supp.2d 168 (D.D.C. 2005). The district court's attempt to permit the *Alejandre* plaintiffs to execute a portion of their judgment against debts owed by U.S. businesses to a Cuban telecommunications company pursuant to § 1610(a)(7) was reversed on grounds that the Cuban company was an entity separate from the Cuban Government and thus not liable for its debts. Alejandre v. Telefonica Larga Distancia de Puerto Rico, *et al.*, 183 F.3d 1277 (11th Cir.1999).

Libya raised some interesting due process questions in *Rein*, arguing that its designation as a "sponsor of state terrorism" prejudiced its ability to mount a defense to the claims and requesting that the court review the Secretary of State's designation under strict scrutiny. The District Court held that the designation merely related to immunity and not to the merits, and that foreign sovereign immunity is a "matter of grace and comity" and thus within the foreign affairs powers of the political branches. 995 F.Supp. at 330. On appeal, the Second Circuit rejected Libya's argument that § 1605(a)(7) unconstitutionally delegates power to the Secretary of State to determine the jurisdiction of the federal courts because of her discretion to designate state sponsors of terrorism. Are Libya's objections to § 1605(a)(7) well-taken? Have the District Court and Court of Appeals misunderstood the separation of powers aspects of the FSIA?

For a listing of other case trends and new legislation, see "U.S. Judgments Against Terrorist States," Contemporary Practice of the United States, 95 AM. J. INT'L L. 134–39 (2001). A Victims of Trafficking and Violence Protection Act of 2000, Pub. L. No. 106–386, 114 Stat. 1464, 1542–43, § 2002, amends the FSIA to provide claimants with certain final judgments against Cuba or Iran (but not other states such as Iraq, Libya, or Syria) two new options for redress of merely compensatory damages and interest. Under the new options, they can obtain funds from the U.S. Treasury Department, but must waive claims to punitive damages. See § 2002(a). Alternatively, they can pursue execution against the foreign states. However, the legislation also delegates powers to the President to prevent certain forms of attachment or execution against terrorist-state properties located within the U.S. See § 2002 (f), amending 28 U.S.C. § 1610(f).

Note that § 1605(a)(7) has two important limits: (1) the foreign state must be designated by the U.S. Government as an official sponsor of terrorism, and (2) the plaintiff must have been a national of the United States at the time of the tortious acts. Did Congress respond inappropriately to narrow political interests in enacting § 1605(a)(7)? Is § 1605(a)(7) the codification of a customary international norm? Or, does the 1996 amendment represent a genuine effort to balance interests in justice for victims of terrorism against the need for sensitivity to comity and foreign policy concerns? At the time of enactment, states designated as sponsors of terrorism were Cuba, Iraq, Iran, Libya, North Korea, Sudan, and Syria. *See, e.g.*, David MacKusick, *Human Rights vs. Sovereign Rights: The State Sponsored Terrorism Exception to the Foreign Sovereign Immunities Act*, 10 EMORY INT'L L.J. 741, 743 n.21 (1996).

6. *A Jus Cogens or "Iniquity" Exception*

One intriguing issue that has emerged is the claim that foreign states should not enjoy sovereign immunity for any act that constitutes a violation of, at least, a *jus cogens* norm of international law. The concept of *jus cogens* is explained in Chapter 1 and also by Judge Fletcher in *Siderman de Blake* and Judges Ginsburg and Wald in *Princz, infra*. The House of Lords ruled that no state immunity could attach to a former head of state for certain acts of torture, because "the commission of a crime which is an international crime against humanity and *jus cogens* . . . cannot be a state function." Regina v. Bartle and the Commissioner of Police for the Metropolis and Others, *Ex Parte* Pinochet, Judgment of 24 March 1999 (opinion of Lord Browne–Wilkinson). The *Pinochet* judgment is further discussed in Sections 2 B and 4 F, *infra*. Gross violations of human rights were not among the concerns expressly addressed by Congress when enacting the FSIA in 1976, and the 1996 AEDPA amendments are highly selective (see Section 1 C 5). Nevertheless, does the "international agreement" exception in §§ 1330(a) and 1604 or the "implied waiver" exception of § 1605(a)(1) provide a statutory basis for a *jus cogens* exception? and more? *See, e.g.*, JORDAN J. PAUST, INTERNATIONAL LAW AS LAW OF THE UNITED STATES 236–38, 321 (2 ed. 2003). Did the Supreme Court err when stating in *Amerada Hess* that the FSIA's codified exceptions are the exclusive basis for rejecting claims to foreign sovereign immunity? Have the lower courts exaggerated the significance of *Amerada Hess*? At least the Court recognized the existence of the international agreements exception.

If the restrictive principle is a doctrine of public international law, does it necessarily incorporate international legal doctrines limiting or delineating the scope of sovereignty? If so, is the concept of *jus cogens* a recognized limit on sovereignty? The article by Adam C. Belsky, Mark Merva, Naomi Roht–Arriaza, *Implied Waiver Under the FSIA: A Proposed Exception to Immunity for Violations of Peremptory Norms of International Law*, 77 CAL. L. REV. 365 (1989), is generally regarded as the leading expositor of the implied waiver theory. *See also Draft Brief Concerning Claims to Foreign Sovereign Immunity and Human Rights*, 8 HOUS. J. INT'L L. 49, 65–67 (1985).

In Prefecture of Voiotia v. Federal Republic of Germany, extract addressed in 92 AM. J. INT'L L. 765 (1999), a 1997 decision of a Greek court allowed litigation against Germany with respect to atrocities committed by German occupation forces during World War II to proceed when *jus cogens* norms were allegedly violated. The Greek court ruled, among other points:

(1) When a state is in breach of *jus cogens* rules, it cannot *bona fide* expect that it will be granted immunity privileges. Therefore, it is assumed that it tacitly waives the privilege (constructive waiver through the operation of law).

(2) The acts of a state that violate *jus cogens* norms do not have the character of sovereign acts. In such cases it is considered that the accused state did not act within the ambit of its capacity as a sovereign.

(3) Acts contrary to *jus cogens* norms are null and void, and cannot constitute a source of legal rights or privileges, such as the claim to

immunity, according to the general principle of law *ex injuria jus non oritur*.

(4) The recognition of immunity by a national court for an act that is contrary to *jus cogens* would be tantamount to collaboration by the national court in an act that is strongly condemned by the international community.

See 92 AM. J. INT'L L. at 766. In 2000, the Hellenic Supreme Court upheld the decision of nonimmunity, noting that the murders in question were crimes against humanity and an abuse of sovereign power that were not protectable acts under customary international law as well as acts "in breach of rules of peremptory international law (Article 46 of the [1907 Hague Convention No. IV, Annex] Regulations, and they were not acts *jure imperii*." See 95 AM. J. INT'L L. 198 (2001).

SIDERMAN DE BLAKE v. REPUBLIC OF ARGENTINA

965 F.2d 699 (9th Cir.1992), *cert. denied*, 507 U.S. 1017 (1993).

[The facts are summarized at pp. 722–723]

II. A. *JUS COGENS*

The Sidermans contend that Argentina does not enjoy sovereign immunity with respect to its violation of the *jus cogens* norm of international law condemning official torture. While we agree with the Sidermans that official acts of torture of the sort they allege Argentina to have committed constitute a *jus cogens* violation, we conclude that *Amerada Hess* forecloses their attempt to posit a basis for jurisdiction not expressly countenanced by the FSIA.

As defined in the Vienna Convention on the Law of Treaties, a *jus cogens* norm, also known as a "peremptory norm" of international law, "is a norm accepted and recognized by the international community of states as a whole as a norm from which no derogation is permitted and which can be modified only by a subsequent norm of general international law having the same character." Vienna Convention on the Law of Treaties, art. 53, May 23, 1969, 1155 U.N.T.S. 332, 8 I.L.M. 679 [hereinafter "Vienna Convention"]; see also RESTATEMENT [(THIRD) FOREIGN RELATIONS LAW OF THE UNITED STATES § 102 Reporters' Note 6. *Jus cogens* is related to customary international law (the direct descendant of the law of nations), which the Restatement defines as the "general and consistent practice of states followed by them from a sense of legal obligation." RESTATEMENT § 102(2). Courts seeking to determine whether a norm of customary international law has attained the status of *jus cogens* ... must ... determine whether the international community recognizes the norm as one "from which no derogation is permitted." Committee of U.S. Citizens Living in Nicaragua v. Reagan, 859 F.2d 929, 940 (D.C.Cir.1988) [hereinafter "*CUSCLIN*"] (*quoting* Vienna Convention, art. 53). In *CUSCLIN*, the only reported federal decision to give extended treatment to *jus cogens*, the court described *jus cogens* as an elite subset of the norms recognized as customary international law. *Id.*

While *jus cogens* and customary international law are related, they differ in one important respect. Customary international law, like international law defined by treaties and other international agreements, rests on the consent of states. A state that persistently objects to a norm of customary international law that other states accept is not bound by that norm, see RESTATEMENT § 102, cmt. d, just as a state that is not party to an international agreement is not bound by the terms of that agreement. International agreements and customary international law create norms known as *jus dispositivum*, the category of international law that "consists of norms derived from the consent of states" and that is founded "on the self-interest of the participating states."

Whereas customary international law derives solely from the consent of states, the fundamental and universal norms constituting *jus cogens* transcend such consent, as exemplified by the theories underlying the judgments of the Nuremberg tribunals following World War II.... The legitimacy of the Nuremberg prosecutions rested not on the consent of the Axis Powers and individual defendants, but on the nature of the acts they committed: acts that the laws of all civilized nations define as criminal.... In the words of the International Court of Justice, these norms, which include "principles and rules concerning the basic rights of the human person," are the concern of all states; "they are obligations *erga omnes*." The Barcelona Traction, Light & Power Co. (Belgium v. Spain), 1970 I.C.J. 3, 32.

[W]hile not all customary international law carries with it the force of a *jus cogens* norm, the prohibition against official torture has attained that status. In *CUSCLIN*, 859 F.2d at 941–42, the D.C. Circuit announced that torture is one of a handful of acts that constitute violations of *jus cogens*.... Supporting this case law is the Restatement, which recognizes the prohibition against official torture as one of only a few *jus cogens* norms. RESTATEMENT § 702 cmt. n (also identifying *jus cogens* norms prohibiting genocide, slavery, murder or causing disappearance of individuals, prolonged arbitrary detention, and systematic racial discrimination). Finally, there is widespread agreement among scholars that the prohibition against official torture has achieved the status of a *jus cogens* norm....

Given this extraordinary consensus, we conclude that the right to be free from official torture is fundamental and universal, a right deserving of the highest status under international law, a norm of *jus cogens*. The crack of the whip, the clamp of the thumb screw, the crush of the iron maiden, and, in these more efficient modern times, the shock of the electric cattle prod are forms of torture that the international order will not tolerate. To subject a person to such horrors is to commit one of the most egregious violations of the personal security and dignity of a human being. That states engage in official torture cannot be doubted, but all states believe it is wrong, all that engage in torture deny it, and no state claims a sovereign right to torture its own citizens.... Under international law, any state that engages in official torture violates *jus cogens*.

The question in the present case is what flows from the Sidermans' allegation that Argentina tortured Jose Siderman and thereby violated a *jus cogens* norm. The Sidermans contend that when a foreign state's act violates *jus cogens*, the state is not entitled to sovereign immunity with respect to that act. This argument begins from the principle that *jus cogens* norms "enjoy the highest status within international law," *CUS-CLIN*, 859 F.2d at 940, and thus "prevail over and invalidate ... other rules of international law in conflict with them," RESTATEMENT § 102 cmt. k. The Sidermans argue that since sovereign immunity itself is a principle of international law, it is trumped by *jus cogens*. In short, they argue that when a state violates *jus cogens*, the cloak of immunity provided by international law falls away, leaving the state amenable to suit.

As a matter of international law, the Sidermans' argument carries much force. We previously have recognized that "[s]overeign immunity is a principle of international law." International Ass'n of Machinists & Aerospace Workers (IAM) v. Organization of Petroleum Exporting Countries (OPEC), 649 F.2d 1354, 1359 (9th Cir.1981), *cert. denied*, 454 U.S. 1163 ... (1982). Chief Justice Marshall identified the foundation of the doctrine of sovereign immunity as the "perfect equality and absolute independence of sovereigns," a state of affairs making it improper for one state to subject another to its jurisdiction. *The Schooner Exchange*, 11 U.S. (7 Cranch) at 137. As described by one scholar of international law, the doctrine of foreign sovereign immunity "is rooted in two bases of international law, the notion of sovereignty and the notion of the equality of sovereigns." Riesenfeld, *Sovereign Immunity in Perspective*, 19 VAND. J. TRANSNAT'L L. 1 (1986). When Jack Tate, writing on behalf of the State Department, issued his famous letter in 1952, the United States was recognizing the trend in international law toward adoption of the restrictive principle of foreign sovereign immunity, under which states receive immunity for their sovereign acts (*jure imperii*) but not their private acts (*jure gestionis*). With the enactment of the FSIA, Congress explicitly adopted the restrictive principle, identifying its origin in international law. 28 U.S.C. § 1602 (findings and declaration of purpose); see also H.R. Rep. No. 1487, 94th Cong., 2d Sess. 7, *reprinted in* 1976 U.S. Code Cong. & Admin. News 6604, 6605 (FSIA "would codify the so-called 'restrictive' principle of sovereign immunity, as presently recognized in international law"); *id.* at 8, 1976 U.S. Code Cong. & Admin. News at 6606 ("Sovereign immunity is a doctrine of international law under which domestic courts, in appropriate cases, relinquish jurisdiction over a foreign state."); *id.* at 9, 1976 U.S. Code Cong. & Admin. News at 6608 ("[S]overeign immunity is a question of international law to be determined by the courts.").

The Sidermans posit that because sovereign immunity derives from international law, *jus cogens* supersedes it. "*Jus cogens* norms represent the fundamental duties incident to international life. They are an essential component of the modern law definition of sovereignty." [Belsky, *et al.* at 392.] International law does not recognize an act that violates *jus cogens* as a sovereign act. A state's violation of the *jus cogens* norm prohibiting official torture therefore would not be entitled to the immunity afforded by international law.

Unfortunately, we do not write on a clean slate. We deal not only with customary international law, but with an affirmative Act of Congress, the FSIA. We must interpret the FSIA through the prism of *Amerada Hess*. Nothing in the text or legislative history of the FSIA explicitly addresses the effect violations of *jus cogens* might have on the FSIA's cloak of immunity. Argentina contends that the Supreme Court's statement in *Amerada Hess* that the FSIA grants immunity "in those cases involving alleged violations of international law that do not come within one of the FSIA's exceptions," 488 U.S. at 436, precludes the Sidermans' reliance on *jus cogens* in this case. Clearly, the FSIA does not specifically provide for an exception to sovereign immunity based on *jus cogens*. In *Amerada Hess*, the Court had no occasion to consider acts of torture or other violations of the peremptory norms of international law, and such violations admittedly differ in kind from transgressions of *jus dispositivum*, the norms derived from international agreements or customary international law with which the *Amerada Hess* Court dealt. However, the Court was so emphatic in its pronouncement "that immunity is granted in those cases involving alleged violations of international law that do not come within one of the FSIA's exceptions," *Amerada Hess*, 488 U.S. at 436, and so specific in its formulation and method of approach, id. at 439 ("Having determined that the FSIA provides the sole basis for obtaining jurisdiction over a foreign state in federal court, we turn to whether any of the exceptions enumerated in the Act apply here"), that we conclude that if violations of *jus cogens* committed outside the United States are to be exceptions to immunity, Congress must make them so. The fact that there has been a violation of *jus cogens* does not confer jurisdiction under the FSIA.

PRINCZ v. FEDERAL REPUBLIC OF GERMANY

26 F.3d 1166 (D.C.Cir.1994), *cert. denied*, 513 U.S. 1121 (1995).

GINSBURG, J.

Hugo Princz, a Holocaust survivor, brought suit in the district court against the Federal Republic of Germany to recover money damages for the injuries he suffered and the slave labor he performed while a prisoner in Nazi concentration camps....

We now hold, for the reasons set out below, that the district court does not have subject matter jurisdiction of Mr. Princz's claims. Assuming that the Foreign Sovereign Immunities Act of 1976, 28 U.S.C. §§ 1330, 1602–1611, applies retroactively to events occurring in 1942–1945, no exception to the general grant of sovereign immunity in that statute applies in this case....

When the United States declared war against Nazi Germany in 1942, Hugo Princz, an American and a Jew, was living with his parents, his sister, and his two brothers in what is now Slovakia. The Slovak police arrested the entire Princz family as enemy aliens and turned them over to the Nazi SS. Rather than allow the Princz family to return to the United States as part of the civilian prisoner exchange then being conducted by the Red Cross, because they were Jews the SS sent them to concentration camps. Mr. Princz's parents and his sister were murdered at Treblinka, while Mr. Princz and his two younger brothers were sent to Auschwitz and then to Birkenau, where they were forced to work at an I.G. Farben chemical plant. After being injured at work, Mr. Princz's brothers were starved to death in the "hospital" at Birkenau. Mr. Princz was later marched to Dachau, where he was forced to work in a Messerschmidt factory. When United States soldiers liberated Mr. Princz at the end of the war, he was in a freight car full of concentration camp prisoners en route to another camp for extermination. The other liberated prisoners were sent to displaced persons camps, but because Mr. Princz is an American he was sent to an American military hospital for treatment.

After the war the government of the new Federal Republic of Germany established a program of reparations for Holocaust survivors. The German government denied Mr. Princz's 1955 request for reparations, however, because Mr. Princz was neither a German citizen at the time of his imprisonment nor a "refugee," within the meaning of the Geneva Convention [relating to the Status of Refugees], after the war. It appears that Mr. Princz would have qualified for reparations when the German government changed the criteria for eligibility in 1965, but he did not apply again before the statute of limitations ran in 1969.

[Various efforts to obtain compensation through diplomatic channels failed.]

In 1992, Mr. Princz finally resorted to federal district court, filing this action against Germany for false imprisonment, assault and battery, and negligent and intentional infliction of emotional distress, as well as recovery *quantum meruit* for the value of his labor in the I.G. Farben and Messerschmidt plants....

The district court held that it had jurisdiction of the case on the ground that the FSIA "has no role to play where the claims alleged involve undisputed acts of barbarism committed by a one-time outlaw nation which demonstrated callous disrespect for the humanity of an American citizen, simply because he was Jewish." 813 F. Supp. 22, 26 (D.D.C.1992). As we shall see below, that is not the law.

We do not have to decide whether the FSIA applies to pre–1952 events ... in order to resolve this case. For as will be seen in Part II. B below, even if the FSIA does apply here, none of the statutory exceptions to foreign sovereign immunity applies....

II. B. The Foreign Sovereign Immunities Act of 1976

... Mr. Princz invokes both the international agreement provision and two of the listed exceptions, *viz.* the exception for instances "in which the foreign state has waived its immunity either explicitly or by implication" [§ 1605(a)(1)], and the exception for cases in which the claim arises from the foreign state's "commercial activity" [§ 1605(a)(2).]

1. [The commercial activity exception was found inapplicable. The Court reasoned that, even if leasing slaves to commercial entities is a commercial activity, Germany's acts in this case did not have a direct effect in the United States.]

2. The waiver exception of § 1605(a)(1)

Not surprisingly, there is no sovereign immunity in a case "in which the foreign state has waived its immunity either explicitly or by implication," 28 U.S.C. § 1605(a)(1).... Here the *amici* argue that the Third Reich impliedly waived Germany's sovereign immunity under the FSIA by violating *jus cogens* norms of the law of nations. In their own words: "A foreign state that violates these fundamental requirements of a civilized world thereby waives its right to be treated as a sovereign." With respect, we do not think that the waiver exception to the FSIA can be read so broadly.

... [T]he *amici's jus cogens* theory of implied waiver is incompatible with the intentionality requirement implicit in § 1605(a)(1). *See* Foremost–McKesson, Inc. v. Islamic Republic of Iran, 905 F.2d 438, 444 (D.C.Cir.1990), *quoting* Frolova v. Union of Soviet Socialist Republics, 761 F.2d 370, 377 (7th Cir.1985).... That requirement is also reflected in the examples of implied waiver set forth in the legislative history of § 1605(a)(1), all of which arise either from the foreign state's agreement (to arbitration or to a particular choice of law) or from its filing a responsive pleading without raising the defense of sovereign immunity. *See* H.R. Rep. 1487 ... (1976).

Wald, J., dissenting

Due to Germany's unequivocal refusal to enter into any settlement with Princz, this appeal is his last resort. Contrary to my colleagues, who would deny Princz the opportunity even to present his claims in federal court, I would affirm the district court's order denying Germany's motion to dismiss on grounds of foreign sovereign immunity. I believe that Germany's treatment of Princz violated *jus cogens* norms of the law of nations, and that by engaging in such conduct, Germany implicitly waived its immunity from suit within the meaning of § 1605(a)(1) of the FSIA. Accordingly, in my view, the federal courts have jurisdiction to entertain Princz's claims.

Germany waived its sovereign immunity by violating the *jus cogens* norms of international law condemning enslavement and genocide....

One need not pause long before concluding that the international community's denunciation of both genocide and slavery are accepted norms of customary international law and, in particular, are *jus cogens* norms.... What could be more fundamental than an individual's right to be free from the infliction of cruel and sadistic terrors designed with the sole purpose of destroying the individual's psyche and person because of the national, ethnic, racial, or religious community to which he belongs? What could be more elementary than a prohibition against eviscerating a person's human dignity by thrusting him into the shackles of slavery? Germany clearly violated *jus cogens* norms by forcibly extracting labor from Princz at the I.G. Farben and Messerschmidt factories and by subjecting him to unconscionable physical and mental abuse at the Auschwitz and Dachau concentration camps.

... The Nuremberg Principles crystallized the pre-existing international condemnation of persecution and enslavement of civilians on the basis of race or religious belief, with the widescale atrocities committed by Hitler's Germany driving home the concept that certain fundamental rights may never be transgressed under international law....

The principle of nonderogable peremptory norms evolved due to the perception that conformance to certain fundamental principles by all states is absolutely essential to the survival of the international community.... Were the conscience of the international community to permit derogation from these norms, ordered society as we know it would cease. Thus, to preserve the international order, states must abdicate any "right" to ignore or violate such norms. As the German Supreme Constitutional Court has explained, *jus cogens* norms are those that "are indispensable to the existence of the law of nations as an international legal order, and the observance of which can be required by *all* members of the international community." Comment, *Jus Dispositivum and Jus Cogens in International Law: In the Light of a Recent Decision of the German Supreme Constitutional Court*, 60 AM. J. INT'L L. 511, 513 (1966) (emphasis added). Unlike general rules of customary international law (*jus dispositivum*), *jus cogens* norms are binding upon all nations; whereas states are not constricted by customary international law norms to which they continuously object, *jus cogens* norms do not depend on the consent of any individual state for their validity.... Therefore, *jus cogens* norms have significant implications for the law of sovereign immunity, which hinges on the notion that a state's consent to suit is a necessary prerequisite to another state's exercise of jurisdiction.

... While Justice Marshall's seminal opinion [in *The Schooner Exchange*] is most often cited for the proposition that foreign sovereigns enjoy virtually absolute immunity from suit in United States courts, *see, e.g., Verlinden*, 461 U.S. at 486, the decision in fact focused on the *exceptions* to exclusive territorial jurisdiction, which stem from a state's explicit or implicit consent to be intruded upon. *See The Schooner Exchange*, 11 U.S. (7 Cranch) at 136–42.... Such consent derives from the interest in interstate relations, "which humanity dictates and its wants require." *Id.* at 136.... Even in the early nineteenth century, therefore, states recognized that, to facilitate international relations, they must on occasion allow infringements on their exclusive territorial jurisdiction.

Because the Nuremberg Charter's definition of "crimes against humanity" includes what are now termed *jus cogens* norms, a state is never entitled to immunity for any act that contravenes a *jus cogens* norm, regardless of where or against whom that act was perpetrated. The rise of *jus cogens* norms limits state sovereignty "in the sense that the 'general will' of the international community of states, and other actors, will take precedence over the individual wills of states to order their relations." Mary Ellen Turpel & Phillipe Sands, *Peremptory International Law and Sovereignty: Some Questions*, 3 CONN. J. INT'L L. 364, 365 (1988). *Jus cogens* norms are by definition nonderogable, and thus when a state thumbs its nose at such a norm, in effect overriding the collective will of the entire international community, the state cannot be performing a sovereign act entitled to immunity....

It is a well-established canon of statutory construction that, because "[i]nternational law is part of our law," *Paquete Habana*, 175 U.S. at 700, we must, wherever possible, interpret United States law consistently with international law.... Indeed, the legislative history of the FSIA indicates that Congress intended the Act to create "a statutory regime which incorporates standards recognized under international law." H.R.Rep. No. 1487, 94th Cong., 2d Sess. at 14 (1976). The only way to reconcile the FSIA's presumption of foreign sovereign immunity with international law is to interpret § 1605(a)(1) of the Act as encompassing the principle that a foreign state implicitly waives its right to sovereign immunity in United States courts by violating *jus cogens* norms.

Construing § 1605(a)(1) to include as an implied waiver a foreign state's breach of a *jus cogens* norm is not at odds with the language and legislative history of the FSIA, which supply scant guidance as to the provision's meaning....

Moreover, I disagree with my colleagues that the "*jus cogens* theory of implied waiver is incompatible with the intentionality requirement implicit in § 1605(a)(1)." ... The implicit intentionality requirement stems from several decisions that have limited the implied waiver exception to cases in which the foreign sovereign "contemplated" the involvement of United States courts. *See, e.g.*, Seetransport Wiking Trader v. Navimpex Centrala, 989 F.2d 572, 578–79 (2d Cir.1993).... In inflicting theretofore unimaginable atrocities on innocent civilians during the Holocaust, Germany could not have helped but realize that it might one day be held accountable for its heinous actions by any other state, including the United States....

An exercise of jurisdiction over a foreign state for claims of genocide and enslavement does not awaken traditional comity concerns, particularly where, as here, both of the political branches of government have voiced strong support for the plaintiff.

Notes and Questions

1. The Second Circuit joined the Ninth and the D.C. Circuits in rejecting a *jus cogens* exception to the FSIA in Smith v. Socialist People's Libyan Arab Jamahiriya, 101 F.3d 239 (2d Cir.1996), *cert. denied*, 520 U.S. 1204 (1997). Survivors of three victims of the 1988 bombing of Pan Am flight 103 over Lockerbie, Scotland, had sued the Government of Libya and several of its agents and instrumentalities, alleging that they had instigated the bombing. Acknowledging that "[t]he contention that a foreign state should be deemed to have forfeited its sovereign immunity whenever it engages in conduct that violates fundamental humanitarian standards is an appealing one," Chief Judge Newman found no evidence in the text of § 1605(a)(1) or in the FSIA's legislative history to support a general *jus cogens* exception. *Id.* at 242–44. Although finding the concept of implied waiver to be ambiguous, the Second Circuit concluded that "Congress's concept of an implied waiver, as used in the FSIA, cannot be extended so far as to include a state's existence in the community of nations...." *Id.* at 244. Chief Judge Newman noted that implied waiver logically might be deduced in three different situations: (1) subjectively, where an actor intends to waive immunity but fails to say so explicitly; (2) objectively, where an actor behaves in a manner that an observer would interpret as indicating an intent to waive immunity; or (3) in the manner of a forfeiture, where the actor behaves in a manner that the law deems to strip him of his immunity. *Id.* at 243.

The narrowness of the 1996 AEDPA amendments was found to suggest "that Congress is not necessarily adverse to permitting some violations of *jus cogens* to be redressed through channels other than suits against foreign states in United States courts." *Id. See also* Hirsh v. State of Israel, 962 F.Supp. 377 (S.D.N.Y.1997), *aff'd by* 133 F.3d 907 (2d Cir.1997), *cert. denied sub nom.*, Berkowitz v. State of Israel, 523 U.S. 1062 (1998), *reh'g denied*, 523 U.S. 1134 (1998) (suit by Holocaust victims seeking reparations under 1952 Luxembourg Agreement dismissed under FSIA). Should plaintiffs use the international agreements exception as an alternative? What hurdles does the Rehnquist opinion in *Amerada Hess* seek to impose?

Hwang Geum Joo v. Japan, 172 F.Supp.2d 52 (D.D.C. 2001) found that no FSIA exception existed regarding suits by comfort women against Japan and that no case is known to have found that a violation of a *jus cogens* norm constitutes an implied waiver.

2. Princz and ten other U.S. concentration camp survivors reached a settlement with Germany in 1995 for $2.1 million. In 1999, the U.S. Department of State negotiated an $18 million settlement with Germany for 235 other U.S. concentration camp survivors.

3. If a posited *jus cogens* exception has a firm logical basis in public international law, why has Congress failed to codify it? Is it partly codified in §§ 1330(a) and 1604 of the FSIA? Given the notoriety of *Siderman de Blake*, *Princz*, and *Smith*, can Congress be unaware of the concern regarding *jus cogens*? How does this square with the general rule that acts of Congress are to be construed consistently with international law?

4. In a case involving torture inflicted against a dual U.K./Kuwait citizen in Kuwait, the British Court of Appeal found that the tort exception in section 5 of the U.K. State Immunity Act 1978 did not apply and rejected

plaintiff's argument that the Act should be read to include an implicit *jus cogens* exception. Al–Adsani v. Government of Kuwait, [1996] Times L.R. (29 March 1996). Section 5 of the U.K. Act provides: "A State is not immune as respects proceedings in respect of—(a) death or personal injury; or (b) damage or loss of tangible property, caused by an act or omission in the United Kingdom." However, Richardson, J., of the New Zealand Court of Appeal, applying a common law version of the restrictive principle, held that concepts of "iniquity" and public policy should inform decisions whether to extend sovereign immunity to illegal conduct substantially affecting the forum state. Controller and Auditor–General v. Davison, [1996] 2 NZLR 278, 304–307, 36 I.L.M. 721, 736–37 (1997).

7. *Expropriation*

Read 28 U.S.C. § 1605(a)(3) in the Documents Supplement.

According to one court, the plaintiff must not have been a national of the expropriating state at the time of the expropriation. *See, e.g.*, Chuidian v. Philippine Nat'l Bank, 912 F.2d 1095, 1105 (9th Cir.1990) ("[e]xpropriation by a sovereign state of the property of its own nationals does not implicate settled principles of international law"). *See also* de Sanchez v. Banco Central de Nicaragua, 770 F.2d 1385, 1395 (5th Cir.1985). Relatively few cases have considered the international takings exception. *See, e.g., Siderman de Blake, supra*, 965 F.2d at 711–13 (finding that Susana Siderman de Blake, a U.S. citizen, had made sufficient allegations to survive a motion to dismiss her claim under the international takings exception).

Altmann v. Republic of Austria, 317 F.3d 954 (9th Cir. 2002), amended, 327 F.3d 1246 (9th Cir. 2003), involved retroactive application of the FSIA to cover Nazi era "complicity in and perpetuation of the discriminatory expropriation" of artwork in violation of the 1907 Hague Convention on the Laws and Customs of War in a case where the U.S. Department of State would likely have denied immunity and Austria could not legitimately have expected that immunity would attach. *Altmann* also quoted West v. Multibanco Comermex, S.A., 807 F.2d 820, 826 (9th Cir. 1987) ("violations of international law are not 'sovereign' acts"), *cert. denied*, 507 U.S. 1017 (1993). The Supreme Court in *Altmann* affirmed the fact that the FSIA applies retroactively. 541 U.S. 677, 692–95, 701 (2004). However, the Court would not decide whether the district court was correct that § 1605(a)(3) provided nonimmunity. Thus, the Court ducked the issue involving obvious war crime activity with respect to confiscation, pillage, or thievery during war and the broader issue of illegal confiscation of property in time of peace or war. *See also* Ware v. Hylton, 3 U.S. (3 Dall.) 199, 229 (1796); Banco Nacional de Cuba v. Farr, Whitlock & Co., 383 F.2d 166, 170–72 (2d Cir. 1967); Republic of Iraq v. First Nat'l City Bank, 353 F.2d 47, 50–52 (2d Cir. 1965); O'Neill v. Central Leather Co., 94 A. 789 (N.J.Err. & App. 1915); Hawkins v. Nelson, 40 Ala. 553, 556 (1867).

8. *Arbitration*

28 U.S.C. § 1605(a)(6) provides for the enforcement of arbitral awards against foreign states where the arbitration takes place or is intended to take place in the United States, the agreement or award is governed by a treaty of the United States calling for the enforcement of arbitral awards, the underlying claim could have been brought in a U.S. court, or where the foreign state has explicitly or implicitly waived its immunity. This exception was added by Congress in 1988 (Pub. L. No. 100–669) out of a concern that the waiver provision of § 1605(a)(1) might not be construed as widely as Congress preferred with respect to arbitral agreements or awards. *See* Libyan American Oil Co. v. Socialist People's Libyan Arab Jamahirya, 482 F.Supp. 1175 (D.D.C.1980), *vacated*, 684 F.2d 1032 (D.C.Cir.1981).

E. *Immunity from Attachment and Execution of Judgment*

28 U.S.C. § 1609 provides that the property of foreign states shall be immune from attachment and execution except as provided in §§ 1610 and 1611. § 1609, however, contains its own international agreements exception concerning attachments and execution. Specific provisions for service of process upon foreign states and their entities were provided in § 1608 in order to replace the prior practice of commencing litigation by attachment of a foreign state's property. Prior to the enactment of the FSIA, the property of foreign states was absolutely immune from execution, even after the Tate Letter announced U.S. adherence to the restrictive principle of foreign sovereign immunity from judgment.

There remains a significant discongruity between immunity from judgment and immunity from execution under the FSIA. After the victims of an assassination in Washington. D.C. by agents of Chile secured a default judgment against Chile, they were unable to execute it against property of Chile's state-owned airline, because their cause of action was not sufficiently linked to conduct of the airline. De Letelier v. Republic of Chile, 748 F.2d 790 (2d Cir.1984), *cert. denied*, 471 U.S. 1125 (1985); *see also* Alejandre v. Telefonica Larga Distancia de Puerto Rico, *et al.*, 183 F.3d 1277 (11th Cir.1999). Some argue that *Letelier* suggests that, in general, the property against which the judgment is executed must be connected with the plaintiff's cause of action. Note, however, that under § 1610(a)((6) and (7), any commercial property of a foreign state located in the United States may be subject to execution for judgments entered pursuant to §§ 1605(a)(6) and (7). Pursuant to § 1610(b)(2), the U.S.-located property of a foreign state agency and instrumentality, engaged in commercial activity in the United States, is subject to execution of judgments entered under §§ 1605(a)(2), (3), (5) or (7), "regardless of whether the property is or was involved in the act upon which the claim is based."

Reread Section 1610(b)(2). Does the judgment have to be based on a claim against the agency as such (as *Letelier* suggests) or merely a judgment that "relates to a claim for which the agency ... is not immune" if it had been sued?

FIRST NATIONAL CITY BANK v. BANCO PARA EL COMERCIO EXTERIOR DE CUBA

462 U.S. 611 (1983).

O'CONNOR, J.

In 1960 the Government of the Republic of Cuba established respondent Banco Para el Comercio Exterior de Cuba (Bancec) to serve as "[a]n official autonomous credit institution for foreign trade ... with full juridical capacity ... of its own...." Law No. 793, Art. 1 (1960).... In September 1960 Bancec sought to collect on a letter of credit issued by petitioner First National City Bank (now Citibank) in its favor in support of a contract for delivery of Cuban sugar to a buyer in the United States. Within days after Citibank received the request for collection, all of its assets in Cuba were seized and nationalized by the Cuban Government. When Bancec brought suit on the letter of credit in United States District Court, Citibank counterclaimed, asserting a right to set off the value of its seized Cuban assets. The question before us is whether Citibank may obtain such a setoff, notwithstanding the fact that Bancec was established as a separate juridical entity. Applying principles of equity common to international law and federal common law, we conclude that Citibank may apply a setoff.

I

Bancec's stated purpose was "to contribute to, and collaborate with, the international trade policy of the Government and ... Cuba's central bank (Banco Nacional).... Bancec was empowered to act as the Cuban Government's exclusive agent in foreign trade. The Government supplied all of its capital and owned all of its stock. The General Treasury of the Republic received all of Bancec's profits, after deduction of amounts for capital reserves....

In contracts signed on August 12, 1960, Bancec agreed to purchase a quantity of sugar from El Institutio Nacional de Reforma Agraria (INRA), an instrumentality of the Cuban Government which owned and operated Cuba's nationalized sugar industry, and to sell it to the Cuban Canadian Sugar Company. The latter sale agreement was supported by an irrevocable letter of credit in favor of Bancec issued by Citibank on August 18, 1960, which Bancec assigned to Banco Nacional for collection.

Meanwhile, in July 1960 the Cuban Government enacted Law No. 851, which provided for the nationalization of the Cuban properties of United States citizens. By Resolution No. 2 of September 17, 1960, the Government ordered that all of the Cuban property of three United States banks, including Citibank, be nationalized through forced expropriation....

On or about September 15, 1960, before the banks were nationalized, Bancec's draft was presented to Citibank for payment by Banco Nacional. The amount sought was $193,280.30 for sugar delivered at Pascagoula, Miss. On September 20, 1960, after its branches were nationalized, Citibank credited the requested amount to Banco Nacional's account and applied the balance in Banco Nacional's account as a setoff against the value of its Cuban branches.

On February 1, 1961, Bancec brought this diversity action to recover on the letter of credit in the United States District Court for the Southern District of New York....

[Bancec was dissolved in 1961 and its capital was split between Banco Nacional and Empresa, which was empowered to conduct all commercial export transactions formerly conducted by Bancec. Later Empresa was dissolved and Bancec's rights relating to foreign commerce in sugar were assigned to Cubazucar, a state trading company.]

Apparently the case lay dormant until May 1975, when respondent filed a motion seeking an order substituting Cubazucar as plaintiff. [The District Court granted judgment in favor of Citibank, rejecting Bancec's contention that its separate juridical status shielded it from liability for the acts of the Cuban Government. Without determining the exact value of Citibank's assets seized by Cuba, the court held that the value of the confiscated branches substantially exceeded the set-off and entered judgment dismissing the complaint.]

The United States Court of Appeals for the Second Circuit reversed. 658 F.2d 913 (1981). While expressing agreement with the District Court's "descriptions of Bancec's functions and its status as a wholly-owned instrumentality of the Cuban government," the court concluded that "Bancec was not an alter ego of the Cuban government for the purpose of [Citibank's] counterclaims." *Id.*, at 917. It stated that, as a general matter, courts would respect the independent identity of a governmental instrumentality created as "a separate and distinct juridical entity under the laws of the state that owns it"—except "when the subject matter of the counterclaim assertable against the state is state conduct in which the instrumentality had a key role." *Id.*, at 918....

II. A

As an initial matter, Bancec contends that the Foreign Sovereign Immunities Act of 1976, 28 U.S.C. §§ 1602–1611 (FSIA), immunizes an instrumentality owned by a foreign government from suit on a counterclaim based on actions taken by that government. Bancec correctly concedes that, under 28 U.S.C. § 1607(c), an instrumentality of a foreign state bringing suit in a United States court is not entitled to immunity "with respect to any counterclaim ... to the extent that the counterclaim does not seek relief exceeding in amount or differing in kind from that sought by the [instrumentality]." It contends, however, that as a substantive matter the FSIA prohibits holding a foreign instrumentality owned and controlled by a foreign government responsible for actions taken by that government.

We disagree. The language and history of the FSIA clearly establish that the Act was not intended to affect the substantive law determining the liability of a foreign state or instrumentality, or the attribution of liability among instrumentalities of a foreign state. Section 1606 of the FSIA provides in relevant part that "[a]s to any claim for relief with respect to which a foreign state is not entitled to immunity . . . , the foreign state shall be liable in the same manner and to the same extent as a private individual under like circumstances. . . ."

Thus, we conclude that the FSIA does not control the determination of whether Citibank may set off the value of its seized Cuban assets against Bancec's claim. Nevertheless, our resolution of that question is guided by the policies articulated by Congress in enacting the FSIA. . . .

II. B

We must next decide which body of law determines the effect to be given to Bancec's separate juridical status. Bancec contends that internationally recognized conflict-of-law principles require the application of the law of the state that establishes a government instrumentality—here Cuba—to determine whether the instrumentality may be held liable for actions taken by the sovereign.

We cannot agree. As a general matter, the law of the state of incorporation normally determines issues relating to the *internal* affairs of a corporation. . . . Different conflicts principles apply, however, where the rights of third parties *external* to the corporation are at issue. . . . To give conclusive effect to the law of the chartering state in determining whether the separate juridical status of its instrumentality should be respected would permit the state to violate with impunity the rights of third parties under international law while effectively insulating itself from liability in foreign courts. . . .

Bancec contends in the alternative that international law must determine the resolution of the question presented. Citibank, on the other hand, suggests that federal common law governs. The expropriation claim against which Bancec seeks to interpose its separate juridical status arises under international law, which, as we have frequently reiterated, "is part of our law. . . ." *The Paquete Habana*, 175 U.S. 677, 700 (1900). . . . [T]he principles governing this case are common to both international law and federal common law, which in these circumstances is necessarily informed both by international law principles and by articulated congressional policies.

III. A

Increasingly during this century, governments throughout the world have established separately constituted legal entities to perform a variety of tasks. The organization and control of these entities vary considerably, but many possess a number of common features. A typical government instrumentality, if one can be said to exist, is created by an enabling statute that prescribes the powers and duties of the instrumentality, and specifies that it is to be managed by a board selected by the government in a manner consistent with the enabling law. The instrumentality is typically established as a separate juridical entity, with the powers to hold and sell property and to sue and be sued. Except for appropriations to provide capital or to cover losses, the instrumentality is primarily responsible for its own finances. The instrumentality is run as a distinct economic enterprise; often it is not subject to the same budgetary and personnel requirements with which government agencies must comply.

These distinctive features permit government instrumentalities to manage their operations on an enterprise basis while granting them a greater degree of flexibility and independence from close political control than is generally enjoyed by government agencies. These same features frequently prompt governments in developing countries to establish separate juridical entities as the vehicles through which to obtain the financial resources needed to make large-scale national investments.

Provisions in the corporate charter stating that the instrumentality may sue and be sued have been construed to waive the sovereign immunity accorded to many governmental activities, thereby enabling third parties to deal with the instrumentality knowing that they may seek relief in the courts. Similarly, the instrumentality's assets and liabilities must be treated as distinct from those of its sovereign in order to facilitate credit transactions with third parties....

Freely ignoring the separate status of government instrumentalities would result in substantial uncertainty over whether an instrumentality's assets would be diverted to satisfy a claim against the sovereign, and might thereby cause third parties to hesitate before extending credit to a government instrumentality without the government's guarantee. As a result, the efforts of sovereign nations to structure their governmental activities in a manner deemed necessary to promote economic development and efficient administration would surely be frustrated. Due respect for the actions taken by foreign sovereigns and for principles of comity between nations ... leads us to conclude ... that government instrumentalities established as juridical entities distinct and independent from their sovereign should normally be treated as such.

We find support for this conclusion in the legislative history of the FSIA. During its deliberations, Congress clearly expressed its intention that duly created instrumentalities of a foreign state are to be accorded a presumption of independent status. In its discussion of FSIA § 1610(b), the provision dealing with the circumstances under which a judgment creditor may execute upon the assets of an instrumentality of a foreign government, the House Report states:

> Section 1610(b) will not permit execution against the property of one agency or instrumentality to satisfy a judgment against another, unrelated agency or instrumentality. There are compelling reasons

> for this. If U.S. law did not respect the separate juridical identities of different agencies or instrumentalities, it might encourage foreign jurisdictions to disregard the juridical divisions between different U.S. corporations or between a U.S. corporation and its independent subsidiary. However, a court might find that property held by one agency is really the property of another.

H.R. Rep. No. 94–1487, pp. 29–30 (1976) (citation omitted).

III. C

... Giving effect to Bancec's separate juridical status in these circumstances, even though it has long been dissolved, would permit the real beneficiary of such an action, the Government of the Republic of Cuba, to obtain relief in our courts that it could not obtain in its own right without waiving its sovereign immunity and answering for the seizure of Citibank's assets—a seizure previously held by the Court of Appeals to have violated international law. We decline to adhere blindly to the corporate form where doing so would cause such an injustice....

IV

Our decision today announces no mechanical formula for determining the circumstances under which the normally separate juridical status of a government instrumentality is to be disregarded. Instead, it is the product of the application of internationally recognized equitable principles to avoid the injustice that would result from permitting a foreign state to reap the benefits of our courts while avoiding the obligations of international law.

... The judgment of the Court of Appeals is reversed, and the case is remanded for further proceedings consistent with this opinion.

STEVENS, J. (with whom BRENNAN and BLACKMUN, J.J., join), concurring in part and dissenting in part.

Today the Court correctly rejects the contention that American courts should readily "pierce the corporate veils" of separate juridical entities established by foreign governments to perform governmental functions. Accordingly, I join Parts I, II, III–A, and III–B of the Court's opinion. But I respectfully dissent from Part III–C, in which the Court endeavors to apply the general principles it has enunciated. Instead I would vacate the judgment and remand the case to the Court of Appeals for further proceedings.

Note

1. The *Bancec* case is noteworthy for its stress upon the significance of the separate legal personality of a foreign state and its entities, its determination that the FSIA did not provide a clear answer to the issue presented, and its attention to international law to inform the meaning of federal common law. *Bancec*'s approach to the "alter ego" question has been applied by lower courts analyzing FSIA immunity. *See, e.g.*, Arriba Ltd. v. Petroleos Mexicanos, 962 F.2d 528, 533–34 (5th Cir.), *cert. denied,* 506 U.S. 956 (1992).

SECTION 2. HEAD OF STATE IMMUNITY

A. *Current Head of State*

Revisit the Introductory Problem on pp. 674–675.

Some U.S. courts have developed a common law or comity-based concept of head of state immunity. Is the common law notion of head of state immunity anachronistic, reflecting a personalized concept of sovereignty similar to that expressed by Chief Justice Marshall in *The Schooner Exchange*, at pp. 676–679? Should the approach of Justice Story in *The Santissima Trinidad* be continued—that if the sovereign comes personally within our limits, he may become liable to judicial process regarding violations of the law of nations, especially in view of international law and nonimmunity at the international level (*e.g.*, as recognized by the I.M.T. at Nuremberg; and Principles of the Nuremberg Charter and Judgment, and the "Rome" Statute of the ICC)? Or does the need to avoid international conflict mandate personal immunity for foreign chief executives, even for conduct otherwise regarded as nonimmune under the restrictive principle of sovereign immunity? Does the FSIA leave any scope for the operation of a common law doctrine of head of state immunity? Should courts rewrite legislation under the guise of interpreting words contained, for example, in § 1603(b) of the FSIA? Should the Executive Branch, rather than an independent judiciary implementing a statutory text, determine the availability of head of state immunity? Is head of state immunity more properly seen as a species of diplomatic immunity? *See generally*, Jerrold L. Mallory, *Resolving the Confusion over Head of State Immunity: the Defined Rights of Kings*, 86 COLUM. L. REV. 169 (1986); Shobha Varughese George, *Head-of-State Immunity in the United States: Still Confused After All These Years*, 64 FORDHAM L. REV. 1051 (1995) (proposing amendment to FSIA); Jordan J. Paust, *It's No Defense:* Nullum Crimen, *International Crime and the Gingerbread Man*, 60 ALBANY L. REV. 657, 660–61 n.11 (1997); Arthur Watts, *The Legal Position in International Law of Heads of State, Heads of Government and Foreign Ministers*, 247 RECUEIL DES COURS 13 (1994–III).

LAFONTANT v. ARISTIDE

844 F.Supp. 128 (E.D.N.Y.1994).

WEINSTEIN, J.

[Editors' note: Plaintiff, a resident of Queens, New York, sought money damages for the killing of her husband, Dr. Roger Lafontant, by Haitian soldiers, allegedly acting on the orders of the President of Haiti, Jean–Bertrand Aristide. Lafontant was arrested in July 1991 on suspicion of complicity in a coup plot against Aristide. He was killed, while in detention, in September 1991 during a later successful coup that forced Aristide's exile to the United States.]

The question posed by this case is whether the recognized head of a state who has violated the civil rights of a person by having him killed can avoid civil prosecution in this country by virtue of his status. The answer is yes.

Defendant submitted a suggestion of immunity under 22 U.S.C. § 254d claiming that President Aristide is immune from suit because of his status as the head-of-state of the Republic of Haiti. He asks the court to quash service of process and dismiss the action....

The United States government has consistently recognized Jean–Bertrand Aristide as the current lawful head-of-state of the Republic of Haiti.... Exec. Order No. 12775, 56 Fed. Reg. 50641, § 3(a) (*Prohibiting Certain Transactions with Respect to Haiti*, Oct. 4, 1991) ("The term 'de facto regime in Haiti' means those who seized power illegally from the democratically elected government of President Jean–Bertrand Aristide on September 30, 1991"); ... Notice of Sept. 30, 1993, 58 Fed. Reg. 51563 (*Continuation of Haitian Emergency*) (President Clinton refers to "President Aristide, the democratically elected head of the Government of Haiti")....

In reply to defendant's suggestion of immunity, plaintiff submitted what purports to be a letter signed by President Aristide on September 30, 1991, relinquishing his title as President of the Republic of Haiti. She also relies on the fact that on October 6, 1991, the parliament of Haiti applied Article 149 of the Constitution of Haiti which governs succession in the event of a presidential vacancy. On October 8, 1991 a judge of the Supreme Court of Haiti, Joseph Nerette, was sworn in as temporary President of Haiti.... On October 16 the new government was approved by the parliament....

The Justice Department submitted a suggestion of immunity letter. It states in pertinent part:

> The United States has an interest and concern in this action against President Aristide insofar as the action involves the question of immunity from the Court's jurisdiction of the head-of-state of a friendly foreign state. The United States' interest arises from a determination by the Executive Branch of the Government of the United States, in the implementation of its foreign policy and in the conduct of its international relations, that permitting this action to proceed against President Aristide would be incompatible with the United States' foreign policy interests.

II. Law

A. *Common Law Head–of–State Immunity*

A head-of-state recognized by the United States government is absolutely immune from personal jurisdiction in United States courts unless that immunity has been waived by statute or by the foreign government recognized by the United States. A visiting head-of-state is generally immune from the jurisdiction of a foreign state's courts. *See, e.g.*, Saltany v. Reagan, 702 F. Supp. 319 (D.D.C. 1988), *order aff'd in part, reversed in part (on other grounds)*, 886 F.2d 438 (D.C.Cir.1989), *cert. denied*, 495 U.S. 932 (1990) (granting head-of-state immunity to Prime Minister of England in suit alleging violations of international law); Kilroy v. Windsor, Civ. No. C–78–291 (N.D. Ohio 1978), (Prince Charles, The Prince of Wales, granted immunity from suit alleging human rights violations in Northern Ireland), *excerpted in* 1978 DIG. U.S. PRAC. INT'L L. 641–43; Psinakis v. Marcos, Civ. No. C–75–1725 (N.D. Cal.1975), *excerpted in* 1975 DIG. U.S. PRAC. INT'L L. 344–45 (immunity granted to then-President Marcos following suggestion of immunity by the Executive Branch); Kendall v. Saudi Arabia, 65 Adm. 885 (S.D.N.Y. 1965), *reported in* 1977 DIG. U.S. PAC. INT'L L. 1017, 1053–34 [sic].

Head-of-state immunity, like foreign sovereign immunity, is premised on the concept that a state and its ruler are one for purposes of immunity. As early as 1812 the Supreme Court embraced the notion, grounded in customary international law, that a head-of-state is absolutely "exempted" from the jurisdiction of the receiving state's courts. Schooner Exchange v. M'Faddon, 11 U.S. (7 Cranch) 116 ... (1812).

This absolute form of immunity is based on the notion that all states are equal and that no one state may exercise judicial authority over another. The foreign head-of-state, as representative of his nation, enjoys extraterritorial status when traveling abroad because he would not intend "to subject himself to a jurisdiction incompatible with his dignity, and the dignity of his nation." *Id.* at 137....

Head-of-state immunity is also supported by the doctrine of comity—that is to say, each state protects the immunity concept so that its own head-of-state will be protected when he or she is abroad....

Like the related doctrine of diplomatic immunity, head-of-state immunity is required to safeguard mutual respect among nations.... Heads of state must be able to freely perform their duties at home and abroad without the threat of civil and criminal liability in a foreign legal system....

The immunity extends only to the person the United States government acknowledges as the official head-of-state. Recognition of a government and its officers is the exclusive function of the Executive Branch. Whether the recognized head-of-state has *de facto* control of the government is irrelevant; the courts must defer to the Executive determination.... Presidential decisions to recognize a government are binding on the courts, and the courts must give them legal effect....

Since determination of who qualifies as a head-of-state is made by the Executive Branch, it is not a factual issue to be determined by the courts. No judicial hearing or factual determination aside from receipt of the State Department's communication is warranted.

The government of a foreign state which is recognized by the Executive Branch may waive its head-of-state immunity. *In re* Grand Jury Proceedings, 817 F.2d 1108 (4th Cir.1987), *cert. denied*, 484 U.S. 890 ... (1987), Ferdinand and Imelda Marcos, the former leaders of the Philippines, were found civilly liable for failing to comply with federal grand jury subpoenas. The court held that the doctrine of head-of-state immunity is not an individual right but an "attribute of state sovereignty," a privilege that can be revoked by the foreign state.... The court honored President Aquino's waiver [of Marcos's immunity].

Similarly, the court held that the foreign government waived immunity in Paul v. Avril, 812 F. Supp. 207 (S.D.Fla.1993).... The court held that the Haitian government then recognized by the United States could waive head-of-state immunity of the former head of military government, and that waiver extends to whatever "residual" head-of-state immunity defendant possessed. *Id.*

Waiver of head-of-state immunity is analogous to waiver provisions in the Vienna Convention of Diplomatic Relations, April 18, 1961, 23 U.S.T. 3227, T.I.A.S. No. 7502, 500 U.N.T.S. 95, Articles 31(a), 31(2), and 29, which provide that the immunity of diplomatic agents may be waived by the sending state. Such waiver must be explicit....

B. Application of Common Law Immunity to Facts

... The United States government does not recognize the *de facto* military rulers of Haiti. It has repeatedly condemned their regime. The United Nations has also severely criticized their illegal seizure of power.... Because the United States does not recognize the *de facto* government, that government does not have the power to waive President Aristide's immunity.

Granting President Aristide head-of-state immunity will further the goals of comity. The State Department, in its suggestion of immunity letter, states that "permitting this action to proceed against President Aristide would be incompatible with the United States' foreign policy interests."

The United States foreign policy goal of encouraging democratic elections is strengthened by recognizing President Aristide as the democratically elected head of Haiti. Numerous Executive Orders supporting President Aristide establish that the Republic of Haiti is a "friendly foreign state."

Even, however, if the goal of the United States were less lofty, it would make no difference. In this matter the courts are bound by executive decision.

C. Lack of Statutory Modification of Immunity Law

No statute has modified the long standing rule of international and common law. The two statutes which need to be considered are the Foreign Sovereign Immunities Act and the Torture Victim Protection Act.

1. Foreign Sovereign Immunities Act

... There is some support for the application of immunity under the FSIA to individuals as "instrumentalities" of foreign states.... No case has, however, construed "agency or instrumentality" to include a head-of-state.

The legislative history of the FSIA does not directly address the issue of head-of-state immunity. . . .

The view that the FSIA is inapplicable to a head-of-state comports with both the history of the FSIA and the underlying policy of comity. The FSIA was not designed to apply to diplomatic or other consular officials. Instead, it was crafted primarily to allow state-owned companies, which had proliferated in the communist world and in the developing countries, to be sued in United States courts in connection with their commercial activities. The FSIA took these cases out of the political arena of the State Department, while leaving traditional head-of-state and diplomatic immunities untouched. Scholars have argued that the willingness of the State Department, which co-authored the FSIA, to continue issuing suggestions of immunity for heads-of-state, and the willingness of courts to defer to such suggestions evidences the FSIA's nonapplicability to heads of state. . . . Both comity and the Executive's plenary role in fashioning foreign policy suggest that the State Department needs to retain decisive control of grants of head-of-state immunity, by preserving the pre-FSIA "absolute" theory of immunity. The language and legislative history of the FSIA, as well as case law, support the proposition that the pre–1976 suggestion of immunity procedure survives the FSIA with respect to heads-of-state.

2. Torture Victim Protection Act

Plaintiff argues that President Aristide should be denied immunity because head-of-state immunity extends only to official acts, and the alleged extrajudicial killing is not an official act under color of law. The scope of head-of-state immunity in this regard has not been conclusively established. . . .

The legislative history of the [Torture Victim Protection Act] lends ample support for the proposition that the Act was not intended to trump diplomatic and head-of-state immunities. *See e.g.*, Sen. Comm. on the Judiciary, The Torture Victim Protection Act of 1991, S. Rep. No. 249, 102nd Cong., 1st Sess. 7–8 (1991) ("The TVPA is not intended to override traditional diplomatic immunities which prevent the exercise of jurisdiction by U.S. courts over foreign diplomats. . . . Nor should visiting heads of state be subject to suits under the TVPA."); House Comm. on the Judiciary, The Torture Victims Protection Act of 1991, H.R. Rep. No. 367, 102nd Cong., 1st Sess., Pt. 1 (1991), 1992 U.S. Code Cong. and Admin. News 84, 88 ("nothing in the TVPA overrides the doctrines of diplomatic and head-of-state immunity. . . . These doctrines would generally provide a defense to suits against foreign heads of state and other diplomats visiting the United States on official business."). . . .

We need not consider whether an act of President Aristide in ordering the killing would be official or private because he now enjoys head-of-state immunity. The courts are barred from exercising personal jurisdiction over him.

III. Conclusion

The State Department has submitted a letter of immunity. It speaks for the President of the United States. Its suggestion of immunity is controlling with respect to President Aristide. The court must defer to the Executive on this matter.

This court has subject matter jurisdiction, but it cannot exercise *in personam* jurisdiction over defendant because of his head-of-state immunity.

Notes and Questions

1. Was the district court's read of *The Schooner Exchange* correct? Recall also The Santissima Trinidad, 20 U.S. (7 Wheat.) 283, 352–53 (1822) (Story, J., noting that even if a foreign sovereign "comes personally within our limits, although he generally enjoys a personal immunity, he may be liable to judicial process" for violations of international law); 9 Op. Att'y Gen. 356, 362–63 (1859). *In re* Doe v. United States, 860 F.2d 40 (2d Cir.1988) declared: "there is respectable authority for denying head-of-state immunity to a former head-of-state for private or criminal acts in violation of American law," *citing* The Schooner Exchange, 11 U.S. (7 Cranch) at 135, 144; *In re* Grand Jury Proceedings, Doe No. 700, 817 F.2d 1108, 1111 (4th Cir.), *cert. denied*, 484 U.S. 890 (1987); Republic of the Philippines v. Marcos, 806 F.2d 344, 360 (2d Cir. 1986), and adding that head of state immunity is animated by "comity". Nonetheless, should "American law" form the basis for exceptions? foreign law? international law? Why do you suspect that *Lafontant v. Aristide* failed to address these cases?

2. The control by the Executive Branch over the availability of head of state immunity is emphasized in *Lafontant*. Is there a constitutional basis for this deference in Article II, Section 3 ("[The President] shall receive Ambassadors and other public Ministers.")? Is there a constitutional basis for independent judicial power or is this a matter for the courts to decide? In United States v. Noriega, 117 F.3d 1206, 1212 (11th Cir.), *reh'g and reh'g en banc denied*, 128 F.3d 734 (1997), *and cert. denied*, 523 U.S. 1060 (1998), the Eleventh Circuit noted that "[b]ecause the FSIA addresses neither head-of-state immunity, nor foreign sovereign immunity in the criminal context, head-of-state immunity could attach in cases, such as this one, only pursuant to" direction from the Executive, and also noted the previous practice of the Fifth Circuit: "where the Executive Branch either expressly grants or denies a request to suggest immunity, courts must follow that direction, but ... courts should make an independent determination regarding immunity when the Executive Branch neglects to convey clearly its position on a particular immunity request." The position of the Executive Branch in *Noriega* was unambiguously negative on head of state immunity. The Eleventh Circuit noted that, if it were to make an independent determination, it would be influenced by the fact that Noriega had never been the constitutional leader of Panama, that Panama did not seek head of state immunity for him, and

that his actions relevant to the prosecution involved the private pursuit of personal enrichment.

With respect to lawsuits against a sitting Pope, a case in Texas decided that suit against Pope John Paul II should be dismissed in view of a suggestion of immunity by the Executive. Guardian F. v. Archdiocese of San Antonio, Case No. 93–CI–11345 (Tex. Dist. Ct. 1994). A case in California against the Vatican Bank, *et al.* proceeded with respect to claims concerning conversion, unjust enrichment, and restitution of property during the Nazi era in the face of "political question" challenges. See Alperin v. Vatican Bank, 410 F.3d 532 (9th Cir. 2005).

3. In Tachiona v. Mugabe, 386 F.3d 205, 210 (2d Cir. 2004), the Second Circuit noted that the district court below had "concluded that the executive branch's suggestion of immunity, not the FSIA, governed immunity of heads of state, and that the suggestion mandated dismissal" of claims against Zimbabwe's dictator, President Robert Mugabe, and Foreign Minister, Stan Mudenge. *Id.* at 210, citing 169 F. Supp.2d 259, 297 (S.D.N.Y. 2001); see also Wei Ye v. Jiang Zemin, 383 F.3d 620 (7th Cir. 2004). The court agreed to immunity, adding: "We have some doubt as to whether the FSIA was meant to supplant the 'common law' of head-of-state immunity, which generally entailed deference to the executive branch's suggestion of immunity.... For one thing, the FSIA applies only to foreign states, which are defined [in § 1603(a)].... Moreover, the only references to head of state or other foreign officials in the FSIA's legislative history suggest that their immunity is not governed by the Act.... In light of our conclusion that the claims against Mugabe and Mudenge were properly dismissed on the basis of diplomatic immunity, however, we have no occasion to decide whether Mugabe and Mudenge were protected from suit by head-of-state immunity–whether under the terms of the FSIA or because of the Government's suggestion of immunity." *Id.* at 220–21. The district court had allowed the suit to proceed against Zimbabwe's ruling party even though service had been made on the ruler, Mugabe. *See* 234 F. Supp.2d 401 (S.D.N.Y. 2002).

4. Is there a constitutional basis for nonimmunity when issues of international law are at stake, in Article III, Section 2, and Article VI, clause 2 [extracts are in Chapter 2]? See also Article III, Section 2, clause 1 regarding lawsuits against ambassadors, public ministers, and foreign states. Should immunity be available merely regarding violations of ordinary domestic laws?

5. The Second Circuit in Kadic v. Karadzic, 70 F.3d 232 (2d Cir.1995), *cert. denied*, 518 U.S. 1005 (1996), denied head of state immunity to Radovan Karadzic, self-proclaimed President of the Republika Srpska, in two suits brought under the ATCA and TVPA. "[T]he mere possibility that Karadzic might at some future date be recognized by the United States as the head of state of a friendly nation and might thereby acquire head-of-state immunity does not transform the appellants' claims into a nonjusticiable request for an advisory opinion, as the District Court intimated. Even if such future recognition, determined by the Executive Branch ... would create head-of-state immunity ... , it would be entirely inappropriate for a court to create the functional equivalent of such an immunity based on speculation about what the Executive Branch *might* do in the future." *Id.* at 248 (emphasis in

original). *See also* Jordan J. Paust, *Suing Karadzic*, 10 LEIDEN J. INT'L L. 89 (1997). Just as potential future heads of state find it difficult to invoke a personal immunity, former heads of state are at risk that a successor regime may waive their immunity. *In re* Grand Jury Proceedings, Doe No. 700, 817 F.2d 1108 (4th Cir.1987), *cert. denied*, 484 U.S. 890 (1987) (former President Ferdinand Marcos of the Philippines). *See also* Jimenez v. Aristeguieta, 311 F.2d 547, 557–58 (5th Cir.1962), *cert. denied sub nom.*, Jimenez v. Hixon, 373 U.S. 914, *reh'g denied*, 374 U.S. 858 (1963) (re: extradition and an "act of state" claim of a former dictator); *infra* Section 2 B.

6. In his discussion of the Torture Victim Protection Act, Judge Weinstein rejected plaintiff's argument that head of state immunity could only attach to official acts and that extrajudicial killings could not be official acts. Was this appropriate? *See generally* cases in Chapter 2, Section 2 D 2; Xuncax v. Gramajo, 886 F.Supp. 162, 176 (D.Mass.1995); Letelier v. Republic of Chile, 488 F.Supp. 665, 673 (D.D.C.1980). Related issues have arisen with respect to a *jus cogens* exception to the FSIA (*see* Section 1 C 6), the scope of authority of individuals who claim status as foreign states under the § 1603(b) of the FSIA (*see* Section 1 D 1) and the "public act" concept of the act of state doctrine as applied to gross violations of human rights (*see* Section 4 F, *infra*).

The Senate Report on the TVPA also stated: "The purpose of this legislation is to provide a federal cause of action against any individual who.... This legislation will carry out the intent of the Convention Against Torture and Other Cruel, Inhuman or Degrading Treatment or Punishment.... The Convention obligates state parties to adopt measures to ensure that torturers within their territories are held legally accountable for their acts. This legislation will do precisely that–by making sure that torturers and death squads will no longer have a safe haven in the United States.... A state that practices torture and summary executions is not one that adheres to the rule of law. Consequently, the ... [TVPA] is designed to respond to this situation by providing a cause of action in U.S. courts...." How does this part of the legislative history square with that quoted by Judge Weinstein?

7. If other courts adopt head of state immunity, should there also be exceptions to head of state immunity? What sort of exceptions? *See also* questions 8–10.

8. Since head of state immunity is a judicially-created doctrine of common law or comity, can it be trumped by congressional legislation? *See, e.g.*, Paust, *Suing Karadzic*, *supra* at 97–98 & n.52. Should it be trumped by treaty law? Head of state immunity potentially raises a tension among branches of the federal government. The Executive has exclusive authority to recognize (as such) foreign governments; courts create, modify, and apply judicially created common law; and Congress can legislate on the subject, and arguably did in enacting the FSIA (without explicit reference to head of state immunity) and TVPA (with express coverage of persons acting under foreign state authority).

9. Should treaties trump mere common law doctrine? Consider the nonimmunity of public actors required in Article 2(3)(a) of the International Covenant on Civil and Political Rights and Articles 1 and 14 of the Conven-

tion Against Torture and Other Cruel, Inhuman or Degrading Treatment or Punishment. See also American Convention on Human Rights, art. 25 (1); European Convention for the Protection of Human Rights and Fundamental Freedoms, art. 13; Inter–American Convention on the Forced Disappearance of Persons, arts. II, IX.

10. In 1998, the "Rome" Statute of the International Criminal Court (ICC) (U.N. Doc. A/CONF.183/9) created a permanent international criminal court with jurisdiction over genocide, certain crimes against humanity, and certain war crimes. See also Documents Supplement. Article 27 of this statute, entitled "Irrelevance of official capacity," declares that no head of state immunity shall apply for violations of its statute:

> 1. This Statute shall Apply equally to all persons without any distinction based on official capacity. In particular, official capacity as a Head of State or Government, a member of a Government or parliament, an elected representative or a government official shall in no case exempt a person from criminal responsibility under this Statute, nor shall it, in and of itself, constitute a ground for reduction of sentence.
>
> 2. Immunities or special procedural rules which may attach to the official capacity of a person, whether under national or international law, shall not bar the Court from exercising its jurisdiction over such a person.

Article 75 of the treaty also provides for reparations, restitution, compensation, and rehabilitation for victims. See Documents Supplement.

11. Prior to and since the Charters of the I.M.T.s at Nuremberg (1945) and the Far East (1946), which reflect similar international norms of nonimmunity for heads of state and other officials, there has been recognition of nonimmunity under international law with respect to heads of state, diplomats, or other government officials who engage in violations of customary international criminal law. *See, e.g.*, PAUST, BASSIOUNI, *ET AL.*, INTERNATIONAL CRIMINAL LAW 27–33, 38, 53, 63, 73, 79, 132, 134, 136, 169–71, 621–22, 625–26, 660, 677–78, 702–06, 717, 741–48, 821 (2 ed. 2000); Chapter 8. The I.M.T. at Nuremberg declared: "The principle of international law, which under certain circumstances protects the representatives of a state, cannot be applied to acts which are condemned as criminal by international law. The authors of these acts cannot shelter themselves behind their official position," and one "cannot claim immunity while acting in pursuance of the authority of the State if the State in authorizing action moves outside its competence under international law." Opinion and Judgment, I.M.T. (1946).

In The Prosecutor v. Tadic, ICTY–94–1–AR72 (2 Oct. 1995), the Appeals Chamber of the International Criminal Tribunal for Former Yugoslavia recognized: "It would be a travesty of law and a betrayal of the universal need for justice, should the concept of State sovereignty be allowed to be raised successfully against human rights. Borders should not be considered as a shield against the reach of the law and as a protection for those who trample underfoot the most elementary rights of humanity." *Id.* para. 58. In The Prosecutor v. Milosevic, ICTY–99–37–PT (Nov. 8, 2001), the Trial Chamber ruled that Milosevic had no immunity from alleged international crimes as a head of state and that Article 7 of the Statute of the ICTY, rejecting head of state immunity, "reflects a rule of customary international law." *Id.* at paras. 26–34. *See also* The Prosecutor v. Furundzija, ICTY–95–17/1, para. 140 (10 Dec. 1998).

Professor Paust notes that international crimes are nonimmune and is of the view that acts in violation of international law are beyond lawful authority or discretion and are recognizably nonimmune, especially other violations of human rights and other *obligatio erga omnes*. Professor Fitzpatrick had noted that violations of norms *jus cogens* are nonimmune.

B. Former Head of State

Just as there is an important difference between the immunity of the state and immunity of individuals, there is an equally critical difference between the immunity accorded to a sitting head of state and that given to a former head of state. For purposes of immunity from legal process, United States courts distinguish between heads of state visiting the country on official business and former heads of state. Current heads of state are "generally given the same personal inviolability and immunities as are accorded to members of special missions, especially those of an accredited diplomat," Restatement of the Foreign Relations Law of the United States, § 464, RN 14 (3 ed. 1987). However, a former head of state "would have no immunity from [U.S. court's] jurisdiction to adjudicate" claims arising out of their acts while in office. *Id. See, e.g., In re* Doe v. United States of America, 860 F.2d 40, 45 (2d Cir.1988) ("there is respectable authority for denying head-of-state immunity to a former head-of-state for private or criminal acts in violation of American law.").

This distinction is made because one of the principal reasons for granting immunity to heads of state does not apply to former heads of state. One rationale for head of state immunity is that "[t]he inviolability of the head of state's person coheres with the basic rules of diplomatic intercourse, which allow government officials to perform their functions unencumbered by the threat or possibility of arrest or detention." Note, *Resolving the Confusion over Head of State Immunity: The Defined Rights of Kings*, 86 Colum. L. Rev. 169, 195 (1986). Because the former head of state no longer has official government duties to perform, the defendant would not automatically be entitled to immunity.[2]

The House of Lords observed under English law in the *Pinochet* extradition case (excerpts *infra*) that a sitting head of state has absolute immunity *ratione personae*, while a former head of state may only enjoy

2. The claim of head of state immunity is presented pursuant to 22 U.S.C. Section 254d. The U.S. State Department may file a "suggestion of immunity" letter pursuant to 28 U.S.C. Section 517. *See* Lafontant v. Aristide, 844 F.Supp. 128 (E.D.N.Y.1994) (dismissing lawsuit based on U.S. recognition of defendant as the current President of Haiti). Some U.S. courts may grant immunity to a former head of state for violations of foreign law, even though it is not required by international law, if suggested by the Executive Branch on foreign policy grounds. *See* Restatement, *supra*. For reasons developed below, however, it is doubtful that the Executive would suggest immunity for a former head of state in a case involving alleged violations of internationally-protected human rights and others seriously question whether judicial deference to foreign policy is proper when international law forms the basis of a plaintiff's claim.

a limited immunity *ratione materiae* for acts performed within the scope of his or her official functions.

Former heads of state do not enjoy immunity for a broad range of acts that violate international, U.S., or foreign law. *In re* Doe v. United States of America, 860 F.2d 40, 45 (2d Cir.1988) (quoted above), *citing*, among other cases, *The Schooner Exchange*, 11 U.S. (7 Cranch) at 135, 144. *See also* The Santissima Trinidad, 20 U.S. (7 Wheat.) 283, 350–55 (1822) (international law); United States v. Noriega, 746 F.Supp. 1506, 1519, n. 11 (S.D.Fla.1990) (observing in dictum that "there is ample doubt whether head of state immunity extends to private or criminal acts in violation of U.S. law."); *id.* 117 F.3d at 1212 (11th Cir. 1997) ("the FSIA addresses neither head-of-state immunity, nor foreign sovereign immunity in the criminal context...."); Jimenez v. Aristeguieta, 311 F.2d 547, 557–58 (5th Cir.1962) (foreign law). In particular, former heads of state have generally not been granted immunity from prosecution for gross human rights violations, including systematic torture, disappearance, summary execution or prolonged arbitrary detention. For example, United States courts have upheld jurisdiction in a variety of suits against former Philippine President Ferdinand Marcos and his wife, Imelda, despite the defendants' claims of immunity. Several lawsuits were filed in 1986, shortly after the Marcos' arrived in the United States after being ousted from power. The cases involved a class action of nearly 10,000 persons who alleged systematic torture, disappearances and summary execution. In addition, approximately 25 direct action plaintiffs asserted these and other claims, including prolonged arbitrary detention. *See* Republic of the Philippines v. Marcos, 806 F.2d 344 (2d Cir.1986); Hilao v. Marcos (*In re* Estate of Ferdinand E. Marcos Human Rights Litigation), 25 F.3d 1467 (9th Cir.1994), *cert. denied*, 513 U.S. 1126 (1995); United States v. Noriega, 746 F.Supp. 1506, 1519, n. 11 (S.D.Fla.1990); Chapter 2, Section 2 D 3. *But see* Wei Ye v. Jiang Zemin, 383 F.3d 620 (7th Cir. 2004) (following a State Department suggestion of immunity).

In Republic of the Philippines v. Marcos, 806 F.2d 344 (2d Cir.1986), the Second Circuit Court of Appeals rejected the Marcos' claim of sovereign immunity, holding that they lacked standing to raise the defense. The court also expressed doubt "that the immunity of a foreign state, though it extends to its head of state, ... goes so far as to render a former head of state immune as regards his private acts." *Id.* at 360. The Ninth Circuit Court of Appeals also rejected Marcos' claim of head of state and sovereign immunity in the *Marcos Human Rights Litigation* cases. In Hilao v. Marcos (*In re* Estate of Ferdinand E. Marcos Human Rights Litigation, 25 F.3d 1467 (9th Cir.1994), the court held that Marcos was not immune from suit under the FSIA, because acts such as torture and illegal execution cannot be deemed an exercise of sovereign authority. Instead, those actions "should be treated as taken without official mandate pursuant to [Marcos'] own authority." Hilao v. Marcos, *supra,* 25 F.3d at 1470–71. The Ninth Circuit later affirmed damage awards of nearly $2 billion in favor of the plaintiff class and direct action plaintiffs against the Marcos Estate and affirmed its previous denial of immunity to former President Marcos. Hilao v. Estate of Marcos, 103 F.3d 767, 771–72 (9th Cir.1996).

REGINA v. BARTLE AND THE COMMISSIONER OF POLICE FOR THE METROPOLIS AND OTHERS, *EX PARTE* PINOCHET

House of Lords (24 March 1999).

BROWNE-WILKINSON, L.J.

. . . [T]his case concerns an attempt by the Government of Spain to extradite Senator Pinochet from this country to stand trial in Spain for crimes committed (primarily in Chile) during the period when Senator Pinochet was head of state in Chile. . . .

Since the Nazi atrocities and the Nuremberg trials, international law has recognised a number of offences as being international crimes. Individual states have taken jurisdiction to try some international crimes even in cases where such crimes were not committed within the geographical boundaries of such states. The most important of such international crimes for present purposes is torture which is regulated by the International Convention Against Torture and other Cruel, Inhuman or Degrading Treatment or Punishment, 1984. The obligations placed on the United Kingdom by that Convention (and on the other 110 or more signatory states who have adopted the Convention) were incorporated into the law of the United Kingdom by section 134 of the Criminal Justice Act 1988. That Act came into force on 29 September 1988. Section 134 created a new crime under United Kingdom law, the crime of torture. As required by the Torture Convention "all" torture wherever committed world-wide was made criminal under United Kingdom law and triable in the United Kingdom. No one has suggested that before section 134 came into effect torture committed outside the United Kingdom was a crime under United Kingdom law. Nor is it suggested that section 134 was retrospective so as to make torture committed outside the United Kingdom before 29 September 1988 a United Kingdom crime. Since torture outside the United Kingdom was not a crime under U.K. law until 29 September 1988, the principle of double criminality which requires an Act to be a crime under both the law of Spain and of the United Kingdom cannot be satisfied in relation to conduct before that date if the principle of double criminality requires the conduct to be criminal under United Kingdom law *at the date it was committed*. . . .

This question, although raised, was not decided in the Divisional Court. At the first hearing in this House it was apparently conceded that all the matters charged against Senator Pinochet were extradition crimes. It was only during the hearing before your Lordships that the importance of the point became fully apparent. As will appear, in my view only a limited number of the charges relied upon to extradite Senator Pinochet constitute extradition crimes since most of the conduct relied upon occurred long before 1988. In particular, I do not consider that torture committed outside the United Kingdom before 29 September 1988 was a crime under U.K. law. It follows that the main question discussed at the earlier stages of this case—is a former head of state entitled to sovereign immunity from arrest or prosecution in the U.K. for acts of torture—applies to far fewer charges. But the question of state immunity remains a point of crucial importance since, in my view, there is certain conduct of Senator Pinochet (albeit a small amount) which does constitute an extradition crime and would enable the Home Secretary (if he thought fit) to extradite Senator Pinochet to Spain unless he is entitled to state immunity....

[U]nder the Act of 1870 the double criminality rule required the conduct to be criminal under English law at the conduct date not at the request date....

Finally, Lord Hope's analysis shows that the charge of conspiracy in Spain to murder in Spain (charge 9) and such conspiracies in Spain to commit murder in Spain, and such conspiracies in Spain prior to 29 September 1988 to commit acts of torture in Spain, as can be shown to form part of the allegations in charge 4 are extradition crimes.

I must therefore consider whether, in relation to these two surviving categories of charge, Senator Pinochet enjoys sovereign immunity. But first it is necessary to consider the modern law of torture.

Torture

... [T]he Republic of Chile accepted before your Lordships that the international law prohibiting torture has the character of *jus cogens* or a peremptory norm, *i.e.*, one of those rules of international law which have a particular status.

The *jus cogens* nature of the international crime of torture justifies states in taking universal jurisdiction over torture wherever committed. International law provides that offences *jus cogens* may be punished by any state because the offenders are "common enemies of all mankind and all nations have an equal interest in their apprehension and prosecution": *Demjanjuk v. Petrovsky* (1985) 603 F. Supp. 1468; 776 F. 2d 571 [6th Cir. 1985].

... [T]he objective was to ensure a general jurisdiction so that the torturer was not safe wherever he went. For example, in this case it is alleged that during the Pinochet regime torture was an official, although unacknowledged, weapon of government and that, when the regime was about to end, it passed legislation designed to afford an amnesty to those who had engaged in institutionalised torture. If these allegations are true, the fact that the local court had jurisdiction to deal with the international crime of torture was nothing to the point so long as the totalitarian regime remained in power: a totalitarian regime will not permit adjudication by its own courts on its own shortcomings. Hence the demand for some international machinery to repress state torture which is not dependent upon the local courts where the torture was committed. In the event, over 110 states (including Chile, Spain and the United Kingdom) became state parties to the Torture Convention.... The Torture Convention was agreed not in order to create an international crime which had not previously existed but to provide an international system under which the international criminal—the torturer—could find no safe haven.

The Torture Convention

Under Article 5(1) each state party has to establish its jurisdiction over torture (a) when committed within territory under its jurisdiction (b) when the alleged offender is a national of that state, and (c) in certain circumstances, when the victim is a national of that state. Under Article 5(2) a state party has to take jurisdiction over any alleged offender who is found within its territory. Article 6 contains provisions for a state in whose territory an alleged torturer is found to detain him, inquire into the position and notify the states referred to in Article 5 (1) and to indicate whether it intends to exercise jurisdiction. Under Article 7 the state in whose territory the alleged torturer is found shall, if he is not extradited to any of the states mentioned in Article 5 (1), submit him to its authorities for the purpose of prosecution. Under Article 8(1) torture is to be treated as an extraditable offence and under Article 8(4) torture shall, for the purposes of extradition, be treated as having been committed not only in the place where it occurred but also in the state mentioned in Article 5(1).

Who is an "Official" for the Purposes of the Torture Convention?

The first question on the Convention is to decide whether acts done by a head of state are done by "a public official or a person acting in an official capacity" within the meaning of Article 1. The same question arises under section 134 of the Criminal Justice Act 1988. The answer to both questions must be the same. In his judgment at the first hearing (at pp. 1476G–1477E) Lord Slynn held that a head of state was neither a public official nor a person acting in an official capacity within the meaning of Article 1: he pointed out that there are a number of international conventions (for example the Yugoslav War Crimes Statute and the Rwanda War Crimes Statute) which refer specifically to heads of state when they intend to render them liable....

It became clear during the argument that both the Republic of Chile and Senator Pinochet accepted that the acts alleged against Senator Pinochet, if proved, were acts done by a public official or person acting in an official capacity within the meaning of Article 1.... In my judgment it would run completely contrary to the intention of the Convention if there was anybody who could be exempt from guilt. The crucial question is not whether Senator Pinochet falls within the definition in Article 1: he plainly does. The question is whether, even so, he is procedurally immune from process....

State Immunity

This is the point around which most of the argument turned.... [I]t will be the first time so far as counsel have discovered when a local domestic court has refused to afford immunity to a head of state or former head of state on the grounds that there can be no immunity against prosecution for certain international crimes.

It is a basic principle of international law that one sovereign state (the forum state) does not adjudicate on the conduct of a foreign state. The foreign state is entitled to procedural immunity from the processes of the forum state. This immunity extends to both criminal and civil liability.... This immunity enjoyed by a head of state in power and an ambassador in post is a complete immunity attaching to the person of the head of state or ambassador and rendering him immune from all actions or prosecutions whether or not they relate to matters done for the benefit of the state. Such immunity is said to be granted *ratione personae*.

What then when the ambassador leaves his post or the head of state is deposed?....

The continuing partial immunity of the ambassador after leaving post is of a different kind from that enjoyed *ratione personae* while he was in post. Since he is no longer the representative of the foreign state he merits no particular privileges or immunities as a person. However in order to preserve the integrity of the activities of the foreign state during the period when he was ambassador, it is necessary to provide that immunity is afforded to his *official* acts during his tenure in post.... This limited immunity, *ratione materiae*, is to be contrasted with the former immunity *ratione personae* which gave complete immunity to all activities whether public or private.

In my judgment at common law a former head of state enjoys similar immunities, *ratione materiae*, once he ceases to be head of state. He too loses immunity *ratione personae* on ceasing to be head of state.... As ex head of state he cannot be sued in respect of acts performed whilst head of state in his public capacity....

The correct way in which to apply Article 39(2) of the Vienna Convention [on Diplomatic Relations, 1961] to a former head of state is baffling. To what "functions" is one to have regard? Is a former head of state's immunity limited to the exercise of the functions of a member of the mission?.... [A] former head of state has immunity in relation to acts done as part of his official functions when head of state. Accordingly, in my judgment, Senator Pinochet as former head of state enjoys immunity *ratione materiae* in relation to acts done by him as head of state as part of his official functions as head of state.

The question then which has to be answered is whether the alleged organisation of state torture by Senator Pinochet (if proved) would constitute an act committed by Senator Pinochet as part of his official functions as head of state.... Actions which are criminal under the local law can still have been done officially and therefore give rise to immunity *ratione materiae*. . . .

Can it be said that the commission of a crime which is an international crime against humanity and *jus cogens* is an act done in an official capacity on behalf of the state? I believe there to be strong ground for saying that the implementation of torture as defined by the Torture Convention *cannot be a state function* [emphasis added]. . . .

The jurisdiction being established by the Torture Convention and the Hostages Convention is one where existing domestic courts of all the countries are being authorised and required to take jurisdiction. . . .

Not until there was some form of universal jurisdiction for the punishment of the crime of torture could it really be talked about as a fully constituted international crime. But in my judgment the Torture Convention did provide what was missing: a worldwide universal jurisdiction. . . . How can it be for international law purposes an official function to do something which international law itself prohibits and criminalises?. . . . [A]ll defendants in torture cases will be state officials. Yet, if the former head of state has immunity, the man most responsible will escape liability while his inferiors (the chiefs of police, junior army officers) who carried out his orders will be liable. I find it impossible to accept that this was the intention. . . .

Immunity *ratione materiae* applies not only to ex-heads of state and ex-ambassadors but to all state officials who have been involved in carrying out the functions of the state. . . . Therefore the whole elaborate structure of universal jurisdiction over torture committed by officials is rendered abortive and one of the main objectives of the Torture Convention—to provide a system under which there is no safe haven for torturers—will have been frustrated. In my judgment all these factors together demonstrate that the notion of continued immunity for ex-heads of state is inconsistent with the provisions of the Torture Convention.

As to the charges of murder and conspiracy to murder, no one has advanced any reason why the ordinary rules of immunity should not apply and Senator Pinochet is entitled to such immunity.

Goff of Chieveley, L.J.

. . . The functions of, for example, a head of state are governmental functions, as opposed to private acts; and the fact that the head of state performs an act, other than a private act, which is criminal does not deprive it of its governmental character. This is as true of a serious crime, such as murder or torture, as it is of a lesser crime. . . .

[N]ot only is there no mention of state immunity in the [Torture] Convention, but in my opinion it is not inconsistent with its express provisions that, if steps are taken to extradite him or to submit his case to the authorities for the purpose of prosecution, the appropriate state should be entitled to assert state immunity. In this connection, I comment that it is not suggested that it is inconsistent with the Convention that immunity *ratione personae* should be asserted; if so, I find it difficult to see why it should be inconsistent to assert immunity *ratione materiae*....

State immunity *ratione materiae* operates therefore to protect former heads of state, and (where immunity is asserted) public officials, even minor public officials, from legal process in foreign countries in respect of acts done in the exercise of their functions as such, including accusation and arrest in respect of alleged crimes.... Preservation of state immunity is therefore a matter of particular importance to powerful countries whose heads of state perform an executive role, and who may therefore be regarded as possible targets by governments of states which, for deeply felt political reasons, deplore their actions while in office.... It is not beyond the bounds of possibility that a state whose government is imbued with this opinion might seek to extradite from a third country, where he or she happens to be, a responsible Minister of the Crown, or even a more humble public official such as a police inspector, on the ground that he or she has acquiesced in a single act of physical or mental torture in Northern Ireland....

For these reasons I am of the opinion that the proposed implication must be rejected not only as contrary to principle and authority, but also as contrary to common sense....

Hope of Craighead, L.J.

... The question then is to what extent does the immunity which Article 39.2 [of the Vienna Convention on Diplomatic Relations] gives to former diplomats have to be modified in its application to former heads of state?.... In its application to a former head of state this provision raises two further questions: (1) does it include functions which the head of state performed outside the receiving state from whose jurisdiction he claims immunity, and (2) does it include acts of the kind alleged in this case ... ?

... In my opinion the functions of the head of state are those which his own state enables or requires him to perform in the exercise of government.... The test is whether they were private acts on the one hand or governmental acts done in the exercise of his authority as head of state on the other. It is whether the act was done to promote the state's interests—whether it was done for his own benefit or gratification or was done for the state.... The fact that acts done for the state have involved conduct which is criminal does not remove the immunity.... A head of state needs to be free to promote his own state's interests during the entire period when he is in office without being subjected to the prospect of detention, arrest or embarrassment in the foreign legal system of the receiving state....

There are only two exceptions to this approach which customary international law has recognised. The first relates to criminal acts which the head of state did under the colour of his authority as head of state but which were in reality for his own pleasure or benefit. The examples which Lord Steyn gave [1998] 3 W.L.R. 1456, 1506B–C of the head of state who kills his gardener in a fit of rage or who orders victims to be tortured so that he may observe them in agony seem to me plainly to fall into this category and, for this reason, to lie outside the scope of the immunity. The second relates to acts the prohibition of which has acquired the status under international law of *jus cogens*....

But even in the field of such high crimes as have achieved the status of *jus cogens* under customary international law there is as yet no general agreement that they are outside the immunity to which former heads of state are entitled from the jurisdiction of foreign national courts. There is plenty of source material to show that war crimes and crimes against humanity have been separated out from the generality of conduct which customary international law has come to regard as criminal....

The Torture Convention and Loss of Immunity

... The Torture Convention does not contain any provision which deals expressly with the question whether heads of state or former heads of state are or are not to have immunity from allegations that they have committed torture.

But there remains the question whether the effect of the Torture Convention was to remove the immunity by necessary implication....

It would also be a strange result if the provisions of the Convention could not be applied to heads of state who, because they themselves inflicted torture or had instigated the carrying out of acts of torture by their officials, were the persons primarily responsible for the perpetration of these acts....

The *jus cogens* character of the immunity enjoyed by serving heads of state *ratione personae* suggests that, on any view, that immunity was not intended to be affected by the Convention. But once one immunity is conceded it becomes harder, in the absence of an express provision, to justify the removal of the other immunities....

These considerations suggest strongly that it would be wrong to regard the Torture Convention as having by necessary implication removed the immunity *ratione materiae* from former heads of state in regard to every act of torture of any kind which might be alleged against him falling within the scope of Article 1....

Nevertheless there remains the question whether the immunity can survive Chile's agreement to the Torture Convention if the torture which is alleged was of such a kind or on such a scale as to amount to an international crime. Sir Arthur Watts in his Hague Lectures, p. 82 states that the idea that individuals who commit international crimes are internationally accountable for them has now become an accepted part of international law....

The allegations which the Spanish judicial authorities have made against Senator Pinochet fall into that category.... [W]e are not dealing in this case—even upon the restricted basis of those charges on which

Senator Pinochet could lawfully be extradited if he has no immunity—with isolated acts of official torture.... This is because he is said to have been involved in acts of torture which were committed in pursuance of a policy to commit systematic torture within Chile and elsewhere as an instrument of government....

I would not regard this as a case of waiver. Nor would I accept that it was an implied term of the Torture Convention that former heads of state were to be deprived of their immunity *ratione materiae* with respect to all acts of official torture as defined in article 1. It is just that the obligations which were recognised by customary international law in the case of such serious international crimes by the date when Chile ratified the Convention are so strong as to override any objection by it on the ground of immunity *ratione materiae* to the exercise of the jurisdiction over crimes committed after that date which the United Kingdom had made available.

I consider that the date as from which the immunity *ratione materiae* was lost was 30 October 1988, which was the date when Chile's ratification of the Torture Convention on 30 September 1988 took effect. Spain had already ratified the Convention.... The Convention was ratified by the United Kingdom on 8 December 1988 following the coming into force of section 134 of the Criminal Justice Act 1988....

Conclusion

It follows that I would hold that, while Senator Pinochet has immunity *ratione materiae* from prosecution for the conspiracy in Spain to murder in Spain ... and such conspiracies in Spain prior to 8 December 1988 to commit acts of torture in Spain ... , he has no immunity from prosecution for the charges of torture and of conspiracy to torture which relate to the period after that date....

HUTTON, L.J.

... The alleged acts of torture by Senator Pinochet were carried out under colour of his position as head of state, but they cannot be regarded as functions of a head of state under international law when international law expressly prohibits torture as a measure which a state can employ in any circumstances whatsoever and has made it an international crime....

In my opinion there has been no waiver of the immunity of a former head of state in respect of his functions as head of state. My conclusion that Senator Pinochet is not entitled to immunity is based on the view that the commission of acts of torture is not a function of a head of state, and therefore in this case the immunity to which Senator Pinochet is entitled as a former head of state does not arise in relation to, and does not attach to, acts of torture....

Therefore I consider that a single act of torture carried out or instigated by a public official or other person acting in a official capacity constitutes a crime against international law, and that torture does not become an international crime only when it is committed or instigated on a large scale. Accordingly I am of opinion that Senator Pinochet cannot claim that a single act of torture or a small number of acts of torture carried out by him did not constitute international crimes and did not constitute acts committed outside the ambit of his functions as head of state....

Therefore for the reasons which I have given I am of opinion that Senator Pinochet is not entitled to claim immunity in the extradition proceedings in respect of conspiracy to torture and acts of torture alleged to have been committed by him after 29 September 1988 and to that extent I would allow the appeal....

Saville of Newdigate, L.J.

... To my mind it must follow in turn that a head of state, who for state purposes resorts to torture, would be a person acting in an official capacity within the meaning of this Convention. He would indeed to my mind be a prime example of an official torturer.

It does not follow from this that the immunity enjoyed by a serving head of state, which is entirely unrelated to whether or not he was acting in an official capacity, is thereby removed in cases of torture. In my view it is not, since immunity *ratione personae* attaches to the office and not to any particular conduct of the office holder.

On the other hand, the immunity of a former head of state does attach to his conduct whilst in office and is wholly related to what he did in his official capacity.

So far as the states that are parties to the Convention are concerned, I cannot see how, so far as torture is concerned, this immunity can exist consistently with the terms of that Convention. Each state party has agreed that the other state parties can exercise jurisdiction over alleged official torturers found within their territories, by extraditing them or referring them to their own appropriate authorities for prosecution; and thus to my mind can hardly simultaneously claim an immunity from extradition or prosecution that is necessarily based on the official nature of the alleged torture.

I do not reach this conclusion by implying terms into the Torture Convention, but simply by applying its express terms.... If there were states that wished to preserve such immunity in the face of universal condemnation of official torture, it is perhaps not surprising that they kept quiet about it.

For the same reasons it seems to me that the wider arguments based on Act of State or nonjusticiability must also fail, since they are equally inconsistent with the terms of the Convention agreed by these state parties.

Millett, L.J.

State immunity is not a personal right. It is an attribute of the sovereignty of the state....

Senator Pinochet is not a serving head of state. If he were, he could not be extradited....

Immunity *ratione materiae* is very different. This is a subject-matter immunity. It operates to prevent the official and governmental acts of one state from being called into question in proceedings before the courts of another, and only incidentally confers immunity on the individual.... It is an immunity from the civil and criminal jurisdiction of foreign national courts but only in respect of governmental or official acts. The exercise of authority by the military and security forces of the state is the paradigm example of such conduct. The immunity finds its rationale in the equality of sovereign states and the doctrine of noninterference in the internal affairs of other states: see Duke of Brunswick v. King of Hanover (1848) 2 H.L.Cas. 1; Hatch v. Baez (1876) 7 Hun. 596 U.S.; Underhill v. Hernandez (1897) 168 U.S. [250]....

Given its scope and rationale, it is closely similar to and may be indistinguishable from aspects of the Anglo–American Act of State doctrine. As I understand the difference between them, state immunity is a creature of international law and operates as a plea in bar to the jurisdiction of the national court, whereas the Act of State doctrine is a rule of domestic law which holds the national court incompetent to adjudicate upon the lawfulness of the sovereign acts of a foreign state....

The immunity is available whether the acts in question are illegal or unconstitutional or otherwise unauthorised under the internal law of the state, since the whole purpose of state immunity is to prevent the legality of such acts from being adjudicated upon in the municipal courts of a foreign state....

Whether conduct contrary to the peremptory norms of international law attracted state immunity from the jurisdiction of national courts, however, was largely academic in 1946, since the criminal jurisdiction of such courts was generally restricted to offences committed within the territory of the forum state or elsewhere by the nationals of that state....

In 1946 the General Assembly had entrusted the formulation of the principles of international law recognised in the Charter of the Nuremberg Tribunal and the Judgment of the Tribunal to the International Law Commission. It reported in 1954. It rejected the principle that international criminal responsibility for crimes against humanity should be limited to crimes committed in connection with war crimes or crimes against peace. It was, however, necessary to distinguish international crimes from ordinary domestic offences. For this purpose, the Commission proposed that acts would constitute international crimes only if they were committed at the instigation or the toleration of state authorities. This is the distinction which was later adopted in the Convention against Torture (1984). In my judgment it is of critical importance in relation to the concept of immunity *ratione materiae*. The very official or governmental character of the acts which is necessary to found a claim to immunity *ratione materiae*, and which still operates as a bar to the civil jurisdiction of national courts, was now to be the essential element which made the acts an international crime. It was, no doubt, for this reason that the Commission's draft code provided that: "The fact that a person acted as head of state or as a responsible Government official does not relieve him of responsibility for committing any of the offences defined in the code." ...

The case [of Attorney General of Israel v. Eichmann (1962) 36 INT'L L. REPTS. 5] is authority for three propositions:

(1) There is no rule of international law which prohibits a state from exercising extraterritorial criminal jurisdiction in respect of crimes committed by foreign nationals abroad.

(2) War crimes and atrocities of the scale and international character of the Holocaust are crimes of universal jurisdiction under customary international law.

(3) The fact that the accused committed the crimes in question in the course of his official duties as a responsible officer of the state and in the exercise of his authority as an organ of the state is no bar to the exercise of the jurisdiction of a national court.

... The Republic of Chile accepts that by 1973 the use of torture by state authorities was prohibited by international law, and that the prohibition had the character of *jus cogens* or obligation *erga omnes*. But it insists that this does not confer universal jurisdiction or affect the immunity of a former head of state *ratione materiae* from the jurisdiction of foreign national courts.

In my opinion, crimes prohibited by international law attract universal jurisdiction under customary international law if two criteria are satisfied. First, they must be contrary to a peremptory norm of international law so as to infringe a *jus cogens*. Secondly, they must be so serious and on such a scale that they can justly be regarded as an attack on the international legal order. Isolated offences, even if committed by public officials, would not satisfy these criteria....

The jurisdiction of the English criminal courts is usually statutory, but it is supplemented by the common law. Customary international law is part of the common law, and accordingly I consider that the English courts have and always have had extra-territorial criminal jurisdiction in respect of crimes of universal jurisdiction under customary international law....

In my opinion, the systematic use of torture on a large scale and as an instrument of state policy had joined piracy, war crimes and crimes against peace as an international crime of universal jurisdiction well before 1984. I consider that it had done so by 1973. For my own part, therefore, I would hold that the courts of this country already possessed extra-territorial jurisdiction in respect of torture and conspiracy to torture on the scale of the charges in the present case and did not require the authority of statute to exercise it....

I turn finally to the plea of immunity *ratione materiae* in relation to the remaining allegations of torture, conspiracy to torture and conspiracy to murder. I can deal with the charges of conspiracy to murder quite shortly. The offences are alleged to have taken place in the requesting state. The plea of immunity *ratione materiae* is not available in respect of an offence committed in the forum state, whether this be England or Spain.

The definition of torture, both in the Convention and section 134, is in my opinion entirely inconsistent with the existence of a plea of immunity *ratione materiae*. The offence can be committed *only* by or at the instigation of or with the consent or acquiescence of a public official or other person acting in an official capacity. The official or governmental nature of the act, which forms the basis of the immunity, is an essential ingredient of the offence. No rational system of criminal justice can allow an immunity which is co-extensive with the offence....

... The international community had created an offence for which immunity *ratione materiae* could not possibly be available. International law cannot be supposed to have established a crime having the character of a *jus cogens* and at the same time to have provided an immunity which is co-extensive with the obligation it seeks to impose....

I see nothing illogical or contrary to public policy in denying the victims of state sponsored torture the right to sue the offending state in a foreign court while at the same time permitting (and indeed requiring) other states to convict and punish the individuals responsible if the offending state declines to take action. This was the very object of the Torture Convention....

In future those who commit atrocities against civilian populations must expect to be called to account if fundamental human rights are to be properly protected. In this context, the exalted rank of the accused can afford no defence....

PHILLIPS OF WORTHMATRAVERS, L.J.

What seems inherently unlikely is that a foreign head of state should commit a criminal offence in the performance of his official functions while on a visit and subsequently return after ceasing to be head of state. Certainly this cannot have happened with sufficient frequency for any custom to have developed in relation to it.... For these reasons I do not believe that custom can provide any foundation for a rule that a former head of state is entitled to immunity from criminal process in respect of crimes committed in the exercise of his official functions....

There would seem to be two explanations for immunity *ratione materiae*. The first is that to sue an individual in respect of the conduct of the state's business is, indirectly, to sue the state.... This reasoning has no application to criminal proceedings. The second explanation for the immunity is the principle that it is contrary to international law for one state to adjudicate upon the internal affairs of another state. Where a state or a state official is impleaded, this principle applies as part of the explanation for immunity.... [T]he English and American courts have nonetheless, as a matter of judicial restraint, held themselves not competent to entertain litigation that turns on the validity of the public acts of a foreign state, applying what has become known as the act of state doctrine....

It is contended on behalf of the respondent that the question of whether an official is acting in a public capacity does not depend upon whether he is acting within the law of the state on whose behalf he purports to act, or even within the limits of international law. His conduct in an official capacity will, whether lawful or unlawful, be conduct of the state and the state will be entitled to assert immunity in respect of it. In the field of civil litigation these propositions are supported by authority.... What was in issue was whether the criminality of the conduct deprived the state of immunity and on that issue the plaintiffs failed. Counsel for the Respondent provided us with an impressive, and depressing, list of such cases: Saltany v. Reagan (1988) 702 F. Supp. 319 (claims of assassination and terrorism); Siderman de Blake v. Republic of Argentina (1992) 965 F.2d 699 (claim of torture); Princz v. Federal Republic of Germany (1994) 26 F.3d 1166 (D.C.Cir.1994) (claim in respect of the holocaust); Al–Adsani v. Government of Kuwait (1996) 107 I.L.R. 536 (claim of torture); Sampson v. Federal Republic of Germany, 975 F. Supp. 1108 (N.D. Ill. 1997) (claim in respect of the holocaust); Smith v. Libya, 886 F. Supp. [4]06 (E.D.N.Y. 1995)[;] 101 F.3d 239 (2d Cir.1996) (claim in respect of Lockerbie bombing); Persinger v. Islamic Republic of Iran, 729 F.2d 835, (D.C.Cir.1984) (claim in relation to hostage taking at the U.S. Embassy).

... In each case immunity from civil suit was afforded by statute—in America, the Foreign Sovereign Immunities Act and, in England, the State Immunity Act 1978. In each case the court felt itself precluded by the clear words of the statute from acceding to the submission that state immunity would not protect against liability for conduct which infringed international law....

The submission advanced on behalf of the respondent in respect of the effect of public international law can, I believe, be summarised as follows:

1. One state will not entertain judicial proceedings against a former head of state or other state official of another state in relation to conduct performed in his official capacity.

2. This rule applies even if the conduct amounts to a crime against international law. 3. This rule applies in relation to both civil and criminal proceedings....

In the latter part of this century there has been developing a recognition among states that some types of criminal conduct cannot be treated as a matter for the exclusive competence of the state in which they occur....

My Lords, this is an area where international law is on the move and the move has been effected by express consensus recorded in or reflected by a considerable number of international instruments.... There are some categories of crime of such gravity that they shock the consciousness of mankind and cannot be tolerated by the international community. Any individual who commits such a crime offends against international law. The nature of these crimes is such that they are likely to involve the concerted conduct of many and liable to involve the complicity of the officials of the state in which they occur, if not of the state itself. In these circumstances it is desirable that jurisdiction should exist to prosecute individuals for such conduct outside the territory in which such conduct occurs.

I believe that it is still an open question whether international law recognises universal jurisdiction in respect of international crimes.... They have however, on occasion, agreed by conventions, that their national courts should enjoy jurisdiction to prosecute for a particular category of international crime wherever occurring....

Where states, by convention, agree that their national courts shall have jurisdiction on a universal basis in respect of an international crime, such agreement cannot implicitly remove immunities *ratione personae* that exist under international law. Such immunities can only be removed by express agreement or waiver. Such an agreement was incorporated in the Convention on the Prevention and Suppression of the Crime of Genocide 1948, which provides:

> "Persons committing genocide or any of the other acts enumerated in Article III shall be punished, whether they are constitutionally responsible rulers, public officials, or private individuals."

Had the Genocide Convention not contained this provision, an issue could have been raised as to whether the jurisdiction conferred by the Convention was subject to state immunity *ratione materiae*. Would international law have required a court to grant immunity to a defendant upon his demonstrating that he was acting in an official capacity? In my view it plainly would not. I do not reach that conclusion on the ground that assisting in genocide can never be a function of a state official. I reach that conclusion on the simple basis that no established rule of international law requires state immunity *ratione materiae* to be accorded in respect of prosecution for an international crime. International crimes and extra-territorial jurisdiction in relation to them are both new arrivals in the field of public international law. I do not believe that state immunity *ratione materiae* can co-exist with them....

There are only two possibilities. One is that the States Parties to the [Torture] Convention proceeded on the premise that no immunity could exist *ratione materiae* in respect of torture, a crime contrary to international law. The other is that the States Parties to the Convention expressly agreed that immunity *ratione materiae* should not apply in the case of torture. I believe that the first of these alternatives is the correct one, but either must be fatal to the assertion by Chile and Senator

Pinochet of immunity in respect of extradition proceedings based on torture ...

... I do not consider that Section 20 of the [U.K. State Immunity] Act of 1978 has any application to conduct of a head of state outside the United Kingdom. Such conduct remains governed by the rules of public international law....

If I am mistaken in this view and we are bound by the Act of 1978 to accord to Senator Pinochet immunity in respect of all acts committed "in performance of his functions as head of state", I would not hold that the course of conduct alleged by Spain falls within that description....

Insofar as Part III of the Act of 1978 entitles a former head of state to immunity in respect of the performance of his official functions I do not believe that those functions can, as a matter of statutory interpretation, extend to actions that are prohibited as criminal under international law. In this way one can reconcile, as one must seek to do, the provisions of the Act of 1978 with the requirements of public international law.

Notes and Questions

1. Which arguments or points are most persuasive? Why?

2. When Millet stated that in his opinion international crimes over which there is universal jurisdiction "must be contrary to a peremptory norm ... *jus cogens*," was he correct? Recall cases and opinions in Chapters 1, 2 and 3. When Millet stated that such crimes must also "be so serious and on such a scale that they can justly be regarded as an attack on the international legal order" and that "isolated offences" do not constitute such international crimes, was he correct? Consider, for example, the crimes of piracy, aircraft hijacking, aircraft sabotage, assaults on foreign ambassadors, breaches of neutrality, isolated war crimes, the definition of genocide in Article II of the Genocide Convention, and other crimes by private and public perpetrators addressed in Chapters 1, 3. When he noted that immunity "finds its rationale" in state equality and the doctrine of noninterference in "internal affairs" of other states, can you posit an argument that, in view of such a rationale, acts of genocide and other human rights violations should be nonimmune?

3. Did the Lords refer to the Charters or Judgments and Opinions of the I.M.T. at Nuremberg and the I.M.T. for the Far East; Control Council Law No. 10 (art. II(2), (4)(a)); the Principles of the Nuremberg Charter and Judgment (Principles I and III) and other General Assembly resolutions on universal responsibility over war crimes, genocide, and other crimes against humanity; the 1919 Report of the Responsibilities Commission; the Treaty of Versailles which publicly indicted the Kaiser of Germany for international crimes (see Chapter 8, and see other examples of public official responsibility there and in Chapter 1); the Statutes of the ICTY (art. 7(2)) or ICTR (art. 6(2)); or the Statute of the ICC, art. 27? Do any of the above international instruments or opinions distinguish between notions *ratione personae* and *ratione materiae*? Do *any* international legal instruments? What is the consistent recognition concerning head of state or other public official

responsibility in each of the above instruments or opinions? Also see Report of the Secretary–General Pursuant to Paragraph 2 of Security Council Resolution 808, paras. 55, 59 (1993), U.N. Doc. S/25704 (1993).

Do you think that acts of a head of state that are international crimes under customary or treaty-based international law are immune? Do you think that only crimes *jus cogens* are nonimmune? Or do you agree with Lord Hope that "serving" head of state immunity from international crime is a *jus cogens* norm? Do you think that a head of state is immune from prosecution for crimes such as hostage-taking, torture, or aircraft sabotage, if a relevant treaty recognizes international criminal responsibility for "any person" or "a person" who commits such a crime if the treaty does not also address head of state or public official immunity or nonimmunity? Also recall the portion of the Opinion and Judgment of the I.M.T. at Nuremberg on the lack of official "immunity," and lack of state competence, for acts made "criminal by international law," quoted earlier in this chapter. Is nonimmunity for international crime based merely on express provisions of Charters and treaties?

Are there other indications of ahistorical statements in the opinions?

4. Read Article 1 of the Convention Against Torture, in the Documents Supplement. Who is expressly covered? Is there immunity expressed in any form? Is the treaty really "silent" on nonimmunity? *See also* the Principles of the Nuremberg Charter and Judgment, in the Documents Supplement; Gunther Handl, *The Pinochet Case, Foreign State Immunity and the Changing Constitution of the International Community*, in DEVELOPMENT AND DEVELOPING INTERNATIONAL AND EUROPEAN LAW 59, 62 n.15, 65–66, 74 (W. Benedek ed. 1999); PAUST, BASSIOUNI, *ET AL.*, *supra*, at 27–30, *passim*. Also consider Article 2(3)(a) of the International Covenant on Civil and Political Rights, Article 25(1) of the American Convention on Human Rights, and Article IX of the Inter–American Convention on the Forced Disappearance of Persons, in the Documents Supplement.

Can torture also constitute a crime against humanity or genocide? See relevant instruments in the Documents Supplement. If so, does this establish universal jurisdictional responsibilities that prohibit the granting of immunity? Also recall *Filartiga*, affirming that torture is a violation of customary human rights law, such rights are guaranteed to all persons through the United Nations Charter, and "the torturer has become–like the pirate and slave trader before him–*hostis humani generis*, an enemy of all mankind." *See also Demjanjuk* ("enemies of all people"), in Chapter 3. Is such a status determinative of the question whether a torturer should enjoy head of state or former head of state immunity?

5. In the 1999 decision, the House of Lords narrowed the charges upon which General Augusto Pinochet Ugarte could be extradited from the United Kingdom to Spain. This was based on a questionable interpretation of the timing element of the dual criminality rule of extradition law. Nevertheless, its 6–1 holding that a former head of state's acts of official torture cannot be immunized from universal criminal jurisdiction (as established by a treaty domestically incorporated into U.K. law) is highly significant.

6. Judge Garzón was the Spanish magistrate who issued orders seeking the extradition of Pinochet to Spain for genocide, terrorism, and acts of

torture that are a part of the crime of genocide. These efforts were opposed by Spain's public prosecutor. In November, 1988, the Criminal Division of the Spanish National Court (*Audiencia Nacional*) unanimously held that Spain had universal jurisdiction over crimes alleged in the extradition warrants. Article 23(4) of the Judicial Branch Act of 1985 grants Spanish courts jurisdiction over acts committed abroad by either Spanish or foreign nationals when such acts are likely to be considered, according to the Spanish criminal legislation, any of the following crimes: genocide, terrorism, piracy, or "any other which according to international treaties or conventions must be prosecuted by Spain." The legislation does not specifically refer to torture or to crimes against humanity as such. The Spanish National Court held that the allegations of torture could be subsumed under the concepts of genocide or terrorism. *See* María del Carmen Márquez Carrasco, Joaquín Alcaide Fernández, *In re Pinochet*, 93 AM. J. INT'L L. 690, 690–93 & ns.5, 14 (1999).

Do you see any difficulty in characterizing Pinochet's crimes as genocide or terrorism? Is the concluding phrase in Article 23(4) sufficient to cover acts of torture committed in Chile?

7. In the first decision of the House of Lords on November 25, 1998 (deciding 3–2 that Pinochet was not entitled to immunity regarding torture or hostage-taking), Lord Slynn noted that the Spanish request for extradition "set out a large number of alleged murders, disappearances and cases of torture ... in breach of Spanish law relating to genocide, to torture and to terrorism;" that Spain claimed universal jurisdiction under international law and internal legislation; but stated that the U.K.'s Genocide Act of 1969 did not enact Article IV of the Genocide Convention "as part of domestic law" (although Article IV covers heads of state). He added that the acts covered by the definition of genocide in Article II of the Convention were made a domestic criminal offense in the U.K. under the Genocide Act. See 37 I.L.M. at 1302, 1305, 1311, 1315 (1998). He also assumed that Article IV of the Convention makes heads of state liable to punishment (as opposed to merely recognizing nonimmunity or responsibility for any person). *Id.* at 1315. Lord Lloyd added that Parliament omitted Article IV from the English Act because it probably intended, "or at least contemplated," head of state immunity. *Id.* at 1324. Using such logic, would the omission of Article IV mean that no person can be responsible for genocide under the English Act, since Article IV addresses the responsibility of all persons, including other public officials and private persons? Such logic also leads to the conclusion that England is in breach of Articles I and V of the Genocide Convention (see Documents Supplement), as well as customary international law. See Chapters 1 and 3, Sections 2 and 4 A. Article V expressly affirms the duty to enact legislation needed "to give effect to the provisions of the ... Convention and, in particular, to provide effective penalties for persons guilty...."

If a lack of dual criminality concerning domestic laws of the U.K. and Spain exists, should the U.K. rightly claim that it will not extradite Pinochet for genocide because of its breach of the Genocide Convention? Should the consequence of such a breach enlarge a functional immunity for genocide in the U.K. to an immunity from prosecution for genocide in Spain because of the doctrines of dual criminality and speciality, thus imposing the consequences of the U.K.'s breach on other states? Would this not be inconsistent with a universal jurisdictional competence and responsibility concerning international crimes? Recall Chapters 1 and 3.

8. Is the opinion limited to criminal jurisdiction? Should this decision affect other courts' understanding of the international agreements, customary international law, or *jus cogens* exceptions to immunity from civil damages liability for acts of official torture? Only against former heads of state, or against the state itself?

Note that Chile (unlike Haiti in the *Avril* case or the Philippines in the various *Marcos* cases) did not waive General Pinochet's head of state immunity but vigorously asserted it as an intervenor in the House of Lords appeal.

9. Is there a relationship between former head of state immunity and the act of state doctrine? If there is, what limits or exceptions to immunity might apply?

10. Does the *Pinochet* extradition case illuminate connections between head of state immunity and diplomatic immunity? Diplomatic immunity relates to acts committed within the state to which the diplomat is posted. *See* Section 3. Where a head of state visits a foreign state to perform diplomatic functions, similar protections *rationae personae* apply, whether derived from principles of sovereign immunity or diplomatic immunity. The *Pinochet* case is especially interesting because the U.K. State Immunity Act 1978 makes several convoluted and obscure efforts to assimilate head of state immunity to diplomatic immunity. The difficulty comes, as the *Pinochet* case illustrates, where the head of state is called to account criminally or civilly, not for acts he committed in the state he is visiting, but in his own or another state. Where he is the recognized head of state, he is immunized under the absolute principles derived from both doctrines of sovereign immunity and conventional rules on diplomatic immunity. But where he has left office, his lingering immunities for acts not committed in the state he is visiting are more contestable. Diplomats have lingering immunities only for official acts performed in the state of their former posting. Should the same rule be applied to former heads of state vacationing (or seeking medical treatment) in foreign states? Should either be immune for violations of international law?

11. On March 2, 2000, the U.K. let Pinochet fly back to Chile because he was supposedly too ill and mentally incompetent to stand trial. The day he landed in Chile he walked among and spoke to many who greeted his return. On March 3rd, the International Criminal Tribunal for Former Yugoslavia sentenced Croatian General Blaskic to 45 years imprisonment for war crimes and crimes against humanity. In August, 2000 the Supreme Court of Chile ruled that Pinochet is no longer protected by an earlier domestic amnesty previously placed in the Chilean Constitution.

SECTION 3. IMMUNITIES OF DIPLOMATS, CONSULS AND INTERNATIONAL ORGANIZATIONS

A. *Diplomatic Privileges and Immunities*

The law of diplomatic privileges and immunities is one of the most ancient strands of customary international law. As Chief Justice Marshall noted in *Schooner Exchange*, diplomatic immunity shares common roots with foreign sovereign immunity. The diplomat, though present in the territory of the receiving state to perform her function, maintains her loyalty to her own sovereign. An act of hostility against or interference with a diplomat's functions can be an affront to the sending state and a threat to peaceful intercourse among nations. *See generally*, BISWANATH SEN, A DIPLOMAT'S HANDBOOK OF INTERNATIONAL LAW AND PRACTICE (3 ed. 1988); ERNEST M. SATOW, SATOW'S GUIDE TO DIPLOMATIC PRACTICE (Gore–Booth ed., 5 ed. 1979).

Traditionally, there have been three theories justifying the grant of diplomatic privileges and immunities: "representative character," "extraterritoriality," and "functional necessity". *See* J. CRAIG BARKER, THE ABUSE OF DIPLOMATIC PRIVILEGES AND IMMUNITIES: A NECESSARY EVIL? 35–65 (1996). The "extraterritoriality" theory, which posits that the diplomat occupies an imaginary territory of the sending state while physically present in the receiving state, is more successful as a metaphor than as an actual guide to state practice. In recent times, the "extraterritoriality" theory is increasingly perceived as misleading and risky. Current norms are largely informed by a pragmatic shared understanding of the protections necessary for the successful discharge of the diplomatic function (the "functional necessity" theory) and, to a lesser extent, continued recognition that a diplomat stands in a representative character to her sovereign (the "representative character" theory). *Id.* In the modern era, diplomatic privileges and immunities are largely governed by multilateral conventions, particularly the 1961 Vienna Convention on Diplomatic Relations (see Documents Supplement) based on a set of draft articles prepared by the International Law Commission, and by national statutes implementing the 1961 Convention. *See, e.g.*, Diplomatic Relations Act, 22 U.S.C. § 254(a)-(e).

1. The Principle of Inviolability

The central norm of diplomatic privileges and immunities is the principle of inviolability. Simply put, diplomats cannot be subjected to ordinary criminal, civil or administrative processes in the receiving state, unless their diplomatic immunity has been waived or if they commit international crimes, as noted below. The principle of inviolability embraces a number of complex rules, including the designation of persons, places and objects (such as the diplomatic bag) that enjoy it;[3] the scope of exemptions from certain regulations of the receiving state;[4] the mechanisms by which immunity from judgment and execution may be waived;[5]

3. 1961 Convention arts. 14, 19, 24, 27, 37, 38.

4. For example, accredited diplomats and members of their households are exempt from the customs, tax, social security and military service laws of the receiving state. 1961 Convention, arts. 23, 28, 33, 34, 35, 36, 37.

5. 1961 Convention art. 32. Waiver must be by the state (art. 32(1)) and must be express (art. 32(2)); a separate waiver is necessary for execution of any judgment (art. 32(4)). A diplomatic agent, by initiating proceedings in the receiving state, will be treated as waiving immunity with respect to any counterclaims directly connected to the principal claim (art. 32(3)).

and the consequences of a refusal by the sending state to waive immunity.[6] However, under international law, diplomats are not immune from prosecution for international crimes.

Two well-publicized cases illustrate the operation of diplomatic privileges and immunities with respect to ordinary domestic offenses. While in general the rate of criminal conduct by diplomats is low, traffic accidents, including fatal collisions involving alcohol, are not uncommon.[7] Two diplomats who in 1996 and 1997 caused fatal traffic accidents in France[8] and the United States,[9] respectively, were subjected to criminal prosecution after their diplomatic immunity was formally waived by their sending states under strong pressure of public opinion. If immunity

6. The primary mechanism is the withdrawal of the diplomat by the sending state, sometimes following a declaration of *persona non grata* by the receiving state. 1961 Convention, art. 9. 1961 Convention art. 31(4) provides that a diplomat is not immune from the jurisdiction of her sending state for acts committed in the receiving state, but there is no requirement that the sending state provide relief to those aggrieved by the diplomat's conduct.

7. A study by the U.K. Foreign and Commonwealth Office of incidents between 1974 and 1983 involving diplomats, technical and administrative staff, and family members thereof attached to missions in London, indicated 546 occasions in which such persons escaped arrest because of the immunity granted by Articles 29 and 31 of the 1961 Convention. Of these, 228 were traffic offenses and 233 were theft offenses, primarily shoplifting. Additionally, in 1983 alone 102,210 parking fines were ignored by persons protected by the Convention in the U.K. Barker, *supra* at 8–9. In the United States, a Department of State study of the period between August 1982 and February 1988 disclosed 147 criminal cases in which diplomatic immunities were invoked, and an additional 44 criminal cases involving persons attached to United Nations missions in New York (not including traffic offenses). *Id.* at 10.

8. Zaire's ambassador to France, Ramazani Baya, speeding to a meeting with then-President Mobutu Sese Seko at his holiday home, caused the deaths of two boys in a crosswalk. Julian Nundy, *Diplomat Kills French Boy in Pedestrian Crossing*, Daily Telegraph, Nov. 26, 1996. Baya's diplomatic immunity was waived by Zaire two months after the accident, under public pressure. See Anne Swardson, *No Jail Time Proposed for Zairian Envoy*, Wash. Post, Mar. 26, 1997.

9. In January 1997 a senior diplomat from Georgia, Gueorgui Makharadze, was involved in a five-car collision in Washington, D.C., that resulted in the death of a 16 year old girl. While early reports indicated that the Georgian Government intended to withdraw Makharadze, instead his diplomatic immunity was waived by President Eduard Shevardnadze following a personal appeal by Secretary of State Warren Christopher. Steven Lee Myers, *Georgia Prepared to Waive Immunity of Top Diplomat*, N.Y. Times, Jan. 11, 1997. Members of Congress, including Senator Judd Gregg (R.-N.H.), had threatened to suspend foreign assistance to Georgia if Makharadze's immunity was not waived. U.S. Department of State Daily Press Briefing, Jan. 13, 1997, M2 Presswire. Such waivers are rarely granted, the most common resolution being the withdrawal of the diplomat, or in some minor cases the suspension of their diplomatic driving licenses. *Russia, Kyrgyzstan Won't Lift Diplomats' Immunity*, Reuters North American Wire, May 14, 1997. In 1995, the Department of State requested waivers of diplomatic immunity in nine serious cases and fifty-three misdemeanors; fifteen requests were granted, all involving misdemeanors. Brooke A. Masters, *Former Diplomat Faces Sexual Assault Trial*, Wash. Post, April 16, 1997. In 1989, a Belgian soldier assigned as a clerk at the Belgian embassy in Washington was convicted of murder in Florida after Belgium agreed to waive his diplomatic immunity, on the condition that he not be sentenced to the death penalty. *Belgian Soldier Convicted of Murder in Florida*, Reuters, Aug. 16, 1989. The general practice of the United States regarding U.S. diplomats involved in traffic offenses is similarly to withdraw the diplomat rather than to waive immunity. U.S. Department of State Daily Press Briefing, August 20, 1997, *available at* http://www.state.gov (involving withdrawal of U.S. diplomat whose car struck a pedestrian in Moscow, prior to any request for waiver of his diplomatic immunity).

had not been waived in these cases, the receiving state could have requested the sending state to withdraw the diplomat or, even more pointedly, declare the diplomat *persona non grata*, essentially requiring his departure. 1961 Convention, art. 9.

Diplomats are declared *persona non grata* only in rare cases. This was done, for example, in a notorious case in the United Kingdom in 1984 where a police officer was killed by shots fired from the premises of the Libyan mission; the mission was closed and all personnel departed the United Kingdom under a grant of safe passage, but no one was prosecuted for the constable's murder. See BARKER, *supra* at 1–4. A dispute between Turkey and Switzerland involving the shooting death of a Kurdish demonstrator in Bern, killed by shots fired from the Turkish embassy, resulted in the withdrawal of the Turkish ambassador and five other staff members (despite Swiss requests for waiver of their diplomatic immunity), and the retaliatory expulsion of the Swiss ambassador and two aides from Turkey. See *Turkey Expels Swiss Ambassador, Moves Berne Envoy*, Reuters N. Am. Wire, Aug. 24, 1993.

Diplomatic immunity protects family members of accredited diplomats, administrative and technical staff and, to a lesser extent, servants of diplomats. See 1961 Conv. art. 37. It generally extends to personal conduct as well as to acts committed as part of the diplomatic function, though the 1961 Convention specifies that no immunity is enjoyed for commercial and professional activity in the receiving state, not related to the diplomatic function. See *id.* art. 42. The "diplomatic bag" by which communications are sent between the mission and the sending state is also largely inviolable, despite risks that it can be abused for criminal, terrorist, and subversive activities. See *id.* art. 27. The duration of diplomatic immunity is geared to the period of appointment.[10] Courts in the United States generally suspend processes brought against diplomats for nonimmune conduct committed prior to the acquisition of diplomatic status. *See, e.g.*, Arcaya v. Paez, 145 F.Supp. 464 (S.D.N.Y.1956), *aff'd*, 244 F.2d 958 (2d Cir.1957) (libel action).

RESTATEMENT OF THE FOREIGN RELATIONS LAW OF THE UNITED STATES § 464 (3 ed. 1987)

A diplomatic agent of a state, accredited to and accepted by another state, is immune

(1) from the exercise by the receiving state of jurisdiction to prescribe in respect of acts or omissions in the exercise of the agent's official functions, as well as from other regulation that would be incompatible with the agent's diplomatic status; and

(2) from arrest, detention, criminal process, and, in general, civil process in the receiving state.

10. Diplomatic immunity, for example, is lost when the receiving state withdraws recognition of the sending state's embassy. The U.S. Department of State ordered the closing of the embassy of Afghanistan in August 1997 because of controversy and confusion over competing claims to power among Afghan factions. U.S. Department of State Daily Press Briefing, Aug. 14, 1997, *available at* http://www.state.gov.

Note

1. The *Restatement* draws an important distinction between immunity from the receiving state's jurisdiction to prescribe (which includes exemptions from taxes, military service, etc.) and a diplomat's immunity from the receiving state's jurisdiction to adjudicate, which is much broader. It should be noted that diplomats have an obligation to obey the laws of the receiving state, particularly its criminal law, and this obligation is explicitly affirmed in Article 41(1) of the 1961 Convention.Because diplomats have an obligation to obey these laws, their immunity from criminal processes is subject to waiver at the discretion of the sending state. 1961 Convention, art. 32. Concerning civil liability, *see also id.* art. 31(1)(c).

Problem

The Mayor of New York City provoked a heated controversy during 1997 by announcing a plan to crack down on parking violations committed by diplomatic personnel attached to foreign missions located in New York and accredited to the United Nations. An incident in December 1996, during which two diplomats from Russia and Belarus had a violent encounter with New York police over a parked car with diplomatic plates, contributed to the Mayor's insistence that a crackdown was imperative.[11] The key points in the Mayor's proposal[12] were the following:

1. The plan would apply to vehicles with federally-issued license plates of the "D" (members of diplomatic staff of permanent missions to the U.N.), "A" (senior U.N. officials enjoying diplomatic status in the U.S.) and "C" (consular corps) categories.

2. New York would insure that each mission would have two designated parking spaces for the mission and one additional space for the ambassador's residence.

3. New York would establish a "hot line" by which mission personnel could report unauthorized vehicles in reserved diplomatic spaces, to be towed by police.

4. New York would establish a special office in its Department of Finance to review parking tickets issued to vehicles with "D," "A," or "C" plates, to insure that invalid tickets would be dismissed. Valid tickets would be reported on a monthly basis to each mission. Drivers would be required either to pay the ticket or to contest it in a timely fashion.

5. New York would designate as "scofflaws" those drivers with one or more outstanding violations for a period of 12 months. The State Department would request the surrender of the diplomatic plates of any such

11. In June 1997, the U.S. Department of State formally requested the waiver of diplomatic immunity for the two envoys to stand charges for driving while intoxicated, resisting arrest and disorderly conduct. Russia's UN ambassador characterized the event quite differently, as a police beating. Evelyn Leopold, *State Dep't Seek Immunity Waiver for U.N. Diplomats*, Reuters N. Am. Wire, June 5, 1997. News reports indicate that New York issued 116,345 parking tickets in 1996 to diplomatic personnel, most of which went unpaid. *Parking: Giuliani Says U.N. Can Hit Road*, SEATTLE TIMES, Apr. 11, 1997, at A10.

12. The proposal was circulated as a U.N. document by the Chairman of the Committee on Relations with the Host Country of the General Assembly. New York City Diplomatic Parking Programme, U.N. Doc. A/Ac.154/305 (1997).

vehicle, which could not be legally operated until adjudication of the outstanding violation. If a "scofflaw" vehicle is towed, the plates would be removed and the vehicle would be impounded. The vehicle could not legally be operated until properly registered in conformity with State Department regulations.

6. Vehicles that have been ticketed for parking in front of a fire hydrant after 1 January 1997 would be placed in "scofflaw" status if an additional health and safety violation remained unadjudicated for a period of 30 days, subjecting it to treatment as outlined above.

Implementation of this policy was delayed because of strenuous objections by members of the U.N. General Assembly Committee on Relations with the Host Country. At the request of the Committee, the U.N. Legal Counsel issued an opinion on the consistency of New York's plan with pertinent international norms, including the 1961 Convention.[13] The Legal Counsel noted the following:

> [R]emoval of license plates from vehicles towed to a place of safe keeping, and non-release of a diplomatic vehicle for operation until certain conditions are met, such as payment of a fine and/or a charge for its towing or safe keeping ... would appear to be enforcement measures and amount to an exercise of jurisdiction and, therefore, inconsistent with article 31 of the Vienna Convention, article IV and V of the 1946 Convention[14] and article V of the Headquarters Agreement.[15]
>
> In general, measures aimed at depriving a diplomatic agent of the right to drive by withdrawal of license plates, registration or other pertinent legal documents ... are tantamount to an exercise of jurisdiction of the host country and thus are in contravention of the relevant provisions of article 31 of the Vienna Convention.... More importantly, they would be inconsistent with the host country's obligation to facilitate the functioning of the missions accredited to the United Nations and of their members.

The Legal Counsel acknowledged that the requirements of public safety justify the towing of diplomatic vehicles parked in a manner creating a public hazard, but any such vehicle must be made available when reclaimed, "and payment of a fine or charge cannot be made a precondition for its recovery." Letter, *id.* at para. 27. Tickets for ordinary parking violations may be issued, but any payments are voluntary and do not amount to a

13. Letter Dated 21 March 1997 from the Chairman of the Committee on Relations with the Host Country Addressed to the Members of the Committee, U.N. Doc. A/AC.154/307, annex (1997).

14. The 1946 Convention on the Privileges and Immunities of the United Nations, 1 U.N.T.S. 15, provides, in Article IV, section 11(g), that representatives of U.N. member states are entitled to the privileges, immunities and facilities "as diplomatic envoys enjoy." Article V, section 19 provides that the Secretary–General and other senior U.N. officials are entitled the "the privileges and immunities, exemptions and facilities accorded to diplomatic envoys, in accordance with international law."

15. The 1947 Headquarters Agreement between the United Nations and the United States, 11 U.N.T.S. 11, provides in its Article V, section 15 that ambassadors and accredited diplomats at missions accredited to the U.N. "shall ... be entitled in the territory of the United States to the same privileges and immunities, subject to corresponding conditions and obligations, as it accords to diplomatic envoys accredited to it."

waiver of diplomatic immunity. *Id.* at para. 26. Implementation of New York's program was deferred while the United States attempted to respond to the Legal Counsel's concerns. U.N. Press Release HQ/577, 2 July 1997, *available at* http://www.un.org.

In your opinion, did New York's proposal envision the imposition of "enforcement" measures inconsistent with Article 31 of the 1961 Convention?

Notes and Questions

1. Does Section 464(1) of the Restatement imply an exception to immunity with respect to non-official acts or acts *ultra vires*? Should there be such an exception? The Restatement notes that Article 41(1) of the Consular Convention extends general immunity from pretrial arrest and detention, " 'except in the case of a grave crime and pursuant to a decision by the competent judicial authority.' " *Id.* § 465, cmt. b; *see also id.* cmts. c-d. *See also* Ali Aidi, *et al.* v. Yaron, Civ. Action No. 87–1216, slip. op. (D.D.C. 1987), *reprinted in part in* Paust, Bassiouni, *et al.*, International Criminal Law 79 (2 ed. 2000). Article 31(1)(c) of the 1961 Vienna Convention on Diplomatic Relations addresses an exception concerning "an action [in the receiving state] relating to any professional or commercial activity ... outside his official functions."

2. In the French case of *Abetz*, it was held that diplomatic immunity was not relevant to a war crimes prosecution, since the legal basis for prosecution rests with offenses against the community of nations. See 46 Am. J. Int'l L. 161, 162 (1952) (French Cour de Cassation 1950). See also Paust, Bassiouni, *et al.*, International Criminal Law 27–31, 33, 53, 79, 136, 1010 (2 ed. 2000); United States v. Weizsaecker, *et al.* (The Ministries Case), 16 Int'l L. Rpts. 361 (1949), XII, XIII, XIV Trials of War Criminals (1950–51) (diplomatic immunity applies only to legitimate acts of state and not to violations of international law); United States v. Furlong (The Pirates), 18 U.S. (5 Wheat.) 184, 201–02 (1820) (fact person who violated international law had a commission from a foreign government did not allow immunity from criminal sanctions); 2 Op. Att'y Gen. 725, 726 (1835) (Vattel [1758] thinks that a foreign consul should be immune " 'unless he violate the law of nations by some enormous crime' "); Triquet v. Bath, 3 Burr. 1478 (K.B. 1764) ("This privilege of foreign ministers ... depends upon the law of nations"). Also recall Article 27 of the Statute of the ICC.

3. Why do the U.S. Constitution, Article III, Section 2, clause 1, and the Judiciary Act of 1789, ch. 20, § 13, 1 Stat. 73 (1789), address suits "against ambassadors," "public ministers," and "foreign States"?

4. During the NATO bombing of Yugoslavia in May 1999, the Chinese embassy in Belgrade was damaged and three Chinese nationals were killed. The United States explained that the bombing was a mistake, its military having relied on inaccurate four-year old maps. If so, did the bombing violate the 1961 Vienna Convention on Diplomatic Relations? Did the subsequent attacks on the U.S. embassy compound in Beijing by Chinese civilians engaged in while Chinese police stood by and official Chinese accusations had aroused the crowd?

The United States voluntarily paid $4.5 million to the families of those killed and to other victims of the bombing of the Chinese embassy. China and the U.S. agreed to pay for damage to each other's diplomatic premises through bilateral negotiations.

2. *Obligation to Protect Diplomatic Personnel*

The principle of inviolability is not only a negative restraint upon enforcement action by the receiving state, but under modern standards imposes an affirmative obligation of protection. Article 29 of the 1961 Convention requires receiving states to treat diplomats "with due respect" and to "take all appropriate steps to prevent any attack on [their] person, freedom or dignity." The obligation of protection was further elaborated in the 1973 Convention on the Prevention and Punishment of Crimes Against Internationally Protected Persons, including Diplomatic Agents, 1035 U.N.T.S. 167, 28 U.S.T. 1975, T.I.A.S. No. 8532. Implementing the latter Convention, the United States has made it a crime to assault, strike, wound, imprison or inflict violence upon any internationally protected person. 18 U.S.C. § 112. The Iranian hostage crisis of 1979–1980 involved a notorious episode of violence against internationally protected persons, providing the International Court of Justice an opportunity to elucidate the obligation of protection assumed by states parties under the 1961 Convention. The Court had jurisdiction pursuant to the Optional Protocol to the 1961 Convention, to which both the United States and Iran were parties and which provides for compulsory jurisdiction over disputes arising under the 1961 Convention.

U.S. DIPLOMATIC AND CONSULAR STAFF IN TEHRAN CASE (UNITED STATES v. IRAN)

1980 I.C.J. 3.

[In November 1979, armed militants overran the premises of the United States embassy in Tehran, Iran, taking its personnel hostage and seizing its property and archives. The ICJ held, by 13 votes to 2, that Iran had violated and was in continuing violation of international law; unanimously, that Iran must release the hostages immediately; and by 12 votes to 3, that Iran must pay reparations to the United States. Iran did not comply directly with the Judgment. The hostages were released in January 1981 pursuant to a bilateral agreement between the United States and Iran.]

58. No suggestion has been made that the militants, when they executed their attack on the Embassy, had any form of official status as recognized "agents" or organs of the Iranian State. Their conduct in mounting the attack, overrunning the Embassy and seizing its inmates as hostages cannot, therefore, be regarded as imputable to that State on that basis....

61. The conclusion just reached ... does not mean that Iran is, in consequence, free of any responsibility in regard to those attacks; for its

own conduct was in conflict with its international obligations. By a number of provisions of the Vienna Conventions of 1961 and 1963 [1963 Vienna Convention on Consular Relations, 596 U.N.T.S. 261, extracts in the Documents Supplement; see also Section 3 C 2], Iran was placed under the most categorical obligations, as a receiving State, to take appropriate steps to ensure the protection of the United States Embassy and Consulates, their staffs, their archives, their means of communication and the freedom of movement of the members of their staffs....

63. [T]he Iranian Government failed altogether to take any "appropriate steps" to protect the premises, staff and archives of the United States' mission against attack by the militants, and to take any steps either to prevent this attack or to stop it before it reached its completion....

67. This inaction by the Iranian Government by itself constituted clear and serious violation of Iran's obligations to the United States under the provisions of Article 22, paragraph 2, and Articles 24, 25, 26, 27 and 29 of the 1961 Vienna Convention on Diplomatic Relations....

69. The second phase of the events which are the subject of the United States' claims comprises the whole series of facts which occurred following the completion of the occupation.... [T]he action required of the Iranian Government by the Vienna Conventions and by general international law was manifest. Its plain duty was at once to make every effort, and to take every appropriate step, to bring these flagrant infringements of the inviolability of the premises, archives and diplomatic and consular staff of the United States Embassy to a speedy end, ... and in general to re-establish the status quo and to offer reparation for the damage....

73. The seal of official government approval was finally set on this situation by a decree issued on 17 November 1979 by the Ayatollah Khomeini.... [He declared] that the premises of the Embassy and the hostages would remain as they were until the United States had handed over the former Shah for trial and returned his property to Iran....

74. The policy thus announced by the Ayatollah Khomeini ... was complied with by other Iranian authorities and endorsed by them repeatedly.... The result of that policy was fundamentally to transform the legal nature of the situation created by the occupation of the Embassy and the detention of its diplomatic and consular staff as hostages. The approval given to these facts by the Ayatollah Khomeini and other organs of the Iranian State, and the decision to perpetuate them, translated continuing occupation of the Embassy and detention of the hostages into acts of that State. The militants, authors of the invasion and jailers of the hostages, had now become agents of the Iranian State for whose acts the State itself was internationally responsible....

76. [The actions of the Iranian authorities] clearly gave rise to repeated and multiple breaches of the applicable provisions of the Vienna Conventions even more serious than those which arose from their failure

to take any steps to prevent the attacks on the inviolability of these premises and staff....

77. In the first place, these facts constituted breaches additional to those already committed of paragraph 2 of Article 22 of the 1961 Vienna Convention on Diplomatic Relations which requires Iran to protect the premises of the mission against any intrusion or damage and to prevent any disturbance of its peace or impairment of its dignity. Paragraphs 1 and 3 of that Article have also been infringed, and continue to be infringed, since they forbid agents of a receiving State to enter the premises of a mission without consent, or to undertake any search, requisition, attachment or like measure on the premises. Secondly, they constitute continuing breaches of Article 29 of the Convention which forbids any arrest or detention of a diplomatic agent and any attack on his person, freedom or dignity. Thirdly, the Iranian authorities are without doubt in continuing breach of the provisions of Articles 25, 26 and 27 of the 1961 Vienna Convention ... concerning facilities for the performance of functions, freedom of movement and communications for diplomatic and consular staff....

86. The rules of diplomatic law, in short, constitute a self-contained regime which, on the one hand, lays down the receiving State's obligations regarding the facilities, privileges and immunities to be accorded to diplomatic missions and, on the other, foresees their possible abuse by members of the mission and specifies the means at the disposal of the receiving State to counter any such abuse. These means are, by their nature, entirely efficacious, for unless the sending State recalls the member of the mission objected to forthwith, the prospect of the almost immediate loss of his privileges and immunities, because of the withdrawal by the receiving State of his recognition as a member of the mission, will in practice compel that person, in his own interest, to depart at once. But the principle of the inviolability of the persons of diplomatic agents and the premises of diplomatic missions is one of the very foundations of this long-established régime.... The fundamental character of the principle of inviolability is, moreover, strongly underlined by the provisions of Article 44 and 45 of the Convention of 1961....

Even in the case of armed conflict or in the case of a breach in diplomatic relations those provisions require that both the inviolability of the members of a diplomatic mission and of the premises, property and archives of the mission must be respected by the receiving State....

Notes and Questions

1. Violence against or interference with diplomats, mission premises, or the diplomatic bag is a tempting tactic for political groups with grievances against either the sending or receiving state. Examples include hostage-taking by guerrillas of the Tupac Amaru at the Japanese embassy in Lima,

Peru in 1997;[16] the bombing of the Israeli embassy in London in July 1994;[17] and action by members of a postal union in Australia to halt or delay delivery of mail (including in one instance the diplomatic bag) to the French embassy and consulates, in protest against France's resumption of nuclear testing in the Pacific in 1995.[18] Do the provisions of the 1961 Convention provide adequate guidance concerning the scope of the affirmative obligation of the receiving state to prevent such violence and interference?

2. Read Articles 22(2) and 29 of the 1961 Convention in the Documents Supplement. Did Peru breach the 1961 Convention by waiting four months prior to storming the Japanese embassy and freeing the hostages?

B. Consular Immunities

Like diplomatic relations, consular relations are established by bilateral agreement. However, a severance of diplomatic relations or closure of an embassy does not necessarily sever consular relations. RESTATEMENT § 465, RN 2. Consular functions are varied and may be exercised at embassies or at separate consular posts. The widely ratified 1963 Vienna Convention on Consular Relations provides a comprehensive codification of principles relating to consular privileges and immunities. See Documents Supplement. Article 5 of that Convention lists a wide variety of consular functions, and includes protecting the nationals of the sending state; furthering economic, commercial, cultural and scientific relations; issuing passports and travel documents; safeguarding the interests of nationals in inheritance matters, and of nationals who are minors or incompetent; representing or obtaining representation for nationals before tribunals of the receiving state; transmitting judicial and other official documents; and supervising ships and aircraft and providing assistance to their crews. Consular privileges and immunities resemble diplomatic privileges and immunities.

RESTATEMENT OF THE FOREIGN RELATIONS LAW OF THE UNITED STATES § 465 (3 ed. 1987)

(1) A consular officer of a state, commissioned to and accepted by another state, is immune

(a) from an exercise by the receiving state of jurisdiction to prescribe that interferes with the officer's official functions, and

16. Calvin Sims, *Rescue in Peru*, N.Y. TIMES, Apr. 24, 1997.

17. *Bombing in London Hits Israeli Embassy*, N.Y. TIMES, July 27, 1994.

18. See *Consideration of Effective Measures to Enhance the Protection, Security and Safety of Diplomatic and Consular Missions and Representatives, Report of the Secretary–General*, U.N. Doc. A/INF/50/3 at 11–12 (1995) (in a letter to the Secretary–General, France's Minister for Foreign Affairs stated that Australia's failure to prevent interference with diplomatic correspondence and blockages of the entrance to the embassy violated arts. 22(2), 25 and 27 of the 1961 Convention). *See also Consideration of Effective Measures to Enhance the Protection, Security and Safety of Diplomatic and Consular Missions and Representatives, Report of the Secretary–General*, U.N. Doc. A/51/257 at 6–7 (containing Australia's reply, indicating that negotiations with the unions had restored mail service to the French embassy and consulates and that several persons were being prosecuted for breaking into the grounds of the embassy, but that picketing at its entrance involved "no breaches of the law" and would not be restrained by Australia).

from other regulation that would be unreasonable to apply to persons of such status; and

(b) from arrest, detention, and criminal or civil process in respect of acts or omissions in the exercise of the officer's official functions.

(2) Where Subsection (1)(b) provides no immunity from criminal process, a consular officer is subject to arrest and detention pending trial only in a case of a grave crime and pursuant to a decision of a competent judicial authority, in which case criminal proceedings must be instituted with a minimum of delay.

Note

1. The primary difference between consular and diplomatic immunities is the limitation of the former to acts within the scope of the consul's official functions. See 1963 Convention, art. 43(1). A consular officer may be required to appear in criminal or civil proceedings in order to plead and prove that her acts were committed within the scope of her consular duties. While the U.S. Department of State will provide a certification of consular status, it is ordinarily left to the courts to determine whether the act giving rise to the criminal or civil proceedings was within the scope of official duties. *See* RESTATEMENT § 465, RN 1; Koeppel & Koeppel v. Federal Republic of Nigeria, 704 F.Supp. 521 (S.D.N.Y.1989) (summary judgment granted to Nigerian consul general because his grant of permission to Nigerian national to spend night in consulate, which was forbidden by the lease and resulted in fire damage to the premises, was an exercise of his consular duties); *see generally,* LUKE T. LEE, CONSULAR LAW AND PRACTICE (2d ed. 1991). Consuls perform important functions in assisting their nationals who are facing criminal prosecution in a state and must have access to an accused in order to perform certain functions.

C. Immunities of International Organizations

The immunities of international organizations and their officials is one aspect of the growing body of international law on their identity and personality. The theoretical basis for immunities for international organizations differs somewhat from that of diplomatic or consular immunity, because of the absence of the traditional dynamic of reciprocity in the relationship between the organization and the receiving state. The issue of the immunity of international organizations and their officials is of especial importance to those states, including the United States, within which the organizations have their headquarters and greatest concentration of personnel.

The immunities of international organizations and their representatives are specified in their charters (for example, in Article 105 of the United Nations Charter); treaties specifically addressing their immunities (for example, the 1946 Convention on the Privileges and Immunities of the United Nations, *supra*); in agreements with host states (for example, the Agreement Between the United Nations and the United States Regarding the Headquarters of the United Nations, 11 U.N.T.S.

11, T.I.A.S. No. 1676); and in statutes (for example, the International Organizations Immunities Act, 22 U.S.C. § 288). *See generally,* C.W. JENKS, INTERNATIONAL IMMUNITIES (1961); DEREK BOWETT, THE LAW OF INTERNATIONAL INSTITUTIONS (4th ed. 1982).

The immunities of international organizations and their officials are essentially functional (*i.e.,* limited to those immunities necessary to the performance of the organization's functions). *See* RESTATEMENT §§ 467–469. In contrast, diplomats representing states before those organizations generally are entitled to full diplomatic immunity. *Id.* § 470. *See supra* Section 3 A. 1 for a discussion of the controversy over parking enforcement against members of missions accredited to the UN in New York.

The treatment of the immunities of international organizations in the United States is illustrated by cases such as Mendaro v. World Bank, 717 F.2d 610 (D.C.Cir.1983), which dismissed a sexual harassment lawsuit filed under Title VII of the Civil Rights Act of 1964, reading the Bank's waiver of immunity in its Articles of Agreement narrowly to encompass only those cases necessary to facilitate its banking activities.

United Nations officials are increasingly the target of violent action in situations of unrest or armed conflict, such as the violence after the independence vote organized by the U.N. in East Timor in 1999. Between 1992 and 1999, 180 U.N. staff were killed on duty.[19]

The I.C.J. issued an advisory opinion finding that the Special Rapporteur of the U.N. Commission on Human Rights on the Independence of Judges and Lawyers was immune from judicial process in Malaysia for remarks he made during a magazine interview concerning alleged favoritism in the Malaysian courts. Four lawsuits were filed against him by companies and lawyers who claimed that his remarks had libeled them. The Malaysian courts had refused to dismiss despite the U.N. Secretary General's finding that the Special Rapporteur's interview had been conducted as part of his United Nations duties and was therefore immune under the Convention on the Privileges and Immunities of the United Nations, which Malaysia has ratified. Further, Malaysian courts ordered the Special Rapporteur to pay sizeable costs related to his unsuccessful motion to dismiss on grounds of immunity. The I.C.J. rendered its advisory opinion at the request of the Economic and Social Council, the I.C.J. finding that the Special Rapporteur had been an expert on a mission within the meaning of Article VI, Section 22(b) of the Convention, and that the Malaysian Government was obliged to insure that its courts expeditiously dismiss the proceedings against him and hold him harmless. Difference Relating to Immunity from Legal Process of a Special Rapporteur of the Commission on Human Rights, 1999 I.C.J. ___ (29 Apr.), *reprinted in* 38 I.L.M. 873 (1999).

19. Judith Miller, *U.N.'s Workers Become Targets in Angry Lands*, N.Y. TIMES, Sept. 19, 1999, at A1.

SECTION 4. THE ACT OF STATE DOCTRINE

The act of state doctrine shares common roots with the principle of foreign sovereign immunity, but it is a distinct barrier to litigation. The act of state doctrine is a principle of comity, used by national courts to withhold judgment on the legality of public acts undertaken by a foreign government within its own territory. It is more deeply rooted in conflicts of laws principles[20] and constitutional separation of powers theory than in norms of public international law. Despite the Supreme Court's categorization of the act of state doctrine as a norm of federal common law in *Sabbatino*, it is not a uniquely American principle.[21]

The act of state doctrine may serve as the basis for dismissal of a civil suit, even where all requirements of subject matter and personal jurisdiction have been met, and even where none of the parties is a foreign state. Some of the prominent exceptions to foreign sovereign immunity under the restrictive theory have parallels in the act of state doctrine, for example "commercial activity" and "treaty" exceptions (*see infra* Sections 4 D and 4 E). Although the FSIA has significantly limited the role of the Executive Branch in determining questions of foreign sovereign immunity, the extent to which courts should seek and defer to the advice of the Executive in applying the act of state doctrine is one of the most contested issues surrounding the doctrine, badly splintering the U.S. Supreme Court in cases such as *First National City Bank, infra*, Section 4 C.

The act of state doctrine has many vocal critics, who regard it as an unwarranted abnegation of the judiciary's responsibility to provide justice to the victims of illegal acts of foreign states. *See, e.g.,* Michael Bazyler, *Abolishing the Act of State Doctrine*, 134 U. PA. L. REV. 325 (1986). Litigation involving expropriation and human rights effectively exposes the tension between the value of comity and competing claims

20. *See* Louis Henkin, *Act of State Today: Recollections in Tranquility*, 6 COLUM. J. TRANSNAT'L L. 175, 178 (1967) (observing that the act of state doctrine is in essence an exception to the general conflict of law principle permitting the forum state to refuse to give effect to a foreign law that is contrary to the public policy of the forum).

21. RESTATEMENT § 443, RN 12, surveys some leading decisions of foreign courts adopting a pose of judicial restraint especially where the legality of expropriation is in issue, *citing* A.M. Luther v. James Sagor & Co. (U.K.), [1921] 3 K.B. 532 (C.A.); Anglo–Iranian Oil Co. Ltd. v. S.U.P.O.R. Co. (Italy), [1955] INT'L L. RPTS. 23 (Civ. Ct. Rome, Sept., 13, 1954); Soc. Minera El Teniente, S.A. v. A.G. Norddeutsche Affinerie (Germ. Fed. Rep.), 12 I.L.M. 251 (Hamburg, Langericht Jan. 22, 1973). The U.K. House of Lords has adopted the U.S. Supreme Court's approach toward the act of state doctrine in expropriation cases. *See* Buttes Gas & Oil Co. v. Hammer, [1982] A.C. 888 (H.L.(E.)); Williams & Humbert Ltd. v. W.H. Trademarks (Jersey) Ltd., [1986] 2 W.L.R. 24 (H.L.(E.)). For commentary on the competing analyses of foreign practice by Justice Harlan and Justice White in *Sabbatino, see, e.g.,* William H. Reeves, *The Act of State—Foreign Decisions Cited in the* Sabbatino *Case: A Rebuttal and Memorandum of Law*, 33 FORDHAM L. REV. 599 (1965). The act of state doctrine did not bar the United Kingdom from finding General Augusto Pinochet of Chile extraditable to Spain for acts of official torture. *See* Section 2.B *supra*. Nor does it bar prosecution of those accused of international crime. *See, e.g.,* International Military Tribunal at Nuremberg, Opinion and Judgment (1946), *quoted in* PAUST, BASSIOUNI, *ET AL.*, INTERNATIONAL CRIMINAL LAW 28, 31 (2 ed. 2000); *id.* at 27–33, 38, 132, 171.

for redress for violations of international norms, contributing to an apparent erosion in the doctrine.

A. *Foundations: Underhill and Sabbatino*

The U.S. Supreme Court's opinions in *Underhill* and *Sabbatino* respectively locate the historical and theoretical basis for the act of state doctrine and delineate its modern contours. Did *Sabbatino* expose a deep division on the Court with respect to the U.S. judiciary's role in policing breaches of international law by foreign states or was there significant disagreement whether relevant international legal standards actually existed?

UNDERHILL v. HERNANDEZ

168 U.S. 250 (1897).

FULLER, C.J.

[Editors' note: Underhill was a U.S. citizen who had contracted with the government of Venezuela to construct and operate a system of waterworks for Ciudad Bolivar, Venezuela. In August 1892, the forces of General Hernandez took over the city as part of a revolution led by Crespo. In October 1892 the Crespo forces achieved control over the entire country and were recognized by the United States as Venezuela's legitimate government on October 23rd. Underhill had sought a passport to leave Ciudad Bolivar when Hernandez entered the city, but he did not receive it until several months later and had been detained under house arrest. Having obtained personal jurisdiction over Hernandez by serving him while he was visiting New York, Underhill filed suit in federal court in New York seeking damages for unlawful detention and assault and battery by Hernandez' soldiers.]

Every sovereign State is bound to respect the independence of every other sovereign State, and the courts of one country will not sit in judgment on the acts of the government of another done within its own territory. Redress of grievances by reason of such acts must be obtained through the means open to be availed of by sovereign powers as between themselves.

Nor can the principle be confined to lawful or recognized governments, or to cases where redress can manifestly be had through public channels. The immunity of individuals from suits brought in foreign tribunals for acts done within their own States, in the exercise of governmental authority, whether as civil officers or as military commanders, must necessarily extend to the agents of governments ruling by paramount force as matter of fact. Where a civil war prevails ... generally speaking foreign nations do not assume to judge of the merits of the quarrel.... [A]cts of legitimate warfare cannot be made the basis of individual liability....

[T]he court is bound to take judicial notice ... [and] may consult the Department of State [concerning the facts of the Crespo revolution]....

It is idle to argue that the proceedings of those who thus triumphed should be treated as the acts of banditti or mere mobs.

The decisions cited on plaintiff's behalf are not in point. Cases respecting arrests by military authority in the absence of the prevalence of war; or the validity of contracts between individuals entered into in aid of insurrection; or the right of revolutionary bodies to vex the commerce of the world on its common highway without incurring the penalties denounced on piracy; and the like, do not involve the questions presented here.

We agree with the Circuit Court of Appeals that "the evidence upon the trial indicated that the purpose of the defendant in his treatment of the plaintiff was to coerce the plaintiff to operate his waterworks and his repair works for the benefit of the community and the revolutionary forces," and that "it was not sufficient to have warranted a finding by the jury that the defendant was actuated by malice or any personal or private motive," and we concur in its disposition of the rulings below. The decree of the Circuit Court is affirmed.

BANCO NACIONAL DE CUBA v. SABBATINO

376 U.S. 398 (1964).

HARLAN, J.

The act of state doctrine in its traditional formulation precludes the courts of this country from inquiring into the validity of the public acts a recognized foreign sovereign power committed within its own territory.

I

[In 1960, respondent Farr, Whitlock & Co. contracted to purchase Cuban sugar from Compania Azucarera Vertientes–Camaguey de Cuba (C.A.V.), a corporation organized under Cuban law whose capital stock was owned principally by United States residents. Farr, Whitlock agreed to pay for the sugar in New York. In 1960, Congress authorized and President Eisenhower implemented a reduction in Cuba's sugar quota. The Cuban Council of Ministers adopted Law No. 851, which characterized this reduction as an act of "aggression, for political purposes," justifying countermeasures. The law gave the Cuban Government power to expropriate property in which American nationals had an interest. The State Department found the Cuban law to be "in violation of ... international law ... [because it is] discriminatory, arbitrary and confiscatory." Cuba expropriated all property and enterprises of certain listed companies, including C.A.V. In order to obtain the consent of the Cuban Government to deliver the sugar in New York, Farr, Whitlock entered into contracts, identical to those it had made with C.A.V., with the Banco Para el Comercio Exterior de Cuba, an instrumentality of the Cuban Government.]

[Banco Exterior assigned the bills of lading to petitioner, also an instrumentality of the Cuban Government, which instructed its agent in

New York, Sociéte Générale, to deliver the bills and a sight draft to Farr, Whitlock in return for payment. In return for a promise not to turn the funds over to petitioner or its agent, C.A.V. agreed to indemnify Farr, Whitlock for any loss. Farr, Whitlock subsequently accepted the shipping documents, negotiated the bills of lading to its customer, and received payment for the sugar. However, it refused to hand over the proceeds to Sociéte Générale. Shortly thereafter, Farr, Whitlock was served with an order of the New York Supreme Court, which had appointed Sabbatino as Temporary Receiver of C.A.V.'s New York assets. Following this, Farr, Whitlock transferred the funds to Sabbatino.]

[Petitioner then instituted this action in the Federal District Court for the Southern District of New York to recover the proceeds from Farr, Whitlock and to enjoin the receiver from exercising any dominion over the proceeds. The District Court found the act of state doctrine inapplicable to acts in violation of international law and specifically "found the Cuban expropriation decree to violate such law in three separate respects: it was motivated by a retaliatory and not a public purpose; it discriminated against American nationals; and it failed to provide adequate compensation. Summary judgment against petitioner was accordingly granted." The Court of Appeals affirmed.].... We granted certiorari because the issues involved bear importantly on the conduct of the country's foreign relations and more particularly on the proper role of the Judicial Branch in this sensitive area.... For reasons to follow we decide that the judgment below must be reversed....

IV

The classic American statement of the act of state doctrine, which appears to have taken root in England as early as 1674, Blad v. Bamfield, 3 Swans. 604, 36 Eng.Rep. 992, and began to emerge in the jurisprudence of this country in the late eighteenth and early nineteenth centuries, *see e.g.*, Ware v. Hylton, 3 Dall. 199, 230 ... , is found in Underhill v. Hernandez, 168 U.S. 250, p. 252....

None of this Court's subsequent cases in which the act of state doctrine was directly or peripherally involved manifest any retreat from *Underhill. See* American Banana Co. v. United Fruit Co., 213 U.S. 347 ... ; Oetjen v. Central Leather Co., 246 U.S. 297 ... ; Ricaud v. American Metal Co., 246 U.S. 304 ... ; Shapleigh v. Mier, 299 U.S. 468 ... ; United States v. Belmont, 301 U.S. 324 ... ; United States v. Pink, 315 U.S. 203.... On the contrary in two of these cases, *Oetjen* and *Ricaud*, the doctrine as announced in *Underhill* was reaffirmed in unequivocal terms.

[In *Ricaud*, the Court observed that the act of state doctrine] does not deprive the courts of jurisdiction once acquired over a case. It requires only that when it is made to appear that the foreign government has acted in a given way on the subject-matter of the litigation, the details of such action or the merit of the result cannot be questioned but must be accepted by our courts as a rule for their decision. To accept a ruling authority and to decide accordingly is not a surrender or abandonment of jurisdiction but is an exercise of it.... [246 U.S. at 309]

In deciding the present case the Court of Appeals relied in part upon an exception to the unqualified teachings of *Underhill*, *Oetjen*, and *Ricaud* which that court had earlier indicated. In Bernstein v. Van Heyghen Freres Sociéte Anonyme, 2 Cir., 163 F.2d 246, suit was brought to recover from an assignee property allegedly taken, in effect, by the Nazi Government because plaintiff was Jewish. Recognizing the odious nature of this act of state, the court, through Judge Learned Hand, nonetheless refused to consider it invalid on that ground. Rather, it looked to see if the Executive had acted in any manner that would indicate that United States Courts should refuse to give effect to such a foreign decree. Finding no such evidence, the court sustained dismissal of the complaint. In a later case involving similar facts the same court again assumed examination of the German acts improper, Bernstein v. N.V. Nederlandsche–Amerikaansche Stoomvaart–Maatschappij, 2 Cir., 173 F.2d 71, but, quite evidently following the implications of Judge Hand's opinion in the earlier case, amended its mandate to permit evidence of alleged invalidity, 2 Cir., 210 F.2d 375, subsequent to receipt by plaintiff's attorney of a letter from the Acting Legal Adviser to the State Department written for the purpose of relieving the court from any constraint upon the exercise of its jurisdiction to pass on that question.

This Court has never had occasion to pass upon the so-called *Bernstein* exception, nor need it do so now ... [because the Executive Branch unambiguously supported Cuba's act of state claim before the Supreme Court.]

[Respondents argued, as the District Court and Court of Appeals ruled]: (1) that the doctrine does not apply to acts of state which violate international law, as is claimed to be the case here; (2) that the doctrine is inapplicable unless the Executive specifically interposes it in a particular case; and (3) that, in any event, the doctrine may not be invoked by a foreign government plaintiff in our courts.

V

Preliminarily, we discuss the foundations on which we deem the act of state doctrine to rest, and more particularly the question of whether state or federal law governs its application in a federal diversity case.

We do not believe that this doctrine is compelled either by the inherent nature of sovereign authority ... or by some principle of international law.... While historic notions of sovereign authority do bear upon the wisdom of employing the act of state doctrine, they do not dictate its existence.

That international law does not require application of the doctrine is evidenced by the practice of nations. Most of the countries rendering decisions on the subject fail to follow the rule rigidly [and] ... no claim has ever been raised before an international tribunal that failure to apply the act of state doctrine constitutes a breach of international obligation. [Editors' note: Justice Harlan cited numerous decisions from foreign courts, noting that some refuse to apply the doctrine where the act violates international law or is contrary to public order.] If international law does not prescribe use of the doctrine, neither does it forbid application of the rule even if it is claimed that the act of state in question violated international law.... Because of its peculiar nation-to-nation character the usual method for an individual to seek relief is to exhaust local remedies and then repair to the executive authorities of his own state to persuade them to champion his claim in diplomacy or before an international tribunal.... Although it is, of course, true that United States courts apply international law as a part of our own in appropriate circumstances ... , the public law of nations can hardly dictate to a country which is in theory wronged how to treat that wrong within its domestic borders.

The text of the Constitution does not require the act of state doctrine; it does not irrevocably remove from the judiciary the capacity to review the validity of foreign acts of state.

The act of state doctrine does, however, have "constitutional" underpinnings. It arises out of the basic relationships between branches of government in a system of separation of powers.... The doctrine as formulated in past decisions expresses the strong sense of the Judicial Branch that its engagement in the task of passing on the validity of foreign acts of state may hinder rather than further this country's pursuit of goals both for itself and for the community of nations as a whole in the international sphere. Many commentators disagree with this view; they have striven by means of distinguishing and limiting past decisions and by advancing various considerations of policy to stimulate a narrowing of the apparent scope of the rule....

[W]e are constrained to make it clear that an issue concerned with a basic choice regarding the competence and function of the Judiciary and the National Executive in ordering our relationships with other members of the international community must be treated exclusively as an aspect of federal law. It seems fair to assume that the Court did not have rules like the act of state doctrine in mind when it decided *Erie R. Co. v. Tompkins*. Soon thereafter, Professor Philip C. Jessup, now a judge of the International Court of Justice, recognized the potential dangers were *Erie* extended to legal problems affecting international relations. He cautioned that rules of international law should not be left to divergent and perhaps parochial state interpretations. His basic rationale is equally applicable to the act of state doctrine.

VI

If the act of state doctrine is a principle of decision binding on federal and state courts alike but compelled by neither international law nor the Constitution, its continuing vitality depends on its capacity to reflect the proper distribution of functions between the judicial and political branches of the Government on matters bearing upon foreign affairs. It should be apparent that the greater the degree of codification or consensus concerning a particular area of international law, the more appropriate it is for the judiciary to render decisions regarding it, since the courts can then focus on the application of an agreed principle to circumstances of fact rather than on the sensitive task of establishing a principle not inconsistent with the national interest or with international justice. It is also evident that some aspects of international law touch much more sharply on national nerves than do others; the less important the implications of an issue are for our foreign relations, the weaker the justification for exclusivity in the political branches. The balance of relevant considerations may also be shifted if the government which perpetrated the challenged act of state is no longer in existence, as in the *Bernstein* case, for the political interest of this country may, as a result, be measurably altered. Therefore, rather than laying down or reaffirming an inflexible and all-encompassing rule in this case, we decide only that the (Judicial Branch) will not examine the validity of a taking of property within its own territory by a foreign sovereign government, extant and recognized by this country at the time of suit, in the absence of a treaty or other unambiguous agreement regarding controlling legal principles, even if the complaint alleges that the taking violates customary international law.

There are few if any issues in international law today on which opinion seems to be so divided as the limitations on a state's power to expropriate the property of aliens.... [The opinion then noted the significant disagreement of "communist countries" and "newly independent and underdeveloped countries" with others concerning the content of international "rules" and "standards".]

The disagreement as to relevant international law standards reflects an even more basic divergence between the national interests of capital importing and capital exporting nations and between the social ideologies of those countries that favor state control of a considerable portion of the means of production and those that adhere to a free enterprise system. It is difficult to imagine the courts of this country embarking on adjudication in an area which touches more sensitively the practical and ideological goals of the various members of the community of nations. [At this point, Harlan added the following footnote, #34: There are, of course, areas of international law in which consensus as to standards is greater and which do not represent a battleground for conflicting ideologies. This decision in no way intimates that the courts of this country are broadly foreclosed from considering questions of international law.]

Following an expropriation of any significance, the Executive engages in diplomacy aimed to assure that United States citizens who are harmed are compensated fairly. Representing all claimants of this country, it will often be able, either by bilateral or multilateral talks, by submission to the United Nations, or by the employment of economic and political sanctions, to achieve some degree of general redress. Judicial determinations of invalidity of title can, on the other hand, have only an occasional impact, since they depend on the fortuitous circumstance of the property in question being brought into this country....

Piecemeal dispositions of this sort involving the probability of affront to another state could seriously interfere with negotiations being carried on by the Executive Branch and might prevent or render less favorable the terms of an agreement that could otherwise be reached....

The dangers of such adjudication are present regardless of whether the State Department has, as it did in this case, asserted that the relevant act violated international law....

When articulating principles of international law in its relations with other states, the Executive Branch speaks not only as an interpreter of generally accepted and traditional rules, as would the courts, but also as an advocate of standards it believes desirable for the community of nations and protective of national concerns....

Against the force of such considerations, we find respondents' countervailing arguments quite unpersuasive. Their basic contention is that United States courts could make a significant contribution to the growth of international law, a contribution whose importance, it is said, would be magnified by the relative paucity of decisional law by international bodies. But given the fluidity of present world conditions, the effectiveness of such a patchwork approach toward the formulation of an acceptable body of law concerning state responsibility for expropriations is, to say the least, highly conjectural. Moreover, it rests upon the sanguine presupposition that the decisions of the courts of the world's major capital exporting country and principal exponent of the free enterprise system would be accepted as disinterested expressions of sound legal principle by those adhering to widely different ideologies.

It is suggested that if the act of state doctrine is applicable to violations of international law, it should only be so when the Executive Branch expressly stipulates that it does not wish the courts to pass on the question of validity.... Often the State Department will wish to refrain from taking an official position, particularly at a moment that would be dictated by the development of private litigation but might be inopportune diplomatically.... We do not now pass on the *Bernstein* exception, but even if it were deemed valid, its suggested extension is unwarranted.

VII

Respondents offer another theory for treating the case differently because of Cuba's participation.... An analogy is drawn to the area of sovereign immunity, National City Bank v. Republic of China, 348 U.S. 356, in which, if a foreign country seeks redress in our courts, counterclaims are permissible. But immunity relates to the prerogative right not to have sovereign property subject to suit; fairness has been thought to require that when the sovereign seeks recovery, it be subject to legitimate counterclaims against it. The act of state doctrine, however, although it shares with the immunity doctrine a respect for sovereign states, concerns the limits for determining the validity of an otherwise applicable rule of law....

The judgment of the Court of Appeals is reversed and the case is remanded to the District Court for proceedings consistent with this opinion. It is so ordered.

WHITE, J., dissenting

I am dismayed that the Court has, with one broad stroke, declared the ascertainment and application of international law beyond the competence of the courts of the United States in a large and important category of cases.... This backward-looking doctrine, never before declared in this Court, is carried a disconcerting step further: not only are the courts powerless to question acts of state proscribed by international law but they are likewise powerless to refuse to adjudicate the claim founded upon a foreign law; they must render judgment and thereby validate the lawless act.... No other civilized country has found such a rigid rule necessary for the survival of the executive branch of its government; the executive of no other government seems to require such insulation from international law adjudications in its courts; and no other judiciary is apparently so incompetent to ascertain and apply international law.

II

That the act of state doctrine is rooted in a well-established concept of international law is evidenced by the practice of other countries. These countries ... afford substantial respect to acts of foreign states occurring within their territorial confines. Our act of state doctrine ... carries the territorial concept one step further. It precludes a challenge to the validity of foreign law on the ordinary conflict of laws ground of repugnancy to the public policy of the forum....

[S]uch deference reflects an effort to maintain a certain stability and predictability in transnational transactions, to avoid friction between nations, to encourage settlement of these disputes through diplomatic means and to avoid interference with the executive control of foreign relations....

Contrary to the assumption underlying the Court's opinion, these considerations are relative, their strength varies from case to case, and they are by no means controlling in all litigation involving the public acts of a foreign government....

III

I start with what I thought to be unassailable propositions: that our courts are obliged to determine controversies on their merits, in accordance with the applicable law; and that part of the law American courts are bound to administer is international law.

IV

All legitimate exercises of sovereign power, whether territorial or otherwise, should be exercised consistently with rules of international law.... [A foreign state] cannot with impunity ignore the rules governing the conduct of all nations and expect that other nations and tribunals will view its acts as within the permissible scope of territorial sovereignty.

Of course, there are many unsettled areas of international law, as there are of domestic law, and these areas present sensitive problems of accommodating the interests of nations that subscribe to divergent economic and political systems.... Also, it may be that domestic courts, as compared to international tribunals, or arbitral commissions, have a different and less active role to play in formulating new rules of international law or in choosing between rules not yet adhered to by any substantial group of nations. Where a clear violation of international law is not demonstrated, I would agree that principles of comity underlying the act of state doctrine warrant recognition and enforcement of the foreign act. But none of these considerations relieve a court of the obligation to make an inquiry into the validity of the foreign act, none of them warrant a flat rule of no inquiry at all.

V

There remains for consideration the relationship between the act of state doctrine and the power of the executive over matters touching upon the foreign affairs of the Nation. It is urged that the act of state doctrine is a necessary corollary of the executive's authority to direct the foreign relations of the United States....

A valid statute, treaty or executive agreement could, I assume, confine the power of federal courts to review or award relief in respect of foreign acts or otherwise displace international law as the rule of decision. I would not disregard a declaration by the Secretary of State or the President that an adjudication in the courts of the validity of a foreign expropriation would impede relations between the United States and the foreign government or the settlement of the controversy through diplomatic channels.

VI

Obviously there are cases where an examination of the foreign act and declaration of invalidity or validity might undermine the foreign policy of the Executive Branch and its attempts at negotiating a settlement for a nationalization of the property of Americans.... [But] a blanket presumption of nonreview in each case is inappropriate and a requirement that the State Department render a determination after reasonable notice, in each case, is necessary.

[A]ll the Department of State can legitimately request is nonexamination of the foreign act. It has no proper interest or authority in having courts decide a controversy upon anything less than all of the applicable law or to decide it in accordance with the executive's view of the outcome that best comports with the foreign or domestic affairs of the day.... The proper disposition is to stay the proceedings until circumstances permit an adjudication or to dismiss the action where an adjudication within a reasonable time does not seem feasible. To do otherwise would not be in accordance with the obligation of courts to decide controversies justly and in accordance with the law applicable to the case.

Notes and Questions

1. What type of acts of warfare did *Underhill* consider to be covered by the act of state doctrine? What type of exception to the doctrine is thus implied?

2. Although the act of state doctrine is not a norm of customary international law, both Justice Harlan and Justice White in *Sabbatino* surveyed state practice, drawing different conclusions as to whether other national judiciaries will examine the international illegality of sovereign acts, despite comity concerns. Does the majority opinion in *Sabbatino* categorically reject an "international illegality" exception to the act of state doctrine, at least for norms that are clear and universal? Does it recognize such an exception, contrary to Justice White's protestations? *See also* Kalamazoo Spice Extraction Co. v. Provisional Military Government of Socialist Ethiopia, 729 F.2d 422 (6th Cir.1984), excerpt reprinted below; Filartiga v. Pena–Irala, 630 F.2d 876, 880–81 (2d Cir.1980), in Chapter 2; Paust, *Federal Jurisdiction Over Extraterritorial Acts of Terrorism and Nonimmunity for Foreign Violators of International Law Under the FSIA and the Act of State Doctrine*, 23 VA. J. INT'L L. 191, 242–46 (1983); letter, 18 VA. J. INT'L L. 601 (1978).

3. The *Sabbatino* case was remanded, and both the District and Circuit courts reiterated the violation of international law exception to the act of state doctrine, but also relied alternatively on the First Hickenlooper Amendment. The case was then *cert. denied*: Banco Nacional de Cuba v. Farr, Whitlock & Co., 383 F.2d 166 (2d Cir.1967), *cert. denied*, 390 U.S. 956 (1968). Concerning nonapplicability of the act of state doctrine with respect to such illegal acts, normally because they are not considered to be "public" acts, but acts beyond the scope of lawful authority, see cases in Chapter 2, Section 2 D 2.

4. Chief Justice Fuller in *Underhill* stressed that legitimate acts of warfare are not regarded as unlawful or subject to adjudication in foreign courts. Today, Underhill's trauma might implicate norms of humanitarian and human rights law protecting the physical integrity of civilians during internal armed conflict and prohibiting such conduct as arbitrary detention.

5. Were a modern Underhill to sue Venezuela,[22] he might have difficulty overcoming the jurisdictional bar of § 1605(a)(5) of the FSIA because

22. Suing Hernandez, as the real Underhill did, would raise the murky issue whether individual officials (who are not the head of state) should be considered "agencies and instrumentalities" of a foreign state so as to enjoy immunity under § 1603(b). *See* Section 1 D 1, *supra*. It is interesting that, at a time when the United States retained the absolute doctrine of sovereign immunity, Chief Justice Fuller chose to address the issue as one of act of state rather than sovereign immunity, despite

extraterritorial torts generally do not fit within § 1605(a)(5). If the state is a sponsor of state terrorism, what other portions of § 1605 might be argued? Would the exception in §§ 1330(a) and 1604 be a viable alternative? Is it possible (depending upon the facts concerning the terms of the waterworks contract and the nexus between that contract and Underhill's trauma) that the modern Underhill's claim might be found to be "based upon" commercial activity with a sufficient link to the United States under § 1605(a)(2)? *But see Saudi Arabia v. Nelson, supra* Section 1 C 2 ii (suggesting that torture and arbitrary detention are by their nature noncommercial).

6. Should it be necessary, given the already great complexity posed by the FSIA, for the District Court to make a separate inquiry into the applicability of the act of state doctrine? Given the common roots of foreign sovereign immunity and act of state, should the FSIA provide the exclusive mechanism for balancing the competing concerns of comity and access to justice, at least in suits where the foreign state or state entity is a party? For a discussion of the lower courts' treatment of the act of state doctrine in human rights litigation, *see infra* Section 4 F; Chapter 2, Section 2 D 2.

B. *Second Hickenlooper Amendment*

Congress reacted with hostility to *Sabbatino* in 1964, directing U.S. courts to adjudicate certain expropriation claims notwithstanding the act of state doctrine. The Second Hickenlooper Amendment, codified at 22 U.S.C. § 2370(e)(2),[23] revised a provision in the Foreign Assistance Act of 1962 barring aid to states engaging in expropriations in violation of international law, as defined in the Act.[24] Unlike the later FSIA, the Second Hickenlooper Amendment specifies a direct role for the Executive Branch to notify the courts to withhold judgment out of concern for "foreign policy interests." Application of the Second Hickenlooper Amendment has been fairly grudging. *See, e.g.*, GARY B. BORN, INTERNA-

Hernandez' official, and distinctly nonpersonal (or non-"banditti"), role in Underhill's ordeal.

23. "Notwithstanding any other provision of law, no court in the United States shall decline on the ground of the federal act of state doctrine to make a determination on the merits of giving effect to the principles of international law in a case in which a claim of title or other right to property is asserted by any party including a foreign state (or party claiming through such state) based upon (or traced through) a confiscation or other taking after January 1, 1959, by an act of that state in violation of the principles of international law, including the principles of compensation and the other standards set out in this subsection: *Provided*, That this subparagraph shall not be applicable (1) in any case in which an act of a foreign state is not contrary to international law or with respect to a claim of title or other right to property acquired pursuant to an irrevocable letter of credit of not more than 180 days duration issued in good faith prior to the time of the confiscation or other taking, or (2) in any case with respect to which the president determines that application of the act of state doctrine is required in that particular case by the foreign policy interests of the United States and a suggestion to this effect is filed on his behalf in that case with the court."

24. 22 U.S.C. § 2370(e)(1) deals with instances where a foreign state has (after Jan. 1, 1962) nationalized or expropriated property owned by a U.S. citizen or an entity not less than 50% owned by U.S. citizens; repudiated or nullified contracts with a U.S. citizen or with entities not less that 50% U.S.-owned; or imposed or enforced discriminatory taxes or exactions, or restricted maintenance or operational conditions; or engaged in other actions with the effect of nationalizing or expropriating property so owned, where the foreign government fails within six months to arbitrate or settle the dispute and to provide speedy and adequate compensation.

TIONAL CIVIL LITIGATION IN UNITED STATES COURTS 744 (3d. ed 1996) (collecting cases); RESTATEMENT OF THE FOREIGN RELATIONS LAW OF THE UNITED STATES § 444 & RN 3 (3 ed. 1987).

C. The "Bernstein" Exception

FIRST NATIONAL CITY BANK v. BANCO NACIONAL DE CUBA

406 U.S. 759 (1972).

REHNQUIST, J.

[Editors' note: Petitioner in 1958 loaned $15 million to respondent's predecessor, secured by a pledge of United States Government bonds. The loan was renewed in 1959; in 1960 $5 million was repaid, the $10 million balance renewed for one year. In 1960 the Castro Government seized all of the branches of petitioner located in Cuba. The bank retaliated by selling the collateral securing the loan, and applying the proceeds of the sale to repayment of the principal and unpaid interest. An excess of at least $1.8 million over and above principal and unpaid interest was realized from the sale of the collateral. Respondent sued petitioner in the Federal District Court to recover this excess; petitioner, by way of setoff and counterclaim, asserted the right to recover damages as a result of the expropriation of its property in Cuba.]

We must here decide whether, in view of the substantial difference between the position taken in this case by the Executive Branch and that which it took in *Sabbatino*, the act of state doctrine prevents petitioner from litigating its counterclaim on the merits. We hold that it does not.

In the case now before us ... [t]he Legal Adviser of the Department of State advised ... that as a matter of principle where the Executive publicly advises the Court that the act of state doctrine need not be applied, the Court should proceed to examine the legal issues raised by the act of a foreign sovereign within its own territory as it would any other legal question before it.

The question that we must now decide is whether the so-called *Bernstein* exception to the act of state doctrine should be recognized....

The line of cases from this Court establishing the act of state doctrine justifies its existence primarily on the basis that juridical review of acts of state of a foreign power could embarrass the conduct of foreign relations by the political branches of the government....

The opinion of Scrutton, L.J., in Luther v. James Sagor & Co., (1921) 3 K.B. 532 ..., strongly suggests that under the English doctrine the Executive by representation to the courts may waive the application of the doctrine....

The act of state doctrine is grounded on judicial concern that application of customary principles of law to judge the acts of a foreign sovereign might frustrate the conduct of foreign relations by the political branches of the government. We conclude that where the Executive Branch, charged as it is with primary responsibility for the conduct of foreign affairs, expressly represents to the Court that application of the act of state doctrine would not advance the interests of American foreign policy, that doctrine should not be applied by the courts. In so doing, we of course adopt and approve the so-called *Bernstein* exception to the act of state doctrine....

Our holding is in no sense an abdication of the judicial function to the Executive Branch. The judiciary is ... free to decide the case without the limitations that would otherwise be imposed upon it by the judicially created act of state doctrine.

The act of state doctrine, as reflected in the cases culminating in *Sabbatino*, is a judicially accepted limitation on the normal adjudicative processes of the courts, springing from the thoroughly sound principle that on occasion individual litigants may have to forgo decision on the merits of their claims because the involvement of the courts in such a decision might frustrate the conduct of the Nation's foreign policy. It would be wholly illogical to insist that such a rule, fashioned because of fear that adjudication would interfere with the conduct of foreign relations, be applied in the face of an assurance from that branch of the Federal Government that conducts foreign relations that such a result would not obtain....

We therefore reverse the judgment of the Court of Appeals, and remand the case to it for consideration of respondent's alternative bases of attack on the judgment of the District Court.

DOUGLAS, J., concurring

It would offend the sensibilities of nations if one country, not at war with us, had our courthouse door closed to it. It would also offend our sensibilities if Cuba could collect the amount owed on liquidation of the collateral for the loan and not be required to account for any setoff. To allow recovery without more would permit Cuba to have its cake and eat it too. Fair dealing requires allowance of the setoff to the amount of the claim on which suit is brought....

If the amount of the setoff exceeds the asserted claim, then we would have a *Sabbatino* type of case.... I would disallow the judicial resolution of that dispute for the reasons stated in *Sabbatino* and by Mr. Justice Brennan, in the instant case....

POWELL, J., concurring

Although I concur in the judgment of reversal and remand, my reasons differ from those expressed by Mr. Justice Rehnquist and Mr. Justice Douglas.... [T]he reasoning of *Sabbatino* implicitly rejects [the *Bernstein*] exception. Moreover, I would be uncomfortable with a doctrine which would require the judiciary to receive the Executive's permission before invoking its jurisdiction....

Nor do I think the doctrine of separation of powers dictates such an abdication. To so argue is to assume that there is no such thing as international law but only international political disputes that can be resolved only by the exercise of power. Admittedly, international legal disputes are not as separable from politics as are domestic legal disputes, but I am not prepared to say that international law may never be determined and applied by the judiciary where there has been an "act of state." Until international tribunals command a wider constituency, the courts of various countries afford the best means for the development of a respected body of international law....

... The balancing of interests, recognized as appropriate by *Sabbatino*, requires a careful examination of the facts in each case and of the position, if any, taken by the political branches of government.... Unless it appears that an exercise of jurisdiction would interfere with delicate foreign relations conducted by the political branches, I conclude that federal courts have an obligation to hear cases such as this....

BRENNAN, J. (with whom STEWART, MARSHALL, and BLACKMUN, J.J.J., join), dissenting

Mr. Justice Rehnquist's opinion reasons that the act of state doctrine exists primarily, and perhaps even solely, as a judicial aid to the Executive to avoid embarrassment to the political branch in the conduct of foreign relations. Where the Executive expressly indicates that invocation of the rule will not promote domestic foreign policy interests, his opinion states the view, adopting the "*Bernstein*" exception, that the doctrine does not apply. This syllogism—from premise to conclusion—is, with all respect, mechanical and fallacious....

II

The United States has protested the nationalization by Cuba of property belonging to American citizens as a violation of international law. The United States has also severed diplomatic relations with that government. The very terms of the Legal Adviser's communication to this Court, moreover, anticipate a favorable ruling that the Cuban expropriation of petitioner's properties was invalid....

Sabbatino itself explained why in these circumstances the representations of the Executive in favor of removing the act of state bar cannot be followed: "It is highly questionable whether the examination of validity by the judiciary should depend on an educated guess by the Executive as to probable result and, at any rate, should a prediction be wrong, the Executive might be embarrassed in its dealings with other countries." *Id.*, at 436. Should the Court of Appeals on remand uphold the Cuban expropriation in this case, the Government would not only be embarrassed but would find its extensive efforts to secure the property of United States citizens abroad seriously compromised.

Thus, the assumption that the Legal Adviser's letter removes the possibility of interference with the Executive in the conduct of foreign affairs is plainly mistaken.

III

That, however, is not the crux of my disagreement with my colleagues who would uphold the "*Bernstein*" exception.

In short, *Sabbatino* held that the validity of a foreign act of state in certain circumstances is a "political question" not cognizable in our courts. Only one—and not necessarily the most important—of those circumstances concerned the possible impairment of the Executive's conduct of foreign affairs. Even if this factor were absent in this case because of the Legal Adviser's statement of position, it would hardly follow that the act of state doctrine should not foreclose judicial review of the expropriation of petitioner's properties. To the contrary, the absence of consensus on the applicable international rules, the unavailability of standards from a treaty or other agreement, the existence and recognition of the Cuban Government, the sensitivity of the issues to national concerns, and the power of the Executive alone to effect a fair remedy for all United States citizens who have been harmed all point toward the existence of a "political question".... The Executive Branch, however extensive its powers in the area of foreign affairs, cannot by simple stipulation change a political question into a cognizable claim.

Sabbatino, as my Brother Rehnquist's opinion notes, formally left open the validity of the "Bernstein" exception to the act of state doctrine. But that was only because the issue was not presented there. As six members of this Court recognize today, the reasoning of that case is clear that the representations of the Department of State are entitled to weight for the light they shed on the permutation and combination of factors underlying the act of state doctrine. But they cannot be determinative.

IV

The consequence of adopting the "*Bernstein*" approach would only be to bring the rule of law both here at home and in the relations of nations into disrespect. Indeed, the fate of the individual claimant would be subject to the political considerations of the Executive Branch. Since those considerations change as surely as administrations change, similarly situated litigants would not be likely to obtain even-handed treatment.

Note

1. Five, and possibly six, members of the Court rejected the *Bernstein* exception in *First National City Bank*. Concerning inconsistent lower court use of the exception, *see, e.g.*, Gary B. Born, International Civil Litigation in United States Courts 730 (3 ed. 1996).

D. Public Acts and a "Commercial Activity" Exception

Only sovereign or governmental acts enjoy the insulation from scrutiny provided by the act of state doctrine. The Supreme Court's opinion in *Alfred Dunhill v. Republic of Cuba*, provides some guidance on how to identity public acts of the sovereign, although Justice Marshall, in dissent, asserts that the purported standard is misleading and incomplete. Stressing the common roots of the act of state doctrine and foreign sovereign immunity, Justice White (writing for a plurality of four) embraced the restrictive principle (shortly before Congress enacted the FSIA) and pronounced a "commercial activity" exception to the act of state doctrine analogous to that soon to be codified in 28 U.S.C. § 1605(a)(2). As under the FSIA, excluding an act of state defense in suits involving commercial activity is seen to protect the reasonable expectations of trading partners of states and state entities, to promote stability and to advance rather than to impede the foreign policy interests of the United States. Do you agree?

ALFRED DUNHILL OF LONDON, INC. v. REPUBLIC OF CUBA

425 U.S. 682 (1976).

WHITE, J.

I

[Editors' notes: In 1960 Cuba expropriated the property of five leading Havana cigar manufacturers, most of whose owners were Cuban and none of whom was American. Dunhill, Saks and Faber were the three leading importers of Havana cigars into the United States. They accepted shipments of cigars from the "interventors" the Cuban Government appointed to take over the cigar companies. Many of the owners fled to the United States, and a group of them filed suit against Dunhill, Saks and Faber alleging trademark infringement and seeking compensation for the value of trademarked cigars imported into the United States. The interventors and the Republic of Cuba were permitted to intervene in the litigation, interposing a competing claim to the $700,000 value of cigars shipped following the expropriation. At the time of the expropriation, a sum of $477,200 was owed by the importers for cigars previously shipped. This sum had been paid to the interventors by the importers. The importers now claimed that, because these accounts receivable were located in the United States, Cuba lacked power to expropriate them and the $477,200 was properly owed to the former owners. The importers thus sought to set off the $477,200 previously paid to the interventors against the $700,000 owed for post-expropriation shipments.

[The District Court held that the importers could set off the $477,200 against the $700,000 owed to the interventors. However, Dunhill owed only $93,000 of the $700,000, while it had mistakenly paid $148,000 of the $477,200. Dunhill sought to recover the difference between $148,000 and $93,000 from the interventors. The District Court granted a judgment in Dunhill's favor, but the Court of Appeals reversed. Reasoning that the obligation of the interventors to repay the $477,200 mistakenly paid to them by the importers had a situs in Cuba, the Court of Appeals held that the repudiation of the obligation to repay was an act of state. While permitting a setoff for all three importers under the authority of *First Nat'l City Bank v. Banco Nacional de Cuba*, the Court of Appeals held that the act of state doctrine prevented Dunhill from an affirmative recovery beyond an amount sufficient to set off the $93,000 it owed the interventors.]

II

[In The Gul Djemal, 264 U.S. 90 (1924), a Turkish naval officer interposed a defense of sovereign immunity when the ship was libeled and arrested at the behest of a supplier.] [T]his Court ... held that the master's assertion of sovereign immunity was insufficient because his mere representation of his government as master of a commercial ship furnished no basis for assuming he was entitled to represent the sovereign in other capacities. Here there is no more reason to suppose that the interventors possess governmental, as opposed to commercial, authority than there was to suppose that the master of the *Gul Djemal* possessed such authority....

Nor do we consider *Underhill v. Hernandez*, heavily relied upon by the Court of Appeals, to require a contrary conclusion. In that case ... it was apparently concluded that the facts were sufficient to demonstrate that the conduct in question was the public act of those with authority to exercise sovereign powers and was entitled to respect in our courts. We draw no such conclusion from the facts of the case before us now. As the District Court found, the only evidence of an act of state other than the act of nonpayment by interventors was "a statement by counsel for interventors, during trial, that the Cuban Government and the interventors denied liability and had refused to make repayment".... No statute, decree, order, or resolution of the Cuban Government itself was offered in evidence indicating that Cuba had repudiated its obligations in general or any class thereof or that it had as a sovereign matter determined to confiscate the amounts due three foreign importers....

III

If we assume ... that the Cuban Government itself had purported to exercise sovereign power to confiscate the mistaken payments ..., we are nevertheless persuaded ... that the concept of an act of state should not be extended to include the repudiation of a purely commercial obligation owed by a foreign sovereign or by one of its commercial instrumentalities....

It is the position of the United States, stated in an amicus brief filed by the Solicitor General, that such a line should be drawn in defining the outer limits of the act of state concept.... Attached to the brief of the United States and to this opinion as Appendix I is the letter of November 26, 1975, in which the Department of State, speaking through its Legal Advisor agrees with the brief filed by the Solicitor General and, more specifically, declares that "we do not believe that the *Dunhill* case raises an act of state question because the case involves an act which is commercial, and not public, in nature."

The major underpinning of the act of state doctrine is the policy of foreclosing court adjudications involving the legality of acts of foreign states on their own soil that might embarrass the Executive Branch of our Government in the conduct of our foreign relations. But based on the presently expressed views of those who conduct our relations with foreign countries, we are in no sense compelled to recognize as an act of state the purely commercial conduct of foreign governments in order to avoid embarrassing conflicts with the Executive Branch....

[Justice White noted that with the 1952 Tate Letter, the United States has announced its adherence to the restrictive theory of foreign sovereign immunity, under which "commercial or proprietary actions" are nonimmune.]

Repudiation of a commercial debt cannot, consistent with this restrictive approach to sovereign immunity, be treated as an act of state; for if it were, foreign governments, by merely repudiating the debt before or after its adjudication, would enjoy an immunity which our Government would not extend them under prevailing sovereign immunity principles....

Participation by foreign sovereigns in the international commercial market has increased substantially in recent years. The potential injury to private businessmen—and ultimately to international trade itself—from a system in which some of the participants in the international market are not subject to the rule of law has therefore increased correspondingly....

There may be little codification or consensus as to the rules of international law concerning exercises of governmental powers, including military powers and expropriations, within a sovereign state's borders affecting the property or persons of aliens. However, more discernable rules of international law have emerged with regard to the commercial dealings of private parties in the international market. The restrictive approach to sovereign immunity suggests that these established rules should be applied to the commercial transactions of sovereign states.

For all the reasons which led the Executive Branch to adopt the restrictive theory of sovereign immunity, we hold that the mere assertion of sovereignty as a defense to a claim arising out of purely commercial acts by a foreign sovereign is no more effective if given the label "Act of State" than if it is given the label "sovereign immunity."

POWELL, J., concurring

I join the opinion of the Court. Since the line between commercial and political acts of a foreign state often will be difficult to delineate, I write to reaffirm my view that even in cases deemed to involve purely political acts, it is the duty of the judiciary to decide for itself whether deference to the political branches of Government requires abstention....

STEVENS, J., concurring in part

For reasons stated in Parts I and II of the Court's opinion, I agree that the act of state doctrine does not bar the entry of judgment in favor of Dunhill.

MARSHALL, J. (with whom BRENNAN, STEWART, and BLACKMUN, J.J.J., join), dissenting

Under any realistic view of the facts of this case, the interventors' retention of and refusal to return funds paid to them by Dunhill constitute an act of state, and no affirmative recovery by Dunhill can rest on the invalidity of that conduct....

I do not understand the Court to suggest that the act of state doctrine can be triggered only by a "statute, decree, order, or resolution" of a foreign government, or that the presence of an act of state can only be demonstrated by some affirmative action by the foreign sovereign. While it is true that an act of state generally takes the form if an executive or legislative step formalized in a decree or measure, that is only because duly constituted governments generally act through formal means. When they do not, their acts are no less the acts of a state, and the doctrine, being a practical one, is no less applicable....

Justice White advances a contention, not adopted by the Court, that even if the Cuban Government "had purported to exercise sovereign power to confiscate" the monies at issue ... , the act of state doctrine is inapplicable because of the "purely commercial" nature of the confiscation.... [T]here is no need to consider whether, and under what circumstances, an exception for commercial acts might be appropriate.

[T]he doctrines of sovereign immunity and act of state, while related, differ fundamentally in their focus and in their operation. Sovereign immunity accords a defendant exemption from suit by virtue of its status. By contrast, the act of state doctrine excepts no one from the process of the court. Equally applicable whether a sovereign nation is a party or not, the act of state doctrine merely tells a court what law to apply to a case.... In the absence of "unambiguous agreement regarding controlling ... principles of international law" [*citing Sabbatino*], the act of state doctrine commands that the acts of a sovereign nation committed in its own territory be accorded presumptive validity.

Whatever exceptions there may be to sovereign immunity ought not be transferred automatically, therefore, to the act of state doctrine....

W.S. KIRKPATRICK & CO., INC. v. ENVIRONMENTAL TECTONICS CORP., INT'L

493 U.S. 400 (1990).

SCALIA, J.

[Editors' notes: Kirkpatrick sought a contract with the Government of Nigeria to build a medical center on an airbase. It hired a Nigerian citizen to act as intermediary in securing the contract, agreeing to pay

20% of the contract price as a "commission" that would be disbursed to Nigerian officials as a bribe. Nigerian law prohibits both the payment and the receipt of bribes in connection with the award of a government contract. Environmental Tectonics Corporation, International, an unsuccessful bidder, learned of the 20% "commission" and brought the matter to the attention of the Nigerian Air Force and the United States Embassy in Lagos.]

[Kirkpatrick and its president pleaded guilty to violations of the Foreign Corrupt Practices Act of 1977, 91 Stat. 1495, as amended, 15 U.S.C. § 78dd–1 *et seq*. Environmental Tectonics then brought this civil action in the United States District Court for the District of New Jersey against Kirkpatrick and others, seeking damages under the Racketeer Influenced and Corrupt Organizations Act, 18 U.S.C. § 1961 *et seq*., the Robinson–Patman Act, 49 Stat. 1526, 15 U.S.C. § 13 *et seq*., and the New Jersey Anti–Racketeering Act, N.J.Stat.Ann. § 2C:41–2 *et seq*. (West 1982). The defendants moved to dismiss the complaint under Rule 12(b)(6) of the Federal Rules of Civil Procedure on the ground that the action was barred by the act of state doctrine.]

In this case we must decide whether the act of state doctrine bars a court in the United States from entertaining a cause of action that does not rest upon the asserted invalidity of an official act of a foreign sovereign, but that does require imputing to foreign officials an unlawful motivation (the obtaining of bribes) in the performance of such an official act.

I

[The Court of Appeals reversed the dismissal of the suit on act of state grounds.] The Court of Appeals found particularly persuasive the letter to the District Court from the legal adviser to the Department of State, which had stated that in the opinion of the Department judicial inquiry into the purpose behind the act of a foreign sovereign would not produce the "unique embarrassment, and the particular interference with the conduct of foreign affairs, that may result from the judicial determination that a foreign sovereign's acts are invalid"....

II

This Court's description of the jurisprudential foundation for the act of state doctrine has undergone some evolution over the years. We once viewed the doctrine as an expression of international law, resting upon "the highest considerations of international comity and expediency," Oetjen v. Central Leather Co., 246 U.S. 297, 303–304 (1918). We have more recently described it, however, as a consequence of domestic separation of powers.... Some Justices have suggested possible exceptions to application of the doctrine ... : an exception, for example, for acts of state that consist of commercial transactions, since neither modern international comity nor the current position of our Executive Branch accorded sovereign immunity to such acts ... ; or an exception for cases in which the Executive Branch has represented that it has no objection to denying validity to the foreign sovereign act, since then the courts would be impeding no foreign policy goals, *see* First National City Bank v. Banco Nacional de Cuba, 406 U.S. 759, 768–770 (1972) (opinion of Rehnquist, J.).

The parties have argued at length about the applicability of these possible exceptions, and, more generally, about whether the purpose of the act of state doctrine would be furthered by its application in this case. We find it unnecessary, however, to pursue those inquiries, since the factual predicate for application of the act of state doctrine does not exist. Nothing in the present suit requires the Court to declare invalid ... the official act of a foreign sovereign.

In every case in which we have held the act of state doctrine applicable, the relief sought or the defense interposed would have required a court in the United States to declare invalid the official act of a foreign sovereign performed within its own territory.... In the present case, by contrast, neither the claim nor any asserted defense requires a determination that Nigeria's contract with Kirkpatrick International was, or was not, effective.

Petitioners point out, however, that the facts necessary to establish respondent's claim will also establish that the contract was unlawful. Specifically, they note that in order to prevail respondent must prove that petitioner Kirkpatrick made, and Nigerian officials received, payments that violate Nigerian law, which would, they assert, support a finding that the contract is invalid under Nigerian law. Assuming that to be true, it still does not suffice. The act of state doctrine is not some vague doctrine of abstention.... Act of state issues only arise when a court must decide—that is, when the outcome of the case turns upon—the effect of official action by a foreign sovereign. When that question is not in the case, neither is the act of state doctrine. That is the situation here. Regardless of what the court's factual findings may suggest as to the legality of the Nigerian contract, its legality is simply not a question to be decided in the present suit, and there is thus no occasion to apply the rule of decision that the act of state doctrine requires....

Petitioners insist, however, that the policies underlying our act of state cases—international comity, respect for the sovereignty of foreign nations on their own territory, and the avoidance of embarrassment to the Executive Branch in its conduct of foreign relations—are implicated in the present case because, as the District Court found, a determination that Nigerian officials demanded and accepted a bribe "would impugn or question the nobility of a foreign nation's motivations," and would "result in embarrassment to the sovereign or constitute interference in the conduct of foreign policy of the United States." 659 F. Supp., at 1392–1393. The United States, as *amicus curiae*, favors the same approach to the act of state doctrine, though disagreeing with petitioners as to the outcome it produces in the present case....

The short of the matter is this: Courts in the United States have the power, and ordinarily the obligation, to decide cases and controversies properly presented to them. The act of state doctrine does not establish an exception for cases and controversies that may embarrass foreign governments, but merely requires that, in the process of deciding, the acts of foreign sovereigns taken within their own jurisdictions shall be deemed valid. That doctrine has no application to the present case because the validity of no foreign sovereign act is at issue.

The judgment of the Court of Appeals for the Third Circuit is affirmed.

Notes and Questions

1. Does Justice White's reliance in *Dunhill* on the letter from Department of State Legal Adviser Monroe Leigh concerning the nonapplicability of the act of state doctrine to the *Dunhill* dispute signal that the courts must or will defer to the advice of the Executive Branch? Should they? Justice Powell insisted that applicability of the act of state doctrine is a judicial matter.[25] Recall that one of the key innovations of the FSIA was to oust the Department of State from a controlling position with respect to the availability of foreign sovereign immunity.

2. Justice Powell notes in his *Dunhill* concurrence that the line between commercial and noncommercial activity is often a very murky one. If the courts must autonomously determine the scope of the FSIA's exception for commercial activity, why should they take deferential note of the Executive Branch's assessment of the same distinction in applying the federal common law doctrine of act of state? Is the act of state doctrine simply a variant on the political question doctrine, by which the U.S. courts avoid rendering decisions that will cause the judiciary to stray into the realm of one of the political branches? If so, should courts apply that doctrine when issues of law are directly at stake, since the interpretation and application of law in cases otherwise properly before the courts is a significant judicial power? Do courts need the advice of the Executive Branch to know reliably when their questioning of the conduct of a foreign sovereign will impinge upon a U.S. foreign policy interest? Does such deference to foreign policy pose serious threats to judicial independence and to the rule of law? In this regard, would you distinguish between claims under a commercial acts exception and a violation of international law exception?

3. Do you think *Kirkpatrick*'s limitation of the act of state doctrine to cases where the legal validity of the foreign state's act is directly in question will significantly narrow the doctrine's scope?

25. Justice Powell provided the fifth vote for Parts I and II of Justice White's opinion (Justice Stevens refusing to join in Part III's explication of a commercial activity exception). The four dissenters disagreed that Cuba's actions were commercial rather than public acts of state, indicating that they were not inclined to defer to Mr. Leigh's assessment.

E. A "Treaty" Exception

KALAMAZOO SPICE EXTRACTION CO. v. PROVISIONAL MILITARY GOVERNMENT OF SOCIALIST ETHIOPIA

729 F.2d 422 (6th Cir.1984).

KEITH, J.

. . . Kal–Spice, as well as the United States Departments of State, Treasury, Justice, and the American Bar Association, as *amici curiae*, request that this Court recognize a "treaty exception" to the act of state doctrine. According to appellant and *amici*, the following language in *Sabbatino* provides the basis for a treaty exception:

> [T]he Judicial Branch will not examine the validity of a taking of property within its own territory by a foreign sovereign government, extant and recognized by this country at the time of suit, *in the absence of a treaty or other unambiguous agreement regarding controlling legal principles*, even if the complaint alleges that the taking violates customary international law (emphasis added).

The treaty in existence between the United States and Ethiopia is the 1953 Treaty of Amity and Economic Relations (Treaty of Amity). Article VIII, paragraph two of that treaty provides:

> Property of nationals and companies of either High Contracting Party, including interests in property, shall receive the most constant protection and security within the territories of the other High contracting party. *Such property shall not be taken except for a public purpose, nor shall it be taken without prompt payment of just and effective compensation* (emphasis added).

We do not agree with the district court's decision that the provision of the treaty requiring payment of prompt, just and effective compensation fails to provide a controlling legal standard. To the contrary, we find that this is a controlling legal standard in the area of international law.

Numerous treaties employ the standard of compensation used in the 1953 Treaty of Amity between Ethiopia and the United States. Undoubtedly, the widespread use of this compensation standard is evidence that it is an agreed upon principle in international law.... [The court added that the *Sabbatino* decision, among others, "requires a reversal of the district court decision that the 1953 Treaty of Amity was too ambiguous to be susceptible to judicial interpretation," and quoted *Sabbatino* concerning " 'the greater the degree of codification or consensus concerning a particular area of international law,' " etc.]

Nor will adjudication in this matter interfere with any efforts by the Executive branch to resolve this matter. In fact, the Executive branch has also intervened in this matter through the Departments of State, Treasury, and Justice who have filed a joint *amicus* brief urging that the 1953 Treaty of Amity makes the act of state doctrine inapplicable....

Additionally, there is a great national interest to be served in this case, *i.e.*, the recognition and execution of treaties that we enter into with foreign nations. Article VI of the Constitution provides that treaties made under the authority of the United States shall be the supreme law of the land.... The failure of this court to recognize a properly executed treaty would indeed be an egregious error because of the position that treaties occupy in our body of laws.

Notes and Questions

1. Does the existence of a treaty provision governing the foreign state conduct specifically challenged in the litigation provide the kind of clarity the Supreme Court found missing in *Sabbatino* with respect to alleged customary international norms on expropriation?

2. The "treaty" exception to the act of state doctrine shares some features with the "waiver" exception to the FSIA, § 1605(a)(1), and, especially, the "international agreement" exception in §§ 1330(a) and 1604. The foreign state's anticipation that it could be sued in the United States would not appear to be crucial in the act of state context. *See* RESTATEMENT § 443, RN 5.

3. In Callejo v. Bancomer, S.A., 764 F.2d 1101, 1116–21 (5th Cir.1985), the Fifth Circuit cautioned that *Sabbatino*'s reference to a treaty exception was posed in the negative (*i.e.*, the absence in *Sabbatino* of a relevant treaty or other unambiguous norm ("codification or consensus")), and stated that courts should examine the foreign policy implications of judicial inquiry into acts of foreign states and that mere existence of a treaty does not require that a court not apply the doctrine. Yet, the court stressed the difference between treaties setting forth "unambiguous rules" and those with "broad but vague pronouncements." The opinion added: "The treaty exception was intended to allow courts to apply international law where consensus exists; it was not intended to allow courts to upset a preexisting consensus regarding the validity of a foreign state act...." *Id.* Where such exists, should courts apply clearly identifiable international law and not venture into examination of foreign policy?

4. Do you agree with the approach in *Kalamazoo Spice* or that in *Callejo*? Are foreign acts that violate international law legitimate sovereign acts? What are the foreign policy implications if U.S. courts do not apply international law? What are the implications for judicial integrity and independence? Do treaties normally trump mere common law doctrines?

5. Does Article 2(3)(a) of the International Covenant on Civil and Political Rights form the basis for a treaty exception? Do Articles 1 and 14 of the Convention Against Torture and Other Cruel, Inhuman or Degrading Treatment or Punishment?

F. Application of the Act of State Doctrine in Human Rights Litigation

Some violations of international human rights law, classically the norms against piracy, war crimes, genocide, other crimes against humanity, and slavery, do not require any proof of state action or complicity. *See, e.g.*, Kadic v. Karadzic, 70 F.3d 232, 239 (2d Cir.1995), *cert. denied*, 518 U.S. 1005 (1996). However, the types of gross human rights violations that have figured in litigation under the Alien Tort Claims Act (ATCA) and the Torture Victim Protection Act (TVPA) often involve persons acting in an official capacity. Many of the cases of torture, arbitrary detention, and extrajudicial killing brought under the ATCA involved defendants who were officials of, or otherwise claimed to be exercising authority delegated by, a foreign state. *See, e.g.*, cases in Chapter 2, Section 2 D 2.

Foreign states have generally been successful in asserting sovereign immunity under the FSIA during certain types of human rights litigation (*see, e.g.*, this chapter, Sections 1 C 2 and 1 C 4, *supra*, concerning the nature of commercial activity under 28 U.S.C. § 1605(a)(2) and the territorial limitation concerning § 1605(a)(5)). Claims to immunity under the FSIA for individual officials, whether or not appropriate, have succeeded less often (*see* Section 1 D 1, *supra*, concerning interpretations of § 1603(b)). In some of the early cases reviving the ATCA, no act of state defense was asserted. A noteworthy example of this failure to interpose an act of state defense is Filartiga v. Pena–Irala, 630 F.2d 876 (2d Cir.1980). The Second Circuit, in *dictum*, nevertheless observed that the clear international consensus on the illegality of torture and the disinclination of foreign states to formally ratify human rights violations committed by their agents made it highly unlikely that an act of state defense would be available in suits under § 1350 involving allegations of torture. *Id.* at 889. As the number and prominence of human rights suits increased during the 1980s and 1990s, defendants began more frequently to assert that their acts were nonjusticiable under the act of state doctrine. These defendants cautioned that granting relief to human rights plaintiffs would require the court to find that breaches of international law (and sometimes also violations of the law of the foreign state) had been committed, offending the foreign state and impinging on the authority of the Executive Branch to conduct foreign policy. Because the act of state doctrine is supplementary to the FSIA, this defense has been asserted even where the acts of the foreign state fall within an FSIA exception or where an individual human rights violator is not a "foreign state."

Issues of justiciability and liability in human rights litigation may require a court, for several distinct purposes, to explore the official capacity and scope of authority exercised by an individual defendant at the time of the claimed human rights violation. These issues might include the discretionary function limitation to the tort exception in § 1605(a)(5)(A) (recall *Letelier v. Republic of Chile*), the "color of law" or "apparent authority" requirements of the TVPA (recall *Kadic v. Karadzic*), the attribution rules of the principle of *respondeat superior* or command responsibility (recall *Xuncax v. Gramajo*), as well as the "public act" concept of the act of state doctrine. At times, these different ways of assessing the links between the individual perpetrator and the foreign state may appear to be on a collision course with each other, in that a close link between the individual defendant and the foreign state may suggest culpability while also pointing toward immunity or nonjusticiability. How have the cases noted above generally approached such relationships or issues? Recall Chapter 2, Section 2 D 2.

U.S. courts have generally rejected claims by former heads of state that the act of state doctrine bars adjudication of human rights violations. Several courts have held that gross human rights violations are not lawful or authoritative public acts requiring application of the act of state doctrine. *See, e.g., Hilao v. Marcos, supra*, 25 F.3d at 1471; Paul v. Avril, 812 F.Supp. 207, 212 (S.D.Fla.1993); Forti v. Suarez–Mason, 672 F.Supp. 1531, 1546 (N.D.Cal.1987). Significantly, courts have applied this analysis even when defendants were sued for conduct committed while they were heads of state, reasoning that "the illegal acts of a dictator are not 'official acts' unreviewable by federal courts." *Hilao v. Marcos, supra*, 25 F.3d at 1471, *citing* Jimenez v. Aristeguieta, 311 F.2d 547, 557–58 (5th Cir.1962), *cert. denied sub nom.*, Jimenez v. Hixon, 373 U.S. 914, *reh'g denied*, 374 U.S. 858 (1963). The *Pinochet* case in the House of Lords was similarly resolved. *See* Section 2 B. According to the Senate Report on the Torture Victim Protection Act, the act of state doctrine does not apply to torture and similar violations of international law. "Since this doctrine applies only to public acts, and no state commits torture as a matter of public policy, this doctrine cannot shield former officials from liability under this legislation." S. Rep. No. 249, 102nd Cong., 1st Sess. 8 (1992).

Motions to dismiss human rights suits on act of state grounds have been temporarily successful in some cases. *See, e.g.,* Liu v. Republic of China, 892 F.2d 1419 (9th Cir.1989), *cert. dismissed*, 497 U.S. 1058 (1990) (reversing dismissal on act of state grounds); *Siderman de Blake, supra* (same). However, the clear trend among lower U.S. courts is to reject the act of state defense in cases involving violations of internationally protected human rights, especially where *jus cogens* norms have been violated, a successor regime has repudiated the human rights violations of former officials, or the Executive Branch signals that it does not regard the litigation as contrary to U.S. foreign policy objectives. According to some, this also suggests that a *jus cogens* limitation on the act of state doctrine may be embraced more readily by the courts than a similar, implicit limitation on FSIA immunity. The dominant theoretical basis for rejecting the act of state defense in these suits has been a refinement of the "public act" requirement to stress limits on official authority to commit acts that violate clearly established human rights norms or the formal law of the foreign state. This "public act" approach shares some common features with the *ultra vires* basis for rejecting FSIA immunity claims by individual officials in human rights cases when courts otherwise misread § 1603(b) (*see* Section 1 D 1). Also recall the International Military Tribunal at Nuremberg Opinion and Judgment, stating, in response to a claim of immunity for "an act of State," that immunity "cannot be applied to acts which are condemned as criminal by international law" and one "cannot obtain immunity while acting in pursuance of the authority of the State if the State in authorizing action moves outside its competence under international law;" and the Principles of the Nuremberg Charter and Judgement, *supra* and in Chapter 1. Moreover, acts taken in violation of a state's domestic law are *ultra vires* and cannot be lawful public acts under the domestic law of such country (which thereby negates one of the elements of an act of state defense: (1) lawful public acts, (2) completed within its territory).

A signal of the trend toward rejection of the act of state doctrine for acts beyond the scope of proper governmental authority was the Second Circuit's opinion in Republic of Philippines v. Marcos, 806 F.2d 344 (2d Cir.1986), *cert. denied sub nom.*, New York Land Co. v. Republic of the Philippines, 481 U.S. 1048 (1987) (Marcos I), and the Ninth Circuit's *en banc* decision in Republic of the Philippines v. Marcos, 862 F.2d 1355 (9th Cir.1988) (*en banc*), *cert. denied*, 490 U.S. 1035 (1989) (Marcos II). Although these cases involved claims that former President Marcos had looted the Philippine treasury, rather than his commission of human rights violations, they are significant in their rejection of a broad application of the act of state doctrine,[26] their deference to the assessment of foreign policy implications of the suits by the Governments of the Philippines and the United States, and their reliance upon a distinction drawn earlier in *Jimenez v. Aristeguieta, supra*, between the official and private acts (*e.g.*, theft of public monies) of a former Venezuelan dictator.

Forti v. Suarez–Mason, supra, held that acts of torture, extrajudicial execution and arbitrary detention by a former member of the junta conducting Argentina's "dirty war" were not acts of state. Although these acts were somewhat "official," they were not governmental, "public," or "public official" acts, nor "ratified," but were "illegal" acts. *See also* Letelier v. Republic of Chile, 488 F.Supp. at 673–74. The Ninth Circuit's unreported decisions reversing the dismissal of several human rights suits against President Marcos on act of state grounds continued this trend. See Hilao v. Marcos, 878 F.2d 1438 (9th Cir.1989); Trajano v. Marcos, 878 F.2d 1439 (9th Cir.1989) (table decisions).

The inapplicability of the act of state doctrine was further explored by the Ninth Circuit in *Liu v. Republic of China, supra*, which involved a plot by the head of the secret police of Taiwan to assassinate a critic in California. The Republic of China was not immune from suit because the tort had been committed within U.S. territory. Even though the FSIA posed no difficulties, the Ninth Circuit carefully explored the availability of an act of state defense, after having found that the actions of the secret police chief should be attributed to the Republic of China under *respondeat superior,* even though the perpetrators had been tried and convicted under Taiwanese law. The Ninth Circuit resolved the act of state question by noting that the assassination was not an act in the

26. The *en banc* Ninth Circuit vacated a panel decision suggesting that virtually all acts of a dictator would be immunized under the act of state doctrine. In Republic of the Philippines v. Marcos, 818 F.2d 1473, 1489 (9th Cir.1987), the vacated panel decision had stated: [I]t is difficult to see what law to apply to Mr. Marcos' actions. By its nature, dictatorial rule is arbitrary and unrestrained by legal authority; martial law is a suspension of the normal rule of law. Offensive as such absolute government may be to our sense of justice, no legal restraints can prevail against dictatorial power. A dictator can do whatever he can get away with. A court of law in this country simply cannot second-guess how that power is exercised.

"public interest" of the Republic of China; that a strong international consensus exists that murder is illegal; that the U.S. Government would not be embarrassed or likely to make differing pronouncements if the court adjudicated the claims; and that the criminal judgments of Taiwan's courts would not be questioned in the civil litigation. *Id.* at 1432–1433.

Notes and Questions

1. The TVPA does not permit suit against foreign states, but only against individual defendants. The Senate Report, S.Rep. No. 249, 102nd Cong., 1st Sess. 8 (1991), specifically noted that the act of state doctrine "applies only to 'public' acts, and no state commits torture as a matter of public policy," adding: "[a] state that practices torture and summary execution is not one that adheres to the rule of law. Consequently, the [TVPA] is designed to respond to this situation by providing a civil cause of action in US courts," and that the Senate Judiciary "Committee does not intend the 'act of state' doctrine to provide a shield from lawsuit...." Thus, Congress signaled its awareness and approval of a distinction between "official" and "public" acts, for purposes of the act of state doctrine. This nod encouraged the courts to continue the trend toward rejection of act of state defenses mounted by individual defendants in ATCA and TVPA litigation. *See, e.g.,* Kadic v. Karadzic, 70 F.3d at 250; Xuncax v. Gramajo, 886 F.Supp. at 175–76.

2. Even where the foreign sovereign is dismissed from the suit under the FSIA because its conduct (*e.g.,* torture, forced displacement and forced labor) is "sovereign" rather than "commercial" in nature, an act of state defense asserted by private joint venturers may be rejected. *See, e.g.,* Doe v. Unocal Corp., 963 F.Supp. 880, 892–95 (C.D.Cal.1997):

> Because nations do not, and cannot under international law, claim a right to torture or enslave their own citizens, a finding that a nation has committed such acts, particularly where, as here, that finding comports with the prior conclusions of the coordinate branches of government, should have no detrimental effect on the policies underlying the act of state doctrine. Accordingly, the Court need not apply the act of state doctrine in this case.

3. Where the foreign state (generally, a successor regime) has repudiated the acts of the individual defendant, the courts are disinclined to recognize an act of state defense. *See, e.g.,* Paul v. Avril, 812 F.Supp. 207 (S.D.Fla.1993), adding:

> "[d]efendant's ... argument ... [regarding] act of state ... is completely devoid of merit. The acts, as alleged in the complaint, if true, would hardly qualify as official public acts." *Id.* at 212.

4. For discussion of the inapplicability of the act of state defense to human rights litigation, *see, e.g.,* Restatement § 443, cmt. c & RN 5; Jordan J. Paust, International Law as Law of the United States 236, 305–08 n.547 (2 ed. 2003); Tom Lininger, *Overcoming Immunity Defenses to Human Rights Suits in U.S. Courts,* 7 Harv. Hum. Rts. J. 177 (1994); Lynn E. Parseghian, *Defining the "Public Act" Requirement in the Act of State Doctrine,* 58 U.

CHI. L. REV. 1151 (1991); Jordan J. Paust, *Suing Karadzic*, 10 LEIDEN J. INT'L L. 91, 97–98 & n.52 (1997); Andrew Saindon, Note, *The Act of State Doctrine and International Human Rights Cases in United States Courts*, 7 MD. J. CONTEMP. L. ISSUES 287 (1995/96); *but see* Anne–Marie Burley, *Law Among Liberal States: Liberal Internationalism and the Act of State Doctrine*, 92 COLUM. L. REV. 1907 (1992) (arguing that international relations theory of "liberal internationalism" requires insulating human rights violations of "nonliberal" states and their agents from judicial scrutiny in courts of "liberal" states).

Chapter Five

COOPERATION IN TRANSNATIONAL ENFORCEMENT

SECTION 1. OBTAINING EVIDENCE ABROAD

RESTATEMENT OF THE FOREIGN RELATIONS LAW OF THE UNITED STATES (3 ed. 1987)

§ 473. Obtaining Evidence in Foreign State

(1) Under international law, a state may determine the conditions for taking evidence in its territory in aid of litigation in another state, but the state of the forum may determine its admissibility, probative value, and effect.

(2) Under the Hague Evidence Convention,

(a) each contracting state is required to designate a Central Authority to which letters or request for assistance in obtaining evidence for use in civil or commercial litigation may be addressed by courts of other contracting states . . . ;

(b) a contracting state may determine the conditions for taking evidence in its territory, without compulsion, by diplomatic or consular officers, or by commissions designated by a court in another contracting state, for use in civil or commercial litigation pending in that state.

(3) A person required or requested to give evidence for use in a foreign state, whether pursuant to the Hague Evidence Convention or through other arrangements for judicial assistance, may refuse to do so insofar as he has a privilege or a duty of nondisclosure under either the law of the state or origin of the request or of the state in which the evidence is sought.

Comment *a*. *Admissibility of evidence obtained in foreign state*. In general, . . . the admissibility of evidence lawfully obtained in one state for use in litigation in another state is determined by the law of the forum state. . . .

Comment *b*. *Scope and purpose of Hague Evidence Convention*. The Hague Evidence Convention provides for gathering of evidence . . . (i) by letters of request (or letters rogatory), addressed by the court of the requesting state to a Central Authority designated by the requested state, seeking assistance in obtaining evidence through compulsory process, Subsection (2)(a); and (ii) by commissions issued by the court to consular officers of the requesting state, or to specially appointed persons, directing them to take evidence in a foreign state, generally without compulsory process, Subsection (2)(b). Execution of letters of request from courts of another contracting state is required under the Convention. . . . However, since taking of evidence is a function regarded by many states as an official act of the foreign state, the Convention provides that contracting states may refuse to permit execution of commissions in their territory, or may give permission subject to conditions. . . .

Comment *c*. *Civil or commercial matters*. The Hague Evidence Convention, like the Hague Service Convention, applies only in aid of civil or commercial litigation. . . .

Comment *d*. *Judicial Authority*. The Hague Evidence Convention applies only to requests transmitted by or on behalf of a judicial authority, and only in respect of evidence to be used in judicial proceedings. . . .

§ 474. Obtaining Evidence in or for Use in Foreign State: Law of the United States

(1) A United States district court may execute a letter rogatory issued by a foreign tribunal by ordering a person residing or found in the district to give testimony or to produce a document or other thing for use in a proceeding in the foreign tribunal.

(2) A United States district court, in order to obtain evidence for use in a proceeding before it, may:

> (a) issue a commission to a United States consul, or to any other person not related to the parties or their attorneys, to take testimony in a foreign state;
>
> (b) issue a letter rogatory requesting a court or other appropriate authority in a foreign state to direct the taking of evidence in that state; or
>
> (c) issue a subpoena ordering a national or resident of the United States in a foreign state to give evidence as directed by the court,

provided the procedure is not inconsistent with the law of the state where the evidence is to be taken.

Comment *h*. *International judicial assistance and criminal proceedings*. The provisions for international judicial assistance in 28 U.S.C. §§ 1781–82 make no distinction between civil and criminal proceedings, and United States courts have full authority to execute letters rogatory in aid of foreign criminal proceedings. Similarly, the authority of United States courts to issue letters rogatory or commission, Fed.R.Civ.P. 28(b), is not limited to civil actions. Traditionally, United States courts and prosecutors seeking evidence located abroad have resorted only to subpoenas directed to United States nationals or residents. However, efforts to trace funds or other evidence of transnational crime, such as trafficking in drugs and terrorism, have led to increased international cooperation in law enforcement, pursuant to treaties of mutual assistance in criminal matters, by greater use of letters rogatory, and by a variety of less formal arrangements among governments and law enforcement agencies.

SOCIETE NATIONALE INDUSTRIELLE AEROSPATIALE v. UNITED STATES, COURT FOR THE SOUTHERN DISTRICT OF IOWA

482 U.S. 522 (1987).

STEVENS, J.

The United States, the Republic of France, and 15 other Nations have acceded to the Hague Convention on the Taking of Evidence Abroad in Civil or Commercial Matters, opened for signature, Mar. 18, 1970, 23 U.S.T. 2555, T.I.A.S. No. 7444. This Convention—sometimes referred to as the "Hague Convention" or the "Evidence Convention"—prescribes certain procedures by which a judicial authority in one contracting state may request evidence located in another contracting state. The question presented in this case concerns the extent to which a federal district court must employ the procedures set forth in the Convention when litigants seek answers to interrogatories, the production of documents, and admissions from a French adversary over whom the court has personal jurisdiction.

I

The two petitioners are corporations owned by the Republic of France. They are engaged in the business of designing, manufacturing, and marketing aircraft. One of their planes, the "Rallye," was allegedly advertised in American aviation publications as "the World's safest and most economical STOL plane." On August 19, 1980, a Rallye crashed in Iowa, injuring the pilot and a passenger. Dennis Jones, John George, and Rosa George brought separate suits based upon this accident in the United States District Court for the Southern District of Iowa, alleging that petitioners had manufactured and sold a defective plane and that they were guilty of negligence and breach of warranty. Petitioners answered the complaints, apparently without questioning the jurisdiction of the District Court....

Initial discovery was conducted by both sides pursuant to the Federal Rules of Civil Procedure without objection. When plaintiffs served a second request for the production of documents pursuant to Rule 34, a set of interrogatories pursuant to Rule 33, and requests for admission pursuant to Rule 36, however, petitioners filed a motion for a protective order.... The motion alleged that because petitioners are "French corporations, and the discovery sought can only be found in a foreign state, namely France," the Hague Convention dictated the exclusive procedures that must be followed for pretrial discovery.... In addition, the motion stated that under French penal law, the petitioners could not respond to discovery requests that did not comply with the Convention.... [1]

II

In the District Court and the Court of Appeals, petitioners contended that the Hague Evidence Convention "provides the exclusive and mandatory procedures for obtaining documents and information located within the territory of a foreign signatory." 782 F.2d, at 124.[2] We are satisfied that the Court of Appeals correctly rejected this extreme position. We believe it is foreclosed by the plain language of the Convention. Before discussing the text of the Convention, however, we briefly review its history.

The Hague Conference on Private International Law, an association of sovereign states, has been conducting periodic sessions since 1893. S. Exec. Doc. A, 92d Cong., 2d Sess., p. v (1972) (S. Exec. Doc. A). The United States participated in those sessions as an observer in 1956 and 1960, and as a member beginning in 1964 pursuant to congressional authorization. In that year Congress amended the Judicial Code to grant foreign litigants, without any requirement of reciprocity, special assistance in obtaining evidence in the United States. In 1965 the Hague Conference adopted a Convention on the Service Abroad of Judicial and Extrajudicial Documents in Civil or Commercial Matters (Service Convention), 20 U.S.T. 361, T.I.A.S. No.6638, to which the Senate gave its advice and consent in 1967. The favorable response to the Service Convention, coupled with the longstanding interest of American lawyers in improving procedures for obtaining evidence abroad, motivated the United States to take the initiative in proposing that an evidence convention be adopted.... The Conference organized a special commission to prepare the draft convention, and the draft was approved without a dissenting vote on October 26, 1968.... It was signed on behalf of the United States in 1970 and ratified by a unanimous vote of the Senate in 1972. The Convention's purpose was to establish a system for obtaining

1. [Court's n.6] Article 1A of the French "blocking statute," French Penal Code Law No. 80–538, provides:

"Subject to treaties or international agreements and applicable laws and regulations, it is prohibited for any party to request, seek or disclose, in writing, orally or otherwise, economic, commercial, industrial, financial or technical documents or information leading to the constitution of evidence with a view to foreign judicial or administrative proceedings or in connection therewith...."

2. [Court's n.11] The Republic of France likewise takes the following position in this case: "The Hague Convention is the exclusive means of discovery in transnational litigation among the Convention's signatories unless the sovereign on whose territory discovery is to occur chooses otherwise." Brief for Republic of France as Amicus Curiae 4.

evidence located abroad that would be "tolerable" to the state executing the request and would produce evidence "utilizable" in the requesting state....

... The Convention was fairly summarized in the Secretary of State's letter of submittal to the President:

"The willingness of the Conference to proceed promptly with work on the evidence convention is perhaps attributable in large measure to the difficulties encountered by courts and lawyers in obtaining evidence abroad from countries with markedly different legal systems. Some countries have insisted on the exclusive use of the complicated, dilatory and expensive system of letters rogatory or letters of request. Other countries have refused adequate judicial assistance because of the absence of a treaty or convention regulating the matter. The substantial increase in litigation with foreign aspects arising, in part, from the unparalleled expansion of international trade and travel in recent decades had intensified the need for an effective international agreement to set up a model system to bridge differences between the common law and civil law approaches to the taking of evidence abroad.

"Civil law countries tend to concentrate on commissions rogatoires, while common law countries take testimony on notice, by stipulation and through commissions to consuls or commissioners. Letters of request for judicial assistance from courts abroad in securing needed evidence have been the exception, rather than the rule. The civil law technique results normally in a resume of the evidence, prepared by the executing judge and signed by the witness, while the common law technique results normally in a verbatim transcript of the witness's testimony certified by the reporter.

"Failure by either the requesting state or the state of execution fully to take into account the differences of approach to the taking of evidence abroad under the two systems and the absence of agreed standards applicable to letters of request have frequently caused difficulties for courts and litigants. To minimize such difficulties in the future, the enclosed convention, which consists of a preamble and forty-two articles, is designed to:

"1. Make the employment of letters of request a principal means of obtaining evidence abroad;

"2. Improve the means of securing evidence abroad by increasing the powers of consuls and by introducing in the civil law world, on a limited basis, the concept of the commissioner;

"3. Provide means for securing evidence in the form needed by the court where the action is pending; and

"4. Preserve all more favorable and less restrictive practices arising from internal law, internal rules of procedure and bilateral or multilateral conventions.

"What the convention does is to provide a set of minimum standards with which contracting states agree to comply. Further, through articles

27, 28 and 32, it provides a flexible framework within which any future liberalizing changes in policy and tradition in any country with respect to international judicial cooperation may be translated into effective change in international procedures. At the same time it recognizes and preserves procedures of every country which now or hereafter may provide international cooperation in the taking of evidence on more liberal and less restrictive bases, whether this is effected by supplementary agreements or by municipal law and practice." *Id.*, p. VI.

III

In arguing their entitlement to a protective order, petitioners correctly assert that both the discovery rules set forth in the Federal Rules of Civil Procedure and the Hague Convention are the law of the United States.... This observation, however, does not dispose of the question before us; we must analyze the interaction between these two bodies of federal law. Initially, we note that at least four different interpretations of the relationship between the federal discovery rules and the Hague Convention are possible. Two of these interpretations assume that the Hague Convention by its terms dictates the extent to which it supplants normal discovery rules. First, the Hague Convention might be read as requiring its use to the exclusion of any other discovery procedures whenever evidence located abroad is sought for use in an American court. Second, the Hague Convention might be interpreted to require first, but not exclusive, use of its procedures. Two other interpretations assume that international comity, rather than the obligations created by the treaty, should guide judicial resort to the Hague Convention. Third, then, the Convention might be viewed as establishing a supplemental set of discovery procedures, strictly optional under treaty law, to which concerns of comity nevertheless require first resort by American courts in all cases. Fourth, the treaty may be viewed as an undertaking among sovereigns to facilitate discovery to which an American court should resort when it deems that course of action appropriate, after considering the situations of the parties before it as well as the interests of the concerned foreign state. In interpreting an international treaty, we are mindful that it is "in the nature of a contract between nations," Trans World Airlines, Inc. v. Franklin Mint Corp., 466 U.S. 243, 253 (1984), to which "general rules of construction apply." *Id.*, at 262. See Ware v. Hylton, 3 Dall. 199, 240–241 (1796) (opinion of Chase, J.). We therefore begin "with the text of the treaty and the context in which the written words are used." Air France v. Saks, 470 U.S. 392, 397 (1985). The treaty's history, " 'the negotiations, and the practical construction adopted by the parties' " may also be relevant. *Id.*, at 396 (*quoting* Choctaw Nation of Indians v. United States, 318 U.S. 423, 431–432 (1943)). We reject the first two of the possible interpretations as inconsistent with the language and negotiating history of the Hague Convention. The preamble of the Convention specifies its purpose "to facilitate the transmission and execution of Letters of Request" and to "improve mutual judicial cooperation in civil or commercial matters." 23 U.S.T., at

2557, T.I.A.S. No. 7444. The preamble does not speak in mandatory terms which would purport to describe the procedures for all permissible transnational discovery and exclude all other existing practices. The text of the Evidence Convention itself does not modify the law of any contracting state, require any contracting state to use the Convention procedures, either in requesting evidence or in responding to such requests, or compel any contracting state to change its own evidence-gathering procedures.

The Convention contains three chapters. Chapter I, entitled "Letters of Requests," and chapter II, entitled "Taking of Evidence by Diplomatic Officers, Consular Agents and Commissioners," both use permissive rather than mandatory language. Thus, Article 1 provides that a judicial authority in one contracting state "may" forward a letter of request to the competent authority in another contracting state for the purpose of obtaining evidence. Similarly, Articles 15, 16, and 17 provide that diplomatic officers, consular agents, and commissioners "may . . . without compulsion," take evidence under certain conditions. The absence of any command that a contracting state must use Convention procedures when they are not needed is conspicuous.

Two of the Articles in chapter III, entitled "General Clauses," buttress our conclusion that the Convention was intended as a permissive supplement, not a pre-emptive replacement, for other means of obtaining evidence located abroad. Article 23 expressly authorizes a contracting state to declare that it will not execute any letter of request in aid of pretrial discovery of documents in a common-law country. Surely, if the Convention had been intended to replace completely the broad discovery powers that the common-law courts in the United States previously exercised over foreign litigants subject to their jurisdiction, it would have been most anomalous for the common-law contracting parties to agree to Article 23, which enables a contracting party to revoke its consent to the treaty's procedures for pretrial discovery. In the absence of explicit textual support, we are unable to accept the hypothesis that the common-law contracting states abjured recourse to all pre-existing discovery procedures at the same time that they accepted the possibility that a contracting party could unilaterally abrogate even the Convention's procedures. Moreover, Article 27 plainly states that the Convention does not prevent a contracting state from using more liberal methods of rendering evidence than those authorized by the Convention. Thus, the text of the Evidence Convention, as well as the history of its proposal and ratification by the United States, unambiguously supports the conclusion that it was intended to establish optional procedures that would facilitate the taking of evidence abroad. . . .

An interpretation of the Hague Convention as the exclusive means for obtaining evidence located abroad would effectively subject every American court hearing a case involving a national of a contracting state to the internal laws of that state. Interrogatories and document requests are staples of international commercial litigation, no less than of other suits, yet a rule of exclusivity would subordinate the court's supervision of even the most routine of these pretrial proceedings to the actions or, equally, to the inactions of foreign judicial authorities.... The Hague Convention, however, contains no such plain statement of a pre-emptive intent. We conclude accordingly that the Hague Convention did not deprive the District Court of the jurisdiction it otherwise possessed to order a foreign national party before it to produce evidence physically located within a signatory nation.[3]....

V

Petitioners contend that even if the Hague Convention's procedures are not mandatory, this Court should adopt a rule requiring that American litigants first resort to those procedures before initiating any discovery pursuant to the normal methods of the Federal Rules of Civil Procedure. *See, e.g.*, Laker Airways, Ltd. v. Pan American World Airways, 103 F.R.D. 42 (D.D.C. 1984); Philadelphia Gear Corp. v. American Pfauter Corp., 100 F.R.D. 58 (E.D.Pa.1983). The Court of Appeals rejected this argument because it was convinced that an American court's order ultimately requiring discovery that a foreign court had refused under Convention procedures would constitute "the greatest insult" to the sovereignty of that tribunal. 782 F.2d, at 125–126. We disagree with the Court of Appeals' view. It is well known that the scope of American discovery is often significantly broader than is permitted in other jurisdictions, and we are satisfied that foreign tribunals will recognize that the final decision on the evidence to be used in litigation conducted in American courts must be made by those courts. We therefore do not believe that an American court should refuse to make use of Convention procedures because of a concern that it may ultimately find it necessary to order the production of evidence that a foreign tribunal permitted a party to withhold. Nevertheless, we cannot accept petitioners' invitation to announce a new rule of law that would require

3. [Court's n.25] The opposite conclusion of exclusivity would create three unacceptable asymmetries. First, within any lawsuit between a national of the United States and a national of another contracting party, the foreign party could obtain discovery under the Federal Rules of Civil Procedure, while the domestic party would be required to resort first to the procedures of the Hague Convention. This imbalance would run counter to the fundamental maxim of discovery that "mutual knowledge of all the relevant facts gathered by both parties is essential to proper litigation." Hickman v. Taylor, 329 U.S. 495, 507 (1947).

Second, a rule of exclusivity would enable a company which is a citizen of another contracting state to compete with a domestic company on uneven terms, since the foreign company would be subject to less extensive discovery procedures in the event that both companies were sued in an American court. Petitioners made a voluntary decision to market their products in the United States. They are entitled to compete on equal terms with other companies operating in this market. But since the District Court unquestionably has personal jurisdiction over petitioners, they are subject to the same legal constraints, including the burdens associated with American judicial procedures, as their American competitors. A general rule according foreign nationals a preferred position in pretrial proceedings in our courts would conflict with the principle of equal opportunity that governs the market they elected to enter.

Third, since a rule of first use of the Hague Convention would apply to cases in which a foreign party is a national of a contracting state, but not to cases in which a foreign party is a national of any other foreign state, the rule would confer an unwarranted advantage on some domestic litigants over others similarly situated.

first resort to Convention procedures whenever discovery is sought from a foreign litigant. Assuming, without deciding, that we have the lawmaking power to do so, we are convinced that such a general rule would be unwise. In many situations the Letter of Request procedure authorized by the Convention would be unduly time consuming and expensive, as well as less certain to produce needed evidence than direct use of the Federal Rules. A rule of first resort in all cases would therefore be inconsistent with the overriding interest in the "just, speedy, and inexpensive determination" of litigation in our courts. See Fed. Rule Civ. Proc. 1.

Petitioners argue that a rule of first resort is necessary to accord respect to the sovereignty of states in which evidence is located. It is true that the process of obtaining evidence in a civil-law jurisdiction is normally conducted by a judicial officer rather than by private attorneys. Petitioners contend that if performed on French soil, for example, by an unauthorized person, such evidence-gathering might violate the "judicial sovereignty" of the host nation. Because it is only through the Convention that civil-law nations have given their consent to evidence-gathering activities within their borders, petitioners argue, we have a duty to employ those procedures whenever they are available.... We find that argument unpersuasive. If such a duty were to be inferred from the adoption of the Convention itself, we believe it would have been described in the text of that document. Moreover, the concept of international comity[4] requires in this context a more particularized analysis of the respective interests of the foreign nation and the requesting nation than petitioners' proposed general rule would generate.[5] We therefore

4. [Court's n.27] Comity refers to the spirit of cooperation in which a domestic tribunal approaches the resolution of cases touching the laws and interests of other sovereign states. This Court referred to the doctrine of comity among nations in Emory v. Grenough, 3 Dall. 369, 370, n. (1797) (dismissing appeal from judgment for failure to plead diversity of citizenship, but setting forth an extract from a treatise by Ulrich Huber (1636–1694), a Dutch jurist):

" 'By the courtesy of nations, whatever laws are carried into execution, within the limits of any government, are considered as having the same effect every where, so far as they do not occasion a prejudice to the rights of the other governments, or their citizens....

" 'Nothing would be more inconvenient in the promiscuous intercourse and practice of mankind, than that what was valid by the laws of one place, should be rendered of no effect elsewhere, by a diversity of law....' " *Ibid.* (*quoting* 2 U. Huber, *Praelectiones Juris Romani et hodiemi*, bk. 1, tit. 3, pp. 26–31 (C. Thomas, L. Menke, & G. Gebauer eds. 1725)). See also Hilton v. Guyot, 159 U.S. 113, 163–164 (1895):

" 'Comity,' in the legal sense, is neither a matter of absolute obligation, on the one hand, nor of mere courtesy and good will, upon the other. But it is the recognition which one nation allows within its territory to the legislative, executive or judicial acts of another nation, having due regard both to international duty and convenience, and to the rights of its own citizens or of other persons who are under the protection of its laws."

5. [Court's n.28] The nature of the concerns that guide a comity analysis is suggested by the Restatement of Foreign Relations Law of the United States (Revised) § 437(1)(c) (Tent. Draft No. 7, 1986) (approved May 14, 1986) (Restatement). While we recognize that § 437 of the Restatement may not represent a consensus of international views on the scope of the district court's power to order foreign discovery in the face of objections by foreign states, these factors are relevant to any comity analysis:

"(1) the importance to the ... litigation of the documents or other information requested;

decline to hold as a blanket matter that comity requires resort to Hague Evidence Convention procedures without prior scrutiny in each case of the particular facts, sovereign interests, and likelihood that resort to those procedures will prove effective.[6]

Some discovery procedures are much more "intrusive" than others. In this case, for example, an interrogatory asking petitioners to identify the pilots who flew flight tests in the Rallye before it was certified for flight by the Federal Aviation Administration, or a request to admit that petitioners authorized certain advertising in a particular magazine, is certainly less intrusive than a request to produce all of the "design specifications, line drawings and engineering plans and all engineering change orders and plans and all drawings concerning the leading edge slats for the Rallye type aircraft manufactured by the Defendants." ... Even if a court might be persuaded that a particular document request was too burdensome or too "intrusive" to be granted in full, with or

"(2) the degree of specificity of the request;

"(3) whether the information originated in the United States;

"(4) the availability of alternative means of securing the information; and

"(5) the extent to which noncompliance with the request would undermine important interests of the United States, or compliance with the request would undermine important interests of the state where the information is located." *Ibid.*

6. [Court's n.29] The French "blocking statute," n. 6, *supra*, does not alter our conclusion. It is well settled that such statutes do not deprive an American court of the power to order a party subject to its jurisdiction to produce evidence even though the act of production may violate that statute. See Societe Internationale Pour Participations Industrielles et Commerciales, S.A. v. Rogers, 357 U.S. 197, 204–206 (1958). Nor can the enactment of such a statute by a foreign nation require American courts to engraft a rule of first resort onto the Hague Convention, or otherwise to provide the nationals of such a country with a preferred status in our courts. It is clear that American courts are not required to adhere blindly to the directives of such a statute. Indeed, the language of the statute, if taken literally, would appear to represent an extraordinary exercise of legislative jurisdiction by the Republic of France over a United States district judge, forbidding him or her to order any discovery from a party of French nationality, even simple requests for admissions or interrogatories that the party could respond to on the basis of personal knowledge. It would be particularly incongruous to recognize such a preference for corporations that are wholly owned by the enacting nation. Extraterritorial assertions of jurisdiction are not one-sided. While the District Court's discovery orders arguably have some impact in France, the French blocking statute asserts similar authority over acts to take place in this country. The lesson of comity is that neither the discovery order nor the blocking statute can have the same omnipresent effect that it would have in a world of only one sovereign. The blocking statute thus is relevant to the court's particularized comity analysis only to the extent that its terms and its enforcement identify the nature of the sovereign interests in nondisclosure of specific kinds of material.

The American Law Institute has summarized this interplay of blocking statutes and discovery orders: "When a state has jurisdiction to prescribe and its courts have jurisdiction to adjudicate, adjudication should (subject to generally applicable rules of evidence) take place on the basis of the best information available.... [Blocking] statutes that frustrate this goal need not be given the same deference by courts of the United States as substantive rules of law at variance with the law of the United States." See Restatement § 437, Reporter's Note 5, pp. 41, 42. "On the other hand, the degree of friction created by discovery requests ... and the differing perceptions of the acceptability of American-style discovery under national and international law, suggest some efforts to moderate the application abroad of U.S. procedural techniques, consistent with the overall principle of reasonableness in the exercise of jurisdiction." *Id.*, at 42.

without an appropriate protective order, it might well refuse to insist upon the use of Convention procedures before requiring responses to simple interrogatories or requests for admissions. The exact line between reasonableness and unreasonableness in each case must be drawn by the trial court, based on its knowledge of the case and of the claims and interests of the parties and the governments whose statutes and policies they invoke.

American courts, in supervising pretrial proceedings, should exercise special vigilance to protect foreign litigants from the danger that unnecessary, or unduly burdensome, discovery may place them in a disadvantageous position. Judicial supervision of discovery should always seek to minimize its costs and inconvenience and to prevent improper uses of discovery requests. When it is necessary to seek evidence abroad, however, the district court must supervise pretrial proceedings particularly closely to prevent discovery abuses. For example, the additional cost of transportation of documents or witnesses to or from foreign locations may increase the danger that discovery may be sought for the improper purpose of motivating settlement, rather than finding relevant and probative evidence. Objections to "abusive" discovery that foreign litigants advance should therefore receive the most careful consideration. In addition, we have long recognized the demands of comity in suits involving foreign states, either as parties or as sovereigns with a coordinate interest in the litigation. See Hilton v. Guyot, 159 U.S. 113 (1895). American courts should therefore take care to demonstrate due respect for any special problem confronted by the foreign litigant on account of its nationality or the location of its operations, and for any sovereign interest expressed by a foreign state. We do not articulate specific rules to guide this delicate task of adjudication. . . .

Notes and Questions

1. Recall that service of process within a foreign state implicates enforcement jurisdictional competence. See Chapter 3, Section 3 A. The Restatement notes that service in states not party to the 1965 Convention on the Service Abroad of Judicial and Extrajudicial Documents in Civil or Commercial Matters, 658 U.N.T.S. 163, 20 U.S.T. 361 (the Hague Service Convention) is generally accomplished pursuant to a letter rogatory or request for judicial assistance by a court of one state to a court or other competent authority of another state. RESTATEMENT, *supra* § 471, cmt. b and RN 1. *See also id.* § 472. Some states also authorize their consuls to serve judicial process within foreign states that consent to such service. See *id.* § 471, RN 2.

2. Federal statutes and rules of procedure concerning the obtaining and use of evidence abroad as well as assistance to foreign and international tribunals include: 28 U.S.C. §§ 1781–1784; Federal Rules of Civil Procedure 28(b), 45 (e); Federal Rules of Criminal Procedure 15(d), 17(e). For general discussion, see Bernard H. Oxman, *The Choice Between Direct Discovery and Other Means of Obtaining Evidence Abroad: The Impact of the Hague*

Evidence Convention, 37 U. Miami L. Rev. 733 (1983); Harold G. Maier, *Extraterritorial Discovery: Cooperation, Coercion and the Hague Evidence Convention*, 19 Vand. J. Transnat'l L. 239 (1986).

3. In the U.S., the Department of State receives letters rogatory issued by a foreign court and also transmits letters rogatory from a U.S. court to courts or entities abroad. *See* 28 U.S.C. § 1781.

4. The Restatement notes that letters rogatory are essentially the same as letters of request under the Hague Evidence Convention, "but execution of letters rogatory [outside the Hague Convention] is voluntary or depends on bilateral arrangements and ordinarily involves diplomatic channels, while execution of letters or request is required by [the Hague] treaty and does not involve diplomatic channels." Restatement, *supra* § 473, RN 1.

5. Other cases requiring production of evidence abroad despite foreign laws include: Doe v. United States, 487 U.S. 201 (1988); *In re* Grand Jury Proceedings (United States v. Bank of Nova Scotia), 691 F.2d 1384 (11th Cir.1982); 740 F.2d 817 (11th Cir.1984), *cert. denied*, 469 U.S. 1106 (1985); *In re* Grand Jury (Union Bank of Switzerland v. United States), 948 F.2d 1298 (11th Cir.1991) (suggestion for rehearing *en banc* denied), *cert. denied*, 502 U.S. 1092 (1992).

6. Many countries have made declarations under Article 23 of the Hague Evidence Convention concerning pretrial discovery of documents. The Restatement notes that Article 23 "applies only to letters of request for discovery of documents, and does not preclude examination before trial of witnesses pursuant to a letter of request," *e.g.*, by depositions and interrogatories. Restatements § 473, cmt. h. Also, statements in the letter that evidence requested is sought "for trial" or "tied to issues in the trial," and not mere pretrial discovery, can provide exceptions to such declarations. *Id.* RNs 4, 7(i).

7. What sort of evidence can one obtain from a consular officer, employee or service staff who is located within the United States? See the Vienna Convention on Consular Relations (in the Documents Supplement).

8. Concerning trends in mutual assistance in criminal matters, *see, e.g.*, Section 2 of this chapter; Jordan J. Paust, M. Cherif Bassiouni, *et al.*, International Criminal Law chpt. 6 (2 ed. 2000).

SECTION 2. MUTUAL LEGAL ASSISTANCE

A. *Letters Rogatory*

28 U.S.C. § 1782. Assistance to Foreign and International Tribunals and to Litigants Before Such Tribunals.

(a) The district court of the district in which a person resides or is found may order him to give his testimony or statement or to produce a document or other thing for use in a proceeding in a foreign or international tribunal. The order may be made pursuant to a letter rogatory issued, or request made, by a foreign or international tribunal or upon the application of an interested person.

Notes and Questions

1. The letters rogatory process is initiated with the submission through diplomatic channels of a request from a foreign court that seeks assistance from a U.S. court in obtaining witness testimony, documents, or other evidence. The Department of State acts as a conduit in the receipt and transmission of such requests and forwards the letter rogatory to the Department of Justice. The Office of International Affairs in the Criminal Division of the Department of Justice reviews the judicial assistance request for sufficiency and to insure that the request can be executed under United States law. Upon completion of the review, the request is sent to the Office of the U.S. Attorney in the federal judicial district where the witness or evidence requested is located. The U.S. Attorney's Office then makes the necessary application to a U.S. district court for the execution of the request. 28 U.S.C. § 1782 states that a court "may" order testimony or document production. Thus, it is not required to provide assistance in response to a letter rogatory. If it decides to grant the request for judicial assistance, it will ordinarily appoint an Assistant U.S. Attorney as a commissioner to administer any oaths and to take the testimony of a witness or receive documents. When necessary, the court will utilize compulsory process (*i.e.*, subpoenas) to compel the production of documents or the presence of a witness for a deposition hearing before the commissioner. This process is time consuming, often taking as long as three to six months to complete.

2. What constitutes a "proceeding in a foreign or international tribunal" for purposes of 28 U.S.C. § 1782? Would a criminal investigation that had not yet reached the indictment stage qualify? Would a proceeding before an administrative agency, such as a foreign version of the IRS or SEC? The legislative history indicates that "[t]he word 'tribunal' is used to make it clear that assistance is not confined to proceedings before conventional courts." H.R. Rep. 1052, 88th Cong., 1st Sess., at 9 (1963), 1964 U.S. Code Cong. & Admin. News 3788. In *In re* Request From Ministry of Legal Affairs of Trinidad and Tobago, 848 F.2d 1151 (11th Cir.1988), the Eleventh Circuit held that the statute gives the district courts discretion to grant judicial assistance in connection with a criminal investigation even before a judicial proceeding has begun.

3. U.S. courts also have authority to send letters rogatory through diplomatic channels to foreign courts for judicial assistance in criminal cases. *See* United States v. Steele, 685 F.2d 793 (3d Cir.), *cert. denied*, 459 U.S. 908 (1982). In such cases, U.S. courts have held that a deposition of a prosecution witness taken abroad in a manner different from that which would be required of a deposition taken in the United States may be admitted in evidence and used against a defendant in a U.S. criminal prosecution. *See, e.g.*, United States v. Salim, 855 F.2d 944 (2d Cir.1988).

B. International Criminal Treaties

Many of the newer international criminal law treaties have specific provisions concerning mutual cooperation and assistance.

CONVENTION AGAINST TORTURE AND OTHER CRUEL, INHUMAN OR DEGRADING TREATMENT OR PUNISHMENT

Dec. 10, 1984, 39 U.N. GAOR, Supp. No. 51, at 197, U.N. Doc. A/39/51.

Article 9

1. States Parties shall afford one another the greatest measure of assistance in connection with criminal proceedings brought in respect of any of the offenses referred to in Article 4, including the supply of all evidence at their disposal necessary for the proceedings.

2. States Parties shall carry out their obligations under paragraph 1 of this article in conformity with any treaties on mutual judicial assistance that may exist between them.

Article 14

1. Each State Party shall ensure in its legal system that the victim of an act of torture obtains redress and has an enforceable right to fair and adequate compensation, including the means for as full rehabilitation as possible. In the event of the death of the victim as a result of an act of torture, his dependents shall be entitled to compensation.

2. Nothing in this article shall affect any right of the victim or other persons to compensation which may exist under national law.

1971 MONTREAL CONVENTION FOR THE SUPPRESSION OF UNLAWFUL ACTS AGAINST THE SAFETY OF CIVIL AVIATION

974 U.N.T.S. 177, 24 U.S.T. 564, T.I.A.S. 7570.

Article 11

1. Contracting States shall afford one another the greatest measure of assistance in connection with criminal proceedings brought in respect of the offenses. The law of the State requested shall apply in all cases.

2. The Provisions of paragraph 1 of this article shall not affect obligations under any other treaty, bilateral or multilateral, which governs or will govern, in whole or in part, mutual assistance in criminal matters.

Article 12

Any Contracting State having reason to believe that one of the offenses mentioned in Article 1 will be committed shall, in accordance with its national law, furnish any relevant information in its possession to those states which it believes would be the states mentioned in Article 5, paragraph 1 [which have jurisdiction over an offense].

STATUTE OF THE INTERNATIONAL CRIMINAL TRIBUNAL [FOR THE FORMER YUGOSLAVIA]

U.N. Doc. S/25704 (May 3, 1993), Annex.

Article 29

Cooperation and judicial assistance

1. States shall cooperate with the International Tribunal in the investigation and prosecution of persons accused of committing serious violations of international humanitarian law.

2. States shall comply without undue delay with any request for assistance or an order issued by a Trial Chamber, including, but not limited to:

(a) the identification and location of persons;

(b) the taking of testimony and the production of evidence;

(c) the service of documents;

(d) the arrest or detention of persons;

(e) the surrender or the transfer of the accused to the International Tribunal.

Rules of Procedure and Evidence [of the ICT for the Former Yugoslavia (1994)]

Rule 56

Cooperation of States

The State to which a warrant of arrest is transmitted shall act promptly and with all due diligence to ensure proper and effective execution thereof, in accordance with Article 29 of the Statute.

Rule 57

Procedure after Arrest

Upon the arrest of the accused, the State concerned shall detain him, and shall promptly notify the Registrar. The transfer of the accused to the seat of the Tribunal shall be arranged between the State authorities concerned and the Registrar.

Rule 58

National Extradition Provisions

The obligations laid down in Article 29 of the Statute shall prevail over any legal impediment to the surrender or transfer of the accused to the Tribunal which may exist under the national law or extradition treaties of the State concerned.

Rule 59

Failure to Execute a Warrant

(A) Where the State to which a warrant of arrest has been transmitted has been unable to execute the warrant, it shall report forthwith its inability to the Registrar, and the reasons therefor.

(B) If, within a reasonable time after the warrant of arrest has been transmitted to the State, no report is made on action taken, this shall be deemed a failure to execute the warrant of arrest and the Tribunal, through the President, may notify the Security Council accordingly.

Rule 60

Advertisement of Indictment

At the request of the Prosecutor, a form of advertisement shall be transmitted by the Registrar to the national authorities of any State or States in whose territory the Prosecutor has reason to believe that the accused may be found, for publication in newspapers having wide circulation in that territory, intimating to the accused that service of an indictment against him is sought.

Rule 61

Procedure in Case of Failure to Execute a Warrant

(A) If a warrant of arrest has not been executed, and personal service of the indictment has consequently not been effected, and the Prosecutor satisfies a Judge of a Trial Chamber that:

(i) he has taken all reasonable steps to effect personal service, including recourse to the appropriate authorities of the State in whose territory or under whose jurisdiction and control the person to be served resides or was last known to him to be; and

(ii) he has otherwise tried to inform the accused of the existence of the indictment by seeking publication of newspaper advertisements pursuant to Rule 60, the Judge shall order that the indictment be submitted by the Prosecutor to the Trial Chamber.

(B) Upon obtaining such an order the Prosecutor shall submit the indictment to the Trial Chamber in open court, together with all the evidence that was before the Judge who initially confirmed the indictment.

(C) If the Trial Chamber is satisfied on that evidence, together with such additional evidence as the Prosecutor may tender, that there are reasonable grounds for believing that the accused has committed all or any of the crimes charged in the indictment, it shall so determine. The Trial Chamber shall have the relevant parts of the indictment read out by the Prosecutor together with an account of the efforts to effect service referred to in Sub-rule (A) above.

(D) The Trial Chamber shall also issue an international arrest warrant in respect of the accused which shall be transmitted to all States.

(E) If the Prosecutor satisfies the Trial Chamber that the failure to effect personal service was due in whole or in part to a failure or refusal of a State to cooperate with the Tribunal in accordance with Article 29 of the Statute, the Trial Chamber shall so certify, in which event the President shall notify the Security Council....

Rule 95

Evidence Obtained by Means Contrary to Internationally Protected Human Rights

Evidence obtained directly or indirectly by means which constitute a serious violation of internationally protected human rights shall not be admissible....

Rule 105

Restitution of Property

(A) After a judgement of conviction containing a specific finding as provided in Sub-rule 88(B), the Trial Chamber shall, at the request of the Prosecutor, or may, at its own initiative, hold a special hearing to determine the matter of the restitution of the property or the proceeds thereof, and may in the meantime order such provisional measures for the preservation and protection of the property or proceeds as it considers appropriate.

(B) The determination may extend to such property or its proceeds, even in the hands of third parties not otherwise connected with the crime of which the convicted person has been found guilty.

(C) Such third parties shall be summoned before the Trial Chamber and be given an opportunity to justify their claim to the property or its proceeds.

(D) Should the Trial Chamber be able to determine the rightful owner on the balance of probabilities, it shall order the restitution either of the property or the proceeds as appropriate.

(E) Should the Trial Chamber not be able to determine ownership, it shall notify the competent national authorities and request them so to determine.

(F) The Registrar shall transmit to the competent national authorities any summonses, orders and requests issued by a Trial Chamber pursuant to Sub-rules (C), (D) and (E).

Rule 106

Compensation to Victims

(A) The Registrar shall transmit to the competent authorities of the States concerned the judgement finding the accused guilty of a crime which has caused injury to a victim.

(B) Pursuant to the relevant national legislation, a victim or persons claiming through him may bring an action in a national court or other competent body to obtain compensation.

(C) For the purposes of a claim made under Sub-rule (B) the judgement of the Tribunal shall be final and binding as to the criminal responsibility of the convicted person for such injury.

Notes and Questions

1. Article 11 of the Montreal Convention is nearly the same as Article 11 of the International Convention Against the Taking of Hostages, 1316 U.N.T.S. 205; and is the same as Article 10 of the 1970 [Hague] Convention for the Suppression of Unlawful Seizure of Aircraft, 860 U.N.T.S. 105, 22 U.S.T. 1641. Article 11 of the Hostages Convention adds with respect to measures of assistance to be afforded: "including the supply of all evidence at their disposal necessary for the proceedings."

2. For further discussion and application of Article 29 of the Statute of the International Criminal Tribunal for Former Yugoslavia and the Rules of Procedure and Evidence, see JORDAN J. PAUST, M. CHERIF BASSIOUNI, *ET AL.*, INTERNATIONAL CRIMINAL LAW 76–77, 79, 759–71, 780, 782–823 (1996). What is the treaty that forms the primary basis for duties recognized in Article 29 of the Statute and in the Rules?

3. These treaties do not address sanctions to be imposed on a state in case of breach. What sorts of sanction response are available under international law? See Chapters 1 and 2; *see also* Vienna Convention on the Law of Treaties, Articles 26, 60; ALONA E. EVANS & JOHN F. MURPHY (EDS.), LEGAL ASPECTS OF INTERNATIONAL TERRORISM, especially chpts. 7, 11–13 and appendix (1978); Jordan J. Paust, *A Survey of Possible Legal Responses to International Terrorism: Prevention, Punishment, and Cooperative Action*, 5 GA. J. INT'L & COMP. L. 431, 445–69 (1975) (also outlining individual and cooperative enforcement efforts concerning education, data sharing and intelligence, warning requirements, investigations, arrests, prosecutions, and other preventive and responsive measures).

4. With respect to war crimes and crimes against humanity, the United Nations General Assembly has also recognized customary and treaty-based responsibilities of states. From the late 1960s to the early 1970s there were a series of United Nations General Assembly resolutions evidencing expectations about universal jurisdiction and the duty to engage in criminal sanction efforts. For example, in a 1973 resolution on principles of international cooperation in the detection, arrest, extradition, and punishment of persons guilty of war crimes and crimes against humanity, it was rightly affirmed:

> 1. War crimes and crimes against humanity, wherever they are committed, shall be subject to investigation and the persons against whom there is evidence that they have committed such crimes shall be subject to tracing, arrest, trial and, if found guilty, to punishment....
>
> 3. States shall co-operate with each other on a bi-lateral and multilateral basis with a view to halting and preventing war crimes and crimes against humanity, and take the domestic and international measures necessary for that purpose.
>
> 4. States shall assist each other in detecting, arresting and bringing to trial persons suspected of having committed such crimes and, if they are found guilty, in punishing them....

> 7. States shall not grant asylum to any person with respect to whom there are serious reasons for considering that he has committed a crime against peace, a war crime or a crime against humanity.

U.N. G.A. Res. 3074, 28 U.N. GAOR, Supp. (No. 30), at 78, U.N. Doc. A/9030 (1973). In other resolutions it was also affirmed that a refusal "to cooperate in the arrest, extradition, trial and punishment" of such persons is contrary to the United Nations Charter "and to generally recognized norms of international law."

It should be noted that there are no statutes of limitation under international law regarding such crimes. Indeed, use of domestic statutes of limitation to inhibit domestic prosecutions would run afoul of the above requirements and the duty under customary international law with respect to international crimes to either initiate prosecution of or extradite those reasonably accused of such a crime who are found within a state's territory *if* such a state does not extradite the accused and cooperate with foreign and/or international tribunal prosecution efforts. *See generally* PAUST, BASSIOUNI, *ET AL.*, INTERNATIONAL CRIMINAL LAW 8, 15, 46, 74–78, 82–84 (1996).

5. After the bombings of U.S. embassies in Kenya and Tanzania on August 7, 1998, the U.N. Security Council condemned the "indiscriminate and outrageous acts of international terrorism" and called upon "all States to adopt, in accordance with international law and as a matter of priority, effective and practical measures for security and cooperation, for the prevention of such acts of terrorism, and for the prosecution and punishment of their perpetrators." U.N. S.C. Res. 1189 (13 Aug. 1998). What might happen if a state did not comply? Also recall the discussions of *Jaffe* and *Alvarez-Machain* and other measure of self-help and self-defense in Chapter 3.

6. The Rome Statute of the International Criminal Court (ICC) adopted by the U.N. Diplomatic Conference July 17, 1998, contains a number of provisions concerning transnational or mutual cooperation and assistance with respect to crimes within the jurisdiction of the ICC (such as genocide, certain crimes against humanity, and certain war crimes), including provisions on awarding money reparations and enforcement of judgments. See Rome Statute on the International Criminal Court, Articles 75, 79 (reparations), 86–100 (cooperation and assistance), 109 (judgments), *reprinted in* 37 I.L.M. 1002 (1998). The U.S. presently has expressed opposition to ratification of this treaty. Some of the opposition involves concerns about subjecting U.S. nationals to an international criminal tribunal and concerns about due process guarantees, although human rights law provides a minimum set of guarantees before the ICC. Given universal jurisdictional competence of every state to prosecute U.S. nationals found in their territory who are accused of having committed crimes within the jurisdiction of the ICC (and the power of each such state to delegate their competence to an international court, as the U.S. did regarding the IMT at Nuremberg and the IMT for the Far East), do you think such opposition is warranted?

C. *Mutual Legal Assistance Treaties*

1990 U.S.–Canada Mutual Legal Assistance Treaty in Criminal Matters

[read the Treaty in the Documents Supplement]

Notes and Questions

1. The first U.S. Mutual Legal Assistance Treaty (MLAT) entered into force with Switzerland in 1977. TIAS No. 8302, 20 U.S.T. 2019, May 25, 1977. The United States now has MLATS with several countries, including: Argentina, the Bahamas, Canada, the Cayman Islands, Italy, Jamaica, Mexico, The Netherlands, Spain, Switzerland, Turkey, the United Kingdom, and Uruguay.

2. Concerning advantages of MLATs over the letters rogatory process, consider the following testimony of Alan Kreczko, Deputy Legal Adviser, U.S. Department of State, before the Senate Committee on Foreign Relations, April 8, 1992:

> Mutual Legal Assistance Treaties are generally intended to enable law enforcement authorities to obtain evidence abroad in a form admissible in our courts. They supplement rather than supplant existing international arrangements on exchange of information and evidence, such as INTERPOL, law enforcement liaison relationships, and judicial assistance/letters rogatory.
>
> One of the most significant U.S. objectives that each of these treaties serves is the establishment of direct, expedited channels of communication through the Central Authorities. This direct channel, generally Justice-to-Justice, is intended to expedite and facilitate the provision of all categories of assistance. This has proved to be of critical importance, particularly with civil law countries (*i.e.*, Argentina, Spain and Uruguay) which traditionally have restricted their willingness to execute legal assistance requests to those submitted by judicial authorities rather than prosecutors. While this practice may be consistent with the investigative role of judges in these countries, it has seriously hampered the ability of the United States to obtain necessary assistance, since parallel responsibility in the United States is assigned to prosecutors rather than judges.
>
> Each of the treaties provides for the same types of assistance which are generally catalogued in the first article. These include service of documents, provision of records, locating persons, taking the testimony of persons, production of documents, execution of requests for search and seizure, and the transfer of persons in custody for testimonial purposes. Some types of assistance available under the MLATs, such as transfer of persons in custody for testimonial purposes, may not be available through letters rogatory. Moreover, MLATs establish a framework that ensures the provision of evidence in admissible form in the requesting state's courts.

Contemporary Practice of the United States Relating to International Law, 86 AM. J. INT'L L. 548 (1992).*

3. Is the duty to provide assistance pursuant to a MLAT less discretionary than the duty to respond to a letter rogatory? The MLAT with Canada permits Canada to deny assistance only when "execution of the request is contrary to its public interest, as determined by its Central Authority." What types of cases might fall within the exception?

4. Is there a duty on the part of the requesting state to use the MLAT rather than unilateral measures? If the requested state denies a MLAT request, does the requesting state have the right to pursue unilateral measures? The U.S.-U.K. MLAT is the only MLAT with a provision requiring "first resort" to the MLAT and the use of consultative procedures prior to the enforcement of unilateral "compulsory measures." An interpretive note that accompanied the MLAT provides that the U.S. Department of Justice shall instruct all federal prosecutors and advise all federal agencies not to seek compulsory measures with respect to any matter for which assistance could be granted under the Treaty unless the U.S. Central Authority has concluded that the consultative mechanisms in Article 18 of the Treaty have been satisfied. See *U.S. Practice: Judicial Assistance*, 89 AM. J. INT'L L. 589 (1995).

5. Can the government use evidence obtained through a MLAT for other matters beyond the scope of the request? In United States v. Johnpoll, 739 F.2d 702 (2d Cir.1984), the Second Circuit held that "[a]s long as the evidence was used to prosecute violations covered by the Treaty, the government was not precluded from also prosecuting other related non-treaty offenses...." *Id.* at 714. Once the evidence is entered into the "public" record at trial, can the evidence be used later to prosecute an unrelated offense?

6. What right does a criminal accused have to use a MLAT to obtain evidence located abroad? The negotiators of MLATs have sought to exclude their use by non-governmental parties. *See, e.g.*, Article II (4) of the U.S.-Canada MLAT. Criminal defendants are expected to use the letters rogatory process, even though it is much slower and subject to the discretion of the foreign court. Is it fair or consistent with due process to allow the government the right to gather incriminating evidence with relative speed but relegate the defendant to much slower methods in order to gather exculpatory evidence?

7. If a criminal defendant cannot use a MLAT directly, can the defendant nevertheless request the court to compel the government to make a request under a MLAT for information that contains exculpatory evidence? In United States v. Sindona, 636 F.2d 792 (2d Cir.1980), *cert. denied*, 451 U.S. 912 (1981), a request for assistance under the treaty with Switzerland was made by the defense, and the court ruled that the request should be complied with or the case would be dismissed.

8. What rights does a criminal accused have to assert that the procedures of a MLAT have been violated? Consider:

UNITED STATES v. DAVIS

767 F.2d 1025 (2d Cir.1985).

PALMIERI, J.

The indictment containing seventeen counts (Davis having been named in fourteen) charged Davis and three co-defendants with various charges arising out of a scheme contrived and executed during the years 1973–1978 which involved the payment of multi-million dollar kickbacks to executives of General Dynamics Corporation in return for the approval of subcontracts awarded by General Dynamics to Frigitemp Corporation of New York City ("Frigitemp"), of which Davis was a Senior Vice President....

The principal actor in the scheme was Davis, who first proposed the payment of kickbacks to Veliotis and Gilliland. A fund of over $5 million to pay the kickbacks was devised by Davis by creating and submitting to Frigitemp for payment a series of fictitious "consulting contracts" and materials invoices in the names of sham Cayman Island corporations, for non-existent consulting services and raw materials.

Davis also organized and supervised the laundering of the kickback fund through an elaborate network of bank accounts in the United States, Canada, the Cayman Islands and Switzerland, and carried out the actual payment of the kickbacks through a series of wire transfers to secret numbered Swiss bank accounts of Veliotis and Gilliland. In the course of carrying out the kickback scheme, Davis secretly diverted nearly half of the $5 million fund to himself.

Davis seeks reversal on three grounds. First, he claims that records of his Swiss bank accounts were procured by the Government in contravention of applicable treaty provisions and were therefore inadmissible....

In October 1981, almost two years before the return of the indictment, the Government availed itself of the Treaty between the United States and Switzerland on Mutual Assistance in Criminal Matters, May 25, 1973, 27 U.S.T. 2019, T.I.A.S. No. 8302 (the "Treaty"), to seek out records of Swiss bank accounts used in the scheme, including those maintained by Davis.

Following the procedure set forth in the Treaty, the Central Authority approved the request and transmitted it to the Examining Magistrate for the canton in which Davis' accounts were located for issuance of orders to the banks to produce the required records. On February 8, 1982, the Swiss Magistrate directed the Swiss Bank Corporation and the Credit Suisse (the two Zurich banks where Davis maintained accounts) to produce the records and to swear to their authenticity as genuine business records maintained in the regular course of business. On February 19, 1982, Davis' Swiss attorney became aware of the October

1981 document request and filed a notice of protest in the Swiss courts. As provided for in the Treaty, a hearing (referred to here for convenience as an authentication hearing) was held in June 1982. At that time, the bank employees produced written affidavits certifying that the documents produced were authentic business records maintained in the regular course of business. In addition, as provided in paragraphs 1 through 3 of Article 18 of the Treaty, the Magistrate before whom the documents were produced examined the bank employees under oath, satisfied himself as to the authenticity of the records, and attested to their authenticity under his official seal....

Davis was not notified of the authentication hearing and was not present at the hearing. Davis made no application to attend the hearing....

Davis contends that the Zurich Bank records were procured in violation of Article 18, paragraph 5 of the Treaty and that the records should therefore have been excluded. That paragraph provides as follows: "Where a request under this Article pertains to pending court proceedings, the defendant, upon his application, may be present or represented by counsel or both, and may examine the person producing the document as to its genuineness and admissibility. In the event the defendant elects to be present or represented, a representative of the requesting State or a state or canton thereof may also be present and put such questions to the witness." (emphasis added.)

At the outset, it must be noted that Davis has no standing to raise this purported Treaty violation before this Court. See United States v. Johnpoll, 739 F.2d 702, 714 (2d Cir.), *cert. denied,* 469 U.S. 1075, 105 S.Ct. 571, 83 L.Ed.2d 511 (1984). Article 37 of the Treaty provides that: "[t]he existence of restrictions in this Treaty shall not give rise to a right on the part of any person to take any action in the United States to suppress or exclude any evidence or to obtain other judicial relief in connection with requests under this Treaty, except with respect to [certain enumerated paragraphs.]" One of the enumerated paragraphs, paragraph 7 of Article 18, provides that "[i]n the event that the genuineness of any document authenticated in accordance with Article is denied by any party" that party shall have the burden of establishing that the document is not genuine. Since Davis has never contested the genuineness of the documents, paragraph 7 is not implicated.

That Davis has no standing to raise a purported violation of Article 18, paragraph 5 of the Treaty in this context is made absolutely clear by both the interpretative letters signed by the United States and Switzerland and by the Technical Analysis of the Treaty. The interpretative letters signed on May 25, 1973 provide that it is the understanding of the United States and Swiss governments that a person alleging a violation of Article 5 of the Treaty (which deals with limitations on the use of information obtained pursuant to the Treaty) "has no standing to have such allegations considered in any proceeding in the United States.... [H]is recourse would be for him to inform the Central

Authority of Switzerland for consideration only as a matter between governments." 27 U.S.T. at 2128–38. The Technical Analysis provides that "restrictions in the Treaty shall not give rise to a right of any person to take action to suppress or exclude evidence or to obtain judicial relief." Technical Analysis of the Treaty between the United States and Switzerland on Mutual Assistance in Criminal Matters (reprinted in Message from the President Transmitting the Treaty with the Swiss Confederation on Mutual Assistance in Criminal Matters, 94th Cong., 2d Sess. at 63–64 (1976)). . . .

Given the clear and unambiguous language in Article 37 of the Treaty reflecting the intention of the signatory states that the Treaty would not—except in certain specifically designated circumstances—confer judicially enforceable rights on individuals and the absence of any protest from either Switzerland or the United States, Davis has no standing to move to exclude or suppress the Swiss Bank records on the basis of a purported violation of Article 18, paragraph 5. . . .

SECTION 3. FOREIGN SOVEREIGN COMPULSION

[recall discussion in Chapter 3, Section 1]

SECTION 4. RECOGNITION OF FOREIGN JUDGMENTS

HILTON v. GUYOT

159 U.S. 113, 202 (1895).

GRAY, J.

In view of all the authorities upon the subject, and of the trend of judicial opinion in this country and in England, following the lead of Kent and Story, we are satisfied that, where there has been opportunity for a full and fair trial abroad before a court of competent jurisdiction, conducting the trial upon regular proceedings, after due citation or voluntary appearance of the defendant, and under a system of jurisprudence likely to secure an impartial administration of justice between citizens of its own country and those of other countries, and there is nothing to show either prejudice in the court, or in the system of laws under which it was sitting, or fraud in procuring the judgment, or any other special reason why the comity of this nation should not allow it full effect, the merits of the case should not, in an action brought in this country upon the judgment, be tried afresh, as on a new trial or an appeal, upon the mere assertion of the party that the judgment was erroneous in law or in fact.

RESTATEMENT OF THE FOREIGN RELATIONS LAW OF THE UNITED STATES (3 ed. 1987)

§ 481. Recognition and Enforcement of Foreign Judgments

(1) Except as provided in § 482, a final judgment of a court of a foreign state granting or denying a sum of money, establishing or

confirming the status of a person, or determining interests in property, is conclusive between the parties, and is entitled to recognition in courts in the United States.

(2) A judgment entitled to recognition under Subsection (1) may be enforced by any party or its successors or assigns against any other party, its successors or assigns, in accordance with the procedure for enforcement of judgments applicable where enforcement is sought.

Comment *a. Recognition and enforcement of judgments as State law.* This section sets forth the prevailing common and statutory law of States of the United States, not rules of federal or international law.... [I]n the absence of a federal statute or treaty or some other basis for federal jurisdiction ... , recognition and enforcement of foreign country judgments is a matter of State law, and an action to enforce a foreign country judgment is not an action arising under the laws of the United States....

d. Reciprocity in enforcement of foreign judgments. A judgment otherwise entitled to recognition will not be denied recognition or enforcement because courts in the rendering state might not enforce a judgment of a court in the United States if the circumstances were reversed....

§ 482. Grounds for Nonrecognition of Foreign Judgments

(1) A court in the United States may not recognize a judgment of the court of a foreign state if:

(a) the judgment was rendered under a judicial system that does not provide impartial tribunals or procedures compatible with due process of law; or

(b) the court that rendered the judgment did not have jurisdiction over the defendant in accordance with the law of the rendering state and with rules set forth in § 421.

(2) A court in the United States need not recognize a judgment of the court of a foreign state if:

(a) the court that rendered the judgment did not have jurisdiction of the subject matter of the action;

(b) the defendant did not receive notice of the proceeding in sufficient time to enable him to defend;

(c) the judgment was obtained by fraud;

(d) the cause of action on which the judgment was based, or the judgment itself, is repugnant to the public policy of the United States or of the State where recognition is sought;

(e) the judgment conflicts with another final judgment that is entitled to recognition; or

(f) the proceeding in the foreign court was contrary to an agreement between the parties to submit the controversy on which the judgment is based to another forum.

Notes and Questions

1. The Restatement notes that subsection (1) relates to mandatory denial of recognition, whereas subsection (2) relates to discretionary denial of recognition. *Id.* § 482, cmt. a. If a lack of impartial tribunals or fair procedure in the foreign judicial system mandates nonrecognition, should the circumstances listed in subsection (2)(b) and (c) also mandate nonrecognition? See also *id.* cmt. b (lack of fair procedure).

Concerning enforcement of foreign judgments more generally, *see, e.g.*, Harold D. Maier, *"Could a Treaty Trump Supreme Court Jurisdictional Doctrine?: A Hague Conference Judgments Convention and United States Courts: A Problem and a Possibility"*, 61 ALB. L. REV.1207 (1998).

2. If a foreign judgment was produced in violation of international law, *e.g.*, human rights to due process or "denial of justice" to an alien, should the foreign judgment be entitled to any recognition? Do not treaty-based and customary international legal norms override inconsistent state law and mere federal common law? *See* Chapter 2, Section 2 F. In addition to the general norm of nondiscrimination, what human rights to due process are discoverable in human rights instruments?

3. Treaties modify or condition judicial discretion concerning recognition of certain foreign judgments among signatory states. *See, e.g.*, The Hague Convention on the Civil Aspects of International Child Abductions, T.I.A.S. No. 11670, reprinted in 19 I.L.M. 1501 (1980); Final Act, 18th Session of the Hague Conference (July 1996), reprinted in 35 I.L.M. 1391 (1996); the United Nations Convention on the Recovery Abroad of Maintenance, 268 U.N.T.S. 3. Within the U.S., there is often comparable federal legislation. *See, e.g.*, Federal Parental Kidnapping Prevention Act, 28 U.S.C. § 1738A, *et seq.*; International Child Abduction Remedies Act, 42 U.S.C. § 11601 *et seq. See also* RESTATEMENT, *supra* §§ 485–486. With respect to international crimes, recall the Rules of Procedure and Evidence of the ICT for the Former Yugoslavia, Rules 105–106, in Section 2 above.

4. The 1958 New York or U.N. Convention on the Recognition and Enforcement of Foreign Arbitral Awards, 330 U.N.T.S. 3, 21 U.S.T. 2517, T.I.A.S. No. 6997, has had significant impact on enforcement of arbitral awards. *See also* 9 U.S.C. §§ 1–14, 201–208; RESTATEMENT, *supra* §§ 487–488. Recall that the Foreign Sovereign Immunities Act also addresses certain agreements to arbitrate and the effect of arbitral awards. See Chapter Four, Section 1 D.

5. It is a "maxim of international law that 'courts of no nation execute the penal laws of another.'" Brady v. Daly, 175 U.S. 148, 155 (1899), *quoting* Huntington v. Attrill, 146 U.S. 657, 666 (1892), *quoting* The Antelope, 23 U.S. (10 Wheat.) 66, 123 (1825) (Marshall, C.J.). See also RESTATEMENT, *supra* § 483, cmt. b and RNs 3–4.

SECTION 5. TRANSFER OF PRISONERS

PFEIFER v. UNITED STATES BUREAU OF PRISONS

615 F.2d 873 (9th Cir.1980).

FARRIS, J.

Pfeifer, who was serving the remainder of a Mexican sentence in a federal penitentiary, filed petition for writ of habeas corpus. The United States District Court for the Southern District of California, Gordon Thompson, Jr., 468 F. Supp. 920, denied relief, and appeal was taken.

Pfeifer was arrested in the Mexico City airport on September 19, 1977. Mexican officials found what appeared to be cocaine in his suitcase and three apparently counterfeit $100 bills on his person. On March 31, 1978 he was found guilty in a Mexican court of importing cocaine and of possessing counterfeit money. He was sentenced to twelve years in prison. Pfeifer alleges that he was made to sign a confession by torture, that he was denied effective assistance of counsel, and that he was denied the right to appeal. At a hearing in Tijuana, Mexico on May 12, 1978 before a United States magistrate, Pfeifer consented to be transferred to the custody of the United States to serve his Mexican sentence in accordance with the provisions of the Treaty. He was transferred to the United States and on June 2, 1978 he filed this petition for habeas corpus.

Pfeifer contends that those portions of the treaty and its implementing legislation that deny transferred prisoners the right to challenge the constitutionality of their foreign convictions in United States courts are unconstitutional. He argues that his conviction was obtained in violation of his due process rights and that he should therefor be released from custody. Alternatively, he contends that, even if the Treaty is constitutional, the provisions of the Treaty were not met in his case because his consent to be transferred was not voluntarily and knowingly given.

We understand but reject Pfeifer's arguments. The Treaty does not create new rights which enable a foreign convict to have a review of an otherwise final foreign judgement. Its sole purpose is to permit persons convicted in foreign countries to serve their incarcerations in the country of which they are citizens. We recognize that the procedures followed in some foreign countries may not meet our constitutional standards. That fact, however, does not render the challenged portions of the Treaty unconstitutional, nor does the fact that we will not recognize a foreign penal judgment which was obtained in a manner that does not comport with due process. Our concern here is the constitutionality of the challenged portions of the Treaty. The constitutionality of the conviction which led to the foreign incarceration is not before us.

The district court held that the United States Constitution has no relation to the validity of Pfeifer's foreign conviction for a foreign crime, relying on Neely v. Henkel, 180 U.S. 109 (1901) and Holmes v. Laird,

148 U.S. App. D.C. 187, 459 F.2d 1211 (D.C.Cir.), *cert. denied*, 409 U.S. 869 (1972). We do not reach that question because the Treaty and its implementing legislation provide that, prior to transfer, an offender must first consent to the conditions of the Treaty. This consent constitutes a waiver of, or at least an agreement not to assert, any constitutional rights the offender might have regarding his or her conviction. The issue is whether this consent is obtained in a manner that meets the constitutional tests for a valid waiver.

A valid waiver of constitutional rights must be voluntarily and knowingly made. McCarthy v. United States, 394 U.S. 459 (1969). The accused must have access to competent counsel. *See* Tollett v. Henderson, 411 U.S. 258 (1973). The validity of the waiver should be determined by a court and an affirmative showing that the waiver was intelligent and voluntary must appear in the record. Boykin v. Alabama, 395 U.S. 238 (1969).

The statute implementing the Treaty provides that a United States magistrate shall verify at a hearing held in the transferring country, that the offender consents to the transfer voluntarily and will full knowledge of the consequences. 18 U.S.C. § 4108. It provides that the offender be advised of his or her right to counsel, that certain specific questions be asked concerning the consequences of transferring, and that a record be made of the verification proceedings. *Id.* Counsel will be appointed for an offender who is financially unable to obtain his or her own. 18 U.S.C. § 4109. An offender's consent to be transferred pursuant to the Treaty is a constitutionally valid waiver of any constitutional rights he or she might have regarding his or her conviction.

Further, the requirement that an offender agree not to challenge his or her conviction in a United States court is not an unconstitutional condition. A constitutional question arises when a party is required to relinquish a vested right as a condition for obtaining a benefit. *See* United States v. Jackson, 390 U.S. 570 (1968); Sherbert v. Verner, 374 U.S. 398 (1963); Smartt v. Avery, 370 F.2d 788 (6th Cir.1967). Americans who are incarcerated in Mexican prisons, however, have no right to relief from United States courts. Those who accept the opportunity presented by the Treaty lose nothing by consenting to limit themselves solely to Mexican remedies after the transfer. See Note, *Constitutional Problems in the Execution of Foreign Penal Sentences: The Mexican–American Prisoner Transfer Treaty*, 90 HARV. L. REV. 1500, 1524–25 (1977). In cases concerning conditional presidential pardons, where the offenders also lose no vested rights in accepting the conditional benefit, the conditions imposed have been upheld. See Schick v. Reed, 419 U.S. 256 (1974); Hoffa v. Saxbe, 378 F. Supp. 1221 (D.D.C.1974). *Cf.* Birzon v. King, 469 F.2d 1241 (2d Cir.1972) (parole conditions upheld).

Pfeifer contends that a waiver under the Treaty cannot be valid because the duress caused by the brutal conditions of Mexican prisons denies the transferring prisoner any real choice. He cites *United States v. Jackson, supra.* There the Court held that the death penalty clause of the Federal Kidnapping Act was unconstitutional because it provided that the death penalty could be awarded only if recommended in the jury's verdict. This provision could be awarded only if recommended in the jury's verdict. This provision needlessly encouraged defendants to waive their rights to jury trial. Crucial to the court's holding was its finding that the statute's purpose could be accomplished in a way that did not encourage a waiver of constitutional rights. See Corbitt v. New Jersey, 439 U.S. 212, 219 n. 9 (1978). The same cannot be said about the Treaty and its implementing statute. The reasoning of Jackson therefore does not apply....

Notes and Questions

1. Other cases include: Mitchell v. United States, 483 F.Supp. 291 (E.D.Wis.1980); Rosado v. Civiletti, 621 F.2d 1179 (2d Cir.1980).

2. Many prisoners who were transferred challenged the constitutionality of transfer of prisoner treaties, especially whether the U.S. can constitutionally incarcerate U.S. citizens denied basic process without the possibility of review by U.S. courts. A related issue is whether a U.S. transferee can be forced to choose between continued mistreatment and "waiver" of her right to attack her foreign conviction collaterally in a U.S. court. The prisoner may be presented with either an unconstitutional condition or an impermissibly coercive situation in making that choice. *See, e.g.*, Abraham Abramovsky & Stephen J. Eagle, *A Critical Evaluation of the Mexican–American Transfer of Penal Sanctions Treaty*, 64 Iowa L. Rev. 314 (1979); Ira P. Robbins, *A Constitutional Analysis of the Prohibition Against Collateral Attack in the Mexican–American Prisoner Exchange Treaty*, 26 U.C.L.A. L. Rev. 8 (1978); *but see* M. Cherif Bassiouni, *Perspectives on the Transfer of Prisoners Between the United States and Mexico and the United States an Canada*, 11 Vand. J. Transnat'l. L. 193 (1978); Detlev F. Vagts, *A Reply* to "*A Critical Evaluation of the Mexican–American Transfer of Penal Sanctions Treaty*", 64 Iowa L. Rev. 325 (1979); Myres S. McDougal, W. Michael Reisman, International Law In Contemporary Perspective 1512 (1981); Jordan J. Paust, M. Cherif Bassiouni, *et al.*, International Criminal Law 596–97 (1996).

3. Functionally, does the U.S. "execute" the penal laws of a foreign country or foreign penal judgments under such treaty-based enforcement processes? Does execution of the foreign conviction and sentence involve the "power of punishment"? *Compare* Rosado v. Civiletti, *supra. See also* Brady v. Daly, 175 U.S. 148, 155 (1899) (it is a "maxim of international law that 'courts of no nation execute the penal laws of another' "), *quoting* Huntington v. Attrill, 146 U.S. 657, 666 (1892), *quoting* The Antelope, 23 U.S. (10 Wheat.) 66, 123 (1825) (Marshall, C.J.).

4. The critical question is not merely whether a prisoner has made a knowing and voluntary waiver (a rights question), but whether the United States Government has the constitutional power to incarcerate persons convicted under foreign domestic laws who have not been convicted of offenses under our law, in our tribunals, with U.S. constitutional safeguards (a powers question not adequately addressed by the courts). It can be argued that there can be no such power conferred by treaty (*citing, e.g., Reid v.*

Covert), the practice involves a subversion of U.S. constitutional guarantees and our system of constitutionally derived federal powers, and serious issues arise when foreign state illegalities exist and the U.S. executes foreign sentences necessarily connected with such improprieties. *See, e.g.*, JORDAN J. PAUST, INTERNATIONAL AS LAW OF THE UNITED STATES 421–38 (1995); *see also* THOMAS M. FRANCK & MICHAEL J. GLENNON, FOREIGN RELATIONS AND NATIONAL SECURITY LAW 311–12 (2 ed. 1993).

5. With respect to execution of transferred sentences in the receiving state, 18 U.S.C. § 4103 provides:

> "All laws of the United States, as appropriate, pertaining to prisoners, probationers, parolees, and juvenile offenders shall be applicable to offenders transferred to the United States, unless a treaty or this chapter provides otherwise."

The effect of this provision is to treat a foreign-imposed sentence as if it were one imposed by a court of the United States, bringing all questions of sentence computation, good time credits, parole release and revocation, and any other related subjects, under United States laws. An example of a treaty provision which may require a different course of action than that which would be available if the sentence had been imposed by a U.S. court is found in article V(3) of the treaty with Mexico, and article IV(3) of the treaty with Canada. Those articles provide "no sentence of confinement shall be enforced by the Receiving State in such a way as to extend its duration beyond the date at which it would have terminated according to the sentence of the court of the transferring (sending) State."

Chapter Six

LAW OF THE SEA

Introductory Problem

A Mexican speed boat, *El Solo*, with Mexican crew, was spotted recently by a U.S. Coast Guard vessel in the Gulf some 30 nautical miles from the west coast of Florida. The Coast Guard had information that *El Solo* was attempting to deliver illegal drugs to persons on shore and sought to stop the foreign vessel in order to "verify" its nationality and registration papers and hopefully, when on board, discover any drugs. When ordered to stop, *El Solo* sped away. A chase began, during which several warning shots were fired by the Coast Guard toward *El Solo*, until one final burst of fire severely damaged *El Solo* as she neared a Turkish flag gambling vessel, the *Wazcourt*. The Mexican and Turkish vessels collided, leading to serious injuries and deaths among several crew and passengers and spillage of numerous packets of illegal narcotics floating on the surface (which were retrieved by the Coast Guard).

Some of the *El Solo* crew were rescued from the water, but arrested for drug trafficking in violation of U.S. law. The Mexican criminal accused have subsequently challenged U.S. jurisdiction on several grounds, including claims that the attempt to stop *El Solo* on suspicion of drug trafficking was impermissible under the law of the sea, that the U.S. cannot unilaterally claim an exclusive economic zone, that the U.S. in any event has no competence in such a zone to enforce its drug laws, and that the arrests were illegal for reasons noted above and because the U.S. used illegal and excessive force in the equivalent of foreign state territory without consent, in violation of customary and treaty-based international law.

Mexico and Turkey have made similar claims against the U.S. at the international level, have demanded compensation for loss of lives and property during the *El Solo–Wazcourt* incident, and have filed *amicus* briefs in support of defense motions to dismiss. Mexican and Turkish survivors and representatives of decedents also seek to file suit in U.S. federal courts or the Court of Claims against the Coast Guard vessel commander and crew as well as the United States.

What legal issues are presented? How should a court rule in the criminal cases? What U.S. statutes noted in Chapter 2 might foreign plaintiffs use? How should a court rule in case of foreign civil suits or claims?

General Introduction

The oceans have served historically as a "commons" to be used by the people of all nations. Hugo Grotius wrote that the seas must be free for navigation and fishing because natural law forbids the ownership of things that seem "to have been created by nature for common use."[1] Because the use of the seas for navigation by one nation does not diminish the potential for the same use by others, he argued, the inherent nature of the ocean is that of a common space or shared resource. In Grotius' time, the fish in the ocean also seemed limitless, but we have seen in our time, with high-technology fishing methods, that the fish of the oceans are definitely exhaustible and that over-fishing by one nation can have a grave impact on the ability of other nations to harvest "their share" of the resource. Given these developments, what is the functional meaning of "freedom" of the seas?

Should ships be free to move freely in all parts of the oceans? Even if they are warships carrying nuclear weapons? Even if they are carrying ultrahazardous radioactive cargoes that impose risks on coastal populations? What law applies when one vessel collides with another one? Or when a crime takes place on a vessel sailing on the high seas or other waters off the coast of a foreign state? Should fishing vessels be free to harvest fish wherever they can be found, or should the people living near the sea have a preference for, or even ownership of, the fish that live near their coasts? Should a different approach be taken regarding fish that "straddle" between adjacent fishing zones, or between a fishing zone and the high seas? Who should own the petroleum and mineral resources found under the sea? Can scientific research be done freely in all parts of the ocean, or in certain parts only with permission of an adjacent country? How should ocean competencies or boundaries be drawn? *See generally* FREEDOM FOR THE SEAS FOR THE 21ST CENTURY 72 (Jon M. Van Dyke, Durwood Zaelke & Grant Hewison eds. 1993).

These questions are now largely answered in the 1982 United Nations Law of the Sea Convention (U.N. LOSC), in the Documents Supplement. President Clinton signed the Convention in July 1994 and submitted it to the Senate for advice and consent to ratification on October 7, 1994, but the U.S. Senate has not yet provided the necessary advice and consent. Nonetheless, as explained in Section 2, the United States adheres to almost all provisions of the Convention as a reflection of binding customary international law. *See, e.g.*, R.M.S. Titanic, Inc. v. Haver, 171 F.3d 943, 965 n.3 (4th Cir.1999). One court has stated that "[a]lthough the ... convention is currently pending ratification [sic] before the Senate, it nevertheless carries the weight of law from the date

1. HUGO GROTIUS, MARE LIBERUM (The Freedom of the Seas) 28 (James B. Scott ed. & Ralph Van Deman Magoffin trans. 1916) (originally published in 1633).

of its submission by the President to the Senate," because such submission "expresses to the international community the United States' ultimate intention to be bound by the pact." United States v. Royal Caribbean Cruises, 24 F.Supp.2d 155, 159 (D.P.R.1997); recall Vienna Convention on the Law of Treaties, art. 18. To understand the terminology used in the Convention, and the reasons why the oceans were divided up as they have been, it is useful to review a few of the key decisions that took place before this Convention was drafted.

SECTION 1. TRADITIONAL JURISDICTIONAL CONCEPTS

THE S.S. LOTUS (FRANCE v. TURKEY)

P.C.I.J., Ser. A, No. 10 (1927).

... By a special agreement signed at Geneva on October 12th, 1926, ... the Governments of the French and Turkish Republics ... have submitted to the Permanent Court of International Justice the question of jurisdiction which has arisen between them following upon the collision which occurred on August 2nd, 1926, between the steamships *Boz-Kourt* and *Lotus*....

THE FACTS

On August 2nd, 1926, just before midnight, a collision occurred between the French mail steamer *Lotus*, proceeding to Constantinople, and the Turkish collier *Boz-Kourt*, between five and six nautical miles to the north of Cape Sigri (Mitylene). The *Boz-Kourt*, which was cut in two, sank, and eight Turkish nationals who were on board perished. After having done everything possible to succour the shipwrecked persons, of whom ten were able to be saved, the *Lotus* continued on its course to Constantinople, where it arrived on August 3rd.

At the time of the collision, the officer of the watch on board the *Lotus* was Monsieur Demons, a French citizen, lieutenant in the merchant service and first officer of the ship, whilst the movements of the *Boz-Kourt* were directed by its captain, Hassan Bey, who was one of those saved from the wreck....

[After Lieutenant Demons had traveled to Turkey for questioning, he was arrested and tried, and on September 15th the Turkish Criminal Court "sentenced Lieutenant Demons to eighty days' imprisonment and a fine of twenty-two pounds, Hassan Bey being sentenced to a slightly more severe penalty." The question presented to the P.C.I.J. was whether Turkey acted contrary to international law in prosecuting Lieutenant Demons for this incident, which occurred outside Turkey's territorial sea in waters that would in 1926 have been considered to be the "high seas."]

THE LAW

I

... The prosecution was instituted because the loss of the *Boz-Kourt* involved the death of eight Turkish sailors and passengers.... [N]o criminal intention has been imputed to either of the officers responsible for navigating the two vessels; it is therefore a case of prosecution for involuntary manslaughter....

... The prosecution was instituted in pursuance of Turkish legislation. The special agreement does not indicate what clause or clauses of that legislation apply. No document has been submitted to the Court indicating on what article of the Turkish Penal Code the prosecution was based; the French Government however declares that the Criminal Court claimed jurisdiction under Article 6 of the Turkish Penal Code, and far from denying this statement, Turkey, in the submissions of her Counter–Case, contends that that article is in conformity with the principles of international law. It does not appear from the proceedings whether the prosecution was instituted solely on the basis of that article.

Article 6 of the Turkish Penal Code, ... runs as follows [*Translation*]:

"Any foreigner who, apart from the cases contemplated by Article 4, commits an offence abroad to the prejudice of Turkey or of a Turkish subject, for which offence Turkish law prescribes a penalty involving loss of freedom for a minimum period of not less than one year, shall be punished in accordance with the Turkish Penal Code provided that he is arrested in Turkey...."

Even if the Court must hold that the Turkish authorities had seen fit to base the prosecution of Lieutenant Demons upon the above-mentioned Article 6, the question submitted to the Court is not whether that article is compatible with the principles of international law; it is more general. The Court is asked to state whether or not the principles of international law prevent Turkey from instituting criminal proceedings against Lieutenant Demons under Turkish law. Neither the conformity of Article 6 in itself with the principles of international law nor the application of that article by the Turkish authorities constitutes the point at issue; it is the very fact of the institution of proceedings which is held by France to be contrary to those principles....

III

The French Government contends that the Turkish Courts, in order to have jurisdiction, should be able to point to some title to jurisdiction recognized by international law in favour of Turkey. On the other hand, the Turkish Government takes the view [it can assert] ... jurisdiction whenever such jurisdiction does not come into conflict with a principle of international law.

International law governs relations between independent States. The rules of law binding upon States therefore emanate from their own free will as expressed in conventions or by usages generally accepted as expressing principles of law and established in order to regulate the relations between these co-existing independent communities or with a view to the achievement of common aims. Restrictions upon the independence of States cannot therefore be presumed.

Now the first and foremost restriction imposed by international law upon a State is that—failing the existence of a permissive rule to the contrary—it may not exercise its power in any form in the territory of another State. In this sense jurisdiction is certainly territorial; it cannot be exercised by a State outside its territory except by virtue of a permissive rule derived from international custom or from a convention.

It does not, however, follow that international law prohibits a State from exercising jurisdiction in its own territory, in respect of any case which relates to acts which have taken place abroad, and in which it cannot rely on some permissive rule of international law. Such a view would only be tenable if international law contained a general prohibition to States to extend the application of their laws and the jurisdiction of their courts to persons, property and acts outside their territory, and if, as an exception to this general prohibition, it allowed States to do so in certain specific cases. But this is certainly not the case under international law as it stands at present. Far from laying down a general prohibition to the effect that States may not extend the application of their laws and the jurisdiction of their courts to persons, property and acts outside their territory, it leaves them in this respect a wide measure of discretion which is only limited in certain cases by prohibitive rules; as regards other cases, every State remains free to adopt the principles which it regards as best and most suitable.

This discretion left to States by international law explains the great variety of rules which they have been able to adopt without objections or complaints on the part of other States; it is in order to remedy the difficulties resulting from such variety that efforts have been made for many years past, both in Europe and America, to prepare conventions the effect of which would be precisely to limit the discretion at present left to States in this respect by international law, thus making good the existing lacunae in respect of jurisdiction or removing the conflicting jurisdictions arising from the diversity of the principles adopted by the various States.

In these circumstances, all that can be required of a State is that it should not overstep the limits which international law places upon its jurisdiction; within these limits, its title to exercise jurisdiction rests in its sovereignty.

It follows from the foregoing that the contention of the French Government to the effect that Turkey must in each case be able to cite a rule of international law authorizing her to exercise jurisdiction, is opposed to the generally accepted international law. . . .

IV

The Court will now proceed to ascertain whether general international law . . . contains a rule prohibiting Turkey from prosecuting Lieutenant Demons. . . .

The arguments advanced by the French Government [include the following]:

... International law does not allow a State to take proceedings with regard to offences committed by foreigners abroad, simply by reason of the nationality of the victim; and such is the situation in the present case because the offence must be regarded as having been committed on board the French vessel....

As has already been observed, the characteristic features of the situation of fact are as follows: there has been a collision on the high seas between two vessels flying different flags, on one of which was one of the persons alleged to be guilty of the offence, whilst the victims were on board the other.

This being so, the Court does not think it necessary to consider the contention that a State cannot punish offences committed abroad by a foreigner simply by reason of the nationality of the victim. For this contention only relates to the case where the nationality of the victim is the only criterion on which the criminal jurisdiction of the State is based. Even if that argument were correct generally speaking—and in regard to this the Court reserves its opinion—it could only be used in the present case if international law forbade Turkey to take into consideration the fact that the offence produced its effects on the Turkish vessel and consequently in a place assimilated to Turkish territory in which the application of Turkish criminal law cannot be challenged, even in regard to offences committed there by foreigners. But no such rule of international law exists. No argument has come to the knowledge of the Court from which it could be deduced that States recognize themselves to be under an obligation towards each other only to have regard to the place where the author of the offence happens to be at the time of the offence. On the contrary, it is certain that the courts of many countries, even of countries which have given their criminal legislation a strictly territorial character, interpret criminal law in the sense that offences, the authors of which at the moment of commission are in the territory of another State, are nevertheless to be regarded as having been committed in the national territory, if one of the constituent elements of the offence, and more especially its effects, have taken place there. French courts have, in regard to a variety of situations, given decisions sanctioning this way of interpreting the territorial principle....

Consequently, once it is admitted that the effects of the offence were produced on the Turkish vessel, it becomes impossible to hold that there is a rule of international law which prohibits Turkey from prosecuting Lieutenant Demons because of the fact that the author of the offence was on board the French ship....

The offence for which Lieutenant Demons appears to have been prosecuted was an act—of negligence or imprudence—having its origin on board the *Lotus*, whilst its effects made themselves felt on board the *Boz-Kourt*. These two elements are, legally, entirely inseparable, so much so that their separation renders the offence non-existent. Neither the exclusive jurisdiction of either State, nor the limitations of the jurisdiction of each to the occurrences which took place on the respective ships would appear calculated to satisfy the requirements of justice and effectively to protect the interests of the two States. It is only natural that each should be able to exercise jurisdiction and to do so in respect of the incident as a whole. It is therefore a case of concurrent jurisdiction....

For these reasons, the Court, having heard both Parties, gives, by the President's casting vote—the votes being equally divided—, judgment to the effect:

(1) that, following the collision which occurred on August 2nd, 1926, on the high seas between the French steamship *Lotus* and the Turkish steamship *Boz-Kourt*, and upon the arrival of the French ship at Stamboul, and in consequence of the loss of the *Boz-Kourt* having involved the death of eight Turkish nationals, Turkey, by instituting criminal proceedings in pursuance of Turkish law against Lieutenant Demons, officer of the watch on board the *Lotus* at the time of the collision, has not acted in conflict with the principles of international law....

(2) that, consequently, there is no occasion to give judgment on the question of the pecuniary reparation which might have been due to Lieutenant Demons if Turkey, by prosecuting him ... , had acted in a manner contrary to the principles of international law.

Notes and Questions

1. As noted in Chapter 1, the Permanent Court of International Justice is the predecessor of the International Court of Justice. These courts have "consensual" jurisdiction, because countries must agree to participate in cases before them. Such agreement can exist through a special *ad hoc* agreement, as in the *Lotus* case.

2. In the *Lotus* case, what was the holding of the court? What was the vote of the Court? Compare Article 55(2) of the I.C.J. Statute.

3. What was the French argument? How did Turkey respond? Why did the Court place the burden on France to show that Turkey had acted contrary to international law? See section III of the opinion. This part of the *Lotus* decision is considered to be a classic description of an older "positivistic" approach toward international law. *See* Chapter 1. But is the Court's conclusion also influenced by whether the result is correct from an equitable perspective?

4. Did the Court state that, because of the absence of any prohibitive rule of international law, any approach adopted by Turkey would be acceptable? Did the court find a positive rule of international law that would allow the exercise of criminal jurisdiction by Turkey over Lieutenant Demons?

Since the *Lotus* case, the international community has tried to limit the circumstances where a state can assert jurisdiction, as addressed in Chapter 3.

5. Did the Court determine whether Article 6 of the Turkish Penal Code is a legitimate assertion of jurisdiction under international law? Suppose a French citizen kills a citizen of Turkey in Paris. If the French citizen

later went to Turkey on a vacation and was arrested and prosecuted for murder, would the I.C.J. uphold the Turkish exercise of jurisdiction?

The P.C.I.J. did not rule on the propriety of use of the passive personality principle and it remains a minority theory and controversial assertion of prescriptive jurisdiction, illustrated by Article 6 of the Turkish Penal Code. The assertion of jurisdiction under this principle will raise problems of overlapping national jurisdiction, and U.S. courts note that this principle "has generally not been accepted in this country as a basis for jurisdiction." United States v. Marino–Garcia, 679 F.2d 1373 (11th Cir.1982).

6. Although the P.C.I.J. in *Lotus* avoided ruling on the "passive personality" theory, it still arises. In United States v. Roberts, 1 F.Supp.2d 601 (E.D.La.1998), the United States prosecuted a citizen of St. Vincent & the Grenadines who was serving as crew member of the Carnival Cruise Lines' vessel *Celebration* for sexual abuse of a minor. The *Celebration* was registered in Liberia and owned by a company incorporated in Panama (but with corporate headquarters in the U.S. and some shareholders who were U.S. citizens). The victim of the assault, which took place 63 miles off the Mexican coast on a voyage that originated and terminated in the United States, was a U.S. citizen. The relevant statutory provisions (18 U.S.C. §§ 2243, 2244, and 7(8)) state that anyone who knowingly engages in a sexual act with a person under the age of 16 is guilty of a criminal act "[t]o the extent permitted by international law," if the act takes place on "any foreign vessel during a voyage having a scheduled departure from or arrival in the United States with respect to an offense committed by or against a national of the United States." Does international law permit the United States to prescribe such a law and enforce it against crew-member Roberts in this situation? Does the objective territorial principle apply? Does Article 92(1) of the U.N. LOSC limit enforcement jurisdiction?

7. Does the territorial principle cover the *Lotus* fact situation? Why was the "act–of negligence" "legally ... inseparable" from the effects on the Turkish vessel in this case? Was there a continual process of negligence?

8. The current approach to jurisdiction over a collision at sea, such as the one involved in the *Lotus* case, is found in Article 97 of the U.N. LOSC. Would the outcome be the same or different under this provision? *See also* Article 218, which permits a nation to assert jurisdiction over a foreign flag ship docked in its port for pollution caused by that ship on the high seas. This principle is referred to as "port state jurisdiction" and is one of the innovations introduced in the 1982 Convention.

9. Could the United States exercise prescriptive jurisdiction over gambling "cruises to nowhere" which leave from and return to U.S. ports, but engage in otherwise-illegal gambling activities once they are outside the U.S. territorial sea? Is the gambling a "process" that has effects in the U.S.? *See also* United States v. Black, 291 F.Supp. 262 (S.D.N.Y.1968) (otherwise emphasizing the statute's reach to U.S. nationals, U.S. residents, or other persons either on U.S. vessels or otherwise subject to the jurisdiction of the U.S., yet the statute's definition of U.S. vessel included vessels "licensed in" the U.S. and those "under effective control, whether by ownership, charter or otherwise, of" U.S. citizens, residents or corporations. 18 U.S.C. § 1081). The current U.S. statute (newer § 1081) permits the ships to engage in

gambling once "beyond the territorial waters of the United States," but disputes still exist regarding whether the "territorial waters" for the purpose of this statute extends three or 12 nautical miles from the coast. *See* United States v. One Big Six Wheel, 166 F.3d 498 (2d Cir.1999) (ruling that although the Antiterrorism and Effective Death Penalty Act of 1996, Pub. L. 104–132, 110 Stat. 1214, extended "federal criminal jurisdiction" from three to 12 nautical miles, it did not amend the Gambling Ship Act, 18 U.S.C. §§ 1081–82, which makes it criminal to gamble only within the first three nautical miles from shore). Does § 1081 incorporate changes in the extent of the U.S. territorial sea, and is international law a useful background for interpretation of the statute?

10. The *Lotus* opinion stated that the "Turkish vessel" was "a place assimilated to Turkish territory in which the application of Turkish criminal law cannot be challenged, even in regard to offences committed there by foreigners." How does a vessel become a "Turkish vessel"? *See* U.N. LOSC, Articles 91–94.

Why might a vessel owned by a Panamanian corporation with headquarters in the United States be registered in Liberia? Why might a vessel owned by a PRC corporation be registered in Panama? Does the country of registration have to have any real contact with a ship flying its flag? Does the country of registration have to exercise any responsibilities to ensure that the ship is safe and sea-worthy and that the working conditions of the sailors are adequate? *See* U.N. LOSC, Article 94.

11. Does the flag state have jurisdiction over activities on a vessel flying its flag no matter where it is located? Even if it is in the territorial sea or internal waters of another country? Does it matter what crime or tort has occurred? *See* U.N. LOSC, Articles 27–28.

12. Do all vessels have a "nationality" or assimilated "territory"? What if a vessel carries two flags and registration papers from two countries in order to evade jurisdiction "through clever use of registration papers and various other indicia of nationality"? *See* United States v. Matute, 767 F.2d 1511 (11th Cir.1985), upholding the seizure on the high seas and conviction of seven individuals carrying 60,000 pounds of marijuana on a vessel that seemed to be registered in both Venezuela and Colombia and had a "hybrid" flag incorporating characteristics of the flags of both countries. Is such a vessel like a "stateless" vessel? *See also* U.N. LOSC, Article 110(1)(d).

In United States v. Maynard, 888 F.2d 918 (1st Cir.1989), the court ruled that a vessel flying the British Virgin Islands flag was not a "stateless" vessel, especially in light of the failure of U.S. authorities to contact the United Kingdom regarding the status of the vessel.

13. A Danish seaman brought suit under the U.S. Jones Act to recover for injuries he suffered while on a Danish flag vessel docked in Havana, Cuba, arguing that the U.S. court should have jurisdiction because the owner of the ship had significant business contacts in New York. What result? *See* Lauritzen v. Larsen, 345 U.S. 571, 584 (1953) ("Perhaps the most venerable and universal rule of maritime law ... is that which gives cardinal importance to the law of the flag.").

14. Do U.S. laws governing the obligation to accommodate individuals with disabilities apply to foreign-flag cruise ships departing from and returning to U.S. ports? *See* Spector v. Norwegian Cruise Line Ltd., 125 S.Ct. 2169 (2005).

FISHERIES CASE (UNITED KINGDOM v. NORWAY)

1951 I.C.J. 116.

On September 28th, 1949, the Government of the United Kingdom of Great Britain and Northern Ireland filed ... an Application instituting proceedings before the Court against the Kingdom of Norway, the subject of the proceedings being the validity or otherwise, under international law, of the lines of delimitation of the Norwegian fisheries zone laid down by the Royal Decree of July 12th, 1935, as amended by a Decree of December 10th, 1937, for that part of Norway which is situated northward of 66 degrees 28.8' (or 66 degrees 28'48') N. latitude. The Application refers to the Declarations by which the United Kingdom and Norway have accepted the compulsory jurisdiction of the Court in accordance with Article 36, paragraph 2, of the Statute....

The historical facts laid before the Court establish that as the result of complaints from the King of Denmark and of Norway, at the beginning of the seventeenth century, British fishermen refrained from fishing in Norwegian coastal waters for a long period, from 1616–1618 until 1906.

In 1906 a few British fishing vessels appeared off the coasts of Eastern Finnmark. From 1908 onwards they returned in greater numbers. These were trawlers equipped with improved and powerful gear. The local population became perturbed, and measures were taken by the Norwegian Government with a view to specifying the limits within which fishing was prohibited to foreigners.

The first incident occurred in 1911 when a British trawler was seized and condemned for having violated these measures. Negotiations ensued between the two Governments. These were interrupted by the war in 1914. From 1922 onwards incidents recurred. Further conversations were initiated in 1924. In 1932, British trawlers, extending the range of their activities, appeared in the sectors off the Norwegian coast west of the North Cape, and the number of warnings and arrests increased. On July 27th, 1933, the United Kingdom Government sent a memorandum to the Norwegian Government complaining that in delimiting the territorial sea the Norwegian authorities had made use of unjustifiable base-lines. On July 12th, 1935, a Norwegian Royal Decree was enacted delimiting the Norwegian fisheries zone north of 66 degrees 28.8′ North latitude.

The United Kingdom made urgent representations in Oslo in the course of which the question of referring the dispute to the Permanent Court of International Justice was raised. Pending the result of the negotiations, the Norwegian Government made it known that Norwegian fishery patrol vessels would deal leniently with foreign vessels fishing a certain distance within the fishing limits. In 1948, since no agreement had been reached, the Norwegian Government abandoned its lenient enforcement of the 1935 Decree; incidents then became more and more frequent. A considerable number of British trawlers were arrested and condemned. It was then that the United Kingdom Government instituted the present proceedings. . . .

The Norwegian Royal Decree of July 12th, 1935, concerning the delimitation of the Norwegian fisheries zone sets out in the preamble the considerations on which its provisions are based. In this connection it refers to "well-established national titles of right", "the geographical conditions prevailing on the Norwegian coasts", "the safeguard of the vital interests of the inhabitants of the northernmost parts of the country"; it further relies on the Royal Decrees of February 22nd, 1812, October 16th, 1869, January 5th, 1881, and September 9th, 1889.

The Decree provides that "lines of delimitation towards the high sea of the Norwegian fisheries zone as regards that part of Norway which is situated northward of 66 degrees 28.8′ North latitude ... shall run parallel with straight base-lines drawn between fixed points on the mainland, on islands or rocks, starting from the final point of the boundary line of the Realm in the easternmost part of the Varangerfjord and going as far as Traena in the County of Nordland". . . .

Although the Decree of July 12th, 1935, refers to the Norwegian fisheries zone and does not specifically mention the territorial sea, there can be no doubt that the zone delimited by this Decree is none other than the sea area which Norway considers to be her territorial sea. That is how the Parties argued the question and that is the way in which they submitted it to the Court for decision. . . .

The coastal zone concerned in the dispute is of considerable length. It lies north of latitude 66 degrees 28.8′ N., that is to say, north of the Arctic Circle, and it includes the coast of the mainland of Norway and all the islands, islets, rocks and reefs, known by the name of the "*skjaergaard*" (literally, rock rampart), together with all Norwegian internal and territorial waters. The coast of the mainland, which, without taking any account of fjords, bays and minor indentations, is over 1,500 kilometres in length, is of a very distinctive configuration. Very broken along its whole length, it constantly opens out into indentations often penetrating for great distances inland: the Porsangerfjord, for instance, penetrates 75 sea miles inland. To the west, the land configuration stretches out into the sea: the large and small islands, mountainous in character, the islets, rocks and reefs, some always above water, others emerging only at low tide, are in truth but an extension of the Norwegian mainland. The number of insular formations, large and small, which make up the "*skjaergaard*", is estimated by the Norwegian Government to be one hundred and twenty thousand. From the southern extremity of the disputed area to the North Cape, the "*skjaergaard*" lies along the whole of the coast of the mainland; east of the North Cape, the "*skjaergaard*" ends, but the coast line continues to be broken by large and deeply indented fjords.

Within the "*skjaergaard*", almost every island has its large and its small bays; countless arms of the sea, straits, channels and mere waterways serve as a means of communication for the local population which inhabits the islands as it does the mainland. The coast of the mainland does not constitute, as it does in practically all other countries, a clear dividing line between land and sea. What matters, what really constitutes the Norwegian coast line, is the outer line of the "*skjaergaard*"....

In these barren regions the inhabitants of the coastal zone derive their livelihood essentially from fishing.

Such are the realities which must be borne in mind in appraising the validity of the United Kingdom contention that the limits of the Norwegian fisheries zone laid down in the 1935 Decree are contrary to international law.

The Parties being in agreement on the figure of 4 miles for the breadth of the territorial sea, the problem which arises is from what base-line this breadth is to be reckoned. The Conclusions of the United Kingdom are explicit on this point: the base-line must be low-water mark on permanently dry land which is a part of Norwegian territory, or the proper closing line of Norwegian internal waters....

The Court finds itself obliged to decide whether the relevant low-water mark is that of the mainland or of the "*skjaergaard*". Since the mainland is bordered in its western sector by the "*skjaergaard*", which constitutes a whole with the mainland, it is the outer line of the "*skjaergaard*" which must be taken into account in delimiting the belt of Norwegian territorial waters. This solution is dictated by geographic realities.

Three methods have been contemplated to effect the application of the low-water mark rule. The simplest would appear to be the method of the trace parallele, which consists of drawing the outer limit of the belt of territorial waters by following the coast in all its sinuosities. This method may be applied without difficulty to an ordinary coast, which is not too broken. Where a coast is deeply indented and cut into, as is that of Eastern Finnmark, or where it is bordered by an archipelago such as the "*skjaergaard*" along the western sector of the coast here in question, the base-line becomes independent of the low-water mark, and can only be determined by means of a geometrical construction. In such circumstances the line of the low-water mark can no longer be put forward as a rule requiring the coastline to be followed in all its sinuosities. Nor can one characterize as exceptions to the rule the very many derogations which would be necessitated by such a rugged coast: the rule would disappear under the exceptions. Such a coast, viewed as a whole, calls for the application of a different method; that is, the method of base-lines which, within reasonable limits, may depart from the physical line of the coast....

It does not at all follow that, in the absence of rules having the technically precise character alleged by the United Kingdom Government, the delimitation undertaken by the Norwegian Government in 1935 is not subject to certain principles which make it possible to judge as to its validity under international law. The delimitation of sea areas has always an international aspect; it cannot be dependent merely upon the will of the coastal State as expressed in its municipal law. Although it is true that the act of delimitation is necessarily a unilateral act, because only the coastal State is competent to undertake it, the validity of the delimitation with regard to other States depends upon international law.

In this connection, certain basic considerations inherent in the nature of the territorial sea, bring to light certain criteria which, though not entirely precise, can provide courts with an adequate basis for their decisions, which can be adapted to the diverse facts in question.

Among these considerations, some reference must be made to the close dependence of the territorial sea upon the land domain. It is the land which confers upon the coastal State a right to the waters off its coasts. It follows that while such a State must be allowed the latitude necessary in order to be able to adapt its delimitation to practical needs and local requirements, the drawing of base-lines must not depart to any appreciable extent from the general direction of the coast.

Another fundamental consideration, of particular importance in this case, is the more or less close relationship existing between certain sea areas and the land formations which divide or surround them. The real question raised in the choice of base-lines is in effect whether certain sea areas lying within these lines are sufficiently closely linked to the land domain to be subject to the regime of internal waters. This idea, which is at the basis of the determination of the rules relating to bays, should be liberally applied in the case of a coast, the geographical configuration of which is as unusual as that of Norway.

Finally, there is one consideration not to be overlooked, the scope of which extends beyond purely geographical factors: that of certain economic interests peculiar to a region, the reality and importance of which are clearly evidenced by a long usage....

In the light of these considerations, and in the absence of convincing evidence to the contrary, the Court is bound to hold that the Norwegian authorities applied their system of delimitation consistently and uninterruptedly from 1869 until the time when the dispute arose.

From the standpoint of international law, it is now necessary to consider whether the application of the Norwegian system encountered any opposition from foreign States....

The general toleration of foreign States with regard to the Norwegian practice is an unchallenged fact. For a period of more than sixty years the United Kingdom Government itself in no way contested it. One cannot indeed consider as raising objections the discussions to which the

Lord Roberts incident gave rise in 1911, for the controversy which arose in this connection related to two questions, that of the four-mile limit, and that of Norwegian sovereignty over the Varangerfjord, both of which were unconnected with the position of base-lines. It would appear that it was only in its Memorandum of July 27th, 1933, that the United Kingdom made a formal and definite protest on this point. . . .

The Court is thus led to conclude that the method of straight lines, established in the Norwegian system, was imposed by the peculiar geography of the Norwegian coast; that even before the dispute arose, this method had been consolidated by a constant and sufficiently long practice, in the face of which the attitude of governments bears witness to the fact that they did not consider it to be contrary to international law. . . .

For these reasons, The Court, rejecting all submissions to the contrary, Finds by ten votes to two, that the method employed for the delimitation of the fisheries zone by the Royal Norwegian Decree of July 12th, 1935, is not contrary to international law; and by eight votes to four, that the base-lines fixed by the said Decree in application of this method are not contrary to international law.

Notes and Questions

1. What does the opinion hold, (a) that Norway's claim was consistent with international law, or (b) that it did not violate international law and hence was permissible? What country had the burden of proof? What sources of law did the Court rely upon? How long had Norway used its base-line method? How had the United Kingdom reacted to the Norwegian claims over the centuries? Should this decision be characterized as "positivist," or "realist," or is it based on equitable (or natural-law) principles, or some combination of these?

2. If a state has a coastline similar to that of Norway's northwestern coast (like that of southern Chile), but had not historically exercised any control of the waters off of its coast, could the state lawfully draw straight baselines connecting the islands along its irregular coast, citing this decision? What if the people of the coastal state had no particular economic dependence upon the resources of the sea? The *Anglo-Norwegian Fisheries* decision established criteria for straight baselines that are now codified in Article 7 of the U.N. LOSC; *cf.* Article 7(1).

3. What does the I.C.J. find to be the "coastline" of Norway? What factors led to the Court's determination? Were they purely geographical? Of what significance was the historical acquiescence of Great Britain to the Norwegian system?

4. What is the method for drawing baselines along an "ordinary" coastline? *See* Articles 4, 5. Upon what grounds did Norway claim that its coastline was not ordinary?

SECTION 2. THE 1982 UNITED NATIONS LAW OF THE SEA CONVENTION

The first claim to an extended maritime zone was made by the United States in 1945, when it claimed sovereign rights and jurisdiction over the nonliving resources on its "**continental shelf**" in 1945 in the Truman Proclamation, Proclamation No. 2667, 10 FED. REG. 12303 (1945), 4 DIGEST OF INTERNATIONAL LAW 756–58 (Margery Whiteman ed. 1965); *see* 2 FOREIGN RELATIONS OF THE UNITED STATES, 1945, at 1502. In making this claim, the U.S. sought to protect its navigational freedoms by distinguishing between the ability to claim resources, on the one hand, and the ability to regulate navigation, on the other, adding: "The character of the waters above the continental shelf and the right to their free and unimpeded navigation are in no way thus affected." Countries that do not have gradually sloping continental shelves off their coasts, such as those on the west coast of Latin America, sought to make a comparable claim with respect to living resources. They claimed territorial seas that extended 200 nautical miles from their coasts and claimed sovereign rights over all the fish in that zone.

In an effort to resolve these competing claims, the international community met in Geneva in 1958 and negotiated four treaties, which reasserted traditional freedoms of fishing and navigation, but accepted coastal state jurisdiction over the continental shelf. Convention on the Territorial Sea and Contiguous Zone, April 29, 1958, 516 U.N.T.S. 205, 15 U.S.T. 1606; Convention on the High Seas, April 29, 1958, 450 U.N.T.S. 82, 13 U.S.T. 2312; Convention on Fishing and Conservation of Living Resources of the High Seas, April 29, 1958, 17 U.S.T. 138, 599 U.N.T.S. 285; Convention on the Continental Shelf, April 29, 1958, 499 U.N.T.S. 311, 15 U.S.T. 471. These treaties allowed coastal states to extend maritime zones and adopt fishery conservation measures over adjacent waters, but they did not define the permissible limits of the territorial sea or fisheries jurisdiction. In addition, because countries could ratify some of the treaties, but not others, a patchwork of treaty law emerged. In 1960, a second conference on the law of the sea was held in Geneva to determine the width of the territorial sea, but it ended in failure.

The nations of the world renewed their effort to develop a comprehensive treaty to govern the oceans after the "discovery" of **polymetallic nodules** on the ocean floor that were thought by some to be a source of future wealth. In 1967, Ambassador Arvid Pardo of Malta told the U.N. General Assembly that vast riches lay scattered across the floor of the deep sea-bed in the form of exploitable soft-ball-sized rocks and offered the "Pardo proposal" urging the creation of a "common heritage" of humankind for the seabed. This idea was also developed in JOHN MERO, THE MINERAL RESOURCES OF THE SEA (1965). Within three years of Ambassador Pardo's speech, an international consensus developed that these nodules should be viewed as the "common heritage" of humankind, that national claims of exclusive rights to seabed resources must be prohibited, that exploitation should take place pursuant to an international legal regime, and that developing nations should share genuine benefits from seabed exploitation. The key international document was the U.N. General Assembly's 1970 Declaration of Principles Governing the Seabed and the Ocean Floor, and the Subsoil Thereof, Beyond the

Limits of National Jurisdiction, G.A. Res. 2749 (XXV), 25 U.N. GAOR, Supp. No. 28, at 24, U.N. Doc. A/8028 (1970). Whether these nodules will ever be commercially exploitable is still being debated. In any event, the creation of an acceptable international legal regime to govern their exploitation has proved to be challenging.

The Third United Nations Conference on the Law of the Sea began in 1974 in Caracas, Venezuela, amid great fanfare and high expectations. The delegations gathered to negotiate a comprehensive treaty that would clarify and bring certainty to the many ocean issues that had divided nations over the years. Eight years later, after long negotiating sessions that alternated between New York and Geneva, the Law of the Sea Convention was completed, and on December 10, 1982, 119 nations signed the document in Montego Bay, Jamaica. The Convention came into force in July 1994 after a sufficient number of ratifications, and as of February 2005, 148 parties had ratified it.

Although the United States had the largest delegation by far in Caracas and played a leading role in negotiating most parts of the Convention, President Reagan refused to allow the U.S. delegation to sign the treaty in 1982. Finally, in 1994, after certain provisions of the Convention had been revised by the "Part XI Agreement," described below, President Clinton signed the treaty, but as of the publication of this Second Edition, advice and consent to ratification is still pending in the U.S. Senate. The United States has stated frequently that the Convention reflects customary international law and U.S. courts have also recognized the central role that the Convention plays in governing ocean affairs. *See, e.g.,* United States v. Alaska, 503 U.S. 569, 588 n.10 (1992) ("The United States has not ratified [the Law of the Sea Convention], but has recognized that its baseline provisions reflect customary international law."); Mayaguezanos por la Salud y el Ambiente v. United States, 198 F.3d 297, 305 n. 14 (1st Cir. 1999) (noting that because it had signed the Convention, even though it had not yet ratified it, the United States "is obliged to refrain from acts that would defeat the object and purpose of the agreement"); Mansel v. Baker Hughes, Inc., 203 F.Supp.2d 745, 746 n.1 (S.D.Texas 2002) (same); Sarei v. Rio Tinto PLC, 221 F.Supp.2d 1116, 1161, 1162 (C.D.Cal. 2002) (explaining that because the Convention has been ratified by most states and signed by the United States, it "thus appears to represent the law of nations," and because it "reflects customary international law, plaintiffs may base an ATCA claim upon it").

What does this Convention contain, and why has it been controversial in the United States? Some articles repeat language from earlier treaties, and many of the articles reflect customary international law. Other sections were new and innovative in 1982, and their status as customary international law remains uncertain. Please begin by reading U.N. LOSC Articles 3–10, 17–19, 33,and 46–85 in the Documents Supplement

Categories of Water

[read U.N. LOSC Articles 3, 33, 55–75 in the Documents Supplement]

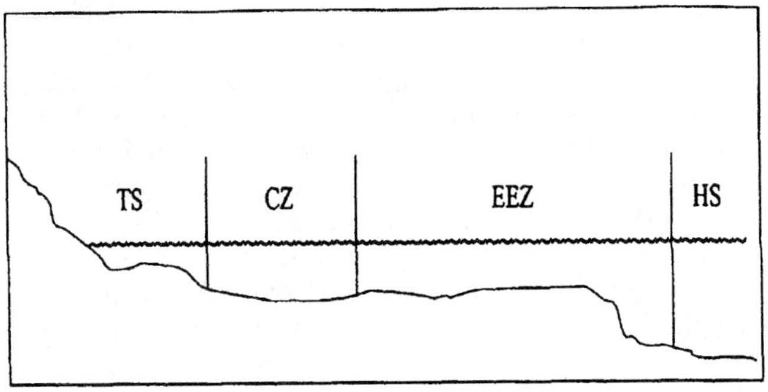

Notes and Questions

1. What is the difference between "**internal waters**" and the waters in the "**territorial sea**"? Compare Articles 2 and 8. Does the right of "innocent passage" exist in "internal waters"? Countries have sovereignty over their internal waters–which include rivers, lakes, bays, harbors, and all water landward of their baselines–just as they have over their land territory. In their internal waters, which are sometimes called "inland waters," "[n]ations may exclude ... even vessels engaged in so-called 'innocent passage'–passage that 'is not prejudicial to the peace, good order or security of the coastal State.'" Alaska v. United States, 125 S.Ct. 2137, 2145 (2005) (*citing* Article 14 of the Convention on the Territorial Sea and the Contiguous Zone).

2. Is a country obliged to allow any foreign-flag vessels to enter their **ports**? *See* U.N. LOSC, Articles 2, 18(1). In April 1974, the United States refused to allow the *M/V Tropwave* to enter the port of Norfolk, Virginia, where it was to pick up a load of coal to take to Spain. The vessel was owned by a Swiss corporation, registered in Singapore, chartered to Canadian Transport, and subchartered to a Belgian corporation. It had a multinational crew, including a Polish master and Polish officers. The Coast Guard refused to allow the ship to enter the port of Norfolk (which is the location of a U.S. Navy base), on the ground that the presence of the Polish nationals posed a risk to U.S. national security. Was this refusal lawful? After the refusal, the vessel went to Baltimore and dropped off the Polish officers, returned to Norfolk to pick up the load of coal, went back to Baltimore to pick up the Polish officers, and then took the coal to Spain. Canadian Transport sought to recover $93,000 in damages attributable to the Baltimore detour. Canadian Transport Co. v. United States, 663 F.2d 1081 (D.C.Cir.1980).

3. In the 1980s, New Zealand enacted legislation prohibiting nuclear-powered and nuclear-weapons-carrying vessels from entering its ports. Was this legislation consistent with international law? What if a vessel carrying a dangerous cargo is in distress? Is it entitled to come into the nearest port for assistance and repair? Can such vessels be kept out of New Zealand's territorial sea? *See* U.N. LOSC, Articles 18(2), 22, 23, 25(2).

4. What laws apply when a vessel is in the territorial sea or docked in the port of a state other than the one whose flag it flies? If a murder occurred on the vessel? If a brawl occurred below deck over a card game? Does it matter if the vessel is a warship or a merchant ship? In Wildenhus's Case, 120 U.S. 1 (1888), the Court ruled that New Jersey could exercise jurisdiction over the murder of a Belgian sailor by another Belgian sailor on a Belgian ship while docked in a New Jersey port. The Court noted that, as a matter of comity, local officials wisely abstain "from interfering with the internal discipline of the ship," but that it is proper to assert jurisdiction "if crimes are committed on board of a character to disturb the peace and tranquility of the country to which the vessel has been brought," a principle reflected in the customary **"peace of the port" doctrine**. *See also* United States v. Diekelman, 92 U.S. 520 (1875) ("The merchant vessels of one country visiting the ports of another for the purposes of trade subject themselves to the laws which govern the port they visit, so long as they remain; and this as well in war as in peace, unless it is otherwise provided by treaty."). Could the United States enforce its laws prohibiting sexual harassment of foreign crew members on a foreign-flag vessel docked in a U.S. port? What if the foreign-flag vessel was sailing through a U.S. territorial sea or exclusive economic zone? See U.N. LOSC, Articles 27, 33, 73(1).

5. What bodies of water qualify as "**bays**" under Article 10 of the U.N. LOSC? Does San Francisco Bay, Monterey Bay, or San Pedro Bay on the coast of California? Does Cook's Inlet in Alaska? Does the Gulf of Sidra along the coast of Libya? Does the Gulf of Toronto on the boot of Italy qualify?

6. How does a body of water qualify as an "**historic bay**" under Article 10(6)? Most tribunals that have examined this question have used criteria similar to those used in the *Anglo-Norwegian Fisheries* case–including a period of asserting sovereign jurisdiction over the ocean space and protesting against intruders, combined with some level of acquiescence and acceptance of the claim by other nations. No universal principles have emerged regarding how long the claim must have been asserted, how active the protests must have been, and how enthusiastic the acquiescence and acceptance must be. Examples of areas that have been accepted as historic waters include the Bohai Bay in northeast China and the Palk Strait between India and Sri Lanka. Areas where such claims have been made, but have not been universally accepted, include Cook Inlet in Alaska, the channel waters between the Hawaiian Islands, Canada's Arctic straits, Libya's Gulf of Sidra, and Italy's Gulf of Toronto.

7. When *Lotus* was decided, most countries claimed "**territorial seas**" of three or four nautical miles. Today, under Article 3 of the U.N. LOSC, countries are authorized to claim a territorial sea that extends 12 nautical miles from its baselines, but in certain crowded locations, countries have limited their claims to territorial seas to only three or six nautical miles. In the Aegean Sea, for instance, Greece and Turkey have each claimed six-nautical-mile territorial seas. *See* Jon M. Van Dyke, *An Analysis of the Aegean Disputes Under International Law*, 36 Ocean Development and International Law 63–117 (2005). (A "nautical mile" is somewhat longer than a land mile, equaling about 1.15 land miles.) President Reagan issued an executive order extending the U.S. territorial sea to 12 nautical miles in December 1988, *infra*, Section 4. Countries have sovereignty over their

territorial seas, but must permit the ships of other countries to exercise "**innocent passage**" in these waters. Airplanes have no rights of innocent passage and cannot pass over the territorial seas of other countries without permission. Compare Articles 2 and 8 of the U.N. LOSC, and see also Articles 17–19.

8. Suppose a cruise ship flying the Norwegian flag dumped 30 gallons of oil into the territorial sea of the United States near the coast of San Juan, Puerto Rico. Is such an action unlawful? *See* U.N. LOSC, Articles 19, 21. Does it matter whether the dumping posed an immediate threat to the environment? *See id., see also id.* Articles 192 and 235. Would the United States or Norway, or both, have prescriptive jurisdiction to allow prosecution of the personnel who discharged the pollutants? What penalties or other sanctions could be imposed? *See* Articles 19, 21, 25, 27, 28, 230(2); United States v. Royal Caribbean Cruises, Ltd., 24 F. Supp.2d 155; *id.*, 30 F. Supp.2d 114 (D.P.R.1997).

9. Article 33 of the U.N. LOSC allows countries to claim the next 12 nautical miles (out to a distance of 24 miles from their coasts) as a "**contiguous zone**," where they can exercise control to enforce violations of its customs, fiscal, immigration or sanitary laws that occurred in its territorial sea. The United States claimed a contiguous zone from 12 to 24 nautical miles from its coasts in 1999. Pres. Proc. 7219, 64 FED. REG. 48701 (1999). This proclamation stated that:

> The contiguous zone of the United States is a zone contiguous to the territorial sea of the United States, in which the United States may exercise the control necessary to prevent infringement of its customs, fiscal, immigration, or sanitary laws and regulations within its territory or territorial sea, and to punish infringement of the above laws and regulations committed within its territory or territorial sea.

As a country that has not ratified the U.N. LOSC, was it lawful for the United States to claim this jurisdiction over its contiguous zone? Can coastal states suppress illegal drug trafficking in the contiguous zone? Concerning coastal state prescriptive and enforcement powers with respect to drug trafficking in its territorial sea, *see* Articles 2, 21(1)(h), and 27(1)(d).

10. Do coastal and island countries have preferential or exclusive rights over the petroleum and minerals beneath their coastal waters? The "**continental shelf**" is the geologic extension of the continental land mass that, in many parts of the world (but not all), slopes gradually from the continent into the sea, until it drops off into the abyssal depths. Most undersea commercially-viable petroleum deposits are found under such continental shelves, and most productive fisheries are found in the waters above them. Under the Law of the Sea Convention, every country has exclusive sovereign rights to the natural resources of the seabed and subsoil of the continental shelf adjacent to its coast and seaward of its territorial sea within 200 nautical miles of its coast, whether or not the sea floor is actually a "geographical" continental shelf, and if the coastal country has a geographical continental shelf that extends beyond this point, it can claim the shelf resources out to 350 nautical miles. The Commission on the Limits of the Continental Shelf, established under Annex II, is now in the process of reviewing claims to extended continental shelves. *See* U.N. LOSC, Articles

76–85. What claims can a country that has not ratified the Convention make with regard to its continental shelf resources?

11. Do coastal and island countries have preferential or exclusive rights to harvest the fish in their coastal waters? Beginning in 1959, Iceland made increasingly expansive claims to an exclusive fishery zone, first claiming all the living resources within 12 nautical miles of its coast and then extending this claim to all the resources in the waters within 50 nautical miles of the island. Iceland justified these claims because of the collapse of the haddock fishery in these waters—the combined British–Icelandic haddock catch dropped from 110,000 tons in 1961 to just over 40,000 tons in 1973. In 1972 and 1973, Icelandic gunboats cut the trawls off of British fishing vessels and, in some cases, fired at them. The United Kingdom, whose fishers had harvested in those waters for many years, objected to Iceland's claims and brought a case in the International Court of Justice. Fisheries Jurisdiction Case (U.K. v. Iceland), 1974 I.C.J. 3. There, the Court recognized that "State practice on the subject of fisheries reveals an increasing and widespread acceptance of the concept of preferential rights for coastal States, particularly in favour of countries or territories in a situation of special dependence on coastal fisheries," such as Iceland. *Id.* paras. 58–59. The Court also ruled by a 10–4 vote, however, that "[t]he concept of preferential rights is not compatible with the exclusion of all fishing activities of other States.... The coastal State has to take into account and pay regard to the position of such other States, particularly when they have established an economic dependence on the same fishing grounds." *Id.* para. 62. Because the United Kingdom had been fishing in the disputed waters for "upward of 50 years" (para. 63), Iceland could not unilaterally exclude them from these waters and was required to negotiate with the United Kingdom to resolve the impasse. Para. 73. In these negotiations, Iceland was entitled to a "preferential share" because of "the special dependence of its people upon the fisheries," but the United Kingdom also has "established rights" based on the dependence of its people on these resources "for their livelihood and economic well-being." *Id.* para. 79. This decision played a role in ameliorating the dispute and in negotiations that led to the 1982 Law of the Sea Convention, but the Court's summary of the law was quickly overtaken by the changes that were included in that treaty, especially the creation of the 200–nautical-mile exclusive economic zone.

12. The United States initially resisted efforts to create an extended fisheries zone, because it was concerned that such a zone could limit navigational freedoms. The United States was particularly concerned about its continuing ability to navigate its warships, including submerged submarines, through key **international straits** such as the Strait of Gibralter (into the Mediterranean Sea), the Strait of Hormuz (into the Persian/Arabian Gulf), the Strait of Bab el Mandeb (into the Red Sea), the Strait of Malacca (connecting the Indian Ocean with the Pacific), the Dover Strait (through the English Channel), the Bering Strait (in the Arctic), and the Strait of Lombok (through the Indonesian archipelago). If countries were allowed to extend their territorial seas to 12 nautical miles, no high-seas corridors would remain in these narrow straits, and control over passage might arguably fall under the control of the countries bordering on these key waterways. The United States maintained that free movement through these

straits was essential to its national security, and protested claims of expanding territorial seas.

13. The compromise that emerged consisted of (A) allowing coastal states to extend their territorial seas to 12 nautical miles, (B) recognizing the right to transit passage through international straits, which is discussed in Section 3 below, and (C) allowing countries to establish an "**exclusive economic zone**" (**EEZ**) up to a distance of 200 nautical miles from its coast, governed by Part V of the U.N. LOSC, Articles 55–75. In this zone, the adjacent or coastal state has sovereign rights over the living and nonliving resources and can exercise certain forms of jurisdiction to protect the marine environment, regulate scientific research, and govern artificial structures, but it must exercise "due regard to the rights and duties of other States" and, in particular, must permit navigational passage. Article 56(2). This zone was thus designed to balance carefully the interests of both the coastal and the maritime states. Professor Bernard H. Oxman of the University of Miami School of Law, who served as vice-chair of the U.S. delegation to the Third U.N. Conference on the Law of the Sea has described this zone as follows:

> The rights of the coastal state in the economic zone are:
>
> • exclusive sovereign rights to control the exploration, exploitation, conservation, and management of living and non-living natural resources in the waters and the seabed and subsoil;
>
> • exclusive sovereign rights to control other activities for the economic exploitation and exploration of the zone, such as the production of energy from the water, currents, and winds;
>
> • the exclusive right to control the construction and use of all artificial islands and installations and structures that are used for economic purposes or may interfere with the coastal state's exercise of its rights in the zone (for example, an oil rig or offshore tanker depot);
>
> • the right to be informed of and participate in proposed marine scientific research projects and to withhold consent for a project in a timely manner under specified circumstances;
>
> • the right to control the dumping of wastes; and
>
> • the right to board, inspect, and, when there is threat of major damage, arrest a merchant ship suspected of discharging pollutants in the zone in violation of internationally approved standards. This right is subject to substantial safeguards to protect shippers, sailors, and consumers. Even if investigation indicates a violation, the ship must be released promptly on reasonable bond. If release is not obtained within ten days, an international court may set the bond and order release "without delay." If so authorized, a private party may seek this release order on behalf of the flag state. The convention establishes a time limit for prosecution, requires that the coastal state observe "recognized rights of the accused," prohibits punishments other than monetary fines, and restricts successive trials by different states for the same offense.
>
> The right of all states in the economic zone are:

- the high seas freedoms of navigation, overflight, and the laying of submarine cables and pipelines; and

- other internationally lawful uses of the sea related to these freedoms, such as those associated with the operation of ships, aircraft, and submarine cables and pipelines. This category may cover a gamut of uses—for example, recreational swimming, weather monitoring, and various naval operations.

This allocation of rights is accompanied by extensive duties.

Because both the coastal state and other states have independent rights to use the economic zone, each is required to ensure that its rights are exercised with "due regard" to the rights and duties of the other.

Flag states must ensure that their ships observe generally accepted international antipollution regulations.

The coastal state must take measures to ensure that activities under its jurisdiction or control do not cause pollution damage to other states.

The coastal state is required to ensure the conservation of living resources in the waters of the economic zone. Except with respect to marine mammals, it also must promote the optimum utilization of these resources by determining its harvesting capacity and granting access under reasonable conditions to foreign vessels to fish for the surplus, if any, that remains under this conservation limits. Neighboring states with small enclosed coastlines, or none at all, enjoy some priority of access to this surplus. International protection of whales and other marine mammals is required, as is regional regulation of migratory species.

If the economic zones or continental shelves of neighboring coastal states overlap, they are to be delimited by agreement between those states on the basis of international law in order to achieve an equitable solution. This general provision should be read against the background of an increasing number of bilateral agreements and international judicial and arbitral decisions on offshore boundary delimitation.

Bernard H. Oxman, *The New Law of the Sea,* 69 A.B.A.J. 156 (Feb. 1983) (reprinted by permission of the ABA Journal and Professor Oxman).

14. Under Articles 56 and 57 of the U.N. LOSC, what rights does Iceland have to the fishing resources in its exclusive economic zone (EEZ)? Based on its historic fishing activities, does the United Kingdom have any continuing rights to fish in Iceland's EEZ? *See* U.N. LOSC, Article 62 (1)-(3). May other states construct artificial islands or conduct research without the permission of the coastal state within the coastal state's exclusive economic zone?

15. Articles 46–49 of the Law of the Sea Convention describe the concept of "**archipelagic waters**." These provisions specify that countries made up exclusively of islands and that have a water-to-land ratio of between 9:1 and 1:1 can become "archipelagic states" exercise unique jurisdiction over the waters within their islands. These provisions apply to

countries such as the Bahamas, Fiji, Indonesia, Papua New Guinea, the Philippines, the Solomon Islands, and Vanuatu. Are the waters between the Hawaiian Islands "archipelagic waters"? Why? What difference would it make if they were? Are the provisions in the Convention governing archipelagic waters now part of customary international law? *See* the 1983 U.S. Oceans Policy Statement, *infra*. How are archipelagic baselines drawn? Does a nonratifying nation have the same right to use the archipelagic sea lanes as a ratifying nation? How do "archipelagic waters" differ from the waters in the "territorial sea" and the "exclusive economic zone? *See* Articles 50, 52–53. Can submarines pass through archipelagic waters without surfacing?

16. The ocean areas beyond the exclusive economic zone are the "**high seas**." See Article 87, which protects the "freedom of navigation" and certain other freedoms, but also recognizes that all freedoms must be exercised "with due consideration for the interests of other States." It is now a "well-established norm of international law that no nation has sovereignty over the high seas." R.M.S. Titanic v. Haver, 171 F.3d 943 (4th Cir.1999) (citing Article 89 of the U.N. LOSC). Earlier, the high seas were recognized as "the common property of all nations." The Vinces, 20 F.2d 164, 172 (E.D.S.C.1927). Under the earlier approach, all nations had free access to these waters, their resources were shared, rights could be "exercised by all nations, and the assertion by any nation of exclusive sovereignty would interfere with those rights." R.M.S. Titanic, *supra*. Today, see U.N. LOSC, Articles 86–90, 136–141, *passim*. Article 66 of the Law of the Sea Convention has eliminated free high seas fishing for salmon and other anadromous species and Article 65 says that such freedoms can also be eliminated or restricted for whales and other marine mammals.

Under certain U.S. statutes, such as the Death on the High Seas Act, the term "high seas" has been defined as those waters beyond the territorial sea of the United States. *In re* Air Crash Off Long Island, N.Y. on July 17, 1996, 209 F.3d 200, 207 (2d Cir. 2000). In the context of this statute, this term has also included foreign territorial waters and the U.S. Pacific possession of Johnston Atoll. *See In re* Air Crash Disaster Near Peggy's Cove, Nova Scotia on Sept. 2, 1998, 210 F.Supp.2d 570, 586 (E.D.Pa. 2002); Jacobson v. Kalama Services, 128 F.Supp.2d 644 (D.Hawaii 2000).

17. Can states ratifying the 1982 Convention file reservations to those provisions that they do not like? See Articles 309–310. Also recall Vienna Convention on the Law of Treaties, arts. 2(1)(d), 19. Was the Convention a "package deal" that resulted from compromises between competing camps? Did any group of states get everything they wanted from this Convention? Concerning formal amendments to the Convention, especially with respect to the Sea Bed Area, see Articles 312, 314, 316. Concerning supplemental or "modifying" agreements, see Article 311(3) (such agreements shall not be "incompatible with the effective execution of the object and purpose" of the Convention, and "provided further that such agreements shall not affect the application of the basic principles") and (6) ("shall be no amendments to the basic principle relating to the common heritage of mankind set forth in Article 136"). Can supplemental agreements legally modify the "Principles Governing the Area" found in Articles 136–137?

18. What parts of the Convention are particularly beneficial to the United States? Which parts are not beneficial to the interests of the United States? Taken as a whole, is this Convention beneficial to the United States? Would you recommend to your Senators that they vote for ratification?

SECTION 3. NAVIGATIONAL FREEDOMS

The free movement of ships, including warships, was a central issue during the negotiations that led to the Law of the Sea Convention. Under earlier legal principles, countries have the right of "**innocent passage**" through the territorial seas of other countries during peacetime, but this right can be suspended in times of conflict, and submarines must surface in order to be passing through the territorial sea "innocently." *See* U.N. LOSC, Article 20. In order to ensure that its warships could move without restrictions even as the territorial sea expanded to 12 nautical miles, the maritime nations insisted that the Convention recognize the right of "**transit passage through international straits**." *See* Articles 37–45.

Notes and Questions

1. What is the right of "innocent passage" and does it apply to aircraft? *See* Articles 2(2), 17–20. How does it differ from the right of transit passage through international straits? *See* Articles 37–39 and 42. Are military aircraft covered under the right of transit passage? Do military vessels have more free transit rights through straits than they might through a mere territorial sea? What acts are noninnocent? Is any act of espionage, any research, any form of pollution, or any fishing not "innocent"?

2. What other coastal regulations of passage are permissible? See Articles 21–24.

3. If a merchant vessel is not engaged in innocent passage, what enforcement powers does the coastal state have under the Convention? See Article 25; see also Articles 27–28. Must enforcement "steps" under Article 25 be necessary or merely reasonable or useful? Is that standard similar to the enforcement standard in the contiguous zone (CZ) and EEZ? See Articles 33(1), 73. Is it similar to standards (express or implicit) in Articles 105, 108(2), 109(3), and 110(1), which apply to enforcement on the high seas? What justifications might exist for different standards (e.g., proximity to land territory, types of activities regulated)? What is the coastal state's enforcement power with respect to foreign warships in its territorial sea? See Articles 30–32.

4. Can the right of innocent passage be suspended in times of war or crisis? See Article 25(3).

5. Do warships have the same rights of innocent passage in a territorial sea as merchant ships? See Articles 17, 20, 29–32. Before World War II, the United States argued that warships did not have the right of innocent passage through the territorial sea, because the right was established to promote commerce. During an international negotiation in 1910, the U.S. representative Elihu Root said that "warships may not pass without consent . . . because they threaten. Merchant ships may pass because they do not threaten." See PHILIP JESSUP, THE LAW OF TERRITORIAL WATERS AND MARITIME

JURISDICTION 120 (1927); 1 D.P. O'CONNELL, THE INTERNATIONAL LAW OF THE SEA 275, 282 (I.A. Shearer ed. 1982). Yet, after World War II, the U.S. position on this issue changed, and its negotiators worked to establish the right of innocent passage for warships. The 1958 Conventions and the 1982 Convention make no major distinctions between warships and merchant ships, allowing the United States to argue that no new restrictions can be imposed upon the exercise of innocent passage by warships. See United States v. Conroy, 589 F.2d 1258 (5th Cir.1979) ("At least between the parties to the [1958 Convention], a warship of one nation may enter the territorial waters of another without first giving notification and receiving authorization."). When the Netherlands ratified the Law of the Sea Convention on June 28, 1996, it filed a Declaration containing the following paragraph:

> Innocent passage in the territorial sea.
>
> The Convention permits innocent passage in the territorial sea for all ships, including foreign warships, nuclear-powered ships and ships carrying nuclear or hazardous waste, without any prior consent or notification, and with due observance of special precautionary measures established for such ships by international agreements.

NILOS NEWSLETTER No. 14, at 5 (June 1997). However, a number of countries still require prior notification or prior authorization before a warship can pass through their territorial waters. *See, e.g.*, Shao Jin, *The Question of Innocent Passage of Warships—After UNCLOS III*, 13 MARINE POLICY 56 (1989); K. Hakapaa, E.J. Molenaar, *Innocent Passage—Past and Present*, 23 MARINE POLICY 131 (1999).

6. On March 13, 1986, the U.S. guided missile cruiser Yorktown and the U.S. destroyer Caron sailed through the territorial sea of the Soviet Union in the Black Sea, passing within six nautical miles of the a Soviet Naval Base at Sevastopol in the Crimea. The U.S. vessels were not heading to any particular destination, and because both ships were capable of sophisticated electronic intelligence gathering, it was suspected by some that the U.S. mission included eavesdropping. Does the right of innocent passage include random sailing toward no particular destination, or is it like an easement-of-necessity over private land to an otherwise inaccessible plot, limited to travel necessary to reach a specific destination? *See* Articles 18–19.

7. In September 1989, the United States and the Soviet Union issued a joint statement, known as the Jackson Hole Agreement, which states that "[a]ll ships, including warships, regardless of cargo, armament or means of propulsion, enjoy the right of innocent passage through the territorial sea in accordance with international law, for which neither prior notification nor authorization is required." The agreement refers to Part II, Section 3 of the Law of the Sea Convention as stating relevant rules of international law. What is the effect of such an agreement? Is it binding on other nations?

8. When can a coastal state exercise criminal enforcement jurisdiction on board a foreign flag vessel in its territorial sea? *See* Articles 2(1), 24–25, 27. Article 27 provides consent in advance by treaty for certain enforcement measures. What other forms of consent are covered by Article 27(1)(c)? Can the coastal state arrest persons on board a foreign flag vessel in its territorial sea for crimes committed prior to entry of the vessel? What about international crimes committed in violation of, for example, the International

Convention Against the Taking of Hostages (*see* Articles 6(1), 8), the Convention Against Torture and Other Cruel, Inhuman or Degrading Treatment or Punishment (*see* Articles 6(1), 7(1)), or the Montreal Convention for the Suppression of Unlawful Acts Against the Safety of Civil Aviation (*see* Articles 6(1), 7)? In case of a clash, which treaties should prevail?

9. If a foreign flag vessel suspected of violating laws or regulations of the coastal state in its internal waters, territorial sea, or contiguous zone escapes out onto the high seas, can the coastal state pursue the foreign flag vessel? *See* Article 111. What is the burden of proof in 111(1)? How must pursuit occur and when must it end?

10. When can a coastal state exercise civil jurisdiction over persons on board a foreign flag vessel in its territorial sea? *See* Articles 2 (1), 24–25, 28. Can the coastal state enjoin a foreign flag vessel from leaving its territorial sea with persons on board who seek asylum in accordance with human rights law or who are refugees? Does the U.N. Charter, Article 103, override limits found in the U.N. LOSC? If the asylum seeker is being held in captivity below deck, does Article 27 add to coastal state competence?

11. Does the Convention protect the ability of the United States and other maritime powers to move their military warships freely through the narrow straits that provide key waterways connecting the world's oceans? Examine Articles 20, 37–44, 45.

12. Do vessels have the right to pass through **straits** that connect larger bodies of water? In 1946, the United Kingdom sent four warships through the Corfu Channel, which separates the Greek island of Corfu and the Albanian coast. Several of the vessels were seriously damaged by mines in the channel, and a number of British sailors were killed. Albania argued that the channel was not a necessary route between two parts of the high seas and therefore that no right of passage existed. The International Court of Justice agreed that it was not a necessary route, but said that "[i]t has nevertheless been a useful route for international maritime traffic," and hence that "the North Corfu Channel should be considered as belonging to the class of international highways through which passage cannot be prohibited by a coastal State in time of peace." As long as the passage through the waterway is innocent, passage of warships is permissible and the coastal state cannot require prior authorization. Corfu Channel Case (United Kingdom v. Albania), 1949 I.C.J. 4.

The I.C.J. also noted that British warships could pass through with crew and guns at the ready when Albanian shore batteries had previously fired at British ships, since "the measure of precaution" was not "unreasonable" under the circumstances. The Court ruled, however, that subsequent sweeping of the Corfu Channel of mines without Albanian consent was an impermissible use of force or enforcement jurisdiction in Albanian territorial waters. Especially unpersuasive was a British claim that it was acting to gather evidence (before it disappeared) concerning the illegal placement of mines in the channel.

Would Britain have had a viable claim under the U.N. Charter, Articles 51 and 103? Can a ship lawfully use force to destroy a mine that is in its immediate path?

13. What straits qualify under Article 37 of the Law of the Sea Convention as "straits which are used for international navigation"? Must they have been historically used for international navigation, or only be capable of such use? Is the Detroit River, which forms the border between the United States and Canada and connects Lake St. Clair with Lake Erie a international strait? *See In re* J.W. Westcott Co., 266 F.Supp.2d 601 (E.D.Mich. 2003).

14. As noted, submarines have the right to travel submerged when passing through straits used for international navigation. *See* Articles 38–39. Do they have the same right in straits used for archipelagic sea lanes passage? *See* Article 53(3). What is the "normal mode" of transit for a submarine?

15. If a vessel is exercising its right of transit passage through the Strait of Malacca, passing through waters that are in Malaysia's territorial sea, does the vessel have the right to allow its passengers to participate in gambling activities that violate Malaysian law? Can Malaysia enact regulations to protect the waters in the strait from vessel-source pollution?

16. Are all of the Convention's provisions on transit passage through straits (Articles 34–45) customary international law? How is that status achieved? Can transit passage be denied to nations that fail to ratify the Convention?

17. Do airplanes have the right to fly over straits? *See* Articles 38–39, 45.

18. Can states engage in military maneuvers, including the firing of weapons, on the high seas? *See* Articles 87(1)(a), (b), and (2), and 95. How does Article 88 condition such activity?

19. Can countries engage in military maneuvers, including the firing of weapons, in the exclusive economic zone of another country? *See* Article 58(1). When Brazil signed the Convention on December 10, 1982, it issued a Declaration containing the following language:

> (2) The Brazilian Government understands that the regime which is applied in practice in maritime areas adjacent to the coast of Brazil is compatible with the provisions of the Convention.
>
> (3) The Brazilian Government understands that the provisions of Article 301, which prohibits "any threat or use of force against the territorial integrity or political independence of any State, or in any other manner inconsistent with the principles of international law embodied in the Charter of the United Nations", apply, in particular, to the maritime areas under the sovereignty or the jurisdiction of the coastal State.
>
> (4) The Brazilian Government understands that the provisions of the Convention do not authorize other States to carry out in the exclusive economic zone military exercises or manoeuvres, in particular those that imply the use of weapons or explosives, without the consent of the coastal State.

Is Brazil's interpretation correct? What is the effect of such a "declaration" or "understanding"? Recall the Vienna Convention on the Law of Treaties, art. 2(1)(d), in Chapter 1. What is the effect of Articles 2(4) and 103 of the U.N. Charter? Could a coastal state rightly require that it be notified prior to military maneuvers occurring in its EEZ?

20. When the question of military activities in the EEZ came up at a meeting in Honolulu in 1984, Tommy T.B. Koh, who represented Singapore and served as the second and final President of the Third United Nations Conference on the Law of the Sea, analyzed this problem as follows:

> The question of military activities in the exclusive economic zone is a very difficult one. Bernie Oxman will remember that the status of the exclusive economic zone was one of the last questions to be wrapped up in the negotiations in Committee Two. We finally succeeded in wrapping up this question of the status of the exclusive economic zone thanks to the personal initiative of our friend Jorge Castaneda of Mexico. Before he became foreign minister, he was the leader of the Mexican delegation. In 1977, I believe, Jorge Castaneda invited about 20 of us to dinner one evening. After dinner was over, he asked that the table be cleared and said,
>
> . . . [W]e have been grappling for the last three years with the question of the status of the exclusive economic zone. I have invited you here because I believe you represent a cross section of the points of view of the Conference and you are the leaders of the Conference. I suggest, if you all agree, that we commence informal consultations on this question.
>
> We agreed and sat down and worked, in fact, all night long. And we began to negotiate every night for two weeks and eventually wrapped up the issue.
>
> *Military Activities in the EEZ: Unstated But Understood*
>
> The solution in the Convention text is very complicated. Nowhere is it clearly stated whether a third state may or may not conduct military activities in the exclusive economic zone of a coastal state. But, it was the general understanding that the text we negotiated and agreed upon would permit such activities to be conducted. I therefore would disagree with the statement made in Montego Bay by Brazil, in December 1982, that a third state may not conduct military activities in Brazil's exclusive economic zone. . . .
>
> *Provisions Are Slipping Away Through Interpretations*
>
> David Colson (Assistant Legal Adviser for Oceans and International Environmental and Scientific Affairs, U.S. Dept. of State): . . . From a United States political perspective, I am sure our politicians would be asking this kind of question: "How can the United States have confidence in the deep seabed mining provisions of this Convention when we see basic and fundamental aspects of the nonseabed provisions that were negotiated slipping away." The Brazilian declaration has already been mentioned. I could mention others. It was frankly outrageous that some states could make those statements in good faith and sign the Convention saying that they intended to ratify the Convention. We have heard statements about prior notification and authorization of warships in the territorial sea. We have heard statements about the meaning or possible

> interpretation of the phrase "normal mode." ... They want to see [the Convention] come into force, but yet their statements clearly indicate to us that they are not really very serious about the law that the Convention would seem to create.

CONSENSUS AND CONFRONTATION: THE UNITED STATES AND THE LAW OF THE SEA CONVENTION 303–04 (Jon M. Van Dyke ed. 1985). Does the text support the result articulated by Ambassador Koh? Is this interpretation binding on contracting parties? When it ratified the Law of the Sea Convention on June 28, 1996, the Netherlands filed a Declaration that included the following paragraph:

> *Military exercises in the Exclusive Economic Zone*
>
> The Convention does not authorize the coastal state to prohibit military exercises in its EEZ. The rights of the coastal state in its EEZ are listed in Article 56 of the Convention, and no such authority is given to the coastal state. In the EEZ all states enjoy the freedoms of navigation and overflight, subject to the relevant provisions of the Convention.

NILOS NEWSLETTER No. 14, at 5 (June 1997).

21. What pollution control measures can a coastal state impose upon vessels passing through its EEZ beyond its TS and CZ? *See* Article 211, 220, 230.

22. A hydrographic survey involves the mapping of the sea floor in order to facilitate navigational safety, particularly for submarines. The position of the United States and other maritime states has been that military intelligence-gathering activities and military hydrographic surveys are distinct from marine scientific research and are not governed by Article 246 of the Law of the Sea Convention, which says that marine scientific research can be conducted only with the consent of the coastal state. *See, e.g.,* Bernard Oxman, *The Regime of Warships Under the United Nations Convention on the Law of the Sea,* 24 VA. J. INT'L L. 809 (1984); J. ASHLEY ROACH AND ROBERT W. SMITH, UNITED STATES RESPONSES TO EXCESSIVE MARITIME CLAIMS 425–26, 448–49 (2nd ed. 1996). According to this view, military intelligence gathering is different, because it is not related to resource exploitation. Is this view persuasive, and, if so, is the distinction between surveillance and surveying and scientific research clear enough to be sure what is permitted and what is prohibited? *See generally* Jon M. Van Dyke, *Military Ships and Planes Operating in the Exclusive Economic Zone of Another Country,* 28 MARINE POLICY 29 (2004).

SECTION 4. WHY DID THE UNITED STATES REJECT THE CONVENTION?

When Ronald Reagan became President in January 1981, he reassigned or fired most of the U.S. diplomats who had been conducting negotiations at the Third U.N. Law of the Sea Conference, and ordered his aides to undertake a year-long review of the Draft Convention. Two negotiating sessions were held that year, but no serious talks took place, because the United States refused to participate in substantive discussions.

In early 1982, President Reagan said the United States would return to the Conference, but would insist on specific changes before it would accept the Convention. His statement of January 29, 1982, explains the position of the United States (from U.S. Department of State Bureau of Public Affairs, Current Policy No. 371):

> The world's oceans are vital to the United States and other nations in diverse ways. They represent waterways and airways essential to preserving the peace and to trade and commerce; are major sources for meeting increasing world food and energy demands and promise further resource potential. They are a frontier for expanding scientific research and knowledge, a fundamental part of the global environmental balance, and a great source of beauty, awe, and pleasure for mankind.
>
> Developing international agreement for this vast ocean space, covering over half of the Earth's surface, has been a major challenge confronting the international community. Since 1973 scores of nations have been actively engaged in the arduous task of developing a comprehensive treaty for the world's oceans at the Third U.N. Conference on Law of the Sea. The United States has been a major participant in this process.
>
> Serious questions had been raised in the United States about parts of the draft convention and, last March, I announced that my Administration would undertake a thorough review of the current draft and the degree to which it met U.S. interests in the navigation, overflight, fisheries, environmental, deep seabed mining, and other areas covered by that convention. We recognize that the last two sessions of the conference have been difficult, pending the completion of our review. At the same time, we consider it important that a Law of the Sea treaty be such that the United States can join in and support it. Our review has concluded that while most provisions of the draft convention are acceptable and consistent with U.S. interests, some major elements of the deep seabed mining regime are not acceptable.
>
> I am announcing today that the United States will return to those negotiations and work with other countries to achieve an acceptable treaty. In the deep seabed mining area, we will seek changes necessary to correct those unacceptable elements and to achieve the goal of a treaty that:
>
> • Will not deter development of any deep seabed mineral resources to meet national and world demand;
>
> • Will assure national access to these resources by current and future qualified entities to enhance U.S. security of supply, to avoid monopolization of the resources by the operating arm of the international Authority, and to promote the economic development of the resources;

- Will provide a decisionmaking role in the deep seabed regime that fairly reflects and effectively protects the political and economic interests and financial contributions of participating states;

- Will not allow for amendments to come into force without approval of the participating states, including in our case the advice and consent of the Senate;

- Will not set other undesirable precedents for international organizations; and

- Will be likely to receive the advice and consent of the Senate. In this regard, the convention should not contain provisions for the mandatory transfer of private technology and participation by and funding for national liberation movements.

The United States remains committed to the multilateral treaty process for reaching agreement on law of the sea. If working together at the conference we can find ways to fulfill these key objectives, my Administration will support ratification.

I have instructed the Secretary of State and my Special Representative for the Law of the Sea Conference, in coordination with other responsible agencies, to embark immediately on the necessary consultations with other countries and to undertake further preparations for our participation in the conference.

During the spring 1982 session, intense negotiations were held in an effort to bridge the gap between the United States and the nations of the developing world. The United States was given a virtually guaranteed seat on the governing body of the International Sea–Bed Authority (Article 161(1)(a)) and a resolution was passed protecting the investments already made by the mining consortia interested in deep seabed mining and guaranteeing to them access to the polymetallic nodules of the deep seabed.

These actions did not satisfy the Reagan Administration, however, and on April 30, 1982, the U.S. Ambassador to the Conference insisted that a vote be taken on the Convention as a whole. 130 nations voted for the Convention, 4 voted against (Israel, Turkey, the United States, and Venezuela), and 17 abstained. The abstaining nations included the Eastern European nations, who thought the United States had been given too much in the spring 1982 negotiating session, plus several Western European nations.

On July 9, 1982, President Reagan announced that the United States would not sign the Convention, citing the following problems as forming the basis for this decision:

- Provisions that would actually deter future development of deep seabed mineral resources, when such development should serve the interest of all countries;

- A decisionmaking process that would not give the United States or others a role that fairly reflects and protects their interests;

- Provisions that would allow amendments to enter into force for the United States without its approval; this is clearly incompatible with the U.S. approach to such treaties;
- Stipulations relating to mandatory transfer of private technology and the possibility of national liberation movements sharing in benefits; and
- The absence of assured access for future qualified deep seabed miners to promote the development of these resources.

Statement of President Ronald Reagan, July 9, 1982, (reprinted in U.S. State Department Bureau of Public Affairs Current Policy No. 416). Articles that explain the dynamics of how the decision not to sign was reached include: Leigh Ratiner, *The Law of the Sea: A Crossroads for American Foreign Policy*, 60 FOREIGN AFFAIRS 5:1006 (1982); Nossiter, *Underwater Treaty: The Fascinating Story of How the Law of the Sea was Sunk*, BARRON'S 10 (July 26, 1982).

On March 10, 1983, President Reagan issued a Proclamation establishing an exclusive economic zone for the United States and an Oceans Policy Statement announcing U.S. policy on related oceans issues, and then on December 27, 1988, President Reagan issued another proclamation extending the U.S. territorial sea to 12 nautical miles:

PROCLAMATION NO. 5030

48 FED. REG. 10,605 (1983).

Whereas the Government of the United States of America desires to facilitate the wise development and use of the oceans consistent with international law;

Whereas international law recognizes that, in a zone beyond its territory and adjacent to its territorial sea, known as the Exclusive Economic Zone, a coastal State may assert certain sovereign rights over natural resources and related jurisdiction; and

Whereas the establishment of an Exclusive Economic Zone by the United States will advance the development of ocean resources and promote the protection of the marine environment, while not affecting other lawful uses of the zone, including the freedoms of navigation and overflight, by other States;

Now, Therefore, I, Ronald Reagan, by the authority vested in me as President by the Constitution and laws of the United States of America, do hereby proclaim the sovereign rights and jurisdiction of the United States of America and confirm also the rights and freedoms of all States within an Exclusive Economic Zone, as described herein.

The Exclusive Economic Zone of the United States is a zone contiguous to the territorial sea, including zones contiguous to the territorial sea of the United States, the Commonwealth of Puerto Rico, the Commonwealth of the Northern Mariana Islands (to the extent consistent with the Covenant and the United Nations Trusteeship Agreement), and

United States overseas territories and possessions. The Exclusive Economic Zone extends to a distance 200 nautical miles from the baseline from which the breadth of the territorial sea is measured. In cases where the maritime boundary with a neighboring State remains to be determined, the boundary of the Exclusive Economic Zone shall be determined by the United States and other State concerned in accordance with equitable principles.

Within the Exclusive Economic Zone, the United States has, to the extent permitted by international law, (a) sovereign rights for the purpose of exploring, exploiting, conserving and managing natural resources, both living and non-living, of the seabed and subsoil and the superjacent waters and with regard to other activities for the economic exploitation and exploration of the zone, such as the production of energy from the water, currents and winds; and (b) jurisdiction with regard to the establishment and use of artificial islands, and installations and structures having economic purposes, and the protection and preservation of the marine environment.

This Proclamation does not change existing United States policies concerning the continental shelf, marine mammals and fisheries, including highly migratory species of tuna which are not subject to United States jurisdiction and require international agreements for effective management.

The United States will exercise these sovereign rights and jurisdiction in accordance with the rules of international law.

Without prejudice to the sovereign rights and jurisdiction of the United States, the Exclusive Economic Zone remains an area beyond the territory and territorial sea of the United States in which all States enjoy the high seas freedoms of navigation, overflight, the laying of submarine cables and pipelines, and other internationally lawful uses of the sea....

OCEANS POLICY STATEMENT BY THE PRESIDENT

March 10, 1983.

The United States has long been a leader in developing customary and conventional law of the sea. Our objectives have consistently been to provide a legal order that will, among other things, facilitate peaceful, international uses of the oceans and provide for equitable and effective management and conservation of marine resources. The United States also recognizes that all nations have an interest in these issues.

Last July I announced that the United States will not sign the United Nations Law of the Sea Convention that was opened for signature on December 10. We have taken this step because several major problems in the Convention's deep seabed mining provisions are contrary to the interests and principles of industrialized nations and would not help attain the aspirations of developing countries.

The United States does not stand alone in those concerns. Some important allies and friends have not signed the Convention. Even some signatory States have raised concerns about these problems.

However, the Convention also contains provisions with respect to traditional uses of the oceans which generally confirm existing maritime law and practice and fairly balance the interests of all States.

Today I am announcing three decisions to promote and protect the oceans interests of the United States in a manner consistent with those fair and balanced results in the Convention and international law.

First, the United States is prepared to accept and act in accordance with the balance of interests relating to traditional uses of the oceans—such as navigation and overflight. In this respect, the United States will recognize the rights of other States in the waters off their coasts, as reflected in the Convention, so long as the rights and freedoms of the United States and others under international law are recognized by such coastal States.

Second, the United States will exercise and assert its navigation and overflight rights and freedoms on a worldwide basis in a manner that is consistent with the balance of interests reflected in the Convention. The United States will not, however, acquiesce in unilateral acts of other States designed to restrict the rights and freedoms of the international community in navigation and overflight and other related high seas uses.

Third, I am proclaiming today an Exclusive Economic Zone in which the United States will exercise sovereign rights in living and non-living resources within 200 nautical miles of its coast. This will provide United States jurisdiction for mineral resources out to 200 nautical miles that are not on the continental shelf. Recently discovered deposits there could be an important future source of strategic minerals.

Within this Zone all nations will continue to enjoy the high seas rights and freedoms that are not resource-related, including the freedoms of navigation and overflight. My Proclamation does not change existing United States policies concerning the continental shelf, marine mammals and fisheries, including highly migratory species of tuna which are not subject to United States jurisdiction. The United States will continue efforts to achieve international agreements for the effective management of these species. The Proclamation also reinforces this government's policy of promoting the United States fishing industry.

While international law provides for a right of jurisdiction over marine scientific research within such a zone, the Proclamation does not assert this right. I have elected not to do so because of the United States interest in encouraging marine scientific research and avoiding any unnecessary burdens. The United States will nevertheless recognize the right of other coastal States to exercise jurisdiction over marine scientific research within 200 nautical miles of their coasts, if that jurisdiction is exercised reasonably in a manner consistent with international law.

The Exclusive Economic Zone established today will also enable the United States to take limited additional steps to protect the marine environment. In this connection, the United States will continue to work through the International Maritime Organization and other appropriate international organizations to develop uniform international measures for the protection of the marine environment while imposing no unreasonable burdens on commercial shipping.

The policy decisions I am announcing today will not affect the application of existing United States law concerning the high seas or existing authorities of any United States government agency.

In addition to the above policy steps, the United States will continue to work with other countries to develop a regime, free of unnecessary political and economic restraints, for mining deep seabed minerals beyond national jurisdiction. Deep seabed mining remains a lawful exercise of the freedom of the high seas open to all nations. The United States will continue to allow its firms to explore for and, when the market permits, exploit these resources....

TERRITORIAL SEA OF THE UNITED STATES OF AMERICA

Proclamation 5928 (Dec. 27, 1988).

International law recognizes that coastal nations may exercise sovereignty and jurisdiction over their territorial seas.

The territorial sea of the United States is a maritime zone extending beyond the land territory and internal waters of the United States over which the United States exercises sovereignty and jurisdiction, a sovereignty and jurisdiction that extends to the airspace over the territorial sea, as well as to its bed and subsoil.

Extension of the territorial sea by the United States to the limits permitted by international law will advance the national security and other significant interests of the United States.

Now, Therefore, I, Ronald Reagan, by the authority vested in me as President by the Constitution of the United States of America, and in accordance with international law, do hereby proclaim the extension of the territorial sea of the United States of America, the Commonwealth of Puerto Rico, Guam, American Samoa, the United States Virgin Islands, the Commonwealth of the Northern Mariana Islands, and any other territory or possession over which the United States exercises sovereignty.

The territorial sea of the United States henceforth extends to 12 nautical miles from the baselines of the United States determined in accordance with international law.

In accordance with international law, as reflected in the applicable provisions of the 1982 United Nations Convention on the Law of the Sea, within the territorial sea of the United States, the ships of all countries enjoy the right of innocent passage and the ships and aircraft of all countries enjoy the right of transit passage through international straits.

Nothing in this Proclamation:

(a) extends or otherwise alters existing Federal or State law or any jurisdiction, rights, legal interests, or obligations derived therefrom; or

(b) impairs the determination, in accordance with international law, of any maritime boundary of the United States with a foreign jurisdiction....

Notes and Questions

1. Was the extension of the U.S. territorial sea from 3 to 12 nautical miles an action that a president can take unilaterally without congressional authority? Can the President "execute" international law? *See* Douglas W. Kmiec, *Legal Issues Raised by the Proposed Presidential Proclamation to Extend the Territorial Sea,* 1 TERRITORIAL SEA J. 1 (1990); Jack H. Archer, Joan M. Bondareff, *The Role of Congress in Establishing U.S. Sovereignty Over the Expanded Territorial Sea,* 1 TERRITORIAL SEA J. 117 (1990); David M. Forman, M. Casey Jarman, & Jon M. Van Dyke, *Filling in a Jurisdictional Void: The New U.S. Territorial Sea,* 2 TERRITORIAL SEA J. 1, 7–17 (1992).

2. What is the meaning of proviso (a) in the 1988 Territorial Sea Proclamation? The 1953 Submerged Lands Act, 43 U.S.C. §§ 1301–15, granted to the states (within the U.S.) authority over the resources in the first three nautical miles from their coasts (a few states were given broader jurisdiction for historical reasons), but this Act gave the federal government jurisdiction and responsibility over all resources beyond this three-mile limit. This division remains unchanged by the 1988 Proclamation. What criminal jurisdiction for environmental or resource protection applies in the 3–12 nautical mile zone?

3. Does customary international law permit the United States to establish an EEZ if it has not ratified the Law of the Sea Convention? If so, how did the EEZ concept become recognized under customary international law? *See* Koru North America v. United States, 701 F.Supp. 229, 232 n. 6 (U.S. Ct. Int'l Trade 1988):

> The concept of an EEZ has been given legitimacy in international law. The number of States claiming such a zone, fifty-nine as of 1985, represents two-thirds of all coastal States, including all industrial maritime States. Most EEZs generally conform to the regime set out in the United Nations Convention on the Law of the Sea and such widespread acceptance provides the necessary elements for international legal acceptance. The United States not only proclaims its own EEZ, but also recognizes the claims of foreign nations to an EEZ.

Is this analysis sufficient to establish the proposition?

4. Is the U.S. EEZ claim identical to the juridical concept of the EEZ established in the Law of the Sea Convention, or does it differ in some important respects?

5. If the United States does not ratify the Convention, how will disputes between the navigational claims of maritime nations and the environmental interests of U.S. coastal areas be resolved?

6. What enforcement powers does a coastal state have within its EEZ? *See* Articles 56, 58, 73. Do these include the stopping and search of foreign flag vessels reasonably suspected of engaging in drug smuggling into the coastal state? *See* also Articles 108, 110.

SECTION 5. FISHING DISPUTES

The recognition of exclusive economic zones (EEZs) in the Law of the Sea Convention transferred most of the productive fishing areas from the high seas where fishing freedoms are recognized to the exclusive jurisdiction of the adjacent coastal or island community. This transfer was based on the views, recognized in the Anglo–Norwegian Fisheries Case, that coastal communities tend to have an economic dependence on their nearby fisheries and that they are more likely to manage these resources carefully to protect them for future generations. Management under this new regime has not always been enlightened or orderly, however, and new disputes have arisen, particularly when fish stocks overlap or "straddle" between an EEZ and its adjacent high seas zone. In areas such as the productive fisheries off the east coast of Canada, European fishing vessels have harvested just outside the 200–nautical-mile EEZ in a way that impacts the stocks within the EEZ. This activity has led to disputes, such as the Estai incident, infra, and also led in 1995 to the creation of a new agreement designed to reduce such conflicts.

How do the principles of international law designed to protect the environment apply to the international law of fisheries? The provisions of the 1982 U.N. Law of the Sea Convention are general in nature but nonetheless clearly articulate an overarching duty to cooperate in all situations involving shared fisheries. Article 56 gives the coastal state sovereignty over the living resources in the 200–nautical-mile EEZ, but Articles 61, 62, 69 and 70 require the coastal state: (a) to cooperate with international organizations to ensure that species are not endangered by over-exploitation, (b) to manage species in a manner that protects "associated or dependent species" from over-exploitation, ©) to exchange data with international organizations and other nations that fish in its EEZ, and (d) to allow other states (particularly developing, land-locked, and geographically disadvantaged states) to harvest the surplus stocks in its EEZ. Article 63 addresses stocks (or stocks of associated species) that "straddle" adjacent EEZs, or an EEZ and an adjacent high seas area, and requires the states concerned to agree either directly or through an organization on the measures necessary to ensure the conservation of such stocks. Article 64 requires coastal states and distant-water fishing states that harvest highly migratory stocks such as tuna to cooperate either directly or through an organization to ensure the conservation and optimum utilization of such stocks. Article 65 contains strong language requiring nations to "work through the appropriate international organization" to conserve, manage, and study whales and dolphins. Article 66 gives the states of origin primary responsibility for anadromous stocks (i.e., salmon), but requires the states of origin to cooperate with other states whose nationals have traditionally harvested such stocks and states whose waters these fish migrate through.

On the high seas, Articles 118 and 119 require states to cooperate with other states whose nationals exploit identical or associated species. Article 118 is mandatory in stating that nations "shall enter into negotiations with a view to taking the measures necessary for the conservation of the living resources concerned," and suggests creating regional fisheries organizations, as appropriate (emphasis added). Article 120 states that the provisions of Article 65 on marine mammals also apply on the high seas.

These provisions thus reinforce the duty to cooperate that has always existed in customary international law. Because they are not specific enough to resolve conflicts that have arisen as species have been over-exploited, the 1995 Straddling and Migratory Stocks Agreement was negotiated.

CASE CONCERNING FISHERIES JURISDICTION (SPAIN v. CANADA)

I.C.J., Judgment of December 4, 1998.

[Editors' notes: The waters above the continental shelf extending off the east coast of Canada have been a particularly productive fishery over the years. The shelf of Canada's Grand Bank extends beyond 200 nautical miles in two locations (the Nose and the Tail), and the fish stocks in those waters—which swim both within Canada's EEZ and outside it—are called "straddling stocks," because the straddle between the EEZ and the high seas. Fishing vessels from Spain have aggressively harvested the fish outside the 200 nautical mile zone. Canada also overfished within its EEZ, but finally started taking measures to restore the fishery when the extent of overfishing became evident. Canada imposed strict limits on the activities of Canadian fishers, but Spanish fishers continued their harvesting without restraint.

[Spanish fishing led to one of the most dramatic recent confrontation over fishing rights. On May 12, 1994, Canada amended the Canadian Coastal Fisheries Protection Act to restrict fishing for the straddling stocks and on March 9, 1995, a Canadian patrol boat boarded, seized, and impounded the Spanish fishing trawler Estai, which was beyond Canada's EEZ, on the high seas. Canadian gunboats also cut the nets of another Spanish boat for allegedly exceeding its quotas for Greenland halibut (also known as turbot) established by the Northwest Atlantic Fisheries Organization (NAFO). Because of the dramatic decline in fish stocks, NAFO's Fishery Commission had reduced the total catch in its "Regulatory Area" (i.e., the area beyond national jurisdiction) from 60,000 tons to 27,000 tons annually, and allotted only about 13% of this amount (3,400 tons) to the European Union (EU). The EU issued an objection to this allocation under Article XII of the NAFO Convention, arguing that it had a historical dependence on this fishery, and allocated to itself about two-thirds (18,000 tons) of the overall allowable catch of 27,000 tons. Canada responded unilaterally by imposing a moratorium on EU vessels fishing for Greenland halibut in this area, and by taking action against the Estai and the other Spanish vessel.

[On March 28, 1995, Spain filed an application instituting proceedings in the International Court of Justice against Canada, arguing that Canada had violated the freedom of navigation and freedom of fishing on the high seas, and had also infringed the right of exclusive jurisdiction of the flag state over its ships on the high seas. On the merits, Canada argued in response that Spain violated its duties under Articles 63 and 117 of the Law of the Sea Convention to carry out necessary conservation measures and to cooperate in the management of straddling stocks. Both Canada and Spain had previously filed declarations with the International Court of Justice accepting the compulsory jurisdiction of the Court (under Article 36, para. 2 of the Court's Statute). However, on May 10, 1994, Canada modified its declaration to state that the Court had compulsory jurisdiction "over all disputes ... other than ... disputes arising out of or concerning conservation and management measures taken by Canada with respect to vessels fishing in [NAFO's] Regulatory Area ... and the enforcement of such measures". By a 12–5 vote, the Court ruled that it did not have jurisdiction over the dispute because it fell within Canada's conservation and management measures.]

Notes and Questions

1. If the I.C.J. had reached the merits of the Estai dispute, how should it have ruled? Does a nation have the right to harvest just outside another nation's EEZ without regard to the impact of such harvesting on the fish stocks within the EEZ? *See* Article 63 of the U.N. LOSC.

2. Is a coastal state free to take unilateral steps to protect its fish stocks, or does it have to cooperate with distant-water fishing nations to develop arrangements to protect straddling stocks?

3. After a period of political posturing, the dispute was resolved peacefully. Canada acknowledged that it does not have the right unilaterally to seize vessels on the high seas and allowed the European Union (EU) nations to harvest 41% of the allowable 27,000 tons in the NAFO Regulatory Area. The EU agreed that independent observers should be placed on all vessels fishing within the Regulatory Area and that satellite tracking devices should be placed on at least 35% of them.

JON M. VAN DYKE, *THE STRADDLING AND MIGRATORY STOCKS AGREEMENT AND THE PACIFIC*

11 INT'L J. MARINE & COASTAL L. 406 (1996).[2]

On December 4, 1995, the nations of the world settled on the text of an important document with the cumbersome title of "Agreement for the Implementation of the Provisions of the United Nations Convention on the Law of the Sea of 10 December 1982 Relating to the Conservation and Management of Straddling Fish Stocks and Highly Migratory Fish Stocks," UN Doc. A/CONF.164/37, 34 I.L.M. 1542 (1995). The goal of this document is to stop the dramatic overfishing that has decimated the fish stocks in many parts of the world. It builds on existing provisions in the 1982 United Nations Law of the Sea Convention, but it also introduces a number of new strategies that will require the fishing industry to change its mode of operation in a number of significant ways.

The Duty to Cooperate. The guiding principle that governs the 1995 Agreement is the duty to cooperate. This venerable notion is given specific new meaning, and the coastal nations and distant-water fishing nations of each region will be required to share data and manage the straddling fisheries together. Article 7(2) requires that "[c]onservation and management measures established for the high seas and those adopted for areas under national jurisdiction shall be compatible in order to ensure conservation and management of the straddling fish stocks and highly migratory fish stocks in their entirety" (emphasis added). This duty gives the coastal state a leadership role in determining the catch allowed to be taken from a stock that is found both within and outside its exclusive economic zone, as evidenced by the requirement in Article 7(2)(a) that contracting parties "take into account" the conservation measures established by the coastal state under Article 61 of the Law of the Sea Convention for the exclusive economic zone "and ensure that measures established in respect of such stocks for the high seas do not undermine the effectiveness of such measures." This polite diplomatic language indicates clearly that catch rates outside a 200–nautical-mile exclusive economic zone cannot differ significantly from those within the EEZ.

The Duty to Work Through an Existing or New Fisheries Organization. Article 64 of the 1982 Law of the Sea Convention requires coastal and distant-water nations that fish for highly migratory species to "co-operate directly or through appropriate international organizations" to ensure conservation and promote optimum utilization of these species. In 1979, the independent Pacific Island nations formed the Forum Fisheries Agency (FFA) to govern access to the highly migratory tuna in their 200–nautical-mile exclusive economic zones. Membership in this organization is limited to the 16 independent Pacific Island nations.

2. Reproduced with kind permission from Kluwer Law International, © 1996.

During the 1978 meetings that led to the creation of FFA, the members of the South Pacific Forum examined a draft that would have also allowed distant-water fishing nations to join, but they explicitly rejected that model in favor of an organization limited to the independent island nations.... [In 2000, a new Commission for the Conservation and Management of Highly Migratory Fish Stocks in the Western and Central Pacific Ocean was established, as described below.]

Article 11 addresses the difficult question whether new distant-water fishing nations must be allowed into such an organization once established. Do the nations that have established fishing activities in the region have to allow new entrants? The language of Article 11 does not give a clear answer to this question, but it seems to indicate that some new entrants could be excluded if the current fishing nations have developed a dependency on the shared fish stock in question. Furthermore, developing nations from the region would appear to have a greater right to enter the fishery than would developed nations from outside the region.

The 1995 Agreement emphasizes the need to cooperate, and it requires the coastal and island nations to cooperate with the distant-water fishing nations operating in the adjacent high-seas areas to the same extent that the distant-water fishing nations must cooperate with the coastal and island nations.

The Duty to Apply the Precautionary Principle. The "precautionary principle" has gained almost universal acceptance during the past decade as the basic rule that should govern activities that affect the ocean environment. This principle requires users of the ocean to exercise caution by undertaking relevant research, developing nonpolluting technologies, and avoiding activities that present uncertain risks to the marine ecosystem. Although the precautionary principle has been phrased in many ways in recent agreements and commentaries, perhaps the phrasing in Principle 15 of the 1992 Rio Declaration on Environment and Development, A/CONF.151/5/Rev.1 (June 13, 1992), best captures the essence of this principle:

> In order to protect the environment, the precautionary approach shall be widely applied by States according to their capabilities. Where there are threats of serious or irreversible damage, lack of full scientific certainty shall not be used as a reason for postponing cost-effective measures to prevent environmental degradation.

What specific burdens does this principle impose users of the ocean? It requires policy makers to be alert to risks of environmental damage, and the "greater the possible harm, the more rigorous the requirements of alertness, precaution and effort." David Freestone, *The Precautionary Principle*, in INTERNATIONAL LAW AND GLOBAL CLIMATE CHANGE 21, 36 (Robin Churchill & David Freestone eds. 1991). It rejects the notion that the oceans have an infinite or even a measurable ability to assimilate wastes or support living resources, and it instead recognizes that our knowledge about the ocean's ecosystems may remain incomplete and that policy makers must err on the side of protecting the environment. It certainly means at a minimum that a thorough evaluation of the environmental impacts must precede actions that may affect the marine environment. All agree that it requires a vigorous pursuit of a research agenda in order to overcome the uncertainties that exist.

Some commentators have explained the precautionary principle by emphasizing that it shifts the burden of proof: "[W]hen scientific information is in doubt, the party that wishes to develop a new project or change the existing system has the burden of demonstrating that the proposed changes will not produce unacceptable adverse impacts on existing resources and species." FREEDOM FOR THE SEAS IN THE 21ST CENTURY 477 (Jon M. Van Dyke, Durwood Zaelke & Grant Hewison eds. 1993). Others have suggested that the principle has an even more dynamic element, namely that it requires all users of the ocean commons to develop alternative nonpolluting or nonburdensome technologies.

The precautionary principle is given center stage as the primary basis for decisionmaking in the new Straddling and Migratory Stocks Agreement. Article 5©) lists the "precautionary approach" among the general principles that governing conservation and management of the straddling and migratory fish stocks, and Article 6 explains this approach in some detail. States are required to improve their data collection, and to share their information widely with others. When "information is uncertain, unreliable or inadequate," states must be "more cautious" (Article 6 (2)) and they must take "uncertainties" into account when establishing management goals (Article 6(3)©)). Species thought to be under stress shall be subjected to "enhanced monitoring in order to review their status and the efficacy of conservation and management measures" (Article 6(5)). If "new or exploratory fisheries" are opened, precautionary conservation measures must be established "as soon as possible" (Article 6(6)).

Then in Annex II, the Agreement explains a specific procedure that must be used to control exploitation and monitor the effects of the management approach. For each harvested species, a "conservation" or "limit" reference point as well as a "management" or "target" reference must be determined. If stock populations go below the agreed-upon conservation/limit reference point, then "conservation and management action should be initiated to facilitate stock recovery" (Annex II(5)). Over-fished stocks must be managed to ensure that they can recover to the level at which they can produce the maximum sustainable yield (Annex II (7)). The continued use of the maximum sustainable yield approach indicates that the Agreement has not broken out of the cycle that has led to the rapid decline in the world's fisheries. Fishing to attain the maximum sustainable yield inevitably means reducing the abundance of a stock, sometimes by one-half or two-thirds. This reduction can threaten the stock in unforeseeable ways and also will impact on other species in the ecosystem. It is hoped that the conservation/limit reference point will lead to early warning signs of trouble being taken more seriously.

The Duty to Assess and to Collect and Share Data. Article 5(d) reaffirms the duty to "assess the impacts of fishing, other human activities and environmental factors" of stocks, and Articles 14 and 18(3)(e) explain the data collection requirements necessary to facilitate such assessments. Article 14 requires contracting parties to require fishing vessels flying their flags to collect data "in sufficient detail to facilitate effective stock assessment" (Article 14(1)(b)). Annex I then explains the specific information that must be collected, which includes the amount of fish caught by species, the amount of fish discarded, the types of fishing methods used, and the locations of the fishing vessels (Annex I, art. 3(1)). In order to permit stock assessment, each nation must also provide to the regional fishery organization data on the size, weight, length, age, and distribution of its catch, plus "other relevant research, including surveys of abundance, biomass surveys, hydro-acoustic surveys, research on environmental factors affecting stock abundance, and oceanographic and ecological studies" (Annex I, art. 3(2)). These requirements, if taken seriously, will revolutionize the fishing industry, where the competitive nature of the quest for fish has encouraged each nation to hide its activities from others to the extent possible. The data collected "must be shared with other flag States and relevant coastal States through appropriate subregional or regional fisheries management organizations or arrangements" in a "timely manner," although the "confidentiality of nonaggregated data" should be maintained (Annex I, art. 7). Decisionmaking at regional fishery organizations must now be "transparent" under Article 12, and international and nongovernmental organizations must be allowed to participate in meetings and to observe the basis for decisions.

The Methods of Enforcement. Article 18 further requires contracting parties to establish "national inspection schemes," "national observer programmes," and "vessel monitoring systems, including, as appropriate, satellite transmitter systems" to manage their flag fishing vessels with some rigor. Article 21(1) gives these requirements teeth by authorizing the ships of a nation that is party to a regional fisheries agreement to board and inspect on the high seas any ship flying the flag of any other nation that is a party to the same agreement. If the boarded vessel is found to have committed a "serious violation," it can be brought into the "nearest appropriate port" for further inspection (Article 21(8)). The term "serious violation" is defined in Article 21(11) to include using prohibited fishing gear, having improper markings or identification, fishing without a license or in violation of an established quota, and failing to maintain accurate records or tampering with evidence needed for an investigation.

Dispute-Resolution. Part VIII of the Agreement requires contracting parties to settle their disputes peacefully, and extends the dispute-resolution mechanisms of the Law of the Sea Convention to disputes arising under this new Agreement. These procedures are complicated and untested, but should provide flexible and sophisticated mechanisms to allow nations to resolve their differences in an orderly fashion....

Notes and Questions

1. Commentators have discussed whether the precautionary principle has been officially accepted as a norm of customary international law that is formally binding on all nations. The principle has been so universally included in recent treaties that it appears now to have that status. *See generally* Jon M. Van Dyke, *The Evolution and International Acceptance of the Precautionary Principle*, in David D. Caron and Harry N. Scheiber (eds.), BRINGING NEW LAW TO OCEAN WATERS 357 (2004). One commentator has stated that the Organization of Economic Cooperation and Development (OECD) (of which Japan is a member) adopted the precautionary principle as early as 1979, and that today "modern international environmental law is largely precautionary." HAROLD HOHMANN, PRECAUTIONARY LEGAL DUTIES AND PRINCIPLES OF MODERN INTERNATIONAL ENVIRONMENTAL LAW 141, 203, 341–45 (1979)(citing the Declaration of Anticipatory Environmental Policies, adopted by the OECD environment ministers on May 8, 1979). *See also* Daniel Bodansky, *Remarks: New Developments in International Environmental Law*, 85 PROC., AM. SOC'Y INT'L L. 401, 413 (1991)("Indeed, so frequent is its invocation that some commentators are even beginning to suggest that the precautionary principle is ripening into a norm of customary international law"); David Freestone, *The Precautionary Principle*, in INTERNATIONAL LAW AND GLOBAL CLIMATE CHANGE 21, 36 (Robin Churchill & David Freestone eds. 1991). The specific content of the precautionary principle is, however, still controversial. For an analysis of some of the unresolved issues, see James E. Hickey, Jr. & Vern R. Walker, *Refining the Precautionary Principle in International Environmental Law*, 14 VA. ENVT'L L.J. 423 (1995). *See also* Gregory D. Fullem, Comment, *The Precautionary Principle: Environmental Protection in the Face of Scientific Uncertainty*, 31 WILLAMETTE L. REV. 495 (1995).

2. As explained above, the 1995 Straddling and Migratory Stocks Agreement requires countries to work together through regional organizations to regulate fisheries that overlap their exclusive economic zones or that straddle the high seas and exclusive economic zones. Such organizations have been established through treaties in most regions of the world. Among the most innovative of these agreements is the Convention on the Conservation and Management of Highly Migratory Fish Stocks in the Western and Central Pacific Ocean, signed in Honolulu in September 2000. *See generally* Violanda Botet, *Filling in One of the Last Pieces of the Ocean: Regulating Tuna in the Western and Central Pacific Ocean*, 41 VA. J. INT'L L. 787–813 (2001); Jon M. Van Dyke, *Regionalism, Fisheries, and Environmental Challenges in the Pacific*, 6 SAN DIEGO INT'L L.J. 143 (2004). The area encompassed by this treaty is huge in its geographical scope, covering much of the vast Pacific Ocean and governing territorial seas and exclusive economic zones as well as high seas areas. It creates a Commission with authority to set catch limits and allocate catch quotas to fishing nations both within and outside the exclusive economic zones of coastal and island nations. The Commission can also regulate vessel types, fish size, and gear, and can establish area and time limitations. Decisionmaking is by consensus for some issues and by chambered voting on others, with the interests of the distant-water-fishing nations and the island nations both carefully protected. Decisions of the Commission can be reviewed by an arbitral review panel to ensure consistency and protect against discrimination.

This new treaty requires fishing of migratory species in the high seas to be compatible with the regulations that apply within adjacent exclusive economic zones. It relies on the precautionary approach as its basic foundation throughout. It reinforces the importance of the duty to cooperate. It allows Taiwan to participate in decisionmaking (as "Chinese Taipei"), it allows nonselfgoverning territories to participate, and nongovernmental organizations can also participate in appropriate ways. Compliance will be through flag-state and port-state enforcement, boarding and inspection rights, obligatory transponders on all high-seas fisheries, and regional observers on the vessels.

SECTION 6. SALMON

Salmon (which are anadromous) are born in freshwater streams and, after their first year, swim into the open ocean, usually into the high seas beyond the 200–nautical-mile EEZ, and then find their way back to the stream of their birth at the end of their life cycle, when they are about five or six years old. Article 66(1) of the Law of the Sea Convention says that "States in whose rivers anadromous stocks originate shall have the primary interest in and responsibility for such stocks." Yet, how does a country assert jurisdictions over the salmon stocks that spawn in its fresh waters while they are swimming in the high seas? It is scientifically possible to determine the stream that a given salmon originated in, but it is expensive to run such a test on each salmon caught. Countries tend to make rough approximations and divide the stocks in accordance with such estimates.

What happens when states with claims to an overlapping fish stock negotiate in good faith but are not able to agree on how to divide or share the resource? An important case study is provided by the long-running dispute between the United States and Canada over the salmon of the Northeast Pacific. These two countries have had a long record of friendship and cooperative solutions to regional problems, but it took them a long time to resolve this dispute in a satisfactory manner. They agreed upon a treaty in 1985, which established an "equity principle" in Article III(1) saying that each country should "receive benefits equivalent to the production of salmon originating in its waters." Pacific Salmon Treaty Between the United States of America and Canada, Jan. 28, 1985, T.I.A.S. No. 11091, 1985 WL 167273 (Treaty). *See generally* Marian Nash Leich, *U.S.-Canada Treaty on Pacific Salmon*, 79 Am. J. Int'l L. 423 (1985); Joy A. Yanagida, *The Pacific Salmon Treaty*, 81 Am. J. Int'l L. 577 (1987). But the two nations had difficulty agreeing on how to interpret and apply the treaty, because of Canada's assertions that U.S. fishing vessels based in Alaska had greatly exceeded their quotas. As of 1994, 52% of the region's salmon stocks spawned in the Province of British Columbia (Canada), while 17% spawned in States of Oregon and Washington (United States) and another 31% spawned in the State of Alaska (United States). However, U.S. fishing vessels were harvesting about 5 million more Canadian-spawned salmon than U.S.-spawned salmon were caught by Canadians. This imbalance resulted in part because fewer salmon were being produced in the rivers of Oregon and

Washington, and the U.S. fishing vessels focused their energies in the coastal waters adjacent to southeast Alaska, where many of the rivers originate in Canada. The Canadians believed that because they had made great sacrifices to conserve the salmon spawning grounds in their rivers, in contrast to the Oregonians and Washingtonians who had let their rivers deteriorate, they should be rewarded with a greater share of the salmon catch.

To make its position clear and get the attention of U.S. decisionmakers, the Canadians took a number of dramatic steps. In June 1994, they imposed a fee of $1,100 per vessel on U.S. fishing vessels traveling (each way) through Canadian waters on the inland passage between the State of Washington and the southeast tip of Alaska. About 300 U.S. fishing vessels paid the fee before the United States and Canada reopened negotiations. On July 24, 1995, 300 Canadian fishing boats swarmed around an Alaskan ferry to prevent it from docking for three hours at Prince Rupert on British Columbia's north coast. International mediation was unsuccessful during those years, and the United States rejected calls for binding arbitration. In July 1997, more than 100 Canadian fish boats again blocked a U.S. ferry (and its 385 passengers) at Prince Rupert, British Columbia, this time for three days. The U.S. Senate responded on July 23, 1997 by passing a resolution rebuking the Canadian government for allowing this action to occur and urging President Clinton to respond with "appropriate action," such as sending the U.S. Navy to protect Alaskan ferries' "right of innocent passage" through Canadian waters. The State of Alaska then canceled its scheduled ferry stops at Prince Rupert, dealing an economic blow to this Canadian region. The State of Alaska filed suit against the Canadian fishers and the Canadian government for damages of $2.8 million said to have resulted from the ferry blockade. The following week, President Clinton appointed William Ruckelshaus, former administrator of the Environment Protection Agency, to facilitate a solution, and Canada named retiring University of British Columbia President David Strangway to represent its interests.

Also in July 1997, Governor Glen Clark of British Columbia canceled the lease that allowed the United States to test torpedoes at the Nanoose Bay Torpedo Range near Vancouver to retaliate against U.S. overfishing. Not wanting to further antagonize the United States, the Canadian government filed suit in August 1997 against the Province of British Columbia for breach of contract regarding the lease for the base. In September 1997, British Columbia, along with Canadian salmon fishers, filed suit in the U.S. District Court in Seattle against the United States and the States of Alaska and Washington accusing the United States of violating international law by ignoring the terms of the 1985 treaty and seeking compensation for the lost salmon that are not available to Canadians.

This dispute has also taken its toll on the depleted fish stocks. In 1994, the Canadian government urged Canadian fishers to harvest aggressively along the west coast of Vancouver Island and in the Strait of Juan de Fuca in order to intercept Fraser River sockeye before they entered U.S. waters. Canadian fishers also continued to harvest fragile coho and chinook stocks heading south to spawn in U.S. rivers despite the fact that conservation concerns had led Washington and Oregon to close their own offshore coho and chinook fisheries. Fishing interests in Oregon and Washington disagreed with those in Alaska, and lawsuits were filed in U.S. courts that led to an injunction in August 1995 blocking the chinook harvest in southeastern Alaska.

In July 1997, the Canada sent a strong diplomatic note to the U.S. government stating that Alaskan fishers had caught more than three times the sockeye permitted, accusing the U.S. of violating the 1985 treaty, and calling for an immediate end to fishing for salmon in Alaskan waters to preserve Canadian-bound sockeye stocks. In January 1998, William Ruckelshaus and David Strangeway issued a report stating that the Alaskan harvest of fish bound for Canadian waters might have to be reduced, that Canada might have to rethink its position on its entitlement, that an interim two-year fishing agreement should be established, and that during these two years the underlying principles of the 1985 treaty should be reconsidered to provide a practical framework for a long-term solution.

Finally, in June 1999, the two countries reached a complex agreement that set new limits on salmon catches (based on scientific measurements of fish stocks along thousands of miles of coastline), established a conservation fund to buy back fishing licenses (and thus to pay certain fishers not to fish), and began stock restoration efforts in rivers whose spawning areas had been damaged.

Notes and Questions

1. What can one conclude from this awkward confrontation between two nations that have maintained cooperative relations for so long? They "cooperated" by meeting regularly and exchanging data. The dispute was brought to the attention of the country's leaders, and high-level negotiators were appointed to seek a resolution. Finally, an amicable and enlightened agreement was reached.

2. If no agreement was forthcoming, would the Duty to Cooperate have required that Canada and the United States take the next step, which would be to appoint third-party mediators? And then if the mediation did not produce a resolution, would the two nations have to submit the dispute to binding arbitration or a judicial tribunal? Does the Duty to Cooperate inevitably include the duty to reach an accommodation or resolution, through third-party procedures if necessary? Although some states would resist this conclusion, especially when matters of transcendent national security are at stake, the answer in most cases is clear. The Duty to Cooperate must include the duty to reach an agreement, and if compromise becomes impossible (usually because of domestic political pressures), then the disputants should turn to an outside mediator or arbitrator to produce a solution.

3. Does Article 64 of the Convention require that an organization be created with powers to manage tuna in the Pacific, which includes distant-water fishing nations as well as the Pacific island nations? Is Article 64 a constraint on the sovereign rights given to coastal nations under Article 56 such that coastal nations must cooperate with distant-water fishing nations to conserve the migratory species and promote their optimum utilization? Or do coastal countries have the same sovereign rights over the migratory species in their EEZs that they have over other species?

4. What does the language in Article 62(3) of the Law of the Sea Convention require of coastal states in allocating their "surplus" stocks? Must coastal states have a scientific basis for their determinations on "optimum utilization" and their "capacity to harvest" each species? Can these requirements be viewed as part of customary law? Can decisions of the coastal state be challenged? See Article 297.

5. Can a nonratifying state take advantage of the rights given to distant-water fishing states to share in the "surplus" stocks?

6. What rights do land-locked and geographically-disadvantaged countries have in the EEZs of their neighbors? *See* Articles 69–70 of the Law of the Sea Convention. What is a "geographically-disadvantaged State"?

7. In 1989 and 1991, the U.N. General Assembly passed resolutions effectively prohibiting the use of large-scale drift nets on the high seas, because of a concern that these miles-long nets were indiscriminate in their take and were causing damage to marine mammals, birds, and protected and nontarget species. Was this action consistent with the provisions of the Law of the Sea Convention? *See* articles by William T. Burke, James Carr and Matthew Gianni, Kazuo Sumi, and Catherine Floit, in FREEDOM FOR THE SEAS IN THE 21ST CENTURY: OCEAN GOVERNANCE AND ENVIRONMENTAL HARMONY 231–326 (Jon M. Van Dyke, Durwood Zaelke & Grant Hewison eds. 1993).

8. At the beginning of the twenty-first century, explorations of the deep sea floor and of the seamounts that rise from the ocean floor discovered previously-unknown rich ecosystems of plant and animal life. At the same time, fishing vessels called "trawlers" have been scraping off the surfaces of these seamounts, sometimes destroying entire unique ecosystems before they have been studied. Does the U.N. General Assembly have the authority to pass a resolution prohibiting trawling on seamounts? Is there any other practical way a moratorium could be imposed upon this activity?

9. For discussion of the 1995 Straddling and Highly Migratory Stocks Agreement, *see* Moritaka Hayashi, *The 1995 Agreement on the Conservation and Management of Straddling and Highly Migratory Fish Stocks: Significance for the Law of the Sea Convention*, 29 OCEAN & COASTAL MANAGEMENT 51 (1995); Moritaka Hayashi, *Enforcement by Non–Flag States on the High Seas Under the 1995 Agreement on Straddling and Highly Migratory Fish Stocks*, 9 GEO. INT'L ENVT'L L. REV. 1 (1996); Ted L. McDorman, *The Dispute Settlement Regime of the Straddling and Highly Migratory Fish Stocks Convention*, in THE CANADIAN YEARBOOK OF INTERNATIONAL LAW 57 (1997).

SECTION 7. POLYMETALLIC NODULES

Part XI of the Law of the Sea Convention regulates Sea–Bed Mining on the sea floor in the area beyond the exclusive economic zones of coastal countries. The primary resource though potentially to be of some value are the soft-ball sized polymetallic nodules on the sea floor, particularly in the Pacific and Indian oceans, which contain nickel, manganese, cobalt, copper and trace amounts of other metals.

The Convention declared this resource to be "the common heritage" of humankind and established an International Sea–Bed Authority, based in Jamaica, to regulate it. The structure of this Authority was one of the major reasons the Reagan Administration refused to sign the Convention in 1982 and refused to participate in the Preparatory Commission to establish the details of the international regime to govern exploitation of the polymetallic nodules. The dispute over these resources was based in part on a disagreement regarding whether the concept of the "freedom of the seas," which protects navigational freedoms and fishing activities on the high seas, also includes the ability to harvest mineral resources. Because the nodules are on the floor of the abyssal plains in the deep sea-bed, they have never been exploited historically, and the question was not addressed in earlier agreements. Those arguing that seabed mining should be considered to be a high-seas freedom have relied upon Article 2 of the 1958 Convention on the High Seas, which has the following language:

> The high seas being open to all nations, no State may validly purport to subject any part of them to its sovereignty. Freedom of the high seas is exercised under the conditions laid down by these articles and by the other rules of international law. It comprises, inter alia, both for coastal and non-coastal States:
>
> (1) Freedom of navigation;
>
> (2) Freedom of fishing;
>
> (3) Freedom to lay submarine cables and pipelines;
>
> (4) Freedom to fly over the high seas.
>
> These freedoms and others which are recognized by general principles of international law, shall be exercised by all States with reasonable regard to the interests of other States in the exercise of the freedom of the high seas.

The debate on this issue is analyzed in the following:

JON VAN DYKE AND CHRISTOPHER YUEN, *"COMMON HERITAGE" v. "FREEDOM OF THE HIGH SEAS": WHICH GOVERNS THE SEABED?*

9 San Diego L. Rev. 493 (1982).*

. . . The Commentaries to Article 2 [of the 1958 Convention on the High Seas] are elusive but arguably offer some support for the idea that deep seabed mining is one of the freedoms of the high seas. The first Commentary of the International Law Commission included the following language:

> The list of freedoms of the high seas contained in this article is not restrictive; the Commission has merely specified four of the main freedoms. It is aware that there are other freedoms, such as freedom to explore or exploit the subsoil of the high seas and freedom to engage in scientific research therein.... [1]

The second Commentary, prepared for submission to the United Nations General Assembly with the draft articles of all of the Conventions on the Law of the Sea, contained language that seems to recognize the uncertainty of the subject:

> The Commission has not made specific mention of the freedom to explore or exploit the subsoil of the high seas. It considered that apart from the case of the exploitation or exploration of the soil or subsoil of a continental shelf—a case dealt with separately in section III below—such exploitation had not yet assumed sufficient practical importance to justify special regulation.[2]

The "exploitation or exploration of the soil or subsoil of a continental shelf" did not, of course, become a high seas freedom. Instead, it is within the exclusive jurisdiction of the coastal State.[3]

As applied to the deep seabed beyond national jurisdiction, these oft-cited Commentaries are simply ambiguous. Although it is possible to read the Commentaries as stating that deep seabed mining is a freedom of the high seas, that is certainly not the only possible interpretation. More importantly, no evidence exists that this interpretation was adopted in the Convention or that the Commentaries to Article 2 express customary international law.

The history and text of the Commentaries provide further evidence why they should not be used to make sweeping claims about the legal status of the deep seabed. These Commentaries were the product of a struggle of one of the members of the ILC, Professor Georges Scelle, against the continental shelf doctrine. Scelle, a Frenchman, believed that national jurisdiction over the continental shelf violated the traditional freedom of the high seas. When it became clear that he would be unsuccessful in opposing the continental shelf doctrine, Scelle pressed for an explicit limit to the continental shelf, beyond which the regime of the high seas would apply. Scelle also objected to the ILC's failure to include seabed mining as a freedom of the high seas in its draft Article 2. The ambiguous language of the Commentaries was apparently prepared in part to satisfy Scelle's concerns, and he in fact said that he was

1. [1955] 2 Y.B. INT'L L. COMM'N 21–22, U.N. Doc. A/CN.4/Ser. A.

2. Report of ILC to General Assembly, U.N. Doc. A/3159, *also in* U.N. GAOR Supp. No. 9, at 24 (1956).

3. Convention on the Continental Shelf, art. 2, April 29, 1958, 15 U.S.T. 471, T.I.A.S. No. 5578, 499 U.N.T.S. 311 (1964).

"satisfied" with the Commentaries. They in effect side step the issues that divided the members of the Commission....

B. Is the Analogy Logical?

The meaning of Article 2 [should] therefore be examined from the perspective of the nature of usage and logic. Whether seabed mining should be included as a high seas freedom should turn in the final analysis on whether it is logical to do so, in other words, whether seabed mining is analogous to the four listed freedoms in terms of the impact of mining on other competing uses and on the interests of other states. It has been observed that "[t]he relevance of an analogy depends of course on the degree to which common policy is found to underlie both the analogy and the new problem...." With this observation as a guide, it will be seen that to call seabed mining a freedom of the high seas is an unwarranted extension of that doctrine, a total contradiction of the policies and principles underlying the freedom of the seas.

The arguments in favor of the freedoms of the high seas are usually traced to Grotius. He wrote that the seas must be free for navigation and fishing because natural law forbids the ownership of things that seem "to have been created by nature for common use."[4] Things for common use are those that "can be used without loss to anyone else...."[5] For example, the use of the seas for navigation by one nation does not diminish the potential for the same use by others. Since Grotius, the freedom of the seas has outgrown its natural-law roots; now both navigation and fisheries require some regulation. Nevertheless, the rules that developed governing the use of the sea as a common resource were tied to the special character of those uses. For example, States are free today to navigate and fish on the high seas so long as they do not diminish the resource or prejudice the future ability of other nations to use the seas. The new uses that were recognized as freedoms of the seas, such as cable-laying and scientific research, also did not diminish the use of the sea by others.

In contrast, seabed mining for polymetallic nodules is entirely different from any use previously recognized as a high seas freedom. Polymetallic nodules are an exhaustible resource, nonrenewable on any human time frame. Deposits of polymetallic nodules differ dramatically in their economic value, and the deposits that are economically attractive in the near future are limited. If exploited vigorously, the prime mine sites could be completely exhausted within a few decades. Mining could still continue on poorer sites because, as the technology improves, seabed mining should become more competitive with terrestrial mining. But the first miners will take the better sites. Many of these better mine sites have already been identified and explored by scientific groups and by the private seabed mining consortia. For example, Deepsea Ventures, the predecessor of one of the seabed mining consortia, filed a "claim of

4. H. Grotius, Mare Liberum 28 (Magoffin trans. 1916).

5. *Id.* at 27.

discovery" for a 60,000 square kilometer tract of seabed in November 1974. Deepsea's "claim" lies almost entirely within a 180,000 square kilometer area which apparently "is the most promising for seabed mining of all the areas studied." . . .

C. Summary

The "high seas freedom" argument rests upon a questionable interpretation of two Commentaries prepared by the ILC, Commentaries done with inadequate discussion at a time when no one considered the deep seabed to be of practical significance. Because they were not subsequently endorsed at UNCLOS I, the Commentaries are weak legal authority. The deep seabed was not considered part of the high seas in customary international law. The 1958 United Nations Conference on the Law of the Sea left this question unresolved. The treaties prepared by that Conference do not include the deep seabed in definitions of the high seas in a geographical sense, nor do they list seabed mining as one of the freedoms of the high seas. Despite ample opportunity, few nations committed themselves on the seabed issue.

Equally significant is the logical problem that arises if one includes seabed mining as a high seas freedom. All the other high seas freedoms are compatible uses, uses that do not diminish the potential for the same use by others. Polymetallic nodules are a finite resource from an economic perspective. The exploitation of the prime mine sites in the near future by the technologically advanced nations will deny developing nations access to this resource at a later time. Polymetallic nodules do not, therefore, fit into the concept Grotius developed, of things that seem "to have been created by nature for common use."

SECTION 8. THE 1994 PART XI AGREEMENT

The Clinton Administration worked with the international community to modify the provisions of Part XI of the Law of the Sea Convention to address the concerns that had been identified during the Reagan Administration. The modifications made to the regime governing the nonliving resources of the deep seabed are dramatic and reveal a new approach to international decisionmaking and resource sharing. The detailed provisions of Part XI of the 1982 Law of the Sea Convention have been simplified through the "Agreement Relating to the Implementation of Part XI of the United Nations Convention of the Law of the Sea of December 30, 1982," which was signed by many nations on July 29, 1994. See Documents Supplement. Some of the provisions of Part XI are put on hold for the time being, others are scaled down or altered to meet new perceptions of the economic potential of the seabed minerals and the greater acceptance of free market principles by the world community. The Agreement is effectively an amendment to the Law of the Sea Convention, although it creation was not in compliance with the Convention's provisions on amendments, reservations or modifying agreements.

Perhaps the most significant change for the United States concerned decisionmaking within the International Sea–Bed Authority. Article 161 of the Convention established a sophisticated decisionmaking procedure calling for different levels of enhanced majorities depending was being made. Section 3 of the new Agreement restructures this procedure by establishing a system of "chambered voting" within the Sea–Bed Authority's governing Council, to protect minority interests while at the same time allowing majority rule under an one-nation one-vote system. This approach was originally advocated by the Nixon Administration when it outlined a system of decisionmaking for the body that eventually became the International Sea–Bed Authority.

As modified, the Council, which is the main decisionmaking body of the International Sea–Bed Authority, will consist of 35 members and within that number will have four distinct "chambers" of nations representing different interest groups. One chamber will consist of four of the nations with the world's largest economies, with a specific seat allocated to the United States and one reserved for an Eastern European nation. The second chamber will consist of four of the nations that have made the largest investments in deep seabed mining. The third chamber will include four of the nations that are net exporters of the minerals to be mined from the sea floor, including at least two developing countries that rely heavily on the income from these minerals. And the fourth chamber will consist of all the other developing nations that are elected to the Council.

All questions of substance must be adopted by a two-thirds majority of the entire Council and cannot be opposed by a majority in any of the chambers. In other words, each chamber can veto any decision and block action. Certain key decisions can only be made if there is "consensus" of the entire Council.

Another change affecting decisionmaking is the establishment of a Finance Committee, made up of representatives of 15 countries, that has the power to control the budget of the International Sea–Bed Authority. The United States will have a guaranteed seat on the Finance Committee, as one of the five largest financial contributors to the Authority which are automatically elected to the committee. Because decisions of the Committee on substance must be made by consensus, the United States (along with the other members of the Committee) will effectively have a veto on the budget of the International Sea–Bed Authority. This change has been important in the Clinton Administration's decision to sign and support ratification of the 1982 Convention.

Other changes of importance concern the articles on transfer of technology, the Review Conference, production policies, and the financial terms of contracts. With regard to the mandatory provision on these topics in the 1982 Law of the Sea Convention, the new Agreement says simply that the text of the Convention "shall not apply."

Pioneer investors who have registered their claims are protected under the New Agreement, and they have 36 months from the entry into force of the convention to submit their plan of work of exploration. Mining consortia licensed under U.S. law would also be eligible to attain pioneer investor status on the basis of terms and conditions "similar to and no less favorable than" those granted to companies registered with the Preparatory Commission. Fees owed by pioneer investors may also be waived for a period of time under this new scheme.

It should also be emphasized that the fundamental principle that the resources of the seabed are the common heritage of humankind, first established in 1970, remains unchanged, and that the obligation to share these resources, particularly with the least developed nations, remains firm.

Notes and Questions

1. Read Article 137 of the U.N. LOSC, which vests title to the minerals of the deep seabed in "mankind as a whole" and prohibits any nation from claiming sovereignty over these resources. What will be the law on this question if the United States never ratifies the Convention? Can the Convention's Article 137 become customary law? The treaty negotiating process can develop law in two ways: (a) by creating new norms that become law through consent, and (b) by destroying, rejecting, or discarding old norms that are no longer appropriate. Even if the Convention's new norm does not become law in this instance, can the negotiating process be deemed to have rejected any contrary position, thus leaving the matter ambiguous and creating a situation of uncertainty and instability?

2. Can the Law of the Sea Convention bind the United States even if it never ratifies? If a U.S. company mines the seabed's resources with U.S. government authorization and another state challenges this activity in the International Court of Justice, where would the I.C.J. find the governing law and how should it rule?

3. What are the practical problems that would be raised by a state that sought to mine the resources of the deep seabed outside the regime established by the Convention? Could it make an exclusive claim for a mine site? If so, how large a claim? How would poachers be dealt with?

4. What if a seamount containing cobalt crusts is partially within a state's EEZ and partially outside it in international waters? Can the coastal nation claim the entire seamount, either for its own exclusive benefit or as a management trustee for the international community? If such a claim were made, how could other nations effectively challenge it?

5. Can the concept that the resources of the deep seabed are the "common heritage" of humankind be viewed as customary law? If so, what does this concept mean? Examine Articles 136 and 137. Do they require that developing countries receive genuine benefits from seabed exploitations? What would constitute "genuine benefits"?

6. Should the "common heritage" principle set forth in Articles 136–137 apply to Antarctica, or portions thereof? Should it apply to outer space, e.g., to space and the moon? *See* Chapter 7.

7. During the Reagan Administration, U.S. negotiators suggested that "weighted voting" be used in the Council. Would this have been a viable approach?

8. Could the U.S. have ratified the 1982 Convention with reservations that protect its interests? *See* Articles 309–310. Does the 1994 Agreement function as a valid modification of or reservation to the 1982 Convention? Could the U.S. ratify the 1982 Convention and be assured of obtaining amendments that it prefers? Does the 1994 Agreement function as a valid amendment? If the 1994 Agreement is not accepted by all signatories to the 1982 Convention, how should the clash of duties, rights, and interests of states be resolved?

SECTION 9. DISPUTE RESOLUTION

The dispute-resolution provisions in Part XV of the Law of the Sea Convention are innovative and are carefully crafted to maintain the Convention's delicate balances between competing interests. Article 287 instructs each ratifying nation to pick from among four possible means of settling disputes over the interpretation of the Convention: the International Tribunal for the Law of the Sea (ITLOS) (a 21–judge court located in Hamburg, Germany, established according to Annex VI), the International Court of Justice (in The Hague, Netherlands), an arbitral tribunal established pursuant to Annex VII, or a special arbitral tribunal established pursuant to Annex VIII to deal with specialized scientific issues. If the disputing countries have picked different procedures and cannot agree on a procedure, their dispute will be resolved through an Annex VII arbitration.

According to Article 297, controversies subject to mandatory dispute-resolution procedures include those involving coastal state environmental regulations that limit navigation (Article 297(1)(a) & (b)), allegations that a coastal state is violating internationally-established environmental regulations (Article 297(1)(c)), and allegations that a coastal state has improperly seized a vessel flying the flag of another country (Article 292). Coastal states are not required to submit to these dispute-resolution procedures their decisions regarding marine scientific research on their continental shelf and exclusive economic zone (Article 297(2)) and their decisions regarding management of their EEZ fisheries and the allocation of their surplus catch (Article 297(3)). Ratifying countries have the option of withdrawing from mandatory dispute resolution disagreements over maritime boundaries (Article 298(1)(a)), disputes concerning military activities (Article 298(1)(b)), and disputes that are pending before the U.N. Security Council (Article 298(1)(c)). Disputes relating to deep seabed mining are subject to a special regime, and the Sea–Bed Disputes Chamber of ITLOS will deal with most of these controversies. The following case was the first presented to the International Tribunal for the Law of the Sea (ITLOS):

THE M/V SAIGA CASE (SAINT VINCENT AND THE GRENADINES v. GUINEA)

International Tribunal for the Law of the Sea, July 1, 1999.

[Editors' note: On October 28, 1997, Guinea seized and detained the M/V Saiga a commercial vessel registered in Saint Vincent and the Grenadines, and prosecuted and convicted its master. On December 22, 1997, Saint Vincent and the Grenadines instituted an arbitral proceeding against Guinea in accordance with Annex VII of the Law of the Sea Convention in respect of a dispute relating to the Saiga. On February 20, 1998, the two countries agreed to transfer the arbitration proceedings to the International Tribunal for the Law of the Sea. On March 11, 1998, the Tribunal issued a "provisional measure" under Article 290(1) of the Convention instructing Guinea to refrain from taking any enforcement action against the ship, its master, or crew members. From March 8 to March 20, the Tribunal held 18 public sessions hearing witnesses presented by the two parties, and receiving documentary evidence.]

Factual background

31. The Saiga is an oil tanker. At the time of its arrest on 28 October 1997, it was owned by Tabona Shipping Company Ltd. of Nicosia, Cyprus, and managed by Seascot Shipmanagement Ltd. of Glasgow, Scotland. The ship was chartered to Lemania Shipping Group Ltd. of Geneva, Switzerland. The Saiga was provisionally registered in Saint Vincent and the Grenadines on 12 March 1997. The Master and crew of the ship were all of Ukrainian nationality. There were also three Senegalese nationals who were employed as painters. The Saiga was engaged in selling gas oil as bunker and occasionally water to fishing and other vessels off the coast of West Africa. The owner of the cargo of gas oil on board was Addax BV of Geneva, Switzerland.

32. Under the command of Captain Orlov, the Saiga left Dakar, Senegal, on 24 October 1997 fully laden with approximately 5,400 metric tons of gas oil. On 27 October 1997, between 0400 and 1400 hours and at a point 10°25'03'N and 15°42'06'W, the Saiga supplied gas oil to three fishing vessels, the Giuseppe Primo and the Kriti, both flying the flag of Senegal, and the Eleni S, flying the flag of Greece. This point was approximately 22 nautical miles from Guinea's island of Alcatraz. All three fishing vessels were licensed by Guinea to fish in its exclusive economic zone. The Saiga then sailed in a southerly direction to supply gas oil to other fishing vessels at a pre-arranged place. Upon instructions from the owner of the cargo in Geneva, it later changed course and sailed towards another location beyond the southern border of the exclusive economic zone of Guinea.

33. At 0800 hours on 28 October 1997, the Saiga, according to its log book, was at a point 09°00'01'N and 14°58'58'W. It had been drifting since 0420 hours while awaiting the arrival of fishing vessels to which it was to supply gas oil. This point was south of the southern limit of the

exclusive economic zone of Guinea. At about 0900 hours the Saiga was attacked by a Guinean patrol boat (P35). Officers from that boat and another Guinean patrol boat (P328) subsequently boarded the ship and arrested it. On the same day, the ship and its crew were brought to Conakry, Guinea, where its Master was detained. . . .

35. On 13 November 1997, Saint Vincent and the Grenadines submitted to this Tribunal a Request for the prompt release of the Saiga and its crew under Article 292 of the Convention. On 4 December 1997, the Tribunal delivered Judgment on the Request. The Judgment ordered that Guinea promptly release the Saiga and its crew upon the posting of a reasonable bond or security by Saint Vincent and the Grenadines. The security consisted of the gas oil discharged from the Saiga by the authorities of Guinea plus an amount of US$400,000 to be posted in the form of a letter of credit or bank guarantee or, if agreed by the parties, in any other form.

[The trial court in Conakry, Guinea convicted the Master of the Saiga on December 17, 1997 of fraudulently importing diesel oil into Guinean territory without declaring the merchandise and paying the necessary taxes. The court fined the Master 15,354,024,040 Guinean francs and confiscated the vessel and its cargo as a guarantee for payment of the fine. On February 3, 1998, this judgment was affirmed by the Court of Appeal in Conakry, which confirmed the penalty and also imposed a six month suspended sentence on the Master. Guinea argued that Saint Vincent and the Grenadines did not have "legal standing" to bring claims on behalf of the Saiga because the registration of the vessel had temporarily lapsed. The Tribunal analyzed this issue by applying the criteria in Article 91 of the Law of the Sea Convention.]

63. Article 91 leaves to each State exclusive jurisdiction over the granting of its nationality to ships. In this respect, Article 91 codifies a well-established rule of general international law. Under this article, it is for Saint Vincent and the Grenadines to fix the conditions for the grant of its nationality to ships, for the registration of ships in its territory and for the right to fly its flag. These matters are regulated by a State in its domestic law. Pursuant to Article 91, paragraph 2, Saint Vincent and the Grenadines is under an obligation to issue to ships to which it has granted the right to fly its flag documents to that effect. The issue of such documents is regulated by domestic law. . . .

66. The Tribunal considers that the nationality of a ship is a question of fact to be determined, like other facts in dispute before it, on the basis of evidence adduced by the parties. [After reviewing the facts, the Tribunal stated that the country challenging the registration had the burden of proof. Given the statements by Saint Vincent and the Grenadines that the vessel remained properly registered according to its laws, the Tribunal ruled that Guinea had not succeeded in convincing the Tribunal that the vessel was not properly registered.]

Genuine link

75. The next objection to admissibility raised by Guinea is that there was no genuine link between the Saiga and Saint Vincent and the Grenadines. Guinea contends that "without a genuine link between Saint Vincent and the Grenadines and the M/V 'Saiga', Saint Vincent and the Grenadines' claim concerning a violation of its right of navigation and the status of the ship is not admissible before the Tribunal vis-à-vis Guinea, because Guinea is not bound to recognise the Vincentian nationality of the M/V 'Saiga', which forms a prerequisite for the mentioned claim in international law." ...

79. Article 91, paragraph 1, of the Convention provides: "There must exist a genuine link between the State and the ship." Two questions need to be addressed in this connection. The first is whether the absence of a genuine link between a flag State and a ship entitles another State to refuse to recognize the nationality of the ship. The second question is whether or not a genuine link existed between the Saiga and Saint Vincent and the Grenadines at the time of the incident....

83. The conclusion of the Tribunal is that the purpose of the provisions of the Convention on the need for a genuine link between a ship and its flag State is to secure more effective implementation of the duties of the flag State, and not to establish criteria by reference to which the validity of the registration of ships in a flag State may be challenged by other States....

86. In the light of the above considerations, the Tribunal concludes that there is no legal basis for the claim of Guinea that it can refuse to recognize the right of the Saiga to fly the flag of Saint Vincent and the Grenadines on the ground that there was no genuine link between the ship and Saint Vincent and the Grenadines.

87. With regard to the second question, the Tribunal finds that, in any case, the evidence adduced by Guinea is not sufficient to justify its contention that there was no genuine link between the ship and Saint Vincent and the Grenadines at the material time....

Exhaustion of local remedies

[Guinea argued that Saint Vincent and the Grenadines could not bring an action before an international tribunal until it had exhausted local remedies pursuant to Article 295 of the Law of the Sea Convention.]

100. In the opinion of the Tribunal, whether there was a necessary jurisdictional connection between Guinea and the natural or juridical persons in respect of whom Saint Vincent and the Grenadines made claims must be determined in the light of the findings of the Tribunal on the question whether Guinea's application of its customs laws in a customs radius was permitted under the Convention. If the Tribunal were to decide that Guinea was entitled to apply its customs laws in its customs radius, the activities of the Saiga could be deemed to have been

within Guinea's jurisdiction. If, on the other hand, Guinea's application of its customs laws in its customs radius were found to be contrary to the Convention, it would follow that no jurisdictional connection existed. The question whether Guinea was entitled to apply its customs laws is dealt with in paragraphs 110 to 136. For reasons set out in those paragraphs, the Tribunal concludes that there was no jurisdictional connection between Guinea and the natural and juridical persons in respect of whom Saint Vincent and the Grenadines made claims. Accordingly, on this ground also, the rule that local remedies must be exhausted does not apply in the present case.

101. In the light of its conclusion that the rule that local remedies must be exhausted does not apply in this case, the Tribunal does not consider it necessary to deal with the arguments of the parties on the question whether local remedies were available and, if so, whether they were effective....

Arrest of the Saiga

110. Saint Vincent and the Grenadines asserts that the arrest of the Saiga and the subsequent actions of Guinea were illegal. It contends that the arrest of the Saiga was unlawful because the ship did not violate any laws or regulations of Guinea that were applicable to it. It further maintains that, if the laws cited by Guinea did apply to the activities of the Saiga, those laws, as applied by Guinea, were incompatible with the Convention....

116. The main charge against the Saiga was that it violated Article 1 of Law L/94/007 by importing gas oil into the customs radius (rayon des douanes) of Guinea....

126. The Tribunal needs to determine whether the laws applied or the measures taken by Guinea against the Saiga are compatible with the Convention. In other words, the question is whether, under the Convention, there was justification for Guinea to apply its customs laws in the exclusive economic zone within a customs radius extending to a distance of 250 kilometres from the coast.

127. The Tribunal notes that, under the Convention, a coastal State is entitled to apply customs laws and regulations in its territorial sea (Articles 2 and 21). In the contiguous zone, a coastal State may exercise the control necessary to:

> (a) prevent infringement of its customs, fiscal, immigration or sanitary laws and regulations within its territory or territorial sea;
>
> (b) punish infringement of the above laws and regulations committed within its territory of territorial sea. (Article 33, paragraph 1)

In the exclusive economic zone, the coastal State has jurisdiction to apply customs laws and regulations in respect of artificial islands, installations and structures (Article 60, paragraph 2). In the view of the Tribunal, the Convention does not empower a coastal State to apply its customs laws in respect of any other parts of the exclusive economic zone not mentioned above....

129. The Tribunal finds it necessary to distinguish between the two main concepts referred to in the submissions of Guinea. The first is a broad notion of "public interest" or "self-protection" which Guinea invokes to expand the scope of its jurisdiction in the exclusive economic zone, and the second is "state of necessity" which it relies on to justify measures that would otherwise be wrongful under the Convention.

130. The main public interest which Guinea claims to be protecting by applying its customs laws to the exclusive economic zone is said to be the "considerable fiscal losses a developing country like Guinea is suffering from illegal off-shore bunkering in its exclusive economic zone". Guinea makes references also to fisheries and environmental interests. In effect, Guinea's contention is that the customary international law principle of "public interest" gives it the power to impede "economic activities that are undertaken [in its exclusive economic zone] under the guise of navigation but are different from communication".

131. According to Article 58, paragraph 3, of the Convention, the "other rules of international law" which a coastal State is entitled to apply in the exclusive economic zone are those which are not incompatible with Part V of the Convention. In the view of the Tribunal, recourse to the principle of "public interest", as invoked by Guinea, would entitle a coastal State to prohibit any activities in the exclusive economic zone which it decides to characterize as activities which affect its economic "public interest" or entail "fiscal losses" for it. This would curtail the rights of other States in the exclusive economic zone. The Tribunal is satisfied that this would be incompatible with the provisions of Articles 56 and 58 of the Convention regarding the rights of the coastal State in the exclusive economic zone.

132. It remains for the Tribunal to consider whether the otherwise wrongful application by Guinea of its customs laws to the exclusive economic zone can be justified under general international law by Guinea's appeal to "state of necessity".

133. In the Case Concerning the Gabíkovo-Nagymaros Project (Gabíkovo-Nagymaros Project (Hungary/Slovakia), Judgment, I.C.J. Reports 1997, pp.40 and 41, paragraphs 51 and 52), the International Court of Justice noted with approval two conditions for the defence based on "state of necessity" which in general international law justifies an otherwise wrongful act. These conditions, as set out in Article 33, paragraph 1, of the International Law Commission's Draft Articles on State Responsibility, are:

(a) the act was the only means of safeguarding an essential interest of the State against a grave and imminent peril; and

(b) the act did not seriously impair an essential interest of the State towards which the obligation existed.

134. In endorsing these conditions, the Court stated that they "must be cumulatively satisfied" and that they "reflect customary international law".

135. No evidence has been produced by Guinea to show that its essential interests were in grave and imminent peril. But, however essential Guinea's interest in maximizing its tax revenue from the sale of gas oil to fishing vessels, it cannot be suggested that the only means of safeguarding that interest was to extend its customs laws to parts of the exclusive economic zone.

136. The Tribunal, therefore, finds that, by applying its customs laws to a customs radius which includes parts of the exclusive economic zone, Guinea acted in a manner contrary to the Convention. Accordingly, the arrest and detention of the Saiga, the prosecution and conviction of its Master, the confiscation of the cargo and the seizure of the ship were contrary to the Convention.

Hot pursuit

[Guinea argued that it had the right to seize the Saiga pursuant to the right of hot pursuit recognized in Article 111 of the Law of the Sea Convention.]

149. The Tribunal has already concluded that no laws or regulations of Guinea applicable in accordance with the Convention were violated by the Saiga. It follows that there was no legal basis for the exercise of the right of hot pursuit by Guinea in this case.

150. For these reasons, the Tribunal finds that Guinea stopped and arrested the Saiga on 28 October 1997 in circumstances which did not justify the exercise of the right of hot pursuit in accordance with the Convention....

Use of force

155. In considering the force used by Guinea in the arrest of the Saiga, the Tribunal must take into account the circumstances of the arrest in the context of the applicable rules of international law. Although the Convention does not contain express provisions on the use of force in the arrest of ships, international law, which is applicable by virtue of Article 293 of the Convention, requires that the use of force must be avoided as far as possible and, where force is unavoidable, it must not go beyond what is reasonable and necessary in the circumstances. Considerations of humanity must apply in the law of the sea, as they do in other areas of international law.

156. These principles have been followed over the years in law enforcement operations at sea. The normal practice used to stop a ship at sea is first to give an auditory or visual signal to stop, using internationally recognized signals. Where this does not succeed, a variety of actions may be taken, including the firing of shots across the bows of the ship. It is only after the appropriate actions fail that the pursuing vessel may, as a last resort, use force. Even then, appropriate warning

must be issued to the ship and all efforts should be made to ensure that life is not endangered (S.S. "I'm Alone" case (Canada/United States, 1935), U.N.R.I.A.A., Vol. III, p. 1609; The Red Crusader case (Commission of Enquiry, Denmark—United Kingdom, 1962), I.L.R., Vol.35, p. 485). The basic principle concerning the use of force in the arrest of a ship at sea has been reaffirmed by the Agreement for the Implementation of the Provisions of the United Nations Convention on the Law of the Sea of 10 December 1982 Relating to the Conservation and Management of Straddling Fish Stocks and Highly Migratory Fish Stocks.

Article 22, paragraph 1(f), of the Agreement states:

1. The inspecting State shall ensure that its duly authorized inspectors:

(f) avoid the use of force except when and to the degree necessary to ensure the safety of the inspectors and where the inspectors are obstructed in the execution of their duties. The degree of force used shall not exceed that reasonably required in the circumstances.

157. In the present case, the Tribunal notes that the Saiga was almost fully laden and was low in the water at the time it was approached by the patrol vessel. Its maximum speed was 10 knots. Therefore it could be boarded without much difficulty by the Guinean officers. At one stage in the proceedings Guinea sought to justify the use of gunfire with the claim that the Saiga had attempted to sink the patrol boat. During the hearing, the allegation was modified to the effect that the danger of sinking to the patrol boat was from the wake of the Saiga and not the result of a deliberate attempt by the ship. But whatever the circumstances, there is no excuse for the fact that the officers fired at the ship itself with live ammunition from a fast-moving patrol boat without issuing any of the signals and warnings required by international law and practice.

158. The Guinean officers also used excessive force on board the Saiga. Having boarded the ship without resistance, and although there is no evidence of the use or threat of force from the crew, they fired indiscriminately while on the deck and used gunfire to stop the engine of the ship. In using firearms in this way, the Guinean officers appeared to have attached little or no importance to the safety of the ship and the persons on board. In the process, considerable damage was done to the ship and to vital equipment in the engine and radio rooms. And, more seriously, the indiscriminate use of gunfire caused severe injuries to two of the persons on board.

159. For these reasons, the Tribunal finds that Guinea used excessive force and endangered human life before and after boarding the Saiga, and thereby violated the rights of Saint Vincent and the Grenadines under international law....

Reparation

169. Article 111, paragraph 8, of the Convention provides:

> Where a ship has been stopped or arrested outside the territorial sea in circumstances which do not justify the exercise of the right of hot pursuit, it shall be compensated for any loss or damage that may have been thereby sustained.

Reparation may also be due under international law as provided for in Article 304 of the Convention, which provides:

> The provisions of this Convention regarding responsibility and liability for damage are without prejudice to the application of existing rules and the development of further rules regarding responsibility and liability under international law.

170. It is a well-established rule of international law that a State which suffers damage as a result of an internationally wrongful act by another State is entitled to obtain reparation for the damage suffered from the State which committed the wrongful act and that "reparation must, as far as possible, wipe out all the consequences of the illegal act and reestablish the situation which would, in all probability, have existed if that act had not been committed" (Factory at Chorzów, Merits, Judgment No. 13, 1928, P.C.I.J., Series A, No. 17, p. 47).

171. Reparation may be in the form of "restitution in kind, compensation, satisfaction and assurances and guarantees of non-repetition either singly or in combination" (Article 42, paragraph 1, of the Draft Articles of the International Law Commission on State Responsibility). Reparation may take the form of monetary compensation for economically quantifiable damage as well as for non-material damage, depending on the circumstances of the case. The circumstances include such factors as the conduct of the State which committed the wrongful act and the manner in which the violation occurred. Reparation in the form of satisfaction may be provided by a judicial declaration that there has been a violation of a right.

172. In the view of the Tribunal, Saint Vincent and the Grenadines is entitled to reparation for damage suffered directly by it as well as for damage or other loss suffered by the Saiga, including all persons involved or interested in its operation. Damage or other loss suffered by the Saiga and all persons involved or interested in its operation comprises injury to persons, unlawful arrest, detention or other forms of ill-treatment, damage to or seizure of property and other economic losses, including loss of profit....

175. After a careful scrutiny of invoices and other documents submitted, the Tribunal decides to award compensation in the total amount of US$2,123,357 (United States Dollars Two Million One Hundred and Twenty–Three Thousand Three Hundred and Fifty–Seven) with interest, as indicated below:

(a) Damage to the Saiga, including costs of repairs, in the sum of US$202,764; with interest at the rate of 6%, payable from 31 March 1998;

(b) Loss with respect to charter hire of the Saiga, in the sum of US$650,250; with interest at the rate of 6%, payable from 1 January 1998;

(c) Costs related to the detention of the Saiga in Conakry, in the sum of US$256,892; with interest at the rate of 6%, payable from 1 January 1998;

(d) Value of 4,941.322 metric tons of gas oil discharged in Conakry, in the sum of US$875,256; with interest at the rate of 8%, payable from 28 October 1997;

(e) Detention of Captain Orlov, the Master, in the sum of US$17,-750; with interest at the rate of 3%, payable from 1 October 1999;

(f) Detention of members of the crew and other persons on board the Saiga, in the sum of US$76,000, computed as specified in the Annex; with interest at the rate of 3%, payable from 1 October 1999;

(g) Medical expenses of Second Officer Klyuyev, in the sum of US$3,130; with interest at the rate of 6%, payable from 1 January 1998;

(h) Medical expenses of Mr. Djibril Niasse, in the sum of US$6,315; with interest at the rate of 6%, payable from 1 January 1998;

(i) Injury, pain and suffering of Second Officer Klyuyev, in the sum of US$10,000; with interest at the rate of 3%, payable from 1 October 1999;

(j) Injury, pain, suffering, disability and psychological damage of Mr. Djibril Niasse, in the sum of US$25,000; with interest at the rate of 3%, payable from 1 October 1999.

176. With regard to the claims of Saint Vincent and the Grenadines for compensation for violation of its rights in respect of ships flying its flag, the Tribunal has declared in paragraphs 136 and 159 that Guinea acted wrongfully and violated the rights of Saint Vincent and the Grenadines in arresting the Saiga in the circumstances of this case and in using excessive force. The Tribunal considers that these declarations constitute adequate reparation.

177. Saint Vincent and the Grenadines requests the Tribunal to award compensation for the loss of registration revenue resulting from the illegal arrest of the Saiga by Guinea, and for the expenses resulting from the time lost by its officials in dealing with the arrest and detention of the ship and its crew. The Tribunal notes that no evidence has been produced by Saint Vincent and the Grenadines that the arrest of the Saiga caused a decrease in registration activity under its flag, with resulting loss of revenue. The Tribunal considers that any expenses incurred by Saint Vincent and the Grenadines in respect of its officials must be borne by it as having been incurred in the normal functions of a flag State. For these reasons, the Tribunal does not accede to these requests for compensation made by Saint Vincent and the Grenadines.

[Judges Warioba and Ndiaye dissented from the substantive elements of the Tribunal's decision and filed dissenting opinions. Nine other separate opinions were also filed by judges in the majority.]

Notes and Questions

1. Is there any procedure whereby a nonratifying state can use the dispute-resolution mechanisms in the Law of the Sea Convention? To what extent are these mechanisms improvements on existing methods of resolving disputes?

2. For discussion of the Tribunal's December 1997 decision in this case concerning the "prompt release" requirement under Article 292 of the Law of the Sea Convention, *see, e.g.*, E.D. Brown, *The M/V "Saiga" Case on Prompt Release of Detained Vessels: the First Judgment of the International Tribunal for the Law of the Sea*, 22 MARINE POLICY 307 (1998); Hee Kwon Park, Note, 92 AM. J. INT'L L. 278 (1998).

3. The second case submitted under the Law of the Sea Convention's dispute resolution procedures was brought by Australia and New Zealand against Japan for alleged overfishing of the prized southern bluefin tuna. Southern Bluefin Tuna Cases (New Zealand and Australia v. Japan) (ITLOS, provisional measures, Aug. 27, 1999), 38 I.L.M. 1624 (1999), available at <www.itlos.org>. The Tribunal acted under Article 290 of the Convention, which authorizes it to prescribe "provisional measures" pending final outcome, whenever "appropriate under the circumstances to preserve the respective rights of the parties to the dispute or to prevent serious harm to the marine environment...." After hearing testimony and receiving legal memoranda, the Tribunal ordered Japan to "refrain from conducting an experimental fishing programme involving the taking of a catch of southern bluefin tuna," unless the catch from such a program is deducted from Japan's annual national allocation as agreed upon with Australia and New Zealand. The Tribunal thus tried to freeze the status quo, and ordered Japan to stop its unilateral "experimental fishing" in order to give the bluefin tuna a chance to recover while the countries developed new management arrangements. In its order, the Tribunal stated that:

> ... parties should in the circumstances act with prudence and caution to ensure that effective conservation measures are taken to prevent serious harm to the stock of southern bluefin tuna.... [Although there is] scientific uncertainty regarding measures to be taken to conserve the stock of southern bluefin tuna and ... although the Tribunal cannot conclusively assess the scientific evidence presented by the parties, it finds that measure should be taken as a matter of urgency to preserve the rights of the parties and to avert further deterioration.

Paras. 77, 79, 80. Judge Alexander Yankov, one of the 21 members of the Tribunal, later wrote that "there are some statements of the Tribunal in the Order which appear to reveal its stand in favor of essential elements of the precautionary approach." Alexander Yankov, *Irregularities in Fishing Activities and the Role of the International Tribunal for the Law of the Sea,* in LIBER AMICORUM JUDGE SHIGERU ODA 773, 780 (N. Ando, E. McWhinney and R. Wolfrum eds. 2002).

The merits of the case were then transferred to an arbitral panel established pursuant to Annex VII of the Convention, which reached the surprising conclusion that it lacked jurisdiction over the case because of conflicting dispute resolution provisions in the relevant treaties. 39 I.L.M. 1359 (2000), available at <www.worldbank.org/icsid/bluefintuna/0508icsi.pdf>. During the year that the provisional measures ordered by the Tribunal remained in place, they produced "great benefits in environmental protection." L. Sturtz, *Southern Bluefin Tuna Case: Australia and New Zealand v. Japan,* 28 Ecology L.Q. 455, 459 (2001).

4. The third case to come before the Tribunal was The *Camouco* Case (Panama v. France) (ITLOS, Feb. 7, 2000), involving a fishing vessel registered in Panama and licensed by it to catch Patagonian toothfish by longline in the South Indian Ocean. On September 28, 1999, a French helicopter spotted the vessel in the EEZ that France had claimed around the remote Crozet Islands, which are uninhabited French possessions between Madagascar and Antarctica. The French escorted the fishing vessel to Reunion, a French island near Madagascar. The ship's master was arrested and put under court supervision, and the French court said the boat would be released only upon a payment of 20 million French francs. On January 17, 2000, Panama filed an application before the Tribunal, seeking a prompt release of the vessel under Article 292 of the Convention. On February 7, 2000, the Tribunal ordered the vessel released on the condition that Panama provided a bank guarantee to France of 8 million French francs, basing that figure on the gravity of the alleged offenses and the value of the detained vessel and its cargo.

5. In The MOX Plant Case (United Kingdom v. Ireland) (ITLOS 2001), 41 I.L.M. 405 (2002), the Tribunal stated in its Order of 3 December 2001 that "the duty to cooperate is a fundamental principle in the prevention of pollution of the marine environment under Part XII of the [Law of the Sea] Convention and general international law and that rights arise therefrom which the Tribunal may consider appropriate to preserve under article 290 of the Convention." This Order instructed the United Kingdom to consult and cooperate with Ireland on possible consequences resulting from the proposed expansion of the MOX (mixed plutonium/uranium oxide) plant at Sellafield on the UK's Cumbrian Coast facing the Irish Sea, to exchange information regarding these risks, to monitor risks, and to devise measures to prevent pollution. The Tribunal's Order underscored the obligation to consult under international law. This case has not yet proceeded to any further decisions on its merits because of jurisdictional issues that have been raised. MOX Plant Case (Ireland v. U.K.), (Perm. Ct. Arbitration), Order No. 3 (June 24, 2003), available at website of Permanent Court of Arbitration (suspending the proceeding pending a resolution of issues related to the possibly conflicting jurisdiction of the European Court of Justice, but also calling for more formalized arrangements to ensure cooperation and consultation between the two countries).

6. In the *Volga* case (Russian Federation v. Australia), Application for Prompt Release, Judgment (ITLOS, Dec. 23, 2002), available at <www.itlos.org> , the Tribunal addressed the nature of the bond that can be required by a coastal State before it is obliged to release a vessel accused of fishing illegally in the coastal state's EEZ. The Tribunal said that the bond

could be set by the coastal State, Australia, at the full value of the vessel, fuel, lubricants, and fishing equipment, which came to US$1,082,000. But it rejected Australia's effort to charge another US$563,000 as a "good behavior bond" to ensure that the vessel carried a fully operational vessel monitoring system (VMS) and observed the conservation measures of the 1980 Convention for the Conservation of Antarctic Marine Living Resources (CCAMLR), 1329 UNTS 47. The Tribunal said that it "understands the international concerns about illegal, unregulated and unreported fishing and appreciates the objectives behind the measures taken by States, including the States Parties to CCAMLR, to deal with the problem." But it nonetheless gave a narrow textual ruling, saying that the "bond or other security" allowed in Article 73(2) of the LOS Convention must be reasonable in light of its purpose, which "is to provide the flag State with a mechanism for obtaining the prompt release of a vessel and crew ... by posting a security of a financial nature whose reasonableness can be assessed in financial terms."

7. Article 297(1)(b) of the U.N. LOSC authorizes coastal and island states to bring claims against shipping nations whenever "it is alleged that a State in exercising [its navigational] freedoms, rights, or uses has acted in contravention of this Convention or of laws or regulations adopted by the coastal State in conformity with this Convention and other rules of international law not incompatible with this Convention."

Could a claim be brought under this provision by coastal states concerned about the shipments of radioactive materials against France, Japan, and the United Kingdom contending that these nations have violated: (a) their duties under Articles 204–206 to prepare and disseminate an environmental impact statement (because "planned activities under their jurisdiction or control may cause substantial pollution of or significant and harmful changes to the marine environment"), (b) their duty to consult affected states, including specifically their duty under Article 199 to "jointly develop and promote contingency plans for responding to pollution incidents in the marine environment," (c) their general duty under Articles 192 and 235 to "protect and preserve the marine environment," including the more specific duty under Article 194(5) "to protect and preserve rare or fragile ecosystems as well as the habitat of depleted, threatened or endangered species and other forms of marine life," and (d) their more specific duty under Article 235(3) to create an appropriate liability regime, including the "development of criteria and procedures for payment of adequate compensation, such as compulsory insurance or compensation funds"? *See generally* Jon M. Van Dyke, *The Legal Regime Governing Sea Transport of Ultrahazardous Radioactive Materials,* 33 Ocean Dev. & Int'l L. 77 (2002).

SECTION 10. IMPORTANT UNRESOLVED OCEAN LAW ISSUES

A. *Maritime Boundary Delimitation*

The extended maritime zones recognized in the 1982 Law of the Sea Convention have required all coastal and island nation to delimit new maritime boundaries with all of their neighbors. The overwhelming majority of these new maritime boundaries between opposite and adjacent states have been drawn in a spirit of cooperation and good neighborliness through face-to-face negotiations. Many imaginative solutions have been devised for unique geographical situations. In about a dozen situations, countries have agreed to establish joint development zones in disputed areas where both countries have been reluctant to abandon their claims but nonetheless wish to cooperate with their neighbor and want to develop the marine resources for the benefit of the people of both countries. *See, e.g.,* MARK J. VALENCIA, JON M. VAN DYKE & NOEL A. LUDWIG, SHARING THE RESOURCES OF THE SOUTH CHINA SEA 183–87 (1997); David M. Ong, *The 1979 and 1990 Malaysia–Thailand Joint Development Agreements: A Model for International Legal Co-operation in Common Offshore Petroleum Deposits?* 14 INT'L J. MAR. & COASTAL L. 207 (1999). Some difficult boundaries have been submitted to the International Court of Justice or to an arbitral tribunal for resolution. In these cases the decisions of the court have been accepted by the parties and implemented without further controversy. These decisions have articulated a rich and relatively coherent set of standards that can be applied to the relatively few boundaries that remain to be delimited.

The first modern maritime boundary delimitation case was the North Sea Continental Shelf Case (W. Germany v. Denmark, W. Germany v. Netherlands), 1969 I.C.J. 3, which rejected the notion that a geographically rigid equidistance or median line must be drawn to resolve each boundary dispute. Instead, it accepted Germany's argument that boundary lines should follow the "natural prolongation" of the land areas. Germany was thus allocated a pie-shaped area extending into the middle of the North Sea, instead of being limited to the smaller zone advocated by Denmark and the Netherlands. Although the "natural prolongation" idea has not received much attention in more recent adjudications, the idea that boundaries should be resolved in an "equitable" manner is now codified in Articles 74 and 83 of the Law of the Sea Convention and has been followed in all the recent boundary delimitations.

CASE CONCERNING DELIMITATION OF THE MARITIME BOUNDARY IN THE GULF OF MAINE AREA (CANADA v. UNITED STATES)

1984 I.C.J. 246.

[Editors' note: By special agreement, Canada and the United States submitted their dispute over the maritime boundary in the Gulf of Maine to a specially constituted "chamber" of the International Court of Justice. The judges in this chamber were designated by the parties and consisted of Judges Ago (Italy), Gros (France), Mosler (Federal Republic of Germany), Schwebel (United States), and Judge ad hoc Cohen (Canada). Competing contentions of the two nations are depicted in what the chamber designated as Maps No. 2 and 3.

[The Canadian line in Map 3 is based on an equidistant line dividing the waters equally in half; the basepoints used by the Canadians in this division ignore all of Cape Cod, Massachusetts, which it characterizes as a "geographical anomaly" that should not affect the division of ocean space. The U.S. line is based in part on its view of the "natural prolongation" of the continental shelf, and hence follows the Northeast Channel which separates Georges Bank from Brown Bank. The United States also argued that it should receive the larger share of the disputed ocean space because (a) the coastline on the U.S. side of the Gulf is longer than on the Canadian side, (b) the population of the U.S. coastal areas facing the Gulf is considerably higher than that of the Canadian coastal areas and hence that citizens of the United States have relied on and continue to need the resources of this region more than the Canadian citizens, (c) that Americans have historically fished the Georges Bank area in much greater numbers than have Canadians, and (d) that it is preferable to keep unified ecosystems within one nation's control (and hence that all of Georges Bank should be awarded to the United States).

[Both states asked the Chamber to draw a single maritime line that would apply both to the continental shelf and to the water above and its living resources. The major known resource in dispute was the fish and shellfish in the Georges Bank region. The Chamber adopted its own line, as illustrated in the final map herein. The segment from points A to B is essentially an equidistance line between the upper part of the Gulf. The segment between B and D allocates greater ocean space to the United States according to a ratio of 1.32 to 1. This figure was determined by the court to correspond to the relative lengths of coastline of the two countries in the Gulf. Canada's coastline included the coast of the Bay of Fundy, excluding only those areas in the mouth where the Bay narrows to 12 miles.

[The Chamber concluded that the governing international law standard was one of "equity," and that the language of Article 6 of the 1958 Convention on the Continental Shelf and Articles 74 and 83 of the 1982 Law of the Sea Convention, along with judicial decisions and state practices all pointed in that general direction. The Chamber stated that the parts of the 1982 Convention on the exclusive economic zone "may ... be regarded as consonant at present with general international law on the question" (para. 94). The Chamber also recognized that notions of equity are elusive and mentioned some of the criteria that have been used to reach equitable results:]

157. There has been no systematic definition of the equitable criteria that may be taken into consideration for an international maritime delimitation, and this would in any vent be difficult a priori, because of their highly variable adaptability to different concrete situations. Codification efforts have left this field untouched. Such criteria have however been mentioned in the arguments advanced by the parties in cases concerning the determination of continental shelf boundaries, and in the judicial or arbitral decisions in those cases. There is, for example, the criterion expressed by the classic formula that the land dominates the sea; the criterion advocating, in cases where no special circumstances require correction thereof, the equal division of the areas of overlap of the maritime and submarine zones appertaining to the

respective coasts of neighbouring States; the criterion that, whenever possible, the seaward extension of a State's coast should not encroach upon areas that are too close to the coast of another State; the criterion of preventing, as far as possible, any cut-off of the seaward projection of the coast or of part of the coast of either of the States concerned; and the criterion whereby, in certain circumstances, the appropriate consequences may be drawn from any inequalities in the extent of the coasts of two States into the same area of delimitation.

[None of these criteria are automatic or always applicable, and the Chamber concluded that equality of ocean space should be the starting point for decision and that it should be modified in this case only to correspond to the difference in the lengths of the coasts between the two nations. The Chamber rejected any modification based on historical use or greater dependence because it found that the residents of both nations had historically used the area and continued to rely on it. It rejected the U.S. claim based on keeping the ecological units intact, because it found that different ecological considerations applied to the continental shelf from those that applied to the living resources and that the requirement that it draw a single maritime line prevented it from looking at such considerations. In its closing section, the Chamber analyzed its solution in light of the impact on the division of resources and concluded that because each nation received part of the Georges Bank, the division would not impose serious economic consequences on either nation.

[Judge Schwebel wrote a separate opinion, agreeing with the approach taken by the majority, but disagreeing that the shores of the Bay of Fundy should have been included in the determination of the proportionality ratio based on the respective coastlines. Judge Schwebel's approach would lead to a different solution as depicted in his map.

[Judge Gros dissented, arguing that "equity" does not have any known meaning, and that the court should simply have drawn the equidistant line between the two coastal areas. His approach was depicted in a map attached to his opinion.]

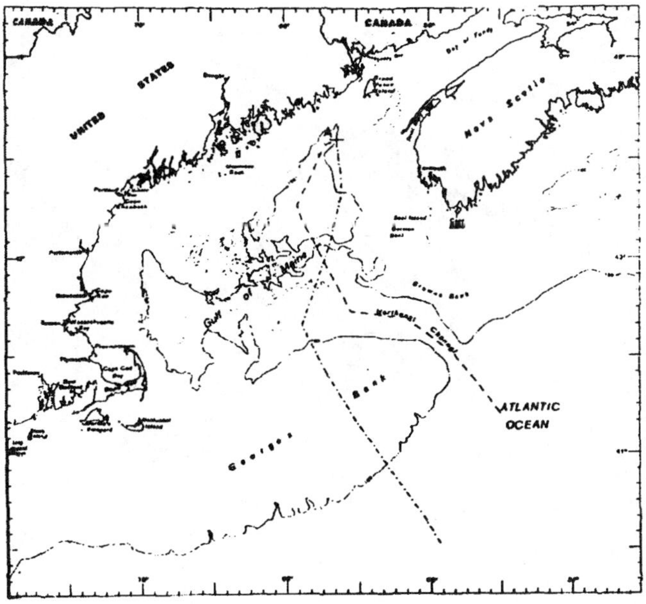

Map 2. Limits of Fishery Zones and Continental Shelf Claimed by Parties 1 March 1977—broken bars line by U.S.; alternating dots and lines line by Canada.

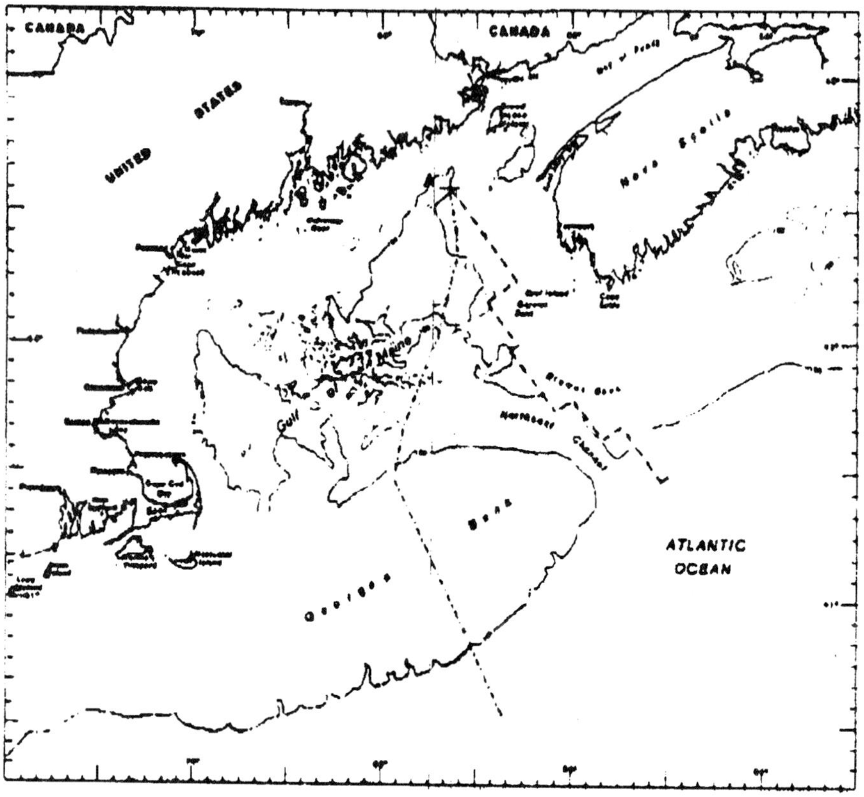

Map 3. Delimitation lines proposed by parties before the Chamber.

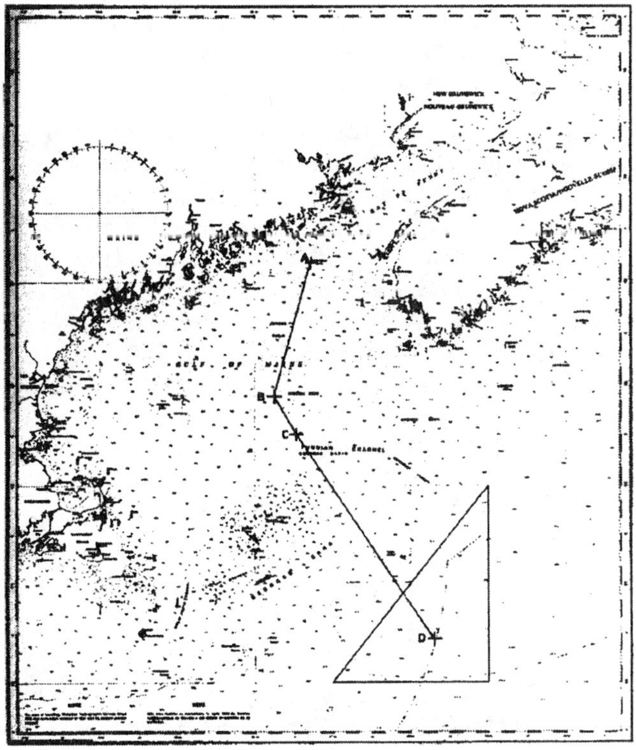

Map 4. Delimitation line drawn by Chamber.

B. *Equitable Principles Governing Maritime Boundaries*

Although many ocean boundaries have been delimited amicably, two locations have defied resolution because of the deep political divisions in these regions and the challenge presented by the geography. In the South China Sea and in the Aegean Sea, the countries bordering on these seas have deep differences of viewpoints that do not appear to be susceptible to logical resolution. In the South China Sea, the problem is aggravated by the two dozen or so tiny Spratly islets that have never been inhabited, but now have garrisons of soldiers clinging to their limited land area in order to support their nation's claims. China, Taiwan, Vietnam, Malaysia, Brunei, and the Philippines all have claims to all or some of these islets and to the maritime space in the South China Sea. *See* MARK J. VALENCIA, JON M. VAN DYKE & NOEL A. LUDWIG, SHARING THE RESOURCES OF THE SOUTH CHINA SEA 17–76 (1997).

In the Aegean, islands also create part of the problem, but in this case the islands have long been inhabited by Greeks. The problem is that they are nestled close to the Turkish mainland and that if they were permitted to generate full maritime zones, Turkey would be left with almost no maritime space of its own in the Aegean. In fact, Turkey has insisted that Greece claim a territorial sea of no more than six miles around its islands so that Turkey will not have to fly over or sail through Greek territorial seas in order to get into the Mediterranean.

In both these situations, the most logical solution might be to establish a joint-development or shared zone of some sort to recognize the rights of all claimants, diffuse the tension, and allow whatever resources may exist to be developed. In the South China Sea, the claimants are reluctant or even unable to abandon their claims because of domestic pressures, and potentially important hydrocarbon reserves remain untapped. In the Aegean, the resources appear to be more limited, but the security and navigational interests of both nations are strong and deserve to be recognized and protected. In both situations, a pragmatic approach would recognize the importance of the claims of the other claimant(s), and devise a shared regime that will serve the interests of each party.

The "equitable principles" that have emerged from the decisions of the International Court of Justice are explained in the following excerpt, which applies them to the dispute between Greece and Turkey in the Aegean Sea.

JON M. VAN DYKE, *THE AEGEAN SEA DISPUTE: OPTIONS AND AVENUES*

20 MARINE POLICY 397, 398–401 (1996).*

A Single Maritime Line Should Be Drawn to Divide the Continental Shelves and the Exclusive Economic Zones. All recent maritime boundary disputes have been resolved with the drawing of a single line.[1] In the Jan Mayen dispute, the parties did not request a single zone, and the Court addressed the continental shelf and exclusive economic zone issues separately, but nonetheless found the analysis to be identical and came up with a single line for both issues.[2]

The Equidistance Approach Can Be Used as an Aid to Analysis, But It Is Not to Be Used as a Binding or Mandatory Principle. In the Libya/Malta case,[3] the Gulf of Maine case, and most recently the Jan Mayen case, the I.C.J. examined the equidistance line as an aid to its preliminary analysis, but then adjusted the line in light of the differences

* Reprinted from MARINE POLICY, vol. 20, Jon M. Van Dyke, *The Aegean Sea Dispute: Options and Avenues*, pp. 398–401, Copyright 1996, with permission from Elsevier Science. *See also* Jon M. Van Dyke, *An Analysis of the Aegean Disputes Under International Law*, 36 OCEAN DEVELOPMENT AND INTERNATIONAL LAW 63–117 (2005).

1. *See* Jonathan I. Charney, *Progress in International Maritime Boundary Delimitation Law*, 88 AM. J. INT'L L. 227, 245–47 (1994).

2. Case Concerning Maritime Delimitation in the Area Between Greenland and Jan Mayen (Den. v. Nor.), 1993 I.C.J. 38, 61–62 paras. 52–53, 69–70 para. 71, 79 para. 90 [hereafter cited as the *Jan Mayen* case].

3. Continental Shelf (Libya/Malta), 1985 I.C.J. 13 [hereafter cited as *Libya/Malta* case].

in the length of the coastlines of the contending parties. The Court has made it clear in all these cases that the equidistance line is not mandatory or binding.

The Proportionality of Coasts Must Be Examined to Determine if a Maritime Boundary Delimitation Is "Equitable." It has now become well established that an essential element of a boundary delimitation is the calculation of the relative lengths of the relevant coastlines. If this ratio is not roughly comparable to the ratio of the provisionally delimited relevant water areas, then the tribunal will generally make an adjustment to bring the ratios into line with each other.[4] In the recent Jan Mayen case, the I.C.J. determined that the ratio of the relevant coasts of Jan Mayen (Norway) to Greenland (Denmark) was 1:9, and ruled that this dramatic difference required a departure from reliance on the equidistance line. The final result was perhaps a compromise between an equidistance approach and a proportionality-of-the-coasts approach, with Denmark (Greenland) receiving three times as much maritime space as Norway (Jan Mayen).

Geographical considerations will govern maritime boundary delimitations and nongeographic considerations will only rarely have any relevance. The Gulf of Maine case was perhaps the most dramatic example of the Court rejecting submissions made by the parties regarding nongeographic considerations, such as the economic dependence of coastal communities on a fishery, fisheries management issues, and ecological data.

The concept of the continental shelf as a "natural prolongation" of the adjacent continent is a geographical notion, but it has not received prominence in recent decisions.[5] But it is used in Article 76 of the 1982 Law of the Sea Convention, and thus may continue to be of some relevance in the Aegean dispute. To some extent, the Principle of Non–Encroachment, discussed below, has taken the place of the natural-prolongation idea.

The Principle of Non–Encroachment. This principle is stated explicitly in Article 7(6) of the 1982 U.N. Law of the Sea Convention, which says that no state can use a system of straight baselines "in such a manner as to cut off the territorial sea of another State from the high seas or an exclusive economic zone." It has recently been relied upon more expansively in the Jan Mayen case, where the Court emphasized the importance of avoiding cutting-off the extension of a coastal state's entry into the sea. Even though Norway's tiny Jan Mayen island was minuscule in

4. This approach has been used particularly in the *Gulf of Maine* case, excerpted above, and the *Libya/Malta* case, *supra*, and has been used more recently in the *Jan Mayen* case, *supra* note 89, and the Delimitation of the Maritime Areas Between Canada and France (St. Pierre and Miquelon), 31 I.L.M. 1149 (1992) [hereafter cited as the *St. Pierre and Miquelon* case]. *See generally* Charney, *supra*, at 241–43.

5. The natural prolongation claim was recognized in the 1969 North Sea Continental Shelf Case (Fed. Rep. of Germany v. Denmark; F.R.G. v. Netherlands), 1969 I.C.J. 3, but it appears to have been rejected in the Case Concerning the Continental Shelf (Tunisia v. Libya), 1982 I.C.J. 18 [hereafter cited as *Libya/Tunisia* case], and the *Libya/Malta*, *supra*, and the *Gulf of Maine* cases.

comparison with Denmark's Greenland, Norway was allocated a maritime zone sufficient to give it equitable access to the important capelin fishery that lies between the two land features.

The unusual 16–nautical-mile-wide and 200–nautical-mile-long corridor drawn in the St. Pierre and Miquelon case also appears to have been based on a desire to avoid cutting off these islands' coastal fronts into the sea. But, at the same time, the arbitral tribunal accepted Canada's argument that the French islands should not be permitted to cut off the access of Canada's Newfoundland coast to the open ocean.

The Principle of Maximum Reach. This principle first emerged in the North Sea Continental Shelf Case, where Germany received a pie-shaped wedge to the equidistant point even though this wedge cut into the claimed zones of Denmark and the Netherlands. Professor Charney reports that this approach has been followed in all the later cases: "No subsequent award or judgment has had the effect of fully cutting off a disputant's access to the seaward limit of any zone."[6] The recent cases have reconfirmed this trend. In the Gulf of Fonseca case, the Court recognized the existence of an undivided condominium regime in order to give all parties access to the maritime zone and its resources,[7] and in the St. Pierre and Miquelon case France was given a narrow corridor connecting its territorial sea with the outlying high seas.

The geographical configuration in the Jan Mayen case presented different issues, but even there the Court gave Norway more than it "deserved" given the small coastline and tiny size of Jan Mayen island, apparently to enable it to have at least "limited geographical access to the middle of the disputed area,"[8] which contained a valuable fishery.

Professor Charney identifies several interests that are served by the Maximum Reach Principle—"status" (by recognizing that even geographically disadvantaged countries have rights to maritime resources), the right "to participate in international arrangements as an equal," navigational freedoms, and "security interests in transportation and mobility."[9]

Similarly, in the Libya/Malta Continental Shelf Case, the I.C.J. started with the median lines between the countries, but then adjusted the line northward through 18' of latitude to take account of the "very marked difference in coastal lengths"[10] between the two countries. The Court then confirmed the appropriateness of this solution by examining the "proportionality" of the length of the coastlines of the two countries and the "equitableness of the result."[11]

6. Charney, *supra*, at 247.

7. Land, Island and Maritime Frontier Dispute (El Salvador/Honduras; Nicaragua intervening), 1992 I.C.J. 351, 606–09 paras. 415–20.

8. Charney, *supra*, at 248.

9. *Id.* at 249.

10. *Libya/Malta* case, *supra*, 1985 I.C.J. at 49, para. 66.

11. *Id.* para. 75.

In the Delimitation of the Maritime Boundary between Guinea and Guinea–Bissau, 25 I.L.M. 252 (1986), the arbitral tribunal also evaluated the "proportionality" of the coasts to determine whether an "equi-

Each Competing Country Is Allocated Some Maritime Area. This principle is similar to the Non–Encroachment and Maximum–Reach Principles, but must be restated in this form to emphasize how the I.C.J. has operated in recent years. Although the Court has attempted to articulate consistent governing principles, its approach to each dispute submitted to it has, in fact, been more akin to the approach of an arbitrator than that of a judge. Instead of applying principles uniformly without regard to the result they produce, the Court has tried to find a solution that gives each competing country some of what it has sought, and that each country can live with. In that sense, the Court has operated like a court of equity, or as a court that has been asked to give a decision ex aequo et bono. Perhaps such an approach is inevitable, and even desirable, given that the goal of a maritime boundary delimitation is to reach an "equitable solution."

Islands Have a Limited Role in Resolving Maritime Boundary Disputes. Islands can generate maritime zones,[12] but they do not generate full zones when they are competing directly against continental land areas. This conclusion has been reached consistently by the Court and arbitral tribunals in the North Sea Continental Shelf[13] case, the Anglo–French[14] arbitration, the Libya/Tunisia Continental Shelf case, the Libya/Malta Continental Shelf case, the Gulf of Maine case, the Guinea/Guinea–Bissau case, the Jan Mayen case, and the St. Pierre and Miquelon arbitration.

The Vital Security Interests of Each Nation Must Be Protected. This principle was also recognized in the Jan Mayen case, where the Court refused to allow the maritime boundary to be too close to Jan Mayen island, and it can be found in the background of all the recent decisions. The refusal of tribunals to adopt an "all-or-nothing" solution in any of these cases illustrates their sensitivity to the need to protect the vital security interests of each nation.

Turkey's security interests include the right of unimpeded navigation and the right of overflight. Turkey is also concerned about limiting the militarization of the Greek islands adjacent to its shores.

With regard to navigation, the right of innocent passage of course exists through the territorial seas of other nations, but for Turkey this right does not provide sufficient protection for its ships. Turkey needs a right of unimpeded passage to gain access to the Mediterranean and the

table solution" had been achieved by the boundary line chosen. *Id.* para. 120.

12. Law of the Sea Convention, art. 121; the I.C.J. ruled in the *Jan Mayen* case that tiny Jan Mayen could generate an exclusive economic zone and continental shelf even though this barren islet has never sustained a permanent population. *Jan Mayen* case, *supra*, 1993 I.C.J. at 69, 73–74, paras. 70, 80.

13. *North Sea Continental Shelf* case, *supra*, at para. 101(d) ("the presence of islets, rocks, and minor coastal projections, the disproportional distorting effects of which can be eliminated by other means" should be ignored in continental shelf delimitations).

14. Case Concerning the Delimitation of the Continental Shelf Between the United Kingdom of Great Britain and Northern Ireland, and the French Republic, 18 U.N. Rpts. Int'l Arb. Awards 74 (1977), *reprinted in* 18 I.L.M. 397 (1979) [hereafter cited as *Anglo-French* arbitration].

open ocean. In addition, airplanes do not share the right of innocent passage, and Turkey needs rights of passage for its aircraft.

Turkey now engages in naval and aerial military maneuvers in the Aegean in order to maintain defense preparedness. Turkey's concern is that if Greece expands its territorial sea to 12 nautical miles or establishes continental shelf and exclusive economic zone rights to the bulk of the Aegean, Turkey will lose its right to move its ships and aircraft freely.

Turkey also has valid environmental concerns, because if the waters of the Aegean are not managed properly, the coasts of Turkey and its coastal fisheries will be impacted negatively. Ultimately, Turkey's interests might be best served if a joint management or condominium arrangement were established, whereby Turkey would be able to continue its shared navigational uses of the region and would also be able to participate in management decisions affecting the environment and the resources.

In fact, it could be argued that Greece and Turkey have established a de facto joint use zone, particularly in the northern sector of the Aegean, where military exercises, navigation, and fishing, have been carried out by each country without interference by the other. The unusual decision of the I.C.J. Chamber in the El Salvador–Honduras Maritime Frontier Dispute concluding that El Salvador, Honduras, and Nicaragua hold undivided interests in the maritime zones seaward of the closing line across the Gulf of Fonseca[15] may provide a useful precedent in the Aegean case. It has also become increasingly common for countries to establish joint development areas in disputed maritime regions, and such a joint zone may provide the logical solution in the northern part of the Aegean.

Notes and Questions

1. Does the Chamber's reasoning in the Gulf of Maine case provide guidance for other nations seeking to resolve their boundary disputes? Should the equidistance principle govern? What about the "proportionality" of the coasts? How should a court evaluate the "natural prolongation" of the land masses and which "special circumstances" in the geographical configuration should it consider? When agreements are made, in "practice ... the equidistance line has played a major role in boundary delimitation agreements." Jonathan I. Charney and Lewis M. Alexander, International Maritime Boundaries xlii-xlv (1993).

2. How should **islands** be treated when drawing boundaries? Article 121 of the Law of the Sea Convention defines an island as "a naturally formed area of land, surrounded by water, which is above water at high tide." This article also says that islands are entitled to all maritime zones unless they are "rocks which cannot sustain human habitation or economic life of their own," in which case they can have a territorial sea but no EEZ

15. *See* Charney, *supra*, at 230 and 235 (discussing Land, Island and Maritime Frontier Dispute (El Salvador/Honduras: Nicaragua intervening), 1992 I.C.J. 351, 606–09, paras. 415–20).

or continental shelf. The terms in this provision are not defined elsewhere in the Convention, and commentators have debated whether a geological feature must literally be a "**rock**" to be denied an EEZ or continental shelf or whether all features that "cannot sustain human habitation or economic life of their own" are in this category. *See, e.g.,* Jon M. Van Dyke and Robert Brooks, *Uninhabited Islands: Their Impact on the Ownership of the Oceans' Resources,* 12 OCEAN DEV. & INT'L L. 265 (1983); Jon M. Van Dyke, Joseph R. Morgan, and Jonathan Gurish, *The Exclusive Economic Zone of the Northwestern Hawaiian Islands: When Do Uninhabited Islands Generate an EEZ,* 25 SAN DIEGO L. REV. 425 (1988); Barbara Kwiatkowska and Alfred H.A. Soons, *Entitlement to Maritime Areas of Rocks Which Cannot Sustain Human Habitation or Economic Life of Their Own*, 21 NETHERLANDS YEARBOOK OF INTERNATIONAL LAW 153 (1990). Judge Budislav Vukas of the International Tribunal for the Law of the Sea has recently explained that the latter interpretation should be viewed as the correct one, because of the underlying purposes of establishing the exclusive economic zone regime.*"Volga" (Russian Federation v. Australia), Prompt Release, Judgment,* Declaration of Judge Vukas, ITLOS Reports 2002, <http://www.itlos.org/start2_en.html>. According to Judge Vukas, the reason for giving exclusive rights to coastal states was to protect the economic interests of their coastal communities that depended on the resources of the sea, and thus to promote their economic development and enable them to feed themselves. This rationale does not apply to uninhabited islands, because they have no coastal fishing communities that require such assistance. The EEZ regime may also be "useful for the more effective preservation of the marine resources," Judge Vukas acknowledged, but he explained that it is not necessary to give exclusive rights to achieve this goal, because multilateral solutions such as 1980 Convention on the Conservation of Antarctic Marine Living Resources can serve to protect fragile resources.

An important example of "state practice" relevant to the meaning of Article 121(3) occurred in 1997 when the United Kingdom renounced any claim to an EEZ or continental shelf around its barren granite feature named Rockall which juts out of the ocean northwest of Scotland. Fishery Limits Order (United Kingdom), S.I. 1997, No. 1750; *see generally* D.H. Anderson, *British Accession to the UN Convention on the Law of the Sea*, 46 International and Comparative Law Quarterly 761, 778 (1997)(*citing* House of Commons Hansard, vol. 298, written answers, col. 397). Rockall is a towering granite feature measuring about 200 feet (61 meters) in circumference, which is about seventy feet (21 meters) high.

An earlier example of state practice on this issue occurred in 1970, when the Republic of China (Taiwan) issued a reservation when ratifying the 1958 Convention on the Continental Shelf, apparently with reference to the Daioyu–Dao (Senkakus), stating that in "determining the boundary of the continental shelf of the Republic of China, exposed rocks and islets shall not be taken into account." *See* CLIVE SYMMONS, THE MARITIME ZONES OF ISLANDS IN INTERNATIONAL LAW 136 and 270 n. 539 (1979)(*citing* Allen & Mitchell, *The Legal Status of the Continental Shelf of the East China Sea*, 51 OREGON LAW REVIEW 789, 808 (1972)). One prominent scholar from the People's Republic of China has reported that the position of the PRC is similar: "China holds that the Diaoyudao Islands are small, uninhabited, and cannot sustain economic life of their own, and that they are not entitled to have a continental shelf.'' Ji Guoxing, *The Diaoyudao (Senkaku) Disputes and Prospects for Settlement*, 6 Korean Journal of Defense Analysis 285, 306 (1994). *See also* Ji Guoxing, *Maritime Jurisdiction in the Three China Seas: Options for Equitable Settlement* (before footnote 22) (Institute on Global Conflict and Cooperation, University of California at San Diego, Policy Paper No. 19, October 1995)(''China holds that the Senkaku Islands are small, uninhabited, and cannot sustain economic life of their own, and that they are not entitled to have continental shelf.'').

3. Do artificial islands have the capacity to generate any maritime zones? *See* Article 60(8). What if a ''rock'' within the meaning of Article 121(3) is artificially developed into a substantial land area that can sustain human habitation? Is it then entitled to generate an EEZ?

4. Many maritime boundaries remain unresolved. For discussions of some of them, *see* Jon M. Van Dyke, *Regionalism, Fisheries, and Environmental Challenges in the Pacific*, in 6 San Diego International Law Journal 143–78 (2004); Jon M. Van Dyke, *The Republic of Korea's Maritime Boundaries*, 18 Int'l J. Marine & Coastal L. 509–40 (2003); Jon M. Van Dyke, Mark J. Valencia, and Jenny Miller Garmendia, *The North/South Korea Boundary Dispute in the Yellow (West) Sea*, 27 Marine Policy 143–58 (2003); Jon M. Van Dyke, *Northeast Asian Seas–Conflicts, Accomplishments, and the Role of the United States*, 17 International Journal of Marine and Coastal Law 397 (2002).

C. *Exercising Jurisdiction on the High Seas*

Notes and Questions

1. What actions can the United States lawfully use to enforce its drug laws against ships smuggling illegal cargo on the high seas? Recall that Article 92(1) of the Convention states that a ship is under the ''exclusive jurisdiction'' of the country whose flag it flies. Article 6 of the 1958 Convention on the High Seas, which the United States has ratified, contains this same language. Read Article 108 of the Convention. Does paragraph 1 impliedly provide treaty-based consent to board suspect vessels? Article 110 of the Convention (repeating much of the language of Article 22 of the 1958 Convention on the High Seas) recognizes the ''right of visit'' on the high seas in situations involving reasonable suspicion of piracy, slave trade, illegal broadcasting, sailing without a ''nationality,'' or ''though flying a foreign flag or refusing to show its flag'' a vessel is in reality of the same nationality as the visiting vessel. The ''right of visit'' or ''approach'' is a doctrine of customary international law ''that bestows a nation's warship with the authority to hail and board an unidentified vessel to ascertain its nationality.'' United States v. Romero–Galue, 757 F.2d 1147 (11th Cir.1985), adding that even if the captain declares his vessel's state of registry, the warship ''may board the vessel and search for registration papers or other identification in order to verify the vessel's nationality.'' Does Article 110(1)(d) or (e) authorize boarding for purposes of interdicting drug smuggling?

The following description of U.S. recent practice is offered by David Colson, Assistant Legal Adviser for Oceans and International Environmental and Scientific Affairs, U.S. State Department:

Arrest Procedure

The way we deal with these issues is that when a U.S. Coast Guard vessel comes across a non-U.S. flag vessel that is suspected of intending to smuggle narcotics into the United States, the Coast Guard vessel radios the Coast Guard commandant's office in Washington, and a conference call is put together between the State Department, the Department of Justice, and the Coast Guard to determine how to proceed. The Coast Guard vessel asks the suspected smuggler for the vessel's identification and where it is home-ported, under the right of approach set forth in the 1958 High Seas Convention. The vessel normally responds with that information. For example, let us say the vessel says, "I am British and I am registered in the Grand Caymans." Absent an agreement, we would then immediately notify our embassy in the claimed flag country and request that the embassy contact the local shipping authorities to determine whether that claim was valid. If the claim was valid, we would then institute a discussion with the flag state government to ask it to do one of two things: One is to allow the United States to board the vessel as its agent and to take action under the law of that particular country; the alternative is to board the vessel under the authority of the flag state but, if violations of U.S. law are found, to act in accordance with U.S. law at that point.

Depending on the country concerned, we receive different responses. Some countries wish us to board simply as their agent and to hold the vessel and to turn the vessel and the crew over to that government. Others are more inclined simply to wash their hands of the issue and to authorize the boarding but also to allow the United States, once on board, to take whatever action it wishes under U.S. law. Of course, under the law of the sea, if the vessel is legitimately registered in the state, and the state does not wish to cooperate with us, we have to break off the matter.

We sometimes find that the vessel has claimed a registry that is clearly invalid and has not given us the true story. Therefore, under the law of the sea, that vessel is not entitled to the protection of any flag under international law, and the United States can proceed against the vessel as a stateless vessel.

We have had a number of interesting cases over the years. We are now able to deal with these kinds of situations rather routinely with about a dozen different governments. Occasionally we run into a situation with a maritime state with which we have not had this problem before. We have gone so far as to take the flag state consular officer out to the suspected vessel by helicopter so that he can board the vessel in the name of the flag state in order to ensure that the flag state jurisdiction over vessels on the high seas has not been questioned. It has cost the U.S. government money and effort to deal with the issue in this way, but it is an example of how one can deal with a new problem in the law of the sea within the bounds of traditional legal concepts, without requiring or claiming that the only way that a new problem can be dealt with is by defining a new zone of jurisdiction.

CONSENSUS AND CONFRONTATION: THE UNITED STATES AND THE LAW OF THE SEA CONVENTION 307–09 (Jon M. Van Dyke ed. 1985).

2. What is the effect of Article 108(1) of the Law of the Sea Convention, a new provision, which states: "All States shall co-operate in the suppression of illicit traffic in narcotic drugs and psychotropic substances engaged in by ships on the high seas contrary to international conventions"? Does this duty to cooperate in "suppression," combined with Article 110(1)(e) (which allows boarding on the high seas vessels whose flags are nonexistent or ambiguous) provide a right to seize suspicious ships? Article 110 is based on Article 22 of the 1958 Convention on the High Seas. Professor Louis Sohn states that such a right does not exist, unless a separate treaty or agreement has been established: "Under the ... LOS Convention, Articles 99, 108, and 110, seizure is not an available remedy for the prevention of slave trade or illicit drug traffic, unless specially provided by treaty." LOUIS B. SOHN, KRISTEN GUSTAFSON, THE LAW OF THE SEA 20 (1984). Is consent through radio communication sufficient to justify a seizure? Examples of U.S. practice in obtaining ad hoc consent are found in United States v. Gonzalez, 776 F.2d 931 (11th Cir.1985) (holding that no treaty is necessary and that arrangements can "be informal, as long as there is a clear indication of consent by the foreign nation"); United States v. Crews, 605 F.Supp. 730 (S.D.Fla.1985); United States v. Romero–Galue, 757 F.2d 1147 (11th Cir.1985); United States v. Cardales, 168 F.3d 548 (1st Cir.1999). In March 1999, the International Convention on Arrest of Ships was negotiated in Geneva, U.N. Doc. A/CONF.188/6. This Convention permits arrests, under court supervision, for a variety of maritime claims, but drug smuggling is not included in the list of such claims. Article 17 of the 1990 Convention Against Illicit Traffic in Narcotic Drugs and Psychotropic Substances states that signatories "shall co-operate to the fullest extent possible to suppress illicit traffic by sea, in conformity with the international law of the sea."

3. In United States v. Postal, 589 F.2d 862 (5th Cir. 1979), the U.S. Coast Guard boarded a vessel registered in the Grand Cayman Islands (a territory of the United Kingdom) more than 12 miles from the U.S. coast in the Caribbean. The court ruled that this action violated the provisions of the 1958 Convention on the High Seas, but also ruled that the defendants could not take advantage of this breach because the treaty provisions were not "self-executing." *See also* United States v. Roberts, 1 F. Supp.2d 601 (E.D.La.1998) (same). Recall the discussion of self-executing treaties in Chapter 2. What factors determine whether a treaty is self-executing? Is it logical to conclude that this treaty is not self-executing? Suppose the United Kingdom had protested the actions of the U.S. Coast Guard? Would that have changed the outcome of this case?

4. Was the result in Postal correct, but the reasoning incorrect? Does an individual have standing to challenge U.N. LOSC treaty violations or do such violations merely cause damage to the flag state's sovereignty and thereby limit individual standing if the flag state does not raise an objection? *See, e.g.*, United States v. Bush, 794 F.Supp. 40, 43 (D.P.R.1992) (rejecting a motion to suppress evidence under the Fourth Amendment after a seizure of a Venezuelan-flag vessel, with Venezuela's consent, because "our Circuit finds that the principles of international law, regarding freedom of navigation, are designed to protect the rights of foreign sovereigns, not the privacy

rights of individual sailors."). Should Articles 110(3) and 111(8) condition one's answer? Who has the right to compensation under those articles? Compare Article 106 in the case of seizure of a suspected piratical vessel without adequate grounds. Are law of the sea treaties the only relevant international law? Recall RESTATEMENT §§ 431–433, in Chapter 3.

In November 1986, a U.S. Coast Guard cutter arrested the vessel Don Yeyo, which was registered in Honduras, in international waters east of the Bahamas. At trial, the government produced a letter signed by the Commander General of the Honduran Navy consenting to the U.S. exercise of jurisdiction over the *Don Yeyo*. 46 U.S.C. § 1903 states that "[a] claim of failure to comply with international law in the enforcement of this chapter may be invoked solely by a foreign nation." The court nonetheless allowed defendants to challenge the domestic-law requirement that a vessel being apprehended was "subject to the jurisdiction of the United States," but ruled that the search had been reasonable and affirmed the convictions. *See* United States v. Mena, 863 F.2d 1522 (11th Cir.1989).

5. Is the central question under the LOS treaty whether the treaty provisions are self-executing or whether an individual has standing to challenge a violation of the treaty? In these cases, are those questions functionally the same, or should they remain different types of issues?

6. What is the burden of proof concerning searches or seizures of vessels in Articles 105–106 (regarding piracy), and 110? If the U.S. searches to "verify the flag" and, while doing so, discovers illegal drugs, can the search and discovery be lawful?

7. 21 U.S.C. § 955a prohibits any person on board a "vessel subject to the jurisdiction of the United States" from possessing illegal drugs with the intent to distribute them, and 21 U.S.C. § 955b(d) defines vessels without nationality as being "subject to the jurisdiction of the United States." Does it violate international law for the United States to board on the high seas and seize vessels without nationality? *See* United States v. Marino–Garcia, 679 F.2d 1373, 1382 (11th Cir.1982) ("Vessels without nationality are international pariahs.").

8. On December 9, 2002, Spain stopped and search a North Korean vessel on the high seas near Yemen. The vessel and cargo, including some scud missiles that had been purchased by Yemen, were seized and delivered to U.S. authorities in the area. Assuming that the boarding of the vessel and discovery of scud missiles were reasonable, was it proper to seize the scud missiles? What if the missiles had been headed for delivery to members of Al Qaeda involved in continual attacks on the United States and its nationals?

9. Who has authority to regulate the salvage of the R.M.S. Titanic, which was not a U.S. flag vessel and sits under 12,500 feet of water about 400 miles off the coast of Newfoundland, Canada? In 1994, the U.S. District Court for Eastern Virginia awarded exclusive salvage rights to R.M.S. Titanic, Inc., a Florida corporation, and four years later the court issued an injunction preventing others from coming near the wrecked ship for inspection or tourism purposes. R.M.S. Titanic, Inc. v. The Wrecked and Abandoned Vessel, 9 F.Supp.2d 624, 626 (E.D.Va.1998). Should this ruling be affirmed on appeal? Did the U.S. court have jurisdiction under international law? *See* U.N. LOSC, Article 303; R.M.S. Titanic, Inc. v. Haver, 171 F.3d 943

(4th Cir.1999); James A.R. Nafziger, *The Titanic Revisited,* 30 J. MAR. L. & COMMERCE 311 (1999).

10. Does a state have the right to stop and search merchant vessels in any sea areas in response to an ongoing process of armed attack on that state? *See* U.N. Charter, Articles 51, 103.

11. When using forceful measures of enforcement against foreign flag vessels, must the measure be reasonably proportionate in view of the harm posed by the foreign vessel activity? *See* The I'm Alone, 3 U.N. RPT. INT'L ARB. AWARDS 1609 (1935) (U.S. destruction by intentional sinking of a Canadian rum-running vessel that was trying to escape after ignoring warning shots was excessive and actionable).

D. Environmental Protection

1. The London (Dumping) Convention

The transformation of the London Dumping Convention[1] is one of the most impressive success stories of the environmental movement in the Nineties. This Convention was drafted shortly after the 1972 Stockholm meeting that launched international environmental consciousness. As originally written, it contained a "black list" of materials (such as high-level radioactive wastes) that could never be dumped into the ocean and a "grey list" of items (such as low-level radioactive wastes) that could be dumped in appropriate locations if proper governmental permits were obtained. This treaty was a step forward, but it still permitted a substantial amount of dumping, and efforts were made at its annual meetings to tighten its provisions, so that no radioactive materials whatsoever could be dumped[2] and that the dumping of other hazardous materials would similarly be prohibited. Although the developed nations resisted restrictions on their ability to dump low-level radioactive wastes for a number of years,[3] after many debates and many preliminary meetings, a new Protocol was adopted in 1996 that dramatically altered the treaty. In fact, the name of this treaty was even changed, because the contracting parties did not want the public to think that it authorized dumping, and now it is titled simply "London Convention, 1972."

Under the new Protocol, the presumptions are reversed, and the dumping of all wastes are prohibited unless the item to be dumped is

1. The London Dumping Convention has the formal name of The Convention on the Prevention of Marine Pollution by Dumping of Wastes and Other Matter, *reprinted in* 11 I.L.M. 129 (1973).

2. *See, e.g.,* Jon M. Van Dyke, *Ocean Disposal of Nuclear Wastes,* 12 MARINE POLICY 82 (1988); W. Jackson Davis and Jon M. Van Dyke, *Dumping of Decommissioned Nuclear Submarines at Sea: a Technical and Legal Analysis,* 14 MARINE POLICY 467 (1990).

3. During the Seventh Consultative Meeting in 1983, the contracting parties passed a resolution imposing a moratorium on the dumping of all low-level radioactive wastes, but the Soviet Union, China, Belgium, France, the United Kingdom, and the United States voted against the resolution and a number of other industrialized nations abstained. The dissenting nations did not feel that they were bound by this resolution, and the British government sought to continue its dumping program; but the British unions refused to load the low-level wastes on the British ship in 1985, and thus the British were forced to adhere to the moratorium by their own people. Van Dyke, *Ocean Disposal of Nuclear Wastes, id.*, at 82.

explicitly listed in Annex I. Even these materials, which include dredged material, sewage sludge, vessels, and ocean platforms, cannot be dumped without a permit. Permits can be granted only after assessments are undertaken that evaluate options and describe the potential effects of the dumping. Incineration at sea and the dumping of industrial wastes are completely prohibited. This new Protocol is thus based on the precautionary approach[4] as well as the polluter-pays principle.[5] The burden has thus shifted from those that challenged the dumping to the dumper, who now must demonstrate that no alternatives exist to the dumping option.

This remarkable makeover of the London Convention illustrates the "greening" of the international community and the new spirit of shared responsibility for the common areas of the planet. As of June 1997, 76 countries had become contracting parties to the London Convention, and under Article 210(6) of the Law of the Sea Convention, parties to the Law of the Sea Convention are bound by the requirements of the London Convention even if they are not parties to that treaty.

Notes and Questions

1. As explained above, following the completion of appropriate studies, the contracting parties to the London Convention agreed in 1993 to amend Annexes I and II to ban the dumping into the ocean of all radioactive wastes, high, intermediate, and low. This legally binding prohibition entered into force on February 20, 1994. As of early 2005, 21 of the 80 countries that are contracting parties to the London Convention had ratified the 1996 Protocol. The five additional ratifications needed to bring the Protocol into force are expected during 2005.

2. Article 192 of the Law of the Sea Convention states that "States have the obligation to protect and preserve the marine environment." U.S. Ambassador Elliot L. Richardson stated that if this and its accompanying environmental provisions survived in a treaty that was widely ratified, it "would represent one of the most significant accomplishments in the history of international environmental law." Press conference, Geneva, Switzerland, April 27, 1979. Does this article create a new obligation or codify a previously existing one? Is the Article 235 obligation of international responsibility for environmental harm a codification of existing norms or a new obligation? Which of the environmental protection provisions in the Convention codify

4. Protocol, art. 3(1):

In implementing this Protocol, Contracting Parties shall apply a precautionary approach to environmental protection from dumping of wastes or other matter whereby appropriate preventative measures are taken when there is reason to believe that wastes or other matter introduced into the marine environment are likely to cause harm even when there is no conclusive evidence to prove a causal relation between inputs and their effects.

5. *Id.*, art. 3(2):

Taking into account the approach that the polluter should, in principle, bear the cost of pollution, each Contracting Party shall endeavor to promote practices whereby those it has authorized to engage in dumping or incineration at sea bear the cost of meeting the pollution prevention and control requirements for the authorized activities, having due regard to the public interest.

existing customary international law, and which introduce new norms for the world community?

3. No international organization to monitor environmental problems is created by the Convention, and most of the burden of pollution regulation is imposed on the states themselves. Examine Articles 207–20. Can a coastal state regulate pollution from vessels in its exclusive economic zone? *See* Article 211. How can such regulations be enforced? *See* Articles 217–20. Do you suspect that the compulsory dispute resolution provisions (Articles 279–99) are essential to the acceptance by the coastal states of reduced jurisdiction over environmental protection and navigation in their EEZs?

4. Are the powers of the coastal states to adopt laws to control pollution in Article 211 new powers, or is the article a codification of previously recognized rights? Can the careful (precarious?) balance between coastal state jurisdiction and navigational freedoms in the exclusive economic zone, as developed in the Convention, be incorporated into customary international law, or is this series of compromises doomed to eventual collapse? Will coastal states begin to assert greater jurisdiction over their 200–mile zones?

5. Is "port-state jurisdiction" a developing customary norm, or is it a new principle of international law introduced by the Convention? *See* Article 218. Can a nonratifying state properly assert "port-state jurisdiction" today?

6. If a foreign flag vessel engages in illegal dumping (in violation of the London Convention, 1972) 150 miles off the coast of the United States, what enforcement measures can be taken against the vessels? *See* Articles 216 and 228. What if the illegal dumping occurs 300 miles from the nearest land area? What penalties can be applied? Can the master and crew be imprisoned? *See* Article 230.

7. What if the vessel that engaged in the illegal dumping came into a U.S. port for repairs? Could the U.S. exercise jurisdiction over the vessel? Could the U.S. do so regarding illegal dumping that had occurred in the EEZ of another country?

8. Can a coastal state detain and inspect a vessel passing through its territorial sea or exclusive economic zone if the vessel is suspected of polluting these waters? See Articles 220 and 224 of the Law of the Sea Convention. Can foreign flag warships be detained and inspected? See Articles 236 and 95–96. What if the detention is unjustified and causes damage to the vessel? When can the dispute-resolution procedures in Articles 279–99 be invoked?

9. Residents of the island of Bougainville in Papua New Guinea alleged that the operators of the Rio Tinto Mine dumped toxic-mine-waste tailings into the Jaba River which flowed into the Empress Augusta Bay causing the fish to disappear and die. Does this allegation state a claim based on a violation of customary international law reflected in the U.N. LOSC sufficient to allow plaintiffs to bring a claim for damages under the Alien Tort Claims Act, 28 U.S.C. sec. 1350? *See* Sarei v. Rio Tinto PLC, 221 F.Supp.2d 1116, 1162 (C.D.Cal. 2002).

JON M. VAN DYKE, *SHARING OCEAN RESOURCES ... IN A TIME OF SCARCITY AND SELFISHNESS*

in THE LAW OF THE SEA: INHERITED DOCTRINE AND A REGIME FOR THE COMMON HERITAGE (Harry Scheiber ed. 2000).*

Sea Transport of Ultrahazardous Radioactive Materials

Many coastal communities have expressed substantial fears of environmental disasters that could result from the sea shipments of large cargoes of highly toxic radioactive materials. In November 1992, Japan shipped 2200 pounds (one metric ton) of plutonium in a refitted freighter called the Akatsuki Maru from France to Japan, going around the Cape of Good Hope in Africa and then south of Australia and New Zealand before turning north to traverse the Pacific to Japan. In February 1995, the British vessel Pacific Pintail carried 28 canisters of high-level vitrified nuclear waste in glass blocks, each weighing 1,000 pounds, going around Cape Horn at the tip of South America and then across the Pacific. In early 1997, the British vessel Pacific Teal carried 40 such canisters, going around Africa and then up through the Tasman Sea. In January 1998, the British vessel Pacific Swan carried 60 canisters, going through the Panama Canal. The Pacific Swan made a similar voyage in early 1999, departing France on February 26, carrying 40 cylinders of reprocessed vitrified nuclear wastes through the Mona Passage (between Puerto Rico and the Dominican Republic) and then through the Panama Canal. Later in 1999, from July to September, the Pacific Pintail and the Pacific Teal traveled from France to Japan carrying 446 kilograms in 40 nuclear fuel elements of the highly-dangerous mixed plutonium-uraniumoxide (MOX), going around the Cape of Good Hope in South Africa, through the Southern Ocean, and then up through the Tasman Sea and the western Pacific Islands to Japan. French officials estimate that one or two such shipments will be made each year for the next 15 years.

These shipments present risks of a magnitude totally different from any previous ocean cargoes. Each of the 60 canisters on the Pacific Swan contained 17,000 terabecquerels in beta-gamma activity. These highly-toxic and long-lived poisons could endanger large coastal populations or create an ecologically dead zone in the ocean for thousands of years. They are extremely difficult to handle, and the equipment necessary to salvage them in the event of an accident have not yet been developed. British representatives acknowledged that in the event of a vessel sinking "it was quite apparent that recovery from some places would not be possible."[1] If a vessel carrying such a cargo collided with another vessel causing an intensely hot and long-lasting shipboard fire, then

* Reproduced with kind permission from Kluwer Law International, © 2000. *See also* Jon M. Van Dyke, *The Legal Regime Governing Sea Transport of Ultrahazardous Radioactive Materials,* 33 OCEAN DEV. & INT'L L. 77 (2002).

1. Maritime Safety Committee, Matters Related to the INF Code, March 27, 1997, at 2 (MSC 68/15/Add.2 (statement attributed to United Kingdom delegation).

radioactive particles could become airborne, putting all nearby life forms in grave danger of catastrophic health impacts. Brazil, Argentina, and Chile exerted every possible pressure to keep the Pacific Pintail from traveling through their territorial waters and exclusive economic zones in 1995,[2] and in August 1998 Argentina and Chile conducted joint naval exercises to prepare for a hypothetical accident in which a ship carrying ultrahazardous radioactive materials collided with an iceberg.

These cargoes are not, therefore, just another "dangerous goods." They are truly "ultrahazardous," and require a focused and comprehensive legal regime designed to internalize the real costs of the shipments, and to ensure that the risks they create are not transferred from those that benefit from these shipments to those who gain nothing from them.

In March 1996, the International Maritime Organization (IMO) held a Special Consultative Meeting during which governmental and nongovernmental organizations presented their views on the risks created by these transports and the legal regime that applies to them. After that meeting assignments were given to various international bodies to address these issues. A few issues have been satisfactorily resolved, but many of them require further examination and discussion.

The international community appears to have agreed that the Code for the Safe Carriage of Irradiated Nuclear Fuel, Plutonium, and High–Level Radioactive Wastes in Flasks Aboard Ships (the INF Code)[3] should become binding and obligatory, although the United States' view is that this Code should apply only to commercial vessels. The Marine Safety Committee of the International Maritime Organization (IMO) has formally recommended that the Code, as amended, should become mandatory, and its text is being revised to reflect this change.

The IMO's Marine Environment Protection Committee (MEPC) has developed Guidelines for Developing Shipboard Emergency Plans, which are designed to be added to the INF Code. The Committee recognized the need for consultation with coastal states in the development of these shipboard emergency plans. It is unclear, however, whether coastal nations will be fully informed of these plans, in order to develop coordinated shore-based emergency plans.

Although the Duty to Consult is one of the most venerable and well-established principles of international law, the shipping and nuclear nations are reluctant to acknowledge that they must consult with affected coastal nations regarding these ultrahazardous shipments. They argue that such consultation would interfere with their freedom of navigation and may assist terrorists who wish to attack the shipments. These arguments are spurious. Consultation regarding route-selection

2. *See generally* Jon M. Van Dyke, *Applying the Precautionary Principle to Ocean Shipments of Radioactive Materials*, 27 Ocean Dev. & Int'l L. 379 (1996)[hereafter Van Dyke, *Precautionary Principle*].

3. IMO Resolution A 18/Res. 748, Annex, adopted by the 18th Assembly of the International Maritime Organization on November 4, 1993.

and emergency-planning is in everyone's best interest and can only serve to make these shipments safer for all concerned.

Proper international consultation has several elements. The first step is to disclose the nature of the project with its attendant risks and safety measures to those states that may be affected by the activity. Preparing an environmental impact assessment is a logical way to fulfill this obligation, and preparing such a document is required in any event by Articles 204–206 of the U.N. Law of the Sea Convention. The second step is to listen to the concerns expressed by the affected nations along with their suggestions for reducing the risks. Suggestions that are helpful and constructive should of course be accepted and acted upon. If the shipping states reject a suggestion, they should explain why they have rejected it.

This procedure entails no risks and can only lead to safer voyages. The coastal states may have ideas regarding shipping lanes and weather patterns that can reduce the risks to these voyages. The areas of the Western Pacific are, for instance, subject to intense typhoons during certain times of the year. The coastal states' understanding of the shipments and their cargoes can enable them to use their rescue equipment in a manner that is more likely to be helpful in an emergency. Preparing contingency plans for coastal emergencies can only be done after a full understanding of the risks involved.

A nation that is consulted about a project outside its borders that may affect it does not have a veto power over that project. But it does have the right to understand the risks it is being subjected to and to offer constructive advice to reduce those risks.

The shipping and nuclear nations argue that prior notification is inconsistent with the freedom of navigation guaranteed under the U.N. Law of the Sea Convention. But in fact the shipping and nuclear nations currently do provide notification, at least to their close allies and the nations that they trust.[4] The Japanese stated on December 18, 1997, that it would announce the route for its 1998 shipment the day after it left France. The British provided advance notification to the Panama Canal Commission regarding the 1998 shipment through the Canal. The smaller Pacific and Caribbean nations have been, however, left in the dark regarding these shipments, creating a two-tiered situation whereby some affected nations are treated as second-class citizens without the right to learn what is going on. Obviously such a situation is unfair and unacceptable.

Prior notification is useful in reducing the alarm that results from unsubstantiated rumors as well as ensuring that contingency plans for dealing with coastal emergencies can be prepared in time. Prior notification for transboundary movement of hazardous materials is standard in

4. Jean-Louis Ricaud, vice-president of the French nuclear company Cogema, has said that the shippers had "informed everybody who needed to be informed" about the 1998 shipment. Ann MacLachlan, *It's Official: Japan-Bound Waste Ship Will Move Through the Panama Canal*, NUCLEAR FUEL, Jan. 26, 1998, at 5, 6.

a number of conventions, including the Basel Convention (see below), the Bamako Convention,[5] the IAEA Code of Practice on the International Transboundary Movement of Radioactive Waste,[6] and the IAEA Regulations for the Safe Transport of Radioactive Material.[7]

Other important initiatives are to require the shipping nations to work with the affected coastal and island nations to develop contingency plans for shore emergencies and salvage operations. Efforts should also be undertaken through the IMO to continue the effort to identify particularly sensitive sea area that must be avoided altogether by ships carrying these ultrahazardous cargoes.

The IAEA Standing Committee on Liability for Nuclear Damage has recommended to the Agency's Board of Governors that a diplomatic conference be held to amend the 1963 Vienna Convention on Civil Liability for Nuclear Damage and to adopt a Convention on Supplementary Funding. Liability remains an outstanding issue, which should be addressed both through the IMO and the IAEA.

The provisions in the Law of the Sea Convention relevant to shipments of ultrahazardous cargoes point in different directions. Although the freedom of navigation is protected in Articles 17–19 and 34–45, the duty to protect the marine environment is also clearly articulated in Article 192. The Convention recognizes in Articles 22 and 23 that ships carrying nuclear cargoes are different and do require special precautionary measures. Articles 204–06 require the preparation of environmental assessments in situations that might lead to "substantial pollution of or significant and harmful changes to the marine environment" (Article 206). The drafters of the Convention did not anticipate the current shipments of ultrahazardous radioactive cargoes, but the language in the Convention indicates that they recognized that a unique regime should apply to such shipments. All parts of the Convention must be viewed as equally important and the duty to protect and preserve the marine environment is just as much an international norm as the rights to innocent and transit passage. Because the relevant provisions of the Convention seem somewhat contradictory, a new regime establishing clear rules must be developed to explain how they are to be reconciled. The recent practices of states provide some guidance, and it is instructive that the shipping and nuclear nations are now engaged in a process of consultation and notification with regard to many of the affected coastal states. They undertake this practice based on their view that it is the responsible and appropriate action to take, required by norms of

5. Bamako Convention on the Ban of the Import into Africa and the Control of Transboundary Movement and Management of Hazardous Wastes within Africa, Jan. 29, 1991, 30 I.L.M. 773 (1991).

6. International Atomic Energy Agency, General Conference Resolution on Code of Practice on the International Transboundary Movement of Radioactive Waste, Sept. 21, 1990, 30 I.L.M. 556 (1991).

7. These regulations, first promulgated in 1961, and revised in 1964, 1967, 1973, 1985, and 1996, are discussed on pages 6–7 of the April 1998 Report of the IAEA Secretariat. The latest version, approved by the IAEA Board of Governors in September 1996, has been published by the IAEA as "Safety Standards Series No. ST–1."

international law and comity. It is also instructive to remember that the 1995 shipment of the Pacific Pintail did change its course and leave the exclusive economic zones of the South American countries after their strong protests.[8] A new international document recognizing the rights of the coastal states and the responsibilities of the shipping and nuclear states is needed to protect those concerned coastal states that are left out of the current informal consultative process.

This process should not be seen as an adversarial situation between the shipping and nuclear nations on the one hand and the concerned coastal states on the other. It is in everyone's interest to protect the marine environment and coastal populations. If these shipments are to continue in the future, agreements must also be reached regarding the duty to prepare environmental impact assessments, the duty to consult with and notify affected states, the duty to prepare shore-emergency and salvage contingency plans, the duty to protect sensitive sea areas, and the liability regime that would govern damages resulting from accidents. Until agreements are reached on these important matters, the shipment of these extremely-dangerous materials will continue to violate fundamental norms of international law and comity, because they place coastal nations that receive no benefit from the shipments at grave risk of environmental disaster without any legal protections.

DUNCAN E.J. CURRIE AND JON M. VAN DYKE, *RECENT DEVELOPMENTS IN THE INTERNATIONAL LAW GOVERNING SHIPMENTS OF NUCLEAR MATERIALS AND WASTES AND THEIR IMPLICATIONS FOR SIDS*[9]

14:2 Review of European Community & International Environmental Law (RECIEL) 117 (2005).

As coastal nations understand the risks created by shipments of hazardous materials, frequently on unseaworthy vessels, they have been asserting the right to reduce the risks created by these shipments as they pass through their exclusive economic zones and coastal waters. Developments in the past several years have confirmed that many coastal countries believe they have the necessity and the right, individually and in groups, to take steps to address these shipments based on the cargo and type of ship, and have increasingly asserted the right to do so. *See generally* Jon M. Van Dyke, *The Disappearing Right to Navigational Freedom in the Exclusive Economic Zone*, 29 MARINE POLICY 107–21 (2005).

European Restrictions on Navigational Freedoms

When future histories of navigational rights are written, they will probably point to the November 2002 breakup of the oil tanker *Prestige*

8. *See* Van Dyke, *Precautionary Principle, supra*, at 386–87.

9. This excerpt has been adapted, with permission, from the Review of European Community & International Environmental Law (RECIEL).

off the coast of Spain as the defining moment that changed perceptions and the governing principles of international law. When this aged single-hull tanker started foundering and leaking its oil cargo, Spain refused to permit the crippled vessel to come into a Spanish port for "safe haven." And then, when the tanker was towed out into the open ocean, it broke apart causing a dramatic and destructive spillage of its cargo. After more than 17,000 tons of oil washed up along the beautiful and resource-rich coasts of Spain, Portugal, and France, France and Spain issued a decree that said:

> A. All oil tankers traveling through these two countries' EEZs will have to provide advance notice to the coastal countries about their cargo, destination, flag, and operators.
>
> B. All single-hulled tankers more than 15 years old traveling through the EEZs of Spain and France will be subject to spot inspections by coastal maritime authorities while in the adjacent EEZs and will be expelled from the EEZs if they are determined, after inspection, to be not seaworthy.

Shortly after the Spanish–French decree, Portugal announced that it would also take the same position on this issue. Then Morocco announced that single hull oil tankers more than 15 years old carrying heavy fuel, tar, asphaltic bitumen or heavy crude oil would be subject to the requirement that they provide prior notification and adhere to strict safety regulations. Spain also issued a decree banning single-hulled oil tankers from entering its ports.

In early 2003, following these unilateral steps, the European Union banned large single-hulled tankers carrying heavy grade oil from coming into any European ports, and on April 3, 2003, the French National Assembly unanimously adopted a new law asserting the right to intercept ships out to a distance 90 miles from its Mediterranean coast that release polluting ballast waters and also imposing stricter controls on transient oil tankers. Captains of vessels violating these new French rules can be sentenced to up to four years in prison and fined up to $600,000. About this same time, Spain, France, and Portugal were joined by Belgium and the United Kingdom in submitting a petition to the International Maritime Organization (IMO) to declare virtually their entire EEZs to be "particularly sensitive sea areas" that would be completely off-limits for single-hulled oil tankers and other cargo vessels transporting dangerous cargoes. The IMO agreed to designate this area as a particularly sensitive sea area, but did not completely prohibit passage of single-hulled oil tankers, establishing instead a reporting and emergency-response system.

The San Onofre Nuclear Reactor

Another defining moment in the tension between navigational freedom and the right of coastal states to restrict the movement of ships through their exclusive economic zones based on the nature of the ship and its cargo was the US announcement on February 3, 2004 that it was abandoning its plan to ship the 770–ton decommissioned nuclear reactor from the San Onofre nuclear plant in Southern California around Cape Horn at the tip of South America to South Carolina for burial. This plan, which had previously been approved by the U.S. Department of Transportation despite conflicting views within the U.S. government, was to put the reactor on a barge that would make a 90–day journey around South America. This journey would thus include the transiting of Drake's Passage at the continent's tip, which is one of the world's most dangerous nautical passages, where gale force winds blow 200 days each year. Although logic would have favored burial in California, or Hanford, Washington, or transporting the reactor across the United States by train, these options had all been rejected because of U.S. laws governing the disposal of nuclear wastes and because of liability concerns.

Chile's Nuclear Safety Law. The first hurdle faced by the proposed shipment concerned Chile's "Law for Nuclear Safety" which had been modified in October 2002 to require prior authorization for any transport of "nuclear substances" and "radioactive materials" through Chile's exclusive economic zone. The law explained that such authorization would be granted only if the transporter establishes that the shipment will "keep[] the environment free of contamination" and only after information has been provided regarding the date and route of the shipment, the "characteristics of the load," and the "safety and contingency measures" that are being utilized.

The U.S. State Department had originally instructed Southern California Edison that it "should not apply for Chilean authorization for the passage because it was concerned that our doing so would set an unfavorable precedent for future shipments." Subsequently, however, the U.S. Transportation Department indicated that it thought consultations with Chile would be logical because of the potential risks and the advantages of having emergency contingency plans in place. The Department of Transportation also urged Southern California Edison to develop more realistic plans for salvage in the case of a sinking.

These concerns seemed to have resonated in the State Department because two weeks later the State Department said that "a number of significant issues" needed to be resolved before the reactor could be shipped, and stated specifically that Southern California Edison should consider another route around South America, explain in detail its salvage contingency plans, and show that it has adequate liability insurance. Finally, however, the Department of Transportation did issue a permit for the shipment on December 1, 2003. Southern California Edison said that "the ocean journey will be made in international shipping lanes hundreds of miles off the coasts of Central and South America." It was never clear whether the vessel was going to try to avoid passing through Chile's EEZ altogether by staying more than 200 nautical miles from the Chilean coast, but the shippers did consider several potential safe harbors, including a number in Chile.

Argentina's Court Decision. A second hurdle was presented by a January 2004 court decision in Argentina, which prohibited the passage of the reactor through Argentina's EEZ. This decision issued by Argentine federal judge Jorge Pfleger cited the Basel Convention on the Control of Trans–Boundary Movements of Hazardous Wastes and Their Disposal, signed at Basel March 22,1989, entered into force May 5, 1992, UNEP Doc. T/BSL/000, 28 I.L.M. 657 (1989), as authorizing coastal countries to block such shipments. After this decision, Argentine officials stated that if the shipment passed through Argentina's exclusive economic zone "the load will be intercepted by the military and escorted out of the nation's territorial waters." This action would have been in line with Argentina's declaration to the Law of the Sea Convention that the transit by sea of vessels carrying highly radioactive substances would be duly regulated. This important decision set the stage for a significant international incident if the shipment had taken place and had transited within 200 nautical miles of Argentina's coast.

Opposition to Nuclear Cargoes from Other Countries. The decision to abandon the effort to ship the reactor by sea, and thus to leave it in place in Southern California, avoided confrontations, and also reinforced the view that countries can act to protect their coastal populations and coastal resources by preventing passage of particularly dangerous cargoes and unseaworthy ships through their coastal waters. Numerous states have previously declared that the shipments of ultrahazardous nuclear cargoes should not transit through their EEZs. In 1992, for instance, South Africa, and Portugal explicitly requested that Japan's shipment of plutonium stay out of their EEZs, and in response to an inquiry from Australia, Japan stated that "in principle" the ship would stay outside the 200–nautical-mile zone of all nations. In 1995, Brazil, Argentina, Chile, South Africa, Nauru, and Kiribati all expressly banned the British nuclear cargo ship *Pacific Pintail* from their EEZs and Chile sent its ships and aircraft to force the ship out of its EEZ. In 1999, New Zealand issued a strong statement protesting these shipments and stating that they should not be permitted through New Zealand's EEZ because of the " 'precautionary principle' enshrined in the Rio Declaration."

U.S. Restrictions on Navigational Freedoms

Environmental Restrictions. The United States has imposed some restrictions on navigational freedoms to protect its environmental and security interests. In December 1998, for instance, the International Maritime Organization (IMO) approved a U.S. proposal to require ships transiting through the northeast and southeast coasts of the United States to report their locations and travel plans in order to protect the northern right whale from being hit by ships. This whale species was hunted almost to extinction because of its oil, and is now thought to be the rarest whale species in the world. This mandatory ship reporting area joins nine others that have been established by IMO to protect other fragile environmental areas.

Security Restrictions. The U.S. and allied "military intercept operations" during the past decade have also imposed restrictions on navigational movement. Blockades have been used historically in wartime, and the United States imposed a "quarantine" around Cuba during the October 1962 Cuban Missile Crisis. During the 1982 Falklands/Malvinas War, the United Kingdom declared a 200–nautical-mile military exclusion zone around the islands, which some military lawyers viewed "as a bad mistake" because it "strengthened the trend by which a zone 200 miles from the shore is seen to have security as well as legal implications."

Since then, the United Nations has authorized military intercept operations in connection with the 1991 Gulf War, the civil war in the former Yugoslavia in 1991–93, the internal conflict in Haiti in 1993–94, and the civil war in Sierra Leone in 1997. After the September 11, 2001 attacks, the United States began boarding vessels in the Indian Ocean, the Red Sea, the Strait of Hormuz and elsewhere in search of Osama bin Laden and his Al Qaeda associates. Attempts have been made to undertake these boarding operations with the consent of the masters of the vessels, but "the US notification made to the maritime industry made it clear that vessels suspected of transporting or assisting bin Laden and senior al Qaeda leadership would be subject to the use of force to compel a boarding." Although the specific legal basis for these searches has never been articulated, U.S. President George W. Bush has said generally that U.S. actions to respond to the attacks by Al Qaeda are "acts of self-defense."

On December 9, 2002, a North Korean cargo vessel, the *M/V So San*, said to be registered variously in Cambodia or Singapore, was forcibly stopped in the Gulf of Aden 600 miles east of the Horn of Africa by two Spanish warships, who discovered 23 containers filled with 15 Scud missiles hidden beneath 40,000 sacks of cement. After some confusion and high level negotiations involving U.S. Vice President Richard Cheney and Secretary of State Colin Powell talking with Yemen President Ali Abdullah Salih, the United States "[a]cknowledg[ed] that the purchase of the missiles was not unlawful," and the vessel was released to continue its voyage to Yemen.

The Proliferation Security Initiative. Since then, the United States has shown an increased interest in using its naval muscle to stop ships that it views as presenting a security threat. In a speech delivered in Poland May 31, 2003, U.S. President George W. Bush outlined the "Proliferation Security Initiative," whereby the United States is mobilizing "like-minded states" to prepare for and participate in naval intercept operations designed to inspect ships thought to be carrying nuclear materials to or from "rogue" states, notably North Korea and perhaps also Iran. The countries most actively supporting this U.S.-initiative are Spain, France, the United Kingdom, Portugal, Australia, Germany, Italy, Japan, the Netherlands, and Poland.

The countries coordinating these efforts met several times during 2003 and 2004 and held a number of joint exercises to practice interdiction techniques. Related to these efforts were the seizure by Taiwan of

150 barrels of dual-use chemicals from a North Korean freighter when it stopped in Kaohsiung to refuel, the confiscation of 22–tons of ultra-strong dual-use aluminum tubing bound for North Korea on the French-flagged vessel *Ville de Virgo* when it was about to enter the Suez Canal on April 12, 2003, and Japan's searches of the cargoes of North Korean ferries when they are in Japanese ports.

Changing the Law. Although the public statements have said that these endeavors would be undertaken in a manner that is consistent with international law, it is also clear that the United States and its allies are seeking to expand international law to permit more active interception when warranted. President Bush's National Security Advisor Condoleezza Rice explained recently that:

> While all actions will be taken consistent with existing national and international legal authorities, *we are also seeking ways to expand those authorities.* And it is for this reason that the President proposed in his September address to the United Nations that the Security Council adopt a resolution calling on all states to criminalize proliferation activities, establish effective export controls, and ensure the safety and security of sensitive materials and technologies.

Australia's Foreign Minister Alexander Downer also has expressed support for changing the law permitting free navigation on the high seas in order to stop North Korea's shipping of missiles, nuclear materials, and drugs to its allies or customers. In January 2004, the Japanese press reported that the Japanese government was planning to submit a bill to the Japanese Diet that would allow the Japanese Maritime Self–Defense Force to stop foreign vessels and inspect their cargo in Japanese territorial waters or on the high seas near Japan during periods of emergency or conflict in the areas surrounding Japan.

Australia's 1000 Mile Maritime Identification Zone

In a proposal exemplifying the global trend recognizing the requirements of prior notification and consultation, Australia announced in December 2004 its intention to establish a Maritime Identification Zone, which will extend up to 1,000 nautical miles from Australia's coastline. Upon entering this Zone, vessels proposing to enter Australian ports will be required to provide comprehensive information regarding its identity, crew, cargo, location, course, speed, and intended port of arrival. Australia's goal is thus to identify all vessels, other than day recreational boats, that are navigating within its 200–nautical-mile exclusive economic zone. Malaysia, New Zealand, and Indonesia have expressed concern at the plan, while New Zealand's understanding is that vessels transiting the zone but not traveling to an Australian port will be asked to provide information on a voluntary basis.

Initiatives of the Small Island States

At the Pacific Islands Forum in August 2004, the independent island states of the Pacific sought to develop a region-specific environmental impact assessment of nuclear shipments, and restated their concerns about a possible economic loss after an incident involving a nuclear shipment that did not result in a release of measurable radioactivity but nonetheless caused fears that led to declines in the tourism and fishery industries. These small island states have long been concerned about the possibility of economic losses to their fragile tourism and fishing interests which may follow from a nuclear incident or accident in the region, regardless of actual contamination, thus leaving coastal states without compensation. The Permanent Representative of the Federated States of Micronesia, Masao Nakayama, stated at the United Nations in November 2004 that "[t]he continued shipment of plutonium and radioactive wastes through our Exclusive Economic Zones remains of great concern. Our Pacific Ocean is a vital breadbasket for the entire planet. Any transshipment accident could have a serious impact on the livelihood of our peoples, our economies, and would be felt far beyond our shores, for many generations to come."

The Caribbean nations have been equally united in their opposition to the shipments of ultrahazardous cargoes. Their coordinating body, the Caribbean Community (CARICOM) explained in its statement to the 2004 Prepcom of the Nuclear Proliferation Treaty that:

> In addition to the provision of information regarding the shipment of radioactive materials, CARICOM States continue to call for the establishment of a comprehensive regulatory framework, to promote state responsibility with respect to disclosure, prior informed consent, liability and compensation in the event of accidents. While we appreciate the steps undertaken by States to prevent the likelihood of accidents, we cannot overstate the damage that would be done to the ecosystems of our countries, and the potentially catastrophic impact on our vulnerable economies should an accident occur.

On January 14, 2005, at the UN meeting on Small Island Developing States (SIDS) in Mauritius, these small island states and the rest of the international community participating in this event adopted the Mauritius Declaration and a companion strategy to implement the Barbados Programme of Action for their sustainable development. The SIDS, composed of islands in the Caribbean, the Pacific, and the AIMS region (Atlantic, Indian Ocean, and Mediterranean and South China Seas), were united in their opposition to the transport of radioactive material through their regions. The statement that emerged from this important meeting recognized that the cessation of transport of radioactive materials through SIDS regions is the ultimate desired goal of SIDS and some other countries (which was recognized to include New Zealand, which was chairing the negotiating meeting). The statement also recognized that concerns remained regarding the need to develop and strengthen international regulatory regimes to enhance safety, disclosure, liability, security and compensation in relation to such transport.

Conclusion

Although it is not yet clear how all these conflicting initiatives will be resolved, it is clear that we are in a period of reassessment and transition and that many coastal countries believe they need to and are entitled to take steps to address the risks created by ships carrying dangerous cargoes near their shores. The law of the sea has always been created through the give-and-take process of states make conflicting claims, which are ultimately resolved through negotiation, a decision rendered by a tribunal or international organization, military force, or a pattern of practice that emerges and is accepted as obligatory by those concerned about the issue. *See, e.g.*, Myres McDougal and Norbert Schlei, *The Hydrogen Bomb Tests in Perspective: Lawful Measures for Security,* 64 YALE L.J. 648, 659–60 (1955). We are in a particularly active law-making period at present, and it appears that the law that will emerge will impose allow coastal countries to impose restrictions on navigation near their shores.

Notes and Questions

1. Do foreign-flag vessels carrying ultrahazardous cargoes have the right to pass through the territorial sea of the United States? For a list of countries that have asserted the right to restrict passage of hazardous cargoes through their maritime zones, see K. Hakapaa and E.J. Molenaar, *Innocent Passage—Past and Present*, 23 MARINE POLICY 131, 142 (1999). In Mayaguezanos por la Salud y el Ambiente v. United States, 198 F.3d 297, 305 n.15 (1st Cir. 1999), the Court dismissed a challenge by a citizen group to a shipment carrying nuclear wastes, but said specifically that "we disavow" the broad statements made by the District Court that the doctrine of innocent passage "meant that the United States could not exercise power over transport of nuclear waste even through its territorial waters."

2. What restrictions can coastal states impose on the passage of nuclear-powered or nuclear-cargo vessels? See U.N. LOSC, Articles 22, 23, and 41. Are the Chilean law and the Argentine decision described in the article above consistent with the Law of the Sea Convention? Are the restrictions established by European nations after the *Prestige* disaster?

3. How can the environmental assessment requirements in Articles 204–206 of the LOSC be enforced?

4. Is the duty to consult a requirement under international law? What are the components of this duty? How can it be enforced?

2. *Whales, Environmental Protection, and Free Trade*

JON M. VAN DYKE, *SHARING OCEAN RESOURCES ... IN A TIME OF SCARCITY AND SELFISHNESS*

in THE LAW OF THE SEA: INHERITED DOCTRINE AND A REGIME FOR THE COMMON HERITAGE (Harry Scheiber ed. 2000).*

Article 65 of the U.N. Law of the Sea Convention is explicit in requiring states to "work through the appropriate international organizations for [the] conservation, management and study" of cetaceans (whales and dolphins). The International Whaling Commission (IWC)[1]—established in 1946—would appear to be the "appropriate international organization" and it has maintained a moratorium on all harvesting of whales since 1986, except for limited kills allocated to indigenous people, mostly in the Arctic region. Because they wished to continue harvesting whales, Norway, Iceland, the Faroe Islands (Denmark), and Greenland (Denmark) created the North Atlantic Marine Mammal Commission (NAMMCO) in 1992. Norway has consistently objected to the moratorium established by the IWC and has been harvesting minke whales in the North Atlantic under the blessing of NAMMCO.[2] In addition, Canada, which is not a member of either the IWC or NAMMCO but sends observers to meetings of both organizations, has authorized its Inuit natives to harvest limited numbers of bowhead whales.

Can the obligation in Article 65 to "work through" an appropriate international organization be so easily circumvented as Norway and Iceland have tried to do by simply creating their own small regional organization? What is left of the duty to cooperate if Canada can authorize its citizens to harvest whales while not being a member of any organization? Although the duty to cooperate does not necessarily include the duty to agree, it certainly includes the duty to sit with the other party and exchange views, listening respectfully to the other position. Countries that walk out of the global organization and form their own regional body, or that refuse to join any organization, appear to be in violation of their duty to cooperate.

Do indigenous people have special rights to harvest whales? The International Whaling Commission has authorized some limited whaling to indigenous communities, but this action has been vigorously protested by Japan, Iceland, and Norway who have argued that their nonindigenous whaling villagers have just as much right to harvest whales as do indigenous communities in the United States and elsewhere.

In the winter of 1998–99, the Makah Indians embarked on a whale hunt pursuant to an 1855 treaty with the United States that guarantees their right to hunt whales, in search of their quota of five whales during each of the next five years. From their 32–foot ceder canoe, using a steel harpoon and a .50 caliber rifle, they will search for the gray whale, which can weigh up to 40 tons and be much larger than the Indians' canoe. Environmental groups are vigorously protesting this effort because they believe it is part of a campaign to reinstate commercial whaling. No living Makah has been part of a whale hunt, and the current generation views this effort as an important step in restoring their culture and

1. The International Whaling Commission (IWC) was created by the International Convention for the Regulation of Whaling, Dec. 2, 1946, 161 U.N.T.S. 72.

2. *See generally* Harry N. Scheiber, *Historical Memory, Cultural Claims, and Environmental Ethics in the Jurisprudence of Whaling Regulation,* 38 OCEAN & COASTAL MANAGEMENT 5 (1998); David D. Caron, *The International Whaling Commission and the North Atlantic Marine Mammal Commission: The Institutional Risks of Coercion in Consensual Structures,* 89 AM. J. INT'L L. 154 (1995); Trond Bjorndal and Jon M. Conrad, *A Report on the Norwegian Minke Whale Hunt,* 22 MARINE POLICY 161 (1998).

heritage. The gray whale was removed from the endangered species list in 1994, and it is thought that 23,000 of them inhabit the Pacific.

Indigenous people tend to have a heightened awareness of the connections within ecosystems and the need to exercise proper respect for all living creatures. One Maori commentator has described the jurisprudence of indigenous law as one of "nurturance and use," and has described the Maori approach as follows:

> For the Maori people, te tikanga o te moana, or the law of the sea, is predicated on four basic precepts deeply rooted in Maori cultural values. First, the sea is part of a global environment in which all parts are interlinked. Second, the sea, as on of the taonga, or treasures of Mother Earth, must be nurtured and protected. Third, the protected sea is a koha, or gift, which humans may use. Fourth, that use is to be controlled in a way that will sustain its bounty.[3]

How is this dispute over whaling to be resolved? International law increasingly recognizes indigenous people as separate actors with rights to participate in international decisionmaking. Some scholars now argue that the whales also have rights that need to be considered. The duty to cooperate imposes a particularly difficult challenge in this situation, because the dispute concerns whether whales are a "resource" that should be shared or are beings with rights. Even among those who do not agree that whales themselves have rights, many argue that the ban on commercial whaling must continue because so much abuse occurred until the moratorium went into effect in 1986 that whalers and whaling nations simply cannot be trusted to adhere to any guidelines.

One commentator asserts that "To the extent that whales are a res communis resource, no individual nation, or group of nations, has the right to exploit them for economic gain when to do so may preclude humankind's enjoying the alternative benefits that cetaceans may offer.... Therefore, under the doctrine of res communis, the world community can demand a permanent moratorium on commercial whaling." These "alternative benefits" include whale watching, which is commercially quite important in communities (like Hawaii) that rely economically on tourism, but for some these "alternative benefits" also include more profound interactions with the whales and many now view the effort to save the whales as one of the most important crusades of our time. Because of this moral dimension and the sharply conflicting views that humans have toward whales, because of the "inevitable and excruciating choice between environmental protection ... and aboriginal rights,"[4] as well as the dispute between the countries that view whales as a legitimate ocean resource and those that do not, this dispute eludes any easy or obvious resolution.

3. Moana Jackson, *Indigenous Law and the Sea*, in FREEDOM FOR THE SEAS IN THE 21ST CENTURY 41, 46 (Jon M. Van Dyke, Durwood Zaelke, Grant Hewison eds. 1993).

4. Alma Soongi Beck, *The Makah's Decision to Reinstate Whaling*, 11 J. ENVT'L L. & LITIG. 359, 408 (1996).

Notes and Questions

1. The United States has enacted several statutes designed to protect marine mammals and other endangered and threatened species by barring the sale in the United States of seafood products that are harvested by nations that violate international conservation programs. These embargos have been challenged by other nations as a unilateral violation of the free-trade rules established under the General Agreement on Trade and Tariffs (GATT) and the World Trade Organization (WTO). How should such disputes be resolved? Are there other strategies that can be used to give teeth to international conservation programs? What about the dispute resolution procedures established in the Law of the Sea Convention? *See, e.g.*, Melinda P. Chandler, *Recent Developments in the Use of International Trade Restrictions as a Conservation Measure for Marine Resources*, in FREEDOM FOR THE SEAS IN THE 21ST CENTURY: OCEAN GOVERNANCE AND ENVIRONMENTAL HARMONY 327 (Jon M. Van Dyke, Durwood Zaelke, and Grant Hewison eds. 1993); Richard J. McLaughlin, *UNCLOS and the Demise of the United States' Use of Trade Sanctions to Protect Dolphins, Sea Turtles, Whales, and Other International Marine Living Resources*, 21 ECOLOGY L.Q. 1 (1994); John A. Duff, *Recent Applications of United States Laws to Conserve Marine Species Worldwide: Should Trade Sanctions Be Mandatory?* 2 OCEAN & COASTAL L.J. 1 (1996); Richard J. McLaughlin, *Settling Trade–Related Disputes Over the Protection of Marine Living Resources: UNCLOS or the WTO?* 10 GEO. INT'L ENVT'L L. REV. 29 (1997).

2. In May 1996, the U.S. State Department, following congressional statutes and court decisions, prohibited the importation of shrimp and shrimp products from all countries that do not require their commercial shrimp trawlers to use turtle-excluder devices (TEDs) to permit endangered sea turtles to escape from the nets to avoid drowning. In January 1997, Malaysia, Pakistan, and Thailand challenged this decision before the World Trade Organization, arguing that it violated the ban on quantitative import restrictions in the GATT. The United States argued that its ban was permitted by Article XX of the GATT, which contains the following language:

> Subject to the requirement that such measures are not applied in a manner which would constitute a means of arbitrary or unjustifiable discrimination between countries where the same conditions prevail, or a disguised restriction on international trade, nothing in this Agreement shall be construed to prevent the adoption or enforcement by any contracting party of measures: ...
>
> (b) necessary to protect human, animal or plant life or health; ...
>
> (g) relating to the conservation of exhaustible natural resources if such measures are made effective in conjunction with restrictions on domestic production or consumption.

The Appellate Body of the WTO agreed that the U.S. efforts were designed to conserve "exhaustible natural resources"; but in engaging in the "delicate balance" required by the introductory phrases in Article XX, the Body nonetheless ruled that the U.S. program violated the GATT because the U.S. program was too rigid in requiring one specific method of protecting turtles, rather than allowing each nation to develop its own strategies, and in banning all shrimp products from nations that do not require TEDs, even the shrimp products caught by those trawlers that do use TEDs. United States—Import Prohibition of Certain Shrimp and Shrimp Products, WTO Appellate Body, WTO Doc. WT/DS58/AB/R (Oct. 12, 1998); *see* 93 Am. J. Int'l L. 507 (1999).

3. In response to this decision of the WTO Appellate Body, the U.S. Department of State issued Revised Guidelines to permit the importation of TED-caught shrimp from states that do not have a comprehensive program requiring TEDs. The U.S. Court of International Trade ruled in April 1999 that this revision violated the governing congressional enactment, but stayed its decision until full government reports could be examined. Earth Island Institute v. Daley, 48 F. Supp.2d 1064 (C.I.T. 1999). If a congressional statute is unavoidably inconsistent with treaty-based international law articulated by a body established through a treaty the United States has ratified, which law governs at the international level and which law governs domestically? Recall Chapter 2.

4. The United States and other NATO countries have sought to use low-frequency active sonar to detect enemy submarines. This technology involves lowering loudspeakers into the oceans that emit sounds that are among the loudest ever put into the ocean and which have the capability of traveling for vast distances without much dissipation. Training exercises using this technology has led to strandings of marine mammals in various locations. What law governs the use of a new technology that may serve some military purpose but which appears likely to cause substantial damage to marine mammals and other marine creatures? *See* Jon M. Van Dyke, Emily A. Gardner, and Joseph R. Morgan, *Whales, Submarines, and Active Sonar*, in 18 Ocean Yearbook 330 (2004).

Chapter Seven

LAW OF AIRSPACE AND OUTER SPACE

SECTION 1. AIRSPACE

A. *Previous Legal Concepts and Early Norms*

Roman theory had considered ownership of air space to extend above owned territory to the outer reaches of the heavens. These concepts remained with the advent of balloons used for observation and travel in the Nineteenth Century and states claimed absolute sovereignty of the air space above their territory. Later theories would analogize to developments in the law of the sea and offer concepts of belts of air space where private international navigation would be permitted without special consent of the territorial state. World War I led to increased use of air space and recognition of the need for a multilateral agreement concerning territorial state controls and relative freedoms of air flight.

In 1919, the Paris Convention recognized in Article 1 thereof that "every Power has complete and exclusive sovereignty over the air space above its territory," a principle affirmed in the 1944 Chicago Convention, as noted below. Article 2 of the Paris Convention also recognized: "Each contracting State undertakes in time of peace to accord freedom of innocent passage above its territory to the aircraft of the other contracting states, provided that the conditions laid down in the present Convention are observed." Such conditions included the competence of the territorial state to prescribe routes and require aircraft to land for "reasons of general security." The freedom thus recognized, by consent among the treaty signatories, was a freedom of transit across a state (what would later be known as the first freedom) and not the freedom to land (what would later be known as the second freedom). In 1929, the Convention was amended to recognize: "Every contracting State may make conditional on its prior authorization the establishment of international airways and the creation and operation of regular international air navigation lines, with or without landing, on its territory." *See* Michael S. Simons, *Aviation Alliances: Implications for the Qantas–BA Alliance in the Asia Pacific Region*, 62 J. AIR L. & COM. 841 (1997); Jeswald W.

Salacuse, *The Little Prince and the Businessman: Conflicts and Tensions in Public International Air Law*, 45 J. Air L. & Com. 807 (1980).

Prior to the conference in Chicago in November of 1944 which led to the Chicago Convention, theories arose concerning the two freedoms and several others as well as various regimes that might be useful concerning commercial airlines. Five possible freedoms had been identified: (1) to fly across territory nonstop, (2) to land for non-traffic purposes (*e.g.*, merely to buy local fuel), (3) to take traffic (*e.g.*, passengers or cargo taken on for compensation) from the carrier's country to another country, (4) to bring traffic from a foreign country to the carrier's country, and (5) to pick up and discharge traffic at intermediate points between the carrier's country and a foreign country. The United States was in a clear position of dominance of the airline industry and was pressing for generally free competition and access to markets, while the British and others pressed for state controls or relative controls of commercial air transportation. Differences arose concerning scheduled and non-scheduled airline flights and landings for traffic (*e.g.*, to take on passengers and cargo for compensation) and non-traffic purposes (*e.g.*, to merely stop and purchase local fuel). These differences would be worked out over time with the adoption of the Chicago Convention (considered in subsection B 2), the International Air Services Transit Agreement (IASTA) (considered in subsection B 3), and various bilateral agreements among states. To generalize, the bilateral agreements would provide agreement in advance concerning routes and landings for traffic purposes. Patterns of bilateral arrangements still evidence disagreement whether a newer U.S. policy of freer competition should prevail or an older pattern involving significant state control of routes, frequency of flights and capacity (*i.e.*, number of seats) of aircraft.

B. *Allocation of Competencies and Privileges*

1. *Air Defense Identification Zones*

Beginning in the 1950s, states claimed the right to establish Air Defense Identification Zones (ADIZs) extending outward from their land territory, sometimes up to one hundred or two hundred miles. By analogy, similar defensive zones are claimed around a fleet of warships on the high seas. Foreign, or any, aircraft entering such a zone are required to identify themselves or be subject to "misidentification" and the use of force reasonably needed to force an unidentified aircraft to land or, if need be, to destroy the aircraft.

Are such zones consistent with the United Nations Charter? Are they consistent with the Law of the Sea Convention when an ADIZ extends beyond a coastal state's contiguous zone? When reading the materials below, consider whether provisions in the Chicago Convention or the International Air Services Transit Agreement change your answer. The International Civil Aviation Organization (ICAO) created by the Chicago Convention has developed detailed rules to be followed in cases of aerial interception, including those related to attempts to communicate with an unidentified aircraft. ICAO has also passed resolutions condemning states for their failure to comply with standards and practices during certain incidents.

Incidents involving the use of force have included the targeting of aircraft that had been warned away but continued to fly towards a potential military target or sensitive security facility. When Libyan fighter aircraft were headed for a U.S. military fleet in the Mediterranean Sea in an area claimed as a territorial sea by Libya extending far beyond a 24 mile territorial sea and contiguous zone, and would not divert, they were fired upon by U.S. vessels. Was the targeting of Libyan aircraft permissible? Would you like to know more facts?

What guidance exists in Article 51 of the U.N. Charter concerning the propriety of use of force to destroy what appears to be a civilian aircraft that is inside a coastal state's ADIZ, has been apparently warned by radio communication and military aircraft of the coastal state to turn and leave or land, but continues to fly towards a city containing a naval and air base? Would your answer be different if the apparently civilian aircraft had been ordered to land but turned around and was heading out of the ADIZ at the time that force was used to destroy the aircraft?

The targeting of Korean Air Lines flight 007 by Soviet fighter aircraft over the Sea of Japan in 1983 involved claims consistent with the last hypothetical. Would your answer change if the KAL 007 flight had involved more than a strayed passenger aircraft and super sensitive data was photographed or otherwise recorded during its flight over a secret Russian base, but the aircraft was leaving Russian airspace and was beyond a Russian territorial sea at the time of targeting? In 1984, the ICAO Council established under the Chicago Convention condemned the Soviet Union for the downing of KAL 007. *See* Resolution Adopted by the Council of the ICAO, March 6, 1984, *reprinted in* 23 I.L.M. 937 (1984). A similar incident in 1973 led to ICAO condemnation of Israel for the downing of a Libyan airliner that had strayed over occupied territory and, when confronted, had turned to fly out. Israel denied liability but paid some $30,000 to each family of the deceased in settlement of private claims.

In 1988, the U.S. vessel USS Vincennes shot down an Iranian airliner that had recently taken off from Teheran and was heading at high altitude over a U.S. naval fleet in the Persian Gulf. The destruction of the airliner led to the deaths of 290 persons. Iran brought a case against the U.S. in the I.C.J. The U.S. had claimed that it acted in self-defense, targeting a misidentified aircraft flying toward its naval fleet. Iran claimed that the U.S. used unlawful force. In 1996, the U.S. and Iran agreed to a settlement whereby the U.S. would pay $300,000 to the survivors of each wage-earning victim and $150,000 to the survivors of each non-wage-earning victim. See Iran Air ICJ Case and Certain Iran–

U.S. Claims Tribunal Bank Claims–Settlement, 90 Am. J. Int'l L. 278 (1996). If the I.C.J. case had gone forward, what sort of facts would you, as a Justice deciding the case, have liked to know? How might you have ruled, why?

2. *The Chicago Convention*

[read the Convention on International Civil Aviation (The Chicago Convention) in the Documents Supplement]

Introductory Problem

RedEx Airline, from Cuba, has recently flown its aircraft into Florida on an ad hoc basis. The RedEx aircraft have picked up mail and cargo from the United States and delivered such to Cuba, paying local airport fees and using local refueling and repair facilities. Some RedEx aircraft also fly across the U.S. to land in Toronto on an ad hoc basis for similar purposes. Airlines from Mexico and a few other Caribbean countries are engaged in the same activities.

A U.S. Senator from North Carolina is eager to stop or limit such flights and has introduced legislation to ban RedEx airline flights from U.S. airspace.

Are there any international legal issues presented by the legislative proposal? Can RedEx be banned or limited? Cuba and the U.S. have ratified the Chicago Convention.

Notes and Questions

1. Under the Chicago Convention, are military aircraft permitted to transit nonstop on a nonscheduled mission across the territory of another signatory? Are civilian airlines that are owned by the foreign state? Are balloon flights? See Article 3.

2. What types of flights are covered under Article 5?

3. Can a scheduled commercial airliner enter and land when it is in serious distress? See Articles 5 and 6. Article 25 adds: "Each contracting State undertakes to provide such measures of assistance to aircraft in distress in its territory as it may find practicable, and to permit, subject to control by its own authorities, the owners of aircraft or authorities of the State in which the aircraft is registered to provide such measures of assistance as may be necessitated by the circumstances. Each contracting State, when undertaking search for missing aircraft, will collaborate in coordinated measures which may be recommended from time to time pursuant to this Convention."

4. Does ICAO have delegated power under Articles 37 and 54 to set standards that bind contracting states that might disagree with such standards?

3. The International Air Services Transit Agreement

INTERNATIONAL AIR SERVICES TRANSIT AGREEMENT (IASTA)

84 U.N.T.S. 389, 59 Stat. 1693 (1944).

Article I

Section 1

Each contracting State grants to the other contracting States the following freedoms of the air in respect of scheduled international air services:

(1) The privilege to fly across its territory without landing;

(2) The privilege to land for non-traffic purposes.

The privileges of this section shall not be applicable with respect to airports utilized for military purposes to the exclusion of any scheduled international air services. In areas of active hostilities or of military occupation, and in time of war along the supply routes leading to such areas, the exercise of such privileges shall be subject to the approval of the competent military authorities....

Section 4

Each contracting State may, subject to the provisions of this Agreement,

(1) Designate the route to be followed within its territory by any international air service and the airports which any such service may use;

(2) Impose or permit to be imposed on any such service just and reasonable charges for the use of such airports and other facilities; these charges shall not be higher than would be paid for the use of such airports and facilities by its national aircraft engaged in similar international services: provided that, upon representation by an interested contracting State, the charges imposed for the use of airports and other facilities shall be subject to review by the Council of the International Civil Aviation Organization established under the [Chicago] Convention, which shall report and make recommendations thereon for the consideration of the State or States concerned....

Section 5

Each contracting State reserves the right to withhold or revoke a certificate or permit to an air transport enterprise of another State in any case where it is not satisfied that substantial ownership and effective control are vested in nationals of a contracting State, or in case of failure of such air transport enterprise to comply with the laws of the State over which it operates, or to perform its obligations under this Agreement....

Notes and Questions

1. In view of Article I, Sec. 1, of IASTA, can a territorial state require an airliner to land when reasonably necessary for public safety or national security? If under the Chicago Convention a territorial state can require such a landing does that affect your interpretation of IASTA?

2. Under the Chicago Convention and/or IASTA, can the United States preclude a Cuban airliner from either scheduled or nonscheduled flights across the U.S. to land in Canada? All three countries are signatories to both treaties.

3. Under the Chicago Convention and/or IASTA, can a private U.S. citizen fly her plane from Seattle to land in Toronto during her vacation?

4. No-fly zones over Iraq and Bosnia–Herzegovina in the 1990s were established pursuant to United Nations Security Council resolutions. In case of a clash between such no-fly zone regulations and the Chicago Convention and/or IASTA, which competencies prevail? Why?

4. The Warsaw Convention and Liability

Introductory Problem

Hope Eternal purchased an E-ticket for a flight on Land Air from San Francisco to Singapore with a return through Alaska back to San Francisco. While traveling back from Alaska to San Francisco, the aircraft suddenly dropped 2,000 feet, greatly frightening Hope and the other passengers. Later during the ill-fated flight, it was announced that there was an electric fire onboard and that the aircraft may have to crash land in Canada because of a noticeable loss of power. This also greatly frightened the passengers. Even later, the aircraft did make a nonscheduled emergency landing in Canada during which Hope was seriously injured with head, neck and upper body injuries. Two weeks after the mishap, Hope also had a miscarriage, losing her three-month old fetus.

Hope has consulted you for advice as to the type and amount of liability that Land Air has with respect to her injuries. She wants to obtain money for her medical expenses, general injuries, pain and suffering, emotional stress and continuous emotional suffering, other losses, as well as damages sufficient to punish the airline. What would you advise?

CONVENTION FOR THE UNIFICATION OF CERTAIN RULES RELATING TO INTERNATIONAL TRANSPORTATION BY AIR [THE WARSAW CONVENTION]

[read the extracts of the Convention in the Documents Supplement]

Notes and Questions

1. Is a flight on a U.S. air carrier from New York, with a stop in Toronto, Canada, to Anchorage, Alaska covered by the Warsaw Convention?

2. Subsequently, a special contract under the Convention entered into by private air carriers, the Montreal Intercarrier Agreement, functionally

amended the Warsaw Convention's extent and limits of liability concerning passengers and baggage (*e.g.*, Articles 20–22). The limits concerning loss of life or injury to passengers has been presently increased to $75,000 per passenger. Check your next international air ticket for the fine print concerning "Advice to International Passengers on Limitation of Liability." As a "trade off" the carriers are now liable without fault. *See, e.g.*, *In re* Korean Air Lines Disaster of September 1, 1983, 664 F.Supp. 1463 (D.D.C. 1985), *aff'd*, 829 F.2d 1171 (D.C.Cir.1987), *aff'd sub nom.*, Chan v. Korean Air Lines, 490 U.S. 122 (1989).

In that case, plaintiffs tried to avoid liability limits by arguing that a ticket with notice of the limits of liability printed in type smaller than 10–point type did not comply with the Montreal Intercarrier Agreement and did not provide adequate notice to passengers and, thus, that a ticket was not delivered within the meaning of Article 3 of the Warsaw Convention. The U.S. Supreme Court overturned an "American rule" (requiring adequate notice) adopted in several other circuits that would have supported plaintiff's arguments and the Court affirmed the decisions below that a ticket had been "delivered" within the meaning of Article 3.

3. What articles in the Warsaw Convention other than article 3 might allow a claim to avoid limits of liability? What must be proven?

4. Under Article 17 of the Convention, are damages for emotional stress permissible? The U.S. Supreme Court has held that mere mental anguish, without additional physical injury or physical manifestation of injury, is not recoverable under the Warsaw Convention's phrase (in the authoritative French) *lésion corporelle*, which the Court concluded to mean bodily injury. See Eastern Airlines v. Floyd, 499 U.S. 530 (1991).

5. Under Article 17 of the Convention, are punitive damages permissible? The Second and D.C. Circuits have held that damages under Article 17 are limited to compensatory damages. *See, e.g.*, *In re* Air Disaster at Lockerbie, Scotland, 928 F.2d 1267 (2d Cir.1991); *In re* Korean Air Lines Disaster of September 1, 1983, 932 F.2d 1475 (D.C.Cir.1991).

If Article 25 is applicable, are punitive damages excluded or permissible?

ZICHERMAN v. KOREAN AIR LINES CO., LTD.

516 U.S. 217 (1996).

SCALIA, J.

This action presents the question whether, in a suit brought under Article 17 of the Warsaw Convention ... , a plaintiff may recover damages for loss of society resulting from the death of a relative in a plane crash on the high seas.

On September 1, 1983, Korean Air Lines Flight KE007, en route from Anchorage, Alaska, to Seoul, South Korea, strayed into air space of the Soviet Union and was shot down over the Sea of Japan. All 269 persons on board were killed, including Muriel Kole. Petitioners Marjorie Zicherman and Muriel Mahalek, Kole's sister and mother, respectively, sued respondent Korean Air Lines Co., Ltd. (KAL), in the United States

District Court for the Southern District of New York. Petitioners' final amended complaint contained three counts, entitled, respectively, "Warsaw Convention," "Death on the High Seas Act," and "Conscious Pain and Suffering." At issue here is only the Warsaw Convention count, in which petitioners sought "judgment against KAL for their pecuniary damages, for their grief and mental anguish, for the loss of the decedent's society and companionship, and for the decedent's conscious pain and suffering."

Along with other federal-court actions arising out of the KAL crash, petitioners' case was transferred to the United States District Court for the District of Columbia for consolidated proceedings on common issues of liability. There, a jury found that the destruction of Flight KE007 was proximately caused by "willful misconduct" of the flight crew, thus lifting the Warsaw Convention's $75,000 cap on damages. See Warsaw Convention, Art. 25, 49 Stat. 3020; Order of Civil Aeronautics Board Approving Increases in Liability Limitations of Warsaw Convention and Hague Protocol, reprinted in note following 49 U.S.C. App. § 1502 (1988 ed.). The jury awarded $50 million in punitive damages against KAL. The Court of Appeals for the District of Columbia Circuit upheld the finding of "willful misconduct," but vacated the punitive damages award, holding that the Warsaw Convention does not permit the recovery of punitive damages. *In re* Korean Air Lines Disaster of Sept. 1, 1983, 932 F.2d 1475, 1479–1481, 1484–1490, *cert. denied*, 502 U.S. 994 (1991). The individual cases were then remanded by the Judicial Panel on Multidistrict Litigation to the original transferor courts for trial of compensatory damages issues.

At petitioners' damages trial in the Southern District of New York, KAL moved for determination that the Death on the High Seas Act (DOHSA), 41 Stat. 537, 46 U.S.C. App. § 761 *et seq.* (1988 ed.), prescribed the proper claimants and the recoverable damages, and that it did not permit damages for loss of society. The District Court denied the motion and held, *inter alia*, that petitioners could recover for loss of "love, affection, and companionship." *In re* Korean Air Lines Disaster of Sept. 1, 1983, 807 F. Supp. 1073, 1086–1088 (1992). The jury awarded loss-of-society damages in the amount of $70,000 to Zicherman and $28,000 to Mahalek.

The Court of Appeals for the Second Circuit set aside this award. Applying its prior decisions in *In re* Air Disaster at Lockerbie, Scotland, on Dec. 21, 1988, 928 F.2d 1267, 1278–1279 (Lockerbie I), *cert. denied sub nom.*, Rein v. Pan American World Airways, Inc., 502 U.S. 920 ... (1991), and *In re* Air Disaster at Lockerbie, Scotland, on Dec. 21, 1988, 37 F.3d 804 (1994) (Lockerbie II), *cert. denied sub nom.*, Pan American World Airways, Inc. v. Pagnucco, 513 U.S. 1126 ... (1995), it held that general maritime law supplied the substantive law of compensatory damages to be applied in an action under the Warsaw Convention. 43 F.3d 18, 21–22 (1994). Then, following its decision in Lockerbie II, it held that, under general maritime law, a plaintiff is entitled to recover loss-of-society damages, but only if he was a dependent of the decedent at the time of death. 43 F.3d at 22. The court concluded that as a matter of law Mahalek had not established that status, and therefore vacated her award; it remanded to the District Court for determination of whether Zicherman was a dependent of Kole. *Ibid.*

In their petition for certiorari, petitioners contended that under general maritime law dependency is not a requirement for recovering loss-of-society damages. In a cross-petition, KAL contended that the Warsaw Convention does not allow loss-of-society damages in this case, regardless of dependency. We granted certiorari. 514 U.S. 1062 (1995).

Article 17 of the Warsaw Convention, as set forth in the official American translation of the governing French text, provides as follows: "The carrier shall be liable for *damage sustained* in the event of the death or wounding of a passenger or any other bodily injury suffered by a passenger, if the accident which caused the damage so sustained took place on board the aircraft or in the course of any of the operations of embarking or disembarking." 49 Stat. 3018 (emphasis added).

The first and principal question before us is whether loss of society of a relative is made recoverable by this provision.

It is obvious that the English word "damage" or "harm"—or in the official text of the Convention, the French word "*dommage*"—can be applied to an extremely wide range of phenomena, from the medical expenses incurred as a result of Kole's injuries (for which every legal system would provide tort compensation) to the mental distress of some stranger who reads about Kole's death in the paper (for which no legal system would provide tort compensation). It cannot seriously be maintained that Article 17 uses the term in this broadest sense, thus exploding tort liability beyond what any legal system in the world allows, to the farthest reaches of what could be denominated "harm." We therefore reject petitioners' initial proposal that we simply look to English dictionary definitions of "damage" and apply that term's "plain meaning."

There are only two thinkable alternatives to that. First, what petitioners ultimately suggest: that "*dommage*" means what French law, in 1929, recognized as *legally cognizable* harm, which petitioners assert included not only "*dommage matériel*" (pecuniary harm of various sorts) but also "*dommage moral*" (nonpecuniary harm of various sorts, including loss of society). In support of that approach, petitioners point out that in a prior case involving Article 17 we were guided by French legal usage: Air France v. Saks, 470 U.S. 392 . . . (1985) (interpreting the term "*accident*"). See also Eastern Airlines, Inc. v. Floyd, 499 U.S. 530 . . . (1991) (interpreting the Article 17 term "*lésion corporelle*"). What is at issue here, however, is not simply whether we will be guided by French legal usage *vel non*. Because, as earlier discussed, the dictionary meaning of the term "*dommage*" embraces harms that no legal system would compensate, it must be acknowledged that the term is to be understood in its distinctively *legal* sense—that is, to mean only *legally cognizable* harm. The nicer question, and the critical one here, is whether the word "*dommage*" establishes as the content of the concept "*legally cognizable harm*" what French law accepted as such in 1929. No case of ours provides precedent for the adoption of French law in such detail. In *Floyd,* we looked to French law to determine whether "*lésion corporelle*" indeed meant (as it had been translated) "bodily injury"—not to determine the subsequent question (equivalent to the question at issue here) whether "bodily injury" encompassed psychic injury. See *id.* at 536–540. And in *Saks,* once we had determined that in French legal terminology the word "*accident*" referred to an unforeseen event, we did not further inquire whether French courts would consider the event at issue in the case unforeseen; we made that judgment for ourselves. See 470 U.S. at 405–407.

It is particularly implausible that "the shared expectations of the contracting parties," 470 U.S. at 399, were that their mere use of the French language would effect adoption of the precise rule applied in France as to what constitutes legally cognizable harm. Those involved in the negotiation and adoption of the Convention could not have been ignorant of the fact that the law on this point varies widely from jurisdiction to jurisdiction, and even from statute to statute within a single jurisdiction. Just as we found it "unlikely" in *Floyd* that Convention signatories would have understood the general term "*lésion corporelle*" to confer a cause of action available under French law but unrecognized in many other nations, see 499 U.S. at 540, so also in the present case we find it unlikely that they would have understood Article 17's use of the general term "*dommage*" to require compensation for elements of harm recognized in France but unrecognized elsewhere, or to forbid compensation for elements of harm *unrecognized* in France but recognized elsewhere. Many signatory nations, including Czechoslovakia, Denmark, Germany, the Netherlands, the Soviet Union, and Sweden, did not, even many years after the Warsaw Convention, recognize a cause of action for nonpecuniary harm resulting from wrongful death. See 11 International Encyclopedia of Comparative Law: Torts, ch. 9, pp. 15–18 (A. Tunc ed. 1972); *Floyd, supra,* 499 U.S. at 544–545, n.10.

The other alternative, and the only one we think realistic, is to believe that "*dommage*" means (as it does in French legal usage) "legally cognizable harm," but that Article 17 leaves it to adjudicating courts to specify what harm is cognizable....

The post-ratification conduct of the contracting parties displays the same understanding that the damages recoverable—so long as they consist of compensation for harm incurred ("*dommage survenu*")—are to be determined by domestic law. Some countries, including England, Germany and the Netherlands, have adopted domestic legislation to govern the types of damages recoverable in a Convention case. See Haanappel, *The right to sue in death cases under the Warsaw Convention,* 6 Air Law 66, 72, 74 (1981); E. Giemulla, R. Schmid, & P. Ehlers, Warsaw Convention 39, n.5 (1992); German Law Concerning Air Navigation (Luft VG) of Jan. 10, 1959, Arts. 35–36, 38, *reprinted in* 1 Senate Committee on Commerce, Air Laws and Treaties of the World, 89th

Cong., 1st Sess., 766–768 (Comm. Print 1965); R. Mankiewicz, The Liability Regime of the International Air Carrier ¶ 187, pp. 160–161 (1981). Canada has adopted legislation setting forth who may bring suit under Article 24(2), but has left the question of what types of damages are recoverable to provincial law. Haanappel, *supra*, at 70–71. The Court of Appeals of Quebec has rejected the argument that Article 17 permits damages unrecoverable under domestic Quebec law. Dame Surprenant v. Air Canada, [1973] C.A. 107, 117–118, 126–127 (opinion of Deschenes, J.). *But see* Preston v. Hunting Air Transport Ltd., [1956] 1 Q.B. 454, 461–462 (granting damages under Convention, but without considering Article 24). Finally, the expert commentators are virtually unanimous that the type of harm compensable is to be determined by domestic law. *See, e.g.*, H. Drion, Limitation of Liabilities in International Air Law ¶ 111, pp. 125–126 (1954); Giemulla, Schmid, & Ehlers, *supra*, at 33; D. Goedhuis, National Airlegislations and the Warsaw Convention 269 (1937); Mankiewicz, *supra*, ¶ 187, pp. 160–161; G. Miller, Liability in International Air Transport: The Warsaw System in Municipal Courts 125 (1977); *see also* Cha, *The Air Carrier's Liability to Passengers in International Law*, 7 Air L. Rev. 25, 56–57 (1936). . . .

We conclude that Articles 17 and 24(2) of the Warsaw Convention permit compensation only for legally cognizable harm, but leave the specification of what harm is legally cognizable to the domestic law applicable under the forum's choice-of-law rules. Where, as here, an airplane crash occurs on the high seas, DOHSA supplies the substantive United States law. Because DOHSA permits only pecuniary damages, petitioners are not entitled to recover for loss of society. We therefore need not reach the question whether, under general maritime law, dependency is a prerequisite for loss-of-society damages. . . .

Notes and Questions

1. Can a new treaty set standards "beyond what any legal system in the world allows"? In view of your answer, would you have decided the last case differently?

2. Should the "ordinary" or "plain" meaning of the terms of a treaty be used for interpretation purposes? Recall Vienna Convention on the Law of Treaties, art. 31. When inquiring into the "shared expectations" of the treaty signatories, is it enough to identify what "many," as opposed to most, states expect or do? Further, is it enough to identify what they expect or do as a matter of domestic law?

3. Should domestic law govern types of recovery under a multilateral treaty? Is such consistent with the general goal of uniformity? Articles 21 and 25(1) allow some forms of domestic law to be used.

4. The Warsaw Convention is a self-executing treaty which requires no implementing legislation. *See, e.g.*, Trans World Airlines, Inc. v. Franklin Mint Corp., 466 U.S. 243, 252 (1984).

EL AL ISRAEL AIRLINES, LTD. v. TSENG

525 U.S. 155 (1999).

GINSBURG, J.

Plaintiff-respondent Tsui Yuan Tseng was subjected to an intrusive security search at John F. Kennedy International Airport in New York before she boarded an El Al Israel Airlines May 22, 1993 flight to Tel Aviv. Tseng seeks tort damages from El Al for this occurrence. The episode-in-suit, both parties now submit, does not qualify as an "accident" within the meaning of the treaty popularly known as the Warsaw Convention, which governs air carrier liability for "all international transportation." Tseng alleges psychic or psychosomatic injuries, but no "bodily injury," as that term is used in the Convention. Her case presents a question of the Convention's exclusivity: When the Convention allows no recovery for the episode-in-suit, does it correspondingly preclude the passenger from maintaining an action for damages under another source of law, in this case, New York tort law?

The exclusivity question before us has been settled prospectively in a Warsaw Convention protocol (Montreal Protocol No. 4) recently ratified [sic] by the Senate. [Montreal Protocol No. 4 to Amend the Convention for the Unification of Certain Rules Relating to International Carriage By Air, signed at Warsaw on October 12, 1929, as amended by the Protocol Done at the Hague on September 8, 1955 (hereinafter Montreal Protocol No. 4), reprinted in S. Exec. Rep. No. 105–20, pp. 21–32 (1998)] In accord with the protocol, Tseng concedes, a passenger whose injury is not compensable under the Convention (because it entails no "bodily injury" or was not the result of an "accident") will have no recourse to an alternate remedy. We conclude that the protocol, to which the United States has now subscribed, clarifies, but does not change, the Convention's exclusivity domain. We therefore hold that recovery for a personal injury suffered "on board [an] aircraft or in the course of any of the operations of embarking or disembarking," Art. 17, 49 Stat. 3018, if not allowed under the Convention, is not available at all....

I

We have twice reserved decision on the Convention's exclusivity. In Air France v. Saks, 470 U.S. 392 ... (1985), we concluded that a passenger's injury was not caused by an "accident" for which the airline could be held accountable under the Convention, but expressed no view whether that passenger could maintain "a state cause of action for negligence." *Id.* at 408. In Eastern Airlines, Inc. v. Floyd, 499 U.S. 530 ... (1991), we held that mental or psychic injuries unaccompanied by physical injuries are not compensable under Article 17 of the Convention, but declined to reach the question whether the Convention "provides the exclusive cause of action for injuries sustained during international air transportation." *Id.* at 553. We resolve in this case the question on which we earlier reserved judgment.

At the outset, we highlight key provisions of the treaty we are interpreting. Chapter I of the Warsaw Convention, entitled "Scope–Definitions," declares in Article 1(1) that the "Convention shall apply to all international transportation of persons, baggage, or goods performed by aircraft for hire." 49 Stat. 3014. Chapter III, entitled "Liability of the Carrier," defines in Articles 17, 18, and 19 the three kinds of liability for which the Convention provides. Article 17 establishes the conditions of liability for personal injury to passengers. . . .

II

With the key treaty provisions as the backdrop, we next describe the episode-in-suit. On May 22, 1993, Tsui Yuan Tseng arrived at John F. Kennedy International Airport (hereinafter JFK) to board an El Al Israel Airlines flight to Tel Aviv. In conformity with standard El Al preboarding procedures, a security guard questioned Tseng about her destination and travel plans. The guard considered Tseng's responses "illogical," and ranked her as a "high risk" passenger. Tseng was taken to a private security room where her baggage and person were searched for explosives and detonating devices. She was told to remove her shoes, jacket, and sweater, and to lower her blue jeans to midhip. A female security guard then searched Tseng's body outside her clothes by hand and with an electronic security wand.

After the search, which lasted 15 minutes, El Al personnel decided that Tseng did not pose a security threat and allowed her to board the flight. Tseng later testified that she "was really sick and very upset" during the flight, that she was "emotionally traumatized and disturbed" during her month-long trip in Israel, and that, upon her return, she underwent medical and psychiatric treatment for the lingering effects of the body search. . . .

Tseng filed suit against El Al in 1994 in a New York state court of first instance. Her complaint alleged a state law personal injury claim based on the May 22, 1993 episode at JFK. Tseng's pleading charged, *inter alia*, assault and false imprisonment, but alleged no bodily injury. El Al removed the case to federal court. . . .

[from the Court's footnote 9: The District Court, "using the flexible application prescribed by the Supreme Court," concluded that El Al's search of Tseng was an "accident": "[A] routine search, applied erroneously to plaintiff in the course of embarking on the aircraft, is fairly accurately characterized as an accident." 919 F. Supp. 155, 158 (S.D.N.Y. 1996).]

The Court of Appeals disagreed. That court described security searches as "routine" in international air travel, part of a terrorism-prevention effort that is "widely recognized and encouraged in the law," and "the price passengers pay for the degree of airline safety so far afforded them." 122 F.3d at 103. The court observed that passengers reasonably should be aware of "routine operating procedures" of the kind El Al conducts daily. *Ibid.* The risk of mistakes, *i.e.*, that innocent persons will be erroneously searched, is "inherent in any effort to detect malefactors," the court explained. *Ibid.* Tseng thus encountered "ordinary events and procedures of air transportation," the court concluded, and not "an unexpected or unusual event." *Id.* at 104.

It is questionable whether the Court of Appeals "flexibly applied" the definition of "accident" we set forth in *Saks*. Both parties, however, now accept the Court of Appeals' disposition of that issue. In any event, even if El Al's search of Tseng was an "accident," the core question of the Convention's exclusivity would remain. The Convention provides for compensation under Article 17 only when the passenger suffers "death, physical injury, or physical manifestation of injury," Eastern Airlines, Inc. v. Floyd, 499 U.S. 530, 552 ... (1991), a condition that both the District Court and the Court of Appeals determined Tseng did not meet, see 919 F. Supp. at 158; 122 F.3d 99 at 104. The question whether the Convention precludes an action under local law when a passenger's claim fails to satisfy Article 17's conditions for liability does not turn on which of those conditions the claim fails to satisfy.

Article 24 of the Convention, the Court of Appeals said, "clearly states that resort to local law is precluded only where the incident is 'covered' by Article 17, meaning where there has been an accident, either on the plane or in the course of embarking or disembarking, which led to death, wounding or other bodily injury." *Id.* at 104–105. The court found support in the drafting history of the Convention, which it construed to "indicate that national law was intended to provide the passenger's remedy where the Convention did not expressly apply." *Id.* at 105. The Second Circuit also rejected the argument that allowance of state-law claims when the Convention does not permit recovery would contravene the treaty's goal of uniformity. The court read our decision in Zicherman v. Korean Air Lines Co., 516 U.S. 217 ... (1996), to "instruct specifically that the Convention expresses no compelling interest in uniformity that would warrant ... supplanting an otherwise applicable body of law." 122 F.3d at 107.

III

We accept it as given that El Al's search of Tseng was not an "accident" within the meaning of Article 17, for the parties do not place that Court of Appeals conclusion at issue.... We also accept, again only for purposes of this decision, that El Al's actions did not constitute "wilful misconduct"; accordingly, we confront no issue under Article 25 of the Convention.... The parties do not dispute that the episode-in-suit occurred in international transportation in the course of embarking.

Our inquiry begins with the text of Article 24, which prescribes the exclusivity of the Convention's provisions for air carrier liability. "It is our responsibility to give the specific words of the treaty a meaning consistent with the shared expectations of the contracting parties." *Saks*, 470 U.S. at 399. "Because a treaty ratified by the United States is not only the law of this land, see U.S. Const., Art. II, § 2, but also an agreement among sovereign powers, we have traditionally considered as aids to its interpretation the negotiating and drafting history (*travaux préparatoires*) and the postratification understanding of the contracting parties." *Zicherman*, 516 U.S. at 226. Article 24 provides that "cases covered by article 17"—or in the governing French text, "*les cas prevus a l'article 17*"—may "only be brought subject to the conditions and limits set out in the Convention." 49 Stat. 3020. That prescription is not a model of the clear drafter's art. We recognize that the words lend themselves to divergent interpretation.

In Tseng's view, and in the view of the Court of Appeals, "*les cas prevus a l'article 17*" [in the authoritative French version of Article 24(2): "the cases anticipated by Article 17"] means those cases in which a passenger could actually maintain a claim for relief under Article 17. So read, Article 24 would permit any passenger whose personal injury suit did not satisfy the liability conditions of Article 17 to pursue the claim under local law.

In El Al's view, on the other hand, and in the view of the United States as *amicus curiae*, "*les cas prevus a l'article 17*" refers generically to all personal injury cases stemming from occurrences on board an aircraft or in embarking or disembarking, and simply distinguishes that class of cases (Article 17 cases) from cases involving damaged luggage or goods, or delay (which Articles 18 and 19 address). So read, Article 24 would preclude a passenger from asserting any air transit personal injury claims under local law, including claims that failed to satisfy Article 17's liability conditions, notably, because the injury did not result from an "accident," see *Saks*, 470 U.S. at 405, or because the "accident" did not result in physical injury or physical manifestation of injury, see *Floyd*, 499 U.S. at 552. Respect is ordinarily due the reasonable views of the Executive Branch concerning the meaning of an international treaty. See Sumitomo Shoji America, Inc. v. Avagliano, 457 U.S. 176, 184–185 ... (1982) ("Although not conclusive, the meaning attributed to treaty provisions by the Government agencies charged with their negotiation and enforcement is entitled to great weight."). We conclude that the Government's construction of Article 24 is most faithful to the Convention's text, purpose, and overall structure.

The cardinal purpose of the Warsaw Convention, we have observed, is to "achieve uniformity of rules governing claims arising from international air transportation." *Floyd*, 499 U.S. at 552; see *Zicherman*, 516 U.S. at 230. The Convention signatories, in the treaty's preamble, specifically "recognized the advantage of regulating in a uniform manner the conditions of ... the liability of the carrier." ... Given the Convention's comprehensive scheme of liability rules and its textual emphasis on uniformity, we would be hard put to conclude that the delegates at Warsaw meant to subject air carriers to the distinct, nonuniform liability rules of the individual signatory nations.

The Court of Appeals looked to our precedent for guidance on this point, but it misperceived our meaning. It misread our decision in

Zicherman to say that the Warsaw Convention expresses no compelling interest in uniformity that would warrant preempting an otherwise applicable body of law, here New York tort law. See 122 F.3d at 107.... *Zicherman* acknowledges that the Convention centrally endeavors "to foster uniformity in the law of international air travel." 516 U.S. at 230. It further recognizes that the Convention addresses the question whether there is airline liability *vel non*. See *id.* at 231. The *Zicherman* case itself involved auxiliary issues: who may seek recovery in lieu of passengers, and for what harms they may be compensated. See *id.* at 221, 227. Looking to the Convention's text, negotiating and drafting history, contracting states' postratification understanding of the Convention, and scholarly commentary, the Court in *Zicherman* determined that Warsaw drafters intended to resolve whether there is liability, but to leave to domestic law (the local law identified by the forum under its choice of law rules or approaches) determination of the compensatory damages available to the suitor. See *id.* at 231.

A complementary purpose of the Convention is to accommodate or balance the interests of passengers seeking recovery for personal injuries, and the interests of air carriers seeking to limit potential liability. Before the Warsaw accord, injured passengers could file suits for damages, subject only to the limitations of the forum's laws, including the forum's choice of law regime. This exposure inhibited the growth of the then-fledgling international airline industry. See *Floyd*, 499 U.S. at 546; Lowenfeld & Mendelsohn, *The United States and the Warsaw Convention*, 80 HARV. L. REV. 497, 499–500 (1967). Many international air carriers at that time endeavored to require passengers, as a condition of air travel, to relieve or reduce the carrier's liability in case of injury. See Second International Conference on Private Aeronautical Law, October 4–12, 1929, Warsaw, Minutes 47 (R. Horner & D. Legrez transls. 1975) (hereinafter Minutes). The Convention drafters designed Articles 17, 22, and 24 of the Convention as a compromise between the interests of air carriers and their customers worldwide. In Article 17 of the Convention, carriers are denied the contractual prerogative to exclude or limit their liability for personal injury. In Articles 22 and 24, passengers are limited in the amount of damages they may recover, and are restricted in the claims they may pursue by the conditions and limits set out in the Convention. Construing the Convention, as did the Court of Appeals, to allow passengers to pursue claims under local law when the Convention does not permit recovery could produce several anomalies. Carriers might be exposed to unlimited liability under diverse legal regimes, but would be prevented, under the treaty, from contracting out of such liability. Passengers injured physically in an emergency landing might be subject to the liability caps of the Convention, while those merely traumatized in the same mishap would be free to sue outside of the Convention for potentially unlimited damages. The Court of Appeals' construction of the Convention would encourage artful pleading by plaintiffs seeking to opt out of the Convention's liability scheme when local law promised recovery in excess of that prescribed by the treaty.

See Potter v. Delta Air Lines, Inc., 98 F.3d 881, 886 (C.A.5 1996). Such a reading would scarcely advance the predictability that adherence to the treaty has achieved worldwide....

The drafting history of Article 17 is consistent with our understanding of the preemptive effect of the Convention. The preliminary draft of the Convention submitted to the conference at Warsaw made air carriers liable "in the case of death, wounding, or any other bodily injury suffered by a traveler." Minutes 264; see *Saks*, 470 U.S. at 401. In the later draft that prescribed what is now Article 17, airline liability was narrowed to encompass only bodily injury caused by an "accident." See Minutes 205. It is improbable that, at the same time the drafters narrowed the conditions of air carrier liability in Article 17, they intended, in Article 24, to permit passengers to skirt those conditions by pursuing claims under local law.

Inspecting the drafting history, the Court of Appeals stressed a proposal made by the Czechoslovak delegation to state in the treaty that, in the absence of a stipulation in the Convention itself, " 'the provisions of laws and national rules relative to carriage in each [signatory] State shall apply.' "122 F.3d at 105 (*quoting* Minutes 176). That proposal was withdrawn upon amendment of the Convention's title to read: "Convention for the Unification of Certain Rules Relating to International Transportation by Air" 49 Stat. 3014; see 122 F.3d at 105. The Second Circuit saw in this history an indication "that national law was intended to provide the passenger's remedy where the Convention did not expressly apply." 122 F.3d at 105.

The British House of Lords, in Sidhu v. British Airways plc, [1997] 1 All E.R. 193, considered the same history, but found it inconclusive. Inclusion of the word "certain" in the Convention's title, the Lords reasoned, accurately indicated that "the Convention is concerned with certain rules only, not with all the rules relating to international carriage by air." *Id.* at 204. For example, the Convention does not say "anything ... about the carrier's obligations of insurance, and in particular about compulsory insurance against third party risks." *Ibid.* The Convention, in other words, is "a partial harmonization, directed to the particular issues with which it deals," *ibid.*, among them, a carrier's liability to passengers for personal injury. As to those issues, the Lords concluded, "the aim of the Convention is to unify." *Ibid.* Pointing to the overall understanding that the Convention's objective was to "ensure uniformity," *id.* at 209, the Lords suggested that the Czechoslovak delegation may have meant only to underscore that national law controlled "chapters of law relating to international carriage by air with which the Convention was not attempting to deal." *Ibid.* In light of the Lords' exposition, we are satisfied that the withdrawn Czechoslovak proposal will not bear the weight the Court of Appeals placed on it.

Montreal Protocol No. 4, ratified [sic] by the Senate on September 28, 1998, amends Article 24 to read, in relevant part: "In the carriage of passengers and baggage, any action for damages, however founded, can only be brought subject to the conditions and limits set out in this Convention...." [Court's footnote 15]: Article 24, as amended by Montreal Protocol No. 4, provides:

"1. In the carriage of passengers and baggage, any action for damages, however founded, can only be brought subject to the conditions and limits set out in this Convention, without prejudice to the question as to who are the persons who have the right to bring suit and what are their respective rights.

"2. In the carriage of cargo, any action for damages, however founded, whether under this Convention or in contract or in tort or otherwise, can only be brought subject to the conditions and limits of liability set out in this Convention without prejudice to the question as to who are the persons who have the right to bring suit and what are their respective rights. Such limits of liability constitute maximum limits and may not be exceeded whatever the circumstances which gave rise to the liability." [S. Exec. Rep. No. 105–20, at 29.] Both parties agree that, under the amended Article 24, the Convention's preemptive effect is clear: The treaty precludes passengers from bringing actions under local law when they cannot establish air carrier liability under the treaty. Revised Article 24, El Al urges and we agree, merely clarifies, it does not alter, the Convention's rule of exclusivity.

Supporting the position that revised Article 24 provides for preemption not earlier established, Tseng urges that federal preemption of state law is disfavored generally, and particularly when matters of health and safety are at stake. See Brief for Respondent 31–33. See also post ... ("[A] treaty, like an Act of Congress, should not be construed to preempt state law unless its intent to do so is clear.") (Stevens, J., dissenting). Tseng overlooks in this regard that the nation-state, not subdivisions within one nation, is the focus of the Convention and the perspective of our treaty partners. Our home-centered preemption analysis, therefore, should not be applied, mechanically, in construing our international obligations. Decisions of the courts of other Convention signatories corroborate our understanding of the Convention's preemptive effect. In *Sidhu*, the British House of Lords considered and decided the very question we now face concerning the Convention's exclusivity when a passenger alleges psychological damages, but no physical injury, resulting from an occurrence that is not an "accident" under Article 17. See 1 All E.R., at 201, 207. Reviewing the text, structure, and drafting history of the Convention, the Lords concluded that the Convention was designed to "ensure that, in all questions relating to the carrier's liability, it is the provisions of the Convention which apply and that the passenger does not have access to any other remedies, whether under the common law or otherwise, which may be available within the particular country where he chooses to raise his action." *Ibid.* Courts of other nations bound by the Convention have also recognized the treaty's encompassing preemptive effect. The "opinions of our sister signatories," we have observed, are "entitled to considerable weight." *Saks*, 470 U.S. at 404 (internal quotation marks omitted). The text, drafting history, and underlying purpose of the Convention, in sum, counsel us to adhere to a view of the treaty's exclusivity shared by our treaty partners.

For the reasons stated, we hold that the Warsaw Convention precludes a passenger from maintaining an action for personal injury damages under local law when her claim does not satisfy the conditions for liability under the Convention. Accordingly, we reverse the judgment of the Second Circuit....

STEVENS, J., dissenting

My disagreement with the Court's holding today has limited practical significance, not just because the issue has been conclusively determined for future cases by the recent amendment to the Warsaw Convention, ... but also because it affects only a narrow category of past cases. The decision is nevertheless significant because, in the end, it rests on the novel premise that preemption analysis should be applied differently to treaties than to other kinds of federal law.... Because I disagree with that premise, I shall briefly explain why I believe the Court has erred.

I agree with the Court that the drafters of the Convention intended that the treaty largely supplant local law. Article 24 preempts local law in three major categories: (1) personal injury claims arising out of an accident; (2) claims for lost or damaged baggage; and (3) damage occasioned by transportation delays. Those categories surely comprise the bulk of potential disputes between international air carriers and their passengers.

The Convention, however, does not preempt local law in cases arising out of "wilful misconduct." Article 25 expressly provides that a carrier shall not be entitled to avail itself of the provisions of the Convention that "exclude or limit" its liability if its misconduct is willful. Moreover, the question whether the carrier's wrongful act "is considered to be equivalent to wilful misconduct" is determined by "the law of the court to which the case is submitted." *Ibid.* Accordingly, the vast majority of the potential claims by passengers against international air carriers are either preempted by Article 24 or unequivocally governed by local law under Article 25.

Putting these cases aside, we are left with a narrow sliver of incidents involving personal injury that arise neither from an accident nor willful misconduct....

The overriding interest in achieving " 'uniformity of rules governing claims arising from international air transportation,' " ... will be accommodated in the situations explicitly covered by Article 24, regardless of how the Court decides this case. In those circumstances, the Convention's basic tradeoff between the carriers' interest in avoiding unlimited liability and the passengers' interest in obtaining compensation without proving fault will be fully achieved.

On the other hand, the interest in uniformity is disregarded in the category of cases that involve willful misconduct. Under the treaty, a reckless act or omission may constitute willful misconduct. See Koirala v. Thai Airways Int'l, Ltd., 126 F.3d 1205, 1209–1210 (C.A.9 1997); [L.] GOLDHIRSCH, [THE WARSAW CONVENTION ANNOTATED: A LEGAL HANDBOOK] 121 [1988] (stating that most civil law jurisdictions have found that gross negligence satisfies Article 25). This broad definition increases the number of cases not preempted by the Convention. In these circumstances, the delegates at Warsaw did decide "to subject air carriers to the distinct, nonuniform liability rules of the individual signatory nations." . . .

Thus, the interest in uniformity would not be significantly impaired if the number of cases not preempted, like those involving willful misconduct, was slightly enlarged to encompass those relatively rare cases in which the injury resulted from neither an accident nor a willful wrong. That the interest in uniformity is accommodated in one category of cases but not the other simply raises, without resolving, the question whether the drafters of the treaty intended to treat personal injury nonaccident cases as though they involved accidents. A plaintiff in such a case, unlike those injured by an accident, receives no benefit from the treaty, and normally should not have a claim that is valid under local law preempted, unless the treaty expressly requires that result.

Everyone agrees that the literal text of the treaty does not preempt claims of personal injury that do not arise out of an accident. It is equally clear that nothing in the drafting history requires that result. On the contrary, the amendment to the title of the Convention made in response to the proposal advanced by the Czechoslovak delegation, . . . suggests that the parties assumed that local law would apply to all nonaccident cases. I agree with the Court that that inference is not strong enough, in itself, to require that the ambiguity be resolved in the plaintiff's favor. It suffices for me, however, that the history is just as ambiguous as the text. I firmly believe that a treaty, like an Act of Congress, should not be construed to preempt state law unless its intent to do so is clear. . . . For this reason, I respectfully dissent.

Notes and Questions

1. When considering a treaty's preemption of local law, what guidance is offered in Article VI, cl. 2 of the United States Constitution?

2. Do you favor the majority's or dissent's approach to interpretation? Does the majority's interpretation of Article 24 (in those cases where Articles 17, 19 and 25 do not apply) result in a blanket immunity from any passenger injury claims not caused by an "accident," "delay," or "wilful" (including "reckless" or "gross negligence") conduct? Does Article 17 use the word "only"? Was the search prior to boarding "in the course of . . . embarking"?

Does the title to the Warsaw Convention potentially cover non-"accident" cases? Consider the words "relating to" and "transportation."

Does the Montreal Protocol No. 4 only apply to the "carriage" of passengers, and not to "embarking or disembarking"? Does the limitation on liability in Article 22(1) apply to embarkation or disembarkation?

PITTMAN v. GRAYSON, *ET AL.*

869 F.Supp. 1065 (S.D.N.Y. 1994).

SCHWARTZ, District Judge

[Editors' note: Plaintiffs Fred Pittman and his minor daughter brought actions against the child's mother and others alleged to have assisted in smuggling the child out of the U.S. in violation of Florida court orders. The action against Icelandair alleged that the airline participated in intentional interference with custodial rights, intentional infliction of emotional distress, and false imprisonment based on Icelandair's role in smuggling his daughter out of the U.S.]

Defendant Icelandair, Inc. ("Icelandair") moves to dismiss this action pursuant to 12(b)(1) of the Federal Rules of Civil Procedure ... for lack of subject matter jurisdiction based on the Warsaw Convention ... [among other claims]....

Icelandair argues that because plaintiffs' claims arise from "international transportation," as defined by Article 1(2) of the Warsaw Convention ("Convention"), the conditions and limits of the Convention automatically apply, including the forum limitations of Article 28....

Icelandair further argues that if the Court determines that a claim falling under Article 1(2) of the Convention has not been brought in accordance with the forum limitations of Article 28, the court should dismiss the complaint without further inquiry into the Convention's liability provisions. Plaintiffs concede that their claims arise out of "international transportation," as defined by Article 1(2) of the Convention. Plaintiffs, however, maintain that the forum limitations of Article 28 are applicable only to claims falling within the liability provisions of the Convention. Plaintiffs further content that Article 17 is the Convention's only potentially applicable liability provisions.... Plaintiffs argue that their claims fall under neither Article 17 nor any of the other substantive liability provisions of the Convention and consequently that the Convention is inapplicable to their claims. For the reasons set forth below, we find for plaintiffs on this issue.

The Warsaw Convention was designed to effectuate two central public policy goals: (1) to establish uniformity in the aviation industry with respect to claims arising out of international transportation, as well as uniformity as to documentation, and (2) to limit air carriers' potential liability in the event of accidents. *In re* Disaster at Lockerbie, Scotland, 928 F.2d 1267, 1270 (2d Cir. 1991). State law claims which fall within the scope of the Convention are preempted by the Convention. *Id.* At 1273. However, "[t]he text of the Warsaw Convention does not state that it is exclusive as to all causes of action arising out of international air flight; rather, it merely states that it is exclusive as to causes of action governed by its liability provisions." Walker v. Eastern Air Lines, 785 F. Supp. 1168, 1170 (S.D.N.Y. 1992)....

Accordingly, we now turn to the issue of whether the Warsaw Convention's substantive liability provisions apply to plaintiff's claims. Article 17 establishes the liability of international air carriers for harm to passengers. Air France v. Saks, 470 U.S. 392, 396 ... (1985). Under Article 17, an air carrier is liable for passenger injury only when three conditions are satisfied: (1) there have been an accident, in which (2) the passenger suffered death, wounding or other bodily injury and (3) the accident occurred on board the aircraft or in the course of embarking or disembarking. Eastern Airlines, Inc. v. Floyd, 499 U.S. 530, 535 ... (1991).

Plaintiffs argue that the case at bar does not meet the criteria of Article 17, because the events alleged by plaintiffs do not constitute an "accident" nor do plaintiffs' claims include "bodily injury." In *Air France v. Saks*, the Supreme Court held that an "accident" triggering liability under Article 17 "arises only if a passenger's injury is caused by an unexpected or unusual event or happening that is external to the passenger." *Saks*, 470 U.S. at 405.... The Court further noted that this definition of accident "should be flexibly applied after an assessment of all the circumstances surrounding a passenger's injuries." *Id.* Recently, this Court determined whether an alleged incident was an "accident" by considering whether such occurrence was a "risk characteristic of air travel." See Curley v. American Airlines, Inc., 846 F. Supp. 280, 283 (S.D.N.Y. 1994).

The history of the Convention suggests that the drafters intended the word "accident" to include incidents occurring while airplanes are in motion or on route and particularly to provide for events such as air disasters. *Walker*, 785 F. Supp. at 1172. Article 17 has also been interpreted by some courts to include torts committed by terrorists or fellow passengers. *Saks*, 470 U.S. at 405.... The Second Circuit recently affirmed its position that hijacking qualifies as an accident under Article 17. *Pflug* [v. Egyptair Corp.], 961 F.2d at 29.

Instances found by this Court to fall outside the meaning of "accident" range from deaths due to natural causes to injuries sustained by inebriated plaintiffs. *Curley*, 846 F. Supp. at 283 (passenger's injuries while being detained and searched by Mexican authorities, after the captain of his flight falsely identified him as having smoked marijuana on the flight, were not caused by an "accident" under Article 17); *Walker*, 785 F. Supp. at 1170 (passenger who died of natural causes during an international flight did not fit the meaning of "accident" under Article 17); Price v. British Airways, 1992 WL 170679, *1, 3 (S.D.N.Y.) (plaintiff who voluntarily consumed alcoholic beverages during a flight and subsequently suffered injuries when punched by a fellow passenger could not recover under Article 17, because his injuries were not caused by an "accident"); Padilla v. Olympic Airways, 765 F. Supp. 835, 836, 838 (S.D.N.Y. 1991) (plaintiff's injuries as a result of falling in an aircraft lavatory after voluntarily consuming alcoholic beverages during a flight were not due to an "accident" under Article 17).

Here, plaintiffs claim that Icelandair conspired to intentionally interfere with a custodial relationship, intentionally inflicted emotional distress on plaintiff Fred Pittman and falsely imprisoned plaintiff Elizabeth Pittman. Plaintiffs' claims arise from allegations that Icelandair hid Elizabeth and anna in JFK International and then smuggled Elizabeth and Anna onto an Icelandic aircraft by boarding them onto the aircraft from an entrance different from that of the other passengers and boarding them without passports....

While the issue of whether Icelandair's conduct qualifies as an "accident" is a close question, inasmuch as the alleged action is literally "unexpected," "unusual" and "external to the passenger," a thorough examination of relevant legal precedent persuades us that defendant's conduct should not be regarded as an "accident" under the Warsaw Convention. First, in applying the *Saks* test, courts have focused on whether the alleged conduct constitutes a "risk inherent in air travel." See *Curley*, 846 F. Supp. at 283. This criteria both explains why instances such as aircraft collisions, terrorist activities, or even intentional torts by other passengers qualify as accidents, and renders defendant's reference to decisions involving such conduct tenuous at best. The risk that airline personnel will smuggle a passenger onto an international flight in violation of a court order, or will otherwise commit intentional torts against a passenger, hardly constitutes a "risk inherent in air travel." ...

... Accordingly, because state law causes of action arising from an international flight remain viable where, as here, they do not fall under the Convention, *Lockerbie*, 928 F.2d at 1273, plaintiffs' state law claims with respect to defendant Icelandair ... survive Icelandair's motion to dismiss based on the Convention.

Notes and Questions

1. Consider Articles 28 and 32 of the Convention. Where are the places that plaintiff-survivors of an airline crash (or their estate or representatives) can permissibly file actions against the airline?

Where can a U.S. plaintiff injured over El Salvadorian airspace sue a Guatemalan passenger airline, which does substantial business within the United States (both in terms of traffic and revenue), when the U.S. plaintiff, pursuant to the ticket delivered by the carrier's agent, boarded a flight in Mexico City which had departed from Los Angeles and landed in Mexico City with continuations through Guatemala to the passenger's destination in Nicaragua, although the flight's ultimate destination was in Costa Rica? If the U.S. plaintiff had flown from Mexico City to Guatemala but while there, without receiving a new ticket but having received a new boarding pass, boarded a different aircraft with a different flight number, which had originated in Miami (with an ultimate flight destination in Costa Rica), for the passenger's destination in Nicaragua, all at the convenience and request of the carrier, would your answer be different? *See also* Article 3 of the Convention. Nicaragua is not a signatory to the Warsaw Convention.

2. Note that the places listed for suit in Article 28 concern nation-states (such as the U.S.) and not areas within a nation-state (such as Florida). See Mertens v. Flying Tiger Line, Inc., 341 F.2d 851, 855 (2d Cir.1965).

3. Does the phrase "must ... at the option of the plaintiff" allow the plaintiff's selection of a forum to prevail over attempts to change the forum on the ground of forum non conveniens, especially if the defendant air carrier argues that a forum not covered by Article 28 is available and would be more convenient? Consider also Article 32. In general, how should rights under a treaty be interpreted? Recall Chapters 1 and 2.

Note that the forum non conveniens doctrine is a common law doctrine which involves inquiry into an available, adequate, and convenient alternative foreign forum. *See, e.g.*, Piper Aircraft Co. v. Reyno, 454 U.S. 235, 249 n. 13, 253 (1981); Gulf Oil Corp. v. Gilbert, 330 U.S. 501, 507 (1947) ("the common law worked out techniques and criteria"); Mendes Junior Int'l Co. v. Banco do Brasil, 15 F. Supp.2d 332, 337 (S.D.N.Y.1998); Reed v. Fina Oil & Chem. Co., 995 F.Supp. 705, 714 (E.D.Tex.1998); Chapter 3, Section 1. As such, it should yield when it is inconsistent with or impairs the policy or provisions of a U.S. treaty, since treaty law of the U.S. (like a federal statute) trumps mere common law. Also, a federal statute can render forum non conveniens inapplicable when the language and purpose are inconsistent with forum non conveniens dismissal or when the power of choice of a forum is vested in the plaintiff. *See, e.g.*, United States v. National City Lines, Inc., 334 U.S. 573, 596–97 (1948); Industrial Investment Development Corp. v. Mitsui & Co., 671 F.2d 876 (5th Cir.1982), *vacated on other gds.*, 460 U.S. 1007 (1983). Does the Warsaw Convention's express and plain language guarantee a power of choice of the forum in plaintiffs? No known intent of the drafters of the Warsaw Convention supports preclusion of a plaintiff's express guarantee of choice of a forum by application of a domestic procedural doctrine. Further, domestic law is no excuse for failure to perform a treaty in good faith. *See, e.g.*, Vienna Convention on the Law of Treaties, Article 27 ("A party may not invoke the provisions of its internal law as justification for its failure to perform a treaty."); Restatement § 321, cmt. a.

One case has ruled that the express right of choice guaranteed in Article 28 does not preclude use of forum non conveniens. See *In re* Air Crash Disaster Near New Orleans, La., 821 F.2d 1147 [,1162] (5th Cir.1987), *vacated on other gds. and remanded sub nom.*, Pan American World Airways, Inc. v. Lopez, 490 U.S. 1032 (1989), *reinstated on remand sub nom., In re* Air Crash Disaster Near New Orleans, La., 883 F.2d 17 (5th Cir.1989) (per curiam). The court noted that plaintiffs' position that Article 28 of the treaty prevailed over the common law doctrine of forum non conveniens, vesting the absolute choice of forum in a plaintiff, "is a unique argument which our research indicates has never been addressed much less decided." *Id.* at 1160; *see also id.* at 1161 n.22 ("We recognize that the above-cited cases do not involve forum non conveniens motions to transfer or dismiss after a Warsaw Convention forum has been selected.... Our research indicates no such cases exist. We believe however...."), 1162 ("We simply do not believe...."). The court did not identify or use international legal rules that are to be applied when interpreting a treaty; address U.S. Supreme Court standards for treaty interpretation; or address the U.S. Supreme Court mandate that a treaty must be interpreted in a broad manner to protect rights, express or implied, that may be claimed under a treaty (as noted in Chapter 2). Further, the opinion did not address the fact that treaty law of the United States trumps inconsistent common law.

When the court addressed what the delegates to the treaty conference might have had in mind, the court concluded that delegates had "recognized that the Convention's provisions would have to be applied and adopted to a variety of legal systems, so they provided in Article 28(2) that" questions of procedure shall be governed by the law of the forum. *Id.* at 1161 (citing no treaty conference documents or other legislative history). Does the recognition that the treaty's "provisions would have to be applied and adopted to a variety of legal systems" support dismissal of a case brought by a plaintiff at plaintiff's option, which is admittedly the express and clear right of plaintiffs under Article 28(1) of the treaty? *See id.* at 1161 ("The party initiating the action enjoys the prerogative of choosing between these [four] possible national forums...."). Does the fact that the treaty must be "applied" in and "adopted" to domestic systems necessarily mean that the treaty can be obviated or thwarted? The treaty drafters did identify four fora, at least, that have "an actual interest in the matter." *Compare id.* at 1162 *with* Warsaw Convention, *supra* Article 28(1).

The circuit case has been followed per dictum, in a footnote, by a district court case in New York, Feng Zhen Lu v. Air China Int'l Corp., 1992 WL 453646, *1 n. 1 (E.D.N.Y. 1992).

SECTION 2. OUTER SPACE

A. *Previous Legal Concepts and Newer Claims*

Recall that Roman theory had considered both airspace and outer space sectors above a territorial state to be the province of the state. With the advent of sputnik in 1957, states began to contemplate what sort of regime outer space law should be patterned after, *e.g.*, control by the "territorial" state, something more akin to freedom of the seas, or something related to use and controls for the benefit of all humankind (not to mention the interests of other possible life forms yet to be discovered).

Balloons and rocket technology had demonstrated the need for some advance agreement on the use of outer space. Aircraft would soon "fly" into outer space (and U.S. aircraft crew would receive "astronaut" wings), rendering theories concerning the boundaries between airspace and outer space based on flight of aircraft obsolete. Various state and human interests could also be identified: access to resources in space or on the moon, radio waves and possible disruption, surveillance and espionage, sensing of earth resources, coordination of satellite orbits, coordination of rocket flight paths, damage to earth, safe return of astronauts, and military uses of satellites as well as space and celestial bodies more generally. Prior to extensive use of outer space, it was recognized that general principles should be agreed upon for use in the common interest and to avoid unnecessary disputes. A number of U.N. General Assembly resolutions preceded the drafting of the primary treaty to date, the 1967 "Outer Space Treaty," for example, the 1963 Resolution Regarding Weapons of Mass Destruction in Outer Space, U.N. G.A. Res. 1884, 18 U.N. GAOR, Supp. No. 15, at 13, U.N. Doc. A/5515 (1964), and U.N. G.A. Res. 1721A (20 Dec. 1961), which set forth the expectation that exploration and use of outer space should be only for the "betterment of mankind." Already, the 1963 Treaty Banning Nuclear Weapons Tests in the Atmosphere, in Outer Space and Under Water, 480 U.N.T.S. 43, 14 U.S.T. 1313, T.I.A.S. No. 5433, reflected agreement among the signatories that the testing of nuclear weapons in outer space must be banned.

Today, the orbit theory concerning the delimitation between airspace and outer space is the widely accepted legal precept. Accordingly, outer space begins where a satellite can orbit the earth—approximately 100 to 110 kilometers above the earth. A few states, notably the equatorial states, disagreed and made "territorial" claims concerning geostationary orbits and use of information gathered from space above their territories, especially with respect to resources within their earth boundaries that were "sensed" by satellite.

B. The Outer Space Treaty

[read the Treaty on Principles Governing the Activities of States in the Exploration and Use of Outer Space, Including the Moon and Other Celestial Bodies, in the Documents Supplement]

Introductory Problem

A private launch of a rocket and satellite from Texas has not gone well. In fact, negligence caused its diversion from its flight plan and crash in Mexico, destroying property and killing some twenty Mexican nationals. Who is liable under the Outer Space Treaty? What standard of liability pertains, negligence or strict liability?

Can Mexican claimants sue the private parties responsible for the negligent launch in a U.S. federal court under the Alien Tort Claims Act, using the Outer Space Treaty or customary international law as a basis for liability under international law? Can the Mexican claimants also sue the United States as the launch site state? By ratifying the treaty, has the U.S. waived any immunity it might otherwise claim?

Would your answer be the same if the rocket crashed in Louisiana killing local residents?

Notes and Questions

1. Under customary international law, a state is generally liable for foreseeable death, injury or suffering under a fault theory of liability. Recall the general standards of liability mentioned in the Law of the Sea Convention. *See also* The Trail Smelter Case (United States v. Canada), Arbitral Tribunal (1941), addressed in Chapter 3 with respect to jurisdiction in connection with transnational pollution. The tribunal in *Trail Smelter* held that "no state has the right to use or permit the use of its territory in such a manner as to cause injury by fumes in or to the territory of another or the

properties or persons therein, when the case is of serious consequence and the injury is established by clear and convincing evidence." With respect to transnational pollution, the Restatement also notes: "A State is responsible . . . for both its own activities and those of individuals or private or public corporations under its jurisdiction. The state may be responsible, for instance, for not enacting necessary legislation, for not enforcing its laws . . . , or for not preventing or terminating an illegal activity, or for not punishing the person responsible. . . . In general, the applicable international rules and standards do not hold a state responsible when it has taken the necessary and practicable measures; some international agreements provide also for responsibility regardless of fault in case of discharge of highly dangerous (radioactive, toxic, etc.) substances, or an abnormally dangerous activity (*e.g.*, launching of space satellites)." RESTATEMENT, *supra* § 601, cmt. d.

2. Does Article I of the treaty reflect the same sort of regime found in Articles 136–137 of the U.N. Law of the Sea Convention? Does Article II of the Space Treaty? Is exploitation prohibited? Who owns the "moon rocks" on display at NASA in Houston?

3. Are "fixed" or stationary orbits of satellites used for telecommunication impermissible uses of outer space in view of Articles I and II? How does Article IX affect your conclusion?

There are limited positions above the earth for geostationary and geosynchronous orbit (the latter allowing some 120 slots about 22,300 miles above earth around the equator) due to limited space and interference when satellites are too close to each other. Low orbit slots for lighter telecommunications satellites are also limited. The International Telecommunications Union's (ITU) World Administrative Radio Conferences (WARC) have produced agreements allocating at least one geostationary orbit slot to each member of the ITU. *See, e.g.*, Milton L. Smith, *The Space WARC Concludes*, 83 AM. J. INT'L L. 596 (1989). Low orbit slots for telecommunication are also being allocated among members of the ITU.

4. Is the use of satellites for military communications or military surveillance, photography, or sensing on earth impermissible?

5. Are nuclear weapons entirely banned from space under the treaty? Would it be permissible to place nuclear devices on a space station beyond the moon's orbit for potential use against errant meteors endangering the earth?

6. Is the use of a satellite with defensive particle-beam or laser capabilities banned under the treaty? Would a "star wars" network of satellites capable of targeting nuclear missiles launched against North America be impermissible?

7. What are "national activities" within the meaning of Article VI? Are private launch and other private space activities covered? How are they affected by state responsibility?

Article II prohibits "national appropriation" of space and celestial bodies. Does Article VI condition the meaning or reach of Article II prohibitions? More specifically, are private commercial entities free to mine or capture and control mineral resources from space and celestial bodies? If treaties are otherwise silent, do prohibitions therein concerning state signatories generally bind nationals of the signatories? Recall Chapters 1 and 2.

A private person or entity can also be independently responsible for damage caused to others. The standard of liability may vary under domestic law, but the general fall-back is fault theory.

8. If a French governmental entity's rocket is launched from Canadian territory, is Canada liable for damage caused by the crash of such a rocket in the United States? Is France?

9. If we contact other life forms in space, will the treaty provide useful normative guidance? What new provisions might you recommend?

C. The Convention on International Liability for Damage Caused by Space Objects

[read the Convention on International Liability for Damage Caused by Space Objects, in the Documents Supplement]

Introductory Problem

A Peoples' Republic of China (PRC) governmental entity launched a rocket with a Chinese commercial satellite on board and the rocket and satellite crashed in California injuring U.S. and Mexican nationals.

In domestic suits filed by U.S. and foreign plaintiffs against the PRC entity, the defendant has made the following claims:

1. There is no prescriptive jurisdiction in U.S. courts (recall Chapter 3).

2. Private claimants have no rights to a remedy under the 1972 Convention on International Liability or the 1967 Outer Space Treaty.

3. Any standard of absolute liability reflected in a treaty is not a standard under customary international law, and private claimants have no lawful claim or right to a remedy under customary international law.

4. The treaties are not self-executing.

5. U.S. claimants have no basis for subject matter jurisdiction and foreign claimants cannot use the Alien Tort Claims Act (ATCA) because there are no private rights under either treaty or customary international law.

6. If either treaty allows private claims, the private claimants must first exhaust available remedies in the PRC or have their state present a claim through diplomatic channels.

7. The PRC has not waived sovereign immunity by ratifying either treaty (recall Chapter 4), and other exceptions to immunity in the Foreign Sovereign Immunities Act (FSIA) are inapplicable (especially §§ 1604, 1605(a)(2) and (a)(5)).

How should plaintiffs respond? What provisions of the treaties are relevant? How should a U.S. court rule on the defendant's claims? Why? Has the defendant waived immunity by making a general appearance?

Notes and Questions

1. Does the term "damage" include emotional distress? Does it include pain and suffering? Does it include punitive damages such as those awarded under international law in *The I'm Alone* (see Chapter 2)? Consider also Article XII.

What sort of liability might pertain under international law against nonsignatory perpetrators?

2. If, within the U.S., Russia and the United States jointly launch a U.S. rocket carrying Russian material for a space station and the rocket explodes causing damage to U.S. nationals, can the U.S. nationals properly claim damages under the Liability Convention or the Outer Space Treaty?

3. Is there a "statute of limitations" within the Liability Convention? Are domestic statutes of limitation operative or changed by the treaty?

4. Under the Liability Convention, what standard of liability would pertain with respect to damage to a U.S.-Russian space station caused by an errant rocket owned and fired by the Peoples' Republic of China? What standard would apply with respect to an errant PRC rocket that kills fifteen Japanese nationals in Japan? What standard would apply concerning each incident under the Outer Space Treaty?

5. Would the results be different if the PRC was the launching or launch site state but the rocket was owned by France? Does Article II apply or would the standard be fault or negligence? Compare Article VII of the Outer Space Treaty.

6. Are signatory states free to ignore consequences of space debris from their former space objects? Compare the Outer Space Treaty.

7. Under the Liability Convention, who is liable for damage caused by private launch or space activities? Are private entities immune from liability under customary international law? Compare the Outer Space Treaty.

8. Is a state required to present an international claim (state-to-state) under Articles 8(1) or 11?

9. Do Articles 2, 3, 5, and 12 and the preamble to the Liability Convention constitute a waiver of or treaty-based exception to any immunity in domestic courts? Does Article 11(2)? Recall §§ 1330(a) and 1604 of the FSIA. How might § 1605(a)(2) and (a)(5) of the FSIA apply to launch and space activities?

10. Under either treaty, are states free to broadcast and/or relay information from satellites or space stations to any place on earth? Alternatively, can territorial states lawfully claim the right to control information broadcast into their territories, especially pornographic images or culturally imperialistic information? Can they lawfully charge fees or taxes with respect to broadcast activities?

Consider also the customary prescriptive competencies of states under objective territorial and protective jurisdiction. Compare the transnational freedom of speech documented, for example, in Article 19 of the Universal Declaration of Human Rights and Articles 18–20 of the International Covenant on Civil and Political Rights. Does it matter that such rights are derogable? Are they nonetheless norms *jus cogens*? Would Article 103 of the

United Nations Charter condition your consideration of relevant legal policies at stake?

11. Under either treaty, are states free to use satellites to sense data from anywhere on earth? if the data is of significant value militarily? commercially? Can sensing states retain such information or sell it at their pleasure, must they share it with sensed states?

Chapter Eight

WAR POWERS AND THE USE OF FORCE

SECTION 1. INTERNATIONAL PROSCRIPTIONS

Introductory Problem

The state of Uwalk has recently developed nuclear weapons, shifting the regional balance of power and posing a significant security threat to its neighbors. More recently, Uwalk shot down military aircraft from its regional neighbor Turlock, which had been flying at high altitudes over Uwalk territory while attempting to locate and photograph nuclear weapon emplacements allegedly aimed at Turlockish cities.

In retaliation, Turlock destroyed three Uwalkian naval vessels near its coast and suspended all trade between the two countries. Uwalk responded by suspending such trade and declaring a holy war "in defense of Uwalk" and in the name of its predominant religious sect. Uwalk also proceeded to send arms to an insurgent group in Turlock attempting to overthrow the Turlockish government.

Has there been any threat or use of force in violation of international law? Any permissible use of force? What additional facts might be helpful? Does the U.N. Security Council have legal competence to order measures involving the use of force to restore peace in the region? If so, what sort of measures?

A. *Impermissible Use of Force*

1. *Historic Background*

Prior to World War II, individuals, including what we might term public officials or heads-of-state, had been prosecuted for initiating an unjust war or for administering territories through acts of cruel oppression. For example, Conradin von Hohenstafen, Duke of Suabia, was tried in 1268 for initiating an unjust war, and he was executed Oct. 29, 1268. In 1474, Peter von Hagenbach, who served as Governor of territory under the Duke of Burgundy, was tried at Breisach for his improper administration of pledged territories on the Upper Rhine. He was tried at the order of the Archduke of Austria in a tribunal presided over by twenty-eight judges from allied towns. Although his crimes took place during peacetime, he was found guilty of murder, rape, a reign of terror, pillage, perjury and other crimes said to constitute violations of the "law of God and man." In 1818, the Congress at Aix–La–Chapelle decided to detain Napoleon for waging wars against peace; and in 1818, there occurred a famous trial in America of two Englishmen, Arbuthnot and Ambrister, for incitement of the Creek Indians and the levying of war against the United States in violation of the law of nations and the laws of war. See PAUST, BASSIOUNI, *ET AL.*, INTERNATIONAL CRIMINAL LAW 279–80 (2 ed. 2000); TELFORD TAYLOR, NUREMBERG AND VIETNAM: AN AMERICAN TRAGEDY 81–82 (1970). There had also been other examples of trials of persons for initiating or contributing to the initiation of aggressive force or war before World War II. *See also* early U.S. cases in Chapter 2, Section 2 B 2 a.

In addition to these applications of legal norms proscribing crimes against peace, were there other recognitions of individual responsibility, even for officials, with respect to crimes against peace and the laws of humanity prior to the prosecutions at Nuremberg?

HENFIELD'S CASE, 11 F. Cas. 1099 (C.C.D.Pa.1793)

[recall, from Chapter 2, Section 2 B 2, at pp. 139–144]

COMMISSION ON THE RESPONSIBILITY OF THE AUTHORS OF THE WAR AND ON ENFORCEMENT OF PENALTIES, REPORT PRESENTED TO THE PRELIMINARY PEACE CONFERENCE, MARCH 29, 1919

(members: Belgium, British Empire, France, Greece, Italy, Japan, Poland, Roumania, Serbia, United States).

reprinted in 14 AM. J. INT'L L. 95 (1920).*

The Commission was charged to inquire into and report upon the following points:

1. The responsibility of the authors of the war.

2. The facts as to breaches of the laws and customs of war committed by the forces of the German Empire and their Allies, on land, on sea, and in the air during the present war.

3. The degree of responsibility for these offences attaching to particular members of the enemy forces, including members of the General Staffs, and other individuals, however highly placed.

4. The constitution and procedure of a tribunal appropriate for the trial of these offences.

5. Any other matters cognate or ancillary to the above which may arise in the course of the enquiry, and which the Commission finds it useful and relevant to take into consideration....

RESPONSIBILITY OF THE AUTHORS OF THE WAR

On the question of the responsibility of the authors of the war, the Commission, after having examined a number of official documents relating to the origin of the World War, and to the violations of neutrality and of frontiers which accompanied its inception, has determined that the responsibility for it lies wholly upon the Powers which declared war in pursuance of a policy of aggression, the concealment of which gives to the origin of this war the character of a dark conspiracy against the peace of Europe.

This responsibility rests first on Germany and Austria, secondly on Turkey and Bulgaria. The responsibility is made all the graver by reason of the violation by Germany and Austria of the neutrality of Belgium and Luxemburg, which they themselves had guaranteed. It is increased, with regard to both France and Serbia, by the violation of their frontiers before the declaration of war.

I. PREMEDITATION OF THE WAR

A. Germany and Austria

... On the 28th June, 1914, occurred the assassination at Sarajevo of the heir-apparent of Austria. "It is the act of a little group of madmen," said Francis Joseph. The act, committed as it was by a subject of Austria–Hungary on Austro–Hungarian territory, could in no wise compromise Serbia, which very correctly expressed its condolences and stopped public rejoicing in Belgrade. If the Government of Vienna thought that there was any Serbian complicity, Serbia was ready to seek out the guilty parties. But this attitude failed to satisfy Austria and still less Germany, who, after their first astonishment had passed, saw in this royal and national misfortune a pretext to initiate war.

At Potsdam a "decisive consultation" took place on the 5th July, 1914. Vienna and Berlin decided upon this plan: "Vienna will send to Belgrade a very emphatic ultimatum and a very short limit of time."

The Bavarian Minister, von Lerchenfeld, said in a confidential despatch dated the 18th July, the facts stated in which have never been officially denied: "It is clear that Serbia cannot accept the demands, which are inconsistent with the dignity of an independent state." Count Lerchenfeld reveals in this report that, at the time it was made, the ultimatum to Serbia had been jointly decided upon by the Governments of Berlin and Vienna; that they were waiting to send it until President Poincare and M. Viviani should have left for St. Petersburg; and that no illusions were cherished, either at Berlin or Vienna, as to the consequences which this threatening measure would involve. It was perfectly well known that war would be the result....

At midday on the 18th Austria declared war on Serbia. On the 29th the Austrian Army commenced the bombardment of Belgrade, and made its dispositions to cross the frontier....

On the 3rd August von Schoen went to the Quai d'Orsay with the declaration of war against France. Lacking a real cause of complaint, Germany alleged, in her declaration of war, that bombs had been dropped by French aeroplanes in various districts in Germany. This statement was entirely false. Moreover, it was either later admitted to be so or no particulars were ever furnished by the German Government....

CONCLUSIONS

1. *The war was premeditated by the Central Powers together with their Allies, Turkey and Bulgaria, and was the result of acts deliberately committed in order to make it unavoidable.*

2. *Germany, in agreement with Austria–Hungary, deliberately worked to defeat all the many conciliatory proposals made by the Entente Powers and their repeated efforts to avoid war.*

II. VIOLATION OF THE NEUTRALITY OF BELGIUM AND LUXEMBURG

A. *Belgium*

Germany is burdened by a specially heavy responsibility in respect of the violation of the neutrality of Belgium and Luxemburg. Article 1 of the Treaty of London of the 19th April, 1839, after declaring that Belgium should form a "perpetually neutral State," had placed this neutrality under the protection of Austria, France, Great Britain, Russia and Prussia. On the 9th August, 1870, Prussia had declared "her fixed determination to respect Belgian neutrality." On the 22nd July, 1870, Bismarck wrote to the Belgian Minister at Paris, "This declaration is rendered superfluous by existing treaties."

It may be of interest to recall that the attributes of neutrality were specifically defined by the fifth Hague Convention, of the 18th October, 1907. That convention was declaratory of the law of nations, and contained these provisions—"The territory of neutral Powers is inviolable" (Article 1). "Belligerents are forbidden to move troops or convoys, whether of munitions of war or of supplies, across the territory of a neutral Power" (Article 2). "The fact of a neutral Power resisting, even by force, attempts against its neutrality cannot be regarded as a hostile act" (Article 10).

There can be no doubt of the binding force of the treaties which guaranteed the neutrality of Belgium. There is equally no doubt of Belgium's sincerity or of the sincerity of France in their recognition and respect of this neutrality.

On the 29th July, 1914, the day following the declaration of war by Austria–Hungary against Serbia, Belgium put her army on its reinforced peace strength, and so advised the Powers by which her neutrality was guaranteed and also Holland and Luxemburg. . . .

At Paris the reply was categorical: "The French Government are resolved to respect the neutrality of Belgium, and it would only be in the event of some other Power violating that neutrality that France might find herself under the necessity, in order to assure the defence of her own security, to act otherwise."

On the same day as this reply was made at Paris, the French Minister at Brussels made the following communication to M. Davignon, the Belgian Minister of Foreign Affairs: "I am authorized to declare that, in the event of an international war, the French Government, in accordance with the declarations they have always made, will respect the neutrality of Belgium. In the event of this neutrality not being respected by another Power, the French Government, to secure their own defence, might find it necessary to modify their attitude".

At this point is may be recalled that the pretext invoked by Germany in justification of the violation of Belgian neutrality, and the invasion of Belgian territory, seemed to the German Government itself of so little weight, that in Sir Edward Goschen's conversations with the German Chancellor, von Bethmann Hollweg, and with von Jagow, the Secretary of State, it was not a question of aggressive French intentions, but a "matter of life and death to Germany to advance through Belgium and violate the latter's neutrality," and of "a scrap of paper." Further, in his speech on the 4th August, the German Chancellor made his well-known avowal: "Necessity knows no law. Our troops have occupied Luxemburg, and perhaps have already entered Belgian territory. Gentlemen, that is a breach of international law. . . . We have been obliged to refuse to pay attention to the justifiable protests of Belgium and Luxemburg. The wrong—I speak openly—the wrong we are thereby committing we will try to make good as soon as our military aims have been attained. He who is menaced, as we are, and is fighting for his all can only consider how he is to hack his way through." To this avowal of the German Chancellor there is added and overwhelming testimony of Count von Lerchenfeld, who stated in a report of the 4th August, 1914, that the German General Staff considered it "necessary to cross Belgium: France can only be successfully attacked from that side. At the risk of bringing about the intervention of England, Germany cannot respect Belgian neutrality."

As for the Austrian Government, it waited until the 18th August to declare war on Belgium, but as early as the middle of the month "the motor batteries sent by Austria have proved their excellence in the battles around Namur, as appears from a proclamation of the German general who at the time was in command of the fortress of Liege, which German troops had seized. Consequently, the participation of Austria–Hungary in the violation of Belgian neutrality is aggravated by the fact that she took part in that violation without any previous declaration of war.

B. *Luxemberg*

The neutrality of Luxemburg was guaranteed by Article 2 of the Treaty of London, 11 May, 1867, Prussia and Austria–Hungary being two of the guarantor Powers. On the 2nd August, 1914, German troops penetrated the territory of the Grand Duchy. Mr. Eyschen, Minister of State of Luxemburg, immediately made an energetic protest.

The German Government alleged "that military measures have become inevitable, because trustworthy news had been received that French forces were marching on Luxemburg." This allegation was at once refuted by Mr. Eyschen.

CONCLUSION

The neutrality of Belgium, guaranteed by the treaties of the 19th April, 1839, and that of Luxemburg, guaranteed by the treaty of the 11th May, 1867, were deliberately violated by Germany and Austria–Hungary.

III. PERSONAL RESPONSIBILITY

The third point submitted by the Conference is thus stated:

> *The degree of responsibility for these offences attaching to particular members of the enemy forces, including members of the General Staffs and other individuals, however highly placed.*

For the purpose of dealing with this point, it is not necessary to wait for proof attaching guilt to particular individuals. It is quite clear from the information now before the Commission that there are grave charges which must be brought and investigated by a court against a number of persons.

In these circumstances, the Commission desire to state expressly that in the hierarchy of persons in authority, there is no reason why rank, however exalted, should in any circumstances protect the holder of it from responsibility when that responsibility has been established before a properly constituted tribunal. This extends even to the case of heads of states. An argument has been raised to the contrary based upon the alleged immunity, and in particular the alleged inviolability, of a sovereign of a state. But this privilege, where it is recognized, is one of practical expedience in municipal law, and is not fundamental. However, even if, in some countries, a sovereign is exempt from being prosecuted in a national court of his own country the position from an international point of view is quite different.

We have later on in our Report proposed the establishment of a high tribunal composed of judges drawn from many nations, and included the possibility of the trial before that tribunal of a former head of state with the consent of that state itself secured by articles in the Treaty of Peace. If the immunity of a sovereign is claimed to extend beyond the limits above stated, it would involve laying down the principle that the greatest outrages against the laws and customs of war and the laws of humanity, if proved against him, could in no circumstances be punished. Such a conclusion would shock the conscience of civilized mankind.

In view of the grave charges which may be preferred against—to take one case—the ex-Kaiser—the vindication of the principles of the laws and customs of war and the laws of humanity which have been violated would be incomplete if he were not brought to trial and if other offenders less highly placed were punished. Moreover, the trial of the offenders might be seriously prejudiced if they attempted and were able to plead the superior orders of a sovereign against whom no steps had been or were being taken.

There is little doubt that the ex-Kaiser and others in high authority were cognizant of and could at least have mitigated the barbarities committed during the course of the war. A word from them would have brought about a different method in the action of their subordinates on land, at sea and in the air.

We desire to say that civil and military authorities cannot be relieved from responsibility by the mere fact that a higher authority might have been convicted of the same offence. It will be for the court to decide whether a plea of superior orders is sufficient to acquit the person charged from responsibility.

CONCLUSION

All persons belonging to enemy countries, however high their position may have been, without distinction of rank, including Chiefs of States, who have been guilty of offences against the laws and customs of war or the laws of humanity, are liable to criminal prosecution. . . .

Any tribunal appropriate to deal with the other offences to which reference is made might hardly be a good court to discuss and deal decisively with such a subject as the authorship of the war. The proceedings and discussions, charges and counter-charges, if adequately and dispassionately examined, might consume much time, and the result might conceivably confuse the simpler issues into which the tribunal will be charged to inquire. While this prolonged investigation was proceeding some witnesses might disappear, the recollection of others would become fainter and less trustworthy, offenders might escape, and the moral effect of tardily imposed punishment would be much less salutary than if punishment were inflicted while the memory of the wrongs done was still fresh and the demand for punishment was insistent.

We therefore do not advise that the acts which provoked the war should be charged against their authors and made the subject of proceedings before a tribunal.

There can be no doubt that the invasion of Luxemburg by the Germans was a violation of the Treaty of London of 1867, and also that the invasion of Belgium was a violation of the Treaties of 1839. These treaties secured neutrality for Luxemburg and Belgium and in that term were included freedom, independence and security for the population living in those countries. They were contracts made between the high contracting parties to them, and involve an obligation which is recognized in international law. . . .

And thus a high-handed outrage was committed upon international engagements, deliberately, and for a purpose which cannot justify the conduct of those who were responsible.

The Commission is nevertheless of opinion that no criminal charge can be made against the responsible authorities or individuals (and notably the ex-Kaiser) on the special head of these breaches of neutrality, but the gravity of these gross outrages upon the law of nations and international good faith is such that the Commission thinks they should be the subject of a formal condemnation by the Conference.

CONCLUSIONS

1. The acts which brought about the war should not be charged against their authors or made the subject of proceedings before a tribunal.

2. On the special head of the breaches of the neutrality of Luxemburg and Belgium, the gravity of these outrages upon the principles of the law of nations and upon international good faith is such that they should be made the subject of a formal condemnation by the Conference.

3. On the whole case, including both the acts which brought about the war and those which accompanied its inception, particularly the violation of the neutrality of Belgium and Luxemburg, it would be right for the Peace Conference, in a matter so unprecedented, to adopt special measures, and even to create a special organ in order to deal as they deserve with the authors of such acts.

4. It is desirable that for the future penal sanctions should be provided for such grave outrages against the elementary principles of international law.

TREATY OF PEACE WITH GERMANY

(Versailles, June 28, 1919)

PENALTIES

Article 227

The Allied and Associated Powers publicly arraign William II of Hohenzollern, formerly German Emperor, for a supreme offence against international morality and the sanctity of treaties.

A special tribunal will be constituted to try the accused, thereby assuring him the guarantees essential to the right of defence. It will be composed of five judges, one appointed by each of the following were: namely the United States of America, Great Britain, France, Italy and Japan.

In its decision the tribunal will be guided by the highest motives of international policy, with a view of vindicating the solemn obligations of international undertakings and the validity of international morality. It will be its duty to fix the punishment which it considers should be imposed.

The Allied and Associated Powers will address a request to the Government of the Netherlands for the surrender to them of the ex-Emperor in order that he may be put on trial.

Article 228

The German Government recognizes the right of the Allied and Associated Powers to bring before military tribunals persons accused of having committed acts in violation of the laws and customs of war. Such persons shall, if found guilty, be sentenced to punishments laid down by law. This provision will apply notwithstanding any proceedings or prosecution before a tribunal in Germany or in the territory of her allies.

The German Government shall hand over to the Allied and Associated Powers, or to such one of them as shall so request, all persons accused of having committed an act in violation of the laws and customs of war, who are specified either by name or by the rank, office or employment which they held under the German authorities.

Article 229

Persons guilty of criminal acts against the nationals of one of the Allied and Associate Powers will be brought before the military tribunals of that Power.

Persons guilty of criminal acts against the nationals of more than one of the Allied and Associated Powers will be brought before military tribunals composed of members of the military tribunals of the Powers concerned.

In every case the accused will be entitled to name his own counsel.

Article 230

The German Government undertakes to furnish all documents and information of every kind, the production of which may be considered necessary to ensure the full knowledge of the incriminating acts, the discovery of offenders, and the just appreciation of responsibility.

Notes and Questions

1. The Treaty of Peace Between the Allied and Associated Powers and Austria (September 10, 1919) was similar.

2. Do you agree with the Commission's Report with respect to the trial of persons for violations of treaties of neutrality and aggressive war? Was there precedent of some sort for the trial of Kaiser William II of Germany?

3. William II had fled to the Netherlands and was not surrendered for prosecution. Lists of other alleged offenders were compiled by the Allied Governments and presented to Germany in 1920, but Germany proposed to try the accused before its highest court at Leipzig, which proposal was

accepted. Of the more than 1,000 persons accused of war crimes, only a few were actually tried. See PAUST, BASSIOUNI, *ET AL.*, INTERNATIONAL CRIMINAL LAW 623–24 (2 ed. 2000). A list of war crimes compiled by the 1919 Responsibilities Commission is contained in the Documents Supplement.

4. Did the court in *Tel-Oren*, in Chapter 1, seem to be sufficiently aware of early 20th century history concerning expectations about individual responsibility for offenses against the laws of humanity, war crimes, and other international crimes? For examples of early expectation concerning crimes against humanity, also see PAUST, BASSIOUNI, *ET AL.*, *supra* at 856–57.

5. After World War I, certain treaties recognized the prohibition of certain uses of force. Do these reaffirm prior trends or set new precedent binding only among treaty signatories? Consider the following:

TREATY PROVIDING FOR THE RENUNCIATION OF WAR AS AN INSTRUMENT OF NATIONAL POLICY

(Paris, August 27, 1928) (The "Kellogg–Briand Pact")

46 Stat. 2343, T.S. No. 796, 2 Bevans 732, 94 L.N.T.S. 57.
[Germany, United States, Belgium, France, Great Britain, India, Italy, Japan, Poland, Czechoslovakia].

Deeply sensible of their solemn duty to promote the welfare of mankind:

Persuaded that the time has come when a frank renunciation of war as an instrument of national policy should be made to the end that the peaceful and friendly relations now existing between their peoples may be perpetuated;

Convinced that all changes in their relations with one another should be sought only by pacific means and be the result of a peaceful and orderly process, and that any signatory Power which shall hereafter seek to promote its national interests by resort to war should be denied the benefits furnished by this Treaty;

Hopeful that, encouraged by their example, all the other nations of the world will join in this humane endeavor and by adhering to the present Treaty as soon as it comes into force bring their peoples within the scope of its beneficent provisions, thus uniting the civilized nations of the world in a common renunciation of war as an instrument of their national policy: . . .

Article I. The High Contracting Parties solemnly declare in the names of their respective peoples that they condemn recourse to war for the solution of international controversies and renounce it as an instrument of national policy in their relations with one another.

Article II. The High Contracting Parties agree that the settlement or solution of all disputes or conflicts of whatever nature or of whatever origin they may be, which may arise among them, shall never be sought except by pacific means. . . .

Notes and Questions

1. Does the treaty mention duties of individuals, crimes, or criminal sanctions? Did the treaties addressed by the 1919 Commission? Are such necessary?

2. By WWII, 63 states had ratified the Kellog–Briand Pact.

JUDGMENT AND OPINION, INTERNATIONAL MILITARY TRIBUNAL (NUREMBERG), Oct. 1, 1946

[Twenty-two accused were tried before the IMT at Nuremberg for crimes against peace, war crimes, and crimes against humanity, with Count One of the Indictment also charging a separate crime of participation in the formation and execution of a common plan or conspiracy to commit such crimes. Three were found not guilty of any crimes charged. Others were convicted on various counts and were given sentences ranging from ten years to life imprisonment and death.]

On August 8, 1945, an Agreement was concluded in London between the Governments of Great Britain and Northern Ireland, of the United States of America, of France, and of the Union of Soviet Socialist Republics, acting in the interest of all the United Nations. That Agreement provided for the establishment of an international Military Tribunal for the trial of war criminals whose offences had no particular geographical location. The constitution, jurisdiction and function of the Tribunal were defined in the Charter annexed to the Agreement.

Article 6 of the Charter provided:

> "The Tribunal established by the Agreement referred to in Article I hereof for the trial and punishment of the major war criminals of the European Axis countries shall have the power to try and punish persons who, acting in the interests of the European Axis countries, whether as individuals or as members of organizations, committed any of the following crimes.

"The following acts, or any of them, are crimes coming within the jurisdiction of the Tribunal for which there shall be individual responsibility:

> (a) *Crimes against peace:* namely, planning, preparation, initiation or waging of a war of aggression, or a war in violation of international treaties, agreements or assurances, or participation in a common plan or conspiracy for the accomplishment of any of the foregoing.... "

The Common Plan of Conspiracy and Aggressive War

The Tribunal now turns to the consideration of the Crimes against Peace charged in the Indictment. Count One of the Indictment charges the defendants with conspiring or having a common plan to commit crimes against peace. Count Two of the Indictment charges the defendants with committing specific crimes against peace by planning, preparing, initiating, and waging wars of aggression against a number of other States. It will be convenient to consider the question of the existence of a common plan and the question of aggressive war together, and to deal later in this Judgment with the question of the individual responsibility of the defendants.

The charges in the Indictment that the defendants planned and waged aggressive wars are charges of the utmost gravity. War is essentially an evil thing. Its consequences are not confined to the belligerent States alone, but affect the whole world.

To initiate a war of aggression, therefore, is not only an international crime; it is the supreme international crime differing only from other war crimes in that it contains within itself the accumulated evil of the whole.

The first acts of aggression referred to in the Indictment are the seizure of Austria and Czechoslovakia; and the first war of aggression charged in the Indictment is the war against Poland begun on September 1939.

Before examining that charge it is necessary to look more closely at some of the events which preceded these acts of aggression. The war against Poland did not come suddenly out of an otherwise clear sky; the evidence has made it plain that this was a war of aggression, as well as the seizure of Austria and Czechoslovakia, was premeditated and carefully prepared, and was not undertaken until the moment was thought opportune for it to be carried through as a definite part of the preordained scheme and plan. For the aggressive design of the Nazi Government were not accidents arising out of the immediate political situation in Europe and the world; they were a deliberate and essential part of Nazi foreign policy.

From the beginning, the National Socialist movement claimed that its object was to unite the German People in the consciousness of their mission and destiny, based on inherent qualities of race, and under the guidance of the Fuhrer.

For its achievement, two things were deemed to be essential: the disruption of the European order as it had existed since the Treaty of Versailles, and the creation of a Greater Germany beyond the frontiers of 1914. This necessarily involved the seizure of foreign territories.

War was seen to be inevitable, or at the very least, highly probable, if these purposes were to be accomplished. The German people, therefore, with all their resources, were to be organized as a great political-military army, schooled to obey without question any policy decreed by the State. . . .

The Seizure of Austria

The invasion of Austria was a pre-meditated aggressive step in furthering the plan to wage aggressive wars against other countries. As a result Germany's flank was protected, that of Czechoslovakia being greatly weakened. The first step had been taken in the seizure of "Lebensraum"; many new divisions of trained fighting men had been acquired; and with the seizure of foreign exchange reserves, the re-armament program had been greatly strengthened.

On 21 May 1935 Hitler announced in the Reichstag that Germany did not intend either to attach Austria or to interfere in her internal affairs. On 1 May 1935 he publicly coupled Czechoslovakia with Austria in his avowal of peaceful intentions; and so late as 11 July 1936 he recognized by treaty the full sovereignty of Austria.

Austria was in fact seized by Germany in the month of March 1938....

The Seizure of Czechoslovakia

The conference of 5 November 1937 made it quite plain that the seizure of Czechoslovakia by Germany had been definitely decided upon. The only question remaining was the selection of the suitable moment to do it. On 4 March 1938 the Defendant Von Ribbentrop wrote to the Defendant Keitel with regard to a suggestion made to Von Ribbentrop by the Hungarian Ambassador in Berlin, that possible war aims against Czechoslovakia should be discussed between the German and Hungarian Armies. In the course of this letter Von Ribbentrop said:

> "I have many doubts about such negotiations. In case we should discuss with Hungary possible war aims against Czechoslovakia, the danger exists that other parties as well would be informed about this." ...

The Invasion of Denmark and Norway

The aggressive war against Poland was but the beginning. The aggression of Nazi Germany quickly spread from country to country. In point of time the first two countries to suffer were Denmark and Norway.

On 31 May 1939 a Treaty of Non–Aggression was made between Germany and Denmark, and signed by the Defendant Von Ribbentrop. It was there solemnly stated that the parties to the Treaty were "firmly resolved to maintain peace between Denmark and Germany under all circumstances." Nevertheless, Germany invaded Denmark on 9 April 1940.

On 2 September 1939, after the outbreak of war with Poland, Germany sent a solemn assurance to Norway....

From this narrative it is clear that as early as October 1939 the question of invading Norway was under consideration. The defense that has been made here is that Germany was compelled to attack Norway to forestall an Allied invasion, and her action was therefore preventive.

It must be remembered that preventive action in foreign territory is justified only in case of "an instant and overwhelming necessity for self-defense, leaving no choice of means, and no moment of deliberation"

(The *Caroline* Case, Moore's *Digest of International Law*, II, 412). How widely the view was held in influential German circles that the Allies intended to occupy Norway cannot be determined with exactitude....

Violations of International Treaties

The [I.M.T.] Charter defines as a crime the planning or waging of war that is a war of aggression or a war in violation of international treaties. The Tribunal has decided that certain of the defendants planned and waged aggressive wars against 12 nations, and were therefore guilty of this series of crimes. This makes it unnecessary to discuss the subject in further detail, or even to consider at any length the extent to which these aggressive wars were also "wars in violation of international treaties, agreements, or assurances."

These treaties are set out in Appendix C of the Indictment. Those of principal importance are the following.

Hague Conventions

In the 1899 Convention the signatory powers agreed: "before an appeal to arms ... to have recourse, as far as circumstances allow, to the good offices or mediation of one or more friendly powers." A similar clause was inserted in the Convention for Pacific Settlement of International Disputes of 1907. In the accompanying Convention Relative to Opening of Hostilities, Article I contains this far more specific language: "The Contracting Powers recognize that hostilities between them must not commence without a previous and explicit warning, in the form of either a declaration of war, giving reasons, or an ultimatum with a conditional declaration of war." Germany was a party to these conventions.

Versailles Treaty

Breaches of certain provisions of the Versailles Treaty are also relied on by the Prosecution—Not to fortify the left bank of the Rhine (Articles 42–44); to "respect strictly the independence of Austria" (Article 80); renunciation of any rights in Memel (Article 99); and the Free City of Danzig (Article 100); the recognition of the independence of the Czechoslovak State; and the military, naval, and air clauses against German rearmament found in Part V. There is no doubt that action was taken by the German government contrary to all these provisions....

On 21 May 1935 Germany announced that, whilst renouncing the disarmament clauses of the Treaty, she would still respect the territorial limitations, and would comply with the Locarno Pact. (With regard to the first five breaches alleged, therefore, the Tribunal finds the allegation proved.)

Treaties of Mutual Guarantee, Arbitration, and Non–Aggression

It is unnecessary to discuss in any detail the various treaties entered into by Germany and with other Powers. Treaties of mutual guarantee were signed by Germany at Locarno in 1925, with Belgium, France,

Great Britain, and Italy, assuring the maintenance of the territorial *status quo*. Arbitration treaties were also executed by Germany at Locarno with Czechoslovakia, Belgium, and Poland.

Article I of the latter treaty is typical, providing: "All disputes of every kind between Germany and Poland ... which it may not be possible to settle amicably by the normal methods of diplomacy, shall be submitted for decision to an arbitral tribunal...."

Conventions of Arbitration and Conciliation were entered into between Germany, the Netherlands, and Denmark in 1926; and between Germany and Luxembourg in 1929. Non-aggression treaties were executed by Germany with Denmark and Russia in 1939.

Kellogg–Briand Pact

The Pact of Paris was signed on 27 August 1928 by Germany, the United States, Belgium, France, Great Britain, Italy, Japan, Poland, and other countries; and subsequently by other powers. The Tribunal has made full reference to the nature of this Pact and its legal effect in another part of this judgment. It is therefore not necessary to discuss the matter further here, save to state that in the opinion of the Tribunal this Pact was violated by Germany in all the cases of aggressive war charged in the Indictment. It is to be noted that on 26 January 1934 Germany signed a Declaration for the Maintenance of Permanent Peace with Poland, which was explicitly based on the Pact of Paris, and in which the use of force was outlawed for a period of ten years.

The Tribunal does not find it necessary to consider any of the other treaties referred to in the Appendix, or the repeated agreements and assurances of her peaceful intentions entered into by Germany.

The Law of the Charter

The jurisdiction of the Tribunal is defined in the Agreement and Charter, and the crimes coming within the jurisdiction of the Tribunal, for which there shall be individual responsibility, are set out in Article 6. The law of the Charter is decisive, and binding upon the Tribunal.

The making of the Charter was the exercise of the sovereign legislative power by the countries to which the German Reich unconditionally surrendered; and the undoubted right of these countries to legislate for the occupied territories has been recognized by the civilized world. The Charter is not an arbitrary exercise of power on the part of the victorious Nations, but in the view of the Tribunal, as will be shown, it is the expression of international law existing at the time of its creation; and to that extent is itself a contribution to international law.

The Signatory Powers created this Tribunal, defined the law it was to administer, and made regulations for the proper conduct of the Trial. In doing so, they have done together what any one of them might have done singly; for it is not to be doubted that any nation has the right to set up special courts to administer law. With regard to the constitution of the Court, all that the defendants are entitled to ask is to receive a fair trial on the facts and law.

The Charter makes the planning or waging of a war of aggression or a war in violation of international treaties a crime; and it is therefore not strictly necessary to consider whether and to what extent aggressive war was a crime before the execution of the London Agreement. But in view of the great importance of the questions of law involved, the Tribunal has heard full argument from the Prosecution and the Defense, and will express its view on the matter....

This view is strongly reinforced by a consideration of the state of international law in 1939, so far as aggressive war is concerned. The General Treaty for the Renunciation of War of 27 August 1928, more generally known as the Pact of Paris or the Kellog–Briand Pact, was binding on 63 nations, including Germany, Italy and Japan at the outbreak of war in 1939....

The question is, what was the legal effect of this Pact? The nations who signed the Pact or adhered to it unconditionally condemned recourse to war for the future as an instrument of policy, and expressly renounced it. After the signing of the Pact, any nation resorting to war as an instrument of national policy breaks the Pact. In the opinion of the Tribunal, the solemn renunciation of war as an instrument of national policy necessarily involves the proposition that such a war is illegal in international law; and that those who plan and wage such a war, with its inevitable and terrible consequences, are committing a crime in so doing. War for the solution of international controversies undertaken as an instrument of national policy certainly includes a war of aggression, and such a war is therefore outlawed by the Pact.... But it is argued that the Pact does not expressly enact that such wars are crimes, or set up courts to try those who make such wars. To that extent the same is true with regard to the laws of war contained in the Hague Convention. The Hague Convention of 1907 prohibited resort to certain methods of waging war. These included the inhumane treatment of prisoners, the employment of poisoned weapons, the improper use of flags of truce, and similar matters. Many of these prohibitions had been enforced long before the date of the Convention; but since 1907 they have certainly been crimes, punishable as offenses against the law of war; yet the Hague Convention nowhere designates such practices as criminal, nor is any sentence prescribed, nor any mention made of a court to try and punish offenders. For many years past, however, military tribunals have tried and punished individuals guilty of violating the rules of land warfare laid down by this Convention. In the opinion of the Tribunal, those who wage aggressive war are doing that which is equally illegal, and of much greater moment than a breach of one of the rules of the Hague Convention. In interpreting the words of the Pact, it must be remembered that international law is not the product of an international legislature, and that such international agreements as the Pact of Paris have to deal with general principles of law, and not with administrative matters of procedure. The law of war is to be found not only in treaties, but in the customs and practices of states which gradually obtained universal recognition, and from the general principles of justice applied by jurists and practised by military courts. This law is not static, but by continual adaptation follows the needs of a changing world. Indeed, in many cases treaties do no more than express and define for more accurate reference the principles of law already existing.

The view which the Tribunal takes of the true interpretation of the Pact is supported by the international history which preceded it. In the year 1923 the draft of a Treaty of Mutual Assistance was sponsored by the League of Nations. In Article I the Treaty declared "that aggressive war is an international crime," and that the parties would "undertake that no one of them will be guilty of its commission." The draft treaty was submitted to 29 states, about half of whom were in favor of accepting the text. The principal objection appeared to be in the difficulty of defining the acts which would constitute "aggression," rather than any doubt as to the criminality of aggressive war. The preamble to the League of Nations 1924 Protocol for the Pacific Settlement of International Disputes ("Geneva Protocol") after "recognising the solidarity of the Members of the international community," declared that "a war of aggression constitutes a violation of this solidarity and is an international crime." It went on to declare that the contracting parties were "desirous of facilitating the complete application of the system provided in the Covenant of the League of Nations for the pacific settlement of disputes between the States and of ensuring the repression of international crimes." The Protocol was recommended to the members of the League of Nations by a unanimous resolution in the assembly of the 48 members of the League. These members included Italy and Japan, but Germany was not then a member of the League.

Although the Protocol was never ratified, it was signed by the leading statesmen of the world, representing the vast majority of the civilized states and peoples, and may be regarded as strong evidence of the intention to brand aggressive war as an international crime.

At the meeting of the Assembly of the League of Nations on 24 September 1927, all the delegations then present (including the German, the Italian, and the Japanese), unanimously adopted a declaration concerning wars of aggression. The preamble to the declaration stated:

> "The Assembly:
>
> Recognizing the solidarity which unites the community of nations; Being inspired by a firm desire for the maintenance of general peace; Being convinced that a war of aggression can never serve as a means of settling international disputes, and is in consequence an international crime.... "

The unanimous resolution of 18 February 1928 of 21 American republics at the Sixth (Havana) Pan-American Conference, declared that "war of aggression constitutes an international crime against the human species."

All these expressions of opinion, and others that could be cited, so solemnly made, reinforce the construction which the Tribunal placed upon the Pact of Paris, that resort to a war of aggression is not merely illegal, but is criminal. The prohibition of aggressive war demanded by the conscience of the world, finds its expression in the series of pacts and treaties to which the Tribunal has just referred.

It is also important to remember that Article 227 of the Treaty of Versailles provided for the constitution of a special Tribunal, composed of representatives of five of the Allied and Associated Powers which had been belligerents in the First World War opposed to Germany, to try the former German Emperor "for a supreme offense against international morality and the sanctity of treaties." The purpose of this trial was expressed to be "to vindicate the solemn obligations of international undertakings, and the validity of international morality." In Article 228 of the Treaty, the German Government expressly recognized the right of the Allied Powers "to bring before military tribunals persons accused of having committed acts in violation of the laws and customs of war." . . .

Notes and Questions

1. Does the Judgment attempt to define "aggression"? Is there sufficient guidance from the Judgment for future prosecutions of those involved in "wars of aggression"?

2. Do you agree with the Tribunal that there was adequate precedent for notice to German leaders that crimes against peace had been proscribed? What sort of precedential matters were identified?

3. Do you agree with the Tribunal that Germany had no lawful right to invade Norway and Denmark? Had this sort of claim been raised by Germany before?

PRINCIPLES OF THE NUREMBERG CHARTER AND JUDGMENT

formulated by the International Law Commission, 5 U.N. GAOR, Supp. No. 12, at 11–14, para. 99, U.N. Doc. A/1316 (1950), UNPAC.*

I. Any person who commits an act which constitutes a crime under international law is responsible therefor and liable to punishment.

II. The fact that internal law does not impose a penalty for an act which constitutes a crime under international law does not relieve the person who committed the act from responsibility under international law.

III. The fact that a person who committed an act which constitutes a crime under international law acted as Head of State or responsible

* In 1946, the United Nations General Assembly affirmed "the principles of international law recognized by the Charter of the Nuremberg Tribunal and the judgment of the Tribunal." G.A. Res. 95(I), U.N. Doc. A/64/Add. 1 (unanimous). The General Assembly had also requested the International Law Commission to formulate such principles, which it did in 1950.

Government official does not relieve him from responsibility under international law....

IV. The crimes hereinafter set out are punishable as crimes under international law:

a. Crimes against peace:

(i) Planning, preparation, initiation or waging of a war of aggression, or a war in violation of international treaties, agreements or assurances;

(ii) Participation in a common plan or conspiracy for the accomplishment of any of the acts mentioned under (i)....

VII. Complicity in the commission of a crime against peace, a war crime, or a crime against humanity as set forth in Principle VI is a crime under international law.

Question

1. Can a nation-state lawfully benefit from its own wrong? Consider: Aboitiz & Co. v. Price, 99 F.Supp. 602, 612 (D. Utah 1951); Factory at Chorzow Case, 1927 P.C.I.J., Ser. A, No. 9, at 31; Article 5 (3) of the 1974 Definition of Aggression, *infra.*

2. U.N. Charter Precepts

CHARTER OF THE UNITED NATIONS

(June 26, 1945), 59 Stat. 1031.

[read the preamble to the Charter and Articles 1–2, 33, 39, 51, in the Documents Supplement]

Notes and Questions

1. What is the use of "armed force ... in the common interest" within the meaning of the preamble to the Charter?

2. Are all threats or uses of force prohibited by the language of Article 2, paragraph 4 of the Charter?

3. Is merely "armed" "force" prohibited or regulated under Article 2 (4)? *See also* JORDAN J. PAUST & ALBERT P. BLAUSTEIN, THE ARAB OIL WEAPON (1977); RICHARD B. LILLICH, ECONOMIC COERCION AND THE NEW INTERNATIONAL ECONOMIC ORDER (1976).

4. After the deadlock of the U.N. Security Council during the Korean Conflict, the U.N. General Assembly carved out a special competence to meet threats to the peace and acts of "aggression" in its 1950 Uniting for Peace Resolution. *See* U.N. G.A. Res. 377A, 5 U.N. GAOR, Supp. (No. 20) 10, U.N. Doc. A/1775 (1951). Such competence was confirmed indirectly by the International Court of Justice. *See* Certain Expenses of the United Nations, 1962 I.C.J. 151.

5. Is the Judgment at Nuremberg of precedential import with respect to the application of U.N. Charter proscriptions to individuals for criminal

sanction purposes? Is there any mention of individual responsibility, crimes, or criminal sanctions in the U.N. Charter?

6. Scholars have been in sharp disagreement whether the U.S. intervention in Vietnam in the 1960s and early 1970s was (or whether those of the People's Republic of China and the Soviet Union were) legally permissible. *See, e.g.*, vols. I–IV, THE VIETNAM WAR AND INTERNATIONAL LAW (R. Falk ed., 1968, 1969, 1972, 1976); LOUIS HENKIN, HOW NATIONS BEHAVE 304–08 (1979).

7. If you could rewrite Article 2 of the Charter, would you? If so, how, why?

8. For further clarification of U.N. Charter norms, read the 1970 Declaration on Principles of International Law, in the Documents Supplement. The 1970 Declaration was the most significant attempt to provide further clarification of the principles of the U.N. Charter for the first 25 years of its existence. Although General Assembly resolutions as such are not binding per se, this declaration, on principles of international law, is considered to be an authoritative, legally relevant guide to the content of U.N. Charter norms, if not also partly reflective of customary international law. More generally, recall Vienna Convention on the Law of Treaties, art. 31, in Chapter 1.

9. The norm of nonintervention reflected partly in U.N. Charter Article 2(7) is elaborated upon in the Declaration. In this regard, what is an "affair of" a particular state as opposed to that of the international community? Is "intervention" as such proscribed or are there distinctions to be made between permissible and impermissible intervention? *See also* Advisory Opinion on Nationality Decrees in Tunis and Morocco (France and Great Britain), 1923 P.C.I.J., Ser. B, No. 4, at 24 (considering art. 15 (8) of the Covenant of the League of Nations); John Norton Moore, *Toward an Applied Theory for the Regulation of Intervention,* in LAW & CIVIL WAR IN THE MODERN WORLD 3 (J.N. Moore ed. 1974); J.N. Moore, *Intervention: A Monochromatic Term for a Polychromatic Reality*, in 2 THE VIETNAM WAR AND INTERNATIONAL LAW 1061 (R. Falk ed. 1969); Myres S. McDougal & W. Michael Reisman, *Rhodesia and the United Nations: The Lawfulness of International Concern,* 62 AM. J. INT'L L. 1 (1968).

10. Is the unilateral use of force to prevent genocidal extermination of groups of people by their own government impermissible under the U.N. Charter, as amplified by the Declaration on Principles of International Law? Are other forms of humanitarian intervention permissible? *See also* the preamble to and Article I of the Convention on the Prevention and Punishment of the Crime of Genocide, in the Documents Supplement; RICHARD B. LILLICH, HURST HANNUM, INTERNATIONAL HUMAN RIGHTS 613–64 (3 ed. 1995), and references cited; FERNANDO R. TESON, HUMANITARIAN INTERVENTION: AN INQUIRY INTO LAW AND MORALITY (1988); Anthony A. D'Amato, *The Invasion of Panama Was a Lawful Response to Tyranny*, 84 AM. J. INT'L L. 516 (1990); Jordan J. Paust, Albert P. Blaustein, *War Crimes Jurisdiction and Due Process: The Bangladesh Experience*, 11 VAND. J. TRANSNAT'L. L. 1, 11–12 n.39, 20 n.69 (1978).

11. In view of the above, was such a use of force by NATO in Kosovo in 1999 permissible under the U.N. Charter, or other international law? Consider this question again in subsection C with respect to U.N. Security

Council powers and NATO's competence under Chapter VIII of the U.N. Charter.

12. Is the use of force to overthrow a foreign government absolutely impermissible under the U.N. Charter, as amplified by the 1970 Declaration? See U.N. S.C. Res. 940 (July 31, 1994) (re: Haiti); U.N. G.A. Res. 39/2 (Sept. 28, 1984) (re: illegal regime in South Africa and self-determination assistance, "recognizing the legitimacy of their struggle to eliminate apartheid and establish a society based on majority rule with equal participation by all the people ... [and] Urges all Governments and organizations ... to assist the oppressed people of South Africa in their legitimate struggle for national liberation...."); U.N. G.A. Res. 3314, Resolution on the Definition of Aggression, art. 7 (noted below); African Charter on Human and Peoples' Rights, art. 20 (2) ("oppressed peoples shall have the right to free themselves from the bonds of domination by resorting to any means recognized by the international community"), (3) ("All peoples shall have the right to assistance of the States parties to the present Charter in their liberation struggle against foreign domination, be it political, economic or cultural."), done in Banjul, June 26, 1981, O.A.U. Doc. CAB/LEG/67/3 Rev. 5; panel, *The United Nations Charter and the Use of Force: Is Article 2(4) Still Workable?*, 78 Proceedings, Am. Soc. Int'l L. 68 (1984); Paust, *The Human Right to Participate in Armed Revolution and Related Forms of Social Violence: Testing the Limits of Permissibility*, 32 Emory L.J. 545, 560–67 (1983); Paust, *Aggression Against Authority: The Crime of Oppression, Politicide and Other Crimes Against Human Rights*, 18 Case W. Res. J. Int'l L. 283, 297–98 (1986); W.M. Reisman, *Coercion and Self–Determination*, 78 Am. J. Int'l L. 642 (1984).

13. Read Articles 1, 2, 33, 39, 51–54 of the U.N. Charter. During the Cuban missile crisis in 1962, the Soviet Union was attempting to deliver nuclear weapons to Cuba but the United States interdicted the weapons using U.S. naval vessels that were deployed to stop and search Soviet vessels heading to Cuba. The U.S. was careful not to use the term "blockade," which would communicate that an act of war had been undertaken. On October 23, 1962, the O.A.S. General Assembly has passed a resolution authorizing member states to participate in the interdiction. The U.S. position was that use of naval vessels in such an instance was permissible under the U.N. Charter as "collective measures" permitted under Article 52. The then Legal Adviser to the State Department noted "The President in his speech did not invoke Article 51 or the right of self-defense. And the O.A.S. acted not under Article 3 [of the Rio Treaty], covering cases of armed attack, but under Article 6, covering threats to the peace other than armed attack." Abram Chayes, The Legal Case for U.S. Action in Cuba, 47 Dep't State Bull. 763, 764 (1962). The U.N. Security Council made no formal decision concerning the matter. Was this permissible regional action? Would it have been permissible self-defense under Article 51 of the U.N. Charter?

14. When NATO authorized the use of force by various states in Kosovo in 1999 to stop "ethnic cleansing" of Kosovo Albanians, the U.N. Security Council was veto-deadlocked or unable to authorize "enforcement action" to stop genocidal conduct in Kosovo. Some argued that subsequent use of force by NATO members was illegal under the U.N. Charter. Some argued that it was illegal but necessary. Some argued that it was permissible

humanitarian intervention. Was NATO's use of force in Kosovo and against the Federal Republic of Yugoslavia in 1999 permissible under the U.N. Charter? *See generally* 33 U.N. L. Rpts. 111–24 (No. 9 May 1999) (remarks of D'Amato (permissible humanitarian intervention, not prohibited under Articles 2 (4) or 2 (7)), Paust (permissible "regional action" under Articles 52–53, not impermissible under Articles 2 (4) or 2 (7)), Conlon, Megret, Damrosch, Wippman, Delbruck, Hoffman, Chayes, Kirgis, Simma, Cassese, Carey), reprinted in 2 Translex, Special Supp. (May 1999); editorial comments of Henkin, Wedgwood, Charney, Chinkin, Falk, Franck, Reisman, in 93 AM. J. INT'L L. 824–62 (1999); http://www.msu.edu/course/pls/364/stein/364–IntLaw-and-Force.htm; Julie Mertus, *Reconsidering the Legality of Humanitarian Intervention: Lessons from Kosovo*, 41 Wm. & Mary L. Rev. 1743, 1772 (2000).

15. If the use of force in self-defense and certain forms of armed intervention are permissible—indeed, if even other forms of "self-help" or "self-determination assistance" are permissible—does the 1970 Declaration adequately clarify what constitutes an impermissible "war of aggression" (which "constitutes a crime against peace")?

RESOLUTION ON THE DEFINITION OF AGGRESSION

[read the Resolution, in the Documents Supplement]

Notes and Questions

1. Is application of the Definition of Aggression nearly self-operative? Consider Articles 1, 2, and 3(a), (b), and (d) in connection with the 1986 bombing of Libya by the United States and the 1998 missile attacks on alleged terrorist sites in Afghanistan and the Sudan by the United States in response to bombings of U.S. embassies in Kenya and Tanzania. *See also* symposium, 8 Whittier L. Rev. no. 3 (1986).

2. Is the 1974 Definition too limited, *e.g.*, with respect to types of actors, types of force, in other ways?

3. Is an accused on sufficient notice of what might be labeled a "war of aggression" in every instance? *See* 1974 Definition of Aggression, Articles 2 and 4. *See also id.*, Arts. 6–8.

4. President Truman, in 1950, had noted that the United States had opposed attempts to define "aggression" during the formation of the U.N. Charter. As the President noted:

> The United States opposed this proposal. It took the position that a definition of aggression cannot be so comprehensive as to include all cases of aggression and cannot take into account the various circumstances which might enter into the determination of aggression in a particular case. Any definition of aggression is a trap for the innocent and an invitation to the guilty. The United States position prevailed at San Francisco, and the Charter adopted a system whereby the appropriate U.N. organ, in the first instance the Security Council, would determine on the basis of the facts of a particular case whether aggression has taken place.

5 Whiteman, Digest of International Law 740 (1965).

Do you agree with the former President? *See also* MYRES S. MCDOUGAL & FLORENTINO P. FELICIANO, LAW AND MINIMUM WORLD PUBLIC ORDER 61–62 (1961).

5. In 1970, the International Court of Justice recognized that obligations "towards the international community as a whole ... are obligations *erga omnes*. Such obligations derive, for example, in contemporary international law, from the outlawing of acts of aggression, and of genocide, as also from the principles and rules concerning the basic rights of the human person...." Case Concerning the Barcelona Traction, Light and Power Company, Limited (Belgium v. Spain), 1970 I.C.J. 3, paras. 33–34. In the 1976 I.L.C. Draft Convention on State Responsibility, it was also recognized that "an international crime may result ... from" an international obligation "prohibiting aggression."

6. Did the government of South Africa during the apartheid regime meet the standard of legitimacy found in Article 21 of the Universal Declaration of Human Rights? Article 21(3) of the Universal Declaration reads:

> "The will of the people shall be the basis of the authority of government; this will shall be expressed in periodic and genuine elections which shall be by universal and equal suffrage and shall be held by secret vote or by equivalent free voting procedures."

Does the 1970 Declaration on Principles of International Law reaffirm this type of standard? *See also* Western Sahara Advisory Opinion, 1975 I.C.J. 3, 4, 12, 31–33, 36; U.N. S.C. Res. 940 (July 31, 1994); U.N. G.A. Res. 39/2 (Sept. 28, 1984).

7. Would U.S. support of South African rebels have been legally permissible? What provisions of the U.N. Charter, the 1970 Declaration on Principles of International Law, and the 1974 Definition of Aggression are relevant? *See also* U.N. G.A. Res. 2, 39 U.N. GAOR, Supp. No. 51, at 14–15, U.N Doc. A/39/51 (Sept. 28, 1984) (vote: 133–0–2); panel, *Permissible Measures and Obligations for Outside States and Internal Peoples Toward Minority Rule in South Africa*, 80 PROC., AM. SOC. INT'L L. 308 (1986). Consider also Paust & Blaustein, *War Crimes Jurisdiction and Due Process: The Bangladesh Experience,* 11 VAND. J. TRANS. L. 1, 11–12 n. 39, 18–20 & n.69, 30–31 (1978). *But see* Intentional Commission of Jurists, THE EVENTS IN EAST PAKISTAN, 1971 (Geneva 1972).

8. Despite the Nuremberg Opinion and Judgment, the 1950 Principles, and the General Assembly Resolution on the Definition of Aggression (U.N. G.A. Res. 3314), debate concerning the definability of the crime of aggression continues. Relevant developments include the International Law Commission's Draft Statute for an International Criminal Court, *Report of the International Law Commission on Its Forty-sixth Session*, U.N. GAOR, 49th Sess., Supp. No. 10, at 43, U.N. Doc. A/49/10 (1994) [ILC Draft Statute]; the International Law Commission's Draft Code of Crimes Against the Peace and Security of Mankind, *Report of the International Law Commission on Its Forty-eight Session*, U.N. GAOR, 51st Sess., Supp. No. 10, at 9, U.N. Doc. A/51/10 (1996) [ILC Draft Code of Crimes]; and the Rome Statute of the International Criminal Court, adopted by the United Nations Diplomatic Conference of Plenipotentiaries on the Establishment of an International Criminal Court on 17 July 1998, U.N. Doc. A/CONF. 183/9 (1998) [ICC

Statute]. In the ILC Draft Statute, Article 20 included the crime of aggression, but the ILC provided no definition of aggression. In its commentary the ILC noted that it would seem "retrogressive to exclude individual criminal responsibility for aggression (in particular, acts directly associated with the waging of a war of aggression) 50 years after Nürnberg." ILC Draft Statute, at 72. In Article 23 (2) of the Draft Statute, the ILC proposed that "[a] complaint of or directly related to an act of aggression may not be brought under this Statute unless the Security Council has first determined that a State has committed the act of aggression which is the subject of the complaint." *Id.* at 84. In the ILC Draft Code of Crimes, Article 16 provides:

> An individual who, as leader or organizer, actively participates in or orders the planning, preparation, initiation or waging of aggression committed by a State shall be responsible for a crime of aggression.

The ILC in its commentary noted that this provision defines individual criminal responsibility, but that a court determining guilt under Article 16 would be required to determine whether the state had violated Article 2 (4) of the U.N. Charter and whether the conduct was a sufficiently serious violation as to implicate individual criminal responsibility.

In the negotiations leading up to the adoption of the ICC Statute, several serious disagreements prevented the immediate inclusion of the crime of aggression. Consider the following:

REPORT OF THE PREPARATORY COMMITTEE ON THE ESTABLISHMENT OF AN INTERNATIONAL CRIMINAL COURT

U.N. GAOR, 51st Sess., Supp. No. 22, U.N. Doc. A/51/22, vol. I (1995).

65. There were different views concerning the inclusion of aggression.

66. Some delegations were of the view that aggression should be included to avoid a significant gap in the jurisdiction of the Court, as aggression was one of the most serious crimes of concern to the entire international community, and that it should be regarded as a core crime under general international law; to create a deterrent and to avoid the impunity of the responsible individuals by providing a forum for their prosecution; to enhance the role and stature of the Court; to avoid any negative inference concerning individual criminal responsibility under customary law contrary to the Nürnberg Tribunal precedent affirmed by the General Assembly; and to avoid adopting a retrogressive statute 50 years after the Nürnberg and Tokyo tribunals and the adoption of the Charter of the United Nations.

67. Some delegations supported the inclusion of this crime if general agreement could be reached on its definition and on the appropriate balance of the respective roles and functions of the Court and the Security Council, without delaying the establishment of the Court.

68. Still other delegations were of the view that it should not be included because there was no generally accepted definition of aggression for the purpose of determining individual criminal responsibility; there was no precedent for individual criminal responsibility for acts of aggression in contrast to wars of aggression; it would be difficult and inappropriate to attempt to elaborate a sufficiently clear, precise and comprehensive defini-

tion of aggression; any attempt to elaborate a generally acceptable definition would substantially delay the establishment of the Court; the crime of aggression necessarily involved political and factual issues (such as territorial claims) that were inappropriate for adjudication by a criminal court; its inclusion could subject the Court to the struggle for political influence among states; the Court would still have jurisdiction over other crimes that often accompanied acts of aggression; it would be difficult to achieve an appropriate relationship between the judicial functions of the Court and the political functions entrusted to the Security Council under the Charter of the United Nations ... ; and its inclusion could jeopardize the general acceptance or universality of the Court.

69. Some delegations expressed support for providing a review mechanism under which aggression might be added at a later stage to avoid delaying the establishment of the Court pending the completion of a generally accepted definition. Other delegations were opposed to that view. The view was also expressed that appropriate language could be added to the preamble or an operative provision to avoid any negative inferences regarding individual criminal responsibility for such crimes under customary law....

70. Several delegations noted the absence of a generally agreed definition of aggression for the purpose of determining individual criminal responsibility under treaty law....

71. Some delegations were of the view that the Nürnberg Charter provided a precise definition of particularly serious offenses resulting in individual criminal responsibility under customary law, while others described the definition contained therein as too imprecise for these purposes, or too restrictive or outdated.

72. Some delegations expressed the view that the General Assembly resolution provided a generally accepted definition of aggression and contained elements that could be included in the definition of this crime. Other delegations expressed the view that the resolution did not contain a definition for the purpose of individual criminal responsibility; or indicate the acts that were of sufficient gravity for this purpose; or address a number of fundamental issues that could arise in criminal proceedings, including questions relating to exceptional situations involving the lawful use of force; or deal with possible defenses, including self-defense.

73. Some delegations suggested that it might be easier to reach agreement on a general definition similar to the [ILC Draft Code]. Other delegations expressed a preference for a general definition accompanied by an enumeration of acts.... Some delegations which had recommended that no definition of aggression should be included in the Statute proposed that a provision should be inserted which specified that ... the Security Council would determine whether or not a situation could be considered aggression. The role of the Court would then be to establish whether or not that situation had given rise to the commission of crimes involving individual responsibility. On the role of the Security Council ... , some delegations pointed out the need to avoid a situation in which the use of the veto in the Council might preclude the prosecution of a person by the Court for the commission of such a crime.

Notes and Questions

1. The draft Statute submitted to the Rome Conference by the Preparatory Committee reflected these differences. Three competing definitions of the crime of aggression were proposed: (1) one based on the Nuremberg definition of crimes against peace; (2) one based on General Assembly Resolution 3314 of 1974; and (3) one limited to armed attack against a state that results in occupation or annexation of territory. Draft Statute of the International Criminal Court, *Report of the Preparatory Committee on the Establishment of an International Criminal Court*, U.N. Doc. A/CONF. 183/2/Add.1, at 12–14 (1998). Delegations to the 1998 Rome Conference remained divided on the role of the Security Council as well. Since no final consensus on a definition of aggression could be reached, the Conference chose the compromise reflected in Articles 5 (1) and 5 (2) of the ICC Statute. See the Documents Supplement.

The Rome Conference also created a Preparatory Commission which is charged *inter alia* with preparing proposals for a definition of the crime of aggression and the conditions under which the ICC should exercise jurisdiction over it. These proposals will be submitted to a Review Conference of the states parties for possible amendment to the Statute. Final Act of the United Nations Diplomatic Conference of Plenipotentiaries on the Establishment of an International Criminal Court, Annex I, Resolution F, U.N. Doc. A/CONF. 183/10 (1998).

2. Do the results of the Rome Conference cast doubt on the proposition that the crime of aggression exists as a matter of customary international law? Are there some core areas of consensus and practice despite disagreement concerning the possible further reach of such a crime? Is there precedent for criminal responsibility for acts of aggression not amounting to wars of aggression? Recall Chapters 1 and 2. Does the phrasing of Article 5 (1) adequately prevent retrogression feared by the ILC if the crime of aggression had not been included in the Draft Statute and the ILC Draft Code of Crimes?

Why do you think the definition of aggression and the potential role of the Security Council with respect to prosecutions for this crime have been so contentious? Is there concern about frivolous claims or that leaders of countries with a veto in the Security Council might be subject to the same law prosecuted at Nuremberg and Tokyo? Are you optimistic that the Preparatory Commission established at the Rome Conference will succeed in resolving disagreements to the satisfaction of a future Review Conference on the ICC Statute?

3. In view of your approach(es) to the last questions, was the continuing U.S. support of the *Contras* against the government of Nicaragua legally permissible? *See also* Appraisals of the ICJ Decision: Nicaragua v. United States (Merits), 81 AM. J. INT'L L. 77 (1987); J.N. Moore, *The Secret War in Central America and the Future of World Order*, 80 AM. J. INT'L L. 43 (1986); J. Rowles, *"Secret Wars," Self-Defense and the Charter—A Reply to Professor Moore*, 80 AM. J. INT'L L. 568 (1986). In general, the United States was concerned about Nicaraguan support of insurgents in El Salvador, claiming that such was a violation of prohibitions concerning the use of force, including the general norm of non-intervention, and also constituted an

attack within the meaning of Article 51 of the Charter. Nicaragua was concerned about responsive force engaged in by the United States against Nicaragua, including support of the *Contras* (who were seeking to overthrow the government of Nicaragua). Portions of the International Court's decision follow in the next section.

B. *Self-Defense*

UNITED NATIONS CHARTER

[read Articles 51–52, in the Documents Supplement]

Notes and Questions

1. Prior to the U.N. Charter, the famous *Caroline* incident, on December 29, 1837, led to an exchange of letters in 1842 by Lord Ashburton of the U.K. (then in control of Canada) and U.S. Secretary of State Webster. The incident had involved an attack on the *Caroline* (a small steamer that had been used to support insurgent acts against Canada) in U.S. territory by a small force led by a British officer. The attack resulted in the death of one U.S. citizen, the wounding of several others, one person being missing, and the loss of the burning vessel over Niagara Falls. The U.K. denied violating international law but apologized for the invasion of U.S. territory. Secretary Webster wrote in response:

> The President sees with pleasure that your Lordship fully admits those great principles of public international law, applicable to cases of this kind, which this government has expressed; and that on your part, as on ours, respect for the inviolable character of the territory of independent states is the most essential foundation of civilization.... [W]hile it is admitted that exceptions growing out of the great law of self-defense do exist, those exceptions should be confined to cases in which the "necessity of that self-defense is instant, overwhelming, and leaving no choice of means, and no moment for deliberation."

2. Is preemptive or anticipatory self-defense permissible under the Charter? What standards and limits are articulated? How would these have applied in the circumstance of German claims to invade Belgium in the World War I era, to invade Norway and Denmark during World War II? *See also* Mary Ellen O'Connell, The Myth of Preemptive Self-Defense, at http://www.asil.org/taskforce/oconnell.pdf; Jordan J. Paust, *Use of Armed Force against Terrorists in Afghanistan, Iraq, and Beyond*, 35 CORNELL INT'L L.J. 533, 536–38 (2002); Jordan J. Paust, *Responding Lawfully to International Terrorism: The Use of Force Abroad*, 8 WHITTIER L. REV. 711, 716–19, 729–32 (1986).

In 2002, the Bush Administration's National Security Strategy indicated that a general goal is to prevent "our enemies from threatening us, our allies, and our friends, with weapons of mass destruction" and claimed that the U.S. must "stop rogue states and their terrorist clients before they are able to threaten or use" such weapons, although the U.S. "will not use force in all cases to preempt emerging threats." Nevertheless, it states, the U.S. "has long maintained the option of preemptive actions to counter a sufficient threat to our national security ... even if uncertainty exists as to the time and place of the enemy's attack." National Security Strategy (Sept. 17, 2002), available at http:www.usinfo.state.gov. Would certain effectuations of such a policy be impermissible? Could they be criminal?

3. What is an "armed attack" within the meaning of the Charter? Does it include a process of attack over time? The French version of Article 51 includes the phrase *agression armee*. Would armed "aggression" involve a broader circumstance than armed "attack"?

4. An armed attack on one's military forces abroad or on one's nationals abroad has been considered to be included within Article 51. *Compare* Louis Henkin, The Missile Attack on Baghdad and its Justifications, ASIL Newsletter 3 (June–Aug. 1993) *with* Jordan J. Paust, Response to President's Notes on Missile Attack on Baghdad, ASIL Newsletter 4 (Sept.-Oct. 1993); Paust, *Responding Lawfully*, *supra* at 716, 728–29.

5. Prior to the U.N. Charter, reprisals involving military force had sometimes been permissible. The *Naulilaa* arbitration between Germany and Portugal in 1928 had identified the nature of permissible reprisals. The alleged reprisal occurred after a small German force invaded Portuguese South–West Africa, Portuguese forces shot and killed three of the Germans, and then, in response, Germany sent in a new force to punish the Portuguese at their post of Naulilaa, which it did and thereafter withdrew. The Tribunal declared:

Reprisals are acts of self-help by the injured State, acts in retaliation for acts contrary to international law on the part of the offending State, which have remained unaddressed after a demand for amends. In consequence of such measures, the observance of this or that rule of international law is temporarily suspended, in the relations between the two States. They are limited by considerations of humanity and the rules of good faith, applicable in the relations between States. They are illegal unless they are based upon a previous act contrary to international law. They seek to impose on the offending State reparation for the offence, the return to legality and the avoidance of new offences....

(1) The *sine qua non* of a legitimate resort to reprisals is that there should have been a previous violation of international law by the other party and in this case the previous act had been not a breach of international law but an accident.

(2) Reprisals are only legitimate when they have been preceded by an unsuccessful demand for redress and in this case there had been no attempt to obtain satisfaction by legal means. The employment of force is only justifiable by a necessity to use it.

(3) Reprisals, when taken, must be reasonably proportionate to the injury suffered and in this case were out of all proportion to the injury.

Reported at 2 U.N. Rep. Int'l Arb. Awards 1011 (1949).

6. After creation of the U.N. Charter, are reprisals permissible? Recall the 1970 Declaration on Principles of International Law; *see also* symposium, 8 Whittier L. Rev. no. 3 (1986).

CASE CONCERNING MILITARY AND PARAMILITARY ACTIVITIES IN AND AGAINST NICARAGUA (NICARAGUA v. UNITED STATES)

1986 I.C.J. 14.

[Editors' note: In 1984, the U.S. had argued, among other things, that the I.C.J. lacked jurisdiction to hear claims by Nicaragua against the U.S. concerning impermissible use of force and intervention in Nicaragua–including support of the *Contras* to overthrow the government of Nicaragua, attacks on Nicaraguan vessels and territory, and the mining of Nicaraguan waters (see lists of such acts in the Court's opinion, para. 292). When generally agreeing in 1946 to the competence of the I.C.J. to hear claims by or against the U.S., the United States consent had excluded "disputes arising under a multilateral treaty." Thus, the Court could not base its rulings on the U.N. Charter as such, but the Court found authority to address customary international law. Having lost the 1984 case on jurisdiction, the U.S. refused to participate in the proceedings on the merits and also terminated its general declaration of acceptance of the competence of the I.C.J. on October 7, 1985. The Court retained jurisdiction despite the lack of further U.S. participation and made its ruling on the merits.]

113. The question of the degree of control of the contras by the United States government is relevant to the claim of Nicaragua attributing responsibility to the United States for activities of the contras whereby the United States has, it is alleged, violated an obligation of international law not to kill, wound or kidnap citizens of Nicaragua. The activities in question are said to represent a tactic which includes "the spreading of terror and danger to non-combatants as an end in itself with no attempt to observe humanitarian standards and no reference to the concept of military necessity." In support of this, Nicaragua has catalogued numerous incidents....

115. The Court has taken the view ... that United States participation, even if preponderant or decisive in the financing, organizing, training, supplying and equipping of the contras, the selection of its military or paramilitary targets, and the planning of the whole of its operation, is still insufficient in itself, on the basis of the evidence in the possession of the Court, for the purpose of attributing to the United States the acts committed by the contras in the course of their military and paramilitary operations in Nicaragua. All the forms of United States participation mentioned above, and even the general control by the respondent State over a force with a high degree of dependency on it, would not in themselves mean, without further evidence, that the United States directed or enforced the perpetration of the acts contrary to human rights and humanitarian law alleged by the applicant State. Such acts could well be committed by members of the contras without the control of the United States. For this conduct to give rise to legal responsibility of the United States, t would in principle have to be

proved that the State had effective control of the military or paramilitary operations in the course of which the alleged violations were committed. . . .

174. In its Judgment of 26 November 1984, the Court . . . [c]ontrary to the views advanced by the United States, . . . affirmed that it "cannot dismiss the claims of Nicaragua under principles of customary and general international law simply because such principles have been enshrined in the texts of the conventions relied upon by Nicaragua. The fact that the above mentioned principles, recognized as such, have been codified or embodied in multilateral conventions does not mean that they cease to exist and to apply as principles of customary law, even as regards countries that are parties to such conventions. Principles such as those of the non-use force, non-intervention, respect for the independence and territorial integrity of States, and the freedom of navigation, continue to be binding as part of customary international law, despite the operation of provisions of conventional law in which they have been incorporated." (*I.C.J. Reports 1984* p. 424, para. 73.). . . .

176. As regards the suggestion that the areas covered by the two sources of law are identical, the Court observes that the United Nations Charter, the convention to which most of the United States argument is directed, by no means covers the whole area of the regulation of the use of force in international relations. On one essential point, this treaty itself refers to pre-existing customary international law; this reference to customary law is contained in the actual text of Article 51, which mentions the "inherent right" (in the French text the "*droit naturel*") of individual or collective self-defence, which "nothing in the present Charter shall impair" and which applies in the event of an armed attack. The Court therefore finds that Article 51 of the Charter is only meaningful on the basis that there is a "natural" or "inherent" right of self-defence, and it is hard to see how this can be other than of a customary nature, even if its present content has been confirmed and influenced by the Charter. Moreover the Charter, having itself recognized the existence of this right, does not go on to regulate directly all aspects of its content. For example, it does not contain any specific rule whereby self-defence would warrant only measures which are proportional to the armed attack and necessary to respond to it, a rule well established in customary international law. Moreover, a definition of the "armed attack" which, if found to exist, authorizes the exercise of the "inherent right" of self-defence, is not provided in the Charter, and is not part of treaty law. It cannot therefore be held that Article 51 is a provision which "subsumes and supervenes" customary international law. It rather demonstrates that in the field in question, the importance of which for the present dispute need hardly be stressed, customary international law continues to exist alongside treaty law. The areas governed by the two sources of law thus do not overlap exactly, and the rules do not have the same content. This could also be demonstrated for other subjects, in particular for the principle of non-intervention. . . .

181. ... [O]n the question of the use of force, the United States itself argues for a complete identity of the relevant rules of customary international law with the provisions of the Charter. The Court has not accepted this extreme contention, having found that on a number of points the areas governed by the two sources of law do not exactly overlap, and the substantive rules in which they are framed are not identical in content (paragraph 174 above). However, so far from having constituted a marked departure from a customary international law which still exists unmodified, the Charter gave expression in this field to principles already present in customary international law, and that law has in the subsequent four decades developed under the influence of the Charter, to such an extent that a number of rules contained in the Charter have acquired a status independent of it. The essential consideration is that both the Charter and the customary international law flow from a common fundamental principle outlawing the use of force in international relations. The differences which may exist between the specific content of each are not in the Court's view, such as to cause a judgment confined to the field of customary international law to be ineffective or inappropriate, or a judgment not susceptible to compliance or execution.

182. The Court concludes that it should exercise the jurisdiction conferred upon it by the United States declaration of acceptance under Article 36, paragraph 2, of the Statute, to determine the claims of Nicaragua based upon customary international law notwithstanding the exclusion from its jurisdiction of disputes "arising under" the United Nations and Organization of American States Charters.

183. In view of this conclusion, the Court has next to consider what are the rules of customary international law applicable to the present dispute. For this purpose, it has to direct its attention to the practice and *opinio juris* of States; as the Court recently observed.

> "it is of course axiomatic that the material of customary international law is to be looked for primarily in the actual practice and *opinio juris* of States, even though multilateral conventions may have an important role to play in recording and defining rules deriving from custom, or indeed in developing them." *(Continental Shelf (Libyan Arab Jamahiriya/ Malta), I.C.J. Reports 1985*, pp. 29–30, para. 27.)

In this respect the Court must not lose sight of the Charter of the United Nations and that of the Organization of American States, notwithstanding the operation of the multilateral treaty reservation. Although the Court has no jurisdiction to determine whether the conduct of the United States constitutes a breach of those conventions, it can and must take them into account in ascertaining the content of the customary international law which the United States is also alleged to have infringed.

184. The Court notes that there is in fact evidence, to be examined below, of a considerable degree of agreement between the Parties as to the content of the customary international law relating to the non-use of

force and non-intervention. This concurrence of their views does not however dispense the Court from having itself to ascertain what rules of customary international law are applicable. The mere fact that States declare their recognition of certain rules is not sufficient for the Court to consider these as being part of customary international law, and as applicable as such to those States. Bound as it is by Article 38 of its Statute to apply, *inter alia*, international custom "as evidence of a general practice accepted as law", the Court may not disregard the essential role played by general practice. Where two States agree to incorporate a particular rule in a treaty, their agreement suffices to make that rule a legal one, binding upon them; but in the field of customary international law, the shared view of the Parties as to the content of what they regard as the rule is not enough. The Court must satisfy itself that the existence of the rule in the *opinio juris* of States is confirmed by practice.

185. In the present dispute, the Court, while exercising its jurisdiction only in respect of the application of the customary rules of non-use of force and non-intervention, cannot disregard the fact that the Parties are bound by these rules as a matter of treaty law and of customary international law. Furthermore, in the present case, apart from the treaty commitments binding the Parties to the rules in question, there are various instances of their having expressed recognition of the validity thereof as customary international law in other ways. It is therefore in the light of this "subjective element"—the expression used by the Court in its 1969 Judgment in the *North Sea Continental Shelf* cases (*I.C.J. Reports 1969*, p. 44)—that the Court has to appraise the relevant practice.

186. It is not to be expected that in the practice of States the application of the rules in question should have been perfect, in the sense that States should have refrained, with complete consistency, from the use of force or from intervention in each other's internal affairs. The Court does not consider that, for a rule to be established as customary, the corresponding practice must be in absolutely rigorous conformity with the rule. In order to deduce the existence of customary rules, the Court deems it sufficient that the conduct of States should, in general, be consistent with such roles, and that instances of State conduct inconsistent with a given rule should generally have been treated as breaches of that rule, not as indications of the recognition of a new rule. If a State acts in a way prima facie incompatible with a recognized rule, but defends its conduct by appealing to exceptions or justifications contained within the rule itself, then whether or not the State's conduct is in fact justifiable on that basis, the significance of that attitude is to confirm rather than to weaken the rule.

187. The Court must therefore determine, first, the substance of the customary rules relating to the use of force in international relations, applicable to the dispute submitted to it. The United States has argued that, on this crucial question of the lawfulness of the use of force in inter-State relations, the rules of general and customary international

law, and those of the United Nations Charter, are in fact identical. In its view this identity is so complete that, as explained above (paragraph 173), it constitutes an argument to prevent the Court from applying this customary law, because it is indistinguishable from the multilateral treaty law which it may not apply. In its Counter–Memorial on jurisdiction and admissibility the United States asserts that "Article 2(4) of the Charter *is* customary and general international law". It quotes with approval an observation by the International Law Commission to the effect that

> "the great majority of international lawyers today unhesitatingly hold that Article 2, paragraph 4, together with other provisions of the Charter, authoritatively declares the modern customary law regarding the threat or use of force" *(ILC) Yearbook*, 1966, Vol. II, p. 247).

The United States points out that Nicaragua has endorsed this view, since one of its counsel asserted that "indeed it is generally considered by publicists that Article 2, paragraph 4, of the United Nations Charter is in this respect an embodiment of existing general principles of international law". And the United States concludes:

> "In sum, the provisions of Article 2(4) with respect of the lawfulness of the use of force *are* 'modern customary law' (International Law Commission, *loc. cit.*) and the 'embodiment of general principles of international law' (counsel for Nicaragua, Hearing of 25 April 1994, morning, *loc. cit.*). There is no other 'customary and general international law' on which Nicaragua can rest its claims."
>
> "It is, in short, inconceivable that this Court could consider the lawfulness of an alleged use of armed force without referring to the principal source of the relevant international law—Article 2(4) of the United Nations Charter."

As for Nicaragua, the only noteworthy shade of difference in its view lies in Nicaragua's belief that

> "in certain cases the rule of customary law will not necessarily be identical in content and mode of application to the conventional rule".

188. The Court thus finds that both Parties take the view that the principles as to the use of force incorporated in the United Nations Charter correspond, in essentials, to those found in customary international law. The Parties thus both take the view that the fundamental principle in this area is expressed in the terms employed in Article 2, paragraph 4, of the United Nations Charter. They therefore accept a treaty-law obligation to refrain in their international relations from the threat or use of force against the territorial integrity or political independence of any State, or in any other manner inconsistent with the purposes of the United Nations. The Court has however to be satisfied that there exists in customary international law an *opinio juris* as to the binding character of such abstention. This *opinio juris* may, though with

all due caution, be deduced from, *inter alia*, the attitude of the Parties and the attitude of States towards certain General Assembly resolutions, and particularly resolution 2625 (XXV) entitled "Declaration of Principles on International Law concerning Friendly Relations and Co-operation among States in accordance with the Charter of the United Nations". The effect of consent to the text of such resolutions cannot be understood as merely that of a "reiteration or elucidation" of the treaty commitment undertaken in the Charter. On the contrary, it may be understood as an acceptance of the validity of the rule or set of rules declared by the resolution by themselves. The principle of non-use of force, for example, may thus be regarded as a principle of customary international law, not as such conditioned by provisions relating to collective security, or to the facilities or armed contingents to be provided under Article 43 of the Charter. It would therefore seem apparent that the attitude referred to expresses an *opinio juris* respecting such rule (or set of rules), to be thenceforth treated separately from the provisions, especially those of an institutional kind, to which it is subject on the treaty-law plane of the Charter. . . .

190. A further confirmation of the validity as customary international law of the principle of the prohibition of the use of force expressed in Article 2, paragraph 4, of the Charter of the United Nations may be found in the fact that it is frequently referred to in statements by State representatives as being not only a principle of customary international law but also a fundamental or cardinal principle of such law. The International Law Commission, in the course of its work on the codification of the law of treaties, expressed the view that "the law of the Charter concerning the prohibition of the use of force in itself constitutes a conspicuous example of a rule in international law having the character of *jus cogens*" (paragraph (1) of the commentary of the Commission to Article 50 of its draft Articles on the Law of Treaties, *ILC Yearbook*, 1966–II, p. 247). Nicaragua in its Memorial on the Merits submitted in the present case states that the principle prohibiting the use of force embodied in Article 2, paragraph 4, of the Charter of the United Nations "has come to be recognized as *jus cogens*". The United States, in its Counter–Memorial on the questions of jurisdiction and admissibility, found it material to quote the views of scholars that this principle is a "universal norm", a "universal international law", a "universally recognized principle of international law", and a "principle of *jus cogens*".

191. As regards certain particular aspects of the principle in question, it will be necessary to distinguish the most grave forms of the use of force (those constituting an armed attack) from other less grave forms. In determining the legal rule which applies to these latter forms, the Court can again draw on the formulations contained in the Declaration on Principles of International Law concerning Friendly Relations and Co-operation among States in accordance with the Charter of the United Nations (General Assembly resolution 2625 (XXV), referred to above). As already observed, the adoption by States of this text affords

an indication of their *opinio juris* as to customary international law on the question. Alongside certain descriptions which may refer to aggression, this text includes others which refer only to less grave forms of the use of force....

192. Moreover, in the part of this same resolution devoted to the principle of non-intervention in matters within the national jurisdiction of States, a very similar rule is found:

> "Also, no State shall organize, assist, foment, finance, incite or tolerate subversive, terrorist or armed activities directed towards the violent overthrow of the regime of another State, or interfere in civil strife in another State."

In the context of the inter-American system, this approach can be traced back at least to 1928 (Convention on the Rights and Duties of States in the Event of Civil Strife, Art. 1 (1)); it was confirmed by resolution 78 adopted by the General Assembly of the Organization of American States on 21 April 1972. The operative part of this resolution reads as follows:

> *"The General Assembly Resolves:*
>
> 1. To reiterate solemnly the need for the member states of the Organization to observe strictly the principles of nonintervention and self-determination of peoples as a means of ensuring peaceful coexistence among them and to refrain from committing any direct or indirect act that might constitute a violation of these principles.
>
> 2. To reaffirm the obligation of those states to refrain from applying economic, political, or any other type of measures to coerce another state and obtain from it advantages of any kind.
>
> 3. Similarly, to reaffirm the obligation of these states to refrain from organizing, supporting, promoting, financing, instigating, or tolerating subversive, terrorist, or armed activities against another state and from intervening in a civil war in another state or in its internal struggles."

193. The general rule prohibiting force allows for certain exceptions. In view of the arguments advanced by the United States to justify the acts of which it is accused by Nicaragua, the Court must express a view on the content of the right of self-defence, and more particularly the right of collective self-defence. First, with regard to the existence of this right, it notes that in the language of Article 51 of the United Nations Charter, the inherent right (or "*droit naturel*") which any State possesses in the event of an armed attack, covers both collective and individual self-defence. Thus, the Charter itself testifies to the existence of the right of collective self-defence in customary international law. Moreover, just as the wording of certain General Assembly declarations adopted by States demonstrates their recognition of the principle of the prohibition of force as definitely a matter of customary international law, some of the wording in those declarations operates similarly in respect of the right of self-defence (both collective and individual). Thus, in the declaration quoted above on the Principles of International Law concern-

ing Friendly Relations and Co-operation among States in accordance with the Charter of the United Nations, the reference to the prohibition of force is followed by a paragraph stating that:

> "nothing in the foregoing paragraphs shall be construed as enlarging or diminishing in any way the scope of the provisions of the Charter concerning cases in which the use of force is lawful".

This resolution demonstrates that the States represented in the General Assembly regard the exception to the prohibition of force constituted by the right of individual or collective self-defence as already a matter of customary international law.

194. With regard to the characteristics governing the right of self-defence, since the Parties consider the existence of this right to be established as a matter of customary international law, they have concentrated on the conditions governing its use. In view of the circumstances in which the dispute has arisen, reliance is placed by the Parties only on the right of self-defence in the case of an armed attack which has already occurred, and the issue of the lawfulness of a response to the imminent threat of armed attack has not been raised. Accordingly the Court expresses no view on that issue. The Parties also agree in holding that whether the response to the attack is lawful depends on observance of the criteria of the necessity and the proportionality of the measures taken in self-defence. Since the existence of the right of collective self-defence is established in customary international law, the Court must define the specific conditions which may have to be met for its exercise, in addition to the conditions of necessity and proportionality to which the Parties have referred.

195. In the case of individual self-defence, the exercise of this right is subject to the State concerned having been the victim of an armed attack. Reliance on collective self-defence of course does not remove the need for this. There appears now to be general agreement on the nature of the acts which can be treated as constituting armed attacks. In particular, it may be considered to be agreed that an armed attack must be understood as including not merely action by regular armed forces across an international border, but also "the sending by or on behalf of a State of armed bands, groups, irregulars or mercenaries, which carry out acts of armed force against another State of such gravity as to amount to"*(inter alia)* an actual armed attack conducted by regular forces, "or its substantial involvement therein". This description, contained in Article 3, paragraph *(g)*, of the Definition of Aggression annexed to General Assembly resolution 3314 (XXIX), may be taken to reflect customary international law. The Court sees no reason to deny that, in customary law, the prohibition of armed attacks may apply to the sending by a State of armed bands to the territory of another State, if such an operation, because of its scale and effects, would have been classified as an armed attack rather than as a mere frontier incident had it been carried out by regular armed forces. But the Court does not believe that the concept of "armed attack" includes not only acts by

armed bands where such acts occur on a significant scale but also assistance to rebels in the form of the provision of weapons or logistical or other support. Such assistance may be regarded as a threat or use of force, or amount to intervention in the internal or external affairs of other States. It is also clear that it is the State which is the victim of an armed attack which must form and declare the view that it has been so attacked. There is no rule in customary international law permitting another State to exercise the right of collective self-defence on the basis of its own assessment of the situation. Where collective self-defence is invoked, it is to be expected that the State for whose benefit this right is used will have declared itself to be the victim of an armed attack....

202. The principle of non-intervention involves the right of every sovereign State to conduct its affairs without outside interference; though examples of trespass against this principle are not infrequent, the Court considers that it is part and parcel of customary international law. As the Court has observed: "Between independent States, respect for territorial sovereignty is an essential foundation of international relations" *(I.C.J. Reports 1949,* p. 35), and international law requires political integrity also to be respected. Expressions of an *opinio juris* regarding the existence of the principle of non-intervention in customary international law are numerous and not difficult to find. Of course, statements whereby States avow their recognition of the principles of international law set forth in the United Nations Charter cannot strictly be interpreted as applying to the principle of non-intervention by States in the internal and external affairs of other States, since this principle is not, as such, spelt out in the Charter. But it was never intended that the Charter should embody written confirmation of every essential principle of international law in force. The existence in the *opinio juris* of States of the principle of non-intervention is backed by established and substantial practice. It has moreover been presented as a corollary of the principle of the sovereign equality of States. A particular instance of this is General Assembly resolution 2625 (XXV), the Declaration of the Principles of International Law concerning Friendly Relations and Co-operation among States. In the *Corfu Channel* case, when a State claimed a right of intervention in order to secure evidence in the territory of another State for submission to an international tribunal *(I.C.J. Reports 1949,* p. 34), the Court observed that:

> "the alleged right of intervention is the manifestation of a policy of force, such as has, in the past, given rise to most serious abuses and such as cannot, whatever be the present defects in international organization, find a place in international law. Intervention is perhaps still less admissible in the particular form it would take here; for, from the nature of things, it would be reserved for the most powerful States, and might easily lead to perverting the administration of international justice itself." *(I.C.J. Reports 1949,* p. 35.) ...

208. In particular, as regards the conduct towards Nicaragua which is the subject of the present case, the United States has not claimed that its intervention, which it justified in this way on the

political level, was also justified on the legal level, alleging the exercise of a new right of intervention regarded by the United States as existing in such circumstances. As mentioned above, the United States has, on the legal plane, justified its intervention expressly and solely by reference to the "classic" rules involved, namely, collective self-defence against an armed attack. Nicaragua, for its part, has often expressed its solidarity and sympathy with the opposition in various States, especially in El Salvador. But Nicaragua too has not argued that this was legal basis for an intervention, let alone an intervention involving the use of force.

209. The Court therefore finds that no such general right of intervention, in support of an opposition within another State, exists in contemporary international law. The Court concludes that acts constituting a breach of the customary principle of non-intervention will also, if they directly or indirectly involve the use of force, constitute a breach of the principle of non-use of force in international relations. . . .

211. The Court has recalled above (paragraphs 193 to 195) that for one State to use force against another, on the ground that that State has committed a wrongful act of force against a third State, is regarded as lawful, by way of exception, only when the wrongful act provoking the response was an armed attack. Thus the lawfulness of the use of force by a State in response to a wrongful act of which it has not itself been the victim is not admitted when this wrongful act is not an armed attack. In the view of the Court, under international law in force today—whether customary international law or that of the United Nations system—States do not have a right of "collective" armed response to acts which do not constitute an "armed attack". Furthermore, the Court has to recall that the United States itself is relying on the "inherent right of self-defence" (paragraph 126 above), but apparently does not claim that any such right exists as would, in respect of intervention, operate in the same way as the right of collective self-defence in respect of an armed attack. In the discharge of its duty under Article 53 of the Statute, the Court has nevertheless had to consider whether such a right might exist; but in doing so it may take note of the absence of any such claim by the United States as an indication of *opinio juris*. . . .

263. The finding of the United States Congress also expressed the view that the Nicaraguan Government had taken "significant steps towards establishing a totalitarian Communist dictatorship". However the regime in Nicaragua be defined, adherence by a State to any particular doctrine does not constitute a violation of customary international law; to hold otherwise would make nonsense of the fundamental principle of State sovereignty, on which the whole of international law rests, and the freedom of choice of the political, social, economic and cultural system of a State. Consequently, Nicaragua's domestic policy options, even assuming that they correspond to the description given of them by the Congress finding, cannot justify on the legal plane the various actions of the Respondent complained of. The Court cannot contemplate the creation of a new rule opening up a right of intervention

by one State against another on the ground that the latter has opted for some particular ideology or political system.

264. The Court has also emphasized the importance to be attached, in other respects, to a text such as the Helsinki Final Act, or, on another level, to General Assembly resolution 2625 (XXV) which, as its name indicates, is a declaration on "Principles of International Law concerning Friendly Relations and Co-operation among States in accordance with the Charter of the United Nations". Texts like these, in relation to which the Court has pointed to the customary content of certain provisions such as the principles of the non-use of force and non-intervention, envisage the relations among States having different political, economic and social systems on the basis of coexistence among their various ideologies; the United States not only voiced no objection to their adoption, but took an active part in bringing it about....

267. The Court also notes that Nicaragua is accused by the 1985 finding of the United States Congress of violating human rights. This particular point requires to be studied independently of the question of the existence of a "legal commitment" by Nicaragua towards the Organization of American States to respect these rights; the absence of such a commitment would not mean that Nicaragua could with impunity violate human rights. However, where human rights are protected by international conventions, that protection takes the form of such arrangements for monitoring or ensuring respect for human rights as are provided for in the conventions themselves. The political pledge by Nicaragua was made in the context of the Organization of American States, the organs of which were consequently entitled to monitor its observance. The Court has noted above (paragraph 168) that the Nicaraguan Government has since 1979 ratified a number of international instruments on human rights, and one of these was the American Convention on Human Rights (the Pact of San José, Costa Rica). The mechanisms provided for therein have functioned. The Inter–American Commission on Human Rights in fact took action and compiled two reports (OEA/Ser.L/V/11.53 and 62) following visits by the Commission to Nicaragua at the Government's invitation. Consequently, the Organization was in a position, if it so wished, to take a decision on the basis of these reports.

268. In any event, while the United States might form its own appraisal of the situation as to respect for human rights in Nicaragua, the use of force could not be the appropriate method to monitor or ensure such respect. With regard to the steps actually taken, the protection of human rights, a strictly humanitarian objective, cannot be compatible with the mining of ports, the destruction of oil installations, or again with the training, arming and equipping of the *contras*. The Court concludes that the argument derived from the preservation of human rights in Nicaragua cannot afford a legal justification for the conduct of the United States, and cannot in any event be reconciled with the legal strategy of the respondent State, which is based on the right of collective self-defence....

292. For these reasons,

THE COURT . . .

(3) By twelve votes to three,

Decides that the United States of America, by training, arming, equipping, financing and supplying the *contra* forces or otherwise encouraging, supporting and aiding military and paramilitary activities in and against Nicaragua, has acted, against the Republic of Nicaragua, in breach of its obligation under customary international law not to intervene in the affairs of another State;

(4) By twelve votes to three,

Decides that the United States of America, by certain attacks on Nicaraguan territory in 1983–1984, namely attacks on Puerto Sandino on 13 September and 14 October 1983; an attack on Corinto on 10 October 1983; an attack on Potosi Naval Base on 4/5 January 1984; an attack on San Juan del Sur on 7 March 1984; attacks on patrol boats at Puerto Sandino on 28 and 30 March 1984; and an attack on San Juan del Norte on 9 April 1984; and further by those acts of intervention referred to in subparagraph (3) hereof which involve the use of force, has acted, against the Republic of Nicaragua, in breach of its obligation under customary international law not to use force against another State;

(5) By twelve votes to three,

Decides that the United States of America, by directing or authorizing overflights of Nicaraguan territory, and by the acts imputable to the United States referred to in subparagraph (4) hereof, has acted, against the Republic of Nicaragua, in breach of its obligation under customary international law not to violate the sovereignty of another State;

(6) By twelve votes to three,

Decides that, by laying mines in the internal or territorial waters of the Republic of Nicaragua during the first months of 1984, the United States of America has acted, against the Republic of Nicaragua, in breach of its obligations under customary international law not to use force against another State, not to intervene in its affairs, not to violate its sovereignty and not to interrupt peaceful maritime commerce;

(7) By fourteen votes to one,

Decides that, by acts referred to in subparagraph (6) hereof, the United States of America has acted, against the Republic of Nicaragua, in breach of its obligations under Article XIX of the Treaty of Friendship, Commerce and Navigation between the United States of America and the Republic of Nicaragua signed at Managua on 21 January 1956; . . .

(12) By twelve votes to three,

Decides that the United States of America is under a duty immediately to cease and to refrain from all such acts as may constitute breaches of the foregoing legal obligations;

(13) By twelve votes to three,

Decides that the United States of America is under an obligation to make reparation to the Republic of Nicaragua for all injury caused to Nicaragua by the breaches of obligations under customary international law enumerated above....

Dissenting Opinion of Judge Schwebel

... I. The Court's Conclusion is Inconsistent with the General Assembly's Definition of Aggression

162. While the conclusion which the Court has reached on this question is inconsistent with the large and authoritative body of State practice and United Nations interpretation to which the Nicaraguan Memorial adverts, the Court is not the first to maintain that acts of armed subversion—of "indirect aggression"—by one State against another cannot be tantamount to armed attack. In the long debates that ultimately culminated in the adoption by the United Nations General Assembly of the Definition of Aggression, opinion on this question was divided. The Soviet Union, a leading proponent of the adoption of a definition of aggression, in its draft definition enumerated among the acts of "*armed* aggression (direct or indirect)":

> "The use by a State of armed force by sending armed bands, mercenaries, terrorists or saboteurs to the territory of another State and engagement in other forms of subversive activity involving the use of armed force with the aim of promoting an internal upheaval in another State ..."(A/8719, p. 8; emphasis supplied.)
>
> Six Powers—Australia, Canada, Italy, Japan, the United Kingdom and the United States—proposed that the use of force in international relations, "overt or covert, direct or indirect" by a State against the territorial integrity or political independence of another State may constitute aggression when effected by means including:
>
> "(6) Organizing, supporting or directing armed bands or irregular or volunteer forces that make incursions or infiltrate into another State;
>
> (7) Organizing, supporting or directing violent civil strife or acts of terrorism in another State; or
>
> (8) Organizing, supporting or directing subversive activities aimed at the violent overthrow of the Government of another State." (A/8719, pp.11–12)

163. In marked contrast to these approaches of "East" and "West", 13 small and middle Powers put forward a draft definition of aggression which did not include indirect as well as direct uses of force. Their definition spoke only of "the use of armed force by a State against

another State". Their list of acts of aggression conspicuously failed to include acts of force effected by indirect means....

164. As Professor Julius Stone—widely recognized as one of the century's leading authorities on the law of the use of force in international relations—concluded in respect of the Thirteen–Power proposals:

> "to take away the right of individual and collective self-defence ... was, of course, the precise purpose of the Thirteen Power provision.... It sought to achieve this purpose, both by withholding the stigma of aggression, and by express statement. Acceptance of such a provision would have been at odds with the Charter and general international law as hitherto accepted in a number of respects.
>
> First ... international law imputed responsibility to a State knowingly serving as a base of such para-military activities, and gave the victim State rather wide liberties of self-defence against them.
>
> Second, none of the Charter provisions dealing with unlawful use of force, whether armed or not, offers any basis for distinguishing between force applied by the putative aggressor, or indirectly applied by him through armed bands, irregulars and the like....
>
> Third ... the General Assembly has more than once included at least some species of "indirect" aggression within its description of "aggression".
>
> Fourth, it may be added that from at least the Spanish Civil War onwards, the most endemic and persistent forms of resorts to armed force ... have been in contexts caught as "aggression" by the Soviet and Six Power drafts, but condoned more or less fully by the "Thirteen Power Draft". (*Conflict through Consensus*, 1977, pp. 89–90).

It will be observed that the essential legal rationale of the Judgment of the Court in the current case appears to be well expressed by these Thirteen–Power proposals which Professor Stone characterized as "at odds with the Charter and general international law ...".

165. The Thirteen–Power proposals were not accepted by the United Nations Special Committee on the Question of Defining Aggression. They were not accepted by the General Assembly. On the contrary, the General Assembly by consensus adopted a Definition of Aggression which embraces not all, but still the essence of the proposals of the Six Powers and the Soviet Union. Its list in Article 3 of the acts which shall "qualify as an act of aggression" includes:

> "(g) The sending by or on behalf of a State of armed bands, groups, irregulars or mercenaries, which carry out acts of armed force against another State of such gravity as to amount to the acts listed above, *or its substantial involvement therein*". (emphasis supplied)....

166. It has been demonstrated above and in the appendix to this opinion that the Nicaraguan Government is "substantially involved" in the sending of armed bands, groups and irregulars to El Salvador. Nicaragua apparently has not "sent" Nicaraguan irregulars to fight in

El Salvador, but it has been "substantially involved" in the sending of leadership of the Salvadoran insurgency back and forth. As has been shown by the admissions of a principal witness of Nicaragua, Mr. MacMichael, and other evidence, leadership of the Salvadoran insurgency has been established in and operated from Nicaragua, and moved into and out of El Salvador from and to its Nicaraguan bases with the full support of the Nicaraguan Government, a situation which in substance equates with Nicaragua's "sending" of that leadership to direct the insurgency in El Salvador.... Nicaragua's substantial involvement further takes the forms of providing arms, munitions, other supplies, training, command-and-control facilities, sanctuary and lesser forms of assistance to the Salvadoran insurgents. Those insurgents, in turn, carry out acts of armed force against another State, namely, El Salvador. Those acts are of such gravity as to amount to the other acts listed in Article 3 of the Definition of Aggression, such as invasion, attack, bombardment and blockade. The many thousands of El Salvadorans killed and wounded, and the enormous damage to El Salvador's infrastructure and economy, as a result of insurgent attacks so supported by Nicaragua is ample demonstration of the gravity of the acts of the insurgents....

170. The Court's reasoning is open to criticism, in terms of the Definition of Aggression and under customary international law—not to speak of the realities of modern warfare. Article 3 (*g*) does not confine its definition of acts that qualify as acts of aggression to the sending of armed bands; rather, it specifies as an act of aggression a State's "substantial involvement" in the sending of armed bands....

K. The Court's Views on Counter–Intervention and its Implied Support for "Wars of Liberation"

174. When the Court's Judgment comes to deal with questions of intervention, it finds that the United States has committed "a clear breach of the principle of non-intervention" by its support of the *Contras*. The Court at the same time finds it possible—remarkably enough—to absolve Nicaragua of any act of intervention in El Salvador, despite its multiple acts of intervention in El Salvador in support of the Salvadoran insurgents....

175. While this conclusion may be treated as *obiter dictum* in view of the fact that there is no plea of counter-intervention before the Court, it is no more correct because it is unnecessary. In my view, its errors are conspicuous. The Court appears to reason this way. Efforts by State A (however insidious, sustained, substantial and effective), to overthrow the government of State B, if they are not or do not amount to an armed attack upon State B, give rise to no right of self-defence by State B and hence, to no right of State C to join State B in measures of collective self-defence. State B, the victim State, is entitled to take counter-measures against State A, of a dimension the Court does not specify. But State C is not thereby justified in taking counter-measures against State A which involve the use of force.

176. In my view, the Court's reasoning certainly as it applies to the case before the Court, is erroneous for the following reasons: (a) A State is not necessarily and absolutely confined to responding in self-defence only if it is the object of armed attack. (b) Armed attack in any event is not only the movement of regular armed forces across international frontiers; it is not only the sending by State A of armed bands across an international frontier to attack State B or overthrow its government; it is, as the Definition of Aggression puts it, "substantial involvement therein"—for example, the very sort of substantial involvement which Nicaragua's multifaceted involvement in promoting and sustaining the Salvadoran insurgency illustrates. (c) In a case such as the case before the Court, where Nicaragua has carried out and continues to carry out the acts of support of armed insurgency against the Government of El Salvador which El Salvador which El Salvador and the United States have charged and the appendix to this opinion establishes, the Government of El Salvador has had the choice of acting in self-defense or capitulating. Lesser measures of counter-intervention could not suffice. It has chosen to act in self-defence, but it lacks the power to carry the battle to the territory of the aggressor, Nicaragua. (d) In such a case, El Salvador is entitled to seek assistance in collective self-defence. Such assistance may in any event take place on the territory of El Salvador, as by the financing, provisioning and training of its troops by the United States. But, as shown below, contemporary international law recognizes that a third State is entitled to exert measures of force against the aggressor on its own territory and against its own armed forces and military resources.

177. I find the Court's enunciation of what it finds to be the law of counter-intervention as applied to this case unpersuasive for all these reasons. More generally, I believe that it raises worrisome questions. Let us suppose that State A's support of the subversion of State B, while serious and effective enough to place the political independence of State B in jeopardy, does not amount to an armed attack upon State B. Let us further suppose that State A acts against State B not only on its behalf but together with a Great Power and an organized international movement with a long and successful history of ideology and achievement in the cause of subversion and aggrandizement, and with the power and will to stimulate further the progress of what that movement regards as historically determined. If the Court's *obiter dictum* were to be treated as the law to which States deferred, other Great Powers and other States would be or could be essentially powerless to intervene effectively to preserve the political independence of State B and all other similarly situated States, most of which will be small. According to the Court, State B could take counter-measures against State A, but whether they would include measures of force is not said. What is said is that third States could not use force, whether or not the preservation of the political independence—or territorial integrity—of State B depended on the exertion of such measures. In short, the Court appears to offer—quite gratuitously—a prescription for overthrow of weaker governments

by predatory governments while denying potential victims what in some cases may be their only hope of survival....

S. The United States Has not Unlawfully Intervened in the Internal or External Affairs of Nicaragua

241. Relying on the same factual allegations which it has advanced against the United States in respect of the use of force against it, Nicaragua also maintains that the United States stands in breach of its obligations under the Chapter of the Organization of American States, as contained in Articles 18, 19, 20 and 21, and under customary international law. The essence of its claim is that the United States has unlawfully intervened in the internal and external affairs of Nicaragua by attempting to change the policies of its Government or the Nicaraguan Government itself.

242. In view of the comprehensive and categorical injunctions of the OAS Charter against intervention, and the much narrower but significant rules of non-intervention of customary international law, Nicaragua's prima facie case appears to be considerable. On analysis, however, it is inadequate, and for two reasons (in addition to those posed by the multilateral treaty reservation). The first of those reasons goes a long way towards countering Nicaraguan contentions of unlawful intervention. The second vitiates them.

243. It has been shown that, in order to extract from the OAS and its Members their recognition of the Junta of National Reconstruction in place of the Government of President Somoza, the Junta, in response to the OAS resolution of 23 June 1979, gave undertakings to the OAS and its Members to govern in accordance with specified democratic standards and policies (see paras. 8–13 of the appendix to this opinion). It has also been shown that the Nicaraguan Government has failed so to govern, and has so failed deliberately and willfully, as a matter of State policy (ibid.)....

245. The Permanent Court of International Justice in its advisory opinion on *Nationality Decrees Issued in Tunis and Morocco (P.C.I.J., Series B, No. 4,* p. 24) dealt with what is a matter of domestic jurisdiction in classic terms:

> "The question whether a certain matter is or is not solely within the jurisdiction of a State is an essentially relative question; it depends on the development of international relations ... it may well happen that, in a matter which ... is not, in principle, regulated by international law, the right of a State to use its discretion is nevertheless restricted by obligations which it may have undertaken towards other States. In such a case, jurisdiction which, in principle, belongs solely to the State, is limited by the rules of international law".

There is nothing to debar a state—or a revolutionary junta entitled to bind the State—from undertaking obligations towards other States in respect of matters which otherwise would be within its exclusive jurisdiction. Thus, under the Statute of the Council of Europe, every Member of the Council of Europe "must accept the principles of the rule of law and of the enjoyment by all persons within its jurisdiction of human rights and fundamental freedoms" (Art.3). Any Member which has seriously violated Article 3 may be suspended from its rights of representation. The history of the Council of Europe demonstrates that these international obligations are treated as such by the Council; they may not be avoided by pleas of domestic jurisdiction and non-intervention.

246. The Nicaraguan Junta of National Reconstruction, by the undertakings it entered into not only with the OAS but with its Members, among them, the United States (which individually and in consideration of those undertakings treated with the Junta as the Government of the Republic of Nicaragua), has not dissimilarly placed within the domain of Nicaragua's international obligations its domestic governance and foreign policy to the extent of those undertakings. Thus, what otherwise would be "the right" of Nicaragua "to use its discretion is nevertheless restricted by obligations" which it has undertaken towards those States, including the United States. It follows that, when the United States demands that Nicaragua perform its undertakings given to the OAS and its Members, including the United States, to observe human rights, to enforce civil justice, to call free elections; when it demands that the Junta perform its promises of "a truly democratic government ... with full guaranty of human rights" and "fundamental liberties" including "free expression, reporting" and trade union freedom and "an independent foreign policy of non-alignment" (appendix to this opinion, paras. 8–11), the United States does not "intervene" in the internal or external affairs of Nicaragua. Such demands are not a "form of interference or attempted threat against the personality of the State" of Nicaragua. They are legally well-grounded efforts to induce Nicaragua to perform its international obligations.

247. The Court, however, has found that, by its 1979 communications to the OAS and its Members, Nicaragua entered into no commitments. It may be observed that that conclusion is inconsistent not only with the views of the United States quoted in the Court's Judgment, but apparently with the views of Nicaragua (appendix to this opinion, para. 53). In my view, the commitment of Nicaragua is clear: essentially, in exchange for the OAS and its Members stripping the Somoza Government of its legitimacy and bestowing recognition upon the Junta as the Government of Nicaragua, the Junta extended specific pledges to the OAS and its Members which it bound itself to "implement"....

248. It is of course obvious that the Junta did not, by its written undertakings to the OAS and its Members, conclude an international agreement in treaty form. But, as the Vienna Convention on the Law of Treaties recognized (Art. 3), and as the Permanent Court of International Justice held in the *Legal Status of Eastern Greenland, Judgment, 1933 P.C.I.J. Series A/B, No. 53*, page 71, an international commitment binding upon a State need not be made in written, still less particularly formal, form. The question is simply, did the authority of the State

concerned give an assurance, or extend an undertaking, which, in the particular circumstances, is to be regarded as binding upon it? When a revolutionary government, soliciting recognition, has given assurances to foreign governments, such assurances have repeatedly been treated by foreign governments as binding the revolutionary government and its successors.... As the Inter–American Commission on Human Rights recognized, the OAS deprived the Somoza Government of legitimacy. The OAS offered recognition to the Junta on bases which the Junta accepted. The Junta in reply indeed prescribed that, immediately following its installation inside Nicaragua, "the Member States of the OAS ... will proceed to recognize it as the legitimate Government of Nicaragua" and that it in turn "will immediately proceed" to decree its Fundamental Statute and Organic Law and implement its Program (appendix, para. 10). The OAS and its Members performed; the Government of Nicaragua did not. Not only was the creation of an international obligation clear; so was its breach....

250. This brings us to the second, and dispositive, consideration. The United States claims that the measures of force which it has exerted, directly and indirectly, against Nicaragua, are measures of collective self-defence. If that claim is good—and, for the reasons expounded above, I believe that it is—it is a defence not only to Nicaraguan charges of the unlawful use of force against it but of intervention against it. That is demonstrated by the terms of the OAS Charter. Articles 21 and 22 provide:

> "Article 21
>
> The American States bind themselves in their international relations not to have recourse to the use of force, except in the case of self-defence in accordance with existing treaties or in fulfillment thereof.
>
> Article 22
>
> Measures adopted for the maintenance of peace and security in accordance with existing treaties do not constitute a violation of the principles set forth in Articles 18 and 20".

As has been shown above, the use of force by the United States comports not only with the United Nations Charter but with the Rio Treaty—one of the "existing treaties" to which Articles 21 and 22 of the Charter of the OAS refer. The "measures adopted for the maintenance of peace and security in accordance with existing treaties" by the United States and El Salvador, in exercise of their inherent right of collective self-defence, thus "do not constitute a violation of the principles set forth in Articles 18 and 20" of the OAS Charter. Nor do they transgress customary international law. If a State charged with intervention actually acted in collective self-defence, its measures are treated not as unlawful intervention but as measures of justified counter-intervention or self-defence.

Notes and Questions

1. Do you agree with the Court's opinion (all of it) or the dissenting opinion (all of it), or what?

2. Would you have made any different claims before the Court on behalf of the United States (which did not appear), or Nicaragua?

3. Was the Court correct that "sovereignty" or self-determination of a people is equivalent to or consistent with "adherence by a State to any particular doctrine ... ideology or political system"? Consider U.N. Charter, arts. 1(2) and (3), 55(c), 56; U.N. G.A. Res. 2625 (XXV); Universal Declaration of Human Rights, art. 21(3); Western Sahara Advisory Opinion, 1975 I.C.J. 12, 31–33, 36; U.N. S.C. Res. 940 (July 31, 1994); U.N. G.A. Res. 39/2 (Sept. 28, 1984); American Convention on Human Rights, preamble and art. 29(c); American Declaration of the Rights and Duties of Man, art. XX.

4. On August 20, 1998, President Clinton declared "war on terrorism" and the United States fired cruise missiles into Afghanistan and the Sudan to target an alleged terrorist training center under the control of Mr. Osama bin Laden and an alleged chemical weapons facility in Khartoum, the Sudan. Each target was alleged to have been connected to bomb attacks on the U.S. Embassy compounds in Nairobi, Kenya, and in Dar Es Salaam, Tanzania, that killed more than 250 persons (including 12 U.S. nationals) and injured more than 5,500 people. The U.S. claimed that the use of force was in "self-defense" and that "terrorist-related facilities" were a "threat ... to our national security," President Clinton adding: "We have compelling information that additional attacks were planned," that groups under bin Laden were "seeking to acquire chemical weapons," and that governments in the Sudan and Afghanistan had been warned for years not to be safe havens for terrorists. The Government of the Sudan complained to the U.N. Security Council of a U.S. act of "aggression".

Do you think that self-defense was a proper claim? Were new attacks continuing attacks or just imminent? Was the U.S. action merely preemptive self-defense? Was it merely a reprisal? Is the use of force justified if a foreign government cannot or will not comply with international law to stop terrorist interventions and attacks from its territory? *See also* symposium, 8 WHITTIER L. REV. no. 3 (1986).

When reading the materials in Section 2, consider also whether the President's actions were appropriate under the United States Constitution. What does a "war" on "terrorism" mean?

5. With respect to alleged U.S. responsibility for acts by the Contras against Nicaragua because of U.S. "financing, organizing, training, supplying and equipping of the Contras, the selection of its military and paramilitary targets, and the planning of the whole of its operation," recall that the Court stated that it would "have to be proved that the State had effective control of the military and paramilitary operations" of the Contras for state responsibility of the U.S. to arise and there was insufficient evidence that the U.S. "directed or enforced the perpetration of the acts" under investigation. *Id.* at para. 115. Later, the International Criminal Tribunal for Former Yugoslavia declared that "in addition to financing, training and equipping or providing operational support," the state should have a "role in organizing,

coordinating or planning the military actions of the'' non-state group. See The Prosecutor v. Tadic, Opinion and Judgment, IT–94–1–T, para. 137 (7 May 1997). *See also* Paust, *Use of Armed Force against Terrorists in Afghanistan, Iraq, and Beyond*, 35 CORNELL INT'L L.J. 533, 540–44 (2002). State responsibility leading to political, diplomatic, economic, or juridical sanctions can also arise if a state adopts non-state actor conduct as its own. *See, e.g.*, United States Diplomatic and Consular Staff in Tehran (United States v. Iran), 1980 I.C.J. 3; Responsibility of States for Internationally Wrongful Acts, art. 11 (''if and to the extent that the State acknowledges and adopts the conduct in question as its own''), U.N. G.A. Res. 56/83, U.N. GAOR, 56th Sess., Annex, Supp. No. 10, U.N. Doc. A/56/83 (2001). Even where it exists, state responsibility is not the same as an ''armed attack'' triggering self-defense but could allow diplomatic, political, economic, and juridic sanctions.

6. Was the use of force by the United States in Afghanistan on October 7, 2001 permissible self-defense in response to the September 11th al Qaeda attacks on the World Trade Center and the Pentagon? Is Article 51 triggered by non-state actor armed attacks? Was the use of force by the U.S. permissible against the Taliban regime in Afghanistan on October 7, 2001? See also Section 2 B 5, *infra*.

7. Are there any other current events to which the Judgment of the Court might be relevant? Do you foresee the likelihood of criminal sanctions being employed?

C. Security Council Measures

UNITED NATIONS CHARTER

[read Articles 24–25, 33, 39–49 of the U.N. Charter].

Notes and Questions

1. Who determines what constitutes a threat to the peace, breach of the peace, or act of aggression?

2. Must a ''threat to the peace'' involve a violation of Article 2, paragraph 4, of the Charter?

3. Can the International Court of Justice review the legality of a Security Council decision made under Article 39 (or Chapter VII) of the Charter in a case before the Court? *See also* U.N. Charter, Articles 24–25, 55 (c), 56, 92, 96; Statute of the I.C.J., Article 38 [in Chapter 1, Section 1 B]; Further Requests for the Indication of Provisional Measures, 1993 I.C.J. (Sept. 13) (Separate Opinion of Judge Lauterpacht) paras. 99–100; Questions of Interpretation and Application of the 1971 Montreal Convention Arising from the Aerial Incident at Lockerbie (Libya v. U.K.; Libya v. U.S.) 1992 I.C.J. 3 (Apr. 14) at 129 (Judge Oda), 138 (Judge Lachs), 142 (Judge Shahabuddeen); Certain Expenses of the United Nations, 1962 I.C.J. 150–51 (July 20); Thomas M. Franck, *The ''Powers of Appreciation'': Who Is the Ultimate Guardian of UN Legality?*, 86 AM. J. INT'L L. 519, 522–23 (1992); Vera Gowlland–Debbas, *Security Council Enforcement Action and Issues of State Responsibility*, 43 INT'L & COMP. L.Q. 55, 94, 96–98 (1994); Jordan J. Paust, *Peace-Making and Security Council Powers: Bosnia–Herzegovina*

Raises International and Constitutional Questions, 19 So. Ill. U.L.J. 131, 138–42 (1994); Michael Reisman, *The Constitutional Crisis in the United Nations*, 87 Am. J. Int'l L. 83, 92, 94 (1993).

4. What sort of measures can the Security Council decide to impose in order to give effect to its decisions under Article 39? See U.N. Charter, Articles 1, 40–42.

5. Are decisions of the Security Council binding on U.N. members? See U.N. Charter, Articles 1, 24–25, 40–42, 48–49, 51, 52–53, 55 (c), 56; recall question 3 above.

In the *Lockerbie* case (question 3 above), Libya claimed that it had discretion under Article 7 of the Montreal Air Sabotage Convention whether to prosecute those accused of aircraft sabotage or to extradite them and that a U.N. Security Council resolution ordering extradition was *ultra vires* and could not obviate such discretion under the Montreal Convention. How would you rule on such a claim?

If, in the name of regional peace and security, the Security Council approves the dismemberment of a state and orders a cease-fire that would prevent the state from using force in self-defense to reclaim territory controlled by an insurgent group, should the Security Council resolution prevail? If the Security Council had ordered that Kosovo should become independent of Yugoslavia in 1999? How might consideration of self-determination and human rights affect your answer?

6. Should Security Council decisions deny what Article 51 of the Charter refers to as "the inherent right of individual or collective self-defense if an armed attack occurs against a Member of the United Nations"? Does the language in Article 51 which reads "until the Security Council has taken measures necessary to maintain international peace and security" mean that the inherent right is lost once the Security Council takes any measures to maintain peace and security? Must the measures be needed (*i.e.*, "necessary"), generally effective, and not merely be for peace, but also for security? Does additional language in Article 51 which reads "[m]easures taken by Members ... shall not in any way affect the authority and responsibility of the Security Council under the present Charter to take at any time such action as it deems necessary in order to maintain and restore international peace and security" contemplate action by both the state attacked and the Security Council, but necessarily allow a controlling authority in the Security Council even to the point where reasonable use of force in self-defense can be ordered to cease?

7. After the invasion of Kuwait by Iraq in 1990 and various other incidents and threats involving military force, the Security Council issued, among others, Resolution 678, Nov. 29, 1990:

> *The Security Council*, ...
>
> *Acting* under Chapter VII of the Charter,
>
> 1. *Demands* that Iraq comply fully with resolution 660 (1990) [re: immediate withdrawal from Kuwait] and all subsequent relevant resolutions, and decides, while maintaining all its decisions, to allow Iraq one final opportunity, as a pause of goodwill, to do so;

2. *Authorizes* Member States co-operating with the Government of Kuwait, unless Iraq on or before 15 January 1991 fully implements, as set forth in paragraph 1 above, the foregoing resolutions, to use all necessary means to uphold and implement resolution 660 (1990) and all subsequent relevant resolutions and to restore international peace and security in the area;

3. *Requests* all States to provide appropriate support for the actions undertaken in pursuance of paragraph 2 of the present resolution . . . ;

5. *Decides* to remain seized of the matter.

8. What types of military action are authorized by the resolution? What sorts of limitation exist, and what sorts do not exist? For example, can the establishment of no-fly zones over Iraqi territory be permissible? Is the use of force to target Iraqi weapons of mass destruction permissible, even in December of 1998?

9. Could the use of force to capture Saddam Hussein in Iraq and try him for aggressive war and war crimes be permissible? Could a special tribunal be set up for his trial? *See also* JORDAN J. PAUST, M. CHERIF BASSIOUNI, *ET AL.*, INTERNATIONAL CRIMINAL LAW 654–66, 672–88, 698–708 (2 ed. 2000).

10. How would authorizations contained in the 1990 resolution come to an end?

D. Case Study of Iraq, 2003

On March 20, 2003, the United States used military force against the Iraqi regime of Saddam Hussein and became an occupying power in Iraq. Was the use of armed force permissible under U.N. S.C. Res. 678 (1990), as supplemented by U.N. S.C. Res. 1441 (2002)?

U.N. Security Res. 1441 (8 Nov. 2002)

The Security Council,

Recalling all its previous relevant resolutions, in particular its resolutions 661 (1990) . . . , 678 (1990) . . . , 686 (1991) . . . , 687 (1991) . . . , 688 (1991) . . . , 707 (1991) . . . , 715 (1991) . . . , 986 (1995) . . . , and 1284 (1999) of 17 December 1999, and all the relevant statements of its President,

Recalling also its resolution 1382 (2001) of 29 November 2001 and its intention to implement it fully,

Recognizing the threat Iraq's non-compliance with Council resolutions and proliferation of weapons of mass destruction and long-range missiles poses to international peace and security,

Recalling that its resolution 678 (1990) authorized Member States to use all necessary means to uphold and implement its resolution 660 (1990) of 2 August 1990 and all relevant resolutions subsequent to resolution 660 (1990) and to restore international peace and security in the area,

Further recalling that its resolution 687 (1991) imposed obligations on Iraq as a necessary step for achievement of its stated objective of restoring international peace and security in the area, . . .

Deploring also that the Government of Iraq has failed to comply with its commitments pursuant to resolution 687 (1991) with regard to terrorism, pursuant to resolution 688 (1991) to end repression of its civilian population and to provide access by international humanitarian organizations to all those in need of assistance in Iraq, and pursuant to resolutions 686 (1991), 687 (1991), and 1284 (1999) to return or cooperate in accounting for Kuwaiti and third country nationals wrongfully detained by Iraq, or to return Kuwaiti property wrongfully seized by Iraq,

Recalling that in its resolution 687 (1991) the Council declared that a ceasefire would be based on acceptance by Iraq of the provisions of that resolution, including the obligations on Iraq contained therein,

Determined to ensure the full and immediate compliance by Iraq without conditions or restrictions with its obligations under resolution 687 (1991) and other relevant resolutions and recalling that the resolutions of the Council constitute the governing standard of Iraqi compliance, . . .

Determined to secure full compliance with its decisions,

Acting under Chapter VII of the Charter of the United Nations,

1. *Decides* that Iraq has been and remains in material breach of its obligations under relevant resolutions, including resolution 687 (1991), in particular through Iraq's failure to cooperate with United Nations inspectors and the IAEA, and to complete the actions required under paragraphs 8 to 13 or resolution 687 (1991);

2. *Decides*, while acknowledging paragraph 1 above, to afford Iraq, by this resolution, a final opportunity to comply with its disarmament obligations under relevant resolutions of the Council; and accordingly decides to set up an enhanced inspection regime with the aim of bringing to full and verified completion the disarmament process established by resolution 687 (1991) and subsequent resolutions of the Council;

3. *Decides* that, in order to begin to comply with its disarmament obligations, in addition to submitting the required biannual declarations, the Government of Iraq shall provide to UNMOVIC, the lARA, and the Council, not later than 30 days from the date of this resolution, a currently accurate, full, and complete declaration of all aspects of its programmes to develop chemical, biological, and nuclear weapons, ballistic missiles, and other delivery systems such as unmanned aerial vehicles and dispersal systems designed for use on aircraft. including any holdings and precise locations of such weapons, components, sub-components, stocks of agents, and related material and equipment, the locations and work of its research, development and production facilities, as well as all other chemical, biological, and nuclear programmes, including

any which it claims are for purposes not related to weapon production or material;

4. *Decides* that false statements or omissions in the declarations submitted by Iraq pursuant to this resolution and failure by Iraq at any time to comply with, and cooperate fully in the implementation of, this resolution shall constitute a further material breach of Iraq's obligations and will be reported to the Council for assessment in accordance with paragraphs 11 and 12 below;

5. *Decides* that Iraq shall provide UNMOVIC and the lARA immediate, unimpeded, unconditional, and unrestricted access to any and all, including underground, areas, facilities, buildings, equipment, records, and means of transport which they wish to inspect, as well as immediate, unimpeded, unrestricted, and private access to all officials and other persons whom UNMOVIC or the IAEA wish to interview in the mode or location of UNMOVIC's or the IAEA's choice pursuant to any aspect of their mandates; further decides that UNMOVIC and the IAEA may at their discretion conduct interviews inside or outside of Iraq, may facilitate the travel of those interviewed and family members outside of Iraq, and that, at the sole discretion of UNMOVIC and the IAEA, such interviews may occur without the presence of observers from the Iraqi Government; and instructs UNMOVIC and requests the lAEA to resume inspections no later than 45 days following adoption of this resolution and to update the Council 60 days thereafter; . . .

8. *Decides* further that Iraq shall not take or threaten hostile acts directed against any representative or personnel of the United Nations or the IAEA or of any Member State taking action to uphold any Council resolution;

9. *Requests* the Secretary–General immediately to notify Iraq of this resolution, which binding on Iraq; demands that Iraq confirm within seven days of that notification its intention to comply fully with this resolution; and demands further that Iraq cooperate immediately, unconditionally, and actively with UNMOVIC and the IAEA;

10. *Requests* all Member States to give full support to UNMOVIC and the IAEA in the discharge of their mandates, including by providing any information related to prohibited programmes or other aspects of their mandates, including on Iraqi attempts since 1998 to acquire prohibited items, and by recommending sites to be inspected, persons to be interviewed, conditions of such interviews, and data to be collected, the results of which shall be reported to the Council by UNMOVIC and the IAEA;

11. *Directs* the Executive Chairman of UNMOVIC and the Director–General of the IAEA to report immediately to the Council any interference by Iraq with inspection activities, as well as any failure by Iraq to comply with its disarmament obligations, including its obligations regarding inspections under this resolution;

12. *Decides* to convene immediately upon receipt of a report in accordance with paragraphs 4 or 11 above, in order to consider the situation and the need for full compliance with all of the relevant Council resolutions in order to secure international peace and security;

13. *Recalls,* in that context, that the Council has repeatedly warned Iraq that it will face serious consequences as a result of its continued violations of its obligations;

14. *Decides* to remain seized of the matter.

Notes and Questions

1. Was the U.S. use of force in Iraq in 2003 permissible under S.C. Res. 1441? Textwriters and states are split on this issue, although most seem to assume that the U.S. use of force was impermissible. Compare Kirgis, Security Council Resolution 1441 on Iraq's Final Opportunity to Comply with Disarmament Obligations, at http://www.asil.org/insights/insigh92.htm; Mary Ellen O'Connell, Addendum to Armed Force in Iraq: Issues of Legality, at http://www.asil.org/insights/insigh92a.htm; with Paust, *Use of Armed Force against Terrorists in Afghanistan, Iraq, and Beyond*, 35 CORNELL INT'L L.J. 533, 549–50, 556 (2002).

2. Did S.C. Res. 1441 (2002) revitalize S.C. Res. 678 (1990)? Were the authorizations to use force in resolution 678 ever terminated? Was the 1991 war ever terminated?

3. S.C. Res. 687 (1991) adopted a cease-fire (which does not end war but suspends active hostilities), but warfare continued soon thereafter, especially concerning no-fly zones, and intensified in 1993 and 1998. What did S.C. Res. 1441 (2002) declare in connection with resolution 687?

4. S.C. Res. 687 (1991) recognized the "threat that all weapons of mass destruction pose to peace and security in the area," decided "that Iraq shall unconditionally accept the destruction, removal, or rendering harmless, under international supervision," various chemical and biological weapons and ballistic missiles, and decided "that Iraq shall unconditionally agree not to acquire or develop nuclear weapons or nuclear-usable-material," among others. Was resolution 687 a "relevant" subsequent resolution? No weapons of mass destruction were subsequently found in Iraq. Does that make a difference?

5. S.C. Res. 688 (1991) condemned the Iraqi regime's "repression of the Iraqi civilian population in many parts of Iraq, including most recently in Kurdish-populated areas, the consequences of which threaten international peace and security in the region." Was resolution 688 a "relevant" subsequent resolution? Was use of force for a regime change under resolutions 1441 and 688 permissible?

6. How long did Iraq have to comply with Res. 1441? Who decides?

E. Security Council Measures Other Than Force

THE PROSECUTOR v. DUSKO TADIC A/K/A "DULE" DECISION ON THE DEFENCE MOTION FOR INTERLOCUTORY APPEAL ON JURISDICTION

Appeals Chamber of the ICTY, IT–94–1–AR 72 (2 Oct. 1995).

CASSESE, J.

26. Many arguments have been put forward by Appellant in support of the contention that the establishment of the International Tribunal is invalid under the Charter of the United Nations or that it was not duly established by law....

27. The Trial Chamber summarized the claims of the Appellant as follows:

> "It is said that, to be duly established by law, the International Tribunal should have been created either by treaty, the consensual act of nations, or by amendment of the Charter of the United Nations, not by resolution of the Security Council. Called in aid of this general proposition are a number of considerations: that before the creation of the International Tribunal in 1993 it was never envisaged that such an ad hoc criminal tribunal might be set up; that the General Assembly, whose participation would at least have guaranteed full representation of the international community, was not involved in its creation; that it was never intended by the Charter that the Security Council should, under Chapter VII, establish a judicial body, let alone a criminal tribunal; that the Security Council had been inconsistent in creating this Tribunal while not taking a similar step in the case of other areas of conflict in which violations of international humanitarian law may have occurred; that the establishment of the International Tribunal had neither promoted, nor was capable of promoting, international peace, as the current situation in the former Yugoslavia demonstrates; that the Security Council could not, in any event, create criminal liability on the part of individuals and that this is what its creation of the International Tribunal did; that there existed and exists no such international emergency as would justify the action of the Security Council; that no political organ such as the Security Council is capable of establishing an independent and impartial tribunal; that there is an inherent defect in the creation, after the event, of ad hoc tribunals to try particular types of offences and, finally, that to give the International Tribunal primacy over national courts is, in any event and in itself, inherently wrong." (Decision at Trial, at para. 2.)....

29. What is the extent of the powers of the Security Council under Article 39 and the limits thereon, if any?

The Security Council plays the central role in the application of both parts of the Article. It is the Security Council that makes the determination that there exists one of the situations justifying the use of the "exceptional powers" of Chapter VII. And it is also the Security Council that chooses the reaction to such a situation: it either makes recommendations (*i.e.*, opts not to use the exceptional powers but to continue to operate under Chapter VI) or decides to use the exceptional powers by ordering measures to be taken in accordance with Articles 41 and 42 with a view to maintaining or restoring international peace and security.

30. It is not necessary for the purposes of the present decision to examine any further the question of the limits of the discretion of the Security Council in determining the existence of a "threat to the peace"....

[A]n armed conflict (or a series of armed conflicts) has been taking place in the territory of the former Yugoslavia since long before the decision of the Security Council to establish this International Tribunal. If it is considered an international armed conflict, there is no doubt that it falls within the literal sense of the words "breach of the peace" (between the parties or, at the very least, would be a as a "threat to the peace" of others).

But even if it were considered merely as an "internal armed conflict", it would still constitute a "threat to the peace" according to the settled practice of the Security Council and the common understanding of the United Nations membership in general. Indeed, the practice of the Security Council is rich with cases of civil war or internal strife which it classified as a "threat to the peace" and dealt with under Chapter VII, with the encouragement or even at the behest of the General Assembly, such as the Congo crisis at the beginning of the 1960s and, more recently, Liberia and Somalia. It can thus be said that there is a common understanding, manifested by the "subsequent practice" of the membership of the United Nations at large, that the "threat to the peace" of Article 39 may include, as one of its species, internal armed conflicts....

32. ... In its resolution 827, the Security Council considers that "in the particular circumstances of the former Yugoslavia", the establishment of the International Tribunal "would contribute to the restoration and maintenance of peace" and indicates that, in establishing it, the Security Council was acting under Chapter VII (S.C. Res. 827, U.N. Doc. S/RES/827 (1993)). However, it did not specify a particular Article as a basis for this action.

33. The establishment of an international criminal tribunal is not expressly mentioned among the enforcement measures provided for in Chapter VII, and more particularly in Articles 41 and 42....

34. *Prima facie*, the International Tribunal matches perfectly the description in Article 41 of "measures not involving the use of force"....

36. Logically, if the Organization can undertake measures which have to be implemented through the intermediary of its Members, it can

a fortiori undertake measures which it can implement directly via its organs, if it happens to have the resources to do so....

In sum, the establishment of the International Tribunal falls squarely within the powers of the Security Council under Article 41....

65. Appellant's third ground of appeal is the claim that the International Tribunal lacks subject-matter jurisdiction over the crimes alleged. The basis for this allegation is Appellant's claim that the subject-matter jurisdiction under Articles 2, 3 and 5 of the Statute of the International Tribunal is limited to crimes committed in the context of an international armed conflict. Before the Trial Chamber, Appellant claimed that the alleged crimes, even if proven, were committed in the context of an internal armed conflict. On appeal an additional alternative claim is asserted to the effect that there was no armed conflict at all in the region where the crimes were allegedly committed.

Before the Trial Chamber, the Prosecutor responded with alternative arguments that: (a) the conflicts in the former Yugoslavia should be characterized as an international armed conflict; and (b) even if the conflicts were characterized as internal, the International Tribunal has jurisdiction under Articles 3 and 5 to adjudicate the crimes alleged. On appeal, the Prosecutor maintains that, upon adoption of the Statute, the Security Council determined that the conflicts in the former Yugoslavia were international and that, by dint of that determination, the International Tribunal has jurisdiction over this case....

B. Does the Statute Refer Only to International Armed Conflicts?

1. Literal Interpretation of the Statute

71. On the face of it, some provisions of the Statute are unclear as to whether they apply to offences occurring in international armed conflicts only, or to those perpetrated in internal armed conflicts as well. Article 2 refers to "grave breaches" of the Geneva Conventions of 1949, which are widely understood to be committed only in international armed conflicts, so the reference in Article 2 would seem to suggest that the Article is limited to international armed conflicts. Article 3 also lacks any express reference to the nature of the underlying conflict required. A literal reading of this provision standing alone may lead one to believe that it applies to both kinds of conflict. By contrast, Article 5 explicitly confers jurisdiction over crimes committed in either internal or international armed conflicts. An argument *a contrario* based on the absence of a similar provision in Article 3 might suggest that Article 3 applies only to one class of conflict rather than to both of them. In order better to ascertain the meaning and scope of these provisions, the Appeals Chamber will therefore consider the object and purpose behind the enactment of the Statute.

2. Teleological Interpretation of the Statute

72. In adopting resolution 827, the Security Council established the International Tribunal with the stated purpose of bringing to justice

persons responsible for serious violations of international humanitarian law in the former Yugoslavia, thereby deterring future violations and contributing to the re-establishment of peace and security in the region. The context in which the Security Council acted indicates that it intended to achieve this purpose without reference to whether the conflicts in the former Yugoslavia were internal or international.

As the members of the Security Council well knew, in 1993, when the Statute was drafted, the conflicts in the former Yugoslavia could have been characterized as both internal and international, or alternatively, as an internal conflict alongside an international one, or as an internal conflict that had become internationalized because of external support, or as an international conflict that had subsequently been replaced by one or more internal conflicts, or some combination thereof. The conflict in the former Yugoslavia had been rendered international by the involvement of the Croatian Army in Bosnia–Herzegovina and by the involvement of the Yugoslav National Army ("JNA") in hostilities in Croatia, as well as in Bosnia–Herzegovina at least until its formal withdrawal on 19 May 1992. To the extent that the conflicts had been limited to clashes between Bosnian Government forces and Bosnian Serb rebel forces in Bosnia–Herzegovina, as well as between the Croatian Government and Croatian Serb rebel forces in Krajina (Croatia), they had been internal (unless direct involvement of the Federal Republic of Yugoslavia (Serbia–Montenegro) could be proven). It is notable that the parties to this case also agree that the conflicts in the former Yugoslavia since 1991 have had both internal and international aspects....

73. ... Taken together, the agreements reached between the various parties to the conflict(s) in the former Yugoslavia bear out the proposition that, when the Security Council adopted the Statute of the International Tribunal in 1993, it did so with reference to situations that the parties themselves considered at different times and places as either internal or international armed conflicts, or as a mixed internal-international conflict....

77. On the basis of the foregoing, we conclude that the conflicts in the former Yugoslavia have both internal and international aspects, that the members of the Security Council clearly had both aspects of the conflicts in mind when they adopted the Statute of the International Tribunal, and that they intended to empower the International Tribunal to adjudicate violations of humanitarian law that occurred in either context. To the extent possible under existing international law, the Statute should therefore be construed to give effect to that purpose.

78. With the exception of Article 5 dealing with crimes against humanity, none of the statutory provisions makes explicit reference to the type of conflict as an element of the crime; and, as will be shown below, the reference in Article 5 is made to distinguish the nexus required by the Statute from the nexus required by Article 6 of the London Agreement of 8 August 1945 establishing the International Military Tribunal at Nuremberg. Since customary international law no

longer requires any nexus between crimes against humanity and armed conflict (*see below*, paras. 140 and 141), Article 5 was intended to reintroduce this nexus for the purposes of this Tribunal. As previously noted, although Article 2 does not explicitly refer to the nature of the conflicts, its reference to the grave breaches provisions suggest that it is limited to international armed conflicts. It would however defeat the Security Council's purpose to read a similar international armed conflict requirement into the remaining jurisdictional provisions of the Statute. Contrary to the drafters' apparent indifference to the nature of the underlying conflicts, such an interpretation would authorize the International Tribunal to prosecute and punish certain conduct in an international armed conflict, while turning a blind eye to the very same conduct in an internal armed conflict. To illustrate, the Security Council has repeatedly condemned the wanton devastation and destruction of property, which is explicitly punishable only under Articles 2 and 3 of the Statute. Appellant maintains that these Articles apply only to international armed conflicts. However, it would have been illogical for the drafters of the Statute to confer on the International Tribunal the competence to adjudicate the very conduct about which they were concerned, only in the event that the context was an international conflict, when they knew that the conflicts at issue in the former Yugoslavia could have been classified, at varying times and places, as internal, international, or both.

Thus, the Security Council's object in enacting the Statute—to prosecute and punish persons responsible for certain condemned acts being committed in a conflict understood to contain both internal and international aspects—suggests that the Security Council intended that, to the extent possible, the subject-matter jurisdiction of the International Tribunal should extend to both internal and international armed conflicts.

79. ... Although the language of the [Geneva] Conventions might appear to be ambiguous and the question is open to some debate (*see, e.g.*, [*Amicus Curiae*] Submission of the Government of the United States ...), it widely contended that the grave breaches provisions establish universal mandatory jurisdiction only with respect to those breaches of the Conventions committed in international armed conflicts. Appellant argues that, as the grave breaches enforcement system only applies to international armed conflicts, reference in Article 2 of the Statute to the grave breaches provisions of the Geneva Conventions limits the International Tribunal's jurisdiction under that Article to acts committed in the context of an international armed conflict.

80. ... The international armed conflict requirement was a necessary limitation on the grave breaches system in light of the intrusion on State sovereignty that such mandatory universal jurisdiction represents. State parties to the 1949 Geneva Conventions did not want to give other States jurisdiction over serious violations of international humanitarian law committed in their internal armed conflicts—at least not the mandatory universal jurisdiction involved in the grave breaches system.

81. The Trial Chamber is right in implying that the enforcement mechanism has of course not been imported into the Statute of the International Tribunal, for the obvious reason that the International Tribunal itself constitutes a mechanism for the prosecution and punishment of the perpetrators of "grave breaches." However, the Trial Chamber has misinterpreted the reference to the Geneva Conventions contained in the sentence of Article 2: "persons or property protected under the provisions of the relevant Geneva Conventions." (Statute of the Tribunal, art. 2.) For the reasons set out above, this reference is clearly intended to indicate that the offences listed under Article 2 can only be prosecuted when perpetrated against persons or property regarded as "protected" by the Geneva Conventions under the strict conditions set out by the Conventions themselves. This reference in Article 2 to the notion of "protected persons or property" must perforce cover the persons mentioned in Articles 13, 24, 25 and 26 (protected persons) and 19 and 33 to 35 (protected objects) of Geneva Convention I; in Articles 13, 36, 37 (protected persons) and 22, 24, 25 and 27 (protected objects) of Convention II; in Article 4 of Convention III on prisoners of war; and in Articles 4 and 20 (protected persons) and Articles 18, 19, 21, 22, 33, 53, 57 etc. (protected property) of Convention IV on civilians. Clearly, these provisions of the Geneva Conventions apply to persons or objects protected only to the extent that they are caught up in an international armed conflict. By contrast, those provisions do not include persons or property coming within the purview of common Article 3 of the four Geneva Conventions.

83. We find that our interpretation of Article 2 is the only one warranted by the text of the Statute and the relevant provisions of the Geneva Conventions, as well as by a logical construction of their interplay as dictated by Article 2. However, we are aware that this conclusion may appear not to be consonant with recent trends of both State practice and the whole doctrine of human rights—which, as pointed out below (see paras. 97–127), tend to blur in many respects the traditional dichotomy between international wars and civil strife. In this connection the Chamber notes with satisfaction the statement in the *amicus curiae* brief submitted by the Government of the United States, where it is contended that:

> "the 'grave breaches' provisions of Article 2 of the International Tribunal Statute apply to armed conflicts of a non-international character as well as those of an international character." (U.S. *Amicus Curiae* Brief, at 35.)

This statement, unsupported by any authority, does not seem to be warranted as to the interpretation of Article 2 of the Statute. Nevertheless, seen from another viewpoint, there is no gainsaying its significance: that statement articulates the legal views of one of the permanent members of the Security Council on a delicate legal issue; on this score it provides the first indication of a possible change in *opinio juris* of States. Were other States and international bodies to come to share this view, a change in customary law concerning the scope of the "grave breaches" system might gradually materialize. Other elements pointing in the same direction can be found in the provision of the German Military Manual mentioned below (para. 131), whereby grave breaches of international humanitarian law include some violations of common Article 3. In addition, attention can be drawn to the Agreement of 1 October 1992 entered into by the conflicting parties in Bosnia–Herzegovina. Articles 3 and 4 of this Agreement implicitly provide for the prosecution and punishment of those responsible for grave breaches of the Geneva Conventions and Additional Protocol I. As the Agreement was clearly concluded within a framework of an internal armed conflict (see above, para. 73), it may be taken as an important indication of the present trend to extend the grave breaches provisions to such category of conflicts. One can also mention a recent judgement by a Danish court. On 25 November 1994 the Third Chamber of the Eastern Division of the Danish High Court delivered a judgement on a person accused of crimes committed together with a number of Croatian military police on 5 August 1993 in the Croatian prison camp of Dretelj in Bosnia (*The Prosecution v. Refik Saric*, unpublished (Den. H.Ct. 1994)). The Court explicitly acted on the basis of the "grave breaches" provisions of the Geneva Conventions, more specifically Articles 129 and 130 of Convention III and Articles 146 and 147 of Convention IV (*The Prosecution v. Refik Saric*, Transcript, at 1 (25 Nov. 1994)), without however raising the preliminary question of whether the alleged offences had occurred within the framework of an international rather than an internal armed conflict (in the event the Court convicted the accused on the basis of those provisions and the relevant penal provisions of the Danish Penal Code. (see *id.* at 7–8)) This judgement indicates that some national courts are also taking the view that the "grave breaches" system may operate regardless of whether the armed conflict is international or internal.

84. Notwithstanding the foregoing, the Appeals Chamber must conclude that, in the present state of development of the law, Article 2 of the Statute only applies to offences committed within the context of international armed conflicts....

(b) Article 3

86. Article 3 of the Statute declares the International Tribunal competent to adjudicate violations of the laws or customs of war.... As explained by the Secretary–General in his Report on the Statute, this provision is based on the 1907 Hague Convention (IV) Respecting the Laws and Customs of War on Land, the Regulations annexed to that Convention, and the Nuremberg Tribunal's interpretation of those Regulations. Appellant argues that the Hague Regulations were adopted to regulate interstate armed conflict, while the conflict in the former Yugoslavia is *in casu* an internal armed conflict; therefore, to the extent that the jurisdiction of the International Tribunal under Article 3 is based on the Hague Regulations, it lacks jurisdiction under Article 3 to adjudicate alleged violations in the former Yugoslavia. Appellant's argu-

ment does not bear close scrutiny, for it is based on an unnecessarily narrow reading of the Statute....

88. That Article 3 does not confine itself to covering violations of Hague law, but is intended also to refer to all violations of international humanitarian law (subject to the limitations just stated), is borne out by the debates in the Security Council that followed the adoption of the resolution establishing the International Tribunal....

89. In light of the above remarks, it can be held that Article 3 is a general clause covering all violations of humanitarian law not falling under Article 2 or covered by Articles 4 or 5, more specifically: (i) violations of the Hague law on international conflicts; (ii) infringements of provisions of the Geneva Conventions other than those classified as "grave breaches" by those Conventions; (iii) violations of common Article 3 and other customary rules on internal conflicts; (iv) violations of agreements binding upon the parties to the conflict, considered qua treaty law, *i.e.*, agreements which have not turned into customary international law (on this point *see below,* para. 143)....

(iii) Customary Rules of International Humanitarian Law Governing Internal Armed Conflicts

a. General

96. Whenever armed violence erupted in the international community, in traditional international law the legal response was based on a stark dichotomy: belligerency or insurgency. The former category applied to armed conflicts between sovereign States (unless there was recognition of belligerency in a civil war), while the latter applied to armed violence breaking out in the territory of a sovereign State. Correspondingly, international law treated the two classes of conflict in a markedly different way: interstate wars were regulated by a whole body of international legal rules, governing both the conduct of hostilities and the protection of persons not participating (or no longer participating) in armed violence (civilians, the wounded, the sick, shipwrecked, prisoners of war). By contrast, there were very few international rules governing civil commotion, for States preferred to regard internal strife as rebellion, mutiny and treason coming within the purview of national criminal law and, by the same token, to exclude any possible intrusion by other States into their own domestic jurisdiction. This dichotomy was clearly sovereignty-oriented and reflected the traditional configuration of the international community, based on the coexistence of sovereign States more inclined to look after their own interests than community concerns or humanitarian demands.

97. Since the 1930s, however, the aforementioned distinction has gradually become more and more blurred, and international legal rules have increasingly emerged or have been agreed upon to regulate internal armed conflict. There exist various reasons for this development. First, civil wars have become more frequent, not only because technological progress has made it easier for groups of individuals to have access to

weaponry but also on account of increasing tension, whether ideological, inter-ethnic or economic; as a consequence the international community can no longer turn a blind eye to the legal regime of such wars. Secondly, internal armed conflicts have become more and more cruel and protracted, involving the whole population of the State where they occur: the all-out resort to armed violence has taken on such a magnitude that the difference with international wars has increasingly dwindled (suffice to think of the Spanish civil war, in 1936–39, of the civil war in the Congo, in 1960–1968, the Biafran conflict in Nigeria, 1967–70, the civil strife in Nicaragua, in 1981–1990 or El Salvador, 1980–1993). Thirdly, the large-scale nature of civil strife, coupled with the increasing interdependence of States in the world community, has made it more and more difficult for third States to remain aloof: the economic, political and ideological interests of third States have brought about direct or indirect involvement of third States in this category of conflict, thereby requiring that international law take greater account of their legal regime in order to prevent, as much as possible, adverse spill-over effects. Fourthly, the impetuous development and propagation in the international community of human rights doctrines, particularly after the adoption of the Universal Declaration of Human Rights in 1948, has brought about significant changes in international law, notably in the approach to problems besetting the world community. A State-sovereignty-oriented approach has been gradually supplanted by a human-being-oriented approach. Gradually the maxim of Roman law *hominum causa omne jus constitutum est* (all law is created for the benefit of human beings) has gained a firm foothold in the international community as well. It follows that in the area of armed conflict the distinction between interstate wars and civil wars is losing its value as far as human beings are concerned. Why protect civilians from belligerent violence, or ban rape, torture or the wanton destruction of hospitals, churches, museums or private property, as well as proscribe weapons causing unnecessary suffering when two sovereign States are engaged in war, and yet refrain from enacting the same bans or providing the same protection when armed violence has erupted "only" within the territory of a sovereign State? If international law, while of course duly safeguarding the legitimate interests of States, must gradually turn to the protection of human beings, it is only natural that the aforementioned dichotomy should gradually lose its weight.

98. The emergence of international rules governing internal strife has occurred at two different levels: at the level of customary law and at that of treaty law. Two bodies of rules have thus crystallised, which are by no means conflicting or inconsistent, but instead mutually support and supplement each other. Indeed, the interplay between these two sets of rules is such that some treaty rules have gradually become part of customary law. This holds true for common Article 3 of the 1949 Geneva Conventions, as was authoritatively held by the International Court of Justice (*Nicaragua Case*, at para. 218), but also applies to Article 19 of the Hague Convention for the Protection of Cultural Property in the

Event of Armed Conflict of 14 May 1954, and, as we shall show below (para. 117), to the core of Additional Protocol II of 1977.

99. Before pointing to some principles and rules of customary law that have emerged in the international community for the purpose of regulating civil strife, a word of caution on the law-making process in the law of armed conflict is necessary. When attempting to ascertain State practice with a view to establishing the existence of a customary rule or a general principle, it is difficult, if not impossible, to pinpoint the actual behaviour of the troops in the field for the purpose of establishing whether they in fact comply with, or disregard, certain standards of behaviour. This examination is rendered extremely difficult by the fact that not only is access to the theatre of military operations normally refused to independent observers (often even to the ICRC) but information on the actual conduct of hostilities is withheld by the parties to the conflict; what is worse, often recourse is had to misinformation with a view to misleading the enemy as well as public opinion and foreign Governments. In appraising the formation of customary rules or general principles one should therefore be aware that, on account of the inherent nature of this subject-matter, reliance must primarily be placed on such elements as official pronouncements of States, military manuals and judicial decisions. . . .

102. Subsequent State practice indicates that the Spanish Civil War was not exceptional in bringing about the extension of some general principles of the laws of warfare to internal armed conflict. While the rules that evolved as a result of the Spanish Civil War were intended to protect civilians finding themselves in the theatre of hostilities, rules designed to protect those who do not (or no longer) take part in hostilities emerged after World War II. In 1947, instructions were issued to the Chinese "peoples' liberation army" by Mao Tse–Tung who instructed them not to "kill or humiliate any of Chiang Kai–Shek's army officers and men who lay down their arms." (*Manifesto of the Chinese People's Liberation Army,* in Mao Tse–Tung, 4 SELECTED WORKS (1961) 147, at 151.) He also instructed the insurgents, among other things, not to "ill-treat captives", "damage crops" or "take liberties with women." (*On the Reissue of the Three Main Rules of Discipline and the Eight Points for Attention—Instruction of the General Headquarters of the Chinese People's Liberation Army,* in *id.*, 155.)

In an important subsequent development, States specified certain minimum mandatory rules applicable to internal armed conflicts in common Article 3 of the Geneva Conventions of 1949. The International Court of Justice has confirmed that these rules reflect "elementary considerations of humanity" applicable under customary international law to any armed conflict, whether it is of an internal or international character. (*Nicaragua Case*, at para. 218). Therefore, at least with respect to the minimum rules in common Article 3, the character of the conflict is irrelevant.

103. Common Article 3 contains not only the substantive rules governing internal armed conflict but also a procedural mechanism inviting parties to internal conflicts to agree to abide by the rest of the Geneva Conventions. As in the current conflicts in the former Yugoslavia, parties to a number of internal armed conflicts have availed themselves of this procedure to bring the law of international armed conflicts into force with respect to their internal hostilities. For example, in the 1967 conflict in Yemen, both the Royalists and the President of the Republic agreed to abide by the essential rules of the Geneva Conventions. Such undertakings reflect an understanding that certain fundamental rules should apply regardless of the nature of the conflict.

104. Agreements made pursuant to common Article 3 are not the only vehicle through which international humanitarian law has been brought to bear on internal armed conflicts. In several cases reflecting customary adherence to basic principles in internal conflicts, the warring parties have unilaterally committed to abide by international humanitarian law....

108. In addition to the behaviour of belligerent States, Governments and insurgents, other factors have been instrumental in bringing about the formation of the customary rules at issue. The Appeals Chamber will mention in particular the action of the ICRC, two resolutions adopted by the United Nations General Assembly, some declarations made by member States of the European Community (now European Union), as well as Additional Protocol II of 1977 and some military manuals.

109. As is well known, the ICRC has been very active in promoting the development, implementation and dissemination of international humanitarian law. From the angle that is of relevance to us, namely the emergence of customary rules on internal armed conflict, the ICRC has made a remarkable contribution by appealing to the parties to armed conflicts to respect international humanitarian law. It is notable that, when confronted with non-international armed conflicts, the ICRC has promoted the application by the contending parties of the basic principles of humanitarian law. In addition, whenever possible, it has endeavoured to persuade the conflicting parties to abide by the Geneva Conventions of 1949 or at least by their principal provisions. When the parties, or one of them, have refused to comply with the bulk of international humanitarian law, the ICRC has stated that they should respect, as a minimum, common Article 3. This shows that the ICRC has promoted and facilitated the extension of general principles of humanitarian law to internal armed conflict. The practical results the ICRC has thus achieved in inducing compliance with international humanitarian law ought therefore to be regarded as an element of actual international practice; this is an element that has been conspicuously instrumental in the emergence or crystallization of customary rules.

110. The application of certain rules of war in both internal and international armed conflicts is corroborated by two General Assembly

resolutions on "Respect of human rights in armed conflict." The first one, resolution 2444, was unanimously adopted in 1968 by the General Assembly: "[r]ecognizing the necessity of applying basic humanitarian principles in all armed conflicts," the General Assembly "affirm[ed]"

> "the following principles for observance by all governmental and other authorities responsible for action in armed conflict: (a) That the right of the parties to a conflict to adopt means of injuring the enemy is not unlimited; (b) That it is prohibited to launch attacks against the civilian populations as such; (c) That distinction must be made at all times between persons taking part in the hostilities and members of the civilian population to the effect that the latter be spared as much as possible." (G.A. Res. 2444, U.N. GAOR., 23rd Session, Supp. No. 18 U.N. Doc. A/7218 (1968).)

It should be noted that, before the adoption of the resolution, the United States representative stated in the Third Committee that the principles proclaimed in the resolution "constituted a reaffirmation of existing international law" (U.N. GAOR, 3rd Comm., 23rd Sess., 1634th Mtg., at 2, U.N. Doc. A/C.3/SR.1634 (1968)). This view was reiterated in 1972, when the United States Department of Defence pointed out that the resolution was "declaratory of existing customary international law" or, in other words, "a correct restatement" of "principles of customary international law." (See 67 AM. J. INT'L L. (1973), at 122, 124.)

111. Elaborating on the principles laid down in resolution 2444, in 1970 the General Assembly unanimously adopted resolution 2675 on "Basic principles for the protection of civilian populations in armed conflicts."

112. Together, these resolutions played a twofold role: they were declaratory of the principles of customary international law regarding the protection of civilian populations and property in armed conflicts of any kind and, at the same time, were intended to promote the adoption of treaties on the matter, designed to specify and elaborate upon such principles.

113. That international humanitarian law includes principles or general rules protecting civilians from hostilities in the course of internal armed conflicts has also been stated on a number of occasions by groups of States. For instance, with regard to Liberia, the (then) twelve Member States of the European Community, in a declaration of 2 August 1990, stated:

> "In particular, the Community and its Member States call upon the parties in the conflict, in conformity with international law and the most basic humanitarian principles, to safeguard from violence the embassies and places of refuge such as churches, hospitals, etc., where defenceless civilians have sought shelter." (6 European Political Cooperation Documentation Bulletin, at 295 (1990).)

114. A similar, albeit more general, appeal was made by the Security Council in its resolution 788 (in operative paragraph 5 it called

upon "all parties to the conflict and all others concerned to respect strictly the provisions of international humanitarian law") (S.C. Res. 788 (19 November 1992)), an appeal reiterated in resolution 972 (S.C. Res. 972 (13 January 1995)) and in resolution 1001 (S.C. Res. 1001 (30 June 1995)).

Appeals to the parties to a civil war to respect the principles of international humanitarian law were also made by the Security Council in the case of Somalia and Georgia. As for Somalia, mention can be made of resolution 794 in which the Security Council in particular condemned, as a breach of international humanitarian law, "the deliberate impeding of the delivery of food and medical supplies essential for the survival of the civilian population") (S.C. Res. 794 (3 December 1992)) and resolution 814 (S.C. Res. 814 (26 March 1993)). As for Georgia, see Resolution 993, (in which the Security Council reaffirmed "the need for the parties to comply with international humanitarian law") (S.C. Res. 993 (12 May 1993))....

116. It must be stressed that, in the statements and resolutions referred to above, the European Union and the United Nations Security Council did not mention common Article 3 of the Geneva Conventions, but adverted to "international humanitarian law", thus clearly articulating the view that there exists a corpus of general principles and norms on internal armed conflict embracing common Article 3 but having a much greater scope.

117. Attention must also be drawn to Additional Protocol II to the Geneva Conventions. Many provisions of this Protocol can now be regarded as declaratory of existing rules or as having crystallised emerging rules of customary law or else as having been strongly instrumental in their evolution as general principles....

118. That at present there exist general principles governing the conduct of hostilities (the so-called "Hague Law") applicable to international and internal armed conflicts is also borne out by national military manuals....

119. So far we have pointed to the formation of general rules or principles designed to protect civilians or civilian objects from the hostilities or, more generally, to protect those who do not (or no longer) take active part in hostilities. We shall now briefly show how the gradual extension to internal armed conflict of rules and principles concerning international wars has also occurred as regards means and methods of warfare. As the Appeals Chamber has pointed out above (see para. 110), a general principle has evolved limiting the right of the parties to conflicts "to adopt means of injuring the enemy"....

Indeed, elementary considerations of humanity and common sense make it preposterous that the use by States of weapons prohibited in armed conflicts between themselves be allowed when States try to put down rebellion by their own nationals on their own territory. What is inhumane, and consequently proscribed, in international wars, cannot but be inhumane and inadmissible in civil strife.

120. This fundamental concept has brought about the gradual formation of general rules concerning specific weapons, rules which extend to civil strife the sweeping prohibitions relating to international armed conflicts....

124. It is therefore clear that, whether or not Iraq really used chemical weapons against its own Kurdish nationals—a matter on which this Chamber obviously cannot and does not express any opinion—there undisputedly emerged a general consensus in the international community on the principle that the use of those weapons is also prohibited in internal armed conflicts.

125. State practice shows that general principles of customary international law have evolved with regard to internal armed conflict also in areas relating to methods of warfare. In addition to what has been stated above, with regard to the ban on attacks on civilians in the theatre of hostilities, mention can be made of the prohibition of perfidy....

126. The emergence of the aforementioned general rules on internal armed conflicts does not imply that internal strife is regulated by general international law in all its aspects. Two particular limitations may be noted: (i) only a number of rules and principles governing international armed conflicts have gradually been extended to apply to internal conflicts; and (ii) this extension has not taken place in the form of a full and mechanical transplant of those rules to internal conflicts; rather, the general essence of those rules, and not the detailed regulation they may contain, has become applicable to internal conflicts....

127. Notwithstanding these limitations, it cannot be denied that customary rules have developed to govern internal strife. These rules, as specifically identified in the preceding discussion, cover such areas as protection of civilians from hostilities, in particular from indiscriminate attacks, protection of civilian objects, in particular cultural property, protection of all those who do not (or no longer) take active part in hostilities, as well as prohibition of means of warfare proscribed in international armed conflicts and ban of certain methods of conducting hostilities.

(iv) Individual Criminal Responsibility In Internal Armed Conflict

128. Even if customary international law includes certain basic principles applicable to both internal and international armed conflicts, Appellant argues that such prohibitions do not entail individual criminal responsibility when breaches are committed in internal armed conflicts; these provisions cannot, therefore, fall within the scope of the International Tribunal's jurisdiction. It is true that, for example, common Article 3 of the Geneva Conventions contains no explicit reference to criminal liability for violation of its provisions. Faced with similar claims with respect to the various agreements and conventions that formed the basis of its jurisdiction, the International Military Tribunal at Nuremberg concluded that a finding of individual criminal responsibility is not

barred by the absence of treaty provisions on punishment of breaches. (See The Trial of Major War Criminals: Proceedings of the International Military Tribunal Sitting at Nuremberg Germany, Part 22, at 445, 467 (1950).) The Nuremberg Tribunal considered a number of factors relevant to its conclusion that the authors of particular prohibitions incur individual responsibility: the clear and unequivocal recognition of the rules of warfare in international law and State practice indicating an intention to criminalize the prohibition, including statements by government officials and international organizations, as well as punishment of violations by national courts and military tribunals (*id.*, at 445–47, 467). Where these conditions are met, individuals must be held criminally responsible, because, as the Nuremberg Tribunal concluded:

> [c]rimes against international law are committed by men, not by abstract entities, and only by punishing individuals who commit such crimes can the provisions of international law be enforced." (*id.*, at 447.)

129. Applying the foregoing criteria to the violations at issue here, we have no doubt that they entail individual criminal responsibility, regardless of whether they are committed in internal or international armed conflicts. Principles and rules of humanitarian law reflect "elementary considerations of humanity" widely recognized as the mandatory minimum for conduct in armed conflicts of any kind. No one can doubt the gravity of the acts at issue, nor the interest of the international community in their prohibition.

(v) Conclusion

137. In the light of the intent of the Security Council and the logical and systematic interpretation of Article 3 as well as customary international law, the Appeals Chamber concludes that, under Article 3, the International Tribunal has jurisdiction over the acts alleged in the indictment, regardless of whether they occurred within an internal or an international armed conflict. Thus, to the extent that Appellant's challenge to jurisdiction under Article 3 is based on the nature of the underlying conflict, the motion must be denied.

(c) Article 5

138. Article 5 of the Statute confers jurisdiction over crimes against humanity....

140. As the Prosecutor observed before the Trial Chamber, the nexus between crimes against humanity and either crimes against peace or war crimes, required by the Nuremberg Charter, was peculiar to the jurisdiction of the Nuremberg Tribunal.... The obsolescence of the nexus requirement is evidenced by international conventions regarding genocide and apartheid, both of which prohibit particular types of crimes against humanity regardless of any connection to armed conflict....

141. It is by now a settled rule of customary international law that crimes against humanity do not require a connection to international

armed conflict. Indeed, as the Prosecutor points out, customary international law may not require a connection between crimes against humanity and any conflict at all. Thus, by requiring that crimes against humanity be committed in either internal or international armed conflict, the Security Council may have defined the crime in Article 5 more narrowly than necessary under customary international law. There is no question, however, that the definition of crimes against humanity adopted by the Security Council in Article 5 comports with the principle of *nullum crimen sine lege*.

ABI-SAAB, J., concurring in part

. . . I consider, on the basis of the material presented in the Decision itself, that a strong case can be made for the application of Article 2 (of the ICTY Statute], even when the incriminated act takes place in an internal conflict.

Admittedly the traditional view, as far as the interpretation of the Geneva Conventions is concerned, has been that the "grave breaches" regime does not apply to internal armed conflicts. But the minority view that it does is not devoid of merit if we go by the texts alone and their possible teleological interpretation.

Regardless, however, of the outcome of this initial debate, if we consider the recent developments which are aptly presented in the Decision, we can draw two conclusions from them. The first is that a growing practice and *opinio juris* both of States and international organizations, has established the principle of personal criminal responsibility for the acts figuring in the grave breaches articles as well as for the other serious violations of the *jus in bello*, even when they are committed in the course of an internal armed conflict. The second conclusion is that in much of this accumulating practice and *opinio juris*, the former acts are expressly designated as "grave breaches" (see Decision para. 83). . . .

The legal significance of this substance can be understood in at least two ways other than the one followed by the Decision, in order to bring the acts committed in internal conflicts within the reach of the grave breaches regime in the Geneva Conventions, and consequently of Article 2 of the Statute.

As a matter of treaty interpretation—and assuming that the traditional reading of "grave breaches" has been correct—it can be said that this new normative substance has led to a new interpretation of the Conventions as a result of the "subsequent practice" and *opinio juris* of the States parties: a teleological interpretation of the Conventions in the light of their object and purpose to the effect of including internal conflicts within the regime of "grave breaches". The other possible rendering of the significance of the new normative substance is to consider it as establishing a new customary rule ancillary to the Conventions, whereby the regime of "grave breaches" is extended to internal conflicts. But the first seems to me as the better approach. And under either, Article 2 of the Statute applies—the same as Articles 3, 4 and 5—in both international and internal conflicts.

This construction of Article 2 is supported by the fact that it coincides with the understanding of the parties to the conflict themselves of the legal situation....

Notes and Questions

1. The Statutes and the judgments of the two *ad hoc* tribunals established by the Security Council have contributed to development of international humanitarian law. Among the noteworthy aspects of the *Tadic* judgment is its ruling that individual criminal responsibility under international law attaches to offenses committed during internal armed conflict (thus clarifying that "war crimes" can be committed both in international and internal armed conflict) and its observation that Article 5 of its Statute is narrower than required and limits the Tribunal's jurisdiction over crimes against humanity to those linked to armed conflict. Article 3 of the Statute of the International Criminal Tribunal for Rwanda (ICTR) permits prosecution for crimes against humanity "when committed as part of a widespread or systematic attack against any civilian population on national, political, ethnic, racial or religious grounds," thus severing the link to armed conflict but limiting the crimes against humanity within the ICTR's reach. *Compare* the customary international legal instruments in the Documents Supplement and the 1919 Report of the Responsibilities Commission, *supra*, concerning offenses against the laws of humanity. Note that Article 5 (c) of the Charter of the I.M.T. for the Far East applied to "acts committed before or during the war," and the prohibition of genocide under the Genocide Convention, a form of crime against humanity, applies also in time of relative peace.

The Rome Statute of the ICC also recognizes crimes against humanity in time of peace, although it contains significant limitations concerning the crimes against humanity that are prosecutable before the new ICC. Unlike the customary instruments, Article 7 of the ICC Statute provides a more limiting definition of crimes against humanity; fuses the two basic types (inhumane acts against civilians and persecutions) together, while also limiting ICC jurisdiction over each type to circumstances involving attacks "directed against any civilian population"; and requires proof of a "widespread or systematic" attack directed against a civilian population and an element of "knowledge of the attack." *See* the Documents Supplement; PAUST, BASSIOUNI, *ET AL.*, *supra*, at 861, 864–65, 889–90, 905–07, 909. The definition of "attack" is also limited to "multiple commission of acts." These limitations are compounded by an additional requirement in Article 7 (2) (a) that a covered attack be engaged in "pursuant to or in furtherance of a State or organizational policy." Thus needlessly excluded are customary crimes against humanity perpetrated by governmental actors whose crimes are not "pursuant to or in furtherance of" a State or organizational policy, private unorganized actors, and private actors who do not act pursuant to or in furtherance of a State or "organizational" policy.

The ICC list of crimes against humanity expressly includes rape, sexual slavery, enforced prostitution, forced pregnancy, enforced sterilization, enforced disappearance and a definition of persecution ("intentional and severe deprivation of fundamental rights contrary to international law by reason of the identity of the group or collectivity"). Control Council Law No. 10 also included "rape."

Article 8 of the ICC Statute also contains a very limited definition of war crimes, separately listed for international and internal armed conflicts. *See also* ICC Statute, arts. (1), 10, 22 (3). Especially limiting are standards in Article 8 concerning attacks or bombardments that hinge on knowledge or "intentionally directing" attacks, whereas customary laws of war can sometimes reach "wanton" or reckless disregard of consequences. *See, e.g.*, PAUST, BASSIOUNI, *ET AL.*, *supra*, at 33, 87, 92, 96, 821–22, 844, 851–53; Jordan J. Paust, *Crimes Within the Limited Jurisdiction of the International Criminal Court*, in INTERNATIONAL HUMANITARIAN LAW: ORIGINS AND PROSPECTS (J. Carey & R.J. Pritchard eds. 2005); 1919 List of War Crimes prepared by the Responsibilities Commission, Nos. 18, 20; Principles of the Nuremberg Charter and Judgment ("wanton destruction"); Geneva Civilian Convention, art. 147 (in Chapter 2, Section 2 B 4); *see also* 1907 Hague Convention No. IV, Annex, art. 23 (e) ("it is especially forbidden . . . (e) To employ arms, projectiles, or material of a nature as to cause unnecessary suffering"–from the authoritative French version); Geneva Protocol I, arts. 35 (1) ("of a nature to cause superfluous injury or unnecessary suffering"), (3) ("which are intended, or may be expected, to cause"), 51 (5) ("which may be expected to cause")—in the Documents Supplement. Starvation under Article 8 (2) (b) (xxv) is also incomplete. *Compare* 1919 List of War Crimes, No. 4; Geneva Protocol I, art. 54; PAUST, BASSIOUNI, *ET AL.*, *supra*, at 850–51; Jordan J. Paust, *The Human Rights to Food, Medicine and Medical Supplies and Freedom from Arbitrary and Inhumane Detention and Controls in Sri Lanka*, 31 VAND. J. TRANS. L. 617, 622–30 (1998).

As noted *supra*, the ICC Statute does not include a definition of the crime of aggression, because of the inability of the delegates to agree. The ICC Statute's definition of genocide (in Article 6) does not develop the concept beyond the 1948 Genocide Convention, to the disappointment of observers who had hoped to see recognition of the concepts of cultural genocide or political genocide.

2. Do you accept the Appeals Chamber's decision in *Tadic* that the Security Council has authority under Chapter VII of the United Nations Charter to establish *ad hoc* criminal tribunals and to define the crimes they may adjudicate? Should additional *ad hoc* tribunals be established for Cambodia, East Timor or other conflict zones, or should future development occur under the auspices of the ICC, even though the ICC will not have retrospective jurisdiction, and perhaps regional tribunals?

SECTION 2. U.S. CONSTITUTIONAL ALLOCATIONS OF POWER

Introductory Problem

Last week, a terrorist group in Yemen seized twenty U.S. tourists, including the U.S. ambassador to Saudi Arabia, held them hostage, and threatened to kill them the morning after negotiations between the government of Yemen and the terrorist group broke down.

The President of the United States ordered a special antiterrorist evacuation mission the evening before the scheduled execution, which entered Yemen without the consent of its government and freed and evacuated the hostages—having killed two Yemenese soldiers at an airport, all of the hostage-takers, and, unavoidably, two Yemenese police officials and a government negotiator at the hostage site. While a U.S. military aircraft was heading out, a Yemenese antiaircraft unit fired at the U.S. plane but was destroyed by U.S. support aircraft.

In response, Yemen declared "war" against the United States. Thereafter, the U.S. President broke off all diplomatic relations with Yemen and issued an executive "war measure" suspending all trade between the two countries.

Were the President's actions legally permissible?

A. *Congressional Powers*

1. *U.S. Constitutional Provisions*

[recall U.S. Const., Art. I, addressed in Chapter 2, Section 2 A]

Questions

1. Is the express congressional power to issue letters of marque and reprisal evidence of a shared or exclusive power to authorize reprisal actions? *See, e.g.*, The Nereide, 13 U.S. (9 Cranch) 388, 421 (1815) (Congress must order reprisals); United States v. The Tropic Wind, 28 F. Cas. 218, 220 (C.C.D.C.1861) (No. 16,541a); The Joseph, 13 F. Cas. 1126, 1130–31 (C.C.D.Mass.1813); United States v. Smith, 27 F. Cas. 1192, 1211, 1230 (C.C.D.N.Y.1806) (No. 16,342); Henfield's Case, 11 F. Cas. 1099, 1109 (C.C.D.Pa.1793) (No. 6,360); W. Wormuth & E. Firmage, To Chain the Dog of War 37, 41–43, 200 (1986); Paust, *Responding Lawfully to International Terrorism: The Use of Force Abroad*, 8 Whittier L. Rev. 711, 718–19 n.21 (1986).

2. Since reprisals as such are now impermissible under the U.N. Charter, does it matter?

3. There is overwhelming agreement that the power to declare war is exclusive in Congress. *See, e.g.*, Jordan J. Paust, International Law as Law of the United States 457 (2 ed. 2003): ". . . [i]n the *Prize Cases,* Justice Grier declared that '[b]y the Constitution, Congress alone has the power to declare a national or foreign war,' adding that the President 'has no power to initiate or declare a war.' [67 U.S. (2 Black) 635, 668 (1863)] In his dissent, Justice Nelson agreed that 'Congress alone can determine whether war exists or should be declared,' adding: "this power belongs exclusively to the congress of the United States." [*Id.* at 693, 698]. Indeed, in 1806 Chief Justice Paterson had recognized that the '[p]ower of making war . . . is exclusively vested in congress.' [United States v. Smith, 27 F. Cas. 1192, 1230 (C.C.D.N.Y.1806) (No. 16,342)] Presumably then the power to declare war is exclusive in Congress, not shared with the President or subject to presentment and presidential veto, and, when exercised by Congress, it is completed upon the making of a declaration." For other cases, see *id.* at 470 n.25. *See also* D'Amato, Velvel, Sager, Van Dyke, Freeman, Cummings, *Brief*

for Constitutional Lawyers' Committee on Undeclared War as Amicus Curiae, Massachusetts v. Laird, 17 WAYNE L. REV. 67 (1971).

Does it follow that only Congress can authorize "war"? or the use of armed force abroad? Can the President? Can a treaty as law of the land? Does international law set limits to such powers? Can Congress properly set limits to the conduct of war?

BAS v. TINGY

4 U.S. (4 Dall.) 37 (1800).

[Editors' note: Tingy, defendant in error, as commander of the public armed vessel *Ganges*, filed a libel against the ship *Eliza*, John Bas (her master and plaintiff in error), her cargo, etc., claiming that salvage due was governed by a statute of March 2, 1799 (and not an earlier statute), applicable to vessels "re-taken from the enemy. . . ." Controversy arose as to the meaning of "enemy" in the statute and whether Congress, or the President alone, could involve the U.S. in an undeclared war to which the word "enemy" would apply. The case also has relevance as an exposition of the meaning of terms like "war" and "hostilities" near the time of the Founders.]

MOORE, J.

This case depends on the construction of the act [of March 2, 1799], for the regulation of the navy. It is objected, indeed, that the act applies only to future wars; but its provisions are obviously applicable to the present situation of things, and there is nothing to prevent an immediate commencement of its operation.

It is, however, more particularly urged, that the word "enemy" cannot be applied to the French; because the section in which it is used, is confined to such a state of war, as would authorise a re-capture of property belonging to a nation in amity with the United States, and such a state of war, it is said, does not exist between America and France. A number of books have been cited to furnish a glossary on the word enemy; yet, our situation is so extraordinary, that I doubt whether a parallel case can be traced in the history of nations. But, if words are the representatives of ideas, let me ask, by what other word the idea of the relative situation of America and France could be communicated, than by that of hostility, or war? And how can the characters of the parties engaged in hostility or war, be otherwise described than by the denomination of enemies? It is for the honour and dignity of both nations, therefore, that they should be called enemies; for, it is by that description alone, that either could justify or excuse, the scene of bloodshed, depredation and confiscation, which has unhappily occurred; and, surely, congress could only employ the language of the act of June 13, 1798, towards a nation whom she considered as an enemy. . . .

WASHINGTON, J.

It is admitted, on all hands, that the defendant in error is entitled to some compensation; but the plaintiff in error contends, that the compensation should be regulated by the act of the 28th June 1798, (4 vol. p. 154. s. 2.) which allows only one-eighth for salvage; while the defendant in error refers his claim to the act of the 2d March, (ibid. 456. s.7.) which makes an allowance of one-half, upon a re-capture from the enemy, after an adverse possession of ninety-six hours.

If the defendant's claim is well founded, it follows, that the latter law must virtually have worked a repeal of the former; but this has been denied, for a variety of reasons:

1st. Because the former law relates to re-captures from the French, and the latter law relates to re-captures from the enemy; and, it is said, that "the enemy" is not descriptive of France, or of her armed vessels, according to the correct and technical understanding of the word.

The decision of this question must depend upon another; which is, whether, at the time of passing the act of congress of the 2d of March 1799, there subsisted a state of war between the two nations? It may, I believe, be safely laid down, that every contention by force between two nations, in external matters, under the authority of their respective governments, is not only war, but public war. If it be declared in form, it is called solemn, and is of the perfect kind; because one whole nation is at war with another whole nation; and all the members of the nation declaring war, are authorised to commit hostilities against all the members of the other, in every place, and under every circumstance. In such a war all the members act under a general authority, and all the rights and consequences of war attach to their condition.

But hostilities may subsist between two nations more confined in its nature and extent; being limited as to places, persons, and things; and this is more properly termed imperfect war; because not solemn, and because those who are authorised to commit hostilities, act under special authority, and can go no farther than to the extent of their commission. Still, however, it is public war, because it is an external contention by force, between some of the members of the two nations, authorised by the legitimate powers. It is a war between the two nations, though all the members are not authorised to commit hostilities such as in a solemn war, where the government restrain the general power.

Now, if this be the true definition of war, let us see what was the situation of the United States in relation to France. In March 1799, congress had raised an army; stopped all intercourse with France; dissolved our treaty; built and equipt ships of war; and commissioned private armed ships; enjoining the former, and authorising the latter, to defend themselves against the armed ships of France, to attack them on the high seas, to subdue and take them as prize, and to re-capture armed vessels found in their possession. Here, then, let me ask, what were the technical characters of an American and French armed vessel, combating on the high seas, with a view the one to subdue the other, and to make prize of his property? They certainly were not friends, because there was a contention by force; nor were they private enemies, because the contention was external, and authorised by the legitimate authority of the two governments. If they were not our enemies, I know not what constitutes an enemy.

2d. But, secondly, it is said, that a war of the imperfect kind, is more properly called acts of hostility, or reprisal, and that congress did not mean to consider the hostility subsisting between France and the United States, as constituting a state of war.

In support of this position, it has been observed, that in no law prior to March 1799, is France styled our enemy, nor are we said to be at war. This is true; but neither of these things were necessary to be done: because as to France, she was sufficiently described by the title of the French republic; and as to America, the degree of hostility meant to be carried on, was sufficiently described without declaring war, or declaring that we were at war. Such a declaration by congress, might have constituted a perfect state of war, which was not intended by the government....

CHASE, J.

... The decree of the Circuit Court (in which I presided) passed by consent; but although I never gave an opinion, I have never entertained a doubt on the subject. Congress is empowered to declare a general war, or congress may wage a limited war; limited in place, in objects and in time. If a general war is declared, its extent and operations are only restricted and regulated by the *jus belli*, forming a part of the law of nations; but if a partial war is waged, its extent and operation depend on our municipal laws.

What, then, is the nature of the contest subsisting between America and France? In my judgment, it is a limited, partial, war. Congress has not declared war in general terms; but congress has authorised hostilities on the high seas by certain persons in certain cases. There is no authority given to commit hostilities on land; to capture unarmed French vessels, nor even to capture French armed vessels lying in a French port; and the authority is not given, indiscriminately, to every citizen of America, against every citizen of France; but only to citizens appointed by commissions, or exposed to immediate outrage and violence. So far it is, unquestionably, a partial war; but, nevertheless, it is a public war, on account of the public authority from which it emanates....

Having, then, no hesitation in pronouncing, that a partial war exists between America and France, and that France was an enemy, within the meaning of the act of March 1799, my voice must be given for affirming the decree of the Circuit Court.

PATERSON, J.

... The United States and the French republic are in a qualified state of hostility. An imperfect war, or a war, as to certain objects, and to a certain extent, exists between the two nations; and this modified warfare is authorised by the constitutional authority of our country. It is a war quoad hoc. As far as congress tolerated and authorised the war on our part, so far may we proceed in hostile operations. It is a maritime war; a war at sea as to certain purposes. The national armed vessels of France attack and capture the national armed vessels of the United States; and the national armed vessels of the United States are expressly authorised and directed to attack, subdue, and take, the national armed vessels of France, and also to re-capture American vessels. It is therefore a public war between the two nations, qualified, on our part, in the manner prescribed by the constitutional organ of our country. In such a state of things, it is scarcely necessary to add, that the term "enemy," applies; it is the appropriate expression, to be limited in its signification, import, and use, by the qualified nature and operation of the war on our part. The word enemy proceeds the full length of the war, and no farther....

TALBOT v. SEEMAN

5 U.S. (1 Cranch) 1, 28, 41 (1801).

MARSHALL, C.J.

The whole powers of war being, by the constitution of the United States, vested in congress, the acts of that body can alone be resorted to as our guides in this enquiry. It is not denied, nor in the course of the argument has it been denied, that congress may authorize general hostilities, in which case the general laws of war apply to our situation; or partial hostilities, in which case the laws of war, so far as they actually apply to our situation, must be noticed....

[Capture of a vessel by France in] violation of the law of nations ... does not justify its violation by another; but ... remonstrance is the proper course to be pursued, and this is the course which has been pursued ... , but remonstrance having failed, [the U.S.] appealed to a higher tribunal, and authorized limited hostilities. This was not violating the law of nations, but conforming to it.

DELLUMS v. SMITH

577 F.Supp. 1449, 1450–53 (N.D.Cal.1984), *rev'd on other grounds*, 797 F.2d 817 (9th Cir.1986).

WEIGEL, J.

Plaintiffs filed suit to require the Attorney General to conduct a preliminary investigation as to whether the President, the Secretary of State, the Secretary of Defense and other federal executive officers have violated the Neutrality Act, a federal criminal law, by supporting paramilitary operations against Nicaragua. The Neutrality Act, 18 U.S.C. § 960, declares that:

> Whoever, within the United States, knowingly begins or sets on foot or provides or prepares a means for or furnishes the money for, or takes part in, any military or naval expedition or enterprise to be carried on from thence against the territory or dominion of any

foreign prince or state, or any colony, district, or people with whom the United States is at peace, shall be fined not more than $3,000 or imprisoned not more than three years, or both.

Plaintiffs' complaint was founded upon the Ethics in Government Act. 28 U.S.C. §§ 591–598, which directs the Attorney General to conduct a preliminary investigation upon receiving specific information from a credible source that federal criminal law has been violated by any federal official designated in the statute.

The Court found, and the Attorney General has since admitted, that the information presented by plaintiffs was sufficiently specific and that it came from a sufficiently credible source. *Dellums v. Smith*, 573 F. Supp. 1489 at 1504–1505 (N.D.Cal.1983). The Court also determined that officials covered by the Ethics in Government Act *may* have violated the Neutrality Act. *See id.* at 1502 n.11. For these reasons, the Court ordered the Attorney General to conduct a preliminary investigation as required by the Ethics in Government Act. *Id.* at 1504–1505. Pursuant to the same statute, the Court also ordered that unless the Attorney General makes a determination within ninety days that there are no reasonable grounds to believe that further investigation is warranted, he must apply for the appointment of independent counsel. *Id.* at 1505.

Defendants, in opposing plaintiffs' motion for summary judgment and moving for dismissal of the action, argued that plaintiffs lack standing to sue, that the Ethics in Government Act does not grant a private right of action to plaintiffs, that the ruling sought requires an impermissible advisory opinion, and that the action presents a non-justiciable political question. The Court rejected each of these contentions and granted plaintiffs' motion for summary judgment....

The contention that the Neutrality Act reaches executive officials is at least as persuasive as defendant's claim that it does not. The statute itself contains no exception for any person or official. Thus, the doctrine espoused by defendants finds no support on the face of the statute. Consideration of the English statutes upon which the Neutrality Act was modeled supports the conclusion that the American statute's broad language was chosen purposefully. The English statutes provide express exceptions for acts done with leave or license of the crown, i.e., the executive. *See* Lobel, *The Rise and Decline of the Neutrality Act: Sovereignty and Congressional War Powers in United States Foreign Policy*, 24 HARV. INT'L L.J. 1, 31–33 (1983) (hereinafter cited as "Lobel"). The absence of such provisions from the American Act reflects a decision to retain and protect the Constitution's delegation of war power to the legislative branch. *See* U.S. Const. art. I, § 8. In addition, uncontradicted authority holds that the President cannot aid or authorize private expeditions against foreign nations without the approval of Congress.

In 1806, two civilians were indicted and tried for aiding an attempt to launch an expedition against Spanish America in violation of the Neutrality Act. United States v. Smith, 27 F. Cas. 1192 (C.C.N.Y. 1807) (No. 16,342). As part of their defense, they sought to subpoena Secretary of State James Madison and other federal executive officials to prove their claim that their acts had been authorized by President Jefferson. *Id.* at 1228.

The Court declined to issue the requested subpoenas on the ground that such testimony of the cabinet members was immaterial. William Paterson, a Supreme Court Justice and participant in the Constitutional Convention, presided over the trial and handed down the court's opinion. He first examined the Neutrality Act and found that is "is expressed in general, unqualified terms; it contains no condition no exception; it invests no dispensing power in any officer or person whatsoever." Justice Paterson then determined that the Constitution itself does not create such an exception for the President. "This instrument [the Constitution], which measures out the powers and defines the duties of the President, does not vest in him any authority to set on foot a military expedition against a nation with which the United States is at peace." *Id.* at 1229–30. In conclusion, Justice Paterson stated that "the law under consideration is absolute" and "requires universal obedience." *Id.* at 1231.

This conclusion is well-supported by the history of the Neutrality Act. One of its major purposes was to protect the constitutional power of Congress to declare war or authorize private reprisal against foreign states. *See* Lobel, *supra,* at 27–37. This purpose was recognized by early presidents. "[W]hether the interest or honor of the United States requires that they should be made a party to any such struggle, and by inevitable consequence to the war which is waged in its support, is a question which by our Constitution is wisely left to Congress alone to decide. It is by the laws already made criminal in our citizens to embarrass or anticipate that decision by unauthorized military operations on their part." President Martin Van Buren, Second Annual Message to Congress (Dec. 3, 1838), *reprinted in* 3 MESSAGES & PAPERS OF THE PRESIDENTS 483, 487 (J. Richardson ed. 1896); *see also* Inaugural Address of President John Adams (Marsh 4, 1797), *reprinted in* 1 MESSAGES & PAPERS OF THE PRESIDENTS, *supra,* at 231.

Believing that the Neutrality Act bound the President, congressional opponents of the law attempted unsuccessfully to amend it during the 1800s. For example, in 1854, Senator Slidell introduced a resolution seeking to amend the Neutrality Act by allowing the President to suspend its operation during any recess of Congress for up to 12 months when, "in his opinion, the public interests require" such a suspension. Cong. Globe, 33d Cong., 1st Sess. 1021, 1023–24 (1854). Slidell's proposed amendment failed. Similarly, in 1858, Senator Slidell introduced a resolution to amend the Neutrality Act to permit presidential suspension during recesses. Cong. Globe, 35th Cong., 1st Sess. 462 (1858). This proposal also failed. The Neutrality Act remains today substantially the same as it appeared in the original enactment of 1794. The failure of Senator Slidell's proposed amendments fortifies the view that the Neutrality Act grants no executive discretion to authorize paramilitary expeditions against foreign governments with which this nation is not at war.

To support their claim that the executive officials are immune from the coverage of the act, defendants refer to provisions of the 1794 Act empowering the President to take certain actions to enforce the statute's prohibitions. *See* Act of June 5, 1794, § 8, 1 Stat. 381, 384 (1794). The existence of such enforcement powers does not preclude application of the Act to the Executive. For example, Attorney General Robert Jackson rendered the opinion that section 3 of the 1917 reenactment of the Act applied to the President and prevented the President from releasing to the British Government boats then under construction for the United States Navy. 29 Op. Atty. Gen. 484, 494–96 (1940). Attorney General Jackson reached this conclusion even though he acknowledged the provision authorizing presidential enforcement of the prohibition. *See id.* of 494.

Similarly misguided is defendants' reference to the President's powers and duties as "Commander in Chief of the Army and Navy of the United States," and to various military operations conducted by these forces. The paramilitary operations challenged by plaintiffs were not alleged to have been conducted by the armed forces of the United States. The legislative history of the statute indicates that it was not intended to cover the use of regular United States armed forces. *See* Lobel, *supra*, at 31 n.159. Plaintiffs alleged that the named officials may have violated the Neutrality Act by supporting *private* expeditions. Justice Paterson ruled in *Smith* that such expeditions do not lose the taint of illegality merely because authorized by the Executive. No substantial legal authority contradicts this construction of the Neutrality Act.

The same distinction vitiates defendants' citation to the War Powers Resolution as an illustration of the President's plenary authority to intervene militarily in foreign countries. That resolution is directed to the President's power to introduce the "United States Armed Forces," not paramilitary or other private forces. 50 U.S.C. §§ 1541(a); 1541(c); 1547(c)....

The history of the Neutrality Act and judicial precedent demonstrate the reasonableness of the view that the Act applies to all persons, including the President. The Court reaffirms its original determination that the "Executive actions alleged by plaintiffs, if true, *may* violate federal law." Consequently, in this case, a preliminary investigation may not be refused....

Notes

1. The case was reversed on the grounds that plaintiffs lacked standing. A footnote in the district court's opinion states: "A memorandum authored by the Department of Justice Office of Legal Counsel has been submitted by defendants as an exhibit to their reply memorandum.... This memorandum deals primarily with another statute that was part of the Neutrality Act, 18 U.S.C. § 959(a), and concludes that the provision is not

violated when CIA agents serve in the employ of a foreign military service. 18 U.S.C. § 960 and *Smith* are distinguished as follows:

> We understand this case to stand for the proposition that where an activity is not otherwise within the authority of the Executive Branch, it could not authorize a private individual to engage in it. Since the Executive cannot constitutionally wage war on a nation against which there has been no congressional declaration of war, the President's "authorization" to a private citizen is simply immaterial. By contrast, where an activity is otherwise within the province of the Executive as is the case with intelligence gathering, we think that sovereign authorization would be found a good defense.... "

2. One of those tried in *United States v. Smith* for a violation of the Neutrality Act of 1794 was the son-in-law of John Adams, William S. Smith. He had been helping to finance, outfit, and provide men for a local revolutionary effort to oust the Spaniards from Venezuela, which had failed. Part of Smith's defense was that his participation was with the "knowledge and approbation" of President Jefferson and Secretary Madison. He sought the testimony of Secretary of State Madison, Secretary of the Navy Robert Smith, and others, but Justice Paterson, on circuit, ruled that the testimony would not be relevant, since "[t]he president of the United States cannot control the statute, nor dispense with its execution, and still less can he authorize a person to do what the law forbids. If he could, he would render the execution of the laws dependent on his will and pleasure; which is a doctrine that has not been set up, and will not meet with any supporters in our government." Justice Paterson added:

"If, then, the president knew and approved of the military expedition set forth in the indictment against a prince with whom we are at peace, it would not justify the defendant in a court of law, nor discharge him from the binding force of the act of congress; because the president does not possess a dispensing power. Does he possess the power of making war? That power is exclusively vested in congress; for, by the eighth section of the 1st article of the constitution, it is ordained, that congress shall have power to declare war, grant letters of marque and reprisal, raise and support armies, provide and maintain a navy, and to provide for calling forth the militia to execute the laws of the Union, suppress insurrections, and repel invasions. And we accordingly find, that congress have been so circumspect and provident in regard to the last three particulars, that they have from time to time vested the president of the United States with ample powers.

"Thus, by the act of the 28th of February, 1795 (3 Swift's Laws, 188 [1 Stat. 424]), it is made lawful for the president to call forth the militia to repel invasions, suppress insurrections, and execute the laws of the Union. Abstractedly from this constitutional and legal provision, the right to repel invasions arises from self-preservation and defence, which is a primary law of nature, and constitutes part of the law of nations. It therefore becomes the duty of a people, and particularly of the executive magistrate, who is at their head, the commander-in-chief of the forces by sea and land, to repel an invading foe. But to repel aggressions and invasions is one thing, and to commit them against a friendly power is another. It is obvious that if the United States were at war with Spain at the time that the defendant is charged with the offence in the indictment, then he does not come within the purview of the statute, which makes the basis of the offence to consist in beginning or preparing the means to carry on a military expedition or enterprise against a nation with which the United States are at peace. If, indeed, a foreign nation should invade the territories of the United States, it would I apprehend, be not only lawful for the president to resist such invasion, but also to carry hostilities into the enemy's own country; and for this plain reason, that a state of complete and absolute war actually exists between the two nations. In the case of invasive hostilities, there cannot be war on the one side and peace on the other. What! in the storm of battle, and, perhaps, in the full tide of victory, must we stop short at the boundary between the two nations, and give over the conflict and pursuit? Will it be an offence to pass the line of partition, and smite the invading foe on his own ground? No; surely no. To do so would be a duty, and cannot be perverted into a crime. There is a manifest distinction between our going to war with a nation at peace, and a war being made against us by an actual invasion, or a formal declaration. In the former case, it is the exclusive province of congress to change a state of peace into a state of war. A nation, however, may be in such a situation as to render it more prudent to submit to certain acts of a hostile nature, and to trust to negotiations for redress, than to make an immediate appeal to arms. Various considerations may induce to a measure of this kind; such as motives of policy, calculations of interest, the nature of the injury and provocation, he relative resources, means and strength of the two nations, & c. and, therefore, the organ intrusted with the power to declare war, should first decide whether it is expedient to go to war, or to continue in peace; and until such a decision be made, no individual ought to assume an hostile attitude; and to pronounce, contrary to the constitutional will, that the nation is at war, and that he will shape his conduct and act according to such a state of things. This conduct is clearly indefensible, and may involve the nation, of which he is a member, in all the calamities of a long and expensive war."

See United States v. Smith, 27 F. Cas. 1192, 1228–31 (C.C.D.N.Y.1806) (No. 16,342). Portions of this case also appear in Chapter 2, Section 2 D 1.

After a trial, the jury met for some two hours and then returned a verdict of not guilty.

2. The War Powers Resolution

THE WAR POWERS RESOLUTION

50 U.S.C. §§ 1541–1548.

Joint Resolution Concerning the war powers of Congress and the President.

Resolved by the Senate and House of Representatives of the United States of America in Congress assembled, . . .

PURPOSE AND POLICY

Sec. 2. (a) It is the purpose of this joint resolution to fulfill the intent of the framers of the Constitution of the United States and insure that the collective judgment of both the Congress and the President will apply to the introduction of United States Armed Forces into hostilities, or into situations where imminent involvement in hostilities, is clearly indicated by the circumstances, and to the continued use of such forces in hostilities or in such situations.

(b) Under article I, section 8, of the Constitution, it is specifically provided that the Congress shall have the power to make all laws necessary and proper for carrying into execution, not only its own powers but also all other powers vested by the Constitution in the Government of the United States, or in any department of officer thereof.

(c) The constitutional powers of the President as Commander-in-Chief to introduce United States Armed Forces into hostilities, or into situations where imminent involvement in hostilities is clearly indicated by the circumstances, are exercised only pursuant to (1) a declaration of war, (2) specific statutory authorization, or (3) a national emergency created by attack upon the United States, its territories or possessions, or its armed forces.

CONSULTATION

Sec. 3. The President in every possible instance shall consult with Congress before introducing United States Armed Forces into hostilities or into situations where imminent involvement is hostilities is clearly indicated by the circumstances, and after every such introduction shall consult regularly with Congress until United States Armed Forces are no longer engaged in hostilities or have been removed from such situations.

REPORTING

Sec. 4. (a) In the absence of a declaration of war, in any case in which United States Armed Forces are introduced—

(1) into hostilities or into situations where imminent involvement in hostilities is clearly indicated by the circumstances;

(2) into the territory, airspace or waters of a foreign nation, while equipped for combat, except for deployments which relate solely to supply, replacement, repair, or training of such forces; or

(3) in numbers which substantially enlarge United States Armed Forces equipped for combat already located in a foreign nation; the President shall submit within 48 hours to the Speaker of the House of Representatives and to the President pro tempore of the Senate a report, in writing, setting forth—

(A) the circumstances necessitating the introduction of United States Armed Forces;

(B) the constitutional and legislative authority under which such introduction took place; and

(C) the estimated scope and duration of the hostilities or involvement....

Congressional Action

Sec. 5. . . .

(b) Within sixty calendar days after a report is submitted or is required to be submitted pursuant to section 4 (a)(1), whichever is earlier, the President shall terminate any use of United States Armed Forces with respect to which such report was submitted (or required to be submitted), unless the Congress (1) has declared war or has enacted a specific authorization for such use of United States Armed Forces, (2) has extended by law such sixty-day period, or (3) is physically unable to meet as a result of an armed attack upon the United States. Such sixty-day period shall be extended for not more than an additional thirty days if the President determines and certifies to the Congress in writing that unavoidable military necessity respecting the safety of United States Armed Forces requires the continued use of such armed forces in the course of bringing about a prompt removal of such forces.

(c) Notwithstanding subsection (b), at any time that United States Armed Forces are engaged in hostilities outside the territory of the United States, its possessions and territories without a declaration of war or specific statutory authorization, such forces shall be removed by the President if the Congress so directs by concurrent resolution. . . .

Interpretation of Joint Resolution

Sec. 8. (a) Authority to introduce United States Armed Forces into hostilities or into situations wherein involvement in hostilities is clearly indicated by the circumstances shall not be inferred—

(1) from any provision of law (whether or not in effect before the date of the enactment of this joint resolution), including any provision contained in any appropriation Act, unless such provision specifically authorizes the introduction of United States Armed Forces into hostilities or into such situations and states that it is intended to constitute specific statutory authorization within the meaning of this joint resolution; or

(2) from any treaty heretofore or hereafter ratified unless such treaty is implemented by legislation specifically authorizing the introduction of United States Armed Forces into hostilities or into such situations and states that it is intended to constitute specific statutory authorization within the meaning of this joint resolution.

(b) Nothing in this joint resolution shall be construed to require any further specific statutory authorization to permit members of United States Armed Forces to participate jointly with members of the armed forces of one or more foreign countries in the headquarters operations of high-level military commands which were established prior to the date of enactment of this joint resolution and pursuant to the United Nations Charter or any treaty ratified by the United States prior to such date.

(c) For purposes of this joint resolution, the term "introduction of United States Armed Forces" includes the assignment of members of such armed forces to command, coordinate, participate in the movement of, or accompany the regular or irregular military forces of any foreign country or government when such military forces are engaged, or there exists an imminent threat that such forces will become engaged, in hostilities.

(d) Nothing in this joint resolution—

(1) is intended to alter the constitutional authority of the Congress or the President, or the provisions of existing treaties; or

(2) shall be construed as granting any authority to the President with respect to the introduction of United States Armed Forces into hostilities or into situations wherein involvement in hostilities is clearly indicated by the circumstances which authority he would not have had in the absence of this joint resolution.

SEPARABILITY CLAUSE

Sec. 9. If any portion of this joint resolution or the application thereof to any person or circumstance is held invalid, the remainder of the joint resolution and the application of such provision to any other person or circumstance shall not be affected thereby....

Notes and Questions

1. Within the meaning of Section 2 (b), is the President "the Government of the United States, or any department or officer thereof"?

2. Section 2 (c) merely addresses the President's power as "Commander-in-Chief". Does the President have other powers to introduce U.S. military forces into hostilities? For an Executive view, *see, e.g.*, THOMAS M. FRANCK & MICHAEL J. GLENNON, FOREIGN RELATIONS AND NATIONAL SECURITY LAW 606 (2 ed. 1993), quoting testimony of Monroe Leigh, Legal Adviser to the Secretary of State, during hearings before the House Committee on International Relations, 94th Cong., 1st Sess. (1975): "Besides the three situations listed in subsection 2(c) . . . , it appears that the President has the constitutional authority to use the Armed Forces to rescue American citizens abroad, to rescue foreign nationals where such action directly facilitates the rescue of U.S. citizens abroad, to protect U.S. Embassies and Legations abroad, to suppress civil insurrection, to implement and administer the terms of an armistice or cease-fire designed to terminate hostilities involving the United States, and to carry out the terms of security commitments contained in treaties." *See also* Jordan J. Paust, *Peace-Making and Security Council Powers: Bosnia–Herzegovina Raises International and Constitutional Questions*, 19 SO. ILL. U. L.J. 131, 144 (1994); Eugene Rostow, *"Once More Unto the Breach:" The War Powers Resolution Revisited*, 21 VAL. U. L. REV. 1 (1986). Do you agree?

3. Section 2 (c) does not address the power to protect or rescue U.S. nationals in case of an armed attack on such persons outside the United States. Does the President have the power to protect U.S. nationals by use of force in such a circumstance without prior approval of Congress? *See, e.g.*, G. Sidney Buchanan, *A Proposed Model for Determining the Validity of the Use of Force Against Foreign Adversaries Under the United States Constitution*,

29 HOUS. L. REV. 379, 400–05 (1992); Abraham D. Sofaer, *The Sixth Annual Waldemar A. Solf Lecture in International Law: Terrorism, the Law, and the National Defense*, 126 MIL. L. REV. 89 (1989); Section 2 B 3–5 of this chapter; question 2 above.

4. What is the meaning of the words "hostilities" or "combat" found in Section 4 (a)? Is international law relevant to the meaning of such terms? Consider also the testimony of Abraham Sofaer, Legal Adviser to the Secretary of State, before the House Committee on Foreign Affairs, 99th Cong., 2d Sess. (1986), quoted in FRANCK & GLENNON, *supra* at 619: regarding nonstate terrorist activities, "the President may decide to deploy specially-trained anti-terrorist units in an effort to secure the release of the hostages or to capture the terrorists who perpetrated the act.... [W]here no confrontation is expected between our units and forces of another state ... such units can reasonably be distinguished from 'forces equipped for combat' and their actions against terrorists differ greatly from the 'hostilities' contemplated by the Resolution...." Do you agree? *See also* Paust, *supra* at 145–46.

5. If the United States used military force in Panama in 1989 with the consent of the lawfully elected President of Panama, was the U.S. involved in any "hostilities" or "combat" with troops loyal to the former dictator Noriega?

On December 21, 1989, President Bush presented the following Report concerning U.S. use of force in Panama:

"On December 15, 1989, at the instigation of Manuel Noriega, the illegitimate Panamanian National Assembly declared that a state of war existed between the Republic of Panama and the United States. At the same time, Noriega gave a highly inflammatory anti-American speech. A series of vicious and brutal acts directed at U.S. personnel and dependents followed these events.

"On December 16, 1989, a U.S. Marine officer was killed without justification by Panama Defense Forces (PDF) personnel. Other elements of the PDF beat a U.S. Naval officer and unlawfully detained, physically abused, and threatened the officer's wife. These acts of violence are directly attributable to Noriega's dictatorship, which created a climate of aggression that places American lives and interests in peril.

"These and other events over the past two years have made it clear that the lives and welfare of American citizens in Panama were increasingly at risk, and that the continued safe operation of the Panama Canal and the integrity of the Canal Treaties would be in serious jeopardy if such lawlessness were allowed to continue.

"Under these circumstances, I ordered the deployment of approximately 11,000 additional U.S. Forces to Panama. In conjunction with the 13,000 U.S. Forces already present, military operations were initiated on December 20, 1989, to protect American lives, to defend democracy in Panama, to apprehend Noriega and bring him to trial on the drug-related charges for which he was indicted in 1988, and to ensure the integrity of the Panama Canal Treaties.

"In the early morning of December 20, 1989, the democratically elected Panamanian leadership announced formation of a government, assumed power in a formal swearing-in ceremony, and welcomed the assistance of U.S. Armed Forces in removing the illegitimate Noriega regime.

"The deployment of U.S. Forces is an exercise of the right of self-defense recognized in Article 51 of the United Nations Charter and was necessary to protect American lives in imminent danger and to fulfill our responsibilities under the Panama Canal Treaties. It was welcomed by the democratically elected government of Panama. The military operations were ordered pursuant to my constitutional authority with respect to the conduct of foreign relations and as Commander in Chief.

"In accordance with my desire that Congress be fully informed on this matter, and consistent with the War Powers Resolution, I am providing this report on the deployment of U.S. Armed Forces to Panama.

"Although most organized opposition has ceased, it is not possible at this time to predict the precise scope and duration of the military operations or how long the temporary increase of U.S. Forces in Panama will be required. Nevertheless, our objectives are clear and largely have been accomplished. Our additional Forces will remain in Panama only so long as their presence is required."

Do you think the use of force by the U.S. was permissible under international law? Was it permissible in light of the War Powers Resolution? *See also* panels, *The Panamanian Revolution: Diplomacy, War and Self–Determination in Panama, (I) Self–Determination and Intervention in Panama, (II) Extraterritorial Law Enforcement and the "Receipt" and Trial of Noriega*, 84 PROC., AM. SOC. INT'L L. 182, 236 (1990); *Agora: U.S. Forces in Panama: Defenders, Aggressors or Human Rights Activists?*, 84 AM. J. INT'L L. 494 (1990) (remarks of Ved P. Nanda, Tom J. Farer, Anthony D'Amato); Louis Henkin, *The Invasion of Panama Under International Law: A Gross Violation*, 29 COLUM. J. TRANSNAT'L L. 293 (1991); Abraham D. Sofaer, *The Legality of United States Action in Panama*, *id.* at 281.

6. Does Section 5 (b) functionally permit the President to use military force abroad as long as the duration is relatively short? *Compare* Thomas M. Franck, *After the Fall: The New Procedural Framework for Congressional Control Over the War Power*, 71 AM. J. INT'L L. 605, 626–27 (1977); Paust, *supra*, at 145 *with* Buchanan, *A Proposed Model*, *supra*, at 386, 405–11.

7. Is Section 5 (c) constitutional? *See* Immigration and Naturalization Service v. Chadha, 462 U.S. 919 (1983); JOHN E. NOWAK & RONALD D. ROTUNDA, CONSTITUTIONAL LAW 226 (4 ed. 1991); G. Sidney Buchanan, *In Defense of the War Powers Resolution:* Chadha *Does Not Apply*, 22 HOUS. L. REV. 1155 (1985); Michael J. Glennon, *The War Powers Resolution Ten Years Later: More Politics Than Law*, 78 AM. J. INT'L L. 571, 577 (1984).

8. If the President does not file a report, can the courts step in? *See, e.g.*, Crockett v. Reagan, 720 F.2d 1355 (D.C.Cir.1983), *cert. denied*, 467 U.S. 1251 (1984); Conyers v. Reagan, 578 F.Supp. 324 (D.D.C.1984); Sanchez–Espinoza v. Reagan, 568 F.Supp. 596 (D.D.C.1983), *aff'd*, 770 F.2d 202 (D.C.Cir.1985). In Raines v. Byrd, 521 U.S. 811 (1997), the Supreme Court rejected standing for a group of congresspersons who did not allege a

"sufficiently concrete injury" during a constitutional challenge to legislation that they had voted against (the Line Item Veto Act).

9. Despite Section 8 (a) (1), can the Congress of 1973 bind any future Congress? If not, how is one to interpret a claim of implied authorization to use force from relevant money appropriations in the context of some future involvement in hostilities initiated by the President and known to the world? Is the existence of Section 8 (a) (1) part of a relevant context and presumed will of Congress? *See also* MICHAEL J. GLENNON, CONSTITUTIONAL DIPLOMACY 100–02 (1990).

How does Section 8 (a) (1) compare with Justice Frankfurter's remarks in Youngstown Sheet & Tube Co. v. Sawyer, 343 U.S. 579, 610–11 (1952) (Frankfurter, J., concurring): "Deeply embedded traditional ways of conducting government cannot supplant the Constitution or legislation, but they give meaning to the words of a text or supply them ... the gloss.... In short, a systematic, unbroken, executive practice, long pursued to the knowledge of the Congress and never before questioned ... may be treated as a gloss on 'executive Power' vested in the President by § 1 of Art. II." Which approach is preferable?

10. If Section 8 (a) (2) was applied to a future treaty, would Section 8 (a) (2) wipe out the independent treaty power? Would the last in time rule be applicable?

11. Is there an inconsistency between Section 8 (a) (2) and (d)?

12. Does Section 8 (b) recognize the power of the President to use military force in connection with a joint NATO or U.N. "headquarters operation"? If so, was U.S. participation in NATO's use of force in Kosovo and the Republic of Yugoslavia in 1999 covered? Consider also U.S. participation in Bosnia–Herzegovina in 1994, the Gulf War in 1990 before congressional authorization in 1991, and in Korea in the 1950s; Paust, *supra*, at 144–50; and part B, Presidential Powers, below.

3. *The United Nations Participation Act*

UNITED NATIONS PARTICIPATION ACT

22 U.S.C. § 287(d); Pub. Law No. 79–264, ch. 583, 59 Stat. 619 (1945).

287d. Use of armed forces; limitations

The President is authorized to negotiate a special agreement or agreements with the Security Council which shall be subject to the approval of the Congress by appropriate Act or joint resolution, providing for the numbers and types of armed forces, their degree of readiness and general location, and the nature of facilities and assistance, including rights of passage, to be made available to the Security Council on its call for the purpose of maintaining international peace and security in accordance with article 43 of said Charter. The President shall not be deemed to require the authorization of the Congress to make available to the Security Council on its call in order to take action under article 42 of said Charter and pursuant to such special agreement or agreements the armed forces, facilities, or assistance provided for therein: Provided,

That, except as authorized in section 7 of this Act [§ 287d–1], nothing herein contained shall be construed as an authorization to the President by the Congress to make available to the Security Council for such purpose armed forces, facilities, or assistance in addition to the forces, facilities, and assistance provided for in such special agreement or agreements.

Notes and Questions

1. What is the status of U.S. forces made available to the Security Council pursuant to Article 43 of the Charter?

2. Although U.S. forces were under a U.N. flag and command during the Korean War, they remained under the functional command of the President of the United States, especially because the Commander of U.N. forces was a U.S. General. There was no "Article 43" agreement.

3. Did Section 287d of the United Nations Participation Act apply regarding U.S. forces involved in the Gulf war in the 1990s? In the Bosnia–Herzegovina peacemaking activities in the 1990s?

4. Is the Act subject to being trumped by a treaty-executive agreement?

B. Presidential Powers

1. U.S. Constitutional Provisions

[recall U.S. Const., Art. II, addressed in Chapter 2, Section 2 A]

2. Commander-In-Chief Powers

ALEXANDER HAMILTON, THE FEDERALIST PAPERS NO. 69

The President will have only the occasional command of such part of the militia of the nation as by legislative provision may be called into the actual service of the Union.... [The Commander-in-Chief power] would amount to nothing more than the command and direction of the military and naval forces, as first general and admiral of the Confederacy.

FLEMING v. PAGE

50 U.S. (9 How.) 603, 614 (1850).

TANEY, C.J.

[T]he genius and character of our institutions are peaceful, and the power to declare war was not conferred upon Congress for the purposes of aggression or aggrandizement, but to enable the general government to vindicate by arms, if it should become necessary, its own rights and the rights of its citizens....

As Commander-in-Chief he is authorized to direct the movements of the naval and military forces placed by law at his command, and to employ them in the manner he may deem most effectual to harass and conquer and subdue the enemy. He may invade the hostile country and subject it to the sovereignty and authority of the United States.

EX PARTE MILLIGAN

71 U.S. 2, 139 (1866).

CHASE, C.J., dissenting

Congress has the power not only to raise and support and govern armies but to declare war. It has, therefore, the power to provide by law for carrying on war. This power necessarily extends to all legislation essential to the prosecution of war with vigor and success, except such as interferes with the command of the forces and the conduct of campaigns. That power and duty belong to the President as commander-in-chief. Both these powers are derived from the Constitution, but neither is defined by that instrument. Their extent must be determined by their nature, and by the principles of our institutions.

The power to make the necessary laws is in Congress; the power to execute in the President. Both powers imply many subordinate and auxiliary powers. Each includes all authorities essential to its due exercise. But neither can the President, in war more than in peace, intrude upon the proper authority of Congress, nor Congress upon the proper authority of the President. Both are servants of the people, whose will is expressed in the fundamental law.

UNITED STATES v. SWEENY

157 U.S. 281, 284 (1895).

BROWN, J.

... [T]he object of the [Commander-in-Chief] provision is evidently to vest in the President the supreme command over all the military forces—such supreme and undivided command as would be necessary to the prosecution of a successful war. The regular army dates its birth from the act of September 29, 1789, c. 25, 1 stat. 95, which continued in the service of the United States a small military force, which had been held subject to the authority of Congress when the Constitution took effect.

SWAIM v. UNITED STATES

28 Ct.Cl. 173, 221 (1893), *aff'd*, 165 U.S. 553 (1897).

Congress may increase the Army, or reduce the Army, or abolish it altogether; but so long as we have a military force, Congress cannot take away from the President the supreme command. It is true that the Constitution has conferred upon Congress the exclusive power "to make rules for the government and regulation of the land and naval forces"; but the two powers are distinct; neither can trench upon the other; the President cannot, under the disguise of military orders, evade the legislative regulations by which he in common with the Army must be governed; and Congress cannot in the disguise of "rules for the government" of the Army impair the authority of the President as commander in chief.

3. Powers of Protection

DURAND v. HOLLINS

8 F. Cas. 111 (C.C.S.D.N.Y. 1860) (No. 4,186).

NELSON, J.

[Editors' note: The Secretary of the Navy had ordered George Hollins, the commander of the *Cayne*, to bombard San Juan del Norte (Greytown), Nicaragua, in 1854 following an attack on a U.S. diplomat. Durand, a U.S. citizen, sued Hollins for damages suffered from destruction of his property during a fire created by the bombardment. Defendant Hollins claimed that he was bound to obey that lawful orders of the President and of the Secretary of the Navy, that the community of Greytown had forcibly taken possession of the town and had erected an independent government not recognized by the United States, that they had committed acts of violence against citizens of the United States, and that he had demanded redress, which was refused, and that he was thereafter ordered to bombard the town.]

The principal ground of objection to the pleas, as a defense of the action, is, that neither the president nor the secretary of the navy had authority to give the orders relied on to the defendant, and, hence, that they afford no ground of justification.

The executive power, under the constitution, is vested in the president of the United States (article 2, § 1). He is commander-in-chief of the army and navy, (*Id.* § 2), and has imposed upon him the duty to "take care that the laws be faithfully executed" (*Id.* § 3). In organizing a government under the constitution, an executive department, called the "Department of Foreign Affairs," was established, and a principal officer, called the "Secretary for the Department of Foreign Affairs," placed at its head, to "execute such duties as shall, from time to time, be enjoined on or intrusted to him by the president of the United States, agreeable to the constitution, relative to correspondences, commissions, or instructions to or with public ministers or consuls from the United States or to negotiations with public ministers from foreign states or princes, or to memorials or other applications from foreign public ministers or other foreigners, or to such other matters respecting foreign affairs as the president of the United States shall assign to the said department; and, furthermore, that the said principal officer shall conduct the business of the said department in such manner as the president of the United States shall from time to time order or instruct." Act Cong. July 27, 1789, § 1 (1 Stat. 28). By a subsequent act, this department has been denominated the "Department of State," and the head of it the "Secretary of State." There was also established another executive department, denominated the "Department of the Navy," the chief officer of which is called the "Secretary of the Navy," "whose duty it shall be to execute such orders as he shall receive from the president of the United States, relative to the procurement of naval stores and materials, and the construction, armament, equipment and employment of vessels of war, as well as all other matters connected with the naval establishment of the United States." Act Cong. April 30, 1798, § 1 (1 Stat. 553).

As the executive head of the nation, the president is made the only legitimate organ of the general government, to open and carry on correspondence or negotiations with foreign nations, in matters concerning the interests of the country or of its citizens. It is to him, also, the citizens abroad must look for protection of person and of property, and for the faithful execution of the laws existing and intended for their protection. For this purpose, the whole executive power of the country is placed in his hands, under the constitution, and the laws passed in pursuance thereof; and different departments of government have been organized, through which this power may be most conveniently executed, whether by negotiation or by force—a department of state and a department of the navy.

Now, as it respects the interposition of the executive abroad, for the protection of the lives or property of the citizen, the duty must, of necessity, rest in the discretion of the president. Acts of lawless violence, or of threatened violence to the citizen or his property, cannot be anticipated and provided for; and the protection, to be effectual or of any avail, may, not unfrequently, require the most prompt and decided action. Under our system of government, the citizen aboard is an much entitled to protection as the citizen at home. The great object and duty of government is the protection of the lives, liberty, and property of the people composing it, whether abroad or at home; and any government failing in the accomplishment of the object, or the performance of the duty, is not worth preserving.

I have said, that the interposition of the president abroad, for the protection of the citizen, must necessarily rest in his discretion; and it is quite clear that, in all cases where a public act or order rests in executive discretion neither he nor his authorized agent is personally civilly responsible for the consequences. As was observed by Chief Justice Marshall, in Marbury v. Madison, 1 Cranch [5 U.S. 137,] 165: "By the constitution of the United States, the president is invested with certain important political powers, in the exercise of which he is to use his own discretion, and is accountable only to his country in his political character, and to his own conscience. To aid him in the performance of these duties, he is authorized to appoint certain officers, who act by his authority, and in conformity with his orders. In such cases, their acts are his acts, and, whatever opinion may be entertained of the manner in which executive discretion may be used, still there exists, and can exist, no power to control that discretion. The subjects are political. They respect the nation, not individual rights, and, being intrusted to the executive, the decision of the executive is conclusive." This is a sound principle, and governs the present case. The question whether it was the duty of the president to interpose for the protection of the citizens at Greytown against an irresponsible and marauding community that had established itself there, was a public political question, in which the government, as well as the citizens whose interests were involved, was concerned, and which belonged to the executive to determine; and his decision is final and conclusive, and justified the defendant in the execution of his orders given through the secretary of the navy.

Judgment for defendant.

IN RE NEAGLE (CUNNINGHAM v. NEAGLE)

135 U.S. 1 (1890).

MILLER, J.

[Editors' note: David S. Terry was killed by David Neagle, deputy United States marshal, while Neagle was guarding the life of U.S. Supreme Court Justice Field. While on circuit in September of 1888, Justice Field (with Judges Sawyer and Sabin) had ruled against Mr. and Mrs. Terry in a different matter. Mrs. Terry had previously assaulted Judge Sawyer. While the circuit decision was being delivered by Justice Field, the Terrys engaged in conduct which led to sentences of imprisonment for contempt, Mr. Terry even brandishing a bowie-knife against Marshal Neagle and striking Marshal Franks "so violent as to knock out a tooth."]

... From that time until his death the denunciations by Terry and his wife of Mr. Justice Field were open, frequent, and of the most vindictive and malevolent character. While being transported from San Francisco to Alameda, where they were imprisoned [for contempt], Mrs. Terry repeated a number of times that she would kill both Judge Field and Judge Sawyer. Terry, who was present, said nothing to restrain her, but added that he was not through with Judge Field yet; and, while in jail at Alameda, Terry said that after he got out of jail he would horsewhip Judge Field; and that he did not believe he would ever return to California, but this earth was not large enough to keep him from finding Judge Field and horsewhipping him; and, in reply to a remark that this would be a dangerous thing to do, and that Judge Field would resent it, he said: "If Judge Field resents it I will kill him." And while in jail Mrs. Terry exhibited to a witness Terry's knife, at which he laughed, and said, "Yes, I always carry that," and made a remark about judges and marshals, that "they were all a lot of cowardly curs," and he would "see some of them in their graves yet." Mrs. Terry also said that she expected to kill Judge Field some day....

We have no doubt that Mr. Justice Field when attacked by Terry was engaged in the discharge of his duties as Circuit Justice of the Ninth Circuit, and was entitled to all the protection under those circumstances which the law could give him.

It is urged, however, that there exists no statute authorizing any such protection as that which Neagle was instructed to give Judge Field in the present case, and indeed no protection whatever against a vindictive or malicious assault growing out of the faithful discharge of his official duties; and that the language of section 753 of the Revised

Statutes, that the party seeking the benefit of the writ of habeas corpus must in this connection show that he is "in custody for an act done or omitted in pursuance of a law of the United States," makes it necessary that upon this occasion it should be shown that the act for which Neagle is imprisoned was done by virtue of an act of Congress. It is not supposed that any special act of Congress exists which authorizes the marshals or deputy marshals of the United States in express terms to accompany the judges of the Supreme Court through their circuits, and act as a body-guard to them, to defend them against malicious assaults against their persons. But we are of opinion that this view of the statute is an unwarranted restriction of the meaning of a law designed to extend in a liberal manner the benefit of the writ of habeas corpus to persons imprisoned for the performance of their duty. And we are satisfied that if it was the duty of Neagle, under the circumstances, a duty which could only arise under the laws of the United States, to defend Mr. Justice Field from a murderous attack upon him, he brings himself within the meaning of the section we have recited. This view of the subject is confirmed by the alternative provision, that he must be in custody "for an act done or omitted in pursuance of a law of the United States or of an order, process, or decree of a court or judge thereof, or is in custody in violation of the Constitution or of a law or treaty of the United States."

In the view we take of the Constitution of the United States, any obligation fairly and properly inferable from that instrument, or any duty of the marshal to be derived from the general scope of his duties under the laws of the United States, is "a law" within the meaning of this phrase. It would be a great reproach to the system of government of the United States, declared to be within its sphere sovereign and supreme, if there is to be found within the domain of its powers no means of protecting the judges, in the conscientious and faithful discharge of their duties, from the malice and hatred of those upon whom their judgments may operate unfavorably. . . .

. . . The Constitution, section 3, Article 2, declares that the President "shall take care that the laws be faithfully executed," and he is provided with the means of fulfilling this obligation by his authority to commission all the officers of the United States, and, by and with the advice and consent of the Senate, to appoint the most important of them and to fill vacancies. He is declared to be commander-in-chief of the army and navy of the United States. The duties which are thus imposed upon him he is further enabled to perform by the recognition in the Constitution, and the creation by acts of Congress, of executive departments, which have varied in number from four or five to seven or eight, the heads of which are familiarly called cabinet ministers. These aid him in the performance of the great duties of his office, and represent him in a thousand acts to which it can hardly be supposed his personal attention is called, and thus he is enabled to fulfil the duty of, his great department, expressed in the phrase that "he shall take care that the laws be faithfully executed."

Is this duty limited to the enforcement of acts of Congress or of treaties of the United States according to their express terms, or does it include the rights, duties and obligations growing out of the Constitution itself, our international relations, and all the protection implied by the nature of the government under the Constitution?

One of the most remarkable episodes in the history of our foreign relations, and which has become an attractive historical incident, is the case of Martin Koszta, a native of Hungary, who, though not fully a naturalized citizen of the United States, had in due form of law made his declaration of intention to become a citizen. While in Smyrna he was seized by command of the Austrian consul general at that place, and carried on board the Hussar, an Austrian vessel, where he was held in close confinement. Captain Ingraham, in command of the American sloop of war St. Louis, arriving in port at that critical period, and ascertaining that Koszta had with him his naturalization papers, demanded his surrender to him, and was compelled to train his guns upon the Austrian vessel before his demands were complied with. It was, however, to prevent bloodshed, agreed that Koszta should be placed in the hands of the French consul subject to the result of diplomatic negotiations between Austria and the United States. The celebrated correspondence between Mr. Marcy, Secretary of State, and Chevalier Hulsemann, the Austrian minister at Washington, which arose out of this affair and resulted in the release and restoration to liberty of Koszta, attracted a great deal of public attention, and the position assumed by Mr. Marcy met the approval of the country and of Congress, who voted a gold medal to Captain Ingraham for his conduct in the affair. Upon what act of Congress then existing can any one lay his finger in support of the action of our government in this matter?. . . .

We cannot doubt the power of the President to take measures for the protection of a judge of one of the courts of the United States, who, while in the discharge of the duties of his office, is threatened with a personal attack which may probably result in his death, and we think it clear that where this protection is to be afforded through the civil power, the Department of Justice is the proper one to set in motion the necessary means of protection. The correspondence already recited in this opinion between the marshal of the Northern District of California, and the Attorney General, and the district attorney of the United States for that district, although prescribing no very specific mode of affording this protection by the Attorney General, is sufficient, we think, to warrant the marshal in taking the steps which he did take, in making the provisions which he did make, for the protection and defense of Mr. Justice Field.

But there is positive law investing the marshals and their deputies with powers which not only justify what Marshal Neagle did in this matter, but which imposed it upon him as a duty. In chapter fourteen of the Revised Statutes of the United States, which is devoted to the appointment and duties of the district attorneys, marshals, and clerks of the courts of the United States, section 788 declares: "The marshals and their deputies shall have, in each State, the same powers, in executing the laws of the United States, as the sheriffs and their deputies in such State may have, by law, in executing the laws thereof."

If, therefore, a sheriff of the State of California was authorized to do in regard to the laws of California what Neagle did, that is, if he was authorized to keep the peace, to protect a judge from assault and murder, then Neagle was authorized to do the same thing in reference to the laws of the United States.... [The Court found that a sheriff was so authorized]

The result at which we have arrived upon this examination is, that in the protection of the person and the life of Mr. Justice Field while in the discharge of his official duties, Neagle was authorized to resist the attack of Terry upon him; that Neagle was correct in the belief that without prompt action on his part the assault of Terry upon the judge would have ended in the death of the latter; that such being his well-founded belief, he was justified in taking the life of Terry, as the only means of preventing the death of the man who was intended to be his victim; that in taking the life of Terry, under the circumstances, he was acting under the authority of the law of the United States, and was justified in so doing; and that he is not liable to answer in the courts of California on account of his part in that transaction.

We therefore affirm the judgment of the Circuit Court authorizing his discharge from the custody of the sheriff of San Joaquin County.

MR. JUSTICE FIELD did not sit at the hearing of this case, and took no part in its decision.

Notes and Questions

1. Does *In re Neagle* support presidential power to use force to implement treaties? to protect U.S. nationals abroad?

2. In 1868, Congress created the Hostage Act, 22 U.S.C. § 1732, which declares:

"Whenever it is made known to the President that any citizen of the United States has been unjustly deprived of his liberty by or under the authority of any foreign government, it shall be the duty of the President forthwith to demand of that government the reasons of such imprisonment; and if it appears to be wrongful and in violation of the rights of American citizenship, the President shall forthwith demand the release of such citizen, and if the release so demanded is unreasonably delayed or refused, the President shall use such means, not amounting to acts of war, as he may think necessary and proper to obtain or effectuate the release; and all the facts and proceedings relative thereto shall as soon as practicable be communicated by the President to Congress."

3. Does the Hostage Act violate the separation of powers in any respect?

4. Would the Act have precluded executive use of force in circumstances addressed in *Durand*? What are "acts of war" within the meaning of the statute?

5. Does the United Nations Charter prevail over the statute domestically?

4. *Powers to Use Other Force*

Does Congress or the President have the power to authorize the initiation of military force to control vessels or other property, to engage in armed reprisals, or to defend the United States from outside attack? Can Congress control the Executive in such cases? What is the effect of a declaration of war, or lack thereof, in such cases?

LITTLE v. BARREME (THE FLYING FISH)

6 U.S. (2 Cranch) 170 (1804).

[Editors' note: During an undeclared limited war with France, sanctified by Congress, U.S. frigates Boston and General Greene captured the Danish brigantine Flying Fish on Dec. 2, 1799. The Danish vessel was found to be neutral property and not subject to seizure under an Act of Congress of Feb. 9, 1799, suspending traffic and commerce between France and the United States.]

MARSHALL, C.J.

It is by no means clear that the President of the United States, whose high duty it is to "take care that the laws be faithfully executed," and who is commander in chief of the armies and navies of the United States, might not, without any special authority for that purpose, in the then existing state of things, have empowered the officers commanding the armed vessels of the United States, to seize and send into port for adjudication, American vessels which were forfeited by being engaged in this illicit commerce. But when it is observed that the general clause of the first section of the ... [act declares that such vessels may be seized, in the Court's view, within the United States, and the fifth section of the act] gives a special authority to seize on the high seas, and limits that authority to the seizure of vessels ... the legislature seems to have prescribed the manner in which this law shall be carried into execution.... Of consequence, however strong the circumstances might be, which induced Captain Little [of a U.S. vessel] to suspect the Flying Fish to be an American vessel, they could not excuse the detention of her, since he would not have been authorized to detain her had she been really American.

... [Orders had been] given by the executive, under the construction of the act of Congress made by the department to which its execution was assigned [the Secretary of the Navy to the captains of the U.S. vessels] ... , [but] the instructions cannot change the nature of the transaction, or legalize an act which, without those instructions, would have been a plain trespass.... Captain Little, then, must be answerable in damages to the owner of this neutral vessel....

BROWN v. UNITED STATES

12 U.S. (8 Cranch) 110 (1814).

MARSHALL, C.J.

The Emulous owned by John Delano and others citizens of the United States, was chartered to a company carrying on trade in Great Britain, one of whom was an American citizen, for the purpose of carrying a cargo from Savannah to Plymouth. After the cargo was put on board, the vessel was stopped in port by the embargo of the 4th of April, 1812. On the 25th of the same month, it was agreed between the master of the ship and the agent of the shippers, that she should proceed with her cargo to New Bedford, where her owners resided, and remain there without prejudice to the charter party. In pursuance of this agreement, the Emulous proceeded to New Bedford, where she continued until after the declaration of war. In October or November, the ship was unloaded and the cargo; except the pine timber, was landed. The pine timber was floated up a salt water creek, where, at low tide, the ends of the timber rested on the mud, where it was secured from floating out with the tide, by impediments fastened in the entrance of the creek. On the 7th of November, 1812, the cargo was sold by the agent of the owners, who is an American citizen, to the Claimant, who is also an American citizen. On the 19th of April, a libel was filed by the attorney for the United States, in the district Court of Massachusetts, against the said cargo, as well on behalf of the United States of America as for and in behalf of John Delano and of all other persons concerned. It does not appear that this seizure was made under any instructions from the president of the United States; nor is there any evidence of its having his sanction, unless the libels being filed and prosecuted by the law officer who represents the government, must imply that sanction.

On the contrary, it is admitted that the seizure was made by an individual, and the libel filed at his instance, by the district attorney who acted from his own impressions of what appertained to his duty. The property was claimed by Armitz Brown under the purchase made in the preceding November.

The district Court dismissed the libel. The Circuit Court reversed this sentence, and condemned the pine timber as enemy property forfeited to the United States. From the sentence of the Circuit Court, the Claimant appealed to this Court.

The material question made at bar is this. Can the pine timber, even admitting the property not to be changed by the sale in November, be condemned as prize of war? . . .

Respecting the power of government no doubt is entertained. That war gives to the sovereign full right to take the persons and confiscate the property of the enemy wherever found, is conceded. The mitigations of this rigid rule, which the humane and wise policy of modern times has introduced into practice, will more or less affect the exercise of this right, but cannot impair the right itself. That remains undiminished, and when the sovereign authority shall choose to bring it into operation, the judicial department must give effect to its will. But until that will shall be expressed, no power of condemnation can exist in the Court.

The questions to be decided by the Court are:

1st. May enemy's property, found on land at the commencement of hostilities, be seized and condemned as a necessary consequence of the declaration of war?

2d. Is there any legislative act which authorizes such seizure and condemnation?

Since, in this country, from the structure of our government, proceedings to condemn the property of an enemy found within our territory at the declaration of war, can be sustained only upon the principle that they are instituted in execution of some existing law, we are led to ask,

Is the declaration of war such a law? Does that declaration, by its own operation, so vest the property of the enemy in the government, as to support proceedings for its seizure and confiscation, or does it vest only a right, the assertion of which depends on the will of the sovereign power?

The universal practice of forbearing to seize and confiscate debts and credits, the principle universally received, that the right to them revives on the restoration of peace, would seem to prove that war is not an absolute confiscation of this property, but simply confers the right of confiscation.

Between debts contracted under the faith of laws, and property acquired in the course of trade, on the faith of the same laws, reason draws no distinction; and, although, in practice, vessels with their cargoes, found in port at the declaration of war, may have been seized, it is not believed that modern usage would sanction the seizure of the goods of an enemy on land, which were acquired in peace in the course of trade. Such a proceeding is rare, and would be deemed a harsh exercise of the rights of war. But although the practice in this respect may not be uniform, that circumstance does not essentially affect the question. The enquiry is, whether such property vests in the sovereign by the mere declaration of war, or remains subject to a right of confiscation, the exercise of which depends on the national will: and the rule which applies to one case, so far as respects the operation of a declaration of war on the thing itself, must apply to all others over which war gives an equal right. The right of the sovereign to confiscate debts being precisely the same with the right to confiscate other property found in the country, the operation of a declaration of war on debts and on other property found within the country must be the same. What then is this operation?

Even Bynkershoek, who maintains the broad principle, that in war every thing done against an enemy is lawful; that he may be destroyed, though unarmed and defenseless; that fraud, or even poison, may be employed against him; that a most unlimited right is acquired to his person and property; admits that war does not transfer to the sovereign a debt due to his enemy; and, therefore, if payment of such debt be not exacted, peace revives the former right of the creditor; because, "he says, 'the occupation which is had by war consists more in fact than in law.' "He adds to his observations on this subject, "let it not, however, be supposed that it is only true of actions, that they are not condemned *ipso jure*, for other things also belonging to the enemy may be concealed and escape condemnation."

Vattel says, that "the sovereign can neither detain the persons nor the property of those subjects of the enemy who are within his dominions at the time of the declaration."

It is true that this rule is, in terms, applied by Vattel to the property of those only who are personally within the territory at the commencement of hostilities; but it applies equally to things in action and to things in possession; and if war did, of itself, without any further exercise of the sovereign will, vest the property of the enemy in the sovereign, his presence could not exempt it from this operation of war. Nor can a reason be perceived for maintaining that the public faith is more entirely pledged for the security of property trusted in the territory of the nation in time of peace, if it be accompanied by its owner, than if it be confided to the care of others....

The modern rule then would seem to be, that tangible property belonging to an enemy and found in the country at the commencement of war, ought not to be immediately confiscated; and in almost every commercial treaty an article is inserted stipulating for the right to withdraw such property.

This rule appears to be totally incompatible with the idea, that war does of itself vest the property in the belligerent government. It may be considered as the opinion of all who have written on the *jus belli*, that war gives the right to confiscate, but does not itself confiscate the property of the enemy; and their rules go to the exercise of this right.

The constitution of the United States was framed at a time when this rule, introduced by commerce in favor of moderation and humanity, was received throughout the civilized world. In expounding that constitution, a construction ought not lightly to be admitted which would give to a declaration of war an effect in this country it does not possess elsewhere, and which would fetter that exercise of entire discretion respecting enemy property, which may enable the government to apply to the enemy the rule that he applies to us.

If we look to the constitution itself, we find this general reasoning much strengthened by the words of that instrument.

That the declaration of war has only the effect of placing the two nations in a state of hostility, of producing a state of war, of giving those rights which war confers; but not of operating, by its own force, any of those results, such as a transfer of property, which are usually produced by ulterior measures of government, is fairly deducible from the enumeration of powers which accompanies that of declaring war. "Congress shall have power"—"to declare war, grant letters of marque and reprisal, and make rules concerning captures on land and water."

It would be restraining this clause within narrower limits than the words themselves import, to say that the power to make rules concerning captures on land and water, is to be confined to captures which are exterritorial. If it extends to rules respecting enemy property found within the territory, then we perceive an express grant to congress of the power in question as an independent substantive power, not included in that of declaring war.

The acts of congress furnish many instances of an opinion that the declaration of war does not, of itself, authorize proceedings against the persons or property of the enemy found, at the time, within the territory.

War gives an equal right over persons and property: and if its declaration is not considered as prescribing a law respecting the person of an enemy found in our country, neither does it prescribe a law for his property. The act concerning alien enemies, which confers on the president very great discretionary powers respecting their persons, affords a strong implication that he did not possess those powers by virtue of the declaration of war.

The "act for the safe keeping and accommodation of prisoners of war," is of the same character.

The act prohibiting trade with the enemy ... [is similar in effect] ... ; and the authority which the act confers on the president, is manifestly considered as one which he did not previously possess.

The proposition that a declaration of war does not, in itself, enact a confiscation of the property of the enemy within the territory of the belligerent, is believed to be entirely free from doubt. Is there in the act of congress, by which war is declared against Great Britain, any expression which would indicate such an intention?

That act, after placing the two nations in a state of war, authorizes the president of the United States to use the whole land and naval force of the United States to carry the war into effect, and "to issue to private armed vessels of the United States, commissions or letters of marque and general reprisal against the vessels, goods and effects of the government of the united kingdom of Great Britain and Ireland, and the subjects thereof."

That reprisals may be made on enemy property found within the United States at the declaration of war, if such be the will of the nation, has been admitted; but it is not admitted that, in the declaration of war, the nation has expressed its will to that effect....

It is urged that, in executing the laws of war, the executive may seize and the Courts condemn all property which, according to the modern law of nations, is subject to confiscation, although it might require an act of the legislature to justify the condemnation of that property which, according to modern usage, ought not to be confiscated.

This argument must assume for its basis the position that modern usage constitutes a rule which acts directly upon the thing itself by its own force, and not through the sovereign power. This position is not allowed. This usage is a guide which the sovereign follows or abandons at his will. The rule, like other precepts of morality, of humanity, and even of wisdom, is addressed to the judgment of the sovereign; and although it cannot be disregarded by him without obloquy, yet it may be disregarded.

The rule is, in its nature, flexible. It is subject to infinite modification. It is not an immutable rule of law, but depends on political considerations which may continually vary.

... When war breaks out, the question, what shall be done with enemy property in our country, is a question rather of policy than of law. The rule which we apply to the property of our enemy, will be applied by him to the property of our citizens. Like all other questions of policy, it is proper for the consideration of a department which can modify it at will; not for the consideration of a department which can pursue only the law as it is written. It is proper for the consideration of the legislature, not of the executive or judiciary.

It appears to the Court, that the power of confiscating enemy property is in the legislature, and that the legislature has not yet declared its will to confiscate property which was within our territory at the declaration of war. The Court is therefore of opinion that there is error in the sentence of condemnation pronounced in the Circuit Court in this case, and both direct that the same be reversed and annulled, and that the sentence of the District Court be affirmed.

STORY, J., dissenting

... The act of 26th June, 1812, ch. 107, provides that in all cases of captured vessels, goods and effects which shall be brought within the jurisdiction of the United States, the district Court shall have exclusive original cognizance thereof, as in civil causes of admiralty and maritime jurisdiction. The act of 18th June, 1812, ch. 102, declaring war, authorizes the president to issue letters of marque and reprisal to private armed ships against the vessels, goods and effects of the British government and its subjects; and to use the whole land and naval force of the United States to carry the war into effect. In neither of these acts is there any limitation as to the places where captures may be made on the land or on the seas; and, of course, it would seem that the right of the Courts to adjudicate respecting captures would be co-extensive with such captures, wherever made, unless the jurisdiction conferred is manifestly confined by the former act to captures made by private armed vessels....

The next question is, whether congress (for with them rests the sovereignty of the nation as to the right of making war, and declaring its limits and effects) have authorized the seizure of enemies' property afloat in our ports. The act of 18th June, 1812, ch. 102, is in very general terms, declaring war against Great Britain, and authorizing the president to employ the public forces to carry it into effect. Independent of such express authority, I think that, as the executive of the nation, he must, as an incident of the office, have a right to employ all the usual and customary means acknowledged in war, to carry it into effect. And there being no limitation in the act, it seems to follow that the executive may authorize the capture of all enemies' property, wherever, by the law of nations, it may be lawfully seized. In cases where no grant is made by congress, all such captures, made under the authority of the executive, must enure to the use of the government. That the executive is not restrained from authorizing captures on land, is clear from the provisions of the act. He may employ and actually has employed the land forces for that purpose; and no one has doubted the legality of the conduct. That captures may be made, within our own ports, by commissioned ships, seems a natural result of the language—of the generality of expression in relation to the authority to grant letters of marque and reprisal to private armed vessels, which the act does not confine to captures on the high seas, and is supported by the known usage of Great Britain in similar cases. It would be strange indeed, if the executive could not authorize or ratify a capture in our own ports, unless by granting a commission to a public or private ship. I am not bold enough to interpose a limitation where congress have not chosen to make one; and I hold, that, by the act declaring war, the executive may authorize all captures which, by the modern law of nations, are permitted and approved. It will be at once perceived, that in this doctrine I do not mean to include the right to confiscate debts due to enemy subjects. This, though a strictly national right, is so justly deemed odious in modern times, and is so generally discountenanced, that nothing but an express act of congress would satisfy my mind that it ought to be included among the fair objects of warfare; more especially as our own government have declared it unjust and impolitic. But if congress should enact such a law, however much I might regret it, I am not aware that foreign nations, with whom we have no treaty to the contrary, could, on the footing of the rigid law of nations, complain, though they might deem it a violation of the modern policy....

[There] are ... [congressional] acts which confer powers, or make provisions touching the management of the war. In no one of them is there the slightest limitation upon the executive powers growing out of a state of war; and they exist, therefore, in their full and perfect vigour. By the constitution, the executive is charged with the faithful execution of the laws; and the language of the act declaring war authorizes him to carry it into effect. In what manner, and to what extent, shall he carry it into effect? What are the legitimate objects of the warfare which he is to wage? There is no act of the legislature defining the powers, objects or mode of warfare: by what rule, then, must he be governed? I think the only rational answer is by the law of nations as applied to a state of war.

Whatever act is legitimate, whatever act is approved by the law, or hostilities among civilized nations, such he may, in his discretion, adopt and exercise; for with him the sovereignty of the nation rests as to the execution of the laws. If any of such acts are disapproved by the legislature, it is in their power to narrow and limit the extent to which the rights of war shall be exercised; but until such limit is assigned, the executive must have all the right of modern warfare vested in him, to be exercised in his sound discretion, or he can have none. Upon what principle, I would ask, can be have an implied authority to adopt one and not another? The best manner of annoying, injuring and pressing the enemy, must, from the nature of things, vary under different circumstances; and the executive is responsible to the nation for the faithful discharge of his duty, under all the changes of hostilities.

But it is said that a declaration of war does not, of itself, import a right to confiscate enemies' property found within the country at the commencement of war. I cannot admit this position in the extent in which it is laid down. Nothing, in my judgment, is more clear from authority, than the right to seize hostile property afloat in our ports at the commencement of war. It is the settled practice of nations, and the modern rule of Great Britain herself, applied (as appears from the affidavits in this very cause) to American property in the present war; applied, also, to property not merely on board of ships, but to spars floating alongside of them—I forbear, however, to press this point, because my opinion in the Court below contains a full discussion of it.

It is also said that a declaration of war does not carry with it the right to confiscate property found in our country at the commencement of war, because the constitution itself, in giving congress the power "to declare war, grant letters of marque and reprisal, and make rules concerning captures on land and water," has clearly evinced that the power to declare war did not, *ex vi terminorum*, include a right to capture property every where, and that the power to make rules concerning captures on land and water, may well be considered as a substantive power as to captures of property within our own territory. In my judgment, if this argument prove any thing, it proves too much. If the power to make rules respecting captures, & c. be substantive power, it is equally applicable to all captures, wherever made, on land or on water. The terms of the grant import no limitation as to place; and I am not aware how we can place around them a narrower limit than the terms import. Upon the same construction, the power to grant letters of marque and reprisal is a substantive power; and a declaration of war could not, of itself, authorize any seizure whatsoever of hostile property, unless this power was called into exercise. I cannot, therefore, yield assent to this argument. The power to declare war, in my opinion, includes all the powers incident to war, and necessary to carry it into effect. If the constitution had been silent as to letters of marque and captures, it would not have narrowed the authority of congress. The authority to grant letters of marque and reprisal, and to regulate captures, are ordinary and necessary incidents to the power of declaring war. It would be utterly ineffectual without them. The expression, therefore, of that which is implied in the very nature of the grant, cannot weaken the force of the grant itself. The words are merely explanatory, and introduced *ex abundanti cautela*. It might be as well contended; that the power "to provide and maintain a navy," did not include the power to regulate and govern it, because there is in the constitution an express provision to this effect. And yet I suppose that no person would doubt that congress, independent of such express provision, would have the power to regulate and govern the navy; and if they should authorize the executive "to provide and maintain a navy," it seems to me as clear that he must have the incidental power to make rule for its government. In truth, it is by no means unfrequent in the constitution to add clauses of a special nature to general powers which embrace them, and to provide affirmatively for certain powers, without meaning thereby to negative the existence of powers of a more general nature. The power to provide "for the common defence and general welfare," could hardly be doubted to include the power "to borrow money;" the power "to coin money," to include the power "to regulate the value thereof;" and the power "to raise and support armies," to include the power "to make rules for the government and regulation" thereof. On the other hand, the affirmative power "to define and punish piracies and felonies committed on the high seas," has never been supposed to negative the right to punish other offences on the high seas; and congress have actually legislated to a more enlarged extent. I cannot therefore persuade myself that the argument against the doctrine for which I contend, is at all affected by any provision in the constitution....

The act declaring war has authorized the executive to employ the land and naval force of the United States, to carry it into effect. When and where shall he carry it into effect? Congress have not declared that any captures shall be made on land; and if this be a substantive power, not included in a declaration of war, how can the executive make captures on land, when congress have not expressed their will to this effect? The power to employ the army and navy might well be exercised in preventing invasion, and in the common defence, without unnecessarily including a right to capture, if the right to capture be not an incident of war: and upon what ground, then, can the executive plan and execute foreign expeditions or foreign captures? Upon what ground can he authorize a Canadian campaign, or seize a British fort or territory, and occupy it by right of capture and conquest I am utterly at a loss to perceive, unless it be that the power to carry the war into effect, gives every incidental power which the law of nations authorizes and approves in a state of war. I am at a loss to perceive how the power exists, to seize and capture enemy's property which was without our territory at the commencement of the war, and not the power to seize that which was within our territory at the same period. Neither are expressly given nor denied (except as to private armed ships,) and how can either be assumed except as an incident of war, acknowledged upon national and public principles? It may be suggested that the executive, "as commander in chief of the army and navy," has the power to make foreign conquests. But this is utterly inadmissible, if the right to authorize captures resides as a substantive power in congress, and does not follow as an incident of a declaration of war: and certainly the rights of the "commander in chief" must be restrained to such acts as are allowed by the laws. Besides, the same difficulty meets us here as in the former case; if his powers, as commander in chief, authorize him to make captures without the territory, why not within the territory? . . .

It has been supposed that my opinion assumes for its basis the position, that modern usage constitutes a rule which acts directly on the thing itself by its own force, and not through the sovereign power. . . . My argument proceeds upon the ground, that when the legislative authority, to whom the right to declare war is confided, has declared war in its most unlimited manner, the executive authority, to whom the execution of the war is confided, is bound to carry it into effect. He has a discretion vested in him, as to the manner and extent; but he cannot lawfully transcend the rules of warfare established among civilized nations. He cannot lawfully exercise powers or authorize proceedings which the civilized world repudiates and disclaims. The sovereignty, as to declaring war and limiting its effects, rests with the legislature. The sovereignty, as to its execution, rests with the president. If the legislature do not limit the nature of the war, all the regulations and rights of general war attach upon it. I do not, therefore, contend that modern usage of nations constitutes a rule acting on enemies' property, so as to produce confiscation of itself, and not through the sovereign power: on the contrary, I consider enemies' property in no case whatsoever confiscated by the mere declaration of war; it is only liable to be confiscated at the discretion of the sovereign power having the conduct and execution of the war. The modern usage of nations is resorted to merely as a limitation of this discretion, not as conferring the authority to exercise it. The sovereignty to execute it is supposed already to exist in the president, by the very terms of the constitution. . . .

THE PRIZE CASES

67 U.S. (2 Black) 635 (1862).

GRIER, J.

There are certain propositions of law which must necessarily affect the ultimate decision. . . .

They are, 1st. Had the President a right to institute a blockade of ports in possession of persons in armed rebellion against the Government, on the principles of international law, as known and acknowledged among civilized States?

2d. Was the property of persons domiciled or residing within those States a proper subject of capture on the sea as "enemies' property?"

I. Neutrals have a right to challenge the existence of a blockade *de facto*, and also the authority of the party exercising the right to institute it. They have a right to enter the ports of a friendly nation for the purposes of trade and commerce, but are bound to recognize the rights of a belligerent engaged in actual war, to use this mode of coercion, for the purpose of subduing the enemy.

That a blockade *de facto* actually existed, and was formally declared and notified by the President on the 27th and 30th of April, 1861, is an admitted fact in these cases.

That the President, as the Executive Chief of the Government and Commander-in-chief of the Army and Navy, was the proper person to make such notification, has not been, and cannot be disputed.

The right of prize and capture has its origin in the "*jus belli*," and is governed and adjudged under the law of nations. To legitimate the capture of a neutral vessel or property on the high seas, a war must exist *de facto*, and the neutral must have a knowledge or notice of the intention of one of the parties belligerent to use this mode of coercion against a port, city, or territory, in possession of the other.

Let us enquire whether, at the time this blockade was instituted, a state of war existed which would justify a resort to these means of subduing the hostile force.

War has been well defined to be, "That state in which a nation prosecutes its right by force."

The parties belligerent in a public war are independent nations. But it is not necessary to constitute war, that both parties should be acknowledged as independent nations or sovereign States. A war may exist where one of the belligerents, claims sovereign rights as against the other.

Insurrection against a government may or may not culminate in an organized rebellion, but a civil war always begins by insurrection against the lawful authority of the Government. A civil war is never solemnly declared; it becomes such by its accidents—the number, power, and organization of the persons who originate and carry it on. When the party in rebellion occupy and hold in a hostile manner a certain portion of territory; have declared their independence; have cast off their allegiance; have organized armies; have commenced hostilities against their former sovereign, the world acknowledges them as belligerents, and the contest a war. They claim to be in arms to establish their liberty and independence, in order to become a sovereign State, while the sovereign party treats them as insurgents and rebels who owe allegiance, and who should be punished with death for their treason.

The laws of war, as established among nations, have their foundation in reason, and all tend to mitigate the cruelties and misery produced by the scourge of war. Hence the parties to a civil war usually concede to each other belligerent rights. They exchange prisoners, and adopt the other courtesies and rules common to public or national wars....

As a civil war is never publicly proclaimed, *eo nomine* against insurgents, its actual existence is a fact in our domestic history which the Court is bound to notice and to know....

By the Constitution, Congress alone has the power to declare a national or foreign war. It cannot declare was against a State, or any number of States, by virtue of any clause in the Constitution. The Constitution confers on the President the whole Executive power. He is bound to take care that the laws be faithfully executed. He is Commander-in-chief of the Army and Navy of the United States, and of the militia of the several States when called into the actual service of the United States. He has no power to initiate or declare a war either against a foreign nation or a domestic State. But by the Acts of Congress of February 28th, 1795, and 3d of March, 1807, he is authorized to call out the militia and use the military and naval forces of the United States in case of invasion by foreign nations, and to suppress insurrection against the government of a State or of the United States.

If a war be made by invasion of a foreign nation, the President is not only authorized but bound to resist force by force. He does not initiate the war, but is bound to accept the challenge without waiting for any special legislative authority. And whether the hostile party be a foreign invader, or States organized in rebellion, it is none the less a war, although the declaration of it be "unilateral." Lord Stowell (1 Dodson, 247) observes, "It is not the less a war on that account, for war may exist without a declaration on either side. It is so laid down by the best writers on the law of nations. A declaration of was by one country only, is not a mere challenge to be accepted or refused at pleasure by the other."

The battles of Palo Alto and Resaca de la Palma had been fought before the passage of the Act of Congress of May 13th, 1846, which recognized "a state of war as existing by the act of the Republic of Mexico." This act not only provided for the future prosecution of the war, but was itself a vindication and ratification of the Act of the President in accepting the challenge without a previous formal declaration of war by Congress.

This greatest of civil wars was not gradually developed by popular commotion, tumultuous assemblies, or local unorganized insurrections. However long may have been its previous conception, it nevertheless sprung forth suddenly from the parent brain, a Minerva in the full panoply of war. The President was bound to meet it in the shape it presented itself, without waiting for Congress to baptize it with a name; and no name given to it by him or them could change the fact.

It is not the less a civil war, with belligerent parties in hostile array, because it may be called an "insurrection" by one side, and the insurgents be considered as rebels or traitors. It is not necessary that the independence of the revolted province or State be acknowledged in order to constitute it a party belligerent in a war according to the law of nations. Foreign nations acknowledge it as war by a declaration of neutrality. The condition of neutrality cannot exist unless there be two belligerent parties. In the case of the *Santissima Trinidad*, (7 Wheaton, 337,) this Court say; "The Government of the United States has recognized the existence of a civil war between Spain and her colonies, and has avowed her determination to remain neutral between the parties. Each party is therefore deemed by us a belligerent nation, having, so far as concerns us, the sovereign rights of war." (See also 3 Binn., 252.)

As soon as the news of the attack on Fort Sumter, and the organization of a government by the seceding States, assuming to act as belligerents, could become known in Europe, to wit, on the 13th of May, 1861, the Queen of England issued her proclamation of neutrality, "recognizing hostilities as existing between the Government of the United States of America and certain States styling themselves the Confederate States of America." This was immediately followed by similar declarations or silent acquiescence by other nations....

Whether the President in fulfilling his duties, as Commander in-chief, in suppressing an insurrection, has met with such armed hostile resistance, and a civil war of such alarming proportions as will compel him to accord to them the character of belligerents, is a question to be decided by him, and this Court must be governed by the decisions and acts of the political department of the Government to which this power was entrusted. "He must determine what degree of force the crisis demands." The proclamation of blockade is itself official and conclusive evidence to the Court that a state of war existed which demanded and authorized a recourse to such a measure, under the circumstances peculiar to the case.

The correspondence of Lord Lyons with the Secretary of State admits the fact and concludes the question.

If it were necessary to the technical existence of a war, that it should have a legislative sanction, we find it in almost every act passed at the extraordinary session of the Legislature of 1861, which was wholly employed in enacting laws to enable the Government to prosecute the war with vigor and efficiency. And finally, in 1861, we find Congress "*ex majore cautela*" and in anticipation of such astute objections, passing an act "approving, legalizing, and making valid all the acts, proclamations, and orders of the President, & c., as if they had been issued and done under the previous express authority and direction of the Congress of the United States."

Without admitting that such an act was necessary under the circumstances, it is plain that if the President had in any manner assumed powers which it was necessary should have the authority or sanction of Congress, that on the well known principle of law, "*omnis ratihabitio retrotrahitur et mandato equiparatur*," this ratification has operated to perfectly cure the defect. In the case of *Brown* vs. *United States*, (8 Cr., 131, 132, 133,) Mr. Justice Story treats of this subject, and cites numerous authorities to which we may refer to prove this position, and concludes, "I am perfectly satisfied that no subject can commence hostilities or capture property of an enemy, when the sovereign has prohibited it. But suppose he did, I would ask if the sovereign may not ratify his proceedings, and thus by a retroactive operation give validity to them?" . . .

The objection made to this act of ratification, that it is *ex post facto*, and therefore unconstitutional and void, might possibly have some weight on the trial of an indictment in a criminal Court. But precedents from that source cannot be received as authoritative in a tribunal administering public and international law.

On this first question therefore we are of the opinion that the President had a right, *jure belli*, to institute a blockade of ports in possession of the States in rebellion, which neutrals are bound to regard. . . .

NELSON, J., dissenting

. . . It has been said that the proclamation, among other grounds, as stated on its face, is founded on the "law of nations," and hence draws after it the law of blockade as found in that code, and that a warning is dispensed with in all cases where the vessel is chargeable with previous notice or knowledge that the port is blockaded. But the obvious answer to the suggestion is, that there is no necessary connection between the authority upon which the proclamation is issued and the terms prescribed as the condition of its penalties or enforcement, and, besides, if founded upon the law of nations, surely it was competent for the President to mitigate the rigors of that code and apply to neutrals the more lenient and friendly principles of international law. We do not doubt but that considerations of this character influenced the President in prescribing these favorable terms in respect to neutrals; for, in his message a few months later to Congress, (4th of July,) he observes: "a proclamation was issued for closing the ports of the insurrectionary districts" (not by blockade, but) "by proceedings in the nature of a blockade." . . .

Another objection taken to the seizure of this vessel and cargo is, that there was no existing war between the United States and the States in insurrection within the meaning of the law of nations, which drew after it the consequences of a public or civil war. A contest by force between independent sovereign States is called a public war; and, when duly commenced by proclamation or otherwise, it entitles both of the belligerent parties to all the rights of war against each other, and as respects neutral nations. Chancellor Kent observes . . . , "as war cannot lawfully be commenced on the part of the United States without an act of Congress, such act is, of course, a formal notice to all the world, and equivalent to the most solemn declaration."

The legal consequences resulting from a state of war between two countries at this day are well understood, and will be found described in every approved work on the subject of international law. The people of the two countries become immediately the enemies of each other—all intercourse commercial or otherwise between then unlawful—all contracts existing at the commencement of the war suspended, and all made during its existence utterly void.... All the property of the people of the two countries on land or sea are subject to capture and confiscation by the adverse party as enemies' property, with certain qualifications as it respects property on land, (*Brown* vs. *United States*, 8 Cranch, 110,) all treaties between the belligerent parties are annulled, The ports of the respective countries may be blockaded, and letters of marque and reprisal granted as rights of war, and the law of prizes as defined by the law of nations comes into full and complete operation, resulting from maritime captures, *jure belli*. War also effects a change in the mutual relations of all States or countries, not directly, as in the case of the belligerents, but immediately and indirectly, though they take no part in the contest, but remain neutral....

By our Constitution this power is lodged in Congress. Congress shall have power "to declare war, grant letters of marque and reprisal, and make rules concerning captures on land and water."

We have thus far been considering the status of the citizens or subjects of a country at the breaking out of a public war when recognized or declared by the competent power.

In the case of a rebellion or resistance of a portion of the people of a country against the established government, there is no doubt, if in its progress and enlargement the government thus sought to be overthrown sees fit, it may by the competent power recognize, or declare the existence of a state of civil war, which will draw after it all the consequences and rights of war between the contending parties as in the case of a public war.... But before this insurrection against the established Government can be dealt with on the footing of a civil war, within the meaning of the law of nations and the Constitution of the United States, and which will draw after it belligerent rights, it must be recognized or declared by the war-making power of the Government. No power short of this can change the legal status of the Government or the relations of its citizens from that of peace to a state of war, or bring into existence all those duties and obligations to neutral third parties growing out of a state of war. The war power of the Government must be exercised before this changed condition of the Government and people and of neutral third parties can be admitted. There is no difference in this respect between a civil or a public war....

... [W]e find ... that to constitute a civil war in the sense in which we are speaking, before in can exist, in contemplation of law, it must be recognized or declared by the sovereign power of the State, and which sovereign power by our Constitution is lodged in the Congress of the United States—civil war, therefore, under our system of government, can exist only by an act of Congress, which requires the assent of two of the great departments of the Government, the Executive and Legislative.

We have thus far been speaking of the war power under the Constitution of the United States, and as known and recognized by the law of nations. But we are asked, what would become of the peace and integrity of the Union in case of an insurrection at home or invasion from abroad if this power could not be exercised by the President in the recess of Congress, and until that body could be assembled?

The framers of the Constitution fully comprehended this question, and provided for the contingency. Indeed, it would have been surprising if they had not, as a rebellion had occurred in the State of Massachusetts while the Convention was in session, and which had become so general that it was quelled only by calling upon the military power of the State. The Constitution declares that Congress shall have power "to provide for calling forth the militia to execute the laws of the Union, suppress insurrections, and repel invasions." Another clause, "that the President shall be Commander-in-chief of the Army and Navy, of the United States, and of the militia of the several States when called into the actual service of the United States;" and, again, "He shall take care that the laws shall be faithfully executed." Congress passed laws on this subject in 1792 and 1795. 1 United States Laws, pp. 264, 424.

The last Act provided that whenever the United States shall be invaded or be in imminent danger of invasion from a foreign nation, it shall be lawful for the President to call forth such number of the militia most convenient to the place of danger, and in case of insurrection in any State against the Government thereof, it shall be lawful for the President, on the application of the Legislature of such State, if in session, or if not, of the Executive of the State, to call forth such number of militia of any other State or States as he may judge sufficient to suppress such insurrection.

The 2d section provides, that when the laws of the United States shall be opposed, or the execution obstructed in any State by combinations too powerful to be suppressed by the course of judicial proceedings, it shall be lawful for the President to call forth the militia of such State, or of any other State or States as may be necessary to suppress such combinations; and by the Act 3 March, 1807, (2 U.S. Laws, 443,), it is provided that in case of insurrection or obstruction of the laws, either in the United States or of any State or Territory, where it is lawful for the President to call forth the militia for the purpose of suppressing such insurrection, and causing the laws to be executed, it shall be lawful to employ for the same purpose such part of the land and naval forces of the United States as shall be judged necessary.

It will be seen, therefore, that ample provision has been made under the Constitution and laws against any sudden and unexpected disturbance of the public peace from insurrection at home or invasion from abroad. The whole military and naval power of the country is put under the control of the President to meet the emergency. He may call out a force in proportion to its necessities, one regiment or fifty, one ship-of-war or any number at his discretion. If, like the insurrection in the State of Pennsylvania in 1793, the disturbance is confined to a small district of country, a few regiments of the militia may be sufficient to suppress it. If of the dimension of the present, when it first broke out, a much larger force would be required. But whatever its numbers, whether great or small, that may be required, ample provision is here made; and whether great or small, the nature of the power is the same. It is the exercise of a power under the municipal laws of the country and not under the law of nations; and, as we see, furnishes the most ample means of repelling attacks from abroad or suppressing disturbances at home until the assembling of Congress, who can, if it be deemed necessary, bring into operation the war power, and thus change the nature and character of the contest. Then, instead of being carried on under the municipal law of 1795, it would be under the law of nations, and the Acts of Congress as war measures with all the rights of war.

It has been argued that the authority conferred on the President by the Act of 1795 invests him with the war power. But the obvious answer is, that it proceeds from a different clause in the Constitution and which is given for different purposes and objects, namely, to execute the laws and preserve the public order and tranquillity of the country in a time of peace by preventing or suppressing any public disorder or disturbance by foreign or domestic enemies. . . .

The Acts of 1795 and 1807 did not, and could not under the Constitution, confer on the President the power of declaring war against a State of this Union, or of deciding that war existed, and upon that ground authorize the capture and confiscation of the property of every citizen of the State whenever it was found on the waters. The laws of war, whether the war be civil or *inter gentes*, as we have seen, convert every citizen of the hostile State into a public enemy, and treat him accordingly, whatever may have been his previous conduct. This great power over the business and property of the citizen is reserved to the legislative department by the express words of the Constitution. It cannot be delegated or surrendered to the Executive. Congress alone can determine whether war exists or should be declared; and until they have acted, no citizen of the State can be punished in his person or property, unless he had committed some offence against a law of Congress passed before the act was committed, which made it a crime, and defined the punishment. The penalty of confiscation for the acts of others with which he had no concern cannot lawfully be inflicted. . . .

Upon the whole, after the most careful consideration of this case which the pressure of other duties has admitted, I am compelled to the conclusion that no civil war existed between this Government and the States in insurrection till recognized by the Act of Congress 13th of July, 1861; that the President does not possess the power under the Constitution to declare war or recognize its existence within the meaning of the law of nations, which carries with it belligerent rights, and thus change the country and all its citizens from a state of peace to a state of war; that this power belongs exclusively to the Congress of the United States, and, consequently, that the President had no power to set on foot a blockade under the law of nations, and that the capture of the vessel and cargo in this case, and in all cases before us in which the capture occurred before the 13th of July, 1861, for breach of blockade, or as enemies' property, are illegal and void, and that the decrees of condemnation should be reversed and the vessel and cargo restored.

5. *Execution of Treaties*

[recall U.N. Security Council Resolution 678 (1990) concerning sanctions against Iraq, at pp. 1030–1031]

AUTHORIZATION FOR USE OF MILITARY FORCE AGAINST IRAQ

H.R.J. Res. 77, 102d Cong., 1st Sess., Pub. L. No. 102–1, 105 Stat. 3 (Jan. 14, 1991).

Joint Resolution

To authorize the use of United States Armed Forces pursuant to United Nations Security Council Resolution 678.

Whereas the Government of Iraq without provocation invaded and occupied the territory of Kuwait on August 2, 1990;

Whereas both the House of Representative (in H.J.Res. 658 of the 101st Congress) and the Senate (in S.Con.Res. 147 of the 101st Congress) have condemned Iraq's invasion of Kuwait and declared their support for international action to reverse Iraq's aggression;

Whereas Iraq's conventional chemical, biological, and nuclear weapons and ballistic missile programs and its demonstrated willingness to use weapons of mass destruction pose a grave threat to world peace;

Whereas the international community has demanded that Iraq withdraw unconditionally and immediately from Kuwait and that Kuwait's independence and legitimate government be restored;

Whereas the United Nations Security Council repeatedly affirmed the inherent right of individual or collective self-defense in response to the armed attack by Iraq against Kuwait in accordance with Article 51 of the United Nations Charter;

Whereas, in the absence of full compliance by Iraq with its resolutions, the United Nations Security Council in Resolution 678 has authorized member states of the United Nations to use all necessary means, after January 15, 1991, to uphold and implement all relevant Security Council resolutions and to restore international peace and security in the area; and

Whereas Iraq has persisted in its illegal occupation of, and brutal aggression against Kuwait:

Now, therefore, be it

Resolved by the Senate and House of Representatives of the United States of America in Congress assembled,

SECTION 1. SHORT TITLE.

This joint resolution may be cited as the "Authorization for Use of Military Force Against Iraq Resolution".

SECTION 2. AUTHORIZATION FOR USE OF UNITED STATES ARMED FORCES.

(a) Authorization.—The President is authorized, subject to subsection (b), to use United States Armed Forces pursuant to United Nations Security Council Resolution 678 (1990) in order to achieve implementation of Security Council Resolutions 660, 661, 662, 664, 665, 666, 667, 669, 670, 674, and 677.

(b) Requirement for Determination That Use of Military Force Is Necessary.—Before exercising the authority granted in subsection (a), the President shall make available to the Speaker of the House of Representatives and the President pro tempore of the Senate his determination that—

(1) the United States has used all appropriate diplomatic and other peaceful means to obtain compliance by Iraq with the United Nations Security Council resolutions cited in subsection (a); and

(2) that those efforts have not been and would not be successful in obtaining such compliance.

(c) War Powers Resolution Requirements.—

(1) Specific Statutory Authorization.—Consistent with section 8(a)(1) of the War Powers Resolution, the Congress declares that this section is intended to constitute specific statutory authorization within the meaning of section 5(b) of the War Powers Resolution.

(2) Applicability of Other Requirements.—Nothing in this resolution supersedes any requirement of the War Powers Resolution.

SECTION 3. REPORTS TO CONGRESS.

At least once every 60 days, the President shall submit to the Congress a summary on the status of efforts to obtain compliance by Iraq with the resolutions adopted by the United Nations Security Council in response to Iraq's aggression.

REPORT OF PRESIDENT RONALD R. REAGAN TO CONGRESS, APRIL 16, 1986

Commencing at about 7:00 p.m. (EST) on April 14, air and naval forces of the United States conducted simultaneous bombing strikes on headquarters, terrorist facilities and military installations that support Libyan subversive activities. These strikes were completed by approximately 7:30 p.m. (EST).

The United States Air Force element, which launched from bases in the United Kingdom, struck targets at Tripoli Military Air Field, Tarabulus (Aziziyah) Barracks, and Sidi Bilal Terrorist Training Camp. The United States Navy element, which launched from the USS Coral Sea and the USS America, struck targets at Benina Military Air Field and Benghazi Military Barracks. One F–111 with its two crew members is missing. These targets were carefully chosen, both for their direct linkage to Libyan support of terrorist activities and for the purpose of minimizing collateral damage and injury to innocent civilians.

These strikes were conducted in the exercise of our right of self-defense under Article 51 of the United Nations Charter. This necessary and appropriate action was a preemptive strike, directed against the Libyan terrorist infrastructure and designed to deter acts of terrorism by Libya, such as the Libyan-ordered bombing of a discotheque in West Berlin on April 5. Libya's cowardly and murderous act resulted in the death of two innocent people—an American soldier and a young Turkish woman—and the wounding of 50 United States Armed Forces personnel and 180 other innocent persons. This was the latest in a long series of terrorist attacks against United States installations, diplomats and citizens carried out or attempted with the support and direction of Muammar Qadhafi.

Should Libyan-sponsored terrorist attacks against United States citizens not cease, we will take appropriate measures necessary to protect United States citizens in the exercise of our right of self-defense.

In accordance with my desire that Congress be informed on this matter, and consistent with the War Powers Resolution, I am providing this report on the employment of the United States Armed Forces. These self-defense measures were undertaken pursuant to my authority under the Constitution, including my authority as Commander in Chief of United States Armed Forces.

Sincerely,

Ronald Reagan

Notes and Questions

1. In 1994, President Clinton stated that the U.N. Security Council had authorized military actions in Bosnia–Herzegovina to enforce a no-fly zone and use force to implement U.N. mandates to protect certain "safe areas." See *NATO Action in Bosnia*, 88 Am. J. Int'l L. 522 (1994). He declared: "I am taking these actions in conjunction with our allies in order to implement the NATO decision and to assist the parties to reach a negotiated settlement to the conflict. It is not now possible to determine the duration of these operations. I have directed the participation by U.S. armed forces in this effort pursuant to my constitutional authority to conduct U.S. foreign relations and as Commander in Chief." *Id.* at 524. He also declared: "This action, part of the NATO effort to enforce the no-fly zone, was conducted under the authority of U.N. Security Council resolutions and in full compliance with NATO procedures." *Id.*

2. Presidential use of armed force abroad without congressional authorization has been controversial and has stimulated various claims and counterclaims concerning presidential constitutional prerogatives. Can international law enhance presidential powers to use force? Consider The Prize Cases, 67 U.S. (2 Black) 635, 671 (1862) (noting that the "[P]resident had a right, *jure belli*," and was "bound" to act by using armed force, but also addressing early statutory authority for presidential use of force); John Hart Ely, War and Responsibility: Constitutional Lessons of Vietnam and its Aftermath 14–15, 155–56 ns.19–20 (1993); Louis Henkin, Foreign Affairs and the Constitution 190–92 (1972); Thomas M. Franck, Faiza Patel, *UN Police*

Action in Lieu of War: "The Old Order Changeth," 85 AM. J. INT'L L. 63, 72, 74 (1991); *but see* Lori Fisler Damrosch, *The Constitutional Responsibility of Congress for Military Engagements*, 89 AM. J. INT'L L. 58, 67 (1995); Michael J. Glennon, *The Constitution and Chapter VII of the United Nations Charter*, 85 AM. J. INT'L L. 74, 75, 81, 88 (1991). One textwriter remarks:

JORDAN J. PAUST, U.N. PEACE AND SECURITY POWERS AND RELATED PRESIDENTIAL POWERS

26 GA. J. INT'L & COMP. L. 15, 19–20, 22–25 (1996).*

What power does the President of the United States possess to assure adequate U.S. participation in U.N. operations such as those mentioned above? First, in view of the President's duty under Article II, section 3 of the U.S. Constitution faithfully to execute the laws and the fact that the United Nations Charter is treaty law of the United States, it is evident that the Charter can enhance presidential powers. In this respect, there is a conjoining of the faithful execution of the laws power and the treaty power. Also relevant are the Executive power, the President's foreign affairs power and, in time of hostilities at least, the commander in chief power. Importantly, only the commander in chief power is addressed in Section 2(c) of the War Powers Resolution [50 U.S.C. §§ 1541–48].

Counterposed to these are the various powers of Congress under Article I, section 8 of the Constitution, including its share of the war power and the far-reaching, but not all-encompassing, "necessary and proper" clause. Additionally, Congress clearly has the potentially inhibiting power of the purse string. With respect to restraints on the treaty power, Congress has the power to pass legislation that can bind the President domestically to act inconsistently with a treaty if: (1) the legislation is last-in-time; (2) the legislation is unavoidably inconsistent with the treaty; (3) there is a clear and unequivocal evidence of congressional intent to supersede the treaty; (4) none of the various exceptions to the last-in-time rule apply; and (5) the legislation is not unconstitutional (for example, as an impermissible infringement on the constitutional separation of powers)....

Indeed, more generally the President has the power and duty to execute a Security Council resolution, as any law, unless an exclusive congressional power is directly at stake or per terms of a particular resolution it requires prior legislative implementation. In fact, one of the express presidential powers, the "Executive" power, is close in name and meaning to the word "execute." The Constitution confirms that the President has the power (Article II, § 1) and the duty (Article II § 3) to execute law. Thus, unless a matter lies directly within the exclusive prerogative of Congress, it is otherwise constitutionally precluded, or

* This article was originally published in 26 GA. J. INT'L & COMP. L. 15 (1996) and is reprinted with permission.

legislation is required by the international instrument, the President must faithfully execute even an otherwise non-self-executing law. Further, whether a resolution is "self-executing" domestically should not inhibit any effect it may have abroad. Thus, even a "non-self-executing" resolution should be binding on the United States in its actions abroad or at the international level if such an effect is consistent with the terms of the resolution considered in context, and the President's powers and responsibilities would thereby be enhanced.

An interesting question arises when the Security Council resolution is not strictly "mandatory" but "authorizes" states to participate in a military action, especially in the context of a "decision" of the Security Council under Chapter VII of the Charter. Such was the case with respect to Iraq and Haiti. Further, this is what the Executive utilized in the case of Bosnia–Herzegovina, the President stating in 1994 that military actions were taken pursuant to his "constitutional authority to conduct foreign relations and as Commander-in-Chief" and as measures taken as part of a "NATO enforcement effort ... under the authority of U.N. Security Council Resolutions."

An Executive claim might be that even an authorizing resolution, as part of a treaty process, is still an authorizing law which the Executive has discretion to execute or comply with on behalf of the United States—that even if the Executive is not bound to implement the resolution, executive power is enhanced because treaties which have the effect of authorizing action (or treaties plus resolutions thereunder which do the same) are laws of the land. The President's duty faithfully to execute legal "mandates" also reaches, and is enhanced by, treaty law and the President's duty is one involving the good faith exercise of discretion conferred by a Security Council resolution. Moreover, such authorizing resolutions are evidently "decisions" of the Security Council (and, in context, not mere "recommendations") within the meaning of Articles 25 and 48 of the U.N. Charter.

The President might also have the power to circumvent ... [prior] legislation by an Executive agreement made pursuant to the U.N. Charter. For example, an Executive agreement pursuant to Article 43 of the Charter to supply U.S. military forces for U.N. peacekeeping and peacemaking operations, as a treaty-executive agreement, might well prevail over previous and inconsistent federal legislation, including the War Powers Resolution and the United Nations Participation Act [22 U.S.C. §§ 287–287(d)].

[Editors note: consider the following materials concerning the propriety of U.S. use of force against al Qaeda in Afghanistan after the September 11, 2001 attacks on the World Trade Center in New York and the Pentagon]

U.N. SECURITY COUNCIL RES. 1373 (28 SEPT. 2001)

The Security Council,

Reaffirming its resolutions 1269 (1999) of 19 October 1999 and 1368 (2001) of 12 September 2001,

Reaffirming also its unequivocal condemnation of the terrorist attacks which took place in New York, Washington, D.C., and Pennsylvania on 11September2001, and expressing its determination to prevent all such acts,

Reaffirming further that such acts, like any act of international terrorism, constitute a threat to international peace and security,

Reaffirming the inherent right of individual or collective self-defence as recognized by the Charter of the United Nations as reiterated in resolution1368(2001),

Reaffirming the need to combat by all means, in accordance with the Charter of the United Nations, threats to international peace and security caused by terrorist acts,

Deeply concerned by the increase, in various regions of the world, of acts of terrorism motivated by intolerance or extremism,

Calling on States to work together urgently to prevent and suppress terrorist acts, including through increased cooperation and full implementation of the relevant international conventions relating to terrorism,

Recognizing the need for States to complement international cooperation by taking additional measures to prevent and suppress, in their territories through all lawful means, the financing and preparation of any acts of terrorism,

Reaffirming the principle established by the General Assembly in its declaration of October 1970 (resolution 2625 (XXV)) and reiterated by the Security Council in its resolution 1189 (1998) of 13 August 1998, namely that every State has the duty to refrain from organizing, instigating, assisting or participating in terrorist acts in another State or acquiescing in organized activities within its territory directed towards the commission of such acts,

Acting under Chapter VII of the Charter of the United Nations,

1. *Decides* that all States shall:

(a) Prevent and suppress the financing of terrorist acts;

(b) Criminalize the wilful provision or collection, by any means, directly or indirectly, of funds by their nationals or in their territories with the intention that the funds should be used, or in the knowledge that they are to be used, in order to carry out terrorist acts;

(c) Freeze without delay funds and other financial assets or economic resources of persons who commit, or attempt to commit, terrorist acts or participate in or facilitate the commission of terrorist acts; of entities owned or controlled directly or indirectly by such persons; and of persons and entities acting on behalf of, or at the direction of such persons and entities, including funds derived or generated from property owned or controlled directly or indirectly by such persons and associated persons and entities;

(d) Prohibit their nationals or any persons and entities within their territories from making any funds, financial assets or economic resources or financial or other related services available, directly or indirectly, for the benefit of persons who commit or attempt to commit or facilitate or participate in the commission of terrorist acts, of entities owned or controlled, directly or indirectly, by such persons and of persons and entities acting on behalf of or at the direction of such persons;

2. *Decides also* that all States shall:

(a) Refrain from providing any form of support, active or passive, to entities or persons involved in terrorist acts, including by suppressing recruitment of members of terrorist groups and eliminating the supply of weapons to terrorists;

(b) Take the necessary steps to prevent the commission of terrorist acts, including by provision of early warning to other States by exchange of information;

(c) Deny safe haven to those who finance, plan, support, or commit terrorist acts, or provide safe havens;

(d) Prevent those who finance, plan, facilitate or commit terrorist acts from using their respective territories for those purposes against other States or their citizens;

(e) Ensure that any person who participates in the financing, planning, preparation or perpetration of terrorist acts or in supporting terrorist acts is brought to justice and ensure that, in addition to any other measures against them, such terrorist acts are established as serious criminal offences in domestic laws and regulations and that the punishment duly reflects the seriousness of such terrorist acts;

(f) Afford one another the greatest measure of assistance in connection with criminal investigations or criminal proceedings relating to the financing or support of terrorist acts, including assistance in obtaining evidence in their possession necessary for the proceedings;

(g) Prevent the movement of terrorists or terrorist groups by effective border controls and controls on issuance of identity papers and travel documents, and through measures for preventing counterfeiting, forgery or fraudulent use of identity papers and travel documents;

3. *Calls upon* all States to:

(a) Find ways of intensifying and accelerating the exchange of operational information, especially regarding actions or movements of terrorist persons or networks; forged or falsified travel documents; traffic in arms, explosives or sensitive materials; use of communications technologies by terrorist groups; and the threat posed by the possession of weapons of mass destruction by terrorist groups;

(b) Exchange information in accordance with international and domestic law and cooperate on administrative and judicial matters to prevent the commission of terrorist acts;

(c) Cooperate, particularly through bilateral and multilateral arrangements and agreements, to prevent and suppress terrorist attacks and take action against perpetrators of such acts;

(d) Become parties as soon as possible to the relevant international conventions and protocols relating to terrorism, including the International Convention for the Suppression of the Financing of Terrorism of 9 December 1999;

(e) Increase cooperation and fully implement the relevant international conventions and protocols relating to terrorism and Security Council resolutions1269 (1999) and 1368 (2001);

(f) Take appropriate measures in conformity with the relevant provisions of national and international law, including international standards of human rights, before granting refugee status, for the purpose of ensuring that the asylum seeker has not planned, facilitated or participated in the commission of terrorist acts;

(g) Ensure, in conformity with international law, that refugee status is not abused by the perpetrators, organizers or facilitators of terrorist acts, and that claims of political motivation are not recognized as grounds for refusing requests for the extradition of alleged terrorists;

4. *Notes* with concern the close connection between international terrorism and transnational organized crime, illicit drugs, money-laundering, illegal arms-trafficking, and illegal movement of nuclear, chemical, biological and other potentially deadly materials, and in this regard *emphasizes* the need to enhance coordination of efforts on national, subregional, regional and international levels in order to strengthen a global response to this serious challenge and threat to international security;

5. *Declares* that acts, methods, and practices of terrorism are contrary to the purposes and principles of the United Nations and that knowingly financing, planning and inciting terrorist acts are also contrary to the purposes and principles of the United Nations;

6. *Decides* to establish, in accordance with rule 28 of its provisional rules of procedure, a Committee of the Security Council, consisting of all the members of the Council, to monitor implementation of this resolution, with the assistance of appropriate expertise, and *calls upon* all States to report to the Committee, no later than 90 days from the date of adoption of this resolution and thereafter according to a timetable to be

proposed by the Committee, on the steps they have taken to implement this resolution;

7. *Directs* the Committee to delineate its tasks, submit a work programme within 30 days of the adoption of this resolution, and to consider the support it requires, in consultation with the Secretary–General;

8. *Expresses* its determination to take all necessary steps in order to ensure the full implementation of this resolution, in accordance with its responsibilities under the Charter;

9. *Decides* to remain seized of this matter.“

PUBLIC LAW 107–40 (SEPT. 18, 2001) AUTHORIZATION FOR USE OF MILITARY FORCE

Joint Resolution

To authorize the use of United States Armed Forces against those responsible for the recent attacks launched against the United States.

Whereas, on September 11, 2001, acts of treacherous violence were committed against the United States and its citizens; and

Whereas, such acts render it both necessary and appropriate that the United States exercise its rights to self-defense and to protect United States citizens both at home and abroad; and

Whereas, in light of the threat to national security and foreign policy of the United States posed by these grave acts of violence; and

Whereas, such acts continue to pose an unusual and extraordinary threat to the national security and foreign policy of the United States; and

Whereas, the President has authority under the Constitution to take action to deter and prevent acts of international terrorism against the United States:

Now, therefore, be it

Resolved by the Senate and House of Representatives of the United States of America in Congress assembled,

Section 1. Short Title.

This joint resolution may be cited as the "Authorization for Use of Military Force."

Section 2. Authorization for Use of United States Armed Forces.

(a) In General.–That the President is authorized to use all necessary and appropriate force against those nations, organizations, or persons he determines planned, authorized, committed, or aided the terrorist attacks that occurred on September 11, 2001, or harbored such organizations or persons, in order to prevent any future acts of international terrorism against the United States by such nations, organizations or persons.

(b) War Powers Resolution Requirements.—

(1) Specific statutory authorization.–Consistent with section 8 (a) (1) of the War Powers Resolution, the Congress declares that this section is intended to constitute specific statutory authorization within the meaning of section 5 (b) of the War Powers Resolution.

(2) Applicability of other requirements.–Nothing in this resolution supercedes any requirement of the War Powers Resolution.

Notes and Questions

1. Does U.N. S.C. Res. 1373 authorize the use of military force? Consider especially the preambular phrase "combat by all means, in accordance with the Charter" and paragraph 3 (2) of the resolution (especially: "Calls upon all States to . . . take action against perpetrators").

2. Regardless of the authority mandated in S.C. Res. 1373, can the U.S. rightly use military force under Article 51 of the U.N. Charter in response to ongoing attacks on the U.S. connected with the September 11, 2001 attack? Was the U.S. attack that was not merely on bin Laden *et al.*, but also on the Taliban on October 7, 2001 permissible? Consider Paust, *Use of Armed Force against Terrorists in Afghanistan, Iraq, and Beyond*, 35 CORNELL INT'L L.J. 533, 540–44 (2002).

3. Does the congressional authorization recognize independent presidential authority to use force? Consider the phrase "deter and prevent." Consider also Section 2 (c) of the War Powers Resolution. [on page 972]

4. Does the word "appropriate" provide a limitation? Is international law relevant to its interpretation?

5. Is the congressional authorization limited to those nations, organizations, and persons involved in the September 11th attack on the U.S.? Is President Bush's proclaimed war against terrorism so limited?

6. Does the congressional authorization allow detention of persons without trial as appropriate under international law? Recall Hamdi v. Rumsfeld, 542 U.S. 507 (2004) in Chapter 2, Section 2 B 4 b.

7. Does the congressional authorization allow use of armed force in Pakistan without Pakistan's consent in order to capture bin Laden?

8. Do the 60/90 day provisions of Section 5 (b) of the War Powers Resolution apply?

9. What are some of the "other requirements" of the War Powers Resolution?

6. Limitations Under International Law

[recall 11 Op. Att'y Gen. 297 (1865), in Chapter 2, Section 2 B 2; Chapter 2, Section 2 B 5 b and 2 D 1 (especially the list of cases recognizing that the President and all members of the executive branch, including the military, are bound by the laws of war); *United States v. Smith*, 27 F. Cas. 1192 (C.C.D.N.Y.1806), in Chapter 2, Section D 1; JORDAN J. PAUST, INTERNATIONAL LAW AS LAW OF THE UNITED STATES, in Chapter 2, Sections D 1 and E 1 a; *The Paquete Habana*, 175 U.S. 677

(1900), in Chapter 2, Section D 1; *Bas v. Tingy*, in this chapter; *Brown v. United States*, in this chapter]

C. Judicial Competencies

[recall cases in Section 2 A–B]

REPORT OF PRESIDENT GEORGE BUSH TO CONGRESS, AUGUST 9, 1990

On August 2, 1990, Iraq invaded and occupied the sovereign state of Kuwait in flagrant violation of the Charter of the United Nations. In the period since August 2, Iraq has massed an enormous and sophisticated war machine on the Kuwait–Saudi Arabian border and in southern Iraq, capable of initiating further hostilities with little or no additional preparation. Iraq's actions pose a direct threat to neighboring countries and to vital U.S. interests in the Persian Gulf region.

In response to this threat and after receiving the request of the Government of Saudi Arabia, I ordered the forward deployment of substantial elements of the United States Armed Forces into the region. I am providing this report on the deployment and mission of our Armed Forces in accordance with my desire that Congress be fully informed and consistent with the War Powers Resolution.

Two squadrons of F–15 aircraft, one brigade of the 82nd Airborne Division, and other elements of the Armed Forces began arriving in Saudi Arabia at approximately 9:00 a.m. (EDT) on August 8, 1990. Additional U.S. air, naval, and ground Forces also will be deployed. The Forces are equipped for combat, and their mission is defensive. They are prepared to take action in concert with Saudi forces, friendly regional forces, and others to deter Iraqi aggression and to preserve the integrity of Saudi Arabia.

I do not believe involvement in hostilities is imminent; to the contrary, it is my belief that this deployment will facilitate a peaceful resolution of the crisis. If necessary, however, the Forces are fully prepared to defend themselves. Although it is not possible to predict the precise scope and duration of this deployment, our Armed Forces will remain so long as their presence is required to contribute to the security of the region and desired by the Saudi government to enhance the capability of Saudi armed forces to defend the Kingdom.

I have taken these actions pursuant to my constitutional authority to conduct our foreign relations and as Commander in Chief. These actions are in exercise of our inherent right of individual and collective self-defense. I look forward to cooperation with the Congress in helping to restore peace and stability to the Persian Gulf region.

Sincerely,

George Bush

DELLUMS v. BUSH

752 F.Supp. 1141 (D.D.C.1990).

GREENE, J.

This is a lawsuit by a number of members of Congress who request an injunction directed to the President of the United States to prevent him from initiating an offensive attack against Iraq without first securing a declaration of war or other explicit congressional authorization for such action....

The factual background is, briefly, as follows. On August 2, 1990, Iraq invaded the neighboring country of Kuwait. President George Bush almost immediately sent United States military forces to the Persian Gulf area to deter Iraqi aggression and to preserve the integrity of Saudi Arabia. The United States, generally by presidential order and at times with congressional concurrence, also took other steps, including a blockade of Iraq, which were approved by the United Nations Security Council, and participated in by a great many other nations.

On November 8, 1990, President Bush announced a substantial increase in the Persian Gulf military deployment, raising the troop level significantly above the 230,000 then present in the area. At the same time, the President stated that the objective was to provide "an adequate offensive military option" should that be necessary to achieve such goals as the withdrawal of Iraqi forces from Kuwait. Secretary of Defense Richard Cheney likewise referred to the ability of the additional military forces "to conduct offensive military operations."

The House of Representatives and the Senate have in various ways expressed their support for the President's past and present actions in the Persian Gulf. However, the Congress was not asked for, and it did not take, action pursuant to Article I, Section 8, Clause 11 of the Constitution "to declare war" on Iraq. On November 19, 1990, the congressional plaintiffs brought this action, which proceeds on the premise that the initiation of offensive United States military action is imminent, that such action would be unlawful in the absence of a declaration of war by the Congress, and that a war without concurrence by the Congress would deprive the congressional plaintiffs of the voice to which they are entitled under the Constitution. The Department of Justice, acting on behalf of the President, is opposing the motion for preliminary injunction, and it has also moved to dismiss. Plaintiffs thereafter moved for summary judgment.

The Department raises a number of defenses to the lawsuit—most particularly that the complaint presents a non-justiciable political question, that plaintiffs lack standing to maintain the action, that their claim violates established canons of equity jurisprudence, and that the issue of the proper allocation of the war making powers between the branches is not ripe for decision. These will now be considered seriatim.

II. Political Question

It is appropriate first to sketch out briefly the constitutional and legal framework in which the current controversy arises. Article I, Section 8, Clause 11 of the Constitution grants to the Congress the power "To declare War." To the extent that this unambiguous direction requires construction or explanation, it is provided by the framers' comments that they felt it to be unwise to entrust the momentous power to involve the nation in a war to the President alone; Jefferson explained that he desired "an effectual check to the Dog of war"; James Wilson similarly expressed the expectation that this system would guard against hostilities being initiated by a single man. Even Abraham Lincoln, while a Congressman, said more than half a century later that "no one man should hold the power of bringing" war upon us.

The congressional power to declare war does not stand alone, however, but it is accompanied by powers granted to the President. Article II, Section 1, Clause 1 and Section 2 provide that "the executive powers shall be vested in a President of the United States of America," and that "the President shall be Commander in Chief of the Army and Navy...."

It is the position of the Department of Justice on behalf of the President that the simultaneous existence of all these provisions renders it impossible to isolate the war-declaring power. The Department further argues that the design of the Constitution is to have the various war-and military-related provisions construed and acting together, and that their harmonization is a political rather than a legal question. In short, the Department relies on the political question doctrine.

That doctrine is premised both upon the separation of powers and the inherent limits of judicial abilities. *See generally*, Baker v. Carr, 369 U.S. 186 ... (1962); Chicago & Southern Air Lines, Inc. v. Waterman Steamship Corp., 333 U.S. 103 ... (1948). In relation to the issues involved in this case, the Department of Justice expands on its basic theme, contending that by their very nature the determination whether certain types of military actions require a declaration of war is not justiciable, but depends instead upon delicate judgments by the political branches. On that view, the question whether an offensive action taken by American armed forces constitutes an act of war (to be initiated by a declaration of war) or an "offensive military attack" (presumably undertaken by the President in his capacity as commander-in-chief) is not one of objective fact but involves an exercise of judgment based upon all the vagaries of foreign affairs and national security.... Indeed, the Department contends that there are no judicially discoverable and manageable standards to apply, claiming that only the political branches are able to determine whether or not this country is at war. Such a determination, it is said, is based upon "a political judgment" about the significance of those facts. Under that rationale, a court cannot make an independent determination on this issue because it cannot take adequate account of these political considerations.

This claim on behalf of the Executive is far too sweeping to be accepted by the courts. If the Executive had the sole power to determine that any particular offensive military operation, no matter how vast, does not constitute war-making but only an offensive military attack, the congressional power to declare war will be at the mercy of a semantic decision by the Executive. Such an "interpretation" would evade the plain language of the Constitution, and it cannot stand.

That is not to say that, assuming that the issue is factually close or ambiguous or fraught with intricate technical military and diplomatic baggage, the courts would not defer to the political branches to determine whether or not particular hostilities might qualify as a "war." However, here the forces involved are of such magnitude and significance as to present no serious claim that a war would not ensue if they became engaged in combat, and it is therefore clear that congressional approval is required if Congress desires to become involved.

Mitchell v. Laird, 159 U.S. App. D.C. 344, 488 F.2d 611, 614 (D.C.Cir.1973), is instructive in that regard. In *Mitchell*, the Court of Appeals for this Circuit ruled there is "no insuperable difficulty in a court determining" the truth of the factual allegations in the complaint: that many Americans had been killed and large amounts of money had been spent in military activity in Indo–China. In the view of the appellate court, by looking at those facts a court could determine "whether the hostilities in Indo–China constitute[d] ... a 'war,' ... within ... the meaning of that term in Article I, Section 8, Clause 11." 488 F.2d at 614. Said the Court:

> Here the critical question to be initially decided is whether the hostilities in Indo–China constitute in the Constitutional sense a "war".... [If the plaintiffs' allegations are true,] then in our opinion, as apparently in the opinion of President Nixon, ... there has been a war in Indo–China. Nor do we see any difficulty in a court facing up to the question as to whether because of the war's duration and magnitude the President is or was without power to continue the war without Congressional approval.

488 F.2d at 614. In short, *Mitchell* stands for the proposition that courts do not lack the power and the ability to make the factual and legal determination of whether this nation's military actions constitute war for purposes of the constitutional War Clause. See also, Orlando v. Laird, 443 F.2d 1039 (2d Cir.1971); Berk v. Laird, 429 F.2d 302 (2d Cir.1970).

Notwithstanding these relatively straightforward propositions, the Department goes on to suggest that the issue in this case is still political rather than legal, because in order to resolve the dispute the Court would have to inject itself into foreign affairs, a subject which the Constitution commits to the political branches. That argument, too, must fail.

While the Constitution grants to the political branches, and in particular to the Executive, responsibility for conducting the nation's foreign affairs, it does not follow that the judicial power is excluded from the resolution of cases merely because they may touch upon such affairs. The court must instead look at "the particular question posed" in the case. Baker v. Carr, 369 U.S. at 211. In fact, courts are routinely deciding cases that touch upon or even have a substantial impact on foreign and defense policy. Japan Whaling Assn. v. American Cetacean Soc., 478 U.S. 221 . . . (1986); Dames & Moore v. Regan, 453 U.S. 654 . . . (1981); Youngstown Sheet & Tube Co. v. Sawyer, 343 U.S. 579 . . . (1952); United States v. Curtiss–Wright Export Corp., 299 U.S. 304 . . . (1936).

The Department's argument also ignores the fact that courts have historically made determinations about whether this country was at war for many other purposes—the construction of treaties, statutes, and even insurance contracts. These judicial determinations of a de facto state of war have occurred even in the absence of a congressional declaration.

Plaintiffs allege in their complaint that 230,000 American troops are currently deployed in Saudi Arabia and the Persian Gulf area, and that by the end of this month the number of American troops in the region will reach 380,000. They also allege, in light of the President's obtaining the support of the United Nations Security Council in a resolution allowing for the use of force against Iraq, that he is planning for an offensive military attack on Iraqi forces.

Given these factual allegations and the legal principles outlined above, the Court has no hesitation in concluding that an offensive entry into Iraq by several hundred thousand United States servicemen under the conditions described above could be described as a "war" within the meaning of Article I, Section 8, Clause 11, of the Constitution. To put it another way: the Court is not prepared to read out of the Constitution the clause granting to the Congress, and to it alone, the authority "to declare war."

III. Standing

The Department of Justice argues next that the plaintiffs lack "standing" to pursue this action.

The Supreme Court has established a two-part test for determining standing under Article III of the Constitution. The plaintiff must allege: (1) that he personally suffered actual or threatened injury, and (2) that the "injury 'fairly can be traced to the challenged action' and 'is likely to be redressed by a favorable decision.' "Valley Forge Christian College v. Americans United for Separation of Church and State, Inc., 454 U.S. 464 . . . (1982); Allen v. Wright, 468 U.S. 737, 751 . . . (1984). . . .

Plaintiffs further claim that their interest guaranteed by the War Clause of the Constitution is in immediate danger of being harmed by military actions the President may take against Iraq. That claim states a legally-cognizable injury, for as the Court of Appeals for this Circuit stated in a leading case, members of Congress plainly have an interest in protecting their right to vote on matters entrusted to their respective chambers by the Constitution. Moore v. United States House of Representatives, 236 U.S. App. D.C. 115, 733 F.2d 946, 950 (D.C.Cir.1984). Indeed, *Moore* pointed out even more explicitly that where a congressional plaintiff suffers "unconstitutional deprivations of [his] constitutional duties or rights ... if the injuries are specific and discernible," a finding of harm sufficient to support standing is justified. *Id.* at 952....

The right asserted by the plaintiffs in this case is the right to vote for or against a declaration of war. In view of that subject matter, the right must of necessity be asserted before the President acts; once the President has acted, the asserted right of the members of Congress—to render war action by the President contingent upon a prior congressional declaration of war—is of course lost.

The Department also argues that the threat of injury in this case is not immediate because there is only a "possibility" that the President will initiate war against Iraq, and additionally, that there is no way of knowing before the occurrence of such a possibility whether he would seek a declaration of war from Congress.

That argument, too, must fail, for although it is not entirely fixed what actions the Executive will take towards Iraq and what procedures he will follow with regard to his consultations with Congress, it is clearly more than "unadorned speculation," ... that the President will go to war by initiating hostilities against Iraq without first obtaining a declaration of war from Congress.

With close to 400,000 United States troops stationed in Saudi Arabia, with all troop rotation and leave provisions suspended, and with the President having acted vigorously on his own as well as through the Secretary of State to obtain from the United Nations Security Council a resolution authorizing the use of all available means to remove Iraqi forces from Kuwait, including the use of force, it is disingenuous for the Department to characterize plaintiffs' allegations as to the imminence of the threat of offensive military action for standing purposes as "remote and conjectural," ... for standing purposes. *But see* Part V–B, *infra.* For these reasons, the Court concludes that the plaintiffs have adequately alleged a threat of injury in fact necessary to support standing.

IV. Remedial Discretion

Another issue raised by the Department which must be addressed briefly is the application to this case of the doctrine of "remedial" discretion developed by the Court of Appeals for this Circuit.

In Riegle v. Federal Open Market Committee, 211 U.S. App. D.C. 284, 656 F.2d 873, 881 (D.C.Cir.1981), the court indicated that "where a congressional plaintiff could obtain substantial relief from his fellow legislators through the enactment, repeal, or amendment of a statute, this court should exercise its equitable discretion to dismiss the legislator's action." *See also*, Melcher v. Federal Open Market Committee, 266 U.S. App. D.C. 397, 836 F.2d 561, 563 (D.C.Cir.1987). The doctrine is said to evidence the "concern for the separation of powers" raised when a member of Congress asks the Court to rule on the constitutionality of a statute merely because he failed to persuade a majority of his colleagues of the wisdom of his views. Barnes v. Kline, 759 F.2d at 28 (D.C. Cir. 1984), *vacated as moot sub nom.*, Burke v. Barnes, 479 U.S. 361 ... (1987).

An analysis of the decisions which have dismissed actions on the basis of the remedial discretion doctrine shows that, virtually invariably, the congressional plaintiffs were involved in intra-congressional battles, *see, e.g.*, Gregg v. Barrett, 248 U.S. App. D.C. 347, 771 F.2d 539 (D.C.Cir.1985) (plaintiffs sought to challenge procedure by which the Congressional Record was published); Moore v. United States House of Representatives, *supra* (plaintiffs challenging the assignment of committee positions), or were seeking a ruling on the constitutionality of a statute. ... In the former situation, the congressional plaintiff has available to him the remedy of changing or enforcing internal rules of Congress, and in the latter, that of repealing or amending the allegedly unconstitutional statute.

The plaintiffs in this case do not have a remedy available from their fellow legislators. While action remains open to them which would make the issues involved more concrete, and hence make the matter ripe for review by the Court, these actions would not remedy the threatened harm plaintiffs assert. A joint resolution counseling the President to refrain from attacking Iraq without a congressional declaration of war would not be likely to stop the President from initiating such military action if he is persuaded that the Constitution affirmatively gives him the power to act otherwise.

Plaintiffs in the instant case, therefore, cannot gain "substantial relief" by persuasion of their colleagues alone. The "remedies" of cutting off funding to the military or impeaching the President are not available to these plaintiffs either politically or practically. Additionally, these "remedies" would not afford the relief sought by the plaintiffs—which is the guarantee that they will have the opportunity to debate and vote on the wisdom of initiating a military attack against Iraq before the United States military becomes embroiled in belligerency with that nation.

V. Ripeness

Although, as discussed above, the Court rejects several of defendant's objections to the maintenance of this lawsuit, and concludes that, in principle, an injunction may issue at the request of Members of Congress to prevent the conduct of a war which is about to be carried on without congressional authorization, it does not follow that these plaintiffs are entitled to relief at this juncture. For the plaintiffs are met with a significant obstacle to such relief: the doctrine of ripeness.

It has long been held that, as a matter of the deference that is due to the other branches of government, the Judiciary will undertake to render decisions that compel action by the President or the Congress only if the dispute before the Court is truly ripe, in that all the factors necessary for a decision are present then and there. The need for ripeness as a prerequisite to judicial action has particular weight in a case such as this. The principle that the courts shall be prudent in the exercise of their authority is never more compelling than when they are called upon to adjudicate on such sensitive issues as those trenching upon military and foreign affairs. Judicial restraint must, of course, be even further enhanced when the issue is one—as here—on which the other two branches may be deeply divided....

A. Actions by the Congress

No one knows the position of the Legislative Branch on the issue of war or peace with Iraq; certainly no one, including this Court, is able to ascertain the congressional position on that issue on the basis of this lawsuit brought by fifty-three members of the House of Representatives and one member of the U.S. Senate. It would be both premature and presumptuous for the Court to render a decision on the issue of whether a declaration of war is required at this time or in the near future when the Congress itself has provided no indication whether it deems such a declaration either necessary, on the one hand, or imprudent, on the other.

For these reasons, this Court has elected to follow the course described by Justice Powell in his concurrence in Goldwater v. Carter, 444 U.S. 996 ... (1979). In that opinion, Justice Powell provided a test for ripeness in cases involving a confrontation between the legislative and executive branches that is helpful here. In *Goldwater*, President Carter had informed Taiwan that the United States would terminate the mutual defense treaty between the two countries within one year. The President made this announcement without the ratification of the Congress, and members of Congress brought suit claiming that, just as the Constitution required the Senate's ratification of the President's decision to enter into a treaty, so too, congressional ratification was necessary to terminate a treaty.

Justice Powell proposed that "a dispute between Congress and the President is not ready for judicial review unless and until each branch has taken action asserting its constitutional authority." *Id.* at 997. He further explained that in *Goldwater* there had been no such confrontation because there had as yet been no vote in the Senate as to what to do in the face of the President's action to terminate the treaty with Taiwan, and he went on to say that the Judicial Branch should not decide issues affecting the allocation of power between the President and Congress until the political branches reach a constitutional impasse.

> Otherwise we would encourage small groups or even individual Members of Congress to seek judicial resolution of issues before the normal political process has the opportunity to resolve the conflict.... It cannot be said that either the Senate or the House has rejected the President's claim. If the Congress chooses not to confront the President, it is not our task to do so.

444 U.S. at 997–98.

Justice Powell's reasoning commends itself to this Court. The consequences of judicial action in the instant case with the facts in their present posture may be drastic, but unnecessarily so. What if the Court issued the injunction requested by the plaintiffs, but it subsequently turned out that a majority of the members of the Legislative Branch were of the view (a) that the President is free as a legal or constitutional matter to proceed with his plans toward Iraq without a congressional declaration of war, or (b) more broadly, that the majority of the members of this Branch, for whatever reason, are content to leave this diplomatically and politically delicate decision to the President?

It would hardly do to have the Court, in effect, force a choice upon the Congress by a blunt injunctive decision, called for by only about ten percent of its membership, to the effect that, unless the rest of the Congress votes in favor of a declaration of war, the President, and the several hundred thousand troops he has dispatched to the Saudi Arabian desert, must be immobilized. Similarly, the President is entitled to be protected from an injunctive order respecting a declaration of war when there is no evidence that this is what the Legislative Branch as such—as distinguished from a fraction thereof—regards as a necessary prerequisite to military moves in the Arabian desert.

All these difficulties are avoided by a requirement that the plaintiffs in an action of this kind be or represent a majority of the Members of the Congress: the majority of the body that under the Constitution is the only one competent to declare war, and therefore also the one with the ability to seek an order from the courts to prevent anyone else, *i.e.*, the Executive, from in effect declaring war. In short, unless the Congress as a whole, or by a majority, is heard from, the controversy here cannot be deemed ripe; it is only if the majority of the Congress seeks relief from an infringement on its constitutional war-declaration power that it may be entitled to receive it.

B. Actions Taken by the Executive

The second half of the ripeness issue involves the question whether the Executive Branch of government is so clearly committed to immediate military operations that may be equated with a "war" within the meaning of Article I, Section 8, Clause 11, of the Constitution that a judicial decision may properly be rendered regarding the application of that constitutional provision to the current situation.

Plaintiffs assert that the matter is currently ripe for judicial action because the President himself has stated that the present troop build-up is to provide an adequate offensive military option in the area. His successful effort to secure passage of United Nations Resolution 678, which authorizes the use of "all available means" to oust Iraqi forces remaining in Kuwait after January 15, 1991, is said to be an additional fact pointing toward the Executive's intention to initiate military hostilities against Iraq in the near future.

The Department of Justice, on the other hand, points to statements of the President that the troops already in Saudi Arabia are a peacekeeping force to prove that the President might not initiate more offensive military actions. In addition, and more realistically, it is possible that the meetings set for later this month and next between President Bush and the Foreign Minister of Iraq, Tariq Aziz, in Washington, and Secretary of State James Baker and Saddam Hussein in Baghdad, may result in a diplomatic solution to the present situation, and in any event under the U.N. Security Council resolution there will not be resort to force before January 15, 1991.

Given the facts currently available to this Court, it would seem that as of now the Executive Branch has not shown a commitment to a definitive course of action sufficient to support ripeness. In any event, however, a final decision on that issue is not necessary at this time.

Should the congressional ripeness issue discussed in Part V–A above be resolved in favor of a finding of ripeness as a consequence of actions taken by the Congress as a whole, there will still be time enough to determine whether, in view of the conditions as they are found to exist at that time, the Executive is so clearly committed to early military operations amounting to "war" in the constitutional sense that the Court would be justified in concluding that the remainder of the test of ripeness has been met. And of course an injunction will be issued only if, on both of the aspects of the doctrine discussed above, the Court could find that the controversy is ripe for judicial decision. That situation does not, or at least not yet, prevail, and plaintiffs' request for a preliminary injunction will therefore not be granted....

Notes and Questions

1. In footnote 12 of the opinion, the district court noted: "The *Mitchell* court found that the hostilities in Vietnam constituted a war for purposes of Article I, Section 8, Clause 11, and that Congress had not authorized the President's unilateral conduct of that war. However, the court went on to hold that under these circumstances the President's only duty was 'to bring the war to an end.' 488 F.2d at 616. The factual determination of whether at the particular time the President was bringing the war to an end or continuing it was held to be a political question for which there were no judicially manageable standards to apply."

2. The court's opinion was dated December 13, 1990. Recall the January 14, 1991 congressional Authorization for Use of Force Against Iraq, above. Did the "deployment" of combat troops by President Bush trigger any portion of the War Powers Resolution? If so, to what effect?

3. Other cases decided concerning the Vietnam War included: Holtzman v. Schlesinger, 484 F.2d 1307 (2d Cir.1973), *cert. denied*, 416 U.S. 936 ... (1974); DaCosta v. Laird, 471 F.2d 1146 (2d Cir.1973); Massachusetts v. Laird, 451 F.2d 26 (1st Cir.1971); Velvel v. Nixon, 415 F.2d 236 (10th Cir.1969); Atlee v. Laird, 347 F.Supp. 689 (E.D.Pa.1972).

4. Other cases involving dismissal of congressional plaintiff suits where legislation could still be enacted to regulate executive actions include: Lowry

v. Reagan, 676 F.Supp. 333 (D.D.C.1987); Conyers v. Reagan, 578 F.Supp. 324 (D.D.C.1984).

5. Are the courts better equipped to decide legal issues concerning incidents during war (*e.g.*, war crimes, improper seizure of vessels and other property, breaches of neutrality, wrongful obedience to illegal orders or executive authorizations, and denial of justice to aliens) than the macro issue of whether the Executive can use force abroad? Or do international law and other relevant legal norms provide a sufficient basis for judicial competence in each case?

D. The Peace Power

LUDECKE v. WATKINS

335 U.S. 160, 161–63, 167–72 (1948).

FRANKFURTER, J.

The Fifth Congress committed to the President these powers:

"Whenever there is a declared war between the United States and any foreign nation or government, or any invasion or predatory incursion is perpetrated, attempted, or threatened against the territory of the United States by any foreign nation or government, and the President makes public proclamation of the event, all natives, citizens, denizens, or subjects of the hostile nation or government, being of the age of fourteen years and upward, who shall be within the United States and not actually naturalized, shall be liable to be apprehended, restrained, secured, and removed as alien enemies. The President is authorized, in any such event, by his proclamation thereof, or other public act, to direct the conduct to be observed, on the part of the United States, toward the aliens who become so liable; the manner and degree of the restraint to which they shall be subject and in what cases, and upon what security their residence shall be permitted, and to provide for the removal of those who, not being permitted to reside within the United States, refuse or neglect to depart therefrom; and to establish any other regulations which are found necessary in the premises and for the public safety." (Act of July 6, 1798, 1 Stat. 577, R. S. § 4067, as amended, 40 Stat. 531, 50 U.S.C. § 21.)

This Alien Enemy Act has remained the law of the land, virtually unchanged since 1798. Throughout these one hundred and fifty years executive interpretation and decisions of lower courts have found in the Act an authority for the President which is now questioned, and the further claim is made that, if what the President did comes within the Act, the Congress could not give him such power. Obviously these are issues which properly brought the case here. 333 U.S. 865.

Petitioner, a German alien enemy, was arrested on December 8, 1941, and, after proceedings before an Alien Enemy Hearing Board on January 16, 1942, was interned by order of the Attorney General, dated February 9, 1942. Under authority of the Act of 1798, the President, on July 14, 1945, directed the removal from the United States of all alien enemies "who shall be deemed by the Attorney General to be dangerous to the public peace and safety of the United States." Proclamation 2655, 10 Fed. Reg. 8947. Accordingly, the Attorney General, on January 18, 1946, ordered petitioner's removal. Denial of a writ of habeas corpus for release from detention under this order was affirmed by the court below. 163 F.2d 143....

And so we reach the claim that while the President had summary power under the Act, it did not survive cessation of actual hostilities. This claim in effect nullifies the power to deport alien enemies, for such deportations are hardly practicable during the pendency of what is colloquially known as the shooting war. Nor does law lag behind common sense. War does not cease with a cease-fire order, and power to be exercised by the President such as that conferred by the Act of 1798 is a process which begins when war is declared but is not exhausted when the shooting stops. See United States v. Anderson, 9 Wall. 56, 70; The Protector, 12 Wall. 700; McElrath v. United States, 102 U.S. 426, 438; Hamilton v. Kentucky Distilleries Co., 251 U.S. 146, 167. "The state of war" may be terminated by treaty or legislation or Presidential proclamation. Whatever the mode, its termination is a political act. *Ibid.* Whether and when it would be open to this Court to find that a war though merely formally kept alive had in fact ended, is a question too fraught with gravity even to be adequately formulated when not compelled. Only a few months ago the Court rejected the contention that the state of war in relation to which the President has exercised the authority now challenged was terminated. Woods v. Miller Co., 333 U.S. 138. Nothing that has happened since calls for a qualification of that view. It is still true, as was said in the opinion in that case which eyed the war power most jealously, "We have armies abroad exercising our war power and have made no peace terms with our allies, not to mention our principal enemies." Woods v. Miller Co., *supra*, at p. 147 (concurring opinion). The situation today is strikingly similar to that of 1919, where this Court observed: "In view of facts of public knowledge, some of which have been referred to, that the treaty of peace has not yet been concluded, that the railways are still under national control by virtue of the war powers, that other war activities have not been brought to a close, and that it can not even be said that the man power of the nation has been restored to a peace footing, we are unable to conclude that the act has ceased to be valid." Hamilton v. Kentucky Distilleries Co., 251 U.S. at 163.

The political branch of the Government has not brought the war with Germany to an end. On the contrary, it has proclaimed that "a state of war still exists." Presidential Proclamation 2714, 12 Fed. Reg. 1; see Woods v. Miller Co., *supra*, at p. 140; Fleming v. Mohawk Wrecking & Lumber Co., 331 U.S. 111, 116. The Court would be assuming the functions of the political agencies of the Government to yield to the suggestion that the unconditional surrender of Germany and the disintegration of the Nazi Reich have left Germany without a government capable of negotiating a treaty of peace. It is not for us to question a belief by the President that enemy aliens who were justifiably deemed fit subjects for internment during active hostilities do not lose their potency for mischief during the period of confusion and conflict which is characteristic of a state of war even when the guns are silent but the peace of Peace has not come. These are matters of political judgment for which judges have neither technical competence nor official responsibility.

This brings us to the final question. Is the statute valid as we have construed it? The same considerations of reason, authority, and history, that led us to reject reading the statutory language "declared war" to mean "actual hostilities," support the validity of the statute. The war power is the war power. If the war, as we have held, has not in fact ended, so as to justify local rent control, a fortiori, it validly supports the power given to the President by the Act of 1798 in relation to alien enemies. Nor does it require protracted argument to find no defect in the Act because resort to the courts may be had only to challenge the construction and validity of the statute and to question the existence of the "declared war," as has been done in this case. The Act is almost as old as the Constitution, and it would savor of doctrinaire audacity now to find the statute offensive to some emanation of the Bill of Rights. The fact that hearings are utilized by the Executive to secure an informed basis for the exercise of summary power does not argue the right of courts to retry such hearings, nor bespeak denial of due process to withhold such power from the courts....

Notes and Questions

1. What powers of Congress and the Executive are relevant to the power to create or promote peace? Do you think that the peace power is shared or is it an exclusive power of one branch? How might international law impact upon the peace power?

2. Is a mere declaration of war by Congress necessarily a "law" binding on the President? Can a congressional declaration of war, even one contained in a statute or joint resolution, be legally avoided by the President in order to promote peace? *See, e.g.*, JORDAN J. PAUST, INTERNATIONAL LAW AS LAW OF THE UNITED STATES 439–68 (1996).

3. Can Congress issue a binding declaration of peace? *See, e.g., id.* at 443, 446, 459–61 n.55. Can the President? *See, e.g., id.* at 444, 446, 459–61 ns.55 and 58, 463 n.60, 465–66 n.63.

4. Can Congress terminate war by an act of legislation? See Ludecke v. Watkins, 335 U.S. 160, 168–69 (1948).

5. Does full "peace" exist because an armistice and cessation of hostilities have occurred? *See, e.g.*, Kahn v. Anderson, 255 U.S. 1, 9 (1921); *see also* Hamilton v. Kentucky Distilleries Co., 251 U.S. 146, 161, 167 (1919); Hijo v. United States, 194 U.S. 315, 323 (1904).

JORDAN J. PAUST, INTERNATIONAL LAW AS LAW OF THE UNITED STATES 444 (1996)

[T]he circumstances in which a President might disagree with Congress are not limited to that where Congress, by a two-thirds majority, has overridden a presidential veto of legislation declaring war, but might include the adoption, by a bare majority, of a mere declaration of war with obvious approval of a President but subsequent disapproval by the same or a new President. Indeed, should a newly-elected President be bound by a mere declaration of war approved by a bare majority of a prior Congress and not opposed by a prior President as if a mere declaration is "law"? Should any President? I think not. Clearly, any President might end any war through use of the treaty power (involving two-thirds of the Senate but not necessarily the House)[1] and any President can refuse to execute any declaration of war (whether it is based in domestic legislation or not) which would, or to the extent that it would, require the United States to violate international law. Without the approval of Congress, the President can also vote for a mandatory U.N. Security Council resolution prohibiting the use of force or restoring peace, and such a resolution should prevail domestically even against prior congressional legislation. It is quite evident then that Congress has no monopoly with respect to the peace power.[2]

1. *See, e.g.*, Ludecke v. Watkins, 335 U.S. at 168 (war "may be terminated by treaty or legislation or Presidential proclamation"); *In re* Yamashita, 327 U.S. 1, 12–13 (1946); Hijo v. United States, 194 U.S. at 323; Cross v. Harrison, 57 U.S.(16 How.) 164, 190 (1853); National Savings & Trust Co. v. Brownell, 222 F.2d at 397–98; First National Bank of Pittsburgh v. Anglo–Oesterreichische Bank, 37 F.2d 564, 567–68 (3d Cir.1930); Japanese Government v. Commercial Cas. Ins. Co., 101 F.Supp. 243, 245 (S.D.N.Y.1951) (war will continue "until a peace treaty is ratified . . . and ratifications have been exchanged" unless President proclaims peace); . . . *see also* Hamilton v. Kentucky Distilleries Co., 251 U.S. at 161, 165–68; McElrath v. United States, 102 U.S. 426, 438 (1880) (re: civil war & pres. proclamation—which is distinguishable and sometimes based also on legislation); The Protector, 79 U.S.(12 Wall.) 700 (1871) (re: same); United States v. Anderson, 76 U.S.(9 Wall.) 56, 70 (1869)(re: same); Ware v. Hylton, 3 U.S.(3 Dall.) 199 (1796) (peace treaty); *id.* at 236 (Chase, J.) ("war . . . can only be concluded by treaty"); Bowles v. Soverinsky, 65 F.Supp. 808, 813 (E.D.Mich.1946) ("war extends to the ratification of the treaty of peace or the proclamation of peace."); 24 Op. Att'y Gen. 570, 571 (1903); 22 Op. Att'y Gen. 191 (1898). . . .

Of course, a peace treaty would be "last-in-time" and prevail even against a prior joint resolution or act of legislation. . . . The treaty would also prevail against subsequent legislation under the war powers exception to the "last-in-time" rule. . . . It is also of interest that Ellsworth had recognized during the Constitutional Convention that "Peace [is often] attended with intricate & secret negotiations." . . . Surely secrecy and speed are often needed or at least useful for the better implementation of presidential peace powers. Each of the wars noted above had actually ended by treaty or a series of treaties, and our first war with Great Britain ended by treaty. . . . Concerning WWI, *compare* . . . First National Bank of Pittsburgh v. Anglo–Oesterreichische Bank, *supra* at 568–69 ("joint resolution of Congress . . . did not terminate the war," peace can be accomplished only by treaty, and later presidential proclamation attempting to operate retrospectively "cannot vary the terms of the treaty" of peace "which specified when it shall take effect." Thus also, international law, as supreme federal law, should condition one's conclusion as to whether and when peace has occurred. See . . . Frabutt v. N.Y., Chicago & St. Louis R. Co., 84 F.Supp. 460, 465 (W.D.Pa.1949). . . .

2. *See* . . . United States v. One Thousand Five Hundred Bales of Cotton, 27 F. Cas. 325, 328–29 (C.C.W.D.Tenn.1872)(No. 15, 958), adding: "all will concede that the safe depositary for this power is with a president and cabinet, and the congress, all of whom being specifically charged with the duty, constantly engage in ascertaining the facts upon which the policy of political action depends, and in full official communication with all the best sources of information, must necessarily be better informed in reference to situations, and better qualified to determine when peaceful relations should be reinstated with public enemies than a single judge"; A. Hamilton, [*Pacifi-*

Moreover, the President may have appropriately secret information that an enemy regime is likely to last only weeks or months and that a new, more democratic regime will serve U.S. and community interests more adequately, but that use of force by the United States in the next several weeks is likely to assure the old regime's survival. The President might also have appropriately secret indications that the near-term "execution" of war by the United States would play havoc with U.S. strategies at the United Nations, before the Organization of American States, and/or with various foreign governments. There may also be appropriately secret efforts to achieve peace and to promote U.S. foreign policy while avoiding a shooting war. In the past, at least one President had even requested special authorization to use force, not to go to war, but to strengthen his hand with the card of war (not yet declared, but expressly authorized and ready to play). If in these circumstances Congress attempts to impeach the President for failing faithfully to "execute" a war declared and extant (if that is possible) by a mere declaration of war, the President might rightly refuse and even present the courts with a viable legal argument, based on separation of powers, that, in such an instance, impeachment should not be allowed.

Question

1. Should the Court have a supervisory power regarding impeachment of a president who refuses to go to war?

cus No. 1 (June 29, 1793)] at 34 (presidential proclamation of neutrality makes known that the country "is in the condition of a Nation at Peace"), 40 (shared powers), 42 (shared or "concurrent authority," adding: "It is the province and duty of the Executive to preserve to the Nation the blessing of peace."). *See also* Woods v. Miller, 333 U.S. 138, 140 (1948) (district court view has been that the war powers of Congress had ended with presidential proclamation that merely hostilities had ended (*i.e.*, with " 'peace-in-fact' "), but the war and war powers still existed; on this precise point, see United States v. One Thousand Five Hundred Bales of Cotton, *supra* at 329 (it is error to suppose that cessation of hostilities is synonymous with peace)); Myers v. United States, 272 U.S. 52, 137 (1926) (Taft, C.J.) (approving Hamilton's view that the executive power provides the President the right to declare neutrality); *but see* Commercial Trust Co. v. Miller, 262 U.S. 51, 57 (1923) (power to declare "cessation" of "the emergency of war . . . is legislative" and president's proclamation of peace was not determinative under the circumstances); Firmage, *Rogue Presidents and the War Powers of Congress,* 11 GEO. MASON U.L. REV. 79, 80 (1988) (Congress has "sole" and "complete power to decide on [or 'for'] war or peace," a point belied by the early and continued use of peace treaties). . . .

Index

References are to pages

References are to pages

References are to pages

References are to pages

References are to pages

References are to pages

†